Quantitative Analysis for Management, Fifth Edition

by Barry Render and Ralph M. Stair, Jr.

We've taken a text renowned for its

- Comprehensive coverage
- Accuracy
- Pedagogy
- Readability
- Annotated Instructor's Edition
- Computer integration
- Integrated videos
- Just-In-Time Publishing Program

And through continuous improvement, bring you these exciting, cutting-edge improvements.

- A new chapter on statistical quality control
- Integrated spreadsheet applications
- Nine new videos
- Thorough content updates with one-third new cases
- Expanded Annotated Instructor's Edition
- A third software option: PC LINDO in addition to AB:QM and STORM software
- New, reorganized treatment of Linear Programming

The proven coverage you've come to expect—
keeping your students on the cutting edge.

Quantitative Analysis for Management has remained true to its original purpose—providing a comprehensive survey of the widely used mathematical tools—while including coverage of the most current topics and applications configured especially for the introductory student.

The Fifth Edition offers this important coverage:

■ **NEW**—A separate chapter on Statistical Quality Control

■ Graphical and computer presentations of Linear Programming are covered first, followed by applications, and then the Simplex Method.

■ Forecasting includes:
Trend Adjusted Exponential
  Smoothing
Seasonality
Standard Errors of the Estimate
Monitoring and Controlling
  the Forecasting

■ **NEW**—A module on Multifactor Decision Making

■ **NEW**—A module on Decision Theory and the Normal Distribution

■ **NEW**—A module documenting how to use AB:QM

7.4   STATISTICAL PROCESS CONTROL (SPC)

Statistical process control is concerned with establishing standards, monitoring standards, making measurements, and taking corrective action as a product or service is being produced. Samples of process outputs are examined; if they are within acceptable limits, the process is permitted to continue. If they fall outside certain specific ranges, the process is stopped and, typically, the assignable cause is located and removed.   *SPC*

Control charts are graphs that show upper and lower limits for the process we want to control. A **control chart** is a graphic presentation of data over time. Control charts are constructed in such a way that new data can be quickly compared to past performance. Upper and lower limits in a control chart can be in units of temperature, pressure, weight, length, and so on. We take samples of the process output and plot the average of these samples on a chart that has the limits on it.   *control chart*

APPLICATIONS OF QA

How Velcro Got Hooked on Quality

4.6   MONITORING AND CONTROLLING FORECASTS

Once a forecast has been completed, it is important that it not be forgotten. No manager wants to be reminded when his or her forecast is horribly inaccurate, but a firm needs to determine why the actual demand (or whatever variable is being examined) differed significantly from that projected.[5]

One way to monitor forecasts to ensure they are performing well is to employ a tracking signal. A *tracking signal* is a measurement of how well the forecast is predicting actual values. As forecasts are updated every week, month, or quarter, the newly available demand data are compared to the forecast values.   *tracking signal*

The tracking signal is computed as the *running sum of the forecast errors* (RSFE) divided by the mean absolute deviation.

$$\text{Tracking signal} = \frac{\text{RSFE}}{\text{MAD}}$$

$$= \frac{\Sigma(\text{Actual demand in period } i - \text{Forecast demand in period } i)}{\text{MAD}}$$

(4-14)

where

$$\text{MAD} = \frac{\Sigma|\text{Forecast errors}|}{n}$$

as seen earlier in Equation 4-5.

Positive tracking signals indicate that demand is greater than the fore-

plus . . .

The Karmarkar Method in Linear Programming

and . . .

Coverage of Expert Systems and Artificial Intelligence has also been updated.

QUANTITATIVE ANALYSIS FOR MANAGEMENT

5E

3 PROBABILITY DISTRIBUTIONS

KEY EQUATIONS

(3-1) $E(X) = \sum_{i=1}^{n} X_i P(X_i)$

This equation computes the expected value of a discrete probability distribution.

(3-2) $\text{Variance} = \sum_{i=1}^{n} (X_i - E(X))^2 P(X_i)$

This equation computes the variance of a discrete probability distribution.

(3-3) $\sigma = \sqrt{\text{Variance}}$

This equation computes the standard deviation from the variance.

(3-4) $f(X) = \begin{cases} \dfrac{1}{b-a} & \text{for } a \le X \le b \\ \\ 0 & \text{otherwise} \end{cases}$

This is the density function of the uniform probability distribution.

(3-5) $\text{Probability} = \dfrac{n!}{r!(n-r)!} p^r q^{n-r}$

This is the binomial probability distribution.

(3-6) $\text{Expected value} = np$

This equation computes the expected value of the binomial probability distribution.

---

4 FORECASTING

SOLVED PROBLEMS

Solved Problem 4-1

Demand for patient surgery at Washington General Hospital has increased steadily in the past few years, as seen in the following table.

YEAR	OUTPATIENT SURGERIES PERFORMED
1	45
2	50
3	53
4	56
5	58
6	

The director of medical services predicted six years ago that demand in year 1 would be 42 surgeries.

Using exponential smoothing with a weight of $\alpha = 0.20$, develop forecasts for years 2 through 6. What is the MAD?

Solution

YEAR	ACTUAL	FORECAST (SMOOTHED)	ERROR	ERROR
1	45	42	−3	3
2	50	42.6 = 42 + .2(45 − 42)	−7.4	7.4

Pedagogy that helps you because it helps your students.

The tested and well-received learning aids from previous editions include

Chapter Outlines

Margin Notes

Glossary

Key Idea Markers

Data Set Problems—with larger amounts of data for more realistic problem solving using a computer

3 levels of End-of-Chapter Problems—with an emphasis on formulation and interpretation, as well as calculation

Key Equations—summary of important equations used in the chapter

Discussion Questions—questions specifically designed to provoke thoughtful and constructive discussions

Solved Problems—serves as a model for students in solving their own problems

Chapter References

Chapter Summaries

NEW—Spreadsheet Appendices— integration of spreadsheet applications as appendicies to all appropriate chapters.

Thorough computer integration as never before!

To make the use of microcomputers more complete and integrated, we have these exciting features:

New — Optional chapter appendices illustrate the use of spreadsheet software in solving management science problems.

Numerous illustrations and problems suitable for use with any spreadsheet software. Appendices include illustrations of how to solve these problems by spreadsheet: Linear Programming (Ch. 10), Inventory Problems (Ch. 8 & 9), Decision Trees and Bayesian Analysis (Ch. 6), Decision Tables (Ch. 5), Markov Analysis (Ch. 19), Network Problems (Ch. 18), Forecasting (Ch. 4), Queuing (Ch. 16), Simulation (Ch. 17).

Key output from commercial software programs—students will see, first-hand, comparisons of the screens and output of such popular programs as STORM, LINDO, and AB:QM.

Large Data Set Problems— identified in the text by its own heading, these new data sets bring students closer to real-world problem solving. They are designed to be solved using AB:QM or any other software package.

End-of-Chapter Problems— identified by a computer icon, they are especially appropriate for computer solution.

Data Disk— Free to qualified adopters, this disk includes the files for all of the data set and computer problems and is designed to save instructors time by minimizing data entry. Adopters are free to make copies for their students.

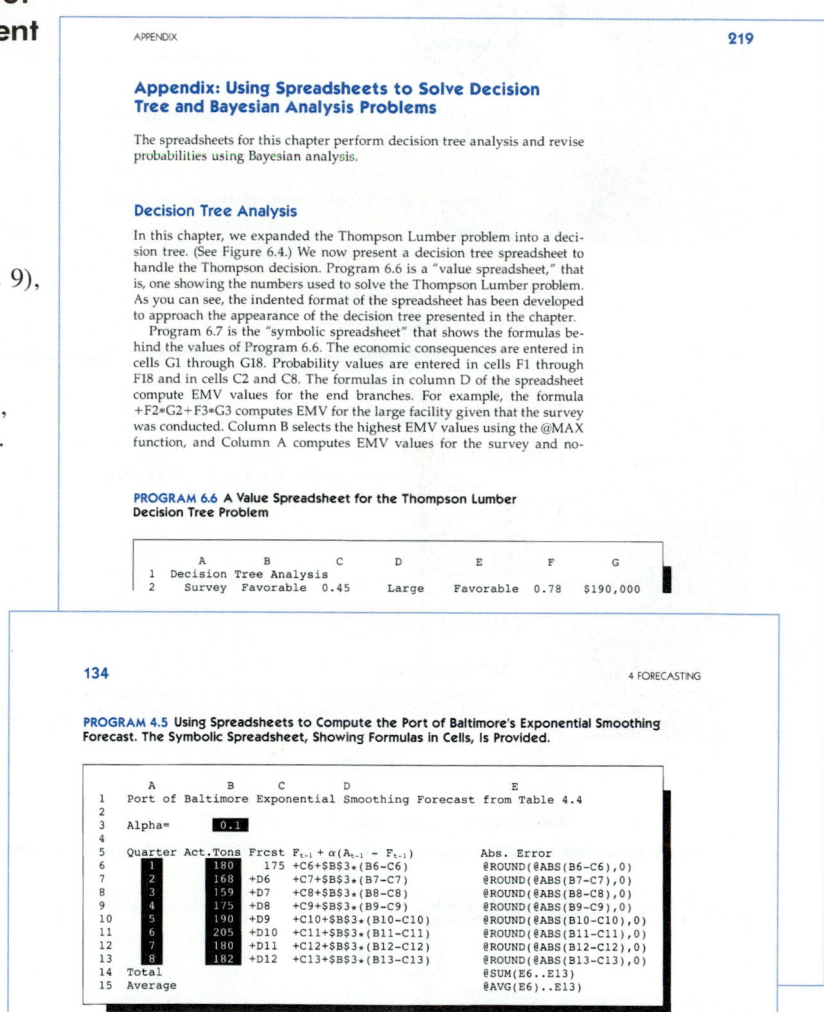

Appendix: Using Spreadsheets to Solve Decision Tree and Bayesian Analysis Problems

The spreadsheets for this chapter perform decision tree analysis and revise probabilities using Bayesian analysis.

Decision Tree Analysis

In this chapter, we expanded the Thompson Lumber problem into a decision tree. (See Figure 6.4.) We now present a decision tree spreadsheet to handle the Thompson decision. Program 6.6 is a "value spreadsheet," that is, one showing the numbers used to solve the Thompson Lumber problem. As you can see, the indented format of the spreadsheet has been developed to approach the appearance of the decision tree presented in the chapter.

Program 6.7 is the "symbolic spreadsheet" that shows the formulas behind the values of Program 6.6. The economic consequences are entered in cells G1 through G18. Probability values are entered in cells F1 through F18 and in cells C2 and C8. The formulas in column D of the spreadsheet compute EMV values for the end branches. For example, the formula +F2*G2+F3*G3 computes EMV for the large facility given that the survey was conducted. Column B selects the highest EMV values using the @MAX function, and Column A computes EMV values for the survey and no-

PROGRAM 6.6 A Value Spreadsheet for the Thompson Lumber Decision Tree Problem

	A	B	C	D	E	F	G
1	Decision Tree Analysis						
2	Survey	Favorable	0.45	Large	Favorable	0.78	$190,000

PROGRAM 4.5 Using Spreadsheets to Compute the Port of Baltimore's Exponential Smoothing Forecast. The Symbolic Spreadsheet, Showing Formulas in Cells, Is Provided.

	A	B	C	D	E
1	Port of Baltimore Exponential Smoothing Forecast from Table 4.4				
2					
3	Alpha=	0.1			
4					
5	Quarter	Act.Tons	Frcst	$F_{t-1} + \alpha(A_{t-1} - F_{t-1})$	Abs. Error
6	1	180	175	+C6+$B$3*(B6-C6)	@ROUND(@ABS(B6-C6),0)
7	2	168	+D6	+C7+$B$3*(B7-C7)	@ROUND(@ABS(B7-C7),0)
8	3	159	+D7	+C8+$B$3*(B8-C8)	@ROUND(@ABS(B8-C8),0)
9	4	175	+D8	+C9+$B$3*(B9-C9)	@ROUND(@ABS(B9-C9),0)
10	5	190	+D9	+C10+$B$3*(B10-C10)	@ROUND(@ABS(B10-C10),0)
11	6	205	+D10	+C11+$B$3*(B11-C11)	@ROUND(@ABS(B11-C11),0)
12	7	180	+D11	+C12+$B$3*(B12-C12)	@ROUND(@ABS(B12-C12),0)
13	8	182	+D12	+C13+$B$3*(B13-C13)	@ROUND(@ABS(B13-C13),0)
14	Total				@SUM(E6..E13)
15	Average				@AVG(E6)..E13)

Spreadsheets now provide another useful feature. We can use the Data Table command to find the value of alpha that provides the lowest MAD. The other way, not very efficient, is to try one alpha after another in cell B3, until we finally locate one that yields the lowest mean error. Program 4.6 illustrates how the MAD for each value of alpha we wish to try is computed. Cell B19 contains the formula to compute the MADs,

Spreadsheet templates are available on a separate disk.

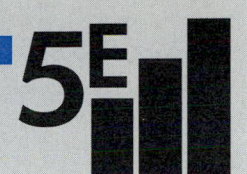
Three Choices of High Quality accompanying software

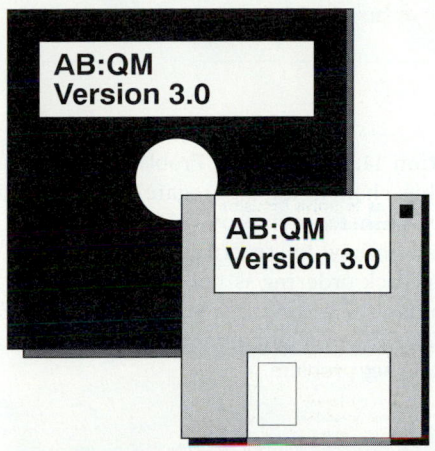

1. Updated—AB:QM Version 3.0
(Allyn & Bacon: Quantitative Methods Software)
by Sang Lee

A tremendous amount of time and effort has been put into developing this enhanced and integrated microcomputer software program for solving real-world problems.
This fast, popular and user friendly program requires no previous computer experience. The text can be purchased by students separately or with the AB:QM on either 5 1/4″ or 3 1/2″ disks.

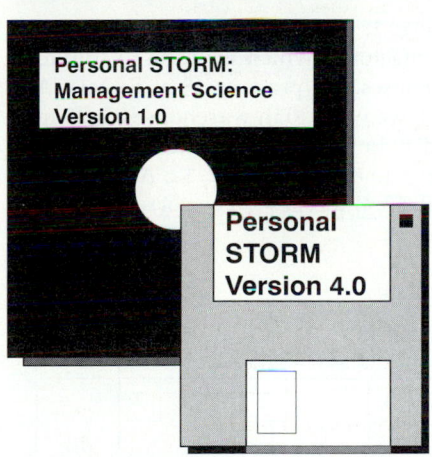

2. Updated—Personal STORM Version 4.0 and Personal STORM: Management Science Version 1.0
(Available exclusively from Paramount Publishing)

Personal STORM is the popular educational version of Professional STORM, which consists of a set of quantitative modeling techniques that can be used in Quantitative Analysis and Operations Management courses. STORM is available at half price when ordered for students, packaged with this text. And for the first time, a separate Personal STORM is available just for Management Science. Each manual includes both 5 1/4″ and 3 1/2″ disks.

3. PC LINDO software with New text/disk pack option!

This fast, easy-to-use modeling and optimization program is popular for solving linear, integer, and quadratic programming problems. PC LINDO helps students to quickly enter, solve, and analyze models—large or small. PC LINDO can now be shrinkwrapped with the text. Available on either 5 1/4″ or 3 1/2″ disks.

Helping you execute the strategy for each class, the Annotated Instructor's Edition combines the Instructor's Section up front followed by the complete student text with instructors' annotations in the margins—all bound together in one comprehensive volume.

This completely integrated and invaluable resource helps you pull together all the course materials and resources included in the extenive instructional package.

Look for these features in the Instructor's Section

Learning objectives

Teaching suggestions—
detailed tips based on the authors' own years of experience in the classroom.

Instructor's video guide—
to help you take full advantage of the text-integrated Edelman Award winning videos from The Institute of Management Sciences (TIMS) and the Consortium for Mathematics and Its Applications (COMAP).

Teaching Suggestion 14.10: Data Set Problem 14-37.

In assigning this challenging aggregate planning problem, you may wish to first provide some background information on how to structure the plan. Remind students that back ordering is not permitted, so very large costs must be inserted in many cells. Note that Problem 14-22 (Mehta Company) is a warm-up exercise for this data set problem.

ALTERNATE EXAMPLES

Alternate Example 14.1: Let us presume a product is made at two of our factories which we wish to ship to three of our warehouses. We produce 18 at Factory A and 22 at Factory B; we want 10 in warehouse #1, 20 in warehouse #2, and 10 in warehouse #3. Per unit transportation costs are: A to #1, $4; A to #2, $2; A to #3, $3; B to #1, $3; B to #2, $2; B to #3, $1. The corresponding transportation table is:

To From	Warehouses #1	#2	#3	Total
	4	2	3	
Factory A				18

NEW—Alternate examples for class lectures—To present your students with a new set of examples other than those they have read in the text, these alternate examples parallel the text material and save you valuable research and preparation time.

Complete solutions to all discussion questions, problems, and cases—fully worked-out solutions including numerical and word answers.

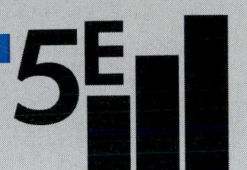

than Point 2, the best decision is to build the large facility. Of course, this is what you would expect as P increases. Point 1 and Point 2 can be computed as follows:

Point 1: EMV (nothing) = EMV (small facility);

$0 = \$120,000P - \$20,000;$ $P = 20,000/120,000 = .167.$

Point 2: EMV (small facility) = EMV (large facility);

$\$120,000P - \$20,000 = \$380,000P - \$180,000;$

$260,000P = 160,000;$ $P = 160,000/260,000 = .62.$

The results of this sensitivity analysis are displayed in the following table.

ACTION	RANGE OF P VALUES
Do nothing	Less than .167
Build small facility	.167 – .62
Build large facility	Greater than .62

Teaching Suggestion 5.5:
Starting the Decision Making Under Uncertainty Material. See the Instructor's Section for details.

no probability data available

Transparency Master 5.4:
Decision Making Under Uncertainty.

Applicable Problems: 5-8, 5-9, 5-12, 5-13, 5-15, 5-17, 5-19, Start Right Case

Alternate Example 5.2

5.5   DECISION MAKING UNDER UNCERTAINTY

When the probability of occurrence of each state of nature can be assessed, the EMV or EOL decision criteria are usually appropriate. When a manager *cannot* assess the outcome probability with confidence or when virtually no probability data are available, other decision criteria are required. This type of problem has been referred to as decision making under uncertainty. The criteria that we will cover in this section include:

1. Maximax.
2. Maximin.
3. Equally likely.
4. Criterion of realism.
5. Minimax.

The first four criteria can be computed directly from the decision table, while the minimax criterion requires the use of the opportunity loss table. Let's take a look at each of the five models and apply them to Thompson Lumber. It is now assumed that no probability information about the two outcomes is available to Thompson.

Maximax

The maximax criterion finds the alternative that *maximizes* the *maximum* outcome or consequence for every alternative. You first locate the maxi-

Annotations are printed in color in the margins of the text. They do not appear in the student edition.

And these guideposts in the annotated text section.

NEW—Applicable Problems— listings of various applicable end-of-chapter homework problems that can be used as homework assignments as you cover each text section.

Answers to Problems— provides answers to all problems. Complete solutions are found in the Instructor's Section.

Case Solutions and references to complete solutions in the Instructor's Section.

Transparency Master References — suggest places for integrating transparencies at specific points in the text.

Video Notes—indicates which application boxes tie into the TIMS and COMAP videos, and refers you to further information in the Instructor's Section.

Teaching Suggestions— indicates where specific suggestions from the Instructor's Section can be used.

Data Disk File Names— provides file names for those problems (including Data Set problems) that are included on the data disks.

Without leaving the classroom, your students will now see how Quantitative Analysis is used in everyday operation of major organizations. LP, simulation, decision theory, dynamic programming, inventory control, and critical path analysis all take on added meaning when seen in real-world situations.

Unique videos from The Institute of Management Sciences (TIMS) and COMAP are now available through Allyn & Bacon. The TIMS video consists of carefully edited tapes from their fabulous library of Edelman Award winners. The COMAP video originally appeared on public television in the series "For All Practical Purposes," produced with major funding by the Annenberg/CPB Project.

1.3 THE QUANTITATIVE ANALYSIS APPROACH

 Video 1.1

5

APPLICATIONS OF QA

The Indispensable Role of Management Science at Reynolds Metals Company

Throughout this book, we will highlight the successful application of management science and quantitative analysis. As the title of this article implies, quantitative approaches can be indispensable in helping companies such as the Reynolds Metals Company. Headquartered in Richmond, Virginia, Reynolds is a Fortune 75 metals producer. Its aluminum operation includes production, mining, and the use of recycled aluminum. Of the company's $6.2 billion in sales in 1989, over 94% was in valued-added fabricated products, including aluminum cans, flexible packaging, and a variety of consumer products.

In order to provide a more effective shipping operation, the Reynolds Metals Company decided to use management science to control shipping and reduce transportation costs. The result was the use of an integer programming model (see Chapter 15) that had the minimization of central dispatch freight cost as a primary objective. Using the annual shipping demand patterns, this quanti-

tative analysis technique was able to improve on-time delivery of shipments and reduce freight costs by over $7 million annually. As a company spokesperson said: "The confidence and respect I have for the management science discipline gave me the resolve to stick to the project plan when others doubted it could be done. I am very pleased to report today that the results that were predicted are being achieved. Management science made the difference between success and failure for this venture." As discussed in this application and other applications presented in this book, quantitative analysis techniques are playing an indispensable role for organizations throughout the world.

Source: William E. Moore, Jr., Janice M. Warmke, and Lonny R. Gorban. "The Indispensable Role of Management Science in Centralizing Freight Operation at Reynolds Metals Company," *Interfaces*, **21**, 1 (January-February 1991): 107–129.

problems to solve cannot be overemphasized. Experience has shown that bad problem definition is a major reason for failure of management science or operations research groups to serve their organizations well.

When the problem is difficult to quantify, it may be necessary to develop *specific, measurable* objectives. A problem might be inadequate health care delivery in a hospital. The objectives might be to increase the number of beds, reduce the average number of days a patient spends in the hospital, increase the doctor-to-patient ratio, and so on. When objectives are used, however, the real problem should be kept in mind. It is important to avoid obtaining specific and measurable objectives that may not solve the real problem.

Developing a Model

Once we select the problem to be analyzed, the next step is to develop a *model*. Simply stated, a model is a representation (usually mathematical) of a situation.

Even though you might not have been aware of it, you have been using models most of your life. You may have developed models about people's behavior. Your model might be that friendship is based on reciprocity, an exchange of favors. If you need a favor like a small loan, your model would suggest that you ask a good friend.

Transparency Master 1.5: Models and the Techniques of Scientific Management.

Transparency Master 1.6: Advantages of Using Models.

Transparency Master 1.7: Using Models: Some Suggestions.

Total Quality Management Video

An in-depth look at how TQM is being implemented at Kurt Manufacturing and how this mid-sized supplier of machine parts changed its culture to make TQM a success.

QUANTITATIVE ANALYSIS FOR MANAGEMENT

---

the use of sensitivity analysis

part of analyzing the results. This type of analysis is called *sensitivity analysis* or *postoptimality analysis*. It determines how much the solution will change if there were changes in the model or the input data. When the solution is sensitive to changes in the input data and the model specification, additional testing should be performed to make sure that the model and input data are accurate and valid. If the model or data are wrong, the solution could be wrong, resulting in financial losses or reduced profits.

Implementing the Results

The final step is to *implement* the results. This is the process of incorporating the solution into the company. This can be much more difficult than you would imagine. Even if the solution is optimal and will result in thousands of dollars in additional profits, if managers resist the new solution, all of the efforts of the analysis are of no value. Experience has shown that a large number of quantitative analysis teams have failed in their efforts because they have failed to implement a good, workable solution properly.

Video 1.2: Polishing the Big Apple.

APPLICATIONS OF QA

Using QA to Clean Up the Big Apple

The Department of Sanitation of New York City faces a number of difficult problems. With about 12,000 employees and a half-billion-dollar annual budget, the department has the responsibility of keeping New York clean. But New York City had a reputation of being dirty. During the mid-1970s, a cleanliness rating system revealed that the city went from a 72% rating concerning its city streets to a very low 56%. In 1980, the department dipped even farther to a 53% overall rating, and it continued to drop in the 1980s. Many workers at the Department of Sanitation believed that street cleaning was low on the city's priority list compared, for example, to refuse collection. In general, staff and employee morale were low. Furthermore, there appeared to be little or no coordination with other agencies when it came to making the city a cleaner place to live. These problems prompted the department to take a closer look at some of the problems and to consider the use of quantitative analysis.

The QA models that were developed clearly showed a strong relationship between personnel levels and overall cleanliness. They also revealed that some districts in New York City had a much better payoff or a better utilization of personnel than others. Some areas, such as Wall Street, required about five times more cleaners than other districts. Some models revealed that illegally parked cars caused problems with keeping the streets clean. Just one fewer car in some circumstances could mean a substantial improvement in the ability to keep streets or certain areas clean. Thus, one proposed solution called for cooperation between the Department of Sanitation and New York's Department of Transportation to coordinate a ticketing program to reduce the number of illegally parked cars.

Part of the overall solution was to develop a plan to improve worker morale. Programs were developed to give recognition to individuals in areas that were able to increase their overall cleanliness rating.

The results of the quantitative analysis approach were remarkable. After being fully implemented, the QA techniques led to near record levels of overall cleanliness and to great improvement in the productivity of the work force. It was also estimated that the techniques saved the city of New York about $12 million annually.

Source: Lucius J. Riccio, Joseph Miller, and Ann Litke, "Polishing the Big Apple: How Management Science Has Helped Make New York Streets Cleaner," *Interfaces,* 16, 1 (January–February 1986): 83–88.

The Institute of Management Sciences, a leading international association in the field of management science, contributes to the video component of this package. The work in the videotapes, representing the best in management science practice, has been excerpted from videotapes of complete presentations from the Institute's Annual Franz Edelman Award for Management Science Achievement.

For further information or a complete catalogue of videos, write to: TIMS, 290 Westminster St., Providence, RI 02903.

Text-integrated videos that enrich and expand upon "Application of QA" boxes.

From the Institute of Management Sciences:

TIMS Volume I
NYC Department of Sanitation (Ch. 1)
United Airlines (Ch. 10)
Canadian National Rails (Ch. 17)
Blue Bell, Inc. (Ch. 8)
The Netherlands Rijkswaterstaat (Ch. 17)
Weyerhauser Company (Module C)

TIMS Volume II
Introduction to Edelman Awards
Reynolds Metals Company (Ch. 1)
Citgo Petroleum
L. L. Bean Company (Ch. 16)

TIMS Volume III
Introduction to Edelman Awards
Columbus-America Discovery Group (Ch. 3)
IBM (Ch. 8)
American Airlines (Ch. 11)
American Airlines Decision Technologies (Ch. 15)
United States Postal Service (Ch. 17)
Military Airlift Command (Module C)

From the Consortium of Mathematics and Its Applications (COMAP):

Management Science Overview (Ch. 1)
Juicy Problems: Linear Programming (Ch. 10)
Juggling Machines: Scheduling Problems Trains, Planes, and Critical Paths (Ch. 18)
Quality Control: A. Frito Lay   B. Deming (Ch. 7)

Additional, powerful supplements— for more flexibility and more support.

In addition to the extensive integrated software and video programs and the Annotated Instructor's Edition presented in the previous pages, we've added these powerful teaching and learning aids to make this the most complete supplements package available.

Test Bank

by Mike Hanna, University of Houston

Provides about 1,000 questions in a variety of formats, including multiple choice questions and problems.

Computerized Testing

A computerized version of the Test Bank featuring the Allyn & Bacon Test Manager Plus software. This programs allows instructors to select and organize existing test questions, as well as to add their own.

Transparency Masters

Over 200 Transparency Masters have been developed and noted in the Annotated Instructor's Edition to help enhance classroom presentations. One-third have been reproduced from the text and the balance have been developed from other sources.

Study Guide

by John Harpell, West Virginia University

Offers additional help for students in the form of key points, and questions with answers, as well as answers to selected text problems.

Now available with Quantitative Analysis for Management, 5/e–

Total Quality Management Paperbacks

Three paperback supplements that highlight actual quality improvement programs from well-known companies—available at a reduced price when ordered for students with this text.

1. *Profiles in Quality: Blueprints for Action from 50 Leading Companies*
2. *Profiles of Malcolm Baldrige Award Winners*
3. *Profile of ISO 9000*

Some restrictions may apply. See your Allyn & Bacon representative for details. All information is accurate as of date of printing.

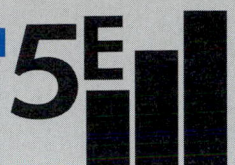
Quantitative Analysis for Management, Fifth Edition can be ordered for students in one of these ways:

Text only
H5379-6   ISBN: 0-205-15379-8

Text w/AB:QM 3.0 Software (3 1/2″ disk)
H5758-1   ISBN: 0-205-15758-0

Text w/AB:QM 3.0 Software (5 1/4″ disk)
H5759-9   ISBN: 0-205-15759-9

Text w/PC LINDO Software (3 1/2″ disk)
H5789-6   ISBN: 0-205-15790-4

Text w/PC LINDO Software (5 1/4″ disk)
H5790-4   ISBN: 0-205-15790-4

Text w/STORM 4.0 Software
(3 1/2″ & 5 1/4″ disks)
H5791-2   ISBN: 0-205-15791-2

Text w/STORM Management Science 1.0 Software
(3 1/2″ & 5 1/4″ disks)
H5792-0   ISBN: 0-205-15792-0

Allyn and Bacon / Ginn Press
JUST-IN-TIME
PUBLISHING PROGRAM
for Decision Sciences

The time is right for Just-In-Time Publishing. And Allyn & Bacon and Ginn Press continue the leadership position they established since starting this revolution, changing forever your limited choice of textbooks.

Using the successful production/operations management strategy of Just-In-Time manufacturing, Allyn & Bacon's innovative program continues to provide you with numerous options for customizing your own text. Through state-of-the-art technology, this program allows you to assemble, in one book, materials selected from a database of several Allyn & Bacon texts, other published sources, and your own materials. With Just-In-Time Publishing, you're no longer limited to the contents of a single title. Now you can combine the best of Quantitative Analysis, Management Science, and Operations Management into one textbook. You become an active participant in the publishing process, selecting the materials, topic sequence, and text length. This means that you produce a textbook that *exactly* fits your individual curriculum.

Quantitative Analysis
for Management

QUANTITATIVE METHODS AND APPLIED STATISTICS SERIES

ALLYN AND BACON

Barry Render, Consulting Editor
Roy E. Crummer Graduate School of Business, Rollins College

Readings in Production and Operations Management: A Productivity Approach
Ahmadian, Afifi, and Chandler

Introduction to Operations Research Techniques, Second Edition
Daellenbach, George, and McNickle

Managing Production: The Adventure
Fulmer

Business Forecasting, Fourth Edition
Hanke and Reitsch

Production and Operations Management: Strategies and Tactics, Third Edition
Heizer and Render

Cases in Business Statistics
Klimberg, Arnold, and Berger

Cases and Readings in Production and Operations Management
Latona and Nathan

Management Science, Fourth Edition
Moore, Lee, and Taylor

Micro Management Science: Microcomputer Applications of Management Science, Second Edition
Lee and Shim

AB:QM Version 3.0 Software
Lee

Service Operations Management
Murdick, Render, and Russell

Applied Statistics, Fourth Edition
Neter, Wasserman, and Whitmore

Microcomputer Software for Management Science and Operations Management, Second Edition
Render, Stair, Attaran, and Foeller

Principles of Operations Management: Building and Managing World Class Operations
Render and Heizer

Quantitative Analysis for Management, Fifth Edition
Render and Stair

Cases and Readings in Management Science, Second Edition
Render, Stair, and Greenberg

Production and Operations Management: A Self-Correcting Approach, Third Edition
Stair and Render

Operations Strategy
Stonebraker and Leong

Introduction to Management Science, Fourth Edition
Taylor

Brief Business Statistics
Watson, Billingsley, Croft, and Huntsberger

Statistics for Management and Economics, Fifth Edition
Watson, Billingsley, Huntsberger, and Croft

AB:POM Version 3.3 Software
Weiss

Production and Operations Management, Second Edition
Weiss and Gershon

A User's Guide to Business MYSTAT
Young

FIFTH EDITION

Annotated Instructor's Edition

Quantitative Analysis for Management

BARRY RENDER

Charles Harwood Distinguished Professor of Management Science
Roy E. Crummer Graduate School of Business, Rollins College

RALPH M. STAIR, Jr.

Professor of Information and Management Sciences
Florida State University

Allyn and Bacon

BOSTON   LONDON   TORONTO   SYDNEY   TOKYO   SINGAPORE

Editor in Chief, Business and Economics: Richard Wohl
Series Editorial Assistant: Jennifer Strada
Production Administrator: Marjorie Payne
Text Designer: Deborah Schneck
Cover Administrator: Linda Dickinson
Composition Buyer: Linda Cox
Manufacturing Buyer: Megan Cochran

ISBN: 0-205-15380-1

Printed in the United States of America

10 9 8 7 6 5 4 3 2 1   99 98 97 96 95 94

Brief Contents

1 Introduction to Quantitative Analysis   1

2 Probability Concepts   25

3 Probability Distributions   47

4 Forecasting   81

5 Fundamentals of Decision Theory   137

6 Decision Trees and Utility Theory   177

7 Statistical Quality Control   223

8 Inventory Control Models: I   249

9 Inventory Control Models: II   277

10 Linear Programming: Graphical and Computer Methods   337

11 Linear Programming Applications: With Computer Analyses in AB:QM, STORM, LINDO and What's*Best!*   387

12 Linear Programming: The Simplex Method   433

13 Linear Programming: Sensitivity Analysis and Duality   479

14 Transportation and Assignment Problems   515

15 Integer Programming, Goal Programming, and the Branch and Bound Method   585

16 Waiting Lines: Queuing Theory   635

17 Simulation   677

18 Network Models   723

19 Markov Analysis   793

MODULES

A Mathematical Tools: Determinants and Matrices   825
B Game Theory   835
C Dynamic Programming   847
D Decision Theory and the Normal Distribution   859
E Multifactor Decision Making   869
F Using AB:QM   881

APPENDIXES   891

Applications of QA Boxes

The Indispensable Role of Management Science at Reynolds Metals Company   5

Using QA to Clean Up the Big Apple   8

Qantas Airways   35

Using Probability Distributions to Search for Sunken Gold   61

Flood Forecasting at NOAA   108

Using Decision Theory in Forest Management   149

Testing Student Athletes for Drug Use: A Decision-Making Model   184

Decision Trees in Selecting Drilling Sites   188

How Velcro Got Hooked on Quality   227

Stalking Six Sigma at Motorola   230

Using Expert Systems in Inventory Management and Logistics   253

Inland Steel Uses Systems Contracts to Control Inventory Costs   261

Blue Bell Trims Its Inventory   265

Using Just-in-Time (JIT) Principles to Improve Ecuador's Health Care Delivery System   308

Linear Programming at New England Apple Products   343

Selecting Tenants in a Shopping Mall   348

Manpower Planning at United Airlines with LP   359

Crew Pairing Optimization at American Airlines   406

Finding Fast Algorithms Means Better Airline Service   465

Linear Programming at Dairyman's Cooperative   491

Optimizing Wood Procurement in Cabinet Manufacturing   494

Transportation Problem for Irish Pharmaceutical Distributor   529

Moving Sand with the Transportation Approach   538

Scheduling American League Umpires with the Assignment Model   556

Selling Seats at American Airlines Using Integer Programming   591

An Integer Programming System for Assigning Classes to Rooms   597

Branch and Bound Technique for Establishing Insurance Sales Territories   606

A Goal Programming Model for Prison Expenditures in Virginia   620

Queuing Theory at Eastman Kodak   642

Queuing up Customers on L. L. Bean's Phone Network   645

Simulating Canadian National Railways Line Capacity   697

Simulating Automation at the U.S. Postal Service   700

The Integration of Simulation and Other Models for Netherlands Water Planning   704

Using Markov Analysis to Forecast Long-Term Care   807

Dynamic Programming at Weyerhaeuser   849

Using Dynamic Programming to Assist in the Scheduling of Operation Desert Storm Airlift Operations   854

Transparency Masters

1-1   Overview of Quantitative Analysis
1-2   The Decision-Making Process
1-3   The Evolution of QA
1-4   The Quantitative Analysis Approach
1-5   Models and the Techniques of Scientific Management
1-6   Advantages of Using Models
1-7   Using Models: Some Suggestions
1-8   Possible Problems
1-9   Roadblocks to Be Faced in Defining a Problem
1-10   Four Difficulties Faced in Using Mathematical Models
1-11   Limitations of Models
1-12   Overview of Artificial Intelligence
1-13   Expert System Development
1-14   The Use of an Expert System

2-1   Chapters That Use Probability
2-2   Fundamental Probability Concepts
2-3   Mutually Exclusive Events
2-4   Addition Law for Events That Are Mutually Exclusive
2-5   Addition Law for Events That Are Not Mutually Exclusive
2-6   Joint Probabilities
2-7   Conditional Probabilities
2-8   Using Bayes's Process

3-1   Examples of Random Variables
3-2   Random Variables for Outcomes That Are Not Numbers
3-3   Probability Distributions
3-4   Continuous Probability Distributions
3-5   Discrete Probability Distributions
3-6   Uniform Probability Density Function
3-7   Binomial Probability Distribution
3-8   Sample Poisson Distribution
3-9   Normal Distribution with Different Values
3-10   Normal Distribution with Different Values

3-11   Three Common Areas Under Normal Curves
3-12   Negative Exponential Distribution

4-1   Outline of Forecasting Topics
4-2   Eight Steps to Forecasting
4-3   The Least Squares Method for Finding the Best Fitting Straight Line
4-4   Four Values of the Correlation Coefficient
4-5   Measures of Accuracy and Error
4-6   Forecasting Time Horizons

5-1   Steps in Decision Theory
5-2   Decision-Making Environments
5-3   Decision Making Under Risk
5-4   Decision Making Under Uncertainty
5-5   Thompson's Maximax Decision
5-6   Thompson's Maximin Decision
5-7   Thompson's Equally Likely Decision
5-8   Thompson's Criterion of Realism Decision
5-9   Joe's Stocking Decision for *Chicago Tribunes*

6-1   Fundamentals of Decision Theory
6-2   Analyzing Problems with Decision Trees: The Five Steps
6-3   Thompson's Decision Tree
6-4   A Decision Involving Conducting a Market Survey
6-5   Probability Revisions Given a Negative Survey
6-6   Standard Gamble and the Utility of $5,000
6-7   Utility Curve for Jane Dickson
6-8   Preferences for Risk

7-1   Definitions of Quality
7-2   The Dimensions of Quality
7-3   The Integral Role of QC in the Organization
7-4   Total Quality Control in the U.S. vs. Japan
7-5   Total Quality Control in the U.S. vs. Japan
7-6   Steps to Follow Using Control Charts

8-1   Inventory Management Techniques
8-2   Inventory as an Important Asset
8-3   Inventory Planning and Control
8-4   The Inventory Process
8-5   The Functions of Inventory
8-6   The Two Basic Questions
8-7   Inventory Cost Factors
8-8   Determining Inventory Holding Costs
8-9   EOQ Basic Assumptions
8-10   Inputs and Outputs of the EOQ Models
8-11   Inventory Level Over Time
8-12   Costs as a Function of Order Quantity
8-13   The Reorder Point (ROP) Curve
8-14   Fixed Period Models

9-1   Inventory Control Models: II
9-2   Inventory Level Over Time: Production Run Model
9-3   EOQ Without the Instantaneous Receipt Assumption
9-4   Quantity Discount Steps
9-5   Total Cost Curve and Computations for Brass Department Store
9-6   Planned Shortages
9-7   The Use of Safety Stock
9-8   Total Cost for ABCO
9-9   Summary of ABC Analysis
9-10   ABC Inventory Analysis
9-11   ABC Inventory Policies
9-12   Benefits of MRP
9-13   Material Structure Tree for Item A
9-14   Net Material Requirements Plan, Including AA
9-15   MRP Schedule
9-16   MRP Planning Sheet
9-17   The Kanban System

10-1   Outline: Linear Programming
10-2   Examples of Successful LP Applications
10-3   Requirements of a Linear Programming Problem
10-4   Table 10.1 Flair Furniture Company Data
10-5   Flair Furniture Company Constraints
10-6   Flair Furniture Company Feasible Region
10-7   Flair Furniture Company Iso-Profit Lines
10-8   Flair Furniture Company Solution
10-9   Special Cases in L.P.
10-10   A Problem with No Feasible Solution
10-11   A Solution Region That Is Unbounded to the Right

10-12   A Problem with a Redundant Constraint
10-13   An Example of Alternate Optimal Solutions

12-1   Simplex Steps for Maximization
12-2   Flair Furniture Company's Feasible Region and Corner Points
12-3   Flair Furniture's Initial Simplex Tableau
12-4   Pivot Row and Pivot Number Identified in the Initial Simplex Tableau
12-5   Completed Second Simplex Tableau for Flair Furniture
12-6   Pivot Row, Pivot Column, and Pivot Number Identified in the Second Simplex Tableau
12-7   Calculating the Nex X_1 Row for Flair's Third Tableau
12-8   Final Simplex Tableau for the Flair Furniture Problem
12-9   Simplex Steps for Minimization

13-1   Sensitivity Analysis
13-2   Changes in the Technological Coefficients for the High Note Sound Company
13-3   Shadow Prices
13-4   A Comparison of the Primal and Dual Optimal Tableaus

14-1   Transportation Solution Techniques
14-2   Transportation Problem
14-3   Transportation Costs
14-4   Transportation Table
14-5   Transportation Table
14-6   Transportation Table
14-7   Initial Solution Using the Northwest Corner Rule
14-8   Transportation Table
14-9   The Stepping-Stone Method
14-10   Stepping-Stone Method: Tracing a Closed Path for the Des Moines to Cleveland Route
14-11   MODI Method: 5 Steps
14-12   Special Problems in Transportation Method
14-13   The Assignment Method Algorithm
14-14   Blank Assignment Table
14-15   Assignment Table
14-16   Assignment Table

15-1   Mathematical Programming Extensions
15-2   Integer Programming Techniques

15-3   Harrison Electric Problem
15-4   Harrison Electric Problem
15-5   Types of Integer Programming Problems
15-6   Goal Programming (vs. LP)
15-7   Analysis of the First Goal
15-8   Analysis of the First and Second Goals
15-9   Analysis of All Four Priority Goals
15-10   The Initial Goal Programming Tableau
15-11   The Second Goal Programming Tableau
15-12   The Final Solution to Harrison Electric's Goal Program

16-1   Outline: Waiting Line Models
16-2   Queuing Costs and Service Levels
16-3   Characteristics of a Waiting Line System
16-4   Two Examples of the Poisson Distribution for Arrival Times
16-5   Basic Queuing System Configurations
16-6   Two Examples of the Exponential Distribution for Service Times
16-7   Assumptions of the Basic Queuing Model
16-8   Measures of Performance of the Queuing System

17-1   Outline: Simulation
17-2   The Process of Simulation
17-3   Advantages of Simulation
17-4   Disadvantages of Simulation
17-5   The Monte Carlo Simulation Technique
17-6   Graphical Representation of the Cumulative Probability Distribution for Radial Tires
17-7   Table of Random Numbers
17-8   Flow Diagram for Simkin's Inventory Example

18-1   Network Models
18-2   Questions That May Be Addressed by PERT and CPM
18-3   Project Planning, Scheduling, and Controlling
18-4   The Six Steps Common to PERT and CPM
18-5   Advantages of PERT/CPM
18-6   Limitations of PERT/CPM
18-7   Network for General Foundry, Inc.
18-8   Beta Probability Distribution with Three Time Estimates
18-9   Time Estimates (in weeks) for General Foundry, Inc.
18-10   General Foundry's Latest Start (LS) and Latest Finish (LF) Times

18-11   Results of PERT; Activities Along Critical Path
18-12   Pert Time Estimates
18-13   PERT Work Sheet
18-14   Probability of Project Completion
18-15   The Importance of Dummy Activities
18-16   PERT and Budgeting
18-17   Budget Ranges for General Foundry, Inc.
18-18   Project Crashing with CPM
18-19   Crash and Normal Times and Costs
18-20   Minimal Spanning Tree
18-21   Maximal Flow
18-22   Shortest Route

19-1   Assumptions of Markov Analysis
19-2   The Markov Process
19-3   Predicting Future States
19-4   Equilibrium Conditions
19-5   Number of Periods to Reach Equilibrium

A-1   Matrix Addition
A-2   Matrix Subtraction
A-3   Matrix Multiplication

B-1   Game Theory Assumptions
B-2   Solution Strategies for Game Theory
B-3   Store X's Payoff Matrix
B-4   The Minimax Procedure
B-5   Mixed Strategy Games
B-6   Procedures for Solving Two-Person, Zero Sum Games

C-1   Steps of Dynamic Programming
C-2   The Highway Map Between Rice and Dixieville
C-3   Solution for the Three-Stage Problem
C-4   Dynamic Programming Terminology

D-1   Marginal Analysis and the Normal Distribution
D-2   Normal Distribution for Barclay's Demand
D-3   Barclay's Opportunity Loss Function
D-4   Expected Value of Perfect Information

E-1   Evaluations of AA, EDS, and PW
E-2   Decision Hierarchy for Computer System Selection
E-3   Scale for Pairwise Comparison

F-1   Main Menu of AB:QM
F-2   AB:QM Commands
F-3   Main Menu for STORM

Preface

About the Annotated Instructor's Edition

Quantitative Analysis for Management, Fifth Edition, was the first book in the field of quantitative methods to have an Annotated Instructor's Edition. This version of the text, available only to instructors, includes the complete student text, with teaching annotations, plus an Instructor's Section. Neither the teaching annotations nor the Instructor's Section appear in the student edition.

We have developed this unique edition so instructors will have all of the information related to their teaching program in one single volume, rather than in a variety of different sources. In addition, this format has allowed us to more fully integrate and coordinate the student text with the many supplements available to instructors.

Instructor's Section

The 273-page Instructor's Section, which appears at the beginning of the Annotated Instructor's Edition, can be readily identified by gray thumb tabs that appear along the outside edges of all pages. We have organized the material in this section by text chapter, each of which is divided into learning objectives, teaching suggestions, notes for using videos, alternate examples, answers to questions and complete solutions to problems, and notes on the case studies.

Teaching Suggestions. The first section within each chapter provides an overview of the chapter contents. We offer suggested lecture topics, ideas for treating particular points that frequently trouble students, and discussions of how much emphasis should be put on special topics.

Instructor's Video Guide. This section provides a summary of each video segment that accompanies the text, along with teaching suggestions for using them with the text and incorporating them into your class.

Answers to Discussion Questions and Solutions to Problems. The third section within each chapter contains answers to questions and complete solutions to all chapter and data set problems, including any appropriate computer printouts. We believe instructors will find this section extremely helpful for responding to students' questions during class.

Case Solutions. The final section of each chapter in the Instructor's Section contains solutions to end-of-chapter cases. We provide a complete solution of each case.

Teaching Annotations

Annotations for instructors are located in color in the margins in the Annotated Instructor's Edition of the text. The notes provide a means for instructors to coordinate the use of all teaching materials quickly and easily. They do not appear in the student edition.

Answers to Problems. Numerical answers are shown in the margin beside problems where appropriate and thus provide a handy reference for instructors. More complete solutions to the problems (including graphs, tableaus and charts) can be found in the Instructor's Section.

Alternate Examples. In the Annotated Instructor's Edition (AIE) are alternate examples. New to this edition, these examples are in place of or in addition to the examples and applications found throughout the book. This should make lecturing easy for both beginning and experienced quantitative analysis instructors. Where to use these alternate examples has been placed in the margin of the AIE.

Applicable Problems. In the margin of most major sections of the annotated instructor's edition (AIE) is a list of the applicable problems. These problems are the ones that require the material in the section to solve. This allows instructors to quickly determine what problems to assign to students after certain material is covered in the book.

Teaching Suggestions. For many topics in the text, the margin notes provide references to specific suggestions in the Instructor's Section. Here, our intent is to help instructors reduce the amount of time required to incorporate the suggestions into class lectures.

Data Disk File Names. Numerous problems in the student edition are marked either with a computer logo or are identified as data set problems. This indicates that the data set for the problem is available on a disk to eliminate the time-consuming task of keying the data into our software progam, AB:QM. The margin notes in the Annotated Instructor's Edition provide the file name next to each problem in order to allow instructors to easily access the files.

Case Notes. Margin notes for the case studies provide cross-references to the case study and solutions found in the Instructor's Section.

Transparency Master References. Margin notes provide references to specific transparency masters at the point where each can be most appropriately used. Both the transparency master title and number is included. Our goal is to facilitate the use of the transparency masters and to enhance classroom discussion of difficult concepts.

Video Notes. Annotations at the appropriate *Applications of QA* boxes tie the material to specific segments in our two video packages: selections from the Edelman Award Winners of The Institute of Management Sciences and selections from "For All Practical Purposes" by the Consortium of Mathematics and Its Applications. Each video is identified by the logo of the appropriate tape. These logos do not appear in the student edition. Our objective here is to assist instructors in incorporating this unique video component into the course.

Author Prepared. It is important to point out that all materials in the Instructor's Section and the margin annotations have been developed by the text authors. By doing so, we have been able to ensure accuracy and consistency throughout the extensive teaching package that is available. Our goal has been to present one complete and fully integrated teaching package.

Additional Supplements for Instructors

In addition to the Annotated Instructor's Edition, *Quantitative Analysis for Management,* Fifth Edition, has numerous other supplements for instructors.

Test Bank. The test bank contains almost 1,000 multiple-choice and true-false questions and problems. Within these questions and problems are a group directly related to interpreting computer output. The test bank was prepared by Michael Hanna at the University of Houston. It has been thoroughly updated to reflect the changes in the fifth edition.

Computerized Test Bank. The test bank items are also available through Allyn and Bacon's computerized testing program, the A&B Test Manager Plus. The computerized test bank can be ordered for IBM and compatible systems in either a $5\frac{1}{4}$" or $3\frac{1}{2}$" format.

Transparency Masters. This package includes more than 200 figures, formulas, and definitions. One-third are from the text, while the remaining two-thirds are new. It is available free to adopters of the text.

Videocassettes. This is the first text in quantitative analysis to provide adopters with free, integrated videos. Tapes from two different sources are available. The first set of tapes, available through an agreement with The Institute of Management Sciences (TIMS) and its College on the Practice of Management Science, consists of three volumes of edited segments from their Franz Edelman Award winning video library. Each is discussed in an *Applications of QA* box in the text. Included are:

Volume I:	Polishing the Big Apple	(Chapter 1)
	Blue Bell Inventory	(Chapter 8)
	United Airlines Manpower	(Chapter 10)
	Netherlands Water Planning	(Chapter 17)
	Canadian Railroad	(Chapter 17)
	Weyerhaeuser	(Module C)
Volume II:	Introduction to Edelman Awards	
	Reynolds Metals Company	(Chapter 1)
	Citgo Petroleum	
	L. L. Bean Company	(Chapter 16)
Volume III:	Introduction to Edelman Awards	
	Columbus-America Discovery Group	(Chapter 3)
	IBM	(Chapter 8)
	American Airlines	(Chapter 11)
	American Airlines Decision Technologies	(Chapter 15)
	United States Postal Service	(Chapter 17)
	Military Airlift Command	(Module C)

An additional video, available through an agreement with the Consortium for Mathematics and Its Applications (COMAP), consists of edited material from their series, "For All Practical Purposes," which was produced for educational television with major funding by The Annenberg/CPB Project. Within this tape, three specific applications have been integrated into the text through *Applications of QA* boxes. These are Apollo 11 Launch (Chapter 1), New England Apple (Chapter 10), Faster Algorithms at American Air (Chapter 12), Quality Control: A. Frito Lay, B. Deming (Chapter 7).

Data Disk. The data disk contains files for all computer-solvable text problems. This data disk is available in either $5\frac{1}{4}''$ or $3\frac{1}{2}''$ formats and can be used with our AB:QM software package. The data disk also can be ordered from Allyn and Bacon by adopters who wish to copy it for student use.

Versions of this Text Available for Students

Quantitative Analysis for Management, Fifth Edition, can be ordered through bookstores in one of these ways:

- Text only
- Text with AB:QM software ($5\frac{1}{4}''$ format)
- Text with AB:QM software ($3\frac{1}{2}''$ format)
- Text with PC LINDO software ($5\frac{1}{4}''$ format)

- Text with PC LINDO software (3 ½″ format)

- Text with Personal STORM 4.0 Software
  (Manual with both 5 ¼″ and 3 ½″ disks)

- Text with STORM Management Science 1.0 Software
  (Manual with both 5 ¼″ and 3 ½″ disks)

Supplement for Students

Study Guide. The *Study Guide* for students has been prepared by John Harpell of West Virginia University. It contains key points and questions (with answers) as well as worked solutions to selected text problems.

1
Introduction to Quantitative Analysis

LEARNING OBJECTIVES

After completing this chapter, students will be able to:

1. Describe the quantitative analysis approach.
2. Understand the application of quantitative analysis in a real situation.
3. Discuss possible problems in using quantitative analysis.
4. Understand how computers can be used to perform quantitative analysis.

TEACHING SUGGESTIONS

Teaching Suggestion 1.1: Importance of Qualitative Factors.

Section 1.2 gives students an overview of quantitative analysis. In this section, a number of qualitative factors, including federal legislation and new technology, are discussed. Students can be asked to discuss other qualitative factors that could have an impact on quantitative analysis. Waiting lines and project planning can be used as examples. This is also a good place to use the overview video of management science.

Teaching Suggestion 1.2: Discussing Other Quantitative Analysis Problems.

Section 1.2 covers an application of the quantitative analysis approach. Students can be asked to describe other problems or areas that could benefit from quantitative analysis.

Teaching Suggestion 1.3: QA Applications in Chapter 1 and Throughout the Book.

Tell students to read the New York City sanitation story in Section 1.3. This is an example of a practical, dirty, down-to-earth problem involving perceptions and morals. Stress that real-world boxes (Applications of QA) will be found in every chapter. These boxes are great motivators and can lead to outside readings, that is, going to the source article and beyond.

Teaching Suggestion 1.4: Discussing Conflicting Viewpoints.

Possible problems in the QA approach are presented in this chapter. A discussion of conflicting viewpoints within the organization can help students understand this problem. For example, how many people should staff a registration desk at a university? Students will want more staff to reduce waiting time, while university administrators will want less staff to save money.

A discussion of these types of conflicting viewpoints will help students understand some of the problems of using quantitative analysis.

Teaching Suggestion 1.5: Difficulty of Getting Input Data.

A major problem in quantitative analysis is getting proper input data. Students can be asked to explain how they would get the information they need to determine inventory ordering or carrying costs. Role-playing with students assuming the parts of the analyst who needs inventory costs and the instructor playing the part of a veteran inventory manager can be fun and interesting. Students quickly learn that getting good data can be the most difficult part of using quantitative analysis.

Teaching Suggestion 1.6: Dealing with Resistance to Change.

Resistance to change is discussed in this chapter. Students can be asked to explain how they would introduce a new system or change within the organization. People resisting new approaches can be a major stumbling block to the successful implementation of quantitative analysis. Students can be asked why some people may be afraid of a new inventory control or forecasting system.

Teaching Suggestion 1.7: Expert Systems.

An important new topic in decision making is expert systems. Students should be aware of some of the major expert systems in medicine, tax analysis, mortgage lending, factory layout, and even in selecting the best forecasting model for a set of data.

VIDEO 1–1

The Indispensable Role of Management Science at Reynolds Metal Company

This TIMS video is based on one of the award-winning papers published in *Interfaces*. The video shows how the Reynolds Metals Company used quantitative analysis. The company, headquartered in Richmond, Virginia, is a Fortune 75 metals producer. In order to provide a more effective shipping operation, the Reynolds Metals Company employed integer programming to control shipping and reduce transportation costs. Using the annual shipping demand patterns, this quantitative analysis technique was able to improve on-time delivery of shipments and reduce freight costs by over $7 million annually.

VIDEO 1–2

Polishing the Big Apple: How Management Science Has Helped Make New York Streets Cleaner

This TIMS video is based on one of the award-winning papers published in *Interfaces*. A brief description of the application follows: Management science has played a critical role in increasing the ability of New York's Department of Sanitation to clean the city's streets. Not only has the department achieved five consecutive years of improved cleanliness ratings, but current levels are near record levels. The program has achieved its goals with a projected savings of about $12 million (refer to Section 1.3).

VIDEO 1–3

Management Science: Overview

This video segment is intended as a motivational overview of the subject of management science (MS). It is a great way to start an MS course because it presents a series of four actual organizations and problems in which MS was applied. Here are the four scenarios:

1. NASA's Apollo Moon Project. NASA Administrator Robert Freitag describes the application of management science systems in the 1969 Apollo 11 lunar mission. MS helped put the 300,000–400,000 pieces of the project together. It managed close to one-half million people in a $20 billion project.

2. Eastern Airlines' Scheduling of Planes. The scene is Logan Airport in Boston, before Eastern declared bankruptcy in 1991, with sixty Eastern flights scheduled each day. With limited personnel and aircraft resources, Eastern needs to turn its flights around and get them in the air quickly and efficiently.

3. Avis Auto Rental, Boston. The transportation problem is introduced in the context of having the right number of cars available in each city. How should Avis plan to accommodate people who return a car to a different city than the one they rented it in? The linear programming approach and Karmarkar's method are mentioned as solution techniques.

4. Store 24, Boston. This chain of 24-hour-a-day convenience stores uses the critical path method to start with a pile of bricks and end up with a fully stocked store in just fourteen weeks.

The video closes with a summary statement of how NASA relied on MS for scheduling, resource allocations, transportation, critical path, and queuing problems. MS replaced guesswork and hope.

Again, a good way to start the course!

SOLUTIONS TO QUESTIONS

1-1. Quantitative analysis involves the use of mathematical equations or relationships in analyzing a particular problem. In most cases, the results of quantitative analysis will be one or more numbers that can be used by managers and decision makers in making better decisions. Calculating rates of return, financial ratios from a balance sheet and profit and loss statement, determining the numbers of units that must be produced in order to break even, and many similar techniques are examples of quantitative analysis. Qualitative analysis involves the investigation of factors in a decision-making problem that cannot be quantified or stated in mathematical terms. The state of the economy, current or pending legislation, perceptions about a potential client, and other similar situations reveal the use of qualitative analysis. In most decision-making problems, both quantitative and qualitative analysis are used. In this book, however, we emphasize the techniques and approaches of quantitative analysis.

1-2. Quantitative analysis is the scientific approach to managerial decision making. This type of analysis is a logical and rational approach to making decisions. Emotions, guesswork, and whim are not part of the quantitative analysis approach. A number of organizations support the use of the scientific approach: the Institute of Management Science, Operation Research Society of America, Decision Sciences Institute, and Academy of Management.

1-3. Quantitative analysis is a step-by-step process that allows decision makers to investigate problems using quantitative techniques. The steps of the quantitative analysis process include defining the problem, developing a model, acquiring input data, developing a solution, testing the solution, analyzing the results, and implementing the results. In every case, the analysis begins with defining the problem. The problem could be too many stockouts, too many bad debts, or determining the products to produce that will result in the maximum profit for the organization. After the problems have been defined, the next step is to develop one or more models. These models could be inventory control models, models that describe the debt situation in the organization, and so on. Once the models have been developed, the next step is to acquire input data. In the inventory problem, for example, such factors as the annual demand, the ordering cost, and the carrying cost would be input data that are used by the model developed in the previous step. In determining the products to produce in order to maximize profits, the input data could be such things as the profitability for all the different products, the amount of time that is available at the various production departments that produce the products, and the amount of time it takes for each product to be produced in each production department. The next step is developing the solution. This requires the manipulation of the model in order to determine the best solution. Next, the results are tested, analyzed, and implemented. In the inventory control problem, this might result in determining and implementing a policy to order a certain amount of inventory at a specified time interval. For the problem of determining the best products to produce, this might mean testing, analyzing, and implementing a decision to produce a certain quantity of given products.

1-4. Although the formal study of quantitative analysis and the refinement of the tools and techniques of the scientific method has only occurred in the recent past, quantitative approaches to decision making have been in existence since the beginning of time. In 1900, Frederick W. Taylor developed the principles of the scientific approach. During World War II, quantitative analysis was intensified and used by the military. Because of the success of these techniques during World War II, increased interest after the war continued. Today, most large organizations employ a staff of operations research or management science personnel.

1-5. Model types include: scale model, physical model, and schematic model (which is a picture or drawing of reality). In this book, mathematical models will be used to describe mathematical relationships in solving quantitative-type problems.

In this question, the student is asked to develop two mathematical models. The student might develop a number of models that relate to finance, marketing, accounting, statistics, or other fields. The purpose of this part of the question is to have the student develop some type of mathematical relationship between variables that the student is familiar with.

1-6. Input data can come from company reports and documents, interviews with employees and other personnel, direct measurement, and sampling procedures. For many problems, a number of different sources are required to obtain data, and in some cases it is necessary to obtain the same data from different sources in order to check the accuracy and consistency of the input data. If the input data are not accurate, the results can be misleading and very costly to the organization. This concept is called "garbage in garbage out."

1-7. Implementation is the process of taking the solution and incorporating it into the company or organization. This is the final step in the quantitative analysis approach, and if a good job is not done with implementation, all of the effort expended on the previous steps can be wasted.

1-8. Sensitivity analysis and postoptimality analysis allow the decision maker to determine how the final solution to the problem will change when the input data or the model changes. This type of analysis is very important when the input data or the model has not been properly specified. A sensitive solution is one in which the results of the solution to the problem will change drastically or by a large amount with small changes in the data or the model. When the model is not sensitive, the results or solutions to the model will not change significantly with changes in the input data or the model. Models that are very sensitive require that the input data and the model itself be thoroughly tested to make sure that both are very accurate and consistent with the problem statement.

1-9. There are a large number of quantitative terms that may not be understood by managers. Examples include PERT, CPM, simulation, Monte Carlo method, mathematical programming, EOQ, and so on. The student should explain each of the four terms selected in his or her own words.

1-10. Many quantitative analysts enjoy building mathematical models and solving them to find the optimal solution to a problem. Others enjoy dealing with other technical aspects, for example, data analysis and collection, computer programming, or computations. The implementation process can involve political aspects, convincing people to trust the new approach or solutions, or the frustrations of getting a simple answer to work in a complex environment. Some people with strong analytical skills have weak interpersonal skills; since implementation challenges these "people" skills, it will not appeal to everyone. If analysts become involved with users and with the implementation environment, and can understand "where managers are coming from," they can better appreciate the difficulties of implementing what they have solved using QA.

1-11. Users need not become involved in technical aspects of the QA technique, *but* they should have an understanding of what the limitations of the model are, how it works (in a general sense), the jargon involved, and the ability to question the validity and sensitivity of an answer handed to them by an analyst.

1-12. Churchman meant that sophisticated mathematical solutions and proofs can be dangerous because people may be afraid to question them. Many people do not want to appear ignorant and question an elaborate mathematical model; yet, the whole model, its assumptions and its approach, may be incorrect.

1-13. An MIS can assist in implementation of QA techniques by its ability to integrate databases needed in forecasting, inventory, linear programming, and other models. It also allows managers to make quicker decisions through online interfaces. The more easily a manager can interact with the QA models, the more likely he or she is to use them.

2
Probability Concepts

LEARNING OBJECTIVES

After completing this chapter, students will be able to:

1. Understand the basic foundations of probability analysis, including the two laws of probability.
2. Understand the difference between mutually exclusive and collectively exhaustive events and be able to provide examples of each.
3. Describe events that are statistically dependent and events that are statistically independent.
4. Apply formulas for joint, marginal, and conditional probabilities under both dependent and independent conditions.
5. Use Bayes's theorem to establish posterior probabilities.

TEACHING SUGGESTIONS

Teaching Suggestion 2.1: Concept of Probabilities Ranging from 0 to 1.

People often misuse probabilities by such statements as, "I'm 110% sure we're going to win the big game." The two basic rules of probability should be stressed.

Teaching Suggestion 2.2: Where Do Probabilities Come From?

Students need to understand where probabilities come from. Sometimes they are subjective and based on personal experiences. Other times they are objectively based on logical observations such as the roll of a die. Often, probabilities are derived from historical data—*if* we can assume the future will be about the same as the past.

Teaching Suggestion 2.3: Confusion Over Mutually Exclusive and Collectively Exhaustive Events.

This concept is often foggy to even the best of students—even if they just completed a course in statistics. Use practical examples and drills to force the point home. The table at the end of Example 3 is especially useful.

Teaching Suggestion 2.4: Addition of Events That Are Not Mutually Exclusive.

The formula for adding events that are not mutually exclusive is $P(A \text{ or } B) = P(A) + P(B) - P(A \text{ and } B)$. Students must understand why we subtract $P(A \text{ and } B)$. Explain that the intersect has been counted twice.

Teaching Suggestion 2.5: Statistical Dependence with Visual Examples.

Figure 2.3 indicates that an urn contains 10 balls. This example works well to explain conditional probability of dependent events. An even better idea is to bring 10 golf balls to class. Six should be white and 4 orange (or green). Mark a big letter or number on each to correspond to Figure 2.3 and draw the balls from a clear bowl to make the point. You can also use the props to stress how random sampling expects previous draws to be replaced.

ALTERNATE EXAMPLES

Alternate Example 2.1: In the past 30 days, Roger's Rural Roundup has sold either 8, 9, 10, or 11 lottery tickets. It never sold fewer than 8 nor more than 11. Assuming the past is similar to the future, here are the probabilities:

SALES	NO. DAYS	PROBABILITY
8	10	.333
9	12	.400
10	6	.200
11	2	.067
Total	30	1.000

Alternate Example 2.2: Grades received for a course have a probability based on the professor's grading pattern. Here are Professor Ernie Forman's BA205 grades for the past five years:

OUTCOME	PROBABILITY
A	.25
B	.30
C	.35
D	.03
F	.02
Withdraw/drop	.05
	1.00

These grades are mutually exclusive and collectively exhaustive.

Alternate Example 2.3:

P(Drawing a 3 from a deck of cards) = 4/52 = 1/3
P(Drawing a club on the same draw) = 13/52 = 1/4

These are neither mutually exclusive nor collectively exhaustive.

Alternate Example 2.4: In Alternate Example 2.3 we looked at 3's and clubs. Here is the probability for 3 *or* club:

$$P(3 \text{ or Club}) = P(3) + P(\text{Club}) - P(3 \text{ and Club})$$
$$= 4/52 + 13/52 - 1/52$$
$$= 16/52 = 4/13$$

Alternate Example 2.5: A class contains 30 students. Ten are female (F) and U.S. citizens (U); 12 are male (M) and U.S. citizens; 6 are female and non-U.S. citizens (N); 2 are male and non-U.S. citizens.

A name is randomly selected from the class roster and it is female. What is the probability the student is a U.S. citizen?

$$P(FU) = 10/30 = .333$$
$$P(FN) = 6/30 = .200$$

$$P(MU) = 12/30 = .400$$
$$P(MN) = 2/30 = .067$$
$$P(F) = P(FU) + P(FN) = .333 + .200 = .533$$
$$P(M) = P(MU) + P(MN) = .400 + .067 = .467$$
$$P(U) = P(FU) + P(MU) = .333 + .400 = .733$$
$$P(N) = P(FN) + P(MN) = .200 + .067 = .267$$

By Bayes's law,

$$P(U \mid F) = \frac{P(FU)}{P(F)} = \frac{.333}{.533} = .625$$

Alternate Example 2.6: Your professor tells you that if you score an 85 or better on your midterm exam, there is a 90% chance you'll get an A for the course. You think you have only a 50% chance of scoring 85 or better. The probability that *both* your score is 85 or better *and* you receive an A in the course is:

$$P(A \text{ and } 85) = P(A \mid 85) \times P(85) = (.90)(.50) = .45$$
$$= 45\%$$

Alternate Example 2.7: An instructor is teaching two sections (classes) of calculus. Each class has 25 students, and on the surface, both classes appear identical. One class, however, consists of students who have all taken calculus in high school. The instructor has no idea which class is which. She knows that the probability of at least half the class getting A's on the first exam is only 25% in an average class, but 50% in a class with more math background.

A section is selected at random and quizzed. More than half the class received A's. Now, what is the revised probability the class was the advanced one?

P(Regular class chosen) = .5
P(Advanced class chosen) = .5
P(> 1/2 A's | regular class) = .25
P(> 1/2 A's | advanced class) = .50

P(> 1/2 A's and regular class)
$$= P(> 1/2 \text{ A's} \mid \text{regular}) \times P(\text{regular})$$
$$= (.25)(.5) = .125$$

P(> 1/2 A's and advanced class)
$$= P(> 1/2 \text{ A's} \mid \text{advanced}) \times P(\text{advanced})$$
$$= (.50)(.5) = .25$$

So, P(> 1/2 A's) = .125 + .25 = .375

$$P(\text{Advanced} \mid > 1/2 \text{ A's}) = \frac{P(\text{Advanced and } > 1/2 \text{ A's})}{P(> 1/2 \text{ A's})}$$

$$= \frac{.25}{.375} = 2/3$$

So there is a 66% chance the class tested was the advanced one.

SOLUTIONS TO DISCUSSION QUESTIONS AND PROBLEMS

2-1. There are two basic laws of probability. First, the probability of any event or state of nature occurring must be greater than or equal to zero and less than or equal to one. Secondly, the sum of the simple probabilities for all possible outcomes of the activity must equal one.

2-2. Events are mutually exclusive if only one of the events can occur on any one trial. Events are collectively exhaustive if the list of outcomes includes every possible outcome. An example of mutually exclusive events can be seen in flipping a coin. The outcome of any one trial can either be a head or a tail. Thus, the events of getting a head and a tail are mutually exclusive because only one of these events can occur on any one trial. This assumes, of course, that the coin does not land on its edge. The outcome of rolling the die is an example of events that are collectively exhaustive. In rolling a standard die, the outcome can be either 1, 2, 3, 4, 5, or 6. These six outcomes are collectively exhaustive because they include all possible outcomes. Again, it is assumed that the die will not land and stay on one of its edges.

2-3. Probability values can be determined both objectively and subjectively. When determining probability values objectively, some type of numerical or quantitative analysis is used. When determining probability values subjectively, a manager's or decision-maker's judgment and experience are used in assessing one or more probability values.

2-4. The probability of the intersection of two events is subtracted in summing the probability of the two events to avoid double counting. For example, if the same event is in both of the probabilities that are to be added, the probability of this event will be added twice unless the intersection of the two events is subtracted from the sum of the probability of the two events.

2-5. When events are dependent, the occurrence of one event does have an effect on the probability of the occurrence of the other event. When the events are independent, on the other hand, the occurrence of one of them has no effect on the probability of the occurrence of the other event. It is important to know whether or not events are dependent or independent because the probability relationships are slightly different in each case. In general, the probability relationships for any kind of independent events are simpler than the more generalized probability relationships for dependent events.

2-6. Bayes's theorem is a probability relationship that allows new information to be incorporated with prior probability values in order to obtain updated or posterior probability values. Bayes's theorem can be used whenever there is an existing set of probability values and new information is obtained that can be used to revise these probability values.

2-7. Probability revisions, using Bayes's theorem, can be useful in terms of managerial decision making. For example, Bayes's theorem can be used to incorporate the results of a marketing survey into existing probability values in order to obtain revised probability values given the results of the marketing survey. Bayes's theorem can also be used to incorporate the results of a pilot study into existing probability values in order to obtain revised probabilities given the outcome of the pilot study. In general, when managers obtain additional information relating to these probability values, Bayes's theorem can usually be used to allow decision makers to revise their probability assessments in light of the new information.

2-8.

GRADE	PROBABILITY
A	$.27\left(=\frac{80}{300}\right)$
B	$.25\left(=\frac{75}{300}\right)$
C	$.30\left(=\frac{90}{300}\right)$
D	$.10\left(=\frac{30}{300}\right)$
F	$.08\left(=\frac{25}{300}\right)$
	1.0

Thus, the probability of a student receiving a C in the course is .30 = 30%.

The probability of a student receiving a C may also be calculated using the following equation:

$$P(\text{of receiving a C}) = \frac{\text{Number of students receiving a C}}{\text{Total number of students}}$$

$$P(C) = \frac{90}{300}$$

$$= .30$$

2-9. **a.** $P(H) = \frac{1}{2} = .5$
  b. $P(T \mid H) = P(T) = .5$
  c. $P(TT) = P(T) \times P(T) = (.5)(.5) = .25$
  d. $P(TH) = P(T) \times P(H) = (.5)(.5) = .25$
  e. We first calculate $P(TH) = .25$, then calculate $P(HT) = (.5)(.5) = .25$. To find the probability of *either* one occurring, we simply add the two probabilities. The solution is .50.

  f. *At least* one head means that we have either *HT*, *TH*, or *HH*. Since each of these have a probability of .25, their total probability of occurring is .75. On the other hand, the complement of the outcome "at least one head" is "two tails." Thus, we could have also computed the probability from $1 - P(TT) = 1 - .25 = .75$.

2-10. The distribution of chips is as follows:

Red	8
Green	10
White	2
Total =	20

  a. Probability of drawing a white chip on the first draw is:

$$P(W) = \frac{2}{20} = \frac{1}{10} = .10$$

  b. Probability of drawing a white chip on the first draw and a red one on the second is:

$$P(WR) = P(W) \times P(R) \quad \text{[The two events are independent.]}$$
$$= \frac{2}{20} \times \frac{8}{20}$$
$$= (.10)(.40)$$
$$= .04$$

  c. $P(GG) = P(G) \times P(G)$
$$= \frac{10}{20} \times \frac{10}{20}$$
$$= (.5)(.5)$$
$$= .25$$

  d. $P(R \mid W) = P(R)$ [The events are independent and hence the conditional probability equals the marginal probability.]
$$= \frac{8}{20}$$
$$= .40$$

2-11. The distribution of the nails is as follows:

TYPE OF NAIL	NUMBER IN BIN
1 inch	651
2 inch	243
3 inch	41
4 inch	451
5 inch	333
Total	1,719

  a. The probability of getting a 4-inch nail is:

$$P(4) = \frac{451}{1,719}$$
$$= .26$$

  b. Probability of getting a 5-inch nail is:

$$P(5) = \frac{333}{1,719}$$
$$= .19$$

  c. Probability of getting a nail 3 inches or shorter is the probability of getting a nail 1 inch, 2 inches, or 3 inches in length. The probability is thus:

$P(1 \text{ or } 2 \text{ or } 3)$
$$= P(1) + P(2) + P(3)$$
$$= \frac{651}{1,719} + \frac{243}{1,719} + \frac{41}{1,719} \quad \begin{array}{l}\text{[The events are}\\ \text{mutually exclusive.]}\end{array}$$
$$= .38 + .14 + .02$$
$$= .54$$

2-12.

Total number of employees	= 1,000
Number involved in exercise	= 500
Number that did no exercising	= 500
Number that had colds	= 200
Number that did no exercising and had colds	= 155
Number that were involved in exercise programs and had colds	= 45

  a. Probability that an employee will have a cold next year is:

$$P(C) = \frac{\text{Number of people who had colds}}{\text{Total number of employees}}$$
$$= \frac{200}{1,000}$$
$$= .20$$

  b. Probability that an employee who is involved in an exercise program will get a cold is:

$$P(C \mid E) = \frac{P(CE)}{P(E)}$$
$$= \frac{45}{500} \quad \text{[by Bayes's theorem]}$$
$$= .09$$

  c. Probability that an employee who is not involved in an exercise program will get a cold is:

$$P(C \mid N) = \frac{P(CN)}{P(N)}$$
$$= \frac{155}{500}$$
$$= .31$$

d. No. If they were independent, then:

$$P(C|E) = P(C), \text{ but}$$

$$P(C|E) = \frac{45}{500} = .09$$

$$P(C) = \frac{200}{1,000}$$

$$= .2$$

Therefore, these events are dependent.

2-13. Probability of winning tonight's game

$$= \frac{\text{Number of wins}}{\text{Number of games}}$$

$$= \frac{12}{20}$$

$$= \frac{6}{10}$$

$$= .60$$

Probability that the team wins tonight is .60. The probability that the team wins tonight and draws a large crowd at tomorrow's game is a joint probability of dependent events. Let probability of winning be $P(W)$ and probability of drawing a large crowd be $P(L)$. Thus:

$$P(WL) = P(L|W) \times P(W)$$ [The probability of
$$= .90 \times .60$$ large crowd is .90 if
$$= .54$$ the team wins tonight.]

Thus, the probability of the team winning tonight and of there being a large crowd at tomorrow's game is .54.

2-14. The second draw is *not* independent of the first because the probabilities of each outcome depend on the rank (sophomore or junior) of the first student's name drawn. Let:

J_1 = junior on first draw
J_2 = junior on second draw
S_1 = sophomore on first draw
S_2 = sophomore on second draw

a. $P(J_1) = \frac{3}{10} = .3$
b. $P(J_2|S_1) = .3$
c. $P(J_2|J_1) = .8$
d. $P(S_1S_2) = P(S_2|S_1) \times P(S_1) = (.7)(.7) = .49$
e. $P(J_1J_2) = P(J_2|J_1) \times P(J_1) = (.8)(.3) = .24$
f. P (1 sophomore and 1 junior regardless of order) is $P(S_1J_2) + P(J_1S_2)$.

$$P(S_1J_2) = P(J_2|S_1) \times P(S_1) = (.3)(.7) = .21$$
$$P(J_1S_2) = P(S_2|J_1) \times P(J_1) = (.2)(.3) = .06$$

hence, $P(S_1J_2) + P(J_1S_2) = .21 + .06 = .27$.

2-15. Without any additional information, we assume that there is an equilikely probability that the soldier wandered into either oasis, so $P(\text{Abu Ilan}) = .50$ and $P(\text{El Kamin}) = .50$. Since the oasis of Abu Ilan has 20 Bedouins and 20 Farimas (a total population of 40 tribesmen), the probability of finding a Bedouin, given that you are in Abu Ilan, is $20/40 = .50$. Likewise, the probability of finding a Bedouin, given that you are in El Kamin, is $32/40 = .80$. Thus, $P(\text{Bedouin}|\text{Abu Ilan}) = .50$ $P(\text{Bedouin}|\text{El Kamin}) = .80$.

We now calculate joint probabilities:

$P(\text{Abu Ilan and Bedouin})$
$$= P(\text{Bedouin}|\text{Abu Ilan}) \times P(\text{Abu Ilan})$$
$$= (.50)(.50) = .25$$

$P(\text{El Kamin and Bedouin})$
$$= P(\text{Bedouin}|\text{El Kamin})$$
$$\times P(\text{El Kamin}) = (.80)(.50)$$
$$= .4$$

The total probability of finding a Bedouin is:

$$P(\text{Bedouin}) = .25 + .40 = .65$$

$P(\text{Abu Ilan}|\text{Bedouin})$
$$= \frac{P(\text{Abu Ilan and Bedouin})}{P(\text{Bedouin})} = \frac{.25}{.65} = .385$$

$P(\text{El Kamin}|\text{Bedouin})$
$$= \frac{P(\text{El Kamin and Bedouin})}{P(\text{Bedouin})} = \frac{.40}{.65} = .615$$

The probability the oasis discovered was Abu Ilan is now only .385. The probability the oasis is El Kamin is .615.

2-16. $P(\text{Abu Ilan})$ is .50; $P(\text{El Kamin})$ is .50.

$$P(\text{2-Bedouins}|\text{Abu Ilan}) = (.50)(.50) = .25$$
$$P(\text{2-Bedouins}|\text{El Kamin}) = (.80)(.80) = .64$$
$P(\text{Abu Ilan and 2-Bedouins})$
$$= P(\text{2-Bedouins}|\text{Abu Ilan}) P(\text{Abu Ilan})$$
$$= (.25)(.50)$$
$$= .125$$
$P(\text{El Kamin and 2-Bedouins})$
$$= P(\text{2-Bedouins}|\text{El Kamin}) P(\text{El Kamin})$$
$$= (.64)(.50)$$
$$= .32$$

Total probability of finding 2-Bedouins is $.125 + .32 = .445$.

$P(\text{Abu Ilan}|\text{2-Bedouins})$
$$= \frac{P(\text{Abu Ilan and 2-Bedouins})}{P(\text{2-Bedouins})} = \frac{.125}{.445} = .281$$

$P(\text{El Kamin}\,|\,\text{2-Bedouins})$

$= \dfrac{P(\text{El Kamin and 2-Bedouins})}{P(\text{2-Bedouins})} = \dfrac{.32}{.445} = .719$

These second revisions indicate that the probability the oasis was Abu Ilan is .281. The probability the oasis found was El Kamin is now .719.

2-17. $P(\text{adjusted}) = .8$; $P(\text{not adjusted}) = .2$

$P(\text{pass}\,|\,\text{adjusted}) = .9$; $P(\text{pass}\,|\,\text{not adjusted}) = .2$

$P(\text{adjusted and pass})$

$= P(\text{pass}\,|\,\text{adjusted}) \times P(\text{adjusted})$

$= (.9)(.8) = .72$

$P(\text{not adjusted and pass})$

$= P(\text{pass}\,|\,\text{not adjusted}) \times P(\text{not adjusted})$

$= (.2)(.2) = .04$

Total probability that part passes inspection

$= .72 + .04 = .76$

$P(\text{adjusted}\,|\,\text{pass})$

$= \dfrac{P(\text{adjusted and pass})}{P(\text{pass})} = \dfrac{.72}{.76} = .947$

The posterior probability the lathe tool is properly adjusted is .947.

2-18. $P(MB \text{ over } K) = \dfrac{3}{5} = .6$

$P(MB \text{ over } M) = \dfrac{4}{5} = .8$

$P(K \text{ over } MB) = \dfrac{2}{5} = .4$ [MB = Mama's Boys,

$P(K \text{ over } M) = \dfrac{1}{5} = .2$ K = The Killers, and

M = The Machos.]

$P(M \text{ over } MB) = \dfrac{1}{5} = .2$

$P(M \text{ over } K) = \dfrac{4}{5} = .8$

a. The probability that K will win every game is:

$P = P(K \text{ over } MB) \text{ and } P(K \text{ over } M)$

$P = (.4)(.2) = .08$

b. The probability that M will win at least one game is:

$P(M \text{ over } K) + P(M \text{ over } MB) - P(M \text{ over } K)$

$\times P(M \text{ over } MB)$

$= (.8) + (.2) - (.8)(.2)$

$= 1 - .16$

$= .84$

c. The probability is:

1. $[P(MB \text{ over } K) \text{ and } P(M \text{ over } MB)]$, or
2. $[P(MB \text{ over } M) \text{ and } P(K \text{ over } MB)]$

$P(1) = (.6)(.2) = .12$

$P(2) = (.8)(.4) = .32$

Probability $= P(1) + P(2)$

$= .12 + .32$

$= .44$

d. Probability $= 1 - $ winning every game

$= 1 - $ answer to part (a)

$= 1 - .08$

$= .92$

2-19. a. Probability $= P(K \text{ over } M) = .2$

b. Probability $= P(K \text{ over } MB) = .4$

c. Probability

$= [P(K \text{ over } M) \text{ and } P(MB \text{ over } K)] \text{ or}$

$[P(K \text{ over } MB) \text{ and } P(M \text{ over } K)]$

$= (.2)(.6) + (.4)(.8)$

$= .12 + .32$

$= .44$

d. Probability $= [P(K \text{ over } MB) \text{ and } P(K \text{ over } M)]$

$= (.4)(.2)$

$= .08$

e. Probability $= P(MB \text{ over } K) \text{ and } P(M \text{ over } K)$

$= (.6)(.8)$

$= .48$

f. No. They do not appear to be a very good team.

2-20. Probability of Dick hitting the bull's-eye:

$P(D) = .90$

Probability of Sally hitting the bull's-eye:

$P(S) = .95$

a. Probability of either Dick or Sally hitting the bull's-eye:

$P(D \text{ or } S) = P(D) + P(S) - P(D)P(S)$

$= .90 + .95 - (.90)(.95)$

$= .995$

b. $P(D \text{ and } S) = P(D)P(S)$

$= (.9)(.95)$

$= .855$

c. It was assumed that the events are independent. This assumption seems to be justified. Dick's performance shouldn't influence Sally's performance.

2-21. In the sample of 1,000, 650 people were from Laketown and 350 from River City. Thirteen of those with cancer were from Laketown. Six of those with cancer were from River City.

a. Probability of a person from Laketown having cancer:

$$P = \frac{13}{650}$$

$$= \frac{1}{50}$$

$$= .020$$

Probability of a person from River City having cancer:

$$P = \frac{6}{350}$$

$$= .017$$

b. I would rather live in River City.

2-22. $P(A \mid B) = \dfrac{P(B \mid A)P(A)}{P(B \mid A)P(A) + P(B \mid \overline{A})P(\overline{A})}$

where A = a fair die,
   $\overline{A}$ = an unfair die, and
   B = getting a 3.

$$P(A \mid B) = P(F \mid 3) = \frac{P(3 \mid F)P(F)}{P(3 \mid F)P(F) + P(3 \mid L)P(L)}$$

$$= \frac{(.166)(.5)}{(.166)(.5) + (.6)(.5)}$$

$$= \frac{.083}{.083 + .3}$$

$$= .22$$

Therefore:

$$P(L) = 1 - .22 = .78$$

3
Probability Distributions

LEARNING OBJECTIVES

After completing this chapter, students will be able to:

1. Describe what a random variable is and provide examples of both discrete and continuous random variables.
2. Explain the difference between discrete and continuous probability distributions.
3. Calculate the expected value and variance of a discrete probability distribution.
4. Use the binomial table to solve problems.
5. State the plus or minus 1, 2, and 3 standard deviation areas under the normal curve.
6. Use the normal table.
7. Explain the meaning of Z in the normal distribution.

TEACHING SUGGESTIONS

Teaching Suggestion 3.1:   Concept of Random Variables.

Students often have problems understanding the concept of random variables. Instructors need to take this abstract idea and provide several examples to drive home the point. Table 3.1 has some useful examples of both discrete and continuous random variables.

Teaching Suggestion 3.2:   Expected Value of a Probability Distribution.

A probability distribution is often described by its mean and variance. These important terms should be discussed with such practical examples as heights or weights of students. But students need to be reminded that even if most of the men in class (or the United States) have heights between 5'6" and 6'2", there is still some small probability of outliers.

Teaching Suggestion 3.3:   Bell-Shaped Curve.

Stress how important the normal distribution is to a large number of processes in our lives (for example, filling boxes of cereal with 32 ounces of cornflakes). Each normal distribution depends on the mean and standard deviation. Discuss Figures 3.7 and 3.8 to show how these relate to the shape and position of a normal distribution.

Teaching Suggestion 3.4:   Three Symmetrical Areas under the Normal Curve.

Figure 3.9 is very important, and students should be encouraged to truly comprehend the meanings of ±1, 2, and 3 standard deviation symmetrical areas. They should especially know that managers often speak of 95% and 99% confidence intervals, which roughly refer to ±2 and 3 standard deviation graphs. Clarify that 95% confidence is actually ±1.96 standard deviations, while ±3 standard deviations is actually a 99.7% spread.

Teaching Suggestion 3.5: Using the Normal Table to Answer Probability Questions.

The I.Q. example in Figure 3.10 is a particularly good way to treat the subject since everyone can relate to it. Students are typically curious about the chances of reaching certain scores. Go through *at least* a half-dozen examples until it's clear that everyone can use the table. Students get especially confused answering questions such as $P(X < 85)$ since the standard normal table shows only right-hand side Z values. The symmetry requires special care.

Teaching Suggestion 3.6: Incentive to Learn These Probability Concepts.

Students need an incentive to retain material in a basic chapter such as this. Remind them that the Poisson and exponential distributions will be seen again and used in Chapter 16, while the normal distribution will be seen in Chapters 7, 9, and 18, and Module D.

VIDEO 3–1

Search for the SS *Central America:* Mathematical Treasure Hunting

This TIMS video is based on one of the award-winning papers published in *Interfaces* in 1992. A brief description follows:

In 1857, while carrying passengers and gold from California to New York, the SS *Central America* sank in a hurricane, taking gold bars and coins worth an estimated 400 million dollars to the ocean bottom almost 8,000 feet below. Some 425 people, including the captain, lost their lives. In 1989, after three summers of effort at sea, the Columbus-America Discovery Group recovered one ton of gold bars and coins from the wreck. In 1985, Lawrence Stone was assigned the task of developing a probability distribution for the location of the *Central America*. This distribution was used to construct the search plan that found the wreck. The methods used to develop the distribution were based on classical OR techniques and included a combination of historical, statistical, analytic, and subjective methods.

ALTERNATE EXAMPLES

Alternate Example 3.1: A statistics class was asked if it believed that all tests on the Monday following the football game win over their archrival should be automatically postponed. The results were:

strongly agree	40
agree	30
neutral	20
disagree	10
strongly disagree	0
	100

We transform the above into a numeric score, using the random variable scale:

strongly agree	5
agree	4
neutral	3
disagree	2
strongly disagree	1

Probability distribution for the results:

OUTCOME	PROBABILITY, PX
strongly agree	0.4 = 40/100
agree	0.3 = 30/100
neutral	0.2 = 20/100
disagree	0.1 = 10/100
strongly disagree	0.0 = 0/100
	1.0 = 100/100

This discrete probability distribution is computed using the relative frequency approach. Probabilities are shown in graph form below.

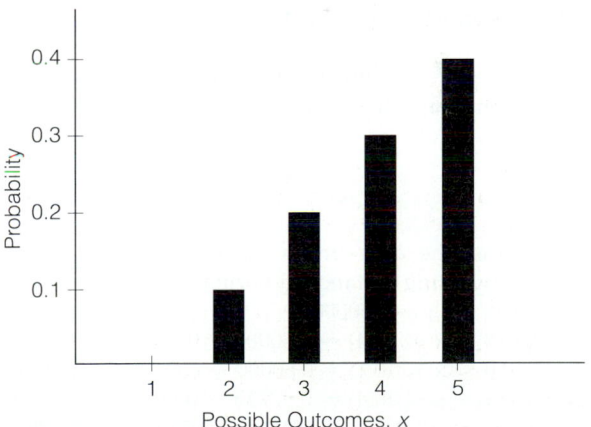

Alternate Example 3.2: Here is how the expected outcome can be computed for the question in Alternate Example 3.1.

$$E(x) = \sum_{i=1}^{5} x_i P(x_i) = x_1 P(x_1) + x_2 P(x_2) + x_3 P(x_3)$$
$$+ x_4 P(x_4) + x_5 P(x_5)$$
$$= 5(0.4) + 4(0.3) + 3(0.2) + 2(0.1) + 1(0)$$
$$= 4.0$$

The expected outcome of 4.0 implies that the average response is "agree."

Alternate Example 3.3: Here is how variance is computed for the question in Alternate Example 3.1.

$$\text{Variance} = \sum_{i=1}^{5} (x_i - E(x))^2 P(x_i)$$

$$= (5 - 4)^2(.4) + (4 - 4)^2(.3) + (3 - 4)^2(.2)$$
$$\quad + (2 - 4)^2(.1)$$

$$= (1)^2(.4) + (0)^2(.3) + (-1)^2(.2) + (-2)^2(.1)$$

$$= 0.4 + 0.0 + 0.2 + 0.4$$

$$= 1.0$$

The standard deviation is

$$\sigma = \sqrt{\text{Variance}}$$
$$= \sqrt{1}$$
$$= 1$$

Alternate Example 3.4: The length of the rods coming out of our new cutting machine can be said to approximate a normal distribution with a mean of 10 inches and a standard deviation of 0.2 inch. Find the probability that a rod selected randomly will have a length

A. of less than 10.0 inches
B. between 10.0 and 10.4 inches
C. between 10.0 and 10.1 inches
D. between 10.1 and 10.4 inches
E. between 9.9 and 9.6 inches
F. between 9.9 and 10.4 inches
G. between 9.886 and 10.406 inches

First compute the standard normal distribution, z-value:

$$z = \frac{x - \mu}{\sigma}$$

Next, find the area under the curve for the given z-value by using a standard normal distribution table.

A. $P(x < 10.0) = 0.50000$
B. $P(10.0 < x < 10.4) = 0.50000 - 0.97725 = 0.47725$
C. $P(10.0 < x < 10.1) = 0.50000 - 0.69146 = 0.19146$
D. $P(10.1 < x < 10.4) = 0.97725 - 0.69146 = 0.28579$
E. $P(9.9 < x < 9.6) = 0.69146 - 0.97725 = 0.28579$
F. $P(9.9 < x < 10.4) = 0.19146 + 0.47725 = 0.66871$
G. $P(9.886 < x < 10.406) = 0.47882 + 0.21566 = 0.69448$

SOLUTIONS TO DISCUSSION QUESTIONS AND PROBLEMS

3-1. A random variable is a function defined over a sample space. There are two types of random variables: discrete and continuous.

The distributions for the price of a product, the number of sales for a salesperson, and the number of ounces in a food container are examples of a probability distribution.

3-2. A probability distribution is a statement of a probability function that assigns all the probabilities associated with a random variable. A discrete probability distribution is a distribution of discrete random variables (that is, random variables with a limited set of values). A continuous probability distribution is concerned with a random variable having an infinite set of values.

3-3. The expected value is the average of the distribution and is computed by using the following formula: $E(X) = \Sigma X \cdot P(X)$ (this is for a discrete probability distribution).

3-4. The variance is a measure of the dispersion of the distribution. The variance of a discrete probability distribution is computed by the following formula:

$$V = \Sigma[(X - E(X)]^2 \cdot P(X).$$

3-5. The Bernoulli process has the following characteristics:
1. For a given number of trials, each trial has only two possible outcomes, usually denoted as success or failure.
2. The probability of the outcome stays the same each time, regardless of how many times the experiment is performed.
3. The trials are statistically independent.

3-6. The binomial probability distribution describes the Bernoulli process. The following values must be known:
1. The proportion of successes, p.
2. The proportion of failures, q (which equals $1 - p$).
3. The number of successes desired.
4. The number of trial performances.

The binomial distribution is a discrete probability distribution. The normal distribution is a continuous probability distribution. The mean and standard deviation completely specify the normal distribution. The mean can be estimated rather easily because it is equivalent to the average. The standard deviation may be found by utilizing the standard normal equation, $Z = \frac{X - \mu}{\sigma}$. By solving for the standard deviation, we get $\sigma = (X - \mu)/Z$.

The normal distribution may be used in determining the risk of a project given a mean and standard deviation. The risk may be estimated in terms of the probability of maintaining production requirements.

3-7. The purpose of this question is to have students name three business processes they know that can be described by a normal distribution. Answers could include sales of a product, project completion time, average weight of a product, and product demand during lead or order time.

3-8. This is an example of a discrete probability distribution. It was most likely computed using historical data. It is important to note that it follows the laws of a probability distribution. The total sums to 1, and the individual values are less than or equal to 1.

3-9. (a) and (c) are probability distributions because the probability values for each event are between 0 and 1, and the sum of the probability values for the events is 1.

3-10.

X	P(X)	X P(X)
0	.05	0.00
1	.15	.15
2	.2	.40
3	.25	.75
4	.20	.80
5	.15	.75
		2.85

Hence, 2.85 loaves will be sold on average.

3-11.

X	P(X)	X · P(X)	X − E(X)	$(X - E(X))^2$	$(X - E(X)^2 P(X))$
1	.05	.05	−4.45	19.803	.99013
2	.05	.1	−3.45	11.903	.59513
3	.10	.3	−2.45	6.003	.6003
4	.10	.4	−1.45	2.103	.2103
5	.15	.75	−.45	.203	.03038
6	.15	.9	.55	.303	.04538
7	.25	1.75	1.55	2.403	.60063
8	.15	1.2	2.55	6.5025	.97538
		5.45			4.04755

$E(X) = \underline{5.45}$

$\sigma^2 = \Sigma[X - E(X)P(X)]$

$\sigma^2 = \underline{4.0476}$

3-12. $\binom{n}{x} p^x q^{n-x}$

$x = 3$

$n = 4$

$q = 15/20 = .75$

$p = 5/20 = .25$

$\binom{4}{3}(.25)^3(.75) =$

$\dfrac{4!}{3!(4-3)!}(.25)^3(.75) =$

$(4)(.0156)(.75) =$

$\underline{.0464}$ [probability that Marie will win 3 games]

$\binom{4}{4}(.25)^4(.75)^0 = \underline{.003906}$ [probability that Marie will win all four games against Jan]

Probability that Marie will be number one is .04694 + .003906 = $\underline{.05086}$.

3-13.

1. $F(x) = \dfrac{1}{b-a} \begin{cases} \text{for } a \le x \le b, \\ 0 \text{ otherwise} \end{cases}$

2. Probability = area under curve = base × height.

3. The height is always $\dfrac{1}{b-a}$, where the range of the distribution is from point a to b.

4. The sum of all intervals (bases) over the range of the distribution must be $b - a$.

5. Therefore, the sum of probability values = sum of the bases × height = $(b - a)$

$\left(\dfrac{1}{b-a}\right) = 1.$

3-14. Probability one will be fined =

$P(2) + P(3) + P(4) + P(5)$

$= 1 - P(0) - P(1)$

$= 1 - \binom{5}{0}(.5)^0(.5)^5 - \binom{5}{1}(.5)^1(.5)^4$

$= 1 - .03125 - .15625$

$= \underline{.8125}$

$\binom{5}{5}(.5)^5(.5)^0 = .5^5$ [probability he'll
foul out all 5 games]

$\quad\quad\quad\quad = \underline{\underline{.03125}}$

$\binom{5}{0}(.5)^0(.5)^5 = \underline{\underline{.03125}}$ [probability that
he'll foul out 0 games]

3-15. P(can will contain 11.5 to 12.5 ounces)

$$\frac{1}{b-a} = \frac{1}{15-11} = 1/4 = .25$$

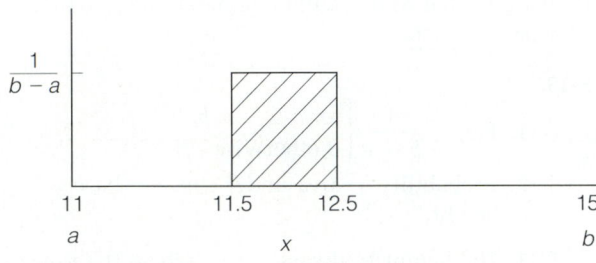

Probability = base × height
$\quad\quad\quad = (12.5 - 11.5) \times 1/4$
$\quad\quad\quad = 1 \cdot 1/4 = 1/4 = .25$

There is a .25 chance that the can will contain between 11.5 to 12.5 ounces of tuna. There is a 0 probability that the can will contain exactly 12 ounces.

3-16. $X = 280$
$\quad\mu = 250$
$\quad\sigma = 25$

$\therefore Z = \dfrac{X - \mu}{\sigma}$

$\quad\quad = \dfrac{280 - 250}{25}$

$\quad\quad = \dfrac{30}{25}$

$\quad\quad = 1.20$ standard deviations

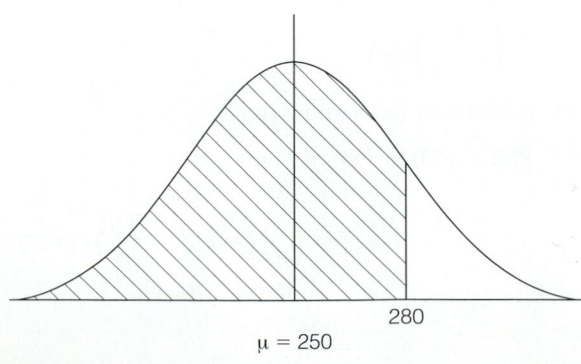

From Table 3.6, the area under the curve corresponding to a Z of 1.20 = .8849. Therefore, the probability that the sales will be less than 280 boats is .8849.

3-17. Probability of sales being over 265 boats:

$\quad X = 265$
$\quad\mu = 250$
$\quad\sigma = 25$

$\quad Z = \dfrac{265 - 250}{25}$

$\quad\quad = \dfrac{15}{25}$

$\quad\quad = .60$

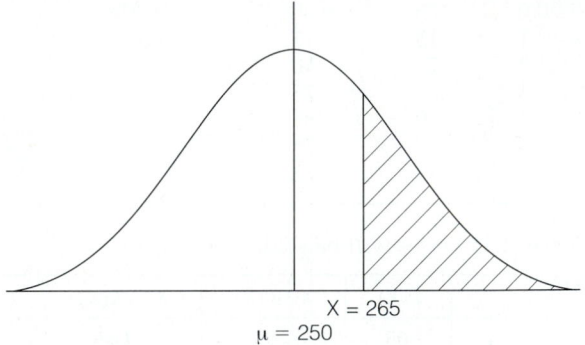

From Table 3.6, we find that the area under the curve, to the left of a $Z = .60$, is .7257. Since we want to find the probability of selling more than 265 boats, we need the area to the right of $Z = .60$. This area is $1 - .7257$, or .2743. Therefore, the probability of selling more than 265 boats = .2743.

For a sale of under 250 boats:

$\quad X = 250$
$\quad\mu = 250$
$\quad\sigma = 25$

However, a sale of 250 boats corresponds to $\mu = 250$. At this point, $Z = 0$. The area under the curve that concerns us is that half of the area lying to the left of $\mu = 250$. This area = .5000. Thus, the probability of selling less than 250 boats = .5.

3-18. $\mu = .55$ inches [average shaft size]
$\quad X = .65$ inches
$\quad\sigma = .10$ inches

Converting to Z values:

$$Z = \frac{X - \mu}{\sigma}$$

$$= \frac{.65 - .55}{.10}$$

$$= \frac{.10}{.10}$$

$$= 1$$

We thus need to look up the area under the curve that lies to the left of 1σ. From Table 3.6, this is seen to be $= .8413$. As seen earlier, the area to the left of μ is $= .5000$.

We are concerned with the area between μ and $\mu + 1\sigma$. This is given by the difference between .8413 and .5000, and it is .3413. Thus, the probability of a shaft size between .55 inch and .65 inch $= .3413$.

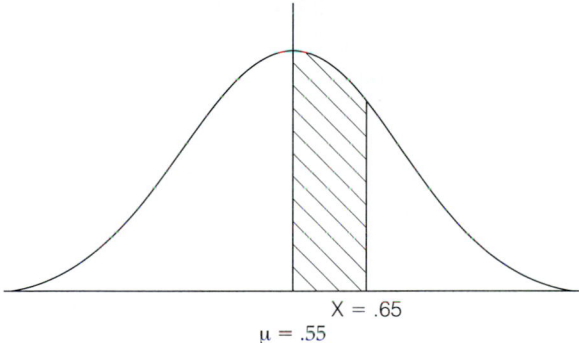

3-19. Greater than .65 inch:

Area to the left of $1\sigma = .8413$

Area to the right of $1\sigma = 1 - .8413$

$$= .1587$$

Thus, the probability of a shaft size being greater than .65 inch is .1587.

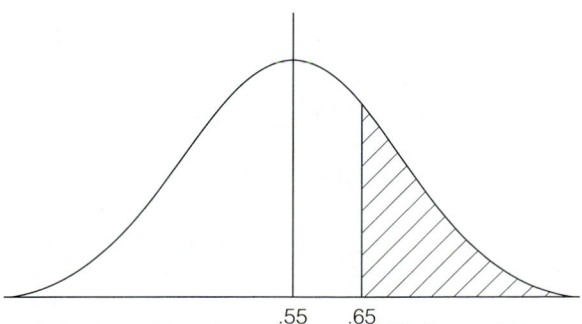

Shaft size between .53 and .59 inch:

$X_2 = .53$ inch

$X_1 = .59$ inch

$\mu = .55$ inch

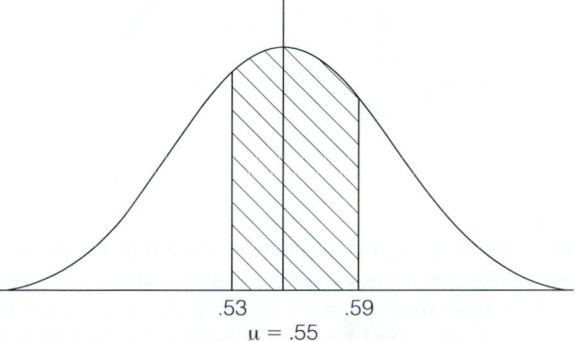

Converting to scores:

$$Z_1 = \frac{X_1 - \mu}{\sigma} \qquad Z_2 = \frac{X_2 - \mu}{\sigma}$$

$$= \frac{.59 - .55}{.10} \qquad = \frac{.53 - .55}{.10}$$

$$= \frac{.04}{.10} \qquad = \frac{-.02}{.10}$$

$$= .4 \qquad = -.2$$

Since Table 3.6 handles only positive Z values, we need to calculate the probability of the shaft size being greater than $.55 + .02 = .57$ inch. This is determined by finding the area to the left of .57, that is, to the left of $.2\sigma$. From Table 3.6, this is .5793. The area to the right of $.2\sigma$ is $1 - .5793 = .4207$. The area to the left of .53 is also .4207 (the curve is symmetrical). The area to the left of $.4\sigma$ is .6554. The area between X_1 and X_2 is $.6554 - .4207 = .2347$. The probability that the shaft will be between .53 inch and .59 inch is .2347.
Under .45 inch:

$$X = .45$$

$$\mu = .55$$

$$\sigma = .10$$

$$Z = \frac{X - \mu}{\sigma}$$

$$= \frac{.45 - .55}{.10}$$

$$= \frac{-.10}{.10}$$

$$= -1$$

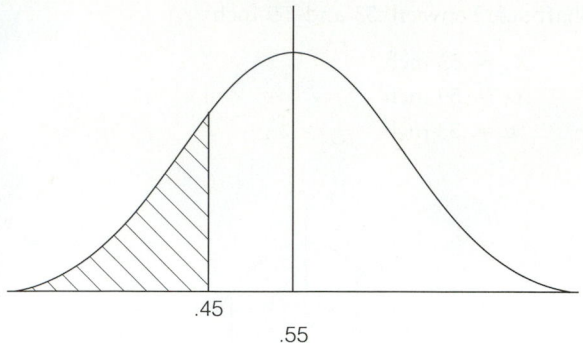

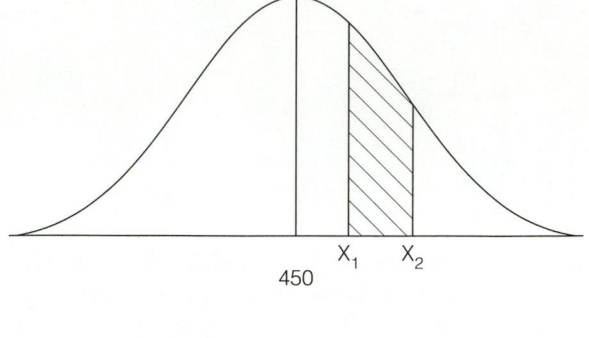

Thus, we need to find the area to the left of 1σ. Again, since Table 3.6 handles only positive values of Z, we need to determine the area to the right of 1σ. This is obtained by $1 - .8413 = .1587$ (.8413 is the area to the left of 1σ). Therefore, the area to the left of $-1\sigma = .1587$ [the curve is symmetrical]. Thus, the probability that the shaft size will be under .45 inch is .1587.

3-20. $\mu = 450$ degrees
$\sigma = 25$ degrees
$X = 475$ degrees

$$Z = \frac{X - \mu}{\sigma} = \frac{475 - 450}{25} = 1$$

$X_1 = 460$
$X_2 = 470$

$$Z_1 = \frac{460 - 450}{25} = \frac{10}{25} = .4$$

area $X_1 = .6554$

$$Z_2 = \frac{470 - 450}{25} = \frac{20}{25} = .8$$

area $X_2 = .7881$

The area between X_1 and X_2 is $.7881 - .6554 = .1327$. Thus, the probability of being between 460 and 470 degrees is $= .1327$.

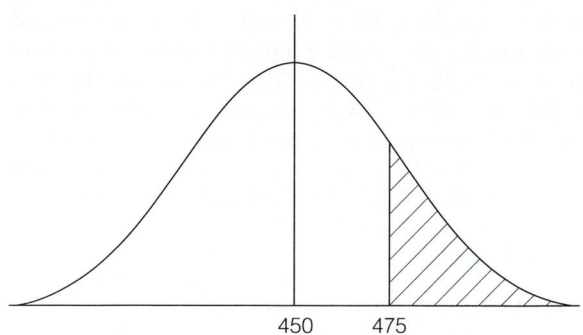

The area to the left of 475 is .8413 from Table 3.6, where $\sigma = 1$. The area to the right of 475 is $1 - .8413 = .1587$. Thus, the probability of the oven getting hotter than 475 is .1587.

To determine the probability of the oven temperature being between 460 and 470, we need to compute two areas.

3-21.

X		$P(X)$
0	$\binom{5}{0}(.2)^0(.8)^5 = .327$	.327
1	$\binom{5}{1}(.2)^1(.8)^{5-1} = .410$	.410
2	$\binom{5}{2}(.2)^2(.8)^{5-2} = .205$	.205
3	$\binom{5}{3}(.2)^3(.8)^{5-3} = .051$	.051
4	$\binom{5}{4}(.2)^4(.8)^{5-4} = .0064$	.0064
5	$\binom{5}{5}(.2)^5(.8)^{5-5} = .00032$	.00032
		1.0

3-22.

$XP(X)$	$X - E(X)$	$(X - E(X))^2$	$(X - E(X))^2 P(X)$
0.0	−.9985	.997	.326
.41	.0015	$2. \times 10^{-6}$	$.9 \times 10^{-7}$
.41	1.0015	1.003	.2056
.153	2.0015	4.006	.2043
.024	3.0015	9.009	.0541
.0015	4.0015	16.012	.0048
.9985			.7948

a. $E(X) = \underline{.9985} \cong 1.0$ $\sigma = \Sigma(X - E(X))^2 P(X)$
$= \underline{.7948} \cong 0.80$

b. $E(R) = NP$
$= (5)(.2) = \underline{1.0}$
$V = NP(1 - P)$
$= 5(.2)(.8)$
$= \underline{0.80}$

c. The equation produced equivalent results.

3-23. a. $n = 10$; $p = .25$; $q = .75$;

$\binom{10}{x} p^x q^{10-x}$	$P(X)$	X
$\binom{10}{0}(.25)^0(.75)^{10-0} =$	.0563	0
$\binom{10}{1}(.25)^1(.75)^{10-1} =$	.1877	1
$\binom{10}{2}(.25)^2(.75)^{10-2} =$	.2816	2
$\binom{10}{3}(.25)^3(.75)^{10-3} =$	.2503	3
$\binom{10}{4}(.25)^4(.75)^{10-4} =$	.1460	4
$\binom{10}{5}(.25)^5(.75)^{10-5} =$	.0584	5
$\binom{10}{6}(.25)^6(.75)^{10-6} =$	.0162	6
$\binom{10}{7}(.25)^7(.75)^{10-7} =$	.0031	7
$\binom{10}{8}(.25)^8(.75)^{10-8} =$	.0004	8
$\binom{10}{9}(.25)^9(.75)^{10-9} =$	.00003	9
$\binom{10}{10}(.25)^{10}(.75)^{10-10} =$	.0000	10

1.000

b. $E(X) = (10).25 = \underline{2.5}$
$V = npq = (10)(.25)(.75)$
$= \underline{1.875}$

c. Expected weekly profit:
$125.
$\times \ 2.5$
$312.50

3-24. a. $\left(\dfrac{1}{13.2 - 9.6}\right) \times (11 - 10) =$
$.2778 \times 1 \qquad = \underline{.2778}$

b. $(.2778) \times (9.8 - 9.6) =$
$.2778 \times .2 \qquad = \underline{.0555}$

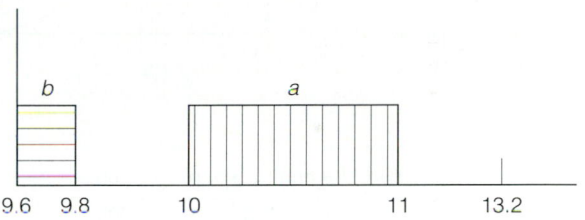

c. The expected value will be the midpoint of the distribution:
$= \dfrac{13.2 + 9.6}{2} = \dfrac{22.8}{2} = 11.4$

3-25. $\mu = 4700$; $\sigma = 500$

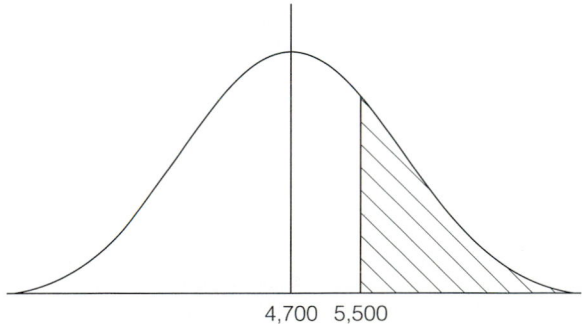

a. The sale of 5,500 oranges ($X = 5,500$) is the equivalent of some Z value which may be obtained from:
$Z = \dfrac{X - \mu}{\sigma}$
$= \dfrac{5,500 - 4,700}{500}$
$= 1.6$

The area under the curve lying to the left of 1.6σ = .94520. Therefore, the area to the right of $1.6\sigma = 1 -$ .94520, or .0548. Therefore, the probability of sales being greater than 5,500 oranges is .0548.

b.

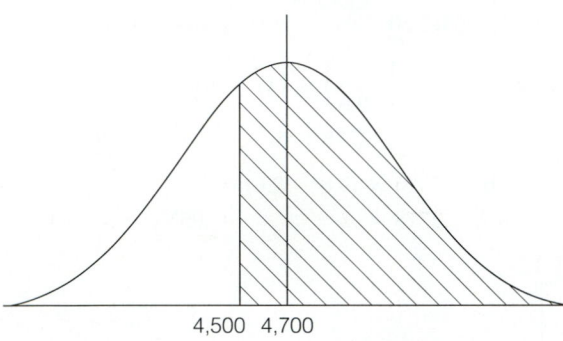

$$Z = \frac{4,500 - 4,700}{500} = -\frac{200}{500} = -.4$$

Area = .6554

Probability = .6554

c.

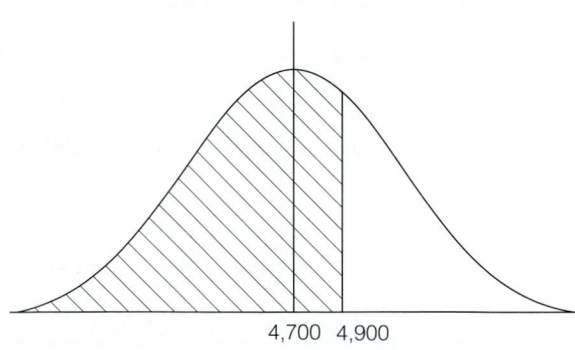

$$Z = \frac{4,900 - 4,700}{500} = \frac{200}{500} = .4$$

Area = .6554 = probability

This answer is the same as the answer to (b) because the normal curve is symmetrical.

d.

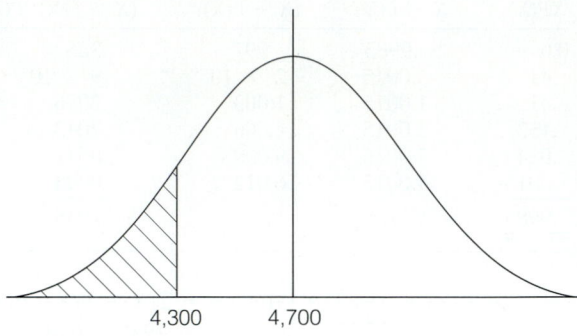

$$Z = \frac{4,300 - 4,700}{500} = -\frac{400}{500} = -.8$$

Area to the right of 4,300 is .788, from Table 3.6. The area to the left of 4,300 is $1 - .788 = .212 =$ the probability that sales will be less than 4,300 oranges.

3-26. $\mu = 87,000$

$\sigma = 4,000$

$X = 81,000$

$$Z = \frac{81,000 - 87,000}{4,000} = -\frac{6}{4} = -1.5$$

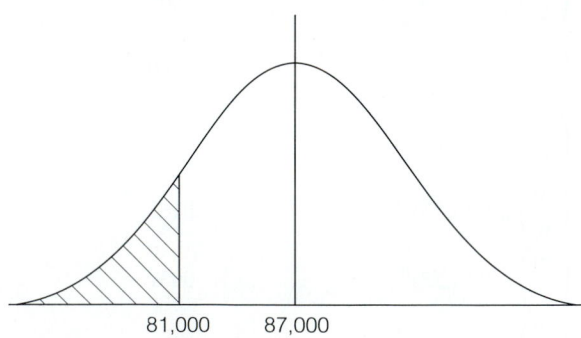

Area to the right of 81,000 = .9332, from Table 3.6, where $Z = 1.5$. Thus, the area to the left of 81,000 = $1 - .9332 = .0668 =$ the probability that sales will be less than 81,000 packages.

3-27.

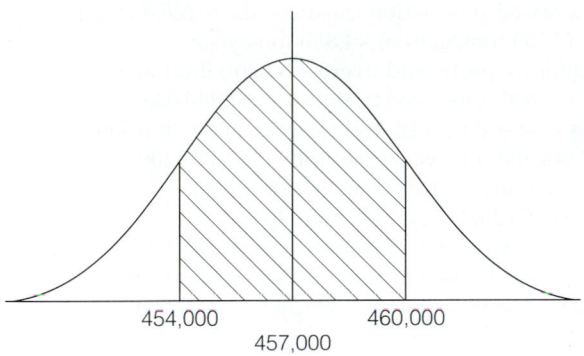

$$\mu = 457,000$$

Ninety percent of the time, sales have been between 460,000 and 454,000 pencils. This means that 10% of the time sales have exceeded 460,000 or fallen below 454,000. Since the curve is symmetrical, we assume that 5% of the area lies to the right of 460,000 and 5% lies to the left of 454,000. Thus, 95% of the area under the curve lies to the left of 460,000. From Table 3.6, we note that the number nearest .9500 is .94950. This corresponds to a Z value of 1.64. Therefore, we may conclude that the Z value corresponding to a sale of 460,000 pencils is 1.64.

Using equation 3-12, we get $Z = \dfrac{X - \mu}{\sigma}$:

$$X = 460,000$$
$$\mu = 457,000$$
$$\sigma \text{ is unknown}$$
$$Z = 1.64$$
$$1.64 = \frac{460,000 - 457,000}{\sigma}$$
$$1.64\sigma = 3000$$
$$\therefore \sigma = \frac{3000}{1.64}$$
$$\therefore \sigma = 1829.27$$

3-28. $\lambda = 5/\text{day}; e^{-\lambda} = .0067$ [from Appendix D]

a. $P(0) = \dfrac{\lambda^x e^{-\lambda}}{X!} = \dfrac{(1)(.0067)}{1} = .0067$

$P(1) = \dfrac{(5)(.0067)}{1} = .0335$

$P(2) = \dfrac{25(.0067)}{2} = .0837$

$P(3) = \dfrac{125(.0067)}{6} = .1396$

$P(4) = \dfrac{625(.0067)}{24} = .1745$

$P(5) = \dfrac{3125(.0067)}{120} = .1745$

b. These sum to .6125, not 1, because there are more possible arrivals. For example, 6 or 7 patients might arrive in one hour.

3-29. $P(X > 3) = 1 - P(X \leq 3) = 1 - [P(0) + P(1) + P(2) + P(3)]$

$= 1 - [.0067 + .0335 + .0837 + .1396]$

$= 1 - .2635 = .7365 = 73.65\%$

3-30. $\mu = 3/\text{hour}$

a. Expected time $= \dfrac{1}{\mu} = \dfrac{1}{3}$ hour $= 20$ minutes

b. Variance $= \dfrac{1}{\mu^2} = \dfrac{1}{9}$

c. $f(1) = 3e^{-\mu x}$

[Using Appendix D, $e^{-\mu x} = e^{-3} = .05$]

So $f(1) = 3(.05) = .15 = 15\% =$ probability of no arrivals for one hour.

Solution to WTVX Case

1. The chances of getting 15 days of rain during the next 30 days can be computed by using the binomial theorem. The problem is well suited for solution by the theorem because there are two and only two possible outcomes (rain or sun) with given probabilities (70% and 30%, respectively). The formula used is:

Probability of r successes $= \dfrac{n!}{r!(n-r)!} p^r(q^{n-r})$

where

$n =$ the number of trials (in this case, the number of days $= 30$),

$r =$ the number of successes (number of rainy days $= 15$),

$p =$ probability of success (probability of rain $= 70\%$), and

$q =$ probability of failure (probability of sun $= 30\%$).

$\dfrac{n!}{r!(n-r)!} p^r(q^{n-r}) = \dfrac{30!}{15!(15!)}(.70)^{15}(.30)^{15} = .0106$

The probability of getting exactly 15 days of rain in the next 30 days is 1.06%.

2. Joe's assumptions concerning the weather for the next 30 days state that what happens on one day is not in any way dependent on what happened the day before; what this says, for example, is that if a cold front passed through yesterday, it will not affect what happens today.

But there are perhaps certain conditional probabilities associated with the weather (for example, given that it rained yesterday, the probability of rain today is 80% as opposed to 70%). Not being familiar with the field of meteorology, we cannot say precisely what these are. However, our contention is that these probabilities do exist and that Joe's assumptions are fallacious.

Solution to Century Chemical Company Case

The stream factor for the chlorine compressor is .92. If the spare compressor also has a stream factor of .92, the compressor "system" stream factor is computed as follows:

Probability that original compressor will fail = .08
Probability that spare compressor will fail = .08
Probability that both original and spare compressor will fail = (.08)(.08) = .0064
Probability that at least one is operable = 1 − .0064 = .9936
Reliability with the spare = .9936
Reliability without the spare = .92
Improved reliability = .0736
Increased operating time = (365 days/year)(.0736) = 26.9 days

As a conservative estimate, it is projected that no more than one change over to the spare would occur in a calendar year. Hence,

Net increased operating time   [12 hours required
    = 26.9 days − .5 day   for change over]
    = 26.4 days

Increased production chlorine = (26.4 days) (1,500 tons/day) = 39,600 tons/year
Increased production caustic soda = (26.4 days) (1,700 tons/day) = 44,880 tons/year
Chlorine profit and overhead contribution = (39,600 tons/year)($50/ton) = $1,980,000
Caustic soda profit and overhead contribution = (44,880 tons/year)($40/ton) = $1,795,200
Contribution after taxes = ($1,980,000 + $1,795,200)(.60) = $2,265,120
Present value for 10-year life = $2,265,120 × 4.192 (present value factor @ 20%) = $9,495,383
Net present value = $9,495,383 − $800,000 = $8,695,383

Obviously, Century Chemical should proceed with the spare compressor installation.

Epilogue to the case: With the obvious advantage of the spare compressor installation, management of Century Chemical launched an inquiry to determine why the spare compressor was not included in the original plant layout. They discovered that the compressor vendor somewhat overstated the capacity and reliability of its machine. Design engineers were led to believe that a .99 reliability was reasonable. A softening of the chlor/alkali market, however, did reduce output in subsequent years. This lowered the projected net present value, but the installation of the spare remained immensely profitable.

4

Forecasting

LEARNING OBJECTIVES

After completing this chapter, students will be able to:

1. Understand different families of forecasting techniques and when each should be used.
2. Compare moving averages, exponential smoothing, and trend time-series models and evaluate the best to use for a set of data.
3. Seasonally adjust data.
4. Understand the concepts of the Delphi and other qualitative decision-making approaches.
5. Compute a variety of error measures.
6. Analyze data by computer and interpret the outputs.

TEACHING SUGGESTIONS

Teaching Suggestion 4.1: Wide Use of Forecasting.

Forecasting is one of the most important tools a student can master because every firm needs to conduct forecasts. It's useful to motivate students with the idea that even as obscure a sounding technique as exponential smoothing is actually widely used in business, and a good manager is expected to understand forecasting. Regression is commonly accepted as a tool in economic and legal cases.

Teaching Suggestion 4.2: Forecasting as an Art and a Science.

Forecasting is as much an art as a science. Students should understand that *qualitative* analysis (judgmental modeling) plays an important role in predicting the future since not every factor can be quantified. Sometimes the best forecast is done by seat-of-the-pants methods.

Teaching Suggestion 4.3: Use of Simple Models.

Many managers want to know what goes on behind the forecast. They may feel uncomfortable with complex statistical models with too many variables. They also need to feel a part of the process.

Teaching Suggestion 4.4: Management Input to the Exponential Smoothing Model.

One of the strengths of exponential smoothing is that it allows decision makers to input constants that give weight to recent data. Most managers want to feel a part of the modeling process and appreciate the opportunity to provide input.

Teaching Suggestion 4.5: Which Is the Independent Variable?

We find that students are often confused about which variable is independent and which is dependent in a regression model. For example, in Triple A's problem, clarify which variable is X and which is Y. When using software, students often enter numbers without understanding which column they should be in.

Teaching Suggestion 4.6: Statistical Correlation Does Not Always Mean Causality.

Students should understand that a high R^2 doesn't always mean one variable will be a good predictor of the other. Explain that skirt lengths and stock market prices may be correlated, but raising one doesn't necessarily mean the other will go up or down.

Teaching Suggestion 4.7: Wide Use of Adaptive Models.

With today's dominant use of computers in forecasting, it is possible for a program to constantly track the accuracy of a model's forecast. It's important to understand that a program can automatically select the best alpha and beta weights in exponential smoothing. Even if a firm has 10,000 products, the constants can be selected very quickly and easily without human intervention.

ALTERNATE EXAMPLES

Alternate Example 4.1:

$$\text{Moving Average} = \frac{\Sigma \text{ Demand in previous } n \text{ periods}}{n}$$

Bicycle sales at Bower's Bikes are shown in the middle column of the following table. A three-week moving average appears on the right.

WEEK	ACTUAL BICYCLE SALES	THREE-WEEK MOVING AVERAGE
1	8	
2	10	
3	9	
4	11	$(8 + 10 + 9)/3 = 9$
5	10	$(10 + 9 + 11)/3 = 10$
6	13	$(9 + 11 + 10)/3 = 10$
7	—	$(11 + 10 + 13)/3 = 11\ 1/3$

Alternate Example 4.2:

Weighted Moving Average

$$= \frac{\Sigma \,(\text{Weight for period } n)\,(\text{Demand in period } n)}{\Sigma \text{ Weights}}$$

Bower's Bikes decides to forecast bicycle sales by weighting the past three weeks as follows:

WEIGHTS APPLIED	PERIOD
3	Last week
2	Two weeks ago
1	Three weeks ago
6	Sum of weights

A three-week weighted moving average appears below.

WEEK	ACTUAL BICYCLE SALES	THREE-WEEK WEIGHTED MOVING AVERAGE
1	8	
2	10	
3	9	
4	11	$[(3 \times 9) + (2 \times 10) + (1 \times 8)]/6 = 9\ 1/6$
5	10	$[(3 \times 11) + (2 \times 9) + (1 \times 10)]/6 = 10\ 1/6$
6	13	$[(3 \times 10) + (2 \times 11) + (1 \times 9)]/6 = 10\ 1/6$
7	—	$[(3 \times 13) + (2 \times 10) + (1 \times 11)]/6 = 11\ 2/3$

Alternate Example 4.3: A firm uses simple exponential smoothing with $\alpha = .1$ to forecast demand. The forecast for the week of January 1 was 500 units, whereas actual demand turned out to be 450 units. The demand forecasted for the week of January 8 is calculated as follows.

$$F_t = F_{t-1} + \alpha(A_{t-1} - F_{t-1})$$
$$= 500 + .1(450 - 500) = 495 \text{ units}$$

Alternate Example 4.4: Exponential smoothing is used to forecast automobile battery sales. Two values of α are examined, $\alpha = .8$ and $\alpha = .5$. To evaluate the accuracy of each smoothing constant we can compute the absolute deviations and MADs. Assume the forecast for January was 22 batteries.

MONTH	ACTUAL BATTERY SALES	ROUNDED FORECAST WITH $\alpha = .8$	ABSOLUTE DEVIATION WITH $\alpha = .8$	ROUNDED FORECAST WITH $\alpha = .5$	ABSOLUTE DEVIATION WITH $\alpha = .5$
January	20	22	2	22	2
February	21	20	1	21	0
March	15	21	6	21	6
April	14	16	2	18	4
May	13	14	1	16	3
June	16	13	3	15	1
Sum of Absolute Deviations			15		16
$\text{MAD} = \dfrac{\Sigma \text{ Deviations}}{n}$			2.5		2.7

On the basis of this analysis, a smoothing constant of $\alpha = .8$ is preferred to $\alpha = .5$ because it has a smaller MAD.

Alternate Example 4.5: Use the sales data given below to determine: (a) the least squares trend line, (b) the predicted value for 1993 sales.

YEAR	SALES (UNITS)
1986	100
1987	110
1988	122
1989	130
1990	139
1991	152
1992	164

To minimize computations, transform the value of x (time) to simpler numbers. In this case, designate 1986 as year 1, 1987 as year 2, and so on.

YEAR	TIME PERIOD	SALES (UNITS)	x^2	xy
1986	1	100	1	110
1987	2	110	4	220
1988	3	122	9	366
1989	4	130	16	520
1990	5	139	25	695
1991	6	152	36	912
1992	7	164	49	1148
	$\Sigma x = 28$	$\Sigma y = 917$	$\Sigma x^2 = 140$	$\Sigma xy = 3971$

$$\bar{x} = \frac{\Sigma x}{n} = \frac{28}{7} = 4 \qquad \bar{y} = \frac{\Sigma y}{n} = \frac{917}{7} = 131$$

$$b = \frac{\Sigma xy - n\bar{x}\bar{y}}{\Sigma x^2 - n\bar{x}^2} = \frac{3971 - (7)(4)(131)}{140 - (7)(4^2)} = \frac{303}{28} = 10.82$$

$$a = \bar{y} - b\bar{x} = 131 - 10.82(4) = 87.72$$

Therefore, the least squares trend equation is,

$$\hat{y} = a + bx = 87.72 + 10.82x$$

To project demand in 1993, we denote the year 1993 as $x = 8$,

Sales in 1993 = 87.72 + 10.82(8) = 174.28

Alternate Example 4.6: The rated power capacity (in hours/week) over the past six years has been:

YEAR	RATED CAPACITY (HRS/WK)
1	115
2	120
3	118
4	124
5	123
6	130

To forecast year 7's capacity using regression:

YEAR	RENUMBERED YEAR (x)*	CAPACITY (y)	x^2	xy
1	-2.5	115	6.25	-287.5
2	-1.5	120	2.25	-180
3	$-.5$	118	.25	-59
4	$+.5$	124	.25	$+62$
5	$+1.5$	123	2.25	$+184.5$
6	$+2.5$	130	6.25	$+325$
	$\Sigma X = 0$	$\Sigma Y = 730$	$\Sigma X^2 = 17.5$	$\Sigma XY = 45$

*Note this alternative way to recode years simplifies the math since $\Sigma X = 0$.

$$b = \frac{\Sigma XY}{\Sigma X^2} = \frac{45}{17.5} = 2.57$$

$$a = \frac{\Sigma Y}{n} = \frac{730}{6} = 121.67$$

$$y = 121.67 + 2.57X$$

Year 7 $= 121.67 + 2.57(3.5)$

$\quad\quad\quad = 131$

Alternate Example 4.7: The sales manager of a large apartment rental complex feels the demand for apartments may be related to the number of newspaper ads placed during the previous month. She has collected the data shown in the accompanying table.

ADS PURCHASED, (x)	APARTMENTS LEASED, (y)
15	6
9	4
40	16
20	6
25	13
25	9
15	10
35	16

We can find a mathematical equation by using the least squares regression approach.

LEASES, y	AD, x	x^2	xy
6	15	225	90
4	9	81	36
16	40	1600	640
6	20	400	120
13	25	625	325
9	25	625	225
10	15	225	150
16	35	1225	560
$\Sigma y = 80$	$\Sigma x = 184$	$\Sigma x^2 = 5006$	$\Sigma xy = 2146$

$$\bar{x} = \frac{184}{8} = 23 \quad\quad \bar{y} = \frac{80}{8} = 10$$

$$b = \frac{\Sigma xy - n\bar{x}\bar{y}}{\Sigma x^2 - n\bar{x}^2} = \frac{2146 - (8)(23)(10)}{5006 - (8)(23^2)} = .395$$

$$a = \bar{y} - b\bar{x} = 10 - .395(23) = .91$$

The estimated regression equation is

$$\hat{y} = .91 + .395x$$

or

Apartments leased $= .91 + .395$ Ads placed

If the number of ads is 30, we can estimate the number of apartments rented with the regression equation:

$.91 + .395(30) = 12.76 \approx 13$ apartments

Alternate Example 4.8: Given the data on ads and apartment rentals in Alternate Example 4.7, compute the standard deviation of regression ($S_{y,x}$). We first find that $\Sigma y^2 = 950$.

$$S_{y,x} = \sqrt{\frac{\Sigma y^2 - a\Sigma y - b\Sigma xy}{n - 2}}$$

$$= \sqrt{\frac{950 - (.91)(80) - (.395)(2146)}{8 - 2}}$$

$$= 2.2 \text{ apartments}$$

Alternate Example 4.9: Alternate Examples 4.7 and 4.8, dealing with ads, x, and apartments leased, y, revealed the following:

$$\Sigma x = 184 \quad\quad \Sigma x^2 = 5006$$
$$\Sigma y = 80 \quad\quad \Sigma y^2 = 950$$
$$\Sigma xy = 2146 \quad\quad n = 8$$

Compute the correlation coefficient.

$$r = \frac{n\Sigma XY - \Sigma X \Sigma Y}{\sqrt{[n\Sigma X^2 - (\Sigma X)^2][n\Sigma Y^2 - (\Sigma Y)^2]}}$$

$$= \frac{8(2,146) - (184)(80)}{\sqrt{[8(5,006) - (184)^2][8(950) - (80)^2]}}$$

$$= \frac{2,448}{\sqrt{7,430,400}}$$

$$= .90$$

This r of .90 appears to be a significant correlation and helps to confirm the closeness of the relationship between the two variables.

Alternate Example 4.10: The forecast demand and actual demand for 10-foot fishing boats are shown below. We compute the tracking signal and MAD.

YEAR	FORECAST DEMAND	ACTUAL DEMAND	ERROR	RSFE	FORECAST ERROR	CUMULATIVE ERROR	MAD	TRACKING SIGNAL
1	78	71	−7	−7	7	7	7.0	−1.0
2	75	80	5	−2	5	12	6.0	−0.3
3	83	101	18	16	18	30	10.0	+1.6
4	84	84	0	16	0	30	7.5	+2.1
5	88	60	−28	−12	28	58	11.6	−1.0
6	85	73	−12	−24	12	70	11.7	−2.1

$$\text{MAD} = \frac{\Sigma \text{ Forecast errors}}{n} = \frac{70}{6} = 11.7$$

$$\text{Tracking Signal} = \frac{\text{RSFE}}{\text{MAD}} = \frac{-24}{11.7} = -2.1 \text{ MADs}$$

SOLUTIONS TO DISCUSSION QUESTIONS AND PROBLEMS

4-1. The steps that are used to develop any forecasting system are:
1. Determine the use of the forecast.
2. Select the items or quantities that are to be forecasted.
3. Determine the time horizon of the forecast.
4. Select the forecasting model.
5. Gather the necessary data.
6. Validate the forecasting model.
7. Make the forecast.
8. Implement the results.

4-2. A time series forecasting model uses historical data to predict future trends.

4-3. The only difference between causal models and time series models is that causal models take into account any factors that may influence the quantity being forecasted. Causal models use historical data as well. Time series models use only historical data.

4-4. Qualitative models incorporate subjective factors into the forecasting model. Judgmental models are useful when subjective factors are important. When quantitative data are difficult to obtain, qualitative models are appropriate.

4-5. Least squares refers to holding the sum of the square of the difference between the observed values and the regression line to a minimum.

4-6. The disadvantages of the moving average forecasting model are that the averages always stay within past levels, and the moving averages require extensive record keeping of past data.

4-7. When the smoothing value, α, is high, more weight is given to recent data. When α is low, more weight is given to past data.

4-8. The Delphi technique involves analyzing the predictions that a group of experts have made, then allowing the experts to review the data again. This process may be repeated several times. After the final analysis, the forecast is developed. The group of experts may be geographically dispersed.

4-9. MAD is a technique for determining the accuracy of a forecasting model by taking the average of the absolute deviations. MAD is important because it can be used to help increase forecasting accuracy.

4-10. $\hat{Y} = 36 + 4.3 \times X_1$
   a. $\hat{Y} = 36 + 4.3(70°)$
      $= 337$
   b. $\hat{Y} = 36 + 4.3(80°)$
      $= 380$
   c. $\hat{Y} = 36 + 4.3(90°)$
      $= 423$

4-11.

MONTH	ACTUAL SHED SALES	4-MONTH MOVING AVERAGE
Jan.	10	
Feb.	12	
Mar.	13	
Apr.	16	
May	19	$(10 + 12 + 13 + 16)/4 = 51/4 = 12.75$
June	23	$(12 + 13 + 16 + 19)/4 = 60/4 = 15$
July	26	$(13 + 16 + 19 + 23)/4 = 70/4 = 17.75$
Aug.	30	$(16 + 19 + 23 + 26)/4 = 84/4 = 21$
Sept.	28	$(19 + 23 + 26 + 30)/4 = 98/4 = 24.5$
Oct.	18	$(23 + 26 + 30 + 28)/4 = 107/4 = 26.75$
Nov.	16	$(26 + 30 + 28 + 18)/4 = 102/4 = 25.5$
Dec.	14	$(30 + 28 + 18 + 16)/4 = 92/4 = 23$

4-12.

MONTH	ACTUAL SHED SALES	3-MONTH FORECAST	3-MONTH ABSOLUTE DEVIATION	4-MONTH FORECAST	4-MONTH ABSOLUTE DEVIATION
Jan.	10				
Feb.	12				
Mar.	13				
Apr.	16	11.66	4.34		
May	19	13.66	5.34	12.75	6.25
June	23	16	7	15	8
July	26	19.33	6.67	17.75	8.5
Aug.	30	22.66	7.34	21	9
Sept.	28	26.33	1.67	24.5	3.5
Oct.	18	28	10	26.75	8.75
Nov.	16	25.33	9.33	25.5	9.5
Dec.	14	20.66	6.66	23	9
			58.35		62.25

3-Month MAD $= \dfrac{58.35}{9} = 6.48$

4-Month MAD $= \dfrac{62.25}{8} = 7.78$

The 3-month moving average appears to be more accurate. However, if weighted moving averages had been used, the results might be different.

4-13.

YEAR	DEMAND	3-YEAR MOVING AVERAGES	WEIGHTED 3-YEAR MOVING AVERAGES
1	4		
2	6		
3	4		sum of the weights
4	5	$(4 + 6 + 4)/3 = 4\frac{2}{3}$	$[(2 \times 4) + 6 + 4]/4 = 4\frac{1}{2}$
5	10	$(6 + 4 + 5)/3 = 5$	$[(2 \times 5) + 4 + 6]/4 = 5$
6	8	$(4 + 5 + 10)/3 = 6\frac{1}{3}$	$[(2 \times 10) + 5 + 4]/4 = 7\frac{1}{4}$
7	7	$(5 + 10 + 8)/3 = 7\frac{2}{3}$	$[(2 \times 8) + 10 + 5]/4 = 7\frac{3}{4}$
8	9	$(10 + 8 + 7)/3 = 8\frac{1}{3}$	$[(2 \times 7) + 8 + 10]/4 = 8$
9	12	$(8 + 7 + 9)/3 = 8$	$[(2 \times 9) + 7 + 8]/4 = 8\frac{1}{4}$
10	14	$(7 + 9 + 12)/3 = 9\frac{1}{3}$	$[(2 \times 12) + 9 + 7]/4 = 10$
11	15	$(9 + 12 + 14)/3 = 11\frac{2}{3}$	$[(2 \times 14) + 12 + 9]/4 = 12\frac{1}{4}$

MAD for 3-year average $= 2.58$
MAD for weighted 3-year average $= 2.32$
The *weighted* moving average appears to be slightly more accurate in its annual forecasts.

4-14.

YEAR	DEMAND	2-YEAR MOVING AVERAGE	4-YEAR MOVING AVERAGE
1	4		
2	6		
3	4	(4 + 6)/2 = 5	
4	5	(6 + 4)/2 = 5	
5	10	(4 + 5)/2 = 4.5	(4 + 6 + 4 + 5)/4 = 4.75
6	8	(5 + 10)/2 = 7.5	(6 + 4 + 5 + 10)/4 = 6.25
7	7	(10 + 8)/2 = 9	(4 + 5 + 10 + 8)/4 = 6.75
8	9	(8 + 7)/2 = 7.5	(5 + 10 + 8 + 7)/4 = 7.5
9	12	(7 + 9)/2 = 8	(10 + 8 + 7 + 9)/4 = 8.5
10	14	(9 + 12)/2 = 10.5	(8 + 7 + 9 + 12)/4 = 9
11	15	(12 + 14)/2 = 13	(7 + 9 + 12 + 14)/4 = 10.5

4-15.

YEAR	ACTUAL DEMAND	2-YEAR MOVING AVERAGE FORECAST	2-YEAR ABSOLUTE DEVIATION	3-YEAR MOVING AVERAGE FORECAST	3-YEAR ABSOLUTE DEVIATION	3-YEAR WEIGHTED AVERAGE	3-YEAR WEIGHTED ABSOLUTE DEVIATION	4-YEAR MOVING AVERAGE	4-YEAR ABSOLUTE DEVIATION
1	4								
2	6								
3	4	5	1						
4	5	5	0	4.66	.34	4.5	.5		
5	10	4.5	5.5	5	5	5	5	4.75	5.25
6	8	7.5	.5	6.33	1.67	7.25	.75	6.25	1.75
7	7	9	2	7.67	.67	7.75	.75	6.75	.25
8	9	7.5	1.5	8.33	.67	8	1	7.5	1.5
9	12	8	4	8	4	8.25	3.75	8.5	3.5
10	14	10.5	3.5	9.33	4.67	10	4	9	5
11	15	13	2	11.66	3.34	12.25	2.75	10.5	4.5
	Total absolute deviations		20.0		20.36		18.5		21.75

$MAD_1 = 20.0/9 = 2.22$ $MAD_3 = 18.5/8 = 2.31$
$MAD_2 = 20.36/8 = 2.54$ $MAD_4 = 21.75/7 = 3.11$

I would use the 2-year weighted moving average because it has the lowest MAD ($MAD_3 = 2.22$).

4-16. $\alpha = .3$. New forecast for year 2 is last period's forecast + α(last period's actual demand − last period's forecast):

New forecast for year 2 = 5,000 + .3(4,000 − 5,000)
$$= 5,000 + .3(-1,000)$$
$$= 5,000 - 300$$
$$= 4,700$$

The calculations are:

YEAR	DEMAND	NEW FORECAST
2	6,000	4,700 = 5,000 + .3(4,000 − 5,000)
3	4,000	5,090 = 4,700 + .3(6,000 − 4,700)
4	5,000	4,763 = 5,090 + .3(4,000 − 5,090)
5	10,000	4,834 = 4,763 + .3(5,000 − 4,763)
6	8,000	6,384 = 4,834 + .3(10,000 − 4,834)
7	7,000	6,869 = 6,384 + .3(8,000 − 6,384)
8	9,000	6,908 = 6,869 + .3(7,000 − 6,869)
9	12,000	7,536 = 6,908 + .3(9,000 − 6,908)
10	14,000	8,875 = 7,536 + .3(12,000 − 7,536)
11	15,000	10,412 = 8,875 + .3(14,000 − 8,875)

The mean absolute deviation (MAD) can be used to determine which forecasting method is more accurate.

YEAR	DEMAND	WEIGHTED MOVING AVERAGE	ABSOLUTE DEVIATION	EXP. SM.	ABSOLUTE DEVIATION
1	4,000			5,000	1,000
2	6,000			4,700	1,300
3	4,000			5,090	1,090
4	5,000	4,500	500	4,763	237
5	10,000	5,000	5,000	4,834	5,166
6	8,000	7,250	750	6,384	1,616
7	7,000	7,750	750	6,869	131
8	9,000	8,000	1,000	6,908	2,092
9	12,000	8,250	3,750	7,536	4,464
10	14,000	10,000	4,000	8,875	5,125
11	15,000	12,250	2,750	10,412	4,588
		Total	18,500		26,808
		Mean	2,312.5		2,437

Thus, the 3-year weighted moving average model appears to be more accurate.

4-17.

Year	1	2	3	4	5	6
Forecast	410.0	422.0	443.9	466.1	495.2	521.8

4-18.

YEAR	SALES	FORECAST USING $\alpha = .6$	FORECAST USING $\alpha = .9$
1	450		
2	495	$410 + .6(450 - 410) = 434$	$410 + .9(450 - 410) = 446$
3	518	$434 + .6(495 - 434) = 470.6$	$446 + .9(495 - 446) = 490.1$
4	563	$470.6 + .6(518 - 470.6) = 499.0$	$490.1 + .9(518 - 490.1) = 515.21$
5	584	$499 + .6(563 - 499) = 537.4$	$515.21 + .9(563 - 515.21) = 558.2$
6	?	$537.4 + .6(584 - 537) = 565.6$	$558.221 + .9(584 - 558.2) = 581.4$

4-19.

YEAR	ACTUAL SALES	$\alpha = .3$ FORECAST	ABSOLUTE DEVIATION	$\alpha = .6$ FORECAST	ABSOLUTE DEVIATION	$\alpha = .9$ FORECAST	ABSOLUTE DEVIATION
1	450	410.0	40.0	410.0	40.0	410.0	40.0
2	495	422.0	73.0	434.0	61.0	446.0	49.0
3	518	443.9	74.1	470.6	47.4	490.1	27.9
4	563	466.1	96.9	499.0	64.0	515.2	47.8
5	584	495.2	88.8	537.4	46.6	558.2	25.8
6	?	521.8	—	565.8	—	581.4	—
	Total absolute deviation		372.8		259.0		190.5

$MAD_{\alpha=.3} = 372.8/5 = 74.56$
$MAD_{\alpha=.6} = 259/5 = 51.8$
$MAD_{\alpha=.9} = 190.5/5 = 38.1$

Because it has the lowest MAD, the smoothing constant $\alpha = .9$ gives the most accurate forecast.

4-20.

YEAR	SALES	3-YEAR MOVING AVERAGE
1	450	
2	495	
3	518	
4	563	$(450 + 495 + 518)/3 = 487.667$
5	584	$(495 + 518 + 563)/3 = 525.333$
6	?	$(518 + 563 + 584)/3 = 555$

4-21.

YEAR	TIME PERIOD X	SALES Y	X^2	XY
1	−2	450	4	−900
2	−1	495	1	−495
3	0	518	0	0
4	+1	563	1	563
5	+2	584	4	1168
		2610	10	336

$b = \Sigma xy/\Sigma xy^2 = 336/10 = 33.6$
$a = \Sigma y/n \quad = 2610/5 = 522$
$y = 522 + 33.6(x)$

Projected sales in year 6, which is this coding scheme, is time period +3.

$y = 522 + 33.6(3)$
$\quad = 622.8$

4-22.

YEAR	ACTUAL SALES	3-YEAR MOVING AVERAGE FORECAST	ABSOLUTE DEVIATION	TIME* SERIES FORECAST	ABSOLUTE DEVIATION
1	450	—	—	454.8	4.8
2	495	—	—	488.4	6.6
3	518	—	—	522.0	4.0
4	563	487.7	75.3	555.6	7.4
5	584	525.3	58.7	589.2	5.2
6	?	555.0	—	622.8	—
	Total absolute deviation		134.0		28.0

$\hat{y} = 522 + 33.6(x)$ [See problem 4-21.]*
$\hat{y} = 522 + 33.6(-2) = 454.8$
$y = 522 + 33.6(-1) = 488.4$
$y = 522 + 33.6(0) \quad = 522.0$
$y = 522 + 33.6(1) \quad = 555.6$
$y = 522 + 33.6(2) \quad = 589.2$
$MAD_{\alpha=.3} = 74.56$ [See problem 4-19.]
$MAD_{\text{moving average}} = 134/2 = 67$
$MAD_{\text{regression}} = 28/5 = 5.6$

Regression is obviously the preferred method because of its low MAD.

4-23. a. Drum sales:

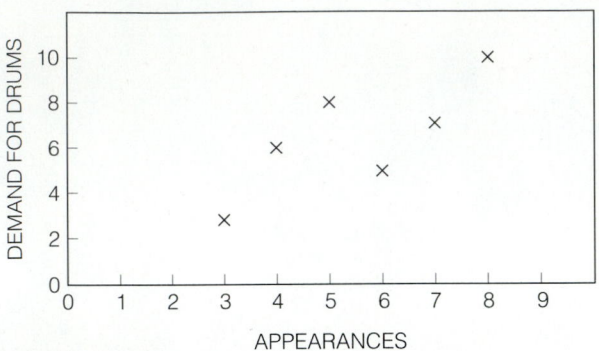

The observations do not form a perfect straight line but approach linearity over the range shown.

b.

DEMAND FOR DRUMS Y	TV APPEARANCES X	X^2	XY
3	3	9	9
6	4	16	24
7	7	49	49
5	6	36	30
10	8	64	80
8	5	25	40
$\Sigma Y = 39$	$\Sigma X = 33$	$\Sigma X^2 = 199$	$\Sigma XY = 232$

$n = 6$ pairs of observations

$\overline{X} = 33/6$

$\overline{Y} = 39/6$

$$b = \frac{\Sigma XY - n\overline{X}\,\overline{Y}}{\Sigma X^2 - n\overline{X}^2}$$

$$= \frac{232 - (6)(33/6)(39/6)}{199 - (6)(33/6)^2} = 1$$

$$a = \overline{Y} - b\overline{X} = 39/6 - (1)(33/6)$$

$$= 6/6 = 1$$

Therefore:

$$\hat{Y} = 1.0 + 1.0X$$

c. If $X = 9$ performances by the *Green Shades,* then estimated sales are:

$$Y = 1.0 + 1.0(9) = 1.0 + 9.0 = 10 \text{ drums}$$

4-24. In order to answer the discussion questions, two forecasting models are required: a three-period moving average and a three-period weighted moving average. Once the actual forecasts have been made, their accuracy can be compared using the mean average differences (MAD).

a, b.

PERIOD	MONTH	DEMAND	AVERAGE	WEIGHTED AVERAGE
4	April	10	13.6667	14.5
5	May	15	13.3333	12.67
6	June	17	13.6667	13.5
7	July	11	14	15.17
8	Aug.	14	14.3333	13.67
9	Sept.	17	14	13.50
10	Oct.	12	14	15
11	Nov.	14	14.3333	14
12	Dec.	16	14.3333	13.83
13	Jan.	11	14	14.67

c. MAD for average is 2.2. MAD for weighted average is 2.72. Moving average forecast for February is 13.6667. Weighted moving average forecast for February is 13.1667.

Because a three-period average forecasting method is used, forecasts start for period four. As can be seen, the MAD for the moving average is 2.2, and the MAD for the weighted moving average is 2.7. Thus, based on this analysis, the moving average appears to be more accurate. The forecast for February is about 14.

d. There are many other factors to consider, including seasonality and any underlying causal variables such as advertising budget.

4-25. a.

WEEK	ACTUAL MILES	FORECAST (F_t)	ERROR	RSFE	SUM OF ABSOLUTE FORECAST ERRORS	MAD	TRACK SIGNAL
1	17	17.00	—	—	—	—	—
2	21	17.00	+4.00	+4.00	4.00	4.00	1
3	19	17.80	+1.20	+5.20	5.20	2.60	2
4	23	18.04	+4.96	+10.16	10.16	3.39	3
5	18	19.03	−1.03	+9.13	11.19	2.80	3.3
6	16	18.83	−2.83	+6.30	14.02	2.80	2.25
7	20	18.26	+1.74	+8.04	15.76	2.63	3.05
8	18	18.61	−0.61	+7.43	16.37	2.34	3.17
9	22	18.49	+3.51	+10.94	19.88	2.49	4.21
10	20	19.19	+0.81	+11.75	20.69	2.30	5.11
11	15	19.35	−4.35	+7.40	25.04	2.50	2.96
12	22	18.48	+3.52	+10.92	28.56	2.60	4.20

b. The total MAD is 2.60.

c. RSFE is consistently positive. Tracking signal exceeds 5 MAD's at week 10.

4-26. a, b. See the accompanying table for a comparison of the calculations for the exponentially smoothed forecasts using constants of .1 and .6.

c. Students should note how stable the smoothed values for the .1 smoothing constant are. When compared to actual week 25 calls of 85, the .6 smoothing constant appears to do a better job. On the basis of the forecast error, the .6 constant is better also. However, other smoothing constants need to be examined. Trend adjustment is also worth an investigation (and is attempted in the next problem).

4-27. To evaluate the trend-adjusted exponential smoothing model, actual week 25 calls are compared to the forecasted values. The model appears to be doing somewhat better, but a seasonality effect may need to be considered. It does not appear that adjusting for trend improves the accuracy of the forecast by much. Other combinations of smoothing constants may help, however. The table on page IS-33 illustrates the calculations for the trend-adjusted forecasts.

4-28. Trend adjusted exponential smoothing: $\alpha = .1$; $\beta = .2$

MONTH	INCOME	INITIAL FORECAST
Feb.	70.0	65.0
Mar.	68.5	$65.0 + .1(70.0 - 65.0) = 65.5$
Apr.	64.8	$65.5 + .1(68.5 - 65.5) = 65.8$
May	71.7	$65.8 + .1(64.8 - 65.8) = 65.7$
June	71.3	$65.7 + .1(71.7 - 65.7) = 66.3$
July	72.8	$66.3 + .1(71.3 - 66.3) = 66.8$
Aug.		$66.8 + .1(72.8 - 66.8) = 67.4$

Solution to 4-26 continued on the next page.

Solution Table for Problem 4-26

WEEK, t	ACTUAL VALUE, A_t	SMOOTHED VALUE, $F_t(\alpha = .1)$	FORECAST ERROR	SMOOTHED VALUE, $F_t(\alpha = .6)$	FORECAST ERROR
1	50	50	—		—
2	35	50	−15	50	−15
3	25	48	−23	41	−16
4	40	46	−6	31	+8
5	45	45	0	37	+9
6	35	45	−10	42	−7
7	20	44	−24	38	−18
8	30	42	−12	27	+3
9	35	41	−6	29	+6
10	20	40	−20	32	−12
11	15	38	−23	25	−10
12	40	36	+4	19	+21
13	55	36	+19	32	+23
14	35	38	−3	46	−11
15	25	38	−13	39	−14
16	55	37	+18	31	+24
17	55	38	+16	45	+10
18	40	40	0	51	−12
19	35	40	−5	44	−10
20	60	40	+20	39	+21
21	75	42	+33	51	+23
22	50	45	+5	66	−16
23	40	45	+9	56	−16
24	65	45	−20	46	+18
25		47		58	

Solution to 4-28 (continued)

MONTH	INCOME	F_t	TREND FORECAST
Feb.	70.0	65.0	0
Mar.	68.5	65.5	$.8(0) + .2(65.5 - 65.0) = .10$
Apr.	64.8	65.8	$.8(.10) + .2(65.8 - 65.5) = .14$
May	71.7	65.7	$.8(.14) + .2(65.7 - 65.8) = .09$
June	71.3	66.3	$.8(.09) + .2(66.3 - 65.7) = .19$
July	72.8	66.8	$.8(.19) + .2(66.8 - 66.3) = .25$
Aug.		67.4	$.8(.25) + .2(67.4 - 66.8) = .32$

MONTH	INCOME	F_t	T_t	FIT_t	ABSOLUTE DEVIATION
Feb.	70.0	—			
Mar.	68.5	65.5	.10	65.6	2.9
Apr.	64.8	65.8	.14	66.0	1.1
May	71.7	65.7	.09	65.8	5.9
June	71.3	66.3	.19	66.5	4.8
July	72.8	66.8	.25	67.0	5.7
Aug.		67.4	.32	67.7	

$$\Sigma = 20.3$$
$$MAD = 4.10$$

Solution Table for Problem 4-27
$\alpha = .3, \beta = .1$

WEEK, t	ACTUAL VALUE, A_t	SMOOTHED VALUE, F_t	TREND ESTIMATE, T_t	FORECAST, FIT_t	FORECAST ERROR
1	50	50.0	—	—	—
2	35	50.0	.0	50.0	−15.0
3	25	45.5	−.5	45.1	−20.0
4	40	39.3	−1.0	38.3	1.7
5	45	39.5	−.9	38.5	6.4
6	35	41.2	−.6	40.3	−5.5
7	20	39.3	−.8	38.3	−18.6
8	30	33.5	−1.3	31.9	−2.2
9	35	32.5	−1.2	30.7	3.8
10	20	33.2	−1.0	31.6	−12.1
11	15	29.3	−1.3	27.2	−12.9
12	40	25.0	−1.6	22.5	16.7
13	55	29.5	−1.0	27.4	26.5
14	35	37.1	−.2	35.9	−2.0
15	25	36.5	−.2	35.1	−11.3
16	55	33.0	−.5	31.4	22.5
17	55	39.6	.2	38.6	15.2
18	40	44.2	.6	43.7	−4.9
19	35	43.0	.7	42.3	−8.4
20	60	40.6	.2	39.6	19.3
21	75	46.4	.7	46.0	27.9
22	50	55.0	1.5	55.5	−6.5
23	40	53.5	1.2	53.8	−14.7
24	65	49.4	0.7	49.4	18.9
25				55.2	

Source of problem: Adapted from J. E. Hanke and A. G. Reitsch, *Business Forecasting,* 2nd ed. (Boston: Allyn & Bacon, Inc., 1989), p. 87.

4-29. Trend adjusted exponential smoothing: $\alpha = .1$; $\beta = .8$

MONTH	INCOME	INITIAL FORECAST
Feb.	70.0	65.0
Mar.	68.5	$65.0 + .1(70.0 - 65.0) = 65.5$
Apr.	64.8	$65.5 + .1(68.5 - 65.5) = 65.8$
May	71.7	$65.8 + .1(64.8 - 65.8) = 65.7$
June	71.3	$65.7 + .1(71.7 - 67.7) = 66.3$
July	72.8	$65.3 + .1(72.8 - 66.3) = 66.8$

MONTH	INCOME	F_t	TREND FORECAST
Feb.	70.0	65.0	0
Mar.	68.5	65.5	$.2(0) + .8(65.5 - 65.0) = .40$
Apr.	64.8	65.8	$.2(.40) + .8(65.8 - 65.5) = .32$
May	71.7	65.7	$.2(.32) + .8(65.7 - 65.8) = .02$
June	71.3	66.3	$.2(.02) + .8(66.3 - 65.7) = .48$
July	72.8	66.8	$.2(.48) + .8(66.8 - 66.3) = .50$
Aug.		67.4	$.2(.50) + .8(67.4 - 66.8) = .58$

MONTH	INCOME	F_t	T_t	FIT_t	ABSOLUTE DEVIATION
Feb.	70.0				
Mar.	68.5	65.5	.40	65.9	2.6
Apr.	64.8	65.8	.32	66.1	1.6
May	71.7	65.7	−.02	65.7	5.4
June	71.3	66.3	.48	66.8	4.0
July	72.8	66.8	.50	67.3	4.6
Aug.		67.4	.58	68.0	

$$\Sigma = 19.9$$
$$\text{MAD} = 3.98$$

Based upon a mean absolute deviation criterion, the exponential smoothing with $\alpha = .1$, $\beta = .8$ is to be preferred over the exponential smoothing with $\alpha = .1$, $\beta = .2$.

4-30. The coefficient of correlation is given by:

$$r = \frac{n\Sigma XY - \Sigma X \Sigma Y}{\sqrt{[n\Sigma X^2 - (\Sigma X)^2][n\Sigma Y^2 - (\Sigma Y)^2]}}$$

$$\therefore r = \frac{5(70) - (15)(20)}{\sqrt{[5(55) - (15)^2][5(130) - (20)^2]}}$$

$$= \frac{5 \times 70 - (15)(20)}{\sqrt{(5 \times 55 - 15 \times 15)(5 \times 130 - 20 \times 20)}}$$

$$= \frac{350 - 300}{\sqrt{(275 - 225)(650 - 400)}}$$

$$= \frac{50}{\sqrt{(50)(250)}}$$

$$= \frac{50}{111.80} = .447 = .45$$

r lies between 0 and 1. This indicates a positive correlation between bank deposits and consumer price indices.

4-31.

Y	X	XY	Y^2	X^2
4	2	8	16	4
1	1	1	1	1
4	4	16	16	16
6	5	30	36	25
5	3	15	25	9
$\Sigma Y = 20$	$\Sigma X = 15$	$\Sigma XY = 70$	$\Sigma Y^2 = 94$	$\Sigma X^2 = 55$

$$\overline{X} = \frac{\Sigma X}{5} = \frac{15}{5} = 3$$

$$\overline{Y} = \frac{\Sigma Y}{5} = \frac{20}{5} = 4$$

$$b = \frac{\Sigma XY - n\overline{X}\,\overline{Y}}{\Sigma X^2 - n\overline{X}^2} = \frac{70 - (5 \times 4 \times 3)}{55 - (5 \times 3^2)}$$

$$= \frac{70 - 60}{55 - (5 \times 9)} = \frac{10}{55 - 45} = \frac{10}{10} = 1.0$$

$$a = \overline{Y} - b\overline{X} = 1$$

a. The regression equation is:

$$\hat{Y} = a + bx$$
$$\hat{Y} = 1 + 1x$$

Coefficient of correlation is:

$$r = \frac{n\Sigma XY - \Sigma X \Sigma Y}{\sqrt{[n\Sigma X^2 - (\Sigma X)^2][n\Sigma Y^2 - (\Sigma Y)^2]}}$$

$$= \frac{5(70) - (15)(20)}{\sqrt{[5(55) - (15)^2][5(94) - (20)^2]}}$$

$$= \frac{350 - 300}{\sqrt{(275 - 225)(470 - 400)}}$$

$$= \frac{50}{\sqrt{50 \times 70}}$$

$$= \frac{50}{\sqrt{3500}} = \frac{50}{59.16} = .845$$

b. Standard error of the estimate:

$$S_{yx} = \text{Standard error of the estimate}$$

$$= \sqrt{\frac{\Sigma y^2 - a\Sigma y - b\Sigma xy}{n - 2}}$$

$$= \sqrt{\frac{94 - (1 * 20) - (1 * 70)}{5 - 2}}$$

$$= \sqrt{\frac{94 - 20 - 70}{3}} = \sqrt{\frac{4}{3}}$$

$$= 1.15$$

4-32. a. It appears from the accompanying graph that the points scatter around a straight line.

b. The values for *a* and *b* are calculated from the accompanying table on page IS-36.

$$b = 1.593$$
$$a = 5.060$$

Thus, the regression relationship is: $y = 5.060 + 1.593x$.

c. For the tourist level of 10,000,000, the model predicts that 2,099,000 riders will use the system. That is:

$$y = 5.060 + 1.593 (10)$$
$$= 20.99, \text{ or } 2,099,000 \text{ people}$$

d. If $x = 0$ tourists, the model produces a ridership of 506,000 people. This is probably a very erroneous forecast, however, because the value $x = 0$ is outside the range of observed values.

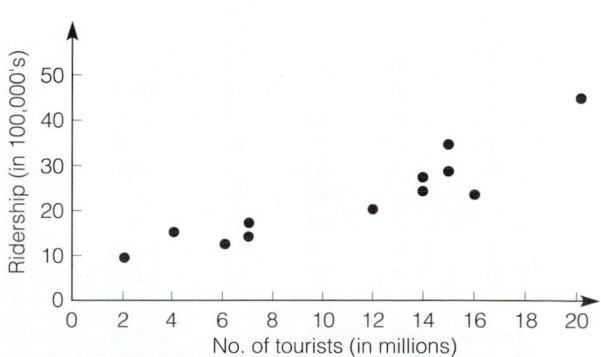

Calculations for Regression Coefficients for Problem 4-32:

x	y	xy	x^2	y^2
7	15	105	49	225
2	10	20	4	100
6	13	78	36	169
4	15	60	16	225
14	25	350	196	625
15	27	405	225	729
16	24	384	256	576
12	20	240	144	400
14	27	378	196	729
20	44	880	400	1,936
15	34	510	225	1,156
7	17	119	49	289
132	271	3,529	1,796	7,159

4-33. The multiple regression equation is:

$$\hat{Y} = \$90.00 + \$48.50X_1 + \$.40X_2$$

a. Thomas Williams:

Number of days on the road: $X_1 = 5$

Distance traveled: $X_2 = 300$ miles

The amount he may be expected to claim is:

$$\hat{Y} = \$90.00 + (\$48.50 \times 5) + (\$.40 \times 300)$$
$$= \$90.00 + \$242.50 + \$120.00$$
$$= \$452.50$$

b. The reimbursement request, according to the model, appears to be too high. The accountants should question Thomas Williams about his expenses.

c. A number of other variables should be included, such as:

1. The type of travel (air or car).
2. Conference fees if any.
3. Entertainment of customers.
4. Other transportation (cab and limousine).

In addition, the coefficient of correlation is only .68. Thus, the validity of the model should be questioned.

4-34.

YEAR	X	Y	PATIENTS X^2	Y^2	XY
1	1	36	1	1,296	36
2	2	33	4	1,089	66
3	3	40	9	1,600	120
4	4	41	16	1,681	164
5	5	40	25	1,600	200
6	6	55	36	3,025	330
7	7	60	49	3,600	420
8	8	54	64	2,916	432
9	9	58	81	3,364	522
10	10	61	100	3,721	610
Totals:	55	478	385	23,892	2,900

Given:

$$Y = a + b * X$$

where

$$b = \frac{\Sigma XY - n\overline{X}\,\overline{Y}}{\Sigma X^2 - n\overline{X}^2}$$

$$a = \overline{Y} - b\overline{X}$$

$$\overline{X} = \frac{55}{10} = 5.5 \quad \overline{Y} = \frac{478}{10} = 47.8$$

Then:

$$b = \frac{2,900 - 10 * 5.5 * 47.8}{385 - 10 * 5.5^2}$$

$$= \frac{2,900 - 2,629}{385 - 302.5} = \frac{271}{82.5}$$

$$= 3.28$$

$$a = 47.8 - 3.28 * 5.5$$

$$= 29.76$$

For:

$$(X = 11): Y = 29.76 + 3.28 * 11 = 65.8$$
$$(X = 12): Y = 29.76 + 3.28 * 12 = 69.1$$
$$(X = 13): Y = 29.76 + 3.28 * 13 = 72.4$$

Therefore:

Year 11 → 65.8 patients

Year 12 → 69.1 patients

Year 13 → 72.4 patients

The model "seems" to fit the data pretty well. One should, however, be more precise in judging the adequacy of the model. Two possible approaches are computation of (1) the correlation coefficient or (2) the mean absolute deviation.

The correlation coefficient:

$r = $ correlation coefficient

$$= \frac{n\Sigma XY - \Sigma X \Sigma Y}{\sqrt{[n\Sigma X^2 - (\Sigma X)^2][n\Sigma Y^2 - (\Sigma Y)^2]}}$$

$$= \frac{10 * 2,900 - 55 * 478}{\sqrt{[10 * 385 - 55^2][10 * 23,892 - 478^2]}}$$

$$= \frac{29,000 - 26,292}{\sqrt{[3,850 - 3,025][238,920 - 228,484]}}$$

$$= \frac{2,708}{\sqrt{825 * 10,436}} = \frac{2,708}{\sqrt{8,609,700}}$$

$$= \frac{2,708}{2,934.2}$$

$$r = .92$$

The correlation coefficient of .92 is quite respectable—indicating that our original judgment of a "good" fit was appropriate.

The mean absolute deviation (MAD):

X	PATIENTS Y	TREND FORECAST	DEVIATION	ABSOLUTE DEVIATION
1	36	$29.7 + 3.28 * 1 = 33.0$	3.0	3.0
2	33	$29.7 + 3.28 * 2 = 36.3$	-3.3	3.3
3	40	$29.7 + 3.28 * 3 = 39.5$	.5	.5
4	41	$29.7 + 3.28 * 4 = 42.8$	-1.8	1.8
5	40	$29.7 + 3.28 * 5 = 46.1$	-6.1	6.1
6	55	$29.7 + 3.28 * 6 = 49.4$	5.6	5.6
7	60	$29.7 + 3.28 * 7 = 52.7$	-7.3	7.3
8	54	$29.7 + 3.28 * 8 = 56.0$	-2.0	2.0
9	58	$29.7 + 3.28 * 9 = 59.2$	1.2	1.2
10	61	$29.7 + 3.28 * 10 = 62.5$	1.5	1.5

$$\Sigma = 32.3$$
$$\text{MAD} = 3.23$$

The MAD is 3.23; this is approximately 6% of the average number of patients and 9% of the minimum number of patients. We also see absolute deviations, for years five, six, and seven, in the range 5.6 to 7.3. The comparison of the MAD with the average and minimum number of patients, and the comparatively large deviations during the middle years, indicate that the forecast model is not exceptionally accurate. It is more useful for predicting general trends than the actual number of patients to be seen in a specific year.

4-35.

YEAR	CRIME RATE X	PATIENTS Y	X^2	Y^2	XY
1	58.3	36	3,398.9	1,296	2,098.8
2	61.1	33	3,733.2	1,089	2,016.3
3	73.4	40	5,358.2	1,600	2,936.0
4	75.7	41	5,730.5	1,681	3,103.7
5	81.1	40	6,577.2	1,600	3,244.0
6	89.0	55	7,921.0	3,025	4,895.0
7	101.1	60	10,221.2	3,600	6,066.0
8	94.8	54	8,987.0	2,916	5,119.2
9	103.3	58	10,670.9	3,364	5,991.4
10	116.2	61	13,502.4	3,721	7,088.2
Totals	854.0	478	76,129.4	23,982	42,558.6

Given:

$$Y = a + b * X$$

where

$$b = \frac{\Sigma XY - n\overline{XY}}{\Sigma X^2 - n\overline{X}^2}$$

$$a = \overline{Y} - b\overline{X}$$

$$\overline{X} = \frac{854}{10} = 85.4 \quad \overline{Y} = \frac{478}{10} = 47.8$$

4-35 (continued)

Then:

$$b = \frac{42{,}558.6 - 10 * 85.4 * 47.8}{76{,}129.4 - 10 * 85.4}$$

$$= \frac{42{,}558.6 - 40{,}821.2}{76{,}129.4 - 72{,}931.6} = \frac{1{,}737.4}{3{,}197.8}$$

$$= .543$$

$$a = 47.8 - .543 * 85.4$$

$$= 1.40$$

For:

$$X = 131.2 : Y = 1.40 + .543 * 131.2 = 72.7$$
$$X = 90.6 : Y = 1.40 + .543 * 90.6 = 50.6$$

Therefore:

Crime rate $= 131.2 \rightarrow 72.7$ patients
Crime rate $= 90.6 \rightarrow 50.6$ patients

4-36. To compute a seasonalized or adjusted sales forecast, we just multiply each seasonal index by the appropriate trend forecast.

$$\hat{Y}_{\text{seasonal}} = \text{Index} * \hat{Y}_{\text{trend forecast}}$$

Hence for:

Quarter I: $\hat{Y}_{\text{I}} = (1.30)(\$100{,}000) = \$130{,}000$
Quarter II: $\hat{Y}_{\text{II}} = (.90)(\$120{,}000) = \$108{,}000$
Quarter III: $\hat{Y}_{\text{III}} = (.70)(\$140{,}000) = \$98{,}000$
Quarter IV: $\hat{Y}_{\text{IV}} = (1.15)(\$160{,}000) = \$184{,}000$

4-37.

$$\frac{\text{Average year 1 - year 2 demand for season}}{} = \frac{\text{Year 1 demand + Year 2 demand}}{2}$$

$$\frac{\text{Average seasonal demand}}{} = \frac{\text{Sum of average year 1 - year 2 demand}}{4}$$

Solution Table for Problem 4-37

SEASON	YEAR 1 DEMAND	YEAR 2 DEMAND	AVERAGE YEAR 1 – YEAR 2 DEMAND	AVERAGE SEASON DEMAND	SEASON INDEX	YEAR 3 DEMAND
Fall	200	250	225.0	250	.90	270
Winter	350	300	325.0	250	1.30	390
Spring	150	165	157.5	250	.63	189
Summer	300	285	292.5	250	1.17	351

4-37 (continued)

$$\text{Season index} = \frac{\text{Average year 1} - \text{year 2 demand}}{\text{Average seasonal demand}}$$

$$\text{Year 3 demand} = \frac{\text{New annual demand}}{4} * \text{Season index}$$

$$= \frac{1,200}{4} * \text{Season index}$$

4-38.

X	Y	X^2	Y^2	XY
421	2.90	177,241	8.41	1,220.9
377	2.93	142,129	8.58	1,104.6
585	3.00	342,225	9.00	1,775.0
690	3.45	476,100	11.90	2,380.5
608	3.66	369,664	13.40	2,225.3
390	2.88	152,100	8.29	1,123.2
415	2.15	172,225	4.62	892.3
481	2.53	231,361	6.40	1,216.9
729	3.22	531,441	10.37	2,347.4
501	1.99	251,001	3.96	997.0
613	2.75	375,769	7.56	1,685.8
709	3.90	502,681	15.21	2,765.1
366	1.60	133,956	2.56	585.6
6,885	36.96	3,857,893	110.27	20,299.5

Given:

$$Y = a + b * X$$

where

$$b = \frac{\Sigma XY - n\overline{XY}}{\Sigma X^2 - n\overline{X}^2}$$

$$a = \overline{Y} - b\overline{X}$$

$$\overline{X} = \frac{6,885}{13} = 529.6$$

$$\overline{Y} = \frac{36.96}{13} = 2.84$$

Then:

$$b = \frac{20,299.5 - 13 * 529.6 * 2.84}{3,857,893 - 13 * 529.6^2}$$

$$= \frac{20,299.5 - 19,552.8}{3,857,893 - 3,646,190} = \frac{746.7}{211,703}$$

$$= .003527$$

$$a = 2.84 - .003527 * 529.6$$

$$= .972$$

and

$$Y = .972 + .0035 * X$$

As an indication of the usefulness of this relationship, we can calculate the correlation coefficient:

$r =$ correlation coefficient

$$= \frac{n\Sigma XY - \Sigma X \Sigma Y}{\sqrt{[n\Sigma X^2 - (\Sigma X)^2][n\Sigma Y^2 - (\Sigma Y)^2]}}$$

$$= \frac{13 * 20,299.5 - 6,885 * 36.96}{\sqrt{[13 * 3,857,893 - 6,885^2][13 * 110.27 - 36.96^2]}}$$

$$= \frac{263,893.5 - 254,469.6}{\sqrt{[50,152,609 - 47,403,225][1,433.5 - 1,366.0]}}$$

$$= \frac{9423.9}{\sqrt{[2,749,384][67.47]}}$$

$$= \frac{9423.9}{1,658.13 * 8.21}$$

or

$$r = .692$$

and

$$r^2 = .479$$

A correlation coefficient of .692 is not particularly high. The coefficient of determination, r^2, indicates that the model explains only 47.9% of the overall variation. Therefore, while the model does provide an estimate of GPA, there is considerable variation in GPA which is as yet unexplained.

For:

$$X = 350 : Y = .972 + .0035 * 350 = 2.197$$
$$X = 800 : Y = .972 + .0035 * 800 = 3.77$$

(In solving this problem, care must be taken to interpret significant digits. The solution presented above was developed on a hand calculator. A solution developed by computer gave: $Y = 1.03 + .0034 X$.)

4-39. a. Students should examine error measures (see printout) and measures of goodness of fit.

b. With older data excluded (and a case can easily be made for doing so), the conclusions may reverse. Trend analysis may have a high r^2, but its projection for year 45 is only 54.39 because of the weight given to old data.

Printout for Problem 4-39 (AB:QM Program Output Excerpts for Shader-Smith Data Set)

```
Program: Forecasting / Exponential Smoothing

Problem Title: SHADER-SMITH DATASET 4.39

***** Input Data *****

Alpha                            :      .600
Initial Estimated Forecast       :      .250
Number of Periods                :       44

Mean Absolute Deviation          :    3.5783
Mean Square Error                :   36.0291     Exponential
Mean Forecast Error              :   -3.4116     Smoothing
Running Sum of Forecast Error : 143.2889
Tracking Signal                  :   40.0436

***** Program Output for Trend *****

Parameter      Coefficient      SE B        t

Intercept       -18.9642       4.1136    -4.6101
   b1             1.6380        .1592    10.2876
                                                     Trend
Coefficient of determination :    .7159
Correlation coefficient      :    .8461
Standard Error               :  13.4115
Mean Absolute Deviation (MAD):  10.8307

***** Program Output for Regression *****

Parameter      Coefficient      SE B

Intercept       -17.6356       4.5042
   b 1           13.5936        1.5019
                                                 Regression
Coefficient of determination :    .6611
Correlation coefficient      :    .8131
Standard Error               :  14.6519
Mean Absolute Deviation (MAD):  10.4936
```

INSTRUCTORS' SECTION

Solution to North-South Airline Case

Northern Airline data:

YEAR	AIRFRAME COST PER AIRCRAFT	ENGINE COST PER AIRCRAFT	AVERAGE AGE (HOURS)
1981	51.80	43.49	6,512
1982	54.92	38.58	8,404
1983	69.70	51.48	11,077
1984	68.90	58.72	11,717
1985	63.72	45.47	13,275
1986	84.73	50.26	15,215
1987	78.74	79.60	18,390

Southern Airline data:

YEAR	AIRFRAME COST PER AIRCRAFT	ENGINE COST PER AIRCRAFT	AVERAGE AGE (HOURS)
1981	13.29	18.86	5,107
1982	25.15	31.55	8,145
1983	32.18	40.43	7,360
1984	31.78	22.10	5,773
1985	25.34	19.69	7,150
1986	32.78	32.58	9,364
1987	35.56	38.07	8,259

Utilizing AB:QM, we can develop the following regression equations for the variables of interest.

Northern Airline—airframe maintenance cost:

$$\text{Cost} = 36.10 + .0025 * \text{Airframe age}$$

Coefficient of determination = .7694

Coefficient of correlation = .8771

Northern Airline—engine maintenance cost:

$$\text{Cost} = 20.57 + .0026 * \text{Airframe age}$$

Coefficient of determination = .6124

Coefficient of correlation = .7825

Southern Airline—airframe maintenance cost:

$$\text{Cost} = 4.60 + .0032 * \text{Airframe age}$$

Coefficient of determination = .3904

Coefficient of correlation = .6248

Southern Airline—engine maintenance cost:

$$\text{Cost} = -.671 + .0047 * \text{Airframe age}$$

Coefficient of determination = .4599

Coefficient of correlation = .6782

The following graphs portray both the actual data and the regression lines for airframe and engine maintenance costs for both airlines.

Note that the two graphs have been drawn to the same scale to facilitate comparisons between the two airlines. Northern Airline: There seem to be modest correlations between maintenance costs and airframe age for Northern Airline. There is certainly reason to conclude, however, that airframe age is not the only important factor. Southern Airline: The relationships

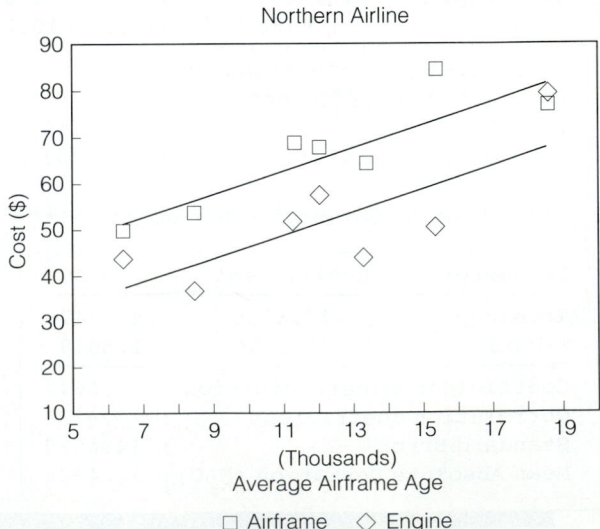

Northern Airline

between maintenance costs and airframe age for Southern Airline are much less well defined. It is even more obvious that airframe age is not the only important factor—perhaps not even the most important factor.

Overall, it would seem that:

1. Northern Airline has the smallest variance in maintenance costs, indicating that the day-to-day management of maintenance is working pretty well.
2. Maintenance costs seem to be more a function of airline than of airframe age.
3. The airframe and engine maintenance costs for Southern Airline are not only lower but more nearly similar than those for Northern Airline, but, from the graphs at least, appear to be rising more sharply with age.
4. From an overall perspective, it appears that Southern Airline may perform more efficiently on sporadic or emergency repairs, and Northern Airline may place more emphasis on preventive maintenance.

Ms. Young's report should conclude that:

1. There is evidence to suggest that maintenance costs *could be made to be a function of airframe age* by implementing more effective management practices.
2. The difference between maintenance procedures of the two airlines should be investigated.
3. The data with which she is presently working does not provide conclusive results.

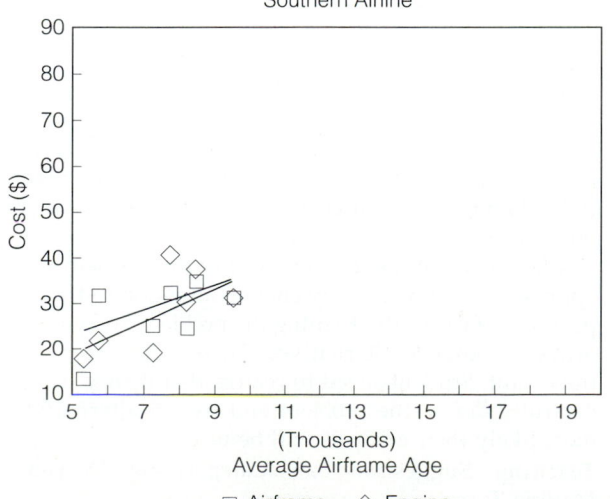

Southern Airline

Solution to Kwik Lube Case

1. The relationship between Kwik Lube sales (y), average industry sales (x), and year (t with $t = 1$ corresponding to 1981) is shown in the table. The x and y values are in thousands of dollars. One could try a multiple regression analysis but the correlation of y with just x is .998 leading one to use the simple linear regression equation: $y = 14.2 + 2.99x$.

t	X	Y
1	220	680
2	250	750
3	240	750
4	260	780
5	330	990
6	350	1040
7	390	1200
8	440	1330

The year 1980 was excluded since the Kwik Lube revenues were not for an entire year. 1988 ($t = 8$) was the last year of Kwik Lube operation without the competition from Speedy Lube. The forecasted sales for 1989 would be estimated using the average industry sales of $470,000 for x:

$$y = 2.99(470) + 14.2 = 1419.5$$

and the forecasted sales for 1990 would use the industry sales of $520,000:

$$y = 2.99(520) + 14.2 = 1,569$$

The estimated lost sales is the difference between the forecasted and actual sales: $(1,419,500 + 1,569,000) - (1,110,000 + 1,110,000) = \$768,500$.

A 95% prediction interval for 1989 is 1419.5 ± 52 and for 1981 is 1569 ± 58. Thus, despite the danger of extrapolation, and the results of a regression outside the range of the data, one can be reasonably certain that the lost sales were at least $658,500.

2. Without the questionnaire study, the best estimate of lost sales would be from the regression of y on t:

$$y = 518 + 93.8t$$

with a somewhat lower correlation. The estimated lost sales would be $598,200, about $200,000 less than the estimate based on average industry sales. Even recovering as little as 10% of this difference would pay for the study.

3. The lawsuit filed by Dick Johnson should discuss two basic areas that will build a sound case for damages being awarded in his favor.

The first factor involves the concept behind setting up a franchise. Franchises are designed so that independent owners can start a business with a well-known name (and consequently, with an already captured market). This, coupled with proven strategies and expertise given to a franchise purchaser by the franchise seller, reduces the usually high probability of a new business going under in its infancy stage. The franchise fee is the cost paid for the reduced risk of a new enterprise.

Naturally, the franchising firm will protect itself against competition in a franchise contract. A franchise holder who violates such clauses has, in essence, gained free proven strategies and has capitalized on it. Thus, the franchising firm has been damaged by the fact that a competitor has gained information without paying for it.

This is the case with Kwik Lube. A franchise owner, T. A. Williams, has benefited from Johnson's expertise more than is justified by the monetary gains earned from franchise fees. This is not simply an economic issue, however, for such a situation was thought of before by Johnson. He had sought to protect himself with a noncompetition clause in his franchised contract. Thus, Williams is legally in the wrong for his breach of contract.

What this first area of discussion in the lawsuit does is to determine that there, in fact, has been damage done to the plaintiff, Johnson. The second area to be discussed in the lawsuit should deal with how those damages can be mitigated by the defendant, Williams.

Usually in lawsuits, there is a problem with measuring the damage done. Johnson, however, can measure his loss by forecasting sales and then comparing actual sales to predicted sales.

In summary, the lawsuit should discuss how damage was incurred to the plaintiff, Johnson, and how said damage should and/or could be mitigated. A well-presented lawsuit or petition to the court should result in a favorable judgment for the owner of Kwik Lube.

5
Fundamentals of Decision Theory

LEARNING OBJECTIVES

After completing this chapter, students will be able to:

1. List the steps of the decision-making process.
2. Describe the types of decision-making environments.
3. Use probability values to make decisions under risk.
4. Make decisions under uncertainty, where there is risk but probability values are not known.
5. Use computers to solve basic decision-making problems.

TEACHING SUGGESTIONS

Teaching Suggestion 5.1: Using the Steps of the Decision-Making Process.

The six steps used in decision theory are discussed in this chapter. Students can be asked to describe a decision they made in the last semester, such as buying a car or selecting an apartment, and describe the steps that were involved. This will help in getting students involved in decision theory. It will also help them realize how this material can be useful to them in making important personal decisions.

Teaching Suggestion 5.2: Importance of Defining the Problem and Listing All Possible Alternatives.

Clearly defining the problem and listing the possible alternatives can be difficult. Students can be asked to do this for a typical decision-making problem, such as constructing a new manufacturing plant. Role-playing can be used to make this exercise more interesting.

Many students get too involved in the mathematical approaches and do not pay enough attention to the importance of carefully defining the problem and considering all possible alternatives. These initial steps are important. Students need to realize that if they do not carefully define the problem and list all alternatives, most likely their analysis will be wrong.

Teaching Suggestion 5.3: Categorizing Decision-Making Types.

Decision-making types are discussed in this chapter; decision making under certainty, risk, and uncertainty are included. Students can be asked to describe an important decision they had to make in the past year and categorize the decision type. A good example can be a financial investment of $1,000. In-class discussion can help students realize the importance of decision theory and its potential use.

Teaching Suggestion 5.4: Starting the EVPI Concept.

The material on the expected value of perfect information (EVPI) can be started with a discussion of how to place a value on information and whether or not new information should be acquired. The use of EVPI to place an upper limit on what you should pay for information is a good way to start the section on this topic.

Teaching Suggestion 5.5: Starting the Decision Making Under Uncertainty Material.

The section on decision making under uncertainty can be started with a discussion of optimistic versus pessimistic decision makers. Students can be shown how maximax is an optimistic approach, while maximin is a pessimistic decision technique. While few people use these techniques to solve real problems, the concepts and general approaches are useful.

Teaching Suggestion 5.6: Use of Marginal Analysis.

Marginal analysis is a practical and time-saving decision technique when the concepts of marginal profit and loss apply. A good way to start this section is to have students develop a decision tree for a problem that requires five or more stocking options and demand levels. This will be a large tree with many branches. Then, you can have students determine the monetary end-values for each branch on the tree. Again, this will take some time. Once students understand what is involved, they will appreciate the simplicity and speed of marginal analysis.

ALTERNATE EXAMPLES

Alternate Example 5-1: Goleb Transport

George Goleb is considering the purchase of two types of industrial robots. The ROB-1 (Alternative 1) is a large robot capable of performing a variety of tasks, including welding, painting, etc. The ROB-2 (Alternative 2) is a smaller and slower robot, but it has all of the capabilities of ROB-1. The robots will be used to perform a variety of repair operations on large industrial equipment. Of course, George can always do nothing and not buy any robot (Alternative 3). The market for the repair could be either favorable (Event 1) or unfavorable (Event 2). George has constructed a payoff matrix showing the expected returns of each alternative

and the probability of a favorable or unfavorable market. The data are presented below:

	EVENT 1	EVENT 2
Probability	0.6	0.4
Alternative 1	50,000	−40,000
Alternative 2	30,000	−20,000
Alternative 3	0	0

This problem can be solved using expected monetary value. The equations are presented below:

EMV (Alternative 1) = ($50,000) (.6) + (−$40,000) (.4)
= $14,000

EMV (Alternative 2) = ($30,000) (.6) + (−$20,000) (.4)
= $10,000

EMV (Alternative 3) = 0.

The best solution is to purchase ROB-1, the large robot.

Alternate Example 5-2: George Goleb is not confident about the probability of a favorable or unfavorable market. (See Alternate Example 5-1.) He would like to determine the equally likely (Laplace), maximax, maximin, coefficient of realism (Hurwicz), and minimax decisions. The Hurwicz alpha coefficient should be .5. The problem data is summarized below:

Hurwicz Alpha Coefficient: 0.5

	EVENT 1	EVENT 2
Alternative 1	50,000.000	−40,000.000
Alternative 2	30,000.000	−20,000.000
Alternative 3	0.000	0.000

The Laplace (Equally Likely) solution is computed assuming that the probabilities are equal (.5). The results are shown below. Alternatives 1 and 2 both give the highest return of $5,000.

EMV (Alternative 1) = ($50,000) (.5) + (−$40,000) (.5)
= $5,000

EMV (Alternative 2) = ($30,000) (.5) + (−$20,000) (.5)
= $5,000

EMV (Alternative 3) = 0.

The maximin decision (pessimistic) maximizes the minimum outcome for every alternative. The solution is to do nothing as seen on page IS-44.

The maximax decision (optimistic) maximizes the maximum outcome for any alternative. The solution is to purchase the large robot.

The Hurwicz approach uses an alpha value of .5. The results will be the same as the equally likely decision. The results are below:

EMV (Alternative 1) = ($50,000) (.5) + (−$40,000) (.5)
= $5,000

EMV (Alternative 2) = ($30,000) (.5) + (−$20,000) (.5)
= $5,000

EMV (Alternative 3) = 0 .

The minimax decision minimizes the maximum opportunity loss. The opportunity loss table for Goleb is presented below:

ALTERNATIVES	FAVORABLE MARKET	UNFAVORABLE MARKET	MAXIMUM IN ROW
ROB 1	0	40,000	40,000
ROB 2	20,000	20,000	20,000
Nothing	50,000	0	50,000

The alternative that minimizes the maximum opportunity loss is the ROB 2. This is seen in the last column in the above table—$20,000. ROB 1 has a maximum opportunity loss of $40,000, and doing nothing has a maximum opportunity loss of $50,000.

Alternate Example 5-3: Joe's Fresh Fruit

Joe Castillo owns and operates a large fresh-fruit stand in Knoxville, Tennessee. Fresh greens are his primary produce. Each case of greens sells for $15. Joe's cost is $5 for each case. Cases that are not sold can be sold for $1 a case at the end of the day to a small grocery store. The probability of sales for cases of greens is below:

DAILY SALES IN CASES	PROBABILITY AT THIS LEVEL
5	.1
6	.1
7	.2
8	.3
9	.2
10	.1

We start the solution by noting that the marginal profit (MP) is $15 − $5 = $10 per case. The marginal loss (ML) is $5 − $1 = $4 per case. In order to solve this problem, we first compute P and construct the cumulative probability distribution. This is done next:

$P \geq ML/(ML + MP) = 4/(4 + 10) = 4/14 = .286$.

DAILY SALES IN CASES	PROBABILITY AT THIS LEVEL	PROBABILITY AT THIS LEVEL OR GREATER
5	.1	1.0 >= .286
6	.1	.9 >= .286
7	.2	.8 >= .286
8	.3	.6 >= .286
9	.2	.3 >= .286
10	.1	.1

As seen above, the best policy is to stock 9 cases each week.

SOLUTIONS TO DISCUSSION QUESTIONS AND PROBLEMS

5-1. The purpose of this question is to make students use a personal experience to distinguish between good and bad decisions. A good decision is based on logic and all of the available information. A bad decision is one that is not based on logic and the available information. It is possible for an unfortunate or undesirable outcome to occur after a good decision has been made. It is also possible to have a favorable or desirable outcome occur after a bad decision.

5-2. The decision-making process includes the following steps: (1) define the problem, (2) list the alternatives, (3) identify the possible outcomes, (4) evaluate the consequences, (5) select an evaluation criterion, and (6) make the appropriate decision. The first four steps or procedures are common for all decision-making problems. Steps five and six, however, depend on the decision-making model used.

5-3. An alternative is a course of action over which we have complete control. A state of nature is an event or occurrence in which we have no control. An example of an alternative is deciding whether or not to take an umbrella to school or work on a particular day. An example of a state of nature is whether or not it will rain on a particular day.

5-4. The basic differences between decision-making models under certainty, risk, and uncertainty depend on the amount of chance or risk that is involved in the decision. A decision-making model under certainty assumes that we know with complete confidence the future outcomes. Decision-making-under-risk models assume that we do not know the outcomes for a particular decision but that we do know the probability of occurrence of those outcomes. With decision making under uncertainty, it is assumed that we do not know the outcomes that will occur, and furthermore, we do not know the probabilities that these outcomes will occur.

5-5. Decision table for Lillich:

	RECESSION	INFLATION	RECESSION AND INFLATION
Invest in real estate			
Invest in stocks			
Invest in certificates of deposit			

5-6. EMV is the expected monetary value. This is the expected return that we would realize if the decision were repeated an infinite number of times. EVwPI is the expected value with perfect information. This is the return or value of making the same decision an infinite number of times when we have perfect or complete information. EVPI is the expected value of perfect information. This is simply the difference between EMV and EVwPI. It is the amount that we would be willing to pay for perfect information.

5-7. The techniques discussed in this chapter used to solve decision problems under uncertainty include maximax, maximin, equally likely, coefficient of realism, and minimax. The maximax decision-making criterion is an optimistic decision-making criterion, while the maximin is a pessimistic decision-making criterion.

5-8. a. Decision making under uncertainty
b. Maximax criterion

c.

EQUIPMENT	FAVORABLE	UNFAVORABLE	ROW MAXIMUM	ROW MINIMUM
SUB 100	300,000	−200,000	(300,000)	−200,000
OILER J	250,000	−100,000	250,000	−100,000
TEXAN	75,000	−18,000	75,000	(−18,000)

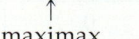

	maximax	maximin

Best alternative: SUB 100

5-9. Maximin criterion: best alternative: TEXAN (see table on page IS-45)

5-10. a. Decision making under risk—maximize expected monetary value

b. EMV (SUB 100) = .7 × 300,000 + .3
$$× (-200,000) = 150,000$$
EMV (OILER J) = .7 × 250,000 + .3
$$× (-100,000)$$
$$= 145,000$$
EMV (TEXAN) = .7 × 75,000 + .3
$$× (-18,000)$$
$$= 47,100$$

Optimal decision: SUB 100

c. (.7)(X) + (.3)(-200,000) = 145,000
$$.7X = 145,000 + 60,000 = 205,000$$
$$X = (205,000)/.7 = 292,857$$

5-11. a.

ALTERNATIVE / MARKET CONDITION	GOOD	FAIR	POOR	EMV
Stock market	1,400	800	0	880
Bank deposit	900	900	900	900
Probabilities of market conditions	.4	.4	.2	

b. Best decision: deposit $10,000 in bank

5-12. a., b.

	FAVORABLE MARKET	UNFAVORABLE MARKET	EOL
Large plant	(400,000 − 400,000) = 0	0 − (−300,000) = 300,000	180,000
Small plant	(400,000 − 80,000) = 320,000	0 − (−10,000) = 10,000	134,000
Don't build	(400,000 − 0) = 400,000	(0 − 0) = 0	160,000
Probabilities	.4	.6	

Using minimum EOL, the best strategy is the small plant

c. EVPI = min EOL = $134,000

5-13. a. Decision under uncertainty

b.

	POPULATION SAME	POPULATION GROWS	ROW AVERAGE
Large wing	−85,000	150,000	32,500
Small wing	−45,000	60,000	7,500
No wing	0	0	0

c. Best alternative: large wing

5-14. a. Expected value *with* perfect information is $1,400 \times .4 + 900 \times .4 + 900 \times .2 = 1,100$ max; EMV = 900. Therefore, Allen should pay at most $(1100 - 900) =$ $200.

b. Yes, Allen should pay $(1,100 \times .4 + 900 \times .4 + 900 \times .2) - 900 = \$80$.

5-15. a.

	POPULATION SAME	POPULATION GROWS	WEIGHTED AVERAGE WITH $\alpha = .75$
Large wing	−85,000	150,000	91,250
Small wing	−45,000	60,000	33,750
No wing	0	0	0

b. Best decision: large wing

c. No

5-16. a.

	DEMAND IS 11 CASES	DEMAND IS 12 CASES	DEMAND IS 13 CASES	EMV
Stock 11 cases	385	385	385	385
Stock 12 cases	329	420	420	379.05
Stock 13 cases	273	364	455	341.25
Probabilities	.45	.35	.2	

b. Stock 11 cases

c. If no loss is involved in excess stock, the recommended course of action is to stock 13 cases and to replenish stock to this level each week. This follows from the following decision table:

STOCK (CASES) \ DEMAND (CASES)	11	12	13	EMV
11	385	385	385	385
12	385	420	420	404.25
13	385	420	455	411.25

5-17. a.

FACILITY \ MARKET	STRONG	FAIR	POOR	ROW MAXIMUM
Large	0	19,000	310,000	310,000
Medium	250,000	0	100,000	250,000
Small	350,000	29,000	32,000	350,000
None	550,000	129,000	0	550,000

minimax

b. Minimax decision: medium-sized facility

5-18. Profit from each case sold is $(95 − 45) = $50.
Loss from each case not sold is $45.

MANU-FACTURE (CASES) \ DEMAND (CASES)	6	7	8	9	EMV
6	300	300	300	300	300
7	255	350	350	350	340.5
8	210	305	400	400	352.5
9	165	260	355	450	317
Probabilities	.1	.3	.5	.1	

John should manufacture 8 cases of cheese spread.

5-19. a.

SIZE OF FIRST STATION \ MARKET	GOOD MARKET	FAIR MARKET	POOR MARKET	ROW MINIMUM	ROW MAXIMUM	ROW AVERAGE	WEIGHT AVERAGE
Small	50,000	20,000	−10,000	(−10,000)	50,000	20,000	38,000
Medium	80,000	30,000	−20,000	−20,000	80,000	30,000	60,000
Large	100,000	30,000	−40,000	−40,000	100,000	30,000	72,000
Very large	300,000	25,000	−160,000	−160,000	(300,000)	(55,000)	(208,000)

↑ maximin   ↑ maximax   ↑ equally likely   ↑ realism (α = .8)

b. Maximax decision: very large size station
c. Maximin decision: small size station
d. Equally likely decision: very large size station
e. Realism decision: very large size station

f.

MARKET SIZE \ MARKET	GOOD	FAIR	POOR	ROW MAXIMUM
Small	250,000	10,000	0	250,000
Medium	220,000	0	10,000	220,000
Large	200,000	0	30,000	200,000
Very large	0	5,000	150,000	(150,000)

opportunity loss table

← minimax

g. Minimax decision: very large station

5-20. a.

	NO CONGESTION	MILD CONGESTION	SEVERE CONGESTION	EXPECTED TIME
Tennessee	15	30	45	25
Backroads	20	25	35	24.17
Expressway	30	30	30	30
Probabilities	(30 days)/ (60 days) = ½	(20 days)/ (60 days) = ⅓	(10 days)/ (60 days) = ⅙	

b. Back roads (minimum time used)

c. Expected time with perfect information:

$15 \times ½ + 25 \times ⅓ + 30 \times ⅙ = 20.83$ minutes.

Time saved is $3⅓$ minutes.

5-21. a. Cost of produced case = \$5

Cost of purchased case = \$16

Selling price   = \$15

Recovered money from each unsold case = \$3

SUPPLY (CASES) \ DEMAND (CASES)	100	200	300	EMV
100	100 × 10 = 1,000	100 × 10 − 100 × (16 − 15) = 900	100 × 10 − 200 × (16 − 15) = 800	1,000 × .3 + 900 × .4 + 800 × .3 = 900
200	100 × 10 − 100 × (5 − 3) = 800	200 × 10 = 2,000	200 × 10 − 100 × (16 − 15) = 1,900	800 × .3 + 2,000 × .4 + 1,900 × .3 = 1,610
300	100 × 10 − 200 × (5 − 3) = 600	200 × 10 − 100 × (5 − 3) = 1,800	300 × 10 = 3,000	600 × .3 + 1,800 × .4 + 3,000 × .3 = 1,800
Probabilities	.3	.4	.3	

b. Produce 300 cases and stock them.

5-22.

DEMAND (CASES)	P
10	1.0
11	.8
12	.5
13	.3
14	.1

$$ML = \$(50 - 75)$$
$$= \$25$$
$$MP = \$(100 - 75) = \$25$$
$$\frac{ML}{MP + ML} = \frac{25}{25 + 25} = .5$$
$$\therefore P \geqq .5$$

Fred should produce 12 cases of E-Z Spread each week.

5-23.

DEMAND (TREES)	P
50	1.0
75	.95
100	.85
125	.65
150	.35
175	.15
200	.05

a. ML = \$6, MP = \$15 − 6 = \$9

$$\therefore P \geqq \frac{6}{6 + 9} = .4$$

$\therefore$ Harry should stock 125 trees.

5-23 (continued)

 b. ML = \$12, MP = \$(15 − 12) = \$3

$$\therefore P \geqq \frac{12}{12 + 3} = .8$$

 ∴ Harry should now stock 100 trees.

 c.

(TREES)	P
50	1.0
75	.75
100	.50
125	.25

ML = \$6
MP = \$(18 − 6) = \$12

$$\therefore P \geqq \frac{6}{6 + 12} = .33$$

∴ Harry should stock 100 trees.

5-24. $P \geqq \dfrac{ML}{MP + ML} = \dfrac{\$.75}{\$(2 - .75) + \$.75}$: $P \geqq .375$

$\mu = 60$ [.625 under curve = .31]

$\sigma = 7$

$$\frac{X^* - 60}{7} = .31$$

$\therefore X^* = 62.17$

∴ Harry should stock 62 bottles.

5-25. $P \geqq \dfrac{ML}{MP + ML} = \dfrac{\$35}{\$35 + \$15} = .7$

[.3 area under curve = −.52]

$\mu = 45,000$

$\sigma = \ 4,450$

$$\frac{X^* - 45,000}{4450} = -.52$$

$X^* = 45,000 - 2314$

$\ \ \ = 42,686$

Bring 42,686 cases to market.

5-26. $\mu = 400$

$$P(X < 450) = P\left(Z < \frac{450 - 400}{\sigma}\right) = .925$$

$Z = 1.44$

$$\therefore \sigma = \frac{50}{1.44} = 34.72$$

$$P \geqq \frac{ML}{ML + MP} = \frac{\$2}{\$2 + \$1} = .67$$

Z of (.33 area under curve) = −.43

$$\frac{X^* - 400}{34.72} = -.43 \text{ or, } X^* = 385$$

∴ Linda should stock 385 cases.

5-27. $\mu = 3000$

$$P[X < 3010] = P\left[Z < \frac{10}{\sigma}\right] = .85$$

$$Z = 1.04 \therefore \sigma = \frac{10}{1.04} = 9.62$$

$$P \geqq \frac{ML}{ML + MP} = \frac{\$15}{\$15 + \$335}$$

$P \geqq .0429$

Z of (.9571 under curve) = 1.72

$X^* = (1.72 \times 9.62) + 3,000$

$\ \ \ \ \ = 3,016.5$

Paula should produce 3,017 reports each week.

5-28. a. The decision table for Chris Dunphy along with the expected profits or expected monetary values (EMVs) for each alternative are shown below.

Table for Problem 5-28a
Return in \$1,000:

NUMBER OF WATCHES	PROBABILITY	EVENT 1 .100	EVENT 2 .200	EVENT 3 .500	EVENT 4 .100	EVENT 5 .100
100,000	Alternative 1	100,000	110,000	120,000	135,000	140,000
150,000	Alternative 2	90,000	120,000	140,000	155,000	170,000
200,000	Alternative 3	85,000	110,000	135,000	160,000	175,000
250,000	Alternative 4	80,000	120,000	155,000	170,000	180,000
300,000	Alternative 5	65,000	100,000	155,000	180,000	195,000
350,000	Alternative 6	50,000	100,000	160,000	190,000	210,000
400,000	Alternative 7	45,000	95,000	170,000	200,000	230,000
450,000	Alternative 8	30,000	90,000	165,000	230,000	245,000
500,000	Alternative 9	20,000	85,000	160,000	270,000	295,000

Expected profit table:

ALTERNATIVE	EXPECTED PROFIT
1	119,500
2	135,500
3	131,500
4	144,500
5	141,500
6	145,000
7	151,500
8	151,000
9	155,500 ⟵ best alternative

For this decision problem, Alternative 9 gives the highest expected profit of $155,500.

b. The expected value with perfect information is $175.50, and the expected value of perfect information (EVPI) is $20.00.

c. The new probability estimates will give more emphasis to event 2 and less to event 5. The overall impact is shown below. As you can see, stocking 400,000 watches is now the best decision with an expected value of $140,700.

Return in $1,000:

	EVENT 1	EVENT 2	EVENT 3	EVENT 4	EVENT 5
PROBABILITY	.100	.280	.500	.100	.020
Alternative 1	100,000	110,000	120,000	135,000	140,000
Alternative 2	90,000	120,000	140,000	155,000	170,000
Alternative 3	85,000	110,000	135,000	160,000	175,000
Alternative 4	80,000	120,000	155,000	170,000	180,000
Alternative 5	65,000	100,000	155,000	180,000	195,000
Alternative 6	50,000	100,000	160,000	190,000	210,000
Alternative 7	45,000	95,000	170,000	200,000	230,000
Alternative 8	30,000	90,000	165,000	230,000	245,000
Alternative 9	20,000	85,000	160,000	270,000	295,000

Expected profit table:

ALTERNATIVE	EXPECTED PROFIT
1	117,100
2	131,500
3	126,300
4	139,700
5	133,900
6	136,200
7	140,700 ⟵ best alternative: stock 400,000 watches
8	138,600
9	138,700

d. Stocking 400,000 is still the best alternative. The results are shown below.

Return in $1,000:

	EVENT 1	EVENT 2	EVENT 3	EVENT 4	EVENT 5
PROBABILITY	.100	.280	.500	.100	.020
Alternative 1	100,000	110,000	120,000	135,000	140,000
Alternative 2	90,000	120,000	140,000	155,000	170,000
Alternative 3	85,000	110,000	135,000	160,000	175,000
Alternative 4	80,000	120,000	155,000	170,000	180,000
Alternative 5	65,000	100,000	155,000	180,000	195,000
Alternative 6	50,000	100,000	160,000	190,000	210,000
Alternative 7	45,000	95,000	170,000	200,000	230,000
Alternative 8	30,000	90,000	165,000	230,000	245,000
Alternative 9	20,000	85,000	160,000	270,000	295,000

Expected profit table:

ALTERNATIVE	EXPECTED PROFIT	
1	117,100	
2	131,500	
3	126,300	
4	139,700	
5	133,900	
6	136,200	
7	140,700	⟵ best alternative:
8	138,600	stock
9	138,700	400,000 watches

Solution to Starting Right Case

This is a decision making under uncertainty problem. There are two events—a favorable market (Event 1) and an unfavorable market (Event 2). There are four alternatives, which include doing nothing (Alternative 1), invest in corporate bonds (Alternative 2), invest in preferred stock (Alternative 3), and invest in common stock (Alternative 4). The decision table is presented below. Note for Alternative 2, the return in a good market is $30,000 \times (1 + .13)^5 = \$55,273$. The return in a good market is $120,000$ ($4 \times \$30,000$) for Alternative 3, and $240,000$ ($8 \times \$30,000$) for Alternative 4.

	EVENT 1	EVENT 2
Alternative 1	0	0
Alternative 2	55,273	−10,000
Alternative 3	120,000	−15,000
Alternative 4	240,000	−30,000

Solutions:

Laplace

ALTERNATIVE	EXPECTED VALUE	
1	0.0	
2	22,636.5	
3	152,500.0	
4	105,000.0	⟵ best

Maximin

ALTERNATIVE	EXPECTED VALUE	
1	0	⟵ best
2	−10,000	
3	−15,000	
4	−30,000	

Maximax

ALTERNATIVE	MAXIMAX PAYOFF	
1	0	
2	55,273	
3	120,000	
4	240,000	⟵ best

Hurwicz Alpha Coefficient: 0.110

Hurwicz

ALTERNATIVE	HURWICZ PAYOFF	
1	0.000	⟵ best
2	−2,819.970	
3	−150.000	
4	−300.000	

Minimax

ALTERNATIVE	MAXIMUM REGRET
1	240,000
2	184,727
3	120,000
4	30,000 ⟵ best

a. Sue Pansky is a risk avoider and should use the maximin decision approach. She should do nothing and not make an investment in Starting Right.

b. Ray Cahn should use a coefficient of realism of .11. The best decision is to do nothing.

c. Lila Battle should eliminate Alternative 1 of doing nothing and apply the maximin criterion. The result is to invest in the corporate bonds.

d. George Yates should use the equally likely decision criterion. The best decision for George is to invest in common stock.

e. Pete Metarko is a risk seeker. He should invest in common stock.

f. Julia Day can eliminate the preferred stock alternative and still offer alternatives to risk seekers (common stock) and risk avoiders (doing nothing or investing in corporate bonds).

6
Decision Trees and Utility Theory

LEARNING OBJECTIVES

After completing this chapter, students will be able to:

1. Develop accurate and useful decision trees.
2. Revise probability estimates using Bayesian analysis.
3. Understand the importance and use of utility theory in decision making.
4. Use computers to solve more complex decision problems.

TEACHING SUGGESTIONS

Teaching Suggestion 6.1: Decision Theory and Life-Time Decisions.

This chapter investigates larger and more complex decisions. During one's life, there are a few very important decisions that have a major impact. Some call these "life-time decisions." Students can be asked to carefully consider these life-time decisions and how decision theory can be used to assist them. Life-time decisions include decisions about what school to attend, marriage, and the first job.

Teaching Suggestion 6.2: Popularity of Decision Trees among Business Executives.

Stress that decision trees are not just an academic subject; they are a technique widely used by top-level managers. Everyone appreciates a graphical display of a tough problem. It clarifies issues and makes a great discussion base. Harvard business students regularly use decision trees in case analysis.

Teaching Suggestion 6.3: Importance of Accurate Tree Diagrams.

Developing accurate decision trees is an important part of this chapter. Students can be asked to diagram several decision situations. The decisions can come from the end-of-chapter problems, the instructor, or from student experiences.

Teaching Suggestion 6.4: Diagramming a Large Decision Problem Using Branches.

Some students are intimidated by large and complex decision trees. To avoid this situation, students can be shown that a large decision tree is like having a number of smaller trees or decisions that can be solved separately, starting at the end branches of the tree. This can help students use decision-making techniques on larger and more complex problems.

Teaching Suggestion 6.5: Using Tables to Perform Bayesian Analysis.

Bayesian analysis can be difficult; the formulas can be hard to remember and use. For many, using tables is the most effective way to learn how to revise probability values. Once students understand how the tables are used, they can be shown that the formulas are making exactly the same calculations.

ALTERNATE EXAMPLES

Alternate Example 6-1: George Goleb is considering the possibility of conducting a survey into the market potential for industrial equipment repair using robots. The cost of the survey is $5,000. George has developed a decision tree that shows the overall decision as seen in the figure on page IS-55.

This problem can be solved using EMV calculations. We start with the end of the tree and work toward the beginning computing EMV values. The results of the calculations are shown in the figure on page IS-56. The conditional payoff of the solution is $18,802.

Alternate Example 6-2: George (in Alternate Example 6-1) would like to determine the expected value of sample information (EVSI). EVSI is equal to the expected value of the best decision *with* sample information, assuming no cost to gather it, minus the expected value of the best decision *without* sample information. Since the cost of the survey is $5,000, the expected value of the best decision *with* sample information, assuming no cost to gather it, is $23,802. The expected value of the best decision *without* sample information is found on the lower branch of the decision tree to be $14,000. Thus, EVSI is $9,802.

Alternate Example 6-3: This example reveals how the conditional probability values for the George Goleb examples (above) have been determined. The probability values about the survey are summarized in the following table:

RESULTS OF SURVEY	FAVORABLE MARKET (FM)	UNFAVORABLE MARKET (UM)
Positive (P)	P(P | FM) = .9	P(P | UM) = .2
Negative (N)	P(N | FM) = .1	P(N | UM) = .8

Using the above values and the fact that P(FM) = .6 and P(UM) = .4, we can compute the conditional probability values of a favorable or unfavorable market given a positive or negative survey result. The calculations are presented in the following two tables.

Probability Revision Given a Positive Survey Result

STATE OF NATURE	CONDI-TIONAL PROB.	PRIOR PROB.	JOINT PROB.	POSTERIOR PROB.
FM	.9	.6	.54	.54/.62 = .871
UM	.2	.4	.08	.08/.62 = .129
		Total	.62	1.00

Probability Revision Given a Negative Survey Result

STATE OF NATURE	CONDI-TIONAL PROB.	PRIOR PROB.	JOINT PROB.	POSTERIOR PROB.
FM	.1	.6	.06	.06/.38 = .158
UM	.8	.4	.32	.32/.38 = .842
		Total	.38	1.00

Alternate Example 6-4: In the section on utility theory, Mark Simkim used utility theory to determine his best decision. What decision would Mark make if he had the following utility values? Is Mark still a risk seeker?

U(−$10,000) = .8

U($0) = .9

U($10,000) = 1

Using the above data, we can determine the expected utility of each alternative as follows:

U(Mark plays the game) = .45(1) + .55(.8) = .89

U(Mark doesn't play the game) = .9

Thus, the best decision for Mark is not to play the game with an expected utility of .9. Given this data, Mark is a risk avoider.

SOLUTIONS TO DISCUSSION QUESTIONS AND PROBLEMS

6-1. A decision tree is preferred to a decision table when a number of sequential decisions are to be made. A sequential decision situation is one in which the outcome of one decision becomes an important factor in making future decisions. For example, if a decision maker is considering the possibility of acquiring additional information and a decision of whether or not to build a new plant, the decision to acquire the new information is made first. Then, based on the results of the new information (if it is gathered) the decision to build the plant is made. Therefore, these decisions are sequential. One is made before the other.

6-2. Probabilities for all states of nature and all monetary outcomes are placed on the decision tree. In addition, intermediate results, such as EMVs for middle branches, can be placed on the decision tree.

6-3. Using the EMV criterion with a decision tree involves starting at the terminal branches of the tree and working toward the origin computing expected monetary values. This is accomplished by multiplying the

Figure for Alternate Example 6-1a

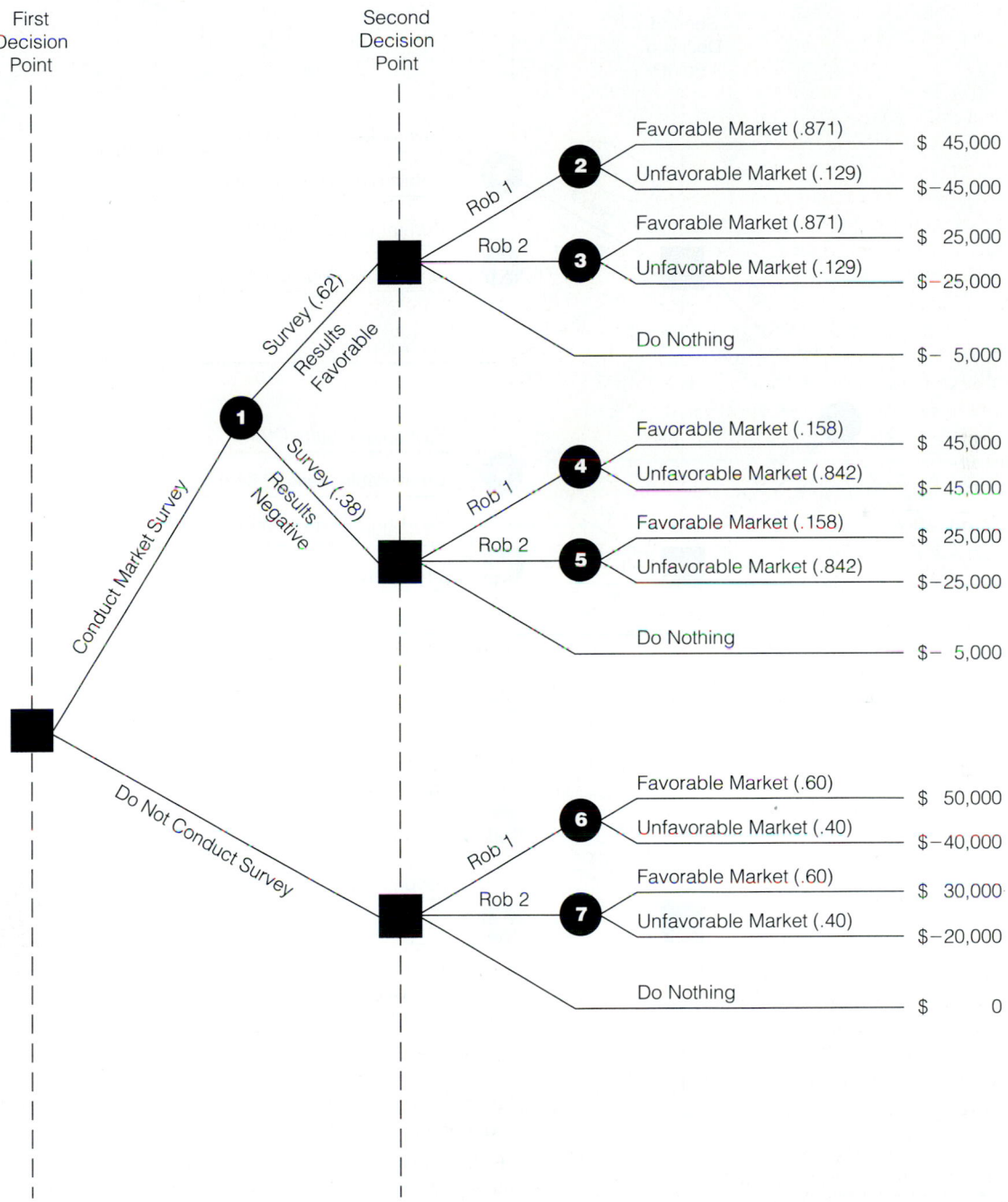

Figure for Alternate Example 6-1b

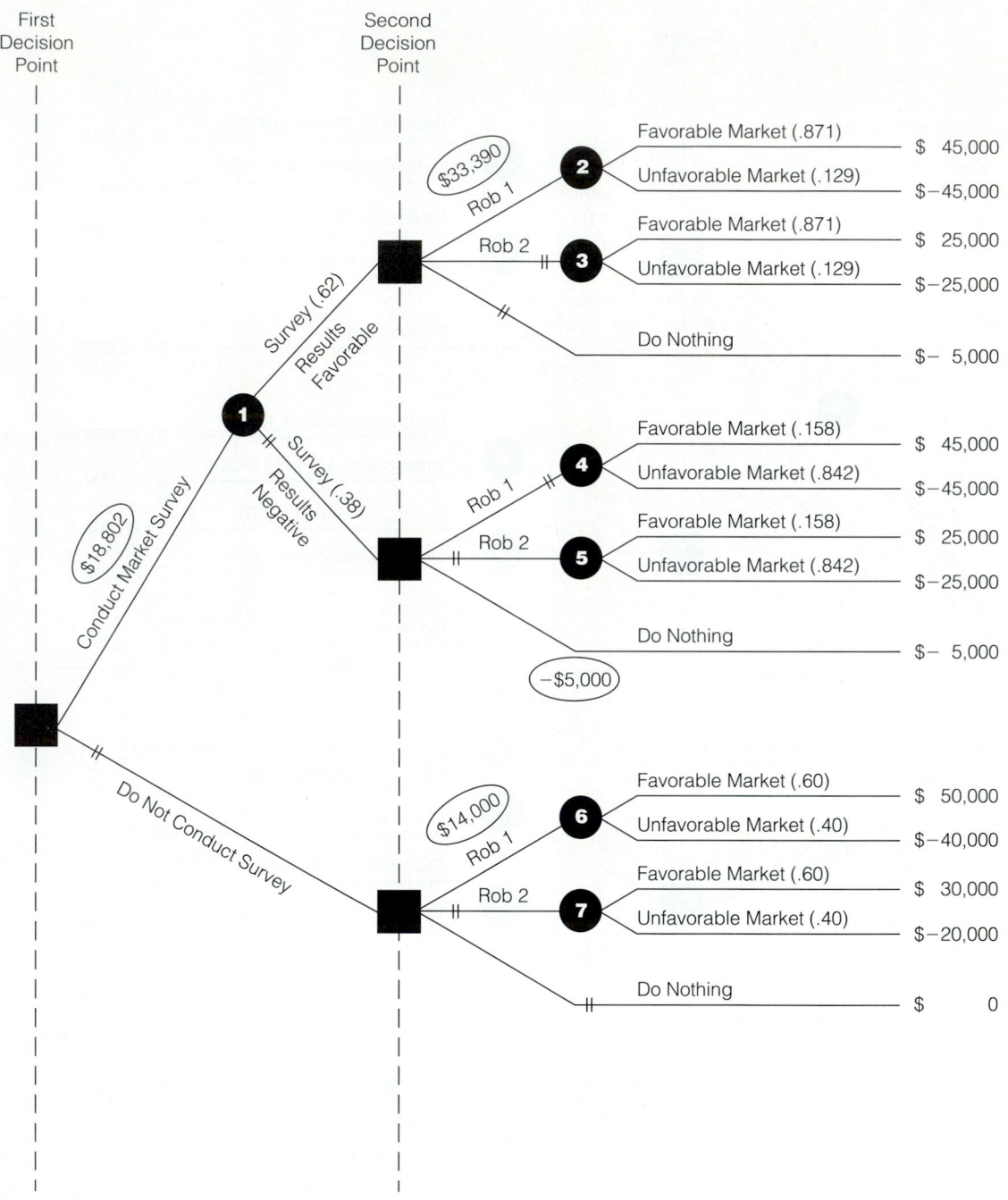

probabilities of the states of nature times the economic consequences and summing the results for each alternative from the terminal branches of the tree to the origin.

6-4. A prior probability is one that exists before additional information is gathered. A posterior probability is one that can be computed based on prior probabilities and additional information.

6-5. The purpose of Bayesian analysis is to determine posterior probabilities based on prior probabilities and new information. Bayesian analysis can be used in the decision-making process whenever additional information is gathered. This information can then be combined with prior probabilities in arriving at posterior probabilities. Once these posterior probabilities are computed, they can be used in the decision-making process as any other probability value.

6-6. Using EMV in the decision-making process can cause several problems. The most severe problem is the EMV criterion assumes that the decision maker is indifferent to risk. In cases where a decision maker is a risk avoider or risk seeker, the EMV criterion is not appropriate. Students are also asked to give an example situation in which EMV is not appropriate. Their answers should lead to an interesting class discussion.

6-7. The overall purpose of utility theory is to incorporate a decision maker's preference for risk in the decision-making process.

6-8. A utility function can be assessed in a number of different ways. A common way is to use a standard gamble. With a standard gamble, the best outcome is assigned a utility of 1, and the worst outcome is assigned a utility of 0. Then, intermediate outcomes are selected and the decision maker is given a choice between having the intermediate outcome for sure and a gamble involving the best and worst outcome. The probability that makes the decision maker indifferent between having the intermediate outcome for sure and a gamble involving the best and worst outcome is determined. This probability then becomes the utility of the intermediate value. This process is continued until utility values for all economic consequences are determined. These utility values are then placed on a utility curve.

6-9. When a utility curve is to be used in the decision-making process, utility values from the utility curve replace all monetary values at the terminal branches in a decision tree or in the body of a decision table. Then, expected utilities are determined in the same way as expected monetary values. The alternative with the highest expected utility is selected as the best decision.

6-10. A risk seeker is a decision maker who enjoys and seeks out risk. A risk avoider is a decision maker who avoids risk even if the economic payoff is higher. The utility curve for a risk seeker increases at an increasing rate. The utility curve for a risk avoider increases at a decreasing rate.

6-11. The utility curve for an individual who is indifferent to risk is linear. This means that the utility curve is a straight line. If a decision maker is indifferent to risk, using utility values will give the same decision as using EMV. Therefore, for a decision maker who is indifferent to risk, it is not necessary to use the values from a utility curve in determining the best decision.

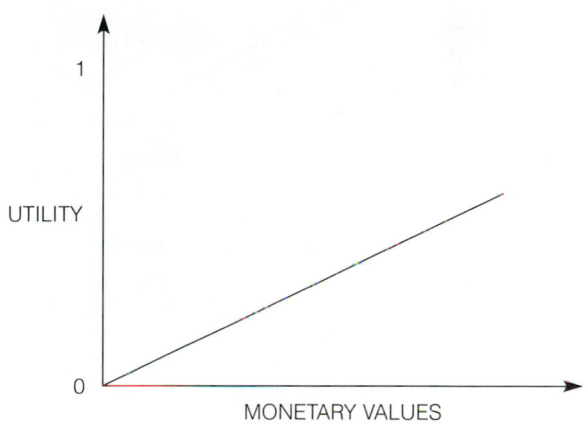

6-12. EMV for node 1 = (.5) ($100,000) + (.5) (−$40,000) = $30,000

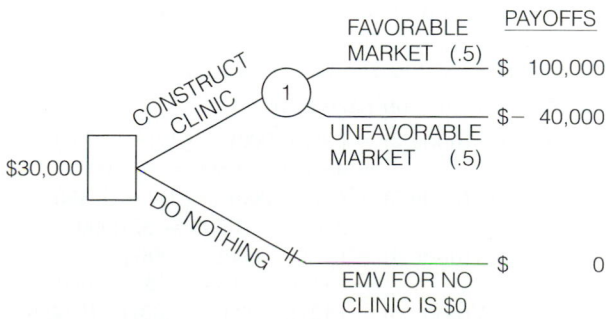

Choose highest EMV; therefore, construct clinic.

6-13. a.

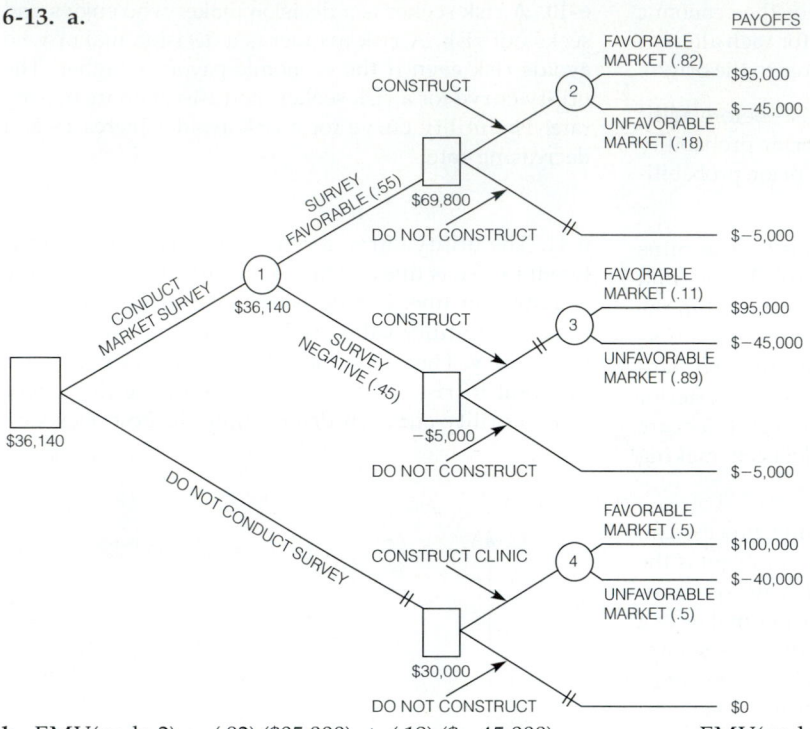

PAYOFFS

b. EMV(node 2) = (.82) ($95,000) + (.18) ($−45,000)
$$= 77,900 − 8,100 = \$69,800$$
EMV(node 3) = (.11) ($95,000) + (.89) ($−45,000)
$$= 10,450 − 40,850 = \$−29,600$$
EMV(node 4) = $30,000
EMV(node 1) = (.55) ($69,800) + (.45) ($−5,000)
$$= 38,390 − 2,250 = \$36,140$$

Survey

EMV (no survey) = (.5) ($100,000) + (.5) (−$40,000)
$$= \$30,000$$
The survey should be taken.

c. EVSI = ($36,140 + $5,000) − $30,000 = $11,140.
Thus, the doctors would pay up to $11,140 more for the survey.

Since EVSI uses the expected value of the best decision with sample information assuming *no* cost to gather it, $5,000 had to be added back to $36,140.

6-14. See figure on page IS-59.

6-15. EMV(node 2) = (.9) (55,000) + (.1) (−45,000)
$$= 49,500 − 4,500 = \$45,000$$
EMV(node 3) = (.9) (25,000) + (.1) (−15,000)
$$= 22,500 − 1,500 = \$21,000$$
EMV(node 4) = (.12) (55,000) + (.88) (−45,000)
$$= 6,600 − 39,600 = \$−33,000$$
EMV(node 5) = (.12) (25,000) + (.88) (−15,000)
$$= 3,000 − 13,200 = \$−10,200$$
EMV(node 6) = (.5) (60,000) + (.5) (−40,000)
$$= 30,000 − 20,000 = \$10,000$$

EMV(node 7) = (.5) (30,000) + (.5) (−10,000)
$$= 15,000 − 5,000 = \$10,000$$
EMV(node 1) = (.6) (45,000) + (.4) (−5,000)
$$= 27,000 − 2,000 = \$25,000$$

Since EMV (market survey) > EMV (no survey), Jerry should conduct the survey.

Since EMV (large shop | favorable survey) > EMV (small shop | favorable survey), and EMV (no shop | favorable survey), Jerry should build a large shop if the survey is favorable. If the survey is unfavorable, Jerry should build nothing since EMV (no shop | unfavorable survey) > EMV (large shop | unfavorable survey) and EMV (small shop | unfavorable survey). (See Figure 6-15 on page IS-59.)

6-16. If no survey, EMV = .5(30,000) + .5(−10,000) = $10,000. To keep Jerry from changing decisions, EMV (survey) must be ≥ EMV (no survey). Thus, X[EMV (favorable survey)] + (1 − X) [EMV (unfavorable survey)] = EMV (no survey) would be the equation. Substituting:

$$X(45,000) + (1 − X) (−5,000) = \$10,000$$

Solving:

$$45,000X − 5,000 + 5,000X = 10,000$$
$$50,000X = 15,000$$
$$X = .3$$

Figure for Problem 6-14

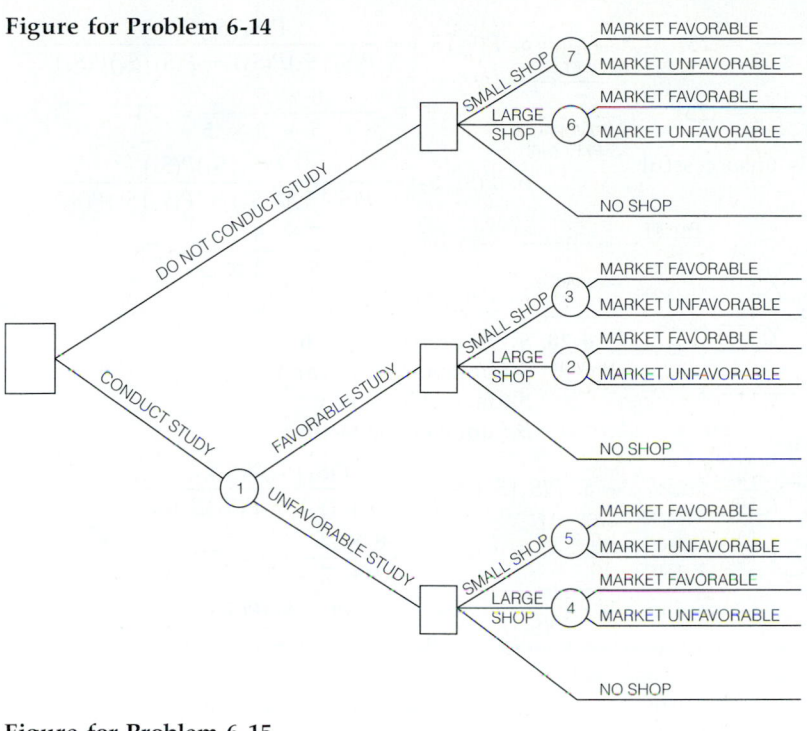

Figure for Problem 6-15

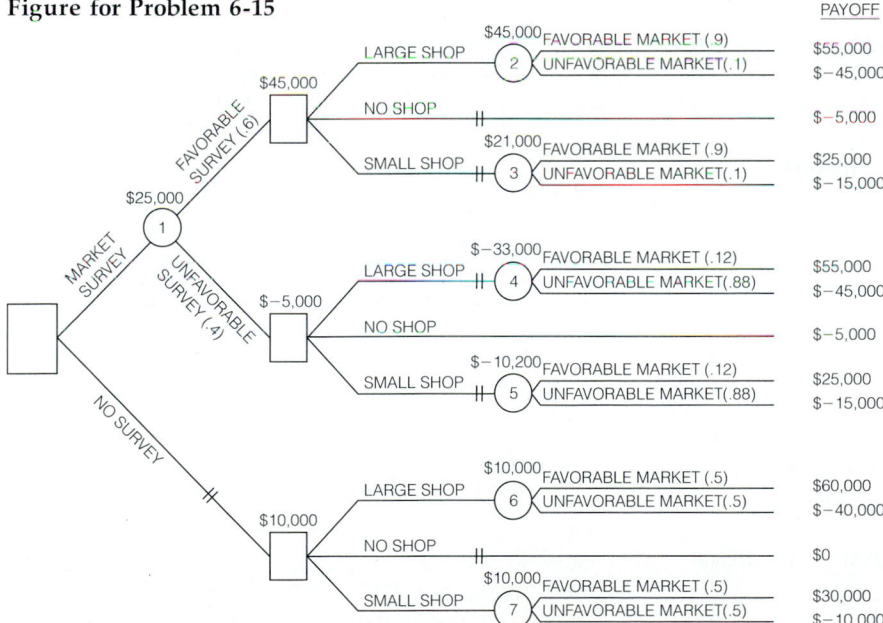

Problem 6-16 (continued)

Thus, the probability of a favorable survey could be as low as .3. Since the marketing professor estimated the probability at .6, the value can deviate −.3 without causing Jerry to change his decision. Jerry's decision in Problem 6-15 is not very sensitive to this probability value.

6-17.

$P(\text{favorable study} \mid \text{SS}) = .9$

$P(\text{unfavorable study} \mid \text{SS}) = .1$

$P(\text{unfavorable study} \mid \text{US}) = .7$

$P(\text{favorable study} \mid \text{US}) = .3 \quad P(\text{SS}) = P(\text{US}) = .5$

$P(\text{SS}\mid\text{favorable study}) = \dfrac{.9 \times .5}{.9 \times .5 + .3 \times .5} = .75$

$P(\text{SS}\mid\text{unfavorable study}) = \dfrac{.1 \times .5}{.1 \times .5 + .3 \times .5} = .25$

where SS is successful shop and US is unsuccessful shop.

6-18.

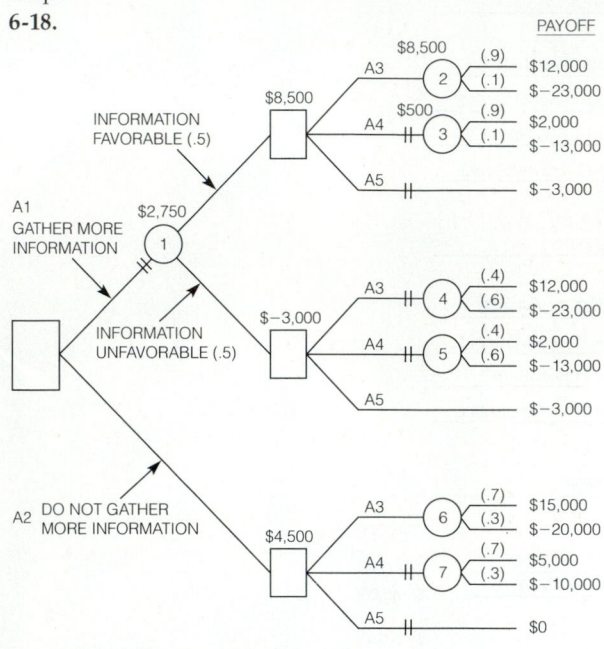

A_1: gather more information
A_2: do not gather more information
A_3: build quadplex
A_4: build duplex
A_5: do nothing

E(node 2) = .9 × 12,000 − .1 × 23,000 = 8,500
E(node 3) = .9 × 2,000 − .1 × 13,000 = 500
E(get information but do nothing) = −3,000
E(node 4) = .4 × 12,000 − .6 × 23,000 = −9,000
E(node 5) = .4 × 2,000 − .6 × 13,000 = −7,000
E(get information but do nothing) = −3,000
∴ (node 1) = 5 × 8,500 − .5 × 3,000 = $2,750
E(build quadplex) = .7 × 15,000 − .3 × 20,000 = $4,500
E(build duplex) = .7 × $5,000 − .3 × 10,000 = $500
E(do nothing) = $0
∴ advice to Bill: Do not gather information and build quadplex.

6-19. S_1: favorable research
S_2: unfavorable research
S_3: store successful
S_4: store unsuccessful

$P(S_3) = P(S_4) = .5$
$P(S_1\mid S_3) = .8 \therefore P(S_2\mid S_3) = .2$
$P(S_2\mid S_4) = .7 \therefore P(S_1\mid S_4) = .3$

a. $P(S_3\mid S_1) = \dfrac{P(S_1\mid S_3)P(S_3)}{P(S_1\mid S_3)P(S_3) + P(S_1\mid S_4)P(S_4)}$

$= \dfrac{.8 \times .5}{.8 \times .5 + .3 \times .5} = .73$

b. $P(S_4\mid S_2) = \dfrac{P(S_2\mid S_4)P(S_4)}{P(S_2\mid S_4)P(S_4) + P(S_2\mid S_3)P(S_3)}$

$= \dfrac{.7 \times .5}{.7 \times .5 + .2 \times .5} = .78$

$\therefore P(S_3\mid S_2) = .22$

6-20. S_1: favorable research
S_2: unfavorable research
S_3: favorable facility
S_4: unfavorable facility

a. $P(S_3\mid S_1) = \dfrac{P(S_1\mid S_3)P(S_3)}{P(S_1\mid S_3)P(S_3) + P(S_1\mid S_4)P(S_4)}$

$= \dfrac{.8 \times .3}{.8 \times .3 + .7 \times .3} = .53$

$P(S_3\mid S_2) = \dfrac{P(S_2\mid S_3)P(S_3)}{P(S_2\mid S_3)P(S_3) + P(S_2\mid S_4)P(S_4)}$

$= \dfrac{.2 \times .3}{.2 \times .3 + .7 \times .7} = .11$

b.

i	$P(S_1\mid S_i) \times P(S_i)$	$P(S_i\mid S_1)$
3	$.8 \times .3 = .24$	$.24/.45 = .53$
4	$.3 \times .7 = \underline{.21}$	$.21/.45 = .47$
	$.45$	

i	$P(S_2\mid S_i) \times P(S_i)$	$P(S_i\mid S_2)$
3	$.2 \times .3 = .06$	$.06/.55 = .11$
4	$.7 \times .7 = \underline{.49}$	$.49/.55 = .89$
	$.55$	

6-21. a.

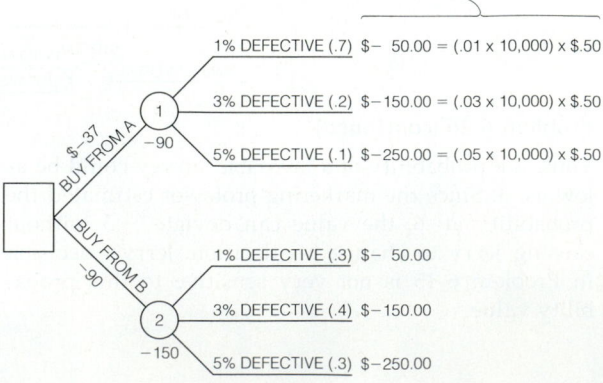

PAYOFF
REPAIR COST = (NO. DEFECTIVE PER BATCH) X REPAIR COST PER UNIT

EMV(node 1) = $(.7) \times (-50) + (.2)(-150)$
$\qquad + (.1)(-250)$
$\qquad = -35 - 30 - 25$
$\qquad = \$-90$

EMV(node 2) = $(.3)(-50) + (.4)(-150)$
$\qquad + (.3)(-250)$
$\qquad = 15 - 60 - 75 = -150$

b. Kuality Komponents should use supplier A (the highest EMV).

c. $\$150 - \$90 = \$60$ less than does supplier A.

Figure for Problem 6-22a

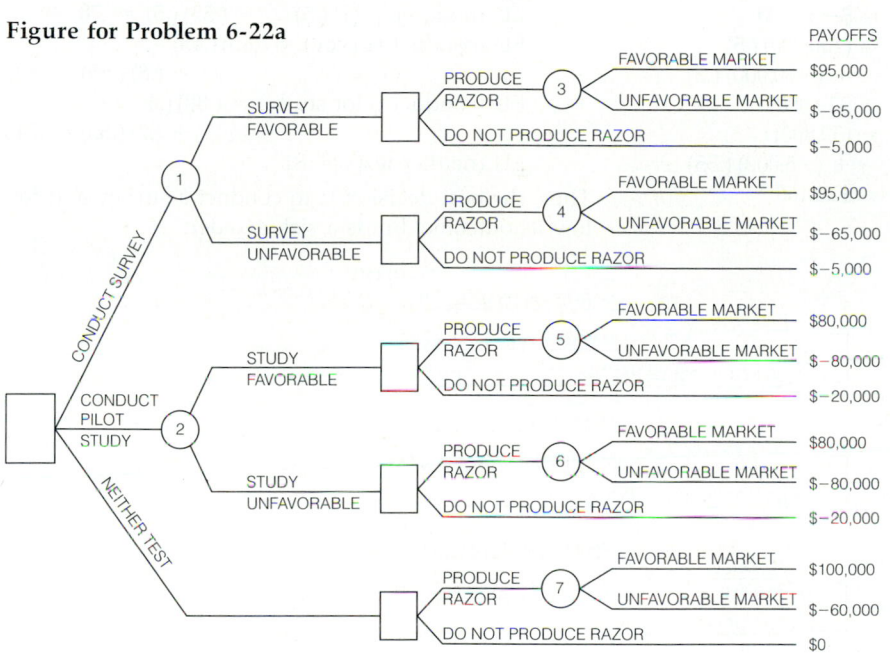

Figure for Problem 6-22b

6-22. **b.** S_1: survey favorable
S_2: survey unfavorable
S_3: study favorable
S_4: study unfavorable
S_5: market favorable
S_6: market unfavorable

$P(S_5|S_1) = \dfrac{(.7 \times .5)}{(.7 \times .5) + (.2 \times .5)} = \dfrac{.35}{.45} = .78$

$P(S_6|S_1) = 1.00 - .78 = .22$

$P(S_5|S_2) = \dfrac{(.3 \times .5)}{(.3 \times .5) + (.8 \times .5)} = \dfrac{.15}{.55} = .27$

$P(S_6|S_2) = 1.00 - .27 = .73$

$P(S_5|S_3) = \dfrac{(.8 \times .5)}{(.8 \times .5) + (.1 \times .5)} = \dfrac{.4}{.45} = .89$

$P(S_6|S_3) = 1.00 - .89 = .11$

$P(S_5|S_4) = \dfrac{(.2 \times .5)}{(.2 \times .5) + (.9 \times .5)} = \dfrac{.1}{.55} = .18$

$P(S_6|S_4) = 1.00 - .18 = .82$

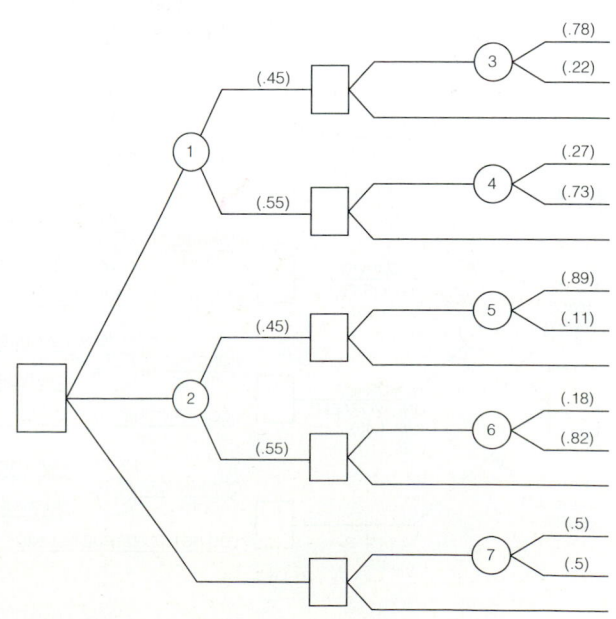

c. EMV (node 3) = (95,000) (.78)
                 + (−65,000) (.22) = $59,800
EMV (node 4) = (95,000) (.27)
             + (−65,000) (.73)
             = $−21,800
EMV (node 5) = (80,000) (.89)
             + (−80,000) (.11)
             = $62,400

EMV (node 6) = (80,000) (.18)
             + (−80,000) (.82)
             = $−51,200
EMV (node 7) = (100,000) (.5)
             + (−60,000) (.5)
             = $20,000
EMV (conduct survey) = (59,800) (.45)
                     + (−5,000) (.55)
                     = $24,160

EMV (conduct pilot survey) = (62,400) (.45)
                           + (−20,000) (.55)
                           = $17,080
EMV (neither test) = 20,000

Therefore, the best decision is to conduct the survey and follow the outcome.

6-23. EU (node 3) = (.95) (.78) + (.5) (.22) = .85
EU (node 4) = (.95) (.27) + (.5) (.73) = .62
EU (node 5) = (.9) (.89) + (0) (.11) = .80
EU (node 6) = (.9) (.18) + (0) (.82) = .16
EU (node 7) = (1) (.5)   + (.55) (.5) = .78
EU (conduct survey) = (.85) (.45)
                    + (.8) (.55) = .823
EU (conduct pilot study) = (.80) (.45)
                         + (.7) (.55) = .745

EU (neither test) = .81

Thus, the best decision is to conduct a survey and follow its outcome. Jim is a risk avoider.

Figure for Problem 6-23

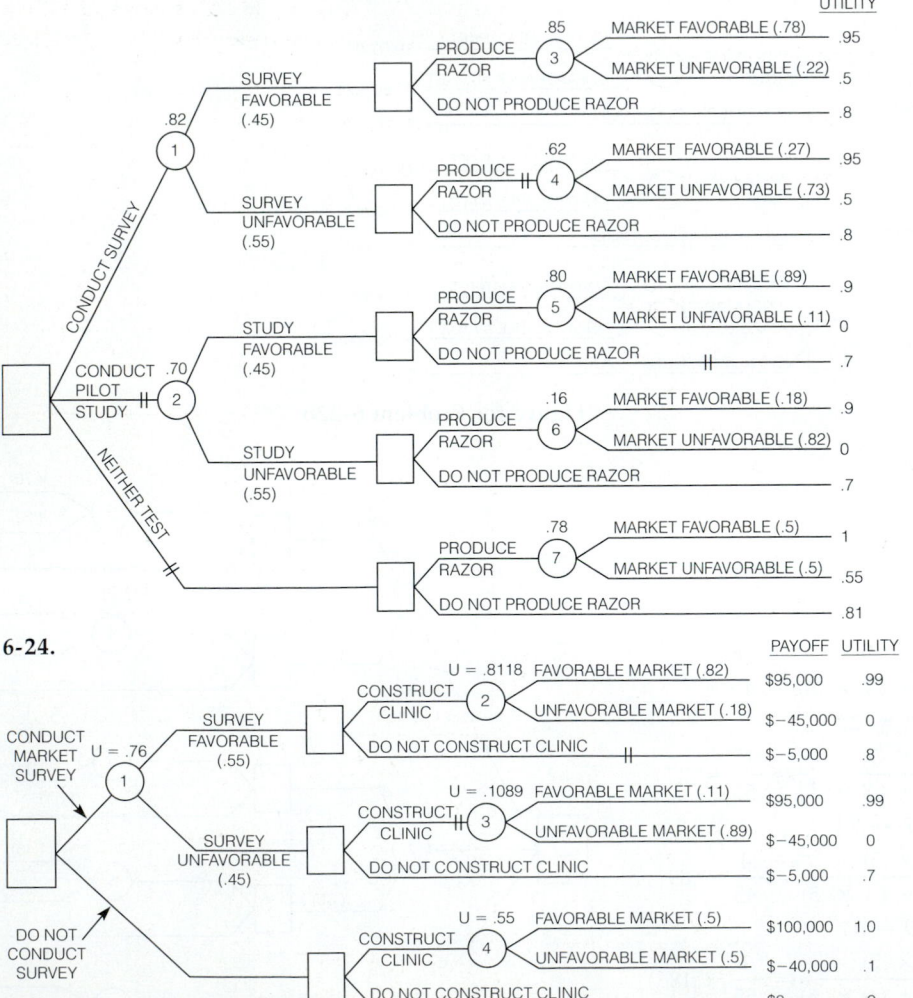

6-24.

EU (node 2) = (.82) (.99) + (.18) (0) = .8118
EU (node 3) = (.11) (.99) + (.89) (0) = .1089
EU (node 4) = (.5) (1) + (.5) (.1) = .55
EU (conduct survey) = (.55) (.8118) + (.45) (.7)
                    = .76149
EU (do not conduct survey) = .9

Therefore, the medical professionals should not conduct the survey and should not construct the clinic. They are risk avoiders.

6-25.

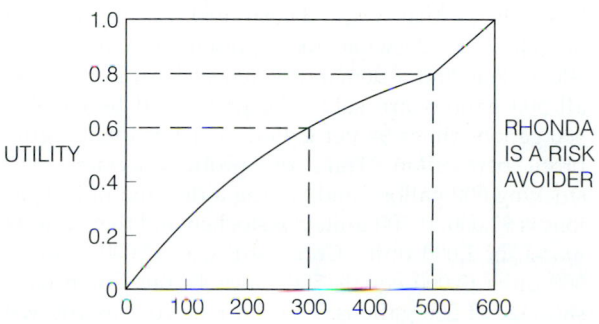

RHONDA IS A RISK AVOIDER

6-26.

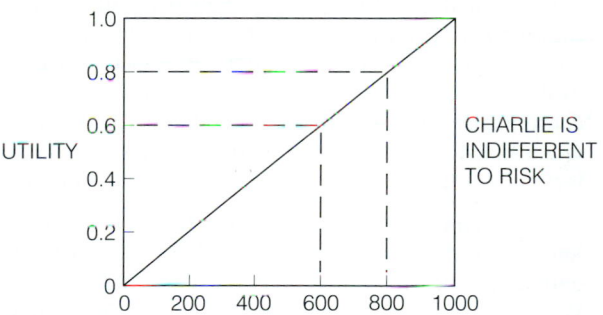

CHARLIE IS INDIFFERENT TO RISK

6-27.

EU(large plant | survey favorable) = (.78) (.95)
                                   + (.22) (0)
                                   = .741
EU(small plant | survey favorable) =
    (.78) (.5) + (.22) (.15) = .39 + .033
                            = .423
EU(no plant | survey favorable) = .2
EU(large plant | survey negative) =
    (.27) (.95) + (.73) (0) = .2565
EU(small plant | survey negative) =
    (.27) (.5) + (.73) (.15) = .135 + .1095
                            = .2445
EU(no plant | survey negative) = .2
EU(large plant | no survey) = (.5) (1) + (.5) (.05)
                            = .5 + .025 = .525
EU(small plant | no survey) = (.5) (.6) + (.5) (.1)
                            = .3 + .05 = .35

EU(no plant | no survey)   = .3
EU(conduct survey)   = (.45) (.741) +
    (.55) (.2565) = .33345 + .1411
                            = .4745
EU(no survey)   = .525

John's decision would change—he would not conduct the survey and build the large plant.

6-28.

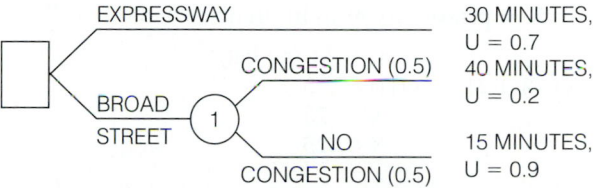

EXPRESSWAY — 30 MINUTES, U = 0.7
CONGESTION (0.5) 40 MINUTES, U = 0.2
BROAD STREET
NO CONGESTION (0.5) 15 MINUTES, U = 0.9

a. Expected travel time on Broad Street = 40 × .5 + 15 × .5, or 27.5 minutes. Broad Street has lower expected travel time.

b. Expected utility on Broad Street = .2 × .5 + .9 × .5 = .55. Therefore, the expressway maximizes utility.

c.

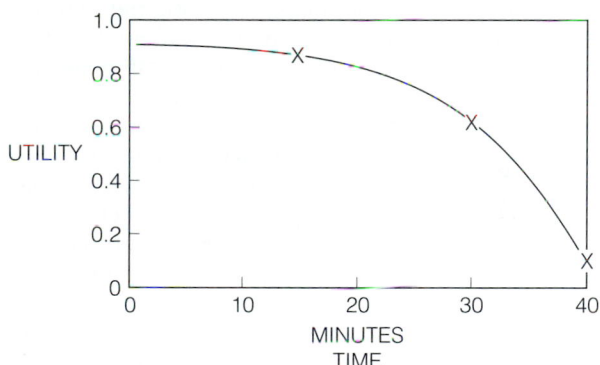

Lynn is a risk avoider.

6-29.

RESTAURANT	UTILITY	
Old Tavern	1	
Big Burger	0	
Ralph's Diner	.5	= .5 × 0 + .5 × 1
Vacation Inn	.75	= .5 × .5 + .5 × 1

6-30.

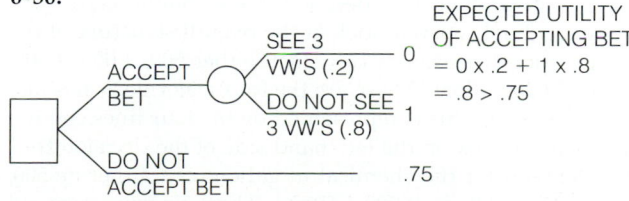

EXPECTED UTILITY OF ACCEPTING BET
= 0 x .2 + 1 x .8
= .8 > .75

ACCEPT BET — SEE 3 VW'S (.2) 0
DO NOT SEE 3 VW'S (.8) 1
DO NOT ACCEPT BET .75

Jack should accept his kids' bet.

6-31.

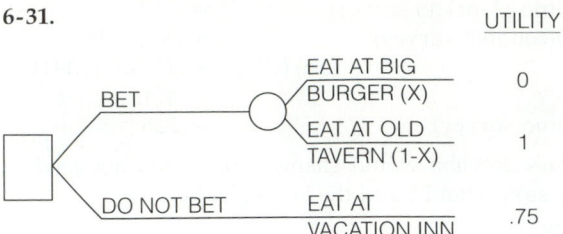

UTILITY

0

1

.75

Let X = probability at indifference, where

$$EU(bet) = EU(no\ bet)$$
$$(X)(0) + (1 - X)(1) = .75$$
$$0 + 1 - X = .75$$
$$X = .25$$

6-32. A decision tree is an excellent way to show the important cost factors and probabilities for the problem facing Coren Chemical Inc. To begin with, there are a number of important costs. The selling price per gallon is $20. From this basic selling price, a number of costs must be subtracted. The manufacturing cost is $12 per gallon, the salvage value is $13, handling costs are $1 per gallon, and advertising costs are $3 per gallon. From this information, marginal profit and marginal loss figures can be computed. The marginal profit is the profit that Coren will receive from selling one gallon of chemical. This is equal to the selling price of $20 minus the manufacturing costs, the handling costs, and the advertising costs. The marginal profit is equal to $20 − $12 − $1 − $3, or $4 per gallon. The marginal loss is the loss incurred if a gallon of chemical is stocked but not sold. This is equal to the salvage value minus the manufacturing cost, the handling cost, and the advertising cost. The marginal loss is equal to $13 − $12 − $1 − $3, or −$3. In addition, there is also a shortage cost. Coren has agreed to fulfill any demand that cannot be met internally. This requires that Coren purchase chemicals from an outside company. Because the cost of obtaining the chemical from the outside company is $25 and the price charged by Coren is $20, there is a shortage cost of $5 per gallon. In other words, Coren will lose $5 for every gallon that is sold that has to be purchased from an outside company due to a shortage.

With the above cost information, a decision tree can be constructed. This decision tree is shown on the next page. First, we will look at the overall structure of the decision tree. Coren can stock either 500, 1,000, 1,500, or 2,000 gallons. These are the four major decisions facing Coren. This is represented by the four lines coming from the box on the left-hand side of the decision tree. Demand for the chemical in gallons can either be 500, 1,000, 1,500, or 2,000 gallons. These various demand

values represent the possible states of nature. These four possible demand values are shown at the end of each stocking decision on the decision tree. As you can see, there is a probability associated with each demand or state of nature. These are enclosed in parentheses. The probability of a demand of 500 gallons is .2. The probability of 1,000, 1,500, or 2,000 gallons is .3, .4, and .1, respectively.

The next step is to compute the monetary values that are associated with any stock and demand level. For this we will need the marginal profit and marginal loss figures that were determined earlier. The top branch of the decision tree represents Coren stocking 500 gallons and a demand of 500 gallons. In this case, all 500 gallons are sold. The profit will be equal to 500 gallons times $4 per gallon, which is the marginal profit per gallon. Thus, the profit associated with stocking 500 gallons and having a demand of 500 gallons is $2,000. If 500 units are stocked and there is a demand for 1,000 units, Coren still gets $2,000 from the 500 units (2,000 equals 500 times 4). But Coren has a shortage of 500 gallons. The shortage cost, as you will recall, is $5. This was determined by subtracting the $25 cost of obtaining each gallon from an outside company from the selling price of $20 per gallon. Thus, the financial consequence of stocking 500 gallons and having a demand of 1,000 gallons is −$500 [−$500 = (500)(4) − (500)(5)]. In a likewise fashion, the economic consequence of a demand for 1,500 and 2,000 gallons when the stocking decision is to stock 500 units is determined. This is shown at the top of the decision tree.

The second stocking decision is to stock 1,000 gallons. If the demand is only 500 gallons, the remaining gallons or the surplus gallons must be sold at a loss. When 1,000 gallons are stocked and only 500 gallons are sold, Coren receives $4 for each of the 500 gallons as a profit, but Coren loses $3 for each of the 500 gallons that are not sold representing the salvage cost. The net result is that Coren will receive $500 if 1,000 gallons are stocked and only 500 gallons are sold. In a likewise fashion, monetary values for all of the other branches on the decision tree can be computed. Four dollars is received for every gallon that is sold, $5 is lost for every gallon that must be purchased from an outside company, and $3 is lost in case there is a surplus or excess of inventory over the demand.

Once these economic consequences are determined and displayed at the end of all the branches on the decision tree, the maximum expected monetary value can be computed. This is done by multiplying the appropriate probabilities times the economic consequences. This is shown in the following table.

Figure for Problem 6-32

DECISION TREE

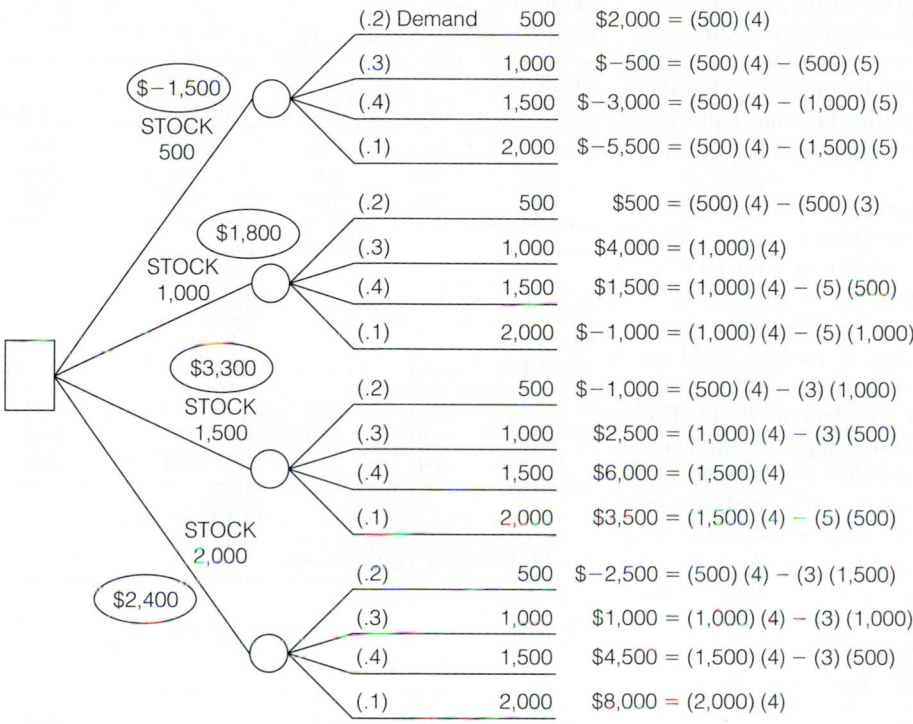

PROBABILITY	DEMAND	STOCK				
		500	1,000	1,500	2,000	MAXIMUM
.2	500	2,000	500	−1,000	−2,500	2,000
.3	1,000	−500	4,000	2,500	1,000	4,000
.4	1,500	−3,000	1,500	6,000	4,500	6,000
.1	2,000	−5,500	−1,000	3,500	8,000	8,000
	EMV	−$1,500	$1,800	$3,300	$2,400	$4,800 = EVwPI

The expected monetary values that are computed in the table are placed and then circled by the appropriate stocking decision on the decision tree. As you can see, the maximum expected monetary value is $3,300, representing a stocking decision of 1,500 gallons. Thus, the decision is to stock 1,500 gallons with an expected monetary value of $3,300.

The expected value of perfect information (EVPI) can be computed by determining the expected value with perfect information and subtracting the maximum expected monetary value from it. The expected value with perfect information is what we would expect if we knew in advance exactly what would happen.

This is determined by multiplying the probabilities for any demand level times the maximum economic outcome for that particular demand level. The maximum economic outcome for every demand level is shown in the right-hand column of the table. The expected value of perfect information can be computed below:

$$\text{EVwPI} = (.2)(2,000) + (.3)(4,000) + (.4)(6,000)$$
$$+ (.1)(8,000) = \$4,800$$
$$\text{EVPI} = \text{EVwPI} - \text{EMV} = 4,800 - 3,300$$
$$\text{EVPI} = \$1,500$$

6-33. Bob has two major decisions to make. First, he must decide whether or not to conduct the survey.

After this decision, he must decide whether to develop a small, medium, or large waste disposal facility. Of course, Bob always has the option of not building any facility, with an expected monetary value of 0. To solve this problem, we will look at a decision tree involving no survey and then another decision tree involving the use of a survey. The decision branches that represent the highest expected monetary value will be the chosen plan of action.

If no survey is to be conducted, the decision tree is fairly straightforward. There are three main decisions, which are building a small, medium, or large facility. Extending from these decision branches are three possible demands, representing the possible states of nature. The demand for this type of facility could be either low, medium, or high. It was given in the problem that the probability for a low demand is .15. The probabilities for a medium and a high demand are .40 and .45, respectively. The problem also gave monetary consequences for building a small, medium, or large facility when the demand could be low, medium, or high for the facility. These data are reflected in a decision tree on the next page. Using the data in the decision tree, we can multiply the appropriate probabilities times the economic consequences for a small, medium, or a large facility. That alternative that maximizes the expected monetary value will be chosen. The results follow.

No survey (analysis values in hundreds of thousands of dollars):

| | | FACILITY | | |
PROBABILITY	DEMAND	SMALL	MEDIUM	LARGE
.15	Low	500	200	−200
.4	Medium	500	700	400
.45	High	500	800	1,000
	EMV	500	670	580

As seen from the above analysis, the expected monetary values for the small, medium, and large facilities are $500,000, $670,000, and $580,000. The medium facility, with an expected monetary value of $670,000, is selected because it represents the highest expected monetary value.

We are still not done with solving the problem. We also have to look at the situation of performing the survey. The most difficult part of this problem is the computation of the revised probabilities using Bayes's law. For each alternative facility, three revised probabilities must be computed, representing low, medium, and high demand for a facility. These probabilities can be computed using tables. One table is used to compute the probabilities for low survey results, another table is

used for medium survey results, and a final table is used for high survey results. These tables are shown below:

For low survey results—A1:

STATE OF NATURE	$P(B_i)$	$P(A_i \mid B_j)$	$P(B_j \text{ and } A_i)$	$P(B_j \mid A_i)$
B1	.150	.700	.105	.339
B2	.400	.400	.160	.516
B3	.450	.100	.045	.145

$$P(A1) = .310$$

For medium survey results—A2:

STATE OF NATURE	$P(B_i)$	$P(A_i \mid B_j)$	$P(B_j \text{ and } A_i)$	$P(B_j \mid A_i)$
B1	.150	.200	.030	.082
B2	.400	.500	.200	.548
B3	.450	.300	.135	.370

$$P(A2) = .365$$

For high survey results—A3:

STATE OF NATURE	$P(B_i)$	$P(A_i \mid B_j)$	$P(B_j \text{ and } A_i)$	$P(B_j \mid A_i)$
B1	.150	.100	.015	.046
B2	.400	.100	.040	.123
B3	.450	.600	.270	.831

$$P(A3) = .325$$

Figure for Problem 6-33

DECISION TREE — SURVEY

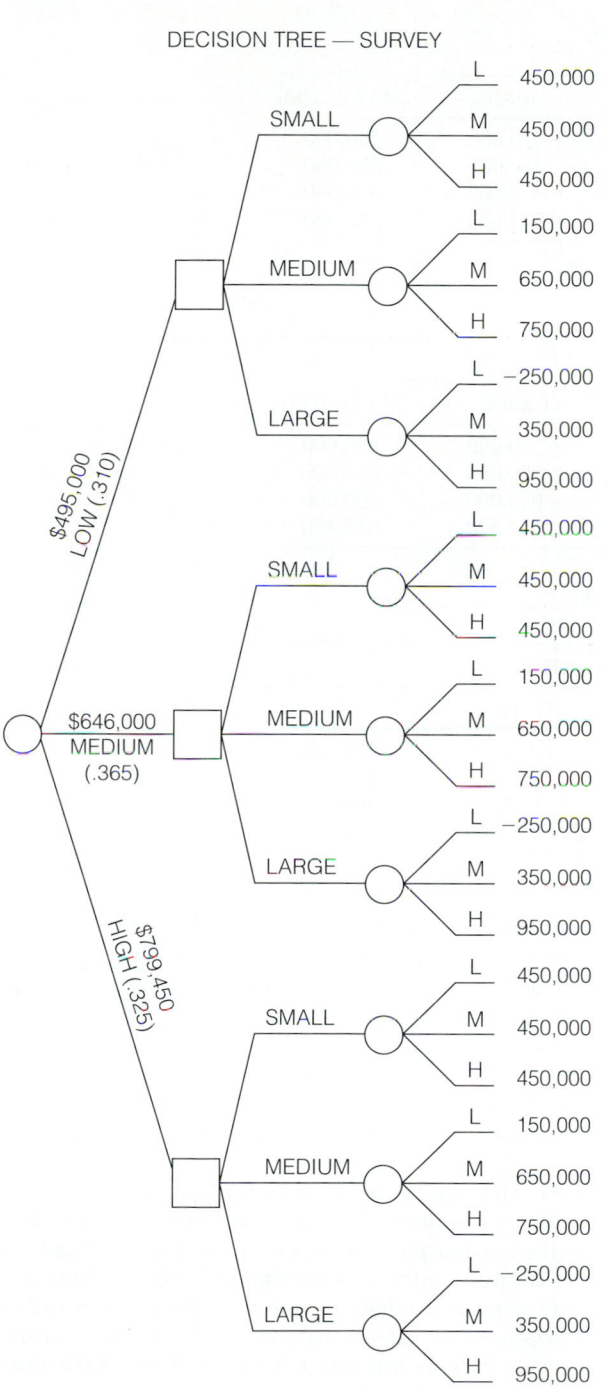

The right-hand sides of these tables contain the needed conditional probabilities that are required in the analysis. You should note that these tables also compute the probability of the various states of nature occurring. The probability of low survey results, for example, is seen at the bottom of the first table to be .310. In a likewise fashion, the probabilities for medium survey results and high survey results are .365 and .325, respectively. These probabilities can then be used along with the conditional probabilities in selecting the best decision. This can be done by determining the expected monetary value for the small, medium, and large facility when the survey results are low, medium, and high.

Figure for Problem 6-33

DECISION TREE — NO SURVEY

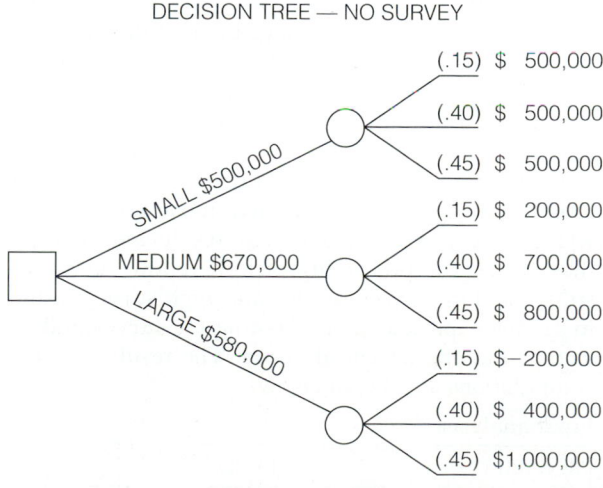

The analysis is shown below.

Survey results are low:

| PROBABILITY | DEMAND | FACILITY | | | |
		SMALL	MEDIUM	LARGE	MAXIMUM
.339	Low	450,000	150,000	−250,000	450,000
.516	Medium	450,000	650,000	350,000	650,000
.145	High	450,000	750,000	950,000	900,000
	EMV	450,000	495,000	233,600	618,450

Maximum EMV = $495,000

Survey results are medium:

| PROBABILITY | DEMAND | FACILITY | | | |
		SMALL	MEDIUM	LARGE	MAXIMUM
.082	Low	450,000	150,000	−250,000	450,000
.548	Medium	450,000	650,000	350,000	650,000
.37	High	450,000	750,000	950,000	900,000
	EMV	450,000	646,000	522,800	618,450

Maximum EMV = $646,000

Survey results are high:

| PROBABILITY | DEMAND | FACILITY | | | |
		SMALL	MEDIUM	LARGE	MAXIMUM
.046	Low	450,000	150,000	−250,000	450,000
.123	Medium	450,000	650,000	350,000	650,000
.831	High	450,000	750,000	950,000	900,000
	EMV	450,000	710,100	821,000	618,450

Maximum EMV = $821,000

If the survey results are low, the best decision is to build the medium facility with an expected return of $495,000. If the survey results are medium, the best decision is also to build the medium plant with an expected return of $646,000. On the other hand, if the survey results are high, the best decision is to build the large facility with an expected monetary value of $821,000. Now, we can take these results and multiply them times the probability of having low survey results, medium survey results, and high survey results to get the expected value of taking the survey and selecting the appropriate decision. The results of these computations are shown below.

Final analysis:

PROBABILITY	DEMAND	
.31	Low	495,000
.365	Medium	646,000
.325	High	821,000

EMV = $656,065

As you can see from the analysis, the expected monetary value is approximately $656,000. This is the expected monetary value for conducting the survey and taking the appropriate action. Because the expected monetary value for not conducting the survey is greater, the decision is not to conduct the survey and to build the medium-sized facility. The expected value from doing this, shown in a previous table, is $670,000.

6-34. The overall purpose of this question is to have students use utility theory in making a decision. One of the hardest parts of this exercise is to construct the actual utility curve. As mentioned in the problem, this may require students to use several rounds of utility assessment to get an accurate and consistent utility curve. Students are asked if they had any difficulties in assessing the utility curve and the overall usefulness of utility assessment and utility theory in general. This can start an in-class discussion concerning some of the many problems and difficulties in determining utility curves. It can be pointed out that it can be very difficult to accurately assess a utility curve. On the other side of the argument, there are many decisions that should be made using non-monetary factors. Life and death decisions at hospitals, decisions concerning the threat of nuclear war, and other very important decisions cannot be made looking at monetary values alone. For these circumstances, such concepts as utility theory and the use of the utility curve can be very important.

6-35. a. The best stocking policy is given in the following table. As you can see, the best decision is to stock 100 trees, with an expected return of $1,000.

Table for Problem 6-35a

NODES	TYPE	PROBA-BILITY	PAYOFF ($)	DECISION
1 ---- 2	Decision	None	1,000	← choice:
1 ---- 3	Decision	None	980	100 trees
1 ---- 4	Decision	None	960	
1 ---- 5	Decision	None	940	
1 ---- 6	Decision	None	880	
2 ---- 7	Event	.100	100	
2 ---- 8	Event	.300	300	
2 ---- 9	Event	.400	400	
2 ---- 10	Event	.100	100	
2 ---- 11	Event	.100	100	
3 ---- 12	Event	.100	80	
3 ---- 13	Event	.300	270	
3 ---- 14	Event	.400	400	
3 ---- 15	Event	.100	110	
3 ---- 16	Event	.100	120	
4 ---- 17	Event	.100	70	
4 ---- 18	Event	.300	240	
4 ---- 19	Event	.400	400	
4 ---- 20	Event	.100	12	
4 ---- 21	Event	.100	130	
5 ---- 22	Event	.100	60	
5 ---- 23	Event	.300	240	
5 ---- 24	Event	.400	400	
5 ---- 25	Event	.100	110	
5 ---- 26	Event	.100	130	
6 ---- 27	Event	.100	50	
6 ---- 28	Event	.300	180	
6 ---- 29	Event	.400	400	
6 ---- 30	Event	.100	120	
6 ---- 31	Event	.100	130	

b. Getting an increase of $100 for each level of demand for stocking 500 trees has the impact shown in the following table. Stocking 100 trees is still the best decision.

Table for Problem 6-35b

NODES	TYPE	PROBA-BILITY	PAYOFF ($)	DECISION
1 ---- 2	Decision	None	1,000	← choice:
1 ---- 3	Decision	None	980	100 trees
1 ---- 4	Decision	None	960	
1 ---- 5	Decision	None	940	
1 ---- 6	Decision	None	980	
2 ---- 7	Event	.100	100	
2 ---- 8	Event	.300	300	
2 ---- 9	Event	.400	400	
2 ---- 10	Event	.100	100	
2 ---- 11	Event	.100	100	
3 ---- 12	Event	.100	80	
3 ---- 13	Event	.300	270	
3 ---- 14	Event	.400	400	
3 ---- 15	Event	.100	110	
3 ---- 16	Event	.100	120	
4 ---- 17	Event	.100	70	
4 ---- 18	Event	.300	240	
4 ---- 19	Event	.400	400	
4 ---- 20	Event	.100	120	
4 ---- 21	Event	.100	130	
5 ---- 22	Event	.100	60	
5 ---- 23	Event	.300	240	
5 ---- 24	Event	.400	400	
5 ---- 25	Event	.100	110	
5 ---- 26	Event	.100	130	
6 ---- 27	Event	.100	60	
6 ---- 28	Event	.300	210	
6 ---- 29	Event	.400	440	
6 ---- 30	Event	.100	130	
6 ---- 31	Event	.100	140	

c. An increase of $200 for each level of demand for stocking 500 trees has the impact shown in the following table. Stocking 500 units is now the best decision, but only by $80.

Table for Problem 6-35c

NODES	TYPE	PROBA-BILITY	PAYOFF ($)	DECISION
1 ---- 2	Decision	None	1,000	
1 ---- 3	Decision	None	980	
1 ---- 4	Decision	None	960	
1 ---- 5	Decision	None	940	
1 ---- 6	Decision	None	1,080	← choice:
2 ---- 7	Event	.100	100	500 trees
2 ---- 8	Event	.300	300	
2 ---- 9	Event	.400	400	
2 ---- 10	Event	.100	100	
2 ---- 11	Event	.100	100	
3 ---- 12	Event	.100	80	
3 ---- 13	Event	.300	270	
3 ---- 14	Event	.400	400	
3 ---- 15	Event	.100	110	

Table for Problem 6-35c (continued)

NODES	TYPE	PROBA-BILITY	PAYOFF ($)	DECISION
3 ---- 16	Event	.100	120	
4 ---- 17	Event	.100	70	
4 ---- 18	Event	.300	240	
4 ---- 19	Event	.400	400	
4 ---- 20	Event	.100	120	
4 ---- 21	Event	.100	130	
5 ---- 22	Event	.100	60	
5 ---- 23	Event	.300	240	
5 ---- 24	Event	.400	400	
5 ---- 25	Event	.100	110	
5 ---- 26	Event	.100	130	
6 ---- 27	Event	.100	70	
6 ---- 28	Event	.300	240	
6 ---- 29	Event	.400	480	
6 ---- 30	Event	.100	140	
6 ---- 31	Event	.100	150	

d. As the increase in profits gets greater, stocking 500 trees is even more attractive as the following table reveals. The expected monetary value is now $1,280.

Table for Problem 6-35d

NODES	TYPE	PROBA-BILITY	PAYOFF ($)	DECISION
1 ---- 2	Decision	None	1,000	
1 ---- 3	Decision	None	980	
1 ---- 4	Decision	None	960	
1 ---- 5	Decision	None	940	
1 ---- 6	Decision	None	1,280 ← choice:	
2 ---- 7	Event	.100	100	500 trees
2 ---- 8	Event	.300	300	
2 ---- 9	Event	.400	400	
2 ---- 10	Event	.100	100	
2 ---- 11	Event	.100	100	
3 ---- 12	Event	.100	80	
3 ---- 13	Event	.300	270	
3 ---- 14	Event	.400	400	
3 ---- 15	Event	.100	110	
3 ---- 16	Event	.100	120	
4 ---- 17	Event	.100	70	
4 ---- 18	Event	.300	240	
4 ---- 19	Event	.400	400	
4 ---- 20	Event	.100	120	
4 ---- 21	Event	.100	130	
5 ---- 22	Event	.100	60	
5 ---- 23	Event	.300	240	
5 ---- 24	Event	.400	400	
5 ---- 25	Event	.100	110	
5 ---- 26	Event	.100	130	
6 ---- 27	Event	.100	90	
6 ---- 28	Event	.300	300	
6 ---- 29	Event	.400	560	
6 ---- 30	Event	.100	160	
6 ---- 31	Event	.100	170	

Solution to the Blake Electronics Case

1. By employing basic decision theory, Steve's problem is quite easily solved. He needs no additional information for its solution. In fact, Iverstine and Kinard's figures are more suitable for manipulation than are MAIs.
2. Steve's problem involves three decisions. First, should he contract the services of an outside research agency? Second, should he employ MAI or Iverstine and Kinard, if a survey is warranted? Third, in any case, should the new product line be introduced?

By using the probabilities stated in the case, some expected values can be derived. Then these expected values can be compared and a decision can be made. This is the basis of decision theory that will be used to reach a conclusion.

To facilitate the solving of this problem, several variables will be defined here.

S_i = *states of nature*
   where $i = 1$ connotes a favorable outcome from the introduction of the product line, and $i = 2$ connotes an unfavorable outcome.

A_j = *decisions*
   where $j = 1$ means survey will be done,
      $j = 2$ means no survey will be undertaken,
      $j = 3$ means MAI will be employed,
      $j = 4$ means Iverstine and Kinard (I&K) will be employed,
      $j = 5$ means product will be introduced, and
      $j = 6$ means product will not be introduced.

I_k = *survey predictions*
   where $k = 1$ means MAI predicts a favorable outcome,
      $k = 2$ means MAI predicts an unfavorable outcome,
      $k = 3$ means I & K predicts a favorable outcome, and
      $k = 4$ means I & K predicts an unfavorable outcome.

$P(I_k|S_i)$ = conditional probability; probability of I_k given S_i.

$P(S_i|I_k)$ = probability of S_i given I_k.

The following tables give the probabilities of pertinent nature:

TABLE A

STATE OF NATURE	PROBABILITY OF OCCURRENCE
S_1 (fav.)	.6
S_2 (unfav.)	.4

The values in Table A were given by Blake Electronics' own research staff. Given that the product line is introduced, it has a 60% chance of success and a 40% chance of failure.

TABLE B
MAIs Conditional Probabilities

| | $P(I_k \mid S_i)$ | |
STATE OF NATURE SURVEY PREDICTIONS	S_1	S_2
I_1	.70	.40
I_2	.30	.60

MAI predicted favorable outcomes 50 out of 100 (50%) times ($35 + 15 = 50$). Given that the actual outcome was successful, MAI predicted that outcome 35 times out of 50 (70%), which means that MAI was wrong 30% of the time ($100\% - 70\%$) it predicted a favorable outcome. Likewise, 30 out of 50 times (60%) MAI correctly predicted an unfavorable outcome. It

follows that 40% of the time, the firm was incorrect in predicting an unfavorable outcome. See Table B.

TABLE C
I & K Conditional Probabilities $P(I_k \mid S_i)$

STATE OF NATURE SURVEY PREDICTIONS	S_1	S_2
I_3	.90**	.20
I_4	.10	.80

It was given in the case that 90% of the time I & K made a correct favorable prediction; and 80% of the time the firm made a correct unfavorable prediction. The other two probabilities follow logically. See Table C.

For simplicity, the entire problem is drawn in decision tree form below.

Using the decision tree, expected values will be found and compared working from right to left.

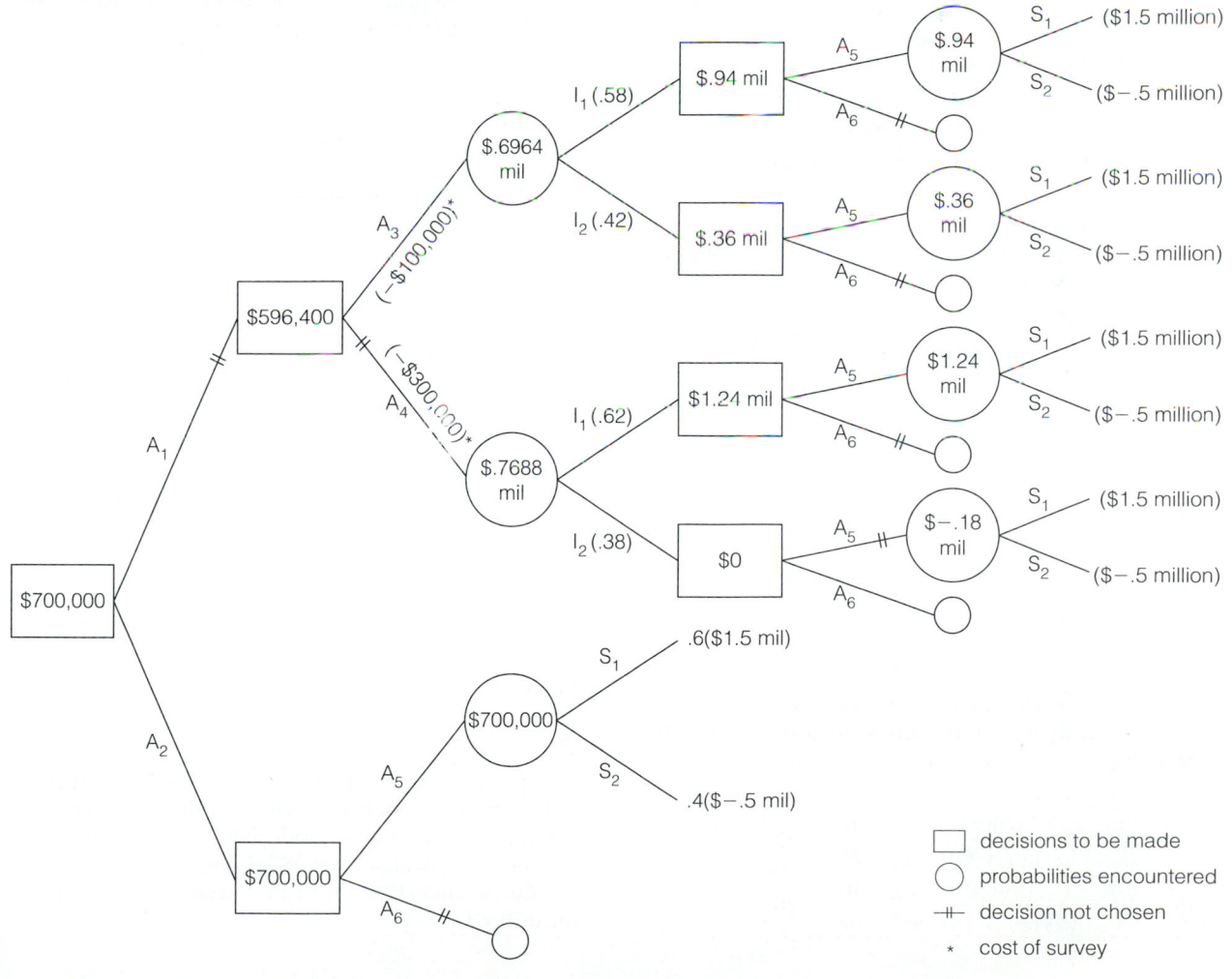

First, assuming that no survey is done (A_2), the expected value of introducing the product line (expected return) can be determined. The case says that sales can be increased by $2 million. However, the cost of developing the product ($500,000) must be subtracted from that figure to arrive at a figure for total benefit for a favorable outcome. That figure is $1,500,000. If the product is introduced and an unfavorable outcome materializes, then the cost of developing the product becomes a loss ($-$500,000). Table D computes the expected return for introducing the product and for not introducing it.

$$P(S_1|I_2) = \frac{(.3)(.6)}{(.3)(.6) + (.6)(.4)} = \frac{.13}{.42} = .43$$

$$P(S_2|I_2) = \frac{(.6)(.4)}{(.3)(.6) + (.6)(.4)} = \frac{.24}{.42} = .57$$

$$P(S_1|I_3) = \frac{(.9)(.6)}{.9(.6) + (.2)(.4)} = \frac{.54}{.62} = .87$$

$$P(S_2|I_3) = \frac{(.2)(.4)}{.9(.6) + (.2)(.4)} = \frac{.08}{.62} = .13$$

TABLE D
PAYOFF TABLE (Profit)

PRIOR PROBABILITIES	STATE OF NATURE	INTRODUCE	DON'T INTRODUCE
.6	S_1	$1,500,000	0
.4	S_2	$-500,000	0
	EXPECTED PROFIT	$ 700,000	0

$$E(P) = .6(1,500,000) + (.4)(-500,000)$$
$$= 900,000 + (-200,000) = \$700,000$$

$$P(S_1|I_4) = \frac{(.1)(.6)}{(.1)(.6) + (.3)(.4)} = \frac{.06}{.38} = .16$$

$$P(S_2|I_4) = \frac{(.3)(.4)}{(.1)(.6) + (.3)(.4)} = \frac{.32}{.38} = .84$$

The expected return for introducing the product is greater than for not introducing it. Therefore, the product should be introduced if no survey is done. (See decision tree for pictorial explanation.)

The problem, however, is still not solved. Two decisions remain: (1) Will a survey help? If so, (2) Who should do the survey? An evaluation of expected returns is necessary here, too. With the surveys, the decision to not introduce the product line still has an expected return of 0 ($E(A_6) = 0$). (See decision tree.) An evaluation of expected returns is necessary and requires Bayes's Law.

$$P(S_i|I_k) = \frac{P(I_k|S_i)(P(S_i))}{P(I_k)}$$

where $P(I_k) = P(I_k|S_1)P(S_1) + P(I_k|S_2)P(S_2)$

The additional probabilities needed are computed below:

$$P(S_1|I_1) = \frac{.70(.6)}{(.7)(.6) + (.4)(.4)} = \frac{.42}{.58} = .72$$

$$P(S_2|I_1) = \frac{.4(.4)}{(.7)(.6) + (.4)(.4)} = \frac{.16}{.38} = .28$$

The expected value can be found on the decision tree.

After an expected return is calculated for each firm, the cost of the study must be subtracted.

E(MAI)	$696,400
Cost of survey	100,000
Actual return	$596,400
E(I&K)	768,800
Cost	300,000
Return	468,800

Since the MAI survey reaps a greater expected profit, its return is compared with that calculated assuming no survey is undertaken ($700,000). Since $700,000 is greater than $596,400, then no survey should be undertaken and the product line should be introduced.

Solution to Sixty-Six-Year-Old Patient with a Hernia Case

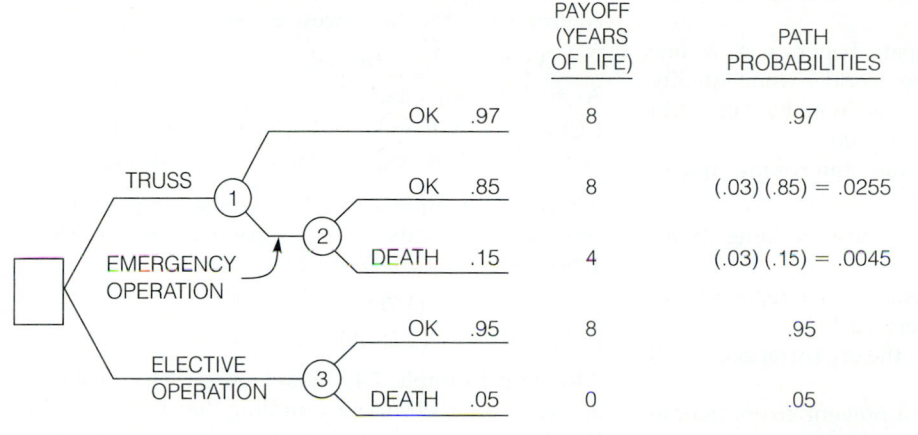

	PAYOFF (YEARS OF LIFE)	PATH PROBABILITIES	EXPECTED VALUE
OK .97	8	.97	7.76
OK .85	8	(.03)(.85) = .0255	.204
DEATH .15	4	(.03)(.15) = .0045	.018
			7.982 YRS
OK .95	8	.95	7.6
DEATH .05	0	.05	0
			7.6 YRS

Expected average survival:

Truss   7.982 years
Elective Operation 7.6   years

 Difference .382 years, or 139.43
             days in favor of truss

Cost of elective operation: $1,500
Possible cost of emergency operation:

$$(.03)\,(\$2,000) = \$\ 60$$
$$\text{Truss:}\qquad\qquad \$\ 50$$
$$\$110$$

Difference: $1,390 in favor of truss

7
Statistical Quality Control

LEARNING OBJECTIVES

After completing this chapter, students will be able to:

1. Define quality of a product or service.
2. Name the six attributes of quality.
3. Develop four types of control charts, i.e., $\bar{x}$, R, p, and c.
4. Understand the basic theoretical underpinnings of statistical quality control, including the central limit theorem.
5. Know if a process is in control or not.

TEACHING SUGGESTIONS

Teaching Suggestion 7.1: Student opinions about quality.

 Certainly every student has an opinion about the problems (or perceived problems) with quality in this country. Open the discussion with a tally of how many American vs. Japanese cars are owned by students, and why.

Teaching Suggestion 7.2: The six dimensions of quality and student perceptions.

Relating these six dimensions of quality to the students' perceptions of quality makes for an interesting classroom discussion.

Teaching Suggestion 7.3: Japan's change in status since WWII.

Remind students that Japan began just a few decades ago with perhaps the world's worst quality and that "Made in Japan" was synonymous with shoddy products just thirty years ago.

Teaching Suggestion 7.4: Four interesting quotes from QC expert Philip Crosby.

1. "The cost of quality is the expense of doing things wrong."
2. "There is absolutely no reason for having errors or defects in any product or service."
3. "If quality isn't ingrained in the organization, it will never happen."
4. "It is much less expensive to prevent errors than to rework, scrap, or service them."

Teaching Suggestion 7.5: Natural vs. assignable variations.

Random chance → "natural"

Specific cause → assignable

Teaching Suggestion 7.6: Mean and range charts.

Mean and range charts tell us what we need to know about the process. Each plays a necessary role.

VIDEO NOTES

VIDEO 7–1   COMAP

Quality Control: Against All Odds (Chapter 7; about 6 minutes)

This segment discusses statistical process control at Frito Lay. The segment provides an introduction to statistical process control via control charts. It also includes several comments by Deming and recognition of the Deming Prize as a premier award in Japan. This is only an introduction to the use of control charts, not a teaching video.

ALTERNATE EXAMPLES

Alternate Example 7.1: Twenty-five engine mountings are sampled each day and found to have an average width of 2", with a standard deviation of 0.1". To set control limits that include 99.7% of sample means (Z = 3),

$$\text{UCL}_{\bar{x}} = \overline{\overline{X}} + Z\sigma_{\bar{x}} = 2 + 3(0.1/\sqrt{25}) = 2 + .06$$
$$= 2.06 \text{ inches}$$
$$\text{LCL}_{\bar{x}} = \overline{\overline{X}} - Z\sigma_{\bar{x}} = 2 - 3(0.1/\sqrt{25}) = 2 - .06$$
$$= 1.94 \text{ inches}$$

Alternate Example 7.2: Several samples of size n = 8 have been taken from today's production of fencing poles. The average pole was 3 yards in length and the average sample range was 0.015 yard. We find 99.7% control limits for the process below:

$\overline{X} = 3$ yds. $\overline{R} = .015$ yd.

$A_2 = .373$ from Table 7.2

$\text{UCL} = \overline{\overline{X}} + A_2\overline{R} = 3 + .373(.015) = 3.006$ yds.

$\text{LCL} = \overline{\overline{X}} - A_2\overline{R} = 3 - .373(.015) = 2.994$ yds.

Alternate Example 7.3: The average range of a process is 10 pounds. The sample size is 10. Using Table 7.2, $D_4 = 1.78$, $D_3 = .22$.

$\text{UCL}_R = D_4\overline{R} = (1.78)(10) = 17.8$ lbs.

$\text{LCL}_R = D_3\overline{R} = (.22)(10) = 2.2$ lbs.

Alternate Example 7.4: Based on samples of 20 IRS auditors, each observed handling 100 files, we find that the total number of mistakes made in handling files is 220. We set 95.45% limits on this process below:

$$\overline{P} = \frac{\text{total \# mistakes}}{\text{total \# files}} = \frac{220}{(100)(20)} = 0.11$$

$$\sigma_P = \sqrt{\frac{(.11)(1 - .11)}{100}} = .03$$

↖ 100 is the size of each sample

$\text{UCL}_P = \overline{P} + Z\sigma_P = .11 + (2)(.03) = .17$

$\text{LCL}_P = \overline{P} - Z\sigma_P = .11 - (2)(.03) = .05$

Alternate Example 7.5: There have been complaints that the sports page of the Dubuque *Register* has lots of typos. The last 6 days have been examined carefully, and the number of typos/page recorded below. Is the process in control, using Z = 2?

DAY	# OF TYPOS
Mon.	2
Tues.	1
Wed.	5
Thurs.	3
Fri.	4
Sat.	0

$\overline{c} = 15/6 = 2.5$

$\text{UCL}_c = \overline{c} + 2\sqrt{\overline{c}} = 2.5 + 2(1.58) = 5.66$

$\text{LCL}_c = \overline{c} - 2\sqrt{\overline{c}} = 2.5 - 2(1.58) = -.66$ (or 0)

All days are in control.

SOLUTIONS TO DISCUSSION QUESTIONS AND PROBLEMS

7-1. The Central Limit Theorem allows us to use the normal curve regardless of the distribution of the population we are trying to control.

7-2. The ultimate goal of the $\bar{x}$ and R-charts is to ascertain, by a sampling procedure, that the process is kept within specified upper and lower bounds. The combination of $\bar{x}$ and the R-charts allows one to determine that both the average or customary value and the extreme deviations are within the limits.

7-3. $\bar{x}$-charts: depict the variation in average value of a variable (weight or diameter, for example)

R-charts: depict the average range of a variable

p-charts: depict the average value of an attribute (percent defective, for example)

c-charts: depict the number of times an attribute (defect, for example) occurs

7-4. A process might become out of control due to such factors as:

tool wear;

a change in raw materials;

a change in working environment (temperature or humidity, for example);

tired or poorly trained labor.

7-5. Any time one samples less than the entire lot of the product, there is the possibility of making an error, which is the acceptance of the lot even though the process is actually out of control.

7-6. n = 6

From Table 7.2, $A_2 = 0.483$, $D_4 = 2.004$, $D_3 = 0$

$$UCL_x = \overline{\overline{X}} + A_2 * \overline{R}$$
$$= 46 + 0.483 * 2$$
$$= 46.966$$
$$LCL_x = \overline{\overline{X}} - A_2 * \overline{R}$$
$$= 46 - 0.483 * 2$$
$$= 45.034$$
$$UCL_R = D_4 * \overline{R}$$
$$= 2.004 * 2$$
$$= 4.008$$
$$LCL_R = D_3 * \overline{R}$$
$$= 0 * 2$$
$$= 0$$

7-7. n = 10

From Table 7.2, $A_2 = 0.308$, $D_4 = 1.777$, $D_3 = 0.223$

$$UCL_x = \overline{\overline{X}} + A_2 * \overline{R}$$
$$= 60 + 0.308 * 3$$
$$= 60.924$$
$$LCL_x = \overline{\overline{X}} - A_2 * \overline{R}$$
$$= 60 - 0.308 * 3$$
$$= 59.076$$
$$UCL_R = D_4 * \overline{R}$$
$$= 1.777 * 3$$
$$= 5.331$$
$$LCL_R = D_3 * \overline{R}$$
$$= 0.223 * 3$$
$$= 0.669$$

7-8. n = 8

From Table 7.2, $A_2 = 0.373$, $D_4 = 1.864$, $D_3 = 0.136$

$$UCL_x = \overline{\overline{X}} + A_2 * \overline{R}$$
$$= 17 + 0.373 * 0.5$$
$$= 17.187$$
$$LCL_x = \overline{\overline{X}} - A_2 * \overline{R}$$
$$= 17 - 0.373 * 0.5$$
$$= 16.814$$
$$UCL_R = D_4 * \overline{R}$$
$$= 1.864 * 0.5$$
$$= 0.932$$
$$LCL_R = D_3 * \overline{R}$$
$$= 0.136 * 0.5$$
$$= 0.068$$

n = 4

From Table 7.2, $A_2 = 0.729$, $D_4 = 2.282$, $D_3 = 0.0$

$$UCL_x = \overline{\overline{X}} + A_2 * \overline{R}$$
$$= 10.04 + 0.729 * 0.52$$
$$= 10.42$$
$$LCL_x = \overline{\overline{X}} - A_2 * \overline{R}$$
$$= 10.04 - 0.729 * 0.52$$
$$= 9.66$$

7-9.

TIME	BOX 1	BOX 2	BOX 3	BOX 4	AVERAGE	RANGE
9 A.M.	9.8	10.4	9.9	10.3	10.10	0.60
10 A.M.	10.1	10.2	9.9	9.8	10.00	0.40
11 A.M.	9.9	10.5	10.3	10.1	10.20	0.60
12 P.M.	9.7	9.8	10.3	10.2	10.00	0.60
1 P.M.	9.7	10.1	9.9	9.9	9.90	0.40
				Average	10.04	0.52

INSTRUCTOR'S SECTION

$$UCL_R = D_4 * \overline{R}$$
$$= 2.282 * 0.52$$
$$= 1.187$$
$$LCL_R = D_3 * \overline{R}$$
$$= 0 * 0.52$$
$$= 0.0$$

The smallest sample mean is 9.9, the largest 10.2. Both are well within the control limits. Similarly, the largest sample range is 0.6, also well within the control limits. Hence, we can conclude that the process is presently within control.

One step the QC department might take would be to increase the sample size to provide a clearer indication as to both control limits *and* whether or not the process is in control.

7-10. See table.

Average X = 2.982

Average R = 1.02375

n = 4

From Table 7.2, $A_2 = 0.729$, $D_4 = 2.282$, $D_3 = 0.0$

$$UCL_x = \overline{\overline{X}} + A_2 * \overline{R}$$
$$= 2.982 + 0.729 * 1.024$$
$$= 3.728$$
$$LCL_x = \overline{\overline{X}} - A_2 * \overline{R}$$
$$= 2.982 - 0.729 * 1.024$$
$$= 2.236$$
$$UCL_R = D_4 * \overline{R}$$
$$= 2.282 * 1.024$$
$$= 2.29$$
$$LCL_R = D_3 * \overline{R}$$
$$= 0 * 1.024$$
$$= 0.0$$

The smallest sample mean is 2.64, the largest 3.39. Both are well within the control limits. Similarly, the largest sample range is 1.61, also well within the control limits. Hence, we can conclude that the process is presently within control.

7-11.
$$UCL_p = \overline{p} + 3\sqrt{\frac{\overline{p}(1-\overline{p})}{n}}$$
$$LCL_p = \overline{p} - 3\sqrt{\frac{\overline{p}(1-\overline{p})}{n}}$$

n = 200

$q = 1 - \overline{p}$

PERCENT DEFECTIVE (p)	q	$\sqrt{pq/n}$	LCL_p	UCL_p
0.01	0.99	0.0070	0.0	0.0311
0.02	0.98	0.0099	0.0	0.0497
0.03	0.97	0.0121	0.0	0.0663
0.04	0.96	0.0139	0.0	0.0817
0.05	0.95	0.0154	0.0038	0.0962
0.06	0.94	0.0168	0.0096	0.1104
0.07	0.93	0.0180	0.0160	0.1240
0.08	0.92	0.0192	0.0224	0.1376
0.09	0.91	0.0202	0.0294	0.1506
0.10	0.90	0.0212	0.0364	0.1636

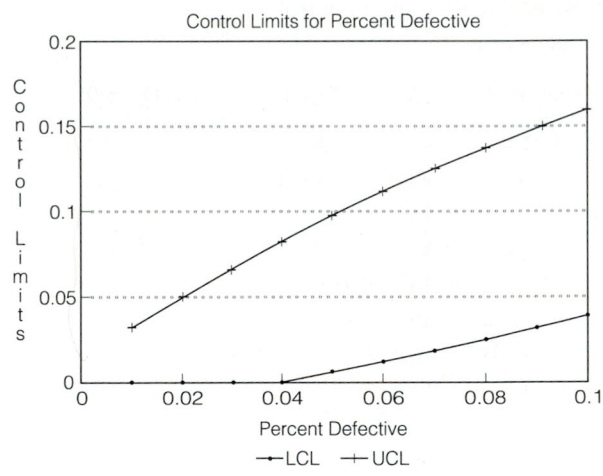

Control Limits for Percent Defective

Table for Problem 7-10

HOUR	$\overline{X}$	$\overline{R}$	HOUR	$\overline{X}$	$\overline{R}$	HOUR	$\overline{X}$	$\overline{R}$
1	3.25	0.71	9	3.02	0.71	17	2.86	1.43
2	3.10	1.18	10	2.85	1.33	18	2.74	1.29
3	3.22	1.43	11	2.83	1.17	19	3.41	1.61
4	3.39	1.26	12	2.97	0.40	20	2.89	1.09
5	3.07	1.17	13	3.11	0.85	21	2.65	1.08
6	2.86	0.32	14	2.83	1.31	22	3.28	0.46
7	3.05	0.53	15	3.12	1.06	23	2.94	1.58
8	2.65	1.13	16	2.84	0.50	24	2.64	0.97

7-12.

SAMPLE NUMBER	SAMPLE RANGE	SAMPLE MEAN
1	1.10	46
2	1.31	45
3	0.91	46
4	1.10	47
5	1.21	48
6	0.82	47
7	0.86	50
8	1.11	49
9	1.12	51
10	0.99	52
11	0.86	50
12	1.20	52

$\overline{R} = 1.049$

$\overline{X} = 48.583$

$n = 12$

From Table 7.2:

$A_2 = 0.266, D_4 = 1.716, D_3 = 0.284$

$LCL_x = \overline{\overline{X}} - A_2 * \overline{R}$

$\qquad = 48.583 - 0.266 * 1.049$

$\qquad = 48.55$

$UCL_x = \overline{\overline{X}} + A_2 * \overline{R}$

$\qquad = 48.583 + 0.266 * 1.049$

$\qquad = 48.86$

$LCL_R = D_3 * \overline{R}$

$\qquad = 0.284 * 1.049$

$\qquad = 0.298$

$UCL_R = D_4 * \overline{R}$

$\qquad = 1.716 * 1.049$

$\qquad = 1.800$

The smallest sample range is 0.82, the largest 1.31. Both are well within the control limits.

The smallest average is 45, the largest 52. Both are outside the proper control limits.

Therefore, while the range is within limits, the average is outside limits, and apparently increasing. Immediate action is needed to correct the problem and get the average within the control limits again.

7-13. See table.

$\overline{X} = 63.45$

$\overline{R} = 1.5$

$n = 4$

From Table 7.2, $A_2 = 0.729, D_4 = 2.282, D_3 = 0$

$UCL_x = \overline{\overline{X}} + A_2 * \overline{R}$

$\qquad = 63.45 + 0.729 * 1.5$

$\qquad = 64.54$

$LCL_x = \overline{\overline{X}} - A_2 * \overline{R}$

$\qquad = 63.45 - 0.729 * 1.5$

$\qquad = 62.36$

$UCL_R = D_4 * \overline{R}$

$\qquad = 2.282 * 1.5$

$\qquad = 3.423$

$LCL_R = D_3 * \overline{R}$

$\qquad = 0 * 1.5$

$\qquad = 0$

7-14. $UCL_p = \bar{p} + 3\sqrt{\dfrac{\bar{p}(1 - \bar{p})}{n}}$

$\qquad LCL_p = \bar{p} - 3\sqrt{\dfrac{\bar{p}(1 - \bar{p})}{n}}$

$\qquad UCL_p = 0.011 + 3\sqrt{\dfrac{0.011 * 0.989}{1000}}$

$\qquad\qquad = 0.0208$

$\qquad LCL_p = 0.011 - 3\sqrt{\dfrac{0.011 * 0.989}{1000}}$

$\qquad\qquad = 0.0011$

Table for Problem 7-13

SAMPLE	$\overline{X}$	R	SAMPLE	$\overline{X}$	R	SAMPLE	$\overline{X}$	R
1	63.5	2.0	10	63.5	1.3	19	63.8	1.3
2	63.6	1.0	11	63.3	1.8	20	63.5	1.6
3	63.7	1.7	12	63.2	1.0	21	63.9	1.0
4	63.9	0.9	13	63.6	1.8	22	63.2	1.8
5	63.4	1.2	14	63.3	1.5	23	63.3	1.7
6	63.0	1.6	15	63.4	1.7	24	64.0	2.0
7	63.2	1.8	16	63.4	1.4	25	63.4	1.5
8	63.3	1.3	17	63.5	1.1			
9	63.7	1.6	18	63.6	1.8			

INSTRUCTOR'S SECTION

7-15.
$$UCL_p = \bar{p} + 3\sqrt{\frac{\bar{p}(1-\bar{p})}{n}}$$

$$LCL_p = \bar{p} - 3\sqrt{\frac{\bar{p}(1-\bar{p})}{n}}$$

$$UCL_p = 0.025 + 3\sqrt{\frac{0.025 * 0.975}{200}}$$

$$= 0.0581$$

$$LCL_p = 0.025 - 3\sqrt{\frac{0.025 * 0.975}{200}}$$

$$= 0.0081$$

7-16. See table.

$$\bar{p} = \frac{\Sigma p_i}{N} = 0.0467$$

$$\sigma_p = \sqrt{\frac{\bar{p}(1-\bar{p})}{n}} = \sqrt{\frac{0.0467 * 0.9533}{100}} = 0.0211$$

For a 3σ p-chart, the upper control level is given by:

$$UCL = \bar{p} + 3\sigma = 0.0467 + 3 * 0.0211 = 0.11$$

The process is in control.

7-17. Average Blemishes/table $= \dfrac{2000}{100} = 20$

Using a Normal approximation to the Poisson distribution:

$$\bar{C} = 20$$
$$\sqrt{\bar{c}} = \sqrt{20} = 4.472$$
$$UCL_C = \bar{C} + 3\sqrt{\bar{c}}$$
$$= 20 + 3 * 4.472$$
$$= 33.4 \text{ or } 33 \text{ blemishes}$$
$$LCL_C = \bar{C} - 3\sqrt{\bar{c}}$$
$$= 20 - 3 * 4.472$$
$$= 6.6 \text{ or } 7 \text{ blemishes}$$

Yes; 42 blemishes is considerably above the upper control limit.

Case Studies

Bayfield Mud Company

The first thing that must be done is to develop quality control limits for the sample means. This can be done as follows. Since the process appears to be unstable, we can use the desired mean as the nominal line.

Desired $\bar{x} = 50.0$

$\sigma_x = 1.2$ (from past results of Wet-Land Drilling)

$\sigma_x = \sigma_x/\sqrt{n} = 1.2/\sqrt{6} = 1.2/2.45 = 0.5$

At a 99.5% confidence interval:
$$UCL_x = \bar{\bar{x}} + 2.81\sigma_x$$
$$= 50 + 2.81 * 0.5$$
$$= 50 + 1.4$$
$$= 51.4$$
$$LCL_x = \bar{\bar{x}} - 2.81\sigma_x$$
$$= 50 - 1.4$$
$$= 48.6$$

Now that we have appropriate control limits, these must be applied to the samples taken on the individual shifts:

(a) Day shift (6:00 A.M.–2:00 P.M.):

$$\frac{\text{Number of means within control limits}}{\text{Total number of means}} = \frac{23}{24} \Rightarrow 96\%$$

(b) Evening shift (2:00 P.M.–10:00 P.M.):

$$\frac{\text{Number of means within control limits}}{\text{Total number of means}} = \frac{12}{24} \Rightarrow 50\%$$

(c) Night shift (10:00 P.M.–6:00 A.M.):

$$\frac{\text{Number of means within control limits}}{\text{Total number of means}} = \frac{12}{24} \Rightarrow 50\%$$

As is now evident, none of the shifts meets the control specifications. Bag weight monitoring needs improvement on all shifts. The problem is much more acute on

Table for Problem 7-16

DAY	NUM. DEFECTIVE	DAY	NUM. DEFECTIVE	DAY	NUM. DEFECTIVE
1	6	8	3	15	4
2	5	9	6	16	5
3	6	10	3	17	6
4	4	11	7	18	5
5	3	12	5	19	4
6	4	13	4	20	3
7	5	14	3	21	7

Day Shift*

TIME	DAY 1			DAY 2			DAY 3		
	AVE	LOW	HIGH	AVE	LOW	HIGH	AVE	LOW	HIGH
6:00	49.6	48.7	50.7	48.6	47.4	52.0	**48.4**	45.0	49.0
7:00	50.2	49.1	51.2	50.0	49.2	52.2	48.8	44.8	49.7
8:00	50.6	49.6	51.4	49.8	49.0	52.4	49.6	48.0	51.8
9:00	50.8	50.2	51.8	50.3	49.4	51.7	50.0	48.1	52.7
10:00	49.9	49.2	52.3	50.2	49.6	51.8	51.0	48.1	55.2
11:00	50.3	48.6	51.7	50.0	49.0	52.3	50.4	49.5	54.1
12:00	48.6	46.2	50.4	50.0	48.8	52.4	50.0	48.7	50.9
1:00	49.0	46.4	50.0	50.1	49.4	53.6	48.9	47.6	51.2

*Bold-faced type indicates a sample outside the quality control limits

Evening Shift

TIME	DAY 1			DAY 2			DAY 3		
	AVE	LOW	HIGH	AVE	LOW	HIGH	AVE	LOW	HIGH
2:00	49.0	46.0	50.6	49.7	48.6	51.0	49.8	48.4	51.0
3:00	49.8	48.2	50.8	**48.4**	47.2	51.7	49.8	48.8	50.8
4:00	50.3	49.2	52.7	**47.2**	45.3	50.9	50.0	49.1	50.6
5:00	51.4	50.0	55.3	**46.8**	44.1	49.0	**47.8**	45.2	51.2
6:00	**51.6**	49.2	54.7	**46.8**	41.0	51.2	**46.4**	44.0	49.7
7:00	**51.8**	50.0	55.6	50.0	46.2	51.7	**46.4**	44.4	50.0
8:00	51.0	48.6	53.2	**47.4**	44.0	48.7	**47.2**	46.6	48.9
9:00	50.5	49.4	52.4	**47.0**	44.2	48.9	**48.4**	47.2	49.5

*Bold-faced type indicates a sample outside the quality control limits

Night Shift

TIME	DAY 1			DAY 2			DAY 3		
	AVE	LOW	HIGH	AVE	LOW	HIGH	AVE	LOW	HIGH
10:00	49.2	46.1	50.7	**47.2**	46.6	50.2	49.2	48.1	50.7
11:00	49.0	46.3	50.8	48.6	47.0	50.0	**48.4**	47.0	50.8
12:00	**48.4**	45.4	50.2	49.8	48.2	50.4	**47.2**	46.4	49.2
1:00	**47.6**	44.3	49.7	49.6	48.4	51.7	**47.4**	46.8	49.0
2:00	**47.4**	44.1	49.6	50.0	49.0	52.2	48.8	47.2	51.4
3:00	**48.2**	45.2	49.0	50.0	49.2	50.0	49.6	49.0	50.6
4:00	**48.0**	45.5	49.1	**47.2**	46.3	50.5	51.0	50.5	51.5
5:00	**48.4**	47.1	49.6	**47.0**	44.1	49.7	50.5	50.0	51.9

*Bold-faced type indicates a sample outside the quality control limits

the evening and night shifts staffed by the more recent hires. See the control chart on page IS-80.

Note also that the number of samples indicating a "short-weight" is much greater than the number indicating excess weight.

With regard to the range, 99.7% of the individual bag weights should lie within $\pm 3\sigma$ of the mean. This would represent a range of 6σ, or 7.2. Only one of the ranges defined by the difference between the highest and lowest bag weights in each sample exceeds this range. It would appear then, that the problem is not due to abnormal deviations between the highest and lowest bag weights, but rather to poor adjustments of the bag weight-feeder causing assignable variations in average bag weights.

The proper procedure is to establish mean and range charts to guide the bag packers. The foreman would then be alerted when sample weights deviate from mean and range control limits. The immediate problem, however, must be corrected by additional bag weight monitoring and weight-feeder adjustments. Short-run declines in bag output may be necessary to achieve acceptable bag weights.

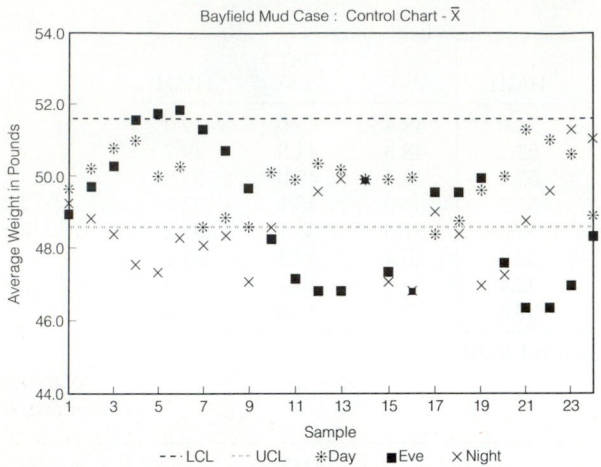

Bayfield Mud Case : Control Chart - X̄

Morristown *Daily Tribune* Case

(1) The overall fraction of errors (p), and the control limits are developed as follows:

$$p = \frac{\text{Total number of errors}}{\text{Number of samples} * \text{Sample size}} = \frac{120}{30 * 100}$$
$$= 0.04$$
$$\sigma = \sqrt{p(1-p)/n} = \sqrt{0.04 * 0.96/100}$$
$$= 0.0196$$

Then the control limits are given (for a 95% confidence interval) by:

$$UCL = p + 1.96\,\sigma$$
$$= 0.04 + 1.96 * 0.0196$$
$$= 0.0784$$

$$LCL = p - 1.96\,\sigma$$
$$= 0.04 - 1.96 * 0.0196$$
$$= 0.0018$$

Both the table presented below and the control chart indicate that the quality requirements of the Morristown *Daily Tribune* are more stringent than those of the industry as a whole. In five instances, the fraction of errors exceeds the firm's upper control limit; in two cases, the industry's upper control limit is exceeded. An investigation, leading to corrective action, is clearly warranted.

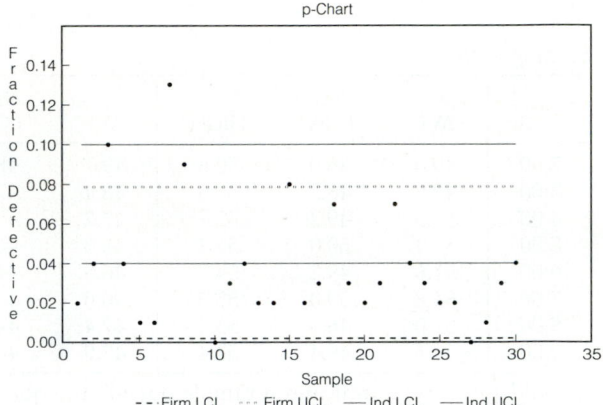

p-Chart

SAMPLE	ERRORS IN SAMPLE	FRACTION* OF ERRORS (n/100)	SAMPLE	ERRORS IN SAMPLE	FRACTION OF ERRORS (n/100)
1	2	0.02	16	2	0.02
2	4	0.04	17	3	0.03
3	10	**0.10**	18	7	0.07
4	4	0.04	19	3	0.03
5	1	0.01	20	2	0.02
6	1	0.01	21	3	0.03
7	13	**0.13****	22	7	0.07
8	9	**0.09**	23	4	0.04
9	11	**0.11****	24	3	0.03
10	0	0.00	25	2	0.02
11	3	0.03	26	2	0.02
12	4	0.04	27	0	0.00
13	2	0.02	28	1	0.01
14	2	0.02	29	3	0.03
15	8	**0.08**	30	4	0.04

*Bold-faced entries indicate sample fractions outside the quality control limits for Morristown *Tribune*.

**Indicates sample fractions outside the industry standard quality control limits.

8
Inventory Control Models: I

LEARNING OBJECTIVES

After completing this chapter, students will be able to:

1. Understand the importance of inventory control.
2. Use the economic order quantity (EOQ) to determine how much to order.
3. Compute the reorder point (ROP) in determining when to order more inventory.
4. Determine other inventory control quantities, including the optimal number of orders per year and the number of days between orders.
5. Perform sensitivity analysis on basic inventory quantities.

TEACHING SUGGESTIONS

Teaching Suggestion 8.1: Importance of Inventory Control.

Inventory control is important to most organizations. This first chapter on inventory control can be introduced to students by a discussion of the consequences of too much and not enough inventory. The high cost of carrying too much inventory and the problems of stockouts, lost customers, and reduced market share as a result of too little inventory can be introduced at the beginning of this chapter. You may want to use a car dealership example. Should the car dealership stock every model and color? How many types of cars should be stocked?

Teaching Suggestion 8.2: Examples of the Functions of Inventory Control.

The importance of inventory to store resources, take advantage of quantity discounts, and avoid stockouts is discussed in this chapter. Students can be asked to give examples of how each of these important functions has been or can be used by organizations. An in-class discussion will help students realize the relevance of inventory control.

Teaching Suggestion 8.3: Importance of Basic Inventory Assumptions.

The assumptions of the basic EOQ model are important. The simple EOQ formula is a direct result of these assumptions. Students can be told that these assumptions will be relaxed in the next chapter, resulting in more complex formulas and inventory procedures.

Teaching Suggestion 8.4: Setting Ordering Cost Equal to Carrying Cost Doesn't Always Work for More Complex Models.

This chapter determines the formula for the basic economic order quantity by setting ordering cost equal to carrying cost. Some students might get the wrong idea that this approach can be used with all inventory problems. Students should be told that calculus procedures can be used to determine the basic EOQ formulas and are needed for more complex inventory situations. Students should be referred to the appendix at the end of this chapter to show them the use of calculus.

Teaching Suggestion 8.5: Other Ways of Looking at Inventory Problems.

In this chapter, students are shown how to compute the optimal number of orders per year and the number of days between orders. This was done so students can see that there are different ways to look at the same inventory problem. This is a good place to point out that there are many ways of solving the same problem. The problems at the end of the chapter ask students to compute related inventory quantities, including the optimal number of orders per month and the optimal number of weeks between orders. These computations can also be done with other inventory problems in the next chapter.

Teaching Suggestion 8.6: Introducing Sensitivity Analysis.

Determining how sensitive the optimal solution is to changes in model parameters is important for every concept discussed in the book. This beginning chapter on inventory control is the formal introduction to this important topic. The section on sensitivity analysis shows that a change in the optimal solution is equal to the square root of a change in a model parameter.

VIDEO 8–1

Using Expert Systems in Inventory Management and Logistics

This TIMS video is based on one of the award-winning papers published in *Interfaces*. The video describes IBM's logistics management system (LMS), which is a real-time expert system that assists with the dispatching function, inventory control, and monitoring of the flow of materials through IBM's semiconductor facility. This facility, which is located near Burlington, Vermont, produces memory and logic chips that are used in a number of computer systems produced by IBM. LMS has the ability to capture and manipulate all manufacturing- and materials-related transactions and activities in a real-time mode. It also allows managers to quickly update various databases and models as required.

VIDEO 8–2

Blue Bell Trims Its Inventory

This TIMS video is based on one of the award-winning papers published in *Interfaces*. A brief description of the application follows: Models for inventory targets, manufacturing requirements, and production scheduling were used with a seasonal demand forecasting technique and diagnostic computer simulation to reduce inventories. Inventory reduction over 21 months was more than $115 million. (See the QA application box in Chapter 8 for details.)

ALTERNATE EXAMPLES

Alternate Example 8-1: Paula Peterson is the inventory manager for Office Supplies, Inc., a large office-supply warehouse. The annual demand for paper punches is 20,000 units. The ordering cost is $100 per order, and the carrying cost is $5 per unit per year. The following equation can be used to compute the economic order quantity.

$$Q^* = \sqrt{\frac{2(20,000)(100)}{5}} = 894 \tag{1}$$

Alternate Example 8-2: Annual demand for a new modem is 5,000 units. The ordering cost is $50 per order, and the carrying cost is $2 per unit per year. What is the optimal number of orders per year?

Given the above data, we can determine the optimal number of orders per year to be 10 orders. The calculations are below:

$$Y^* = \sqrt{\frac{(5,000)(2)}{2(50)}} = 10 \tag{2}$$

Alternate Example 8-3: Given the data presented in Alternate Example 8-2, what is the optimal number of days between orders?

Given the above data, the optimal number of days between orders is 365 divided by 10 or 36.5 days between orders. This value can also be computed directly from the following equation.

$$N^* = \sqrt{\frac{(266,450)(50)}{(5,000)(2)}} = 36.5 \text{ days} \tag{3}$$

Alternate Example 8-4: Fun and Games, Inc., sells a variety of electronic games to children and adults. Annual demand for super Namco games is 360. Holding cost is $1 per game and ordering cost is $100 per order. Fun and Games, Inc., has determined that the economic order quantity should be 268 units given the above data. What happens to the order quantity if annual demand is underestimated by 50%? In other words, what happens if actual annual demand is 540 units?

This is a sensitivity problem. In this case, demand increases by a factor of 1.5 ($540 = 1.5 \times 360$). Thus, the order quantity will increase by the square root of 1.5. The results are shown below: New order quantity = $268 \times \text{SQRT}(1.5) = 268 \times 1.225 = 328.3$.

SOLUTIONS TO DISCUSSION QUESTIONS AND PROBLEMS

8-1. Inventory is an important consideration for managers because as much as 40% of the total assets of a company can be tied up in inventory. Because of this large investment in inventory, controlling inventory becomes extremely important for most organizations. On the one hand, companies will try to reduce the cost of inventory by reducing amounts of inventory on hand. On the other hand, however, companies realize that customer dissatisfaction can be increased significantly due to low inventory levels and stockouts. Thus, it is important to reach a fine balance between low and high inventory levels.

8-2. The purpose of inventory control is to regulate the flow of inventory at the various inventory storage locations within the organization. This can be done by determining how much inventory is to be ordered and when the inventory should be ordered.

8-3. Buying inventory can be used as a hedge against inflation. When inflation of inventory items is high, purchasing inventory at today's prices can be used as a hedge against future inflation of inventory items. In using inventory as a hedge against inflation, however, careful consideration should be given to carrying costs. As more inventory is purchased as a hedge against inflation, higher carrying costs will be paid to hold inventory over a period of time.

8-4. Storing large quantities of inventory can eliminate shortages and stockouts. On the other hand, storing large quantities of inventory can significantly increase the cost of carrying or holding inventory. Therefore, a delicate balance must be sought between increased carrying costs and shortages and stockouts. In determining how much inventory a company should have on hand to avoid shortages and stockouts, the overall objective is to minimize carrying costs and shortage and stockout costs.

8-5. Although there can be many factors to be considered in inventory control, there are basically two fundamental decisions that will have to be made. These decisions are (1) how much to order and (2) when to order. The simplest and the most complex inventory models must answer both of these questions.

8-6. There are a number of assumptions that are made in using the economic order quantity. It is assumed that the cost of the items, the cost of ordering, the cost of holding inventory, and the annual demand are known and constant. It is also assumed that the time it takes to receive an order is known and constant. In the basic economic order quantity model, it is assumed that stockouts can be avoided and that there are no quantity discounts.

8-7. The major costs in determining the economic order quantity include (1) the cost of the items, (2) the cost of ordering, (3) the cost of carrying or holding inventory, (4) the cost of safety, and (5) the cost of stockouts. Under the basic economic order quantity model, it is assumed that there are no stockouts; therefore, the cost of stockouts and the cost of safety stock are not included in the basic model.

8-8. The most commonly used methods in actually determining the equation for the economic order quantity are to use algebra or calculus. When using basic algebra, expressions for ordering costs and carrying costs are determined. These two costs are then set equal to each other, and the equation is solved for Q, the economic order quantity. When calculus is being used, an expression is developed for the total cost. This total cost includes ordering costs and carrying costs. Then the first derivative of this equation is taken and set equal to zero. This equation is solved to determine the economic order quantity. As you would expect, both procedures result in the same equation for the economic order quantity.

8-9. The reorder point specifies when an order is to be placed for new inventory items. When the inventory drops to or below the reorder point, an order is placed.

The reorder point for the basic economic order quantity model is determined by multiplying the demand per period times the lead time for a new order. In most cases, it is determined by multiplying the demand per day times the lead time for a new order in days.

8-10. The fixed-period inventory control system is an approach that is used to answer the "when to order" question. Optimal quantities for the fixed-period inventory control system include the optimal number of orders per year and the optimal number of days between orders.

8-11. The purpose of sensitivity analysis is to determine what effect changes in the annual demand, the ordering cost, and the carrying cost will have on the economic order quantity. In general, sensitivity analysis is used to determine what effect a change in a variable in the model will have on the optimal quantity, such as the economic order quantity.

8-12. Let Y be the optimal number of annual orders.

$$\text{Carrying cost} = \frac{DC_h}{2Y} = \text{ordering cost} = YC_o$$
$$Y = \sqrt{(DC_h)/2C_o}$$

8-13. Let N be optimal number of days between orders.

$$\text{Carrying cost} = \frac{NDC_h}{730} = \text{ordering cost} = \frac{365\,C_o}{N}$$
$$N = \sqrt{\frac{266{,}450C_o}{DC_h}}$$

8-14. Let M be the optimal number of orders per month and W the optimal number of weeks between orders.

$$\text{Carrying cost} = \frac{DC_h}{24M} = \text{ordering cost} = 12MC_o$$
$$M = \sqrt{\frac{DC_h}{288C_o}}$$

Also

$$\text{Carrying cost} = \frac{7WDC_h}{730} = \text{ordering cost} = \frac{365C_o}{7W}$$
$$W = \sqrt{\frac{266{,}450C_o}{49DC_h}} = \sqrt{\frac{5{,}437.76C_o}{DC_h}}$$

8-15. $D = 100{,}000$; $C_o = \$10$; $C_h = \$.005$

$$Q^* = \sqrt{\frac{2 \times 100{,}000 \times 10}{.005}} = 20{,}000 \text{ number 6 screws}$$

8-16. ROP = 8 days $\times$ (500 screws/day) = 4,000 number 6 screws

8-17. $TC = \dfrac{D}{Q}C_o + \dfrac{1}{2}QC_h$

Cost under Lila's policy $= \dfrac{100,000}{20,000} \times \$10 + \dfrac{20,000}{2}$
$$\times \$.005 = \$100$$

Q under brother's policy $= \dfrac{100,000}{2} = 50,000$

Cost under brother's policy $= \dfrac{100,000}{50,000} \times \$10$
$$+ \dfrac{50,000}{2} \times \$.005$$
$$= \$145$$

Extra cost = $45
No effect on ROP

8-18. $D = 4,000$ units
   $C_h = 10\%$ of $90 = $9
   $C_o = $25

a. $Q^* = \sqrt{\dfrac{2 \times 4,000 \times 25}{9}} = 149$ units

b. ROP $= (2 \text{ weeks}) \times (80 \text{ per week}) = 160$

c. Total cost $= \dfrac{4,000}{149} \times \$25 + \dfrac{149}{2} \times \$9 = \$1,341$

d. Optimal number of orders per year $= \dfrac{4,000}{149} \cong 27$

e. Number of days between orders $= \dfrac{365}{27} \cong 13\frac{1}{2}$

8-19. $C_o = $25
   $C_h = 25\%$ of $100 = $25
   $Q^* = 4,000$

$4,000 = \sqrt{\dfrac{2D \times 25}{25}}$, $D = 8$ million loads of plywood

8-20. $D = 500$ sandals
   $C_o = $10

If $Q^* = 100$, $100 = \sqrt{\dfrac{2 \times 500 \times 10}{C_h}}$ or,

   $C_h = $1 which is 20% of cost
If $C_h = 10\%$ of $5 = $0.50,

$Q^* = \sqrt{\dfrac{2 \times 500 \times 10}{.50}} = 141$ sandals

8-21. Optimal order quantity is proportional to the square root of the ordering cost.

When $C_o = $10, $Q^* = 20,000$ screws
   If $C_o = $20, $Q^* = 20,000 \times \sqrt{2} = 28,284$ screws
   If $C_o = $30, $Q^* = 20,000 \times \sqrt{3} = 34,641$ screws
   If $C_o = $40, $Q^* = 20,000 \times \sqrt{4} = 40,000$ screws

8-22. $D = 50,000$ units; $C_o = $10; $C_h = $4

a. $Q^* = \sqrt{\dfrac{2 \times 50,000 \times 10}{4}} = 500$ units

b. ROP $= (25 \text{ days}) \times (250 \text{ units/day}) = 6250$ units
c. Optimal number of orders per year
$$= \dfrac{50,000}{500} = 100$$

d. Optimal number of days between orders
$$= \dfrac{365}{100} = 3.65$$

e. Optimal number of orders per month
$$= \dfrac{100}{12} = 8.33$$

f. Optimal number of weeks between orders
$$= \dfrac{3.65}{7} = .52$$

8-23. $D = 6,000$ units
   $C_o = $10
   $C_h = 15\%$ of $7 = $1.05

$Q^* = \sqrt{\dfrac{2 \times 6,000 \times 10}{1.05}} = 338$

Total cost $= \$7 \times 6,000 + \dfrac{Q^*}{2} \times 1.05 + \dfrac{\$6,000}{Q^*}$
$$\times 10 = \$42,355$$

If new supplier is used, $C_h = 15\%$ of $6.65 \cong $1
$Q = 3,000$

Total cost $= \$6.65 \times 6,000 + \dfrac{3000}{2} \times 1 + \dfrac{6,000}{3,000}$
$$\times \$10 = \$41,416$$

Pampered Pet should use the new supplier and take the discount.

8-24. $C_o = $10; $C_h = $10; $D = 5,000$

$Q^* = \sqrt{\dfrac{2 \times 5,000 \times 10}{10}} = 100$ motors

Cost $= \dfrac{100}{2} \times \$10 + \dfrac{5,000}{100} \times \$10 = \$1000$

Currently, warehouse can hold $\dfrac{5,000 \text{ cu. ft.}}{100 \text{ cu. ft.}} =$
50 motors
They should expand warehouse to 10,000 cu. ft. to hold 100 motors.

Current cost $= \dfrac{50}{2} \times \$10 + \dfrac{5,000}{50} \times \$10$
$$= \$1,250$$

The expansion would be worth $1,250 − $1,000 = $250 per year.

8-25. $D = 50,000$ units; $C_o = \$10$; $C_h = \$16$

a. $Q^* = \sqrt{\dfrac{2 \times 50,000 \times 10}{16}} = 250$ units

b. ROP = (35 days) $\times$ (250 units/day) = 8750 units

c. Optimal number of orders per year = $\dfrac{50,000}{250} = 200$

d. Optimal number of days between orders = $\dfrac{365}{200} = 1.83$

e. Optimal number of orders per month = $\dfrac{200}{12} = 16.67$

f. Optimal number of weeks between orders = $\dfrac{1.83}{7} = .26$

8-26. $D = 12,000$; $C_o = \$30$; $C_h = \$2$

$$Q^* = \sqrt{\dfrac{2 \times 12,000 \times 30}{2}} = 600 \text{ units}$$

Currently, number of lawn mowers that can be stored:

$$= \dfrac{60\% \text{ of } 40 \text{ ft.} \times 25 \text{ ft.} \times 8 \text{ ft.}}{5 \text{ ft.} \times 4 \text{ ft.} \times 2 \text{ ft.}}$$

$$= 120 \text{ units}$$

Current cost $= \dfrac{120}{2} \times \$2 + \dfrac{12,000}{120} \times \$30 = \$3,120$

Optimal cost $= \dfrac{600}{2} \times \$2 + \dfrac{12,000}{600} \times \$30 = \$1,200$

To increase number of units by a factor of 5 ($= 600/120$), the depth should also be increased by a factor of 5, that is, for 40 ft. to 200 ft., increase depth by 160 ft. They would be willing to pay $\$3,120 - \$1,200 = \$1,920$ on a per year basis.

8-27. To begin with, Lisa must determine which costs are not directly related to ordering or carrying costs. The cost of new product development, product advertising, and research and development are not related to ordering or carrying cost. Lisa must also determine which costs are related to ordering and carrying costs. See the following table, which was prepared using Lotus 1-2-3.

Table for Problem 8-27

COST FACTOR	ORDERING COST	CARRYING COST
Taxes		$2,000
Processing and inspection	$1,500	
Bill paying	$500	
Ordering supplies	$50	
Inventory insurance		$600
Spoilage		$750
Sending purchasing orders	$800	
Inventory inquiries	$450	
Warehouse supplies		$280
Purchasing salaries	$3,000	
Warehouse salaries		$2,800
Inventory theft		$800
Purchase order supplies	$500	
Inventory obsolescence		$300
Total	$6,800	$7,530

Next, Lisa needs to determine average ordering cost and carrying cost. Ordering cost is computed by dividing total ordering costs by the number of orders per year. Carrying cost is computed by dividing total carrying costs by the number of inventory items. This is done below:

Number of orders	100
Number of inventory items	10,000
Ordering cost per order	$68.00
Carrying cost per unit per year	$0.75

Given an annual demand of 1,000 for the new product, the EOQ of 424.98 can be computed using the equation presented in this chapter.

8-28. Melinda can solve this problem by determining the probability distribution for ordering cost. This is done by finding the total of the frequency of ordering cost and dividing each number by the total. Melinda can also determine the EOQ value for each possible ordering cost value by using the equation presented in the chapter. In order to determine the EOQ for the average or expected ordering cost, Melinda can multiply the probability of each ordering cost by the EOQ for the ordering cost. This is displayed in the following table under the EXP column. Summing this column will give us the resulting EOQ requested by Melinda's boss. The results, which were computed using Lotus 1-2-3, are below. As you can see, the economic order quantity is 1,890 units.

Table for Problem 8-28

ORDER COST	FREQUENCY	PROBABILITY	EOQ	EXP
$40	24	0.049	1789	88
$41	34	0.070	1811	127
$42	44	0.091	1833	166
$43	56	0.115	1855	214
$44	76	0.156	1876	293
$45	66	0.136	1897	258
$46	64	0.132	1918	253
$47	45	0.093	1939	180
$48	44	0.091	1960	177
$49	23	0.047	1980	94
$50	10	0.021	2000	41
Total	486	1	EOQ = 1,890	

Solution to Sturdivant Sound Systems Case

The optimal order quantity is:

$$Q = \sqrt{\frac{2DC_o}{C_h}}$$

where

Q = optimal order quantity
D = annual demand (5,000)
C_o = procurement costs ($20)
C_h = carrying costs ($6)
d = average daily demand (20)
L = lead time in days (10)
P = cost per unit ($60)

$$Q = \sqrt{\frac{2(5,000)20}{6}} = \sqrt{33,333} = 183 \text{ units}$$

The reorder point is:

$$\begin{aligned} ROP &= dL \\ &= 20(10) \\ &= 200 \end{aligned}$$

Total annual cost under present system (current order level is 400 units):

Cost of equipment = 5,000 units × $60 = $300,000

Procurement costs = $20 per order ×
  12.5 orders = 250

Carrying costs = (400/2) units ×
  $6/unit = 1,200

$301,450

Total annual cost per optimal procurement policy:

$$\begin{aligned} TC &= DP + \frac{D}{Q}C_o + \frac{Q}{2}C_h \\ &= 5,000(60) + \frac{5,000}{183}(20) + \frac{183}{2}(6) \\ &= 300,000 + 546.45^* + 549^* \\ &= \$301,095.45 \end{aligned}$$

*Procurement costs and carrying costs do not equal due to rounding to an even number of units for Q.

Cost savings:

$301,450.00
−301,095.45
$ 354.55

The typical costs associated with procurement of materials include costs of preparing requisitions, writing purchase orders, receiving merchandise, inspecting goods, storage, updating inventory records, and so forth. These costs are usually fixed, regardless of the size of the order. While a large order may require more time, the increase in procurement costs is minimal. As lot size increases, the number of orders decreases (assuming a constant requirement level). Consequently, procurement costs will decrease with increases in lot sizes.

Solution to Western Ranchman Outfitters Case

The computer solution, which appears below, indicates that WRO is following a program very close to the EOQ model. Note that the holding cost is $1.20 per unit per year ($1.20 = 12\% \times \$10.05$ per pair)

```
Program: Inventory Models / EOQ

Problem Title: Western Ranchman

***** Input Data *****

Annual demand     (units/year)            2000.00
Business days     (days/year)              365.00
Lead time         (days)                      .00
Ordering cost     ($/order)                 10.00
Holding cost      ($/unit/year)              1.20

***** Program Output *****

Optimal order quantity  (units/order)  :    182.574
Number of orders        (orders/year)  :     10.954
Inventory cycle         (days)         :     33.320
Maximum inventory level (units)        :    182.574
Average inventory level (units)        :     91.287
Reorder point           (units)        :       .000
Demand rate             (units/day)    :      5.479
Total holding cost      ($/year)       :    109.545
Total ordering cost     ($/year)       :    109.545
Total inventory cost    ($/year)       :    219.089

***** End of Output *****
```

The solution recommends 10.954, or 11, orders per year. WRO orders monthly. The EOQ is about 183 pairs.

There is one remaining problem which the model doesn't solve, but which Mr. Randell has. This is the problem of the unreliability of the supplier. By ordering one extra time (12 orders per year) and by ordering extra quantities, Mr. Randell has managed to keep WRO almost totally supplied with the needed number of Levi 501. Because the actual solution is close to the model solution, Mr. Veta can feel that he is keeping his inventory close to the minimum while still meeting his goal of avoiding stockouts.

The conclusion is that the model has been shown to be practically valid with minor adjustments that compensate for the unreliability of the manufacturer.

This case differs from most in that the EOQ is just a starting point for discussion—students must then develop their own approach and reasoning for why the current policy is acceptable or not.

The case is a perfect illustration of the clothing, or "rag," business, which is known for its lax inventory control procedures. The information provided is based on data from the actual firm, WRO, in Wyoming.

Inventory Control Models: II

LEARNING OBJECTIVES

After completing this chapter, students will be able to:

1. Determine the economic order quantity without the instantaneous receipt assumption.
2. Handle inventory problems that allow quantity discounts or have planned shortages.
3. Understand the use of safety stock with known and unknown stockout costs.
4. Perform ABC analysis and joint ordering.
5. Develop inventory policy for dependent demand situations using material requirements planning (MRP).
6. Describe the importance and use of Kanban.

TEACHING SUGGESTIONS

Teaching Suggestion 9.1: Covering More Complex Models.

This chapter presents more advanced inventory problems. These problems require more sophisticated analysis. Thus, if the class is more applications-oriented, some of the model *derivations* may be skipped. This includes the EOQ model without the instantaneous receipt assumption and planned shortages. Students may need a good math background to understand some of these inventory models.

Teaching Suggestion 9.2: Comparing the Basic EOQ Model with the EOQ Model without the Instantaneous Receipt Assumption.

This chapter computes EOQ for the case where the instantaneous receipt assumption is relaxed. A comparison of the traditional EOQ model and this model can be made. The major difference is the holding cost, which is reduced compared to the traditional EOQ formula. This is due to the change in the average inventory level for this model.

For example, if demand is 50% of production, then the average inventory level will be 50% of what it would be otherwise. This also means that annual holding costs will be 50% lower. Like other inventory formulas, this one makes sense intuitively.

Teaching Suggestion 9.3: Adjusting the Order Quantity Upward.

The quantity discount model is not difficult to apply. The major problem students have is that they forget to adjust the order quantity upward if the quantity

is too low to qualify for the discount. This is step 2 of the quantity discount approach. If this is not done, the results will likely be incorrect. You may have to reinforce the material in the book to make sure students don't make this mistake. Encourage students to run the AB:QM software to check their results.

Teaching Suggestion 9.4: Planned Shortages Model Is More Complex Than Other Inventory Models.

The derivation of the planned shortages model is one of the most complex inventory models presented in the book. If students don't have a good mathematical background, the model formulation may be difficult to understand. Many instructors present the overall approach, the assumptions, and the resulting equations only.

Teaching Suggestion 9.5: Difference between the Planned Shortages Model and the Basic EOQ Model.

The major difference between the planned shortages model and the traditional EOQ model is the inclusion of the back-ordering cost. In the formula for the economic order quantity, a new term has been added. As back-ordering cost increases to infinity, the term approaches 1, and the equation becomes the traditional EOQ equation.

A different term is used to compute the amount back ordered. As the back-ordering cost approaches infinity, this term and the amount back ordered approaches 0.

Teaching Suggestion 9.6: Stockout Cost Calculations May Be Difficult to Understand for Some.

The safety stock calculations with known stockout costs is straightforward. The only area that students may have problems with is the computation of stockout costs. When the safety stock is low, there is a greater possibility of a stockout. In general, stockout costs are the number of units short (short) times the probability (P) times the stockout cost (cost) times the number of orders per year (orders).

Teaching Suggestion 9.7: High Cost of a High Service Level.

The computations for stockout policy without stockout costs are easy to understand. The analysis assumes that demand follows a normal distribution. Students should be told that the same type of analysis can be made with other probability distributions. It is even possible to perform this type of analysis with an observed discrete probability distribution.

It should be noted that the cost of this type of inventory policy increases dramatically with an increase in service level. This is shown in Figure 9.6 in the section. The relationship between service level and total cost should be emphasized. As service level increases, the inventory costs increase exponentially. Discuss the ethical issues of setting service levels of emergency plasma or drug supplies in a hospital.

Teaching Suggestion 9.8: Use of ABC Analysis and Joint Ordering.

ABC analysis and joint ordering are very practical and useful concepts. Although the mathematics is straightforward and easy to understand, these techniques can result in substantial savings. Students can be told that sophisticated and complex analysis does not always result in great savings. Some simple and easy-to-implement policies can be the most effective. Have students go back to Chapter 1 (Section 1.4) to review Churchman's statement that "he who thinks elaborately thinks well" is not always valid.

Teaching Suggestion 9.9: Practical Use of MRP.

MRP is one of the most powerful and highly used inventory techniques today. Since most manufacturing operations face dependent demand situations, MRP computer programs are very popular. This is an excellent place to have students go to the library to investigate the use of MRP. There are many articles in a variety of journals that show the power and popularity of this technique. Students should also be encouraged to visit a local factory that uses MRP to see just how dependent a company can become on the program.

MRP is also tied into other systems within the organization. Aggregate planning, purchasing, and production scheduling are just a few examples. Students can be asked to discuss how MRP is related to these major areas within the organization.

Teaching Suggestion 9.10: Use of Kanban and JIT.

The Kanban approach and just-in-time (JIT) inventory concepts have helped Japan achieve its industrial leadership. In many cases, these inventory concepts are implemented manually. The overall approach is to make the inventory system lean and efficient. Students can be told that the same approach can be used in other areas of the organization.

ALTERNATE EXAMPLES

Alternate Example 9-1: Paula Peterson is considering manufacturing hole punch devices. As in Alternate Example 8-1, the annual demand is 20,000 units. The setup cost is $100 per order, and the carrying cost is $5 per unit per year. The demand rate is 1,000 units per day and the production rate is 1,500 units per day. The following equation can be used to determine the economic lot size.

$$Q^* = \sqrt{\frac{2(2,000)(100)}{5(1 - 1,000/1,500)}} = 1,549$$

Alternate Example 9-2: Paula Peterson (see Alternate Example 9-1) has found a supplier of the hole punches that offers quantity discounts. The annual demand is 20,000 units, the ordering cost is $100 per order, and the carrying cost is .5 of the unit price. For quantities that vary from 0 to 1,999, the unit price is $10. The price is $9.98 for quantities that vary from 2,000 units to 3,999 units and $9.96 for quantities that vary from 4,000 to 10,000 units. Should Paula take the quantity discount?

To solve this problem, we begin by computing the economic order quantity. This is done using the following equation.

$$Q^* = \sqrt{\frac{2(2,000)(100)}{(\$10)(.5)}} = 894 \tag{5}$$

The table below, which was constructed using Lotus 1-2-3, shows the results of the total cost analysis. Note that the order quantity had to be adjusted to 2,000 and 4,000 units for the last two quantity discounts. In this case, the best decision is not to take the quantity discount. The order quantity is 894 units with a total cost of $204,472.

Alternate Example 9-3: Paula Peterson (see above) is considering the possibility of having planned shortages for the hole punch devices. The annual demand is 2,000 units, the ordering cost is $100 per order, and the carrying cost is $5 per unit per year. The back ordering

Table for Alternate Example 9-2

DISCOUNT NUMBER	UNIT PRICE	ORDER QTY.	MATERIAL COST	ORDERING COST	CARRYING COST	TOTAL COST
1	$10	894	$200,000	$2,236	$2,236	$204,472
2	$9.98	2000	$199,600	$1,000	$4,990	$205,590
3	$9.96	4000	$199,200	$500	$9,960	$209,660

or stockout cost is $200. The following equation can be used to compute the order quantity with back ordering.

$$Q^* = \sqrt{\frac{2(2,000)(100)}{5}\left(\frac{5 + 200}{200}\right)} = 906$$

Alternate Example 9-4: Steve Handel has observed the following demand over the lead time for a product.

REORDER POINT	NUMBER OF UNITS	PROBABILITY
	30	.1
	40	.2
ROP →	50	.3
	60	.2
	70	.2
	Total →	1.00

The carrying cost is $30 per unit per year, and the stockout cost is $50 per unit per stockout. There are two orders placed per year. Given this information, Steve would like to determine the best safety stock policy. We begin by developing the following decision table. We also note the following relationships:

Total Cost = 0: When reorder point equals demand over lead time.

Total cost = stockout cost = number of units short times stockout cost per unit times number of orders per year = number of units short times $50 times 2 orders per year: When the reorder point is less than demand over lead time.

Total cost = total additional carrying cost = number of surplus units times the carrying cost = number of surplus units times $30 per unit: When the reorder point is greater than the expected demand over the lead time.

Using the table below and the probability of the demand values over lead time, we can use decision making under risk to determine the total expected cost of every alternative. The AB:QM solution is presented on page IS-91. As you can see, the best alternative is to have a reorder point of 60 units. The total cost is $500. This is equivalent to having a safety stock of 10 units.

Alternate Example 9-5:
Kimberly Caller is in charge of four inventory items. The inventory demand and sales price for each item is summarized in the following table. Using ABC analysis, how should these inventory items be controlled?

	DEMAND	PRICE
Item 1	20000	10.00
Item 2	8000	100.00
Item 3	7000	5.00
Item 4	200	5.00

Using ABC analysis, we can determine the total dollar value of each item. This can be used to categorize each inventory item. The results, computed by AB:QM, are on page IS-91:

As can be seen in the output on page IS-91, Item 2 should be carefully controlled. It is in the A category. Item 1 should be controlled to some extent. It is in the B category. Items 3 and 4 should not be carefully controlled. These items are in the C category.

SOLUTIONS TO DISCUSSION QUESTIONS AND PROBLEMS

9-1. The assumptions made in the production run model are the same assumptions made in the economic order quantity with the exception that the instantaneous receipt of inventory assumption is eliminated. Thus, the assumptions are that the demand is known and constant, the lead time is known and constant, quantity discounts are not allowed, ordering cost and carrying cost are the only variable costs, and stockouts and shortages can be completely eliminated.

9-2. When the daily production rate becomes very large, the production run model becomes identical to the economic quantity model. This is because the fraction d/p approaches zero as the production rate becomes very large.

9-3. In the quantity discount model, the carrying cost is a percentage of the unit cost. This is due to the fact that the unit cost in the quantity discount model is

State of Nature

ALTERNATIVE	30	40	50	60	70
30	$0	$1,000	$2,000	$3,000	$4,000
40	$300	$0	$1,000	$2,000	$3,000
50	$600	$300	$0	$1,000	$2,000
60	$900	$600	$300	$0	$1,000
70	$1,200	$900	$600	$300	$0

Program for Alternate Example 9-4

```
Program: Decision Theory / Decision Making Under Risk

Problem Title: ae9-4

***** Input Data *****

Type of Problem  :  Cost Problem

-----------------------------------------------------------------
              Event 1     Event 2     Event 3     Event 4     Event 5
-----------------------------------------------------------------
Probability     0.100       0.200       0.300       0.400       0.200
-----------------------------------------------------------------
Alternative 1   0.000    1000.000    2000.000    3000.000    4000.000
Alternative 2 300.000       0.000    1000.000    2000.000    3000.000
Alternative 3 600.000     300.000       0.000    1000.000    2000.000
Alternative 4 900.000     600.000     300.000       0.000    1000.000
Alternative 5 1200.000    900.000     600.000     300.000       0.000
-----------------------------------------------------------------

***** Program Output *****

Expected Cost Table
-----------------------------
Alternative      Expected Cost
-----------------------------
     1             2200.000
     2             1330.000
     3              720.000
     4              500.000 <=
     5              540.000
-----------------------------

<= indicate(s) the best alternative(s)
```

Program for Alternate Example 9-5

```
***** Program Output *****

--------------------------------------------------------------------
 Item    Annual    Unit     Annual $    Percentage   Percentage
Number   demand    cost     volume      of items     of cost
--------------------------------------------------------------------
   2      8000   100.000    800000      22.727       77.220
   1     20000    10.000    200000      79.545       96.525
   3      7000     5.000     35000      99.432       99.903
   4       200     5.000      1000     100.000      100.000
--------------------------------------------------------------------
 Total                      1036000
```

allowed to vary or change. Thus, the carrying cost per unit per year is not applicable to quantity discount models.

9-4. Solving a quantity discount model involves several steps. The first step is to compute the economic order quantity for each discount range. The second step is to adjust the order quantity determined in step one if the order quantity is too low to qualify for the discount for any discount level. Furthermore, any economic order quantity values greater than the discount range can be ignored. The third step is to compute the total cost for every discount range. The fourth step is to select that order quantity from step three which has the lowest total inventory cost.

9-5. The assumptions made in the planned shortages model are the same as in the economic order quantity with the exception that shortages or stockouts are allowed. With the planned shortages model, it is assumed that the cost of stocking out is a fixed quantity per unit. This cost is called the back ordering cost. It includes the normal cost of placing an order plus all the costs associated with a stockout or an inventory shortage.

9-6. When the stockout cost is known, the safety stock can be determined by comparing the total cost of each safety stock policy. This method requires that we know the probability of demand over lead time and the cost of a stockout in addition to the traditional costs associated with the economic order quantity. When the stockout cost is not known, a service level policy is established. For this particular model, it is only necessary to know the probability of demand over lead time. This can either be a continuous or a discrete probability function.

9-7. Joint ordering is the process of placing two or more orders from the same vendor or supplier at the same time. The purpose of joint ordering is to reduce ordering cost and thus total inventory cost. ABC analysis is the process of categorizing inventory into three groups. The A group is very important to the organization and requires strict monitoring and control. The B group is not as important and selected items from this group are monitored and controlled. The C group is not as important as group A or group B, and thus sophisticated inventory control techniques are not used in controlling inventory levels for these items.

9-8. $D = 8,000; d = 40; p = 150; C_s = \$100; C_h = \$0.30$

$$Q_p^* = \sqrt{\frac{2 \times 8,000 \times 100}{0.3(1 - 40/150)}} = 2,697 \text{ scissors}$$

9-9. $D = 10,000; d = 50; p = 500; C_o = \$40; C_h = \$0.60$

$$Q^* = \sqrt{\frac{2 \times 10,000 \times 40}{0.60(1 - 50/500)}} = 1,217 \text{ wheel bearings}$$

9-10. $D = 1,000;$ Unit cost $= \$50;$ $C_o = \$40;$ $C_h = 0.25 \times$ Unit cost

$$Q = \sqrt{\frac{2 \times 1,000 \times 40}{.25 \times 50}} = 80$$

With discount, unit cost $= (1 - .03) \times \$50 = \$48.50$

$$Q_d^* = \sqrt{\frac{2 \times 1,000 \times 40}{.25 \times 48.50}} = 81.22 \text{ which should be}$$
adjusted to minimum orderable quantity, i.e., 200

Original total cost $= 1,000 \times 50 + \dfrac{1,000}{80} \times 40$

$$+ \frac{80}{2} \times .25 \times 50$$

$$= \$51,000$$

Discount cost $= 1,000 \times 48.50 + \dfrac{1,000}{200} \times 40$

$$+ \frac{200}{2} \times .25 \times 48 = \$49,912.50$$

Therefore, North Manufacturing should take the discount.

9-11. $D = 3,000; C_o = \$25; C_h = \$4; C_b = 75$

$$Q^* = \sqrt{\frac{2 \times 3,000 \times 25}{4}\left(\frac{4 + 75}{75}\right)} = 198.7 \text{ ranges}$$

$$S^* = Q^*\left(\frac{4}{4 + 75}\right) = 10 \text{ ranges}$$

9-12. $C_c = \$40;$ $C_h = \$5;$ ROP $= 60$ units $\cdot$ Stockout cost $= \$50/$unit

The expected stockout cost is $50 per stockout $\times$ 7 orders per year $\times$ the number of units short. For this problem, there will be 6 alternatives. Alternative 1 is to have a reorder point of 40, Alternative 2 is a reorder point of 50, Alternative 3 is a reorder point of 60, and so on. The additional carrying cost is equal to $5 $\times$ the number of additional inventory items. There are 6 states of nature or events in this problem. Event or state of nature 1 is a demand over lead time of 40 units. Event 2 is a demand of 50, Event 3 is a demand of 60, and so on. The AB:QM solution for this problem is presented on page IS-93. As you can see, the best decision is Alternative 6, which is to have the reorder point plus safety stock equal to 90. If the normal reorder point is 60, the safety stock is 30 units.

9-13. $\mu = 60 \qquad \sigma = 7$

Safety stock for 90% service level
$$= \sigma Z \text{ (at .90)} = 7 \times 1.28 = 8.96 \approx 9$$

Program for Problem 9-12

```
Program: Decision Theory / Decision Making Under Risk

Problem Title: QA9-12

***** Input Data *****

Type of Problem  :  Cost Problem

-----------------------------------------------------------------------
                Event 1    Event 2    Event 3    Event 4    Event 5    Event 6
-----------------------------------------------------------------------
Probability      0.100      0.200      0.200      0.200      0.200      0.100
-----------------------------------------------------------------------
Alternative 1    0.000   3500.000   7000.000  10500.000  14000.000  17500.000
Alternative 2   50.000      0.000   3500.000   7000.000  10500.000  14000.000
Alternative 3  100.000     50.000      0.000   3500.000   7000.000  10500.000
Alternative 4  150.000    100.000     50.000      0.000   3500.000   7000.000
Alternative 5  200.000    150.000    100.000     50.000      0.000   3500.000
Alternative 6  250.000    200.000    150.000    100.000     50.000      0.000
-----------------------------------------------------------------------

***** Program Output *****

Expected Cost Table
-------------------------------
Alternative      Expected Cost
-------------------------------
    1               8750.000
    2               5605.000
    3               3170.000
    4               1445.000
    5                430.000
    6                125.000 <=
-------------------------------

<= indicate(s) the best alternative(s)
```

9-14.

CODE	TOTAL COST = UNIT COST × DEMAND
XX1	$7,008
B66	$5,994
3CP0	$1,003.52
33CP	$82,292.16
R2D2	$2,220
RMS	$1,998.88

Total cost = $100,516.56
70% of total cost = $70,347.92

Items that need strict control are 33CP. Items that should not be strictly controlled are XX1, B66, 3CPO, R2D2, and RMS.

9-15. $D = 3,000$; $C_o = \$35$; $C_h = \$1$; With joint ordering $C_o = \$25$

a. $Q^* = \sqrt{\dfrac{2 \times 3,000 \times 35}{1}} = 458.26$

b. $Q^*_{joint} = \sqrt{\dfrac{2 \times 3,000 \times 25}{1}} = 387.3$

c. Cost saving:

$$TC = \frac{D}{Q} C_o + \frac{Q}{2} C_h$$

$$TC = \left(\frac{3,000}{458}\right)(35) + \left(\frac{458}{2}\right)(1) = \$458$$

$$TC \text{ joint} = \left(\frac{3,000}{387}\right)(25) + \left(\frac{387}{2}\right) = \$387$$

The difference is $71.

9-16. $D = 500$; $C_o = \$4$; $C_h = \$.50$; $C_b = \$10$

a. $Q^* = \sqrt{\dfrac{2 \times 500 \times 4}{.50}} = 89.44$

b. $Q^*_{backordering} = \sqrt{\dfrac{2 \times 500 \times 4}{.50}\left(\dfrac{10 + .50}{10}\right)} = 91.65$

c. ROP $= 10 \times 3 = 30$

d. $S^* = Q^*_{backordering} \times \left(\dfrac{.50}{.50 + 10}\right) = 4.36$

9-17. $C_o = \$60$; $C_h = \$10$; Stockout cost $= \$50/unit$; ROP $= 650$; Number of orders $= 5$

For this problem, the expected stockout cost is $50 per stockout × 5 times per year × the number of units short. There are 11 alternatives. Alternative 1 is to have a reorder point plus safety stock of 600, Alternative 2 is a reorder point of 650, Alternative 3 is a reorder point of 700, and so on. The additional carrying cost is equal to $10 × the number of additional inventory items. There are 11 states of nature or events in this problem. Event or state of nature 1 is a demand over lead time of 600 units. Event 2 is a demand of 650, Event 3 is a demand of 700, and so on. The AB:QM solution for this problem is presented on page IS-95. As you can see, the best decision is Alternative 10, which is to have the reorder point plus safety stock equal to 10,500 units. If the normal reorder point is 650 units, the safety stock is 400 units. The total expected cost is $3,425.

9-18. $D = 5000$; $C_o = \$15$; $C_h = \$0.50$; $d = 100$; $t = 3$

a. $Q^* = \sqrt{\dfrac{2 \times 5,000 \times 15}{.50}} = 547.7$

b. Ordering cost is still $\dfrac{D}{Q}C_o$.

Maximum inventory level = Total order − Total used during lead time

$= Q - 3 \times 100 = Q - 300$

Carrying cost $= \frac{1}{2}(Q - 300)C_h = \dfrac{D}{Q^*}C_o$

Setting the two equal $\frac{1}{2}(Q^* - 300)C_h = \dfrac{D}{Q^*}C_o$

$Q^* - 300 = \dfrac{5,000 \times 15 \times 2}{.50\,Q^*} = \dfrac{300,000}{Q^*}$

$Q^{*2} - 300Q^* - 300,000 = 0$

$Q^* = 717.9$

c. Total cost for instantaneous delivery $= 547.7 \times .50$
$= \$273.85$

Total cost for installment delivery $= .50(717.9 - 300)$
$= .50(417.9) = \$208.95$

Note: Total cost = ordering cost + carrying cost. Since ordering cost = carrying cost, total cost = 2 × carrying cost = $Q^* \times C_h$.

Go for installment delivery.

9-19. $C_h = \$.50$; $\mu = 600$; $\sigma = 7$

Safety stock for 90% service level $\cong 9$

Carrying cost $= 9 \times .5 = \$4.50$

Safety stock for 95% service level $= 7 \times 1.65 \cong 12$

Carrying cost $= \$6.00$

Safety stock for 98% service level $= 7 \times 2.05 \cong 15$

Carrying cost $= \$7.50$

9-20. Maximum inventory level $= Q - 5 \times 100$
$= Q - 500$

Carrying cost $= \frac{1}{2}(Q - 500) \times .50$

Ordering cost $= \dfrac{5,000}{Q} \times 15$

Setting the two equal $Q^* - 500 = \dfrac{300,000}{Q^*}$

$Q^{*2} - 500Q^* - 300,000 = 0$

$Q^* = 852$

Total cost $= (852 - 500) \times .50 = \$176$

Note: Total cost = 2 × carrying cost because ordering cost = carrying cost.

9-21. Item 4 should be carefully controlled:

$Q_4^* = \sqrt{\dfrac{2 \times 560 \times 40}{.15 \times 150}} = 45$

The other items contribute together about 15% of total revenues. They do not need strict quantitative control. If however, items 1 and 2 are controlled using EOQ:

$Q_1^* = \sqrt{\dfrac{2 \times 600 \times 40}{.2 \times 10.6}} = 151$

$Q_2^* = \sqrt{\dfrac{2 \times 450 \times 30}{.25 \times 11.00}} = 99$

Items 3, 4, and 5 are definitely in category C and should be joint ordered.

9-22. $D = 10,000$; $C_o = \$20$; $C_h = \$2$

a. $Q^* = \sqrt{\dfrac{2 \times 10,000 \times 20}{2}} = 447.2$

b. If $C_b = \$40$

$Q^* = \sqrt{\dfrac{2 \times 10,000 \times 20}{2}\left(\dfrac{2 + 40}{40}\right)} = 458$

c. If $C_b = \$100$

$Q^* = \sqrt{200,000\left(\dfrac{2 + 100}{100}\right)} = 452$

Program: Decision Theory / Decision Making Under Risk

Problem Title: QA 9-17

***** Input Data *****

Type of Problem : Cost Problem

	Event 1	Event 2	Event 3	Event 4	Event 5	Event 6
Probability	0.300	0.200	0.100	0.100	0.050	0.050
Alternative 1	0	12500	25000	37500	50000	62500
Alternative 2	500	0	12500	25000	37500	50000
Alternative 3	1000	500	0	12500	25000	37500
Alternative 4	1500	1000	500	0	12500	25000
Alternative 5	2000	1500	1000	500	0	12500
Alternative 6	2500	2000	1500	1000	500	0
Alternative 7	3000	2500	2000	1500	1000	500
Alternative 8	3500	3000	2500	2000	1500	1000
Alternative 9	4000	3500	3000	2500	2000	1500
Alternative 10	4500	4000	3500	3000	2500	2000
Alternative 11	5000	4500	4000	3500	3000	2500

	Event 7	Event 8	Event 9	Event 10	Event 11
Probability	0.050	0.050	0.050	0.030	0.020
Alternative 1	75000	87500	100000	112500	115000
Alternative 2	62500	75000	87500	100000	112500
Alternative 3	50000	62500	75000	87500	100000
Alternative 4	37500	50000	62500	75000	87500
Alternative 5	25000	37500	50000	62500	75000
Alternative 6	12500	25000	37500	50000	62500
Alternative 7	0	12500	25000	37500	50000
Alternative 8	0	0	12500	25000	37500
Alternative 9	1000	500	0	12500	25000
Alternative 10	1500	1000	500	0	12500
Alternative 11	2000	1500	1000	500	0

***** Program Output *****

Expected Cost Table

Alternative	Expected Cost
1	33175
2	24775
3	18775
4	14075
5	10675
6	7925
7	5825
8	4350
9	3575
10	3425 <=
11	3665

<= indicate(s) the best alternative(s)

d. If $C_b = \$500$

$$Q^* = \sqrt{200,000\left(\frac{2 + 500}{500}\right)} = 448$$

e. If $C_b = \$1,000$

$$Q^* = \sqrt{200,000\left(\frac{2 + 1000}{1000}\right)} = 447.7$$

f. If C_b increases, order quantity decreases and approaches the order quantity with no backordering possible.

g. The assumptions are the same as the assumptions of the basic EOQ model, except that back ordering with a C_b cost is allowed.

9-23. $C_o = \$45$; $I = 20\%$; $D = 100$

$$Q_1^* = \sqrt{\frac{2 \times 100 \times 45}{(.2)\,(18)}} = 50$$

$$Q_2^* = \sqrt{\frac{2 \times 100 \times 45}{(.2)\,(17.50)}} = 50.7$$

$$Q_3^* = \sqrt{\frac{2 \times 100 \times 45}{(.2)\,(17.25)}} = 51.1$$

Optimal order quantity would be 51.

$$TC = (100)\,(17.25) + \frac{(100)\,(45)}{51} + \frac{(51)\,(.2)\,(17.25)}{2}$$

$$= 1,725 + 88.24 + 87.98$$

$$= \$1,901.22$$

9-24.
   a., b.

Figure for Problem 9-24

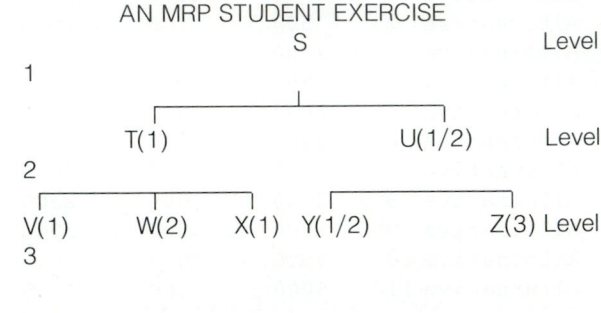

AN MRP STUDENT EXERCISE

Units needed:

S = 100;   T = 100;   U = 50;   V = 100;   W = 200;
X = 100;   Y = 25;   Z = 150

Gross MRP for 100 Units of S (Parent parts are S, T, and U. Component parts are T, V, W, X, U, Y, and Z.):

		WEEK							
		1	2	3	4	5	6	7	
Req. Date	S							100	Lead Time = 2 wks.
Ord. Rel						100			
Req. Date	T					100			Lead Time = 1 wk.
Ord. Rel					100				
Req. Date	U					50			Lead Time = 2 wks.
Ord. Rel				50					
Req. Date	V				100				Lead Time = 2 wks.
Ord. Rel			100						
Req. Date	W				200				Lead Time = 3 wks.
Ord. Rel		200							
Req. Date	X				100				Lead Time = 1 wk.
Ord. Rel				100					
Req. Date	Y			25					Lead Time = 2 wks.
Ord. Rel		25							
Req. Date	Z			150					Lead Time = 1 wk.
Ord. Rel			150						

c. Net material requirements plan:

Item		WEEK							Lead Time
		1	2	3	4	5	6	7	
S	Gross							100	
	On-Hand							20	
	Net							80	2
	Order Receipt							80	
	Order Release					80			
T	Gross					80^S			
	On-Hand					20			
	Net					60			1
	Order Receipt					60			
	Order Release				60				
U	Gross					40^S			
	On-Hand					10			
	Net					30			2
	Order Receipt					30			
	Order Release			30					
V	Gross				60^T				
	On-Hand				30				
	Net				30				2
	Order Receipt				30				
	Order Release		30						
W	Gross				120^T				
	On-Hand				30				
	Net				90				3
	Order Receipt				90				
	Order Release	90							
X	Gross				60^T				
	On-Hand				25				
	Net				35				1
	Order Receipt				35				
	Order Release			35					
Y	Gross				15^U				
	On-Hand				15				
	Net				0				2
	Order Receipt				0				
	Order Release		0						
Z	Gross				90^U				
	On-Hand				10				
	Net				80				1
	Order Receipt				80				
	Order Release		80						

9-25. This is a typical quantity discount problem. It is complicated, however, by the fact that there are drawings for computers and trips, which must be considered as part of the quantity discount. When this is done, a quantity discount table can be developed and used to determine the best inventory policy. The quantity discount table is shown below.

Here is how the quantity discount table was determined. Discount number one represents a quantity

DISCOUNT	DISCOUNT	DISCOUNT	AVERAGE DISCOUNT COST
1	0–199	0	9.90
2	200–299	10 cans	9.39
3	300–399	30 cans	8.90
4	400–499	40 cans	8.89
5	500 and over	50 cans	8.87

ranging from 0 to 199 units. There is no discount, and therefore the cost is simply $9.90. For discount number two, 10 free cans of product are offered. This has a total value of $99. In addition, it is possible to receive a personal computer valued at $3,000. Since there are 1,000 companies that are eligible, the expected monetary value for the personal computer drawing is $3 (3 = 3,000/1,000). This represents a total discount of $102. For 200 cans of product, this represents a 51¢ discount (.51 = 102/200). Therefore, the discount price is $9.39. The same type of computations can be made for discount number three. The 30 cans of free product have a value of $297, and the personal computer drawing has an expected value of $3. The total discount is $300 or $1 per unit. Therefore, the average discount price is $8.90. For discount number four, there is also a drawing for a free trip. This trip has a value of $5,000 and 800 businesses are eligible for the drawing. This represents a $6.25 value ($6.25 = $5,000/800). Adding this to the $396 value for the 40 free cans and the $3 expected monetary value for the personal computer drawing, the total discount is approximately $405. The average discount therefore is $1.01. This represents a discount cost of $8.89. The average discount price for discount number five is computed in the same way. Fifty free cans are valued at $495. Again, the personal computer drawing and the drawing for the trip represent $3 and $6.25, respectively. The drawing for the car is a $15 value (15 = 10,000/600). The total discount is approximately $250. This is a discount per unit of $1.03. Therefore, the average discount cost is $8.87. This information, along with the standard information for inventory control, can be used with our inventory control program to compute a quantity discount. The computer output from this program reveals that the optimal strategy is to order 300 units at a total cost of $9,066.83.

9-26. This is a back ordering or a planned shortage model. The most difficult part of this problem is to determine the input data. The annual demand is for 2,000 gallons of Conradi's Pest Control. For every gallon, two quarts of chemicals are required from an outside supplier. Therefore, there is an annual demand for 4,000 quarts of chemicals from the outside supplier. The 4,000 quarts represent the annual demand for this inventory problem. The normal ordering cost, as given by the problem, is $10. The carrying cost is equal to the spoilage cost of $1 per quart plus the shelving cost of $1.50 per quart. Therefore, the total carrying cost is $2.50 per quart. The other costs, including overhead and advertising allocations, are not a part of carrying costs. The back order cost is the same as the cost of placing a special order. This is $15. From the computer program for the planned shortage model, it can be determined that the number of orders per year is 20.7. This represents a total annual inventory cost, excluding the cost of the goods, of $414.04.

9-27. This safety stock problem can be solved using decision making under risk. The cost of a stockout is $13.05 ($13.05 = $49.95 − $32.90). Carrying cost is $7 per unit per year. The following decision table, which was prepared using Lotus 1-2-3, shows that the best policy is to have a reorder point including safety stock of 600 units. This corresponds to a safety stock of 200 units with a normal reorder point of 400 units.

Frequency	1	2	2	3	4	5	4	4	3	2	2	Total 32
Probability	0.03	0.06	0.06	0.09	0.12	0.15	0.12	0.12	0.09	0.06	0.06	

	STATES OF NATURE											
ALTERNATIVES	300	350	400	450	500	550	600	650	700	750	800	EMV
300	0	653	1305	1958	2610	3263	3915	4568	5220	5873	6525	3466
350	350	0	653	1305	1958	2610	3263	3915	4568	5220	5873	2845
400	700	350	0	653	1305	1958	2610	3263	3915	4568	5220	2287
450	1050	700	350	0	653	1305	1958	2610	3263	3915	4568	1791
500	1400	1050	700	350	0	653	1305	1958	2610	3263	3915	1389
550	1750	1400	1050	700	350	0	653	1305	1958	2610	3263	1112
600	2100	1750	1400	1050	700	350	0	653	1305	1958	2610	993 ← minimum EMV
650	2450	2100	1750	1400	1050	700	350	0	653	1305	1958	998
700	2800	2450	2100	1750	1400	1050	700	350	0	653	1305	1129
750	3150	2800	2450	2100	1750	1400	1050	700	350	0	653	1353
800	3500	3150	2800	2450	2100	1750	1400	1050	700	350	0	1641

Minimum EMV is $993, which corresponds to the alternative of 600 units for the reorder point including safety stock.

9-28. a. The optimal order quantity and the total inventory cost can be solved by computer. The results are shown below.

```
Program: Inventory Models / Quantity Discount

Problem Title: QA9-28

***** Input Data *****

Method type :                          All unit discount

Annual demand    (units/year)                  2000.00
Business days    (days/year)                     365.00
Lead time        (days)                           10.00
Ordering cost    ($/order)                        50.00
Holding cost as a fraction                         0.250
```

	Lower Quantity	Upper Quantity	Unit Price
Price break 1	0.00	10.00	220.00
Price break 2	11.00	20.00	219.99
Price break 3	21.00	30.00	219.98
Price break 4	31.00	40.00	219.97
Price break 5	41.00	50.00	219.96
Price break 6	51.00	60.00	219.95
Price break 7	61.00	70.00	219.94
Price break 8	71.00	80.00	219.93
Price break 9	81.00	90.00	219.92
Price break 10	91.00	100.00	219.91
Price break 11	101.00	110.00	219.90
Price break 12	111.00	120.00	219.89
Price break 13	121.00	130.00	219.88
Price break 14	131.00	140.00	219.87
Price break 15	141.00		219.86

```
***** Program Output *****

ALL UNIT DISCOUNT

Optimal order price      :       219.940
Optimal order quantity   :        61.000
Total inventory cost     :    443196.387
Reorder point            :        54.795

***** End of Output *****
```

As seen in the above analysis, the optimal order quantity is 61. This represents price break 7.

b. The computer solution for a situation where annual demand is equal to 3,000 is presented below:

```
Program: Inventory Models / Quantity Discount

Problem Title: QA9-28

***** Input Data *****

Method type :                               All unit discount

Annual demand (units/year)                        3000.00
All other input is the same.

***** Program Output *****

ALL UNIT DISCOUNT

Optimal order price      :        219.920
Optimal order quantity   :         81.000
Total inventory cost     :     663838.542
Reorder point            :         82.192

***** End of Output *****
```

The computer results reveal that the optimal order quantity is 81. This is Price Break 9.

    c. The computer output below shows the impact of an increase in annual demand to 4,000 frames:

```
Program: Inventory Models / Quantity Discount

Problem Title: QA9-28

***** Input Data *****

Method type :                               All unit discount

Annual demand (units/year)                        4000.00
All other input is the same.

***** Program Output *****

ALL UNIT DISCOUNT

Optimal order price      :        219.910
Optimal order quantity   :         91.000
Total inventory cost     :     884339.278
Reorder point            :        109.589

***** End of Output *****
```

The optimal order quantity is 91 for the above data. This represents Price Break 10.

d. The optimal order quantity increases and total inventory cost increases. As expected, higher demand levels allow the ability to take advantage of quantity discounts.

9-29. This is an ABC inventory problem. We can use AB:QM to determine the total dollar value of each inventory item. This is shown in the following computer output:

```
----------------------------------------------------------------------
  Item     Annual   Unit   Annual $     Percentage     Percentage
 Number    demand   cost    volume      of items        of cost
----------------------------------------------------------------------
    6        5600    400    2240000      15.628          46.941
    8        5400    200    1080000      30.698          69.573
   11         500    400     200000      32.093          73.764
    9        3456     50     172800      41.738          77.385
    4         556    300     166800      43.290          80.880
   12         600    250     150000      44.964          84.024
    1        3200     45     144000      53.894          87.041
   18         345    400     138000      54.857          89.933
    2        5543     23     127489      70.326          92.605
   20        5600     20     112000      85.954          94.952
   17        1000    100     100000      88.745          97.047
   10         456    100      45600      90.018          98.003
    3         123    200      24600      90.361          98.518
   19        2000     10      20000      95.942          98.938
   16         230     60      13800      96.584          99.227
    7         450     30      13500      97.840          99.510
   14         450     20       9000      99.096          99.698
   15          60    145       8700      99.263          99.881
   13          34    100       3400      99.358          99.952
    5         230     10       2300     100.000         100.000
----------------------------------------------------------------------
 Total                     4771989
```

As you can see, Items 6, 8, and 11 represent slightly over 70% total dollar usage. These are **A** items, and they should be carefully controlled. Items 9, 4, 12, 1, and 18 represent an additional 20% of total sales. These are **B** items, and they should be controlled to some extent. The other items are **C** items. The stockout data is not needed in this problem.

Solution to Professional Video Management Case

1. In order to determine the reorder points for the two suppliers, daily demand for the video tape systems must be determined. Since each video system requires two video tape systems that are connected to it, the demand for the video tape units is equal to two times the number of complete systems.

The demand for the complete video system appears to be relatively constant and stable. The monthly demand for the past few months can be averaged, and this value can be used for the average monthly demand. The average monthly sales is equal to $(7{,}970 + 8{,}070 + 7{,}950 + 8{,}010)/4 = 8{,}000$. Therefore, the average monthly demand of the video tape systems is 16,000 units, because two tape units are required for every complete system. Annual demand is 192,000 units $(192{,}000 = 12 \times 16{,}000)$.

We will assume that there are 20 working days per month. In other words, there are 5 working days per week. Making this assumption, we can determine the average daily sales to be equal to the average monthly sales divided by 20. In other words, the daily sales is equal to 800 units per day $(800 = 16{,}000/20)$.

In order to determine the reorder point for Toshiki, we must know the lead time. For Toshiki, it takes 3 months between the time an order is placed and when the order is actually received. In other words, the lead time is 3 months. Again, assuming 20 working days per month, the lead time for Toshiki is 60 days ($60 = 20 \times 3$). In order to determine the reorder point, we multiply the demand expressed as units per day times the lead time in days. For Toshiki, the reorder point is equal to 48,000 units ($48,000 = 800 \times 60$). Because the reorder point will be greater than the EOQ (see #2 for EOQ calculations), the lead time will likely be more important for ordering more inventory.

For Kony, the reorder point can be computed in the same manner. Assuming again that there are 5 working days per week, we can compute the lead time in days. For Kony, it takes 2 weeks between the time an order is placed and when it is received. Therefore, the lead time in days is equal to 10 days ($10 = 2 \times 5$). With the lead time expressed in days, we can compute the reorder point for Kony. This is done by multiplying the lead time in days times the daily demand. Therefore, the reorder point for Kony is 8,000 ($8,000 = 800 \times 10$).

2. In order to make a decision concerning which supplier to use, total inventory cost must be considered for both Toshiki and Kony. Both companies have quantity

discounts. Fortunately, AB:QM can solve this problem for us. All the appropriate data have been entered into this computer program, which determines the best overall policy. Because there are two suppliers, we had to make two separate quantity discount computer runs. The first run was for Toshiki. The second run was for Kony. Toshiki had the lowest total cost of $40,950,895.50. The EOQ for the minimum cost inventory policy was 20,001. Kony had a cost of $42,406,569.

3. Each alternative that Steve is considering would have a direct impact on the quantity discount model and the results. The first strategy is to sell the components separately. If this is done, the demand for video tape systems could change drastically. In addition to selling the video tape units along with the complete system, additional tape units could be demanded. An increase in demand could change the outcome of the quantity discount model. The second strategy would also have an impact on the results of the analysis. At this time, two video tape systems are used for every complete system. If other video tape systems can be used as well, there will be fewer video tape systems ordered when obtaining the complete system. At this time, exactly two video tape systems are sold with every complete system. Implementing the second strategy would cause this ratio to drop below two. Again, this will change the annual demand figures.

10
Linear Programming: Graphical and Computer Methods

LEARNING OBJECTIVES

After completing this chapter, students will be able to:

1. Understand the basic assumptions of linear programming (LP) and the properties of LP problems.
2. Formulate small- to moderate-sized LP problems.
3. Graphically solve any LP problem that has only two variables by both the corner point and iso-line methods.
4. Understand special issues in LP such as infeasiblity, unboundedness, redundancy, and alternative optimal solutions.

TEACHING SUGGESTIONS

Teaching Suggestion 10.1: Linear Programming Relation to Computers.

Many students still think that LP is just another form of computer programming. It pays to invest a minute to explain that the connection between LP and computers relates only to the programmed simplex algorithm.

Teaching Suggestion 10.2: Draw Constraints for a Graphical LP Solution.

Explain constraints of the three types ($\leq$, $=$, $\geq$) carefully the first time you present an example. Show

how to find the X_1, X_2 intercepts so a straight line can be drawn. Then provide some practice in determining which way the constraints point. This can be done by picking a few X_1, X_2 coordinates at random and indicating which direction fulfills the constraints.

Teaching Suggestion 10.3: Feasible Region Is a Convex Polygon.

Explain Dantzing's discovery that all feasible regions are convex (bulge outward) polygons (many-sided figures) and that the optimal solution must lie at one of the corner points. Draw both convex and concave figures to show the difference.

Teaching Suggestion 10.4: Using the Iso-Profit Line Method.

This method can be much more confusing than the corner point approach, but it is faster once students feel comfortable drawing the profit line. Start your first line at a profit figure you know is lower than optimal. Then draw a series of parallel lines, or run a ruler parallel, until the furthest corner point is reached. See Figures 10.6 and 10.7.

Teaching Suggestion 10.5: The Use of Software in Solving LP Problems.

Programs 10.1, 10.2, and 10.3 provide a useful side-by-side comparison of a Flair Furniture's problem solved by AB:QM, LINDO, and STORM. It's important that students feel comfortable with different formats and that they can interpret the output of each program with ease. You can stress the critical role of software in solving problems today and then mention the mainframe packages. Refer the students to Chapter 12's treatment of Karmarkar's method and the reason (large-size problems) why it is so important.

Teaching Suggestion 10.6: Applications of QA Boxes in the LP Chapters.

There are a wealth of motivating tales of real-world applications in Chapters 10–13. The airline industry in particular is a major LP user. See the United Airlines box in this chapter, the section on Karmarkar in Chapter 12, and the American Airlines box in Chapter 11.

Teaching Suggestion 10.7: Feasible Region for the Minimization Problem.

Students often question the open area to the right of the constraints in a minimization problem such as that in Figure 10.10. You need to explain that the area is not unbounded to the right in a minimization problem as it is in a maximization problem.

Teaching Suggestion 10.8: Infeasibility.

This problem is especially common in large LP formulations since many people will be providing input constraints to the problem. This is a real-world problem that should be expected.

Teaching Suggestion 10.9: Alternative Optimal Solutions.

This issue is an important one that can be explained in a positive way. Managers appreciate having choices of decisions that can be made with no penalty. Students can be made aware that alternative optimal solutions will arise again in the transportation model, assignment model, integer programming, and the chapter on network models.

VIDEO 10–1

Management Science: Juicy Problems

This half-hour video segment introduces the subject of linear programming at its most basic level. It does so by dealing with an ingredient mix LP problem—specifically, the blending of fruits into a wide variety of juices at New England Apple Products. (The company is known for its Very Fine line of fruit drinks, see the QA application box in Chapter 10 for details.)

LP is introduced in an intuitive then mathematical manner. Sample constraints are developed by the moderator and then solved graphically. The simplex method is described in a general sense, and N. Karmarkar is shown introducing his new algorithm.

Late in the tape, two other examples of blending are also introduced: gasoline fuel blending and hot dog meat blending.

The final segment is a brief dialogue with Thomas Cook regarding American Airlines' use of LP in airline scheduling. This video should be shown in conjunction with Chapter 10.

VIDEO 10–2

United Airlines Station Manpower Planning System

This TIMS video segment is based on one of the award-winning papers published in *Interfaces*. A brief description of the application follows: A computerized planning system using integer and linear programming and network optimization develops work schedules for 4,000 employees. Eventually, it should cover 20% of the UAL work force in the United States, 10,000 employees. Saving over $6 million annually, the system has been viewed by managers as "magical." (See the QA application box in this chapter for details.)

ALTERNATE EXAMPLES

Alternate Example 10.1: Hal has enough clay to make 24 small vases or 6 large vases. He only has enough of a special glazing compound to glaze 16 of the small vases or 8 of the large vases. Let X_1 = the number of small vases, and X_2 = the number of large vases.

The smaller vases sell for $3 each, while the larger vases would bring $9 each.

a) Formulate the problem.

b) Solve graphically.

SOLUTION:

a) Formulation

OBJECTIVE FUNCTION: $\$3X_1 + \$9X_2$ = MAXIMIZE

$$\text{Clay Constraint:} \quad 1X_1 + 4X_2 \leq 24$$

$$\text{Glaze Constraint:} \quad 1X_1 + 2X_2 \leq 16$$

b) Graphical Solution

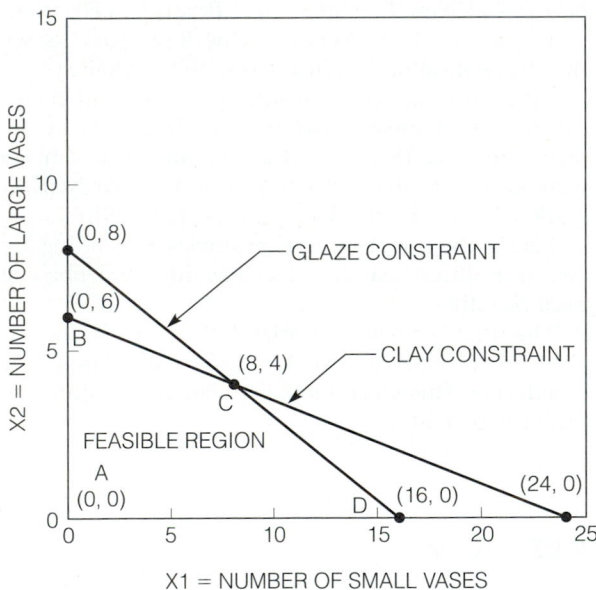

POINT	X_1	X_2	INCOME
A	0	0	0
B	0	6	$54
C	8	4	$60*
D	16	0	$48

*Optimum income of $60 will occur by making and selling eight small vases and four large vases.

Draw an iso-profit line on the above graph from (20, 0) to (0, 6 2/3) as the $60 iso-profit line.

Alternate Example 10.2: A fabric firm has received an order for cloth specified to contain at least 45 pounds of cotton and 25 pounds of silk. The cloth can be woven out on any suitable mix of two yarns (A and B). Material A costs $3 per pound, and B costs $2 per pound. They contain the proportions of cotton and silk (by weight) shown below.

	COTTON %	SILK %
A	30	50
B	60	10

What quantities (pounds) of A and B yarns should be used to minimize the cost of this order?

Objective function: Min. C = 3A + 2B

Constraints: .30A + .60B ≥ 45 lbs.

.50A + .10B ≥ 25 lbs.

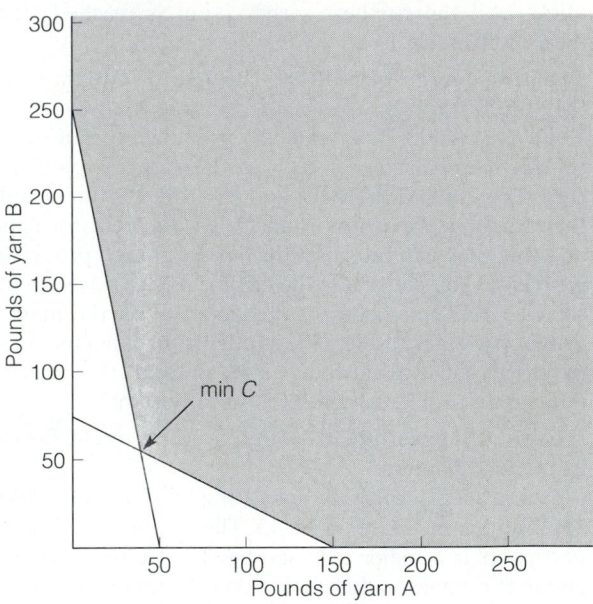

Simultaneous solution of the two constraint equations reveals that A = 39 lbs., B = 55 lbs.

The minimum cost is Min. C = $3A + $2B = 3(39) + 2(55) = $227.

SOLUTIONS TO DISCUSSION QUESTIONS AND PROBLEMS

10-1. Both minimization and maximization LP problems employ the basic approach of developing a feasible solution region by graphing each of the constraint lines. They can also both be solved by applying the corner point method. The iso-profit line method is used for maximization problems, whereas the iso-cost line is applied to minimization problems. Conceptually, iso-profit and iso-cost are the same.

The major differences between minimization and maximization problems deal with the shape of the feasible region and the direction of optimality. In minimization problems, the region must be bounded on the lower left, and the best iso-cost line is the one closest to the zero origin. The region may be unbounded on the top and right and yet be correctly formulated. A maximization problem must be bounded on the top and to the right. The iso-profit line yielding maximum profit is the one furthest from the zero origin.

10-2. The requirements for an LP problem are listed in section two of this chapter. It is also assumed that conditions of certainty exist; that is, coefficients in the objective function and constraints are known with certainty and do not change during the period being studied. Another basic assumption that mathematically sophisticated students should be made aware of is *proportionality* in the objective function and constraints. For example, if one product uses 5 hours of a machine resource, then making 10 of that product uses 50 hours of machine time.

LP also assumes *additivity*. This means that the total of all activities equals the sum of each individual activity. For example, if the objective function is Maximize $P = 6X_1 + 4X_2$, and if $X_1 = X_2 = 1$, then the profit contributions of 6 and 4 must add up to produce a sum of 10.

10-3. Each LP problem that has been formulated correctly *does* have an infinite number of solutions. Only one of the points in the feasible region usually yields the *optimal* solution, but *all* of the points yield a feasible solution. If we consider the region to be continuous and accept noninteger solutions as valid, there will be an infinite number of feasible combinations of X_1 and X_2.

10-4. If a maximization problem has many constraints, then it can be very time-consuming to use the corner point method to solve it. Such an approach would involve using simultaneous equations to solve for each of the feasible region's intersection points. The iso-profit line is much more effective if the problem has numerous constraints.

10-5. A problem can have alternate optimal solutions if the iso-profit or iso-cost line runs parallel to one of the problem's constraint lines (refer to Section 10-7 in the chapter).

10-6. This question involves the student using a little originality to develop his or her own LP constraints that fit the three conditions of (1) unboundedness, (2) infeasibility, and (3) redundancy. These conditions

are discussed in Section 10-7, but each student's graphical displays should be different.

10-7. The manager's statement indeed had merit if the manager understood the deterministic nature of linear programming input data. LP assumes that data pertaining to demand, supply, materials, costs, and resources are known with certainty and are constant during the time period being analyzed. If this production manager operates in a very unstable environment (for example, prices and availability of raw materials change daily, or even hourly) then the model's results may be too sensitive and volatile to be trusted. The application of sensitivity analysis (a subject to be covered in Chapter 13) might be useful to determine whether LP would still be a good approximating tool in decision making.

10-8. The objective function is not linear because it contains the product of X_1 and X_2, making it a second-degree term. The first, second, fourth, and sixth constraints are okay as is. The third and fifth constraints are nonlinear because they contain terms to the second degree and one-half degree, respectively.

10-9.

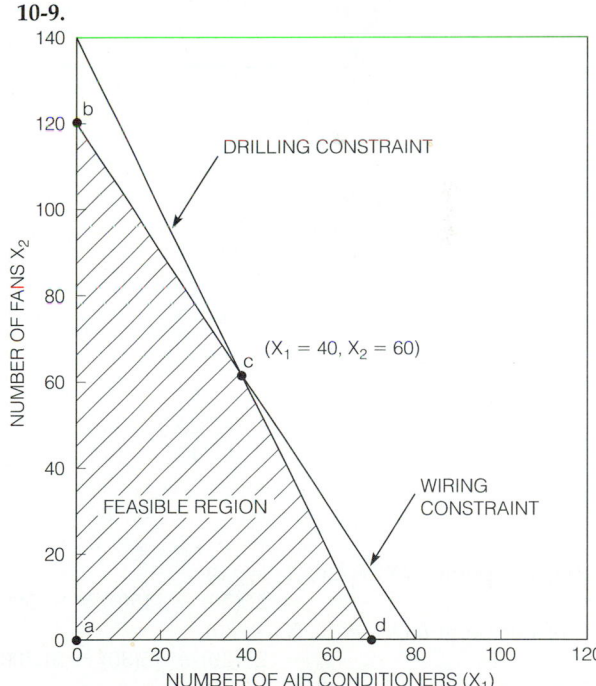

Let: X_1 = number of air conditioners to be produced
X_2 = number of fans to be produced
Maximize profit = $25X_1 + 15X_2$
Subject to:
$\qquad 3X_1 + 2X_2 \leq 240$ (wiring)
$\qquad 2X_1 + 1X_2 \leq 140$ (drilling),
$\qquad X_1, X_2 \geq 0$

Profit at point a ($X_1 = 0$, $X_2 = 0$) $= \$0$
Profit at point b ($X_1 = 0$, $X_2 = 120$)
                  $= 25(0) + 15(120) = \$1,800$
Profit at point c ($X_1 = 40$, $X_2 = 60$)
                  $= 25(40) + 15(60) = \$1,900$
Profit at point d ($X_1 = 70$, $X_2 = 0$)
                  $= 25(70) + 15(0) = \$1,750$

The optimal solution is to produce 40 air conditioners and 60 fans during each production period. Profit will be \$1,900.

10-10. Refer to figure below.

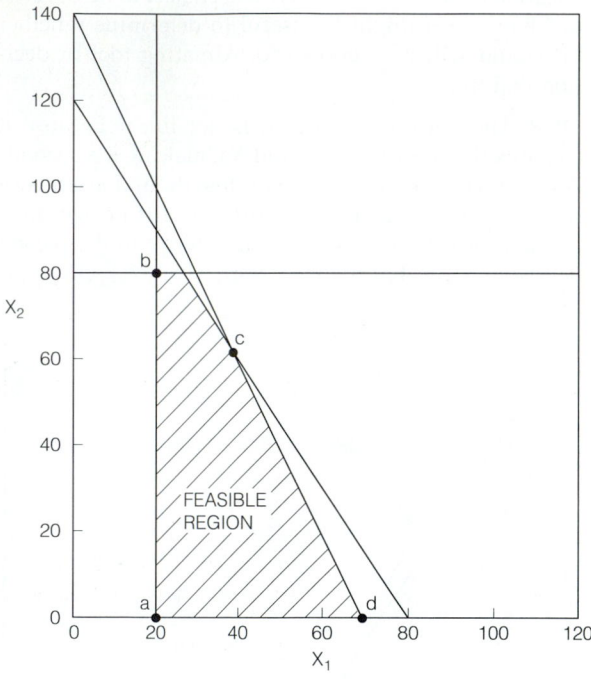

Maximize profit $= 25X_1 + 15X_2$
Subject to: $3X_1 + 2X_2 \leq 240$
                       $2X_1 + 1X_2 \leq 140$
                                $X_1 \geq 20$
                                $X_2 \leq 80$
                         $X_1, X_2 \geq 0$

Profit at point a ($X_1 = 20$, $X_2 = 0$)
                  $= 25(20) + 15(0) = \$\ 500$
Profit at point b ($X_1 = 20$, $X_2 = 80$)
                  $= 25(20) + 15(80) = \$1,700$
Profit at point c ($X_1 = 40$, $X_2 = 60$)
                  $= 25(40) + 15(60) = \$1,900$
Profit at point d ($X_1 = 70$, $X_2 = 0$)
                  $= 25(70) + 15(0) = \$1,750$

Hence, even though the shape of the feasible region changed from Problem 10-9, the optimal solution remains the same.

10-11. Refer to figure below.

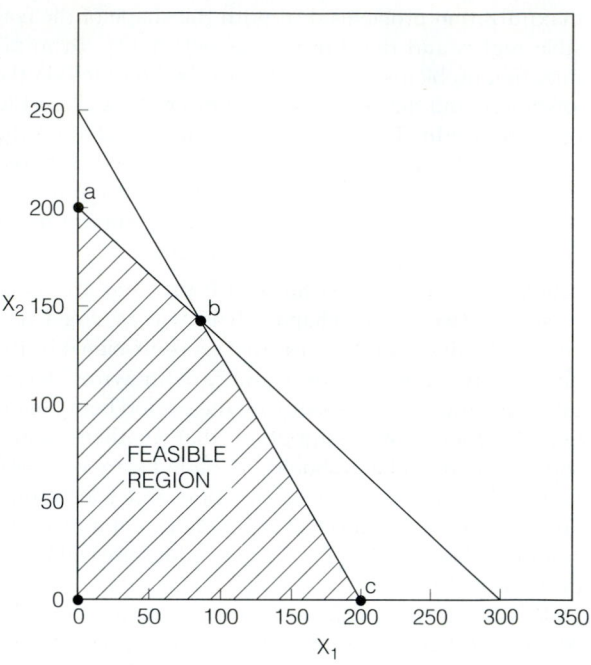

$X_1 =$ number of model A tubs produced
$X_2 =$ number of model B tubs produced
Maximize profit $= 90X_1 + 70X_2$
Subject to: $125X_1 + 100X_2 \leq 25,000$ (steel)
                    $20X_1 + 30X_2 \leq 6,000$ (zinc)
                                $X_1, X_2 \geq 0$
Profit at point a ($X_1 = 0$, $X_2 = 20$) $= \$14,000$
Profit at point b ($X_1 = 85.71$, $X_2 = 142.86$) $= \$17,714.10$
Profit at point c ($X_1 = 100$, $X_2 = 0$) $= \$18,000$
                                    optimal solution

10-12. Refer to figure on next page.

$X_1 =$ number of benches produced
$X_2 =$ number of tables produced
Maximize profit $= \$9X_1 + \$20X_2$
Subject to: $4X_1 + 6X_2 \leq 1,200$ hours
                    $10X_1 + 35X_2 \leq 3,500$ pounds
                                $X_1, X_2 \geq 0$
Profit at point a ($X_1 = 0$, $X_2 = 100$) $= \$2,000$
Profit at point b ($X_1 = 262.5$, $X_2 = 25$) $= \$2,862.50$
Profit at point c ($X_1 = 300$, $X_2 = 0$) $= \$2,700$

Figure for Problem 10-12

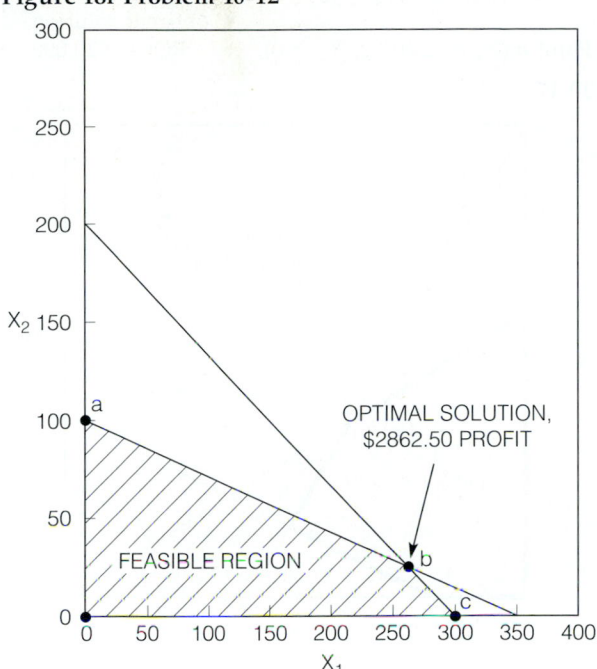

10-13.

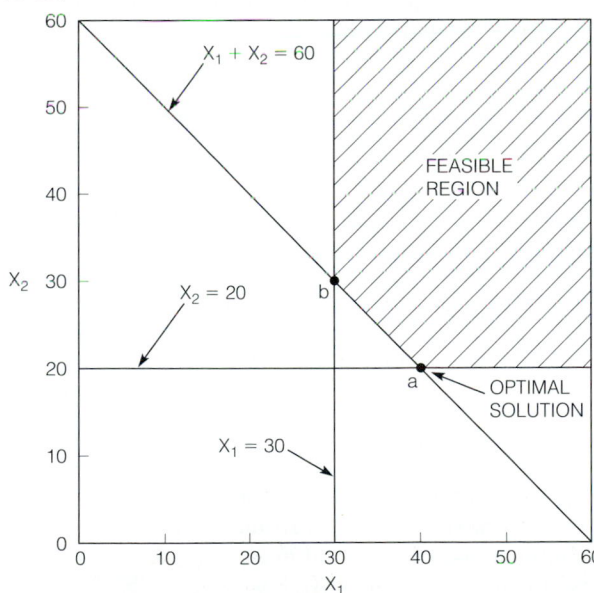

X_1 = number of undergraduate courses
X_2 = number of graduate courses
Minimize cost = $\$2,500X_1 + \$3,000X_2$
Subject to: $\qquad X_1 \geqq 30$
$\qquad\qquad X_2 \geqq 20$
$\qquad X_1 + X_2 \geqq 60$
Total cost at point $a = (X_1 = 40, X_2 = 20)$
$\qquad\qquad = 2,500(40) + 3,000(20)$

$\qquad\qquad = \$160,000$
Total cost at point $b = (X_1 = 30, X_2 = 30)$
$\qquad\qquad = 2,500(30) + 3,000(30)$
$\qquad\qquad = \$165,000$

Point a is optimal

10-14.

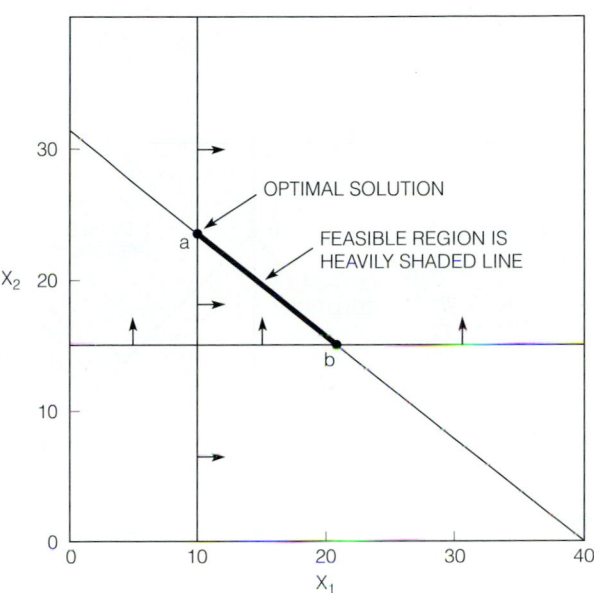

X_1 = number of Alpha 4 computers
X_2 = number of Beta 5 computers
Maximize profit $- \$1,200X_1 + \$1,800X_2$
Subject to: $\qquad\qquad 20X_1 + 25X_2 = 800$ hours
$\qquad\qquad\qquad$ (total hours = 5 workers
$\qquad\qquad\qquad \times$ 160 hours each)
$\qquad\qquad\qquad X_1 \geqq 10$
$\qquad\qquad\qquad X_2 \geqq 15$
Corner points: $\quad a(X_1 = 10, X_2 = 24),$
$\qquad\qquad\qquad$ Profit = \$55,200
$\qquad\qquad\quad b(X_1 = 21\ \frac{1}{4}, X_2 = 15),$
$\qquad\qquad\qquad$ Profit = \$52,500

Point a is optimal.

10-15. Let: X_1 = number of pounds of compost in each
$\qquad\qquad$ bag
$\qquad\qquad X_2$ = number of pounds of sewage waste
$\qquad\qquad$ in each bag
Minimize cost = $5X_1 + 4X_2$
$\quad$ (in cents)
Subject to: $\qquad X_1 + X_2 \geqq 60$ (pounds per bag)
$\qquad\qquad\qquad X_1 \geqq 30$ (pounds compost
$\qquad\qquad\qquad\qquad$ per bag)
$\qquad\qquad\qquad X_2 \leqq 40$ (pounds sewage per
$\qquad\qquad\qquad\qquad$ bag)

Corner point a:
   $(X_1 = 30, X_2 = 40) \Rightarrow$ Cost $= 5(30) + 4(40) = \$3.10$
Corner point b:
   $(X_1 = 30, X_2 = 30) \Rightarrow$ Cost $= 5(30) + 4(30) = \$2.70$
Corner point c:
   $(X_1 = 60, X_2 = 0) \Rightarrow$ Cost $= 5(60) + 4(0) = \$3.00$

10-16.

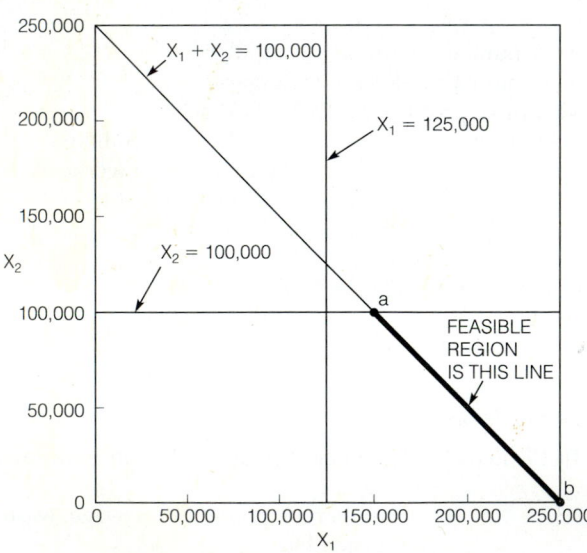

$X_1 = \$$ invested in treasury notes
$X_2 = \$$ invested in bonds
Maximize ROI $= .08X_1 + .09X_2$
$$X_1 \geq \$125,000$$
$$X_2 \leq \$100,000$$
$$X_1 + X_2 = \$250,000$$
$$X_1, X_2 \geq 0$$

Point a ($X_1 = 150,000$, $X_2 = 100,000$), ROI $= \$21,000$ ← optimal solution
Point b ($X_1 = 250,000$, $X_2 = 0$),   ROI $= \$20,000$

10-17.

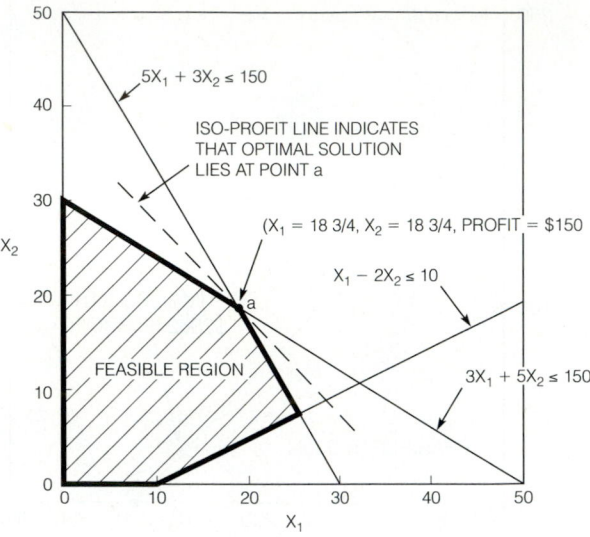

Note that this problem has one constraint with a negative sign. This may cause the beginning student some confusion in plotting the line.

10-18. Refer to figure on next page.
Point a lies at intersection of constraints:

$$3X_1 + 2X_2 = 120$$
$$X_1 + 3X_2 = 90$$

Multiply the second equation by -3 and add it to the first (the method of simultaneous equations):

$$3X_1 + 2X_2 = 120$$
$$\underline{-3X_1 - 9X_2 = -270}$$
$$-7X_2 = -150 \Rightarrow X_2 = 21.43 \text{ and } X_1 = 25.71$$

Cost $= \$1X_1 + \$2X_2 = \$1(25.71) + \$2(21.43) = \$68.57$

10-19. Refer to figure on next page.

$X_1 = \$$ invested in Louisiana Gas and Power
$X_2 = \$$ invested in Trimex Insulation Co.
Minimize total investment $= X_1 + X_2$
Subject to: $\$0.36\,X_1 + \$0.24X_2 \geq \$720$
                      $\$1.67\,X_1 + \$1.50X_2 \geq \$5,000$
                      $.04\,X_1 + \quad .08X_2 \geq \$200$

Investment at a is \$3,333.
Investment at b is \$3,179. ← optimal solution
Investment at c is \$5,000.
Short term growth is \$927.27.
Intermediate term growth is \$5,000.
Dividends are \$200.

Figure for Problem 10-18

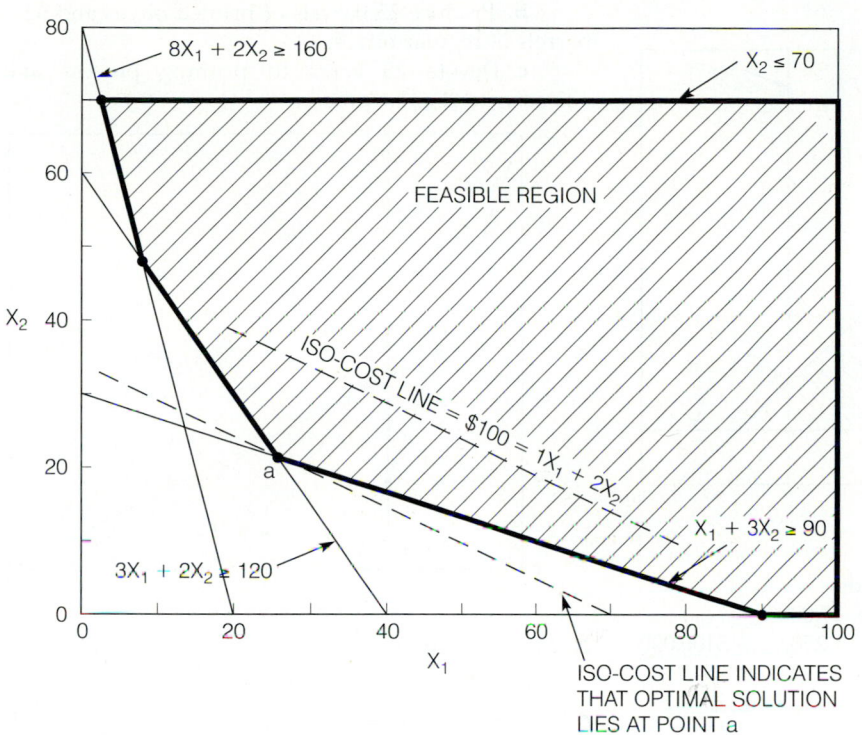

Figure for Problem 10-19

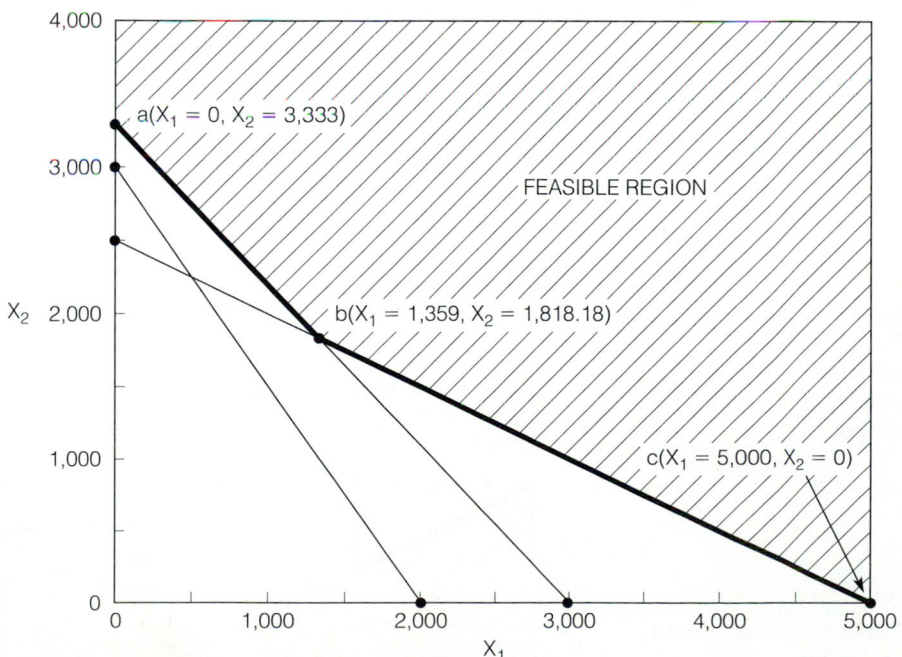

10-20.

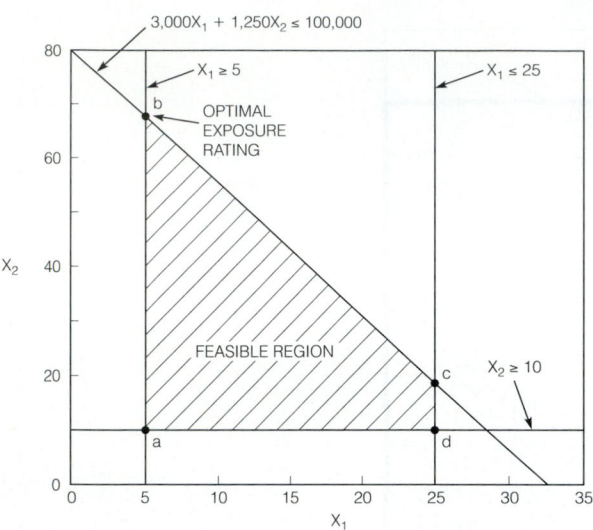

Let: X_1 = number of TV spots
X_2 = number of newspaper ads
Maximize exposures = $35,000X_1 + 20,000X_2$
Subject to: $\qquad 3,000X_1 + 1,250X_2 \leqq \$100,000$
$\qquad\qquad\qquad X_1 \geqq 5$
$\qquad\qquad\qquad X_1 \leqq 25$
$\qquad\qquad\qquad X_2 \geqq 10$
Point a ($X_1 = 5$, $X_2 = 10$), Exposure = 375,000
$\qquad\qquad\qquad\qquad\qquad$ (optimal)
Point b ($X_1 = 5$, $X_2 = 68$), Exposure = 175,000
$\qquad\qquad\qquad\qquad\qquad$ + 1,360,000
$\qquad\qquad\qquad\qquad\qquad$ = 1,535,000
Point c ($X_1 = 25$, $X_2 = 20$), Exposure = 875,000
$\qquad\qquad\qquad\qquad\qquad$ + 400,000
$\qquad\qquad\qquad\qquad\qquad$ = 1,275,000
Point d ($X_1 = 25$, $X_2 = 10$), Exposure = 875,000
$\qquad\qquad\qquad\qquad\qquad$ + 200,000
$\qquad\qquad\qquad\qquad\qquad$ = 1,075,000

10-21. Refer to figure in next column.
Let: X_1 = number barrels of pruned olives
X_2 = number barrels of regular olives
Maximize profit = $\$20X_1 + \$30X_2$
Subject to: $\quad 5X_1 + 2X_2 \leqq 250$ (labor hours)
$\qquad\qquad 1X_1 + 2X_2 \leqq 150$ (acres)
$\qquad\qquad\qquad X_1 \leqq 40$ (barrels)
$\qquad\qquad X_1, X_2 \geqq 0$
a. Corner point $a = (X_1 = 0, X_2 = 0)$,
$\qquad\qquad$ Profit = 0
Corner point $b = (X_1 = 0, X_2 = 75)$,
$\qquad\qquad$ Profit = \$2,250
Corner point $c = (X_1 = 25, X_2 = 62\frac{1}{2})$,
$\qquad\qquad$ Profit = \$2,375 ← optimal profit
Corner point $d = (X_1 = 40, X_2 = 25)$,
$\qquad\qquad$ Profit = \$1,550

Corner point $e = (X_1 = 40, X_2 = 0)$,
$\qquad\qquad$ Profit = \$800
b. Produce 25 barrels of pruned olives and 62 ½ barrels of regular olives.
c. Devote 25 acres to pruning process and 125 acres to regular process.

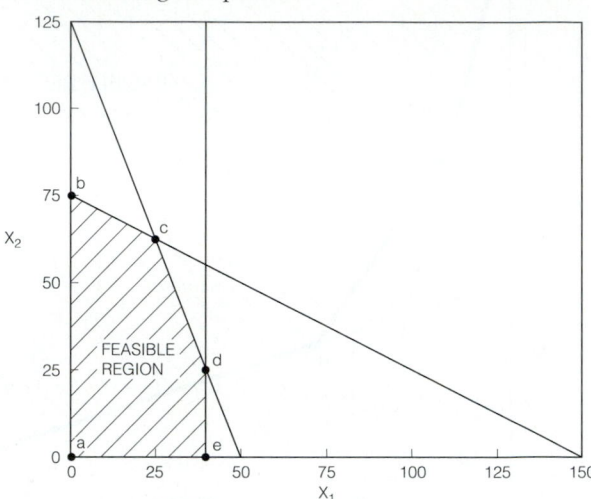

10-22. Formulation 1:

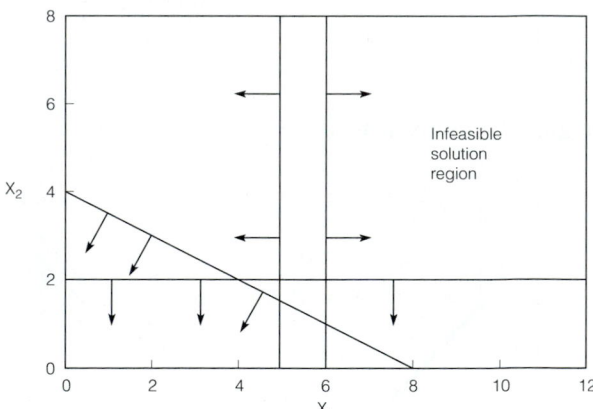

Formulation 2:

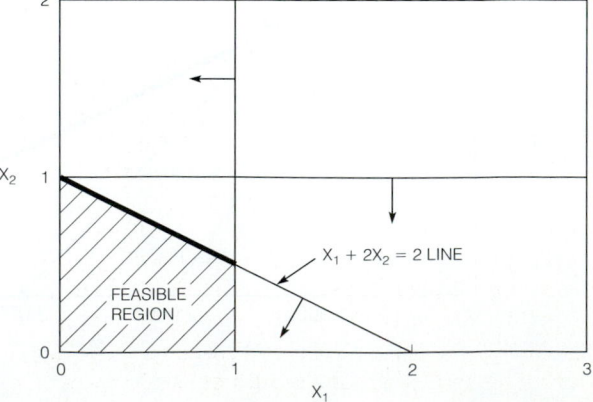

$X_1 + 2X_2 = 2$ line—this is also on the same slope as the iso-profit line $X_1 + 2X_2$ and hence there will be more than one optimal solution.

As a matter of fact, every point along the heavy line will provide an "alternate optimum."

Formulation 3:

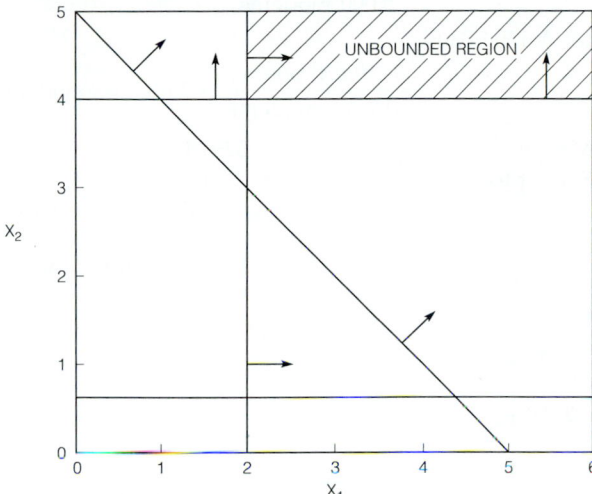

Formulation 4:

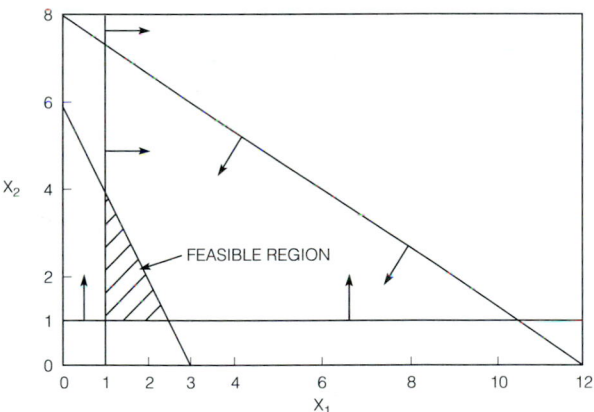

Formulation appears to be proper as is. Note that the constraint $4X_1 + 6X_2 \leq 48$ is redundant.

10-23. Refer to figure in next column.

Let: X_1 = number of coconuts carried
  X_2 = number of skins carried

Maximize profit = $60X_1 + 300X_2$ (in rupees)

Subject to:
$$5X_1 + 15X_2 \leq 300 \text{ pounds}$$
$$\tfrac{1}{8}X_1 + 1X_2 \leq 15 \text{ cubic feet}$$
$$X_1, X_2 \geq 0$$

At point a: ($X_1 = 0$, $X_2 = 15$), $P = 4,500$ rupees
At point b: ($X_1 = 24$, $X_2 = 12$), $P = 1,440 + 3,600$
  $= 5,040$ rupees
At point c: ($X_1 = 60$, $X_2 = 0$), $P = 3,600$ rupees

The three princes should carry 24 coconuts and 12 lions' skins. This will produce a wealth of 5,040 rupees.

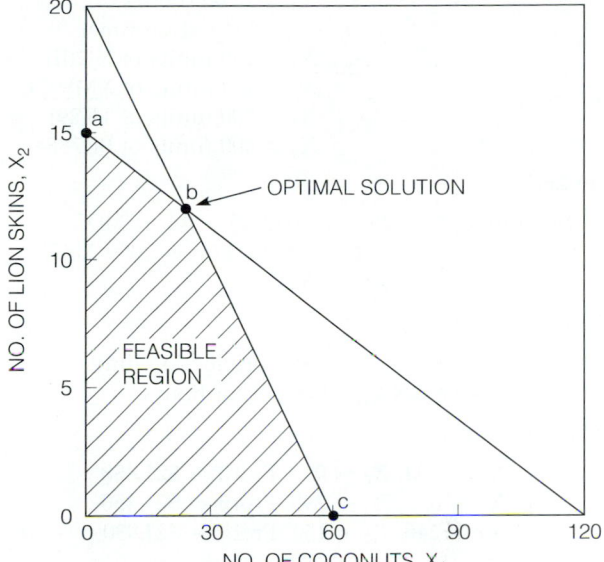

10-24. Let: X_1 = number of pounds of stock X
   purchased per cow each month
  X_2 = number of pounds of stock Y
   purchased per cow each month
  X_3 = number of pounds of stock Z
   purchased per cow each month

Four pounds of ingredient Z per cow can be transformed to:

4 pounds × (16 oz./lb.) = 64 oz. per cow
  5 pounds = 80 oz.
  1 pound = 16 oz.
  8 pounds = 128 oz.

$$3X_1 + 2X_2 + 4X_3 \geq 64 \text{ (ingredient A requirement)}$$
$$2X_1 + 3X_2 + 1X_3 \geq 80 \text{ (ingredient B requirement)}$$
$$1X_1 + 0X_2 + 2X_3 \geq 16 \text{ (ingredient C requirement)}$$
$$6X_1 + 8X_2 + 4X_3 \geq 128 \text{ (ingredient D requirement)}$$
$$X_3 \leq 80 \text{ (stock Z limitation)}$$

Minimize cost = $.02X_1 + .04X_2 + .025X_3$

10-25. Let: X_1 = number units of XJ201 produced
  X_2 = number units of XM897 produced
  X_3 = number units of TR29 produced
  X_4 = number units of BR788 produced

Maximize profit = $9X_1 + 12X_2 + 15X_3 + 11X_4$

Subject to:
$.5X_1 + 1.5X_2 + 1.5X_3 + 1X_4 \leq 15,000$ (hours of
   wiring time
   available)
$.3X_1 + 1X_2 + 2X_3 + 3X_4 \leq 17,000$ (hours of
   drilling time
   available)
$.2X_1 + 4X_2 + 1X_3 + 2X_4 \leq 26,000$ (hours of
   assembly time
   available)

$.5X_1 + 1X_2 + .5X_3 + .5X_4 \leq 1,200$ (hours of
inspection time)
$$X_1 \geq 150 \text{ (units of XJ201)}$$
$$X_2 \geq 100 \text{ (units of XM897)}$$
$$X_3 \geq 300 \text{ (units of TR29)}$$
$$X_4 \geq 400 \text{ (units of BR788)}$$

10-26.

Maximize $Z = [20 - (.45)(220) - 44 - 20]X_1$
$+ [175 - (.40)(175) - 30 - 20]X_2$
$= 57X_1 + 55X_2$

Constraints:

$$X_1 + X_2 \leq 390 \quad \text{production limit}$$
$$2.5X_1 + 2.4X_2 \leq 960 \quad \text{labor hours}$$

Corner points:

$$X_1 = 384, X_2 = 0, \quad \text{Profit} = \$21,888$$
$$X_1 = 0, \quad X_2 = 390, \text{Profit} = \$21,450$$
$$X_1 = 240, X_2 = 150, \text{Profit} = \$21,930$$

Students should point out that those three options are so close in profit that production desires and sensitivity of the RHS and cost coefficient are important issues. This is a good lead-in to the discussion of sensitivity analysis. As a matter of reference, the right-hand side ranging for the first constraint is a production limit from 384 to 400 units. For the second constraint, the hours may range only from 936 to 975 without affecting the solution.

The objective function coefficients, likewise, are very sensitive. The \$57 for X_1 may increase by 29¢ or decrease by \$2. The \$55 for X_2 may increase by \$2 or decrease by 28¢.

10-27. a. Let: X_1 = number of MCA 300 Baud
Modems made and sold in November
X_2 = number of MCA 1200 Baud
Modems made and sold in November

Data needed for variable costs and contribution margin (refer to table below):

Hours needed to produce each modem:

MCA 300 Baud

$$= \frac{5,000 \text{ hours}}{9,000 \text{ modems}} = .555 \text{ hours/modem}$$

MCA 1200 Baud

$$= \frac{10,400 \text{ hours}}{10,400 \text{ modems}} = 1.0 \text{ hours/modem}$$

Maximize profit $= \$22.67X_1 + \$29.01X_2$
Subject to: $.555X_1 + 1.0X_2 \leq 15,400$
direct labor hours
$X_2 \leq 8,000$
1200 Baud Modems

b.

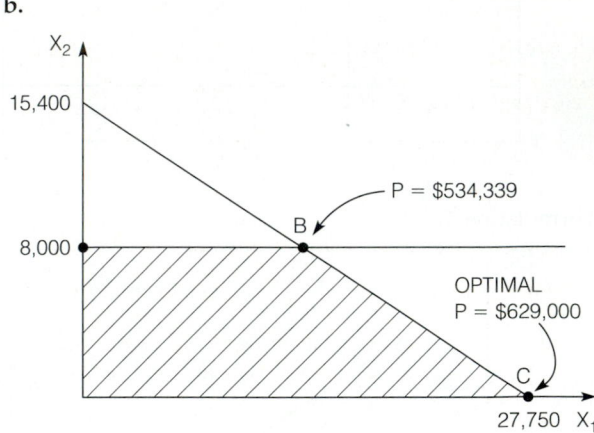

c. The optimal solution suggests making all MCA 300 Baud Modems. Students should discuss the implications of shipping no MCA 1200 models.

Table for Problem 10-27(a)

	MCA 300 BAUD		MCA 1200 BAUD	
	TOTAL	PER UNIT	TOTAL	PER UNIT
Net Sales	\$424,000	\$47.11	\$613,000	\$58.94
Variable Costs*				
Direct labor	60,000	6.67	76,800	7.38
Indirect labor	9,000	1.00	11,520	1.11
Materials	90,000	10.00	128,000	12.31
General expenses	30,000	3.33	35,000	3.37
Sales commissions	31,000	3.44	60,000	5.76
Total variable costs	\$220,000	\$24.44	\$311,320	\$29.93
Contribution Margin	\$204,000	\$22.67	\$301,680	\$29.01

*Depreciation, fixed general expense, and advertising are excluded from the calculations.

Solution to Golding Landscaping and Plants, Inc., Case

Minimize cost = $12X_1 + 9X_2 + 11X_3 + 4X_4$
Subject to:
$$X_1 + X_2 + X_3 + X_4 = 50$$
$$X_4 \geq 7.5$$
$$X_1 + X_2 \geq 22.5$$
$$X_2 + X_3 \leq 15.0$$

Solution:

$$X_1 = 7.5 \text{ pounds of C-30}$$
$$X_2 = 15 \text{ pounds of C-92}$$
$$X_3 = 0 \text{ pounds of D-21}$$
$$X_4 = 27.5 \text{ pounds of E-11}$$

Cost = $3.35

11

Linear Programming Applications: With Computer Analyses in AB:QM, STORM, LINDO and What'sBest!

LEARNING OBJECTIVES

After completing this chapter, students will be able to:

1. Formulate a wide variety of medium- to large-sized LP problems.
2. Understand major application areas, including marketing, production, labor scheduling, fuel blending, and finance.

TEACHING SUGGESTIONS

Teaching Suggestion 11.1: Importance of Formulating Large LP Problems.

Since computers are used to solve virtually all business LP problems, the most important thing a student can do is to get experience in formulating a wide variety of problems. This chapter provides such a variety.

Teaching Suggestion 11.2: Note on Production Scheduling Problems.

The Greenberg Motor example in this chapter is the largest problem in the book in terms of constraints, so it provides a good practice environment. An interesting feature to point out is that LP constraints are capable of tying one production period to the next.

Teaching Suggestion 11.3: Solving Assignment Problems by LP.

The example of the law firm of Ivan and Ivan in this chapter can clearly be solved more quickly using AB:QM's assignment program than by the LP program. Students should be asked why anyone would choose to use the LP approach. There are two answers: (1) many commercial LP programs do not contain assignment algorithms (which are more popular in academic software such as our AB:QM program); and (2) the LP program can provide sensitivity analysis and an economic interpretation which is not available in the assignment module. The assignment problem is treated in Chapter 14.

Teaching Suggestion 11.4: Labor Planning Problem—Arlington Bank.

This example is a good practice tool and lead-in for the Chase Manhattan Bank case at the end of the chapter. Without this example, the case would probably overpower most students.

Teaching Suggestion 11.5: Ingredient Blending Applications.

Three points can be made about the two blending examples in this chapter. First, both the diet and fuel blending problems presented here are tiny compared to huge real-world blending problems. But they do provide some sense of the issues to be faced.

Second, diet problems that are missing the constraints that force variety into the diet can be terribly embarrassing. It has been said that a hospital in New Orleans ended up with an LP solution to feed each patient only castor oil for dinner because analysts neglected to add constraints forcing a well-rounded diet.

Finally, note that the video called "Juicy Problems" deals with the blending of fruit juices. See Chapter 10 of this Instructor's Section for an overview of the film.

VIDEO NOTES

VIDEO 11–1

Crew Pairing at American Airlines

This TIMS video segment is based on one of the award-winning papers in *Interfaces* in 1991. A brief description follows:

Crew pairing optimization, the most important and computationally intensive part of crew assignment, contends with union and FAA work rules and pay guarantees to arrive at a low-cost solution for assigning crews to fly a monthly schedule. The trip reevaluation and improvement program (TRIP) generates annual savings in excess of $20 million. Considered the preeminent solution mechanism for problems of this type, TRIP has been sold to ten major airlines and one railroad.

(See the QA Application box in Chapter 11 for details.)

ALTERNATE EXAMPLES

Alternate Example 11.1:   Natural Furniture Company manufactures three outdoor products, chairs, benches, and tables. Each product must pass through the following departments before it is shipped: sawing, sanding, assembly, and painting. The time requirements (in hours) are summarized in the table below.

The production time available in each department each week and the minimum weekly production requirement to fulfill contracts are as follows:

DEPARTMENT	CAPACITY (IN HOURS)	PRODUCT	MINIMUM PRODUCTION LEVEL
Sawing	450	Chairs	100
Sanding	400	Benches	50
Assembly	625	Tables	50
Painting	550		

The production manager has the responsibility of specifying production levels for each product for the coming week. Let

Table for Alternate Example 11.1:

PRODUCT	SAWING	SANDING	ASSEMBLY	PAINTING	UNIT PROFIT
Chairs	1.5	1.0	2.0	1.5	$15
Benches	1.5	1.5	2.0	2.0	$10
Tables	2.0	2.0	2.5	2.0	$20

X_1 = Number of chairs produced
X_2 = Number of benches produced
X_3 = Number of tables produced

The objective function is

Maximize profit = $15X_1 + 10X_2 + 20X_3$

Constraints

$1.5X_1 + 1.5X_2 + 2.0X_3 \leq 450$ hours of sawing available
$1.0X_1 + 1.5X_2 + 2.0X_3 \leq 400$ hours of sanding available
$2.0X_1 + 2.0X_2 + 2.5X_3 \leq 625$ hours of assembly available
$1.5X_1 + 2.0X_2 + 2.0X_3 \leq 550$ hours of painting available

$X_1 \geq 100$ chairs
$X_2 \geq 50$ benches
$X_3 \geq 50$ tables
$X_1, X_2, X_3 \geq 0$

Alternate Example 11.2:   A phosphate manufacturer produces three grades, A, B, and C, which cost the firm $40, $50, and $60 per kilogram, respectively. The products require the labor and materials per batch that are shown in the table on the next page.

What mix of products would yield minimum cost?

Objective function

Minimize cost = $40A + 50B + 60C$

Constraints

Labor:	$4A + 4B + 5C \leq 80$	
Raw material #1	$200A + 300B + 300C \leq 6000$	
Raw material #2	$600A + 400B + 500C \leq 5000$	

SOLUTIONS TO PROBLEMS

11-1. Since the decision centers about the production of the two different cabinet models, we let:

X_1 = number of French Provincial cabinets produced each day
X_2 = number of Danish Modern cabinets produced each day

Objective: Maximize revenue = $28X_1 + 25X_2$

Table for Alternate Example 11.2:

	GRADE A	GRADE B	GRADE C	AVAILABLE RESOURCES
Labor hours	4	4	5	80 hr
Raw material #1	200	300	300	6000 kg
Raw material #2	600	400	500	5000 kg

11-1. cont.

Subject to:

$$3X_1 + 2X_2 \leqq 360 \text{ hours (carpentry department)}$$
$$1\,1/2X_1 + 1X_2 \leqq 200 \text{ hours (painting department)}$$
$$3/4X_1 + 3/4X_2 \leqq 125 \text{ hours (finishing department)}$$
$$X_1 \geqq 60 \text{ units (contract requirement)}$$
$$X_2 \geqq 60 \text{ units (contract requirement)}$$

Problem 11-1 solved by computer:

Produce 60 French Provincial cabinets (X_1) per day
Produce 90 Danish Modern cabinets (X_2) per day
Profit = $3,930 (in four iterations)

11-2. Let: $X_1 = $ \$ invested in Los Angeles Municipal Bonds
$X_2 = $ \$ invested in Thompson Electronics
$X_3 = $ \$ invested in United Aerospace
$X_4 = $ \$ invested in Palmer Drugs
$X_5 = $ \$ invested in Happy Days Nursing Homes

Maximize return $= .053X_1 + .068X_2 + .049X_3 + .084X_4 + .118X_5$

Subject to: $X_1 + X_2 + X_3 + X_4 + X_5 = \$250,000$
(funds to be invested)
$$X_1 \geqq 50,000$$
(municipal bonds)
$$X_2 + X_3 + X_4 \geqq 100,000$$
(combination of electronics, aerospace and drugs)
$$(X_5 \leqq .5X_1)$$

rewritten as:

$$-.5X_1 + X_5 \leqq 0$$
(nursing home as percent of bonds)

Problem 11-2 solved by computer:

\$50,000 invested in Los Angeles Municipal Bonds (X_1)
\$0 invested in Thompson Electronics (X_2)
\$0 invested in United Aerospace (X_3)
\$175,000 invested in Palmer Drugs (X_4)
\$25,000 invested in Happy Days (X_5)

This produces an annual return on investment of \$20,300 (in six simplex iterations).

11-3. Minimize staff size $= X_1 + X_2 + X_3 + X_4 + X_5 + X_6$

where

$X_i = $ number of workers reporting for start of work at period i (with $i = 1, 2, 3, 4, 5,$ or 6)

$$X_1 + X_2 \geqq 12$$
$$X_2 + X_3 \geqq 16$$
$$X_3 + X_4 \geqq 9$$
$$X_4 + X_5 \geqq 11$$
$$X_5 + X_6 \geqq 4$$
$$X_1 + X_6 \geqq 3$$

The solution is to hire 30 workers:

16 begin at 7 A.M.
9 begin at 3 P.M.
2 begin at 7 P.M.
3 begin at 11 P.M.

An alternate optimum is:

3 begin at 3 A.M.
9 begin at 7 A.M.
7 begin at 11 A.M.
2 begin at 3 P.M.
9 begin at 7 P.M.
0 begin at 11 P.M.

11-4. Let: $X_1 = $ number of pounds of oat product per horse each day
$X_2 = $ number of pounds of enriched grain per horse each day
$X_3 = $ number of pounds of mineral product per horse each day

Minimize cost $= .09X_1 + .14X_2 + .17X_3$
Subject to:

$$2X_1 + 3X_2 + 1X_3 \geqq 6 \text{ (ingredient } A)$$
$$1/2X_1 + 1X_2 + 1/2X_3 \geqq 2 \text{ (ingredient } B)$$
$$3X_1 + 5X_2 + 6X_3 \geqq 9 \text{ (ingredient } C)$$
$$1X_1 + 1\,1/2X_2 + 2X_3 \geqq 8 \text{ (ingredient } D)$$
$$1/2X_1 + 1/2X_2 + 1\,1/2X_3 \geqq 5 \text{ (ingredient } E)$$
$$X_1 + X_2 + X_3 \geqq 6 \text{ (maximum feed/day)}$$

Solution: $X_1 = 1\,1/3$
$X_2 = 0$
$X_3 = 3\,1/3$
Cost $= .687$

11-5. Let: $X_{ij} = 1$ if pitcher i is scheduled to go against opponent j, 0 otherwise where i = 1, 2, 3, 4 stands for Jones, Baker, Parker, and Wilson, respectively, and

j = 1, 2, 3, 4 stands for Des Moines, Davenport, Omaha, and Peoria, respectively.

Objective: Maximize overall probability of winning = Sum of probability of winning each game =

$$.6X_{11} + .8X_{12} + .5X_{13} + .4X_{14}$$
$$+ .7X_{21} + .4X_{22} + .8X_{23} + .3X_{24}$$
$$+ .9X_{31} + .8X_{32} + .7X_{33} + .8X_{34}$$
$$+ .5X_{41} + .3X_{42} + .4X_{43} + .2X_{44}$$

Subject to:

$$X_{11} + X_{12} + X_{13} + X_{14} = 1 \quad \text{("Dead-Arm" Jones)}$$
$$X_{21} + X_{22} + X_{23} + X_{24} = 1 \quad \text{("Spitball" Baker)}$$
$$X_{31} + X_{32} + X_{33} + X_{34} = 1 \quad \text{("Ace" Parker)}$$
$$X_{41} + X_{42} + X_{43} + X_{44} = 1 \quad \text{("Gutter" Wilson)}$$

$$X_{11} + X_{21} + X_{31} + X_{41} = 1 \quad \text{(Des Moines)}$$
$$X_{12} + X_{22} + X_{32} + X_{42} = 1 \quad \text{(Davenport)}$$
$$X_{13} + X_{23} + X_{33} + X_{43} = 1 \quad \text{(Omaha)}$$
$$X_{14} + X_{24} + X_{34} + X_{44} = 1 \quad \text{(Peoria)}$$

Solution: $X_{12} = 1$, $X_{23} = 1$, $X_{34} = 1$, $X_{41} = 1$, Total P = 2.9

11-6. Let: X_1 = number of newspaper ads placed
  X_2 = number of TV spots purchased
Minimize cost = $925X_1 + \$2,000X_2$
Subject to: $.04X_1 + .05X_2 \geq .40$ (city exposure)
  $.03X_1 + .03X_2 \geq .60$ (exposure in northwest suburbs)

Note that the problem is not limited to unduplicated exposure (for example, one person seeing the Sunday newspaper three weeks in a row counts for three exposures).

Problem 11-6 solved by computer:

Buy 20 Sunday newspaper ads (X_1)
Buy 0 TV ads (X_2)

This has a cost of $18,500. Perhaps the paint store should consider a blend of TV and newspaper, not just the latter.

11-7. To formulate this problem, we first add an activity G to represent the end of the project:

Objective = minimize X_G
  $X_A \geq 2$
  $X_B \geq 3$
  $X_C \geq 1$

$$X_D - X_A \geq 4$$
$$X_F - X_B \geq 1$$
$$X_E - X_C \geq 5$$
$$X_E - X_D \geq 5$$
$$X_G - X_E \geq 0$$
$$X_G - X_F \geq 0$$

Solution with AB:QM

X_A = 2
X_B = 10
X_C = 6
X_D = 6
X_E = 11
X_F = 11
X_G = 11

Z = 11

11-8. Let: X_{ij} = number of students bused from sector i to school j

Objective: Minimize total travel miles =

$$5X_{AB} + 8X_{AC} + 6X_{AE}$$
$$+ 0X_{BB} + 4X_{BC} + 12X_{BE}$$
$$+ 4X_{CB} + 0X_{CC} + 7X_{CE}$$
$$+ 7X_{DB} + 2X_{DC} + 5X_{DE}$$
$$+ 12X_{EB} + 7X_{EC} + 0X_{EE}$$

Subject to:

$$X_{AB} + X_{AC} + X_{AE} = 700$$
  (number students in sector A)
$$X_{BB} + X_{BC} + X_{BE} = 500$$
  (number students in sector B)
$$X_{CB} + X_{CC} + X_{CE} = 100$$
  (number students in sector C)
$$X_{DB} + X_{DC} + X_{DE} = 800$$
  (number students in sector D)
$$X_{EB} + X_{EC} + X_{EE} = 400$$
  (number students in sector E)
$$X_{AB} + X_{BB} + X_{CB} + X_{DB} + X_{EB} \leq 900$$
  (school B capacity)
$$X_{AC} + X_{BC} + X_{CC} + X_{DC} + X_{EC} \leq 900$$
  (school C capacity)
$$X_{AE} + X_{BE} + X_{CE} + X_{DE} + X_{EE} \leq 900$$
  (school E capacity)

Solution: X_{AB} = 400
  X_{AE} = 300
  X_{BB} = 500
  X_{CC} = 100
  X_{DC} = 800
  X_{EE} = 400

Distance = 5,400 miles

11-9. Let: X_1 = number of Chaunceys mixed
  X_2 = number of Sweet Italians mixed

X_3 = number of bourbon on the rocks mixed

X_4 = number of Russian martinis mixed

Maximize total drinks = $X_1 + X_2 + X_3 + X_4$

Subject to:

$$1X_1 \qquad\quad + 4X_3 \qquad\qquad \leqq 52 \text{ oz. (bourbon limit)}$$
$$1X_1 + 1X_2 \qquad\qquad\qquad \leqq 38 \text{ oz. (brandy limit)}$$
$$1X_1 \qquad\quad + 2\tfrac{2}{3}X_4 \leqq 64 \text{ oz. (vodka limit)}$$
$$\qquad 1X_2 \quad + 1\tfrac{1}{3}X_4 \leqq 24 \text{ oz. (dry vermouth limit)}$$
$$1X_1 + 2X_2 \qquad\qquad\qquad \leqq 36 \text{ oz. (sweet vermouth limit)}$$

Because a Chauncey (X_1) is ¼ sweet vermouth, it requires 1 oz. of that resource (each drink totals 4 oz.).

Problem 11-9 solved by computer:

Mix 25.99 (or 26) Chaunceys (X_1)
Mix 5.00 (or 5) Sweet Italians (X_2)
Mix 6.50 (or 6 ½) bourbon on the rocks (X_3)
Mix 14.25 (or 14 ¼) Russian martinis (X_4)

This is a total of 51.75 drinks (in five iterations).

11-10. Maximize number of rolls of Supertrex sold = $20X_1 + 6.8X_2 + 12X_3 - 65{,}000X_4$

where X_1 = $ on advertising,
X_2 = $ on store displays,
X_3 = $ in inventory, and
X_4 = percent markup.

Subject to:

$$X_1 + X_2 + X_3 \leq \$17{,}000 \text{ (budgeted)}$$
$$X_1 \qquad\qquad\qquad \geqq \$\ 3{,}000 \text{ (advertising constraint)}$$
$$\qquad X_2 \qquad\quad \geqq .05X_3 \text{ (or } X_2 - .05X_3 \geqq 0)$$
$$\text{(ratio of displays to inventory)}$$
$$X_4 \geqq 0.20$$
$$X_4 \leqq 0.45 \quad \text{(markup ranges)}$$
$$X_1, X_2, X_3, X_4 \geqq 0$$

Problem 11-10 solved by computer:

Spend $17,000 on advertising ($X_1$).
Spend nothing on in-store displays or on-hand inventory (X_2 and X_3).
Take a 20% markup.

The store will sell 327,000 rolls of Supertrex (in six iterations)

This solution implies that no on-hand inventory or displays are needed to sell the product, probably due to an oversight on Mr. Kruger's part. Perhaps a constraint indicating that $X_3 \geqq \$3{,}000$ of inventory should be held might be added.

11-11. Minimize total cost = $\$.60X_1 + 2.35X_2 + 1.15X_3 + 2.25X_4 + .58X_5 + 1.17X_6 + .33X_7$

Subject to:

$$295X_1 + 1{,}216X_2 + 394X_3 + 358X_4 + 128X_5 + 118X_6 + 279X_7 \leqq 1{,}500$$
$$295X_1 + 1{,}216X_2 + 394X_3 + 358X_4 + 128X_5 + 118X_6 + 279X_7 \geqq 900$$
$$.2X_1 + .2X_2 + 4.3X_3 + 3.2X_4 + 3.2X_5 + 14.1X_6 + 2.2X_7 \leqq 4$$
$$16X_1 + 96X_2 + 9X_3 + .5X_4 + .8X_5 + 1.4X_6 + 0.5X_7 \leqq 50$$
$$16X_1 + 81X_2 + 74X_3 + 83X_4 + 7X_5 + 14X_6 + 8X_7 \geqq 26$$
$$22X_1 + 28X_5 + 19X_6 + 63X_7 \leqq 50$$

All $X_i \geqq 0$

Problem 11-11 solved by computer:

The meal plan for the evening is

No milk ($X_1 = 0$)
.499 pound of ground meat (X_2)
.173 pound of chicken (X_3)
No fish ($X_4 = 0$)
No beans ($X_5 = 0$)
.105 pound of spinach (X_6)
.762 pound of white potatoes (X_7)

Each meal has a cost of $1.75 (in six iterations).

The meal is fairly well-balanced (two meats, a green vegetable, and a potato). The weight of each item is realistic. This problem is very sensitive to changing food prices.

Sensitivity analysis when prices change:

Milk increases 10¢/lb.: No change in price or diet
Milk decreases 10¢/lb.: No change in price or diet
Milk decreases 30¢/lb. (to 30¢): Potatoes drop out and milk enters, price = $1.42/meal
Ground meat increases from $2.35 to $2.75: Price = $1.93 and spinach leaves solution
Ground meat increases to $5.25/lb.: Price = $2.07 and meat leaves; milk, chicken, and potatoes in solution
Fish decreases from $2.25 to $2.00/lb.: No change
Chicken increases to $3.00/lb.: Price = $1.91 and meat, fish, spinach, and potatoes in solution

If fish and chicken are omitted from problem, solution becomes:

Meat = .219 lb.
Spinach = .164 lb.
Potatoes = .744 lb.

If meat and fish are omitted;

Chicken = .774 lb.
Milk = 1.891 lb.
Potatoes = .133 lb.

If chicken and meat are omitted;

Fish   = .679 lb.
Spinach = .0988 lb.
Milk   = 2.188 lb.

11-12. a. Let: X_1 = no. of units of internal modems
produced per week
X_2 = no. of units of external modems
produced per week
X_3 = no. of units of circuit boards
produced per week
X_4 = no. of units of floppy disks
produced per week
X_5 = no of units of Winchester drives
produced per week
X_6 = no. of units of memory boards
produced per week

Objective function analysis: First find the time used on each test device:

Hours on test device no. 1

$$= \frac{7X_1 + 3X_2 + 12X_3 + 6X_4 + 18X_5 + 17X_6}{60}$$

Hours on test device no. 2

$$= \frac{2X_1 + 5X_2 + 3X_3 + 2X_4 + 15X_5 + 17X_6}{60}$$

Hours on test device no. 3

$$= \frac{5X_1 + 1X_2 + 3X_3 + 2X_4 + 9X_5 + 2X_6}{60}$$

Thus, the objective function is:

Maximize profit = Revenue − Material cost

− Test cost

$= 200X_1 + 120X_2 + 180X_3 + 130X_4 + 430X_5 + 260X_6$
$- 35X_1 - 25X_2 - 40X_3 - 45X_4 - 170X_5 - 60X_6$
$- 15 \dfrac{[7X_1 + 3X_2 + 12X_3 + 6X_4 + 18X_5 + 17X_6]}{60}$
$- 12 \dfrac{[2X_1 + 5X_2 + 3X_3 + 2X_4 + 15X_5 + 17X_6]}{60}$
$- 18 \dfrac{[5X_1 + 1X_2 + 3X_3 + 2X_4 + 9X_5 + 2X_6]}{60}$

This can be rewritten as:

Maximize profit = $\$161.35X_1 + 92.95X_2 + 135.50X_3$
$+ 82.50X_4 + 249.80X_5 + 191.75X_6$

The constraints are:

$(7X_1 + 3X_2 + 12X_3 + 6X_4 + 18X_5$
$+ 17X_6)/60 \leq 120$ hours
$(2X_1 + 5X_2 + 3X_3 + 2X_4 + 15X_5$
$+ 17X_6)/60 \leq 120$ hours
$(5X_1 + 1X_2 + 3X_3 + 2X_4 + 9X_5 + 2X_6)/60$
≤ 100 hours

b. The solution is:

X_1 = 496.55 internal modems
X_2 = 1,241.38 external modems
X_3 through X_6 = 0
Profit = $195,504.80

c. The shadow prices, as explained in Chapters 10 and 13, for additional time on the three test devices are $21.41, $5.75, and $0, respectively. Time should be added on test device no. 1 only, since $21.41 exceeds the cost of $15 for the extra labor required.

11-13. a. Let: X_i = no. of trained technicians available at start of month i
Y_i = no. of trainees beginning in month i

Minimize total salaries paid = $\$2,000X_1$
$+ 2,000X_2 + 2,000X_3 + 2,000X_4 + 2,000X_5$
$+ 900Y_1 + 900Y_2 + 900Y_3 + 900Y_4 + 900Y_5$

Subject to:

$130X_1 - 90Y_1 \geq 40,000$ (Aug. need, hours)
$130X_2 - 90Y_2 \geq 45,000$ (Sept. need)
$130X_3 - 90Y_3 \geq 35,000$ (Oct. need)
$130X_4 - 90Y_4 \geq 50,000$ (Nov. need)
$130X_5 - 90Y_5 \geq 45,000$ (Dec. need)
$X_1 = 350$ (starting staff on Aug. 1)
$X_2 = X_1 + Y_1 - .05X_1$ (staff on Sept. 1)
$X_3 = X_2 + Y_2 - .05X_2$ (staff on Oct. 1)
$X_4 = X_3 + Y_3 - .05X_3$ (staff on Nov. 1)
$X_5 = X_4 + Y_4 - .05X_4$ (staff on Dec. 1)

All $X_i, Y_i \geq 0$

b. The computer-generated results are:

MONTH	TRAINED TECHNICIANS AVAILABLE	TRAINEES BEGINNING
Aug.	350	13.7 (actually 14)
Sept.	346.2	0
Oct.	328.8	72.2 (actually 72)
Nov.	384.6	0
Dec.	366.4	0

Total salaries paid over the five-month period = $3,627,279.

11-14. Let: $X_{i,j}$ = acres of crop i planted on parcel j
where i = 1 for wheat, 2 for alfalfa, 3 for barley, and
j = 1 to 5 for SE, N, NW, W, and SW parcels.

Irrigation limits:

$1.6X_{11} + 2.9X_{21} + 3.5X_{31} \leq 3,200$ acre-feet in SE
$1.6X_{12} + 2.9X_{22} + 3.5X_{32} \leq 3,400$ acre-feet in N
$1.6X_{13} + 2.9X_{23} + 3.5X_{33} \leq 800$ acre-feet in NW

$1.6X_{14} + 2.9X_{24} + 3.5X_{34} \leqq 500$ acre-feet in W
$1.6X_{15} + 2.9X_{25} + 3.5X_{35} \leqq 600$ acre-feet in SW

$$\sum_{j=1}^{5} 1.6X_{1,j} + \sum_{j=1}^{5} 2.9X_{2,j}$$

$$+ \sum_{j=1}^{5} 3.5X_{3,j} \leqq 7{,}400 \text{ water acre-feet total}$$

Sales limits:

$X_{11} + X_{12} + X_{13} + X_{14} + X_{15}$
$\qquad \leqq 2{,}200$ wheat in acres (= 11,000 bushels)
$X_{21} + X_{22} + X_{23} + X_{24} + X_{25}$
$\qquad \leqq 1{,}200$ alfalfa in acres (= 1,800 tons)
$X_{31} + X_{32} + X_{33} + X_{34} + X_{35}$
$\qquad \leqq 1{,}000$ barley in acres (= 2,200 tons)

Acreage availability:

$X_{11} + X_{21} + X_{31} \leqq 2{,}000$ acres in SE parcel
$X_{12} + X_{22} + X_{32} \leqq 2{,}300$ acres in N parcel
$X_{13} + X_{23} + X_{33} \leqq 600$ acres in NW parcel
$X_{14} + X_{24} + X_{34} \leqq 1{,}100$ acres in W parcel
$X_{15} + X_{25} + X_{35} \leqq 500$ acres in SW parcel

Objective function:

$$\text{Maximize profit} = \sum_{j=1}^{5} \$2(50 \text{ bushels}) X_{1,j}$$

$$+ \sum_{j=1}^{5} \$40(1.5 \text{ tons}) X_{2,j} + \sum_{j=1}^{5} (\$50)(2.2 \text{ tons}) X_{3,j}$$

The solution is to plant:

$X_{12} = 1{,}250$ acres of wheat in N parcel
$X_{13} = \quad 500$ acres of wheat in NW parcel
$X_{14} = \quad 312\frac{1}{2}$ acres of wheat in W parcel
$X_{15} = \quad 137\frac{1}{2}$ acres of wheat in SW parcel
$X_{25} = \quad 131$ acres of alfalfa in SW parcel
$X_{31} = \quad 600$ acres of barley in SE parcel
$X_{32} = \quad 400$ acres of barley in N parcel

Profit will be \$337,862.10.

11-15. Amalgamated's blending problem will have 8 variables and 11 constraints. The 8 variables correspond to the 8 materials available (3 alloys, 2 irons, 3 carbides) that can be selected for the blend. Six of the constraints deal with maximum and minimum quality limits, one deals with the 2,000 pound total weight restriction, and 4 deal with the weight availability limits for alloy 2 (300 lb.), carbide 1 (50 lb.), carbide 2 (200 lb.), and carbide 3 (100 lb.).

Let X_1 through X_8 represent pounds of alloy 1 through pounds of carbide 3 to be used in the blend.

$\text{Minimize cost} \quad = .12X_1 + .13X_2 + .15X_3 + .09X_4$
$\qquad\qquad\qquad + .07X_5 + .10X_6 + .12X_7 + .09X_8$

Subject to:
Manganese quality: ①$.70X_1 + .55X_2 + .12X_3 + .01X_4$
$\qquad + .05X_5 \geq 42$ (2.1% of 2,000)
②$.70X_1 + .55X_2 + .12X_3 + .01X_4$
$\qquad + .05X_5 \leq 46$ (2.3% of 2,000)
Silicon quality: ③$.15X_1 + .30X_2 + .26X_3 + .10X_4$
$\qquad + .025X_5 + .24X_6 + .25X_7$
$\qquad + .28X_8 \geq 86$ (4.3% of 2,000)
④$.15X_1 + .30X_2 + .26X_3 + .10X_4$
$\qquad + .025X_5 + .24X_6 + .25X_7$
$\qquad + .23X_8 \leq 92$ (4.6% of 2,000)
Carbon quality: ⑤$.03X_1 + .01X_2 + .03X_4 + .18X_6$
$\qquad + .20X_7 + .25X_8 \geq 101$
$\qquad$ (5.05% of 2,000)
⑥$.03X_1 + .01X_2 + .03X_4 + .18X_6$
$\qquad + .20X_7 + .25X_8 \leq 107$
$\qquad$ (5.35% of 2,000)

Availability by weight:
⑦ $X_2 \leq 300$
⑧ $X_6 \leq 50$
⑨ $X_7 \leq 200$
⑩ $X_8 \leq 100$

One ton weight:
⑪ $X_1 + X_2 + X_3 + X_4 + X_5 + X_6 + X_7 + X_8$
$\qquad\qquad = 2{,}000$

Solution infeasible

11-16. This problem refers to Problem 11-15's infeasibility. Some investigative work is needed to track down the underlying issues. From a final Simplex tableau, we find that constraints 5 and 11 still have artificial variables in the final solution. The two issues are:

1. Requiring at least 5.05% carbon is not possible.
2. Producing one ton from the materials is not possible.

If the 5th and 11th constraints are relaxed (or removed), one solution is $X_2 = 84$ lbs. (alloy 2), $X_6 = 50$ lbs. (carbide 1), $X_7 = 104$ lbs. (carbide 2), and $X_8 = 100$ lbs. (carbide 3). Cost = \$37.31.

Each student may take a different approach and other recommendations may result.

11-17. X_1 = number of medical patients
$\qquad X_2$ = number of surgical patients

Maximize revenue = $\$2{,}280X_1 + \$1{,}515X_2$

Subject to:

$8X_1 + \quad 5X_2 \leq 32{,}850$ (patient days available
$\qquad\qquad\qquad\qquad = 365 \text{ days} \times 90 \text{ new beds})$
$3.1X_1 + 2.6X_2 \leq 15{,}000$ (lab tests)
$1X_1 + \quad 2X_2 \leq 7{,}000$ (x-rays)
$\qquad\qquad X_2 \leq 2{,}800$ (operations/surgeries)
$\qquad X_1, X_2 \geq 0$

Problem 11-17 solved by computer:

$X_1 = 2,791$ medical patients
$X_2 = 2,105$ surgical patients
Revenue = \$9,551,659 per year

To convert X_1 and X_2 to number of medical versus surgical beds, find the total number of hospital days for each type of patient:

Medical = (2,791 patients) (8 days/patient)
= 22,328 days
Surgical = (2,105 patients) (5 days/patient)
= 10,525 days
Total = 32,853 days

This represents 68% medical days and 32% surgical days, which yields 61 medical beds and 29 surgical beds. (Note that an alternative approach would be to formulate with X_1, X_2 as number of beds.)

See printout on page IS-121.

11-18. This problem, suggested by Professor C. Vertullo, is an excellent exercise in report writing. Here is a chance for students to present management science results in a management format. Basically, the following issues need to be addressed in any report:

a) As seen in Problem 11-17, there should be 61 medical and 29 surgical beds, yielding \$9,551,659 per year.
b) Referring to the printout on page IS-121 from AB:QM, there are no empty beds.
c) There are 876 lab tests of unused capacity.
d) The X ray is used to its maximum and has a \$65.45 shadow price.
e) The operating room still has 695 days of availability.

11-19. Minimize $6X_{11} + 8X_{12} + 10X_{13} + 7X_{21} + 11X_{22} + 11X_{23} + 4X_{31} + 5X_{32} + 12X_{33}$

Subject to:

$$X_{11} + X_{12} + X_{13} \leq 150$$
$$X_{21} + X_{22} + X_{23} \leq 175$$
$$X_{31} + X_{32} + X_{33} \leq 275$$
$$X_{11} + X_{21} + X_{31} \geq 200$$
$$X_{12} + X_{22} + X_{32} \geq 100$$
$$X_{13} + X_{23} + X_{33} \geq 300$$

$X_{11} = 25$, $X_{13} = 125$, $X_{23} = 175$, $X_{31} = 175$, $X_{32} = 100$

Cost = \$4,525

11-20. Minimize time = $12X_{A1} + 11X_{A2} + 8X_{A3} + 9X_{A4} + 6X_{A5} + 6X_{A6} + 6X_{G1} + 12X_{G2} + 7X_{G3} + 7X_{G4} + 5X_{G5} + 8X_{G6} + 8X_{S1} + 9X_{S2} + 6X_{S3} + 6X_{S4} + 7X_{S5} + 9X_{S6}$

Subject to:

$$X_{A1} + X_{A2} + X_{A3} + X_{A4} + X_{A5} + X_{A6} = 200$$
$$X_{G1} + X_{G2} + X_{G3} + X_{G4} + X_{G5} + X_{G6} = 225$$
$$X_{S1} + X_{S2} + X_{S3} + X_{S4} + X_{S5} + X_{S6} = 275$$
$$X_{A1} + X_{G1} + X_{S1} = 80$$
$$X_{A2} + X_{G2} + X_{S2} = 120$$
$$X_{A3} + X_{G3} + X_{S3} = 150$$
$$X_{A4} + X_{G4} + X_{S4} = 210$$
$$X_{A5} + X_{G5} + X_{S5} = 60$$
$$X_{A6} + X_{G6} + X_{S6} = 80$$

Solution:

SOURCE (STATION)	DESTINATION (WING)	NUMBER OF TRAYS
5A	5	60
5A	6	80
5A	3	60
3G	1	80
3G	3	90
3G	4	55
1S	4	155
1S	2	120

Optimal cost = 4,825 minutes

Solution to Chase Manhattan Bank Case

This scheduling problem can be solved most expeditiously using integer linear programming. Let F denote the number of full-time employees. Some number, $F1$, of them will work one hour of overtime between 5 P.M. and 6 P.M. each day and some number, $F2$, of the full-time employees will work overtime between 6 P.M. and 7 P.M. There will be seven sets of part-time employees; Pj will be the number of part-time employees who begin their work day at hour j, $j = 1, 2, \ldots, 7$, with $P1$ being the number of workers beginning at 9 A.M., $P2$ at 10 A.M., $\ldots$, $P7$ at 3 P.M. Note that because part-time employees must work a minimum of four hours, none can start after 3 P.M. since the entire operation ends at 7 P.M. Similarly, some number of part-time employees, Qj, leave at the end of hour j, $j = 4, 5, \ldots, 9$.

The work force requirements for the first two hours, 9 A.M. and 10 A.M., are:

$$F + P1 \geq 14$$
$$F + P1 + P2 \geq 25$$

At 11 A.M. half of the full-time employees go to lunch; the remaining half go at noon. For those hours:

$$.5F + P1 + P2 + P3 \geq 26$$
$$.5F + P1 + P2 + P3 + P4 \geq 38$$

Printout for Problem 11-17

```
Program: Linear Programming

Problem Title: qa11-17

***** Input Data *****

Max. Z = 2280x1 + 1515x2

Subject to

C1   8x1 + 5x2 <= 32850
C2   3.1x1 + 2.6x2 <= 15000
C3   1x1 + 2x2 <= 7000
C4   1x2 <= 2800

***** Program Output *****

Final Optimal Solution At Simplex Tableau : 2

Z  = 9551659.091
```

Variable	Value	Reduced Cost
x 1	2790.909	0.000
x 2	2104.545	0.000

Constraint	Slack/Surplus	Shadow Price
C 1	0.000	276.818
C 2	876.364	0.000
C 3	0.000	65.455
C 4	695.455	0.000

Objective Coefficient Ranges

Variables	Lower Limit	Current Values	Upper Limit	Allowable Increase	Allowable Decrease
x 1	757.500	2280.000	2424.000	144.000	1522.500
x 2	1425.000	1515.000	4560.000	3045.000	90.000

Right-Hand-Side Ranges

Constraints	Lower Limit	Current Values	Upper Limit	Allowable Increase	Allowable Decrease
C 1	25200.000	32850.000	35527.778	2677.778	7650.000
C 2	14123.636	15000.000	No limit	No limit	876.364
C 3	4106.250	7000.000	7956.250	956.250	2893.750
C 4	2104.545	2800.000	No limit	No limit	695.455

```
***** End of Output *****
```

Starting at 1 P.M., some of the part-time employees begin to leave. For the remainder of the straight-time day:

$$F + P1 + P2 + P3 + P4 + P5 - Q4 \geqq 55$$
$$F + P1 + P2 + P3 + P4$$
$$+ P5 + P6 - Q4 - Q5 \geqq 60$$
$$F + P1 + P2 + P3 + P4 + P5$$
$$+ P6 + P7 - Q4 - Q5 - Q6 \geqq 51$$
$$F + P1 + P2 + P3 + P4 + P5 + P6$$
$$+ P7 - Q4 - Q5 - Q6 - Q7 \geqq 29$$

For the two overtime hours:

$$F1 + P1 + P2 + P3 + P4 + P5 + P6$$
$$+ P7 - Q4 - Q5 - Q6 - Q7 - Q8 \geqq 14$$
$$F2 + P1 + P2 + P3 + P4 + P5 + P6 + P7$$
$$- Q4 - Q5 - Q6 - Q7 - Q8 - Q9 \geqq 9$$

If the left-hand sides of these ten constraints are added, one finds that $7F$ hours of full-time labor are used in straight time (although $8F$ are paid for), $F1 + F2$ full-time labor hours are used and paid for at overtime rates, and the total number of part time hours is:

$$10P1 + 9P2 + 8P3 + 7P4 + 6P5 + 5P6 + 4P7 - 6Q4$$
$$- 5Q5 - 4Q6 - 3Q7 - 2Q8 - Q9 \leqq 128.4$$

which is 40% of the day's total requirement of 321 person hours.

This also leads to the objective function. The total daily labor cost which must be minimized is:

$$Z = 8(10.11)F + 8.08(F1 + F2) + 7.82(10P1 + 9P2$$
$$+ 8P3 + 7P4 + 6P5 + 5P6 + 4P7 - 6Q4$$
$$- 5Q5 - 4Q6 - 3Q7 - 2Q8 - Q9)$$

Total overtime for a full-time employee is restricted to five hours or less, an average of one hour or less per day per employee. Thus, the number of overtime hours worked per day cannot exceed the number of full-time employees:

$$F1 + F2 \leqq F.$$

Since part-time employees must work at least four hours per day,

$$Q4 \leqq P1$$

for those leaving at the end of the fourth hour. At the end of the fifth hour, those leaving must be drawn from the $P1 - Q4$ remaining plus the $P2$ that arrived at the start of the second hour:

$$Q5 \leqq P1 + P2 - Q4$$

Similarly, for the remainder of the day:

$$Q6 \leqq P1 + P2 + P3 - Q4 - Q5$$
$$Q7 \leqq P1 + P2 + P3 + P4 - Q4 - Q5 - Q6$$
$$Q8 \leqq P1 + P2 + P3 + P4 + P5$$
$$- Q4 - Q5 - Q6 - Q7$$
$$Q9 \leqq P1 + P2 + P3 + P4 + P5 + P6$$
$$- Q4 - Q5 - Q6 - Q7 - Q8$$

To ensure that all part-timers who began at 9 A.M. do not work more than seven hours:

$$Q4 + Q5 + Q6 + Q7 \geqq P1$$

Similarly:

$$Q4 + Q5 + Q6 + Q7 + Q8 \geqq P1 + P2$$
$$Q4 + Q5 + Q6 + Q7$$
$$+ Q8 + Q9 \geqq P1 + P2 + P3$$

Finally, to ensure that all part-time employees leave at some time:

$$P1 + P2 + P3 + P4 + P5 + P6 + P7$$
$$= Q4 + Q5 + Q6 + Q7 + Q8 + Q9$$

The resulting problem has sixteen integer variables and twenty-two constraints. If integer programming software with sufficient capacity is not available, the linear programming problem can be solved and the solution rounded, making certain that none of the constraints have been violated. Note that the integer programming solution might also need to be adjusted—if F is an odd integer, $.5F$ will not be an integer and the requirement that "half" of the full-time employees go to lunch at 11 A.M. and the other half at noon will have to be altered by assigning the extra employee to the appropriate hour.

1. The least-cost solution requires 29 full-time employees, 9 of whom work two hours of overtime per day. In actuality, 18 of the full-time employees would work overtime on two different days and 9 would work overtime on one day. Fourteen of the full-time workers would take lunch at 11 A.M. and the other 15 would take it at noon. Eleven part-timers would begin at 11 A.M. with 9 of them leaving at 3 P.M. and the other 2 at 4 P.M. Fifteen part-time employees would work from noon until 4 P.M. and 5 would work from 2 P.M. until 6 P.M. The resulting cost of 232 hours of straight time, 18 hours of overtime, and 126 hours of part-time work is $3,476.28 per day.

   This solution is not unique—other work assignments can be found that result in this same cost.

2. The same staffing would be used every day. In fact, one would expect different patterns to present themselves on different days; for example, Fridays are usually much busier bank days than the others. In addition, the person hours required for each hour of the day are assumed to be deterministic. In a real situation, wide fluctuations will be experienced in a stochastic manner.

   The optimal solution results in a considerable amount of idle time, partly caused by the restriction that employees can start at the beginning of an hour and leave at the end. Eliminating this restriction might yield better results at the risk of increasing the problem size.

12

Linear Programming: The Simplex Method

LEARNING OBJECTIVES

After completing this chapter, students will be able to:

1. Convert LP constraints to equalities with slack, surplus, and artificial variables.
2. Set up and solve both maximization and minimization LP problems with simplex tableaus.
3. Interpret the meaning of every number in a simplex tableau.
4. Recognize cases of infeasibility, unboundedness, degeneracy, and multiple optimal solutions in a simplex output.

TEACHING SUGGESTIONS

Teaching Suggestion 12.1: Meaning of Slack Variables.

Slack variables have an important physical interpretation and represent a valuable commodity, such as unused labor, machine time, money, space, and so forth.

Teaching Suggestion 12.2: Initial Solutions to LP Problems.

Explain that all initial solutions begin with $X_1 = 0$, $X_2 = 0$ (that is, the real variables set to zero), and the slacks are the variables with nonzero values. Variables with values of zero are called *nonbasic* and those with nonzero values are said to be *basic*.

Teaching Suggestion 12.3: Substitution Rates in a Simplex Tableau.

Perhaps the most confusing pieces of information to interpret in a simplex tableau are "substitution rates." These numbers should be explained very clearly for the first tableau because they will have a clear physical meaning. Warn the students that in subsequent tableaus the interpretation is the same but will not be as clear because we are dealing with *marginal* rates of substitution.

Teaching Suggestion 12.4: Importance of Shadow Prices.

It pays to stress the interpretation and utility of shadow pricing. This issue arises again when examining tableaus in the next chapter.

Teaching Suggestion 12.5: Hand Calculations in a Simplex Tableau.

It is almost impossible to walk through even a small simplex problem (two variables, two constraints) without making at least one arithmetic error. This can be maddening for students who know what the correct solution should be but can't reach it. We suggest two tips:

1. Encourage students to also solve the assigned problem by computer and to request the detailed simplex output. They can now check their work at each iteration.
2. Stress the importance of interpreting the numbers in the tableau at each iteration. The 0s and 1s in the columns of the variables in the solutions are arithmetic checks and balances at each step.

Teaching Suggestion 12.6: Infeasibility Is a Major Problem in Large LP Problems.

As we noted in Teaching Suggestion 10.7, students should be aware that infeasibility commonly arises in large, real-world-sized problems. Section 12.10 in this chapter deals with how to spot the problem (and is very straightforward), but the real issue is how to correct the improper formulation. This is often a management issue.

VIDEO 12-1 (TIMS)

American Airlines' Use of Linear Programming. This interview of Thomas Cook appears on the same segment as Video 10-1.

ALTERNATE EXAMPLES

Alternate Example 12.1: Simplex Solution to Alternate Example 10.1 (see Chapter 10 for formulation and graphical solution).

1st iteration

$C_j \longrightarrow$	SOLUTION MIX	QUAN-TITY	3	9	0	0
$\downarrow$			X_1	X_2	S_1	S_2
0	S_1	24	1	4	1	0
0	S_2	16	1	2	0	1
	Z_j	0	0	0	0	0
	$C_j - Z_j$		3	9	0	0

2nd iteration

$C_j \longrightarrow$ $\downarrow$	SOLUTION MIX	QUANTITY	3	9	0	0
			X_1	X_2	S_1	S_2
9	X_2	6	$\frac{1}{4}$	1	$\frac{1}{4}$	0
0	S_2	4	$\frac{1}{2}$	0	$-\frac{1}{2}$	1
	Z_j	54	$\frac{9}{4}$	9	$\frac{9}{4}$	0
	$C_j - Z_j$		$\frac{3}{4}$	0	$-\frac{9}{4}$	0

This is not an optimum solution since the X_1 column contains a positive value. More profit remains ($\$\frac{3}{4}$ per #1).

3rd/final iteration

$C_j \longrightarrow$ $\downarrow$	SOLUTION MIX	QUANTITY	3	9	0	0
			X_1	X_2	S_1	S_2
9	X_2	4	0	1	$\frac{1}{2}$	$-\frac{1}{2}$
3	X_1	8	1	0	-1	2
	Z_j	60	3	9	$\frac{3}{2}$	$\frac{3}{2}$
	$C_j - Z_j$		0	0	$-\frac{3}{2}$	$-\frac{3}{2}$

This is an optimum solution since there are no positive values in the $C_j - Z_j$ row. This says to make 4 of item #2 and 8 of item #1 to get a profit of $60.

Alternate Example 12.2: Set up an initial simplex tableau, given the following two constraints and objective function:

$$2X_1 + 4X_2 \geq 8$$
$$3X_1 + 2X_2 \geq 6$$
$$8X_1 + 6X_2 = \text{MINIMIZE}$$

The constraints and objective function may be rewritten as:

$$8 = 2X_1 + 4X_2 - 1S_1 + 0S_2 + 1A_1 + 0A_2$$
$$6 = 3X_1 + 2X_2 + 0S_1 - 1S_2 + 0A_1 + 1A_2$$
$$\text{MINIMIZE} = 8X_1 + 6X_2 + 0S_1 + 0S_2 + MA_1 + MA_2$$

The tableau would be:

$C_j \longrightarrow$ $\downarrow$	SOLUTION MIX	QTY	8	6	0	0	M	M
			X_1	X_2	S_1	S_2	A_1	A_2
M	A_1	8	2	4	-1	0	1	0
M	A_2	6	3	2	0	-1	0	1
	Z_j	14M	5M	6M	$-M$	$-M$	M	M
	$C_j - Z_j$		8−5M	6−6M	M	M	0	0

$C_j \longrightarrow$ $\downarrow$	SOLUTION MIX	QTY	8	6	0	0	M	M
			X_1	X_2	S_1	S_2	A_1	A_2
6	S_2	2	$\frac{1}{2}$	1	$-\frac{1}{4}$	0	$\frac{1}{4}$	0
M	A_2	2	2	0	$\frac{1}{2}$	-1	$-\frac{1}{2}$	1
	Z_j	12+2M	3+2M	6	$-\frac{3}{2}+\frac{1}{2}M$	$-M$	$\frac{3}{2}-\frac{1}{2}M$	M
	$C_j - Z_j$		5−2M	0	$\frac{3}{2}-\frac{1}{2}M$	M	$-\frac{3}{2}+\frac{3}{2}M$	0

$C_j \longrightarrow$ $\downarrow$	SOLUTION MIX	QTY	8	6	0	0	M	M
			X_1	X_2	S_1	S_2	A_1	A_2
6	X_2	$\frac{3}{2}$	0	1	$-\frac{3}{8}$	$\frac{1}{4}$	$\frac{3}{8}$	$-\frac{1}{4}$
8	X_1	1	1	0	$\frac{1}{4}$	$-\frac{1}{2}$	$-\frac{1}{4}$	$\frac{1}{2}$
	Z_j	17	8	6	$-\frac{1}{4}$	$-\frac{5}{2}$	$\frac{1}{4}$	$\frac{5}{2}$
	$C_j - Z_j$		0	0	$\frac{1}{4}$	$\frac{5}{2}$	$M-\frac{1}{4}$	$M-\frac{5}{2}$

A minimal, optimum cost of 17 can be achieved by using 1 of a type #1 and $\frac{3}{2}$ of a type #2.

SOLUTIONS TO DISCUSSION QUESTIONS AND PROBLEMS

12-1. The purpose of the simplex method is to find the optimal solution to LP problems in a systematic and efficient manner. The procedures are described in detail in Section 12.6 of the chapter.

12-2. *Differences* between graphical and simplex methods: (1) Graphical method can be used only when two variables are in model; simplex can handle any dimensions. (2) Graphical method must evaluate all corner points (if the corner point method is used); simplex checks a lesser number of corners. (3) Simplex method can be automated and systematized. (4) Simplex method involves use of surplus, slack, and artificial variables but provides useful economic data as a by-product.

Similarities: (1) Both methods find the optimal solution at a corner point. (2) Both methods require a feasible region and the same problem structure, that is, objective function and constraints.

The graphical method is preferable when the problem has two variables and only two or three constraints (and when no computer is available).

12-3. Discussion of slack variables—see Section 12.2. Surplus and artificial variables—see Section 12.7.

12-4. The number of basic variables (that is, variables in the solution) is always equal to the number of constraints. So in this case there will be eight basic variables. A nonbasic variable is one that is not currently in the solution, that is, not listed in the solution mix column of the tableau. It should be noted that while there will be eight basic variables, the values of some of them may be zero.

12-5. *Pivot column:* Select the variable column with the largest positive $C_j - Z_j$ value (in a maximization problem) or largest negative $C_j - Z_j$ value (in a minimization problem).

Pivot row: Select the row with the smallest quantity-to-column ratio that is a nonnegative number.

Pivot number: Defined to be at the intersection of the pivot column and pivot row.

12-6. Maximization and minimization problems are quite similar in the application of the simplex method. Minimization problems usually include constraints necessitating artificial and surplus variables. In terms of technique, the $C_j - Z_j$ row is the main difference. In maximization problems, the greatest *positive* $C_j - Z_j$ indicates the new pivot column; in minimization problems, it's the greatest *negative* $C_j - Z_j$. The Z_j entry in the "quantity" column stands for profit contribution or cost, in maximization and minimization problems, respectively.

12-7. The minimum ratio criterion used to select the pivot row at each iteration is important because it gives the maximum number of units of the new variable that can enter the solution. By choosing the minimum ratio, we ensure feasibility at the next iteration. Without the rule, an infeasible solution may occur. It also prevents us from choosing negative or undefined (divided by zero) ratios.

12-8. The variable with the largest objective function coefficient should enter as the first "real" variable into the second tableau for a maximization problem. Hence, X_3 (with a value of $12) will enter first. In the minimization problem, the *least-cost* coefficient is X_1, with a $2.5 objective coefficient. X_1 will enter first.

12-9. If an artificial variable is in the final solution, the problem is infeasible. The person formulating the problem should look for the cause, usually conflicting constraints.

12-10. An optimal solution will still be reached if any positive $C_j - Z_j$ value is chosen. This procedure will result in a better (more profitable) solution at each iteration, but it may take more iterations before the optimum is reached.

12-11. **a.** See table below.
  b. $14X_1 + 4X_2 \leq 3{,}360$
     $10X_1 + 12X_2 \leq 9{,}600$
        $X_1, X_2 \geq 0$
  c. Maximization profit $= 900X_1 + 1{,}500X_2$
  d. Basis is $S_1 = 3{,}360$, $S_2 = 9{,}600$.
  e. X_2 should enter basis next.
  f. S_2 will leave next.
  g. 800 units of X_2 will be in the solution at the second tableau.

Table for Problem 12-11a.

$C_j \longrightarrow$ $\downarrow$	SOLU-TION MIX	QUAN-TITY	$900 X_1	$1{,}500 X_2	$0 S_1	$0 S_2
0	S_1	3,360	14	4	1	0
0	S_2	9,600	10	12	0	1
	Z_j	0	0	0	0	0
	$C_j - Z_j$		900	1500	0	0

12-12. **a.** Maximum earnings: $= .8X_1 + .4X_2 + 1.2X_3 - .1X_4 + 0S_1 + 0S_2 - MA_1 - MA_2$
Subject to:

$$X_1 + 2X_2 + X_3 + 5X_4 + S_1 \qquad\qquad = 150$$
$$X_2 - 4X_3 + 8X_4 \qquad\quad + A_1 \qquad = 70$$
$$6X_1 + 7X_2 + 2X_3 - X_4 \qquad - S_2 \qquad + A_2 = 120$$

Table for Problem 12-12b.

$C_j \longrightarrow$ $\downarrow$	SOLUTION MIX	QUANTITY	.8 X_1	.4 X_2	1.2 X_3	-.1 X_4	0 S_1	0 S_2	$-M$ A_1	$-M$ A_2
0	S_1	150	1	2	1	5	1	0	0	0
$-M$	A_1	70	0	1	-4	8	0	0	1	0
$-M$	A_2	120	6	7	2	-1	0	-1	0	1
	Z_j	$-190M$	$-6M$ $+.8$	$-8M$ $+.4$	$2M$ -1.2	$-7M$ $-.1$	0	M	$-M$	$-M$
	$C_j - Z_j$		$6M$	$8M$	$2M$	$7M$	0	$-M$	0	0

12-13. First tableau:

$C_j \longrightarrow$ ↓	SOLU-TION MIX	QUANTITY	$3 X_1	$5 X_2	$0 S_1	$0 S_2
$0	S_1	6	0	1	1	0
$0	S_2	18	3	2	0	1
	Z_j	$ 0	$0	$0	$0	$0
	$C_j - Z_j$		$3	$5	$0	$0

Second tableau:

$C_j \longrightarrow$ ↓	SOLU-TION MIX	QUANTITY	$3 X_1	$5 X_2	$0 S_1	$0 S_2
$5	X_2	6	0	1	1	0
$0	S_2	6	3	0	−2	1
	Z_j	$30	$0	$5	$5	$0
	$C_j - Z_j$		$3	$0	$−5	$0

Third tableau:

$C_j \longrightarrow$ ↓	SOLU-TION MIX	QUANTITY	$3 X_1	$5 X_2	$0 S_1	$0 S_2
$5	X_2	6	0	1	1	0
$3	X_1	2	1	0	$-\frac{2}{3}$	$\frac{1}{3}$
	Z_j	$36	$3	$5	$3	$1
	$C_j - Z_j$		$0	$0	$−3	$−1

$X_1 = 2$, $X_2 = 6$, $S_1 = 0$, $S_2 = 0$, and profit = $36

Graphical solution:

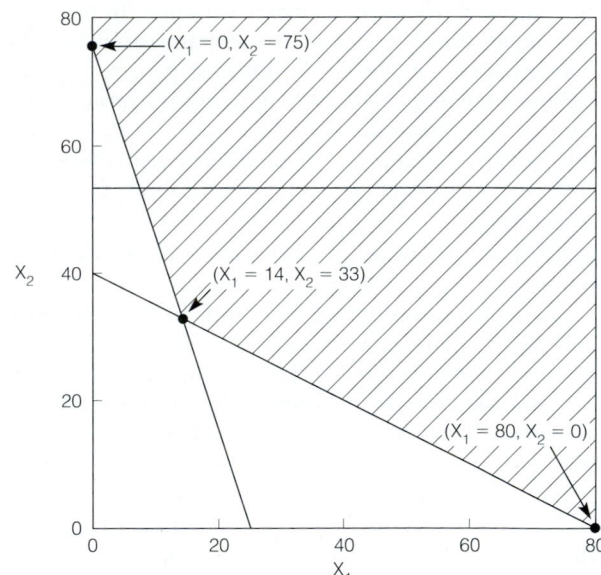

2nd CORNER POINT OF SIMPLEX

(OPTIMAL CORNER POINT OF SIMPLEX)
($X_1 = 2$, $X_2 = 6$; PROFIT = $36)

1st CORNER POINT OF SIMPLEX

12-14. AB:QM is used to solve this problem. The print-out on page IS-127 indicates that $x_1 = 50$, $x_2 = 0$, and profit = $1,000.

12-15. Basis for first tableau: $A_1 = 80$
$\qquad\qquad A_2 = 75$
$\qquad (X_1 = 0, X_2 = 0, S_1 = 0, S_2 = 0)$
Second tableau: $\qquad A_1 = 55$
$\qquad\qquad X_1 = 25$
$\qquad (X_2 = 0, S_1 = 0, S_2 = 0, A_2 = 0)$
Third tableau: $\qquad X_1 = 14$
$\qquad\qquad X_2 = 33$
$\qquad (S_1 = 0, S_2 = 0, A_1 = 0, A_2 = 0)$
Cost = 221 at optimal solution

Graphical solution:

($X_1 = 0$, $X_2 = 75$)

($X_1 = 14$, $X_2 = 33$)

($X_1 = 80$, $X_2 = 0$)

12-16. This problem is infeasible. All $C_j - Z_j$ are 0 or negative, but an artificial variable remains in the basis.

12-17. At the second iteration, the following simplex tableau is found:

$C_j \longrightarrow$ ↓	SOLU-TION MIX	QUANTITY	6 X_1	3 X_2	0 S_1	0 S_2
6	X_1	1	1	−1	$\frac{1}{2}$	0
0	S_2	2	0	0	$\frac{1}{2}$	1
	Z_j	6	6	−6	3	0
	$C_j - Z_j$		0	9	−3	0

At this point, X_2 should enter the basis next. But the two ratios are $1/-1$ = negative and $2/0$ = undefined. Since there is no nonnegative ratio, the problem is *unbounded*.

Printout for Problem 12-14:

```
Program: Linear Programming

Problem Title: PROBLEM 12.14

***** Input Data *****

Max.  Z =   20x1 + 10x2

Subject to

C1  5x1 + 4x2 <= 250
C2  2x1 + 5x2 <= 150

***** Program Output *****

Simplex Tableau: 0
```

\Cj			20.000	10.000	0.000	0.000
Cb \	Basis	Bi	x 1	x 2	s 1	s 2
0.000	s 1	250.000	5.000	4.000	1.000	0.000
0.000	s 2	150.000	2.000	5.000	0.000	1.000
	Zj	0.000	0.000	0.000	0.000	0.000
	Cj-Zj		20.000	10.000	0.000	0.000

```
Simplex Tableau: 1
```

\Cj			20.000	10.000	0.000	0.000
Cb \	Basis	Bi	x 1	x 2	s 1	s 2
20.000	x 1	50.000	1.000	0.800	0.200	0.000
0.000	s 2	50.000	0.000	3.400	-0.400	1.000
	Zj	1000.000	20.000	16.000	4.000	0.000
	Cj-Zj		0.000	-6.000	-4.000	0.000

```
Final Optimal Solution

Z = 1000.000
```

Variable	Value	Reduced Cost
x 1	50.000	0.000
x 2	0.000	6.000

Constraint	Slack/Surplus	Shadow Price
C 1	0.000	4.000
C 2	50.000	0.000

12-18. a. The optimal solution using simplex is $X_1 = 3$, $X_2 = 0$. ROI = \$6. This is illustrated in the problem's final simplex tableau below:

$C_j \longrightarrow$	SOLU-TION MIX	QUAN-TITY	2	3	0	0	$-M$
$\downarrow$			X_1	X_2	S_1	S_2	A_1
0	S_1	6	0	$7/2$	$3/2$	1	-1
2	X_1	3	1	$3/2$	$1/2$	0	0
	Z_j	\$6	2	3	1	0	0
	$C_j - Z_j$		0	0	-1	0	$-M$

b. The variable X_2 has a $C_j - Z_j$ value of \$0, indicating an alternate optimal solution exists by inserting X_2 into the basis.

c. The alternate optimal solution is found in the tableau below to be $X_1 = 3/7 = .42$, $X_2 = 12/7 = 1.7$, ROI = \$6.

$C_j \longrightarrow$	SOLU-TION MIX	QUAN-TITY	2	3	0	0	$-M$
$\downarrow$			X_1	X_2	S_1	S_2	A_1
3	X_2	$12/7$	0	1	$1/7$	$2/21$	$-2/7$
2	X_1	$3/7$	1	0	$-1/21$	$-1/7$	$3/7$
	Z_j	\$6	2	3	$1/3$	0	0
	$C_j - Z_j$		0	0	$-1/3$	0	$-M$

d. The graphical solution is shown below:

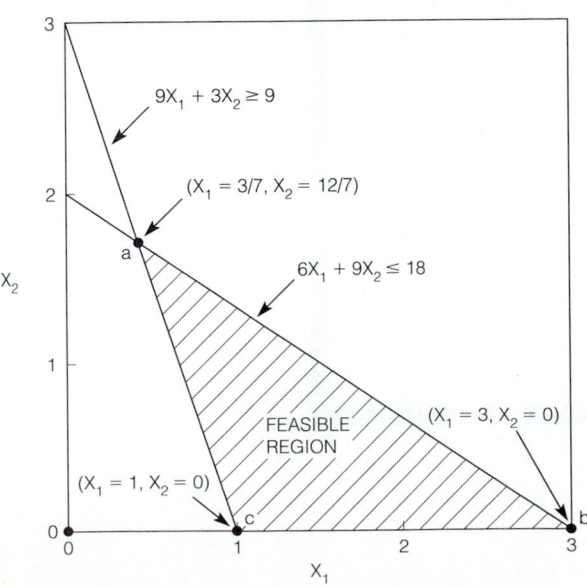

Alternate optimum at a and b, $Z = \$6$.

12-19. This problem is degenerate. Variable X_2 should enter the solution next. But the ratios are as follows:

$$X_3 \text{ row } \frac{5}{1} = 5$$

$$X_1 \text{ row } \frac{12}{-3} = \text{unacceptable}$$

$$S_2 \text{ row } \frac{10}{2} = 5$$

Since X_3 and S_2 are *tied*, we can select one at random, in this case S_2. The optimal solution is shown below. It is $X_1 = 27$, $X_2 = 5$, $X_3 = 0$, Profit = \$177.

$C_j \longrightarrow$	SOLU-TION MIX	QUAN-TITY	6	3	5	0	0	0
$\downarrow$			X_1	X_2	X_3	S_1	S_2	S_3
\$5	X_3	0	0	0	1	$1/2$	$-1/2$	$7/2$
\$6	X_1	27	1	0	0	$3/2$	$3/2$	$-1/2$
\$3	X_2	5	0	1	0	$1/2$	$1/2$	$-1/2$
	Z_j	\$177	6	3	5	13	8	13
	$C_j - Z_j$		0	0	0	-13	-8	-13

12-20. Minimum cost $= 50X_1 + 10X_2 + 75X_3 + 0S_1 + MA_1 + MA_2$

Subject to:
$$1X_1 - 1X_2 + 0X_3 + 0S_1 + 1A_1 + 0A_2 = 1,000$$
$$0X_1 - 2X_2 + 2X_3 + 0S_1 + 0A_1 + 1A_2 = 2,000$$
$$1X_1 + 0X_2 + 0X_3 + 1S_1 + 0A_1 + 0A_2 = 1,500$$

First iteration:

$C_j \rightarrow$	SOLUTION MIX	QUANTITY	50 X_1	10 X_2	75 X_3	0 S_1	M A_1	M A_2
M	A_1	1,000	1	-1	0	0	1	0
M	A_2	2,000	0	-2	2	0	0	1
0	S_1	1,500	1	0	0	1	0	0
	Z_j	3,000M	M	M	$2M$	0	M	M
	$C_j - Z_j$		$-M + 50$	$-M + 10$	$-2M + 75$	0	0	0

Second iteration:

$C_j \rightarrow$	SOLUTION MIX	QUANTITY	50 X_1	10 X_2	75 X_3	0 S_1	M A_1	M A_2
M	A_1	1,000	1	-1	0	0	1	0
75	X_3	1,000	0	1	1	0	0	½
0	S_1	1,500	1	0	0	1	0	0
	Z_j	1,000M + 75,000	M	$-M + 75$	75	0	M	37½
	$C_j - Z_j$		$-M + 50$	$M - 65$	0	0	0	$M - 37½$

Third iteration:

$C_j \rightarrow$	SOLUTION MIX	QUANTITY	50 X_1	10 X_2	75 X_3	0 S_1	M A_1	M A_2
50	X_1	1,000	1	-1	0	0	1	0
75	X_3	1,000	0	1	1	0	0	½
0	S_1	500	0	1	0	1	-1	0
	Z_j	$125,000	50	25	75	0	50	37½
	$C_j - Z_j$		0	-15	0	0	$M - 50$	$M - 37½$

Fourth and final iteration:

$C_j \rightarrow$	SOLUTION MIX	QUANTITY	50 X_1	10 X_2	75 X_3	0 S_1	M A_1	M A_2
50	X_1	1,500	1	0	0	1	0	0
75	X_3	500	0	0	1	-1	1	½
10	X_2	500	0	1	0	1	-1	0
	Z_j	$117,500	50	10	75	-15	65	37½
	$C_j - Z_j$		0	0	0	15	$M - 65$	$M - 37½$

$X_1 = 1500$, $X_2 = 500$, $X_3 = 500$, $C = \$117,500$

12-21. X_1 = number of kilograms of brand A added to
    each batch
  X_2 = number of kilograms of brand B added to
    each batch
  Minimize costs = $9X_1 + 15X_2 + 0S_1 + 0S_2 +$
        $MA_1 + MA_2$

Subject to: $X_1 + 2X_2 - S_1 + A_1 = 30$
    $X_1 + 4X_2 - S_2 + A_2 = 80$

First iteration:

$C_j \longrightarrow$ ↓	SOLUTION MIX	QUANTITY	$9 X_1	$15 X_2	$0 S_1	$0 S_2	M A_1	M A_2
M	A_1	30	1	2	−1	0	1	0
M	A_2	80	1	4	0	−1	0	1
	Z_j	110M	2M	6M	−M	−M	M	M
	$C_j - Z_j$		−2M + 9	−6M + 15	M	M	0	0

Second iteration:

$C_j \longrightarrow$ ↓	SOLUTION MIX	QUANTITY	$9 X_1	$15 X_2	$0 S_1	$0 S_2	M A_1	M A_2
15	X_2	15	½	1	− ½	0	½	0
M	A_2	20	−1	0	2	−1	−2	1
	Z_j	225 + 20M	$15⁄2$ − M	15	− $15⁄2$ + 2M	−M	$15⁄2$ − 2M	M
	$C_j - Z_j$		¾ + M	0	$15⁄2$ − 2M	M	3M − $15⁄2$	0

Third and final iteration:

$C_j \longrightarrow$ ↓	SOLUTION MIX	QUANTITY	$9 X_1	$15 X_2	$0 S_1	$0 S_2	M A_1	M A_2
15	X_2	20	¼	1	0	− ¼	0	¼
0	S_1	10	− ½	0	1	− ½	−1	½
	Z_j	$300	$15⁄4$	15	4	− $15⁄4$	0	$15⁄4$
	$C_j - Z_j$		$21⁄4$	0	0	$15⁄4$	M	M − $15⁄4$

X_1 = 0 kg., X_2 = 20 kg., cost = $300

12-22. X_1 = number of mattresses
  X_2 = number of box springs
  Minimize cost = $20X_1 + 24X_2$
  Subject to: $X_1 + X_2 \geq 30$
        $X_1 + 2X_2 \geq 40$

Initial tableau:

| $C_j \longrightarrow$ | SOLUTION MIX | QUANTITY | $20 | $24 | $0 | $0 | M | M |
			X_1	X_2	S_1	S_2	A_1	A_2
M	A_1	30	1	1	-1	0	1	0
M	A_2	40	1	2	0	-1	0	1
	Z_j	$70M$	$2M$	$3M$	$-M$	$-M$	M	M
	$C_j - Z_j$		$-2M + 20$	$-3M + 24$	M	M	0	0

Second tableau:

| $C_j \longrightarrow$ | SOLUTION MIX | QUANTITY | $20 | $24 | $0 | $0 | M | M |
			X_1	X_2	S_1	S_2	A_1	A_2
M	A_1	10	½	0	-1	½	1	$-$½
$24	X_2	20	½	1	0	$-$½	0	½
	Z_j	$10M + 480$	$\frac{1}{2}M + 12$	24	$-M$	$\frac{1}{2}M - 12$	0	$-\frac{1}{2}M + 12$
	$C_j - Z_j$		$-\frac{1}{2}M + 12$	0	M	$-\frac{1}{2}M + 12$	0	$\frac{3}{2}M - 12$

Final tableau:

| $C_j \longrightarrow$ | SOLUTION MIX | QUANTITY | $20 | $24 | $0 | $0 | M | M |
			X_1	X_2	S_1	S_2	A_1	A_2
$20	X_1	20	1	0	-2	1	2	-1
$24	X_2	10	0	1	1	-1	-1	1
	Z_j	$640	20	24	-16	-4	16	4
	$C_j - Z_j$		0	0	16	4	$M - 16$	$M - 4$

$X_1 = 20, X_2 = 10, \text{Cost} = \$640$

12-23. Maximize profit $= 9X_1 + 12X_2$
Subject to: $X_1 + X_2 \leq 10$
$X_1 + 2X_2 \leq 12$

Initial tableau:

| $C_j \longrightarrow$ | SOLUTION MIX | QUANTITY | $9 | $12 | $0 | $0 |
			X_1	X_2	S_1	S_2
$0	S_1	10	1	1	1	0
$0	S_2	12	1	2	0	1
	Z_j	$0	0	0	0	0
	$C_j - Z_j$		9	12	0	0

Second tableau:

| $C_j \longrightarrow$ | SOLUTION MIX | QUANTITY | $9 | $12 | $0 | $0 |
			X_1	X_2	S_1	S_2
$0	S_1	4	½	0	1	$-$½
$12	X_2	6	½	1	0	½
	Z_j	$72	6	12	0	6
	$C_j - Z_j$		3	0	0	-6

Final tableau:

$C_j \longrightarrow$ $\downarrow$	SOLUTION MIX	QUANTITY	$9 X_1	$12 X_2	$0 S_1	$0 S_2
$4	X_1	8	1	0	2	−1
$12	X_2	2	0	1	−1	1
	Z_j	$96	9	12	6	3
	$C_j - Z_j$		0	0	−6	−3

$X_1 = 8$, $X_2 = 2$, Profit $= \$96$

12-24. Maximize profit $= 8X_1 + 6X_2 + 14X_3$

Subject to: $2X_1 + X_2 + 3X_3 \leq 120$
$2X_1 + 6X_2 + 4X_3 = 240$

Initial Tableau:

$C_j \longrightarrow$ $\downarrow$	SOLUTION MIX	QUANTITY	$8 X_1	$6 X_2	$14 X_3	0 S_1	$-M$ A_1
0	S_1	120	2	1	3	1	0
$-M$	A_2	240	2	6	4	0	1
	Z_j	$-240M$	$-2M$	$-6M$	$-4M$	0	$-M$
	$C_j - Z_j$		$8 + 2M$	$6 + 6M$	$14 + 4M$	0	0

Second Tableau:

$C_j \longrightarrow$ $\downarrow$	SOLUTION MIX	QUANTITY	$8 X_1	$6 X_2	$14 X_3	0 S_1	$-M$ A_1
$0	S_1	80	$\frac{5}{3}$	0	$\frac{7}{3}$	1	$-\frac{1}{6}$
$6	X_2	40	$\frac{1}{3}$	1	$\frac{2}{3}$	0	$\frac{1}{6}$
	Z_j	$240	2	6	4	0	1
	$C_j - Z_j$		6	0	10	0	$-M - 1$

Final Tableau:

$C_j \longrightarrow$ $\downarrow$	SOLUTION MIX	QUANTITY	$8 X_1	$6 X_2	$14 X_3	0 S_1	$-M$ A_1
$14	X_3	$\frac{240}{7}$	$\frac{5}{7}$	0	1	$\frac{3}{7}$	$-\frac{1}{14}$
$6	X_2	$\frac{120}{7}$	$-\frac{1}{7}$	1	0	$-\frac{2}{7}$	$\frac{3}{14}$
	Z_j	$582\frac{6}{7}$	$\frac{64}{7}$	6	14	$\frac{30}{7}$	$+\frac{2}{7}$
	$C_j - Z_j$		−1.1	0	0	$-\frac{30}{7}$	$-M - \frac{2}{7}$

$X_1 = 0$, $X_2 = \dfrac{120}{7}$, $X_3 = \dfrac{240}{7}$, $P = \$582\frac{6}{7}$

(which is $X_1 = 0$, $X_2 = 17.14$, $X_3 = 34.29$,
$P = \$582.86$)

12-25. a.

X_1 = number of deluxe 1-bedroom units converted
X_2 = number of regular 1-bedroom units converted
X_3 = number of deluxe studios converted
X_4 = number of efficiencies converted
Objective: Maximum profit = $8,000X_1 + 6,000X_2 + 5,000X_3 + 3,500X_4$

Subject to:

$$1,100X_1 + 1,000X_2 + 600X_3 + 500X_4 \leq \$35,000$$
$$700X_1 + 600X_2 + 400X_3 + 300X_4 \leq \$28,000$$
$$2,000X_1 + 1,600X_2 + 1,200X_3 + 900X_4 \leq \$45,000$$
$$1,000X_1 + 400X_2 + 900X_3 + 200X_4 \leq \$19,000$$
$$X_1 + X_2 + X_3 + X_4 \leq 50$$
$$X_1 + X_2 + X_3 + X_4 \geq 25$$
$$X_1 + X_2 \geq .40(X_1 + X_2 + X_3 + X_4)$$
$$X_1 + X_2 \leq .70(X_1 + X_2 + X_3 + X_4)$$

These two constraints can be rewritten as:

$$.6X_1 + .6X_2 - .4X_3 - .4X_4 \geq 0$$
$$.3X_1 + .3X_2 - .7X_3 - .7X_4 \leq 0$$

b. Maximize profit = $8,000X_1 + 6,000X_2 + 5,000X_3 + 3,500X_4 + 0S_1 + 0S_2 + 0S_3 + 0S_4 + 0S_5 + 0S_6 + 0S_7 + 0S_8 - MA_1 - MA_2$

Subject to:

$$1,100X_1 + 1,000X_2 + 600X_3 + 500X_4 + S_1 = 35,000$$
$$700X_1 + 600X_2 + 400X_3 + 300X_4 + S_2 = 28,000$$
$$2,000X_1 + 1,600X_2 + 1,200X_3 + 900X_4 + S_3 = 45,000$$
$$1,000X_1 + 400X_2 + 900X_3 + 200X_4 + S_4 = 19,000$$
$$X_1 + X_2 + X_3 + X_4 + S_5 = 50$$
$$X_1 + X_2 + X_3 + X_4 - S_6 + A_1 = 25$$
$$.6X_1 + .6X_2 - .4X_3 - .4X_4 - S_7 + A_2 = 0$$
$$.3X_1 + .3X_2 - .7X_3 - .7X_4 + S_8 = 0$$

12-26. a. The initial formulation is:

Minimize cost = $\$12X_1 + 18X_2 + 10X_3 + 20X_4 + 7X_5 + 8X_6$

Subject to:

$$X_1 - 3X_3 = 100$$
$$25X_2 + X_3 + 2X_4 + 8X_5 \leq 900$$
$$2X_1 + X_2 + 4X_4 + X_6 \geq 250$$
$$18X_1 - 15X_2 - 2X_3 - X_4 + 15X_5 \geq 150$$
$$25X_6 \leq 300$$
$$2X_4 + 6X_5 \geq 70$$

b. Variable X_5 will enter the basis next. (Its $C_j - Z_j$ value is the largest negative number, that is, $-21M + 7$.) Variable A_3 will leave the basis because its ratio (150/15) is the smallest of the three positive ratios.

Solution to Coastal States Chemicals and Fertilizers Case

1. a. For a 20% natural gas curtailment, objective function:

Maximum profit = $60X_1 + 80X_2 + 90X_3 + 100X_4 + 50X_5 + 50X_6 + 65X_7 + 70X_8$

where phosphoric acid $= X_1$
urea $= X_2$
ammonium phosphate $= X_3$
ammonium nitrate $= X_4$
chlorine $= X_5$
caustic soda $= X_6$
vinyl chloride monomer $= X_7$ and
hydrofluoric acid $= X_8$.

Subject to:

Demand constraints:
$$X_1 \leq 320$$
$$X_2 \leq 200$$
$$X_3 \leq 270$$
$$X_4 \leq 300$$
$$X_5 \leq 480$$
$$X_6 \leq 600$$
$$X_7 \leq 300$$
$$X_8 \leq 320$$

20% gas curtailment:

$$5.5X_1 + 7.0X_2 + 8.0X_3 + 10.0X_4 + 15.0X_5 + 16.0X_6 + 12.0X_7 + 11.0X_8 \leq 28,800$$

Note: 36,000 cu. ft. $\times 10^3 \times .80 = 28,800$ cu. ft. $\times 10^3$

For the simplex method, insert a slack variable in each of the nine constraints above.

The problem requires nine tableaus before reaching the optimal solution. With a 20% natural gas curtailment, the following is the production schedule (tons/day):

$$X_1 = 320$$
$$X_2 = 200$$
$$X_3 = 270$$
$$X_4 = 300$$
$$X_5 = 480$$
$$X_6 = 385$$
$$X_7 = 300$$
$$X_8 = 320$$

Objective function = $174,650.00

b. For a 40% percent natural gas curtailment, objective function and demand constraints are the same as for a 20% curtailment. The natural gas constraint is:

$$5.5X_1 + 7.0X_2 + 8.0X_3 + 10.0X_4 + 15.0X_5 + 16.0X_6 + 12.0X_7 + 11.0X_8 \leq 21,600$$

where 36,000 cu. ft. $\times 10^3 \times .60 = 21,600$ cu. ft.

The problem requires eight tableaus before reaching the optimal solution. With a 40% natural gas curtailment, the following is the production schedule (tons/day):

$X_1 = 320$
$X_2 = 200$
$X_3 = 270$
$X_4 = 300$
$X_5 = 410.67$
$X_6 = \ \ \ 0$
$X_7 = 300$
$X_8 = 320$

Objective function value = $151,933.00

Technical note: Chlorine, X_5, and caustic soda, X_6, are coproducts from electrolytic cell operation. For every ton of chlorine produced, approximately 1.1 tons of caustic soda are produced. Hence, alternative disposal methods must be investigated for the caustic soda from the cells prior to a shut down of the caustic soda processing plant.

2. Obviously, those products that have high energy consumption factors must undergo extensive scrutiny to conserve energy. These products include chlorine (15.0) and caustic soda (16.0). Energy consumption is high for these chemicals because they are produced by electrolytic cell operation. The caustic soda also requires extensive steamheated evaporation beyond production at the cells. Energy conservation measures include elimination of steam leaks as well as electrical grounds and proper insulation of equipment.

3. These products are all produced by large volume, capital-intensive plants. Emergency shutdowns often result in loss of raw materials, pollution, potential personnel hazards, and equipment damage. These plants are staffed for normal operations, and emergency rate reductions often require operator manpower beyond normal staffing. Consequently, these plants may be "out of control" during unplanned and drastic rate reductions.

4. Normal profit: $185,400/day

  With 20% curtailment: $174,650/day
  With 40% curtailment: $151,933/day

13
Linear Programming: Sensitivity Analysis and Duality

LEARNING OBJECTIVES

After completing this chapter, students will be able to:

1. Understand the role of sensitivity analysis from a technical and a managerial perspective.
2. Understand the relationship between the primal and dual and when to formulate and use the dual.
3. Solve problems by computer and interpret LP computer programs including AB:QM, LINDO, STORM, and What's*Best!*

TEACHING SUGGESTIONS

Teaching Suggestion 13.1: Importance of Sensitivity Analysis.

Sensitivity analysis should be stressed as one of the most important LP issues. (Actually, the issue should arise for discussion with every model). Here, the issue is the source of data. When accountants tell you a profit contribution is $8.50 per unit, is that figure accurate within 10% or within 10¢? The solution to an LP problem can change dramatically if the input parameters are not exact. Mention that sensitivity analysis also has other names, such as right-hand-side ranging, post-optimality analysis, and parametric programming.

Teaching Suggestion 13.2: Changes in Technological Coefficients.

Advanced management science books provide a mathematical treatment of sensitivity analysis for technological coefficients. But we find the technical treatment to be beyond the abilities of most students, so we treat the issue graphically instead. See Figure 13.3. This visual treatment is more intuitively appealing to students. Transparency Master 13-3 is available to help make the point.

Teaching Suggestion 13.3: Advantage of Duality and Its Role as an LP Topic.

Duality's utility has centered on its computational advantage (when solving problems with few variables but many constraints by hand) and its economic information (opportunity cost). But in this day of speedy software, students are less likely to need to convert a problem to its dual in order to be able to solve it more easily. Consequently, many professors view duality as an optional topic in a crowded quantitative analysis course.

Teaching Suggestion 13.4: Use of Software in Solving LP Problems.

Programs 13.1, 13.2, 13.3, and 13.4 provide a useful side-by-side comparison of the High Note Sound Company problem solved by AB:QM, LINDO, STORM, and What's*Best!* Solved Problem 13-1 is also solved by LINDO and Problem 13-27 involves an interpretation of an AB:QM printout. It's important that students feel comfortable with different formats and that they can interpret the output of each program with ease. You can stress the critical role of software in solving problems today and then mention the mainframe packages. Refer the students back to Chapter 12's treatment of Karmarkar's method and the reason (large-size problems) why it is so important.

ALTERNATE EXAMPLES

Alternate Example 13.1: Referring back to Hal, in Alternate Example 10.1, we had a formulation of:

Maximize Profit = $3X_1$ + $9X_2$

Subject to: $1X_1 + 4X_2 \leq 24$ clay
$1X_1 + 2X_2 \leq 16$ glaze

Where X_1 = small vases made
X_2 = large vases made

The optimal solution was $X_1 = 8$, $X_2 = +$, Profit = $60

Using AB:QM (see the accompanying printout on page IS-136), we can perform a variety of sensitivity analyses on this solution.

Alternate Example 13.2: Levine Micros assembles both laptop and desktop personal computers. Each laptop yields $160 in profit; each desktop $200.

The firm's LP primal is:

Maximize profit = $160X_1$ + $200X_2$
subject to:

$1X_1 + 2X_2 \leq 20$ labor hours
$9X_1 + 9X_2 \leq 108$ RAM chips
$12X_1 + 6X_2 \leq \$120$ royalty fees

where X_1 = no. laptops assembled daily
X_2 = no. desktops assembled daily

Here is the primal optimal solution and final simplex tableau.

$C_j \rightarrow$	SOLUTION MIX	$160 X_1	$200 X_2	0 S_1	0 S_2	0 S_3	QUANTITY
200	X_2	0	1	1	$-\frac{1}{9}$	0	8
160	X_1	1	0	-1	$\frac{2}{9}$	0	4
0	S_3	0	0	6	-2	1	24
	Z_j	160	200	40	$13\frac{1}{3}$	0	$2,240
	$C_j - Z_j$	0	0	-40	$-13\frac{1}{3}$	0	

or $X_1 = 4$, $X_2 = 8$, $S_3 = \$24$ in slack royalty fees paid

Profit = $2,240/day

Here is the *dual* formulation:

Minimize $Z = 20y_1 + 108y_2 + 120y_3$
subject to:

$1y_1 + 9y_2 + 12y_3 \geq 160$
$2y_1 + 9y_2 + 6y_3 \geq 200$

Here is the dual optimal solution and final tableau.

$C_j \rightarrow$	SOLUTION MIX	20 y_1	108 y_2	120 y_3	0 S_1	0 S_2	QUANTITY
108	y_2	0	1	2	$-\frac{2}{9}$	$\frac{1}{9}$	$13\frac{1}{3}$
20	y_1	1	0	-6	1	-1	40
	Z_j	20	108	96	-4	-8	2,240
	$C_j - Z_j$	0	0	$+24$	$+4$	$+8$	

This means

y_1 = marginal value of one more labor hour = $40
y_2 = marginal value of one more RAM chip = $13.33
y_3 = marginal value of one more $1 in royalty fees
   = $0

SOLUTIONS TO DISCUSSION QUESTIONS AND PROBLEMS

13-1. For a discussion of the role and importance of sensitivity analysis in linear programming refer to Section 13-2 of the chapter. It is especially needed when values of the technological coefficients and contribution rates are estimated—a common situation. When all model values are deterministic, that is, known with certainty, sensitivity analysis from the perspective of evaluating parameter accuracy may not be needed. This may be the case in a portfolio selection model in

```
Program: Linear Programming

Problem Title: Alternate Example 13.1

***** Input Data *****

Max. Z = 3x1 + 9x2

Subject to

C1   1x1 + 4x2 <= 24
C2   1x1 + 2x2 <= 16

***** Program Output *****

Simplex Tableau : 2
      \Cj                    3.000     9.000     0.000     0.000
      Cb\      Basis    Bi   x 1       x 2       s 1       s 2
    --------------------------------------------------------------
      9.000    x 2    4.000  0.000     1.000     0.500    -0.500
      3.000    x 1    8.000  1.000     0.000    -1.000     2.000
    --------------------------------------------------------------
               Zj    60.000  3.000     9.000     1.500     1.500
               Cj-Zj         0.000     0.000    -1.500    -1.500

Final Optimal Solution

Z = 60.000

-----------------------------------------------
 Variable          Value       Reduced Cost
-----------------------------------------------
  x 1              8.000          0.000
  x 2              4.000          0.000
-----------------------------------------------
Constraint     Slack/Surplus   Shadow Price
-----------------------------------------------
  C 1              0.000          1.500
  C 2              0.000          1.500
-----------------------------------------------
```

Objective Coefficient Ranges

Variables	Lower Limit	Current Values	Upper Limit	Allowable Increase	Allowable Decrease
x 1	2.250	3.000	4.500	1.500	0.750
x 2	6.000	9.000	12.000	3.000	3.000

Right-Hand-Side Ranges

Constraints	Lower Limit	Current Values	Upper Limit	Allowable Increase	Allowable Decrease
C 1	16.000	24.000	32.000	8.000	8.000
C 2	12.000	16.000	24.000	8.000	4.000

which we select from among a series of bonds whose returns and cash-in values are set for long periods.

13-2. Sensitivity analysis is important in all quantitative modeling techniques. Especially common is the analysis of inventory model results in which we test the model's sensitivity to changes in demand, lead time, cost, and so forth.

13-3. Shadow prices are discussed in detail in Section 13-2. The solutions to the U_i dual variables are the primal's shadow prices. In the primal, the negatives of the $C_j - Z_j$ values in the slack variable columns are the shadow prices.

13-4. The student is to create his or her own data and LP formulation. (a) The meaning of the right-hand-side numbers (resources) is to be explained. (b) The meaning of the constraint coefficient (in terms of how many units of each resource that each product requires) is also to be explained. (c) The problem is to be graphically solved. (d) A simple sensitivity analysis is to be conducted by changing the contribution rate (C_j value) of the X_1 variable. For example, if C_1 was $10 as the problem was originally formulated, the student should resolve with a $15 value and compare solutions.

13-5. A change in a technological coefficient changes the feasible solution region. An increase means that each unit produced requires more of a scarce resource (and may lower the optimal profit). A decrease means that, because of a technological advancement or other reason, less of a resource is needed to produce one unit. Changes in resource availability also change the feasible region shape and can increase or decrease profit.

13-6. The dual will have eight constraints and twelve variables.

13-7. See Section 13.3 of the chapter.

13-8. The student is to write his or her own LP primal problem of the form:

Maximize profit = $C_1X_1 + C_2X_2$
Subject to = $A_{11}X_1 + A_{12}X_2 \leq B_1$
$\qquad\qquad A_{21}X_1 + A_{22}X_2 \leq B_2$

and for a dual of the nature:

Minimize cost = $B_1U_1 + B_2U_2$
Subject to = $A_{11}U_1 + A_{21}U_2 \geq C_1$
$\qquad\qquad A_{12}U_1 + A_{22}U_2 \geq C_2$

13-9. The computer is valuable in (1) solving LP problems quickly and accurately; (2) solving large problems that might take days or months by hand; (3) performing extensive sensitivity analysis automatically; and (4) allowing a manager to try several ideas, models, or data sets.

13-10. Using the iso-profit line or corner point method, we see that point *b* is optimal if the profit = $3X_1 +$ $2X_2$. If the profit changes to $4.50 per unit of X_1, the optimal solution shifts to point *c*. If the objective function becomes $P = $3X_1 + $3X_2$, the corner point *b* remains optimal.

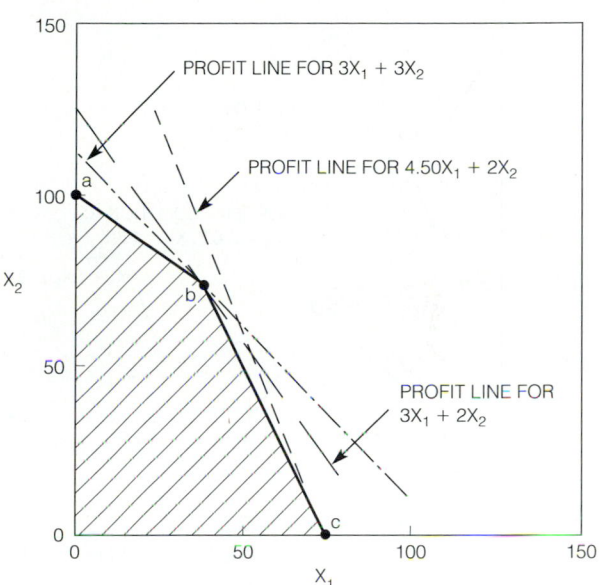

13-11. The optimal solution of $26 profit lies at the point $X_1 = 2$, $X_2 = 3$.

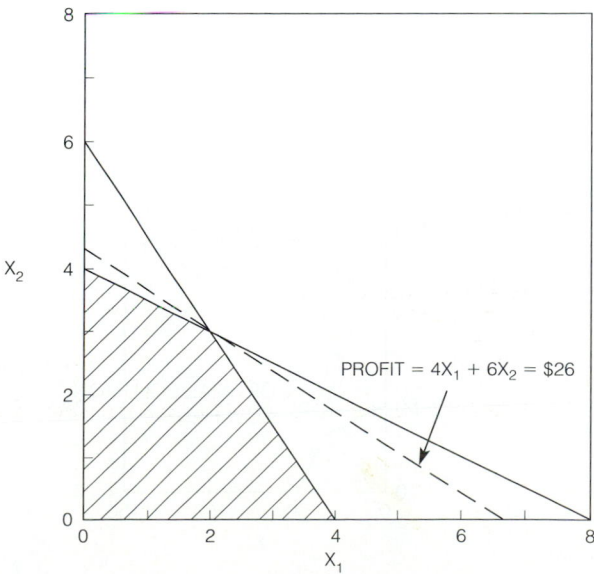

If the first constraint is altered to $1X_1 + 3X_2 \leqq 8$, the feasible region and optimal solution shift considerably, as seen below:

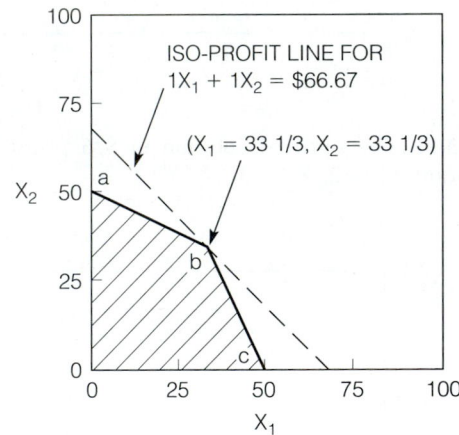

PROFIT = $4X_1 + 6X_2 = \$20\ 2/7$

OPTIMAL SOLUTION AT
$X_1 = 2\ 6/7, X_2 = 1\ 5/7$

$1X_1 + 3X_2 = 8$

13-12. a.

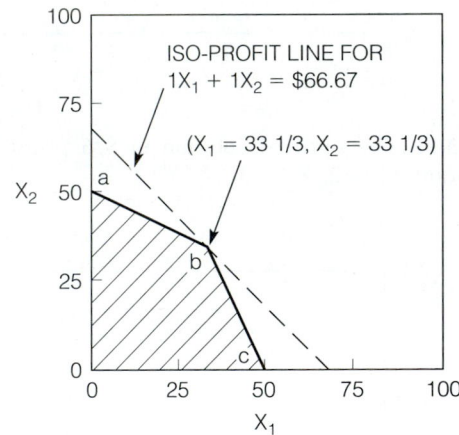

ISO-PROFIT LINE FOR
$1X_1 + 1X_2 = \$66.67$

$(X_1 = 33\ 1/3, X_2 = 33\ 1/3)$

a

b

c

b.

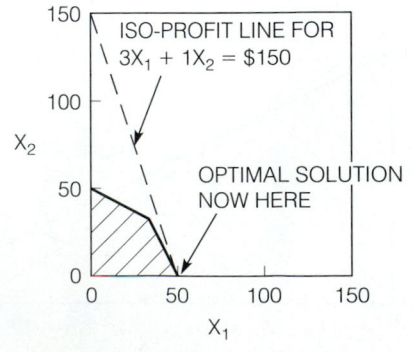

ISO-PROFIT LINE FOR
$3X_1 + 1X_2 = \$150$

OPTIMAL SOLUTION
NOW HERE

c. If X_1's profit coefficient was overestimated, but should only have been \$1.25, it is easy to see graphically that the solution at point b remains optimal.

13-13.

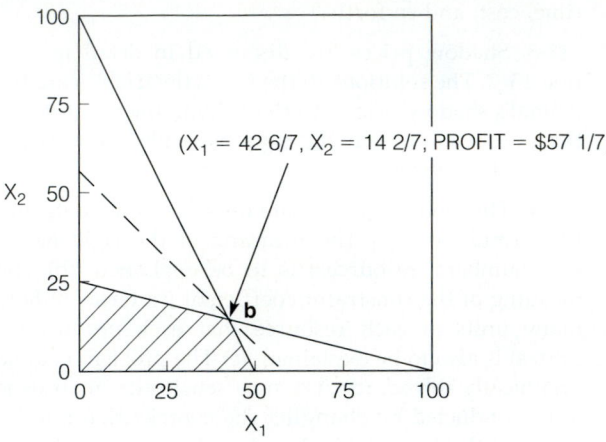

$(X_1 = 42\ 6/7, X_2 = 14\ 2/7; \text{PROFIT} = \$57\ 1/7)$

b

The optimal solution is at point b, but profit has decreased from \$66⅔ to \$57⅐, and the solution has changed considerably.

13-14.

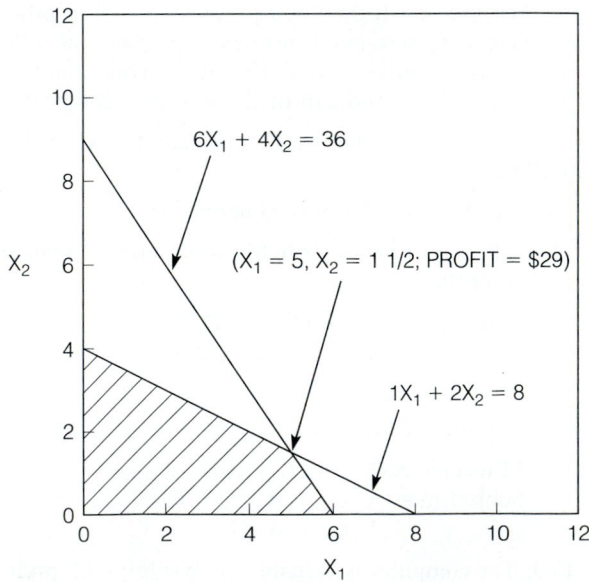

$6X_1 + 4X_2 = 36$

$(X_1 = 5, X_2 = 1\ 1/2; \text{PROFIT} = \$29)$

$1X_1 + 2X_2 = 8$

Using the corner point method, we determine that the optimal solution mix under the new constraint yields a \$29 profit, or an increase of \$3 over the *\$26 profit* calculated.

13-15. a. We change $10 (the C_j coefficient for X_1) to $10 + \Delta$ and note the effect on the $C_j - Z_j$ row in the table below:

$C_j \longrightarrow$	SOLUTION MIX	QUANTITY	$10 + \Delta$	$30	$0	$0
			X_1	X_2	S_1	S_2
$10 + \Delta$	X_1	160	1	4	2	0
$0	S_2	200	0	6	−7	1
	Z_j	$600 + 160\Delta$	$10 + \Delta$	$40 + 4\Delta$	$20 + 2\Delta$	0
	$C_j - Z_j$		0	$-10 - 4\Delta$	$-20 - 2\Delta$	0

From the X_2 column, we require for optimality that:

$$-10 - 4\Delta \leqq 0 \quad \text{or} \quad \Delta \geqq -2\tfrac{1}{2}$$

From the S_1 column, we require that:

$$-20 - 2\Delta \leqq 0 \quad \text{or} \quad \Delta \geqq -10$$

Since the $\Delta \geqq -2\tfrac{1}{2}$ is more binding, the *range of optimality* is:

$$7\tfrac{1}{2} \leqq C_j \text{ (for } X_2\text{)} \leqq \infty$$

b. *Range of insignificance* is:

$$-\infty \leqq C_j \text{ (for } X_2\text{)} \leqq 40$$

c. One more unit of the first scarce resource is worth $20, which is the shadow price in the S_1 column.

d. Another unit of the second resource is worth $0 because there are still 200 unused units ($S_2 = 200$)

13-16.

RESOURCE SOURCE	VALUE OF AN ADDITIONAL HOUR
First constraint (S_1)	$.30
Second constraint (S_2)	$0
Third constraint (S_3)	$3.00

The second resource has a zero shadow price because not all of the resource is currently being used—425 units are still available.

13-17. a. Produce eighteen of Model 102 and four of Model H23.

b. S_1 represents slack time on the soldering machine. S_2 represents available time in the inspection department.

c. Yes—the shadow price of the soldering machine time is $4. Clapper will net $1.50 for every additional hour he rents.

d. No—the profit added for each additional hour of inspection time made available is only $1. Since this shadow price is less than the $1.75 per hour cost, Clapper will lower his profit by hiring the part-timer.

13-18. a. The first shadow price (in the S_1 column) is $.50. The second shadow price (in the S_2 column) is $1.50.

b. The first shadow price represents the value of one more hour in the painting department. The second represents the value of one additional hour in the carpentry department.

c. The range of optimality for tables (X_1) is established from Table 13-18c on page IS-140.

$$-\tfrac{1}{2} - \tfrac{3}{2}\Delta \leqq 0 \quad \text{or} \quad \Delta \geqq -\tfrac{1}{3} \quad \text{from } S_1 \text{ column}$$
$$-\tfrac{3}{2} + \tfrac{1}{2}\Delta \leqq 0 \quad \text{or} \quad \Delta \leqq 3 \quad \text{from } S_2 \text{ column}$$

Hence, the C_j for X_1 must decrease by at least $0.33 to change the optimal solution. It must *increase* by $3 to alter the basis. The range of optimality is $6.67 \leqq C_j \leqq 10.00 for X_1.

d. Range of optimality for X_2. See Table 13-18d on page IS-140.

$$-\tfrac{1}{2} + 2\Delta \leqq 0 \quad \text{or} \quad \Delta \leqq \tfrac{1}{4} \quad \text{from } S_1 \text{ column}$$
$$-\tfrac{3}{2} - \Delta \leqq 0 \quad \text{or} \quad \Delta \geqq -\tfrac{3}{2} \quad \text{from } S_2 \text{ column}$$

Range of optimality for profit coefficient on chairs is from $3.50 (= 5 − \tfrac{3}{2}$) to $5.25 (= 5 + \tfrac{1}{4}$).

e. Ranging for first resource—painting department

QUANTITY	S_1	RATIO
30	$\tfrac{3}{2}$	20
40	−2	−20

Thus, the first resource can be reduced by 20 hours, or increased by 20 hours without affecting the solution. The range is from 80 hours to 120 hours.

Table for Problem 13-18c

$C_j \longrightarrow$	SOLUTION MIX	QUANTITY	$7 + \Delta$	5	0	0
			X_1	X_2	S_1	S_2
$7 + \Delta$	X_1	30	1	0	$\frac{3}{2}$	$-\frac{1}{2}$
5	X_2	40	0	1	-2	1
	Z_j	$\$410 + 30\Delta$	$7 + \Delta$	5	$\frac{1}{2} + \frac{3}{2}\Delta$	$\frac{3}{2} - \frac{1}{2}\Delta$
	$C_j - Z_j$		0	0	$-\frac{1}{2} - \frac{3}{2}\Delta$	$-\frac{3}{2} + \frac{1}{2}\Delta$

Table for Problem 13-18d

$C_j \longrightarrow$	SOLUTION MIX	QUANTITY	7	$5 + \Delta$	0	0
			X_1	X_2	S_1	S_2
7	X_1	30	1	0	$\frac{3}{2}$	$-\frac{1}{2}$
$5 + \Delta$	X_2	40	0	1	-2	1
	Z_j	$\$410 + 40\Delta$	7	$5 + \Delta$	$\frac{1}{2} - 2\Delta$	$\frac{3}{2} + \Delta$
	$C_j - Z_j$		0	0	$-\frac{1}{2} + 2\Delta$	$-\frac{3}{2} - \Delta$

f. Ranging for second resource—carpentry time.

QUANTITY	S_2	RATIO
30	$-\frac{1}{2}$	-60
40	1	40

Range is thus from 200 hours to 300 hours (or $240 - 40$ to $240 + 60$).

13-19. Note that artificial variables may be omitted from the sensitivity analysis since they have no physical meaning.

a. Range of Optimality for X_1 (phosphate):

$C_j \longrightarrow$	SOLUTION MIX	QUANTITY	$\$5 + \Delta$	$\$6$	$\$0$	$\$0$
			X_1	X_2	S_1	S_2
$\$0$	S_2	550	0	0	-1	1
$\$5 + \Delta$	X_1	300	1	0	1	0
$\$6$	X_2	700	0	1	-1	0
	Z_j	$\$5,700 + 300\Delta$	$5 + \Delta$	6	$-1 + \Delta$	0
	$C_j - Z_j$		0	0	$1 - \Delta$	0

$$1 - \Delta \geqq 0 \quad \text{or} \quad \Delta \leqq 1$$

If the C_j value for X_1 *increases* by $1, the basis will change. Hence, $-\infty \leqq C_j$ (for X_1) $\leqq \$6$.

Range of optimality for X_2 (Potassium)

$C_j \longrightarrow$	SOLUTION MIX	QUANTITY	5	$6 + \Delta$	0	0
			X_1	X_2	S_1	S_2
0	S_2	550	0	0	-1	1
5	X_1	300	1	0	1	0
$6 + \Delta$	X_2	700	0	1	-1	0
	Z_j	$\$5{,}700 + 700\Delta$	5	$6 + \Delta$	$-1 - \Delta$	0
	$C_j - Z_j$		0	0	$1 + \Delta$	0

$$1 + \Delta \geqq 0 \quad \text{or} \quad \Delta \geqq -1$$

If the C_j value for X_2 *decreases* by \$1, the basis will change. The range is thus $\$5 \leqq C_j$ (for X_2) $\leqq \infty$.

b. This involves right-hand-side ranging on the slack variables S_1 (which represents number of pounds of phosphate under the 300-pound limit).

QUANTITY	S_2	RATIO
550	-1	-550
300	1	300
700	-1	-700

This indicates that the limit may be *reduced* by 300 pounds (down to zero pounds) without changing the solution.

The question asks if the resources can be increased to 400 pounds without affecting the basis. The smallest negative ratio (-550) tells us that the limit can be raised to 850 pounds without changing the solution mix. However, the values of X_1, X_2, and S_2 would change. X_1 would now be 400, X_2 would be 600, and S_2 would be 450. This is best seen in Figure 12.3 graphically.

13-20. Minimize cost $= 4U_1 + 8U_2$
  Subject to: $1U_1 + 2U_2 \geqq 80$
           $3U_1 + 5U_2 \geqq 75$

The dual of the dual is the original primal.

13-21. Maximize profit $= 50U_1 + 4U_2$
  Subject to: $12U_1 + 1U_2 \leqq 120$
           $20U_1 + 3U_2 \leqq 250$

13-22. $U_1 = \$80$, $U_2 = \$40$, Cost $= \$1{,}000$

13-23. Primal objective function:
  Maximize profit $= .5X_1 + .4X_2$
  Primal constraints: $2X_1 + 1X_2 \leqq 120$
            $2X_1 + 3X_2 \leqq 240$
  Primal solution: $X_1 = 30$, $X_2 = 60$, Profit $= \$39$

13-24.
Maximize
  profit $= 10X_1 + 5X_2 + 31X_3 + 28X_4 + 17X_5$
Subject to: $X_1 + X_2 \qquad\qquad + 12X_5 \leqq 28$
        $2X_2 - 2X_3 \qquad\qquad \leqq 53$
        $X_2 \qquad + 5X_4 + 2X_5 \leqq 70$
     $X_1 \qquad + 5X_3 \qquad - X_5 \leqq 18$
          $X_1, X_2, X_3 \geqq 0$

13-25. a. Machine number 3, as represented by slack variable S_3, still has 62 hours of unused time.

b. There is no unused time when the optimal solution is reached. All three slack variables have been removed from the basis and have zero values.

c. The shadow price of the third machine is the value of the dual variable in column 6. Hence, an extra hour of time on machine number 3 is worth \$0.26.

d. For *each* extra hour of time made available at no cost on machine number 2, profit will increase by \$0.786. Thus, 10 hours of time will be worth \$7.86.

13-26. The dual is:

  Maximize $Z = 120U_1 + 115U_2 + 116U_3$
  Subject to: $8U_1 + 4U_2 + 9U_3 \leqq 23$
          $4U_1 + 6U_2 + 4U_3 \leqq 18$
              $U_1, U_2, U_3 \geqq 0$

$U_1 = \$2.07$ is the price of each test 1.
$U_2 = \$1.63$ is the price of each test 2.
$U_3 = \$0$ is the price of each test 3.

Using the dual objective function:

$$Z = 120U_1 + 115U_2 + 116U_3$$
$$= 120(2.07) + 115(1.63) + 116(0)$$
$$= \$248.4 + \$187.45 + \$0$$
$$= \$435.85$$

Thus, \$435.85 is the maximum the laboratory should be willing to pay an outside resource to conduct the 120 test 1s, 115 test 2s and 116 test 3s per day.

$8U_1 + 4U_2 + 9U_3$ is the value of 8, 4, and 9 of tests 1, 2, and 3, respectively, performed per hour by a bio-chemist. This means that the prices U_1, U_2 and U_3 need to be such that their total value does not exceed the cost per hour to the lab for using one of its own biochemists.

Likewise, $4U_1 + 6U_2 + 4U_3$ is the value of 4, 6, and 4 tests 1, 2, and 3, respectively, performed per hour by a biophysicist. Again, the prices U_1, U_2, and U_3 need to be such that the total value does not exceed the cost per hour for the lab to use one of its own biophysicists.

13-27. a. $X_1 = 27.38$ tables, $X_2 = 37.18$ chairs daily, Profit = $377.58

    b. Not all resources are used. Shadow prices indicate that carpentry hours and painting hours are not fully used. Also, the 40-table maximum is not reached.

    c. The shadow prices relate to the five constraints: $0 value to making more carpentry and painting time available; $6.34 is the value of additional inspection/rework hours; $0.12 is the value of each additional foot of lumber made available.

    d. More lumber *should* be purchased if it costs less than the $0.12 shadow price. More carpenters are not needed at any price.

    e. Flair has a slack (X_4) of 8.056 hours available daily in the painting department. It can spare this amount.

    f. Carpentry hours range: 221 to infinity
Painting hours range: 92 to infinity
Inspection/rework hours range: $19\frac{1}{2}$ to 41

    g. Table profit range: $4.17 to $16.00
Chair profit range: $2.19 to $8.40

13-28. The first AB:QM printout illustrates the model formulation.

    a. Printout 2 provides the optimal solution of $9,683. Only the first product (A158) is not produced.

    b. Printout 2 also lists the shadow prices. The first, for example, deals with steel alloy. The value of one more pound is $2.71.

    c. There is no value to adding more workers, since all 1,000 hours are not yet consumed.

    d. Two tons of steel at a total cost of $8,000 implies a cost per pound of $2.00. It should be purchased since the shadow price is $2.71.

    e. Printout 3 illustrates that profit declines to $8,865 with the change to $8.88.

    f. Printout 4 shows the new constraints. Profit drops to $9,380, and none of the products remain. Previously, only A158 was *not* produced.

Printout 1 for Problem 13-28

Problem Title: DATASET PROBLEM 13-28

***** Input Data *****

Max. Z = 18.79X1 + 6.31X2 + 8.19X3 + 45.88X4 + 63.00X5 + 4.10X6
       + 81.15X7 + 50.06X8 + 12.79X9 + 15.88X10 + 17.91X11 + 49.99X12
       + 24.00X13 + 88.88X14 + 77.01X15

Subject to

C1   4X2 + 6X3 + 10X4 + 12X5 + 10X7 + 5X8 + 1X9 + 1X10 + 2X12
       + 10X14 + 10X15 <= 980
C2   .4X1 + .5X2 + .4X4 + 1.2X5 + 1.4X6 + 1.4X7 + 1.0X8 + .4X9
       + .3X10 + 2X11 + 1.8X12 + 2.7X13 + 1.1X14 <= 400
C3   .7X1 + 1.8X2 + 1.5X3 + 2.0X4 + 1.2X5 + 1.5X6 + 7.0X7 + 5.0X8
       + 1.5X12 + 5.0X13 + 5.8X14 + 6.2X15 <= 600
C4   5.8X1 + 10.3X2 + 1.1X3 + 8.1X5 + 7.1X6 + 6.2X7 + 7.3X8 + 10X9
       + 11X10 + 12.5X11 + 13.1X12 + 15X15 <= 2500
C5   10.9X1 + 2X2 + 2.3X3 + 4.9X5 + 10X6 + 11.1X7 + 12.4X8 + 5.2X9
       + 6.1X10 + 7.7X11 + 5X12 + 2.1X13 + 1X15 <= 1800
C6   3.1X1 + 1X2 + 1.2X3 + 4.8X4 + 5.5X5 + .8X6 + 9.1X7 + 4.8X8
       + 1.9X9 + 1.4X10 + 1.X11 + 5.1X12 + 3.1X13 + 7.7X14
       + 6.6X15 <= 1000
C7   1X1 >= 0
C8   1X2 >= 20
C9   1X3 >= 10
C10   1X4 >= 10
C11   1X5 >= 0
C12   1X6 >= 20
C13   1X7 >= 10
C14   1X8 >= 20
C15   1X9 >= 50
C16   1X10 >= 20
C17   1X11 >= 20
C18   1X12 >= 10
C19   1X13 >= 20
C20   1X14 >= 10
C21   1X15 >= 10

Printout 2 for Problem 13-28

***** Program Output *****

Final Optimal Solution at Simplex Tableau : 18

Z = $9,683.228

Variable	Value	Reduced Cost
X 1	0.000	0.000
X 2	20.000	0.000
X 3	10.000	0.000
X 4	10.000	0.000
X 5	11.507	0.000
X 6	20.000	0.000
X 7	10.000	0.000
X 8	20.000	0.000
X 9	50.000	0.000
X10	20.000	0.000
X11	20.000	0.000
X12	54.946	0.000
X13	20.000	0.000
X14	12.202	0.000
X15	10.000	0.000

Constraint	Slack/Surplus	Shadow Price
C 1	0.000	2.712
C 2	113.866	0.000
C 3	0.000	10.649
C 4	0.000	2.183
C 5	258.885	0.000
C 6	8.530	0.000
C 7	0.000	-1.324
C 8	0.000	-46.187
C 9	0.000	-26.455
C10	0.000	-2.535
C11	11.507	0.000
C12	0.000	-27.370
C13	0.000	-34.041
C14	0.000	-32.676
C15	0.000	-11.749
C16	0.000	-10.842
C17	0.000	-9.374
C18	44.946	0.000
C19	0.000	-29.243
C20	2.202	0.000
C21	0.000	-48.870

(d) Cost is $2.00/lb. for more steel; we should do it.

Printout 3 for Problem 13-28

Problem Title: DATASET PROBLEM 13-28

***** Input Data *****

Max. $Z = 18.79X_1 + 6.31X_2 + 8.19X_3 + 45.88X_4 + 63.00X_5 + 4.10X_6$
$+ 81.15X_7 + 50.06X_8 + 12.79X_9 + 15.88X_{10} + 17.91X_{11}$
$+ 49.99X_{12} + 24.00X_{13} + 8.88X_{14} + 77.01X_{15}$

***** Program Output *****

Final Optimal Solution At Simplex Tableau

$Z = \$8865.500$

Variable	Value	Reduced Cost
X 1	0.000	0.000
X 2	20.000	0.000
X 3	10.000	0.000
X 4	16.993	0.000
X 5	7.056	0.000
X 6	20.000	0.000
X 7	10.000	0.000
X 8	20.000	0.000
X 9	50.000	0.000
X10	20.000	0.000
X11	20.000	0.000
X12	57.698	0.000
X13	20.000	0.000
X14	10.000	0.000
X15	10.000	0.000

Solution to Red Brand Canners Case

1. The main issue in this case is how to allocate 3 million pounds of tomatoes. The overall objective is to maximize total sales less variable costs. These costs include production and selling expenses. Twenty percent of the crop was grade A and the rest was grade B. In setting up the constraints, the amount of grade A tomatoes cannot exceed 20% of 3 million pounds. Thus, not more than 600,000 pounds of grade A tomatoes can be used. Likewise, not more than 2,400,000 pounds of grade B tomatoes can be used. Furthermore, the demand for 50,000 cases of tomato juice and 80,000 cases of tomato paste should be met. The demand for whole tomatoes is not a constraint in this problem. Finally, minimum quality requirements should be met. This includes an average of 8 points per pound for whole tomatoes and 6 points per pound for tomato juice. There is no constraint for tomato paste.

Another issue is whether or not to buy 80,000 additional pounds of grade A tomatoes. This would increase the amount of available grade A tomatoes from 600,000 pounds to 680,000 pounds. In order to answer this question, a new formulation can be made using the new 680,000-pound constraint and a price of 8.5 cents per pound for the 80,000 additional pounds of grade A tomatoes in the objective function. A faster way to resolve this issue is to use postoptimality analysis, or shadow prices. Using this approach, you compare the value of the 80,000 additional tomatoes with the cost, which is 8.5 cents per pound.

Printout 4 for Problem 13–28

```
C7    1X1 >= 0
C8    1X2 >= 0
C9    1X3 >= 0
C10   1X4 >= 0
C11   1X5 >= 0
```

Final Optimal Solution at Simplex Tableau : 21

Z = $9,380.234

Variable	Value	Reduced Cost
X 1	0.000	0.000
X 2	0.000	0.000
X 3	0.000	0.000
X 4	0.000	0.000
X 5	28.723	0.000
X 6	20.000	0.000
X 7	10.000	0.000
X 8	37.517	0.000
X 9	50.000	0.000
X10	20.000	0.000
X11	33.941	0.000
X12	37.485	0.000
X13	20.000	0.000
X14	10.000	0.000
X15	10.277	0.000

2. The problem can be formulated using LP as follows:

X_1 = pounds of whole A tomatoes
X_2 = pounds of whole B tomatoes
X_3 = pounds of juice A tomatoes
X_4 = pounds of juice B tomatoes
X_5 = pounds of paste A tomatoes
X_6 = pounds of paste B tomatoes

Maximize: $.0822X_1 + .0822X_2 + .066X_3 + .066X_4 + .074X_5 + .074X_6$

Subject to:

$$
\begin{aligned}
1X_1 + 1X_2 & \le 14{,}400{,}000 \\
1X_3 + 1X_4 & \le 1{,}000{,}000 \\
1X_5 + 1X_6 & \le 2{,}000{,}000 \\
1X_1 + 1X_3 + 1X_5 & \le 600{,}000 \\
1X_2 + 1X_4 + 1X_6 & \le 2{,}400{,}000 \\
1X_1 - 3X_2 & \ge 0 \\
3X_3 - 1X_4 & \ge 0
\end{aligned}
$$

The first constraint refers to the 14 million pounds of whole tomatoes—800,000 cases at 18 pounds per case—that constitutes maximum demand. Similarly, the maximum demand for tomato juice is 50,000 cases at 20 pounds per case or 1 million pounds, and the maximum demand for tomato paste is 80,000 cases at

25 pounds per case or 2 million pounds, and these are constraints 2 and 3. Constraints 4 and 5 reflect the availability of grade A and grade B tomatoes, respectively, and the last two constraints are the quality constraints. The requirements that canned tomatoes must average at least 8 points means that at least three-fourths of the tomatoes must be grade A:

$$X_1 \geq .75(X_1 + X_2) => X_1 - 3X_2 \geq 0.$$

Similarly, the requirements that tomato juice must average at least 6 points means that at least one-fourth of the tomato juice must be grade A, and that is the last constraint.

The coefficients in the objective function are the unit profits. A case of whole tomatoes (grade A and grade B) sells for $4. The variable cost (less the tomatoes) is $2.52. Since the tomatoes are already on hand (and no salvage appears to be possible), they represent a sunk cost and are not part of the decision process. Since there are 18 pounds per case, the unit profit is $(4.00 - 2.52)/18 = .0822$. Similar analyses hold for the other terms in the objective function.

The solution of the linear programming problem is:

$X_1 = 525,000$	$X_2 = 175,000$
$X_3 = 75,000$	$X_4 = 225,000$
$X_5 = 0$	$X_6 = 2,000,000$

The maximum profit is $225,340.

All of the grade A tomatoes are used. The shadow price for the slack variable in constraint 4 is .0903. Each additional pound of grade A tomatoes costing 8.5 cents will increase profits by $.093 - .0850 = .0053$. A sensitivity analysis indicates that up to an additional 600,000 pounds of grade A tomatoes could be purchased without affecting the solution basis.

14

Transportation and Assignment Problems

LEARNING OBJECTIVES

After completing this chapter, students will be able to:

1. Structure special linear programming problems using the transportation and assignment models.
2. Use the northwest corner method and Vogel's approximation method to find initial solutions to transportation problems.
3. Apply the stepping-stone and MODI methods to find optimal solutions to transportation problems.
4. Solve facility location and other application problems with the transportation model.
5. Solve assignment problems with the Hungarian (matrix reduction) method.
6. Use AB:QM, LINDO, and STORM software to analyze transportation and assignment problems.

TEACHING SUGGESTIONS

Teaching Suggestion 14.1: Transportation Models in the Chapter.

This is a long chapter, in part, because of the four transportation algorithms that are discussed. If time is an issue in your course, select one of the two initial solution methods and one of the two final solution methods to cover in class. The easiest, but *not* most efficient, are the northwest corner and stepping-stone rules.

Teaching Suggestion 14.2: Using the Northwest Corner Rule.

This approach is easily understood by students and is appealing to teach for that very reason. Make sure the students understand the weakness of the algorithm (that is, it ignores costs totally). Ask them to come up with their own approaches that could improve on this. Invariably, a good student will present an approach that comes very close to VAM. Name the student's approach after him (or her) and tell him he could have been famous if he had devised it 50 years earlier.

Teaching Suggestion 14.3: Using the Stepping-Stone Method.

Students usually pick up the concept of a closed path and learn to trace the pluses and minuses fairly quickly. But they run into problems when they have to cross over an empty cell. Stress that the cities in the tableau are just in random order, so crossing an unoccupied box is fine. The big test is Table 14.5. Once students comprehend this tracing, they are usually ready to move on. Use Transparency Master 14-10 to illustrate. Remind students that there is *only one* closed path that can be traced for each unused cell.

Teaching Suggestion 14.4: Dummy Rows and Columns.

Another confusing issue to students is whether to add a dummy row (source) or dummy column (destination) in a transportation problem. A slow and careful explanation is valuable so that students can reach an intuitive understanding as to the correct choice. Also note that the software adds these dummies automatically.

Teaching Suggestion 14.5: Handling Degeneracy in Transportation Problems.

Just as a warning, be aware that students are often confused by the concept of where to place the zero so that the closed paths can be traced. Carefully explain why you chose or didn't choose a certain cell. The choice of cell can affect the number of iterations that follow.

Teaching Suggestion 14.6: Facility Location Problems.

These are an important application of the transportation model and make it easy to compare how a new city will fit into an existing shipping network. It is an application that has intuitive appeal. Both AB:QM and STORM software are easy to run on these problems.

Teaching Suggestion 14.7: Sensitivity Analysis on the Assignment Problem.

This algorithm is easy to use and understand. Tell about solving a large staffing problem, then discuss the cost implications if one worker is not available or insists on doing a particular task. It is easy, with the software, to recompute the answers and conduct a sensitivity analysis. This is the basis of Data Set Problem 14-38.

Teaching Suggestion 14.8: Maximizing Assignment Problems.

This section is needed if students are to solve maximization problems by hand, but AB:QM and STORM software negate the need by handling both types of problems. The section can be skipped if the software is being used.

Teaching Suggestion 14.9: Using LINDO to Solve a Transportation Problem.

Although it is easier to solve transportation problems with AB:QM and STORM's transportation module, the LINDO printout provides interesting shadow price and reduced cost data.

Teaching Suggestion 14.10: Data Set Problem 14-37.

In assigning this challenging aggregate planning problem, you may wish to first provide some background information on how to structure the plan. Remind students that back ordering is not permitted, so very large costs must be inserted in many cells. Note that Problem 14-22 (Mehta Company) is a warm-up exercise for this data set problem.

ALTERNATE EXAMPLES

Alternate Example 14.1: Let us presume a product is made at two of our factories which we wish to ship to three of our warehouses. We produce 18 at Factory A and 22 at Factory B; we want 10 in warehouse #1, 20 in warehouse #2, and 10 in warehouse #3. Per unit transportation costs are: A to #1, $4; A to #2, $2; A to #3, $3; B to #1, $3; B to #2, $2; B to #3, $1. The corresponding transportation table is:

To \ From	Warehouses #1	#2	#3	Total
Factory A	4	2	3	18
Factory B	3	2	1	22
Total	10	20	10	40

The northwest corner approach follows:

To \ From	Warehouses #1	#2	#3	Total
Factory A	10 (4)	8 (2)	(3)	18
Factory B	(3)	12 (2)	10 (1)	22
Total	10	20	10	40

Let us determine the total cost of transportation with this initial northwest corner solution. For each filled cell, simply multiply the number of units being shipped by the unit shipping cost and then add those transhipment costs. Thus, in the order the cells were filled, we have: (10) ($4) + (8) ($2) + (12) ($2) + (10) ($1) = $90.

Using stepping-stone or MODI, we can find the optimal solution (below):

Solution:

To From	Warehouses #1	#2	#3	Total
Factory A	4	2 18	3	18
Factory B	3 10	2 2	1 10	22
Total	10	20	10	40

Cost = (18) ($2) + 10($3) + 2($2) + 10($1) = $80

Alternate Example 14.2: There is often an imbalance between the amount produced and the amounts desired in the warehouses. In Alternate Example 14.1, there were forty units produced and forty units demanded for warehousing. Let us presume that an additional four units are desired at each warehouse, increasing the total demand to 14 + 24 + 14 = 52. The supply shortage of 12 units prevents a solution of this problem until we create a dummy factory which produces a fake 12 units. The cost to ship a false unit from a dummy factory or to a dummy warehouse is zero. After the final optimal solution is computed, the false units and dummy facilities are ignored. Our new example with a dummy warehouse and a northwest corner initial solution would look like this:

To From	Warehouses #1	#2	#3	Total
Factory A	4 14	2 4	3	18
Factory B	3	2 20	1 2	22
Factory C	0	0 12	0	12
Total	14	24	14	52

Alternate Example 14.3: Here is a production application of the transportation problem. Set up the following problem in a transportation format and solve for the minimum-cost plan:

	Period FEB	MAR	APR
Demand...................	55	70	75
Capacity			
Regular	50	50	50
Overtime.................	5	5	5
Subcontract..............	12	12	10
Beginning			
inventory.................	10		
Costs			
Regular time.............	$60 per unit		
Overtime.................	80 per unit		
Subcontract..............	90 per unit		
Inventory			
carrying cost.............	$1 per unit per month		
Back order cost.............	$3 per unit per month		

See page IS-150 for the solution.

Alternate Example 14.4: As an example of an assignment problem, let us assume Susan is a sorority pledge coordinator with four jobs and only three pledges. Susan decides that the assignment problem is appropriate except that she will attempt to minimize total time instead of money (since the pledges aren't paid). Susan also realizes that she will have to create a fictitious fourth pledge and she knows that whatever job gets assigned to that pledge will not be done (this semester, anyhow). She creates estimates for the respective times and places them in a table as:

	Jobs 1	2	3	4
Barb	4	9	3	8
Cindy	7	8	2	6
Donna	3	4	5	7
Zingo	0	0	0	0

Zingo is, of course, a fictitious pledge, so her times are all zero.

a) The first step in this algorithm is to develop the opportunity cost table. This is done by subtracting the smallest number in each row from every other value in that row, then, using these newly created figures, by subtracting the smallest number in each column from every other value in that column. Whenever these

Table for Alternate Example 14.3:   *Transportation solution*

	Supply from	Demand for				Total capacity available (supply)
		FEB	MAR	APR	Unused capacity (dummy)	
Period Beginning inventory		0 — 10	1	2	0	10
FEBRUARY Regular time		60 — 45	61 — 5	62	0	50
Overtime		80	81 — 5	82	0	5
Subcontract		90	91 — 3	92	0 — 9	12
MARCH Regular time		63	60 — 50	61	0	50
Overtime		83	80 — 5	81	0	5
Subcontract		93	90 — 2	91 — 10	0	12
APRIL Regular time		66	63	60 — 50	0	50
Overtime		86	83	80 — 5	0	5
Subcontract		96	93	90 — 10	0	10
Demand		55	70	75	9	209

smallest values are zero, the subtraction results in no change. Susan's resulting matrix is:

	Jobs			
	1	2	3	4
Barb	1	6	0	5
Cindy	5	6	0	4
Donna	0	1	2	4
Zingo	0	0	0	0

No change was produced when dealing with the columns since the smallest values were always the zeros from row four.

b) The next step is to draw lines through all of the zeros. The lines are to be straight and either horizontal or vertical. Furthermore, you are to use as few lines as possible. If it requires four of these lines (four because it is a 4 × 4 matrix), then an optimal assignment is already possible. If it requires fewer than four lines, another step is required before optimal assignments may be made. In our example, draw a line through: row four, column three, either column one or row three. One version of the matrix is:

	Jobs			
	1	2	3	4
Barb	1	6	0	5
Cindy	5	6	0	4
Donna	0	1	2	4
Zingo	0	0	0	0

c) Since the number of lines required was less than the number of assignees, a third step is required (as is normally the case). Looking at the version of the matrix with the lines through it, determine the smallest number. Subtract this smallest number from every number not covered by a line and add it to every number at the intersection of two lines. Repeat the lining out process, with the result:

	Jobs			
	1	2	3	4
Barb	0	5	0	4
Cindy	4	5	0	3
Donna	0	1	3	4
Zingo	0	0	1	0

Which is still not an optimum solution.

d) Since all of the zeros can be lined out with three lines, this is still not optimal. Hence, we repeat the step of finding the smallest uncovered number and both subtracting that quantity from uncovered numbers and adding it to those numbers at line intersections. The resultant matrix, after being lined again, is:

	Jobs			
	1	2	3	4
Barb	0	4	0	3
Cindy	4	4	0	2
Donna	0	0	3	3
Zingo	1	0	2	0

Since this matrix requires four lines to cover all zeros, we have now reached an optimal solution stage.

e) Although there is more than one order for making the assignments, in our example the assignments must be: Cindy, Job 3; Barb, Job 1; Donna, Job 2; Zingo, Job 4. Since Zingo is a dummy row, the job labeled Job 4 does not get completed.

SOLUTIONS TO DISCUSSION QUESTIONS AND PROBLEMS

14-1. The transportation model is an example of decision making under certainty. Under certainty, a decision maker knows beforehand exactly what state of nature will occur (see Chapter 5). In transportation problems, this means that the costs of each shipping route, the demand at each destination, and the supply at each source are all known with certainty.

14-2. Vogel's approximation gives a good initial solution because it makes each allocation on the basis of the opportunity cost, or penalty that would be incurred if that allocation is *not* chosen (see Section 14.5). The northwest corner rule does not take into account the shipping costs associated with each route alternative as does VAM. Nevertheless, the northwest corner rule *could* provide as low-cost an initial solution—*but only* if, by chance, it turned out that the lowest-cost routes happened to be on the initially assigned squares.

14-3. A balanced transportation problem is one in which total demand (from all destinations) is exactly equal to total supply (from all sources). If a problem is *unbalanced,* it is necessary to establish either a dummy source (if demand is greater than supply) or a dummy destination (if demand is less than supply). Refer to Section 14.6 in Chapter 14.

14-4. The major difference between the MODI and stepping-stone methods is in the procedure used to test for optimality. In the stepping-stone method, we first draw a closed path for *each* of the empty squares to calculate its improvement index. Then, the most favorable square (that is, the one with the largest negative index) is identified. In MODI, however, we first identify the most favorable square (by using row and column numbers) and then draw a closed path (only for that path) to direct us in improving the solution.

14-5. A "northeast corner" rule would be directly analogous to the northwest corner rule, but it would simply begin in the upper right-hand corner instead of the upper left-hand corner. We see in the table on page IS-170 that this initial solution is degenerate because only four squares (instead of the expected five) are occupied. The degeneracy condition, by the way, is just a peculiarity of the Executive Furniture Corporation data.

14-6. When $m + n - 1$ squares (where m = number of rows and n = number of columns) are not occupied, the solution is degenerate. Not enough squares are occupied to allow us to draw a closed path for all unused squares. Hence, we would not be able to evaluate all of the unused routes. To handle this problem, we select one empty square, place a zero in it, pretend as if it is occupied, and proceed as in a normal, nondegenerate case. (To bring the number of allocations to $m + n - 1$, it may be necessary to place a zero in more than one empty square).

14-7. The enumeration method is not a practical means of solving 5×5 or 7×7 problems because of the number of possible assignments to be considered. In the

Table for Discussion Question 14-5:

FROM \ TO	ALBU-QUERQUE	BOSTON	CLEVELAND	FACTORY CAPACITY
Des Moines	5	4	3 / 100	100
Evansville	8	4 / 200	3 / 100	300
Fort Lauderdale	9 / 300	7	5	300
Warehouse requirements	300	200	200	700

5×5 case, $5! \ (= 5 \times 4 \times 3 \times 2 \times 1) = 120$ alternatives to be evaluated. In the 7×7 case, there are $7! = 5,040$ alternatives.

14-8. The assignment problem is a special case of the transportation problem and hence can be solved with the approach shown earlier in this chapter. This is illustrated for the Fix-It Shop problem. Notice that the column and row requirements will always be equal to 1.

FROM \ TO	PROJECT 1	PROJECT 2	PROJECT 3	PERSONNEL AVAILABLE
Adams	$11 / 1	$14	$ 6	1
Brown	8	10 / 1	11	1
Cooper	9	12	7 / 1	1
Project needs	1	1	1	3

The above northwest corner initial assignment yields a degenerate solution (only 3 squares are filled instead of the required 5). This will always be a problem when applying the transportation method to assignments. The problem will be degenerate because there will be only one assignment in a given row or column.

14-9. It is not necessary to rework the assignment solution. Changing *each* entry in the cost table will not result in different total opportunity cost tables. The optimal cost will, however, be increased by $25 from $492 to $517 because of the extra $5 charge for each of the five workers.

14-10. To exclude any unwanted or unacceptable assignment from occurring, it is necessary only to place a very high artificial cost in the row and column representing that particular assignment. If, for example, all of the relocation costs for Simmons's firm were in the $1,000–$3,000 range, an artificial cost of $20,000 could be placed on the unwanted assignment. Conversely, if we were dealing with a maximization problem, a very *low* rating would be given to the unacceptable assignment.

14-11. a. Initial solution to modify Executive Furniture Corporation problem using the northwest corner rule:

FROM \ TO	ALBU-QUERQUE		BOSTON		CLEVELAND		FACTORY CAPACITY
Des Moines		5		4		3	
	200		100				300
Evansville		8		4		3	
			100		50		150
Fort Lauderdale		9		7		5	
					250		250
Warehouse requirements	200		200		300		700

Total cost of this initial solution:

$$= 200(\$5) + 100(\$4) + 100(\$4) + 50(\$3)$$
$$+ 250(\$5)$$
$$= 1,000 + 400 + 400 + 150 + 1,250$$
$$= \$3,200$$

b. To see if this initial solution is optimal, we compute improvement indices for each unused square, namely, D–C, E–A, F–A, and F–B:

D–C index path = D–C to E–C to E–B to D–B
$$= \$3 - 3 + 4 - 4 = \$0$$
E–A index path = E–A to E–B to D–B to D–A
$$= \$8 - 4 + 4 - 5 = +\$3$$

F–A index path = F–A to F–C to E–C to E–B to D–B
        to D–A
$$= +\$9 - 5 + 3 - 4 + 4 - 5 = +\$2$$
F–B index path = F–B to F–C to E–C to E–B
$$= +\$7 - 5 + 3 - 4 = +\$1$$

This solution is optimal, so further stepping-stone computations are not necessary.

c. The improvement index for square D–C is zero. This implies the presence of multiple optimal solutions. Practically speaking, management could close the E–C shipping route and send 50 units on the D–C route instead. The table below illustrates the overall changes in this alternative optimal solution.

FROM \ TO	ALBU-QUERQUE		BOSTON		CLEVELAND		FACTORY CAPACITY
Des Moines		5		4		3	
	200		50		50		300
Evansville		8		4		3	
			150		0		150
Fort Lauderdale		9		7		5	
					250		250
Warehouse requirements	200		200		300		700

Total cost of alternate optimal solution:

$$= 200(\$5) + 50(\$4) + 50(\$3) + 150(\$4) + 250(\$5)$$
$$= \$3,200$$

14-12. a. Hardrock's initial solution using the northwest corner rule is shown below.

FROM \ TO	A	B	C	PLANT CAPACITY
1	10 — 40	4 — 30	11	70
2	12	5 — 20	8 — 30	50
3	9	7	6 — 30	30
Project requirements	40	50	60	150

Cost = 40($10) + 30($4) + 20($5) + 30($8) + 30($6)
     = $1,040

Using the stepping-stone method, the following improvement indices are computed:

Plant 1—Project C = $11 − $4 + $5 − $8 = +$4
        (closed path = 1-C to 1-B to 2-B to 2-C)
Plant 2—Project A = +$12 − $5 + $4 − $10 = $1
        (closed path = 2-A to 2-B to 1-B to 1-A)
Plant 3—Project A = +$9 − $6 + $8 − $5 + $4 −
        $10 = $0 (closed path = 3-A to 3-C to 2-C
        to 2-B to 1-B to 1-A)
Plant 3—Project B = +$7 − $6 + $8 − $5 = +$4
        (closed path = 3-B to 3-C to 2-C to 2-B)

Since all indices are greater than or equal to zero, this initial solution provides the optimal transportation schedule, namely, 40 units from 1 to A, 30 units from 1 to B, 20 units from 2 to B, 30 units from 2 to C, and 30 units from 3 to C.

b. There is an alternate optimal solution to this problem. This fact is seen by the index for Plant 3—Project A being equal to zero. The other optimal solution, should you wish for students to pursue it, is as follows:

Plant 1—Project A = 20 units
Plant 1—Project B = 50 units
Plant 2—Project C = 50 units
Plant 3—Project A = 20 units
Plant 3—Project C = 10 units

Total cost remains unchanged at $1,040.

14-13. Hardrock's problem now requires the addition of a dummy project (destination) because supply exceeds demand. The northwest corner initial solution is as follows:

FROM \ TO	A	B	C	DUMMY	CAPACITY
1	10 — 40	4 — 30	11	0	70
2	12	5 — 20	8 — 30	0	50
3	9	7	6 — 30	0 — 30	60
Requirements	40	50	60	30	180

Cost of initial solution = 40($10) + 30($4) + 20($5)
                                  + 30($8) + 30($6) + 30($0)
                                  = $1,040

This is the same initial assignment and cost as that found in Problem 14-12. This coincidence occurs because the change in plant capacity is at the lower right-hand corner of the table and is unaffected by the northwest corner rule.

Testing the unused routes:

Plant 1—Project C index
$$= \$11 - 8 + 5 - 4 = +\$4$$
Plant 1—Dummy index
$$= +\$0 - 0 + 6 - 8 + 5 - 4 = -\$1$$
best $\left.\begin{array}{l}\text{Plant 2—Project } A \text{ index}\\ \qquad = +\$12 - 5 + 4 - 10 = +\$1\\ \text{Plant 2—Dummy index}\\ \qquad = +\$0 - 0 + 6 - 8 = -\$2\end{array}\right.$

best
improve-
ment
index

Plant 2—Project A index
$$= +\$12 - 5 + 4 - 10 = +\$1$$
Plant 2—Dummy index
$$= +\$0 - 0 + 6 - 8 = -\$2$$
Plant 3—Project A index
$$= +\$9 - 6 + 8 - 5 + 4 - 10 = \$0$$
Plant 3—Project B index
$$= +\$7 - 6 + 8 - 5 = +\$4$$

The second table involves bringing the Plant 2—Dummy route into the solution as follows:

FROM \ TO	A		B		C		DUMMY		CAPACITY
1	40	10	30	4		11		0	70
2		12	20	5	0	8	30	0	50
3		9		7	60	6		0	60
Requirements	40		50		60		30		180

Cost of this iteration = $980.

Because two squares became zero by opening the Plant 2—Dummy route, the current solution is *degenerate* (less than 3 rows + 4 columns − 1 squares are occupied). We will need to place an artificial 0 in an unused square (such as Plant 2—Project C) in order to be able to trace all of the closed paths and evaluate where this solution is optimal.

We now trace the closed paths for the six unused squares (we assume the Plant 2—Project C square has a 0 in it). The indices are:

Plant 1—Project C = $+\$11 - 8 + 5 - 4 = +\$4$
Plant 1—Dummy   = $+\$0 - 0 + 5 - 4 = +\$1$

Plant 2—Project A = $+\$12 - 5 + 4 - 10 = +\$1$
Plant 3—Project A = $+\$9 - 6 + 8 - 5 + 4$
$$- 10 = \$0$$
Plant 3—Project B = $+\$7 - 6 + 8 - 5 = +\$4$
Plant 3—Dummy   = $+\$0 - 0 + 8 - 6 = +\$2$

Since all indices are zero or positive, an optimal solution has been reached. Again, note that the Plant 3—Project A route has an improvement index of $0, implying that an alternate optimal solution exists. The alternate optimal solution, whose total cost is also $980, is shown at top of the following page.

TO FROM	A		B		C		DUMMY		CAPACITY
		10		4		11		0	
1	20		50						70
		12		5		8		0	
2					20		30		50
		9		7		6		0	
3	20				40				60
Requirements	40		50		60		30		180

14-14. a. Using the northwest corner rule for the Saussy Lumber Company data, the following initial solution is reached:

TO FROM	CUSTOMER 1		CUSTOMER 2		CUSTOMER 3		CAPACITY
		3		3		2	
Pineville	25						25
		4		2		3	
Oak Ridge	5		30		5		40
		3		2		3	
Mapletown					30		30
Demand	30		30		35		95

Initial cost = 25 ($3) + 5 ($4) + 30 ($2) + 5 ($3)
              + 30 ($3)
          = $260

b. Applying the stepping-stone method, the improvement indices are computed:

best improvement index
$$\left\{ \begin{array}{l} \text{Pineville—Customer 2} \\ \quad = +\$3 - 2 + 4 - 3 = +\$2 \\ \text{Pineville—Customer 3} \\ \quad = +\$2 - 3 + 4 - 3 = \$0 \\ \text{Mapletown—Customer 1} \\ \quad = +\$3 - 3 + 3 - 4 = -\$1 \\ \text{Mapletown—Customer 2} \\ \quad = +\$2 - 3 + 3 - 2 = \$0 \end{array} \right.$$

The improved solution is shown on the following page. Its cost is $255.

TO FROM	CUSTOMER 1	CUSTOMER 2	CUSTOMER 3	CAPACITY
Pineville	25 [3]	[3]	[2]	25
Oak Ridge	[4]	30 [2]	10 [3]	40
Mapletown	5 [3]	[2]	25 [3]	30
Demand	30	30	35	95

Checking improvement indices again, we find that this improved solution is still not optimal. The improvement index for the Pineville—Customer 3 route = +\$2 − 3 + 3 − 3 = −\$1. Hence, another shift is necessary. The third iteration is shown in the following table:

TO FROM	CUSTOMER 1	CUSTOMER 2	CUSTOMER 3	CAPACITY
Pineville	0 [3]	[3]	25 [2]	25
Oak Ridge	[4]	30 [2]	10 [3]	40
Mapletown	30 [3]	[2]	0 [3]	30
Demand	30	30	35	95

The cost of this solution is \$230. Since two squares went to zero simultaneously in this last table, the solution has become degenerate. However, an examination of improvement indices reveals that this current solution is optimal.

14-15. Solving the Saussy Lumber Company problem with MODI, we begin with the same initial solution as found in Problem 14-14:

		K_1	K_2	K_3	
	TO FROM	CUSTOMER 1	CUSTOMER 2	CUSTOMER 3	CAPACITY
R_1	Pineville	25 [3]	[3]	[2]	25
R_2	Oak Ridge	5 [4]	30 [2]	5 [3]	40
R_3	Mapletown	[3]	[2]	30 [3]	30
	Demand	30	30	35	95

$R_1 = 0$
$R_1 + K_1 = C_{11} \Rightarrow 0 + K_1 = 3 \quad \text{or} \quad K_1 = 3$
$R_2 + K_1 = C_{21} \Rightarrow R_2 + 3 = 4 \quad \text{or} \quad R_2 = 1$
$R_2 + K_2 = C_{22} \Rightarrow 1 + K_2 = 2 \quad \text{or} \quad K_2 = 1$
$R_2 + K_3 = C_{23} \Rightarrow 1 + K_3 = 3 \quad \text{or} \quad K_3 = 2$
$R_3 + K_3 = C_{33} \Rightarrow R_3 + 2 = 3 \quad \text{or} \quad R_3 = 1$

Improvement indices are as follows:

Pineville—Customer 2
$= C_{12} - R_1 - K_2 = 3 - 0 - 1 = +2$
Pineville—Customer 3
$= C_{13} - R_1 - K_3 = 2 - 0 - 2 = 0$

best improvement index
Mapletown—Customer 1
$= C_{31} - R_3 - K_1 = 3 - 1 - 3 = -1$
Mapletown—Customer 2
$= C_{32} - R_3 - K_2 = 2 - 1 - 1 = 0$

The final solution is also evaluated using MODI below.

Calculations of the R_i's, K_j's, and improvement indices are shown:

$R_1 + K_1 = C_{11} \Rightarrow 0 + K_1 = 3 \quad \text{or} \quad K_1 = 3$
$R_3 + K_1 = C_{31} \Rightarrow R_3 + 3 = 3 \quad \text{or} \quad R_3 = 0$
$R_1 + K_3 = C_{13} \Rightarrow 0 + K_3 = 2 \quad \text{or} \quad K_3 = 2$
$R_2 + K_3 = C_{23} \Rightarrow R_2 + 2 = 3 \quad \text{or} \quad R_2 = 1$
$R_2 + K_2 = C_{22} \Rightarrow 1 + K_2 = 2 \quad \text{or} \quad K_2 = 1$

Improvement indices:

Pineville—Customer 2
$= C_{12} - R_1 - K_2 = 3 - 0 - 1 = +2$
Oak Ridge—Customer 1
$= C_{21} - R_2 - K_1 = 4 - 1 - 3 = 0$
Mapletown—Customer 2
$= C_{32} - R_3 - K_2 = 2 - 0 - 1 = +1$
Mapletown—Customer 3
$= C_{33} - R_3 - K_3 = 3 - 0 - 2 = +1$

Final solution with R_i and K_j values:

		$K_1 = 3$ CUSTOMER 1	$K_2 = 1$ CUSTOMER 2	$K_3 = 2$ CUSTOMER 3	CAPACITY
$R_1 = 0$	Pineville	3 / 0	3	2 / 25	25
$R_2 = 1$	Oak Ridge	4	2 / 30	3 / 10	40
$R_3 = 0$	Mapletown	3 / 30	2	3	30
	Demand	30	30	35	95

14-16. Krampf Lines Railway Company's initial northwest corner solution is shown below:

		$K_1 = 50$ COAL VALLEY	$K_2 = 30$ COAL-TOWN	$K_3 = -40$ COAL JUNCTION	$K_4 = -90$ COALS-BURG	SUPPLY
$R_1 = 0$	Morgantown	50 / 30	30 / 5	60	70	35
$R_2 = 50$	Youngstown	20	80 / 40	10 / 20	90	60
$R_3 = 120$	Pittsburgh	100	40	80 / 5	30 / 20	25
	Demand	30	45	25	20	120

FROM \ TO	COAL VALLEY $K_1 = 0$	COAL-TOWN $K_2 = 30$	COAL JUNCTION $K_3 = -40$	COALS-BURG $K_4 = 20$	SUPPLY
Morgantown $R_1 = 0$	50 / 30	30 / 5	60	70	35
Youngstown $R_2 = 50$	20	80 / 35	10 / 25	90	60
Pittsburgh $R_3 = 10$	100	40 / 5	80	30 / 20	25
Demand	30	45	25	20	120

Initial solution's total cost

$$= 30 \text{ (50 miles)} + 5 \text{ (30 miles)}$$
$$+ 40 \text{ (80 miles)} + 20 \text{ (10 miles)}$$
$$+ 5 \text{ (80 miles)} + 20 \text{ (30 miles)}$$
$$= 6{,}050 \text{ car-miles}$$

To test for improvement with MODI, we set up an equation for each occupied square:

$R_1 = 0$
$R_1 + K_1 = 50 \quad 0 + K_1 = 50 \quad \text{or} \quad K_1 = 50$
$R_1 + K_2 = 30 \quad 0 + K_2 = 30 \quad \text{or} \quad K_2 = 30$
$R_2 + K_2 = 80 \quad R_2 + 30 = 80 \quad \text{or} \quad R_2 = 50$
$R_2 + K_3 = 10 \quad 50 + K_3 = 10 \quad \text{or} \quad K_3 = -40$
$R_3 + K_3 = 80 \quad R_3 - 40 = 80 \quad \text{or} \quad R_3 = 120$
$R_3 + K_4 = 30 \quad 120 + K_4 = 30 \quad \text{or} \quad K_4 = -90$

$\text{Index}_{13} = C_{13} - R_1 - K_3$
$\quad = 60 - 0 - (-40) = +100$
$\text{Index}_{14} = C_{14} - R_1 - K_4$
$\quad = 70 - 0 - (-90) = +160$
$\text{Index}_{21} = C_{21} - R_2 - K_1$
$\quad = 20 - 50 - 50 = -80$
$\text{Index}_{24} = C_{24} - R_2 - K_4$
$\quad = 90 - 50 - (-90) = +130$
$\text{Index}_{31} = C_{31} - R_3 - K_1$
$\quad = 100 - 120 - 50 = -70$

best improvement index } $\text{Index}_{32} = C_{32} - R_3 - K_2$
$\quad = 40 - 120 - 30 = -110$

$\text{Index}_{13} = C_{13} - R_1 - K_3$
$\quad = 60 - 0 - (-40) = +100$
$\text{Index}_{14} = C_{14} - R_1 - K_4$
$\quad = 70 - 0 - 20 = +50$

best improvement index } $\text{Index}_{21} = C_{21} - R_2 - K_1$
$\quad = 20 - 50 - 50 = -80$
$\text{Index}_{24} = C_{24} - R_2 - K_4$
$\quad = 90 - 50 - 20 = +20$
$\text{Index}_{31} = C_{31} - R_3 - K_1$
$\quad = 100 - 10 - 50 = +40$
$\text{Index}_{33} = C_{33} - R_3 - K_3$
$\quad = 80 - 10 - (-40) = +110$

Second Krampf solution—cost = 5,500 miles:

$R_1 = 0$
$R_1 + K_1 = 50 \Rightarrow K_1 = 50$
$R_1 + K_2 = 30 \Rightarrow K_2 = 30$
$R_2 + K_2 = 80 \Rightarrow R_2 = 50$
$R_2 + K_3 = 10 \Rightarrow K_3 = -40$
$R_3 + K_2 = 40 \Rightarrow R_3 = 10$
$R_3 + K_4 = 30 \Rightarrow K_4 = 20$

Third and optimal Krampf solution—cost = 3,100 miles:

TO / FROM	COAL VALLEY	COAL-TOWN	COAL JUNCTION	COALS-BURG	SUPPLY
Morgantown	50	30 / 35	60	70	35
Youngstown	20 / 30	80 / 5	10 / 25	90	60
Pittsburgh	100	40 / 5	80	30 / 20	25
Demand	30	45	25	20	120

14-17. Jessie Cohen Clothing Group's first VAM assignment table:

TO / FROM	2 A	1 B	2 C	FACTORY AVAILABILITY	
W	4	3	3	35	0
Y	6	7	6	50	0
Z	8 / X	2 / 50	5 / X	50	3
Store demand	30	65	40	135	

In the above initial assignment table, we see that the Z row has the greatest difference (3). We assign the minimum possible number of units (50) to the least-cost route (Z-B) in that row.

Second VAM assignment with B's requirement satisfied:

TO / FROM	2 A	4 B	3 C	AVAILABLE	
W	4	3 / 15	3	35	0
Y	6	7 / X	6	50	0
Z	8 / X	2 / 50	5 / X	50	3̶
Demand	30	65	40	135	

This second VAM table (on the previous page) indicates that the greatest difference is now in the B column (4). We may assign up to 15 units to the W-B square without exceeding the demand at store B.

Third VAM assignment with W's requirement satisfied:

FROM \ TO	A (2)	B (A̶)	C (3)	AVAILABLE	
W	X [4]	15 [3]	20 [3]	35	X̶
Y	[6]	X [7]	[6]	50	0
Z	X [6]	50 [2]	X [5]	50	5̶0̶
Demand	30	65	40	135	

The third VAM table involves assigning 20 units to the W-C route. This is done because column C has the highest difference and square W-C the lowest cost in that column.

Final assignment for Cohen Clothing Group:

FROM \ TO	A (2̶)	B (A̶)	C (3̶)	AVAILABLE	
W	X [4]	15 [3]	20 [3]	35	0
Y	30 [6]	X [7]	20 [6]	50	0
Z	X [8]	50 [2]	X [5]	50	5̶0̶
Demand	30	65	40	135	

The final assignment (above) is made by completing the row and column requirements. This means that 30 units must be assigned to Y-A and 20 units to Y-C.

The total cost of this VAM assignment = (15 units × $3) + (20 units × $3) + (30 units × $6) + (20 units × $6) + (50 units × $2) = $505. A quick check using the stepping-stone index method indicates that this VAM solution is also optimal.

14-18. a. VAM steps are as follows:

1. Assign 30 units to C-W (the W-column has the greatest difference, 7) and place X's in all other row C squares.
2. Assign 20 units to B-X.
3. Assign 10 units to B-W.
4. Assign 20 units to A-Z.
5. Assign 35 units to A-Y and 15 units to B-Y.

FROM \ TO	W	X	Y	Z	EXCESS SUPPLY	
A	12 — X	4 — X	9 — 35	5 — 20	55	4
B	8 — 10	1 — 20	6 — 15	6 — X	45	0
C	1 — 30	12 — X	4 — X	7 — X	30	
Power demand	40	20	50	20	130	

Total VAM Cost = 35(9) + 20(5) + 10(8) + 20(1)
$$+ \ 15(6) + 30(1)$$
$$= 635$$

b. MODI technique to test for optimality:

	$K_1 = 11$	$K_2 = 4$	$K_3 = 9$	$K_4 = 5$	
FROM \ TO	W	X	Y	Z	EXCESS SUPPLY
$R_1 = 0$ A	12	4	9 — 35	5 — 20	55
$R_2 = -3$ B	8 — 10	1 — 20	6 — 15	6	45
$R_3 = -10$ C	1 — 30	12	4	7	30
Power demand	40	20	50	20	130

$R_1 = 0$
$R_1 + K_3 = 9 \quad K_3 = 9$
$R_1 + K_4 = 5 \quad K_4 = 5$
$R_2 + K_3 = 6 \quad R_2 = -3$
$R_2 + K_1 = 8 \quad K_1 = 11$
$R_2 + K_2 = 1 \quad K_2 = 4$
$R_3 + K_1 = 1 \quad R_3 = -10$

$\text{Index}_{11} = C_{11} - R_1 - K_1 = 12 - 0 - 11 = +1$
$\text{Index}_{12} = C_{12} - R_1 - K_2 = 4 - 0 - 4 = 0$
$\text{Index}_{24} = C_{24} - R_2 - K_4 = 6 - (-3) - 5 = +4$
$\text{Index}_{32} = C_{32} - R_3 - K_2 = 12 - (-10) - 4 = +18$
$\text{Index}_{33} = C_{33} - R_3 - K_3 = 4 - (-10) - 9 = +5$
$\text{Index}_{34} = C_{34} - R_3 - K_4 = 7 - (-10) - 5 = +12$

Since all improvement indices are zero or positive, this solution is optimal. An *alternate* optimal solution, however, is: $A\text{-}X = 20$, $A\text{-}Y = 15$, $A\text{-}Z = 20$, $B\text{-}W = 10$, $B\text{-}Y = 35$, $C\text{-}W = 30$, Cost = \$635.

14-19. The initial solution using the northwest corner rule shows that degeneracy exists. The number of rows plus the number of columns minus $1 = 4 + 3 - 1 = 6$. But the number of occupied squares is only 5. To solve the problem a 0 will have to be placed in a square (such as 2-C). This will enable all unused paths to be closed.

FROM \ TO	A		B		C		SUPPLY
1	72	8		9		4	72
	(26)		(15)		(31)		
2	38	5		6		8	38
	(38)						
3		7		9		6	46
	(46)		34		12		
4		5		3		7	19
			(19)		19		
Demand	110		34		31		175

The optimal solution to Problem 14-19, through the use of our computer program is circled. Cost = $1,036.

14-20. Using VAM to find an initial solution, we make the following assignment:

FROM \ TO	HOSPITAL 1		HOSPITAL 2		HOSPITAL 3		HOSPITAL 4		SUPPLY	
Bank 1	50	8	X	9	X	11	X	16	50	X
Bank 2	X	12	70	7	10	5	X	8	80	
Bank 3	40	14	X	10	30	6	50	7	120	1
Demand	90		70		40		50		250	

Cost of VAM assignment = 50($8) + 70($7) + 10($5) + 40($14) + 30($6) + 50($7) = $2,030

Application of the MODI or stepping-stone methods will yield the following solution in one more iteration. The optimal cost is $2,020.

FROM \ TO	HOSPITAL 1		HOSPITAL 2		HOSPITAL 3		HOSPITAL 4		SUPPLY
Bank 1	50	8		9		11		16	50
Bank 2	10	12	70	7		5		8	80
Bank 3	30	14		10	40	6	50	7	120
Demand	90		70		40		50		250

14-21. The optimal solution to the Hall Real Estate decision is shown in the table below:

FROM \ TO	HILL ST.	BANKS ST.	PARK AVE.	DRURY LANE	MAX. AVAIL.
First Homestead	8%	8% $40,000	10% $40,000	11%	$80,000
Commonwealth	9% $60,000	10%	12%	10% $40,000	$100,000
Washington Federal	9%	11%	10% $90,000	9% $30,000	$120,000
Loan needed	$60,000	$40,000	$130,000	$70,000	$300,000

The total interest cost would be $28,300, or an average rate of 9.43%. An alternate optimal solution exists. It is:

First Homestead—Hill Street	30,000
First Homestead—Banks Street	40,000
First Homestead—Park Avenue	10,000
Commonwealth—Hill Street	30,000
Commonwealth—Drury Lane	70,000
Washington Federal—Park Avenue	120,000

14-22. Mehta's production smoothing problem is a good exercise in the formulation of transportation problems and applying them to real-world issues. The problem may be set up as in the table on page IS-165. All squares with X's represent nonfeasible (back-order) solutions. In applying a computer program to solve such a problem, a very large cost (say about $5,000) would be assigned to each of these squares. This would assure that they would not appear in the final solution. The dummy destination (month) is added to balance the problem.

The initial solution has a cost of $65,700.

14-23. To determine which new plant will yield the lowest cost for Ashley in combination with the existing plants, we need to solve two transportation problems.

We begin by setting up a transportation table that represents the opening of the third plant in New Orleans (see table on page IS-165). The northwest corner method is used to provide an initial solution. The total cost of this first solution is seen to be $23,600. You should note that the cost of each individual "plant to distribution center" route is found by adding the distribution costs to the respective unit production costs. Thus, the total production plus shipping cost of one auto top carrier from Atlanta to Los Angeles is $14 ($8 for shipping plus $6 for production).

Table for Problem 14-22

SOURCES	DESTINATION (MONTH)				DUMMY	CAPACITY
	1	2	3	4		
Beginning inventory	10 / 40	20	30	40	0	40
Regular prod. (month 1)	100 / 80	110 / 20	120	130	0	100
Overtime (month 1)	130	140 / 50	150	160	0	50
Regular prod. (month 2)	✕	100 / 90	110 / 10	120	0	100
Overtime (month 2)	✕	130	140 / 50	150	0	50
Regular prod. (month 3)	✕	✕	100 / 100	110	0	100
Overtime (month 4)	✕	✕	130 / 50	140	0	50
Regular prod. (month 4)	✕	✕	✕	100 / 100	0	100
Overtime (month 4)	✕	✕	✕	130	0 / 50	50
Outside purchases	150	150	150 / 30	150	0 / 420	450
Demand	120	160	240	100	470	1,090

Table for Problem 14-23

FROM \ TO	LOS ANGELES	NEW YORK	PRODUCTION CAPACITY
Atlanta	$14 / 600	$11	600
Tulsa	$9 / 200	$12 / 700	900
New Orleans	$9	$10 / 500	500
Demand	800	1,200	2,000

Total Cost = (600 units × $14) + (200 units × $9)
            + (700 units × $12) + (500 units × $10)
          = $8,400 + $1,800 + $8,400 + $5,000
          = $23,600

Is this initial solution optimal? We once again employ the stepping-stone method to test it and to compute improvement indices for unused routes.

Improvement index for Atlanta to New York route:

    +$11 (Atlanta to New York)
    −$14 (Atlanta to Los Angeles)
    + $9 (Tulsa to Los Angeles)
    −$12 (Tulsa to New York)
  = −$6

Improvement index for New Orleans to Los Angeles route:

    + $9 (New Orleans to Los Angeles)
    −$10 (New Orleans to New York)
    +$12 (Tulsa to New York)
    − $9 (Tulsa to Los Angeles)
  = +$2

TO \ FROM	LOS ANGELES	NEW YORK	PRODUCTION CAPACITY
Atlanta	$14	$11 600	600
Tulsa	$9 800	$12 100	900
New Orleans	$9	$10 500	500
Demand	800	1,200	2,000

Since the firm can save $6 for every unit it ships from Atlanta to New York, it will want to improve the initial solution and send as many as possible (600 in this case) on this currently unused route.

You may want to confirm that the total cost is now $20,000, a savings of $3,600 over the initial solution.

Again, we must test the two unused routes to see if their improvement indices are negative numbers.

Index for Atlanta to Los Angeles
            = +$14 − $11 + $12 − $9 = +$6
Index for New Orleans to Los Angeles
            = +$9 − $10 + $12 − $9 = +$2

Since both indices are greater than zero, we have reached an optimal solution. If Ashley selects to open the *New Orleans plant,* the firm's total distribution *system cost will be $20,000.* If the Houston plant site is chosen, the initial solution is as follows:

TO FROM	LOS ANGELES	NEW YORK	PRODUCTION CAPACITY
Atlanta	$14 600	$11	600
Tulsa	$9 200	$12 700	900
Houston	$7	$9 500	500
Demand	800	1,200	2,000

Total cost of initial solution:

$$= \$8,400 + \$1,800 + \$8,400 + \$4,500$$
$$= \$23,100$$

Improvement index for Atlanta to New York:

$$= +\$11 - \$14 + \$9 - \$12$$
$$= -\$6$$

Improvement index for Houston to Los Angeles:

$$= +\$7 - \$9 + \$12 - \$9$$
$$= +\$1$$

The improved solution by opening Atlanta to New York route is shown below.

TO FROM	LOS ANGELES	NEW YORK	PRODUCTION CAPACITY
Atlanta	$14	$11 600	600
Tulsa	$9 800	$12 100	900
Houston	$7	$9 500	500
Demand	800	1,200	2,000

Total cost of improved solution = $19,500.

Improvement indices for Atlanta to New York and Houston to Los Angeles routes are both positive at this point. Hence, an optimal solution has been reached. Upon comparing total costs for the Houston option ($19,500) to those for the New Orleans option ($20,000), we would recommend to Ashley that, all factors being equal, the Houston site should be selected.

14.24 Considering Fontainebleau, we have:

	CANADA	SOUTH AMERICA	PACIFIC RIM	EUROPE	CAPACITY
Waterloo	60	70	75	75	8,000
Pusan	55	55	40	70	2,000
Bogota	60	50	65	70	5,000
Fontainebleau	75	80	90	60	9,000
Market Demand	4,000	5,000	10,000	5,000	

	CANADA	SOUTH AMERICA	PACIFIC RIM	EUROPE	CAPACITY
Waterloo	60 4,000	70	75 4,000	75	8,000
Pusan	55	55	40 2,000	70	2,000
Bogota	60	50 5,000	65	70	5,000
Fontainebleau	75	80	90 4,000	60 5,000	9,000
Market Demand	4,000	5,000	10,000	5,000	

Optimal cost = $1,530,000

Considering Dublin, we have:

	CANADA	SOUTH AMERICA	PACIFIC RIM	EUROPE	CAPACITY
Waterloo	60	70	75	75	8,000
Pusan	55	55	40	70	2,000
Bogota	60	50	65	70	5,000
Dublin	70	75	85	65	9,000
Market Demand	4,000	5,000	10,000	5,000	

	CANADA	SOUTH AMERICA	PACIFIC RIM	EUROPE	CAPACITY
Waterloo	60 / 4,000	70 / 4,000	75	75	8,000
Pusan	55	55 / 1,000	40 / 1,000	70	2,000
Bogota	60	50	65 / 5,000	70	5,000
Dublin	70	75	85 / 4,000	65 / 5,000	9,000
Market Demand	4,000	5,000	10,000	5,000	

	CANADA	SOUTH AMERICA	PACIFIC RIM	EUROPE	CAPACITY
Waterloo	60 / 4,000	70	75 / 4,000	75	8,000
Pusan	55	55	40 / 2,000	70	2,000
Bogota	60	50 / 5,000	65	70	5,000
Dublin	70	75	85 / 4,000	65 / 5,000	9,000
Market Demand	4,000	5,000	10,000	5,000	

Optimal cost = $1,535,000

There is no difference in the routing of shipments, but the Fontainebleau location is $5,000 less expensive than the Dublin location. As a practical matter, changes in exchange rates, subjective factors, or evaluation of future intangibles may overwhelm such a small difference in cost.

14-25. Considering East St. Louis, we have:

Initial Solution—Northwest Corner Rule:

	DECATUR	MINN.	C'DALE	E. ST. L.	DEMAND
Blue Earth	20 / 250	17	21	29	250
Ciro	25 / 50	27 / 150	20	30	200
Des Moines	22	25 / 50	22 / 150	30 / 150	350
Capacity	300	200	150	150	

Optimal Solution:

	DECATUR	MINN.	C'DALE	E. ST. L.	DEMAND
Blue Earth	20 / 50	17 / 200	21	29	250
Ciro	25	27	20 / 150	30 / 50	200
Des Moines	22 / 250	25	22	30 / 100	350
Capacity	300	200	150	150	

Optimal cost using East St. Louis: $17,400

Considering St. Louis, we have:

Initial Solution—Northwest Corner Rule:

	DECATUR	MINN.	C'DALE	ST. LOUIS	DEMAND
Blue Earth	20 / 250	17	21	27	250
Ciro	25 / 50	27 / 150	20	28	200
Des Moines	22	25 / 50	22 / 150	31 / 150	350
Capacity	300	200	150	150	

Optimal Solution:

	DECATUR	MINN.	C'DALE	ST. LOUIS	DEMAND
Blue Earth	20	17 / 200	21	27 / 50	250
Ciro	25	27	20 / 100	28 / 100	200
Des Moines	22 / 300	25	22 / 50	31	350
Capacity	300	200	150	150	

Optimal cost using St. Louis: $17,250

Therefore, St. Louis is $150 per week less expensive than East St. Louis.

14-26. Considering East St. Louis, we have:

Initial Solution—Northwest Corner Rule:

	DECATUR	MINN.	C'DALE	E. ST. L.	DEMAND
Blue Earth	70 ⟶ 250	77	91	69	250
Ciro	75 ⟶ 50	87 ⟶ 150	90	70	200
Des Moines	72	85 ⟶ 50	92 ⟶ 150	70 ⟶ 150	350
Capacity	300	200	150	150	

Optimal Solution:

	DECATUR	MINN.	C'DALE	E. ST. L.	DEMAND
Blue Earth	70 ⟶ 50	77 ⟶ 200	91	69	250
Ciro	75	87	90 ⟶ 150	70 ⟶ 50	200
Des Moines	72 ⟶ 250	85	92	70 ⟶ 100	350
Capacity	300	200	150	150	

Optimal cost using East St. Louis: $60,900

Considering St. Louis, we have:

Initial Solution—Northwest Corner Rule:

	DECATUR	MINN.	C'DALE	ST. LOUIS	DEMAND
Blue Earth	70 ⟶ 250	77	91	77	250
Ciro	75 ⟶ 50	87 ⟶ 150	90	78	200
Des Moines	72	85 ⟶ 50	92 ⟶ 150	81 ⟶ 150	350
Capacity	300	200	150	150	

Optimal Solution:

	DECATUR	MINN.	C'DALE	ST. LOUIS	DEMAND
Blue Earth	70	77	91	77	250
		200		50	
Ciro	75	87	90	78	200
			100	100	
Des Moines	72	85	92	81	350
	300		50		
Capacity	300	200	150	150	

Optimal cost using St. Louis: $62,250

Therefore, East St. Louis is $1350 per week less expensive than St. Louis.

14-27. Step 1—row subtraction:

JOB \ MACHINE	W	X	Y	Z
A12	0	4	6	3
A15	0	1	3	0
B2	0	3	3	2
B9	0	2	4	2

Column subtraction:

JOB \ MACHINE	W	X	Y	Z
A12	0	3	3	3
A15	0	0	0	0
B2	0	2	0	2
B9	0	1	1	2

Step 2—minimum straight lines to cover zeros:

JOB \ MACHINE	W	X	Y	Z
A12	0	3	3	3
A15	0	0	0	0
B2	0	2	0	2
B9	0	1	1	2

Step 3—subtract smallest uncovered from uncovered numbers—add it to numbers at intersections of two lines:

JOB \ MACHINE	W	X	Y	Z
A12	0	2	3	2
A15	1	0	1	0
B2	0	1	0	1
B9	0	0	1	1

Return to Step 2—Cover all zeros:

JOB \ MACHINE	W	X	Y	Z
A12	0	2	3	2
A15	1	0	1	0
B2	0	1	0	1
B9	0	0	1	1

Assignment can be made:

Job A12 to machine W
Job A15 to machine Z
Job B2 to machine Y
Job B9 to machine X
Time = 10 + 12 + 12 + 16 = 50 hours

14-28.

OFFICE MAN	OMAHA	MIAMI	DALLAS
Jones	800	1,100	1,200
Smith	500	1,600	1,300
Wilson	500	1,000	2,300

Row subtraction is done next.

OFFICE MAN	OMAHA	MIAMI	DALLAS
Jones	0	300	400
Smith	0	1,100	800
Wilson	0	500	1,800

Column subtraction is done next.

OFFICE MAN	OMAHA	MIAMI	DALLAS
Jones	0	0	0
Smith	0	800	400
Wilson	0	200	1,400

Cover zeros with lines.

OFFICE MAN	OMAHA	MIAMI	DALLAS
Jones	0	0	0
Smith	0	800	400
Wilson	0	200	1,400

Subtract smallest number.

OFFICE MAN	OMAHA	MIAMI	DALLAS
Jones	200	0	0
Smith	0	600	200
Wilson	0	0	1,200

Cover zeros with lines.

OFFICE MAN	OMAHA	MIAMI	DALLAS
Jones	200	0	0
Smith	0	600	200
Wilson	0	0	1,200

Optimal assignment:

Jones to Dallas
Smith to Omaha
Wilson to Miami
Cost = $1,200 + $500 + $1,000
     = $2,700

14-29. Original problem:

SITE \ CUSTOMER	A	B	C	D
1	7	3	4	8
2	5	4	6	5
3	6	7	9	6
4	8	6	7	4

Row subtraction is done next.

SITE \ CUSTOMER	A	B	C	D
1	4	0	1	5
2	1	0	2	1
3	0	1	3	0
4	4	2	3	0

Column subtraction is done next.

SITE \ CUSTOMER	A	B	C	D
1	4	0	0	5
2	1	0	1	1
3	0	1	2	0
4	4	2	2	0

Cover zeros with lines.

SITE \ CUSTOMER	A	B	C	D
1	4	0	0	5
2	1	0	0	1
3	0	1	2	0
4	4	2	2	0

Optimal assignment:

Taxi at Post 1 to customer C
Taxi at Post 2 to customer B
Taxi at Post 3 to customer A
Taxi at Post 4 to customer D
Total distance traveled = 4 + 4 + 6 + 4 = 18 miles

14-30. Original problem:

SQUAD \ CASE	A	B	C	D	E
1	14	7	3	7	27
2	20	7	12	6	30
3	10	3	4	5	21
4	8	12	7	12	21
5	13	25	24	26	8

Row subtraction is done next.

SQUAD \ CASE	A	B	C	D	E
1	11	4	0	4	24
2	14	1	6	0	24
3	7	0	1	2	18
4	1	5	0	5	14
5	5	17	16	18	0

Column subtraction is done next.

SQUAD \ CASE	A	B	C	D	E
1	10	4	0	4	24
2	13	1	6	0	24
3	6	0	1	2	18
4	0	5	0	5	14
5	4	17	16	18	0

Cover zeros with lines.

SQUAD \ CASE	A	B	C	D	E
1	10	4	0	4	24
2	13	1	6	0	24
3	6	0	1	2	18
4	0	5	0	5	14
5	4	17	16	18	0

Optimal assignment:

Squad 1 to case C
Squad 3 to case B
Squad 5 to case E
Squad 2 to case D
Squad 4 to case A

Total person days projected using this assignment = 3 + 6 + 3 + 8 + 8 = 28 days.

14-31. Because this is a maximization problem, each number is subtracted from 95. The problem is then solved using the minimization algorithm.

ASSIGNMENT	RATING
Anderson—Finance	95
Sweeney—Economics	75
Williams—Statistics	85
McKinney—Management	80
Total rating	335

14-32.

ASSIGNMENT	RATING
Hawkins to Cardiology	18
Condriac to Urology	32
Bardot to Orthopedics	24
Hoolihan to Obstetrics	12
Total "cost scale"	86

14-33. Each rating is subtracted from 27.1 because this is a maximization problem.

ASSIGNMENT	RATING
1–2 P.M. on A	27.1
2–3 P.M. on C	17.1
3–4 P.M. on B	18.5
4–5 P.M. on Independent	12.8
Overall rating	75.5

14-34.

ASSIGNMENT	RATING
C53 at Plant 1	10¢
C81 at Plant 3	4¢
D5 at Plant 4	30¢
D44 at Plant 2	14¢
Total manufacturing cost	58¢

14-35.

ASSIGNMENT	RATING
Adams to Project 3	$ 6
Brown to Project 2	$10
Cooper to Project 1	$ 9
Davis to Dummy	0
	$25

Thus, the optimal solution does not change by adding a fourth member. Davis is assigned to the dummy (nonexistent project). This is because Davis is not the relatively least-cost assignment to any of the first three projects.

14-36. The following optimal assignments can be made:

ASSIGNMENT	COST
Component C53 to Plant 6	.06
Component D5 to Plant 4	.30
Component D44 to Plant 5	.10
Component E35 to Plant 8	.06
Component G99 to Plant 1	.55
Component E2 to Plant 2	.07
Component C81 to Plant 3	.04
Total cost	$1.18

14-37. Students should note the large numbers used to block infeasible production plans (see printout 1).

a. The solution yields a cost of $257,560. The plan is shown in printout 2.

b. Yes, the solution now costs $261,200 with 275 per month in regular time.

c. If overtime rises by $100 per unit to $1,400 per unit, the cost increases, from part a, to $259,450. The production plan remains the same as in printout 2.

Printout 1 for Problem 14-37 (AB:QM Data Entry)

```
Program: Transportation

Problem Title: HAIFA DATASET 14.37

***** Input Data *****

Minimization Problem
```

	1	2	3	4	5	6	7	8	Supply
1	100.0	110.0	120.0	130.0	140.0	150.0	160.0	170.0	235.0
2	130.0	140.0	150.0	160.0	170.0	180.0	190.0	200.0	20.0
3	150.0	160.0	170.0	180.0	190.0	200.0	210.0	220.0	12.0
4	999.0	100.0	110.0	120.0	130.0	140.0	150.0	160.0	255.0
5	999.0	130.0	140.0	150.0	160.0	170.0	180.0	190.0	24.0
6	999.0	150.0	160.0	170.0	180.0	190.0	200.0	210.0	15.0
7	999.0	999.0	100.0	110.0	120.0	130.0	140.0	150.0	290.0
8	999.0	999.0	130.0	140.0	150.0	160.0	170.0	180.0	26.0
9	999.0	999.0	150.0	160.0	170.0	180.0	190.0	200.0	15.0
10	999.0	999.0	999.0	100.0	110.0	120.0	130.0	140.0	300.0
11	999.0	999.0	999.0	130.0	140.0	150.0	160.0	170.0	24.0
12	999.0	999.0	999.0	150.0	160.0	170.0	180.0	190.0	17.0
13	999.0	999.0	999.0	999.0	100.0	110.0	120.0	130.0	300.0
14	999.0	999.0	999.0	999.0	130.0	140.0	150.0	160.0	30.0
15	999.0	999.0	999.0	999.0	150.0	160.0	170.0	180.0	17.0
16	999.0	999.0	999.0	999.0	999.0	100.0	110.0	120.0	290.0
17	999.0	999.0	999.0	999.0	999.0	130.0	140.0	150.0	28.0
18	999.0	999.0	999.0	999.0	999.0	150.0	160.0	170.0	19.0
19	999.0	999.0	999.0	999.0	999.0	999.0	100.0	110.0	300.0
20	999.0	999.0	999.0	999.0	999.0	999.0	130.0	140.0	30.0
21	999.0	999.0	999.0	999.0	999.0	999.0	150.0	160.0	19.0
22	999.0	999.0	999.0	999.0	999.0	999.0	999.0	100.0	290.0
23	999.0	999.0	999.0	999.0	999.0	999.0	999.0	130.0	30.0
24	999.0	999.0	999.0	999.0	999.0	999.0	999.0	150.0	20.0
Demand	255.0	294.0	321.0	301.0	330.0	320.0	345.0	340.0	

Printout 2 for Problem 14-37 (AB:QM Solution to HAIFA)

Optimal Solution by MODI

			1	2	3	4	5	6	7	8	9	Supply
Jan.	RT	1	235.0	0.0	0.0	0.0	0.0	0.0	0.0	0.0	0.0	235.0
	OT	2	20.0	0.0	0.0	0.0	0.0	0.0	0.0	0.0	0.0	20.0
	SUB	3	0.0	12.0	0.0	0.0	0.0	0.0	0.0	0.0	0.0	12.0
Feb.	RT	4	0.0	255.0	0.0	0.0	0.0	0.0	0.0	0.0	0.0	255.0
	OT	5	0.0	24.0	0.0	0.0	0.0	0.0	0.0	0.0	0.0	24.0
	SUB	6	0.0	3.0	0.0	0.0	0.0	0.0	0.0	12.0	0.0	15.0
Mar.	RT	7	0.0	0.0	290.0	0.0	0.0	0.0	0.0	0.0	0.0	290.0
	OT	8	0.0	0.0	26.0	0.0	0.0	0.0	0.0	0.0	0.0	26.0
	SUB	9	0.0	0.0	5.0	0.0	0.0	0.0	0.0	0.0	10.0	15.0
Apr.	RT	10	0.0	0.0	0.0	300.0	0.0	0.0	0.0	0.0	0.0	300.0
	OT	11	0.0	0.0	0.0	1.0	0.0	0.0	0.0	0.0	23.0	24.0
	SUB	12	0.0	0.0	0.0	0.0	0.0	0.0	0.0	0.0	17.0	17.0
May	RT	13	0.0	0.0	0.0	0.0	300.0	0.0	0.0	0.0	0.0	300.0
	OT	14	0.0	0.0	0.0	0.0	30.0	0.0	0.0	0.0	0.0	30.0
	SUB	15	0.0	0.0	0.0	0.0	0.0	0.0	0.0	0.0	17.0	17.0
June	RT	16	0.0	0.0	0.0	0.0	0.0	290.0	0.0	0.0	0.0	290.0
	OT	17	0.0	0.0	0.0	0.0	0.0	28.0	0.0	0.0	0.0	28.0
	SUB	18	0.0	0.0	0.0	0.0	0.0	2.0	0.0	0.0	17.0	19.0
July	RT	19	0.0	0.0	0.0	0.0	0.0	0.0	300.0	0.0	0.0	300.0
	OT	20	0.0	0.0	0.0	0.0	0.0	0.0	30.0	0.0	0.0	30.0
	SUB	21	0.0	0.0	0.0	0.0	0.0	0.0	15.0	0.0	4.0	19.0
Aug.	RT	22	0.0	0.0	0.0	0.0	0.0	0.0	0.0	290.0	0.0	290.0
	OT	23	0.0	0.0	0.0	0.0	0.0	0.0	0.0	30.0	0.0	30.0
	SUB	24	0.0	0.0	0.0	0.0	0.0	0.0	0.0	8.0	12.0	20.0
	Demand		255.0	294.0	321.0	301.0	330.0	320.0	345.0	340.0	100.0	2606.0

14-38. a. Here is the first schedule using AB:QM:

b. The revised schedule is:

Optimal Solution :   96.0

	1	2	3	4	5	6	7	8	9	10
1	0	0	0	0	1	0	0	0	0	0
2	0	0	0	0	0	1	0	0	0	0
3	0	0	0	1	0	0	0	0	0	0
4	0	0	1	0	0	0	0	0	0	0
5	1	0	0	0	0	0	0	0	0	0
6	0	0	0	0	0	0	0	1	0	0
7	0	0	0	0	0	0	0	0	0	1
8	0	0	0	0	0	0	1	0	0	0
9	0	0	0	0	0	0	0	0	1	0
10	0	1	0	0	0	0	0	0	0	0

Optimal Solution :   92.0

	1	2	3	4	5	6	7	8	9	10
1	0	0	0	0	1	0	0	0	0	0
2	0	0	0	0	0	1	0	0	0	0
3	0	0	0	0	0	0	1	0	0	0
4	0	0	1	0	0	0	0	0	0	0
5	1	0	0	0	0	0	0	0	0	0
6	0	0	0	0	0	0	0	1	0	0
7	0	0	0	1	0	0	0	0	0	0
8	0	0	0	0	0	0	0	0	0	1
9	0	0	0	0	0	0	0	0	1	0
10	0	1	0	0	0	0	0	0	0	0

c. Yes, there is a new schedule:

```
Optimum Solution :          93.0

      | 1  2  3  4  5  6  7  8  9  10
 ─────────────────────────────────────
   1  | 0  0  0  0  1  0  0  0  0  0
   2  | 0  0  0  0  0  1  0  0  0  0
   3  | 0  0  0  0  0  0  1  0  0  0
   4  | 0  0  1  0  0  0  0  0  0  0
   5  | 0  0  0  1  0  0  0  0  0  0
   6  | 0  0  0  0  0  0  0  1  0  0
   7  | 1  0  0  0  0  0  0  0  0  0
   8  | 0  0  0  0  0  0  0  0  0  1
   9  | 0  0  0  0  0  0  0  0  1  0
  10  | 0  1  0  0  0  0  0  0  0  0
```

Solution to Custom Vans, Inc. Case

To determine whether the shipping pattern can be improved and where the two new plants should be located, the total costs for the whole transportation system for each combination of plants, as well as the existing shipping pattern costs, will have to be determined.

In the headings identifying the combination being discussed, Gary and Fort Wayne will be omitted since they appear in every possible combination.

Total costs and optimal solutions for each combination are found on the succeeding pages. A summary of the total costs and the respective systems is listed below:

Detroit–Madison　　= $10,200
Madison–Rockford = $10,550
Detroit–Rockford　= $11,400

Since the total cost is lowest in the Gary–Fort Wayne–Detroit–Madison combination ($10,200), the new plants should be located in Detroit and Madison. This system is also an improvement over the existing pattern, which costs $9,000, on a cost per unit basis.

Status quo:　$9,000/450 units = $20/unit
Proposed:　$10,200/750 units = $13.60/unit

Thus, the two new plants would definitely be advantageous, both in satisfying demand and in minimizing transportation costs.

PLANTS \ SHOP	CHICAGO (10)	MILWAUKEE (20)	MINNEAPOLIS (40)	DETROIT (15)	CAPACITIES
Gary	300	X	X	X	300
Fort Wayne	X	X	X	150	150
Dummy	X	100	150	50	300
Demand	300	100	150	200	750 / 750

VAM was used to get an initial solution for the existing shipping pattern in the above tableau. The total cost is (300) ($10) + (100) ($0) + (150) ($0) + (150) ($15) + (50) (0) = $5,250. This is also the optimal solution with no additional plants. The cost of the existing shipping pattern is $9,000 and is shown on the next page. Thus the existing shipping pattern *can* be improved.

Existing Shipping Pattern

PLANTS \ SHOP	CHICAGO	MILWAUKEE	MINNEAPOLIS	DETROIT	CAPACITIES	U_i
Gary	10 / 200	20	40 / 100	25	300	(N/A) 0
Fort Wayne	20	30 / 50	50	15 / 100	150	
Dummy	0 / 100	0 / 50	0 / 50	0 / 100	300	
Demand	300	100	150	200	750	
V_j	(N/A)					

Total costs = 200(10) + 50(30) + 40(100) + 100(15)

= $9,000

The costs for the additional plants are shown below:

Cost Table for Custom Vans, Inc.

	PLANTS \ SHOP	CHICAGO	MILWAUKEE	MINNEAPOLIS	DETROIT	CAPACITIES
Existing	Gary	10	20	40	25	300
	Fort Wayne	20	30	50	15	150
Proposed	Detroit*	26	36	56	1	150
	Madison**	7	2	22	37	150
	Rockford	5	10	30	35	150
	Forecast demand	300	100	150	200	

*Since a plant at Detroit could purchase a gallon of fiberglass for $2 less than any other plant, and one Shower-Rific takes 2 gallons of fiberglass, a systems approach to transportation warrants that (2) (2), $4, be deducted from each price quoted in the case for shipments from Detroit.

**Since a plant at Madison could hire labor for $1 less per hour than the other plants, and one Shower-Rific takes 3 labor hours to build, then $1(3) or $3 may be deducted from each price quoted for shipments from Madison.

Detroit–Madison, iteration no. 1 (Vogel's Approximation Method)

PLANTS \ SHOP	CHICAGO	MILWAUKEE	MINNEAPOLIS	DETROIT	CAPACITIES	U_i	
Gary	10 / 200	20	40 / 100	25	300	0	(10)
Fort Wayne	20 / 100	30	50	15 / 50	150	10	(5) (10)
Detroit	26	36	56	1 / 150	150	−4	(25)
Madison	7	2 / 100	22 / 50	37	150	−18	(5) 15
Demand	300	100	150	200	750		
V_j	10	20	40	5			
	(3)	(18)	(13) 10	(14) 10			

Improvement indices (MODI method):

G to MI:　$20 - 20 - 0 = 0$
G to D:　　$25 - 5 - 0 = +20$
FW to MI:　$30 - 20 - 10 = 0$
FW to Mn:　$50 - 40 - 10 = 0$
D to C:　　$26 - 10 - (-4) = +20$
D to MI:　　$36 - 20 - (-4) = +20$
D to MN:　　$56 - 40 - (-4) = +20$
M to C:　　$7 - 10 - 6(-18) = +15$
M to D:　　$37 - 5 - (-18) = +30$

All solutions are positive; solution is optimal as shown:

G to C:　　200 units
G to Mn:　100 units
FW to C:　100 units
FW to D:　　50 units
D to D:　　150 units
M to MI:　100 units
M to Mn:　　50 units

Total cost $= 200(10) + 100(20) + 2(100) + 40(100)$
　　　　　　$+ 22(50) + 50(15) + 150(1) = \underline{\underline{\$10,200}}$

Madison–Rockford, Iteration No. 1 (Vogel's Approximation Method)

PLANTS \ SHOP	CHICAGO	MILWAUKEE	MINNEAPOLIS	DETROIT	CAPACITIES	U_i	
Gary	10 — 250	20	40	25 — 50	300	0	(10̶)
Fort Wayne	20	30	50	15 — 150	150	−10	(5̶)
Madison	7 — 50	2 — 100	22 — 0*	37	150	−3	(5̶) (1̶5̶)
Rockford	5	10	30 — 150	35	150	5	(1̶)
Demand	300	100	150	200	750		
V_j	10	5	25	25			
	(2̶)	(8̶)	(8̶)	(10̶) (10̶)			

*0 supplied to avoid degeneracy.

Improvement indices (MODI method):

G to MI: $20 - 5 - 0 = +15$
G to Mn: $40 - 25 - 0 = +15$
FW to MI: $30 - 5 - (-10) = +35$
FW to C: $20 - 10 - (-10) = +20$
FW to Mn: $50 - 25 - (-10) = +35$

M to D: $37 - 25 - (-3) = +15$
R to C: $5 - 10 - 5 = -10$ ✓ best improvement
(see iteration no. 2)

R to MI: $10 - 5 - 5 = 0$
R to D: $35 - 25 - 5 = +5$

Madison–Rockford, Iteration No. 2

	PLANTS \ SHOP	CHICAGO 10	MILWAUKEE 15	MINNEAPOLIS 35	DETROIT 25	CAPACITIES	U_i
0	Gary	10 — 250	20	40	25 — 50	300	0
−10	Fort Wayne	20	30	50	15 — 150	150	−10
−13	Madison	7	2 — 100	22 — 50	37	150	−13
−5	Rockford	5 — 50	10	30 — 100	35	150	−5
	Demand	300	100	150	200	750	
	V_j	10	15	35	25		

Improvement indices (MODI method):

G to MI: $20 - 15 - 0 = +5$
G to Mn: $40 - 35 - 0 = +5$
FW to C: $20 - 10 - (-10) = +20$
FW to MI: $30 - 15 - (-10) = +25$
FW to Mn: $50 - 35 - (-10) = +25$
M to C: $7 - 10 - (-13) = +10$
M to D: $37 - 25 - (-13) = +25$
R to MI: $10 - 15 - (-5) = 0$
R to D: $35 - 25 - (-5) = +15$

Optimal Solution:

G to C: 250 units
G to D: 50 units
FW to D: 150 units
M to MI: 100 units
M to Mn: 50 units
R to C: 50 units
R to Mn: 100 units

Total cost = $250(10) + 50(5) + 100(2) + 22(50)$
$+ 100(30) + 50(25) + 150(15)$
$= \$10,550$

Improvement indices (MODI method):

G to Mn: $40 - 40 - 0 = 0$
G to D: $25 - 5 - 0 = +20$
FW to MI: $30 - 20 - 10 = 0$
FW to Mn: $50 - 40 - 10 = 0$
D to C: $26 - 10 - (-4) = +20$
D to MI: $36 - 20 - (-4) = +20$
D to Mn: $56 - 40 - (-4) = +20$
R to C: $5 - 10 - (-10) = +5$
R to D: $35 - 5 - (-10) = +40$

Optimal Solution:

G to C: 200 units
G to MI: 100 units
FW to C: 100 units
D to D: 150 units
FW to D: 50 units
R to Mn: 150 units

Total costs = $200(10) + 20(100) + 20(100) + 50(15)$
$+ 150(1) + 30(150)$
$= \$11,400$

Detroit–Rockford (Vogel's Approximation Method)

		10	30	40	5		
	SHOP / PLANTS	CHICAGO	MILWAUKEE	MINNEAPOLIS	DETROIT	CAPACITIES	U_i
0	Gary	10 / 200	20 / 100	40	25	300	0	(10̶) (30̶)
10	Fort Wayne	20 / 100	30	50	15 / 50	150	10	(5̶) (10̶)
−4	Detroit	26	36	56	1 / 150	150	−4	(25̶)
−10	Rockford	5	10 / 0*	30 / 150	35	150	−10	(5̶)
	Demand	300	100	150	200	750	
	V	10	20	40	5		
		(5̶) (15̶)	(10̶)	(10)	(14̶) (10̶)		

*0 supplied to avoid degeneracy.

Solution to the Old Oregon Wood Store Case

1. The assignment algorithm can be utilized to yield the fastest time to complete a table.

PERSON	JOB	TIME (MINUTES)
Tom	Preparation	100
Cathy	Assembly	70
George	Finishing	60
Leon	Packaging	10
	Total time	240

2. If Randy is used, the assignment problem becomes unbalanced and a dummy job must be added. The optimum assignment would be:

PERSON	JOB	TIME (MINUTES)
George	Preparation	80
Tom	Assembly	60
Leon	Finishing	80
Randy	Packaging	10
	Total time	230

This is a savings of 10 minutes with Cathy becoming the backup.

3. If Cathy is given the preparation task, the solution of the assignment with the remaining three workers assigned the remaining three tasks is:

PERSON	JOB	TIME (MINUTES)
Cathy	Preparation	120
Tom	Assembly	60
George	Finishing	60
Leon	Packaging	10
	Total time	250

If Cathy is assigned to the finishing task, the optimum assignment is:

PERSON	JOB	TIME (MINUTES)
George	Preparation	80
Tom	Assembly	60
Cathy	Finishing	100
Leon	Packaging	10
	Total time	250

4. One possibility would be to combine the packaging operation with finishing. Then, George could build an entire table by himself (in 230 minutes) and Tom could do preparation (100 minutes), Randy the assembly (80 minutes), and Leon the finishing and packaging (90 minutes). This crew could build 4.8 tables in a 480-minute workday, while George himself could build 2.09 tables—a total of almost 7 tables per day.

To utilize all five workers, George and Tom could each build entire tables, 2.09 and 1.75 per day, respectively. Letting Randy do preparation (110 minutes), Cathy the assembly (70 minutes), and Leon the finishing and packaging (90 minutes) allows an additional 4.36 tables per day for a total of 8.2 per day.

Nine tables per day could be achieved by having Tom prepare and assemble 3 tables, George prepare and finish 3 tables, Cathy assemble 6 tables, Leon finish 6 tables, and Randy prepare 3 tables and package all 9. George, Cathy, and Randy would each have 60 minutes per day unutilized and could build 0.6 tables having George do preparation (80 minutes), Cathy assembly and packaging (95 minutes), and Randy the finishing (100 minutes).

15

Integer Programming, Goal Programming, and the Branch and Bound Method

LEARNING OBJECTIVES

After completing this chapter, students will be able to:

1. Understand the difference between LP and integer programming.
2. Apply the cutting plane method to graphically solve integer programming problems.
3. Understand the three types of integer programming problems and be able to solve them using AB:QM, STORM, and LINDO software.
4. Apply the branch and bound method to solve integer programming problems.
5. Graphically solve a goal programming problem that has only two variables.
6. Apply the modified simplex technique to solve goal programming problems.

TEACHING SUGGESTIONS

Teaching Suggestion 15.1: Topics in This Chapter.

The overall purpose of this chapter is to provide a framework for the topics of integer programming, branch and bound, and goal programming. These are fairly advanced topics in a mathematical sense, and the chapter's intention is solely to introduce them through a series of simple graphical problems. Some of the topics are on the cutting edge of QA. For example, in integer programming, no one solution procedure exists to handle all problems.

Teaching Suggestion 15.2: Cutting Plane Method.

Two ideas can be raised at this point: (1) As noted in the Key Idea, students need to be reminded that integer solutions can *never* yield higher profits than the LP solution to the same problem. (2) The cutting plane method's goal is to chop off noninteger points without eliminating an integer solution.

Teaching Suggestion 15.3: Using the Computer to Solve Mixed-Integer Programming Problems.

Note that the LINDO printout in Program 15.1 allows users to specify which variables are integers and which, by default, can be fractional.

Teaching Suggestion 15.4: How the Branch and Bound Method Can Help.

In this section we illustrate how branch and bound is used to solve small assignment and integer programming problems. But its real strength is in dealing with huge problems (for example, thousands of variables/constraints). Branch and bound allows us to divide a large problem into smaller parts, thereby eliminating one-half or two-thirds of the options and reducing the problem to a more manageable level.

Teaching Suggestion 15.5: Applications Box on Assigning Classes.

This is one of those applications that most students can relate to because it addresses classroom scheduling. Note the size of the problem is surprisingly large (26,500 constraints).

Teaching Suggestion 15.6: Multiple Goals.

Ask students what other goals a company might have beyond maximizing profit. Socially conscious firms need to state as their mission a whole series of objectives. Encourage students to research an article showing a goal programming application. There is a wealth of research in journals. One interesting application is in the box later in this section that deals with budgeting for prisons.

Teaching Suggestion 15.7: Deviational Variables Are the Key in Goal Programming.

The concept of deviational variables requires careful explanation to the class. Students are accustomed to the decision variables of X_1 and X_2. Now they need to concentrate on goal achievement. The minus and plus signs on deviational variables need a thoughtful classroom discussion.

Teaching Suggestion 15.8: Difficulty of Graphical Goal Programming.

Solving goal programming problems graphically can be a confusing concept relative to graphical LP. Students often have difficulty with the direction of deviational variables. The use of Transparency Masters 15-7, 15-8, and 15-9 is a good idea.

Teaching Suggestion 15.9: Using the Goal Programming Simplex Method.

Point out the similarities and differences between the simplex method and the modified goal programming tableau. Using Transparency Master 15-10, you can show that the structure is almost the same. The big change is the addition of two rows for each new goal. Surprisingly, the computation is not as difficult as it looks.

VIDEO NOTES

VIDEO 15–1

Yield Management at American Airlines

This TIMS video segment is based on one of the award winning papers published in *Interfaces* in 1992. A brief description follows:

Critical to an airline's operation is the effective use of its reservations inventory. American Airlines began research in the early 1960s in managing revenue from this inventory. Because of the problem's size and difficulty, American Airlines Decision Technologies has developed an integer programming model that effectively reduces the large problem to three much smaller and far more manageable subproblems: overbooking, discount allocation, and traffic management. The results of the subproblem solutions are combined to determine the final inventory levels. American Airlines estimates the quantifiable benefit at $1.4 billion over the last three years and expects an annual revenue contribution of over $500 million to continue into the future.

(See the QA Applications box in Chapter 15 for details.)

ALTERNATE EXAMPLES

Alternate Example 15.1: 0–1 Integer Programming. Indiana's prison budget allows it to consider four new installations next year. They are:

X_1 = maximum security prison in Ft. Wayne
X_2 = minimum security prison in Bloomington
X_3 = half-way house in Indianapolis
X_4 = expanded tri-county jail in South Bend

The state wants to maximize the number of people that can be "served," while only building one of the two prisons (X_1 *or* X_2) and observing cost and space limitations. Here is the formulation:

Maximize Number Served = $3{,}000X_1 + 900X_2 + 4{,}000X_3 + 1{,}500X_4$

subject to:

$X_1 + X_2 \leq 1$ prison
$4X_1 + 2X_2 + 7X_3 + 3X_4 \leq 12$ acres available
$3.5X_1 + 1X_2 + 2.5X_3 + 9X_4 \leq 12$ million dollars budgeted

The solution is: $X_1 = 1$, $X_2 = 0$, $X_3 = 1$, $X_4 = 0$, number served = 7,000

Alternate Example 15.2: The Quality University (QU) is a private non-credit training firm that specializes in Total Quality Management (TQM) courses. QU

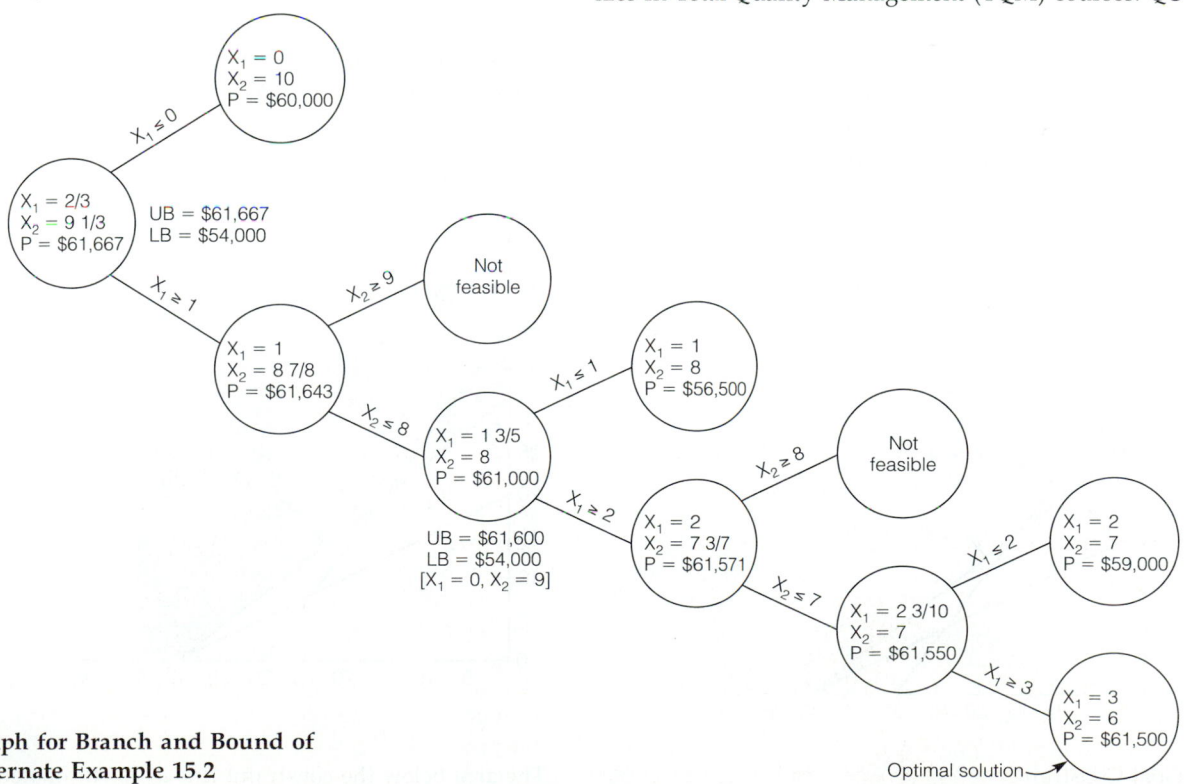

Graph for Branch and Bound of Alternate Example 15.2

wants to determine how many of each of two programs to offer in order to maximize profit. Their integer program can be formulated as follows:

Maximize Profit = $8,500X_1 + $6,000X_2$

Subject to:

$X_1 + X_2 \leq$ courses max. of 10
$\$1,000X_1 + \$700X_2 \leq$ instructor's pay of $7,200
$X_1, X_2 \geq 0$ and are integers

Using LP, the solution is: $X_1 = \frac{2}{3}$, $X_2 = 9\frac{1}{3}$, Profit =
$61,667

Solution

Initial upper bound (UB) = $61,667 ($X_1 = \frac{2}{3}$, $X_2 = 9\frac{1}{3}$)
Initial lower bound (LB) = $54,000 ($X_1 = 0$, $X_2 = 9$)
(See graph on page IS-185.)

All nodes are either integer or infeasible, so the solution is seen to be $X_1 = 3$, $X_2 = 6$, Profit = $61,500.

Alternate Example 15.3: Minimize $P_1d_1^- + P_2d_2^- + P_3d_3^+ + P_4d_1^+$

Subject to

$2x_1 + 4x_2 + d_1^- - d_1^+ = 80$
$2x_1 + 2.5x_2 + d_2^- - d_2^+ = 80$
$2x_1 + 1.5x_2 + d_3^- - d_3^+ = 60$

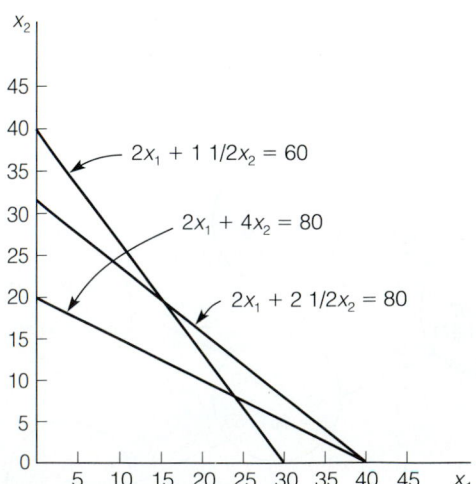

Goal Constraints

The First Priority
Goal: Minimize d_1^-

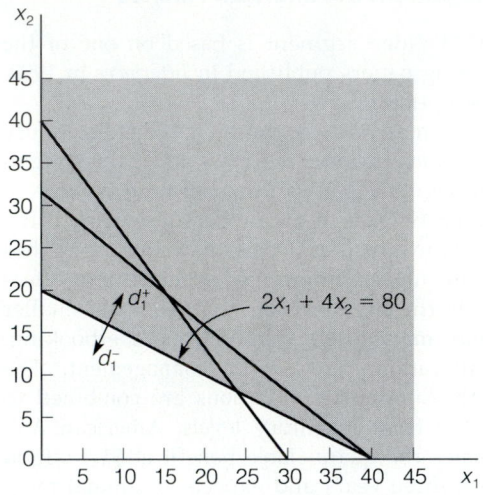

The area below the constraint line d_1^- is eliminated

The Second Priority
Goal: Minimize d_2^-

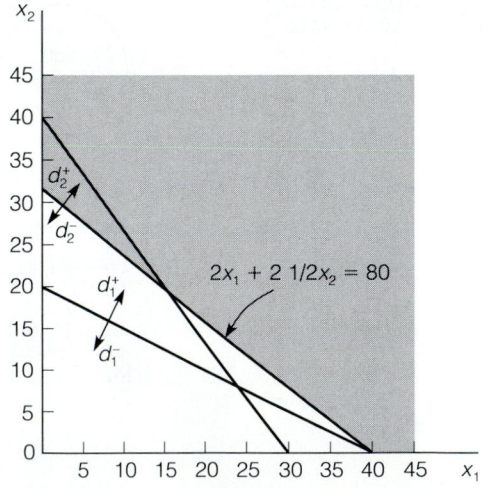

The area below the constraint line d_2^- is eliminated

The Third Priority
Goal: Minimize d_3^+

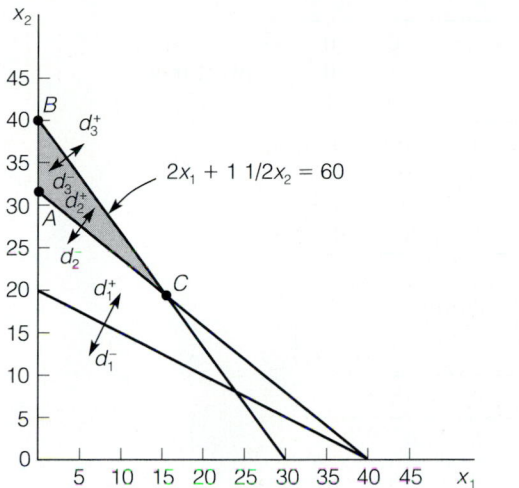

The area above the constraint line $2x_1 + 1\frac{1}{2}x_2 = 60$ is
eliminated

The Fourth Priority
Goal (Minimize d_1^+)
and the Solution

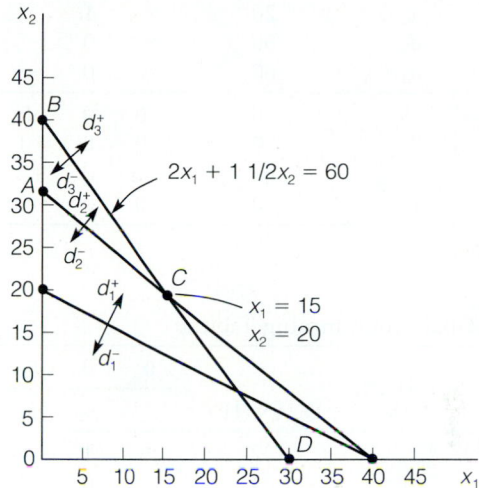

Cannot minimize d_1^+ totally without violating first
two priority goals

Solution:

$$x_1 = 15$$
$$x_2 = 20$$
$$d_1^+ = 15$$

Alternate Example 15.4: Here is the simplex solution
to the goal programming problem in Alternate Example 15.3.

The Initial Goal Programming Tableau

$C_j \longrightarrow$ $\downarrow$	SOLUTION MIX	QUANTITY	0 x_1	0 x_2	P_1 d_1^-	P_2 d_2^-	0 d_3^-	P_4 d_1^+	0 d_2^+	P_3 d_3^+	
P_1	d_1^-	80	2	4	1	0	0	−1	0	0	← pivot row
P_2	d_2^-	80	2	2½	0	1	0	0	−1	0	
0	d_3^-	60	2	1½	0	0	1	0	0	−1	
$C_j - Z_j$	P_4	0	0	0	0	0	0	1	0	0	
	P_3	0	0	0	0	0	0	0	0	1	
	P_2	80	−2	−2½	0	0	0	0	1	0	
	P_1	80	−2	−4	0	0	0	1	0	0	

↑
pivot column

The Second Goal Programming Tableau

$C_j \rightarrow$	SOLUTION MIX	QUANTITY	0 x_1	0 x_2	P_1 d_1^-	P_2 d_2^-	0 d_3^-	P_4 d_1^+	0 d_2^+	P_3 d_3^+	
0	x_2	20	$1/2$	1	$1/2$	0	0	$-1/2$	0	0	
P_2	d_2^-	60	$3/2$	0	$-5/2$	1	0	$5/2$	-1	0	← pivot row
0	d_3^-	60	$5/2$	0	$-3/2$	0	1	$3/2$	0	-1	
$C_j - Z_j$	P_4	0	0	0	0	0	0	1	0	0	
	P_3	0	0	0	0	0	0	0	0	1	
	P_2	60	$-3/2$	0	$+5/2$	0	0	$-5/2$	1	0	
	P_1	0	0	0	1	0	0	0	0	0	

↑ pivot column

The Third Goal Programming Tableau

$C_j \rightarrow$	SOLUTION MIX	QUANTITY	0 x_1	0 x_2	P_1 d_1^-	P_2 d_2^-	0 d_3^-	P_4 d_1^+	0 d_2^+	P_3 d_3^+	
0	x_2	32	$4/5$	1	0	$1/5$	0	0	$-1/5$	0	
P_4	d_1^+	24	$3/5$	0	-1	$2/5$	0	1	$-2/5$	0	
0	d_3^-	24	$8/5$	0	0	$-3/5$	1	0	$3/5$	-1	← pivot row
$C_j - Z_j$	P_4	24	$-3/5$	0	1	$-2/5$	0	0	$2/5$	0	
	P_3	0	0	0	0	0	0	0	0	1	
	P_2	0	0	0	0	1	0	0	0	0	
	P_1	0	0	0	1	0	0	0	0	0	

↑ pivot column

The Final Goal Programming Tableau

$C_j \rightarrow$	SOLUTION MIX	QUANTITY	0 x_1	0 x_2	P_1 d_1^-	P_2 d_2^-	0 d_3^-	P_4 d_1^+	0 d_2^+	P_3 d_3^+
	x_2	20	0	1	0	$1/2$	$-1/2$	0	$-1/2$	$1/2$
P_4	d_1^+	15	0	0	-1	$5/8$	$-3/8$	1	$-5/8$	$3/8$
	x_1	15	1	0	0	$-3/8$	$5/8$	0	$3/8$	$-5/8$
$C_j - Z_j$	P_4	15	0	0	1	$-5/8$	$3/8$	0	$5/8$	$-3/8$
	P_3	0	0	0	0	0	0	0	0	1
	P_2	0	0	0	0	1	0	0	0	0
	P_1	0	0	0	1	0	0	0	0	0

SOLUTIONS TO DISCUSSION QUESTIONS AND PROBLEMS

15-1. a. Linear programming allows only one goal (for example, profit maximization) whereas goal programming permits multiple goals.

b. LP always optimizes; goal programming sometimes only "satisfies."

c. In goal programming, we deal with "deviational variables" as well as real variables.

15-2. The student should provide five realistic examples of integer programming. One good exercise would be to require students to find five articles in the library's *Business Periodic Index* and use those as examples.

15-3. a. Rounding off is the easiest way to solve an integer program, but it can give an infeasible or nonoptimal solution.

b. Enumeration is simple in concept, but it can be very time-consuming in large problems.

c. The cutting plane method reaches an optimal solution, but for most problems it requires the availability of a computer algorithm.

d. The branch and bound method, which can be computerized, is especially useful when solving large problems where enumeration is impractical. It does not always reach an optimal solution in large problems, however.

15-4. The cutting plane method is described in Section 15.2. The student should phrase it in his or her own words.

15-5. The three types of integer programs are also noted in Section 15.2. Mixed integer programs are the most common.

15-6. The upper and lower bounds are limits set at each branch and bound stage on the highest and lowest possible costs of a possible assignment. The process is described in Section 15.3. The bounds help us decide which branches can be discarded.

15-7. *Satisfying* is a term used in goal programming because it is often not possible to "optimize" a multigoal problem. We come as close as possible to reaching goals.

15-8. Deviational variables, similar to slack variables in LP, are the difference between set goals and the current solution. In LP problems, only "real" variables are used, representing physical quantities. This is discussed in Section 15.3.

15-9. A college president's goals might be to: (1) increase enrollments by 1,000 students, (2) stay within budget; (3) keep class sizes down to an average of 25 students, (4) increase faculty salaries, (5) develop 10 new off-campus courses; (6) reduce average teaching loads to 3 courses per semester, and so on. There will be financial, space, tenure, and many other constraints.

15-10. Ranking goals just means more weight can be placed on one goal over another. The higher-ranked goals must be completely achieved before goal programming moves on to meet lower-ranked goals.

15-11. The text details the differences between the regular and modified simplex methods.

15-12. a. Linear
  b. Nonlinear because of $8X_1X_2$ in objective
  c. Goal programming
  d. Nonlinear because X_1^2 in first constraint
  e. Nonlinear and quadratic objective function

15-13. Optimal solution to *linear* program is at $X_1 = 1.46$, $X_2 = 1.69$, profit = \$21.82 (point *b*). First cut is $X_1 \leq 1$, optimal solution is at $X_1 = 1$, $X_2 = 2$, profit = \$20. See the next column for the graph.

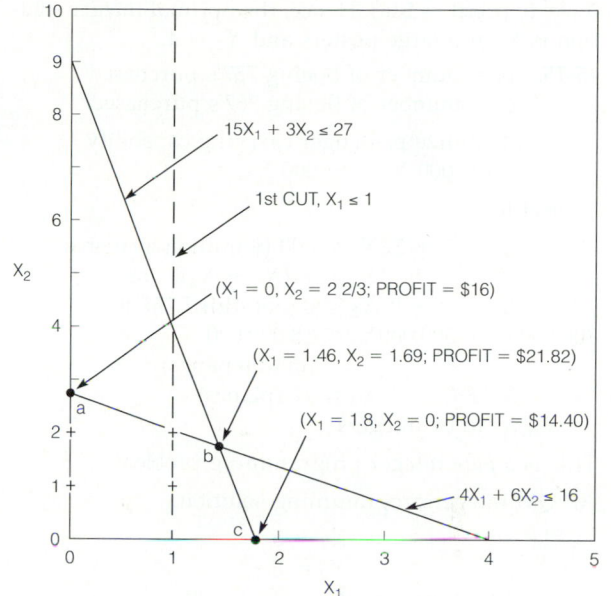

15-14. X_1 = number of larger posters
X_2 = number of smaller posters

Maximize profit = $3X_1 + 2X_2$
Subject to:
$$X_1 \leq 3$$
$$X_2 \leq 5$$
$$2X_1 + X_2 \leq 10$$

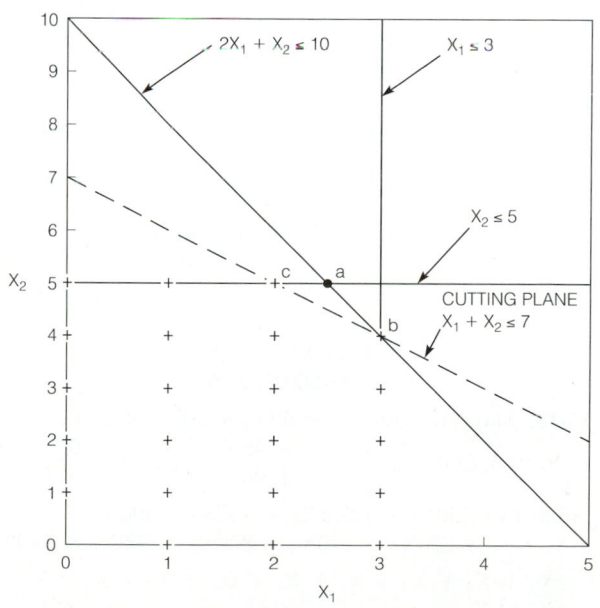

Step 1 Optimal LP solution at *a* is ($X_1 = 2\frac{1}{2}$, $X_2 = 5$, profit = \$17.50). Step 2 Integer solution at *b* is ($X_1 = 3$, $X_2 = 4$, profit = \$17). Integer solution at *c* is ($X_1 = 2$,

$X_2 = 5$, profit = \$16). Hence, the optimal integer solution is $X_1 = 3$ large posters and $X_2 = 4$.

15-15. X_1 = number of Boeing 757's purchased
X_2 = number of Boeing 767's purchased

Maximize passenger carrying capability
= $125{,}000\,X_1 + 81{,}000\,X_2$

Subject to:

$$35X_1 \quad + 22X_2 \leq 400 \text{ (\$ million available)}$$
$$[X_1 \geq \tfrac{1}{3}(X_1 + X_2)] \quad \text{or}$$
$$\tfrac{2}{3}X_1 \quad - \tfrac{1}{3}X_2 \geq 0 \text{ (one-third 757's)}$$
$$800{,}000X_1 + 500{,}000X_2 \leq \$8{,}000{,}000$$
$$\text{(maintenance)}$$
$$X_1 + \quad X_2 \leq 17 \text{ (planes)}$$
$$X_1, X_2 \text{ to be integers}$$

This is a *pure* integer programming problem.

AB:QM integer programming solution:

$$X_1 = 5$$
$$X_2 = 8$$
$$\text{Passengers carried} = 1{,}273{,}000$$

15-16. By LP:

Point a = (4.44, 8.88) $Z = 555{,}000 + 719{,}280$
$\qquad\qquad\qquad\qquad = 1{,}274{,}280$ passengers
Point B = (10, 0) $Z = 1{,}250{,}000$ passengers

First cutting plane is $X_2 \leq 8$, optimal solution is at point C:

$$X_1 = 5, X_2 = 8 \quad Z = 625{,}000 + 648{,}000$$
$$= 1{,}273{,}000 \text{ passengers}$$

See next column for the graph.

15-17.

Let: $X_i = \begin{cases} 1 \text{ if location } i \text{ is selected} \\ 0 \text{ if location } i \text{ is not selected} \end{cases}$

Maximize profit = $\$5{,}000X_1 + 6{,}000X_2 + 10{,}000X_3$
$\qquad\qquad\qquad + 12{,}000X_4 + 8{,}000X_5 + 3{,}000X_6$
$\qquad\qquad\qquad + 9{,}000X_7 + 10{,}000X_8$

Subject to: $\$60{,}000X_1 + 50{,}000X_2 + 82{,}000X_3$
$\qquad\qquad\quad + 103{,}000X_4 + 50{,}000X_5$
$\qquad\qquad\quad + 41{,}000X_6 + 80{,}000X_7$
$\qquad\qquad\quad + 69{,}000X_8 \leq \$300{,}000$

15-18. Maximize return = $50X_1 + 100X_2 + 30X_3$
$\qquad\qquad\qquad\qquad + 45X_4 + 65X_5 + 20X_6$
$\qquad\qquad\qquad\qquad + 90X_7 + 35X_8$

Subject to: $500X_1 + 1{,}000X_2 + 350X_3 + 490X_4$
$\qquad\quad + 700X_5 + 270X_6 + 800X_7 + 400X_8 \leq 3{,}000$

$$X_1 + X_2 + X_3 + X_4 + X_5 + X_6 + X_7 + X_8 \geq 5$$
$$X_1 + X_2 \qquad\qquad\qquad\qquad\quad \leq 1$$
$$X_3 + X_4 + X_5 \qquad\qquad \leq 2$$
$$X_6 + X_7 + X_8 \geq 2$$

All X_i = 0 or 1

Figure for Problem 15-16

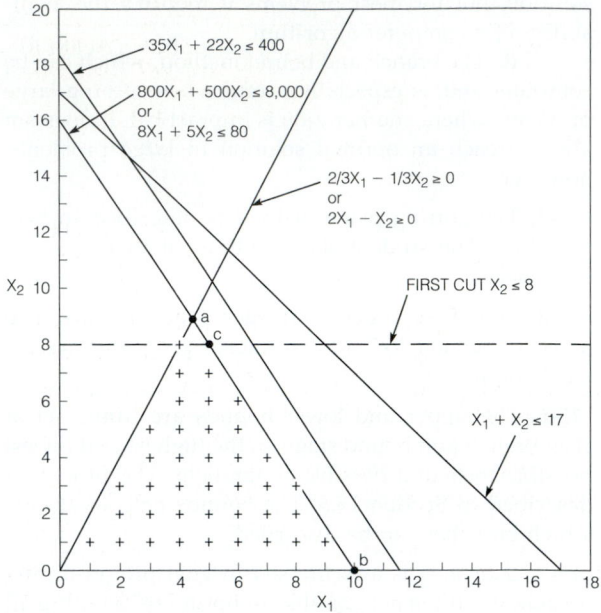

15-19. Maximize profit = $8X_1 + 6X_2$
Subject to: $\qquad 4X_1 + 6X_2 \leq 16$
$\qquad\qquad\qquad\qquad 15X_1 + 3X_2 \leq 27$

1. Solution to LP: $X_1 = 1.46$, $X_2 = 1.69$,
   $P = \$21.82$ [upper bound]
2. Round down both for lower bound: $X_1 = 1$,
   $X_2 = 1$, $P = \$14.00$
3. Branch on X_1 $\prec$
   $\quad A \quad X_1 \geq 2$ [infeasible region]
   $\quad B \quad X_1 \leq 1$

SUBPROBLEM A	SUBPROBLEM B
$4X_1 + 6X_2 \leq 6$	$4X_1 + 6X_2 \leq 16$
$15X_1 + 3X_2 \leq 27$	$15X_1 + 3X_2 \leq 7$
$X_1 \geq 2$	$X_1 \leq 1$
Infeasible area	$X_1 = 1, X_2 = 2,$
(Terminate)	$P = \$20.00$
	Optimal solution reached—
	no more nodes

15-20. Maximize $Z = 125{,}000X_1 + 81{,}000X_2$
Subject to: $\qquad 35X_1 + 22X_2 \leq 400$
$\qquad\qquad\qquad\qquad 2X_1 - \quad X_2 \geq \quad 0$
$\qquad\qquad\qquad\qquad 8X_1 + \quad 5X_2 \leq \quad 80$

1. Solution to LP: $X_1 = 4.44$, $X_2 = 8.88$,
   $Z = 1{,}274{,}280$
2. Round both down for a lower bound $X_1 = 4$,
   $X_2 = 8$, $Z = 1{,}148{,}000$

3. Branch on X_1:

SUBPROBLEM A's NEW CONSTRAINT	SUBPROBLEM B's NEW CONSTRAINT
$X_1 \leq 4$	$X_1 \geq 5$
Solution:	Solution:
$X_1 = 4$	$X_1 = 5$
$X_2 = 8$	$X_2 = 8$
$Z = 1,148,000$	$Z = 1,273,000$
Feasible	Feasible

4. All solutions are integer values. Thus, optimal is reached at $X_1 = 5$, $X_2 = 8$, $Z = 1,273,000$.

15-21. Lower bound set on rows with assignment $A4$ ($10), $B1$ ($6), $C3$ ($5), $D4$ ($25): Total $46

Two optimal solutions (see the figure below) with a total cost of $105:

ASSIGNMENT	COST	ASSIGNMENT	COST
$A4$	$ 10	$A4$	$ 10
$B1$	6	$B2$	15
$C3$	5	$C3$	5
$D2$	84	$D1$	75
	$105		$105

15-22. Maximize profit $= 2X_1 + 3X_2$

Subject to:
$$X_1 + 3X_2 \leq 9$$
$$3X_1 + X_2 \leq 7$$
$$X_1 - X_2 \leq 1$$

1. Solve graphically as an LP problem:

$$X_1 = 1.5$$
$$X_2 = 2.5$$
$$\text{Profit} = \$10.50$$

This provides an upper bound value.

2. Round down to $X_1 = 1$, $X_2 = 2$, profit $= \$8.00$ for a feasible solution. The lower bound is $8.00.

3. Branch on X_2 to begin:

SUBPROBLEM A	SUBPROBLEM B
New constraint: $X_2 \leq 2$	New constraint: $X_2 \geq 3$
Optimal solution: $X_2 = 2$	Optimal solution: $X_2 = 3$
$X_1 = 1.6$	$X_1 = 0$
Profit $= \$9.33$	Profit $= \$9.00$
(new upper bound)	(new lower bound)

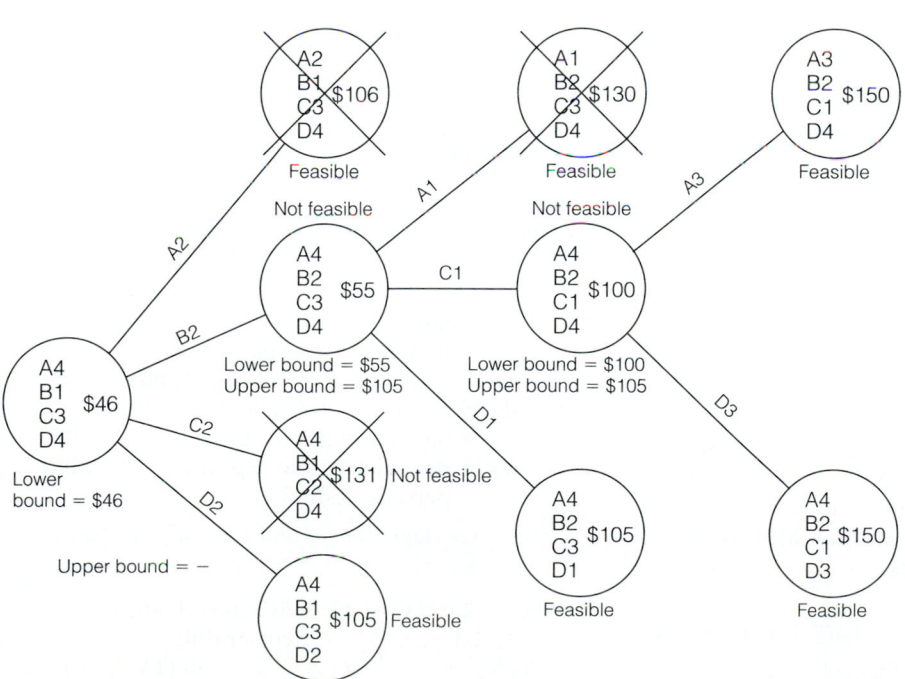

Branch and Bound Solution for Problem 15-21.

4. Branch on X_1 now from Subproblem A:

SUBPROBLEM C	SUBPROBLEM D
New constraints: $X_2 \leq 2$	New constraints: $X_2 \leq 2$
$X_1 \leq 1$	$X_1 \geq 2$
Optimal solution: $X_2 = 2$	Optimal solution: $X_2 = 1$
$X_1 = 1$	$X_1 = 2$
Profit = \$8.00	Profit = \$7.00

5. Both of these subproblems yield all-integer solutions. Comparing them to the lower bound of \$9.00, we see they are both smaller (see graph below). The solution to the problem is:

$$X_1 = 0, X_2 = 3, \text{Profit} = \$9.00.$$

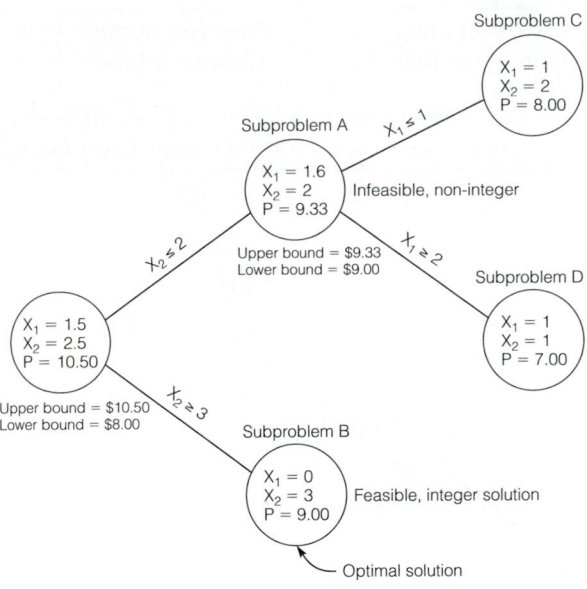

15-23. Let: X_1 = number of 2-drawer cabinets produced each week

X_2 = number of 3-drawer cabinets produced each week

d_1^- = underachievement of profit goal

d_1^+ = overachievement of profit goal

d_2^- = idle time in production capacity

d_3^- = underachievement of sales goal for 2-drawer files

d_4^- = underachievement of sales goal for 3-drawer files

Minimize deviations
$$= P_1 d_1^- + P_1 d_1^+ + P_2 d_2^- + P_3 d_3^- + P_3 d_4^-$$

Subject to:
$$10X_1 + 15X_2 + d_1^- - d_1^+ = \$11,000$$
$$\text{(profit target)}$$

$$1X_1 + 2X_2 + d_2^- = 1,300 \text{ hours}$$
$$\text{(production limit)}$$
$$1X_1 + d_3^- = 600$$
$$\text{(2-drawer sales limit)}$$
$$X_2 + d_4^- = 400$$
$$\text{(3-drawer sales limit)}$$

All X_i, d_i variables ≥ 0

15-24. Because we want to achieve the profit goal as closely as possible (minimize both d_1^- and d_1^+), the line ABC becomes the feasible region. When the P_2 priority is included, the feasible region is reduced to the segment AB. P_3 priority applies to both d_3^- and d_4^-. The 3-drawer goal (d_4^-) is fully attained at point B and the 2-drawer goal (d_3^-) is almost reached.

The best solution is $X_1 = 500$, $X_2 = 400$. The value of $d_3^- = 100$, meaning the 2-drawer sales goal is underachieved by 100 cabinets. See graph below.

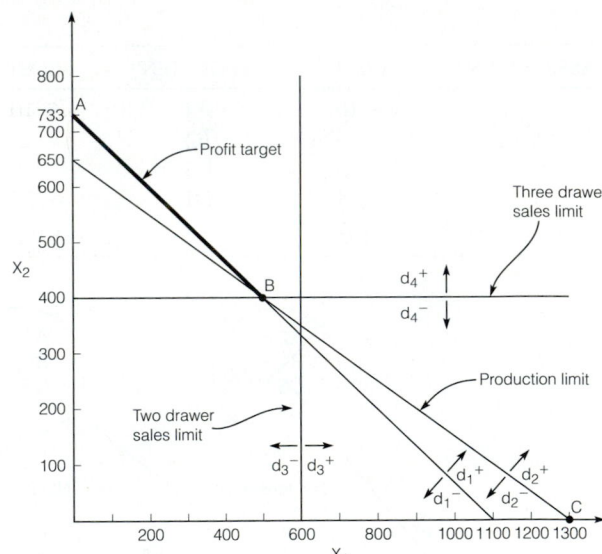

15-25. X_1 = number of TV spots

X_2 = number of newspaper ads

d_1^+ = deviation above budget funds of \$120,000

d_2^- = number of TV spots below 10

d_3^- = number of newspaper ads below 20

d_4^- = deviation below exposure of 9 million persons desired

Minimize deviations $= P_1 d_1^+ + P_2 d_2^- + P_2 d_3^-$
$$+ P_3 d_4^-$$

$$5,000X_1 + 2,000X_2 - d_1^+ = \$120,000 \text{ (budget}$$
$$\text{constraint)}$$
$$X_1 + d_2^- = 10 \text{ (TV spots)}$$
$$X_2 + d_3^- = 20 \text{ (newspaper ads)}$$
$$300,000X_1 + 150,000X_2 + d_4^- = 9,000,000 \text{ (exposures)}$$

15-26. The first two priorities, P_1 and P_2, are fully satisfied by the region ABC. But the P_3 priority requires that we select a solution above the exposure constraint line (minimize d_4^-). Point A comes closest to reaching the P_3 goal. The best solution is:

$X_1 = 10$ TV spots
$X_2 = 35$ newspaper ads

Total exposure here is 8,250,000 people, so $d_4^- = 750,000$ people. In other words, the exposure goal was underachieved by $\frac{3}{4}$ million people.

Notice that in this problem d_2^- and d_3^- are of equal (P_2) priority and, hence, are equally important. See graph below.

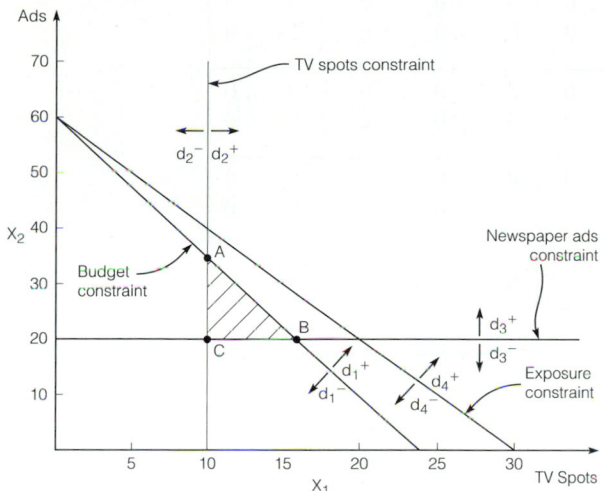

15-27. $X_1 = $ number of 64K chips produced
$X_2 = $ number of 256K chips produced
$X_3 = $ number of 512K chips produced
$d_1^- = $ underfilling customers' orders of 64K chips
$d_2^- = $ underfilling customers' orders of 256K chips
$d_3^- = $ underachievement of sales quotas for 64K chips
$d_4^- = $ underachievement of sales quotas for 256K chips
$d_5^- = $ underachievement of sales quotas for 512K chips
$d_6^- = $ underutilization of plant capacity

Minimize deviations
$$= P_1 d_1^- + P_1 d_2^- + P_2 d_3^- + P_2 d_4^- + P_2 d_5^- + P_3 d_6^-$$

Subject to:

$$X_1 + d_1^- - d_1^+ = 30 \quad \text{(64K chips order)}$$
$$X_2 + d_2^- - d_2^+ = 35 \quad \text{(256K chips order)}$$
$$X_1 + d_3^- - d_3^+ = 40 \quad \text{(64K sales goal)}$$
$$X_2 + d_4^- - d_4^+ = 50 \quad \text{(256K sales goal)}$$
$$X_3 + d_5^- - d_5^+ = 60 \quad \text{(512K sales goal)}$$
$$8X_1 + 13X_2 + 16X_3 + d_6^- = 1{,}200 \quad \text{(hours capacity)}$$

15-28. Third tableau for Harrison Electric:

$C_j \rightarrow$	SOLUTION MIX	QUANTITY	0 X_1	0 X_2	P_1 d_1^-	P_2 d_2^-	0 d_3^-	P_4 d_4^-	0 d_1^+	0 d_2^+	P_3 d_3^+	0 d_4^+	
0	X_1	2	1	0	1/3	−2/3	0	0	−1/3	(2/3)	0	0	← pivot row
0	X_2	8/3	0	1	−2/9	7/9	0	0	2/9	−7/9	0	0	
0	d_3^-	14/3	0	0	−8/9	1/9	1	0	8/9	−1/9	−1	0	
P_4	d_4^-	13/3	0	0	2/9	−7/9	0	1	−2/9	7/9	0	−1	
P_4	Z_j	13/3	0	0	2/9	−7/9	0	1	−2/9	7/9	0	−1	
	$C_j - Z_j$		0	0	−2/9	7/9	0	0	2/9	−7/9	0	+1	
P_3	Z_j	0	0	0	0	0	0	0	0	0	0	0	
	$C_j - Z_j$		0	0	0	0	0	0	0	0	1	0	
P_2	Z_j	0	0	0	0	0	0	0	0	0	0	0	
	$C_j - Z_j$		0	0	0	1	0	0	0	0	0	0	
P_1	Z_j	0	0	0	0	0	0	0	0	0	0	0	
	$C_j - Z_j$		0	0	1	0	0	0	0	0	0	0	

↑
pivot column

Fourth tableau for Harrison Electric:

$C_j \longrightarrow$			0	0	P_1	P_2	0	P_4	0	0	P_3	0
$\downarrow$	SOLUTION MIX	QUANTITY	X_1	X_2	d_1^-	d_2^-	d_3^-	d_4^-	d_1^+	d_2^+	d_3^+	d_4^+
0	d_2^+	3	3/2	0	1/2	−1	0	0	−1/2	1	0	0
0	X_2	5	7/6	1	1/6	0	0	0	−1/6	0	0	0
0	d_3^-	5	1/6	0	−5/6	0	1	0	5/6	0	−1	0
P_4	d_4^-	2	−7/6	0	−1/6	0	0	1	1/6	0	0	−1
P_4	Z_j	2	−7/6	0	−1/6	0	0	1	1/6	0	0	−1
	$C_j - Z_j$		7/6	0	1/6	0	0	0	−1/6	0	0	+1
P_3	Z_j	0	0	0	0	0	0	0	0	0	0	0
	$C_j - Z_j$		0	0	0	0	0	0	0	0	1	0
P_2	Z_j	0	0	0	0	0	0	0	0	0	0	0
	$C_j - Z_j$		0	0	0	1	0	0	0	0	0	0
P_1	Z_j	0	0	0	0	0	0	0	0	0	0	0
	$C_j - Z_j$		0	0	1	0	0	0	0	0	0	0

15-29. a.

$C_j \longrightarrow$			0	0	P_1	P_2	0	P_4	0	P_3	
$\downarrow$	SOLUTION MIX	QUANTITY	X_1	X_2	d_1^-	d_2^-	d_3^-	d_1^+	d_2^+	d_3^+	
P_1	d_1^-	80	2	④	1	0	0	−1	0	0	← pivot row
P_2	d_2^-	320	8	10	0	1	0	0	−1	0	
0	d_3^-	240	8	6	0	0	1	0	0	−1	
P_4	Z_j	0	0	0	0	0	0	0	0	0	
	$C_j - Z_j$		0	0	0	0	0	1	0	0	
P_3	Z_j	0	0	0	0	0	0	0	0	0	
	$C_j - Z_j$		0	0	0	0	0	0	0	1	
P_2	Z_j	320	8	10	0	1	0	0	−1	0	
	$C_j - Z_j$		−8	−10	0	0	0	0	1	0	
P_1	Z_j	80	2	4	1	0	0	−1	0	0	
	$C_j - Z_j$		−2	−4	0	0	0	1	0	0	

$\uparrow$
pivot
column

15-29. b.

$C_j \longrightarrow$ SOLUTION MIX	QUANTITY	0 X_1	0 X_2	P_1 d_1^-	P_2 d_2^-	0 d_3^-	P_4 d_1^+	0 d_2^+	P_3 d_3^+
0 X_2	20	0	1	0	1/4	−1/4	0	−1/4	1/4
P_4 d_1^+	30	0	0	−1	5/8	−3/8	1	−5/8	3/8
0 X_1	15	1	0	0	−3/16	5/16	0	3/16	−5/16
P_4 $\begin{cases} Z_j \\ C_j - Z_j \end{cases}$	30	0 0	0 0	−1 1	5/8 −5/8	−3/8 3/8	1 0	−5/8 5/8	3/8 −3/8
P_3 $\begin{cases} Z_j \\ C_j - Z_j \end{cases}$	0	0 0	0 0	0 0	0 0	0 0	0 0	0 0	0 1
P_2 $\begin{cases} Z_j \\ C_j - Z_j \end{cases}$	0	0 0	0 0	0 0	0 1	0 0	0 0	0 0	0 0
P_1 $\begin{cases} Z_j \\ C_j - Z_j \end{cases}$	0	0 0	0 0	0 1	0 0	0 0	0 0	0 0	0 0

Best solution is:

$$X_1 = 15$$
$$X_2 = 20$$
$$d_1^+ = 30$$

15-30. d_1^- = underachievement of class and study goal
d_1^+ = overachievement of class and study goal
d_2^+ = overachievement of sleeping goal
d_3^- = underachievement of social time goal

Major Bligh's objective function becomes:

Minimize $= d_1^- + d_1^+ + d_2^+ + d_3^-$

Subject to constraints (per week):

$$1X_1 + 1X_2 + 1X_3 + 1X_4 \leq 168$$
$$1X_3 + d_1^- - d_1^+ = 30$$
$$1X_1 - d_2^+ = 49$$
$$1X_4 + d_3^- = 20$$

Since the goals have priority, they can be rewritten in this order, yielding to the absolute completion of each goal before attempting to achieve the next goal. The objective function would become:

Minimize $= P_1 d_1^- + P_1 d_1^+ + P_2 d_2^+ + P_3 d_3^-$

where P_1 = meet class and study goal,
P_2 = meet sleeping goal, and
P_3 = meet socializing goal.

15-31. Maximize profit $= X_1(1800 - 50X_1)$
$+ X_2(2,400 - 70X_2)$
$= 1,800X_1 - 50X_1^2$
$+ 2,400X_2 - 70X_2^2$

Subject to: $100X_1 + 130X_2 \leq 5,000$ hours

15-32. a. $Z = \$665,000$

VARIABLE	VALUE
X_1	0
X_2	0
X_3	0
X_4	0
X_5 (South Orlando)	1
X_6	0
X_7	0
X_8 (Apopka)	1
X_9 (Lake Mary)	1
X_{10} (Cocoa Beach)	1

b. The program output on page IS-196 shows the new set of constraints and final solution. The expected return drops to $625,000. Osceola opens and Cocoa Beach closes.

c. As seen below, with Apopka corrected, the new solution has a return of $635,000, but the same locations as part (a).

$Z = \$635,000$

VARIABLE	VALUE
X_1	0
X_2	0
X_3	0
X_4	0
X_5	1
X_6	0
X_7	0
X_8	1
X_9	1
X_{10}	1

Printout for Problem 15-32 (AB:QM Output)

```
Program: Zero One Programming

Problem Title: FIRST NATIONAL DATASET 15.32

***** Input Data *****

Max.  Z = 120x1 + 100x2 + 110x3 + 140x4 + 155x5 + 128x6 + 145x7 + 190x8
          +170x9 + 150x10

Subject to

     20x1 + 30x2 + 20x3 + 25x4 + 30x5 + 30x6 + 25x7 + 20x8 + 25x9 + 30x10
     <= 110
     15x1 + 5x2 + 20x3 + 20x4 + 5x5 + 5x6 + 10x7 + 20x8 + 5x9 + 20x10
     <= 50
     1x2 + 1x6 + 1x7 + 1x9 + 1x10 <= 3
     1x2 + 1x3 + 1x5 + 1x8 + 1x9 >= 2
     1x1 + 1x3 + 1x10 >= 1
     1x1 + 1x2 + 1x3 + 1x4 + 1x5 + 1x6 + 1x7 + 1x8 + 1x9 + 1x10 <= 4
     1x2 + 1x3 >= 1

                    Z = 625,000
```

VARIABLE	VALUE
x_1	0
x_2	0
x_3	1
x_4	0
x_5	1
x_6	0
x_7	0
x_8	1
x_9	1
x_{10}	0

Solution to Schank Marketing Research Case

1. The first part of this case is an assignment problem that can be formulated with LP. A dummy project manager can be added to create a balanced 4×4 cost matrix.

$$\text{Minimize} = \sum_{j=1}^{n} \sum_{i=1}^{m} C_{ij} X_{ij}$$

where $X_{ij} = \begin{cases} 1 \text{ if project leader } i \text{ is assigned} \\ \quad \text{to client } j \\ 0 \text{ if otherwise} \end{cases}$

$i = 1, 2, 3, 4$ for Gardener, Ruth, Hardgraves, Dummy

$j = 1, 2, 3, 4$ for Hines, NASA, General, CBT

2. This part is a goal programming formulation with five goals, ranked from P_1 (highest) to P_5 (lowest):

P_1: Assign a manager to the NASA account.
P_2: Do not assign Gardener to CBT Television account.
P_3: Meet demands of Hines; they are twice as important as those of General Foundry.
P_4: Place Ruth on a project that will cost $3,000 or more.
P_5: Minimize the total cost of all assignments.

Constraints

For client's demand:

$$X_{11} + X_{21} + X_{31} + d_1^- = 1 \quad \text{Hines}$$
$$X_{12} + X_{22} + X_{32} + d_2^- = 1 \quad \text{NASA}$$

$$X_{13} + X_{23} + X_{33} + d_3^- = 1 \quad \text{General}$$
$$X_{14} + X_{24} + X_{34} + d_4^- = 1 \quad \text{CBT}$$

These constraints assume no more than one assignment per manager.

For project managers:

$$X_{11} + X_{12} + X_{13} + X_{14} + d_5^- - d_5^+ = 1 \quad \text{Gardener}$$
$$X_{21} + X_{22} + X_{23} + X_{24} + d_6^- - d_6^+ = 1 \quad \text{Ruth}$$
$$X_{31} + X_{32} + X_{33} + X_{34} + d_7^- - d_7^+ = 1 \quad \text{Hardgraves}$$

These constraints permit assigning three managers to four clients while minimizing positive and negative deviational variables (d_5, d_6, d_7).

Gardener to CBT restriction:

$$X_{14} - d_8^+ = 0$$

This constraint looks at the deviation of d_8^+ from 0. In other words, the closer d_8^+ is to 0 (not assigning Gardener to CBT), the closer it comes to meeting the restriction.

Ruth earns \$3,000 or more:

$$2{,}700X_{21} + 3{,}200X_{22} + 3{,}000X_{23}$$
$$+ 3{,}100X_{24} + d_9^- - d_9^+ = \$3{,}000$$

Here d_9^- represents underachievement of the goal, while d_9^+ is overachievement. The coefficients are the costs per assignment.

Total costs:

$$\sum_{j=1}^{4} \sum_{i=1}^{3} (C_{ij}X_{ij}) - d_{10}^+ = 0$$

This attempts to minimize total cost, bringing it as close to zero as possible; d_{10}^+ is the deviation from the goal.

Objective function:

$$\text{Minimize } Z = P_1 d_2^- + P_2 d_8^+ + P_3(2d_1^- + d_3^-)$$
$$+ P_4 d_9^- + P_5 d_{10}^+$$

Solution to the Oakton River Bridge Case

For a given set of requirements, the smallest number of toll collectors that will meet them can be obtained from the following integer linear programming problem:

$$\text{Minimize } Z = X_1 + X_2 + X_3 + X_4 + X_5 + X_6 + X_7$$
Subject to:
$$X_1 + X_2 + X_3 + X_4 + X_5 + X_6 + X_7 \geq R_5$$
$$X_1 + X_2 + X_3 + X_4 + X_5 \qquad\qquad \geq R_5$$
$$\qquad X_2 + X_3 + X_4 + X_5 + X_6 \qquad \geq R_6$$
$$\qquad\qquad X_3 + X_4 + X_5 + X_6 + X_7 \geq R_7$$
$$X_1 \qquad\qquad + X_4 + X_5 + X_6 + X_7 \geq R_1$$
$$X_1 + X_2 \qquad\qquad + X_5 + X_6 + X_7 \geq R_2$$
$$X_1 + X_2 + X_3 \qquad\qquad + X_6 + X_7 \geq R_3$$
$$X_1 + X_2 + X_3 + X_4 \qquad\qquad + X_7 \geq R_4$$

where X_j is the number of collectors starting on day j ($j = 1$ is Sunday) and R_j is the number required on day j.

1. The following table summarizes the requirements for shifts A, B, and C for each of the three days of the week along with the allocations that yield the minimum numbers of collectors starting each: 18 for shift A, 16 for shift B, and 18 for shift C.

2. If mixing of shifts is allowed, the daily requirements become the sum of the shift requirements, as shown in the second part of the table. The minimum number of collectors starting each day is shown in the last day. The total 50 is a reduction of two from the total required without allowing for the mixing of shifts.

Toll collector requirements:

DAY	SHIFT	A REQ.	A START	B REQ.	B START	C REQ.	C START	MIX REQ.	MIX START
Sun.		8	0	10	0	15	5	33	3
Mon.		13	3	10	1	13	2	36	9
Tue.		12	5	10	5	13	1	35	8
Wed.		12	0	10	1	12	4	34	6
Thu.		13	5	10	5	12	1	35	9
Fri.		13	1	13	1	13	5	39	7
Sat.		15	4	15	3	8	0	38	8
Total		18		16		18		50	

Note: Alternative optimal solutions for each shift may be possible.

Solution to Puyallup Mall

The problem can be expressed as the following integer linear programming problem with x_i being a 0–1 variable, 1 if store i is to be included and 0 if not:

MAXIMIZE

$$28.1x_1 + 34.6x_2 + 50.0x_3 + 162.0x_4 + 77.8x_5 + 100.4x_6$$
$$+ 45.2x_7 + 80.2x_8 + 51.4x_9 + 62.5x_{10} + 18.0x_{11}$$
$$+ 11.6x_{12} + 50.4x_{13} + 73.6x_{14} + 51.2x_{15}$$

SUBJECT TO

the space constraint

$$1.0x_1 + 1.6x_2 + 2.0x_3 + 3.2x_4 + 1.8x_5 + 2.1x_6 + 1.2x_7$$
$$+ 2.4x_8 + 1.6x_9 + 2.0x_{10} + 0.6x_{11} + 0.5x_{12}$$
$$+ 1.4x_{13} + 2.0x_{14} + 1.0x_{15} \leq 16$$

the annual rent constraint

$$4.4x_1 + 6.1x_2 + 8.3x_3 + 24.0x_4 + 19.5x_5 + 20.7x_6$$
$$+ 7.7x_7 + 19.4x_8 + 11.7x_9 + 15.2x_{10} + 3.9x_{11}$$
$$+ 3.2x_{12} + 11.3x_{13} + 16.0x_{14} + 9.6x_{15} \geq 150$$

the construction cost constraint

$$24.6x_1 + 32.0x_2 + 41.4x_3 + 124.4x_4 + 64.8x_5 + 79.8x_6$$
$$+ 38.6x_7 + 66.8x_8 + 45.1x_9 + 54.3x_{10} + 15.0x_{11}$$
$$+ 13.4x_{12} + 42.0_{13} + 63.7x_{14} + 40.0x_{15} \leq 700$$

at least one clothing store

$$x_1^+ \quad x_2^+ \quad x_3 \quad \geq \quad 1$$

at least one hard goods store

$$x_8^+ \quad x_9^+ \quad x_{10} \quad \geq \quad 1$$

at least one miscellaneous-type store

$$x_{11}^+ \quad x_{12}^+ \quad x_{13}^+ \quad x_{14}^+ \quad x_{15} \quad \geq \quad 1$$

at least two restaurants

$$x_4^+ \quad x_5^+ \quad x_6^+ \quad x_7 \quad \geq \quad 2$$

no more than two clothing stores

$$x_1^+ \quad x_2^+ \quad x_3 \quad \leq \quad 2$$

miscellaneous types cannot exceed total of clothing hard goods

$$x_1^+ \quad x_2^+ \quad x_3^+ \quad x_8^+ \quad x_9^+ \quad x_{10}^- \quad x_{11}^- \quad x_{12}^- \quad x_{13}^- \quad x_{14}^- \quad x_{15} \quad \geq 0.$$

The optimum solution is to include stores 1, 4, 5, 6, 8, 10, 12, 14, and 15. The present value is $645,400, all 16,000 square feet of space will be used, the annual rent is $131,700, and the construction cost is $531,800.

16
Waiting Lines: Queuing Theory

LEARNING OBJECTIVES

After completing this chapter, students will be able to:

1. Describe the trade-off curves for cost of waiting time and cost of service provided.
2. Understand the three parts of a queuing system: the calling population, the queue itself, and the service facility.
3. Describe the basic queuing system configurations.
4. Understand the assumptions of the common models dealt with in this chapter.
5. Analyze by hand and by computer a variety of operating characteristics of waiting lines.

TEACHING SUGGESTIONS

Teaching Suggestion 16.1: Topic of Queuing.

Here is a chapter that all students can relate to. Ask about student experiences in lines. Stress that queues are a part of our everyday lives and how things have changed at banks, post offices, and airports in just the past decade. (We now wait in a common line for the first available server.)

Teaching Suggestion 16.2: Cost of Waiting Time from an Organizational Perspective.

Using Transparency Master 16-2 (Queuing Costs), we can see that a cost of waiting time can be expressed.

Students should realize that different organizations place different values on customer waiting time. Ask students to consider different scenarios, from a drive-through restaurant to a doctor's office to a registration line in their college or motor vehicle office. It becomes clear that organizations place different values on their customers' time (with most colleges and DMVs unfortunately placing minimal cost on waiting time).

Teaching Suggestion 16.3: Use of Poisson and Exponential Probability Distributions to Describe Arrival and Service Rates.

These two distributions are very common in basic models, but students should not take their appropriateness for granted. As a project, ask students to visit a bank or drive-through restaurant and time arrivals to see if they indeed are Poisson distributed. Note that other distributions (such as exponential, normal, or Erlang) are often more valid.

Teaching Suggestion 16.4: Balking and Reneging Assumptions.

Note that most queuing models assume that balking and reneging are not permitted. Since we know they do occur in supermarkets, what can be done? This is one of many places to prepare students for the need for simulation.

Teaching Suggestion 16.5: Use of Queuing Software.

The AB:QM queuing software is among the easiest

models in the program to use since there are so few inputs. Yet students should be reminded of how long it would take to produce Programs 16.1 and 16.2 by hand.
Teaching Suggestion 16.6: Importance of L_q and W_q in Economic Analysis.

Although many parameters are computed for a queuing study, the two most important ones are L_q and W_q when it comes to an actual cost analysis.
Teaching Suggestion 16.7: Waiting Line Tables and Nomographs.

Until the proliferation of microcomputers, tables such as Table 16.3 and nomographs (graphical presentations of the data on those tables) were often used to solve multichannel problems. These days, we strongly encourage the software approach. The use of nomographs will likely follow the path of the slide rule.
Teaching Suggestion 16.8: Teaching the New England Castings Case.

Here is a tip for this very teachable case. About half the students who tackle the case forget that time walking to the counter must be noted *and* that the return time also needs to be added.

VIDEO NOTES

VIDEO 16–1

Allocating Telecommunications Resources at L. L. Bean, Inc.

This TIMS video segment is based on one of the award-winning papers published in *Interfaces* in 1991. A brief description of the application follows:

A model for optimizing the deployment of telemarketing resources was developed at L. L. Bean, a large telemarketer and mail-order catalog house. The deployment levels obtained with economic optimization were significantly different from those formerly determined by service-level criteria, and the resultant cost savings were estimated as $9 to $10 million per year. To develop the economic-optimization approach, queuing theory was used. Management at L. L. Bean has fully accepted this approach, which now explicitly sets optimal levels for the number of telephone trunks (lines) carrying incoming traffic, the number of agents scheduled, and the maximum number of queue positions allowed for customers waiting for a telephone agent.

See the Applications of QA box in Chapter 16 for details.

ALTERNATE EXAMPLES

Alternate Example 16.1: A new shopping mall is considering setting up an information desk manned by one employee. Based upon information obtained from similar information desks, it is believed that people will arrive at the desk at the rate of 20 per hour. It takes an average of 2 minutes to answer a question. It is assumed that arrivals are Poisson and answer times are exponentially distributed.

a. Find the probability that the employee is idle.
b. Find the proportion of the time that the employee is busy.
c. Find the average number of people receiving and waiting to receive information.
d. Find the average number of people waiting in line to get information.
e. Find the average time a person seeking information spends at the desk.
f. Find the expected time a person spends just waiting in line to have a question answered.

ANSWER: $\lambda = 20/\text{hr.}$ $\mu = 30/\text{hr.}$

a. $P_0 = 1 - \dfrac{\lambda}{\mu} = 1 - \dfrac{20}{30} = .33 = 33\%$

b. $\rho = \dfrac{\lambda}{\mu} = .66$

c. $L = \dfrac{\lambda}{\mu - \lambda} = \dfrac{20}{30 - 20} = 2 \text{ people}$

d. $L_q = \dfrac{\lambda^2}{\mu(\mu - \lambda)} = \dfrac{(20)^2}{30(30 - 20)} = 1.33 \text{ people}$

e. $W = \dfrac{1}{\mu - \lambda} = \dfrac{1}{30 - 20} = .1 \text{ hour}$

f. $W_q = \dfrac{\lambda}{\mu(\mu - \lambda)} = \dfrac{20}{30(30 - 20)} = .0667 \text{ hours}$

Alternate Example 16.2: In Alternate Example 16.1, the information desk employee earns $5/hour. The cost of waiting time, in terms of customer unhappiness with the mall, is $12/hour of time spent *waiting* in line. Find the total expected costs over an 8-hour day.

a. The average person waits .0667 hours and there are 160 arrivals per day. So total waiting time = (160) (.0667) = 10.67 hrs. @ $12/hr, implying a waiting cost of $128/day.
b. The salary cost is $40/day.
c. Total costs are $128 + $40 = $168/day.

Alternate Example 16.3: A new shopping mall is considering setting up an information desk manned by two employees. Based upon information obtained from similar information desks, it is believed that people will arrive at the desk at the rate of 20 per hour. It

I N S T R U C T O R' S   S E C T I O N

takes an average of 2 minutes to answer a question. It is assumed that arrivals are Poisson and answer times are exponentially distributed.

a. Find the proportion of the time that the employees are idle.

b. Find the average number of people waiting in the system.

c. Find the expected time a person spends waiting in the system.

ANSWER: $\lambda = 20$/hr. $\mu = 30$/hr. $M = 2$ open channels (servers)

a. $P_0 = \dfrac{1}{\dfrac{1}{0!}\left(\dfrac{20}{30}\right)^0 + \dfrac{1}{1!}\left(\dfrac{20}{30}\right)^1 + \dfrac{1}{2}\left(\dfrac{20}{30}\right)^2\left[\dfrac{2(30)}{2(30) - 20}\right]}$

$= \dfrac{1}{1 + \dfrac{2}{3} + \dfrac{1}{2}\left(\dfrac{4}{9}\right)\left[\dfrac{60}{(60 - 20)}\right]}$

$= \dfrac{1}{1 + \dfrac{2}{3} + \dfrac{1}{3}} = \dfrac{1}{2} = 50\%$

b. $L = \dfrac{(20)(30)(20/30)^2}{(1)[(2)(30) - 20]^2}\left(\dfrac{1}{2}\right) + \dfrac{20}{30}$

$= \dfrac{(800/3)}{1600}\left(\dfrac{1}{2}\right) + \dfrac{2}{3} = \dfrac{1}{12} + \dfrac{8}{12} = \dfrac{9}{12} = \dfrac{3}{4}$ people

c. $W = \dfrac{L}{\lambda} = \dfrac{3/4}{20} = \dfrac{3}{80}$ hr. $= .0375$ hr.

Alternate Example 16.4: Three students arrive per minute at a coffee machine that dispenses exactly 4 cups/minute at a constant rate. Describe the system parameters.

$L_q = \dfrac{\lambda^2}{2\mu(\mu - \lambda)} = 1.125$ people in queue on average

$W_q = \dfrac{\lambda}{2\mu(\mu - \lambda)} = .375$ minutes in the queue waiting

$L = L_q + \dfrac{\lambda}{\mu} = 1.87$ people in the system

$W = W_q + \dfrac{1}{\mu} = .625$ minutes in the system

SOLUTIONS TO DISCUSSION QUESTIONS AND PROBLEMS

16-1. The waiting line problem concerns the question of finding the ideal level of service that an organization should provide (see Section 16-2). The three components of a queuing system—arrivals, waiting line, and service facility—are discussed in Section 16.2.

16-2. The seven underlying assumptions are listed in Section 16.4.

16-3. The seven operating characteristics are listed in Section 16.4 under the heading Queuing Equations.

16-4. If the service rate is not greater than the arrival rate (that is, $\mu > \lambda$), an infinite queue will eventually build up.

16-5. First-in, first-out (FIFO) is often not applicable. Some examples are (1) hospital emergency rooms, (2) an elevator, (3) an airplane trip, (4) a small store where the shopkeeper serves whoever can get his or her attention first, (5) a computer system set to accept priority runs, (6) a college registration system that allows juniors and seniors to register ahead of freshmen and sophomores, (7) a restaurant that may seat a party of 2 before a party of 4 even though the latter group arrived earlier, (8) a garage that repairs cars with minor problems before it works on major overhauls.

16-6. Examples of finite queuing situations include (1) a firm that has only 3 or 4 machines that need servicing, (2) a small airport at which only 10 or 15 flights land each day, (3) a classroom that seats only 30 students for class, (4) a physician who has a limited number of patients, (5) a hospital ward with only 20 patients who need care, (6) a restaurant that can serve only 15 tables per seating and takes no more reservations beyond that number.

16-7. a. Barber shop: usually a single-channel, multiple-service system (if there is more than one barber)

Arrivals = Customers wanting haircuts
Waiting line = Seated customers who informally recognize who arrived first among them.
Service = Haircut, style, shampoo, and so forth; if service involves barber, then shampooist, then manicurist, it becomes a multiphase system.

b. Car wash: usually either a single-channel, single-server system, or else a system with each service bay having its own queue.

Arrivals = Dirty cars or trucks
Waiting time = Cars in one line (or more lines if there are service parallel wash systems). Always FIFO.
Service = Either multiphase (if car first vacuumed, then soaped, then sent through automatic cleaner, then dried by hand) or single-phase if all automatic or performed by one person.

c. Laundromat: basically a single-channel, multi-server, two-phase system.

> Arrivals = Customers with dirty clothes
> Waiting line = Usually first-come, first-served in terms of selecting an available machine.
> Service = First phase consists of washing clothes in wash machines; second-phase is again queuing for the first available drying machine.

d. Small grocery store: Usually a single-channel, single-server system.

> Arrivals = Customers buying food items
> Waiting line = Customers with cart or basket of groceries who arrive first at the cash register. Sometimes not FIFO. Grocer may care for regular customers first or give priority to person making a small, quick, purchase.
> Service = Ringing up sale on cash register, collecting money, and bagging groceries

16-8. Doctor's offices generally have either "grouped" arrivals or else uniform arrivals, unless they extensively treat emergency cases (these tend to be Poisson arrivals). Grouped arrivals means that 10 patients may be scheduled for 9 A.M., 10 for 10 A.M., 10 more for 11 A.M., and so on. Theoretically, patients all arrive at about the same time and are treated by the next hour. Uniform arrivals are common if a doctor schedules one patient every 15 or 20 minutes. (b) Service times are often random and either the exponential or normal distribution may be applied. Some patients take a minute or two, most take 15 to 20 minutes, some take an hour. (c) Service times might be constant if the doctor's job is to perform a standard exam or physical, taking about the same amount of time for each patient.

16-9. The use of Poisson to describe arrivals:

a. Cafeteria: probably not. Most people arrive in groups and eat at the same time.

b. Barbershop: probably acceptable, especially on a weekend, in which case people arrive at the same rate all day long.

c. Hardware store: okay.

d. Dentist's office: usually not. Patients are most likely scheduled at 15- to 30-minute intervals and do not arrive randomly.

e. College class: number of students come in groups at the beginning of class period; very few arrive during the class or very early before class.

f. Movie theater: probably not if only one movie is shown (if there are four or more auditoriums each playing a different movie simultaneously, it may be okay). Patrons all tend to arrive 5 to 20 minutes before a show in batches.

16-10.

	NUMBER OF CHECKOUT CLERKS			
	1	2	3	4
Number of customers	300	300	300	300
Average waiting time per customer	$\frac{1}{6}$ hour (10 minutes)	$\frac{1}{10}$ hour (6 minutes)	$\frac{1}{15}$ hour (4 minutes)	$\frac{1}{20}$ hour (3 minutes)
Total customer waiting time	50 hours	30 hours	20 hours	15 hours
Cost per waiting hour	$5	$5	$5	$5
Total waiting costs	$250	$150	$100	$75
Checkout clerk hourly salary	$4	$4	$4	$4
Total pay of clerks for 8-hour shift	$32	$64	$96	$128
Total expected cost	$282	$214	$196	$203

optimal number of checkout clerks on duty = 3

16-11. a. $\rho = .375$
   b. Downtime $= W = .2$ days $= 1.6$ hours
   c. Machines waiting $= L_q = .225$
   d. Probability more than K machines in system:

K	PROBABILITY
1	.141
2	.053
3	.020
4	.007

16-12. $\lambda = 20$/hour; $\mu = 30$/hour
   a. Average number in line $= L_q = 1.33$
   b. Average waiting time $= W_q = .0667$ hours $= 4$ minutes
   c. Average time in system $= W = .1$ hour $= 6$ minutes
   d. $\rho = .6667$
   e. $P_0 =$ probability system is empty $= .333$

16-13. $\lambda = 210$/hour; $\mu = 280$/hour
   a. Average number in line $= L_q = 2.25$
   b. Utilization rate $= \rho = .75$
   c. Average time in system $= W = .01428$ hours $= .857$ minutes $= 51.4$ seconds
   d. Average time in line $= W_q = .0107$ hours $= .64$ minutes $= 38.6$ seconds
   e. Probability more than 2 people in system $= .4218 = 42\%$
   Probability more than 3 people in system $= .3164 = 32\%$
   Probability more than 4 people in system $= .2373 = 24\%$

16-14. $\lambda = 4$/minute; $\mu = 5$/minute
   a. Probability more than 2 students in system $= 51.2\%$
Probability more than 3 students in system $= 41.0\%$
Probability more than 4 students in system $= 32.8\%$
   b. Probability system is empty $= P_0 = .20$
   c. Average time waiting in line $= W_q = .80$ minutes $= 48$ seconds
   d. Average number in queue $= L_q = 3.2$
   e. Average number in system $= L = 4$
   f. Add a second cashier and reanalyze with multichannel models or tables:

$$P_0 = .429$$
$$W_q = .0380 \text{ minutes} = 2.3 \text{ seconds}$$
$$L_q = .1523$$
$$L = .9523$$

16-15. $\lambda = 30$ trucks/hour; $\mu = 35$ trucks/hour
   a. Average number of trucks in system $= L = 6$

   b. Average time in system $= W = .2$ hours $= 12$ minutes
   c. Utilization rate $= \rho = .857143$
   d. Probability more than 3 trucks in the system $= .54 = 54\%$
   e. Unloading cost $= (16$ hours/day$) \times (30$ trucks/hour$) \times (.2$ hours average time in system$) \times (\$18$/hour$) = \$1,728$/day
   f. Enlarging the bin will cut waiting costs by 50% next year. First, annual costs must be computed:

Annual cost $= (\$1,728$/day$)(14$ days/unloading season$)$
$= \$24,192$

Thus, if the bin is enlarged, next year's waiting cost will be half of this $= \$12,096$. Since the cost of enlarging the bin is $9,000, the cooperative should do so.

16-16. $\lambda = 12$/hour; $\mu = 15$/hour
   a. Average time waiting for the order clerk:

$$= W_q = \frac{\lambda}{\mu(\mu - \lambda)} = \frac{12}{15(3)}$$
$$= .267 \text{ hours} = 16 \text{ minutes}$$

   b. Average number in queue $= L_q = 3.20$ callers
   c. Current total cost/hour:

$= $ service cost $+$ waiting cost
$= \$5$/hour $+ (12$ arrivals/hour$)$
$\qquad (.267$ hours$)(\$25$/hour$)$
$= \$5 + \$80 = \$85$/hour

If a second clerk is added, Ashley's has a second service facility and $L_q = .1523$ (from the table for L_q). L_q is the same as λW_q. Then total cost/hour:

$= (2$ workers $\times \$5$ each/hour$) + (.1523$ callers$)$
$\qquad (\$25$/hour$)$
$= \$10 + 3.81 = \$13.81$/hour

Thus, a second order clerk should definitely be added. The cost savings is $85 - $13.81 = $71.19/hour.

16-17. $\lambda = 12$/hour; $\mu = 4$/hour/barber; $M = 4$ channels
   a. $P_0 = .0377 = 3.8\%$ (from formula)
   b. $L \cong 4.528$
   c. $W \cong .377$ hours $= 22.6$ minutes
   d. $W_q = .127$ hours $= 7.6$ minutes
   e. $L_q = 1.5282$ (from formula)
   f. $\rho = .75 = 75\%$
   g. ρ with $M = 5$ barbers drops to 60%

16-18. a. 9 A.M.–3 P.M.; $\lambda = 6$ patients/hour; $\mu = 5$ patients/hour/doctor

$$\rho = \frac{\lambda}{\mu} = \frac{6}{5} = 1.20$$

Want W_q to be ≤ 5 minutes $= .0833$ hours. Using tables (for $\rho = 1.20$), $W_q \leq .0833$ implies:

$$W_q = \frac{L_q}{\lambda} \le .0833 \text{ or } L_q \le .0833\lambda \text{ or } L_q \le .50$$

Thus, $M = 3$ channels or doctors are needed (with $M = 2$, $L_q = .6748$; with $M = 3$, $L_q = .0904$).

b. 3 P.M.–8 P.M.; $\lambda = 4$ patients/hour; $\mu = 5$ patients/hour/doctor

$$\rho = \frac{4}{5} = .80$$

$W_q \le .0833$ hours implies $\frac{L_q}{\lambda} \le .0833$ or $L_q \le .0833\lambda$ or $L_q \le .03333$. From the queuing table (with $\rho = .80$), this means $M = 2$ doctors.

c. 8 P.M.–midnight; $\lambda = 12$ patients/hour; $\mu = 5$ patients/hour/doctor

$$\rho = \frac{12}{5} = 2.4$$

Want $W_q \le .0833$ hours or $\frac{L_q}{\lambda} \le .0833$ or $L_q \le .0833\lambda$ or $L_q \le 1.00$. From the table (with $\rho = 2.4$), $M = 4$ doctors are needed.

16-19. and 16-20.

	NUMBER OF FRUIT LOADERS	
	1	2
Truck arrival rate (λ)	3/hour	3/hour
Loading rate (μ)	4/hour	8/hour
Average number in system (L)	3 trucks	.6 trucks
Average time in system (W)	1 hour	.2 hours
Average number in queue (L_q)	2.25 trucks	.225 trucks
Average time in queue (W_q)	¾ hour	.075 hours
Utilization rate (ρ)	.75	.375
Probability system empty (P_0)	.25	.625
Probability of more than K trucks in system $\quad K$		
0	.75	.375
1	.56	.141
2	.42	.053
3	.32	.020

These results indicate that when only one loader is employed, the average truck must wait ¾ hour before it is loaded. Furthermore, there are an average of 2.25 trucks waiting in line to be loaded. This situation may be unacceptable to management. Note the decline in the queue when a second loader is employed.

16-21. Referring to the data in Problems 16-19 and 16-20, we note that the average number of trucks in the *system* is 3 when there is only one loader and .6 when two loaders are employed.

	NUMBER OF LOADERS	
	1	2
Truck driver idle time costs (= average number trucks × hourly rate)	(3) ($10) = $30	$ 6 = (.6)($10)
Loading costs	$ 6	$12 = (2) ($6)
Total expected cost per hour	$36	$18

The firm will save $18/hour by adding the second loader.

16-22. $$P_0 = \cfrac{1}{\left[\displaystyle\sum_{n=0}^{1} \frac{1}{n!}\left(\frac{3}{4}\right)^n\right] + \frac{1}{2!}\left(\frac{3}{4}\right)^2 \frac{2(4)}{2(4) - 3}}$$

$$= \cfrac{1}{1 + \frac{3}{4} + \frac{1}{2}\left(\frac{3}{4}\right)^2 \left(\frac{8}{8 - 3}\right)} = .454$$

$$L = \frac{3(4)(3/4)^2}{(1)!(8 - 3)^2}(0.4545) + \frac{3}{4} = .873$$

$$W = \frac{0.873}{3} = .291 \text{ hours}$$

$$L_q = 0.873 - 3/4 = 0.123$$

$$W_q = \frac{0.123}{3} = .041 \text{ hours}$$

By looking back to Problems 16-19 and 16-20, we see that although length of the *queue* and average time in the queue are lowest by opening the second platform, the average number of trucks in the system and average time spent waiting in the system are smallest when two workers are employed loading at a *single* platform. Hence, we would probably recommend not building a second gate.

16-23. a. Average number in line = .666
   b. Average number in system = 1.333
   c. Average wait in line = .1666 minute = 10 seconds

16-24. For $M = 1$:

$$L = \left[\frac{\lambda\mu\left(\frac{\lambda}{\mu}\right)}{1(\mu - \lambda)^2}\right] P_0 + \frac{\lambda}{\mu} = \frac{\lambda^2}{(\mu - \lambda)^2} P_0 + \frac{\lambda}{\mu}$$

But:

$$P_0 = \frac{1}{1 + \left(\dfrac{\lambda}{\mu}\right)\dfrac{\mu}{\mu - \lambda}} = \frac{1}{1 + \dfrac{\lambda}{\mu - \lambda}} = \frac{\mu - \lambda}{\mu}$$

Thus:

$$L = \frac{\lambda^2}{(\mu - \lambda)^2}\left[\frac{(\mu - \lambda)}{\mu}\right] + \frac{\lambda}{\mu} = \frac{\lambda^2}{(\mu - \lambda)(\mu)} + \frac{\lambda}{\mu}$$

$$= \frac{\lambda^2 + \lambda(\mu - \lambda)}{(\mu - \lambda)(\mu)} = \frac{\mu\lambda}{(\mu - \lambda)(\mu)} = \frac{\lambda}{\mu - \lambda}$$

This is the same formula.

16-25. $\lambda = .1667/\text{day} = \frac{1}{6}/\text{day}$
$\mu = 1/\text{day}$
$N = 5 \quad n = 1$

$$P_0 = \frac{1}{1 + 5(\frac{1}{6}) + 20(\frac{1}{6})^2 + 60(\frac{1}{6})^3 + 120(\frac{1}{6})^4 + 120(\frac{1}{6})^5}$$

$P_0 = .36$

a. No. in queue

$$L_q = N - \left(\frac{\lambda + \mu}{\lambda}\right)(1 - P_0) = 5 - 7(1 - .36)$$

$$= 5 - 4.48 = .52 \text{ units}$$

b. No. being served =

$$L = L_q + (1 - P_0) = .52 + (1 - .36)$$
$$= .52 + .64 = 1.16 \text{ in system}$$

c. No. running ok $= N - L = 5 - 1.16 = 3.84$

d. Aver. time in queue =

$$W_q = \frac{L_q}{(N - L)\lambda} = \frac{.52}{(5 - 1.16)(.1667)} = .817 \text{ days}$$

e. Aver. wait in system $= W = W_q + \dfrac{1}{\mu} = .817 + 1$

$$= 1.817 \text{ days}$$

16-26. $\lambda = \dfrac{60}{85} = .706 \text{ hr.} \quad \dfrac{\lambda}{\mu} = .1765$

$\mu = 4/\text{hr.} \quad N = 5 \quad n = 1$

$$P_0 = \frac{1}{\begin{array}{c} 1 + 5(.1765) + 20(.1765)^2 + \\ 60(.1765)^3 + 120(.1765)^4 + 120(.1765)^5 \end{array}}$$

$$= \frac{1}{1 + .88 + .62 + .30 + .12 + .02} = \frac{1}{2.944} = .344$$

a. Aver. no. waiting $= L_q = N - \left(\dfrac{\lambda + \mu}{\lambda}\right)(1 - P_0)$

$$= 5 - \left(\frac{4.706}{.706}\right)(.66) = 5 - 4.4$$

$$= .576$$

b. Aver. no. broken $= L = L_q + (1 - P_0)$
$$= .576 + (1 - .34) = 1.24$$

c. $P_0 = .344$ as seen above

d. Aver. time in queue $= W_q = \dfrac{L_q}{(N - L)\lambda}$

$$= \frac{.576}{(5 - 1.24)(.706)}$$

$$= \frac{.576}{2.65} = .217 \text{ hrs.}$$

e. Aver. syst. time $= W = W_q + \dfrac{1}{\mu} = .217 + .25$

$$= .467 \text{ hrs.}$$

16-27. a. Entering: $\lambda = 84/\text{minute}$; $\mu = 30/\text{minute}$;
$\rho = 2.8$ (for table)
Exiting: $\lambda = 48/\text{minute}$; $\mu = 30/\text{minute}$;
$\rho = 1.6$ (for table)

The manager desires that $W_q \leqq .1$ minute $= 6$ seconds and that $L_q \leqq 8$ customers in queue.

Entering:
If $M = 3$, $L_q = 12.27$ and $W_q = .14$ minutes
      (too high)
If $M = 4$, $L_q = 1.00$ and $W_q = .01$ minutes
      (this is okay)
If $M = 5$, $L_q = .24$ and $W_q = .003$ minutes
      (this is also okay)

So, the manager must open $M = 4$ or more entrances.

Exiting:
If $M = 2$, $L_q = 2.8$, $W_q = .06$ minutes (this is okay)
If $M = 3$, $L_q = .31$, $W_q = .006$ minutes (also okay)

So, the manager must open $M = 2$ or more exits. Since there are only 6 turnstiles, 4 must be used as entrances and 2 as exits.

b. The students should recognize and *question* all the limiting queuing assumptions that have been applied in solving the case. For example, it may be reasonable to assume that arrivals at the *entrance* turnstiles are independent and Poisson. But are *exiting* passengers independent? More realistically, they arrive in batches (as a train arrives), and unless trains unload every minute or two, this assumption may be unreasonable.

Other problems arise as well. If an exiting passenger's card does not have the correct fare, the card is rejected and the passenger must leave the line, go to an "add fare" machine to correct the deficiency, and enter the queue again. This resembles the "reneging" customer.

Note: In the real-world subway station in Washington, D.C., common queues are *not* formed at turnstiles and the problem becomes a multichannel, multiserver system. This topic was not discussed in Chapter 16, but can be explored by the instructor.

Solution to Shader Lane Hotel Case

1. Determine the average amount of time that a guest spends checking in.

The current system has five clerks, each with his or her own waiting line. This can be treated as five independent queues, each with an arrival time of $\lambda = 90/5 = 18$ per hour. The service rate is one every three minutes or $\mu = 20$ per hour. Assuming Poisson arrivals and exponential service times, the average amount of time that a guest spends waiting and checking in is given by:

$$W = 1/(\mu - \lambda) = 1/(20 - 18) = 0.5 \text{ hours or}$$
$$30 \text{ minutes}$$

2. How would this change under each of the stated options?

If 30 percent of the arrivals (that is, $\lambda = 0.8 * 90 = 27$ per hour) are diverted to a quick-serve clerk who can register them in an average of two minutes ($\mu = 30$ per hour) their average time in the system will be 20 minutes. The remaining 63 arrivals per hour would distribute themselves equally among the four remaining clerks ($\lambda = 63/4 = 15.75$ per hour) each of whose mean service time is 3.4 minutes (or 0.5667 hours) so that $\mu = 1/0.5667 = 17.65$ per hour. The average time in the system for these guests will be 0.53 hours or 31.8 minutes. The average time for all arrivals would be $0.3 * 20 + 0.7 * 31.8 = 28.3$ minutes.

A single waiting line for the five clerks yields an M/M/5 queue with $\lambda = 90$ per hour, $\mu = 20$ per hour. The calculation of average time in system gives $W = 7.6$ minutes.

Use of an ATM with the same service rate as the clerks (20 per hour) by 20 percent of the arrivals (18 per hour) gives the same average time for these guests as the current system—30 minutes. The remaining $\lambda = 72$ per hour form an M/M/4 or M/M/5 queuing system. With four servers, the average time in the system is 8.9 minutes, resulting in an overall average of:

$$0.2 * 30 + 0.8 * 8.9 = 13.1 \text{ minutes}$$

With five servers, the average time is 3.9 minutes resulting in an overall average of:

$$0.2 * 30 + 0.8 * 3.9 = 9.1 \text{ minutes}$$

Solution to New England Castings Case

1. To determine how much time the new layout would save, the present system must be compared to the new

system. The amount of time that an employee spends traveling to the maintenance department added to the time he or she spends in the system being serviced and waiting for service presently, compared to this value under the proposed system, will give the savings in time.

Under the present system, there are two service channels with a single line ($M = 2$). The number of arrivals per hour is 7 ($\lambda = 7$). The number of employees that can be serviced in an hour by each channel is 5 ($\mu = 5$). The average time that a person spends in the system is:

$$W = \frac{\mu(\lambda/\mu)^M}{(M - 1)!\,(M\mu - \lambda)^2}P_0 + \frac{1}{\mu}$$

where

$$P_0 = \frac{1}{\left[\displaystyle\sum_{n=0}^{M-1}\frac{1}{n!}\left(\frac{\lambda}{\mu}\right)^n\right] + \frac{1}{M!}\left(\frac{\lambda}{\mu}\right)^M\frac{M\mu}{M\mu - \lambda}}$$

In this problem:

$$P_0 = \frac{1}{\left[\dfrac{1}{1}(1) + \dfrac{1}{1}\left(\dfrac{7}{5}\right)^1\right] + \dfrac{1}{2}\left(\dfrac{7}{5}\right)^2\left[\dfrac{2(5)}{5(2) - 7}\right]} = .18$$

Therefore:

$$W = \frac{5(7/5)^2}{1 \cdot (10 - 7)^2}(.18) + 1/5$$

$$= .396 \text{ hour, or}$$
$$\underline{23 \text{ minutes and 45 seconds}}$$

Added to the travel times involved (6 minutes total for maintenance personnel and 2 minutes total for molding personnel), the total trip takes:

For maintenance—29 minutes and 45 seconds
For molding—25 minutes and 45 seconds

Under the new system, waiting lines are converted to single-channel, single-line operations. Bob will serve the maintenance personnel and Pete will serve the molding personnel.

Bob can now service 6 people per hour ($\mu = 6$). Four people arrive from the maintenance department every hour ($\lambda = 4$). The time spent in Bob's department is:

$$W = \frac{1}{\mu - \lambda} = \frac{1}{6 - 4} = 1/2 \text{ hour, or 30 minutes}$$

The reduced travel time is equal to 2 minutes, making the total trip time equal to $\underline{32 \text{ minutes}}$. This is an increase in time of $\underline{2 \text{ minutes and 15 seconds}}$ for the maintenance personnel.

Pete can now service 7 people per hour ($\mu = 7$). Three people arrive from the molding department every hour ($\lambda = 3$). The time in Pete's department is:

$$W = \frac{1}{7 - 3} = 1/4 \text{ hour, or 15 minutes}$$

The travel time is equal to 2 minutes, making the total trip time equal to <u>17 minutes</u>. This is a decrease in time of <u>8 minutes and 45 seconds</u> per trip for the molding personnel.

2. To evaluate systemwide savings, the times must be monetized. For the maintenance personnel who are paid $9.50 per hour, the $2\frac{1}{4}$ minutes lost per trip costs the company 36 cents per trip ($2\frac{1}{4} \div 60 = .0375$ of an hour; $.0375 (9.50) = \$.36$). For the molding personnel who are paid $11.75 per hour, the 8 minutes and 45 seconds per trip saved saves in monetary terms

$1.71 per trip. The net savings is $1.71 − .36 = $1.35 per trip. (Students may also find the cost savings on an hourly or daily basis.)

Because the net savings for the new layout is small, other factors should be considered before a final decision is made. For example, the cost of changing from the old layout to the new layout could completely eliminate the advantages of operating the new layout. In addition, there may be other factors, some noneconomic, that were not discussed in the case that could cause you to want to stay with the old layout. In general, when the cost savings of a new approach (a new layout in this case) is small, careful analysis should be made of other factors.

17
Simulation

LEARNING OBJECTIVES

After completing this chapter, students will be able to:

1. Tackle a wide variety of problems by simulation.
2. Understand the seven steps of conducting a simulation.
3. Explain the advantages and disadvantages of simulation.
4. Develop random number intervals and use them to generate outcomes.
5. Understand the alternative computer simulation packages available commercially.

TEACHING SUGGESTIONS

Teaching Suggestion 17.1: There Are Many Kinds of Simulations.

This chapter teaches the concepts of Monte Carlo simulation, but it also notes that there are many *physical* kinds of simulation models as well. The idea of

simulation is analogous whether we are conducting a wind tunnel simulation or a math simulation. Ask students to describe a series of real-world business applications in which a math model would be much better than playing with the actual operation of the firm.

Teaching Suggestion 17.2: Examples of Advantages of Simulation.

Section 17.2 lists advantages of simulation. Have students provide an example of numbers 2, 5, 6, 7, 8, and 9 in order to be sure these points are made. Hospitals are especially good cases for number 6—"do not interfere with the real-world system."

Teaching Suggestion 17.3: Use of the Cumulative Probability Distribution in Setting Random Number Intervals.

Some instructors go directly from probability distribution to random number intervals; others use Figure 17.2 as an intermediate step (see Transparency Master 17-6).

Teaching Suggestion 17.4: Starting the Random Number Intervals at 01 or 00.

Either of these is okay, but the text starts at 01 so that the top of each range is the cumulative probability.

Teaching Suggestion 17.5: Another Way to Generate Random Numbers.

Students who have spreadsheet software available find that simulation is easy with the use of the @RAND function. Lotus, and other programs, make simulation a quick and relatively painless process compared to developing a BASIC language program to do the same task.

Teaching Suggestion 17.6: Use of Computers for Speedy Simulations.

You can never point out enough how important computers are in the simulation process. Instead of conducting a simulation once or twice, with computers we can run it hundreds or thousands of times. This also ties in with the issue of time compression mentioned earlier in the chapter.

Teaching Suggestion 17.7: Relating Simulation Back to the Inventory Chapter.

Students should start to see the relationship between simulation and most of the other techniques in the book. Because of all the EOQ limiting assumptions, simulation is an important tool.

Teaching Suggestion 17.8: Gaming in Business Courses.

One type of simulation that students have probably heard of is business gaming (often taught in a policy course). You can now tie the concept of random numbers into how those games operate.

Teaching Suggestion 17.9: Outside Research Articles.

This is a good chapter for students to find down-to-earth published articles on a wide variety of applications. Ask each student to visit the library and find a simulation application to share with the class.

VIDEO 17–1

Expansion of Canadian National Railway's Line Capacity

This TIMS video is based on one of the award-winning papers published in *Interfaces*. A brief description of the application follows: Faced with a call for double track over much of its congested single-track main line, the Canadian National Railway confronted costs of more than $3.5 million per mile in the mountain region. Two what-if simulation models were used to predict train delay under various scenarios and produce a package of cost-effective improvements which allowed the railway to defer capital expenditures of over $350 million

beyond the 1980s. (See the QA application box in Chapter 17 for details.)

VIDEO 17–2

Management Science in Automating Postal Operations

This TIMS video is based on one of the award-winning papers published in 1992 in *Interfaces*. A brief description follows: In 1988, the postal service released its corporate automation plan (CAP), an ambitious program that includes a cumulative capital investment of $12 billion and labor savings of $4 billion per year by 1995. The backbone of the analysis leading to the CAP was performed with a comprehensive simulation model called META (model for evaluating technology alternatives). META blends a variety of management science and software tools to create a decision support system. It has spawned a family of systems for use at both headquarters and field levels of the USPS, accelerating and enhancing the use of management science throughout the organization.

(See the QA Application box in Chapter 17 for details.)

VIDEO 17–3

Planning the Netherlands' Water Resources

This TIMS video is based on one of the award-winning papers published in *Interfaces*. A brief description of the application follows: A comprehensive, integrated system of fifty models was developed to evaluate policies that include mixes of building new facilities and changing operating rules to improve water supply, as well as adjusting prices and regulations to reduce demands. Analysis performed with the system resulted in a new national water management policy, saving hundreds of millions of dollars in investment expenditures and reducing agricultural damage by about $15 million per year, while decreasing thermal and algae pollution. The methodology was adopted by the Dutch government and has been used to train water resource planners from many nations. (See the QA Application box in Chapter 17 for details.)

ALTERNATE EXAMPLES

Alternate Example 17.1: The number of cars arriving at a self-service gasoline station during the last

50 hours of operation are as follows:

NUMBER OF CARS ARRIVING	FREQUENCY
6	10
7	12
8	20
9	8

The following random numbers have been generated: 44, 30, 26, 09, 49, 13, 33, 89, 13, 37. Simulate 10 hours of arrivals at this station. What is the average number of arrivals during this period?

ANSWER:

# CARS	RN
6	01–20
7	21–44
8	45–84
9	85–00

Arrivals: 7, 7, 7, 6, 8, 6, 7, 9, 6, 7

Alternate Example 17.2: Average daily sales of a product are 8 units. The actual number of sales each day is either 7, 8, or 9 with probabilities 0.3, 0.4, and 0.3 respectively. The lead time for delivery averages 4 days, although the time may be 3, 4, or 5 days with probabilities 0.2, 0.6, and 0.2. The company plans to place an order when the inventory level drops to 32 units (based on the average demand and average lead time). The following random numbers have been generated:

60, 87, 46, 63 (set 1)
52, 78, 13, 06, 99, 98, 80, 09, 67, 89, 45 (set 2)

Use set 1 of these to generate lead times and use set 2 to simulate daily demand. Simulate 2 ordering periods with this and determine how often the company runs out of stock before the shipment arrives.

ANSWER:

SALES	RN	LEAD TIME	RN
7	01–30	3	01–20
8	31–70	4	21–80
9	71–00	5	81–00

First order: RN = 60 so lead time = 4 days.

Demand	day 1	8	(RN = 52)
	day 2	9	(RN = 78)
	day 3	7	(RN = 13)
	day 4	7	(RN = 06)

Total demand during lead time = 31. Since the re-order point is 32, there is no stockout.

Alternate Example 17.3: The time between arrivals at a drive-through window of a fast-food restaurant follows the distribution given below. The service time distribution is also given in the table in the next column. Use the random numbers provided to simulate the activity of the first five arrivals. Assume that the window opens at 11:00 A.M. and the first arrival is after this, based on the first interarrival time generated.

TIME BETWEEN ARRIVALS	PROBABILITY	SERVICE TIME	PROBABILITY
1	.2	1	.3
2	.3	2	.5
3	.3	3	.2
4	.2		

Random numbers for arrivals: 14, 74, 27, 03
Random numbers for service times: 88, 32, 36, 24

What time does the fourth customer leave the system?

ANSWER:

TIME BETWEEN ARRIVALS	PROB.	RN	SERVICE TIME	PROB.	RN
1	.2	01–20	1	.3	01–30
2	.3	21–50	2	.5	31–80
3	.3	51–80	3	.2	81–00
4	.2	81–00			

First arrival (RN = 14) at 11:01. Service time 3 (RN = 88). Leaves at 11:04.
Second arrival (RN = 74) at 11:04 (3 minutes after 1st). Service time = 2 (RN = 32). Leaves at 11:06.
Third arrival (RN = 27) at 11:06. Service time = 2 (RN = 36). Leaves at 11:08.
Fourth arrival (RN = 03) at 11:07. Must wait 1 minute for service to start. Service time = 1 minute (RN = 24). Leaves at 11:09.

SOLUTIONS TO DISCUSSION QUESTIONS AND PROBLEMS

17-1. See Section 17.2 of the chapter for a discussion of advantages and disadvantages of simulation.

17-2. a. Inventory ordering policy: May require simulation if lead time and daily demand are not constant. Also useful if data do not follow traditional probability distribution.

b. Ship docking in port to unload: If arrivals and unloadings do not follow Poisson/exponential distributions common to queuing problems, or if other queuing model assumptions are violated (for example, FIFO not observed)

c. Bank teller service windows: If arrivals or service times do not follow standard distributions, or if several waiting lines exist, may be easier to use simulation

d. U.S. economy: Because mathematical equations and relationships are too complex to solve mathematically and because an optimal solution may not exist

17-3. Problems with conditions of certainty can be solved more easily by other QA techniques. Problems that require quick answers that cannot wait for a simulation model to be built are a second category.

17-4. The major steps are outlined in Section 17.1.

17-5. The Monte Carlo method and its five steps are discussed in Section 17.3.

17-6. Random numbers can be generated by:
1. Computer.
2. Spinning a dial on a uniform wheel.
3. Pulling numbers from an urn.
4. Using a random number table.
5. Creating an algorithm such as the mid-square method.

17-7. The results would very likely change, and perhaps significantly, if a longer period was simulated. The ten-day simulation is valid only to illustrate the features of the system. It would not be safe to forecast based on that short a span.

17-8. A computer is necessary for three reasons:
1. It can do time periods or trials in a matter of seconds or minutes.
2. It can quickly examine and allow change in the complex interrelationships being studied.
3. It can internally (through a subroutine or function statement) generate random numbers by the thousands or millions.

17-9. Operational gaming and systems simulation are discussed in Section 17.7.

17-10. Simulation may very well increase in use for several reasons:
1. Computers are more commonplace in all types and sizes of businesses.
2. Simulation languages may be refined and made easier for noncomputer managers to use.

3. The mass of MBA graduates educated in QA entering the corporate world is growing, decreasing resistance to sophisticated techniques.
4. Complex problems will not become fewer in nature.

17-11. FORTRAN and BASIC are common, popular languages. Learning a specialized simulation language can be time-consuming and difficult. For simple simulation, regular languages may suffice. They may take a few extra seconds of computer CPU time (GPSS and SIMSCRIPT are very efficient), but computer time is often a fixed cost to the firm owning its own machine.

17-12.

NUMBER OF FAILURES	RANDOM NUMBER INTERVAL
0	01–06
1	07–19
2	20–44
3	45–72
4	73–92
5	93–99
6	00

SIMULATED PERIOD	RANDOM NUMBER	NUMBER OF A.C. COMPRESSORS SIMULATED TO FAIL THIS YEAR
1	50	3
2	28	2
3	68	3
4	36	2
5	90	4
6	62	3
7	27	2
8	50	3
9	18	1
10	36	2
11	61	3
12	21	2
13	46	3
14	01	0
15	14	1
16	81	4
17	87	4
18	72	3
19	80	4
20	46	3

No, it's *not* common to find three or more years in a row with two or less compressor failures.

17-13. a., b. Lundberg's car wash:

NUMBER OF CARS	PROBABILITY	CUMULATIVE PROBABILITY	RANDOM NUMBER INTERVAL
3 or less	0	.00	—
4	.10	.10	01–10
5	.15	.25	11–25
6	.25	.50	26–50
7	.30	.80	51–80
8	.20	1.00	81–00
9 or more	0	1.00	—
	1.00		

c.

HOUR	RANDOM NUMBER	SIMULATED ARRIVALS
1	52	7
2	37	6
3	82	8
4	69	7
5	98	8
6	96	8
7	33	6
8	50	6
9	88	8
10	90	8
11	50	6
12	27	6
13	45	6
14	81	8
15	66	7
		105

Average number arrivals per hour $= \dfrac{105}{15} = 7.00$ cars

17-14. Higgins plumbing:

HEATER SALES	PROBABILITY	RANDOM NUMBER INTERVALS
3	.02	01–02
4	.09	03–11
5	.10	12–21
6	.15	22–36
7	.25	37–61
8	.12	62–73
9	.12	74–85
10	.10	86–95
11	.05	96–00
	1.00	

a.

WEEK	RANDOM NUMBER	SIMULATED SALES
1	10	4
2	24	6
3	03	4
4	32	6
5	23	6
6	59	7
7	95	10
8	34	6
9	34	6
10	51	7
11	08	4
12	48	7
13	66	8
14	97	11
15	03	4
16	96	11
17	46	7
18	74	9
19	77	9
20	44	7
		139

With a supply of 8 heaters, Higgins will stock out 5 times during the 20-week period (in weeks 7, 14, 16, 18, and 19).

b. Average sales by simulation = total sales/ 20 weeks $= \dfrac{139}{20} = 6.95$ per week. Other simulations by students will yield slightly different results.

c. Using expected values, E(sales) $= (.02)(3) + (.09)(4) + (.10)(5) + (.15)(6) + (.25)(7) + (.12)(8) + (.12)(9) + (.10)(10) + (.05)(11) = 7.16$ heaters. In a longer time simulation, these two approaches will lead to even closer values.

17-15. a.

UNLOADING RATE	NEW RANDOM NUMBER INTERVAL
1	01–03
2	04–15
3	16–55
4	56–83
5	84–95
6	96–00

DAY	NUMBER DELAYED	RANDOM NUMBER	DAILY ARRIVALS	TOTAL TO BE UNLOADED	RANDOM NUMBER	NUMBER UNLOADED
1	—	37	2	2	69	2
2	0	77	4	4	84	4
3	0	13	0	0	12	0
4	0	10	0	0	94	0
5	0	02	0	0	51	0
6	0	18	1	1	36	1
7	0	31	2	2	17	2
8	0	19	1	1	02	1
9	0	32	2	2	15	2
10	0	85	4	4	29	3
11	1	31	2	3	16	3
12	0	94	5	5	52	3
13	2	81	4	6	56	4
14	2	43	2	4	43	3
15	1	31	2	3	26	3
Total	6		31			31

b. Average number delayed $= \dfrac{6}{15} = .40$

Average number arrivals $= \dfrac{31}{15} = 2.07$

Average number unloaded $= \dfrac{31}{15} = 2.07$

The short span simulated (15 days) introduces volatility in the daily arrival rate (from 2.73 arrivals/day in Table 17.12 to only 2.07 in the above simulation). This, coupled with speedier unloading rate, produces a much lower average delay rate (from 1.33/day down to only .40/day).

17-16. $q = 12$ drills; reorder point $= 6$ drills

DAY	UNITS RECEIVED	BEGINNING INVENTORY	RANDOM NUMBER	DEMAND	END INVENTORY	LOST SALES	ORDER?	RANDOM NUMBER	LEAD TIME (DAYS)
1	—	12	07	1	11	0	No		
2	0	11	60	3	8	0	No		
3	0	8	77	4	4	0	Yes	49	2
4	0	4	76	4	0	0	No		
5	0	0	95	5	0	5	No		
6	12	12	51	3	9	0	No		
7	0	9	16	2	7	0	No		
8	0	7	14	1	6	0	Yes	85	3
9	0	6	59	3	3	0	No		
10	0	3	85	4	0	1	No		
				Total	48	6			

Random numbers will differ from student to student. Ours were selected from the right-hand column of Table 17.5.

Daily order cost $=$ ($10) (.2 orders/day)

$\qquad\qquad\quad = \$2.00$

Daily holding cost $=$ ($.50/unit/year) (4.8 units/day)

$\qquad\qquad\quad\ = \$2.40$

Daily stockout cost = ($8/lost sale) (.6 lost sales/day)
= $4.80

Total daily cost = $9.20

This cost is greater than the $Q = 10$, ROP = 5 policy. However, the short period simulated does not really permit a valid analysis and comparison.

17-17. Flow Diagram for Port of New Orleans simulation:

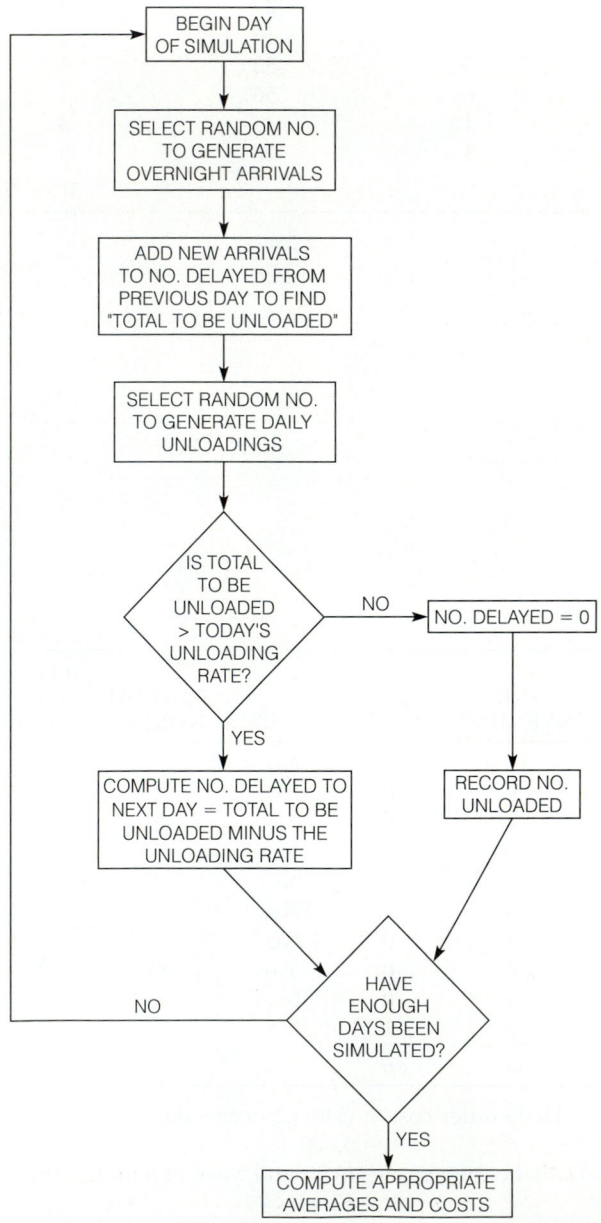

17-18. Three Hills flow diagram:

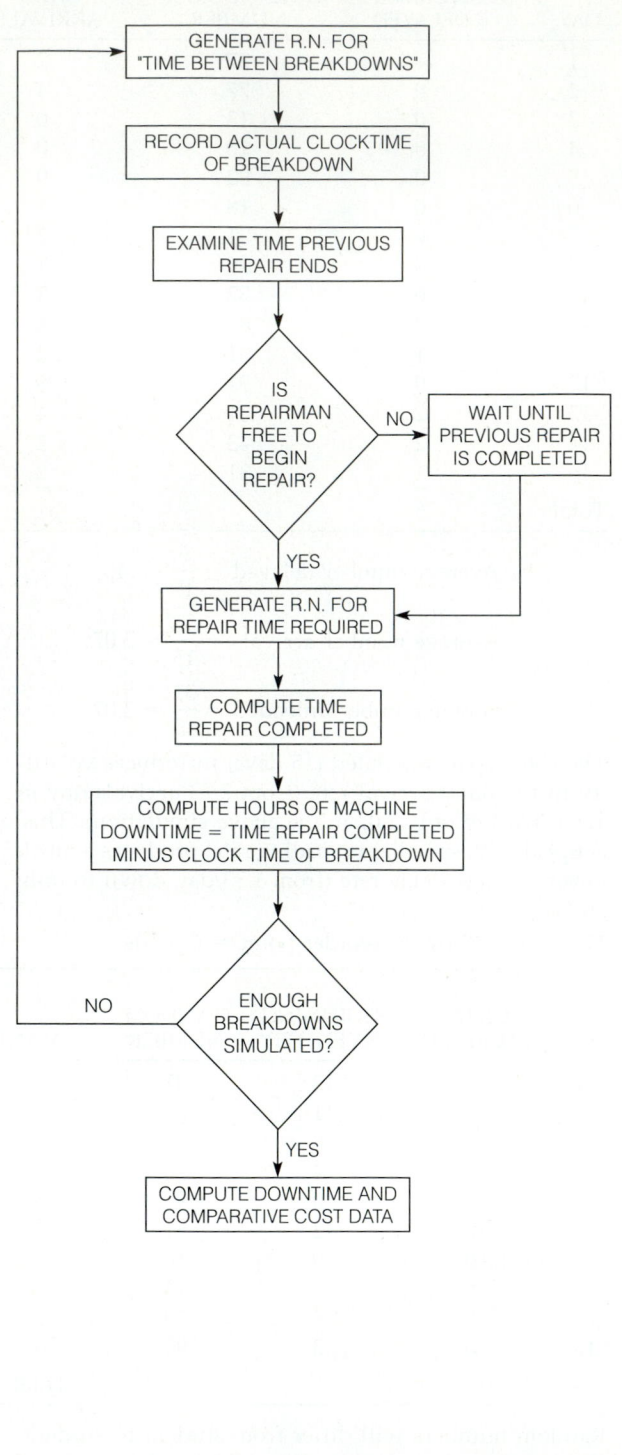

17-19. a. Repair time required with two-person crews:

REPAIR TIME REQUIRED (HOURS)	PROBABILITY	CUMULATIVE PROBABILITY	RANDOM NUMBER INTERVAL
½	.28	.28	01–28
1	.52	.80	29–80
1½	.20	1.00	81–00
	1.00		

BREAK-DOWN NUMBER	RANDOM NUMBER	TIME BETWEEN BREAK-DOWN (HOURS)	TIME OF BREAK-DOWN	TIME REPAIR-PERSON IS FREE TO BEGIN THIS REPAIR	RANDOM NUMBER	REPAIR TIME REQUIRED (HOURS)	TIME REPAIR ENDS	NO. HOURS MACHINE DOWN
1	69	2½	02:30	02:30	37	1	03:30	1
2	84	3	05:30	05:30	77	1	06:30	1
3	12	1½	07:00	07:00	13	½	07:30	½
4	94	3	10:00	10:00	10	½	10:30	½
5	51	2	12:00	12:00	02	½	12:30	½
6	36	2	14:00	14:00	18	½	14:30	½
7	17	1½	15:30	15:30	31	1	16:30	1
8	02	½	16:00	16:30	19	½	17:00	1
9	15	1½	17:30	17:30	32	1	18:30	1
10	29	2	19:30	19:30	85	1½	21:00	1½
11	16	1½	21:00	21:00	31	1	22:00	1
12	52	2	23:00	23:00	94	1½	00:30	1½
13	56	2	01:00	01:00	81	1½	02:30	1½
14	43	2	03:00	03:00	43	1	04:00	1
15	26	1½	04:30	04:30	31	1	05:30	1
								14½

$$\text{Cost of labor hours} = 29\tfrac{1}{2} \text{ hours}$$
$$\begin{pmatrix} 00{:}00 \text{ hours on day 1 to} \\ 05{:}30 \text{ hours on day 2} \end{pmatrix}$$
$$\times \$60/\text{hour}$$
$$= \$1{,}770.00$$
$$\text{Cost of machine downtime} = 14\tfrac{1}{2} \text{ hours} \times \$75/\text{hour}$$
$$= \underline{1{,}087.50}$$
$$\text{Total cost} = \$2{,}857.50$$

b. It is cheaper to hire the second worker each shift. Total cost with only one repairperson was $4,320.

17-20.

MARUGGI'S INCOME	PROBABILITY	CUMUL. PROBABILITY	RANDOM NUMBER INTERVAL
$350	.40	.40	01–40
400	.20	.60	41–60
450	.30	.90	61–90
500	.10	1.00	91–00

MARUGGI'S EXPENSES	PROBABILITY	CUMUL. PROBABILITY	RANDOM NUMBER INTERVAL
$300	.10	.10	01–10
400	.45	.55	11–55
500	.30	.85	56–85
600	.15	1.00	86–00

In this problem, students may select their own random numbers. If the instructor prefers, he or she may assign rows 1 and 2 as we have used on the following page.

MONTH	BEGINNING BALANCE	RANDOM NUMBER	INCOME	RANDOM NUMBER	EXPENSE	ENDING BALANCE
1	$600	52	$400	37	$400	$600
2	600	06	350	63	500	450
3	450	50	400	28	400	450
4	450	88	450	02	300	600
5	600	53	400	74	500	500
6	500	30	350	35	400	450
7	450	10	350	24	400	400
8	400	47	400	03	300	500
9	500	99	500	29	400	600
10	600	37	350	60	500	450
11	450	66	450	74	500	400
12	400	91	500	85	500	400

↑ row 1   ↑ row 2

Maruggi's balance never drops below $400 and he should be able to balance his account.

17-21. a. In this problem, the student must select his or her own random numbers *and* must decide how long a period to simulate. We have selected ten breakdowns for our sample simulations.

HOURS BETWEEN FAILURES IF ONE PEN REPLACED	PROBABILITY	CUMULATIVE PROBABILITY	RANDOM NUMBER INTERVAL
10	.05	.05	01–05
20	.15	.20	06–20
30	.15	.35	21–35
40	.20	.55	36–55
50	.20	.75	56–75
60	.15	.90	76–90
70	.10	1.00	91–00

HOURS BETWEEN FAILURES IF FOUR PENS REPLACED	PROBABILITY	CUMULATIVE PROBABILITY	RANDOM NUMBER INTERVAL
100	.15	.15	01–15
110	.25	.40	16–40
120	.35	.75	41–75
130	.20	.95	76–95
140	.05	1.00	96–00

ONE PEN REPLACED		ALL FOUR PENS REPLACED	
RANDOM NUMBER (COLUMN 8 OF TABLE)	HOURS BETWEEN FAILURES	RANDOM NUMBER (COLUMN 9 OF TABLE)	HOURS BETWEEN FAILURES
47	40	99	140
03	10	29	110
11	20	27	110
10	20	75	120
67	50	89	130
23	30	78	130
89	60	68	120
62	50	64	120
56	50	62	120
74	50	30	110
	380 hours total simulated		1,210 hours total simulated

Total cost = 10 pens × $8
 + 10 repairs at $50/per hour
 (1 hour per repair)
 = $80 + $500 = $580

Cost/hour = $580/380 hours
 = $1.53 per hour

Total cost = 40 pens × $8
 + 10 repairs at $50/per hour
 (2 hours per repair)
 = $320 + $1,000 = $1,320

Cost/hour = $1,320/1,210 hours
 = $1.09 per hour

b. Analytical approach to Brennan Aircraft problem:

Expected number of hours between failures
if one pen replaced = $10(.05) + 20(.15) + 30(.15)$
$+ 40(.20) + 50(.20) + 60(.15)$
$+ 70(.10)$
$= 42$

Cost per breakdown = $8 per pen + $50 per hour = $58

Cost per hour = $58/42 = $1.38 per hour

Expected number of hours between failures if four pens replaced
$= 100(.15) + 110(.25) + 120(.35)$
$+ 130(.2) + 140(.05)$
$= 15 + 27.5 + 42 + 26 + 7$
$= 117.5$

Cost per breakdown $= \$32 + \$100 = \$132$

$$\left(\underset{\text{pens}}{\overset{\uparrow}{4}} \times \underset{\text{pen}}{\overset{}{\$8 \text{ per}}}\right) \left(\underset{\text{hour}}{\overset{\uparrow}{\$50 \text{ per}}} \times \underset{\text{hours}}{\overset{}{2}}\right)$$

Cost per hour = $132/117.5 = $1.12 per hour

Compare to simulation results of $1.53 per hour and $1.09 per hour.

INSTRUCTOR'S SECTION

17-22.

ARRIVAL DISTRIBUTION	PROBABILITY	CUMULATIVE PROBABILITY	RANDOM NUMBER INTERVAL
20 minutes early	.20	.20	01–20
10 minutes early	.10	.30	21–30
On time	.40	.70	31–70
10 minutes late	.25	.95	71–95
20 minutes late	.05	1.00	96–00

EXAM TIME DISTRIBUTION	PROBABILITY	CUMULATIVE PROBABILITY	RANDOM NUMBER INTERVAL
20% faster than expected	.15	.15	01–15
In expected time	.50	.65	16–65
20% later than expected	.25	.90	66–90
40% later than expected	.10	1.00	91–00

PATIENT	RANDOM NUMBER	ARRIVAL TIME (A.M.)	RANDOM NUMBER	EXAM LENGTH (MINUTES)	TIME IN (A.M.)	TIME PATIENT LEAVES
A	60	9:30	80	18	9:30	9:48
B	08	9:25	45	20	9:48	10:08
C	19	9:55	86	18	10:08	10:26
D	29	10:20	99	14	10:26	10:40
E	36	10:45	02	24	10:45	11:09
F	72	11:25	34	15	11:25	11:40
G	30	11:20	87	24	11:40	12:04 P.M.
H	27	11:35	08	12	12:04	12:16 P.M.

        ↑   ↑
  fifth row   fourth row
    from   from
   bottom   bottom

Dr. Greenberg is only 1 minute late so he'll probably make his flight. But you must repeat this simulation several times and take the average schedule.

17-23. Actual distribution:

ORDER (SQ. FT.)	PROBABILITY	CUMULATIVE PROBABILITY	RANDOM NUMBER INTERVAL
8,000	.45	.45	01–45
11,000	.55	1.00	46–00

Demand distribution:

STEEL PER WEEK (SQ. FT.)	PROBABILITY	CUMULATIVE PROBABILITY	RANDOM NUMBER INTERVAL
6,000	.05	.05	01–05
7,000	.15	.20	06–20
8,000	.20	.40	21–40
9,000	.30	.70	41–70
10,000	.20	.90	71–90
11,000	.10	1.00	91–00

Sample Pelnor simulation for twenty weeks:

WEEK	RANDOM NUMBER	SIZE OF ARRIVING SHIPMENT	INVENTORY AT START OF WEEK	RANDOM NUMBER	DEMAND	END OF WEEK INVENTORY
1	84	11,000	11,000	00	11,000	0
2	55	11,000	11,000	59	9,000	2,000
3	25	8,000	10,000	09	7,000	3,000
4	71	11,000	14,000	97	11,000	3,000
5	34	8,000	11,000	69	9,000	2,000
6	57	11,000	13,000	98	11,000	2,000
7	50	11,000	13,000	93	11,000	2,000
8	44	8,000	10,000	49	9,000	1,000
9	95	11,000	12,000	51	9,000	3,000
10	64	11,000	14,000	92	11,000	3,000
11	16	8,000	11,000	92	11,000	0
12	46	11,000	11,000	16	7,000	4,000
13	54	11,000	15,000	84	10,000	5,000
14	64	11,000	16,000	27	8,000	8,000
15	61	11,000	19,000	64	9,000	10,000
16	23	8,000	18,000	94	11,000	7,000
17	01	8,000	15,000	17	7,000	8,000
18	79	11,000	19,000	71	10,000	9,000
19	19	8,000	17,000	94	11,000	6,000
20	50	11,000	17,000	30	8,000	9,000

↑
from third column from right
in random number table

↑
from fourth column from right
in random number table

Pelnor should add more storage capacity if the current policy will be maintained. However, students should recognize that a buildup will continue infinitely. The expected supply is = .45(8,000) + .55(11,000) = 9,650 sq. ft. The expected demand = 8,150 sq. ft. Over the long run, the on-hand supply will grow and grow to an infinite level.

17-24. a. Random number intervals must be set for each from-to combination:

FROM–TO COMBINATION	RANDOM NUMBER INTERVAL
From Initial Exam	
To X-Ray	01–45
To Operating Room	46–60
To Observation	61–70
To Out Processing	71–00
From X-Ray	
To Operating	01–10
To Cast	11–35
To Observation	36–70
To Out Processing	71–00
From Operating Room	
To Cast	01–25
To Observation	26–95
To Out Processing	96–00
From Cast Fitting	
To Observation	01–55
To X-Ray	56–60
To Out Processing	61–00
From Observation	
To Operating	01–15
To X-Ray	16–30
To Out Processing	31–00

Sample simulation using random numbers from Table 17.5, column 1:

	RANDOM NUMBER	FROM	TO
Person no. 1	52	Initial Exam	Operating Room
	37	Operating Room	Observation
	82	Observation	Out Processing
Person no. 2	69	Initial Exam	Observation
	98	Observation	Out Processing
Person no. 3	96	Initial Exam	Out Processing
Person no. 4	33	Initial Exam	X-Ray
	50	X-Ray	Observation
	88	Observation	Out Processing
Person no. 5	90	Initial Exam	Out Processing
Person no. 6	50	Initial Exam	Operating Room
	27	Operating Room	Observation
	45	Observation	Out Processing
Person no. 7	81	Initial Exam	Out Processing
Person no. 8	66	Initial Exam	Observation
	74	Observation	Out Processing
Person no. 9	30	Initial Exam	X-Ray
	59	X-Ray	Observation
	67	Observation	Out Processing
Person no. 10	60	Initial Exam	Operating Room
	60	Operating Room	Observation
	80	Observation	Out Processing

b. Using this very small simulation, no one goes to X-ray twice. It is very possible for this situation to occur, however.

17-25.

TIME BETWEEN ARRIVALS	PROBABILITY	RANDOM NUMBER INTERVAL
1	.20	01–20
2	.25	21–45
3	.30	46–75
4	.15	76–90
5	.10	91–100

SERVICE TIME	PROBABILITY	RANDOM NUMBER INTERVAL
1	.10	01–10
2	.15	11–25
3	.35	26–60
4	.15	61–75
5	.15	76–90
6	.10	91–100

a. Simulation of one teller drive-through:

RANDOM NUMBER	TIME BETWEEN ARRIVALS	ACTUAL TIME	TIME SERVICE BEGINS	RANDOM NUMBER	SERVICE TIME	SERVICE COMPLETE	WAIT TIME (MINUTES)
52	3	1:03	1:03	60	3	1:06	0
37	2	1:05	1:06	60	3	1:09	1
82	4	1:09	1:09	80	5	1:14	0
69	3	1:12	1:14	53	3	1:17	2
98	5	1:17	1:17	69	4	1:21	0
96	5	1:22	1:22	37	3	1:25	0
33	2	1:24	1:25	06	1	1:26	1
50	3	1:27	1:27	63	4	1:31	0
88	4	1:31	1:31	57	3	1:34	0
90	4	1:35	1:35	02	1	1:36	0
50	3	1:38	1:38	94	6	1:44	0
27	2	1:40	1:44	52	3	1:47	4
45	2	1:42	1:47	69	4	1:51	5
81	4	1:46	1:51	33	3	1:54	5
66	3	1:49	1:54	32	3	1:57	5
74	3	1:52	1:57	30	3	2:00	5
30	2	1:54	2:00	48	3	2:03	6
59	3	1:57	2:03	88	5	2:08	6
67	3	2:00					
							40

Yearly waiting costs imputed = (40 minutes/hour)
(7 hours/day) (200 days) ($1/minute) = $56,000.

b. Simulation of two drive-through windows:

RANDOM NUMBER	TIME BETWEEN ARRIVALS	ACTUAL TIME	RANDOM NUMBER	SERVICE TIME	SERVICE STARTS AT #1	SERVICE ENDS AT #1	SERVICE STARTS AT #2	SERVICE ENDS AT #2	WAIT TIME (MINUTES)
52	3	1:03	60	3	1:03	1:06			0
37	2	1:05	60	3			1:05	1:08	0
82	4	1:09	80	5	1:09	1:14			0
69	3	1:12	53	3			1:12	1:15	0
98	5	1:17	69	4	1:17	1:21			0
96	5	1:22	37	3	1:22	1:25			0
33	2	1:24	06	1			1:24	1:25	0
50	3	1:27	63	4	1:27	1:31			0
88	4	1:31	57	3	1:31	1:34			0
90	4	1:35	02	1	1:35	1:36			0
50	3	1:38	94	6	1:38	1:44			0
27	2	1:40	52	3			1:40	1:43	0
45	2	1:42	69	4			1:43	1:47	1
81	4	1:46	33	3	1:46	1:49			0
66	3	1:49	32	3	1:49	1:52			0
74	3	1:52	30	3	1:52	1:55			0
30	2	1:54	48	3			1:54	1:57	0
59	3	1:57	88	5	1:57	2:02			0
67	3	2:00							0
									1

Yearly waiting costs imputed = (1 minute) (7 hours) (200 days) ($1) = $1,400.

      c. Cost alternatives:

Cost/year = Wait cost/year
        + Drive through amortization/year
        + Labor (teller) cost/year

Cost for one teller drive-through = $56,000 + $12,000
          + $16,000
          = $84,000

Cost for two drive-throughs = $1,400 + $20,000
          + $32,000
          = $53,400

Cost savings if two tellers used = $84,000 − $53,400
          = $30,600

The conclusion is to place two teller booths in use. It is *critical* to replicate the simulation for a much longer time period before drawing any firm conclusions, however.

17-26. continued

c.

17-26.

a. Profit = (Amount produced) (Sales price)
    − (Ingredient 1 cost) (Ingredient 1 units)
    − (Ingredient 2 cost) (Ingredient 2 units)
  = 30(Sales price) − $50(25 units)
    − (Ingredient 2 cost) (36 units)
  = 30(Sales price) − $1,250
    − 36(Ingredient 2 cost)

where sales price and ingredient 2 cost are probabilistic.

b. Expected sales price = .2($300) + .5($350)
        + .3($400)
        = $355

Expected ingredient 2 cost = .1($35) + .6($40)
        + .3($45)
        = $41

Expected profit = 30($355) − $1,250 − 36($41)
        = $7,924/day

DAY	RANDOM NUMBER	SALES PRICE	GROSS SALES	RANDOM NUMBER	INGRED. 2 COST/UNIT	DAILY INGRED. 2 COST TOTAL	INGRED. 1 COST	PROFIT
1	52	$350	10,500	37	$40	$1,440	$1,250	$7,810
2	06	300	9,000	66	40	1,440	1,250	6,310
3	50	350	10,500	91	45	1,620	1,250	7,630
4	88	400	12,000	35	40	1,440	1,250	9,310
5	53	350	10,500	32	40	1,440	1,250	7,810
6	30	350	10,500	00	35	1,260	1,250	7,990
7	10	300	9,000	84	45	1,620	1,250	6,130
8	47	350	10,500	57	40	1,440	1,250	7,810
9	99	400	12,000	07	35	1,260	1,250	9,490

Random number intervals for sales price:

    01–20 = $300
    21–70 = $350
    71–00 = $400

Random number intervals for cost 2:

    01–10 = $35
    11–70 = $40
    71–00 = $45

d. Expected profit from simulation = $7,810/day

17-27.

DEMAND FOR MERCEDES	FREQUENCY	PROBABILITY	CUMULATIVE PROBABILITY	RANDOM* NUMBER INTERVAL
6	3	.083	.083	01–08
7	4	.111	.194	09–19
8	6	.167	.361	20–36
9	12	.333	.694	37–69
10	9	.250	.944	70–94
11	1	.028	.972	95–97
12	1	.028	1.000	98–00
	Σ = 36	Σ = 1.000		

*Note that the cumulative probabilities have been rounded to two significant digits when used to develop the random number intervals.

LEAD TIME (MONTHS)	PROBABILITY	CUMULATIVE PROBABILITY	RANDOM NUMBER INTERVAL
1	.44	.44	01–44
2	.33	.77	45–77
3	.16	.93	78–93
4	.07	1.00	94–00

We have arbitrarily chosen a beginning inventory of 14 cars.

TIME PERIOD	BEGINNING INVENTORY	RANDOM NUMBER*	DEMAND	SOLD	END INVENTORY	LOST SALE	PLACE ORDER	RANDOM NUMBER	LEAD TIME
1	14	07	6	6	8	0	Yes	60	2
2	8	77	10	8	0	2	No	—	—
3	0	49	9	0	14	9	No	—	—
4	14	76	10	10	4	0	Yes	95	4
5	4	51	9	4	0	5	No	—	—
6	0	16	7	0	0	7	No	—	—
7	0	14	7	0	0	7	No	—	—
8	0	85	10	0	14	10	No	—	—
9	14	59	9	9	5	0	Yes	85	3
10	5	40	9	5	0	4	No	—	—
11	0	42	9	0	0	9	No	—	—
12	0	52	9	0	14	9	No	—	—
13	14	39	9	9	5	0	Yes	73	2
14	5	89	10	5	0	5	No	—	—
15	0	88	10	0	14	10	No	—	—
16	14	24	8	8	6	0	Yes	01	1
17	6	11	7	6	14	1	No	—	—
18	14	67	9	9	5	0	Yes	62	2
19	5	51	9	5	0	4	No	—	—
20	0	33	8	0	14	8	No	—	—
21	14	08	6	6	8	0	Yes	40	1
22	8	29	8	8	14	0	No	—	—
23	14	75	10	10	4	0	Yes	33	1
24	4	95	11	4	14	7	No	—	—
		Totals Σ	209	112	157	97			16

* Random numbers taken from column 18 of Table 17.5, reading top to bottom, then from column 17, reading bottom to top.

Useful statistics from the simulation:

Average demand:

Simulation $^{209}/_{24} = 8.71$
Theoretical $\quad = 8.75$

Average lead time:

Simulation $^{16}/_{8} = 2.00$
Theoretical $\quad = 1.86$

Average ending inventory:

$^{157}/_{24} = 6.50$

Average number of lost sales:

$^{97}/_{24} = 4.04$

17-28.

C_t = Carrying cost $\quad = \quad 24 * 600 * 6.50 = \quad 93,600$
$\quad$ + Lost sale cost $= 4,350 * 97 \quad\quad = 421,950$
$\quad$ + Order cost $\quad = \quad 8 * 570 \quad\quad = \quad \underline{4,560}$
$\quad\quad\quad\quad\quad\quad\quad\quad\quad\quad\quad\quad\quad\quad\quad\quad 520,110$

$= \$520,110$, or $\$21,671$ per month

17-29. As in problem 17-27, we have arbitrarily chosen a beginning inventory of 14 cars.

TIME PERIOD	BEGINNING INVENTORY	RANDOM NUMBER*	DEMAND	SOLD	END INVENTORY	LOST SALE	PLACE ORDER	RANDOM NUMBER	LEAD TIME
1	14	07	6	6	8	0	Yes	60	2
2	8	77	10	8	0	2	No	—	—
3	0	49	9	0	21	9	No	—	—
4	21	76	10	10	11	0	No	—	—
5	11	95	9	9	2	0	Yes	51	2
6	2	16	7	2	0	5	No	—	—
7	0	14	7	0	0	21	No	—	—
8	21	85	10	10	11	0	No	—	—
9	11	59	9	9	2	0	Yes	85	3
10	2	40	9	2	0	7	No	—	—
11	0	42	9	0	0	9	No	—	—
12	0	52	9	0	21	9	No	—	—
13	21	39	9	9	12	0	No	—	—
14	12	73	10	10	2	0	Yes	89	3
15	2	88	10	2	0	8	No	—	—
16	0	24	8	0	0	8	No	—	—
17	0	01	6	0	21	6	No	—	—
18	21	11	7	7	14	0	No	—	—
19	14	67	9	9	5	0	Yes	62	2
20	5	51	9	5	0	4	No	—	—
21	0	33	6	0	21	6	No	—	—
22	21	08	6	6	15	0	No	—	—
23	15	40	9	9	6	0	Yes	29	1
24	6	29	8	6	21	2	No	—	—
Totals			201	119	214	82			13

* Random numbers taken from column 18 of Table 17.5, reading top to bottom, then from column 17, reading bottom to top.

Useful statistics from the simulation:

Average demand:

Simulation $^{201}/_{24} = 8.38$
Theoretical $= 8.75$

Average lead time:

Simulation $^{13}/_{6} = 2.17$
Theoretical $= 1.86$

Average ending inventory:

$^{214}/_{24} = 8.92$

Average number of lost sales:

$^{82}/_{24} = 3.41$

$C_t =$ Carrying cost $= 24 * 600 * 8.92 = 128,448$
$\quad\quad + $ Lost sale cost $= 4,350 * 82 = 356,700$
$\quad\quad + $ Order cost $= 6 * 570 = \underline{3,420}$
$\quad\quad\quad\quad\quad\quad\quad\quad\quad\quad\quad\quad\quad\quad 488,568$

Order quantity = 14, reorder point = 14
$520,110 or $21,671/month

Order quantity = 21, reorder point = 10
$488,568 or $20,357/month

It would appear the inventory policy of ordering in quantities of 21 using a reorder point of 10 is to be preferred.

Students should be cautioned that the single 24-month period simulation of each condition does not provide sufficient information upon which to base any firm conclusion. It would also be useful, at this point, to discuss with students some of the considerations with regard to choosing random numbers in a way to promote comparability of the two simulations.

Solution to Biales Waste Disposal, GMBH, Case

Costs in German Marks (DM):

Shipment:	DM	900 per load
Loading/unloading	DM	120 per load
Overhead (DM 41,000/25)	DM	1,640 per load
	DM	2,660 per load

Probability distributions:

NUMBER OF BARRELS LOADED	PROBABILITY	RANDOM NUMBER INTERVAL	REVENUE PER BARREL	PROBABILITY	RANDOM NUMBER INTERVAL
26–30 (28)	0.12	01–12	DM50	0.20	01–20
31–35 (33)	0.16	13–28	DM60	0.44	21–64
36–40 (38)	0.24	29–52	DM70	0.28	65–92
41–45 (43)	0.36	53–88	DM80	0.08	93–00
46–50 (48)	0.12	89–00		1.00	
	1.00				

TRUCKLOAD SIMULATION	RANDOM NUMBER	NUMBER OF BARRELS	RANDOM NUMBER	REVENUE PER BARREL	TOTAL REVENUE
1	52	38	06	DM 50	DM 1,990
2	37	38	63	60	2,280
3	82	43	57	60	2,580
4	69	43	02	50	2,150
5	98	48	94	80	3,840
6	96	48	52	60	2,880
7	33	38	69	70	2,660
8	50	38	33	60	2,880
9	88	43	32	60	2,580
10	90	48	30	60	2,880
11	50	38	48	60	2,280
12	27	33	88	70	2,310
13	45	38	14	50	1,900
14	81	43	02	50	2,150
15	66	43	83	70	3,010
16	74	43	05	50	2,150
17	30	38	34	60	2,280
18	59	43	55	60	2,580
19	67	43	09	50	2,150
20	60	43	77	70	3,010
21	60	43	08	50	2,150
22	80	43	45	60	2,580
23	53	43	84	70	3,010
24	69	43	84	70	3,010
25	37	38	77	70	2,660
					DM 63,860

Average income per load = DM 2,544.40
Loss per load = DM 2,660 − 2,554.40 = DM 105.60
Loss per year = 25 ∗ DM 105.60 = DM 2,640

The conclusion, based on just one short simulation, is that money will be lost by continuing service to Italy.

Solution to Abjar Transport Company Case

Table 1 represents a cumulative normal distribution of monthly cargo tonnages. The distribution of cargo between containerized and non-containerized cargo is 25%–75%. It is assumed that the non-containerized shipments will carry the capacity cargo of 60 tons. Hence, daily freight hauled by each truck is 180 tons (60 tons/trips × 3 trips/day).

For containerized cargo:

60% is packaged in 40 ft. containers
20% is packaged in 30 ft. containers
20% is packaged in 20 ft. containers

Cargo weights:

40 ft. handles 60 tons
30 ft. handles 45 tons
20 ft. handles 20 tons

It is noted that a truck can carry two 20-foot containers, so that the total cargo is 40 tons. Thus, average cargo hauled by containerized freight is 53 tons, or $.6 \times 60 + .2 \times 45 \times .2 \times .40$. Daily cargo hauled is: $3 \times 53 = 159$ tons/day.

The following table shows simulated monthly freight shipments. Cargo is then categorized into containerized and non-containerized shipments. The daily truck requirements for each month is projected.

TABLE 1

MO.	RN	FREIGHT	FREIGHT PER DAY (30 DAYS)	75% NONCONTAINERIZED	TRUCKS REQUIRED 3 TRIPS/DAY 60 TONS/TRIP	25% CONTAINERIZED	TRUCKS REQUIRED 3 TRIPS/DAY 53 TONS/TRIP
1	63	171,000	5700	4275	24	1425	9
2	88	197,000	6567	4925	27	1642	10
3	55	165,000	5500	4125	23	1375	9
4	69	176,000	5867	4400	24	1467	9
5	13	124,000	4133	3100	17	1033	7
6	17	131,000	4367	3275	18	1092	7
7	36	150,000	5000	3750	21	1250	8
8	81	186,000	6200	4650	26	1550	10
9	84	190,000	6333	4750	26	1583	10
10	63	172,000	5733	4300	24	1433	9
11	70	177,000	5900	4425	25	1475	9
12	06	110,000	3667	2750	15	917	6

As seen from the simulated year's operation, the daily truck requirement for non-containerized cargo ranges from 15 to 27. For containerized cargo it ranges from 6 to 10 trucks. The maximum number of trucks required to handle the load in any single period is 37. It should be noted that the utilization factor is .96. Hence, the number of trucks should be adjusted upward accordingly.

A discussion of obtaining a simulated "Freight" from a "Random Number" should be highlighted; for example, why does the random number "63" result in a freight of 171,000?

18
Network Models

LEARNING OBJECTIVES

After completing this chapter, students will be able to:

1. Understand how to plan, monitor, and control projects with the use of PERT.
2. Determine earliest start, earliest finish, latest start, latest finish, and slack times for each activity along with the total project completion time.
3. Reduce total project time at the least total cost by crashing the network using manual or linear programming techniques.
4. Connect all points of a network while minimizing total distance using the minimal-spanning tree technique.
5. Determine the maximum flow through a network using the maximal-flow technique.
6. Find the shortest path through a network using the shortest-route technique.
7. Understand the important role of software in project management.

TEACHING SUGGESTIONS

Teaching Suggestion 18.1: Chapter Coverage.

This is one of the largest chapters in the book. It contains information on PERT, CPM, minimal-spanning tree, maximal-flow, and shortest-route techniques. Because of the amount and diversity of material, you may want to break the chapter into smaller units. One approach is to break the chapter into: (1) PERT, (2) CPM, and (3) other network techniques.

Teaching Suggestion 18.2: Importance of PERT.

PERT has rebounded and, due to microcomputer software such as Timeline and Harvard Project Manager, become a highly used quantitative analysis technique. It can be useful for organizations of all sizes and any individuals involved in planning and controlling projects. A good way to start this chapter is to discuss the capabilities of PERT. Students can be asked to contact a local firm (such as a builder) to ask about the use of PERT.

Teaching Suggestion 18.3: Getting Students Involved with PERT.

PERT is a technique that students can apply immediately. For example, students can be asked to use PERT to plan the courses they will need to take and the timing of taking these courses until graduation.

Another approach would be to have students take a typical semester and use PERT to plan the term papers, exams, and assignments that must be finished to successfully complete the semester.

Teaching Suggestion 18.4: Constructing a Network.

One of the most difficult tasks of PERT or CPM is to develop an accurate network that reflects the true situation. Students should be given practice in this important aspect of network analysis as early as possible. Use the end-of-chapter problems. Students can be asked to develop their own networks. We can't stress enough the importance of drawing networks, since many students have a conceptual problem with the task.

Teaching Suggestion 18.5: Using the Beta Distribution.

PERT uses the beta distribution in estimating expected times and variances for each activity. As a matter of fact, it is questionable whether the beta distribution is appropriate. Students should be told that other distributions such as the normal curve can be used. A discrete probability distribution can also be used to determine expected times and variances. Instead of using optimistic, most probable, and pessimistic time estimates, an entire discrete distribution can be used to determine expected times and variances.

Teaching Suggestion 18.6: Finding the Critical Path.

Finding the critical path is not too difficult if the steps given in this chapter are followed. Students should be reminded that in making the forward pass *all* activities must be completed before any activity can be started. In the backward pass, students should be reminded that latest time is computed by making sure that the project would not be delayed for any activity. This means that *all* activities must be completed within the original project completion time.

Teaching Suggestion 18.7: Dummy Activities.

Dummy activities are important in maintaining the accuracy of a network. Without dummy activities, the network may not truly reflect the immediate predecessor relationships. Students should be told that they need to carefully check any network they develop or draw to determine if one or more dummy activities are needed. Not checking may result in wrong answers.

Teaching Suggestion 18.8: Project Crashing.

In manually performing project crashing, the critical path may change. In many cases, two or more critical paths will exist after crashing. Students should be reminded of this problem. Fortunately, the linear programming approach or the use of PERT software, including AB:QM, automatically takes care of this potential problem.

Teaching Suggestion 18.9: Alternate Optimal Solutions in Networks.

The solution techniques for minimal-spanning tree, maximal-flow, and shortest-route techniques are easy and straightforward. Although these techniques obtain an optimal solution, students should be told that other optimal solutions (alternate optimal solutions) may exist. Unlike linear programming, however, these techniques do not alert students to this possibility.

Teaching Suggestion 18.10: Maximal-Flow Technique.

The maximal-flow technique involves subtracting capacity along the path that is picked or selected with some flow. This can be confusing to some students. The capacity is subtracted in the opposite direction of the flow to maintain correct network relationships. You may need to spend some time making this point clear.

VIDEO NOTES

VIDEO 18-1

Management Science: Trains, Planes and Critical Paths

This segment discusses the subjects of network scheduling and the critical path method. The first portion uses a series of examples to illustrate algorithms such as

minimal-cost spanning trees. The video mentions the problem of dealing with combinational explosion, that is, the huge number of possible solutions to even a reasonably sized network problem. (For example, $N = 11$ cities on a route means there are 20 million possible tours).

Other applications mentioned are routes for meter readers, order of installing chips on computer boards, and garbage collection routing.

The video then moves to a simple and straightforward application of critical path scheduling of an Eastern Airlines airplane turnaround problem in Boston. (See the QA Application box in Chapter 18 for details.) It also discusses CPM for building contractors. The tape concludes with a brief interview of Thomas Cook discussing crew scheduling at American Airlines.

ALTERNATE EXAMPLES

Alternate Example 18-1: Sid Orland is involved in planning a scientific research project. The activities are displayed in the following diagram. Optimistic, most likely, and pessimistic time estimates are displayed in the following table, along with activity starting and ending nodes.

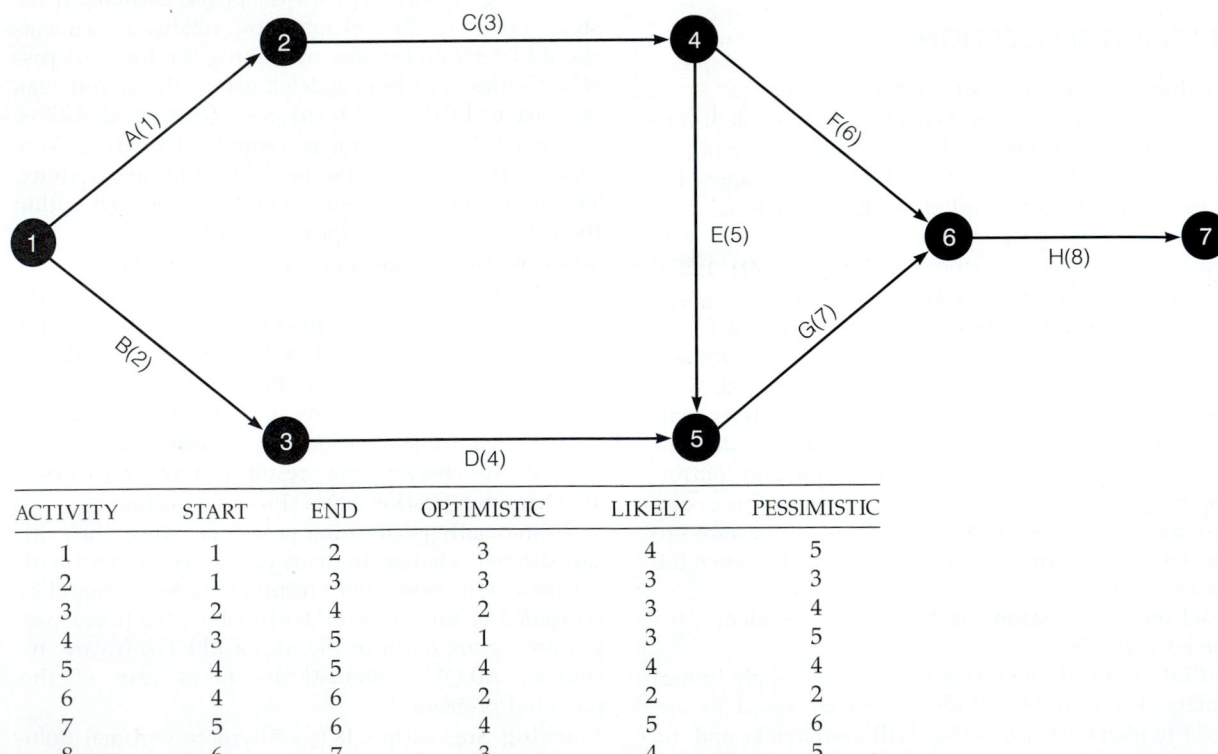

ACTIVITY	START	END	OPTIMISTIC	LIKELY	PESSIMISTIC
1	1	2	3	4	5
2	1	3	3	3	3
3	2	4	2	3	4
4	3	5	1	3	5
5	4	5	4	4	4
6	4	6	2	2	2
7	5	6	4	5	6
8	6	7	3	4	5

The activities along the critical path and the total project completion times are shown in the following figure. The problem is solved using AB:QM as shown below. As can be seen, the total project completion time is 20 weeks. Critical path activities are A(1), C(3), E(5), G(7), and H(8).

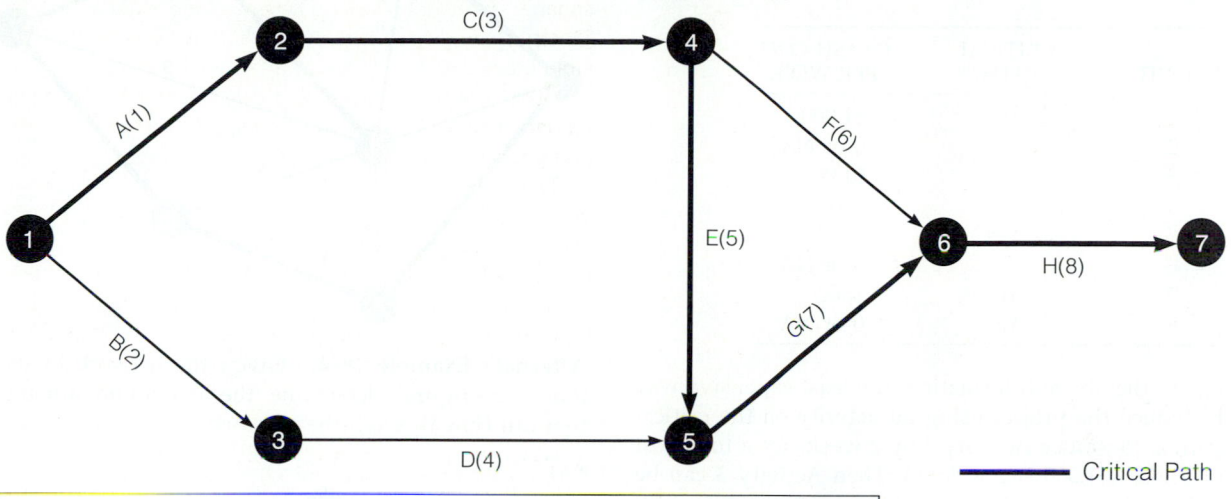

```
------------------------------------------------------------------
Activity       Activity Nodes      Mean      S.D.       Variance
------------------------------------------------------------------
  1*              1 --> 2         4.000      0.333       0.111
  2               1 --> 3         3.000      0.000       0.000
  3*              2 --> 4         3.000      0.333       0.111
  4               3 --> 5         3.000      0.667       0.444
  5*              4 --> 5         4.000      0.000       0.000
  6               4 --> 6         2.000      0.000       0.000
  7*              5 --> 6         5.000      0.333       0.111
  8*              6 --> 7         4.000      0.333       0.111
------------------------------------------------------------------

(* : Critical Path Activities)

Expected Completion Time :    20.000
```

Alternate Example 18-2:   Sid Orland would like to reduce the project completion time for the problem in Alternate Example 18-1 by 3 weeks. The normal and crash times and costs are presented below, along with starting and ending nodes.

			TIME		COST	
ACTIVITY	START	END	NORMAL	CRASH	NORMAL	CRASH
1	1	2	4	3	$2000	$ 3000
2	1	3	3	3	3000	3000
3	2	4	3	2	5000	6000
4	3	5	3	2	5000	5500
5	4	5	4	3	8000	10000
6	4	6	2	2	2000	2000
7	5	6	5	3	3000	4000
8	6	7	4	4	4000	4000

From the above table, the crash cost per week can be determined for each activity. This information is displayed in the following table:

ACTIVITY	CRITICAL PATH?	CRASH COST PER WEEK
1	Yes	$1,000
2		0 or NA
3	Yes	$1,000
4		$500
5	Yes	$2,000
6		0 or NA
7	Yes	$500
8	Yes	0 or NA

Given the above information, the least expensive way to reduce the project using an activity on the critical path is to reduce Activity 7 by 2 weeks for a total cost of $1,000 ($1,000 = 2 × $500). Then Activity 3 can be reduced by one week for an additional $1,000. This will result in the total project completion time being reduced by 3 weeks at a cost of $2,000.

Alternate Example 18-3: Given the following network, perform the minimum spanning tree technique to determine the best way to connect nodes on the network, while minimizing total distance.

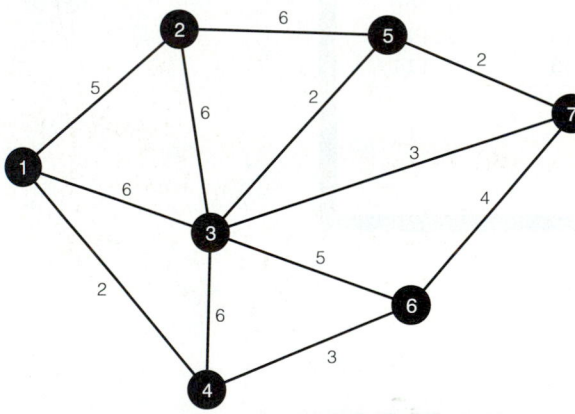

We begin with node 1. Node 4 is the nearest node, and thus we connect node 1 to node 4. Given nodes 1 and 4, node 6 is the nearest, and we connect it to node 4. Now considering nodes 1, 4, and 6, we see that node 7 is the nearest to node 6 and we connect it. Node 5 is connected to node 7, and node 3 is connected to node 3 in the same way.

Using the minimum spanning tree technique, we can see that the total distance required to connect all nodes is 18. The following figure (in the next column) shows the results.

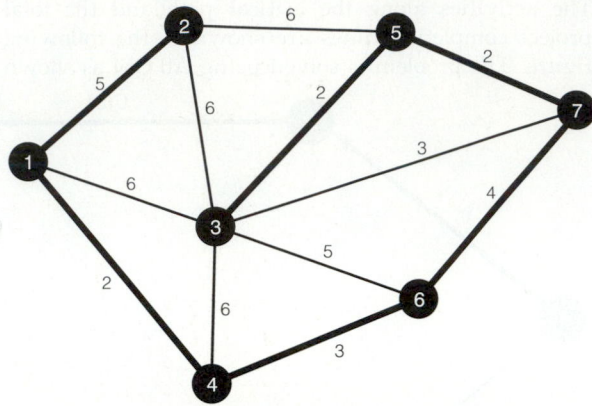

Alternate Example 18-4: Given the network in the following figure, determine the maximum amount that can flow through the network.

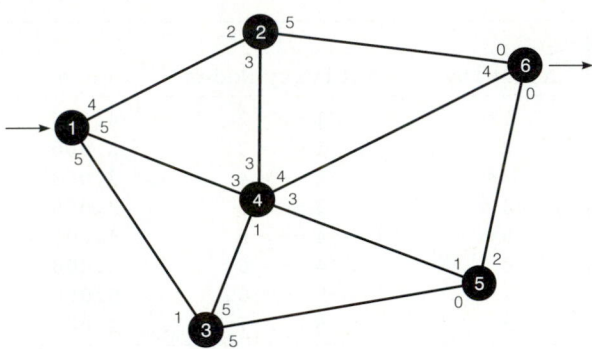

We begin this problem by putting the maximum flow of 4 through nodes 1, 2, and 6. This is shown in the following figure. The flows have been adjusted along this path.

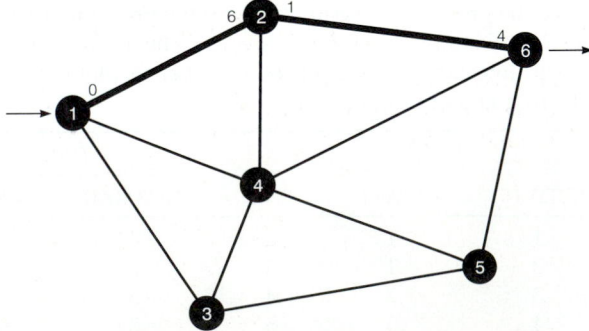

1–2–6   4 units

Next, we will put the maximum flow of 1 through nodes 1, 4, 2, and 6. The adjusted flows are shown in the following figure.

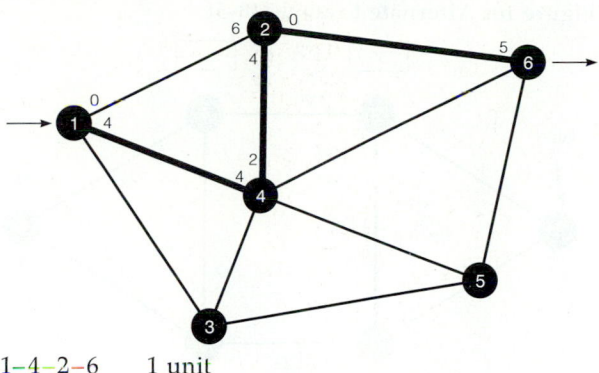

1–4–2–6   1 unit

Next, we put the maximum flow of 4 units through nodes 1, 4, and 6. The adjusted network is shown below:

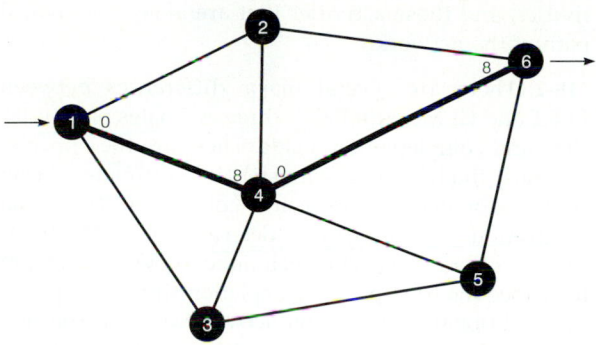

This process continues. We put a maximum of 2 units through nodes 1, 3, 5, and 6. The maximum amount that can flow through the network is 11. The figure below shows the final results.

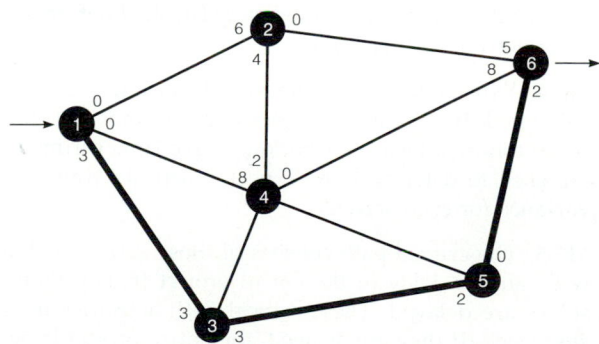

1–2–6	4 units
1–4–2–6	1 unit
1–4–6	4 units
1–3–5–6	2 units
	11

Alternate Example 18-5: Given the network in the following figure, determine the shortest route or path through the network.

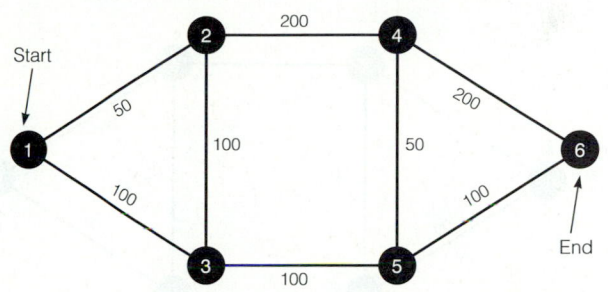

The nearest node to node 1 is node 2. The distance is 50. Thus, we put 50 in a box by node 2. The results of this step are shown in the following figure.

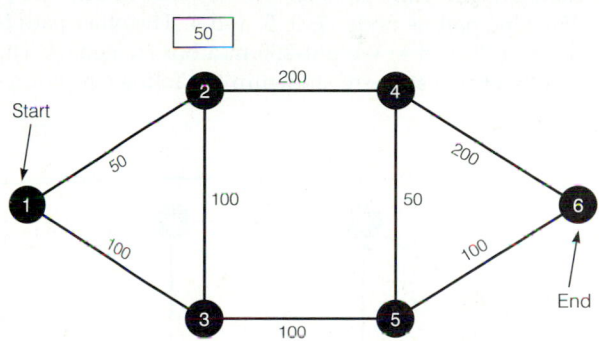

The next nearest node to node 1 is node 3. The distance is 100. Thus, we put 100 in a box by node 3. The results of this step are shown in the following figure.

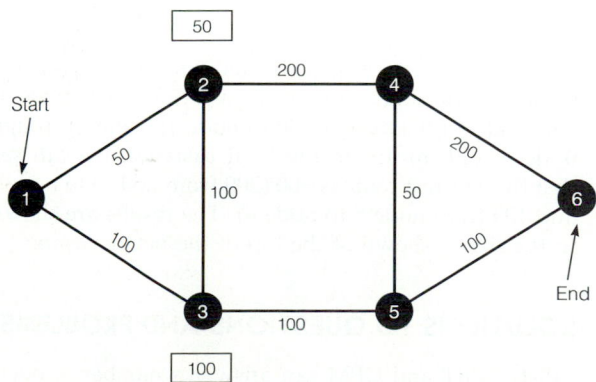

We continue the process. The next nearest node to node 1 is node 5. The distance between node 4 and 5 is 100 and the total distance between node 5 and node 1 is

200. Thus, we put 200 in a box by node 5. The results of this step are shown in the following figure.

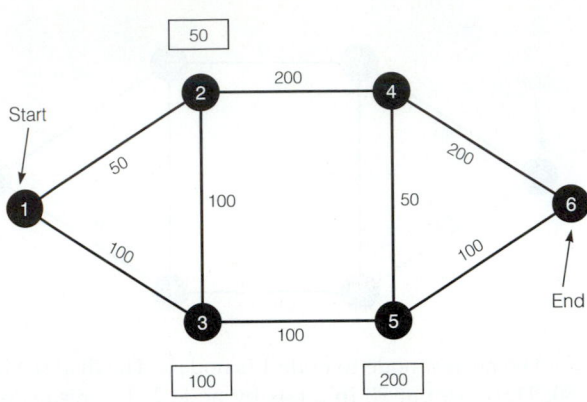

The next nearest node to node 1 is node 4. Actually, there are two paths to node 4 with the same distance of 250. One path is nodes 1, 3, 5, and 4. The other path is nodes 1, 2, and 4. We put 250 in a box by node 4. The results of this step are shown in the following figure.

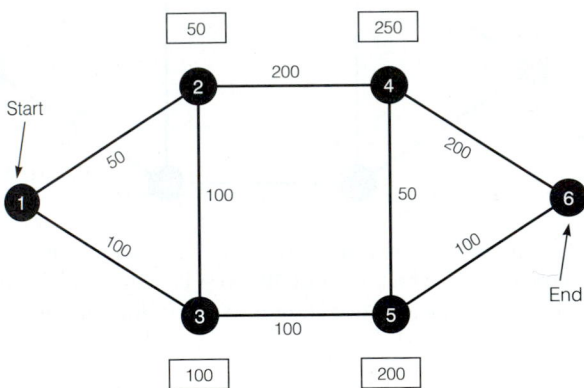

The final step is to consider node 6. We can get to node 6 through node 5 (distance of 200 to node 1) and node 4 (distance of 250 to node 1). Going through node 5 will minimize the total distance. We can see that the shortest route is 300 (200 from node 5 to node 1 and 100 from node 5 to node 6). The results are shown in the figure shown at the top of the next column.

SOLUTIONS TO QUESTIONS AND PROBLEMS

18-1. PERT and CPM can answer a number of questions about a project or the activities within a project. These techniques can determine the earliest start, earliest finish, latest start, and the latest finish times for all activities within a network. Furthermore, these

Figure for Alternate Example 18-5f

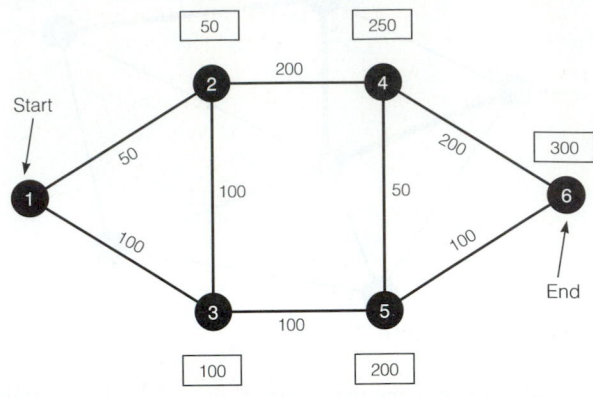

techniques can be used to determine the project completion data for the entire project, the slack for all activities, and those activities that are along the critical path of the network.

18-2. There are several major differences between PERT and CPM. With PERT, three estimates of activity time and completion are made. These are the optimistic, most likely, and pessimistic time estimates. From these estimates, the expected completion time and completion variance can be determined. CPM allows the use of crashing. This technique allows a manager to reduce the total project completion time by expending additional resources on activities within the network. CPM is used in determining the least-cost method of crashing a project or network.

18-3. An activity is a task or something that requires a fixed amount of time and resources to complete. An event is a point in time. Events mark the beginning and ending of activities. An immediate predecessor is an activity that must be completely finished before another activity can be started.

18-4. Expected activity times and variances can be computed by making the assumption that activity times follow a beta distribution. Three time estimates are used to determine the expected activity time and variance for each activity.

18-5. The critical path consists of those activities that will cause a delay in the entire project if they themselves are delayed. These critical path activities have zero slack. If they are delayed, the entire project is delayed. Critical path analysis is a way of determining the activities along the critical path, and the earliest start times, earliest finish times, latest start times, and the latest finish times for every activity. It is important to identify these activities because if they are delayed the entire project will be delayed.

18-6. The earliest activity start time is the earliest time that an activity can be started while all previous activities are completely finished. The earliest activity start times are determined using a forward pass through the network. The latest activity start time represents the latest time that an activity can be started without delaying the entire project. Latest activity start times are determined by making a backward pass through the network.

18-7. Slack is the amount of time that an activity can be delayed without delaying the entire project. If the slack is zero, then the activity cannot be delayed at all without delaying the entire project. For any activity, slack can be determined by subtracting the earliest start from the latest start time, or by subtracting the earliest finish from the latest finish time.

18-8. We can determine the probability that a project will be completed by a certain date by knowing the expected project completion time and variance. The expected project completion time can be determined by adding the activity times for those activities along the critical path. The total project variance can be determined by adding the variance of those activities along the critical path. In most cases, we make the assumption that the project completion times follow a normal distribution. When this is done, we can use a standard normal table in computing the probability that a project will be completed by a certain date.

18-9. PERT/cost is used to monitor and control project cost in addition to the time it takes to complete a particular project. This can be done by making a budget for the entire project using the activity cost estimates and by monitoring the budget as the project takes place. Using this approach we can determine the extent to which a project is incurring a cost overrun or a cost underrun. In addition, we can use the same technique to determine the extent to which a project is ahead of schedule or behind schedule.

18-10. Crashing is the process of reducing the total time it takes to complete a project by expending additional resources. In performing crashing by hand, it is necessary to identify those activities along the critical path and then to reduce those activities which cost the least to reduce or crash. This is continued until the project is crashed to the desired completion date. In doing this, however, two or more critical paths can develop in the same network.

18-11. Linear programming is very useful in CPM crashing because it is a commonly used technique and many computer programs exist that can be easily used to crash a network. In addition, there are many sensi-

tivity and ranging techniques that are available with linear programming.

18-12.

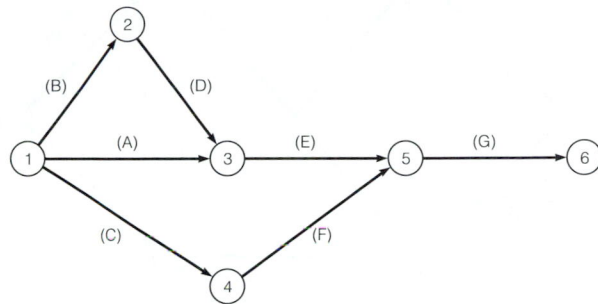

18-13.

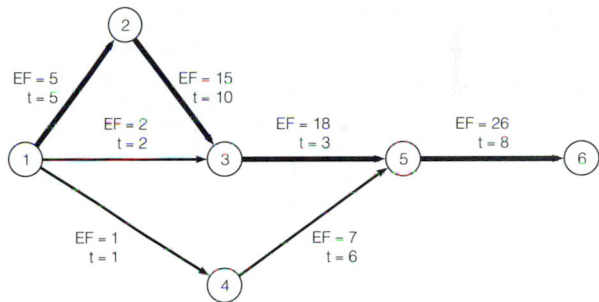

ACTIVITY	ES	EF	LS	LF	S	CRITICAL ACTIVITY
1–2	0	5	0	5	0	Yes
1–3	0	2	13	15	13	No
1–4	0	1	11	12	11	No
2–3	5	15	5	15	0	Yes
3–5	15	18	15	18	0	Yes
4–5	1	7	12	18	11	No
5–6	18	26	18	26	0	Yes

Critical path is 1–2–3–5–6. Project completion time is 26 days.

18-14.

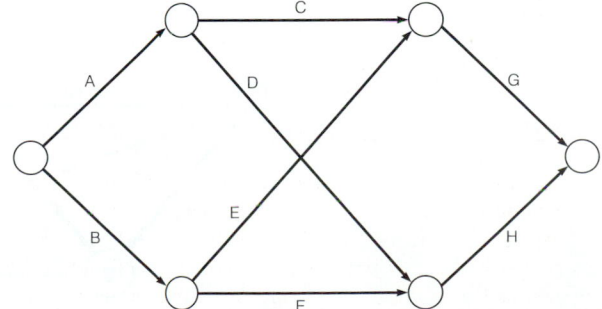

18-15.

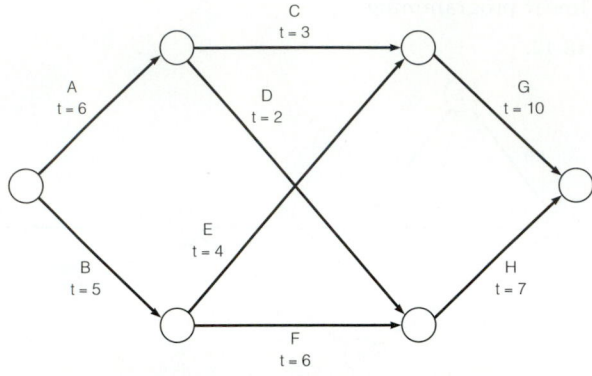

ACTIVITY	TIME (WEEKS)	ES	EF	LS	LF	S	CRITICAL ACTIVITY
A	6	0	6	0	6	0	Yes
B	5	0	5	0	5	0	Yes
C	3	6	9	6	9	0	Yes
D	2	6	8	10	12	4	No
E	4	5	9	5	9	0	Yes
F	6	5	11	6	12	1	No
G	10	9	19	9	19	0	Yes
H	7	11	18	12	19	1	No

There are two critical paths: A–C–G and B–E–G. Project completion time is 19 weeks.

18-16.

ACTIVITY	a	m	b	EXPECTED TIME	VARIANCE
A	3	6	8	5.83	0.69
B	2	4	4	3.67	0.11
C	1	2	3	2.00	0.11
D	6	7	8	7.00	0.11
E	2	4	6	4.00	0.44
F	6	10	14	10.00	1.78
G	1	2	4	2.17	0.25
H	3	6	9	6.00	1.00
I	10	11	12	11.00	0.11
J	14	16	20	16.33	1.00
K	2	8	10	7.33	1.78

18-17. A network for the project is shown in the figure at the bottom of the page.

ACTIVITY	ES	EF	LS	LF	S	CRITICAL PATH
A	0	5.83	7.17	13.00	7.17	No
B	0	3.67	5.33	9.00	5.33	No
C	0	2.00	0	2.00	0	Yes
D	2.00	9.00	2.00	9.00	0	Yes
E	9.00	13.00	9.00	13.00	0	Yes
F	13.00	23.00	13.00	23.00	0	Yes
G	13.00	15.17	15.83	18.00	2.83	No
H	23.00	29.00	23.00	29.00	0	Yes
I	15.17	26.17	18.00	29.00	2.83	No
J	2.00	18.33	20.00	36.33	18.00	No
K	29.00	36.33	29.00	36.33	0	Yes

Critical path is C–D–E–F–H–K. Project completion time is 36.33 days.

Figure for Problem 18-17

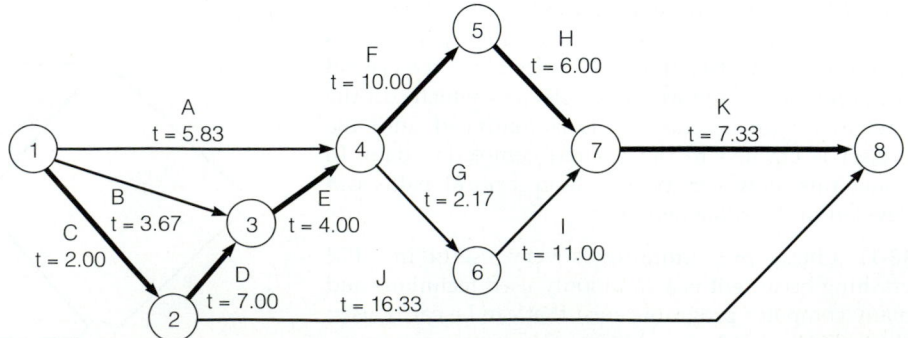

18-18. For the project, expected time = 36.33.

$V_t = .11 + .11 + .44 + 1.78 + 1.00 + 1.78 = 5.22$

Standard deviation = 2.28

Probability of finishing project in less than 40 days:

$$= P\left(Z \le \frac{40 - 36.33}{2.28}\right)$$

$$P(Z \le 1.61) = .9463$$

18-19.

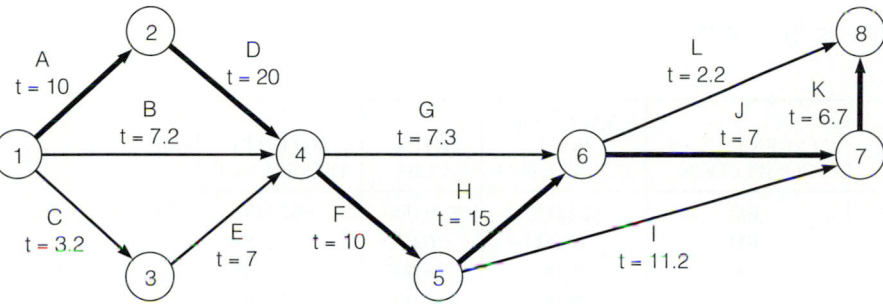

ACTIVITY	a	m	b	t	V	ES	EF	LS	LF	S
A	8	10	12	10.0	0.44	0	10.0	0	10.0	0
B	6	7	9	7.2	0.25	0	7.2	22.8	30.0	22.8
C	3	3	4	3.2	0.03	0	3.2	19.8	23.0	19.8
D	10	20	30	20.0	11.11	10.0	30.0	10.0	30.0	0
E	6	7	8	7.0	0.11	3.2	10.2	23.0	30.0	19.8
F	9	10	11	10.0	0.11	30.0	40.0	30.0	40.0	0
G	6	7	10	7.3	0.44	30.0	37.3	47.7	55.0	17.7
H	14	15	16	15.0	0.11	40.0	55.0	40.0	55.0	0
I	10	11	13	11.2	0.25	40.0	51.2	50.8	62.0	10.8
J	6	7	8	7.0	0.11	55.0	62.0	55.0	62.0	0
K	4	7	8	6.7	0.44	62.0	68.7	62.0	68.7	0
L	1	2	4	2.2	0.25	55.0	57.2	66.5	68.7	11.5

Critical path is A–D–F–H–J–K. Project completion time is 68.7 days. Project variance is .44 + 11.11 + .11 + .11 + .11 + .44 = 12.32.

$$\sigma_t = \sqrt{12.32} = 3.5$$

$$\mu_t = 68.7$$

Probability of finishing in 70 days $= P\left(Z \le \dfrac{70 - 68.7}{3.5}\right) = .644$

Probability of finishing in 80 days $= P\left(Z \le \dfrac{80 - 68.7}{3.5}\right) = .9994$

Probability of finishing in 90 days $= P\left(Z \le \dfrac{90 - 68.7}{3.5}\right) = .9999$

18-20. Assuming normal distribution for project completion time:

a. $P\left(Z \leq \dfrac{17 - 21}{2}\right) = P(Z \leq -2) = 1 - .9772$

$= .0228$

b. $P\left(Z \leq \dfrac{20 - 21}{2}\right) = P(Z \leq -.5) = 1 - .6915$

$= .3085$

c. $P\left(Z \leq \dfrac{23 - 21}{2}\right) = P(Z \leq 1) = .8413$

d. $P\left(Z \leq \dfrac{25 - 21}{2}\right) = P(Z \leq 2) - .9772$

18-21.

ACTIVITY	TOTAL BUDGETED COST	PERCENTAGE OF COMPLETION	VALUE OF WORK COMPLETED	ACTUAL COST	ACTIVITY DIFFERENCE
A	$22,000	100	$22,000	$20,000	−$2,000
B	30,000	100	30,000	36,000	6,000
C	26,000	100	26,000	26,000	0
D	48,000	100	48,000	44,000	−4,000
E	56,000	50	28,000	25,000	−3,000
F	30,000	60	18,000	15,000	−3,000
G	80,000	10	8,000	5,000	−3,000
H	16,000	10	1,600	1,000	−600

After 8 weeks:

Value of work completed = $181,600
Actual cost = $172,000
Cost underrun = $9,600

Using Table 18.5, $212,000 should have been spent using ES times. Using Table 18.6, with LS times $182,000 should have been spent. Hence, the project is behind schedule but there is a cost underrun on the whole.

Table for Problem 8-21

ACTIVITY	ES	LS	t	TOTAL COST (IN $1,000)	COST PER MONTH
A	0	0	6	10	$1,667
B	1	4	2	14	7,000
C	3	3	7	5	714
D	4	9	3	6	2,000
E	6	6	10	14	1,400
F	14	15	11	13	1,182
G	12	18	2	4	2,000
H	14	14	11	6	545
I	18	21	6	18	3,000
J	18	19	4	12	3,000
K	22	22	14	10	714
L	22	23	8	16	2,000
M	18	24	6	18	3,000
				146,000	

Using earliest starting times.

18-22. a. Monthly budget using earliest start times:

ACTIVITY	1	2	3	4	5	6	7	8	9	10	11	12	13	14	15	16	17	18	19	20	21	22	23	24	25	26	27	28	29	30	31	32	33	34	35	36	TOTALS
A	1667	1667	1667	1667	1667	1667																															10,000
B	7000	7000																																			14,000
C			714	714	714	714	714	714	714																												5,000
D			2000	2000	2000																																6,000
E							1400	1400	1400	1400	1400	1400	1400	1400	1400	1400																					14,000
F															1182	1182	1182	1182	1182	1182	1182	1182	1182	1182	1182												13,000
G													2000	2000																							4,000
H															545	545	545	545	545	545	545	545	545	545	545												6,000
I																			3000	3000	3000	3000	3000	3000													18,000
J																			3000	3000	3000	3000															12,000
K																							714	714	714	714	714	714	714	714	714	714	714	714	714	714	10,000
L																							2000	2000	2000	2000	2000	2000	2000	2000							16,000
M																			3000	3000	3000	3000	3000	3000													18,000
Total/month	8667	8667	4381	4381	4381	2381	2114	2114	2114	1400	1400	1400	3400	3400	3127	3127	1727	1727	10727	10727	10727	10727	10441	10441	4441	2714	2714	2714	2714	2714	714	714	714	714	714	714	146,000

b. Monthly budget using latest start times:

ACTIVITY	1	2	3	4	5	6	7	8	9	10	11	12	13	14	15	16	17	18	19	20	21	22	23	24	25	26	27	28	29	30	31	32	33	34	35	36	TOTALS
A	1667	1667	1667	1667	1667	1667																															10,000
B					7000	7000																															14,000
C				714	714	714	714	714	714	714																											5,000
D										2000	2000	2000																									6,000
E							1400	1400	1400	1400	1400	1400	1400	1400	1400	1400																					14,000
F																1182	1182	1182	1182	1182	1182	1182	1182	1182	1182	1182											13,000
G																			2000	2000																	4,000
H															545	545	545	545	545	545	545	545	545	545	545												6,000
I																						3000	3000	3000	3000	3000	3000										18,000
J																				3000	3000	3000	3000														12,000
K																							714	714	714	714	714	714	714	714	714	714	714	714	714	714	10,000
L																								2000	2000	2000	2000	2000	2000	2000	2000						16,000
M																									3000	3000	3000	3000	3000	3000							18,000
Total/ month	1667	1667	1667	2381	9381	9381	2114	2114	2114	4114	3400	3400	1400	1400	1945	3127	1727	1727	3727	6727	4727	7727	8441	7441	10441	9896	8714	5714	5714	5714	2714	714	714	714	714	714	146,000

18-23.

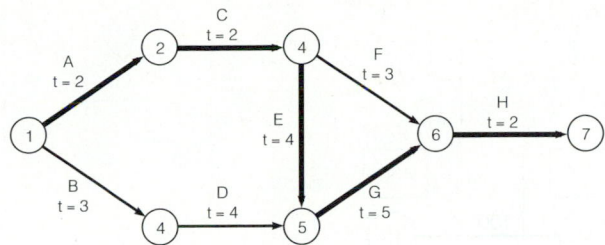

Critical path is A–C–E–G–H. Total time is 15 weeks.

1. Activities A, C, and E all have minimum crash costs per week of $1,000.
2. Reduce activity E by 1 week for a total cost of $1,000. There are now 2 critical paths.
3. The total project completion time is now 14 weeks and the new critical paths are B–D–G–H and A–C–E–G–H.
4. Activities D and E have minimum crashing costs per week for each critical path.
5. Reduce activities D and E by 1 week each for a total cost of $3,000 including the reduction of E by 1 week.
6. The total project completion time is 13 weeks. There are two critical paths: A–C–E–G–H and B–D–G–H.

18-24.

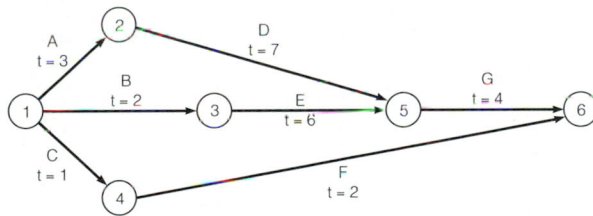

ACTIVITY	t	m	n	C	CRASH COST PER WEEK
A	3	2	$1,000	$1,600	$ 600
B	2	1	2,000	2,700	700
C	1	1	300	300	0
D	7	3	1,300	1,600	100
E	6	3	850	1,000	50
F	2	1	4,000	5,000	1,000
G	4	2	1,500	2,000	250

Project completion date is 14. This project has to be crashed to 10. This is done by the following linear

programming formulation:

If X_i is the time of occurrence at event i where $i = 1, \ldots, 6$, and Y_j is the amount of time reduced for activity j, where

$j = $ A, B, D, E, F, G

Minimize $Z = 600Y_A + 700Y_B + 0Y_C + 100Y_D$
$$+ 50Y_E + 1,000Y_F + 250Y_G$$

Subject to:
$$Y_A \leq 1$$
$$Y_B \leq 1$$
$$Y_C \leq 0$$
$$Y_D \leq 4$$
$$Y_E \leq 3$$
$$Y_F \leq 1$$
$$Y_G \leq 2$$
$$X_6 \leq 10$$

$$X_6 - X_5 + Y_G \geq 4 \qquad X_2 - X_1 + Y_A \geq 3$$
$$X_5 - X_3 + Y_E \geq 6 \qquad X_6 - X_4 + Y_F \geq 2$$
$$X_5 - X_2 + Y_D \geq 7 \qquad X_4 - X_1 + Y_C \geq 1$$
$$X_3 - X_1 + Y_B \geq 2 \qquad X_1 \geq 0$$

18-25.

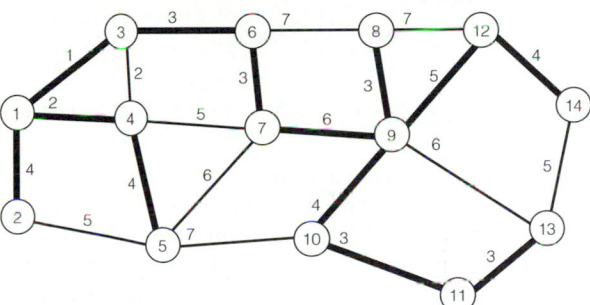

18-26.

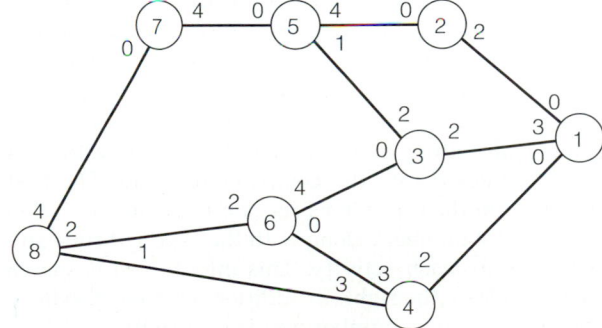

PATH	FLOW (CARS/HOUR)
1–2–5–7–8	200
1–3–6–8	200
1–4–8	100
Total	500

18-27.

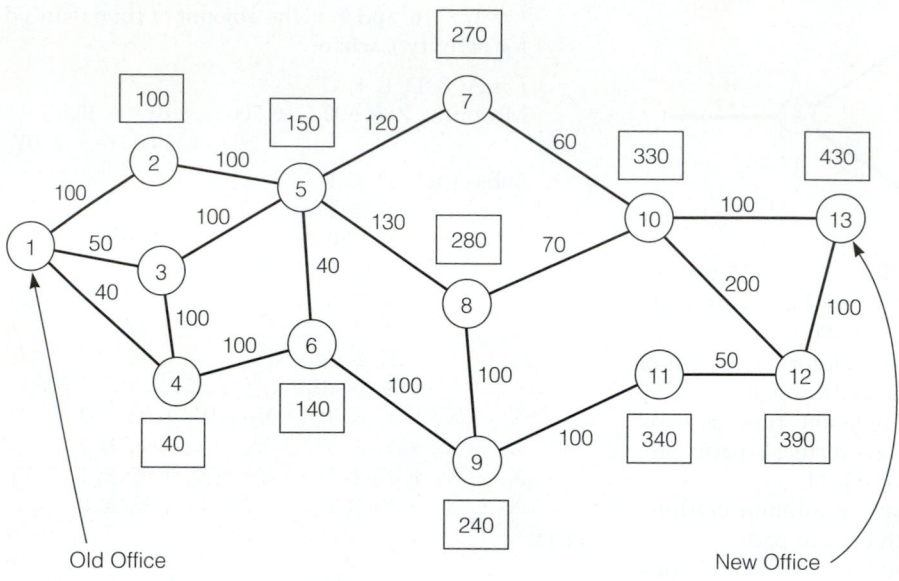

Old Office

New Office

The shortest route is 1–3–5–7–10–13. The distance is 430 miles.

18-28. Before we can determine how long it will take team A to complete its programming assignment, we must develop a PERT diagram and label all activities and beginning and ending node numbers. The beginning and ending node numbers are required to enter the appropriate data into our computer program that will solve this PERT problem. These beginning and ending node numbers will determine the immediate predecessors for any particular activity. The network showing the activities and node numbers is shown in the figure for Problem 18-28 on the next page. Once this network has been constructed, activities, beginning and ending node numbers, and time estimates can be entered into the computer program. The first result from the computer program is a summarization of the node numbers along with the expected time and variance for each activity. This information is shown in the table on the right. In addition, we have also indicated the activity number for every activity:

ACTIVITY	NODES S– –F	TIME	VARIANCE
1	1– –2	4.00	.111
2	2– –3	5.17	.250
3	2– –5	7.83	.250
4	2– –6	3.17	.250
5	2– –7	7.17	.250
6	2– –4	4.00	.111
7	4– –7	3.83	.250
8	6– –7	4.17	.250
9	5– –7	2.17	.250
10	3– –7	2.83	.250
11	7– –8	4.17	.250
12	8– –9	5.83	.250
13	9– –10	8.00	.444
14	10– –11	4.17	.250
15	7– –12	4.00	.111
16	12– –13	4.00	.444
17	11– –13	3.00	.111
18	13– –14	4.83	.250

We can also determine the expected project length and variance. The expected project length is 44 weeks. The variance is 2.1666 weeks. In addition, we can determine the earliest start, earliest finish, latest start, latest finish, and slack time for all activities along the critical path. This information is shown on the following page:

| ACTIVITY | ACTIVITY TIMES | | | | |
S--F	ES	EF	LS	LF	SLACK
1--2	.00	4.00	.00	4.00	.00*
2--3	4.00	9.17	6.00	11.17	2.00
2--5	4.00	11.83	4.00	11.83	.00*
2--6	4.00	7.17	6.67	9.83	2.67
2--7	4.00	11.17	6.83	14.00	2.83
2--4	4.00	8.00	6.17	10.17	2.17
4--7	8.00	11.83	10.17	14.00	2.17
6--7	7.17	11.33	9.83	14.00	2.67
5--7	11.83	14.00	11.83	14.00	.00*
3--7	9.17	12.00	11.17	14.00	2.00
7--8	14.00	18.17	14.00	18.17	.00*
8--9	18.17	24.00	18.17	24.00	.00*
9--10	24.00	32.00	24.00	32.00	.00*
10--11	32.00	36.17	32.00	36.17	.00*
7--12	14.00	18.00	31.17	35.17	17.17
12--13	18.00	22.00	35.17	39.17	17.17
11--13	36.17	39.17	36.17	39.17	.00*
13--14	39.17	44.00	39.17	44.00	.00*

*Indicates critical path activity

As can be seen in the above table, the critical path for this particular problem includes activities 1, 3, 9, 11, 12, 13, 14, 17, and 18. The solution, however, is not complete. Software Development Specialist (SDS) is not sure about the time estimates for activity 5. As indicated in the problem, these time estimates might be as high as 12, 14, and 15 weeks for the optimistic, most likely, and pessimistic times. Now, we must find out what impact this possible increase in expected times would have on the network. Fortunately, our computer program has a convenient rerun capability. We are able to go back to the original data, modify the time estimates for these activities, and resolve the problem. Doing this will result in an expected project completion time of 47.83 weeks. The variance of the project is approximately 1.92 weeks. Will this change the critical

path? The answer is yes. The critical path now includes activities 1, 5, 11, 12, 13, 14, 17, and 18. Activity 5 now lies along the critical path. The earliest start, earliest finish, latest start, latest finish, and slack times for all activities with the new time estimates for activity 5 are shown below:

| ACTIVITY | ACTIVITY TIMES | | | | |
S--F	ES	EF	LS	LF	SLACK
1--2	.00	4.00	.00	4.00	.00*
2--3	4.00	9.17	9.83	15.00	5.83
2--5	4.00	11.83	7.83	15.67	3.83
2--6	4.00	7.17	10.50	13.67	6.50
2--7	4.00	17.83	4.00	17.83	.00*
2--4	4.00	8.00	10.00	14.00	6.00
4--7	8.00	11.83	14.00	17.83	6.00
6--7	7.17	11.33	13.67	17.83	6.50
5--7	11.83	14.00	15.67	17.83	3.83
3--7	9.17	12.00	15.00	17.83	5.83
7--8	17.83	22.00	17.83	22.00	.00*
8--9	22.00	27.83	22.00	27.83	.00*
9--10	27.83	35.83	27.83	35.83	.00*
10--11	35.83	40.00	35.83	40.00	.00*
7--12	17.83	21.83	35.00	39.00	17.17
12--13	21.83	25.83	39.00	43.00	17.17
11--13	40.00	43.00	40.00	43.00	.00*
13--14	43.00	47.83	43.00	47.83	.00*

*Indicates critical path activity

18-29. The Bender Construction Co. problem is one involving 23 separate activities. These activities, their immediate predecessors, and time estimates were given in the problem. One of the most difficult aspects of this problem is to take the data in the table given in the problem and to construct a network diagram. This network diagram is necessary in order to determine beginning and ending node numbers which can be used in the computer program to solve this particular

Figure for Problem 18-28

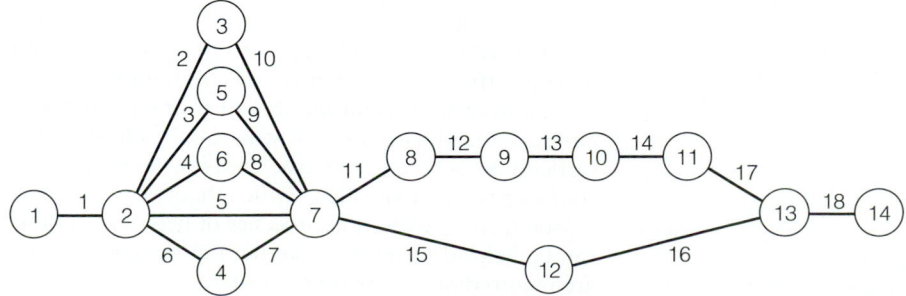

problem. The network diagram for this problem is shown on page IS-241. Once this diagram has been developed, activity numbers, starting and finishing node numbers, and the three time estimates for each activity can be entered into the computer program. The first results of the computer program are the expected time and variance estimates for each activity. These data are shown below:

ACTIVITY	NODES S‑‑F	TIME	VARIANCE
1	1‑‑2	3.67	.444
2	1‑‑3	3.00	.111
3	1‑‑4	4.00	.111
4	1‑‑5	8.00	.111
5	2‑‑6	4.17	.028
6	4‑‑9	2.17	.250
7	5‑‑7	5.00	.111
8	7‑‑8	2.17	.250
9	6‑‑9	3.83	.028
10	3‑‑9	1.17	.028
11	1‑‑9	20.67	1.778
12	8‑‑9	2.00	.111
13	9‑‑10	1.17	.028
14	10‑‑11	.14	.000
15	11‑‑13	.30	.001
16	11‑‑12	1.17	.028
17	12‑‑13	2.00	.111
18	13‑‑14	5.00	.444
19	14‑‑15	.12	.000
20	15‑‑16	.14	.000
21	15‑‑17	3.33	.444
22	16‑‑17	.12	.000
23	17‑‑18	.18	.001

EXPECTED PROJECT LENGTH = 33.77
VARIANCE OF THE PROJECT LENGTH = 2.8339

Next, the computer determines the expected project length, variance, and data for all activities. Like the other network problems, these data include the earliest start time, earliest finish time, latest start time, latest finish time, and slack for all activities. The data are shown in the next column.

ACTIVITY S‑‑F	ACTIVITY TIMES				
	ES	EF	LS	LF	SLACK
1‑‑2	.00	3.67	9.00	12.67	9.00
1‑‑3	.00	3.00	16.50	19.50	16.50
1‑‑4	.00	4.00	14.50	18.50	14.50
1‑‑5	.00	8.00	3.50	11.50	3.50
2‑‑6	3.67	7.83	12.67	16.83	9.00
4‑‑9	4.00	6.17	18.50	20.67	14.50
5‑‑7	8.00	13.00	11.50	16.50	3.50
7‑‑8	13.00	15.17	16.50	18.67	3.50
6‑‑9	7.83	11.67	16.83	20.67	9.00
3‑‑9	3.00	4.17	19.50	20.67	16.50
1‑‑9	.00	20.67	.00	20.67	.00*
8‑‑9	15.17	17.17	18.67	20.67	3.50
9‑‑10	20.67	21.83	20.67	21.83	.00*
10‑‑11	21.83	21.97	21.83	21.97	.00*
11‑‑13	21.97	22.27	24.84	25.14	2.87
11‑‑12	21.97	23.14	21.97	23.14	.00*
12‑‑13	23.14	25.14	23.14	25.14	.00*
13‑‑14	25.14	30.14	25.14	30.14	.00*
14‑‑15	30.14	30.25	30.14	30.25	.00*
15‑‑16	30.25	30.39	33.33	33.47	3.08
15‑‑17	30.25	33.59	30.25	33.59	.00*
16‑‑17	30.39	30.51	33.47	33.59	3.08
17‑‑18	33.59	33.77	33.59	33.77	.00*

* Indicates critical path activity

As you can see, the expected project length is about 34 weeks. The activities along the critical path are activities 11, 13, 14, 16, 17, 18, 19, 21, and 23.

18-30. The overall purpose of Problem 18-30 is to have students use a network approach in attempting to solve a problem that almost all students face. The first step is for students to list all courses that they must take, including possible electives, to get a degree from their particular college or university. For every course, students should list all the immediate predecessors. Then, students are asked to attempt to develop a network diagram that shows these courses and their immediate predecessors or prerequisite courses.

This problem can also point out some of the limitations of the use of PERT. As students try to solve this problem using the PERT approach, they may run into several difficulties. First, it is difficult to incorporate a minimum or maximum number of courses that a student can take during a given semester. In addition, it is difficult to schedule elective courses. Some elective courses have prerequisites, while others may not. Even so, some of the overall approaches of network analysis can be helpful in terms of laying out the courses that are required and their prerequisites.

Figure for Problem 18-29

ACTIVITIES FOR BENDER CONSTRUCTION

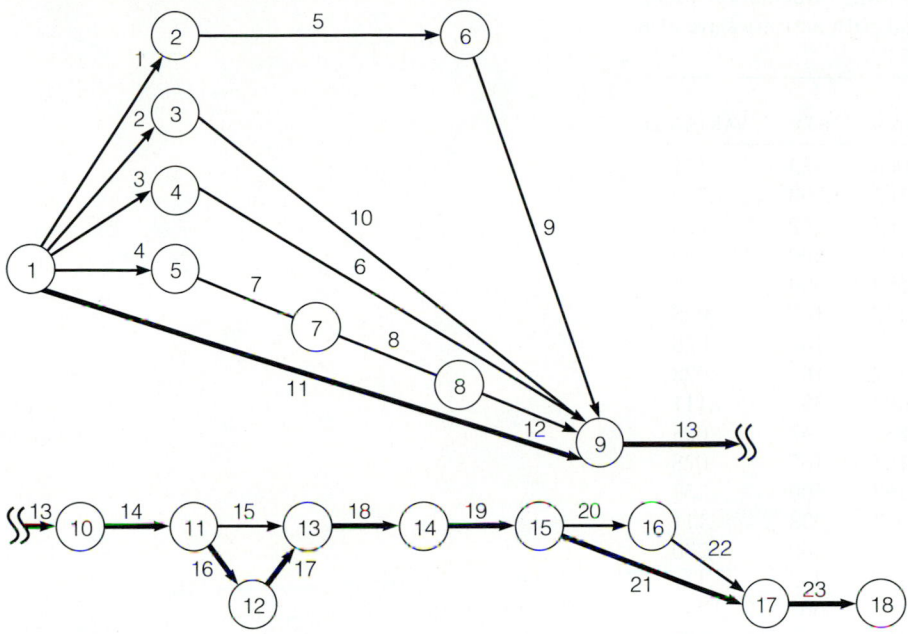

Students can also be asked to think about other quantitative techniques that can be used in solving this problem. One of the most appropriate approaches would be to use linear programming to incorporate many of the constraints, such as minimum and maxi-

mum number of credit hours per semester, that are difficult or impossible to incorporate in a PERT network.

18-31. a. The first step for Jim Sager is to summarize the time estimates for each of the activities. This is shown below:

ACTIVITY	START	END	OPTIMISTIC	LIKELY	PESSIMISTIC
1	1	2	2	3	4
2	1	3	5	6	8
3	1	4	1	1	2
4	1	5	8	9	11
5	2	6	1	1	4
6	3	7	3	3	4
7	3	8	1	2	2
8	4	8	5	5	6
9	5	9	9	10	11
10	5	10	1	2	2
11	6	11	2	2	3
12	7	12	3	4	6
13	8	12	2	2	4
14	9	13	8	9	11
15	9	14	1	1	3
16	10	15	4	4	8
17	11	16	6	6	7
18	12	16	1	2	4
19	13	17	6	6	7
20	14	17	3	3	4
21	15	17	1	2	3
22	16	18	9	10	11
23	17	18	2	4	5

The next step is to compute the average or mean times and the standard deviations (S.D.) for each activity. The table below contains this information along with activity variances. Critical path activities are also shown with an asterisk(*):

ACTIVITY	ACTIVITY NODES	MEAN	S.D.	VARIANCE
1	1– –2	3.000	.333	.111
2	1– –3	6.167	.500	.250
3	1– –4	1.167	.167	.028
4*	1– –5	9.167	.500	.250
5	2– –6	1.500	.500	.250
6	3– –7	3.167	.167	.028
7	3– –8	1.833	.167	.028
8	4– –8	5.167	.167	.028
9*	5– –9	10.000	.333	.111
10	5– –10	1.833	.167	.028
11	6– –11	2.167	.167	.028
12	7– –12	4.167	.500	.250
13	8– –12	2.333	.333	.111
14*	9– –13	9.167	.500	.250
15	9– –14	1.333	.333	.111
16	10– –15	4.667	.667	.444
17	11– –16	6.167	.167	.028
18	12– –16	2.167	.500	.250
19*	13– –17	6.167	.167	.028
20	14– –17	3.167	.167	.028
21	15– –17	2.000	.333	.111
22	16– –18	10.000	.333	.111
23*	17– –18	3.833	.500	.250

* Critical path activities

Earliest and latest start and finish times (ES, EF, LS, and LF) can also be computed for each activity. This is shown below:

ACTIVITY	NODES	ACTIVITY TIMES				
		ES	EF	LS	LF	SLACK
1	1– –2	.00	3.00	15.50	18.50	15.50
2	1– –3	.00	6.17	12.67	18.83	12.67
3	1– –4	.00	1.17	17.50	18.67	17.50
4	1– –5	.00	9.17	.00	9.17	.00*
5	2– –6	3.00	4.50	18.50	20.00	15.50
6	3– –7	6.17	9.33	18.83	22.00	12.67
7	3– –8	6.17	8.00	22.00	23.83	15.83
8	4– –8	1.17	6.33	18.67	23.83	17.50
9	5– –9	9.17	19.17	9.17	19.17	.00*
10	5– –10	9.17	11.00	26.00	27.83	16.83
11	6– –11	4.50	6.67	20.00	22.17	15.50
12	7– –12	9.33	13.50	22.00	26.17	12.67
13	8– –12	8.00	10.33	23.83	26.17	15.83
14	9– –13	19.17	28.33	19.17	28.33	.00*
15	9– –14	19.17	20.50	30.00	31.33	10.83
16	10– –15	11.00	15.67	27.83	32.50	16.83

		ACTIVITY TIMES				
ACTIVITY	NODES	ES	EF	LS	LF	SLACK
17	11– –16	6.67	12.83	22.17	28.33	15.50
18	12– –16	13.50	15.67	26.17	28.33	12.67
19	13– –17	28.33	34.50	28.33	34.50	.00*
20	14– –17	20.50	23.67	31.33	34.50	10.83
21	15– –17	15.67	17.67	32.50	34.50	16.83
22	16– –18	15.67	25.67	28.33	38.33	12.67
23	17– –18	34.50	38.33	34.50	38.33	.00*

The final network results are summarized below:

Expected project length = 38.3333
Variance of the critical path = .8888
Standard deviation = .9428

As seen above, the project will be completed in less than 40 weeks.

b. If activity D has already been completed, activity time for D is 0. The results are shown below. As you can see, Activity D (4) is still on the critical path. The project completion time is now about 29 weeks.

ACTIVITY	ACTIVITY NODES	MEAN	S.D.	VARIANCE
1	1– –2	3.000	.333	.111
2	1– –3	6.167	.500	.250
3	1– –4	1.167	.167	.028
4*	1– –5	.000	.000	.000
5	2– –6	1.500	.500	.250
6	3– –7	3.167	.167	.028
7	3– –8	1.833	.167	.028
8	4– –8	5.167	.167	.028
9*	5– –9	10.000	.333	.111
10	5– –10	1.833	.167	.028
11	6– –11	2.167	.167	.028
12	7– –12	4.167	.500	.250
13	8– –12	2.333	.333	.111
14*	9– –13	9.167	.500	.250
15	9– –14	1.333	.333	.111
16	10– –15	4.667	.667	.444
17	11– –16	6.167	.167	.028
18	12– –16	2.167	.500	.250
19*	13– –17	6.167	.167	.028
20	14– –17	3.167	.167	.028
21	15– –17	2.000	.333	.111
22	16– –18	10.000	.333	.111
23*	17– –18	3.833	.500	.250

*Critical path activities

Expected completion time is 29.167 weeks.

c. The results of having both activity D (4) and I (9) completed is shown in the next column. These activities are no longer on the critical path. The project completion time is now about 26 weeks.

ACTIVITY	ACTIVITY NODES	MEAN	S.D.	VARIANCE
1	1– –2	3.000	.333	.111
2*	1– –3	6.167	.500	.250
3	1– –4	1.167	.167	.028
4	1– –5	.000	.000	.000
5	2– –6	1.500	.500	.250
6*	3– –7	3.167	.167	.028
7	3– –8	1.833	.167	.028
8	4– –8	5.167	.167	.028
9	5– –9	.000	.000	.000
10	5– –10	1.833	.167	.028
11	6– –11	2.167	.167	.028
12*	7– –12	4.167	.500	.250
13	8– –12	2.333	.333	.111
14	9– –13	9.167	.500	.250
15	9– –14	1.333	.333	.111
16	10– –15	4.667	.667	.444
17	11– –16	6.167	.167	.028
18*	12– –16	2.167	.500	.250
19	13– –17	6.167	.167	.028
20	14– –17	3.167	.167	.028
21	15– –17	2.000	.333	.111
22*	16– –18	10.000	.333	.111
23	17– –18	3.833	.500	.250

*Critical path activities

Expected completion time is 25.667 weeks.

d. Changing the immediate predecessor activity will change the structure of the network. Fortunately, AB:QM can handle this situation. The results are shown below. Activity F (6) now goes from node 2 to node 7. Node 2 is the ending node for activity A (1). Thus, activity F now has activity A as an immediate predecessor.

ACTIVITY	ACTIVITY NODES	MEAN	S.D.	VARIANCE
1*	1– –2	3.000	.333	.111
2	1– –3	6.167	.500	.250
3	1– –4	1.167	.167	.028
4	1– –5	.000	.000	.000
5*	2– –6	1.500	.500	.250

ACTIVITY	ACTIVITY NODES	MEAN	S.D.	VARIANCE
6	2--7	3.167	.167	.028
7	3--8	1.833	.167	.028
8	4--8	5.167	.167	.028
9	5--9	.000	.000	.000
10	5--10	1.833	.167	.028
11*	6--11	2.167	.167	.028
12	7--12	4.167	.500	.250
13	8--12	2.333	.333	.111
14	9--13	9.167	.500	.250
15	9--14	1.333	.333	.111
16	10--15	4.667	.667	.444
17*	11--16	6.167	.167	.028
18	12--16	2.167	.500	.250
19	13--17	6.167	.167	.028
20	14--17	3.167	.167	.028
21	15--17	2.000	.333	.111
22*	16--18	10.000	.333	.111
23	17--18	3.833	.500	.250

* Critical path activities

Expected completion time is 22.833 weeks.

Solution to Haygood Brothers Construction Company Case

ACTIVITY	a	m	b	t_c	σ^2
1–2	4	5	6	5	$\frac{1}{9}$
2–3	2	5	8	5	1
3–4	5	7	9	7	$\frac{4}{9}$
3–5	4	5	6	5	$\frac{1}{9}$
4–6	2	4	6	4	$\frac{4}{9}$
6–7	3	5	9	$5\frac{1}{3}$	1
6–8	4	5	6	5	$\frac{1}{9}$
6–9	3	4	7	$4\frac{1}{3}$	$\frac{1}{9}$
6–10	5	7	9	7	$\frac{4}{9}$
10–11	10	11	12	11	$\frac{1}{9}$
11–12	4	6	8	6	$\frac{4}{9}$
11–13	7	8	9	8	$\frac{1}{9}$
13–14	4	5	10	$5\frac{2}{3}$	1
12–15	5	7	9	7	$\frac{4}{9}$
15–16	5	6	7	6	$\frac{1}{9}$
16–17	2	3	4	3	$\frac{1}{9}$

Critical path is 1–2–3–4–6–10–11–12–15–16–17 (61 days).

A delay in the completion of an event on the critical path will delay the entire project by an equal amount of time.

EVENT	T_E	T_L	SLACK
1	0	0	0
2	5	5	0
3	10	10	0
4	17	17	0
5	15	28	13
6	21	21	0
7	$26\frac{1}{3}$	39	$12\frac{2}{3}$
8	26	39	13
9	$25\frac{1}{3}$	39	$13\frac{2}{3}$
10	28	28	0
11	39	39	0
12	45	45	0
13	47	$52\frac{1}{3}$	$5\frac{1}{3}$
14	$52\frac{2}{3}$	58	$5\frac{1}{3}$
15	52	52	0
16	58	58	0
17	61	61	0

$$Z = \frac{T_E - T_S}{\sigma_E} = \frac{61 - 60}{1.92} = .52$$

$$P(T_S) = 30.15\%$$

Solution to Bay Community Hospital Case

ACTIVITY	TIME	ADDED COST
A	2	0
	1	+400
	3	−300
B	4	0
C	3	0
	2	+600
D	4	0
E	8	0
	7	+200
	6	+750
F	2	0

1. Completion time under normal circumstances:

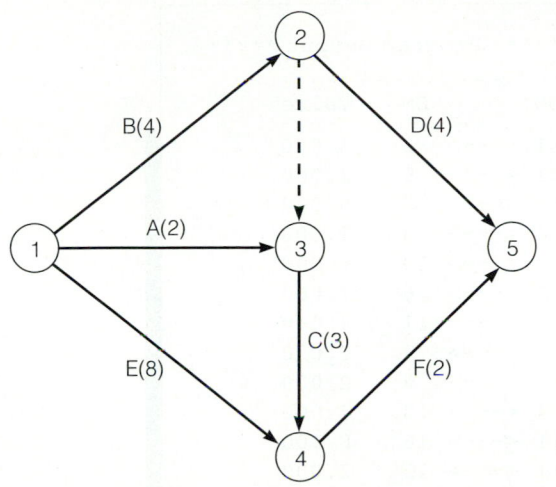

ACTIVITY	TIME	ES	EF	LS	LF	SLACK	CRITICAL?
1––3 (A)	2	0	2	3	5	3	No
1––2 (B)	4	0	4	1	5	1	No
3––4 (C)	3	4	7	5	8	1	No
2––5 (D)	4	4	8	6	10	2	No
1––4 (E)	8	0	8	0	8	0	Yes
4––5 (F)	2	8	10	8	10	0	Yes

Therefore, the minimum time under normal circumstances is 10 weeks. The critical path is: 1–4–5.

2. Shortest possible completion time:

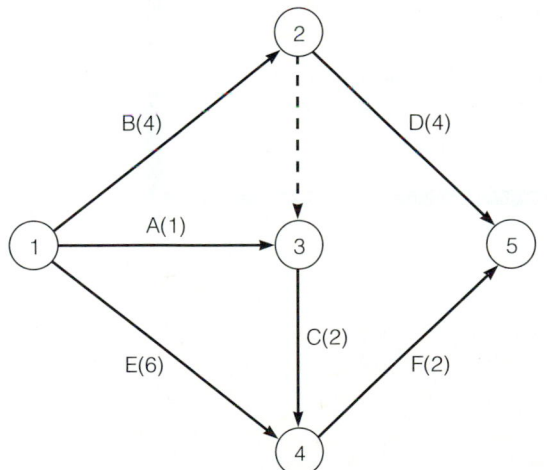

ACTIVITY	TIME	ES	EF	LS	LF	SLACK	CRITICAL?
1––3 (A)	1	0	1	3	4	3	No
1––2 (B)	4	0	4	0	4	0	Yes
3––4 (C)	2	4	6	4	6	0	Yes
2––5 (D)	4	4	8	4	8	0	Yes
1––4 (E)	6	0	6	0	6	0	Yes
4––5 (F)	2	6	8	6	8	0	Yes

The shortest possible completion time is 8 weeks. All activities but A are critical.

3. The lowest-cost schedule with which to accomplish the minimum completion time is achieved by crashing C by one week and E by two weeks and extending A by one week.

Additional cost = +600 + 750 − 300
                = $1,050

Solution to the Ranch Development Project Case

1. The minimum distance that will connect all houses to the water and sewer lines is 10,700 feet (107). The AB:QM solution along with the final network follows:

```
Program: Network Models
/ Minimum Spanning Tree

Problem Title: QA18-RDPA

***** Input Data *****
------------------
SN        EN    Value
------------------
 1 <---->  2     3.00
 4 <---->  3     1.00
 4 <---->  8     5.00
 3 <---->  4     1.00
 3 <---->  8     5.00
 2 <----> 10     6.00
 5 <---->  6     2.00
 5 <----> 10     5.00
 6 <---->  7     2.00
 6 <----> 11     4.00
 7 <----> 12     4.00
 8 <---->  9     2.00
 9 <----> 13     7.00
10 <----> 11     8.00
10 <----> 15    11.00
11 <----> 12     2.00
11 <----> 16     8.00
12 <----> 17     9.00
13 <----> 14     4.00
13 <----> 18     6.00
14 <----> 15     4.00
15 <----> 20     7.00
16 <----> 22     8.00
17 <----> 23     8.00
18 <----> 19     2.00
19 <----> 20     2.00
19 <----> 24     5.00
20 <----> 21     4.00
21 <----> 22     1.00
21 <----> 25     4.00
22 <----> 23     6.00
22 <----> 25     5.00
23 <----> 26     7.00
24 <----> 27    11.00
25 <----> 27     3.00
26 <----> 27    10.00
 1 <---->  5     2.00
------------------
```

Printout for QA18-RDPA (*continued*)

```
***** Program Output *****
------------------
SN        EN    Value
------------------
 1 <---->  2     3.000
 1 <---->  5     2.000
 4 <---->  8     5.000
 4 <---->  3     1.000
 5 <----> 10     5.000
 5 <---->  6     2.000
 6 <----> 11     4.000
 6 <---->  7     2.000
 8 <---->  9     2.000
 9 <----> 13     7.000
11 <----> 16     8.000
11 <----> 12     2.000
13 <----> 18     6.000
13 <----> 14     4.000
14 <----> 15     4.000
16 <----> 22     8.000
17 <----> 23     8.000
18 <----> 19     2.000
19 <----> 24     5.000
19 <----> 20     2.000
20 <----> 21     4.000
21 <----> 25     4.000
21 <----> 22     1.000
22 <----> 23     6.000
23 <----> 26     7.000
25 <----> 27     3.000
------------------

Total Minimum Spanning Tree
  Lengths  :  107.000

***** End of Output *****
```

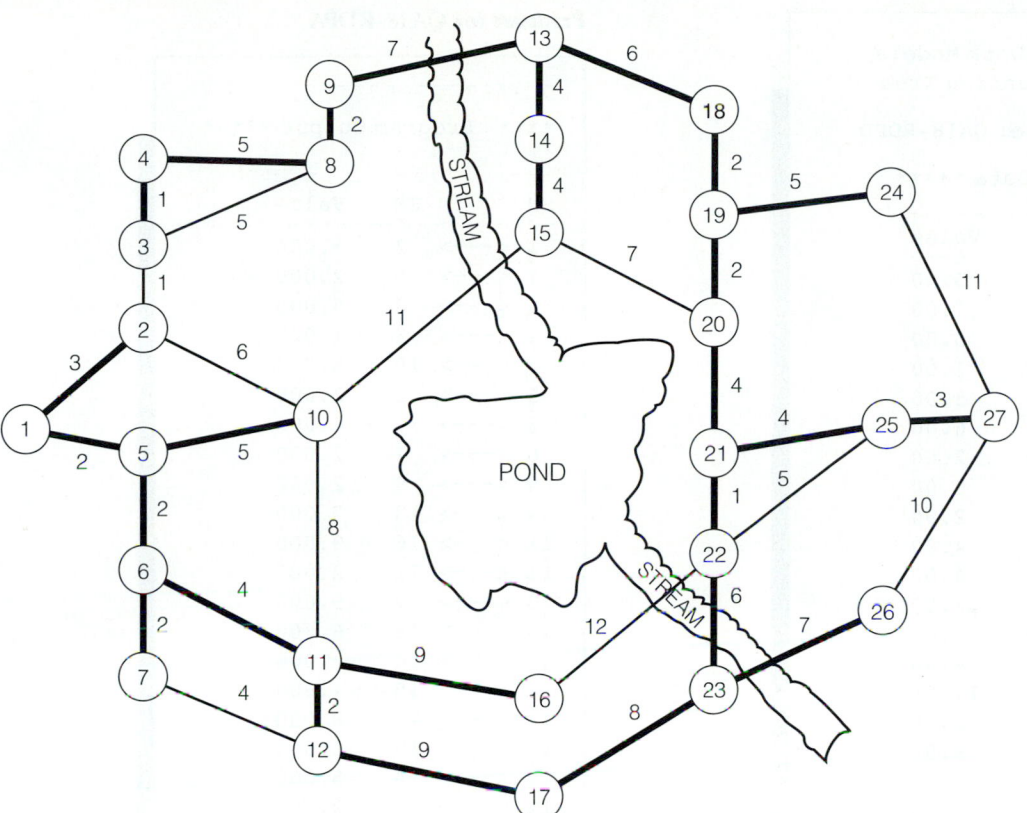

2. Moving footprint number 16 to accommodate the expansion of the pond area has increased the minimum total distance to 10,900 feet (109). A decision now has to be made about whether the increased distance and cost for the water and sewer system is worth the additional expected property prices. The AB:QM solution along with the final network follows.

```
Program: Network Models
/ Minimum Spanning Tree

Program Title: QA18-RDPB

***** Input Data *****
- - - - - - - - - - - - - - - - -
SN          EN    Value
- - - - - - - - - - - - - - - - -
  1 <---> 2      3.00
  4 <---> 3      1.00
  4 <---> 8      5.00
  3 <---> 4      1.00
  3 <---> 8      5.00
  2 <---> 10     6.00
  5 <---> 6      2.00
  5 <---> 10     5.00
  6 <---> 7      2.00
  6 <---> 11     4.00
  7 <---> 12     4.00
  8 <---> 9      2.00
  9 <---> 13     7.00
 10 <---> 11     8.00
 10 <---> 15    11.00
 11 <---> 12     2.00
 11 <---> 16     9.00
 12 <---> 17     9.00
 13 <---> 14     4.00
 13 <---> 18     6.00
 14 <---> 15     4.00
 15 <---> 20     7.00
 16 <---> 22    12.00
 17 <---> 23     8.00
 18 <---> 19     2.00
 19 <---> 20     2.00
 19 <---> 24     5.00
 20 <---> 21     4.00
 21 <---> 22     1.00
 21 <---> 25     4.00
 22 <---> 23     6.00
 22 <---> 25     5.00
 23 <---> 26     7.00
 24 <---> 27    11.00
 25 <---> 27     3.00
 26 <---> 27    10.00
  1 <---> 5      2.00
```

Printout for QA18-RDPA

```
- - - - - - - - - - - - - - - - -

***** Program Output *****

- - - - - - - - - - - - - - - - -
SN          EN    Value
- - - - - - - - - - - - - - - - -
  1 <---> 2      3.000
  1 <---> 5      2.000
  4 <---> 8      5.000
  4 <---> 3      1.000
  5 <---> 10     5.000
  5 <---> 6      2.000
  6 <---> 11     4.000
  6 <---> 7      2.000
  8 <---> 9      2.000
  9 <---> 13     7.000
 11 <---> 16     9.000
 11 <---> 12     2.000
 12 <---> 17     9.000
 13 <---> 18     6.000
 13 <---> 14     4.000
 14 <---> 15     4.000
 17 <---> 23     8.000
 18 <---> 19     2.000
 19 <---> 24     5.000
 19 <---> 20     2.000
 20 <---> 21     4.000
 21 <---> 25     4.000
 21 <---> 22     1.000
 22 <---> 23     6.000
 23 <---> 26     7.000
 25 <---> 27     3.000
- - - - - - - - - - - - - - - - -

Total Minimum Spanning Tree
  Lengths  :  109.000

***** End of Output *****
```

Figure for Problem 18-RDPA

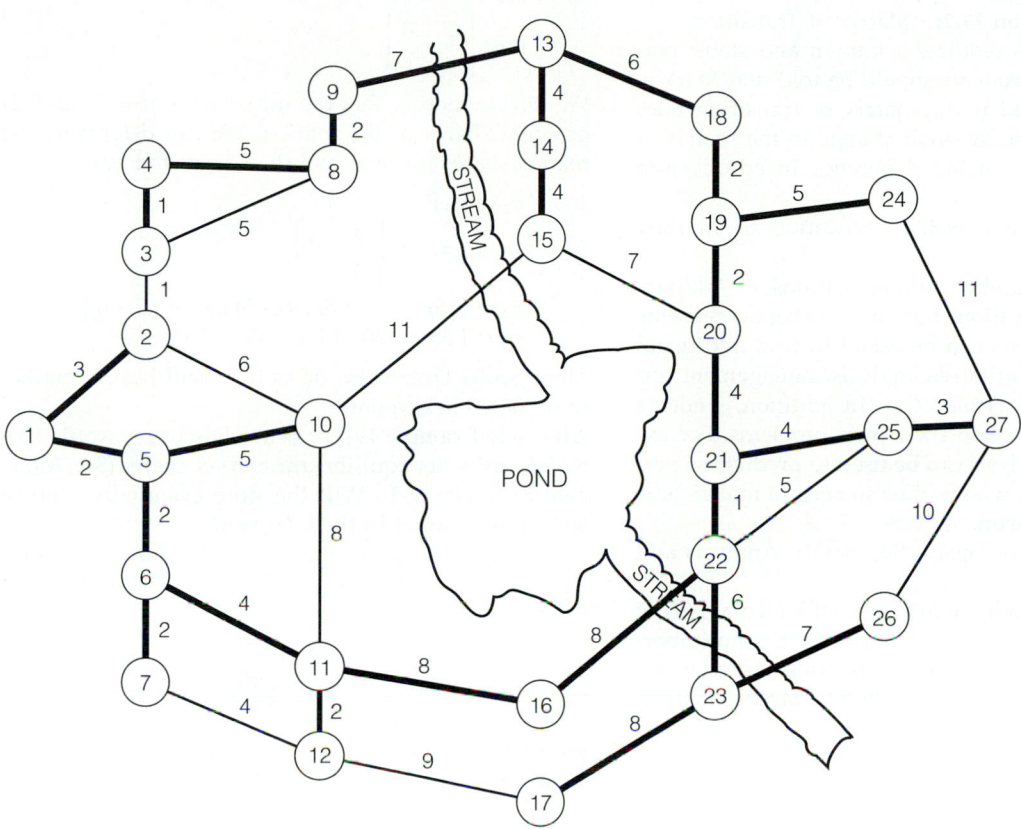

19

Markov Analysis

LEARNING OBJECTIVES

After completing this chapter, students will be able to:

1. Determine future states or conditions using Markov analysis.
2. Compute long-term or steady-state conditions using only the matrix of transition.
3. Understand the use of absorbing state analysis in predicting future conditions.

TEACHING SUGGESTIONS

Teaching Suggestion 19.1: Use of Matrix Algebra.

Markov analysis requires the use of matrix algebra, primarily matrix multiplication. You may want to have students review basic concepts in matrix algebra before the material in the chapter is covered. If you plan to cover absorbing state analysis in detail, more advanced matrix algebra will be needed, including the identity matrix, matrix subtraction, and the inverse of a matrix. See Module A.

Teaching Suggestion 19.2: Matrix of Transition.

Markov analysis requires a known and stable matrix of transition. Students should be told that Markov analysis is not valid if the matrix of transition does not remain the same. A small change in the matrix of transition can make a big difference in equilibrium calculations.

Teaching Suggestion 19.3: Application of Markov Analysis.

There are a number of applications of Markov analysis. The applications box in this chapter presents an example. Students can be asked to find additional applications in quantitative analysis/management science journals such as *Interfaces*. In addition, students can be asked to develop their own problems. For example, Markov analysis can be used to predict the percentage of students who will be in certain majors next year or in the long run.

Teaching Suggestion 19.4: Sensitivity Analysis and Markov Analysis.

Although sensitivity analysis is not a formal part of the material discussed in this chapter, it is an important and interesting topic. Students can be asked to determine how sensitive the results of Markov analysis are to changes in probability values.

Teaching Suggestion 19.5: Equilibrium Conditions and the Beginning State or Condition.

As mentioned in this chapter, equilibrium conditions do not depend on the initial state or condition. The only factor that needs to be considered is the matrix of transition. While this is true, the time or number of periods needed to approach equilibrium is a function of the beginning state. Students can be asked to determine what impact the initial state has on the number of periods it takes to reach equilibrium.

Teaching Suggestion 19.6: Absorbing State Analysis and Matrix Algebra.

Absorbing state analysis requires more complex matrix algebra, including the inverse of the $(I - B)$ matrix. If you plan to get into the mathematics of absorbing state analysis, you may have to spend additional time covering more advanced matrix algebra. An alternative approach is to cover the assumptions and overall approach of the model and leave the computations to the computer.

ALTERNATE EXAMPLES

Alternate Example 19-1: Scuba Discovery (Store 1) currently splits the market for scuba classes with Bob's Dive Shop. Given the matrix of transition proba-

bilities below, what will the market shares be next month (period)?

$$P = \begin{bmatrix} .7 & .3 \\ .4 & .6 \end{bmatrix}$$

We start by noting that the initial state or π_1 is (.5 .5) or equal shares of the market. We can determine the market shares for next month or π_2 as follows:

$$\pi_2 = \pi_1 P$$

$$\pi_2 = (.5 \quad .5) \begin{bmatrix} .7 & .3 \\ .4 & .6 \end{bmatrix}$$

$$\pi_2 = [(.5)(.7) + (.5)(.4), (.5)(.3) + (.5)(.6)]$$
$$\pi_2 = [.35 + .20, .15 + .30] = [.55, .45]$$

Thus, Scuba Discovery, or store 1, will have a market share of .55 next month.

Alternate Example 19-2: Scuba Discovery would like to determine its equilibrium market share. (See Alternate Example 19-1.) Will the store eventually capture 60% of the market in the long run?

To solve this problem, we set up the equilibrium equations and solve for π_1 and π_2. The results are below:

$$\pi_1 = .7\pi_1 + .4\pi_2 \quad \text{(Equation 2)}$$
$$\pi_2 = .3\pi_1 + .6\pi_2 \quad \text{(Equation 1)}$$

We also know that $\pi_1 + \pi_2 = 1$ or $\pi_2 = 1 - \pi_1$. We put this equation for π_2 into Equation 1 and solve for π_1 as follows:

$$\pi_1 = .7\pi_1 + .4(1 - \pi_1) = .7\pi_1 + .4 - .4\pi_1$$
$$\pi_1 - .7\pi_1 + .4\pi_1 = .4; \quad .7\pi_1 = .4$$

$\pi_1 = .4/.7 = 4/7 = 57.14\%$, and thus $\pi_2 = 3/7$. Scuba Discovery will not reach 60% of the market in the long run.

We can put these values back into Equation 2 as a check as follows:

$$\pi_2 = .3\pi_1 + .6\pi_2 = (.3)(4/7) + (.6)(3/7)$$
$$\pi_2 = 1.2/7 + 1.8/7 = 3/7.$$

SOLUTIONS TO DISCUSSION QUESTIONS AND PROBLEMS

19-1. Markov analysis makes the assumption that the propensity to change over time stays the same. This tendency to change is embodied in the matrix of transition. Furthermore, it is assumed that there is a finite number of states or conditions. In addition, we are assuming that we can predict any future state from the previous state and that the size and makeup of the system does not change.

19-2. The vector of state probabilities is a collection of probability values that the particular system will be in a given state. In most cases, it is determined using historical data. For example, if the market shares for three stores are 30%, 50%, and 20%, the probability of being at one of these stores is .3, .5, and .2. The matrix of transition is a probability matrix that reveals the tendency of the system to change from one state to another over a given period of time. Like the vector of state probabilities, the matrix of transition is normally determined using empirical or historical data.

19-3. Future states can be determined by multiplying the current state times the matrix of transition. If we want to determine future market shares in August, we multiply the market shares in July times the matrix of transition. This process can be repeated to determine future states several months or years in the future.

19-4. An equilibrium condition is a condition in which the states or state probabilities do not change from one period to the next. We can compute the equilibrium conditions by setting the unknown equilibrium state probabilities equal to the unknown state probabilities times the matrix of transition. We also include the equation that sets the sum of the state probabilities equal to 1. With this set of equations it is possible to determine the equilibrium conditions.

19-5. An absorbing state is one in which once it is entered it cannot be left. In the matrix of transition, an absorbing state is indicated by a probability value of 1. An example of an absorbing state is paying a bill. Once the bill for a particular item is paid in full, it is impossible to owe on that item in the future.

19-6. The fundamental matrix is equal to the inverse of the identity matrix minus the B matrix. The B matrix is determined by partitioning the matrix of transition. The fundamental matrix is then multiplied times the A matrix, which is another partition of the matrix of transition.

19-7. State 1: start; state 2: not start

a. $P = \begin{bmatrix} .9 & .1 \\ .3 & .7 \end{bmatrix}$

b. If $\pi(0) = (1 \quad 0)$, $\pi(1) = (.9, .1)$
∴Probability of starting is 90%.

c. If $\pi(0) = (0 \quad 1)$, $\pi(1) = (.3, .7)$
∴Probability of starting is 30%.

19-8. a. If $\pi(0) = (1 \quad 0)$, $\pi(1) = (.9, .1)$, $\pi(5)$
     $= (.76944, .23056)$
∴Probability it will not start five days from today is 23.056%.

b. If $\pi(0) = (0 \quad 1)$, $\pi(1) = (.3, .7)$, $\pi(5)$
     $= (.69168, \quad .30832)$
∴Probability it will not start five days from today is 30.832%.

c. In equilibrium $\pi = \pi P$
$$\pi_1 = .9\pi_1 + .3\pi_2$$
$$\pi_2 = .1\pi_1 + .7\pi_2$$
$$\pi_1 + \pi_2 = 1 \text{ or, } \pi_1 = .75, \pi_2 = .25$$

Therefore, long-run probability of starting is 75%.

19-9. If states 1, 2, 3 represent Dress-Rite, Fashion, Inc., and Luxury living customers:

$$P = \begin{bmatrix} .7 & .1 & .2 \\ .05 & .85 & .1 \\ .05 & .05 & .9 \end{bmatrix}$$

If $\pi(0) = (\frac{1}{3} \quad \frac{1}{3} \quad \frac{1}{3}) = \frac{1}{3}(1 \quad 1 \quad 1)$
$\pi(1) = \frac{1}{3}(.8 \quad 1 \quad 1.2) = (\frac{4}{15} \quad \frac{5}{15} \quad \frac{6}{15})$

Market shares after one month are $(\frac{4}{15}, \quad \frac{5}{15}, \quad \frac{6}{15})$:

$$\pi(2) = (.2233 \quad .33 \quad .4467)$$
$$\pi(3) = (.1952 \quad .3252 \quad .4796)$$

After three months, market shares will be 19.52%, 32.52%, and 47.96%.

19-10. Let states 1, 2, 3 correspond to placing 49, 50, and 51 pounds into the bags. Then:

$$P = \begin{bmatrix} .5 & .3 & .2 \\ .1 & .7 & .2 \\ .1 & .4 & .5 \end{bmatrix}$$

a. 70% = the second column (50 pounds)
     of $(0 \quad 1 \quad 0) P$

b. 30% = the second column of $(1 \quad 0 \quad 0) P$

c. 40% = the second column of $(0 \quad 0 \quad 1) P$

19-11.

$$P = \begin{bmatrix} .6 & .2 & .1 & .1 \\ .0 & .7 & .2 & .1 \\ .1 & .1 & .8 & .0 \\ .05 & .05 & .1 & .8 \end{bmatrix}$$

Current market shares are equal, that is, 25% each. Hence, $\pi(0) = (.25 \quad .25 \quad .25 \quad .25)$. Therefore, $\pi(1) = \pi(0) P = (.1875 \quad .2625 \quad .3 \quad .25)$. Hence, market shares for the next period will be 18.75%, 26.25%, 30%, and 25% for University; Bill's, College, and Battle's, respectively.

19-12. a. If $\pi(0) = (0 \quad 1 \quad 0)$
     $\pi(1) = (.1 \quad .7 \quad .2)$, $\pi(2) = (.14 \quad .6 \quad .26)$
     $\pi(3) = (.156 \quad .566 \quad .278)$,
     $\pi(4) = (.1624 \quad .5542 \quad .2834)$
     $\pi(5) = (.1650 \quad .55 \quad .2850)$

Therefore probability of placing 50 pounds is 55%.

b. If $\pi(0) = (1 \quad 0 \quad 0)$, $\pi(1) = (.5 \quad .3 \quad .2)$
     $\pi(2) = (.3 \quad .44 \quad .26)$
     $\pi(3) = (.22 \quad .502 \quad .278)$

$$\pi(4) = (.188 \quad .5286 \quad .2834)$$
$$\pi(5) = (.1752 \quad .5398 \quad .2850)$$

Required probability of placing 50 pounds is 53.98%.

c. If $\pi(0) = (0 \quad 0 \quad 1)$; $\pi(1) = (.1 \quad .4 \quad .5)$,
$$\pi(2) = (.14 \quad .51 \quad .35)$$
$$\pi(3) = (.156 \quad .539 \quad .305),$$
$$\pi(4) = (.1624 \quad .5461 \quad .2915)$$
$$\pi(5) = (.1650 \quad .5475 \quad .2875)$$

Hence, probability of placing 50 pounds = 54.75%.

19-13. In the long run, $\pi = \pi P$. We drop the equation for π_2 and solve.

$$\pi_1 = .6\pi_1 \qquad + .1\pi_3 + .05\pi_4$$
$$\pi_3 = .1\pi_1 + .2\pi_2 + .8\pi_3 + .1\pi_4$$
$$\pi_4 = .1\pi_1 + .1\pi_2 \qquad + .8\pi_4$$
$$1 = \pi_1 \quad + \pi_2 \quad + \pi_3 \quad + \pi_4$$

which simplify to:

$$-8\pi_1 \qquad + 2\pi_3 + \quad \pi_4 = 0$$
$$\pi_1 + 2\pi_2 - 2\pi_3 + \quad \pi_4 = 0$$
$$\pi_1 + \quad \pi_2 \qquad - 2\pi_4 = 0$$
$$\pi_1 + \quad \pi_2 + \pi_3 + \quad \pi_4 = 1$$

The solution for this set of simultaneous equations is $\pi_1 = \frac{4}{31}$; $\pi_2 = \frac{8}{31}$; $\pi_3 = \frac{13}{31}$; $\pi_4 = \frac{6}{31}$. Hence, the long-run market share of the four bookstores can be expected to be 12.90%, 25.81%, 41.94%, and 19.35% respectively.

19-14. Let states 1, 2, 3 represent fair, tolerable, and miserable traffic conditions, respectively:

$$P = \begin{bmatrix} .7 & .2 & .1 \\ .2 & .75 & .05 \\ .3 & .1 & .6 \end{bmatrix}$$

If $\pi(0) = (0 \quad 0 \quad 1)$
$$\pi(1) = (.3 \quad .1 \quad .6)$$
$$\pi(2) = (.41 \quad .195 \quad .395)$$

After two hours, traffic conditions will be fair with a probability of 41% and tolerable with a probability of 19.5%.

19-15. From problem (19-14) we get the transition matrix P. In the long run, $\pi = \pi P$:

$$\pi_1 = .7\pi_1 + .2\pi_2 + .3\pi_3$$
$$\pi_2 = .2\pi_1 + .75\pi_2 + .1\pi_3$$
$$1 = \pi_1 + \quad \pi_2 + \quad \pi_3$$

which reduces to:

$$-3\pi_1 + 2\pi_2 + 3\pi_3 = 0$$
$$4\pi_1 - 5\pi_2 + 2\pi_3 = 0$$
$$\pi_1 + \quad \pi_2 + \quad \pi_3 = 1$$

which has a solution of $\pi_1 = \frac{19}{44}$, $\pi_2 = \frac{18}{44}$, $\pi_3 = \frac{7}{44}$. Therefore, in the long run, traffic conditions will be

fair 43.18%, tolerable 40.91%, and miserable 15.9% of the time.

19-16. Let existence in Lake Jackson denote state 1 and existence in Lake Bradford denote state 2 for an individual tiger minnow. Then:

$$P = \begin{bmatrix} .9 & .1 \\ .05 & .95 \end{bmatrix}$$
$$\pi(0) = (900 \quad 100)$$

In the long run, $\pi = \pi P$

$$\pi_1 = .9\pi_1 + .05\pi_2$$
$$.1\pi_1 = .05\pi_2 \quad \text{or}$$
$$\pi_2 = 2\pi_1$$

Also:

$$\pi_1 + \pi_2 = 1,000$$
$$\pi_1 = 333, \pi_2 = 667$$

In the long run there will be 333 minnows in Lake Jackson and 667 in Lake Bradford.

19-17. a. Original state = $(900 \quad 100) = \pi(0)$

b. Let P = probability of going from Lake Jackson to Lake Bradford.

c. $P = \begin{bmatrix} 1-P & P \\ .05 & .95 \end{bmatrix}$

d. At equilibrium, $\pi = \pi P$

$$(900 \quad 100) = (900 \quad 100) \begin{bmatrix} 1-P & P \\ .05 & .95 \end{bmatrix}$$

which gives us:

$$900 = (900)(1-P) + (100)(.05)$$
$$900 = 900 - 900P + 5$$
$$P = \frac{5}{900} = .005556$$

Here is another way of solving the problem:

$$100 = (900)(P) + (100)(.95)$$
$$100 = 900P + 95$$
$$P = \frac{5}{900} = .005556$$

e. Thus, the probability of going from Lake Jackson to Lake Bradford must be .005556 to restore the original situation.

19-18.

$$P = \begin{bmatrix} 1 & 0 & 0 & 0 \\ 0 & 1 & 0 & 0 \\ .7 & 0 & .2 & .1 \\ .4 & .2 & .2 & .2 \end{bmatrix}$$
$$M = (2000, 5000)$$

$$F = \begin{bmatrix} 1.29 & .181 \\ .322 & 1.29 \end{bmatrix}$$

$$FA = \begin{bmatrix} .967 & .032 \\ .741 & .258 \end{bmatrix}$$

$$MFA = (5645.16, \; 1354.84)$$

Hence, $5,645 will eventually be paid and $1,355 will end up as bad debt.

19-19.

$$P = \begin{bmatrix} 1 & 0 & 0 & 0 \\ 0 & 1 & 0 & 0 \\ .6 & 0 & .1 & .3 \\ .3 & .3 & .2 & .2 \end{bmatrix}$$

$$F = (I\text{-}B)^{-1} = \begin{bmatrix} .9 & -.3 \\ -.2 & .8 \end{bmatrix}^{-1}$$

$$= \begin{bmatrix} 1.21 & .46 \\ .30 & 1.36 \end{bmatrix}$$

$$FA = \begin{bmatrix} 1.21 & .46 \\ .30 & 1.36 \end{bmatrix} \begin{bmatrix} .6 & .0 \\ .3 & .3 \end{bmatrix} = \begin{bmatrix} .864 & .136 \\ .588 & .412 \end{bmatrix}$$

If $\quad M = (50 \quad 30)$

$$MFA = (50 \quad 30) \begin{bmatrix} .864 & .136 \\ .588 & .412 \end{bmatrix} = (61 \quad 19)$$

Hence, 61 will pass and 19 fail the course.

19-20. The Hicourt Industries problem requires some careful thought and analysis. At first glance, it appears that there is insufficient data to solve the problem. Important matrix of transition values are seemingly missing. For this particular problem, we will assume that Hicourt Industries will be state 1, the Printing House will be state 2, and Gandy Printers will be state 3. From the problem, we know that the current market shares are .3, .5, and .2 for these industries. We also know the probabilities that these various states will retain their customer base. This allows us to enter some of the probability values into the matrix of transition. Hicourt has an 80% chance of keeping its customers from one month to another. In other words, the first row and first column of the matrix of transition is .8. In a similar fashion, we know that the second row and second column for the matrix of transition for the Printing House is .7 and that the third row and third column of the matrix of transition for Gandy Printers is .6. These probabilities can be entered into the matrix of transition. We will also use variables $A, B, C, D, E,$ and F to represent unknown probabilities for the matrix of transition. This is shown below:

$$[.3 \quad .5 \quad .2] \begin{bmatrix} .8 & A & B \\ C & .7 & D \\ E & F & .6 \end{bmatrix}$$

Before we can go any further, we must determine a value for the six unknown probabilities in the matrix of transition. As seen above, these probabilities have been represented by the variables, $A, B, C, D, E,$ and F. To begin with, we know that the probabilities for any row in the matrix of transition must sum to one. We also know that the original market shares multiplied times the matrix of transition must be equal to the current market share, which was given in the problem. The current market share for the three printers is .38, .42, and .20. With this information, we can develop the appropriate equations with the appropriate unknowns to solve for the six probabilities that we need in the matrix of transition. Doing this is shown below. We know that:

$$.8 + A + B = 1$$
$$C + .7 + D = 1$$
$$E + F + .6 = 1$$

or

$$B = .2 - A$$
$$D = .3 - C$$
$$F = .4 - E$$

Putting these into the matrix of transition, we get:

$$[.3 \quad .5 \quad .2] \begin{bmatrix} .8 & A & .2 - A \\ C & .7 & .3 - C \\ E & .4 - E & .6 \end{bmatrix} = [.38 \quad .42 \quad .20]$$

Since we know that the matrix of transition probabilities times a previous market share is equal to a future market share, we can solve the above problem and get three equations and three unknowns. These equations can be solved for $A, C,$ and E. These values can then be substituted back into previous equations to determine values for $B, D,$ and F. This will completely specify our matrix of transition probabilities. This is shown below.

1. $(.3)(.8) + (.5)(C) + (.2)E + .38$
2. $(.3)(A) + (.5)(.7) + (.2)(.4 - E) = .42$
3. $(.3)(.2 - A) + (.5)(.3 - C) + (.2)(.6) = .2$

Solving the above, we get:

$$A = .1$$
$$C = .2$$
$$E = .2$$

From this we can compute $B, D,$ and F:

$$B = .2 - A = .1$$
$$D = .3 - C = .1$$
$$F = .4 - E = .2$$

Thus the matrix of transition is:

$$\begin{bmatrix} .8 & .1 & .1 \\ .2 & .7 & .1 \\ .2 & .2 & .6 \end{bmatrix}$$

Once we have determined all of the probability values of the matrix of transition, we can determine the market share for next month and the equilibrium market shares. This was the original objective for the problem. The market shares for next month will be .427, .371, and .2. In other words, George can expect a market share of approximately 42.7% next month. We can also determine the equilibrium probabilities. These are 50% for Hicourt, 30% for Printing House, and 20% for Gandy Printers. This tells us that Hicourt will not be able to completely run Printing House out of business. In the long run, Printing House will have 30% of the market, while Hicourt will have 50% of the market. Gandy Printers will keep 20% of the market.

19-21. In order for John to get the loan that he desires, he must keep at least 35% of the market share in the long run. Currently, John has 26 condominiums, representing 50% of the market ($.50 = {}^{26}/_{52}$). Cleanco has about 28.8% of the market ($.288 = {}^{15}/_{52}$) and Beach Services has about 21.2% of the market ($.212 = {}^{11}/_{52}$). In order for us to determine equilibrium market shares, we must first know the matrix of transition probabilities. Because of a careful survey conducted by John and Bayside laundry, we know that John will keep 18 of his original customers. He will lose 6 to Cleanco and 2 to Beach Services. From these data, we can determine the first row of the matrix of transition probabilities by dividing 18, 6, and 2 by 26. The top row of the matrix of transition probabilities will thus be .692, .231, and .077. We can also determine the second row of the matrix of transition probabilities, which will represent the second state or Cleanco. We already know that Bayside will get one customer from Cleanco. Furthermore, we know that Cleanco will retain 80% of its current customers. This represents 12 customers out of 15. The remaining 2 customers out of the original 15, therefore, must have switched to Beach Services. By dividing the numbers 1, 12, and 2 by 15, we know the second row of the matrix of transition probabilities. Doing this will give us .067, .80, and .133 for the second row of the matrix of transition probabilities. Here, we run into a stumbling block. We know that Beach Services will give up 2 of its customers to Bayside. Since Beach Services has a total of 11 customers, this represents a probability of .182, which is the probability in the third row and first column of the matrix of transition probabilities. Unfortunately, we do not know the last two

probabilities, which are row 3 column 2, and row 3 column 3 of the matrix of transition probabilities. What we know for the matrix of transition probabilities is shown below:

$$\begin{bmatrix} .692 & .231 & .077 \\ .067 & .8 & .133 \\ .182 & X & Y \end{bmatrix}$$

As you can see, all of the probabilities are known but the last two in the third row. These are represented by the variables X and Y. It was also given in the problem that Beach service would keep at least 50% of its current customers. Fifty percent of John's current customers would be 6 customers. Since we know that 2 customers are going to Beach Services and at least 6 customers remain with Beach Services, we know that Beach Services could end up with 6, 7, 8, or 9 customers. The remaining 3, 2, 1, or 0 customers would go to Cleanco. By dividing these values by 11, we can convert these values into 4 possible probability values for X and Y. We can then compute an equilibrium market share for each of the possibilities. The four probabilities for X and Y are shown below:

X	Y	$P(X)$	$P(Y)$
3	6	.273	.545
2	7	.182	.636
1	8	.727	.091
0	9	.818	0

From the above probability values, we can determine the equilibrium market share for each possibility. The results are shown below:

Equilibrium State Probabilities
(Market Shares) $X = 3$, $Y = 6$

For state #1, equil. prob. (share) = .24
For state #2, equil. prob. (share) = .555
For state #3, equil. prob. (share) = .203

Equilibrium State Probabilities
(Market Shares) $X = 2$, $Y = 7$

For state #1, equil. prob. (share) = .252
For state #2, equil. prob. (share) = .508
For state #3, equil. prob. (share) = .239

Equilibrium State Probabilities
(Market Shares) $X = 1$, $Y = 8$

For state #1, equil. prob. (share) = .267
For state #2, equil. prob. (share) = .441
For state #3, equil. prob. (share) = .29

Equilibrium State Probabilities
(Market Shares) $X = 0$, $Y = 9$

For state #1, equil. prob. (share) = .292
For state #2, equil. prob. (share) = .337
For state #3, equil. prob. (share) = .37

As you can see from the analysis, the highest market share that John will achieve would be approximately 29.2% of the market in the long run. This assumes that Beach Services will retain 9 of its current 11 customers and lose none to Cleanco ($X = 0$ and $Y = 9$). The worst circumstances for John would be a situation where Beach Services keeps 6 of its customers and loses 3 to Cleanco. John's market share would be 24%. This represents a situation where $X = 3$ and $Y = 6$. As can be seen in this analysis, there are no circumstances under which John will retain 35% or more of the market in the long run. Therefore, it is unlikely he will be able to get the loan he desires at Bay Bank.

19-22. a. By using the Markov process, Sandy can determine market shares for each of the Quick Oil change operations for next period. The results are summarized below:

STATE	VALUE
1	.36
2	.14
3	.13
4	.16
5	.07
6	.04
7	.02
8	.02
9	.02
10	.02

b. The equilibrium market shares for this problem are as follows:

STATE	PROBABILITY	VALUE
1	.02439	.02
2	.05807	.06
3	.03934	.04
4	.15363	.15
5	.05226	.05
6	.41723	.42
7	.05779	.06
8	.08832	.09
9	.05228	.05
10	.05669	.06

c. The market shares for next period will change, but the equilibrium shares will remain the same. This is shown below:

STATE	VALUE
1	.25
2	.28
3	.11
4	.14
5	.07
6	.06
7	.02
8	.02
9	.02
10	.03

STEADY STATE

STATE	PROBABILITY	VALUE
1	.02439	.02
2	.05807	.06
3	.03934	.04
4	.15363	.15
5	.05226	.05
6	.41723	.42
7	.05779	.06
8	.08832	.09
9	.05228	.05
10	.05669	.06

d. The equilibrium shares for this situation are given below. As you can see, shop 1 will not have 90 percent of the market in the long run.

STEADY STATE

STATE	PROBABILITY	VALUE
1	.50000	.50
2	.04762	.05
3	.01613	.02
4	.06494	.06
5	.02381	.02
6	.22112	.22
7	.02878	.03
8	.04333	.04
9	.02564	.03
10	.02864	.03

19-23. a. This is a typical Markov problem. We assume the same data as presented in Problem 19-22 with the exception that the first row for the matrix of transition (representing Shop 1) will have .99 in the first column and 0's elsewhere except for Shop 7, which will have a .01. The AB:QM solution is given below. While Sandy has increased her market share, it is not 99%. She does not win her bet.

```
Program: Markov Analysis

Problem Title : QA 19-22a

***** Output Data *****

<<Steady State>>

-------------------------------
States    Probability    Value
-------------------------------
  1         0.50000       0.50
  2         0.02381       0.02
  3         0.01613       0.02
  4         0.06494       0.06
  5         0.02381       0.02
  6         0.22112       0.22
  7         0.04519       0.05
  8         0.04546       0.05
  9         0.03039       0.03
 10         0.02916       0.03
-------------------------------
```

b. We make the same types of changes for Chris that we did for Sandy. The seventh row for the matrix of transition (representing Shop 7) will have .99 in the first column and 0's elsewhere except for Shop 1, which will have a .01. The AB:QM solution is given below. As with Part a, Chris has also increased his market share, but it is not 99%. He does not win his bet.

```
Program: Markov Analysis

Problem Title : QA 19-22b

***** Output Data *****

<<Steady State>>

-------------------------------
States    Probability    Value
-------------------------------
  1         0.02439       0.02
  2         0.02763       0.03
  3         0.01872       0.02
  4         0.07060       0.07
  5         0.02182       0.02
  6         0.13449       0.13
  7         0.63934       0.64
  8         0.03019       0.03
  9         0.01342       0.01
 10         0.01941       0.02
-------------------------------
```

c. If both are correct, the market shares will be 50% each as seen in the following AB:QM solution. Perhaps they can get together, each paying for his or her own meal. Neither Sandy or Chris will end up with 99% of the market.

```
Program: Markov Analysis

<<Steady State>>

-------------------------------
States    Probability    Value
-------------------------------
  1         0.50000       0.50
  2         0.00000       0.00
  3         0.00000       0.00
  4         0.00000       0.00
  5         0.00000       0.00
  6         0.00000       0.00
  7         0.50000       0.50
  8         0.00000       0.00
  9         0.00000       0.00
 10         0.00000       0.00
-------------------------------
```

Solution for Rentall Trucks Case

1. In order to determine what the market shares will be in one month Markov analysis must be used. We will define the following states for this case:

State 1—Rentall
State 2—Rentran
State 3—National

The market shares are as follows:

Rentall—   80% =   800
Rentran—   5% =   50
National— 15% =   150
          ----   ----
          100%   1000 people

Therefore

$n(0) = (.8 \quad .05 \quad .15)$

The next step is to determine the matrix of transition. If no changes are made one has:

	CUSTOMERS	RENTALL	RENTRAN	NATIONAL
Rentall	800	520/800 = .65	200/800 = .25	80/800 = .1
Rentran	60	3/60 = .05	51/60 = .85	6/60 = .1
National	140	14/140 = .1	35/140 = .25	91/140 = .65

Thus, $P = \begin{bmatrix} .65 & .25 & .1 \\ .05 & .85 & .1 \\ .1 & .25 & .65 \end{bmatrix}$

To determine the share of the market for next month, we multiply the market shares times the matrix of transition.

$$n(1) = n(0)P$$

$$n(1) = (.8 \quad .05 \quad .15) \begin{bmatrix} .65 & .25 & .1 \\ .05 & .85 & .1 \\ .1 & .25 & .65 \end{bmatrix}$$

$$n(1) = (.5365 \quad .2775 \quad .1760)$$

Thus, the new share of the market is about

Rentall	54%
Rentran	28%
National	18%
	100%

If changes are made:

	CUSTOMERS	RENTALL	RENTRAN	NATIONAL
Rentall	800	680/800 = .85	100/800 = .125	20/800 = .025
Rentran	60	9/60 = .15	45/60 = .75	6/60 = .1
National	140	28/140 = .2	35/140 = .25	77/140 = .55

$P = \begin{bmatrix} .85 & .125 & .025 \\ .15 & .75 & .1 \\ .2 & .25 & .55 \end{bmatrix}$

$$n(1) = n(0)P$$

$$n(1) = (.8 \quad .05 \quad .15) \begin{bmatrix} .85 & .125 & .025 \\ .15 & .75 & .10 \\ .2 & .25 & .55 \end{bmatrix}$$

$$= (.718 \quad .175 \quad .107)$$

Market shares:

Rentall	72%
Rentran	17%
National	11%
	100%

2. With no changes, in two months the market shares will be

$$n(2) = (.5365 \quad .2775 \quad .1760) \begin{bmatrix} .65 & .25 & .1 \\ .05 & .85 & .1 \\ .1 & .25 & .65 \end{bmatrix}$$

$$n(2) = (.3802 \quad .4140 \quad .1958)$$

In three months, the market share will be

$$n(3) = (.3802 \quad .4140 \quad .1958) \begin{bmatrix} .65 & .25 & .1 \\ .05 & .85 & .1 \\ .1 & .25 & .65 \end{bmatrix}$$

$$n(3) = (.28741 \quad .4959 \quad .20669)$$

The approximate market shares after three months are listed below:

Rentall	29%
Rentran	50%
National	21%
	100%

If the changes are made:

$$n(2) = n(1)P$$

$$= (.718 \quad .175 \quad .107) \begin{bmatrix} .85 & .125 & .025 \\ .15 & .75 & .10 \\ .2 & .25 & .55 \end{bmatrix}$$

$$= (.658 \quad .248 \quad .094)$$

$$n(3) = n(2)P$$

$$= (.658 \quad .248 \quad .094) \begin{bmatrix} .85 & .125 & .025 \\ .15 & .75 & .10 \\ .2 & .25 & .55 \end{bmatrix}$$

$$= (.615 \quad .292 \quad .093)$$

Market Shares:

Rentall	62%
Rentran	29%
National	09%
	100%

3. At equilibrium, with these changes

$$n = nP$$
$$n_1 + n_2 + n_3 = 1$$

$$(n_1 \quad n_2 \quad n_3) = (n_1 \quad n_2 \quad n_3) \begin{bmatrix} .85 & .125 & .025 \\ .15 & .75 & .10 \\ .2 & .25 & .55 \end{bmatrix}$$

$$n_1 = .85n_1 + .15n_2 + .2n_3$$
$$n_2 = .125n_1 + .75n_2 + .25n_3$$
$$n_3 = .025n_1 + .1n_2 + .55n_3$$

(1) $-.15n_1 + .15n_2 + .2n_3 = 0$
(2) $.125n_1 - .25n_2 + .25n_3 = 0$
(3) $.025n_1 + .1n_2 - .45n_3 = 0$
(4) $n_1 + n_2 + n_3 = 1$

We have four equations and three unknowns. We will drop equation one and solve equations 2, 3, and 4 for n_1, n_2, and n_3.

The results are shown below:

$$n_1 = .519$$
$$n_2 = .370$$
$$n_3 = \underline{.111}$$
$$1.000$$

The equilibrium market shares are:

Rentall	52%
Rentran	37%
National	11%
	100%

With no changes:

$$(n_1 \quad n_2 \quad n_3) = (n_1 \quad n_2 \quad n_3) \begin{bmatrix} .65 & .25 & .1 \\ .05 & .85 & .1 \\ .1 & .25 & .65 \end{bmatrix}$$

$$n_1 = .65n_1 + .05n_2 + .1n_3$$
$$n_2 = .25n_1 + .85n_2 + .25n_3$$
$$n_3 = .1n_1 + .1n_2 + .65n_3$$

Solving as above, the results are:

$$n_1 = .153$$
$$n_2 = .625$$
$$n_3 = \underline{.222}$$
$$1.000$$

The equilibrium market shares would be:

Rentall	15%
Rentran	63%
National	22%
	100%

A

Mathematical Tools: Determinants and Matrices

LEARNING OBJECTIVES

After completing this module, students will be able to:

1. Understand how matrices and determinants are used as mathematical tools in QA.
2. Compute the value of a determinant.
3. Solve simultaneous equations with determinants.
4. Add, subtract, multiply, and divide matrices.
5. Transpose matrices.

TEACHING SUGGESTIONS

Teaching Suggestion A.1: Why Discuss Matrices and Determinants?

These mathematical tools are needed in Markov analysis, in order to compute absorbing states. In a more advanced treatment of linear programming, matrix manipulation skills are also desired.

Teaching Suggestion A.2: Matrices Can Be Used to Display Data in Tabular Form.

As seen in Section A.3 of the module, a matrix is also a useful tool for presenting data.

SOLUTIONS TO PROBLEMS

A-1. a. Value $= (6)(2) - (-5)(3) = 27$

b. Value $= (3)(-1)(-2) + (7)(2)(4) + (-6)(1)(3) - (4)(-1)(-6) - (3)(2)(3) - (-2)(1)(7)$
$= 6 + 56 - 18 - 24 - 18 + 14 = 16$

A-2.

$$X = \frac{\begin{vmatrix} 4 & 2 & 3 \\ 2 & 3 & 1 \\ 3 & 1 & 2 \end{vmatrix}}{\begin{vmatrix} 5 & 2 & 3 \\ 2 & 3 & 1 \\ 3 & 1 & 2 \end{vmatrix}} = \frac{\begin{matrix}(4)(3)(2) + (2)(1)(3) + (3)(2)(1) \\ - (3)(3)(3) - (1)(1)(4) - (2)(2)(2)\end{matrix}}{\begin{matrix}(5)(3)(2) + (2)(1)(3) + (3)(2)(1) \\ - (3)(3)(3) - (1)(1)(5) - (2)(2)(2)\end{matrix}}$$

$$= \frac{-3}{2}$$

$$Y = \frac{\begin{vmatrix} 5 & 4 & 3 \\ 2 & 2 & 1 \\ 3 & 3 & 2 \end{vmatrix}}{\begin{vmatrix} 5 & 2 & 3 \\ 2 & 3 & 1 \\ 3 & 1 & 2 \end{vmatrix}} = \frac{\begin{matrix}(5)(2)(2) + (4)(1)(3) + (3)(2)(3) \\ - (3)(2)(3) - (3)(1)(5) - (2)(2)(4)\end{matrix}}{2}$$

$$= \frac{1}{2}$$

$$Z = \frac{\begin{vmatrix} 5 & 2 & 4 \\ 2 & 3 & 2 \\ 3 & 1 & 3 \end{vmatrix}}{\begin{vmatrix} 5 & 2 & 3 \\ 2 & 3 & 1 \\ 3 & 1 & 2 \end{vmatrix}} = \frac{\begin{matrix}(5)(3)(2) + (2)(2)(3) + (4)(2)(1) \\ - (3)(3)(4) - (1)(2)(5) - (3)(2)(2)\end{matrix}}{2}$$

$$= \frac{7}{2}$$

To verify, we check to be sure that $5X + 2Y + 3Z = 4$; namely, $5(-\frac{3}{2}) + 2(\frac{1}{2}) + 3(\frac{7}{2}) = \frac{8}{2} = 4$.

A-3. a. Matrix A + matrix B

$$= \begin{pmatrix} 2 & 4 & 1 \\ 3 & 8 & 7 \end{pmatrix} + \begin{pmatrix} 7 & 6 & 5 \\ 0 & 1 & 2 \end{pmatrix} = \begin{pmatrix} 9 & 10 & 6 \\ 3 & 9 & 9 \end{pmatrix}$$

b. Matrix B − matrix $A = \begin{pmatrix} 7 & 6 & 5 \\ 0 & 1 & 2 \end{pmatrix}$

$$- \begin{pmatrix} 2 & 4 & 1 \\ 3 & 8 & 7 \end{pmatrix} = \begin{pmatrix} 5 & 2 & 4 \\ -3 & -7 & -5 \end{pmatrix}$$

c. Matrix C + matrix D

$$= \begin{pmatrix} 3 & 6 & 9 \\ 7 & 8 & 1 \\ 9 & 2 & 4 \end{pmatrix} + \begin{pmatrix} 5 & 1 & 6 \\ 4 & 0 & 6 \\ 3 & 1 & 5 \end{pmatrix} = \begin{pmatrix} 8 & 7 & 15 \\ 11 & 8 & 7 \\ 12 & 3 & 9 \end{pmatrix}$$

d. Matrix C + matrix A: Cannot be added: matrix A is (3×2) and matrix C is (3×3). Only matrices of the *same dimension* can be *added* or *subtracted*.

A-4. a. Matrix A Matrix B Matrix C

$$\begin{pmatrix} 2 \\ 1 \end{pmatrix} \times (3 \quad 4 \quad 5) = \begin{pmatrix} 6 & 8 & 10 \\ 3 & 4 & 5 \end{pmatrix}$$

b. Matrix E Matrix F Matrix G

$$(5 \quad 2 \quad 6 \quad 1) \times \begin{pmatrix} 4 \\ 3 \\ 2 \\ 0 \end{pmatrix} = (20 + 6 + 12 + 0) = (38)$$

c. Matrix R Matrix S Matrix F

$$\begin{pmatrix} 2 & 3 \\ 1 & 4 \end{pmatrix} \times \begin{pmatrix} 1 & 0 \\ 0 & 1 \end{pmatrix} = \begin{pmatrix} 2+0 & 0+3 \\ 1+0 & 0+4 \end{pmatrix} = \begin{pmatrix} 2 & 3 \\ 1 & 4 \end{pmatrix}$$

d. Matrix W

$$\begin{pmatrix} 3 & 5 \\ 2 & 1 \\ 4 & 4 \end{pmatrix} \times \begin{pmatrix} 1 & 4 & 5 & 1 \\ 2 & 3 & 6 & 5 \end{pmatrix}$$

$$= \begin{pmatrix} 3+10 & 12+15 & 15+30 & 3+25 \\ 2+2 & 8+3 & 10+6 & 2+5 \\ 4+8 & 16+12 & 20+24 & 4+20 \end{pmatrix}$$

$$= \begin{pmatrix} 13 & 27 & 45 & 28 \\ 4 & 11 & 16 & 7 \\ 12 & 28 & 44 & 24 \end{pmatrix}$$

A-5. Job matrix   Cost matrix

$$\begin{pmatrix} 50 & 100 & 10 & 20 \\ 70 & 80 & 20 & 30 \\ 20 & 50 & 30 & 10 \end{pmatrix} \times \begin{pmatrix} \$1 \\ \$2 \\ \$3 \\ \$5 \end{pmatrix}$$

$$= \begin{pmatrix} \$50 + 200 + 30 + 100 \\ \$70 + 160 + 60 + 150 \\ \$20 + 100 + 90 + 50 \end{pmatrix} = \begin{pmatrix} \$380 \\ \$440 \\ \$260 \end{pmatrix}$$

Cost of dormitory job is \$380, of office building job is \$440, and of apartment complex job is \$260.

A-6.

$$\text{Transpose of matrix } R = \begin{bmatrix} 6 & 1 & 6 & 3 \\ 8 & 0 & 4 & 1 \\ 2 & 5 & 3 & 2 \\ 2 & 7 & 1 & 7 \end{bmatrix}$$

$$\text{Transpose of matrix } S = \begin{pmatrix} 3 & 2 & 5 \\ 1 & 2 & 4 \end{pmatrix}$$

A-7.

ELEMENT REMOVED	DETERMINANT OF COFACTORS	VALUE OF COFACTOR
Row 1, column 1	$\begin{vmatrix} 0 & 8 \\ 6 & 9 \end{vmatrix} = -48$	−48
Row 1, column 2	$\begin{vmatrix} 2 & 8 \\ 3 & 9 \end{vmatrix} = -6$	+6
Row 1, column 3	$\begin{vmatrix} 2 & 0 \\ 3 & 6 \end{vmatrix} = 12$	12
Row 2, column 1	$\begin{vmatrix} 4 & 7 \\ 6 & 9 \end{vmatrix} = -6$	+6
Row 2, column 2	$\begin{vmatrix} 1 & 7 \\ 3 & 9 \end{vmatrix} = -12$	−12
Row 2, column 3	$\begin{vmatrix} 1 & 4 \\ 3 & 6 \end{vmatrix} = -6$	+6
Row 3, column 1	$\begin{vmatrix} 4 & 7 \\ 0 & 8 \end{vmatrix} = 32$	32
Row 3, column 2	$\begin{vmatrix} 1 & 7 \\ 2 & 8 \end{vmatrix} = -6$	+6
Row 3, column 3	$\begin{vmatrix} 1 & 4 \\ 2 & 0 \end{vmatrix} = -8$	−8

$$\text{Matrix of cofactors} = \begin{pmatrix} -48 & 6 & 12 \\ 6 & -12 & 6 \\ 32 & 6 & -8 \end{pmatrix}$$

$$\text{Adjoint of matrix} = \begin{pmatrix} -48 & 6 & 32 \\ 6 & -12 & 6 \\ 12 & 6 & -8 \end{pmatrix}$$

A-8.

$$\text{Original matrix} = \begin{pmatrix} 1 & 4 & 7 \\ 2 & 0 & 8 \\ 3 & 6 & 9 \end{pmatrix}$$

$$\text{Value of determinant} = 0 + 96 + 84 - 0 - 48 - 72$$

$$= 60$$

$$\text{Adjoint calculation in Problem A-7} = \begin{pmatrix} -48 & 6 & 32 \\ 6 & -12 & 6 \\ 12 & 6 & -8 \end{pmatrix}$$

$$\text{Inverse of matrix} = \begin{pmatrix} -48/60 & 6/60 & 32/60 \\ 6/60 & -12/60 & 6/60 \\ 12/60 & 6/60 & -8/60 \end{pmatrix}$$

To verify, we multiply the original matrix by its inverse. An identity matrix indeed results.

B
Game Theory

LEARNING OBJECTIVES

After completing this module, students will be able to:

1. Understand the principles of zero-sum, two-person games.
2. Analyze pure strategy games and use dominance to reduce the size of a game.
3. Solve mixed strategy games when there is no saddle point.
4. Use linear programming to solve larger games.

TEACHING SUGGESTIONS

Teaching Suggestion B.1: Game Theory and Conflict.

This chapter covers zero-sum, two-person games. The mathematics of more complex games is beyond the scope of this book. Even though students may not perform the techniques covered in this chapter, the overall concepts are interesting and important. Conflict is a part of our world. Students can be asked to discuss the use of conflict analysis and game theory in corporate and political settings.

Teaching Suggestion B.2: Use of Pure Strategy Games and Dominance.

The use of pure strategy games and dominance shows students that some strategies or alternatives can be eliminated from consideration by carefully analyzing the situation. This is an important concept that can be applied to many problems in addition to game theory. Students can be asked to consider situations where the principles of dominance can be applied.

Teaching Suggestion B.3: Use of Linear Programming.

For larger and more complex games, linear programming can be used. Students can be told that all of the features of linear programming can be utilized in analyzing game theory problems. For example, sensitivity analysis and ranging can be used to determine how sensitive the solution is to changes in the values used in the game. In addition, linear programming can be used to determine if there are alternate optimal solutions.

ALTERNATE EXAMPLE

Alternate Example B-1: Melinda (Person A) and Stanley (Person B) are involved in a competitive situation. Both have two strategies (1 and 2) that they can play. A table showing the winnings is presented below.

	STANLEY (B)	
MELINDA (A)	STRATEGY 1	STRATEGY 2
Strategy 1	10	1
Strategy 2	2	7

To solve this game, we determine the strategies for both players. We begin with Melinda (Player A). The equations are below:

For Player A—Melinda:

$$10Q + 2(1 - Q) = 1Q + 7(1 - Q)$$
$$10Q + 2 - 2Q = 1Q + 7 - 7Q$$

$14Q = 5; Q = 5/14 = .357$ − Strategy 1 for Player A—Melinda

$1 - Q = 9/14; Q = .643$ − Strategy 2 for Player A—Melinda

For Player B—Stanley:

$$10P + 1(1 - P) = 2P + 7(1 - P)$$
$$10P + 1 - P = 2P + 7 - 7P$$

$14P = 6; P = 6/14 = .429$ − Strategy 1 for Player B—Stanley

$1 - P = 8/14 = .571$ − Strategy 2 for Player B—Stanley

SOLUTIONS TO DISCUSSION QUESTIONS AND PROBLEMS

B-1. A two-person game is one in which only two players can participate in the game. These players could be people, companies, other organizations, governments, and so on. A zero-sum game means that when one person wins the other person must lose. Therefore, the sum of gains and losses for both players will always be equal to zero because when one player wins, the other player loses.

B-2. The value of the game can be computed by multiplying the percentage that each player plays a given strategy times the game outcomes embodied in the table of the game. Since the optimal strategies for each player are obtained by equating the expected gains of both strategies for each player, there is a short-cut method for determining the value of the game. This short-cut method involves multiplying game outcomes times their probabilities of occurrence for any row or any column.

B-3. A pure strategy is one in which a player will always play one strategy in the game. Dominance can be used in game theory to reduce the size of the game. This is done by eliminating strategies that would never be played by one of the players of the game.

B-4. A mixed game is one in which each player would play every strategy a given percent of the time. In other words, there is no pure strategy in a mixed game. A mixed game can be solved by equating a player's expected winnings for one of the strategies with his or her expected winnings for the other opponent's strategy.

B-5. Linear programming can be used to solve games that are larger than 2×2 by developing the appropriate objective function and constraints. The objective function will be to maximize a player's winnings or to minimize the inverse of the player's winnings. The constraints in the linear programming problem can be formulated by setting the value of any strategy of the game to be less than or equal to the value of the entire game itself. This process is done for every strategy.

B-6. Strategy for $X = X_2$
Strategy for $Y = Y_2$
Value of game $= 6$

B-7. A's strategy $= A_1$
B's strategy $= B_1$
Value of game $= 19$

B-8. X's strategy $= 86Q + 36(1 - Q) = 42Q$
$$+ 106(1 - Q) \quad Q = \frac{35}{57},$$
$$1 - Q = \frac{22}{57}$$
Y's strategy $= 86P + 42(1 - P) = 36P$
$$+ 106(1 - P) \quad P = \frac{32}{57},$$
$$1 - P = \frac{25}{57}$$
Value of game $= 86 \times \frac{35}{57} + 36 \times \frac{22}{57} = 66.70$

B-9. $21Q + 89(1 - Q) = 116Q + 3(1 - Q);$
$$Q = \frac{86}{181}; 1 - Q = \frac{95}{181}$$
Value of game $= \frac{86}{181} \times 21 + \frac{95}{181} \times 89$
$$= 56.69$$

B-10. A_1: A selects $5 bill
A_2: A selects $10 bill
B_1: B selects $1 bill
B_2: B selects $20 bill

a.

	B_1	B_2
A_1	-6	25
A_2	11	-30

b. Strategy for $A = -6Q + 11(1 - Q) = 25Q$
$$- 30(1 - Q) \quad Q = \frac{41}{72},$$
$$1 - Q = \frac{31}{72}$$
Strategy for $B = -6P + 25(1 - P) = 11P$
$$- 30(1 - P) \quad P = \frac{55}{72},$$
$$1 - P = \frac{17}{72}$$

c. Value of game $= -6 \times \frac{41}{72} + 11 \times \frac{31}{72} = 1.32$

Since game value is positive, I'd rather be A.

B-11. a.

	B_1	B_2
A_1	6	-25
A_2	-11	30

b. A's strategy $= 6Q - 11(1 - Q) = -25Q$
$$+30(1 - Q) \quad Q = \frac{41}{72},$$
$$1 - Q = \frac{31}{72}$$
B's strategy $= 6P - 25(1 - P) = -11P$
$$+30(1 - P) \quad P = \frac{55}{72},$$
$$1 - P = \frac{17}{72}$$

So strategies remain identical.

c. Value of game $= 6 \times \frac{41}{72} - 11 \times \frac{31}{72} = -1.32$

Since game value is negative, I'd rather be B.

B-12. The game can be reduced to a 2×2 game, since X would never play X_1 or X_4 since X stands to lose in every eventuality under those two strategies. Thus, the game is:

	Y_1	Y_2
X_2	12	8
X_3	4	12

X's strategy $= 12Q + 4(1 - Q) = 8Q + 12(1 - Q)$
$$Q = \tfrac{2}{3}, 1 - Q = \tfrac{1}{3}$$
Y's strategy $= 12P + 8(1 - P) = 4P + 12(1 - P)$
$$P = \tfrac{1}{3}, 1 - P = \tfrac{2}{3}$$
Value of game $= 12 \times \tfrac{2}{3} + 4 \times \tfrac{1}{3} = 9.33$

B-13. A_1: Shoe Town does no advertising.
A_2: Shoe Town invests $15,000 in advertising.
B_1: Fancy Foot does nothing.
B_2: Fancy Foot invests $10,000 in advertising.
B_3: Fancy Foot invests $20,000 in advertising.

a.

	B_1	B_2	B_3
A_1	0	-2	-5
A_2	3	1	-1

b. Maximize $= \overline{Y}_1 + \overline{Y}_2 + \overline{Y}_3$

Subject to:
$$-2\overline{Y}_2 - 5\overline{Y}_3 \leqq 1$$
$$3\overline{Y}_1 + \overline{Y}_2 - \overline{Y}_3 \leqq 1$$

c. Once optimal $\overline{Y}_1$, $\overline{Y}_2$, and $\overline{Y}_3$ are found, value of the game is:

$$\frac{1}{(\overline{Y}_1 + \overline{Y}_2 + \overline{Y}_3)} \text{ optimal}$$

This particular problem has a saddle point with strategies A_2 and B_3 and game value of -1.

B-14. a.

	B_1	B_2	B_3
A_1	0	$-2,000$	$-5,000$
A_2	3,000	1,000	$-1,000$

b. Maximize $= \overline{Y}_1 + \overline{Y}_2 + \overline{Y}_3$

Subject to: $-2,000Y_2 - 5,000Y_3 \leqq 1$
$$3,000Y_1 + 1,000Y_2 - 1,000Y_3 \leqq 1$$

c. Value of game $= \dfrac{1}{(\overline{Y}_1 + \overline{Y}_2 + \overline{Y}_3)} \text{ optimal}$

Once again we have a saddle point at A_2 and B_3.

B-15. The value of the game is 3.17. The optimal strategies for A and B can be computed along with the value of the game using AB:QM. The results are presented below:

```
***** Program Output *****

- - - - - - - - - - - - -
Mixed Strategy
- - - - - - - - - - - - -

For Player A:

Probability of Strategy   1    0.390
Probability of Strategy   2    0.244
Probability of Strategy   3    0.366
Probability of Strategy   4    0.000
Probability of Strategy   5    0.000
Probability of Strategy   6    0.000

For Player B:

Probability of Strategy   1    0.190
Probability of Strategy   2    0.707
Probability of Strategy   3    0.102

Value for this game is        3.17
```

B-16. This problem can be solved using AB:QM. The best strategy for Petroleum Research is to play Strategy 5 11.1% of the time and Strategy 14 88.9% of the time. Petroleum Research can expect to get a return of $3 million from this approach. These results are summarized below:

```
***** Program Output *****

- - - - - - - - - - - - -
Mixed Strategy
- - - - - - - - - - - - -

For Player A:

Probability of Strategy   1    0.000
Probability of Strategy   2    0.000
Probability of Strategy   3    0.000
Probability of Strategy   4    0.000
Probability of Strategy   5    0.111
Probability of Strategy   6    0.000
Probability of Strategy   7    0.000
Probability of Strategy   8    0.000
Probability of Strategy   9    0.000
Probability of Strategy  10    0.000
Probability of Strategy  11    0.000
Probability of Strategy  12    0.000
Probability of Strategy  13    0.000
Probability of Strategy  14    0.889
Probability of Strategy  15    0.000

For Player B:

Probability of Strategy   1    0.000
Probability of Strategy   2    0.154
Probability of Strategy   3    0.846
Probability of Strategy   4    0.000
Probability of Strategy   5    0.000

Value for this game is        3.00
```

C
Dynamic Programming

LEARNING OBJECTIVES

After completing this module, students will be able to:

1. Understand the overall approach of dynamic programming.
2. Use dynamic programming to solve the shortest-route problem.
3. Develop dynamic programming stages.
4. Describe important dynamic programming terminology.

TEACHING SUGGESTIONS

Teaching Suggestion C.1: Overall Use of Dynamic Programming.

Dynamic programming is a general approach that can be used to solve a number of different problems. The overall approach of breaking a larger problem into smaller stages is an important principle. In addition to being essential for the solution of a dynamic programming problem, this concept is a useful approach for general decision-making problems.

Teaching Suggestion C.2: Use of the Shortest-Route Problem.

Dynamic programming can be a difficult topic for some students to understand. The shortest-route problem was used in this chapter to show students how the principles of dynamic programming can be used to solve a familiar problem. Once students understand the use of dynamic programming to solve the shortest-route problem, more complex and difficult problems can be undertaken.

Teaching Suggestion C.3: Applications Boxes in This Module.

Because dynamic programming is a difficult and advanced topic, we selected applications that might interest the average student.

Teaching Suggestion C.4: Use of Terminology.

Understanding dynamic programming terminology is one approach to handling larger and more complex problems. Learning how the terminology of dynamic programming is applied to the shortest-route problem can help students understand larger and more complex dynamic programming problems.

VIDEO C–1

Weyerhaeuser Decision Simulator Improves Timber Profits

This TIMS video is based on one of the award-winning papers published in *Interfaces*. A brief description of the application follows:

VISION teaches woods buckers to cut tree stems for optimal profits through a video game. The dynamic programming optimization procedure behind the game has revised Weyerhaeuser's cutting policies to improve profits by $100 million. (See the QA application box in this module for details.)

VIDEO C–2

Using Dynamic Programming to Assist in the Scheduling of Operation Desert Storm Airlift Operations

This TIMS video is based on one of the award-winning papers published in *Interfaces*. This video investigates the use of the Airlift Deployment Analysis System (ADANS). The system is a dynamic programming-based airlift scheduling algorithm. Using the dynamic programming approach, the airlift scheduler for ADANS was able to produce schedules for the massive airlift based on the requirements for the airlifts, the available resources that could be deployed, and the overall scheduling of the mission.

ADANS was used in Desert Storm by the Military Airlift Command (MAC). The operation was the largest airlift of cargo and troops in history. More than 25,000 missions had transported 774,000 tons of cargo and 966,000 passengers to the Persian Gulf region by early August of 1991.

ALTERNATE EXAMPLE

Alternate Example C-1: Darrell Washington would like to use dynamic programming to solve the shortest route problem shown in the following figure.

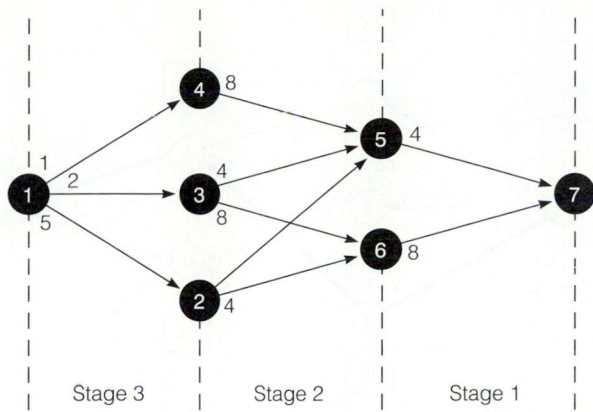

Beginning with Stage 1, we begin to solve the problem. The distance from node 5 to node 7 is 4 and the distance from node 6 is 8. These values are put in boxes by the nodes. The results are shown in the following network.

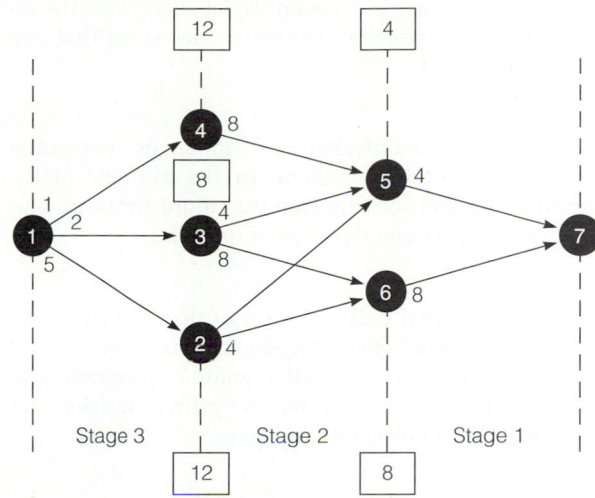

Finally, we solve Stage 3. The minimum distance is through node 3. The distance from node 1 to node 3 is 2, and the minimum distance from node 3 to the end of the network is 8 as seen in the results for Stage 2. Thus, the shortest route through the network is 10.

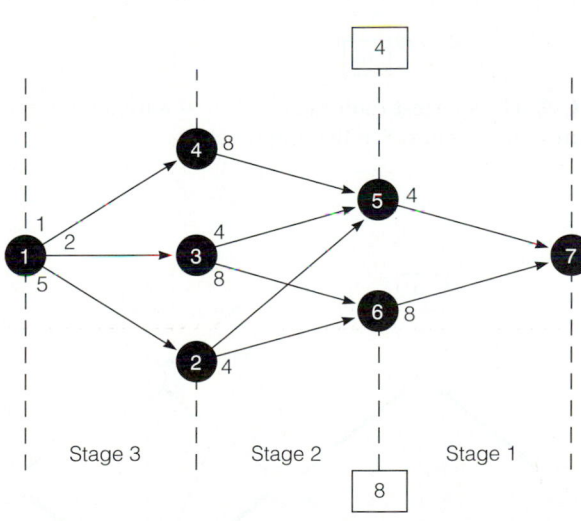

Next, we solve Stage 2. The minimum distances between nodes 2, 3, and 4 and the ending node 7 are 12, 8, and 12. These distances are also put in boxes by the nodes. The results for Stage 2 are shown in the following network.

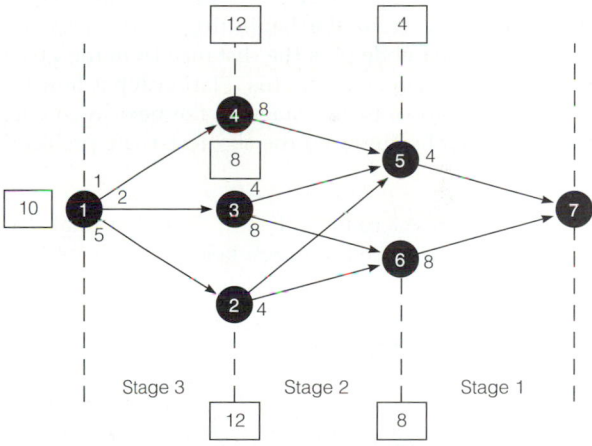

SOLUTIONS TO QUESTIONS AND PROBLEMS

C-1. A stage in dynamic programming is a period or a logical subproblem. Dynamic programming divides problems into a number of decisions stages, whereby the outcome of a decision at one stage affects the decision at each of the next stages.

C-2. State variables include all of the possible beginning situations or conditions of a stage. These have also been called the input variables. Decision variables, on the other hand, represent the alternatives or possible decisions that exist at each stage. Thus, state variables are possible existing situations or conditions at the beginning, while decision variables include the alternatives and possible actions or decisions that can exist at each stage.

C-3. A decision criterion is a statement concerning the objective of the problem. In the example in the module, the decision criterion was to minimize the total distance between two points or nodes.

C-4. The optimal policy is a set of decision rules, developed as a result of the decision criteria. The optimal policy is necessary for all dynamic programming problems to give those problems optimal decisions for any entering condition at any stage.

C-5. A transformation is important for dynamic programming problems because it allows us to determine the relationship between stages. This permits us to go from one stage to the next in solving dynamic programming problems. In the shortest-route problem, the following transformation was used: the distance from the beginning of a given stage to the last node is equal to the distance from the beginning of the previous stage to the last node plus the distance from the given stage to the previous stage. This relationship is how we were able to go from stage to the next in solving for the optimal solution to the shortest-route problem.

C-6. The shortest route is 1–2–6–7 with a total distance of 10 miles. See the graph below.

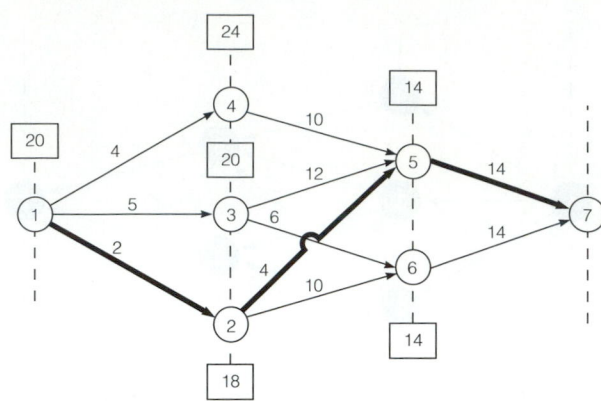

C-8. The shortest route is 1–2–5–7 with a total distance of 14 miles. See the graph below.

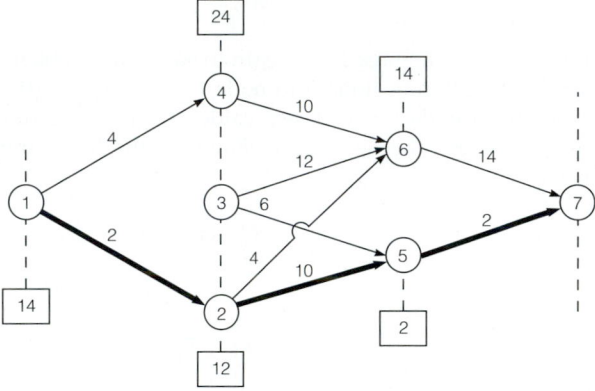

C-9. The shortest route is 1–2–5–8–9 with a total distance of 19 miles. See the graph below.

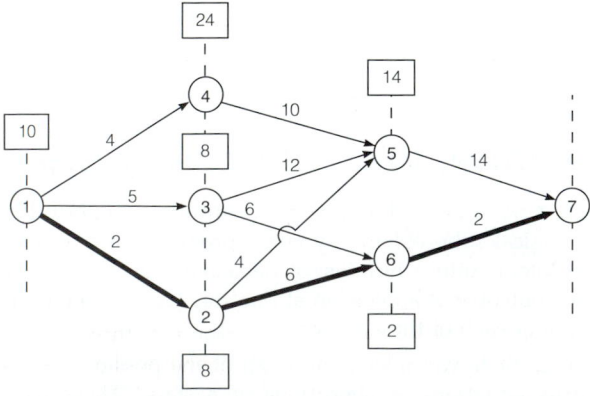

C-7. The shortest route is 1–2–5–7 with a total distance of 20 miles. See the graph at top of next column.

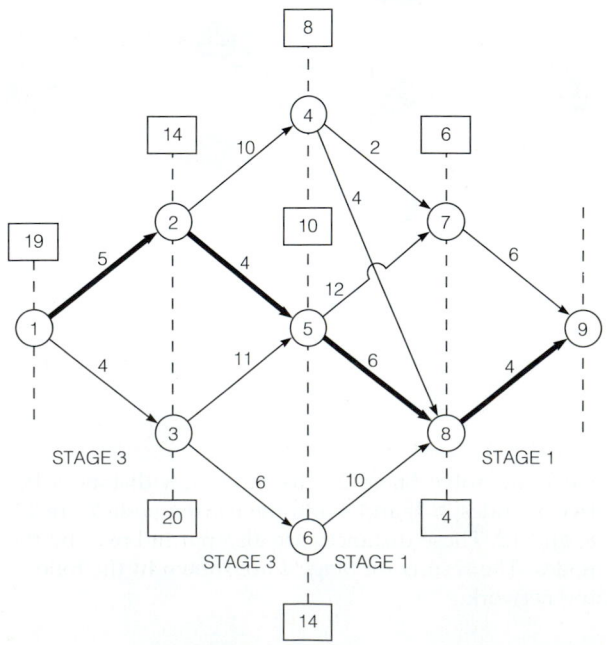

C-10. State variables are node 2 and node 3. Decision variables are route 2–4, route 2–5, route 3–5, and route 3–6. The decision criterion is to minimize the total distance traveled. The optimal policy for any beginning condition is:

ENTERING CONDITION	ARC THAT WILL MINIMIZE TOTAL DISTANCE TO NODE 9
2	2—5
3	3—6

D
Decision Theory and the Normal Distribution

LEARNING OBJECTIVES

After completing this module, students will be able to:

1. Understand how the normal curve can be used in performing break-even analysis.
2. Compute the expected value of perfect information (EVPI) using the normal curve.
3. Perform marginal analysis where products have a constant marginal profit and loss.

TEACHING SUGGESTIONS

Teaching Suggestion D.1: Reviewing the Normal Curve.

Most of the material in this module requires the use of the normal curve. A review of the basic principles of the normal curve found in the probability chapters would be helpful before this module is started.

Teaching Suggestion D.2: Covering Break-Even Analysis First.

Covering break-even calculations first helps students get into decision theory and normal curve analysis. This material will also help students get back into the fundamental principles of normal curve theory. Once break-even analysis has been mastered by students, they should be ready for the rest of the material in this module.

Teaching Suggestion D.3: Spending More Time on EVPI and the Normal Distribution.

EVPI and the normal distribution concepts are difficult for many students. You may need to spend more time on this topic and reinforce the basic steps involved. Some instructors reduce coverage or eliminate this topic.

SOLUTIONS TO QUESTIONS AND PROBLEMS

D-1. The purpose of break-even analysis is to help a manager determine at what point overall revenue will equal overall cost. It can also help the manager to determine at a certain sales volume what revenues will be generated. This knowledge can assist the manager in making decisions as to whether or not to introduce a new product to the market.

D-2. The normal distribution can be used in break-even analysis when sales are symmetrical around the mean expected demand and follow a bell-shaped distribution (when demand is normally distributed), and when there is only one random variable. Usually the normal distribution represents the demand for a new product.

D-3. The relationship between EMV and the state of nature must be linear when you use the computations presented in Equation D-5 in determining EMV from the mean and the standard deviation. When this relationship is not linear, the approach used in computing EMV cannot be used.

D-4. When EVPI is to be computed using a state of nature that follows a normal distribution, three steps are required. The first step is to determine the opportunity loss function. The second step is to determine the opportunity loss using the unit normal loss integral. The third step is to equate the expected value of perfect information to the number you obtained in step two. EVPI will always be equal to EOL.

D-5.

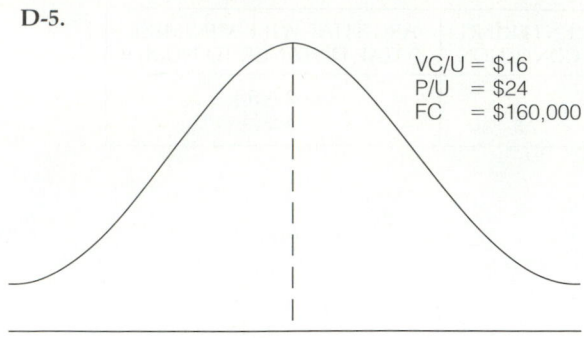

VC/U = $16
P/U = $24
FC   = $160,000

M = 60,000
σ = 10,000

a. $BE = \dfrac{FC}{P/U - VC/U} = \dfrac{160,000}{24 - 16} = 20,000$ books

b. $EMV = (P/U - VC/U)(M) - FC$
$= (24 - 16)(60,000) - 160,000$
$= 480,000 - 160,000 = \$320,000$

D-6. a. $OLF = K(BE - X)$ for $X \leq BE$
$\qquad\qquad\qquad\qquad\qquad X \geq BE$

where

$\qquad K = (P/U - VC/U) = 8$

Thus:

$\qquad EOL = \$8\,(20,000 - X)$ for $X \leq 20,000$
$\qquad\qquad \$0 \qquad\qquad\qquad X \geq 20,000$

where X = sales in units.

b. $EOL = K\sigma N(D)$

with

$\qquad K = \$8$
$\qquad \sigma = 10,000$
$\qquad D = \left| \dfrac{60,000 - 20,000}{10,000} \right| = 4$

and

$\qquad N(D) = .000007145.$

Thus:

$\qquad EOL = (8)(10,000)(.000007145) = \$.57160$

c. $EVPI = \$.57160$, since $EOL = EVPI$

d. $Z = \dfrac{20,000 - 60,000}{10,000} = -4$

[Standard deviations from μ]

A Z value for $+4$ is not found in table, but we used .99997. Thus:

$\qquad P(\text{profit}) = .99997 = 99.99\%$
$\qquad P(\text{loss}) \;\;= .00003 = .003\%$

e. The firm should print the book

D-7.

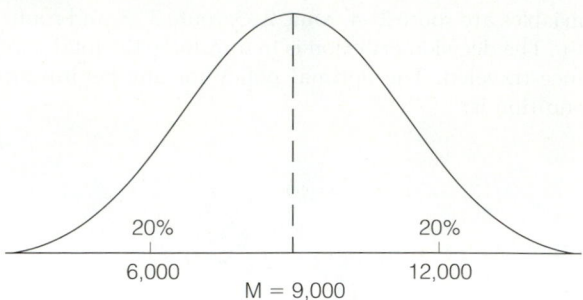

20%   20%
6,000   12,000
M = 9,000

a. $Z = \dfrac{D - M}{\sigma}$
[Area to the left of 12,000 = .80.
From Appendix A,
Z value for .80 = .84.]

Thus:

$\qquad .84 = \dfrac{12,000 - 9,000}{\sigma}$

$\qquad .84\sigma = 3,000$
$\qquad \sigma = 3,571$

b. $Z = \dfrac{6,000 - 9,000}{3,571} = \dfrac{-3,000}{3,571} = -.84$

Using Appendix A:

$\qquad Z(.84) = .79955$
$\qquad 1 - .79955 = .20045$

Thus:

$\qquad P(\text{loss}) \;\;= .20045 = 20.045\%$
$\qquad P(\text{profit}) = .79955 = 79.955\%$

c. $EMV = (P/U - VC/U)(M) - FC$
$= (\$10 - \$4)(9,000) - \$36,000$
$= \$54,000 - \$36,000$
$= \$18,000$

d. $EVPI = EOL$
$\qquad EOL = K\sigma N(D)$
$\qquad K = 6$
$\qquad \sigma = 3,571$
$\qquad D = \left| \dfrac{9,000 - 6,000}{3,571} \right| = .8401$
$\qquad N(.84) = .1120$

Thus, $EOL = (6)(3571)(.1120) = \$2,399.71$ and Rudy should be willing to pay up to \$2,399.71 for a marketing research study.

D-8. $FC = \$24,000$
$\qquad VC/U = \$8$
$\qquad P/U = \$24$

a. $BE = \dfrac{FC}{P/U - VC/U} = \dfrac{24,000}{24 - 8} = 1,500$ sets

b. If $D = 2,000$, True Lens should produce the lenses. The expected profit would be:

Revenue $(2,000 \times \$24/\text{set}) = \$48,000$

Less expenses
Fixed cost   24,000
Variable cost   16,000
$(2,000 \times \$8/\text{set})$ (40,000)
Profit   = $8,000

D-9. $\text{EMV} = (\$28 - \$20)(35,000) - \$16,000$
$= \$264,000$

No effect

D-10.

a. $\text{OLF} = \begin{cases} \$10(30 - x) & \text{For } X < 30 \text{ where } X \text{ is actual sales} \\ 0 & \text{otherwise} \end{cases}$

b. $D = \left| \dfrac{\mu - X}{\sigma} \right| = \left| \dfrac{45 - 30}{30} \right|$
$= .5 \therefore N(D) = N(.5) = .1978$

$\text{EOL} = K\sigma N(D) = \$10 \times 30 \times .1978 = \$59.34$

c. $\text{EVPI} = \text{EOL} = \$59.34$

D-11. $\text{EOL} = K\sigma N(D)$
$K = \$8, \$10, \text{ or } \$15$
$\sigma = 30$
$D = \left| \dfrac{45 - 30}{30} \right| = .5$
$N(D) = .1978$

Thus:

EOL if $K = \$8\ = (8)(30)(.1978)\ = \$47.47$
EOL if $K = \$10 = (10)(30)(.1978) = \$59.34$
EOL if $K = \$15 = (15)(30)(.1978) = \$89.01$

Thus, as the loss per lamp increases, the expected opportunity loss increases.

D-12. a. New $\text{EMV} = (\$28 - \$19)(35,000) - 32,000$
$= \$283,000$

Go ahead with new process.

b. New $\text{EMV} = (\$32 - \$20)(26,000) - 16,000$
$= \$296,000$

Increase selling price.

D-13. $D = \left| \dfrac{\mu - X_b}{\sigma} \right| = \left| \dfrac{350 - 200}{150} \right| = 1$
$N(D) = .0833$

$\text{EVPI} = \text{EOL} = K\sigma N(D) = \$80 \times 150 \times .0833 = \$999.6$
The most Joe would be willing to pay is $999.60.

D-14. $\text{EVPI} = \text{EOL} = K\sigma N(D)$
$\$500 = \$100 \times 50 \times N(D)$
$N(D) = .1; \text{ From OL tables, } D = .9$

$D = \dfrac{\mu - X_b}{\sigma} = \dfrac{5,000 - X_b}{50}\ \ X_b = 4955$

Break-even point is 4,955 pumps.

D-15. $\mu = 700$

$P(X < 750) = P\left(Z < \dfrac{750 - 700}{\sigma} \right) = .60$

$\therefore \sigma = \dfrac{750 - 700}{.25} = 200$

$D = \left| \dfrac{\mu - X_b}{\sigma} \right| = \dfrac{700 - 500}{200} = 1.00$

$N(D) = .08332$
$\text{EVPI} = \text{EOL} = K\sigma N(D)$
$= \$15 \times 200 \times .08332 = \$249.96$

D-16. $\mu = 750; \sigma \text{ still} = 200$

$D = \left| \dfrac{750 - 500}{200} \right|$
$= 1.25; N(D) \text{ decreased to } .05059$
$\text{EOL} = \$15 \times .05059 \times 200 = \$151.77$

E
Multifactor Decision Making

LEARNING OBJECTIVES

After completing this module, students will be able to:

1. Use the multifactor evaluation process in making decisions that involve a number of factors, where importance weights can be assigned.
2. Understand the use of the analytic hierarchy process in decision making.
3. Contrast multifactor evaluation with the analytic hierarchy process.

TEACHING SUGGESTIONS

Teaching Suggestion E.1: Using Multifactor Decision-Making Techniques.

Many decisions students make involve a number of factors. Thus, multifactor decision-making techniques can be useful and practical. This section can be started by having students give examples of decisions that require the analysis of multiple factors. Buying a car or stereo and picking the best job offer are examples. Once students understand the principles of multiplying factor weights times factor evaluations, they will be able to understand the use of AHP. Perhaps in another class there will be a student using the program called Expert Choice; call on that student to demonstrate the program to the class.

Teaching Suggestion E.2: Using AHP.

Have the students describe situations where AHP would be preferred over the multifactor evaluation process. You may want to take one of these situations and show how pairwise comparisons can be made. Students can then be asked to complete the AHP problem and determine the best solution. This can lead to in-class discussions on the AHP process.

SOLUTIONS TO QUESTIONS AND PROBLEMS

E-1. Multifactor decision making is appropriate when a decision involves a number of factors. Deciding to buy a house, for example, can involve the price, location, taxes, utilities, and so forth.

E-2. When using multifactor decision making, each factor receives an importance weight. These weights will sum to 1. Then, every alternative and factor combination will receive a factor evaluation. The factor weights are multiplied by the factor evaluations to get a weighted evaluation for each alternative. The alternative with the highest weighted evaluation is selected.

E-3. The analytic hierarchy process should be used when it is difficult or impossible to subjectively determine factor weights and factor evaluations. In this case, pairwise comparisons are performed to assist in the decision-making process and determining the best alternative.

E-4. Here is an analysis of George's decision.

Factor weights:

FACTOR	IMPORTANCE (WEIGHT)
Price	.4
Color	.1
Warranty	.1
Size	.1
Brand name	.3

Factor Evaluations:

FACTOR	SUN	HITEK	SURGO
Price	.7	.6	.8
Color	.9	.9	.4
Warranty	.8	.9	.4
Size	.8	.8	.2
Brand name	.9	.9	.6

Evaluation of SUN:

FACTOR NAME	FACTOR RATING	FACTOR EVALUATION	WEIGHTED EVALUATION
Price	.4	.7	.28
Color	.1	.9	.09
Warranty	.1	.8	.08
Size	.1	.8	.08
Brand name	.3	.9	.27
Total	1		.80

Evaluation of HITEK:

FACTOR NAME	FACTOR RATING	FACTOR EVALUATION	WEIGHTED EVALUATION
Price	.4	.6	.24
Color	.1	.9	.09
Warranty	.1	.9	.09
Size	.1	.8	.08
Brand name	.3	.9	.27
Total	1		.77

Evaluation of SURGO:

FACTOR NAME	FACTOR RATING	FACTOR EVALUATION	WEIGHTED EVALUATION
Price	.4	.8	.32
Color	.1	.4	.04
Warranty	.1	.4	.04
Size	.1	.2	.02
Brand name	.3	.6	.18
Total	1		.6

SUN is selected with the highest total weighted evaluation of .80.

E-5. Linda's problem can be analyzed as follows:

PRICE	CAR 1	CAR 2	CAR 3
Car 1		2	7
Car 2			4
Car 3			

The following will be the priorities for price:

Priority for car 1 is   .6025.
Priority for car 2 is   .3151.
Priority for car 3 is   .0824.

Consistency information follows:

Weighted sum vector = (1.8096   .9460   .2473)
Consistency vector = (3.0035   3.0019   3.0005)
Lambda = 3.0020
Value of CI = .0010
RI = .5800
CR = .0017

E-6.

WARRANTY	CAR 1	CAR 2	CAR 3
Car 1		1/3	1/8
Car 2			1/5
Car 3			

The following will be the priorities for warranty:

Priority for car 1 is   .0768.
Priority for car 2 is   .1863.
Priority for car 3 is   .7370.

Consistency information follows:

Weighted sum vector = (.2310   .5640   2.2825)
Consistency vector = (3.0088   3.0276   3.0972)
Lambda = 3.0445
Value of CI = .0223
RI = .5800
CR = .0384

E-7.

STYLE	CAR 1	CAR 2	CAR 3
Car 1		1/3	3
Car 2			8
Car 3			

The following will be the priorities for style:

Priority for car 1 is   .2364.
Priority for car 2 is   .6816.
Priority for car 3 is   .0820.

Consistency information follows:

Weighted sum vector = (.7096   2.0468   .2460)
Consistency vector = (3.0011   3.0031   3.0004)
Lambda = 3.0015
Value of CI = .0008
RI = .5800
CR = .0013

E-8.

FACTORS	PRICE	WARRANTY	STYLE
Price		2	9
Warranty			6
Style			

The following will be the priorities for the factors:

Priority for price is   .6049.
Priority for warranty is   .3337.
Priority for style is   .0614.

Consistency information follows:

Weighted sum vector = (1.8246   1.0044   .1842)
Consistency vector = (3.0163   3.0097   3.0016)
Value of CI = .0046
RI = .5800
CR = .0079

The following are the final rankings—Car 1 is selected.

ITEM	RANKING
Car 1	.4045
Car 2	.2946
Car 3	.3008

E-9. The analysis to determine which computer system is to be selected is below:

PRICE	S-1	S-2	S-3
S-1		2	8
S-2			5
S-3			

The following will be the priorities for price:

Priority for system 1 (S-1) is .6039.
Priority for system 2 (S-2) is .3258.
Priority for system 3 (S-3) is .0703.

Consistency information follows:

Weighted sum vector = (1.8178 .9792 .2109)
Consistency vector = (3.0099 3.0056 3.0011)
Lambda = 3.0055
Value of CI = .0028
RI = .5800
CR = .0048

BRAND NAME	S-1	S-2	S-3
S-1		1	6
S-2			4
S-3			

The following will be the priorities for brand name:

Priority for system 1 (S-1) is .4838.
Priority for system 2 (S-2) is .4232.
Priority for system 3 (S-3) is .0930.

Consistency information follows:

Weighted sum vector = (1.4649 1.2789 .2794)
Consistency vector = (3.0278 3.0220 3.0051)
Lambda = 3.0183
Value of CI = .0092
RI = .5800
CR = .0158

MEMORY	S-1	S-2	S-3
S-1		1/2	1/7
S-2			1/6
S-3			

The following will be the priorities for memory:

Priority for system 1 (S-1) is .0919.
Priority for system 2 (S-2) is .1535.
Priority for system 3 (S-3) is .7545.

Consistency information follows:

Weighted sum vector = (.2765 .4631 2.3192)
Consistency vector = (3.0078 3.0164 3.0736)
Lambda = 3.0326
Value of CI = .0163
RI = .5800
CR = .0281

SPEED	S-1	S-2	S-3
S-1		1/3	2
S-2			5
S-3			

The following will be the priorities for speed:

Priority for system 1 (S-1) is .2299.
Priority for system 2 (S-2) is .6479.
Priority for system 3 (S-3) is .1222.

Consistency information:

Weighted sum vector = (.6902 1.9485 .3667)
Consistency vector = (3.0026 3.0071 3.0013)
Lambda = 3.0037
Value of CI = .0018
RI = .5800
CR = .0032

FLEXIBILITY	S-1	S-2	S-3
S-1		1/2	1/8
S-2			1/4
S-3			

Table for Factors for Problem E-9

FACTORS	PRICE	BRAND NAME	MEMORY	SPEED	FLEXIBILITY	PC COMPATIBILITY
Price		9	4	5	3	2
Brand name			1/2	1	1/4	1/5
Memory				2	1/2	1/6
Speed					1/3	1/6
Flexibility						1/2
PC compatible						

The following will be the priorities for flexibility:

Priority for system 1 (S-1) is .0909.
Priority for system 2 (S-2) is .1818.
Priority for system 3 (S-3) is .7273.

Consistency information follows:

Weighted sum vector = (.2727 .5455 2.1818)
Consistency vector = (3.0000 3.0000 3.0000)
Lambda = 3.0000
Value of CI = .0000
RI = .5800
CR = .0000

PC COMPATIBILITY	S-1	S-2	S-3
S-1		8	4
S-2			1/3
S-3			

The following will be the priorities for PC compatibility:

Priority for system 1 (S-1) is .7146.
Priority for system 2 (S-2) is .0789.
Priority for system 3 (S-3) is .2064.

Consistency information follows:

Weighted sum vector = (2.1717 .2371 .6218)
Consistency vector = (3.0389 3.0040 3.0122)
Lambda = 3.0184
Value of CI = .0092
RI = .5800
CR = .0158

The following will be the weights for the factors:

Weight for price is .3849.
Weight for brand name is .0447.
Weight for memory is .0816.
Weight for speed is .0514.
Weight for flexibility is .1493.
Weight for PC compatibility is .2880.

See Table for Factors for Problem E-9.

Consistency information follows:

$$\text{Weighted sum vector} = \begin{pmatrix} 2.3946 & .2746 & .4927 \\ .3117 & .9179 & 1.8008 \end{pmatrix}$$

$$\text{Consistency vector} = \begin{pmatrix} 6.2208 & 6.1480 & 6.0362 \\ 6.0592 & 6.1485 & 6.2518 \end{pmatrix}$$

Value of CI = .0288
RI = 1.2400
CR = .0232

The following are the final rankings—System 1 (S-1) is selected.

ITEM	RANKING
System 1 (S-1)	.4928
System 2 (S-2)	.2400
System 3 (S-3)	.2671

F
Using AB:QM

LEARNING OBJECTIVES

After completing this module, students will be able to:

1. Perform a number of beginning steps, including formatting blank disks, copying files, creating subdirectories, and getting a directory of files on a disk.
2. Use AB:QM in solving quantitative analysis problems.

TEACHING SUGGESTIONS

Teaching Suggestion F.1: Beginning steps.

Have the students start by formatting several blank disks. Students should then start a data disk, make a backup data disk, and make a backup copy of all program disks. Make sure that students understand basic DOS commands and the operation of their microcomputer.

Teaching Suggestion F.2: Beginning AB:QM.

A good way to have students start AB:QM is to have them run one of the problems at the end of one of the chapters where AB:QM is described. Students will not have to worry about formulating a problem or determining what data is needed. Instead, they can concentrate on how AB:QM works.

Quantitative Analysis
for Management

QUANTITATIVE METHODS AND APPLIED STATISTICS SERIES

ALLYN AND BACON

Barry Render, Consulting Editor
Roy E. Crummer Graduate School of Business, Rollins College

Readings in Production and Operations Management: A Productivity Approach
Ahmadian, Afifi, and Chandler

Introduction to Operations Research Techniques, Second Edition
Daellenbach, George, and McNickle

Managing Production: The Adventure
Fulmer

Business Forecasting, Fourth Edition
Hanke and Reitsch

Production and Operations Management: Strategies and Tactics, Third Edition
Heizer and Render

Cases in Business Statistics
Klimberg, Arnold, and Berger

Cases and Readings in Production and Operations Management
Latona and Nathan

Management Science, Fourth Edition
Moore, Lee, and Taylor

Micro Management Science: Microcomputer Applications of Management Science, Second Edition
Lee and Shim

AB:QM Version 3.0 Software
Lee

Service Operations Management
Murdick, Render, and Russell

Applied Statistics, Fourth Edition
Neter, Wasserman, and Whitmore

Microcomputer Software for Management Science and Operations Management, Second Edition
Render, Stair, Attaran, and Foeller

Principles of Operations Management: Building and Managing World Class Operations
Render and Heizer

Quantitative Analysis for Management, Fifth Edition
Render and Stair

Cases and Readings in Management Science, Second Edition
Render, Stair, and Greenberg

Production and Operations Management: A Self-Correcting Approach, Third Edition
Stair and Render

Operations Strategy
Stonebraker and Leong

Introduction to Management Science, Fourth Edition
Taylor

Brief Business Statistics
Watson, Billingsley, Croft, and Huntsberger

Statistics for Management and Economics, Fifth Edition
Watson, Billingsley, Huntsberger, and Croft

AB:POM Version 3.3 Software
Weiss

Production and Operations Management, Second Edition
Weiss and Gershon

A User's Guide to Business MYSTAT
Young

Quantitative Analysis for Management

BARRY RENDER

Charles Harwood Distinguished Professor of Management Science
Roy E. Crummer Graduate School of Business, Rollins College

RALPH M. STAIR, Jr.

Professor of Information and Management Sciences
Florida State University

Allyn and Bacon
BOSTON LONDON TORONTO SYDNEY TOKYO SINGAPORE

Editor in Chief, Business and Economics: Richard Wohl
Series Editorial Assistant: Jennifer Strada
Production Administrator: Marjorie Payne
Text Designer: Deborah Schneck
Cover Administrator: Linda Dickinson
Composition Buyer: Linda Cox
Manufacturing Buyer: Megan Cochran

Library of Congress Cataloging-in-Publication Data

Render, Barry.
 Quantitative analysis for management: annotated instructor's ed.
 /Barry Render, Ralph M. Stair.—5th ed.
  p. cm.
 Includes bibliographical references and index.
 ISBN 0-205-15379-8
 1. Management science. 2. Operations research. I. Stair, Ralph
M. II. Title.
 T56.R544 1993
 658.4′03—dc20   93-24363
                                                                 CIP

ISBN: 0-205-15383-6 (5¼″ disks)
      0-205-15382-8 (3½″ disks)

Printed in the United States of America

10 9 8 7 6 5 4 3 2 1   99 98 97 96 95 94

To our past, present and future students

Brief Contents

1 Introduction to Quantitative Analysis   1

2 Probability Concepts   25

3 Probability Distributions   47

4 Forecasting   81

5 Fundamentals of Decision Theory   137

6 Decision Trees and Utility Theory   177

7 Statistical Quality Control   223

8 Inventory Control Models: I   249

9 Inventory Control Models: II   277

10 Linear Programming: Graphical and Computer Methods   337

11 Linear Programming Applications: With Computer Analysis in AB:QM, STORM, LINDO, and What's*Best!*   387

12 Linear Programming: The Simplex Method   433

13 Linear Programming: Sensitivity Analysis and Duality   479

14 Transportation and Assignment Problems   515

15 Integer Programming, Goal Programming, and the Branch and Bound Method   585

16 Waiting Lines: Queuing Theory   635

17 Simulation   677

18 Network Models   723

19 Markov Analysis   793

Modules

A Mathematical Tools: Determinants and Matrices   825
B Game Theory   835
C Dynamic Programming   847
D Decision Theory and the Normal Distribution   859
E Multifactor Decision Making   869
F Using AB:QM   881

Appendixes   891

Contents

Preface   xv

1 Introduction to Quantitative Analysis   1

1.1 Introduction   2
1.2 What Is Quantitative Analysis?   2
■ **Applications of QA:** *The Indispensable Role of Management Science at Reynolds Metals Company*   5
1.3 The Quantitative Analysis Approach   3
■ **Applications of QA:** *Using QA to Clean Up the Big Apple*   8
1.4 Possible Problems in the QA Approach   9
1.5 Implementation—Not Just the Final Step   12
1.6 Quantitative Analysis and Computer-Based Information Systems   14
1.7 Use of AB:QM, STORM, and Spreadsheets   18
1.8 Summary   22

Glossary   22   Discussion Questions   23
Bibliography   24

2 Probability Concepts   25

2.1 Introduction   26
2.2 Fundamental Concepts   26
2.3 Mutually Exclusive Collectively Exhaustive Events   29
2.4 Statistically Independent Events   31
2.5 Statistically Dependent Events   33
■ **Applications of QA:** *Qantas Airways*   35
2.6 Revising Probabilities with Bayes's Theorem   36
2.7 Further Probability Revisions   38
2.8 Summary   39

Glossary   39   Key Equations   40
Discussion Questions and Problems   41
Bibliography   44   Appendix: Derivation of Bayes's Theorem   45

3 Probability Distributions   47

3.1 Introduction   48
3.2 Random Variables   48
3.3 Probability Distributions   50
3.4 The Binomial Distribution   56
3.5 The Poisson Distribution   59
3.6 The Normal Distribution   61
■ **Applications of QA:** *Using Probability Distributions to Search for Sunken Gold*   61
3.7 The Exponential Distribution   69
3.8 Summary   70

Glossary   71   Key Equations   72
Discussion Questions and Problems   73
Case Studies: WTVX   78   Century Chemical Company   78   Bibliography   79

4 Forecasting   81

4.1 Introduction   82
4.2 Types of Forecasts   83
4.3 Scatter Diagrams   84
4.4 Time Series Forecasting Models   85
4.5 Causal Forecasting Methods   100
4.6 Monitoring and Controlling Forecasts   106
■ **Applications of QA:** *Flood Forecasting at NOAA*   108
4.7 Using the Computer to Forecast   109
4.8 Summary   116

Glossary   118   Key Equations   118   Solved Problems   120   Discussion Questions and Problems   122   Case Studies: The North-South Airline   130   Kwik Lube   131 Bibliography   132   Appendix: Forecasting with Spreadsheets   133

5 Fundamentals of Decision
Theory   137

5.1 Introduction   138
5.2 The Six Steps in Decision Theory   138
5.3 Types of Decision-Making
Environments   140
5.4 Decision Making under Risk   141
5.5 Decision Making under Uncertainty   146
■ **Applications of QA:** *Using Decision
Theory in Forest Management*   149
5.6 Marginal Analysis with a Large Number
of Alternatives and States of Nature   150
5.7 Using the Computer to Solve Decision
Theory Problems   155
5.8 Summary   157

Glossary   158   Key Equations   159   Solved
Problems   159   Discussion Questions and
Problems   162   Case Study: Starting Right
Corporation   170   Bibliography   171
Appendix: Solving Decision Theory Problems
with Spreadsheets   171

6 Decision Trees and Utility
Theory   177

6.1 Introduction   178
6.2 Decision Trees   178
■ **Applications of QA:** *Testing Student
Athletes for Drug Use: A Decision-Making
Model*   184
6.3 How Probability Values Are Estimated by
Bayesian Analysis   185
■ **Applications of QA:** *Decision Trees in
Selecting Drilling Sites*   188
6.4 Utility Theory   188
6.5 Use of AB:QM in Decision Theory   195
6.6 Summary   200

Glossary   200   Key Equations   201   Solved
Problems   201   Discussion Questions and
Problems   206   Case Study: Blake
Electronics   216   Sixty-Six Year-Old Patient
with a Hernia   218   Bibliography   218
Appendix: Using Spreadsheet Analysis to
Solve Decision Tree and Bayesian Analysis
Problems   219

7 Statistical Quality Control   223

7.1 Introduction   224
7.2 Defining and Measuring Quality   224

7.3 Total Quality Management (TQM)   226
7.4 Statistical Process Control (SPC)   227
■ **Applications of QA:** *How Velcro Got
Hooked on Quality*   227
7.5 Control Charts for Variables   229
■ **Applications of QA:** *Stalking Six Sigma at
Motorola*   230
7.6 Control Charts for Attributes   235
7.7 Summary   237

Glossary   238   Key Equations   238   Solved
Problems   239   Discussion Questions and
Problems   240   Case Studies: Bayfield Mud
Company   244   Morristown *Daily
Tribune*   246   Bibliography   247

8 Inventory Control Models: I   249

8.1 Introduction   250
8.2 Importance of Inventory Control   251
■ **Applications of QA:** *Using Expert Systems
in Inventory Management and
Logistics*   253
8.3 The Inventory Decision   253
8.4 Economic Order Quantity (EOQ):
Determining How Much to Order   254
8.5 Reorder Point (ROP): Determining When
to Order   260
8.6 Fixed Period Inventory Control
System   261
■ **Applications of QA:** *Inland Steel Uses
Systems Contracts to Control Inventory
Costs*   261
8.7 Sensitivity Analysis   264
■ **Applications of QA:** *Blue Bell Trims Its
Inventory*   265
8.8 Summary   266

Glossary   267   Key Equations   267   Solved
Problems   268   Discussion Questions and
Problems   269   Case Studies: Sturdivant
Sound Systems   273   Western Ranchman
Outfitters   274   Bibliography   275
Appendix: Determining EOQ with
Calculus   275   Appendix: Using
Spreadsheet Analysis to Solve Basic Inventory
Problems   276

9 Inventory Control Models: II   277

9.1 Introduction   278
9.2 EOQ without the Instantaneous Receipt
Assumption   278

9.3 Quantity Discount Models 282
9.4 Planned Shortages 285
9.5 Use of Safety Stock 290
9.6 ABC Analysis and Joint Ordering 298
9.7 Dependent Demand: The Case for Material Requirements Planning (MRP) 300
9.8 The Kanban System 307
■ **Applications of QA:** *Using Just-in-Time (JIT) Principles to Improve Ecuador's Health Care Delivery System* 308
9.9 Using the Computer to Solve Inventory Control Problems 310
9.10 Summary 319

Glossary 319   Key Equations 320   Solved Problems 321   Discussion Questions and Problems 323   Case Study: Professional Video Management 331   Bibliography 333   Appendix: Solving the Planned Shortages (Back Order) Model with Calculus 333   Appendix: Using Spreadsheets to Solve Inventory Problems 334

10 Linear Programming: Graphical and Computer Methods 337

10.1 Introduction 338
10.2 Requirements of a Linear Programming Problem 338
10.3 Formulating Linear Programming Problems 340
10.4 Graphical Solution to a Linear Programming Problem 342
■ **Applications of QA:** *Linear Programming at New England Apple Products* 343
■ **Applications of QA:** *Selecting Tenants in a Shopping Mall* 348
10.5 Solving Flair Furniture's LP Problem by AB:QM, STORM, LINDO, and What's*Best!* 353
10.6 An Introduction to Sensitivity Analysis 356
10.7 Solving Minimization Problems 358
■ **Applications of QA:** *Manpower Planning at United Airlines with LP* 359
10.8 Summary of the Graphical Solution Method 363
10.9 A Few Special Issues in Linear Programming 365

Glossary 370   Solved Problems 371   Discussion Questions and Problems 374   Case Study: Golding Landscaping and Plants,

Inc. 382   Bibliography 383   Appendix: Linear Programming with Spreadsheet Software 384

11 Linear Programming Applications: With Computer Analyses in AB:QM, STORM, LINDO, and What's*Best!* 387

11.1 Introduction 388
11.2 Marketing Applications 388
11.3 Manufacturing Applications 392
11.4 Employee Scheduling Applications 400
■ **Applications of QA:** *Crew Pairing Optimization at American Airlines* 406
11.5 Financial Applications 408
11.6 Transportation Applications 409
11.7 Ingredient Blending Applications 415

Problems 420   Case Study: Chase Manhattan Bank 431

12 Linear Programming: The Simplex Method 433

12.1 Introduction 434
12.2 How to Set Up the Initial Simplex Solution 434
12.3 Simplex Solution Procedures 440
12.4 The Second Simplex Tableau 441
12.5 Developing the Third Tableau 446
12.6 Review of Procedures for Solving LP Maximization Problems 449
12.7 Surplus and Artificial Variables 450
12.8 Solving Minimization Problems 452
12.9 Review of Procedures for Solving LP Minimization Problems 461
12.10 Special Cases in Using the Simplex Method 461
12.11 Karmarkar's Algorithm 464
■ **Applications of QA:** *Finding Fast Algorithms Means Better Airline Service* 465
12.12 Summary 466

Glossary 466   Key Equation 467   Solved Problems 468   Discussion Questions and Problems 470   Case Study: Coastal States Chemicals and Fertilizers 476   Bibliography 477

13 Linear Programming: Sensitivity Analysis and Duality 479

13.1 Introduction 480
13.2 Sensitivity Analysis 480
13.3 The Dual in Linear Programming 490
■ **Applications of QA:** *Linear Programming at Dairyman's Cooperative* 491
■ **Applications of QA:** *Optimizing Wood Procurement in Cabinet Manufacturing* 494
13.4 The Role of Computer Software in Sensitivity Analysis: Looking at High Note Sound Company with AB:QM, STORM, LINDO, and What'sBest! 495
13.5 Summary 495

Glossary 500   Solved Problem 501
Discussion Questions and Problems 503
Case Study: Red Brand Canners 512

14 Transportation and Assignment Problems 515

14.1 Introduction 516
14.2 Setting Up a Transportation Problem 518
14.3 Developing an Initial Solution: Northwest Corner Rule 520
14.4 Stepping-Stone Method: Finding a Least-Cost Solution 522
■ **Applications of QA:** *Transportation Problem for Irish Pharmaceutical Distributor* 529
14.5 MODI Method 529
14.6 Vogel's Approximation Method: Another Way to Find an Initial Solution 532
14.7 Unbalanced Transportation Problems 536
■ **Applications of QA:** *Moving Sand with the Transportation Approach* 538
14.8 Degeneracy in Transportation Problems 539
14.9 More than One Optimal Solution 542
14.10 Computer Solutions to the Transportation Problem 542
14.11 Facility Location Analysis 546
14.12 Approach of the Assignment Model 547
14.13 Dummy Rows and Dummy Columns 555

■ **Applications of QA:** *Scheduling American League Umpires with the Assignment Model* 556
14.14 Maximization Assignment Problems 557
14.15 Using the Computer to Solve Assignment Problems 558

Glossary 561   Key Equations 562   Solved Problems 562   Discussion Questions and Problems 569   Case Studies: Custom Vans, Inc. 581   Old Oregon Wood Store 583   Bibliography 584

15 Integer Programming, Goal Programming, and the Branch and Bound Method 585

15.1 Introduction 586
15.2 Integer Programming 586
■ **Applications of QA:** *Selling Seats at American Airlines Using Integer Programming* 591
15.3 The Branch and Bound Method 596
■ **Applications of QA:** *An Integer Programming System for Assigning Classes to Rooms* 597
15.4 Goal Programming 605
■ **Applications of QA:** *Branch and Bound Technique for Establishing Insurance Sales Territories* 606
15.5 Nonlinear Programming 616
■ **Applications of QA:** *A Goal Programming Model for Prison Expenditures in Virginia* 620
15.6 Summary 621

Glossary 621   Solved Problems 622
Discussion Questions and Problems 624
Case Studies: Schank Marketing Research 630   The Oakton River Bridge 630   The Puyallup Mall 631
Bibliography 632

16 Waiting Lines: Queuing Theory 635

16.1 Introduction 636
16.2 Waiting Line Costs 636
16.3 Characteristics of a Queuing System 639
■ **Applications of QA:** *Queuing Theory at Eastman Kodak* 642

16.4 Single-Channel Queuing Model with Poisson Arrivals and Exponential Service Times 644

■ **Applications of QA:** *Queuing up Customers on L. L. Bean's Phone Network* 645

16.5 Multiple-Channel Queuing Model with Poisson Arrivals and Exponential Service Times 650

16.6 Constant Service Time Model 655

16.7 Finite Population Model 656

16.8 More Complex Queuing Models and the Use of Simulation 659

16.9 Summary 660

Glossary 660   Key Equations 661   Solved Problems 663   Discussion Questions and Problems 666   Case Studies: The Shader Lane Hotel 672   New England Castings 673   Bibliography 674   Appendix: Queuing Analysis with Spreadsheets 675

17 Simulation 677

17.1 Introduction 678

17.2 Advantages and Disadvantages of Simulation 679

17.3 Monte Carlo Simulation 681

17.4 Simulation and Inventory Analysis 687

17.5 Simulation of a Queuing Problem 692

17.6 Simulation Model for a Maintenance Policy 696

■ **Applications of QA:** *Simulating Canadian National Railways Line Capacity* 697

■ **Applications of QA:** *Simulating Automation at the U.S. Postal Service* 700

17.7 Two Other Types of Simulation Models 701

17.8 Role of Computers in Simulation 703

■ **Applications of QA:** *The Integration of Simulation and Other Models for Netherlands Water Planning* 704

17.9 Summary 705

Glossary 705   Solved Problems 706   Discussion Questions and Problems 709   Case Studies: Biales Waste Disposal, GmbH 718   Abjar Transport Company 719   Bibliography 719   Appendix: Conducting a Simulation with Spreadsheets 720

18 Network Models 723

18.1 Introduction 724

18.2 PERT 726

18.3 PERT/Cost 740

18.4 Critical Path Method 745

18.5 Minimal-Spanning Tree Technique 750

18.6 Maximal-Flow Technique 754

18.7 Shortest-Route Technique 758

18.8 Using the Computer to Solve Network Problems 761

18.9 Summary 772

Glossary 772   Key Equations 774   Solved Problems 774   Discussion Questions and Problems 776   Case Studies: Haygood Brothers Construcion Company 786   Bay Community Hospital 787   The Ranch Development Project 788   Bibliography 789   Appendix: Using Spreadsheets to Solve Network Problems 790

19 Markov Analysis 793

19.1 Introduction 794

19.2 States and State Probabilities: A Grocery Store Example 794

19.3 Matrix of Transition Probabilities 796

19.4 Predicitng Future Market Shares 798

19.5 Markov Analysis of Machine Operations 798

19.6 Equilibrium Conditions 800

19.7 Absorbing States and the Fundamental Matrix: An Accounts Receivable Application 803

■ **Applications of QA:** *Using Markov Analysis to Forecast Long-Term Care* 807

19.8 Solving Markov Analysis Problems by Computer 808

19.9 Summary 810

Glossary 810   Key Equations 810   Solved Problems 811   Discussion Questions and Problems 815   Case Study: Rentall Trucks 821   Bibliography 822   Appendix: Using Spreadsheets to Solve Markov Analysis Problems 823

Modules

 A Mathematical Tools: Determinants and Matrices   825

A.1 Introduction   826
A.2 Determinants   826
A.3 Matrices   827
A.4 Summary   831

Glossary   832   Problems   832
Bibliography   833

 B Game Theory   835

B.1 Introduction   836
B.2 Language of Games   836
B.3 Pure Strategy Games   837
B.4 Minimax Criterion   837
B.5 Mixed Strategy Games   838
B.6 Dominance   840
B.7 Games Larger Than 2 × 2   841
B.8 Using the Computer to Solve Game Theory Problems   843
B.9 Summary   843

Glossary   843   Discussion Questions and Problems   843   Bibliography   846

 C Dynamic Programming   847

C.1 Introduction   848
C.2 A Shortest-Route Problem Solved by Dynamic Programming   848
■ **Applications of QA:** *Dynamic Programming at Weyerhaeuser*   849
C.3 Dynamic Programming Terminology   852
■ **Applications of QA:** *Using Dynamic Programming to Assist in the Scheduling of Operation Desert Storm Airlift Operations*   853
C.4 Using the Computer to Solve Dynamic Programming Problems   854

Glossary   856   Discussion Questions and Problems   856   Bibliography   857

 D Decision Theory and the Normal Distribution   859

D.1 Introduction   860
D.2 Break-Even Analysis and the Normal Distribution   860
D.3 EVPI and the Normal Distribution   863
D.4 Summary   864

Glossary   865   Key Equations   865
Discussion Questions and Problems   865
Appendix: Derivation of Break-Even Point   867

 E Multifactor Decision Making   869

E.1 Introduction   870
E.2 The Multifactor Evaluation Process   870
E.3 The Analytic Hierarchy Process   871
E.4 A Comparison of MFEP and AHP   876
E.5 Summary   876

Glossary   877   Key Equations   877
Discussion Questions and Problems   877
Bibliography   879

F Using AB:QM   881

F.1 Introduction   882
F.2 Basic Requirements for AB:QM   883
F.3 Starting AB:QM   883
F.4 Using AB:QM   884
F.5 A Forecasting Example of AB:QM   886
F.6 Limitations of AB:QM   889

APPENDIXES

A. Areas Under the Standard Normal Table   A-2
B. Unit Normal Loss Integral   A-3
C. Cumulative Binomial Distribution   A-4
D. Values for $e^{-\lambda}$ for use in the Poisson Distribution   A-15

Solutions to Selected Problems   S-1

Preface

Overview

This fifth edition of *Quantitative Analysis for Management* continues to provide the reader with the skills to apply the techniques of quantitative analysis in all kinds of organizational decision-making situations. The chapters cover every major topic in the quantitative analysis/management science field. There is probably more material included than most instructors can cover in a typical first course, but we have found that the resulting flexibility of topic selection is appreciated by instructors who need to tailor their courses to different audiences and curricula.

We show how each technique works, discuss the assumptions and limitations of the models, and illustrate the real-world usefulness of each technique with many applications in both profit-making and nonprofit organizations. We have kept the notation, terminology, and equations standard with other books. As in the first four editions, we have tried to write a text that is easy to understand and use. Algebra is the only mathematics prerequisite.

Features Retained from the Previous Edition

This book is student oriented; the following features have proved to be effective aids to the learning process.

- Key idea markers are placed in the margin to highlight especially important concepts.

- Margin notes highlight other important points.

- QA Application boxes summarize published articles illustrating how real organizations have used quantitative analysis to solve problems.

- History boxes briefly describe how a technique was discovered.

- Glossaries at the end of each chapter define important terms.

- Key equations are listed at the end of each chapter, which summarize the mathematical material.

- Discussion questions at the end of each chapter test the student's understanding of concepts.

- Problems in every chapter are applications-oriented and test the student's ability to solve exam-type problems. They are graded by three levels: introductory (1 dot), moderate (2 dots), and challenging (three dots).

- Case studies at the ends of most chapters provide challenging managerial applications.

- End-of-chapter bibliographies provide a selection of more advanced books and interesting, practical articles.

- Solved problems, included at the ends of chapters, serve as models for students in solving their own homework problems.

- Data set problems, which require the computer to solve larger amounts of data presented, are found in most chapters. These real-world problems are also available to instructors on data disks.

- AB:QM software (standing for Allyn and Bacon: Quantitative Methods), developed by Professor Sang Lee, accompanies this text. The software closely matches the approach and terminology of our book and is documented in Module F and throughout appropriate chapters.

- LINDO and STORM software, which are popular alternatives to AB:QM, are also illustrated throughout the text.

- TIMS and COMAP videos, which tie directly to QA Applications boxes found throughout the book, are available for classroom use. The TIMS videos are edited versions of the award-winning presentations at the annual meeting.

Key Changes in the Fifth Edition

- *New appendixes in many chapters that describe how to solve management science problems by spreadsheet.* These stress the ease of developing spreadsheet formulas to solve problems in selected chapters.

- *Chapter 7 on quality and statistical process control.* New chapter covering quality and statistical process control. This chapter reflects the growing importance of quality control and total quality management. It stresses the four major types of statistical control charts.

- *New and enhanced end-of-chapter problems.* The fifth edition contains a number of new problems. In addition, many of the problems from the previous edition have been updated.

- *New Cases.* There are new cases for many of the chapters. Some of the cases require students to determine what data are needed to solve the case.

Reorganization of the treatment of linear programming. The four chapters on LP (10–13) have been reordered and reorganized to place more emphasis on the formulation of LP problems and the use of software to solve them. The first chapter deals with graphical and computer solutions, illustrating AB:QM, STORM, LINDO and What's*Best!* software. The second (Chapter 11) formulates ten large and diverse problems, then solves each with either AB:QM, STORM, LINDO, or What's*Best!* software. Chapter 12 addresses the simplex method, and the final LP chapter deals with Sensitivity Analysis and Duality. Bundling the book with LINDO is an option. PC LINDO may now be packaged with this text at a substantial discount.

Inclusion of the finite population queuing model in Chapter 16. This waiting line model is added to illustrate a common situation in which the number of arrivals at a service system is limited or finite.

- *Module F on AB:QM software.* A new module on the use of AB:QM software has been included to help students use this powerful set of programs.

- *Expanded and updated coverage of computer-based information systems.* Chapter 1 contains expanded and updated coverage of computer-based information systems (CBIS). The components of a CBIS are covered. In addition, the use of management information systems (MIS), decision support systems (DSS), and expert systems (ES) in quantitative analysis are covered in Chapter 1.

- *New application boxes and videos.* Most chapters have new application boxes that show the use of QA in business and government. In addition, there are seven new TIMS videos. These new videos complement the dozen videos used with the fourth edition.

- *Module E on multifactor decision making.* Module E is a new module on multifactor decision making, including the analytic hierarchy process (AHP). This module takes material from Chapter 6 to reflect the importance that many instructors place on this material today. This makes Chapter 6 shorter and in line with the length of other chapters in the book.

- *Inclusion of marginal analysis in Chapter 5.* Marginal analysis, which was in Chapter 7, has been placed in Chapter 5 on decision theory. This module shows students how marginal analysis can be used to handle large decision-making problems where a marginal profit and loss can be identified.

- *Module D on decision theory and the normal distribution.* Module D contains material on decision theory and the normal distribution. This material was in Chapter 7 in the fourth edition.

SUPPLEMENTS

We have a complete supplement package. Details of the package can be found in the Annotated Instructor's Edition. It includes:

- An Annotated Instructor's Edition
- A Study Guide by John Harpell at West Virginia University

- A Testbank prepared by Michael Hanna at the University of Houston. This testbank is also available on our computerized testing software, the *A&B Test Manager.*

- 200 Transparency Masters

- Two videotapes: one from The Institute of Management Sciences (The Edelman Award Winners) and the other from The Consortium for Mathematics and Its Applications ("For All Practical Purposes") developed with major funding by the Annenberg/CPB Project. Many are new for this edition.

- AB:QM Software in either a 5¼" or 3½" format

- Data Disk for marked problems

- STORM Software is available as an option.

- PC LINDO may be packaged with the text.

ACKNOWLEDGMENTS

We gratefully thank the many users of the previous editions who provided many important suggestions and ideas for this edition. The Roy E. Crummer School of Business at Rollins College and the Department of Information and Management Science at The Florida State University provided support and a conducive environment for development of this text. Professor Jerry Kinard (Dean at Francis Marion College) and the late Professor Joe C. Iverstine contributed several fine cases. Professor Michael Hanna at the University of Houston prepared the test bank. Professor John Harpell at West Virginia University prepared the Study Guide. Thanks to all.

We would also like to express our appreciation to the reviewers of the past and present editions:

Past Editions:
Stephen Achtenhagen, *San Jose University*
Robert Fiore, *Springfield College*
Irwin Greenberg, *George Mason University*
Gordon Jacox, *Weber State College*
Douglas Lonnstrom, *Siena College*
Ralph Miller, *California State Polytechnic University*
David Murphy, *Boston College*
Robert Myers, *University of Louisville*
Alan D. Olinsky, *Bryant College*
Savas Ozatalay, *Widener University*
William Rife, *West Virginia University*
John Swearingen, *Bryant College*
Grover Rodich, *Portland State University*
F. S. Tanaka, *Slippery Rock State University*
Jack Taylor, *Portland State University*
M. Keith Thomas, *Olivet College*

James Vigen, *California State College, Bakersfield*
William Webster, *The University of Texas at San Antonio*
Edward Chu, *California State University, Dominguez Hills*
L.W. Shell, *Nicholls State University*
M. Jill Austin, *Middle Tennesee State University*
Frank G. Forst, *Loyola University of Chicago*
Michael E. Hanna, *University of Houston-Clear Lake*
Darlene R. Lanier, *Louisiana State University*
Jooh Lee, *Glassboro State College*
Harvey Nye, *Central State University*
Ed Gillenwater, *University of Mississippi*
Robert R. Hill, *University of Houston-Clear Lake*

Present Edition:
Rodney L. Carlson, *Tennessee Technological University*
Shad Dowlatshahi, *University of Wisconsin, Platteville*
Wade Ferguson, *Western Kentucky University*
Cy Peebles, *Eastern Kentucky University*
Ranga Ramasesh, *Texas Christian University*
Chris Vertullo, *Marist College*
Larry Weinstein, *Eastern Kentucky University*

 **The Institute of Management Sciences,** a leading international association in the field of management science, contributes to the video component of this package. The work in the videotapes, representing the best in management science practice, has been excerpted from videotapes of complete presentations from the Institute's Annual Franz Edelman Award for Management Science Achievement.

For further information or a complete catalogue of videos, write to: TIMS, 290 Westminster St., Providence, RI 02903.

Introduction to Quantitative Analysis

CHAPTER OUTLINE

1.1 Introduction

1.2 What Is Quantitative Analysis?

1.3 The Quantitative Analysis Approach

1.4 Possible Problems in the QA Approach

1.5 Implementation—Not Just the Final Step

1.6 Quantitative Analysis and Computer-Based Information Systems

1.7 Use of AB:QM, STORM, and Spreadsheets

1.8 Summary

Glossary

Discussion Questions

Bibliography

1.1   INTRODUCTION

People have been using mathematical tools to help solve problems for thousands of years; however, the formal study and application of quantitative techniques to practical decision making is largely a product of the twentieth century. The techniques we will study in this book have been successfully applied to an increasingly wide variety of complex problems in business, government, health care, education, and many other areas. Many such successful uses will be discussed throughout this book.

It isn't enough though just to know the mathematics of how a particular quantitative technique works; you must also be familiar with the limitations, assumptions, and specific applicability of the technique. The successful use of quantitative techniques usually results in a solution that is timely, accurate, flexible, economical, reliable, and easy to understand and use.

1.2   WHAT IS QUANTITATIVE ANALYSIS?

KEY IDEA

quantitative analysis defined

Transparency Master 1.1: Overview of Quantitative Analysis.

Teaching Suggestion 1.1: The Importance of Qualitative Factors. See the Instructor's Section for details.

quantitative analysis, qualitative factors

Transparency Master 1.2: The Decision-Making Process.

Teaching Suggestion 1.2: Discussing Other Quantitative Analysis Problems. See the Instructor's Section for details.

Quantitative analysis is the scientific approach to managerial decision making. Whim, emotions, and guesswork are not part of the quantitative analysis approach. This approach starts with data. Like raw material for a factory, these data are manipulated or processed into information that is valuable to people making decisions. This processing and manipulating of raw data into meaningful information is the heart of quantitative analysis. Computers have been instrumental in the increasing use of quantitative analysis.

In solving a problem, managers must consider both qualitative and quantitative factors. For example, we might consider several different investment alternatives, including certificates of deposit at a bank, investments in the stock market, and an investment in real estate. We can use quantitative analysis to determine how much our investment will be worth in the future when deposited at a bank at a given interest rate for a certain number of years. Quantitative analysis can also be used in computing financial ratios from the balance sheets for several companies whose stock we are considering. Some real estate companies have developed computer programs that use quantitative analysis to analyze cash flows and rates of return for investment property.

In addition to quantitative analysis, *qualitative* factors should also be considered. The weather, state and federal legislation, new technological breakthroughs, the outcome of an election, and so on may all be factors that are difficult to quantify.

Because of the importance of qualitative factors, the role of quantitative analysis in the decision-making process can vary. When there is a lack of qualitative factors and when the problem, model, and input data remain the same, the results of quantitative analysis can *automate* the decision-making process. For example, some companies use quantitative inventory models to determine automatically *when* to order additional new materials.

In most cases, however, quantitative analysis will be an *aid* to the decision-making process. The results of quantitative analysis will be combined with other (qualitative) information in making decisions.

1.3 THE QUANTITATIVE ANALYSIS APPROACH

The quantitative analysis approach consists of defining a problem, developing a model, acquiring input data, developing a solution, testing the solution, analyzing the results, and implementing the results. See Figure 1.1. One step does not have to be completely finished before the next is started; in most cases one or more of these steps will be modified to some extent before the final results are implemented. This would cause all of the subsequent steps to be changed. In some cases, testing the solution might reveal that the model or the input data is not correct. This would mean that all steps that follow defining the problem would need to be modified.

Defining the Problem

The first step in the quantitative approach is to develop a clear, concise statement of the problem. This statement will give direction and meaning to the following steps.

In many cases, defining the problem is the most important and the most difficult step. It is essential to go beyond the symptoms of the problem and identify the true causes. One problem may be related to other problems; solving one problem without regard to other related problems can make the entire situation worse. Thus, it is important to analyze how the solution to one problem impacts on other problems or on the situation in general.

It is likely that an organization will have *several* problems. However, a quantitative analysis group usually cannot deal with all of an organization's problems at one time. Thus, it is usually necessary to concentrate on

concentrate on only a few problems

HISTORY

The Origin of Quantitative Analysis

Quantitative analysis has been in existence since the beginning of recorded history, but it was Frederick W. Taylor who in the 1900s pioneered the principles of the scientific approach to management. During World War II, many new scientific and quantitative techniques were developed to assist the military. These new developments were so successful that after World War II many companies started using similar techniques in managerial decision making and planning. Today, many organizations employ a staff of operations research or management science personnel or consultants to apply the principles of scientific management to problems and opportunities. In this book, we use the terms *management science, operations research,* and *quantitative analysis* interchangeably.

The origin of many of the techniques discussed in this book can be traced to individuals and organizations that have applied the principles of scientific management first developed by Taylor; they are discussed in "history boxes" scattered throughout this text.

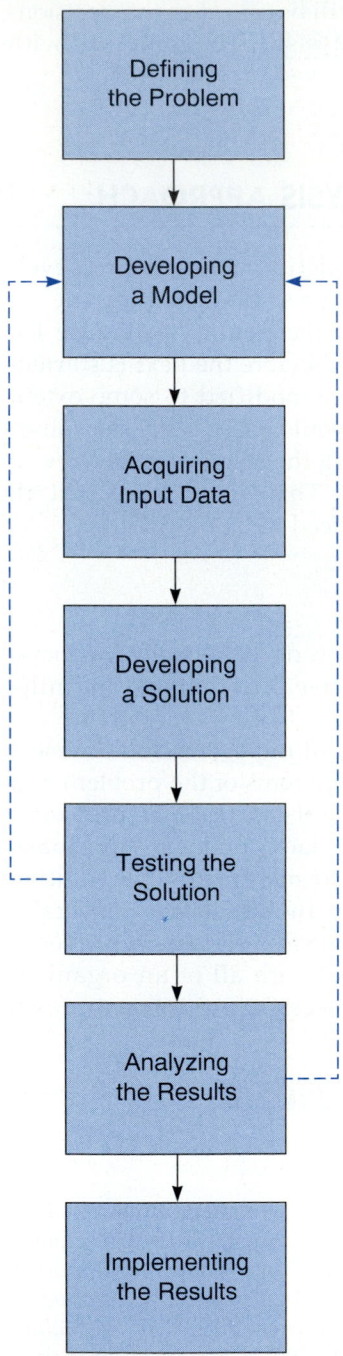

FIGURE 1.1
The Quantitative Analysis Approach

only a few problems. For most companies, this means selecting those problems whose solutions will result in the greatest increase in profits or reduction in costs to the company. The importance of selecting the right

APPLICATIONS OF QA

The Indispensable Role of Management Science at Reynolds Metals Company

Throughout this book, we will highlight the successful application of management science and quantitative analysis. As the title of this article implies, quantitative approaches can be indispensable in helping companies such as the Reynolds Metals Company. Headquartered in Richmond, Virginia, Reynolds is a Fortune 75 metals producer. Its aluminum operation includes production, mining, and the use of recycled aluminum. Of the company's $6.2 billion in sales in 1989, over 94% was in valued-added fabricated products, including aluminum cans, flexible packaging, and a variety of consumer products.

In order to provide a more effective shipping operation, the Reynolds Metals Company decided to use management science to control shipping and reduce transportation costs. The result was the use of an integer programming model (see Chapter 15) that had the minimization of central dispatch freight cost as a primary objective. Using the annual shipping demand patterns, this quantitative analysis technique was able to improve on-time delivery of shipments and reduce freight costs by over $7 million annually. As a company spokesperson said: "The confidence and respect I have for the management science discipline gave me the resolve to stick to the project plan when others doubted it could be done. I am very pleased to report today that the results that were predicted are being achieved. Management science made the difference between success and failure for this venture." As discussed in this application and other applications presented in this book, quantitative analysis techniques are playing an indispensable role for organizations throughout the world.

Source: William E. Moore, Jr., Janice M. Warmke, and Lonny R. Gorban. "The Indispensable Role of Management Science in Centralizing Freight Operation at Reynolds Metals Company," *Interfaces,* **21,** 1 (January-February 1991): 107–129.

problems to solve cannot be overemphasized. Experience has shown that bad problem definition is a major reason for failure of management science or operations research groups to serve their organizations well.

When the problem is difficult to quantify, it may be necessary to develop *specific, measurable* objectives. A problem might be inadequate health care delivery in a hospital. The objectives might be to increase the number of beds, reduce the average number of days a patient spends in the hospital, increase the doctor-to-patient ratio, and so on. When objectives are used, however, the real problem should be kept in mind. It is important to avoid obtaining specific and measurable objectives that may not solve the real problem.

Developing a Model

Once we select the problem to be analyzed, the next step is to develop a *model.* Simply stated, a model is a representation (usually mathematical) of a situation.

Even though you might not have been aware of it, you have been using models most of your life. You may have developed models about people's behavior. Your model might be that friendship is based on reciprocity, an exchange of favors. If you need a favor like a small loan, your model would suggest that you ask a good friend.

Transparency Master 1.5:
Models and the Techniques of Scientific Management.

Transparency Master 1.6:
Advantages of Using Models.

Transparency Master 1.7:
Using Models: Some Suggestions.

types of models

Of course, there are many other types of models. Architects sometimes make a *physical model* of a building that they will construct. Engineers develop *scale models* of chemical plants, called pilot plants. A *schematic model* is a picture, drawing, or chart of reality. Automobiles, lawn mowers, gears, fans, typewriters, and numerous other devices have schematic models (drawings and pictures) that reveal how these devices work. What sets quantitative analysis apart from other techniques is that the models that are used are mathematical. A *mathematical model* is a set of mathematical relationships. In most cases, these relationships are expressed in equations and inequalities.

variables and parameters

While there is considerable flexibility in the development of models, most of the models presented in this book will contain one or more variables and parameters. A *variable*, as the name implies, is a measurable quantity that may vary or is subject to change. Variables can be *controllable* or *uncontrollable*. A controllable variable is also called a *decision variable*. An example would be how many inventory items to order. A *parameter* is a measurable quantity that is inherent in the problem. The cost of placing an order for more inventory items is an example of a parameter. In most cases, variables are unknown quantities, while parameters are known quantities. All models should be carefully developed. They should be solvable, realistic, and easy to understand and modify, and the required input data should be obtainable. The model developer has to be careful to include the appropriate amount of detail to be solvable yet realistic.

Acquiring Input Data

Once we have developed a model, we must obtain the data that are used in the model (input data). Obtaining accurate data for the model is essential, since even if the model is a perfect representation of reality, improper data will result in misleading results. This situation is called garbage in, garbage out (GIGO). For a larger problem, collecting accurate data can be one of the most difficult steps in performing quantitative analysis.

garbage in, garbage out

There are a number of sources that can be used in collecting data. In some cases, company reports and documents can be used to obtain the necessary data. Another source is interviews with employees or other persons related to the firm. These individuals can sometimes provide excellent information, and their experience and judgments can be invaluable. A production foreman, for example, might be able to tell you with a great degree of accuracy the amount of time that it takes to produce a particular product. Sampling and direct measurement provide other sources of data for the model. You may need to know how many pounds of a raw material are used in producing a new photochemical product. This information can be obtained by going to the plant and actually measuring with scales the amount of raw material that is being used. In other cases, statistical sampling procedures can be used to obtain data.

Developing a Solution

Developing a solution involves manipulating the model to arrive at the best (optimal) solution to the problem. In some cases, this requires that an equation be solved for the best decision. In other cases, you can use a *trial and error* method, trying various approaches and picking the one that results in the best decision. For some problems, you may wish to try all posible values for the variables in the model to arrive at the best decision. This is called *complete enumeration.* This book will also show you how to solve very difficult and complex problems by repeating a few simple steps until you find the best solution. A series of steps or procedures that are repeated is called an *algorithm,* named after Algorismus, an Arab mathematician of the ninth century.

The accuracy of the solution depends on the accuracy of the input data and the model. If the input data are accurate to only two significant digits, then the results can be accurate to only two significant digits. For example, the results of dividing 2.6 by 1.4 should be 1.9 and not 1.857142857.

Testing the Solution

Before a solution can be analyzed and implemented, it needs to be completely tested. Because the solution depends on the input data and the model, both require testing.

Testing the input data and the model includes determining the accuracy and completeness of the data used by the model. Inaccurate data will lead to an inaccurate solution. There are several ways to test input data. One method of testing the data is to collect additional data from a different source. If the original data were collected using interviews, perhaps some additional data can be collected by direct measurement or sampling. These additional data can then be compared to the original data, and statistical tests can be employed to determine whether or not there are differences between the original data and the additional data. If there are significant differences, more effort is required to obtain accurate input data. If the data are accurate but the results are inconsistent with the problem, the model may not be appropriate. The model can be checked to make sure it is logical and represents the real situation.

testing the data and model

While most of the quantitative techniques discussed in this book have been computerized, you will most likely be required to solve a number of problems by hand. To help detect both logical and computational mistakes, you should check the results to make sure they are consistent with the structure of the problem. For example, $(1.96)(301.7)$ is close to $(2)(300)$, which is equal to 600. If your computations are significantly different from 600, you know you have made a mistake.

Analyzing the Results

Analyzing the results starts with determining the implications of the solution. In most cases, a solution to a problem will result in some kind of action or change in the way an organization is operating. The implications of these actions or changes must be determined and analyzed before the results are implemented.

Because a model is only an approximation of reality, the sensitivity of the solution to changes in the model and input data is a very important

the use of sensitivity
analysis

part of analyzing the results. This type of analysis is called *sensitivity analysis* or *postoptimality analysis.* It determines how much the solution will change if there were changes in the model or the input data. When the solution is sensitive to changes in the input data and the model specification, additional testing should be performed to make sure that the model and input data are accurate and valid. If the model or data are wrong, the solution could be wrong, resulting in financial losses or reduced profits.

Implementing the Results

Video 1.2: Polishing
the Big Apple.

The final step is to *implement* the results. This is the process of incorporating the solution into the company. This can be much more difficult than you would imagine. Even if the solution is optimal and will result in thousands of dollars in additional profits, if managers resist the new solution, all of the efforts of the analysis are of no value. Experience has shown that a large number of quantitative analysis teams have failed in their efforts because they have failed to implement a good, workable solution properly.

APPLICATIONS OF QA

Using QA to Clean Up the Big Apple

The Department of Sanitation of New York City faces a number of difficult problems. With about 12,000 employees and a half-billion-dollar annual budget, the department has the responsibility of keeping New York clean. But New York City had a reputation of being dirty. During the mid-1970s, a cleanliness rating system revealed that the city went from a 72% rating concerning its city streets to a very low 56%. In 1980, the department dipped even farther to a 53% overall rating, and it continued to drop in the 1980s. Many workers at the Department of Sanitation believed that street cleaning was low on the city's priority list compared, for example, to refuse collection. In general, staff and employee morale were low. Furthermore, there appeared to be little or no coordination with other agencies when it came to making the city a cleaner place to live. These problems prompted the department to take a closer look at some of the problems and to consider the use of quantitative analysis.

The QA models that were developed clearly showed a strong relationship between personnel levels and overall cleanliness. They also revealed that some districts in New York City had a much better payoff or a better utilization of personnel than others. Some areas, such as Wall Street, required about five times more cleaners than other

districts. Some models revealed that illegally parked cars caused problems with keeping the streets clean. Just one fewer car in some circumstances could mean a substantial improvement in the ability to keep streets or certain areas clean. Thus, one proposed solution called for cooperation between the Department of Sanitation and New York's Department of Transportation to coordinate a ticketing program to reduce the number of illegally parked cars.

Part of the overall solution was to develop a plan to improve worker morale. Programs were developed to give recognition to individuals in areas that were able to increase their overall cleanliness rating.

The results of the quantitative analysis approach were remarkable. After being fully implemented, the QA techniques led to near record levels of overall cleanliness and to great improvement in the productivity of the work force. It was also estimated that the techniques saved the city of New York about $12 million annually.

Source: Lucius J. Riccio, Joseph Miller, and Ann Litke, "Polishing the Big Apple: How Management Science Has Helped Make New York Streets Cleaner," *Interfaces,* **16,** 1 (January–February 1986): 83–88.

After the solution has been implemented, it should be closely monitored. Over time, there may be numerous changes that call for modifications of the original solution. A changing economy, fluctuating demand, and model enhancements requested by managers and decision makers are only a few examples of changes that might require the analysis to be modified.

Video 1.3: Management Science Overview

Transparency Master 1.8: Possible Problems.

1.4 POSSIBLE PROBLEMS IN THE QA APPROACH

We have presented the quantitative analysis approach as a logical, systematic means of tackling decision-making problems. Even when these steps are carefully followed, there are many difficulties that can hurt the chances of implementing solutions to real-world problems. We now take a look at what can happen during each of the steps.

Defining the Problem

One view of decision makers is that they sit at a desk all day long waiting until a problem arises and then stand up and attack the problem until it is solved. Once it is solved, they sit down, relax, and wait for the next big problem. In the worlds of business, government, and education, problems are, unfortunately, not easily identified. There are four roadblocks that quantitative analysts face in defining a problem. We use an application, inventory analysis, throughout this section as an example.

Transparency Master 1.9: Roadblocks to Be Faced in Defining a Problem.

KEY IDEA

Conflicting Viewpoints. The first difficulty is that quantitative analysts must often consider conflicting viewpoints in defining the problem. For example, there are at least two views that managers take when dealing with inventory problems. Financial managers usually feel that inventory is too high, as inventory represents cash not available for other investments. Sales managers, on the other hand, often feel that inventory is too low, as high levels of inventory may be needed to fill an unexpected order. If analysts assume either one of these statements as the problem definition, they have essentially accepted one manager's perception and can expect resistance from the other manager when the "solution" emerges. So it's important to consider both points of view before stating the problem.

Teaching Suggestion 1.4: Discussing Conflicting Viewpoints. See the Instructor's Section for details.

Impact on Other Departments. The next difficulty is that problems do not exist in isolation and are not owned by just one department of a firm. Inventory is closely tied with cash flows and various production problems. A change in ordering policy can seriously hurt cash flows and upset production schedules to the point that savings on inventory are more than offset by increased costs for finance and production. The problem statement should thus be as broad as possible and include the input from all departments that have a stake in the solution.

Beginning Assumptions. The third difficulty is that people have a tendency to state problems in terms of solutions. The statement that inventory is too low implies a solution that inventory levels should be raised. The

quantitative analyst who starts off with this assumption will probably indeed find that inventory should be raised. From an implementation standpoint, a "good" solution to the *right* problem is much better than an "optimal" solution to the *wrong* problem.

Solution Outdated. Even with the best of problem statements, however, there is a fourth danger. The problem can change as the model is being developed. In our rapidly changing business environment, it is not unusual for problems to appear or disappear virtually overnight. The analyst who presents a solution to a problem that no longer exists can't expect credit for providing timely help.

Developing a Model

Transparency Master 1.10:
Four Difficulties Faced in
Using Mathematical Models.

Fitting the Textbook Models. One problem in developing quantitative models is that a manager's perception of a problem won't always match the textbook approach. Most inventory models involve minimizing the total of holding and ordering costs. Some managers view these costs as unimportant; instead, they see the problem in terms of cash flow, turnover, and levels of customer satisfaction. Results of a model based on holding and ordering costs are probably not acceptable to such managers.

Transparency Master 1.11:
Limitations of Models.

Understanding the Model. A second major concern involves the trade-off between complexity of the model and ease of understanding. Managers simply will not use the results of a model they do not understand. Complex problems, though, require complex models. One trade-off is to simplify assumptions in order to make the model easier to understand. The model loses some of its reality but gains some acceptance by management.

One simplifying assumption in inventory modeling is that demand is known and constant. This means probability distributions are not needed and it allows us to build simple, easy-to-understand models. Demand, however, is rarely known and constant, so the model we build lacks some reality. Introducing probability distributions provides more realism but may put comprehension beyond all but the most mathematically sophisticated managers. One approach is for the quantitative analyst to start with the simple model and make sure it is completely understood. Later, more complex models can be slowly introduced as managers gain more confidence in using the new approach.

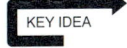
KEY IDEA

Acquiring Input Data

Teaching Suggestion 1.5:
The Difficulty of Getting Input
Data. See the Instructor's
Section for details.

Gathering the data to be used in the quantitative approach to problem solving is often no simple task. One-fifth of all firms in a recent study had difficulty with data access.

Using Accounting Data. One problem is that most data generated in a firm come from basic accounting reports. The accounting department collects its inventory data, for example, in terms of cash flows and turnover.

But quantitative analysts tackling an inventory problem need to collect data on holding costs and ordering costs. If they ask for such data, they may be shocked to find it was just never collected for those specified costs.

Gene Woolsey, former editor of the journal *Interfaces*, tells a story of a young quantitative analyst sent down to accounting to get "the inventory holding cost per item per day for part 23456/AZ." The accountant asked the young man if he wanted the first-in, first-out figure, the last-in, first-out figure, the lower of cost or market figure, or the "how-we-do-it" figure. The young man replied that the inventory model only required one number. The accountant at the next desk said "Hell, Joe, give the kid a number." The kid was given a number and departed.[1]

Validity of Data. A lack of "good, clean data" means that whatever data are available must often be distilled and manipulated (we call it "fudging") before being used in a model. Unfortunately, the validity of the results of a model is no better than the validity of the data that go into the model. You cannot blame a manager for resisting a model's "scientific" results when he or she knows questionable data were used as input.

Developing a Solution

Hard-to-Understand Mathematics. The first concern in developing solutions is that although the mathematical models we use may be complex and powerful, they may not be completely understood. Fancy solutions to problems may have faulty logic or data. The aura of mathematics often causes managers to remain silent when they should be critical. The well-known operations researcher C.W. Churchman cautions that "because mathematics has been so reversed a discipline in recent years, it tends to lull the unsuspecting into believing that he who thinks elaborately thinks well."[2]

Only One Answer Is Limiting. The second problem is that quantitative models usually give just one answer to a problem. Most managers would like to have a *range* of options and not be put in a take-it-or-leave-it position.

We recall the story of the analyst whose job was to find the best location in the city for a new garbage incinerator plant. Her extensive mathematical calculations revealed one best spot: it was centrally located, on the necessary truck lines, and so on. What she neglected to note was that it was also across the street from the home of a city council member—and hence what you might call a less than optimal solution!

A more appropriate strategy is for an analyst to present a range of options, indicating the effect each solution has on the objective function. This gives managers a choice as well as information on how much it will

[1]R.E.D. Woolsey, "The Measure of MS/OR Application or Let's Hear It for the Bean Counters," *Interfaces* **5**, 2 (February 1975).

[2]C.W. Churchman, "Relativity Models in the Social Sciences," *Interfaces* **4**, 1 (November 1973).

cost to deviate from the optimal solution. It also allows problems to be viewed from a broader perspective, since nonquantitative factors can be considered.

Testing the Solution

The results of QA often take the form of predictions of how things will work in the future if certain changes are made now. To get a preview of how well solutions will really work, managers are often asked how good the solution looks to them. The problem is that complex models tend to give solutions that are not intuitively obvious. And such solutions tend to be rejected by managers. The quantitative analyst now has the chance to work through the model and the assumptions with the manager in an effort to convince the manager of the validity of the results. In the process of convincing the manager, the analyst will have to review each and every assumption that went into the model. If there are errors, they may be revealed during this review. In addition, the manager will be casting a critical eye on everything that went into the model and, if he or she can be convinced that the model is valid, there is a good chance that the solution results are also valid.

Analyzing the Results

Once the solution has been tested, the results must be analyzed in terms of how they will affect the total organization. You should be aware that even small changes in organizations are often difficult to bring about. If the results indicate large changes in organization policy, the quantitative analyst can expect resistance. In analyzing the results, the analyst should ascertain who must change and by how much, if the people who must change will be better or worse off, and who has the power to direct the change.

1.5   IMPLEMENTATION—NOT JUST THE FINAL STEP

We have just presented some of the many problems that can affect the ultimate acceptance of the QA approach and use of its models. It should be clear now that implementation isn't just another step that takes place after the modeling process is over. Each one of these steps greatly affects the chances of implementing the results of a quantitative study.

Lack of Commitment and Resistance to Change

Teaching Suggestion 1.6:
Dealing with Resistance to
Change. See the Instructor's
Section for details.

Even though many business decisions can be made intuitively, based on hunches and experience, there are more and more situations in which quantitative models can assist. Some managers, however, fear that the use of a formal analysis process will reduce their decision-making power. Others fear it may expose some previous intuitive decisions as inadequate. Still others just feel uncomfortable about having to reverse their thinking patterns with formal decision making. These managers often argue against the use of quantitative methods.

Gene Woolsey suggests that action-oriented managers do not like the lengthy formal decision-making process, but prefer to get things done quickly. He advocates the use of "quick and dirty" techniques that can yield immediate results and thus slowly indoctrinate the manager to the use of quantitative methods.[3] Once managers see some quick results that have a substantial payoff, the stage is set for convincing them that quantitative analysis is a beneficial tool.

We have known for some time that management support and user involvement are critical to the successful implementation of quantitative analysis projects. A Swedish study found that only 40% of projects suggested by quantitative analysts were ever implemented. But 70% of the quantitative projects initiated by users, and fully 98% of projects suggested by top managers, *were* implemented.

Lack of Commitment by Quantitative Analysts

Just as manager attitudes are to blame for some implementation problems, analysts' attitudes are to blame for others. When the quantitative analyst is not an integral part of the department facing the problem, he or she sometimes tends to treat the modeling activity as an end in itself. That is, the analyst accepts the problem as stated by the manager and builds a model to solve only that problem. When the results are computed, he or she hands them back to the manager and considers the job done. The analyst who does not care whether or not these results help make the final decision is not concerned with implementation.

Successful implementation requires that the analyst not *tell* the users what to do, but work with them and take their feelings into account. An article in *Operations Research* describes an inventory control system that calculated reorder points and order quantities. But instead of insisting that computer-calculated quantities be ordered, a manual override feature was installed. This allowed users to disregard the calculated figures and substitute their own. The override was used quite often when the system was first installed. Gradually, however, as users came to realize that the calculated figures were right more often than not, they allowed the system's figures to stand. Eventually the override feature was used only in special circumstances. This is a good example of how good relationships can aid in model implementation.

---

[3]R. E. D. Woolsey and H. Swanson, *Operations Research for Immediate Application: A Quick and Dirty Manual* (New York: Harper and Row, 1975).

1.6 QUANTITATIVE ANALYSIS AND COMPUTER-BASED INFORMATION SYSTEMS

Quantitative analysis has become an integral part of computer-based information systems. A *computer-based information system (CBIS)* consists of hardware, software, a database, telecommunications, people, and procedures (see Figure 1.2). Computer-based information systems can include management information systems, decision support systems, and the use of artificial intelligence and expert systems. Quantitative analysis models can be used in each of these systems.

Management Information Systems

MIS

A management information system (MIS) is an important tool in business. It is simply an organized way of getting the right information to the right people in the right place at the right time. Getting the right information to

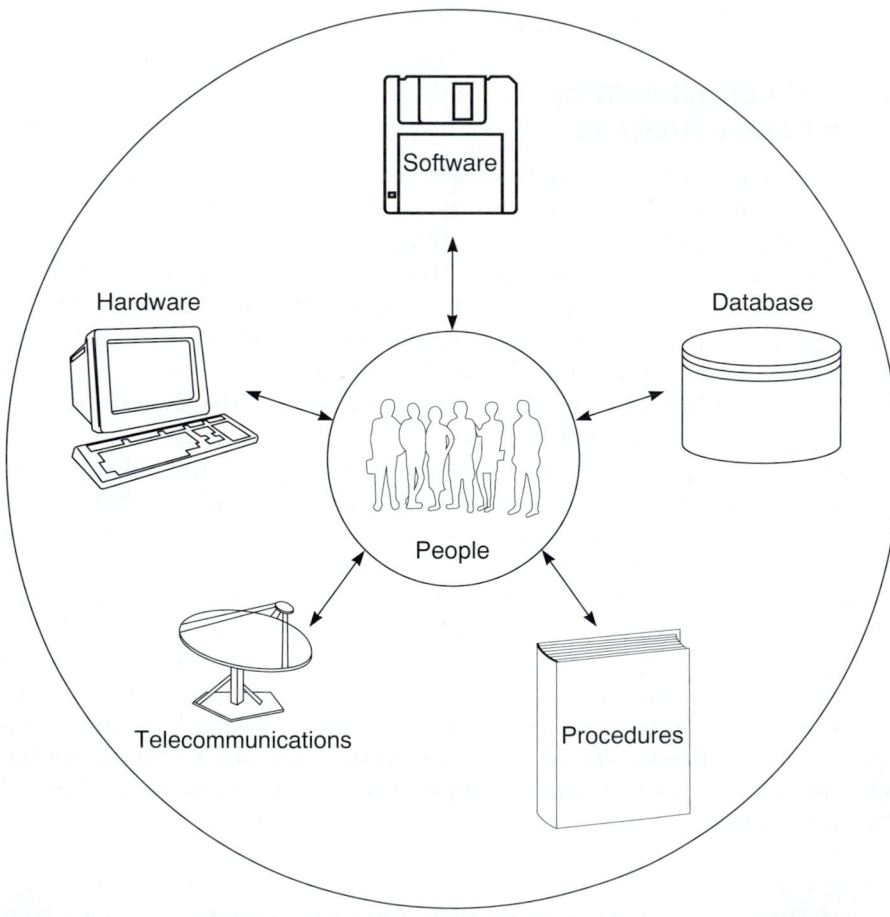

FIGURE 1.2
A Computer-Based Information System

the right manager can often involve using quantitative models. After all, if a manager needs help in ordering and stocking decisions, *forecasting models* to project demand and *inventory models* to compute optimal order policies can be vital.

In order to be able to extract information in the right place at the right time, direct manager-computer interface is becoming popular. This means that computer programs are needed to allow the decision maker to "speak" online to the MIS, usually through terminals or microcomputers. If an application is more complex, the quantitative analyst may act as the interface and handle the data request by writing programs to extract the information.

Decision Support Systems

Along with today's advances in computer technology, we are also seeing the development of decision support systems, expert systems, and artificial intelligence. In a *decision support system (DSS)*, a system is developed to support rather than replace managerial decision making. Typically, decision support systems are oriented toward poorly structured problems. DSS is interactive and allows the use of "what-if" questions. Managers can try out different decisions, alter input data, and quickly see the results of these changes in the solutions to problems. In developing the software that accompanies this book, we have attempted to use the notions of DSS in providing flexible yet powerful decision-making tools.

DSS

Artificial Intelligence

The field of artificial intelligence (AI) began in the mid-1950s at a conference at Dartmouth College. During this conference, concepts and theories related to the use of computer systems and technology to act like or simulate human intelligence were explored. These concepts were called *artificial intelligence.* Since this early beginning, many strides have been made. Artificial intelligence has grown into a number of important and practical subfields with broad implications for quantitative analysis and society in general. Artificial intelligence attempts to develop systems and procedures that mimic or act like intelligent and rational decision makers. These systems may contain components or aspects that are difficult to quantify. Furthermore, large databases or knowledge bases containing expert opinions are captured. An overview of the artificial intelligence field is shown in Figure 1.3.

The three primary components or practical applications of artificial intelligence are expert systems, robotics, and natural languages. *Expert systems* allow us to develop technology that acts and responds like experts in a particular field. Expert systems have been developed to diagnose medical problems, explore for oil, and make good decisions based on available information. The field of *robotics* is concerned with developing devices that have movement and response capabilities far beyond traditional mechanical equipment. With robotics, we can develop mechanical systems to accurately spray paint cars and other products, handle hazardous and

Teaching Suggestion 1.7: Expert Systems. See the Instructor's Section for details.

beginning of artificial intelligence and expert systems

Transparency Master 1.12: Overview of Artificial Intelligence.

KEY IDEA

overview of artificial intelligence

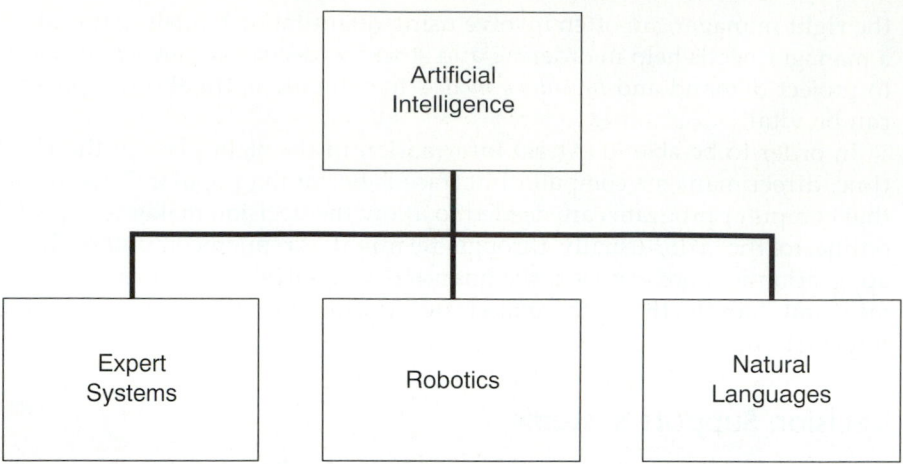

FIGURE 1.3
Overview of Artificial Intelligence

dangerous materials, and perform delicate manipulations that only human beings could perform in the past. *Natural languages* attempt to understand and process statements and commands using language that you would find in normal, everyday conversations. Although these three categories of artificial intelligence are still at the beginning stages of development, positive results have already been achieved.

Applications of Artificial Intelligence. There are numerous examples of developed and installed systems that use the notions of artificial intelligence and expert systems. For example, MYCIN is an expert system started at Stanford University to analyze and propose treatments for various blood infections. AT&T has developed a system that helps to analyze the maintenance of telephone networks and cables. ACE.DELTA, developed by General Electric Corporation, can be used to help analyze repair problems for various types of engines. Atlantic Richfield, a major oil company, uses supercomputers and expert systems to help in oil exploration. Other applications include financial investment planning, external auditing, commercial loan approval, advertising and media selection strategies, inventory control and planning, design and configuration of computer systems, career planning, and a system for developing strategic objectives.

Many strides have been made in the area of robotics. Artificial intelligence has been used to assist in making machines traverse rough and uneven terrain. While everyday activities such as walking or running seem commonplace, developing computer programs and systems to allow machines to perform these functions is difficult and complex. Another area receiving considerable attention in the area of robotics is *vision sciences*. Although most people can look at various objects and quickly determine what is in a room, this process is very difficult for a computer system. Seeing various light and dark shades through lenses and interpreting these patterns as specific objects requires advanced artificial intelligence skills.

use of expert systems

new developments in artificial intelligence

Natural language systems are also being developed and used. Such systems have the ability to understand common English sentences or commands. Instead of developing detailed programs in a language such as COBOL, natural language processors have the ability to understand and then act upon ordinary English sentences.

Use of Expert Systems. One of the most promising applications of artificial intelligence is the use of expert systems on complex or difficult-to-solve problems. An expert system includes all equipment, devices, procedures, and software used to capture the essence of a human expert in a particular field. In order to effectively use an expert system, it must be carefully developed. This development process is shown in Figure 1.4. An expert system is built by one or more individuals called *knowledge engineers.* Knowledge engineers have the expertise and the skill to convert information given to them by experts in a field into computerized systems that act as experts. There are numerous advantages of capturing expertise. For example, use of experience and good judgment can be lost when valued employees retire. With an expert system, their knowledge and experience can be captured and used for generations to come. In addition, the knowledge and experience of valued experts can be used by many individuals in a variety of settings to solve specific problems.

After the expert system has been developed, an effective delivery system must be employed to allow users to gain the benefits of the expert system. The use of an expert system is shown in Figure 1.5. The user goes through an interface system to activate the expert system. As can be seen, the expert system consists of a rule base, a knowledge base, and an inference engine. The *rule base* contains important rules about the particular field that is captured in the expert system. These rules are typically expressed as IF-THEN statements. In general, IF-THEN constructs allow the expert system to capture important rules and judgments. The *knowledge base* consists of data and experience that are captured and placed into the expert system. Finally, the expert system has an *inference engine* that allows the manipulation of the rule base and knowledge base to get meaningful results for the user. The interface consists of people, equipment, procedures, and systems that allow the effective use of the expert system. In many cases, a manager or other decision maker does not have the skills needed to directly access and manipulate the expert system. The interface allows managers and decision makers to gain the benefits of an expert system without spending time becoming technical experts in the use of the

Transparency Master 1.13:
Expert System Development.

development of expert systems

Transparency Master 1.14:
The Use of an Expert System.

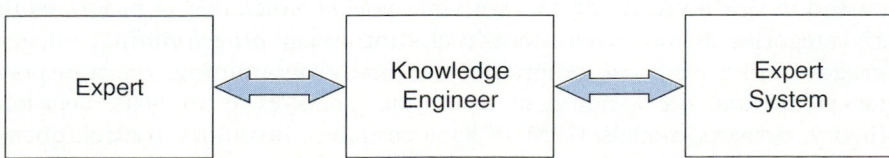

FIGURE 1.4
Expert System Development

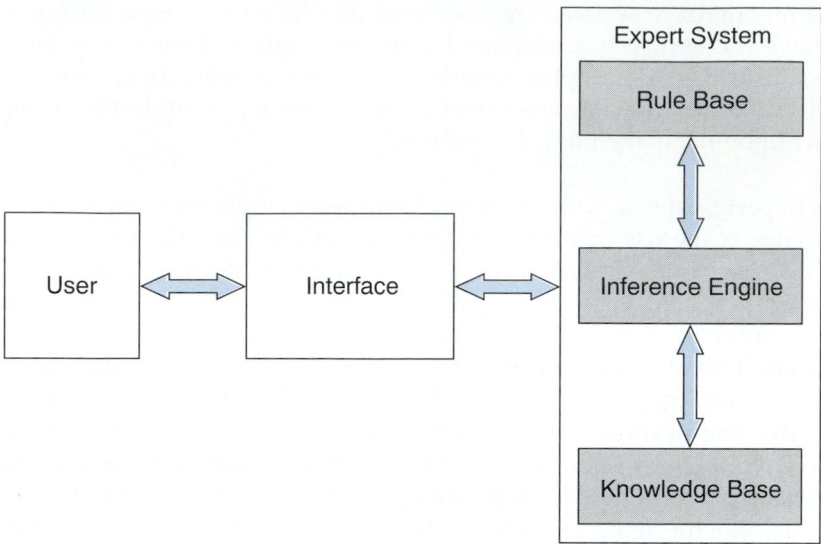

FIGURE 1.5
Use of an Expert System

system. With proper development and careful use, artificial intelligence and expert systems can yield substantial benefits.

1.7   USE OF AB:QM, STORM, AND SPREADSHEETS

Two software packages will be featured throughout this book. AB:QM is a comprehensive software package that accompanies this book. STORM is a popular package that many schools make available to students. In the appropriate chapters, we will illustrate these two packages. Module F contains a more detailed discussion of the use of AB:QM.

This section will also describe the use of spreadsheet models in quantitative analysis. Many of the techniques discussed in this book can be solved using spreadsheet programs and/or spreadsheet add-ins.

Use of AB:QM in Quantitative Analysis

overview of AB:QM

AB:QM (short for Allyn & Bacon: Quantitative Methods) is a software package that allows you to solve many of the quantitative problems discussed in this book. In all, this software package includes 44 programs in 17 categories or menu selections, including linear programming, integer programming, zero-one programming, goal programming, the transportation method, the assignment technique, break-even analysis, decision theory, network models, CPM/PERT techniques, inventory control, queuing theory, dynamic programming, simulation, forecasting, Markov analysis, and game theory. The package is easy to use and does not require previous coursework in computers. The main menu for AB:QM is shown in Program 1.1.

PROGRAM 1.1 MAIN MENU OF AB:QM

```
 ─────────────────────── Menu 1 ───────────────────────
 A    Linear Programming          J    CPM/PERT
 B    All Integer Programming     K    Inventory Models
 C    Zero-One Programming        L    Queuing Theory
 D    Goal Programming            M    Dynamic Programming
 E    Transportation              N    Simulation
 F    Assignment                  O    Forecasting
 G    Break-Even Analysis         P    Markov Analysis
 H    Decision Theory             Q    Game Theory
 I    Network Models            Esc    Exit AB:QM
```

Use of STORM

STORM is an integrated package of programs used to perform a variety of applications in quantitative analysis. This package is relatively easy to use and is popular at many colleges and universities. The complete software package consists of 16 programs or modules. The main menu for STORM displays the 16 programs or modules shown in Program 1.2.

main menu

Although there are a few programs contained in the main menu for STORM that are not appropriate for this book, the following programs in STORM can be used: linear and integer programming, the assignment technique, transportation, distance networks, flow networks, project management, queuing analysis, inventory management, forecasting, and material requirements planning. The use of STORM will be described in the appropriate chapters throughout this book.

PROGRAM 1.2 MAIN MENU FOR STORM

```
  1) Linear & Integer Programming
  2) Assignment
  3) Transportation
  4) Distance Networks (Paths, Tours, Trees)
  5) Flow Networks (Max Flow, Transshipment)
  6) Project Management (PERT/CPM)
  7) Queueing Analysis
  8) Inventory Management
  9) Facility Layout
 10) Assembly Line Balancing
 11) Investment Analysis
 12) Forecasting
 13) Production Scheduling
 14) Material Requirements Planning
 15) Statistical Process Control
 16) Statistics
```

Use of Spreadsheet Models in Quantitative Analysis

A *spreadsheet model,* also called a computerized worksheet, is a collection of computer programs that can be used to make calculations and perform quantitative analysis. Most of the techniques discussed in this chapter can be computerized using a spreadsheet completely or to some extent, and a number of spreadsheets were used in developing chapter material for this book. Although there are a number of spreadsheet programs on the market today, Lotus 1-2-3 is one of the most popular.

A spreadsheet is like a huge piece of paper that consists of hundreds of columns and thousands of rows. The intersection of any row and column is called a *cell.* A name or "label", a number, or a complex formula can be placed in a cell of a spreadsheet. For example, we can place the number 10 in cell A1 and the number 20 in the cell A2. If the cell A3 contains the formula +A1+A2, we will see the result of 30 displayed in the cell. Built-in formulas, such as @SUM for addition and @SQRT for square root, can also be used.

Spreadsheets have a number of very useful features. You can use the *range* command to perform an operation to a range or rectangle of cells. The *move* command can move labels, values, and formulas to other locations, and the *copy* command can be used to copy values, names, and even formulas to other cells with ease. Using the *file* command, you can save or retrieve a worksheet. The *print* command can be used to send the results of a worksheet to the printer or a file, which can be inserted and manipulated in a word processing program. Spreadsheet programs also have *database* capabilities that allow you to sort, merge, find, search and replace, and extract various parts of the spreadsheet. There are even graphics capabilities that allow you to display and print pie charts, line graphs, bar charts, XY graphs, and stack-bar charts. One of the greatest advantages of a spreadsheet is the ability to make changes quickly and see the results immediately. This feature makes spreadsheet analysis a powerful QA modeling tool.

In Chapter 4, we will develop a forecasting model using trend projections and the least squares method. Here is the result of one possible forecasting model:

General Forecasting Model: $Y = a + b(X)$
Forecasting Example: Sales $= 56.70 + 10.54$(Time Period).

For example, if the time period is month 9, the sales projection would be 151.56 ($151.56 = 56.70 + 10.54(9)$). Given this model, we can use a spreadsheet program to forecast sales into the future. Program 1.3 shows the forecast for periods 9 through 12. Note that the value for *a,* which is 56.70, is in cell C15, and the value for *b,* which is 10.54, is in cell C16 of the spreadsheet.

To see the actual formulas used to compute the sales values in Program 1.3, we can use the /**R**ANGE FORMAT **T**EXT or /**RFT** command for the cells that contain the formulas. This is done in Program 1.4. As you can see, the formula to compute the sales value of 151.56 in cell B27 is $C\$15 + \$C\$16*A27$. This formula multiplies 10.54 in cell C15 by the

PROGRAM 1.3 SPREADSHEET SOFTWARE IN QA

```
        A       B       C       D
 1  A sample spreadsheet to forecast demand
 2  Using trend projections
 3
 4
 5  General linear relationship: Y = a + bX
 6
 7          Where:  Y = Sales
 8                  a = Y intercept
 9                  b = slope
10                  X = Time Period
11
12
13  Forecasting Example
14
15              a is     56.7
16              b is    10.54
17
18  Forecasting formula: Sales = 56.7 + 10.54(Time Period)
19
20
21  Forecasting Results for Time Periods 9 through 12
22
23
24    Time    Sales
25  Period
26
27        9   151.56
28       10   162.10
29       11   172.64
30       12   183.18
31
32                6
```

time period, 9, in cell A27 and adds the result to the intercept 56.7 in cell C15. The $'s in the formulas are used to lock in the cells to allow us to copy the formula in cell B27 to the other cells. We will show you spreadsheets, the formulas used in the spreadsheets, or both for many of the techniques described in the book.

In addition to the power of a standard spreadsheet program to solve quantitative analysis problems, specialized programs have been developed to extend its capabilities. These programs are called add-ins. An *add-in* consists of one or more programs that can be directly attached to a spreadsheet to extend its capabilities. Once attached, it can be used as an integral part of the spreadsheet. Examples of add-ins include:

● @What If Solver and @What's*Best!*—solve optimization problems.

● @Project 8-9-10—monitors and controls small projects.

PROGRAM 1.4 "SYMBOLIC" REPRESENTATION OF
PROGRAM 1.3's FORECAST

```
          A               B               C
9
0
1   Forecasting Results for Time Periods 9 through 20
2
3
4    Time                      Sales
5  Period
6
7        9  +$C$15+$C$16*A27
8       10  +$C$15+$C$16*A28
9       11  +$C$15+$C$16*A29
0       12  +$C$15+$C$16*A30
1
2
```

- @Risk—performs Monte Carlo simulations of financial investments.

- @Statplan III—performs advanced statistical calculations.

- @Functions—gives about 40 additional spreadsheet functions that are not currently available.

1.8   SUMMARY

Quantitative analysis is the scientific approach to decision making. The quantitative analysis approach includes defining the problem, developing a model, acquiring input data, developing a solution, testing the solution, analyzing the results, and implementing the results. In using the quantitative approach, however, there can be potential problems, including conflicting viewpoints, the impact of QA models on other departments, beginning assumptions, outdated solutions, fitting textbook models, understanding the model, acquiring good input data, hard-to-understand mathematics, obtaining only one answer, testing the solution, and analyzing the results. In using the QA approach, implementation is not the final step. There can be a lack of commitment to the approach and resistance to change. Today, the QA approach is used as an integral part of many computer-based information systems. QA models can be used with management information, decision support, and expert systems.

GLOSSARY

Artificial Intelligence. The ability of a computer system to act like an expert or intelligent individual.

Quantitative Analysis or **Management Science.** A scientific approach using quantitative techniques as a tool in decision making.

Problem. A statement, which should come from a manager, that indicates a problem to be solved or an objective or goal to be reached.

Decision Support System. A computer system that supports rather than replaces a decision maker.

Model. A representation of reality or of a real-life situation.

Mathematical Model. A model that uses mathematical equations and statements to represent the relationships within the model.

Spreadsheet Model. A collection of computer programs used to make calculations and perform quantitative analysis.

Input Data. Data that are used in the model in arriving at the final solution.

Sensitivity Analysis. Determining how sensitive the solution is to changes in the formulation of the problem.

Algorithm. A set of logical and mathematical operations performed in a specific sequence.

DISCUSSION QUESTIONS

1–1 What is the difference between quantitative and qualitative analysis? Give several examples.

1–2 Define quantitative analysis. What are some of the organizations that support the use of the scientific approach?

1–3 What is the quantitative analysis process? Give several examples of this process.

1–4 Briefly trace the history of quantitative analysis. What happened to the development of quantitative analysis during World War II?

1–5 Give some examples of the different types of models. What is a mathematical model? Develop two examples of mathematical models.

1–6 What are some of the sources of input data?

1–7 What is implementation, and why is it important?

1–8 Describe the use of sensitivity analysis and postoptimality analysis in analyzing the results.

1–9 Managers are quick to claim that quantitative analysts talk to them in a jargon that doesn't sound like English. List four terms that might not be understood by a manager. Then explain in nontechnical terms what each term means.

1–10 Why do you think many quantitative analysts don't like to participate in the implementation process? What could be done to change this attitude?

1–11 Should people who will be using the results of a new quantitative model become involved in the technical aspects of the problem-solving procedure?

1–12 C.W. Churchman once said "mathematics...tends to lull the unsuspecting into believing that he who thinks elaborately thinks well." Do you think that the best QA models are the ones that are most elaborate and complex mathematically? Why?

1–13 How is the implementation of QA models tied to a management information system?

BIBLIOGRAPHY

Ackoff, R. L. *Scientific Method: Optimizing Applied Research Decisions.* New York: John Wiley & Sons, Inc., 1962.

Anderson, J. C., and T. R. Hoffman. "A Perspective on the Implementation of Management Science." *Academy of Management Review* **3**, 3 (July 1978).

Churchman, C.W. "Relativity Models in the Social Sciences." *Interfaces* **4**, 1 (November 1973).

Churchman, C. West. *The Systems Approach.* New York: Delacort Press, 1968.

Fordyce, Kenneth, et al. "Artificial Intelligence and the Management Science Practitioner: One Definition of Knowledge-Based Expert Systems." *Interfaces* **19**, 5 (September-October 1989).

Ginzberg, M. J. "Steps Towards Effective Implementation of MS and MIS." *Interfaces* **8**, 3 (May 1978).

Ginzberg, M. J. "Finding an Adequate Measure of OR/MS Effectiveness." *Interfaces* **8**, 4 (August 1978).

Grayson, C. J. "Management Science and Business Practice." *Harvard Business Review* **51** (1973).

Gupta, J. N. D. "Management Science Implementations: Experiences of a Practicing O. R. Manager." *Interfaces* **7**, 3 (May 1977).

Keeney, Ralph L. "Potential Research Topics in Decision Analysis." *Decision Sciences* **13**, 4 (October 1982).

Liberatore, Matthew J., and George J. Titus. "The Practice of Management Science in R & D Project Management." *Management Sciences* **29**, 8 (August 1983).

Moore, William E., Jr., Janice M. Warmke, and Lonny R. Gorban. "The Indispensable Role of Management Science in Centralizing Freight Operation at Reynolds Metals Company," *Interfaces* **21**, 1 (January-February 1991): 107–129.

Schwenk, Charles R., and Howard Thomas. "Effects of Conflicting Analysis of Managerial Decision Making: A Laboratory Experiment." *Decision Sciences* **14**, 4 (Fall 1983).

Watkins, Paul R. "Perceived Information Structure: Implications for Decision Support System Design." *Decision Sciences* **13**, 1 (January 1982).

Watson, H. J., and P. G. Marett. "A Survey of Management Science Implementations Problems." *Interfaces* **9**, 4 (August 1979).

Woolsey, R. E. D. "The Measure of MS/OR Application or Let's Hear It for the Bean Counters." *Interfaces* **5**, 2 (February 1975).

Wysocki, R. K. "OR/MS Implementation Research: A Bibliography." *Interfaces* **9**, 2 (February 1979).

2

Probability Concepts

CHAPTER OUTLINE

2.1 Introduction

2.2 Fundamental Concepts

2.3 Mutually Exclusive and Collectively Exhaustive Events

2.4 Statistically Independent Events

2.5 Statistically Dependent Events

2.6 Revising Probabilities with Bayes's Theorem

2.7 Further Probability Revisions

2.8 Summary

Glossary

Key Equations

Discussion Questions and Problems

Bibliography

Appendix: Derivation of Bayes's Theorem

2.1 INTRODUCTION

Life would be simpler if we knew without doubt what was going to happen in the future. The outcome of any decision would depend only on how logical and rational the decision was. If you lost money in the stock market, it would be because you failed to consider all of the information or to make a logical decision. If you got caught in the rain, it would be because you simply forgot your umbrella. You could always avoid building a plant that was too large, investing in a company that would lose money, running out of supplies, or losing crops because of bad weather. There would be no such thing as a risky investment. Life would be simpler, but boring.

quantifying risks

It wasn't until the sixteenth century that people started to quantify risks and to apply this concept to everyday situations. Today, the idea of risk or probability is a part of our lives. "There is a 40 percent chance of rain in Omaha today." "The Florida State University Seminoles are favored 2 to 1 over the Louisiana State University Tigers this Saturday." "There is a 50-50 chance that the stock market will reach an all-time high next month."

A probability is a numerical statement about the likelihood that an event will occur. In this and the next chapter on probability we shall examine the basic concepts, terms, and relationships of probability that are useful in solving many quantitative analysis problems. Table 2.1 lists some of the topics covered in this book that rely on probability theory. You can see that the study of quantitative analysis would be quite difficult without it.

KEY IDEA

Transparency Master 2.1:
Chapters That Use Probability.

2.2 FUNDAMENTAL CONCEPTS

There are two basic statements about the mathematics of probability.

KEY IDEA

Teaching Suggestion 2.1:
The Concept of Probabilities
Ranging from 0 to 1. See the
Instructor's Section for
details.

1. The probability, P, of any event or state of nature occurring is greater than or equal to 0 and less than or equal to 1. That is,

$$0 \leq P(\text{Event}) \leq 1 \tag{2-1}$$

A probability of 0 indicates that an event is never expected to occur. A probability of 1 means an event is always expected to occur.

2. The sum of the simple probabilities for all possible outcomes of an activity must equal 1.

Transparency Master 2.2:
Fundamental Probability
Concepts.

Both of these concepts are illustrated in Example 1.

Alternate Example 2.1

Example 1: Two Laws of Probability

Demand for white latex paint at Diversey Paint and Supply has always been 0, 1, 2, 3, or 4 gallons per day. (There are no other possible out-

TABLE 2.1 Chapters in This Book That Use Probability

CHAPTER	TITLE
2	Probability Concepts
3	Probability Distributions
4	Forecasting
5	Fundamentals of Decision Theory
6	Decision Trees and Utility Theory
7	Statistical Quality Control
9	Inventory Control Models: II
16	Waiting Lines: Queuing Theory
17	Simulation
18	Network Models
19	Markov Analysis
Module B	Game Theory
Module D	Decision Theory and the Normal Distribution

comes and when one occurs, no other can.) Over the past 200 working days, the owner notes the following frequencies of demand.

QUANTITY DEMANDED (IN GALLONS)	NUMBER OF DAYS
0	40
1	80
2	50
3	20
4	10
Total	200

Teaching Suggestion 2.2:
Where Do Probabilities Come From? See the Instructor's Section for details.

If this past distribution is a good indicator of future sales, we can find the probability of each possible outcome occurring in the future by converting the data into percentages of the total.

Applicable Problem 2.8

QUANTITY DEMANDED	PROBABILITY
0	.20 $(= {}^{40}/_{200})$
1	.40 $(= {}^{80}/_{200})$
2	.25 $(= {}^{50}/_{200})$
3	.10 $(= {}^{20}/_{200})$
4	.05 $(= {}^{10}/_{200})$
Total	1.00 $(= {}^{200}/_{200})$

past data converted to probabilities

Thus the probability that sales are 2 gallons of paint on any given day is $P(2 \text{ gallons}) = .25 = 25\%$. The probability of any level of sales must be greater than or equal to 0 and less than or equal to 1. Since 0, 1, 2, 3, and 4 gallons exhaust all possible events or outcomes, the sum of their probability values must equal 1.

Types of Probability

There are two different ways to determine probability: the *objective approach* and the *subjective approach*.

objective probability: relative frequency and logical approaches

Objective Probability. Example 1 provided us with an illustration of objective probability assessment. The probability of any paint demand level was the *relative frequency* of occurrence of that demand in a large number of trial observations (200 days in this case). In general,

$$P(\text{Event}) = \frac{\text{Number of occurrences of the event}}{\text{Total number of trials or outcomes}}$$

Objective probability can also be set using what is called the *classical* or *logical method*. Without performing a series of trials, we can often logically determine what the probabilities of various events should be. For example, the probability of tossing a fair coin once and getting a head is:

$$P(\text{Head}) = \frac{1}{2} \quad \begin{array}{l} \textit{number of ways of getting a head} \\ \textit{number of possible outcomes (head or tail)} \end{array}$$

Likewise, the probability of drawing a spade out of a deck of 52 playing cards can be logically set as:

$$P(\text{Spade}) = \frac{13}{52} \quad \begin{array}{l} \textit{number of chances of drawing a spade} \\ \textit{number of total possible outcomes} \end{array}$$

$$= \tfrac{1}{4} = .25 = 25\%$$

subjective probability

Subjective Probability. When logic and past history are not appropriate, probability values can be assessed *subjectively*. The accuracy of subjective probabilities depends on the experience and judgment of the person making the estimates.

A number of probability values cannot be determined unless the subjective approach is used. What is the probability that the price of gasoline will be over four dollars in the next few years? What is the probability that our economy will be in a severe depression in 1998? What is the probability that you will be president of a major corporation within 20 years?

There are several methods for making subjective probability assessments. Opinion polls can be used to help in determining subjective probabilities for possible election returns and potential political candidates. In some cases, experience and judgment must be used in making subjective assessments of probability values. A production manager, for example, might believe that the probability of manufacturing a new product without a single defect is .85. In the Delphi method, a panel of experts is assembled to make their predictions of the future. This approach will be discussed in Chapter 4.

<table>
<tr><td>

2.3 | MUTUALLY EXCLUSIVE AND COLLECTIVELY EXHAUSTIVE EVENTS

</td></tr>
</table>

Events are said to be *mutually exclusive* if only one of the events can occur on any one trial. They are called *collectively exhaustive* if the list of outcomes includes every possible outcome. Many common experiences involve events that have both of these properties. In tossing a coin, for example, the possible outcomes are a head or a tail. Since both of them cannot occur on any one toss, the outcomes head and tail are mutually exclusive. Since obtaining a head and a tail represent every possible outcome, they are also collectively exhaustive.

Example 2: Rolling a Die

Rolling a die is a simple experiment that has six possible outcomes, each listed in the following table with its corresponding probability.

OUTCOME OF ROLL	PROBABILITY
1	$\frac{1}{6}$
2	$\frac{1}{6}$
3	$\frac{1}{6}$
4	$\frac{1}{6}$
5	$\frac{1}{6}$
6	$\frac{1}{6}$
Total	1

These events are both mutually exclusive (on any roll, only one of the six events can occur) and are also collectively exhaustive (one of them must occur and hence they total in probability to 1).

Example 3: Drawing a Card

You are asked to draw one card from a deck of 52 playing cards. Using a logical probability assessment, it is easy to set some of the relationships such as:

$$P(\text{Drawing a 7}) = \frac{4}{52} = \frac{1}{13}$$

$$P(\text{Drawing a heart}) = \frac{13}{52} = \frac{1}{4}$$

We also see that these events (drawing a 7 and drawing a heart) are *not* mutually exclusive since a 7 of hearts can be drawn. They are also *not* collectively exhaustive since there are other cards in the deck besides 7s and hearts.

You can test your understanding of these concepts by going through the following cases.

Transparency Master 2.3:
Mutually Exclusive Events.

toss of a coin has mutually exclusive and collectively exhaustive events

Teaching Suggestion 2.3:
The Confusion over Mutually Exclusive and Collectively Exhaustive Events. See the Instructor's Section for details.

Alternate Example 2.2

Alternate Example 2.3

DRAWS	MUTUALLY EXCLUSIVE?	COLLECTIVELY EXHAUSTIVE?
1. Draw a spade and a club	Yes	No
2. Draw a face card and a number card	Yes	Yes
3. Draw an ace and a 3	Yes	No
4. Draw a club and a nonclub	Yes	Yes
5. Draw a 5 and a diamond	No	No
6. Draw a red card and a diamond	No	No

Adding Mutually Exclusive Events

Often we are interested in whether one event *or* a second event will occur. When these two events are mutually exclusive, the law of addition is simply as follows:

law of addition for mutually exclusive events

$$P(\text{Event } A \text{ or Event } B) = P(\text{Event } A) + P(\text{Event } B)$$

or more briefly,

$$P(A \text{ or } B) = P(A) + P(B) \tag{2-2}$$

For example, we just saw that the events of drawing a spade or drawing a club out of a deck of cards are mutually exclusive. Since $P(\text{Spade}) = {}^{13}/_{52}$, and $P(\text{Club}) = {}^{13}/_{52}$, the probability of drawing either a spade or a club is:

$$P(\text{Spade or Club}) = P(\text{Spade}) + P(\text{Club})$$

$$= {}^{13}/_{52} + {}^{13}/_{52}$$

$$= {}^{26}/_{52} = \frac{1}{2} = .50 = 50\%$$

The *Venn diagram* in Figure 2.1 depicts the probability of the occurrence of mutually exclusive events.

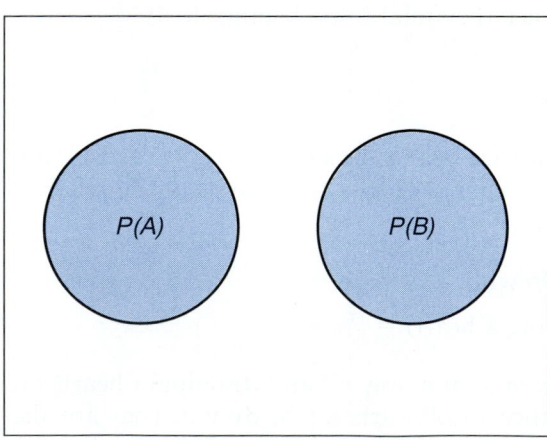

$$P(A \text{ or } B) = P(A) + P(B)$$

FIGURE 2.1
Addition Law for Events That Are Mutually Exclusive

Law of Addition for Events That Are Not Mutually Exclusive

When two events are not mutually exclusive, Equation 2-2 must be modified to account for double counting. The correct equation reduces the probability by subtracting the chance of both events occurring together.

P(Event A or Event B) = P(Event A) + P(Event B)

$\qquad$ − P(Event A and Event B both occurring)

This can be expressed in shorter form as:

$$P(A \text{ or } B) = P(A) + P(B) - P(A \text{ and } B) \qquad \text{(2-3)}$$

Figure 2.2 illustrates this concept of subtracting the probability of outcomes that are common to both events. When events are mutually exclusive, the area of overlap, called the *intersection*, is 0, as shown in Figure 2.1.

Let us consider the events drawing a 5 and drawing a diamond out of the card deck. These events are not mutually exclusive, so Equation 2-3 must be applied to compute the probability of either a 5 or a diamond being drawn.

$$P(\text{Five or Diamond}) = P(\text{Five}) + P(\text{Diamond}) - P(\text{Five and Diamond})$$
$$= {}^4\!/_{52} + {}^{13}\!/_{52} - {}^1\!/_{52}$$
$$= {}^{16}\!/_{52} = {}^4\!/_{13}$$

2.4 STATISTICALLY INDEPENDENT EVENTS

Events may be either independent or dependent. When they are *independent,* the occurrence of one event has no effect on the probability of occurrence

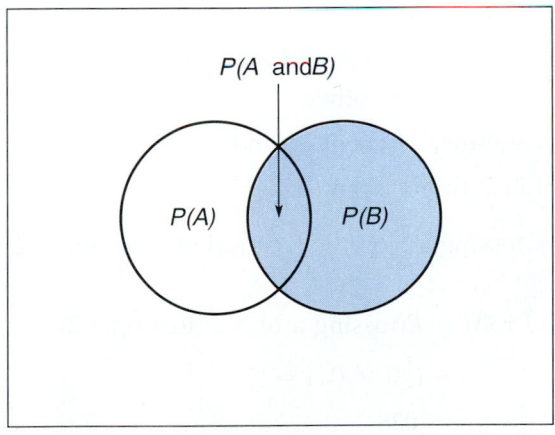

$P(A \text{ or } B) = P(A) + P(B) - P(A \text{ and } B)$

FIGURE 2.2
Addition Law for Events That Are Not Mutually Exclusive

of the second event. Let us examine four sets of events and determine which are independent.

1. (a) Your education
   (b) Your income level   } *Dependent events. Can you explain why?*

2. (a) Draw a jack of hearts from a full 52-card deck
   (b) Draw a jack of clubs from a full 52-card deck   } *Independent events*

3. (a) Chicago Cubs win the National League pennant
   (b) Chicago Cubs win the World Series   } *Dependent Events*

4. (a) Snow in Santiago, Chile
   (b) Rain in Tel Aviv, Israel   } *Independent Events*

The three types of probability under both statistical independence and statistical dependence are (1) marginal, (2) joint, and (3) conditional. When events are independent, these three are very easy to compute, as we shall see.

marginal or simple probability

A *marginal* (or a *simple*) *probability* is just the probability of an event occurring. For example, if we toss a fair die, the marginal probability of a 2 landing face up is P(die is a 2) = ⅙ = .166. Because each separate toss is an independent event (that is, what we get on the first toss has absolutely no effect on any later tosses) the marginal probability for each possible outcome is ⅙.

joint probability for independent events

The *joint probability* of two or more *independent* events occurring is the product of their marginal or simple probabilities. This may be written as:

Transparency Master 2.6:
Joint Probabilities.

$$P(AB) = P(A) \times P(B) \tag{2-4}$$

where

$P(AB)$ = joint probability of events A and B occurring together, or one after the other,

$P(A)$ = marginal probability of event A, and

$P(B)$ = marginal probability of event B.

The probability, for example, of tossing a 6 on the first roll of a die and a 2 on the second roll is:

P(6 on first and 2 on second roll) = P(tossing a 6) × P(tossing a 2)

$$= (⅙) \times (⅙) = \frac{1}{36}$$

$$= .028$$

conditional probability

The third type, *conditional probability,* is expressed as $P(B|A)$, or "the probability of event B, given that event A has occurred." Likewise, $P(A|B)$ would mean the conditional probability of event A, given that event B has taken place. Since when events are independent the occurrence of one *in no way* affects the outcome of another, $P(A|B) = P(A)$ and $P(B|A) = P(B)$.

Transparency Master 2.7:
Conditional Probabilities.

Example 4: Probabilities When Events Are Independent

A bucket contains 3 black balls and 7 green balls. We draw a ball from the bucket, replace it, and draw a second ball. We can determine the probability of each of the following events occurring:

1. A black ball is drawn on the first draw.

$$P(B) = .30 \qquad (\textit{This is a marginal probability.})$$

2. Two green balls are drawn.

$$P(GG) = P(G) \times P(G) = (.7)(.7) = .49$$

(This is a joint probability for two independent events.)

Applicable Problem 2-9

3. A black ball is drawn on the second draw if the first draw is green.

$$P(B \mid G) = P(B) = .30 \qquad (\textit{This is a conditional probability, but}$$
equal to the marginal because the two draws are independent events.)

4. A green ball is drawn on the second draw if the first draw was green.

$$P(G \mid G) = P(G) = .70 \qquad (\textit{This is a conditional probability as above.})$$

2.5   STATISTICALLY DEPENDENT EVENTS

When events are statistically dependent, the occurrence of one event affects the probability of occurrence of some other event. Marginal, conditional, and joint probabilities exist under dependence as they did under independence, but the form of the latter two are changed.

one event affects the chance of another occurring

A *marginal probability* is computed exactly as it was for independent events. Again, the marginal probability of the event A occurring is denoted $P(A)$.

Calculating a *conditional probability* under dependence is somewhat more involved than it is under independence. The formula for the conditional probability of A, given that event B has taken place, is now stated as:

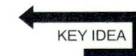
KEY IDEA

$$P(A \mid B) = \frac{P(AB)}{P(B)} \tag{2-5}$$

The use of this important formula, often referred to as *Bayes's law* or *Bayes's theorem*, is best defined by an example.

Example 5: Probabilities When Events Are Dependent

Assume we have an urn containing 10 balls of the following descriptions:

Alternate Example 2.5

> 4 are white (W) and lettered (L)
> 2 are white (W) and numbered (N)
> 3 are yellow (Y) and lettered (L)
> 1 is yellow (Y) and numbered (N)

You randomly draw a ball from the urn and see that it is yellow. What then, we may ask, is the probability that the ball is lettered? (See Figure 2.3.)

Since there are 10 balls, it is a simple matter to tabulate a series of useful probabilities.

Applicable Problems
2-10, 2-11, 2-12, 2-13,
2-14, 2-18, 2-19, 2-21

$$P(WL) = \frac{4}{10} = .4 \qquad P(YL) = \frac{3}{10} = .3$$

$$P(WN) = \frac{2}{10} = .2 \qquad P(YN) = \frac{1}{10} = .1$$

$$P(W) = \frac{6}{10} = .6, \text{ or } P(W) = P(WL) + P(WN) = .4 + .2 = .6$$

$$P(L) = \frac{7}{10} = .7, \text{ or } P(L) = P(WL) + P(YL) = .4 + .3 = .7$$

$$P(Y) = \frac{4}{10} = .4, \text{ or } P(Y) = P(YL) + P(YN) = .3 + .1 = .4$$

$$P(N) = \frac{3}{10} = .3, \text{ or } P(N) = P(WN) = P(YN) = .2 + .1 = .3$$

We may now apply Bayes's law to calculate the conditional probability that the ball drawn is lettered, given that it is yellow.

$$P(L\,|\,Y) = \frac{P(YL)}{P(Y)} = \frac{0.3}{0.4} = .75$$

This equation shows that we divided the probability of *yellow and lettered* balls (*3 out of 10*) by the probability of yellow balls (*4 out of 10*). There is a 0.75 probability that the yellow ball that you drew is lettered.

You may recall that the formula for a joint probability under statistical independence was simply $P(AB) = P(A) \times P(B)$. When events are *depen-*

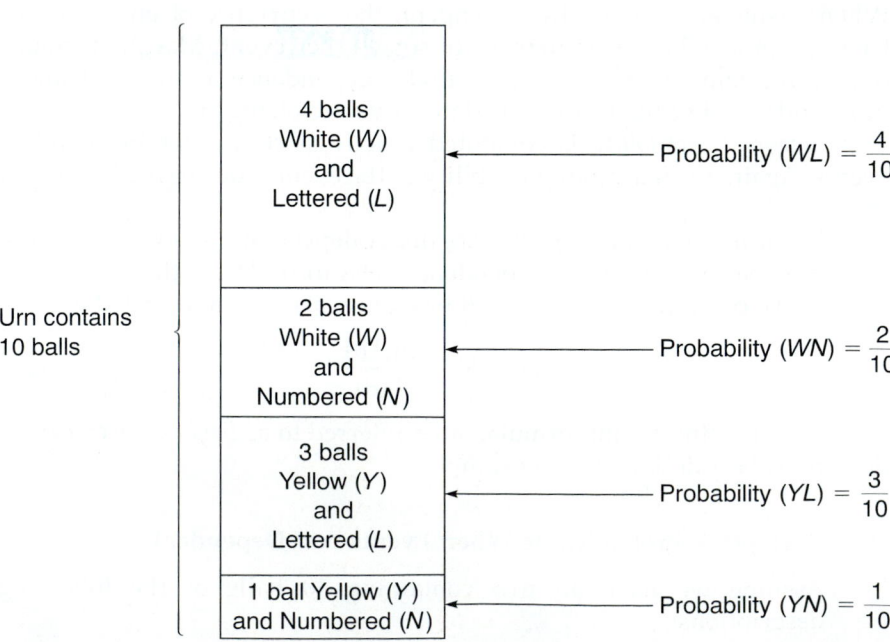

FIGURE 2.3
Example 5's Dependent Events

dent, however, the *joint probability* is derived from Bayes's conditional formula. Equation 2-6 reads as "the joint probability of events *A* and *B* occurring is equal to the conditional probability of event *A*, given that *B* occurred, multiplied by the probability of event *B*."

joint probability for dependent events

$$P(AB) = P(A \mid B) \times P(B) \tag{2-6}$$

We can use this formula to verify the joint probability that $P(YL) = 0.3$, which was obtained by inspection in Example 5, by multiplying $P(L \mid Y)$ times $P(Y)$.

$$P(YL) = P(L \mid Y) \times P(Y) = (.75)(.4) = .3$$

Teaching Suggestion 2.5:
Statistical Dependence with Visual Examples. See the Instructor's Section for details.

Example 6: Joint Probabilities When Events Are Dependent

Your stockbroker informs you that if the stock market reaches the 3,900 point level by January, there is a 70% probability that Tubeless Electronics will go up in value. Your own feeling is that there is only a 40% chance of the market average reaching 3,900 points by January.

Alternate Example 2.6

Can you calculate the probability that *both* the stock market will reach 3,600 points *and* the price of Tubeless Electronics will go up?

Let *M* represent the event of the stock market reaching the 3,900 level, and let *T* be the event that Tubeless goes up in value. Then,

$$P(MT) = P(T \mid M) \times P(M) = (.70)(.40) = .28$$

Thus, there is only a 28% chance that *both* events will occur.

APPLICATIONS OF QA

Qantas Airways

Qantas Airways Limited, the Australian national airline, faced a major cost problem regarding the number of reserve crews needed for aircraft delays. When a plane was delayed, the working hours of the onboard cabin crew sometimes exceeded contract limits and a fresh (reserve) crew was called in as a replacement.

Prior to this study, which used *conditional probabilities,* setting the number of reserve crews was based on experience and guesswork. The objective of the quantitative analysis was to minimize the total costs of both the reserve crews and overnight delays. Since the study, management can estimate the expected number of aircraft overnight delays (and costs) for each of any number of reserve crews.

The probability study of Qantas cost only $3,000 (Australian dollars). The benefits were as follows (all figures are in Australian dollars):

Reduction of 27 cabin crews	$532,000
Training cost savings for 27 flight attendants	84,700
Opportunity cost for return on capital investment (at 10% annually)	61,760
	$678,460

In addition, resulting nonfinancial gains included reduction in reserve duties and management's acceptance of dealing with the risk of overnight delays.

Source: A. Gaballa, "Planning Callout Reserves for Aircraft Delays," *Interfaces,* **9**, 2, Part 2, (February 1979): 78–86.

2.6 REVISING PROBABILITIES WITH BAYES'S THEOREM

Bayes's theorem can also be used to incorporate additional information as it is made available and help create *revised* or *posterior probabilities*. This means that we can take new or recent data, then revise and improve upon our old probability estimates for an event (see Figure 2.4). Let us consider the following example.

Example 7: Posterior Probabilities

Alternate Example 2.7

A cup contains two dice identical in appearance. One, however, is fair (unbiased) and the other is loaded (biased). The probability of rolling a 3 on the fair die is ⅙ or .166. The probability of tossing the same number on the loaded die is .60.

Applicable Problems 2-15, 2-16, 2-17

We have no idea which die is which, but select one by chance and toss it. The result is a 3. Given this additional piece of information, can we find the (revised) probability that the die rolled was fair? Can we determine the probability it was the loaded die that was rolled?

The answer to these questions is *yes,* and we do so by using the formula for joint probability under statistical dependence and Bayes's theorem.

First, we take stock of the information and probabilities available. We know, for example, that since we randomly selected the die to roll, the probability of it being fair or loaded is .50.

$$P(\text{Fair}) = .50 \qquad P(\text{Loaded}) = .50$$

computing posterior probabilities

We also know that

$$P(3\,|\,\text{Fair}) = .166 \qquad P(3\,|\,\text{Loaded}) = .60$$

Transparency Master 2.8: Using Bayes's Process.

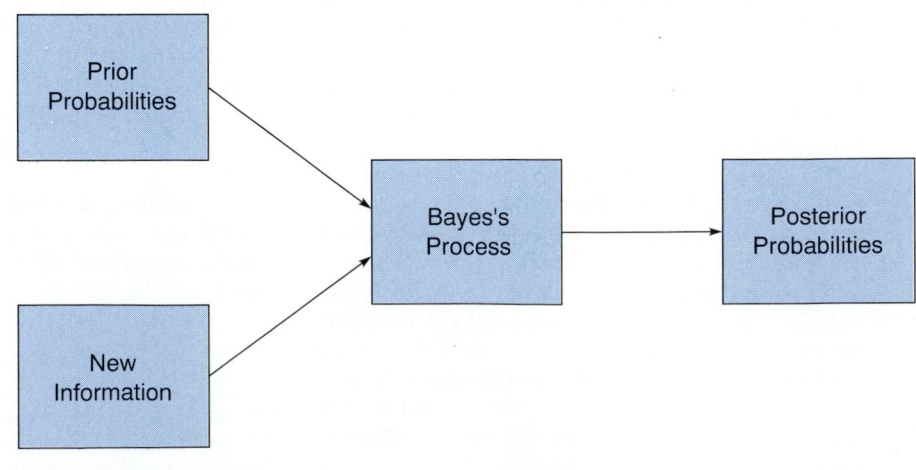

FIGURE 2.4
Using Bayes's Process

Next, we compute joint probabilities P(3 and Fair) and P(3 and Loaded), using the formula $P(AB) = P(A|B) \times P(B)$.

$$P(3 \text{ and Fair}) = P(3|\text{Fair}) \times P(\text{Fair}) = (.166)(.50) = .083$$

$$P(3 \text{ and Loaded}) = P(3|\text{Loaded}) \times P(\text{Loaded}) = (.60)(.50) = .300$$

A 3 can occur in combination with the state "fair die" or in combination with the state "loaded die." The sum of their probabilities gives the unconditional or marginal probability of a 3 on the toss, namely, $P(3) = .083 + .300 = .383$.

If a 3 does occur, and if we do not know which die it came from, the probability that the die rolled was the fair one is:

$$P(\text{Fair}|3) = \frac{P(\text{Fair and 3})}{P(3)} = \frac{.083}{.383} = .22$$

The probability that the die rolled was loaded is:

$$P(\text{Loaded}|3) = \frac{P(\text{Loaded and 3})}{P(3)} = \frac{.300}{.383} = .78$$

These two conditional probabilities are called the revised or posterior probabilities for the next roll of the die.

Before the die was rolled in the preceding example, the best we could say was that there was a 50-50 chance that it was fair (.50 probability) and a 50-50 chance it was loaded. After one roll of the die, however, we are able to revise our *prior probability* estimates. The new posterior estimate is that there is a .78 probability that the die rolled was loaded and only a .22 probability that it was not.

revising prior probability by adding new information

A General Form of Bayes's Theorem

Revised probabilities can also be computed in a more direct way using a *general* form for Bayes's theorem. We originally saw in Equation 2-5 that Bayes's law for the conditional probability of event A, given event B, is:

$$P(A|B) = \frac{P(AB)}{P(B)}$$

However, in the appendix to this chapter we have gone through the mathematical steps to show that:

Applicable Problem 2-22

$$P(A|B) = \frac{P(B|A)P(A)}{P(B|A)P(A) + P(B|\overline{A})P(\overline{A})} \qquad (2\text{-}7)$$

where

$\overline{A}$ = the complement of the event A; for example if A is the event "fair die," then $\overline{A}$ is "unfair" or "loaded die."

Now let's return to Example 7.

Although it may not be obvious to you at first glance, we used this basic equation to compute the revised probabilities. For example, if we want the probability that the fair die was rolled given the first toss was a 3, namely, P(Fair die | 3 rolled), we can let:

Event "Fair die" replace A in Equation 2-7
Event "Loaded die" replace $\overline{A}$ in Equation 2-7
Event "3 rolled" replace B in Equation 2-7

We can then rewrite Equation 2-7 and solve as follows:

$$P(\text{Fair die} \mid 3 \text{ rolled}) = \frac{P(3 \mid \text{Fair})P(\text{Fair})}{P(3 \mid \text{Fair})P(\text{Fair}) + P(3 \mid \text{Loaded})P(\text{Loaded})}$$

$$= \frac{(.166)(.50)}{(.166)(.50) + (.60)(.50)}$$

$$= \frac{.083}{.383} = .22$$

This is the same answer we computed in Example 7. Can you use this alternative approach to show that P(Loaded die | 3 rolled) = .78? Either method is perfectly acceptable, but when we deal with probability revisions again in Chapter 6, we may find that Equation 2-7 is easier to apply.

2.7   FURTHER PROBABILITY REVISIONS

Although one revision of prior probabilities can provide useful posterior probability estimates, additional information can be gained from performing the experiment a second time. If it is financially worthwhile, a decision maker may even decide to make several more revisions.

Example 8: A Second Probability Revision

Returning to Example 7 we now attempt to obtain further information about the posterior probabilities as to whether the die just rolled is fair or loaded. To do so, let us toss the die a second time. Again, we roll a 3. What are the further revised probabilities?

To answer this question, we proceed as before, with only one exception. The probabilities P(Fair) = .50 and P(Loaded) = .50 remain the same, but now we must compute P(3,3 | Fair) = (.166)(.166) = .027 and P(3,3 | Loaded) = (.6)(.6) = .36. With these joint probabilities of two 3s on successive rolls, given the two types of dice, we may revise the probabilities.

$$P(3,3 \text{ and Fair}) = P(3,3 \mid \text{Fair}) \times P(\text{Fair}) = (.027)(.5) = .013$$

$$P(3,3 \text{ and Loaded}) = P(3,3 \mid \text{Loaded}) \times P(\text{Loaded}) = (.36)(.5) = .18$$

Thus, the probability of rolling two 3s, a marginal probability, is .013 + .18 = .193, the sum of the two joint probabilities.

$$P(\text{Fair} \mid 3,3) = \frac{P(3,3 \text{ and Fair})}{P(3,3)} = \frac{.013}{.193} = .067$$

$$P(\text{Loaded}\,|\,3,3) = \frac{P(3,3 \text{ and Loaded})}{P(3,3)} = \frac{.18}{.193} = .933$$

What has this second roll accomplished? Before we rolled the die the first time, we knew only that there was a .50 probability that it was either fair or loaded. When the first die was rolled in Example 7, we were able to revise these probabilities to be:

Probability the die is fair = .22

Probability the die is loaded = .78

Now, after the second roll in Example 8, our refined revisions tell us that:

Probability the die is fair = .067

Probability the die is loaded = .933

*new posterior
probabilities*

This type of information can be extremely valuable in business decision making.

2.8 SUMMARY

This chapter presented the fundamental concepts of probability. Probability values can be obtained objectively or subjectively. A single probability value must be between 0 and 1, and the sum of all probability values for all possible outcomes must sum to 1. In addition, probability values and events can have a number of properties. These properties include mutually exclusive, collectively exhaustive, statistically independent, and statistically dependent events. Rules for computing probability values depend on these fundamental properties. It is also possible to revise probability values when new information becomes available. This can be done using Bayes's theorem.

The topics presented in this chapter and Chapter 3 will be very important in many of the chapters to come. Basic probability concepts and distributions are used for decision theory, inventory control, Markov analysis, quality control, program evaluation and review technique, and simulation.

GLOSSARY

Probability. A statement about the likelihood of an event occurring. It is expressed as a numerical value between 0 and 1, inclusive.

Relative Frequency Approach. An objective way of determining probabilities based on observing frequencies over a number of trials.

Classical or Logical Approach. An objective way of assessing probabilities based on logic.

Subjective Approach. A method of determining probability values based on experience or judgment.

Mutually Exclusive Events. A situation in which only one event can occur on any given trial or experiment.

Collectively Exhaustive Events. A collection of all possible outcomes of an experiment.

Marginal Probability. The simple probability of an event occurring.

Joint Probability. The probability of events occurring together (or one after the other).

Conditional Probability. The probability of one event occurring given that another has taken place.

Independent Events. The situation in which the occurrence of one event has no effect on the probability of occurrence of a second event.

Dependent Events. The situation in which the occurrence of one event affects the probability of occurrence of some other event.

Revised or Posterior Probability. A probability value that results from new or revised information and prior probabilities.

Prior Probability. A probability value determined before new or additional information is obtained. It is sometimes called an *a priori* probability estimate.

Bayes's Theorem. A formula that allows us to compute conditional probabilities when dealing with statistically dependent events.

KEY EQUATIONS

(2-1) $0 \leq P(\text{Event}) \leq 1$
A basic statement of probability.

(2-2) $P(A \text{ or } B) = P(A) + P(B)$
Law of addition for mutually exclusive events.

(2-3) $P(A \text{ or } B) = P(A) + P(B) - P(A \text{ and } B)$
Law of addition for events that are *not* mutually exclusive.

(2-4) $P(AB) = P(A) \times P(B)$
Joint probability for independent events.

(2-5) $P(A \mid B) = \dfrac{P(AB)}{P(B)}$
Bayes's law for conditional probabilities.

(2-6) $P(AB) = P(A \mid B) \times P(B)$
Joint probability for dependent events: a restatement of Bayes's law.

(2-7) $P(A \mid B) = \dfrac{P(B \mid A)P(A)}{P(B \mid A)P(A) + P(B \mid \overline{A})P(\overline{A})}$
A restatement of Bayes's law in general form.

DISCUSSION QUESTIONS AND PROBLEMS

Discussion Questions

2-1 What are the two basic laws of probability?

2-2 What is the meaning of mutually exclusive events; what is meant by collectively exhaustive? Give an example of each.

2-3 Describe the different approaches used in determining probability values.

2-4 Why is the probability of the intersection of two events subtracted in the sum of the probability of two events?

2-5 What is the difference between events that are dependent and events that are independent?

2-6 What is Bayes's theorem and when can it be used?

2-7 How can probability revisions assist in managerial decision making?

Problems

· **2-8** A student taking Management Science 301 at East Haven University will receive one of five possible grades for the course: A, B, C, D, or F. The distribution of grades over the past two years is as follows:

$P(C) = .30$

GRADE	NUMBER OF STUDENTS
A	80
B	75
C	90
D	30
F	25
Total	300

If this past distribution is a good indicator of future grades, what is the probability of a student receiving a C in the course?

· **2-9** A silver dollar is flipped twice. Calculate the probability of each of the following occurring.
  (a) A head on the first flip.   .5
  (b) A tail on the second flip given that the first toss was a head.   .5
  (c) Two tails.   .25
  (d) A tail on the first and a head on the second.   .25
  (e) A tail on the first and a head on the second *or* a head on the first and a tail on the second.   .50
  (f) At least one head on the two flips.   .75

· **2-10** An urn contains 8 red chips, 10 green chips, and 2 white chips. A chip is drawn and replaced, and then a second chip drawn. What is the probability of:
  (a) A white chip on the first draw?   .10
  (b) A white chip on the first draw and a red on the second?   .04

.25   **(c)** Two green chips being drawn?
.40   **(d)** A red chip on the second, given that a white chip was drawn on the first?

· **2-11** Evertight, a leading manufacturer of quality nails, produces 1-, 2-, 3-, 4-, and 5-inch nails for various uses. In the production process, if there is an overrun or if the nails are slightly defective, they are placed in a common bin. Yesterday, 651 of the 1-inch nails, 243 of the 2-inch nails, 41 of the 3-inch nails, 451 of the 4-inch nails, and 333 of the 5-inch nails were placed in the bin.

.26   **(a)** What is the probability of reaching into the bin and getting a 4-inch nail?
.19   **(b)** What is the probability of getting a 5-inch nail?
             (c) If a particular application requires a nail that is 3 inches or shorter, what
.54   is the probability of getting a nail that will satisfy the requirements of the application?

: **2-12** Last year, at Northern Manufacturing Company, 200 people had colds during the year. One hundred fifty-five people who did no exercising had colds, while the remainder of the people with colds were involved in a weekly exercise program. Half of the one thousand employees were involved in some type of exercise.

.20   **(a)** What is the probability that an employee will have a cold next year?
             (b) Given that an employee is involved in an exercise program, what is the
.09   probability that he or she will get a cold?
             (c) What is the probability that an employee that is not involved in an exer-
.31   cise program will get a cold next year?
dependent   **(d)** Are exercising and getting a cold independent events? Explain your answer.

: **2-13** The Springfield Kings, a professional basketball team, has won 12 out of its last 20 games and is expected to continue winning at the same percentage rate. The team's ticket manager is anxious to attract a large crowd to tomorrow's game, but believes that depends on how well the Kings perform tonight against the Galveston Comets. He assesses the probability of drawing a large crowd to be .90, should the team win tonight. What is the probability that the
.54   team wins tonight and that there will be a large crowd at tomorrow's game?

: **2-14** Professor David Mashley teaches two undergraduate statistics courses at Kansas College. The class for Statistics 201 consists of 7 sophomores and 3 juniors. The more advanced course, Statistics 301, has 2 sophomores and 8 juniors enrolled. As an example of a business sampling technique, Professor Mashley randomly selects, from the stack of Statistics 201 registration cards, the class card of one student and then places that card back in the stack. If that student was a sophomore, Mashley draws another card from the Statistics 201 stack; if not, he randomly draws a card from the Statistics 301 group. Are these two draws independent events?

What is the probability of:
.3   **(a)** A junior's name on the first draw?
             (b) A junior's name on the second draw, given that a sophomore's name was
.3   drawn first?
             (c) A junior's name on the second draw, given that a junior's name was
.8   drawn first?
.49   **(d)** A sophomore's name on both draws?
.24   **(e)** A junior's name on both draws?
             (f) One sophomore's name and one junior's name on the two draws, regard-
.27   less of order drawn?

: **2-15** The oasis outpost of Abu Ilan, in the heart of the Negev desert, has a population of 20 Bedouin tribesmen and 20 Farima tribesmen. El Kamin, a nearby oasis, has a population of 32 Bedouins and 8 Farima.

A lost Israeli soldier, accidentally separated from his army unit, is wandering through the desert and arrives at the edge of one of the oases. The soldier has no idea which oasis he has found, but the first person he spots at a distance is a Bedouin. What is the probability that he wandered into Abu Ilan? What is the probability that he is in El Kamin? .385, .615

: **2-16** The lost Israeli soldier mentioned in Problem 2-15 decides to rest for a few minutes before entering the desert oasis he has just found. (He reasons that he may need his strength should the oasis tribesmen be hostile.) Closing his eyes, he dozes off for 15 minutes, wakes, and walks toward the center of the oasis. The first person he spots this time he again recognizes as a Bedouin. What is the posterior probability that he is in El Kamin? .719

: **2-17** Ace Machine Works estimates that the probability their lathe tool is properly adjusted is .8. When the lathe is properly adjusted, there is a .9 probability that the parts produced pass inspection. If the lathe is out of adjustment, however, the probability of a good part being produced is only .2. A part randomly chosen is inspected and found to be acceptable. At this point, what is the posterior probability that the lathe tool is properly adjusted? .947

: **2-18** The Boston South Fifth Street Softball League consists of three teams: Mama's Boys, team 1; The Killers, team 2; and The Machos, team 3. Each team plays the other teams just once during the season. The win-loss record for the past five years is below:

WINNERS	(1)	(2)	(3)
Mama's Boys (1)	X	3	4
The Killers (2)	2	X	1
The Machos (3)	1	4	X

Each row represents the number of wins over the past five years. Mama's Boys beat The Killers 3 times, and beat The Machos 4 times, and so on.

(a) What is the probability that The Killers will win every game next year? .08

(b) What is the probability that The Machos will win at least one game next year? .84

(c) What is the probability that Mama's Boys will win exactly one game next year? .44

(d) What is the probability that The Killers will win less than two games next year? .92

: **2-19** The schedule for The Killers next year is as follows (refer to Problem 2-18):

Game 1   The Machos
Game 2   Mama's Boys

(a) What is the probability that The Killers will win their first game? .2
(b) What is the probability that The Killers will win their last game? .4
(c) What is the probability that The Killers will break even—win exactly one game? .44

.08
.48
No

       (d) What is the probability that The Killers will win every game?
       (e) What is the probability that The Killers will lose every game?
       (f) Would you want to be the coach of The Killers?

: **2-20** The Northside Rifle team has two markspersons, Dick and Sally. Dick hits a bull's-eye 90% of the time, and Sally hits a bull's-eye 95% of the time.

.995
.855

events are independent

       (a) What is the probability that either Dick or Sally or both will hit the bull's-eye if each takes one shot?
       (b) What is the probability that Dick and Sally will both hit the bull's-eye?
       (c) Did you make any assumptions in answering the preceding questions? If you answered yes, do you think that you are justified in making the assumption(s)?

P(Cancer in Laketown) = .02

P(Cancer in River
City) = .017
River City

: **2-21** In a sample of 1,000 representing a survey from the entire population, 650 people were from Laketown, and the rest of the people were from River City. Out of the sample, 19 people had some form of cancer. Thirteen of these people were from Laketown.
       (a) Are the events of living in Laketown and having some sort of cancer independent?
       (b) Which city would you prefer to live in, assuming your main objective was to avoid having cancer?

.78

: **2-22** Compute the probability of "loaded die, given that a 3 was rolled," as shown in Example 7, this time using the general form of Bayes's theorem from Equation 2-7.

BIBLIOGRAPHY

Campbell, S. *Flaws and Fallacies in Statistical Thinking.* Englewood Cliffs, NJ: Prentice-Hall, Inc., 1974.

Feller, W. *An Introduction to Probability Theory and Its Applications* Vols. 1 and 2, New York: John Wiley & Sons, Inc., 1957 and 1968.

Hamburg, Morris. *Statistical Analysis for Decision Making,* 4th ed. San Diego: Harcourt Brace Jovanovich, 1987.

Huff, D. *How to Lie with Statistics.* New York: W.W. Norton & Company, Inc., 1954.

Lapin, Lawrence L. *Statistics for Modern Business Decisions,* 4th ed. San Diego: Harcourt Brace Jovanovich, 1987.

McClave, James T., and P. George Bensen. *Statistics for Business and Economics,* 3rd ed. San Francisco: Dellon Publishing, 1985.

Appendix
Derivation of Bayes's Theorem

Derivation of Bayes's Theorem in the General Form

We know that the following three formulas are correct:

$$P(A\,|\,B) = \frac{P(AB)}{P(B)} \tag{1}$$

$$P(B\,|\,A) = \frac{P(AB)}{P(A)}$$

which can be rewritten as $P(AB) = P(B\,|\,A)P(A)$ (2)

$$P(B\,|\,\overline{A}) = \frac{P(\overline{A}B)}{P(\overline{A})}$$

which can be rewritten as $P(\overline{A}B) = P(B\,|\,\overline{A})P(\overline{A})$ (3)

Furthermore, by definition, we know that:

$$P(B) = P(AB) + P(\overline{A}B)$$

$$= P(B\,|\,A)P(A) + P(B\,|\,\overline{A})P(A) \tag{4}$$

from (2)   *from (3)*

Substituting Equations 2 and 4 into Equation 1, we have

$$P(A\,|\,B) = \frac{P(AB)}{P(B)}$$

from (2)

$$= \frac{P(B\,|\,A)P(A)}{P(B\,|\,A)P(A) + P(B\,|\,\overline{A})P(\overline{A})} \tag{5}$$

from (4)

This is the general form of Bayes's theorem shown as Equation 2-7 in this chapter.

3

Probability Distributions

CHAPTER OUTLINE

3.1 Introduction

3.2 Random Variables

3.3 Probability Distributions

3.4 The Binomial Distribution

3.5 The Poisson Distribution

3.6 The Normal Distribution

3.7 The Exponential Distribution

3.8 Summary

Glossary

Key Equations

Discussion Questions and Problems

Case Studies:

WTVX

Century Chemical Company

Bibliography

3.1 INTRODUCTION

The purpose of this chapter is to bridge the gap between the fundamentals of probability covered in the last chapter and the use of probability in future chapters. For example, in the next two chapters we will need to determine the expected value of a probability distribution to help select the best decision among a number of alternatives. In other chapters, we will need to compute the standard deviation and variance of a probability distribution. An understanding of probability distributions and their use is a prerequisite for about half of the chapters in this book.

The objective of this chapter is to cover the following topics:

1. Random variables.

2. Types of probability distributions.

3. Binomial and Poisson distributions.

4. Normal and exponential distributions.

3.2 RANDOM VARIABLES

In Chapter 2 we discussed various ways of assigning probability values to the outcomes of an experiment. In this chapter, we use this probability information to compute the expected outcome, variance, and standard deviation of the experiment.

outcome numbers can be the random variable

A *random variable* assigns a real number to every possible outcome or event in an experiment. It is normally represented by a letter such as X or Y. When the outcome itself is numerical or quantitative, the outcome numbers can be the random variable. For example, consider refrigerator sales at an appliance store. The number of refrigerators sold during a given day can be the random variable. Using X to represent this random variable, we can express this relationship as follows:

$$X = \text{number of refrigerators sold during the day}$$

In general, whenever the experiment has quantifiable outcomes, it is beneficial to define these quantitative outcomes as the random variable. Examples are given in Table 3.1.

When the outcome itself is not numerical or quantitative, it is necessary to define a random variable that associates each outcome with a unique real number. Several examples are given in Table 3.2.

types of random variables

There are two types of random variables: *discrete random variables* and *continuous random variables.* Developing probability distributions and making computations based on these distributions depends on the type of random variable.

A random variable is a *discrete random variable* if it can assume only a finite or limited set of values. Which of the random variables in Table 3.1 are

TABLE 3.1 Examples of Random Variables

EXPERIMENT	OUTCOME	RANDOM VARIABLES	RANGE OF RANDOM VARIABLES
Stock 50 Christ-mas trees	Number of Christ-mas trees sold	X = number of Christmas trees sold	0, 1, 2, . . . , 50
Inspect 600 items	Number of accept-able items	Y = number of ac-ceptable items	0, 1, 2, . . . , 600
Send out 5,000 sales letters	Number of people responding to the letters	Z = number of people responding to the letters	0, 1, 2, . . . , 5,000
Build an apart-ment building	Percent of building completed after 4 months	R = percent of building completed after 4 months	$0 \le R \le 100$
Test the lifetime of a light bulb (minutes)	Length of time the bulb lasts up to 80,000 minutes	S = time the bulb burns	$0 \le S \le 80,000$

Transparency Master 3.1: Examples of Random Variables.

discrete random variables? Looking at Table 3.1, we can see that stocking 50 Christmas trees, inspecting 600 items, and sending out 5,000 letters are all examples of discrete random variables. Each of these random variables can only assume a finite or limited set of values. The number of Christmas trees sold, for example, can only be integer numbers from 0 to 50. There are 51 values that the random variable X can assume in this example.

A *continuous random variable* is a random variable that has an infinite or an unlimited set of values. Are there any examples of continuous random variables in Table 3.1 or Table 3.2? Looking at Table 3.1, we can see that testing the lifetime of a light bulb is an experiment that can be described with a continuous random variable. In this case, the random variable, S, is the time the bulb burns. It can last for 3,206 minutes, 6,500.7 minutes,

KEY IDEA

TABLE 3.2 Random Variables for Outcomes That Are Not Numbers

EXPERIMENT	OUTCOMES	RANDOM VARIABLES	RANGE OF RANDOM VARIABLES
Students re-spond to a questionnaire	Strongly agree (SA) Agree (A) Neutral (N) Disagree (D) Strongly disagree (SD)	$X = \begin{cases} 5 \text{ if SA} \\ 4 \text{ if A} \\ 3 \text{ if N} \\ 2 \text{ if D} \\ 1 \text{ if SD} \end{cases}$	1, 2, 3, 4, 5
One machine is inspected	Defective Not defective	$Y = \begin{cases} 0 \text{ if defective} \\ 1 \text{ if not} \\ \quad \text{defective} \end{cases}$	0, 1
Consumers re-spond to how they like a product	Good Average Poor	$Z = \begin{cases} 3 \text{ if good} \\ 2 \text{ if average} \\ 1 \text{ if poor} \end{cases}$	1, 2, 3

Transparency Master 3.2: Random Variables for Outcomes That Are Not Numbers

251.726 minutes, or any other value between 0 and 80,000 minutes. In most cases, the range of a continuous random variable is stated as: Lower value $\leq S \leq$ Upper value, such as $0 \leq S \leq 80,000$. The random variable R in Table 3.1 is also continuous. Can you explain why?

3.3 PROBABILITY DISTRIBUTIONS

Transparency Master 3.3:
Probability Distributions

Transparency Master 3.4:
Continuous Probability
Distributions

Transparency Master 3.5:
Discrete Probability
Distributions

In the last chapter, we discussed probability values of an event. In this chapter, we explore the properties of *probability distributions*. We see how popular distributions, such as the uniform, normal, Poisson, binomial, and exponential probability distributions can save us time and effort. Since selection of the appropriate probability distribution depends partially on whether or not the random variable is *discrete* or *continuous*, we consider each of these types separately.

Probability Distribution of a Discrete Random Variable

Applicable Problem 3.9
Alternate Example 3.1

When we have a *discrete random variable*, there is a probability value assigned to each event. These values must be between 0 and 1, and they must sum to 1. Let's look at an example.

The 100 students in Dr. Pat Shannon's statistics class have just completed the instructor evaluations at the end of the course. Dr. Shannon is particularly interested in student response to the textbook because he is in the process of writing a competing statistics book. One of the questions on the evaluation survey was:

"The textbook was well written and helped me acquire the necessary information."

5. Strongly Agree

4. Agree

3. Neutral

2. Disagree

1. Strongly Disagree

The students' response to this question in the survey is summarized in Table 3.3. Also shown is the random variable X and the corresponding probability for each possible outcome. This discrete probability distribution was computed using the relative frequency approach presented in Chapter 2.

assigning a random variable

characteristics of all probability distributions

The distribution follows the three rules required of all probability distributions: (1) the events are mutually exclusive and collectively exhaustive, (2) the individual probability values are between 0 and 1 inclusive, and (3) the total of the probability values sum to 1.

TABLE 3.3 Probability Distribution for Textbook Question

OUTCOME	RANDOM VARIABLE (X)	NUMBER RESPONDING	PROBABILITY P(X)
Strongly agree	5	10	$.1 = {}^{10}/_{100}$
Agree	4	20	$.2 = {}^{20}/_{100}$
Neutral	3	30	$.3 = {}^{30}/_{100}$
Disagree	2	30	$.3 = {}^{30}/_{100}$
Strongly disagree	1	10	$.1 = {}^{10}/_{100}$
		Total 100	$1.0 = {}^{100}/_{100}$

While listing the probability distribution as we did in Table 3.3 is adequate, it can be difficult to get an idea about characteristics of the distribution. To overcome this problem, the probability values are often presented in a graph form. The graph of the distribution in Table 3.3 is shown in Figure 3.1

The graph of this probability distribution gives us a picture of its shape. It helps us identify the central tendency of the distribution, called the *expected value,* and the amount of variability or spread of the distribution, called the *variance.*

Expected Value of a Discrete Probability Distribution

Once we have established a probability distribution, the first characteristic that is usually of interest is the "central tendency," or average of the distribution. The expected value, a measure of central tendency, is computed as a weighted average of the values of the random variable:

$$E(X) = \sum_{i=1}^{n} X_i P(X_i) = X_1 P(X_1) + X_2 P(X_2) + \cdots + X_n P(X_n) \qquad \text{(3-1)}$$

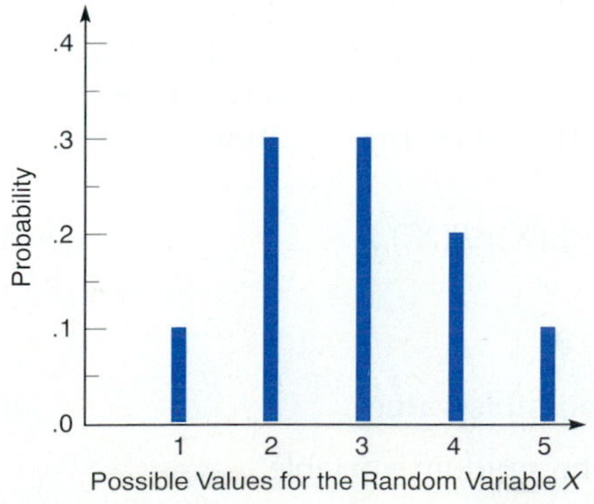

central tendency or the average

Teaching Suggestion 3.2: Expected Value of a Probability Distribution. See the Instructor's Section for details.

Applicable Problems 3-10, 3-11

FIGURE 3.1
Probability Function for Dr. Shannon's Class

where

X_i = the random variable's possible values,

$P(X_i)$ = the probability of each of the random variable's possible values,

$\sum\limits_{i=1}^{n}$ = the summation sign indicating we are adding all n possible values, and

$E(X)$ = the expected value of the random variable.

$E(X)$ for Shannon's class

The expected value of any discrete probability distribution can be computed by multiplying each possible value of the random variable, X_i, times the probability, $P(X_i)$, that outcome will occur, and summing the results, Σ. Here is how the expected value can be computed for the textbook question:

Alternate Example 3.2

$$E(X) = \sum_{i=1}^{5} X_i P(X_i) = X_1 P(X_1) + X_2 P(X_2) + X_3 P(X_3) + X_4 P(X_4) + X_5 P(X_5)$$

$$= (5)(.1) + (4)(.2) + (3)(.3) + (2)(.3) + (1)(.1)$$

$$= 2.9$$

The expected value of 2.9 implies that the mean response is between Disagree (2) and Neutral (3), and that the average response is closer to Neutral, which is 3. Looking at Figure 3.1, this is consistent with the shape of the probability function.

Variance of a Discrete Probability Distribution

In addition to the central tendency of a probability distribution, most people are interested in the variability or the spread of the distribution. If the variability is low, it is much more likely that the outcome of an experiment will be close to the average or expected value. On the other hand, if the variability of the distribution is high, which means that the probability is spread out over the various random variable values, then there is less chance that the outcome of an experiment will be close to the expected value.

The *variance* of a probability distribution is a number that reveals the overall spread or dispersion of the distribution. For a discrete probability distribution, it can be computed using the following equation:

$$\text{Variance} = \sum_{i=1}^{n} (X_i - E(X))^2 P(X_i) \tag{3-2}$$

where

X_i = the random variable's possible values,

$E(X)$ = the expected value of the random variable,

$(X_i - E(X))$ = the difference between each value of the random variable and the expected value, and

$P(X_i)$ = probability of each possible value of the random variable.

To compute the variance, each value of the random variable is subtracted from the expected value, squared, and multiplied times the probability of occurrence of that value. The results are then summed to obtain the variance. Here is how this procedure is done for Dr. Shannon's textbook question:

computing variance for Shannon's class

$$\text{Variance} = \sum_{i=1}^{5} (X_i - E(X))^2 P(X_i)$$

Alternate Example 3.3

$$\text{Variance} = (5 - 2.9)^2(.1) + (4 - 2.9)^2(.2) + (3 - 2.9)^2(.3)$$
$$+ (2 - 2.9)^2(.3) + (1 - 2.9)^2(.1)$$
$$= (2.1)^2(.1) + (1.1)^2(.2) + (.1)^2(.3) + (-.9)^2(.3) + (-1.9)^2(.1)$$
$$= .441 + .242 + .003 + .243 + .361$$
$$= 1.29$$

A related measure of dispersion or spread is the *standard deviation*. This quantity is also used in many computations involved with probability distributions. The standard deviation is just the square root of the variance.

standard deviation

$$\sigma = \sqrt{\text{Variance}} \qquad (3\text{-}3)$$

where

$$\sqrt{} = \text{square root, and}$$
$$\sigma = \text{standard deviation.}$$

The standard deviation for the textbook question is:

$$\sigma = \sqrt{\text{Variance}}$$
$$= \sqrt{1.29} = 1.14$$

Probability Distribution of a Continuous Random Variable

There are many examples of *continuous random variables*. The time it takes to finish a project, the number of ounces in a barrel of butter, the high temperature during a given day, the exact length of a given type of lumber, and the weight of a railroad car of coal are all examples of continuous random variables. Since random variables can take on an infinite number of values, the fundamental probability rules for continuous random variables must be modified.

As with discrete probability distributions, the sum of the probability values must equal 1. Because there are an infinite number of values of the random variables, however, the probability of each value of the random variable must be 0. If the probability values for the random variable values were greater than 0, then the sum would be infinitely large.

probability rules for continuous distributions

With a continuous probability distribution, there is a continuous mathematical function that describes the probability distribution. This function is called the *probability density function* or simply the *probability function*. It is usually represented by $f(X)$.

probability density function

We now look at the sketch of a sample density function in Figure 3.2. This curve represents the probability density function for the weight of a particular machined part. The weight could vary from 5.06 to 5.30 grams, with weights around 5.18 grams being the most likely. The shaded area represents the probability the weight is between 5.22 and 5.26 grams.

If we wanted to know the probability of a part weighing exactly 5.1300000 grams, for example, we would have to compute the area of a slice of width 0. Of course, this would be 0. This result may seem strange, but if we insist on enough decimal places of accuracy, we are bound to find that the weight differs from 5.1300000 grams *exactly,* be the difference ever so slight.

Applicable Problems 3-13, 3-15, 3-24

uniform distribution

Uniform Distributions

The *uniform probability density function* is used to describe a continuous probability distribution that has a range of continuous values from point *a* to point *b*, inclusive. It is described by the following equation:

$$f(X) = \begin{cases} \dfrac{1}{b - a} & \text{for } a \le X \le b \\ 0 & \text{otherwise} \end{cases}$$

(3-4)

This distribution assumes that there is an equally likely chance that any point along this range will occur. Thus, the probability looks like a box, as in Figure 3.3.

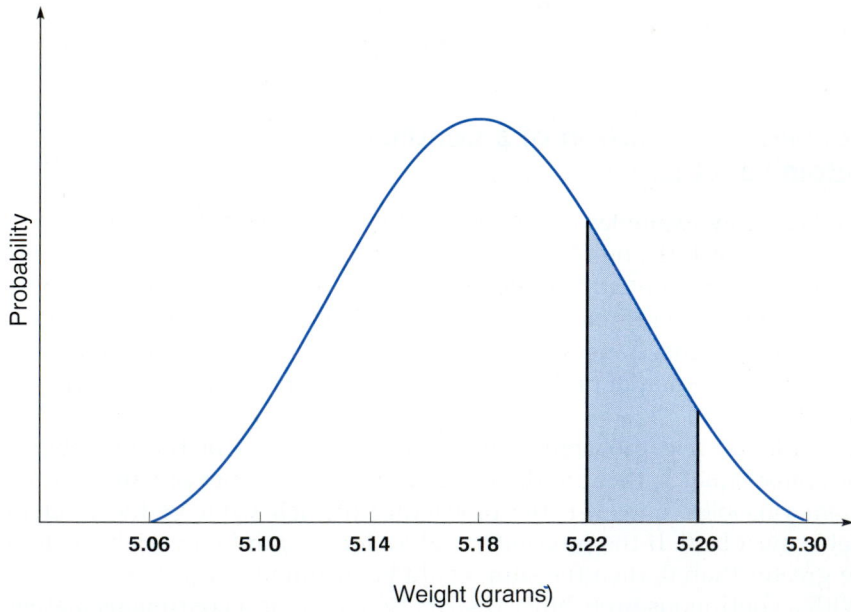

FIGURE 3.2
Sample Density Function

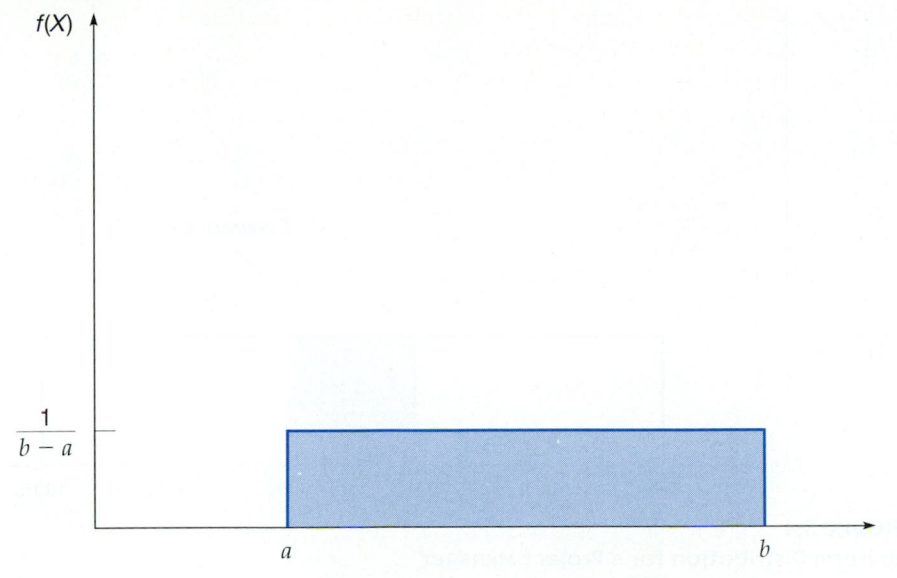

FIGURE 3.3
Uniform Probability Density Function

In order to find the probability that a value will fall within a range or interval inside of a and b, we locate the range and find the area between the range and the top of the probability distribution. Since the area is always a rectangle, this is done by multiplying the base of the rectangle, which is the range or interval, times the height, which is always $1/(b - a)$. Let's look at an example. — **area as a measure of probability**

A project manager would like to determine the probability that a project will be between 70% and 80% complete in six months. At the present time, the project is 50% complete, and the manager believes that project completion follows a uniform probability density function that ranges from 50% complete, which is the current state, to 100% complete. Figure 3.4 graphically represents this situation. — **a uniform distribution example**

In order to get the desired probability, we need to find the shaded area— a rectangle that represents the probability that the project will be between 70% and 80% complete at the end of six months. This area is computed as follows:

$$\text{Probability} = (\text{base}) \cdot (\text{height})$$

$$= (80 - 70)\left(\frac{1}{100 - 50}\right)$$

$$= (10)\left(\frac{1}{50}\right) = 0.20$$

Finding the area under the curve for a uniform probability density function is fairly easy because the area is always a rectangle. Other continuous — **the use of calculus**

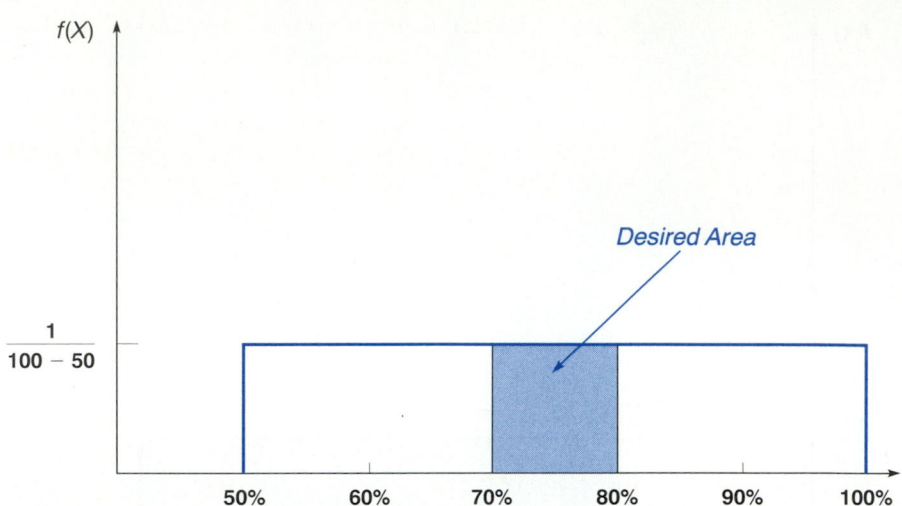

FIGURE 3.4
Uniform Distribution for a Project Manager

probability density functions are not so simple, and finding the area under the curve, the expected value, and the variance may require the use of calculus. Fortunately, the work for some of the popular continuous distributions has already been done for us in tables, as we will see shortly.

In this section, we have investigated the fundamental characteristics and properties of probability distributions in general. In the next four sections, we will introduce two important discrete probability distributions—the binomial distribution and the Poisson distribution—and two useful continuous distributions—the normal distribution and the exponential distribution.

3.4   THE BINOMIAL DISTRIBUTION

Applicable Problems 3-12, 3-14, 3-21, 3-22, 3-23

Many business experiments can be characterized by the *Bernoulli process,* which follows the *binomial probability distribution.* In order to be a Bernoulli process, an experiment must have the following characteristics:

characteristics of the Bernoulli process

1. Each trial in a Bernoulli process has only two possible outcomes— either yes or no, success or failure, heads or tails, pass or fail, and so on.

2. Regardless of how many times the experiment is performed, the probability of the outcome stays the same.

3. The trials are statistically independent.

4. The number of trials is known and is either 1, 2, 3, 4, 5, and so on.

To analyze a Bernoulli process, we need to know the values of: (1) the probability of success on a single trial, p, and the probability of a failure on a single trial, q (which equals $1 - p$); (2) the number of successes desired, r; and (3) the number of trials performed, n.

A common example of a Bernoulli process is flipping a coin. If we wish to compute the probability of getting exactly 4 heads on 5 tosses of a fair coin, the Bernoulli process parameters are:

$$p = \text{probability of heads} = .5$$

$$q = \text{probability of tails (nonheads)} = 1 - p = .5$$

$$r = \text{number of successes desired} = 4$$

$$n = \text{number of trials performed} = 5$$

There are two ways of solving these Bernoulli problems to find the desired probabilities. The first is to apply the formula, called the *binomial probability formula*, given in Equation 3-5.

binomial formula

$$\text{Probability of } r \text{ successes in } n \text{ trials} = \frac{n!}{r!\,(n-r)!}\,p^r q^{n-r} \qquad \textbf{(3-5)}$$

The symbol ! means *factorial*. To compute 5!, for example, we just multiply $5 \times 4 \times 3 \times 2 \times 1 = 120$. Likewise, $4! = 4 \times 3 \times 2 \times 1 = 24$, $1! = 1$, and $0! = 1$.

Although Equation 3-5 works well in small problems, it can become cumbersome when large values of n and r are inserted. The second method is to make use of *binomial distribution tables*. Both approaches are illustrated in the following sections.

Solving Problems with the Binomial Formula

Using the binomial probability formula, we can solve for the probability of getting exactly four heads in five tosses of a coin.

formula approach to solving binomial problems

$$p = .5 \qquad q = .5 \qquad r = 4 \qquad n = 5$$

$$\begin{aligned}\text{Probability of } r \text{ successes in } n \text{ trials} &= \frac{n!}{r!\,(n-r)!}\,p^r q^{n-r} = \frac{5!}{4!\,(5-4)!}\,(.5)^4(.5)^1 \\ &= \frac{5 \times 4 \times 3 \times 2 \times 1}{(4 \times 3 \times 2 \times 1)\,(1)}\,(.5)^4(.5)^1\end{aligned}$$

or

$$\text{Probability} = \frac{120}{(24)\,(1)}\,(.0625)\,(.5) = .15625$$

Thus, the probability that 4 tosses out of 5 will land heads up is .15625 or 16 percent.

Using Equation 3-5, it is also possible to determine the entire probability distribution for a binomial experiment. The probability distribution of flipping a fair coin 5 times is shown in Table 3.4 and then graphed in Figure 3.5.

TABLE 3.4 Binomial Probability Distribution

(NUMBER OF HEADS) (r)	PROBABILITY $= \dfrac{5!}{r!(5-r)!}(.5)^r(.5)^{5-r}$
0	$.03125 = \dfrac{5!}{0!(5-0)!}(.5)^0(.5)^{5-0}$
1	$.15625 = \dfrac{5!}{1!(5-1)!}(.5)^1(.5)^{5-1}$
2	$.3125 = \dfrac{5!}{2!(5-2)!}(.5)^2(.5)^{5-2}$
3	$.3125 = \dfrac{5!}{3!(5-3)!}(.5)^3(.5)^{5-3}$
4	$.15625 = \dfrac{5!}{4!(5-4)!}(.5)^4(.5)^{5-4}$
5	$.03125 = \dfrac{5!}{5!(5-5)!}(.5)^5(.5)^{5-5}$

Solving Problems with Binomial Tables

MSA Electronics is experimenting with the manufacture of a new type of transistor that is very difficult to mass-produce at an acceptable quality

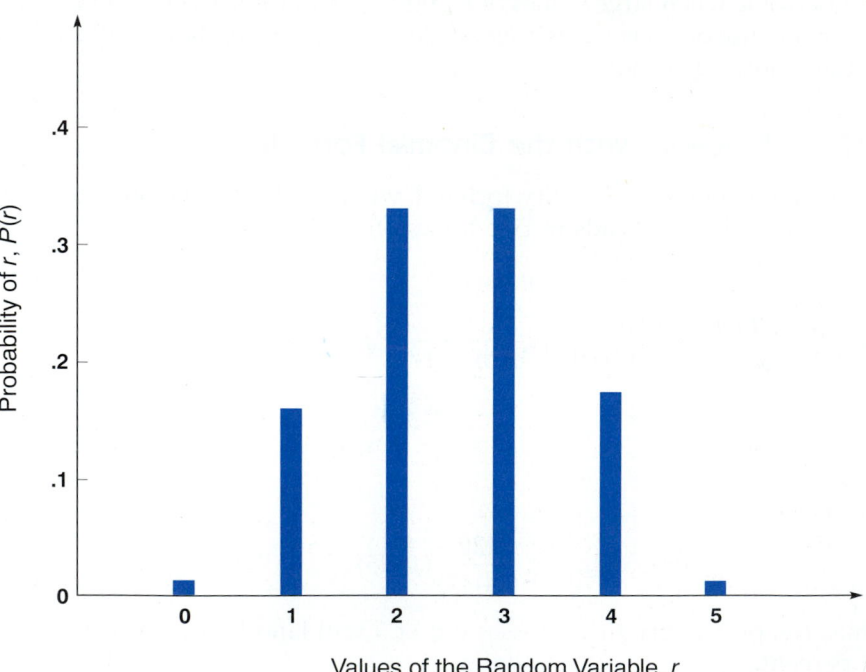

FIGURE 3.5
Binomial Probability Distribution When _n_ = 5,
_p_ = 0.50

level. Every hour a supervisor takes a random sample of 6 transistors produced on the assembly line. The probability that any one transistor is defective is considered to be .13. MSA wants to know the probability of finding 4 or more defects in the lot sampled.

The elements in this problem would be:

$$p = .13 \qquad r = 4 \text{ defects} \qquad n = 6 \text{ trials}$$

The question posed may be easily answered by using a *cumulative* binomial distribution table. Such tables can be very lengthy. For the sake of brevity, we present in Table 3.5 only that portion of a binomial table corresponding to $n = 6$. Appendix C contains a complete binomial table for a broad range of n, r, and p values.

Since the probability of MSA finding any one defect is .13, we look through the $n = 6$ table until we find the column where $p = .13$. We then move down that column until we are opposite the $r = 4$ row. The answer there is found to be 0034, which is interpreted to be a probability of .0034 that there are 4 or more defects in the sample. This value has been shaded in Table 3.5.

There is an easy way to compute the expected value and variance of the binomial distribution. The appropriate equations are:

expected value and variance

$$\text{Expected value} = np \qquad \qquad \textbf{(3-6)}$$

$$\text{Variance} = np(1 - p) \qquad \qquad \textbf{(3-7)}$$

The expected value and variance for MSA Electronics can be computed as follows:

$$\text{Expected value} = np$$

$$= (6)(.13) = .78$$

$$\text{Variance} = np(1 - p)$$

$$= (6)(.13)(1 - .13) = .6786$$

3.5 ## THE POISSON DISTRIBUTION

Applicable Problems 3-28, 3-29

Our second important discrete probability distribution is the *Poisson distribution*.[1] We examine it because of its key role in queuing theory, the topic of Chapter 16. The distribution describes situations in which customers arrive independently during a certain time interval, and the number of arrivals depends on the length of the time interval. Examples are patients arriving at a health clinic, customers arriving at a bank window, passengers arriving at an airport, and telephone calls going through a central exchange.

The formula for the Poisson distribution is:

$$P(X) = \frac{\lambda^X e^{-\lambda}}{X!} \qquad \qquad \textbf{(3-8)}$$

[1]This distribution, derived by Simeon Poisson in 1837, is pronounced "pwah-sahn."

TABLE 3.5 A Sample Table for the Cumulative Binomial Distribution

$P(R \geq r \mid n, p)$

$n = 6$

P\R	01	02	03	04	05	06	07	08	09	10
1	0585	1142	1670	2172	2649	3101	3530	3936	4321	4686
2	0015	0057	0125	0216	0328	0459	0608	0773	0952	1143
3		0002	0005	0012	0022	0038	0058	0085	0118	0159
4					0001	0002	0003	0005	0008	0013
5										0001

P\R	11	12	13	14	15	16	17	18	19	20
1	5030	5356	5664	5954	6229	6487	6731	6960	7176	7397
2	1345	1556	1776	2003	2235	2472	2713	2956	3201	3446
3	0206	0261	0324	0395	0473	0560	0655	0759	0870	0989
4	0018	0025	0034	0045	0059	0075	0094	0116	0141	0170
5	0001	0001	0002	0003	0004	0005	0007	0010	0013	0016
6										0001

P\R	21	22	23	24	25	26	27	28	29	30
1	7569	7748	7916	8073	8220	8358	8487	8607	8719	8824
2	3692	3937	4180	4422	4661	4896	5128	5356	5580	5798
3	1115	1250	1391	1539	1694	1856	2023	2196	2374	2557
4	0202	0239	0280	0326	0376	0431	0492	0557	0628	0705
5	0020	0025	0031	0038	0046	0056	0067	0079	0093	0109
6	0001	0001	0001	0002	0002	0003	0004	0005	0006	0007

P\R	31	32	33	34	35	36	37	38	39	40
1	8921	9011	9095	9173	9246	9313	9375	9432	9485	9533
2	6012	6220	6422	6619	6809	6994	7172	7343	7508	7667
3	2744	2936	3130	3328	3529	3732	3937	4143	4350	4557
4	0787	0875	0969	1069	1174	1286	1404	1527	1657	1792
5	0127	0148	0170	0195	0223	0254	0288	0325	0365	0410
6	0009	0011	0013	0015	0018	0022	0026	0030	0035	0041

P\R	41	42	43	44	45	46	47	48	49	50
1	9578	9619	9657	9692	9723	9752	9778	9802	9824	9844
2	7819	7965	8105	8238	8364	8485	8599	8707	8810	8906
3	4764	4971	5177	5382	5585	5786	5985	6180	6373	6563
4	1933	2080	2232	2390	2553	2721	2893	3070	3252	3438
5	0458	0510	0566	0627	0692	0762	0837	0917	1003	1094
6	0048	0055	0063	0073	0083	0095	0108	0122	0138	0156

Source: Reprinted from Robert O. Schlaifer, *Introduction to Statistics for Business Decisions,* published by McGraw-Hill Book Company, 1961, by permission of the copyright holder, the President and Fellows of Harvard College.

where

$P(X)$ = the probability of exactly X arrivals or occurrences,

λ = the average number of arrivals per unit of time (the mean arrival rate), pronounced "lambda,"

$e = 2.718$, the base of the natural logarithms, and

X = the specific value (0, 1, 2, 3, and so on) of the random variable.

The mean and variance of the Poisson distribution are equal and are simply computed as:

$$\text{Expected value} = \lambda \qquad \textbf{(3-9)}$$

$$\text{Variance} = \lambda \qquad \textbf{(3-10)}$$

A sample distribution for $\lambda = 2$ arrivals is shown in Figure 3.6 (the values plotted are derived from tables in Appendix D). Further examples and details are discussed in Chapter 16.

3.6   THE NORMAL DISTRIBUTION

One of the most popular and useful continuous probability distributions is the *normal distribution*. The probability density function of this distribution is given by the rather complex formula:

**Applicable Problems
3-16, 3-17, 3-18, 3-19.
3-20, 3-25, 3-26, 3-27**

$$f(X) = \frac{1}{\sigma\sqrt{2\pi}} e^{\frac{-\frac{1}{2}(X - \mu)^2}{\sigma^2}} \qquad \textbf{(3-11)}$$

The normal distribution is completely specified when values for the mean, μ, and the standard deviation, σ, are known. Figure 3.7 shows

mean and standard deviation

Video 3.1

APPLICATIONS OF QA

USING PROBABILITY DISTRIBUTIONS TO SEARCH FOR SUNKEN GOLD

In 1857, most people traveling from California to New York sailed by steamer from San Francisco to the west coast of Panama, crossed the isthmus by train, and took a steamship to New York.

The *Central America* operated on the Atlantic side of the Panama route, taking passengers and gold from California to New York. She sank 200 miles off the coast of South Carolina in a hurricane in 1857, taking gold bars and coins worth an estimated $400 million to the ocean bottom almost 8,000 feet below. Some 425 people lost their lives.

In 1985, Lawrence Stone was hired by the Columbus-America Discovery Group to develop a probability distribution map for the location of the *Central America*. The work was to be based on historical information from survivors and ships in the area at the time. The objective was to use the map to design an efficient search plan that would produce a high probability of finding the target. It

would provide specific directions for performing a search and serve as a basis for estimating the amount of time, effort, and money necessary to assure a high probability of success.

Stone's work first involved quantifying all relevant information. He then assigned each scenario a probability distribution and developed the "probability map" as the estimate of the wreck's location from each scenario.

The project was successful. In 1989, the group recovered one ton of gold bars and coins from the wreck. Some thirty-nine insurance companies then filed claims to the recovered gold, but all claims were settled in the favor of the Columbus-America Discovery Group.

Source: Lawrence D. Stone. "Search for the *SS Central America.*" *Interfaces* **22**, 1 (Jan.–Feb. 1992): 32–54.

Transparency Master 3.8:
Sample Poisson Distribution

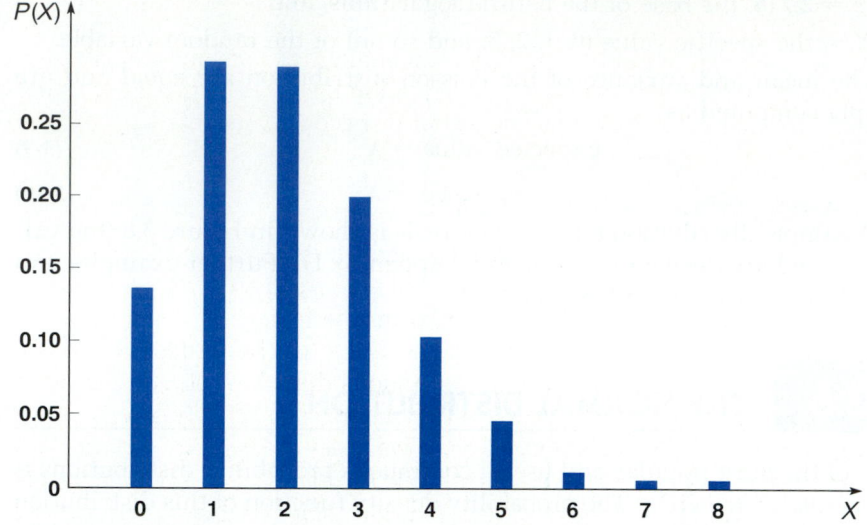

FIGURE 3.6
Sample Poisson Distribution with $\lambda = 2$

several different normal distributions with the same standard deviation and different means.

As shown in Figure 3.7, differing values of μ will shift the average or center of the normal distribution. The overall shape of the distribution remains the same. On the other hand, when the standard deviation is varied,

changes in the mean

Teaching Suggestion 3.3:
The Bell-Shaped Curve.
See the Instructor's Section
for details.

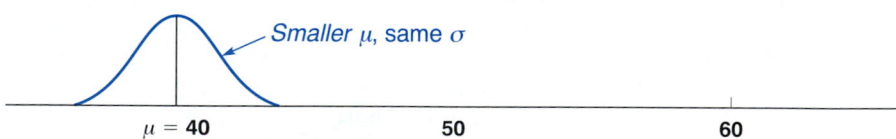

Transparency Master 3.9:
Normal Distribution with
Different Values.

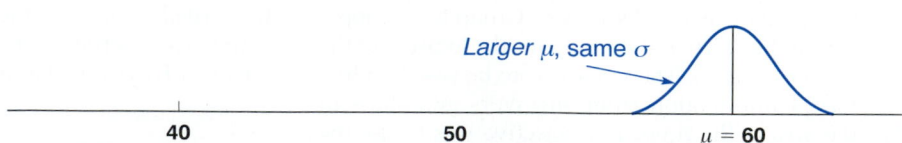

FIGURE 3.7
Normal Distribution with Different Values for μ

the normal curve either flattens out or becomes steeper. This is shown in Figure 3.8.

changes in the standard deviation

As the standard deviation, σ, becomes smaller, the normal distribution becomes steeper. When the standard deviation becomes larger, the normal distribution has a tendency to flatten out or become broader.

The Area under the Normal Curve

Because the normal distribution is symmetrical, its midpoint (and highest point) is at the mean. Values on the X axis are then measured in terms of how many standard deviations they lie from the mean.

As you may recall from our earlier discussion of the uniform distribution, the area under the curve (in a continuous distribution) describes the probability that a random variable has a value in a specified interval. When dealing with the uniform distribution, it was easy to compute the area between any points a and b. The normal distribution requires mathematical calculations beyond the scope of this text, but tables that provide areas or probabilities are readily available. For example, Figure 3.9 illustrates three commonly used relationships that have been derived from standard normal tables (to be discussed shortly). The area from point a to point b in the

commonly used relationships

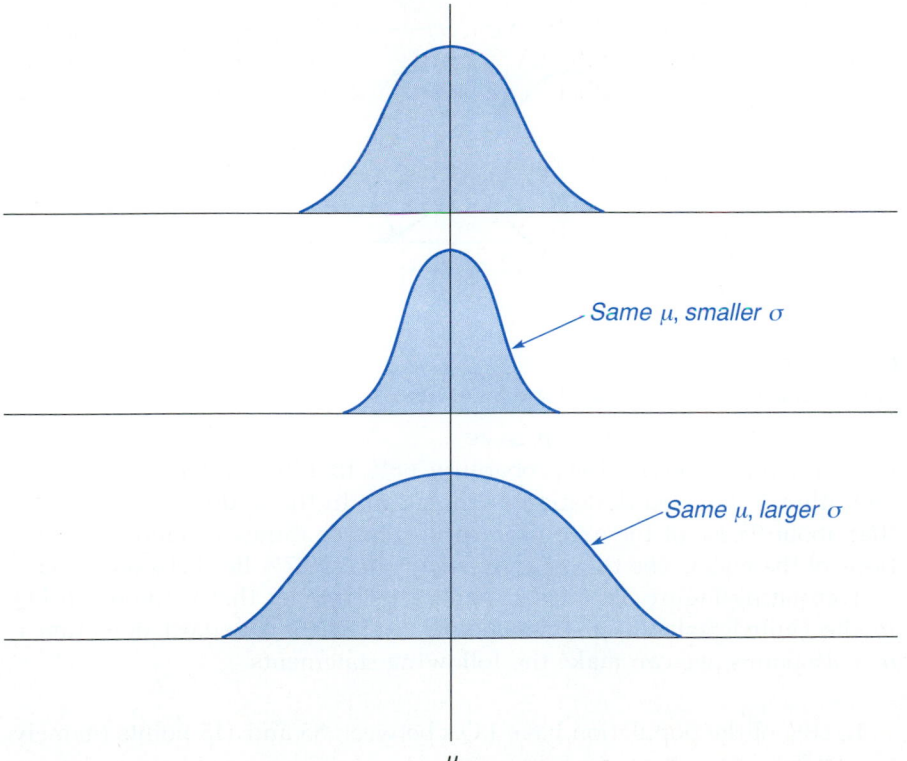

Same μ, smaller σ

Same μ, larger σ

μ

Transparency Master 3.10: Normal Distribution with Different Values.

FIGURE 3.8
Normal Distribution with Different Values for σ

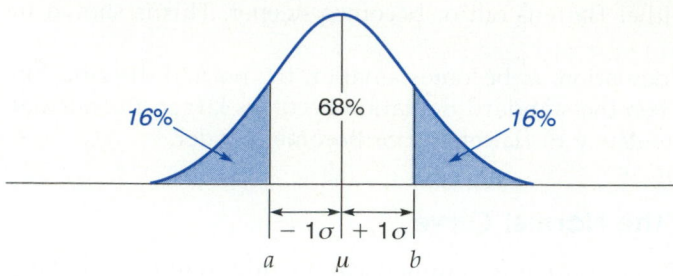

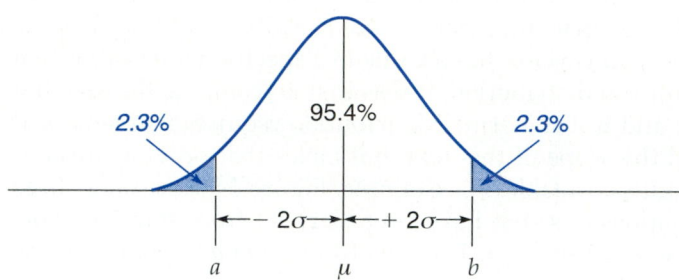

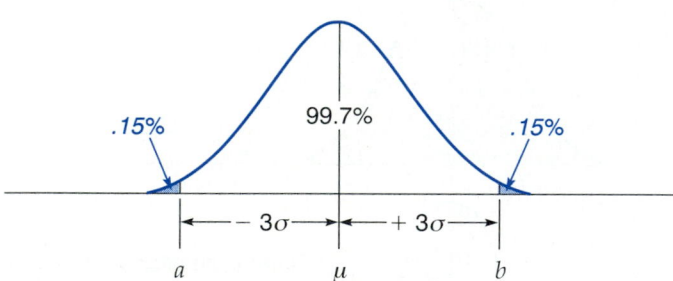

FIGURE 3.9
Three Common Areas under Normal Curves

first drawing represents the probability, 68%, that the random variable will be within 1 standard deviation of the mean. In the middle graph, we see that about 95.4% of the area lies within plus or minus 2 standard deviations of the mean. The third figure shows that 99.7% lies between $\pm 3\sigma$.

Translating Figure 3.9 into an application implies that if the mean I.Q. in the United States is $\mu = 100$ points, and if the standard deviation is $\sigma = 15$ points, we can make the following statements:

1. 68% of the population have I.Q.s between 85 and 115 points (namely, $\pm 1\sigma$).

2. 95.4% of the people have I.Q.s between 70 and 130 points ($\pm 2\sigma$).

3. 99.7% of the population have I.Q.s in the range from 55 to 145 points ($\pm 3\sigma$).

4. Only 16% of the people have I.Q.s greater than 115 points (from first graph, the area to the right of $+1\sigma$).

Many more interesting remarks could likewise be drawn from these data. Can you tell the probability a person selected at random has an I.Q. less than 70? Greater than 145? Less than 145?

Using the Standard Normal Table

To use a table to find normal probability values, we follow two steps.

Step 1: Convert the normal distribution to what we call a *standard normal distribution.* A standard normal distribution is one that has a mean of 0 and a standard deviation of 1. All normal tables are set up to handle random variables with $\mu = 0$ and $\sigma = 1$. Without a standard normal distribution, a different table would be needed for each pair of μ and σ values. We call the new standard random variable Z. The value for Z for any normal distribution is computed from this equation:

use of the standard normal distribution

$$Z = \frac{X - \mu}{\sigma} \qquad \text{(3-12)}$$

where

X = the value of the random variable we want to measure,

Alternate Example 3-4

μ = the mean of the distribution,

σ = the standard deviation of the distribution, and

Z = the number of standard deviations from X to the mean, μ.

For example, if $\mu = 100$, $\sigma = 15$, and we are interested in finding the probability that the random variable X is less than 130, then we want $P(X < 130)$.

$$Z = \frac{X - \mu}{\sigma} = \frac{130 - 100}{15} = \frac{30}{15} = 2 \text{ standard deviations}$$

This means that the point X is 2.0 standard deviations to the right of the mean. This is shown in Figure 3.10.

Step 2: Look up the probability from a table of normal curve areas. Table 3.6, which also appears as Appendix A, is such a table of areas for the standard normal distribution. It is set up to provide the area under the curve to the left of any specified value of Z.

use of normal curves

Let's see how Table 3.6 can be used. The column on the left lists values of Z, with the second decimal place of Z appearing in the top row. For example, for a value of $Z = 2.00$ as just computed, find 2.0 in the left-hand column and .00 in the top row. In the body of the table, we find that the area sought is .97725, or 97.7%. Thus,

$$P(X < 130) = P(Z < 2.00) = 97.7\%$$

This suggests that if the mean I.Q. score is 100 with a standard deviation of 15 points, the probability that a randomly selected person's I.Q. is less than 130 is 97.7%. By referring back to Figure 3.9, we see that this probability could also have been derived from the middle graph. (Note that 1.0 −

Teaching Suggestion 3.5:
Using the Normal Table to
Answer Probability Questions.
See the Instructor's Section
for details.

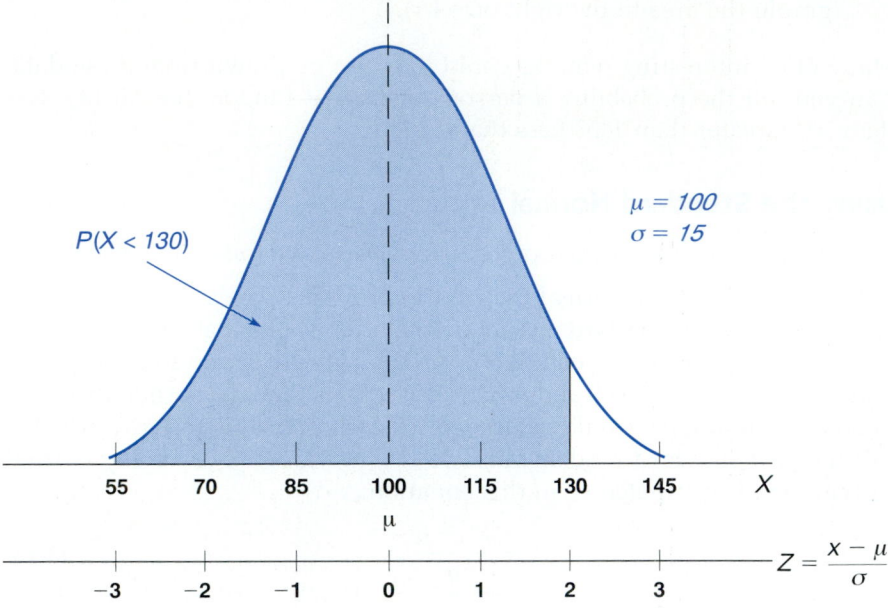

FIGURE 3.10
**Normal Distribution Showing the Relationship
Between Z Values and X Values**

.977 = .023 = 2.3%, which is the area in the right-hand tail of the curve.)

To feel comfortable with the use of the standard normal probability table, we need to work a few more examples. We now use the Haynes Construction Company as a case in point.

Haynes Construction Company Example

Haynes Construction Company builds primarily three- and four-unit apartment buildings (called triplexes and quadraplexes) for investors, and it is believed that the total construction time in days follows a normal distribution. The mean time to construct a triplex is 100 days, and the standard deviation is 20 days. Recently, the president of Haynes Construction signed a contract to complete a triplex in 125 days. Failure to complete the triplex in 125 days would result in severe penalty fees. What is the probability that Haynes Construction will not be in violation of their construction contract? The normal distribution for the construction of triplexes is shown in Figure 3.11.

In order to compute this probability, we need to find the shaded area under the curve. We begin by computing Z for this problem:

$$Z = \frac{X - \mu}{\sigma}$$

$$= \frac{125 - 100}{20}$$

$$= \frac{25}{20} = 1.25$$

TABLE 3.6 The Standardized Normal Distribution Function

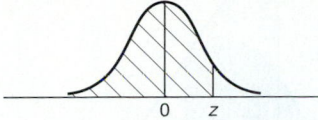

Z	.00	.01	.02	.03	.04	.05	.06	.07	.08	.09
0.0	.50000	.50399	.50798	.51197	.51595	.51994	.52392	.52790	.53188	.53586
0.1	.53983	.54380	.54776	.55172	.55567	.55962	.56356	.56749	.57142	.57535
0.2	.57926	.58317	.58706	.59095	.59483	.59871	.60257	.60642	.61026	.61409
0.3	.61791	.62172	.62552	.62930	.63307	.63683	.64058	.64431	.64803	.65173
0.4	.65542	.65910	.66276	.66640	.67003	.67364	.67724	.68082	.68439	.68793
0.5	.69146	.69497	.69847	.70194	.70540	.70884	.71226	.71566	.71904	.72240
0.6	.72575	.72907	.73237	.73536	.73891	.74215	.74537	.74857	.71575	.75490
0.7	.75804	.76115	.76424	.76730	.77035	.77337	.77637	.77935	.78230	.78524
0.8	.78814	.79103	.79389	.79673	.79955	.80234	.80511	.80785	.81057	.81327
0.9	.81594	.81859	.82121	.82381	.82639	.82894	.83147	.83398	.83646	.83891
1.0	.84134	.84375	.84614	.84849	.85083	.85314	.85543	.85769	.85993	.86214
1.1	.86433	.86650	.86864	.87076	.87286	.87493	.87698	.87900	.88100	.88298
1.2	.88493	.88686	.88877	.89065	.89251	.89435	.89617	.89796	.89973	.90147
1.3	.90320	.90490	.90658	.90824	.90988	.91149	.91309	.91466	.91621	.91774
1.4	.91924	.92073	.92220	.92364	.92507	.92647	.92785	.92922	.93056	.93189
1.5	.93319	.93448	.93574	.93699	.93822	.93943	.94062	.94179	.94295	.94408
1.6	.94520	.94630	.94738	.94845	.94950	.95053	.95154	.95254	.95352	.95449
1.7	.95543	.95637	.95728	.95818	.95907	.95994	.96080	.96164	.96246	.96327
1.8	.96407	.96485	.96562	.96638	.96712	.96784	.96856	.96926	.96995	.97062
1.9	.97128	.97193	.97257	.97320	.97381	.97441	.97500	.97558	.97615	.97670
2.0	.97725	.97784	.97831	.97882	.97932	.97982	.98030	.98077	.98124	.98169
2.1	.98214	.98257	.98300	.98341	.98382	.98422	.98461	.98500	.98537	.98574
2.2	.98610	.98645	.98679	.98713	.98745	.98778	.98809	.98840	.98870	.98899
2.3	.98928	.98956	.98983	.99010	.99036	.99061	.99086	.99111	.99134	.99158
2.4	.99180	.99202	.99224	.99245	.99266	.99286	.99305	.99324	.99343	.99361
2.5	.99379	.99396	.99413	.99430	.99446	.99461	.99477	.99492	.99506	.99520
2.6	.99534	.99547	.99560	.99573	.99585	.99598	.99609	.99621	.99632	.99643
2.7	.99653	.99664	.99674	.99683	.99693	.99702	.99711	.99720	.99728	.99736
2.8	.99744	.99752	.99760	.99767	.99774	.99781	.99788	.99795	.99801	.99807
2.9	.99813	.99819	.99825	.99831	.99836	.99841	.99846	.99851	.99856	.99861
3.0	.99865	.99869	.99874	.99878	.99882	.99886	.99899	.99893	.99896	.99900
3.1	.99903	.99906	.99910	.99913	.99916	.99918	.99921	.99924	.99926	.99929
3.2	.99931	.99934	.99936	.99938	.99940	.99942	.99944	.99946	.99948	.99950
3.3	.99952	.99953	.99955	.99957	.99958	.99960	.99961	.99962	.99964	.99965
3.4	.99966	.99968	.99969	.99970	.99971	.99972	.99973	.99974	.99975	.99976
3.5	.99977	.99978	.99978	.99979	.99980	.99981	.99981	.99982	.99983	.99983
3.6	.99984	.99985	.99985	.99986	.99986	.99987	.99987	.99988	.99988	.99989
3.7	.99989	.99990	.99990	.99990	.99991	.99991	.99992	.99992	.99992	.99992
3.8	.99993	.99993	.99993	.99994	.99994	.99994	.99994	.99995	.99995	.99995
3.9	.99995	.99995	.99996	.99996	.99996	.99996	.99996	.99996	.99997	.99997

Area: Under the Normal Curve

Source: From *Quantitative Approaches to Management,* Fourth Edition, by Richard I. Levin and Charles A. Kirkpatrick. Copyright © 1978, 1975, 1971, 1965 by McGraw-Hill, Inc. Used with the permission of McGraw-Hill Book Company.

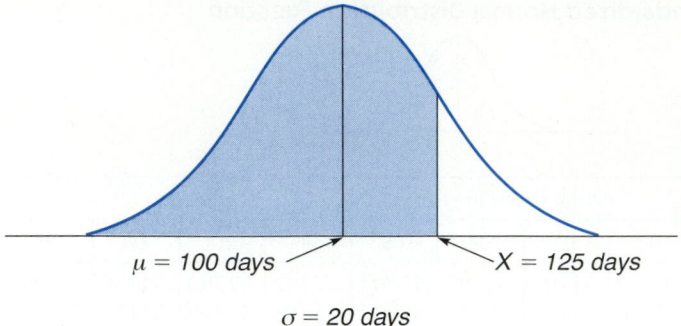

$\mu = 100$ days

$X = 125$ days

$\sigma = 20$ days

FIGURE 3.11

Normal Distribution for Haynes Construction

Looking in Table 3.6 for a Z value of 1.25, we find an area under the curve of .89435. (We do this by looking up 1.2 in the left-hand column of the table, and then moving to the .05 column to find the value for $Z = 1.25$.) Therefore, the probability of not violating the contract is .89435, or about an 89% chance.

Now let us look at the Haynes problem from another perspective. If the firm finishes this triplex in 75 days or less, it will be awarded a bonus payment of $5,000. What is the probability Haynes will receive the bonus?

Figure 3.12 illustrates the probability we are looking for in the shaded area. The first step is again to compute the Z value:

$$Z = \frac{X - \mu}{\sigma} = \frac{75 - 100}{20} = \frac{-25}{20} - -1.25$$

This Z value indicates that 75 days is -1.25 standard deviations to the left of the mean. But the standard normal table is structured to handle only positive Z values. To solve this problem, we observe that the curve is symmetric. The probability Haynes will finish in *less than 75 days* is *equivalent* to the probability it will finish in *more than 125 days*. A moment ago (in Figure 3.11), we found the probability Haynes will finish in less than 125 days. That value was .89435. So the probability it takes more than 125 days is:

$$P(X > 125) = 1.0 - P(X < 125) = 1.0 - .89435 = .10565$$

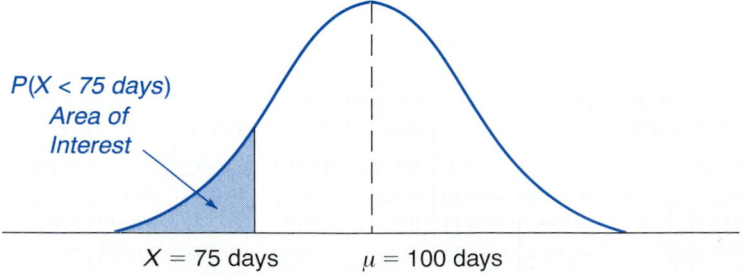

$P(X < 75 \text{ days})$
Area of Interest

$X = 75$ days

$\mu = 100$ days

FIGURE 3.12

Probability Haynes Will Receive the Bonus by Finishing in 75 Days

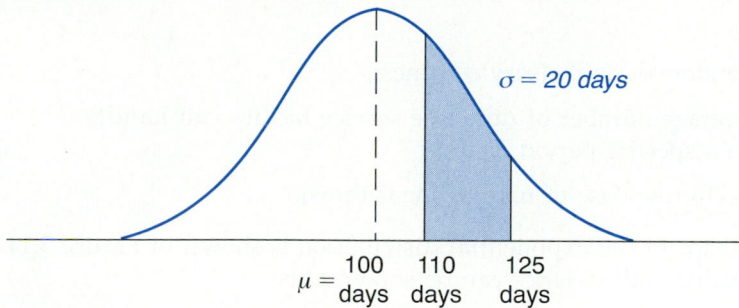

FIGURE 3.13
Probability of Haynes' Completion between 110 and 125 Days

Thus, the probability of completing the triplex in 75 days or less is .10565, or about 10%.

One final example: What is the probability the triplex will take between 110 and 125 days? We see in Figure 3.13 that:

$$P(110 < X < 125) = P(X < 125) - P(X < 110)$$

That is, the shaded area in the graph can be computed by finding the probability of completing the building in 125 days or less *minus* the probability of completing it in 110 days or less.

Recall that $P(X < 125 \text{ days})$ is equal to .89435. To find $P(X < 110 \text{ days})$, we follow the two steps developed earlier.

1. $Z = \dfrac{X - \mu}{\sigma} = \dfrac{110 - 100}{20} = \dfrac{10}{20} = .50$ standard deviations

2. From Table 3.6, the area for $Z = .50$ is .69146. So the probability the triplex can be completed in less than 110 days is .69146. Finally,

$$P(110 < X < 125) = .89435 - .69146 = .20289$$

The probability that it will take between 110 and 125 days is about 20%.

3.7 THE EXPONENTIAL DISTRIBUTION

Applicable Problem 4-30

exponential distribution and queuing theory

The *exponential distribution,* also called the *negative exponential distribution,* is used along with the Poisson distribution in dealing with queuing problems. While the discrete Poisson distribution describes the number of arrivals in a time interval, the exponential distribution describes the service times. The exponential distribution is a continuous distribution. Its probability function is given by:

$$f(X) = \mu e^{-\mu x} \tag{3-13}$$

where

X = random variable (service times),

μ = average number of units the service facility can handle in a specific period of time

e = 2.718 (the base of natural logarithms).

The general shape of the exponential distribution is shown in Figure 3.14. Its expected value and variance can be shown to be:

$$\text{Expected value} = \frac{1}{\mu} \tag{3-14}$$

$$\text{Variance} = \frac{1}{\mu^2} \tag{3-15}$$

The exponential distribution will be illustrated again in Chapter 16.

3.8   SUMMARY

The purpose of this chapter is to bridge the gap between probability theory and the application of probability distributions in future chapters. In this

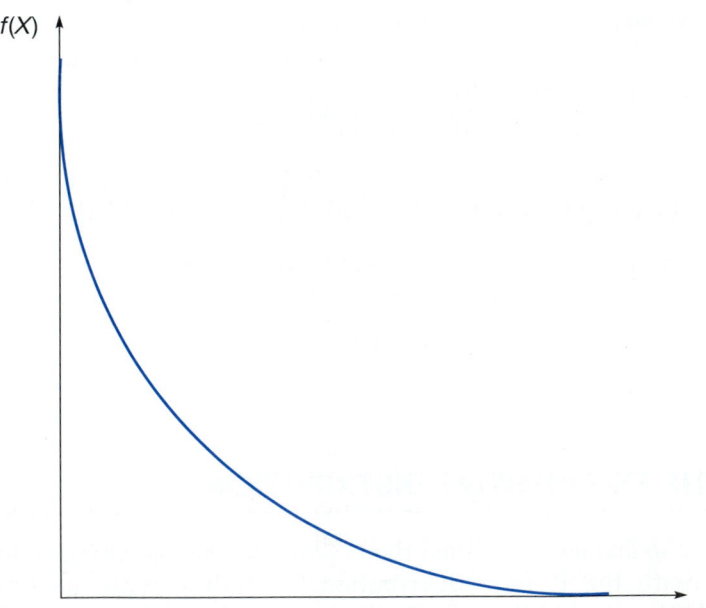

FIGURE 3.14
Negative Exponential Distribution

chapter, we covered the topics of random variables, discrete probability distributions (such as binomial and Poisson), and continuous probability distributions (such as uniform, normal, and exponential).

A probability distribution is any statement of a probability function having a set of collectively exhaustive and mutually exclusive events. All probability distributions follow the probability rules discussed in Chapter 2, namely, that any probability value must be between 0 and 1 and that the sum of the probability values for the events in the probability distribution must sum to 1.

The normal distribution is the most popular and widely used *continuous* probability distribution. Three other chapters and one module will involve normal distribution applications: statistical quality control (Chapter 7), inventory (Chapter 9), PERT (Chapter 18), and decision theory (Module D).

Teaching Suggestion 3.6:
Incentive to Learn the Probability Concepts. See the Instructor's Section for details.

GLOSSARY

Random Variable. A variable that assigns a number to every possible outcome of an experiment.

Discrete Random Variable. A random variable that can only assume a finite or limited set of values.

Continuous Random Variable. A random variable that can assume an infinite or unlimited set of values.

Probability Distribution. The set of all possible values of a random variable and their associated probabilities.

Discrete Probability Distribution. A probability distribution with a discrete random variable.

Continuous Probability Distribution. A probability distribution with a continuous random variable.

Expected Value. The (weighted) average of a probability distribution.

Variance. A measure of dispersion or spread of the probability distribution.

Standard Deviation. The square root of the variance.

Probability Density Function. The mathematical function that describes a continuous probability distribution. It is represented by $f(X)$.

Uniform Probability Distribution. A continous probability function that has a uniform or a flat probability density function.

Binomial Distribution. The distribution of a discrete random variable that describes the number of successes in independent trials.

Poisson Distribution. A discrete probability distribution used in queuing theory.

Normal Distribution. A continuous bell-shaped distribution that is a function of two parameters, the mean and standard deviation of the distribution.

Negative Exponential Distribution. A continuous probability distribution that describes the time between customer arrivals in a queuing situation.

KEY EQUATIONS

(3-1) $\quad E(X) = \sum_{i=1}^{n} X_i P(X_i)$

This equation computes the expected value of a discrete probability distribution.

(3-2) $\quad \text{Variance} = \sum_{i=1}^{n} (X_i - E(X))^2 P(X_i)$

This equation computes the variance of a discrete probability distribution.

(3-3) $\quad \sigma = \sqrt{\text{Variance}}$

This equation computes the standard deviation from the variance.

(3-4) $\quad f(X) = \begin{cases} \dfrac{1}{b-a} & \text{for } a \leq X \leq b \\[2mm] 0 & \text{otherwise} \end{cases}$

This is the density function of the uniform probability distribution.

(3-5) $\quad \text{Probability} = \dfrac{n!}{r!(n-r)!} p^r q^{n-r}$

This is the binomial probability distribution.

(3-6) $\quad \text{Expected value} = np$

This equation computes the expected value of the binomial probability distribution.

(3-7) $\quad \text{Variance} = np(1-p)$

This equation computes the variance of the binomial probability distribution.

(3-8) $\quad P(X) = \dfrac{\lambda^x e^{-\lambda}}{X!}$

The Poisson distribution.

(3-9) $\quad \text{Expected value} = \lambda$

The mean of a Poisson distribution.

(3-10) $\quad \text{Variance} = \lambda$

The variance of a Poisson distribution.

(3-11) $\quad f(X) = \dfrac{1}{\sigma\sqrt{2\pi}} e^{\dfrac{-\frac{1}{2}(X-\mu)^2}{\sigma^2}}$

This is the density function for the normal probability distribution.

(3-12) $Z = \dfrac{X - \mu}{\sigma}$

This equation computes the number of standard deviations, Z, the point X is from the mean μ.

(3-13) $f(X) = \mu e^{-\mu X}$

The exponential distribution.

(3-14) Expected value $= \dfrac{1}{\mu}$

The expected value of an exponential distribution.

(3-15) Variance $= \dfrac{1}{\mu^2}$

The variance of an exponential distribution.

DISCUSSION QUESTIONS AND PROBLEMS

Discussion Questions

3-1 What is a random variable? What are the different types of random variables?

3-2 What is the difference between a discrete probability distribution and a continuous probability distribution? Give your own example of each.

3-3 What is the expected value, and what does it measure? How is it computed for a discrete probability distribution?

3-4 What is the variance, and what does it measure? How is it computed for a discrete probability distribution?

3-5 What is the Bernoulli process? What probability distribution describes the Bernoulli process, and what conditions must be satisfied before this distribution can be used?

3-6 What type of distribution is the binomial distribution? What type of distribution is the normal distribution?

3-7 Name three business processes that can be described by the normal distribution.

3-8 After evaluating student response to a question about a case used in class, the instructor constructed the following probability distribution. What kind of probability distribution is it?

RESPONSE	RANDOM VARIABLE, X	PROBABILITY
Excellent	5	.05
Good	4	.25
Average	3	.40
Fair	2	.15
Poor	1	.15

Problems

(a) and (c) are probability distributions because the probability values for each event are between 0 and 1, and the sum of the probability values for the events is 1.

· **3-9** Which of the following are probability distributions? Why?

(a)

RANDOM VARIABLE X	PROBABILITY
−2	.1
−1	.2
0	.3
1	.25
2	.15

(b)

RANDOM VARIABLE Y	PROBABILITY
1	1.1
1.5	.2
2	.3
2.5	.25
3	−1.25

(c)

RANDOM VARIABLE Z	PROBABILITY
1	.1
2	.2
3	.3
4	.4
5	.0

· **3-10** Harrington Health Food stocks 5 loaves of Neutro-Bread. The probability distribution for the sales of Neutro-Bread is listed in the following table. How many loaves will Harrington sell on the average?

2.85

NUMBER OF LOAVES SOLD	PROBABILITY
0	.05
1	.15
2	.2
3	.25
4	.20
5	.15

· **3-11** What is the expected value and variance of the following probability distribution?

5.45; 4.0476

RANDOM VARIABLE X	PROBABILITY
1	.05
2	.05
3	.10
4	.10
5	.15
6	.15
7	.25
8	.15

· **3-12** This year, Jan Rich, who is ranked number one in women's singles in tennis, and Marie Wacker, who is ranked number three, will play 4 times. If Marie can beat Jan 3 times, she will be ranked number one. The two players have played 20 times before, and Jan has won 15 games. It is expected that this pattern will continue in the future. What is the probability that Marie will be ranked number one after this year? What is the probability that Marie will win all 4 games this year against Jan?

.003906; probability that Marie will be no. 1 = .05086

: **3-13** It was stated in this chapter that the probability values for any probability distribution must sum to 1. Prove that this is the case for the uniform probability distribution.

See Instructor's Section for proof

· **3-14** Over the last two months, the Wilmington Phantoms have been encountering trouble with one of their star basketball players. During the last 30 games, he has fouled out 15 times. The owner of the basketball team has stated that if this player fouls out 2 times in their next 5 games, the player will be fined $200. What is the probability that the player will be fined? What is the probability that the player will foul out of all 5 games? What is the probability that the player will not foul out of any of the next 5 games?

.8125; .03125; .03125

· **3-15** Best of the Sea Tuna processes and packages tuna in a plant located in the state of Washington. Their most popular size is the 12-ounce can. In the past, the processing equipment has placed anywhere from 11 to 15 ounces of tuna in a can. The president of Best of the Sea Tuna believes that this process follows a uniform distribution. What is the probability that a can will contain from 11.5 to 12.5 ounces of tuna? What is the probability that a can will contain exactly 12 ounces of tuna?

.25; 0

· **3-16** Sales for Fast Kat, a 16-foot catamaran sailboat, have averaged 250 boats per month over the last five years with a standard deviation of 25 boats. Assuming that the demand is about the same as past years and follows a normal curve, what is the probability sales will be less than 280 boats?

.8849

: **3-17** Refer to Problem 3-16. What is the probability that sales will be over 265 boats during the next month? What is the probability that sales will be under 250 boats next month?

.2743; .5

· **3-18** Precision Parts is a job shop that specializes in producing electric motor shafts. The average shaft size for the E300 electric motor is 0.55 inch, with a standard deviation of 0.10 inch. It is normally distributed. What is the probability that a shaft selected at random will be between 0.55 and 0.65 inch?

.3413

.1587; .2347; .1587

: **3-19** Refer to Problem 3-18. What is the probability that a shaft size will be greater than 0.65 inch? What is the probability that a shaft size will be between 0.53 and 0.59 inch? What is the probability that a shaft size will be under 0.45 inch?

.1587; .1327

: **3-20** An industrial oven used to cure sand cores for a factory manufacturing engine blocks for small cars is able to maintain fairly constant temperatures. The temperature range of the oven follows a normal distribution with a mean of 450°F and a standard deviation of 25°F. Leslie Larsen, president of the factory, is concerned about the large number of defective cores that have been produced in the last several months. If the oven gets hotter than 475°F, the core is defective. What is the probability that the oven will cause a core to be defective? What is the probability that the temperature of the oven will range from 460 to 470°F?

.327; .410; .205; .051;
.0064; .00032

· **3-21** Wisconsin Cheese Processor, Inc., produces equipment that processes cheese products. Ken Newgren is particularly concerned about a new cheese processor that has been producing defective cheese crocks. The piece of equipment produces 5 cheese crocks during every cycle of the equipment. The probability that any one of the cheese crocks is defective is .2. Ken would like to determine the probability distribution of defective cheese crocks from this new piece of equipment. There can be 0, 1, 2, 3, 4, or 5 defective cheese crocks for any cycle of the equipment.

1.0; 0.80

1.0; 0.80

Yes

: **3-22** Refer to Problem 3-21.
   (a) Determine the expected value and variance of the distribution described in Problem 3-21, using Equations 3-1 and 3-2.
   (b) Determine the expected value and variance of the distribution described in Problem 3-21, using Equations 3-6 and 3-7.
   (c) Compare your answers in (a) and (b) above. Will these equations always be consistent for this type of distribution?

$\binom{10}{X}.25^X.75^{10-X}$

2.5; 1.875
$312.50

: **3-23** Natway, a national distribution company of home vacuum cleaners, recommends that its salespersons make only two calls per day, one in the morning and one in the afternoon. Twenty-five percent of the time a sales call will result in a sale, and the profit from each sale is $125.

   (a) Develop the probability distribution for sales during a five-day week.
   (b) Determine the mean and variance of this distribution.
   (c) What is the expected weekly profit for a salesperson?

.2778

.0555
11.4

· **3-24** The weight in ounces of cans of pears follows a uniform distribution. The range has been from 9.6 to 13.2 ounces.
   (a) What is the probability that the weight will be between 10 and 11 ounces?
   (b) What is the probability that the weight will be between 9.6 and 9.8 ounces?
   (c) What is the expected value of this distribution?

.0548
.6554
.6554
.212

: **3-25** Steve Goodman, production foreman for the Florida Gold Fruit Company, estimates that the average sale of oranges is 4,700 and the standard deviation is 500 oranges. Sales follow a normal distribution.
   (a) What is the probability that sales will be greater than 5,500 oranges?
   (b) What is the probability that sales will be greater than 4,500 oranges?
   (c) What is the probability that sales will be less than 4,900 oranges?
   (d) What is the probability that sales will be less than 4,300 oranges?

: **3-26** Susan Williams has been the production manager of Medical Suppliers, Inc., for the past 17 years. Medical Suppliers, Inc., is a producer of bandages and arm slings. During the past 5 years, the demand for No-Stick bandages has been fairly constant. On the average, sales have been about 87,000 packages of No-Stick. Susan has reason to believe that the distribution of No-Stick follows a normal curve, with a standard deviation of 4,000 packages. What is the probability that sales will be less than 81,000 packages?

.0668

: **3-27** Armstrong Faber produces a standard number two pencil called Ultra-Lite. Since Chuck Armstrong started Armstrong Faber, sales have grown steadily. With the increase in the price of wood products, however, Chuck has been forced to increase the price of the Ultra-Lite pencils. As a result, the demand for Ultra-Lite has been fairly stable over the past six years. On the average, Armstrong Faber has sold 457,000 pencils each year. Furthermore, 90% of the time sales have been between 460,000 and 454,000 pencils. It is expected that the sales follow a normal distribution with a mean of 457,000 pencils. Estimate the standard deviation of this distribution. (*Hint:* Work backward from the normal table to find Z. Then apply Equation 3-12.)

1829.27

: **3-28** Patients arrive at the emergency room of Costa Valley Hospital at an average of 5 per day. The demand for emergency room treatment at Costa Valley follows a Poisson distribution.

.0067; .0335; .0837; .1396; .1745; .1745

  (a) Using Appendix D, compute the probability of exactly 0, 1, 2, 3, 4, and 5 arrivals per day.

  (b) What is the sum of these probabilities, and why is the number less than 1?

.6125; there are more possible arrivals than 5.

: **3-29** Using the data in Problem 3-28, determine the probability of more than 3 visits for emergency room service on any given day.

.7365

: **3-30** Cars arrive at Carla's Muffler shop for repair work at an average of 3 per hour, following an exponential distribution.

  (a) What is the expected time between arrivals?

⅓ hour

  (b) What is the variance of the time between arrivals?

⅑

  (c) What is the probability there are *no* arrivals for a full hour after a random customer has just entered the shop?

.15

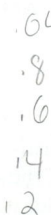

WTVX

WTVX, Channel 6, is located in Eugene, Oregon, home of the University of Oregon's football team. The station was owned and operated by George Wilcox, a former Duck (University of Oregon football player). Although there were other television stations in Eugene, WTVX was the only station that had a weatherperson who was a member of the American Meteorological Society (AMS). Every night, Joe Hummel would be introduced as the only weatherperson in Eugene who was a member of the AMS. This was George's idea, and he believed that this gave his station the mark of quality and helped with market share.

In addition to being a member of AMS, Joe was also the most popular person on any of the local news programs. Joe was always trying to find innovative ways to make the weather interesting, and this was especially difficult during the winter months when the weather seemed to remain the same over long periods of time. Joe's forecast for next month, for example, was that there would be a 70% chance of rain *every* day, and that what happens on one day (rain or shine) was not in any way dependent on what happened the day before.

One of Joe's most popular features of the weather report was to invite questions during the actual broadcast. Questions would be phoned in, and they were answered on the spot by Joe. Once

a ten-year-old boy asked what caused fog, and Joe did an excellent job of describing some of the various causes.

Occasionally, Joe would make a mistake. For example, a high school senior asked Joe what the chances were of getting 15 days of rain in the next month (30 days). Joe made a quick calculation: (70%) × (15 days/30 days) = (70%) (½) = 35%. Joe quickly found out what it was like being wrong in a university town. He had over 50 phone calls from scientists, mathematicians, and other university professors, telling him that he had made a big mistake in computing the chances of getting 15 days of rain during the next 30 days. Although Joe didn't understand all of the formulas the professors mentioned, he was determined to find the correct answer and make a correction during a future broadcast.

Discussion Questions

1. What are the chances of getting 15 days of rain during the next 30 days?

2. What do you think about Joe's assumptions concerning the weather for the next 30 days?

Source: Barry Render and Ralph M. Stair, *Cases and Readings in Quantitative Analysis for Management,* Boston: Allyn and Bacon, Inc., 1982.

.0106; see Instructor's Section for details.

Century Chemical Company

Century Chemical Company, formed in 1955 as a result of the merger of three smaller firms, produces chlorine and caustic soda through the electrolysis of brine. Century's largest plant, located in St. Gabriel, Louisiana, produces approximately 1,500 tons of chlorine and 1,700 tons of caustic soda daily. The St. Gabriel plant operates at capacity; its entire output is sold.

A major problem confronting Century Chemical Corporation is associated with its chlorine collection and handling system. The system incorporates headers that collect chlorine gas from the electrolytic cells. The gas then passes through heat

exchangers for cooling and condensation of water entrapped in the chlorine. Residual water in the chlorine gas is removed by "scrubbing" with concentrated sulfuric acid. Thereafter, the dry chlorine gas is chilled by being bubbled through liquid chlorine before being fed to the chlorine compressor. The chlorine compressor is the "heart" of the handling system. It pulls the gas from the cells through the cooling and drying system. Then it compresses the gas for liquefaction and storage as liquid chlorine.

A major problem for the production manager of Century Chemical is the gradual deterioration of the plant's compressor capacity because of the fouling of component parts. The reliability of Century's centrifugal compressor at its St. Gabriel complex is .92. The 8% downtime includes cleaning and restoration of capacity as well as other mechanical/electrical failures. Heretofore, management at Century has chosen to incur the downtime and lost sales associated with compressor failures. However, from time to time, management considers the installation of a spare compressor. Currently, the cost of such an installation is estimated to total $800,000. The spare compressor is also projected to have a .92 reliability factor.

Approximately 12 hours of downtime are required to change over to an installed spare compressor. Profit and overhead contribution for chlorine is estimated at $50 per ton; the profit and overhead contribution for caustic soda is $40 per ton. Century's cost of capital or opportunity cost is estimated to equal 20%. Useful life of the compressor installation is estimated to be 10 years. Salvage is assumed to be zero. The effective tax rate is 40%.

Discussion Question

Should management of Century Chemical install the spare compressor? Why or why not? (*Hint:* The present value factor of 20% over 10 years is 4.192.)

Source: Dean Jerry Kinard (Francis Marion College).

BIBLIOGRAPHY

Refer to references at end of Chapter 2.

4

Forecasting

CHAPTER OUTLINE

4.1 Introduction

4.2 Types of Forecasts

4.3 Scatter Diagrams

4.4 Time Series Forecasting Models

4.5 Causal Forecasting Methods

4.6 Monitoring and Controlling Forecasts

4.7 Using the Computer to Forecast

4.8 Summary

Glossary

Key Equations

Solved Problems

Discussion Questions and Problems

Case Studies

    The North-South Airline

    Kwik Lube

Bibliography

Appendix: Forecasting with Spreadsheets

Transparency Master 4.1:
Outline of Forecasting Topics.

Teaching Suggestion 4.1:
The Wide Use of Forecasting.
See the Instructor's Section
for details.

KEY IDEA

4.1   INTRODUCTION

Every day managers make decisions without knowing what will happen in the future. Inventory is ordered though no one knows what sales will be, new equipment is purchased though no one knows the demand for products, and investments are made though no one knows what profits will be. Managers are always trying to reduce this uncertainty and to make better estimates of what will happen in the future. Accomplishing this is the main purpose of forecasting.

There are many ways to forecast the future. In numerous firms (especially smaller ones), the entire process is subjective, involving seat-of-the-pants methods, intuition, and years of experience. There are also many *quantitative* forecasting models such as moving averages, exponential smoothing, trend projections, and least squares regression analysis.

Regardless of the method that is used to make the forecast, the same eight overall procedures are used:

forecasting system steps

Transparency Master 4.2:
Eight Steps to Forecasting.

1. Determine the use of the forecast—what objective are we trying to obtain?

2. Select the items or quantities that are to be forecasted.

3. Determine the time horizon of the forecast—is it one to thirty days (short term), one month to one year (medium term), or more than one year (long term)?

4. Select the forecasting model or models.

5. Gather the data needed to make the forecast.

6. Validate the forecasting model.

7. Make the forecast.

8. Implement the results.

These steps present a systematic way of initiating, designing, and implementing a forecasting system. When the forecasting system is to be used to generate forecasts regularly over time, data must be collected routinely, and the actual computations or procedures used to make the forecast can be done automatically. When a computer system is used, computer forecasting files and programs are needed.

no single method is best

There is seldom one single superior forecasting method. One organization may find regression effective, another firm may use several approaches, and a third may combine both quantitative and subjective techniques. Whatever tool works best for a firm is the one that should be used.

4.2 TYPES OF FORECASTS

In this chapter, we consider forecasting models that can be classified into one of three categories. These categories, shown in Figure 4.1, are time series models, causal models, and qualitative models.

Time Series Models

Time series models attempt to predict the future by using historical data. These models make the assumption that what happens in the future is a function of what has happened in the past. In other words, time series models look at what has happened over a period of time and use a series of past data to make a forecast. Thus, if we are forecasting weekly sales for lawn mowers, we use the past weekly sales for lawn mowers in making the forecast. The time series models we examine in this chapter are moving average, exponential smoothing, and trend projections.

Causal Models

Causal models incorporate the variables or factors that might influence the quantity being forecasted into the forecasting model. For example, daily sales of a cola drink might depend on the season, the average temperature,

KEY IDEA

Teaching Suggestion 4.2:
Forecasting as an Art and a Science. See the Instructor's Section for details.

Teaching Suggestion 4.3:
The Use of Simple Models. See the Instructor's Section for details

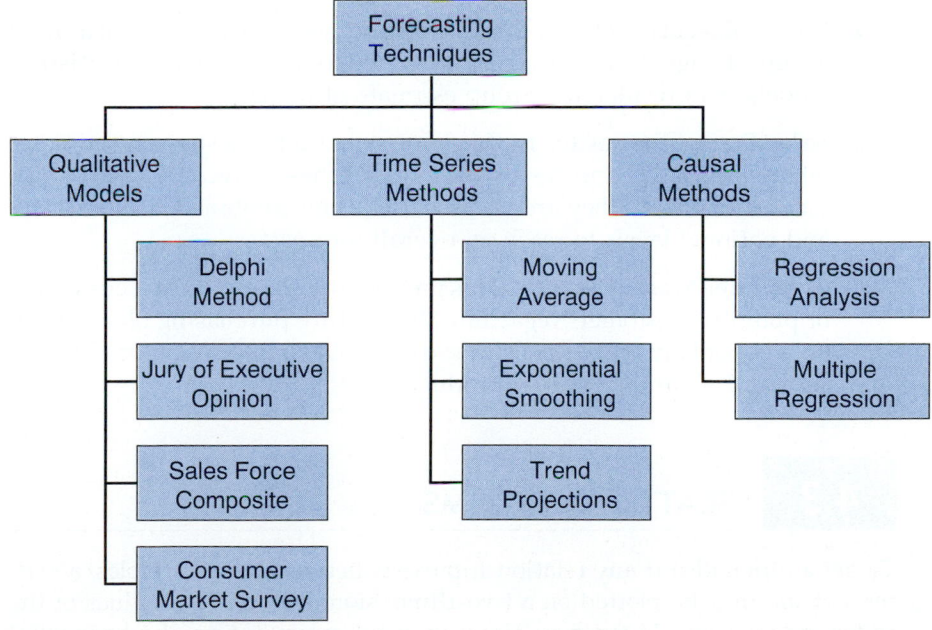

FIGURE 4.1
Forecasting Models Discussed

the average humidity, whether it is a weekend or a weekday, and so on. Thus, a causal model would attempt to include factors for temperature, humidity, season, day of the week, and so on. Causal models may also include past sales data as time series models do.

Qualitative Models

While time series and causal models rely on quantitative data, *qualitative models* attempt to incorporate judgmental or subjective factors into the forecasting model. Opinions by experts, individual experiences and judgments, and other subjective factors may be considered. Qualitative models are especially useful when subjective factors are expected to be very important or when accurate quantitative data is difficult to obtain.

overview of four qualitative or judgemental approaches

Here is a brief overview of four different *qualitative* forecasting techniques.

1. **Delphi Method.** This iterative group process allows experts, who may be located in different places, to make forecasts. There are three different types of participants in the Delphi process: decision makers, staff personnel, and respondents. The decision makers usually consist of a group of five to ten experts who will be making the actual forecast. The staff personnel assist the decision makers by preparing, distributing, collecting, and summarizing a series of questionnaires and survey results. The respondents are a group of people whose judgments are valued and are being sought. This group provides inputs to the decision makers before the forecast is made.

2. **Jury of Executive Opinion.** This method takes the opinions of a small group of high-level managers, often in combination with statistical models, and results in a group estimate of demand.

3. **Sales Force Composite.** In this approach, each salesperson estimates what sales will be in his or her region; these forecasts then are reviewed to ensure they are realistic, and then combined at the district and national levels to reach an overall forecast.

4. **Consumer Market Survey.** This method solicits input from customers or potential customers regarding their future purchasing plans. It can help not only in preparing a forecast but also in improving product design and planning for new products.

4.3   SCATTER DIAGRAMS

obtaining ideas about a relationship

To get a quick idea if any relationship exists between two variables, a *scatter diagram* may be plotted on a two-dimensional graph. The values of the independent variable (such as time) may be measured on the horizontal (X) axis and the proposed dependent variables (such as sales) placed on the vertical (Y) axis. Let us consider the example of a firm that needs to forecast sales for three different products.

TABLE 4.1 Annual Sales of Three Products

YEAR	TELEVISIONS	RADIOS	STEREOS
1	250	300	110
2	250	310	100
3	250	320	120
4	250	330	140
5	250	340	170
6	250	350	150
7	250	360	160
8	250	370	190
9	250	380	200
10	250	390	190

Wacker Distributors notes that annual sales for three of its products—televisions, radios, and stereos—over the past ten years are as shown in Table 4.1.

One simple way to examine these historical data, and perhaps use them to establish a forecast, is to draw a scatter diagram for each product. (See Figure 4.2.) This picture, showing the relationship between sales of a product and time, is useful in spotting trends or cycles. An exact mathematical model that describes the situation can then be developed if it appears reasonable to do so.

**Applicable Problems
4-23a, 4-32a**

4.4 TIME SERIES FORECASTING MODELS

A time series is based on a sequence of evenly spaced (weekly, monthly, quarterly, and so on) data points. Examples include weekly sales of IBM PS/2s, quarterly earnings reports of AT&T stock, daily shipments of Eveready batteries, and annual U.S. consumer price indices. Forecasting time series data implies that future values are predicted *only* from past values (such as we saw in Table 4.1) and that other variables, no matter how potentially valuable, are ignored.

Decomposition of a Time Series

Analyzing time series means breaking down past data into components and then projecting them forward. A time series typically has four components: trend, seasonality, cycles, and random variation.

1. *Trend* (T) is the gradual upward or downward movement of the data over time.

2. *Seasonality* (S) is a pattern of the demand fluctuation above or below the trend line that occurs every year.

3. *Cycles* (C) are patterns in the data that occur every several years. They are usually tied into the business cycle.

**four components of a
time series**

(a)

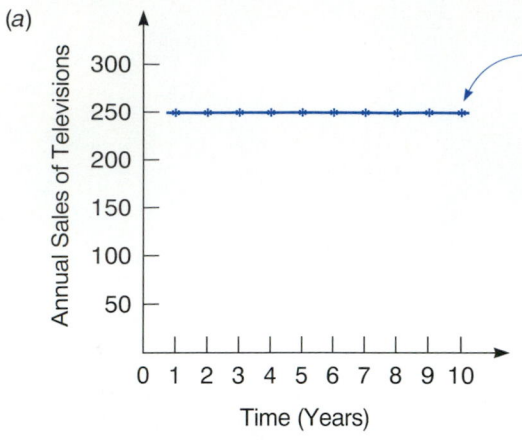

Sales appear to be constant over time. This horizontal line could be described by the equation:

$$Sales = 250$$

That is, no matter what year (1, 2, 3, and so on) we insert into the equation, sales will not change. A good estimate of future sales (in year 11) is 250 televisions!

(b)

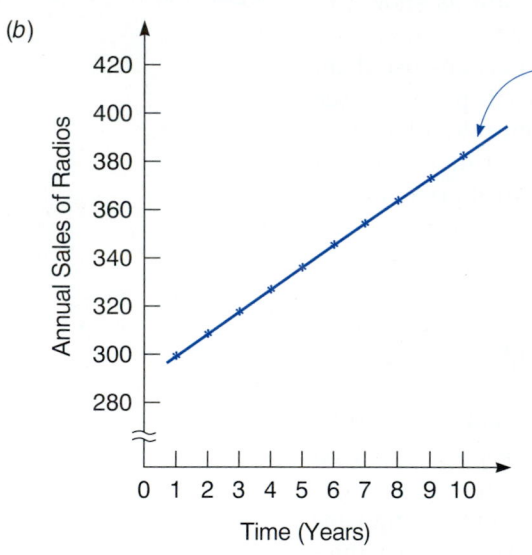

Sales appear to be increasing at a constant rate of ten radios each year. If the line is extended left to the vertical axis, we see that sales would be 290 in year 0. The equation

$$Sales = 290 + 10\,(Year)$$

best describes this relationship between sales and time. A reasonable estimate of radio sales in year 11 is 400, in year 12, 410 radios.

(c)

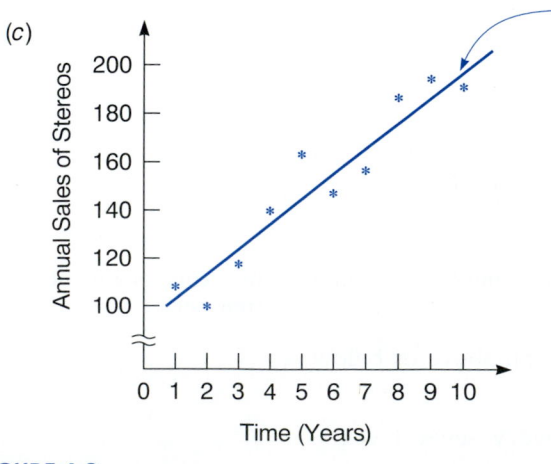

This trend line may not be perfectly accurate because of variation each year. But stereo sales do appear to have been increasing over the past ten years. If we had to forecast future sales, we would probably pick a larger figure each year.

FIGURE 4.2
Scatter Diagram for Sales

4. *Random variations* (R) are "blips" in the data caused by chance and unusual situations; they follow no discernible pattern.

Figure 4.3 shows a time series and its components.

There are two general forms of time series models in statistics. The most widely used is a multiplicative model, which assumes that demand is the product of the four components:

$$\text{Demand} = T \times S \times C \times R$$

An additive model adds the components together to provide an estimate. It is stated as:

$$\text{Demand} = T + S + C + R$$

In most real-world models, forecasters assume that the random variations are averaged out over time. They then concentrate on only the seasonal component and a component that is a combination of trend and cyclical factors.

Moving Averages

Moving averages are useful if we can assume that market demands will stay fairly steady over time. A four-month moving average is found by simply summing the demand during the past four months and dividing by four. With each passing month, the most recent month's data are added to the sum of the previous three months' data, and the earliest month is dropped. This tends to smooth out short-term irregularities in the data series.

meaning of moving averages

**Applicable Problems
4-11, 4-14, 4-20, 4-24a**

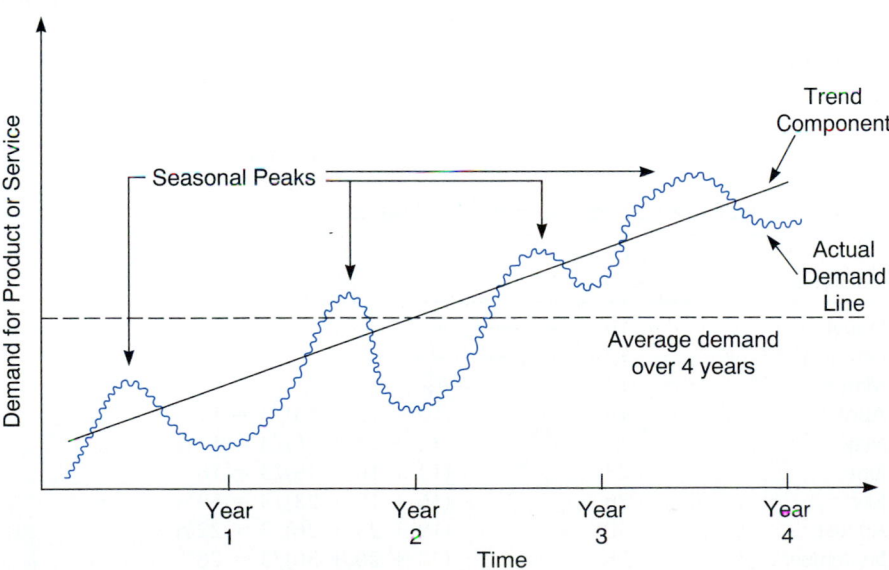

**FIGURE 4.3
Product Demand Charted over Four Years with
Trend and Seasonality Indicated**

Mathematically, the moving average, which serves as an estimate of the next period's demand, is expressed as:

$$\text{Moving average} = \frac{\Sigma \text{ Demand in previous } n \text{ periods}}{n} \qquad (4\text{-}1)$$

where n is the number of period in the moving average—for example, four, five, or six months, respectively, for a four-, five-, or six-period moving average.

Storage shed sales at Wallace Garden Supply are shown in the middle column of Table 4.2. A three-month moving average is indicated on the right.

Alternate Example 4.1
using weights

When there is a trend or pattern, weights can be used to place more emphasis on recent values. This makes the techniques more responsive to changes since latter periods may be more heavily weighted. Deciding which weights to use requires some experience and a bit of luck. Choice of weights is somewhat arbitrary since there is no set formula to determine them. If the latest month or period is weighted too heavily, the forecast might reflect a large unusual change in the demand or sales pattern too quickly.

**Applicable Problems
4-13, 4-24b**

A *weighted moving average* may be expressed mathematically as:

$$\frac{\text{Weighted}}{\text{moving average}} = \frac{\Sigma \text{ (Weight for period } n) \text{ (Demand in period } n)}{\Sigma \text{ Weights}} \qquad (4\text{-}2)$$

Wallace Garden Supply decides to forecast storage shed sales by weighting the past three months as follows:

	Weights Applied	Period
	3	Last month
	2	Two months ago
	1	Three months ago

Alternate Example 4.2

$$\frac{(3) \times \text{Sales last month} + (2) \times \text{Sales two months ago} + (1) \times \text{Sales three months ago}}{(6)}$$

Sum of the weights

TABLE 4.2 Wallace Garden Supply Shed Sales

MONTH	ACTUAL SHED SALES	THREE-MONTH MOVING AVERAGE
January	10	
February	12	
March	13	
April	16	$(10 + 12 + 13)/3 = 11\frac{2}{3}$
May	19	$(12 + 13 + 16)/3 = 13\frac{2}{3}$
June	23	$(13 + 16 + 19)/3 = 16$
July	26	$(16 + 19 + 23)/3 = 19\frac{1}{3}$
August	30	$(19 + 23 + 26)/3 = 22\frac{2}{3}$
September	28	$(23 + 26 + 30)/3 = 26\frac{1}{3}$
October	18	$(26 + 30 + 28)/3 = 28$
November	16	$(30 + 28 + 18)/3 = 25\frac{1}{3}$
December	14	$(28 + 18 + 16)/3 = 20\frac{2}{3}$

The results of this weighted average forecast are shown in Table 4.3. In this particular forecasting situation, you can see that weighting the latest month more heavily provides a much more accurate projection.

Both simple and weighted moving averages are effective in smoothing out sudden fluctuations in the demand pattern in order to provide stable estimates. Moving averages do, however, have three problems. First, increasing the size of *n* (the number of periods averaged) does smooth out fluctuations better, but it makes the method less sensitive to *real* changes in the data. Second, moving averages cannot pick up trends very well. Since they are averages, they will always stay within past levels and will not predict a change to either a higher or lower level. The third problem is that moving averages require extensive record keeping of past data.

problems with moving averages

Exponential Smoothing

Exponential smoothing is a forecasting method that is easy to use and efficiently handled by computers. Although it is a type of moving average technique, it involves little record keeping of past data. The basic exponential smoothing formula can be shown as follows:

New forecast = Last period's forecast

$$+ \alpha \text{ (Last period's actual demand} - \text{Last period's forecast)} \quad \textbf{(4-3)}$$

where α is a weight (or *smoothing constant*) that has a value between 0 and 1, inclusive. Equation 4-3 can also be written mathematically as:

$$F_t = F_{t-1} + \alpha(A_{t-1} - F_{t-1}) \quad \textbf{(4-4)}$$

where

$$F_t = \text{the new forecast,}$$

$$F_{t-1} = \text{the previous forecast,}$$

$$\alpha = \text{smoothing constant } (0 \le \alpha \le 1), \text{ and}$$

$$A_{t-1} = \text{previous period's actual demand.}$$

Teaching Suggestion 4.4:
Management Input to the Exponential Smoothing Model. See Instructor's Section for details.

Applicable Problems
4-16, 4-17, 4-18, 4-25, 4-26, 4-39

TABLE 4.3 Weighted Moving Average Forecast for Wallace Garden Supply

MONTH	ACTUAL SHED SALES	THREE-MONTH WEIGHTED MOVING AVERAGE
January	10	
February	12	
March	13	
April	16	$[(3 \times 13) + (2 \times 12) + (10)]/6 = 12\frac{1}{6}$
May	19	$[(3 \times 16) + (2 \times 13) + (12)]/6 = 14\frac{1}{3}$
June	23	$[(3 \times 19) + (2 \times 16) + (13)]/6 = 17$
July	26	$[(3 \times 23) + (2 \times 19) + (16)]/6 = 20\frac{1}{2}$
August	30	$[(3 \times 26) + (2 \times 23) + (19)]/6 = 23\frac{5}{6}$
September	28	$[(3 \times 30) + (2 \times 26) + (23)]/6 = 27\frac{1}{2}$
October	18	$[(3 \times 28) + (2 \times 30) + (26)]/6 = 28\frac{1}{3}$
November	16	$[(3 \times 18) + (2 \times 28) + (30)]/6 = 23\frac{1}{3}$
December	14	$[(3 \times 16) + (2 \times 18) + (28)]/6 = 18\frac{2}{3}$

The concept here is not complex. The latest estimate of demand is equal to our old estimate adjusted by a fraction of the difference between the last period's actual demand and the old estimate.

smoothing constant

The *smoothing constant, α,* can be changed to give more weight to recent data, when it is high, or more weight to past data, when it is low. For example, when $\alpha = .5$, it can be shown mathematically that the new forecast is based almost entirely on demand in the last three periods. When $\alpha = .1$, the forecast places little weight on recent demand and takes *many* periods (about 19) of historic values into account.[1]

In January, a demand for 142 of a certain car model for February was predicted by a dealer. Actual February demand was 153 autos. Using a smoothing constant of $\alpha = .20$, we can forecast the March demand using the exponential smoothing model. Substituting into the formula, we obtain:

Alternate Example 4.3

$$\text{New forecast (for March demand)} = 142 + .2(153 - 142)$$

$$= 144.2$$

Thus, the demand forecast for the cars in March is 144.

Suppose actual demand for the cars in March was 136. A forecast for the demand in April, using the exponential smoothing model with a constant of $\alpha = .20$, can be made.

$$\text{New forecast (for April demand)} = 144.2 + .2(136 - 144.2)$$

$$= 142.6, \text{ or } 143 \text{ autos}$$

Selecting the Smoothing Constant. The exponential smoothing approach is easy to use, and it has been successfully applied by banks, manufacturing companies, wholesalers, and other organizations. The appropriate value of the smoothing constant, α, however, can make the difference between an accurate forecast and an inaccurate forecast. In picking a value for the smoothing constant, the objective is to obtain the most accurate forecast. The overall accuracy of a forecasting model can be determined by comparing the forecasted values with the actual or observed values.

forecast error

The forecast error is defined as:

$$\text{Forecast error} = \text{Demand} - \text{Forecast}$$

One measure of the overall forecast error for a model is the *mean absolute deviation* (MAD). This is computed by taking the sum of the absolute values of the individual forecast errors and dividing by the number of periods of data (n):

$$\text{MAD} = \frac{\Sigma |\text{Forecast errors}|}{n} \tag{4-5}$$

MAD example

Let us apply this concept with a trial-and-error testing of two values of α in the following example. The Port of Baltimore has unloaded large

---

[1] The term *exponential smoothing* is used because the weight that any one period's demand makes in a forecast demand decreases exponentially over time. See an advanced forecasting book for an algebraic proof.

quantities of grain from ships during the past eight quarters. The port's operations manager wants to test the use of exponential smoothing to see how well the technique works in predicting tonnage unloaded. He assumes that the forecast of grain unloaded in the first quarter was 175 tons. Two values of α are examined, $\alpha = .10$ and $\alpha = .50$. Table 4.4 shows the *detailed* calculations for $\alpha = .10$ only.

To evaluate the accuracy of each smoothing constant we can compute the absolute deviations and MADs (see Table 4.5). Based on this analysis, a smoothing constant of $\alpha = .10$ is preferred to $\alpha = .50$ because its MAD is smaller.

Besides the mean absolute deviations, there are three other measures of the accuracy of historical errors in forecasting that are sometimes used. *Mean squared error* (MSE) is the average of the squared differences between the forecasted and observed values. *Mean absolute percent error* (MAPE) is the absolute difference between the forecasted and observed values expressed as a percentage of the observed values. *Bias* tells whether the fore-

Applicable Problems 4-12, 4-15, 4-24d, 4-19, 4-22

MSE and MAPE error measures

Alternate Example 4.4

TABLE 4.4 Port of Baltimore Exponential Smoothing Forecasts for $\alpha = .10$ and $\alpha = .50$

QUARTER	ACTUAL TONNAGE UNLOADED	ROUNDED FORECAST USING $\alpha = .10^*$	ROUNDED FORECAST USING $\alpha = .50^*$
1	180	175	175
2	168	$176 = 175.00 + .10(180 - 175)$	178
3	159	$175 = 175.50 + .10(168 - 175.50)$	173
4	175	$173 = 174.75 + .10(159 - 174.75)$	166
5	190	$173 = 173.18 + .10(175 - 173.18)$	170
6	205	$175 = 173.36 + .10(190 - 173.36)$	180
7	180	$178 = 175.02 + .10(205 - 175.02)$	193
8	182	$178 = 178.02 + .10(180 - 178.02)$	186
9	?	$179 = 178.22 + .10(182 - 178.22)$	184

* Forecasts rounded to the nearest ton.

TABLE 4.5 Absolute Deviations and MADs for Port of Baltimore Example

QUARTER	ACTUAL TONNAGE UNLOADED	ROUNDED FORECAST WITH $\alpha = .10$	ABSOLUTE DEVIATIONS FOR $\alpha = .10$	ROUNDED FORECAST WITH $\alpha = .50$	ABSOLUTE DEVIATION FOR $\alpha = .50$
1	180	175	5	175	5
2	168	176	8	178	10
3	159	175	16	173	14
4	175	173	2	166	9
5	190	173	17	170	20
6	205	175	30	180	25
7	180	178	2	193	13
8	182	178	4	186	4
		Sum of absolute deviations	84		100

$$MAD = \frac{\Sigma|\text{deviations}|}{n} = 10.50 \qquad\qquad MAD = 12.50$$

cast is too high or too low, and by how much. In effect, bias provides the average total error and its direction.

Applicable Problems
4-27, 4-28, 4-29

Exponential Smoothing with Trend Adjustment. As with any moving average technique, simple exponential smoothing fails to respond to trends. To illustrate a more complex exponential smoothing model, let us consider one that adjusts for trend. The idea is to compute a simple exponential smoothing forecast as illustrated and then adjust for positive or negative lag in trend. The formula is:

Forecast including trend (FIT_t) = New forecast (F_t) + Trend correction (T_t)

To smooth out the trend, the equation for the trend correction uses a smoothing constant, β, in the same way the simple exponential model uses α. T_t is computed by

$$T_t = (1 - \beta)T_{t-1} + \beta(F_t - F_{t-1}) \tag{4-6}$$

where

$$T_t = \text{smoothed trend for period } t,$$

$$T_{t-1} = \text{smoothed trend for previous period,}$$

$$\beta = \text{trend smoothing constant that we select,}$$

$$F_t = \text{simple exponential smoothed forecast for period } t, \text{ and}$$

$$F_{t-1} = \text{forecast for previous period.}$$

There are three steps to compute a trend-adjusted forecast.

Step 1. Compute a simple exponential forecast for time period t (F_t).

Step 2. Compute the trend by using the equation:

$$T_t = (1 - \beta)T_{t-1} + \beta(F_t - F_{t-1})$$

To start step 2 for the first time, an initial trend value must be inserted (either by a good guess or by observed past data). After that, the trend is computed.

Step 3. Calculate the trend adjusted exponential smoothing forecast (FIT_t) by this formula:

$$FIT_t = F_t + T_t$$

As an example, we consider a large Portland manufacturer that uses exponential smoothing to forecast demand for a pollution control equipment product. It appears that a trend is present.

MONTH	DEMAND	MONTH	DEMAND
1	12	6	26
2	17	7	31
3	20	8	32
4	19	9	36
5	24		

Smoothing constants are assigned the values of $\alpha = .2$ and $\beta = .4$. Assume the initial forecast for month 1 was 11 units.

Step 1. Forecast for month 2 (F_2) = Forecast for month 1 (F_1) + α (Month 1 demand − Forecast for month 1):

$$F_2 = 11 + .2(12 - 11) = 11.0 + .2 = 11.2 \text{ units}$$

Step 2. Compute the trend present. Assume an initial trend adjustment of zero, that is, $T_1 = 0$.

$$T_2 = (1 - \beta)T_1 + \beta(F_2 - F_1)$$
$$= 0 + .4(11.2 - 11.0)$$
$$= .08$$

Step 3. Compute the forecast including trend (FIT):

$$FIT_2 = F_2 + T_2$$
$$= 11.2 + .08$$
$$= 11.28 \text{ units}$$

We will do the same calculations for the third month also.

Step 1. $F_3 = F_2 + \alpha$ (Demand in month 2 − F_2)
$$= 11.2 + .2(17 - 11.2) = 12.36$$

Step 2. $T_3 = (1 - \beta)T_2 + \beta(F_3 - F_2) = (1 - .4).08 + .4(12.36 - 11.2) = .51$

Step 3. $FIT_3 = F_3 + T_3 = 12.36 + .51 = 12.87$

So the simple exponential forecast (without trend) for month 2 was 11.2 units, and the trend-adjusted forecast was 11.28 units. In month 3, the simple forecast (without trend) was 12.36 units, and the trend-adjusted forecast was 12.87 units. Naturally, different values of T_1 and β can produce even better estimates.

Table 4.6 completes the forecasts for the nine-month period. Figure 4.4 compares actual demand, forecast without trend (F_t), and forecast with trend (FIT_t).

The value of the trend smoothing constant, β, resembles the α constant in that a high β is more responsive to recent changes in trend. A low β gives less weight to the most recent trends to smooth out the trend present. Values of β can be found by the trial-and-error approach, with the MAD used as a measure of comparison.

β's responsiveness

Simple exponential smoothing is often referred to as first-order smoothing, and trend-adjusted smoothing is called second-order, or double smoothing. Other advanced exponential smoothing models are also in use; they include seasonal-adjusted and triple smoothing, but these are beyond the scope of this book.[2]

---

[2] For more details, see E. S. Gardner, "Exponential Smoothing: The State of the Art," *Journal of Forecasting* **4**, 1 (March 1985) or R. Brown, *Smoothing, Forecasting and Prediction*, Englewood Cliffs, NJ: Prentice-Hall, 1973.

TABLE 4.6 Portland Manufacturer's Data for Trend-Adjusted Exponential Smoothing

MONTH	ACTUAL DEMAND	FORECAST, F_t (WITHOUT TREND)	TREND	ADJUSTED FIT_t
1	12	11.00	0	—
2	17	11.20	.08	11.28
3	20	12.36	.51	12.87
4	19	13.89	.92	14.81
5	24	14.91	.96	15.87
6	26	16.73	1.30	18.03
7	31	18.58	1.52	20.10
8	32	21.07	1.91	22.98
9	36	23.25	2.02	25.27

Trend Projections

**Applicable Problems
4-21, 4-34, 4-39**

The last time series forecasting method we discuss in this section is *trend projection*. This technique fits a trend line to a series of historical data points, and then projects the line into the future for medium- to long-range forecasts. There are several mathematical trend equations that can be developed (for example, exponential and quadratic), but in this section we look at linear (straight line) trends only.

Let us consider the case of Midwestern Manufacturing Company; that firm's demand for electrical generators over the period 1987–1993 is shown in Table 4.7.

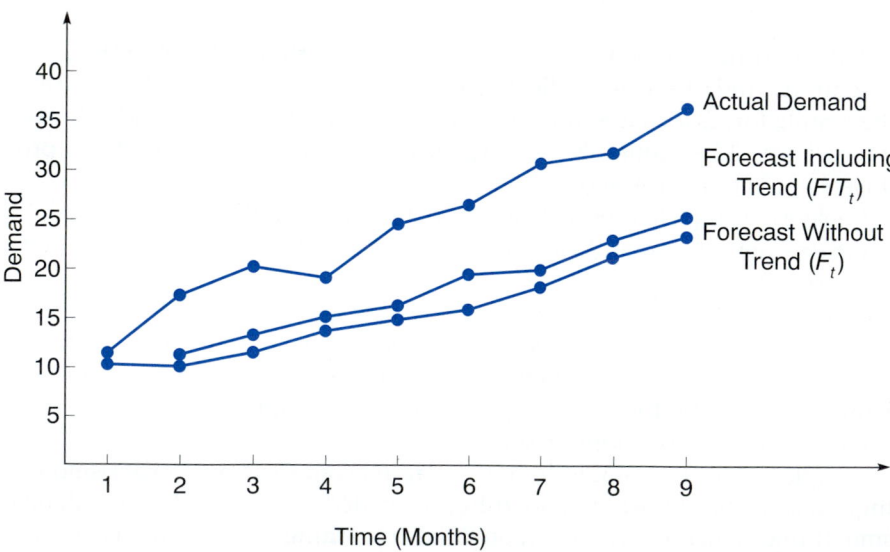

FIGURE 4.4
Comparison of Portland Manufacturer's Actual Demand, Forecast with Trend (FIT_t), and Forecast without Trend (F_t)

TABLE 4.7 Midwestern Manufacturing's Demand

YEAR	ELECTRICAL GENERATORS SOLD
1987	74
1988	79
1989	80
1990	90
1991	105
1992	142
1993	122

Alternate Example 4.5
Alternate Example 4.6

If we decide to develop a linear trend line by a precise statistical method, as opposed to "eyeballing" the line as we did in Figure 4.2(c), the *least squares method* may be applied. This approach results in a straight line that minimizes the sum of the squares of the vertical differences from the line to each of the actual observations. Figure 4.5 illustrates the least squares approach.

A least squares line is described in terms of its Y-intercept (the height at which it intercepts the Y-axis) and its slope (the angle of the line). If we can compute the Y-intercept and slope, the line can be expressed by the following equation:

$$\hat{Y} = a + bX \tag{4-7}$$

least squares method

Transparency Master 4.3:
The Least Squares Method for Finding the Best Fitting Straight Line.

need to solve for Y-intercept and slope

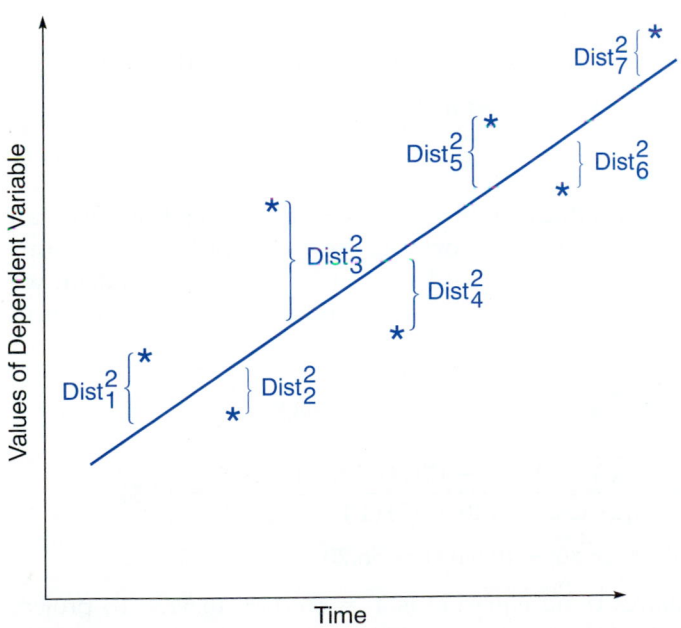

FIGURE 4.5
Least Squares Method for Finding the Best Fitting Straight Line

where

$\hat{Y}$ (pronounced Y-hat) = computed value of the variable to be predicted (called the dependent variable),

a = Y-axis intercept,

b = slope of the least squares line (or the rate of change in Y for given changes in X), and

X = the independent variable.

Statisticians have developed equations that we can use to find the values of a and b for any straight line. The slope, b, is found by:

the slope equation *b*

$$b = \frac{\Sigma XY - n\overline{X}\overline{Y}}{\Sigma X^2 - n\overline{X}^2}$$ (4-8)

where

b = slope of the straight line,

Σ = summation sign for n data points,

X = values of the independent variable, time here,

Y = values of the dependent variable, generator sales,

$\overline{X}$ = the average of the values of the Xs,

$\overline{Y}$ = the average of the values of the Ys, and

n = the number of data points or observations, 7 in this case.

The Y-intercept, a, is then computed as follows:

the intercept equation *a*

$$a = \overline{Y} - b\overline{X}$$ (4-9)

Transforming Time Variables. With a series of data over time, we can minimize the computations by transforming the values of X (time) to simpler numbers. Thus, in the case of Midwestern Manufacturing's data, we can designate 1987 as year 1, 1988 as year 2, and so on. This is shown in Table 4.8.

$$\overline{X} = \frac{\Sigma X}{n} = \frac{28}{7} = 4 \qquad \overline{Y} = \frac{\Sigma Y}{n} = \frac{692}{7} = 98.86$$

$$b = \frac{\Sigma XY - n\overline{X}\overline{Y}}{\Sigma X^2 - n\overline{X}^2} = \frac{3,063 - (7)(4)(98.86)}{140 - (7)(4^2)} = \frac{295}{28} = 10.54$$

$$a = \overline{Y} - b\overline{X} = 98.86 - 10.54(4) = 56.70$$

Hence, the least squares trend equation is $\hat{Y} = 56.70 + 10.54X$. To project demand in 1994, we first denote the year 1994 in our new coding system as $X = 8$:

(Sales in 1994) = 56.70 + 10.54(8)

= 141.02, or 141 generators

TABLE 4.8 Midwestern Manufacturing's Trend Calculations

YEAR	TIME PERIOD	GENERATOR DEMAND	X^2	XY
1987	1	74	1	74
1988	2	79	4	158
1989	3	80	9	240
1990	4	90	16	360
1991	5	105	25	525
1992	6	142	36	852
1993	7	122	49	854
	$\Sigma X = 28$	$\Sigma Y = 692$	$\Sigma X^2 = 140$	$\Sigma XY = 3,063$

We can estimate demand for 1995 by inserting $X = 9$ in the same equation:

$$(\text{Sales in 1995}) = 56.70 + 10.54(9)$$

$$= 151.56, \text{ or } 152 \text{ generators}$$

To check the validity of the model, we plot historical demand and the trend line in Figure 4.6. In this case, we may wish to be cautious and try to understand the 1992-1993 swings in demand.

Seasonal Variations. Time series forecasting such as that in the example of Midwestern Manufacturing involves looking at the *trend* of data over a series of time observations. Sometimes, however, recurring variations at certain seasons of the year make a *seasonal* adjustment in the trend line

**Applicable Problems
4-36, 4-37**

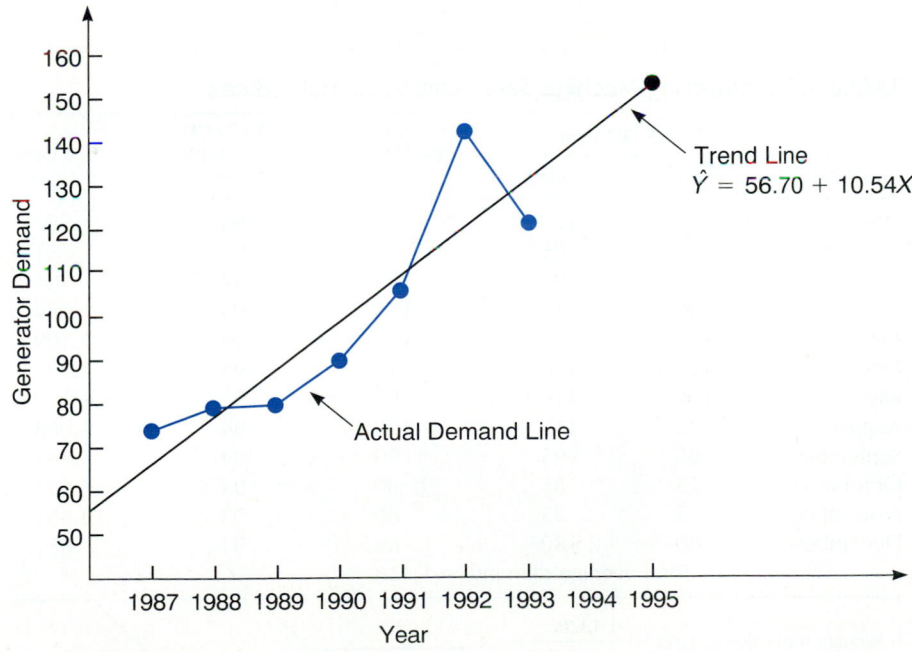

**FIGURE 4.6
Electrical Generators and the Computed
Trend Line**

forecast necessary. Demand for coal and fuel oil, for example, usually peaks during cold winter months. Demand for golf clubs or suntan lotion may be highest in summer. Analyzing data in monthly or quarterly terms usually makes it easy to spot seasonal patterns. Seasonal indices can then be developed by several common methods. The next example illustrates one way to compute seasonal factors from historical data.

Monthly sales of one brand of telephone answering machine at Eichler Supplies are shown in Table 4.9 for the two most recent years.

Using the seasonal indices from Table 4.9, if we expected the third year's annual demand for answering machines to be 1,200 units, we would forecast the monthly demand as follows:

Jan.	$\frac{1,200}{12} \times .957 = 96$	July	$\frac{1,200}{12} \times 1.117 = 112$
Feb.	$\frac{1,200}{12} \times .851 = 85$	Aug.	$\frac{1,200}{12} \times 1.064 = 106$
Mar.	$\frac{1,200}{12} \times .904 = 90$	Sept.	$\frac{1,200}{12} \times .957 = 96$
Apr.	$\frac{1,200}{12} \times 1.064 = 106$	Oct.	$\frac{1,200}{12} \times .851 = 85$
May	$\frac{1,200}{12} \times 1.309 = 131$	Nov.	$\frac{1,200}{12} \times .851 = 85$
June	$\frac{1,200}{12} \times 1.223 = 122$	Dec.	$\frac{1,200}{12} \times .851 = 85$

TABLE 4.9 Answering Machine Sales and Seasonal Indices

MONTH	SALES DEMAND		AVERAGE TWO-YEAR DEMAND	AVERAGE MONTHLY DEMAND*	SEASONAL INDEX†
	YEAR 1	YEAR 2			
January	80	100	90	94	.957
February	75	85	80	94	.851
March	80	90	85	94	.904
April	90	110	100	94	1.064
May	115	131	123	94	1.309
June	110	120	115	94	1.223
July	100	110	105	94	1.117
August	90	110	100	94	1.064
September	85	95	90	94	.957
October	75	85	80	94	.851
November	75	85	80	94	.851
December	80	80	80	94	.851
			Total average demand = 1,128		

* Average monthly demand $= \dfrac{1,128}{12 \text{ months}} = 94$

† Seasonal index $= \dfrac{\text{Average two-year demand}}{\text{Average monthly demand}}$

For simplicity, trend calculations were ignored in the previous example. The following example illustrates how indices that have already been prepared can be applied to adjust trend line forecasts and seasonal adjustments.

A San Diego hospital used 66 months of adult inpatient hospital days to reach the following equation:

$$\hat{Y} = 8{,}091 + 21.5X$$

where

$$\hat{Y} = \text{patient days, and}$$

$$X = \text{time, in months.}$$

Based on this model, the hospital forecasts patient days for the next month (period 67) to be:

$$\text{Patient days} = 8{,}091 + 21.5(67) = 9{,}530 \qquad \text{(trend only)}$$

As well as this model recognized the slight upward trend line in the demand for inpatient services, it ignored the seasonality that the administration knew to be present. Table 4.10 provides seasonal indices based on the same 66 months. Such seasonal data, by the way, were found to be typical of hospitals nationwide. Note that January, March, July, and August seem to exhibit significantly higher patient days on average, while February, September, November, and December experience lower patient days.

To correct the time series extrapolation for seasonality, the hospital multiplied the monthly forecast by the appropriate seasonality index. Thus, for period 67, which was a January,

$$\text{Patient days} = (9{,}530)(1.0436) = 9{,}946 \text{ (trend and seasonal)}$$

TABLE 4.10 Seasonality Indices for Adult Inpatient Days at San Diego Hospital

MONTH	SEASONALITY INDEX
January	1.0436
February	0.9669
March	1.0203
April	1.0087
May	0.9935
June	0.9906
July	1.0302
August	1.0405
September	0.9653
October	1.0048
November	0.9598
December	0.9805

Source: W. E. Sterk and E. G. Shryock, "Modern Methods Improve Hospital Forecasting," *Healthcare Financial Management* (March 1987): 97.

Using this method, patient days were forecasted for January through June (periods 67 through 72) as 9,946, 9,236, 9,768, 9,678, 9,554, and 9,547. This study led to better forecasts as well as to more accurate forecast budgets.

4.5 CAUSAL FORECASTING METHODS

Causal forecasting models usually consider several variables that are related to the variable being predicted. Once these related variables have been found, a statistical model is built and used to forecast the variable of interest. This approach can be more powerful than the time series methods that use only the historic values of the forecasted variable.

**dependent and
independent variables**

Many factors can be considered in a causal analysis. For example, the sales of a product might be related to the firm's advertising budget, the price charged, competitor's prices, promotional strategies, and even the economy and unemployment rates. In this case, sales would be called the *dependent variable*, while the other variables would be called *independent variables*. Our job as quantitative analysts is to develop the best statistical relationship between sales and the set of independent variables. The most common quantitative causal forecasting model is *regression analysis.*

Using Regression Analysis to Forecast

**Applicable Problems
4-10, 4-23b, c, 4-31,
4-32, 4-35, 4-38, 4-39,
North-South case,
Kwik-Lube case**

Triple A Construction Company renovates old homes in Albany. Over time, the company has found that its dollar volume of renovation work is dependent on the Albany area payroll. The figures for Triple A's revenues and the amount of money earned by wage earners in Albany for the past six years are presented in Table 4.11.

Triple A wants to establish a mathematical relationship that will help predict sales. Just as we did with the least squares method of trend projection, we can let Y represent the dependent variable that we want to forecast, sales in this case. But now the independent variable, X, is not time; it is the Albany area payroll.

Alternative Example 4.7

Least squares regression analysis may now be used to establish the statistical model. The same basic model applies:

$$\hat{Y} = a + bX$$

TABLE 4.11 Triple A Construction Company Sales

Teaching Suggestion 4.5:
Which is the Independent
Variable? See the Instructor's
Section for details.

Y TRIPLE A'S SALES ($100,000's)	X LOCAL PAYROLL ($100,000,000's)
2.0	1
3.0	3
2.5	4
2.0	2
2.0	1
3.5	7

where

$\hat{Y}$ = value of the dependent variable, sales here,

a = Y-axis intercept,

b = slope of the regression line, and

X = the independent variable, payroll.

The calculations for a and b follow:

SALES Y	PAYROLL X	X^2	XY
2.0	1	1	2.0
3.0	3	9	9.0
2.5	4	16	10.0
2.0	2	4	4.0
2.0	1	1	2.0
3.5	7	49	24.5
$\Sigma Y = 15.0$	$\Sigma X = 18$	$\Sigma X^2 = 80$	$\Sigma XY = 51.5$

$$\overline{X} = \frac{\Sigma X}{6} = \frac{18}{6} = 3$$

determining a and b

$$\overline{Y} = \frac{\Sigma Y}{6} = \frac{15}{6} = 2.5$$

$$b = \frac{\Sigma XY - n\overline{X}\,\overline{Y}}{\Sigma X^2 - n\overline{X}^2} = \frac{51.5 - (6)(3)(2.5)}{80 - (6)(3^2)} = .25$$

$$a = \overline{Y} - b\overline{X} = 2.5 - (.25)(3) = 1.75$$

The estimated regression equation therefore is:

$$\hat{Y} = 1.75 + .25X$$

or

$$\text{Sales} = 1.75 + .25 \text{ (payroll)}$$

If the local Chamber of Commerce predicts that the Albany area payroll will be six hundred million dollars next year, an estimate of sales for Triple A is found with the regression equation.

making the forecast

$$\text{Sales (\$100,000's)} = 1.75 + .25(6) = 1.75 + 1.50 = 3.25$$

or

$$\text{Sales} = \$325,000$$

The final part of Triple A's problem illustrates a central weakness of causal forecasting methods such as regression. We see that even once a regression equation is computed, it is necessary to provide a forecast of the independent variable, payroll, before estimating the dependent variable (Y) for the next time period. Although not a problem in the case of all forecasts, you can imagine the difficulty of determining future values of

weakness of regression

some common independent variables (such as unemployment rates, gross national product, price indices, and so on).

Standard Error of the Estimate

Applicable Problem 4-31b

The forecast of $325,000 for Triple A's sales in the preceding example is called a *point estimate* of Y. The point estimate is really the mean, or expected value, of a distribution of possible values of sales. Figure 4.7 illustrates this concept.

To measure the accuracy of the regression estimates we need to compute the *standard error of the estimate, $S_{Y,X}$*. This is called the *standard deviation of the regression*. Equation 4-10 is the same expression found in most statistics books for computing the standard deviation of an arithmetic mean:

Alternate Example 4.8

$$S_{Y,X} = \sqrt{\frac{\Sigma(Y - Y_c)^2}{n - 2}} \tag{4-10}$$

where

Y = the Y-value of each data point,

Y_c = the computed value of the dependent variable, from the regression equation,

n = the number of data points.

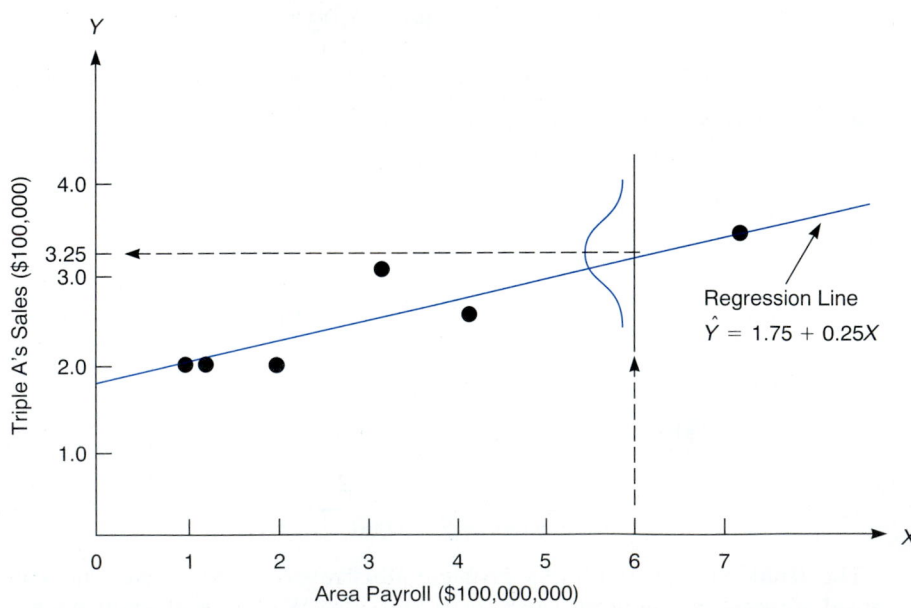

FIGURE 4.7
Distribution about the Point Estimate of $6 Hundred Million Payroll

Equation 4-11 may look more complex, but it is actually an easier-to-use version of Equation 4-10. Either formula provides the same answer and can be used in setting up prediction intervals around the point estimate.[3]

$$S_{Y,X} = \sqrt{\frac{\Sigma Y^2 - a\Sigma Y - b\Sigma XY}{n - 2}} \qquad \text{(4-11)}$$

Let us compute the standard error of the estimate for Triple A's data in the previous section. The only number we will need that is not available to solve for $S_{Y,X}$ is ΣY^2. Some quick addition in Table 4.12 reveals $\Sigma Y^2 = 39.5$. Therefore,

$$
\begin{aligned}
S_{Y,X} &= \sqrt{\frac{\Sigma Y^2 - a\Sigma Y - b\Sigma XY}{n - 2}} \\
&= \sqrt{\frac{39.5 - 1.75(15.0) - 0.25(51.5)}{6 - 2}} \\
&= \sqrt{0.09375} = 0.306 \text{ (in \$ hundred thousands)}
\end{aligned}
$$

The standard error of the estimate is then $30,600 in sales.

Correlation Coefficients for Regression Lines

The regression equation is one way of expressing the nature of the relationship between two variables.[4] The equation shows how one variable relates to the value and changes in another variable.

Another way to evaluate the relationship between two variables is to compute the *coefficient of correlation*. This measure expresses the degree or strength of the linear relationship. It is usually identified as r and can be any number between and including $+1$ and -1. Figure 4.8 illustrates what different values of r might look like.

Teaching Suggestion 4.6: Statistical Correlation Does Not Always Mean Causality. See the Instructor's Section for details.

measuring the strength of the linear relationship

Applicable Problem 4-30

TABLE 4.12 Triple A's Calculations Including New Column for Y^2

Y	X	X^2	XY	Y^2	
2.0	1	1	2.0	4.0	
3.0	3	9	9.0	9.0	
2.5	4	16	10.0	6.25	New
2.0	2	4	4.0	4.0	column
2.0	1	1	2.0	4.0	
3.5	7	49	24.5	12.25	
$\Sigma Y = 15.0$	$\Sigma X = 18$	$\Sigma X^2 = 80$	$\Sigma XY = 51.5$	$\Sigma Y^2 = 39.5$	

[3] When the sample size is large ($n > 30$), the prediction interval for an individual value of Y can be computed using normal tables. When the number of observations is small, the *t*-distribution is appropriate. See any good statistics textbook for details, such as Neter, Wasserman, and Whitmore's *Applied Statistics*, 3rd ed., Newton, Mass.: Allyn and Bacon, 1988.

[4] Regression lines are not always cause-and-effect relationships. In general, they describe the relationship between the movement of variables.

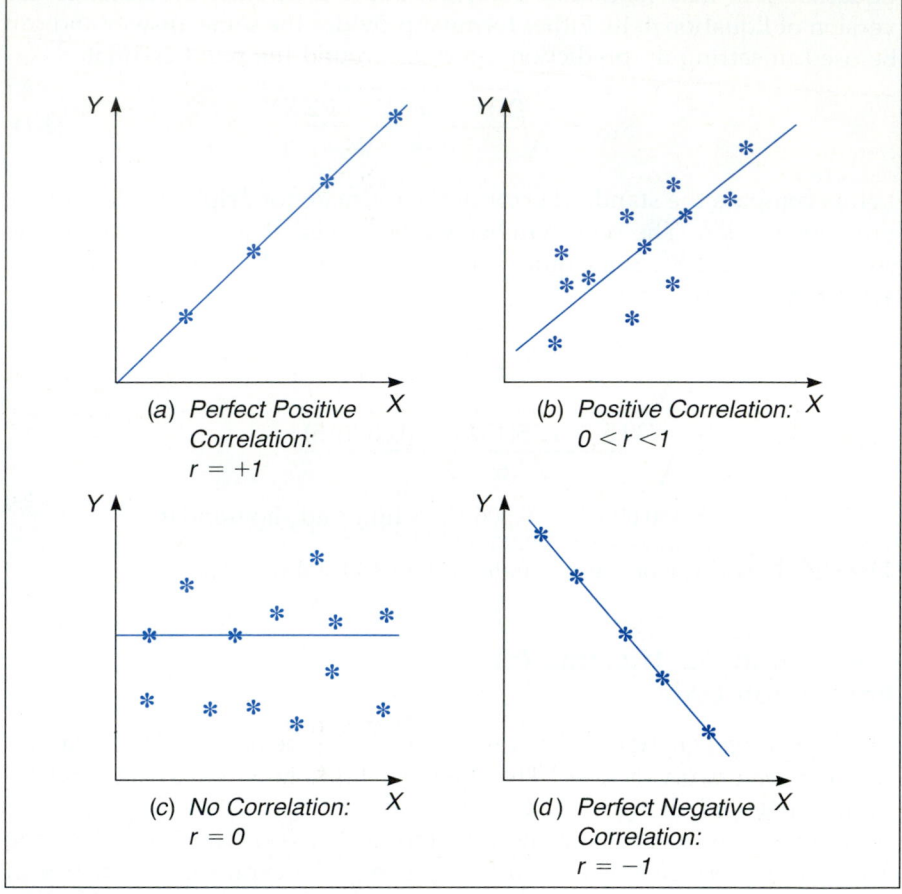

FIGURE 4.8
Four Values of the Correlation Coefficient

To compute r we use much of the same data needed earlier to calculate a and b for the regression line. The rather lengthy equation for r is:

$$r = \frac{n\sum XY - \sum X \sum Y}{\sqrt{[n\sum X^2 - (\sum X)^2][n\sum Y^2 - (\sum Y)^2]}} \qquad (4\text{-}12)$$

Alternate Example 4.9

Using the data in Table 4.12 we can compute the coefficient of correlation for Triple A Construction Company.

$$r = \frac{(6)(51.5) - (18)(15.0)}{\sqrt{[(6)(80) - (18)^2][(6)(39.5) - (15.0)^2]}} = \frac{309 - 270}{\sqrt{(156)(12)}} = \frac{39}{\sqrt{1872}}$$

$$= \frac{39}{43.3} = .901$$

This r of .901 appears to be a significant correlation and helps to confirm the closeness of the relationship of the two variables.

Although the coefficient of correlation is the most commonly used measure to describe the relationship between two variables, another measure does exist—the *coefficient of determination*. This is simply the square of the coefficient of correlation, namely, r^2. The value of r^2 will always be a positive number in the range of $0 \leq r^2 \leq 1$. The coefficient of determination is the percent of variation in the dependent variable (Y) that is explained by the regression equation. In Triple A's case, the value of r^2 is .81, indicating that 81% of the total variation is explained by the regression equation.

Multiple Regression Analysis

Multiple regression is a practical extension of the model we just observed. It allows us to build a model with several independent variables. For example, if Triple A Construction wanted to include average annual interest rates in its model to forecast renovation sales, the proper equation would be:

adding another independent variable

$$\hat{Y} = a + b_1X_1 + b_2X_2 \qquad \text{(4-13)}$$

Applicable Problem 4-33

where

$$\hat{Y} = \text{the dependent variable, sales,}$$

$$a = Y\text{-intercept,}$$

$$X_1 \text{ and } X_2 = \text{values of the two independent variables, area payroll and interest rates, respectively, and}$$

$$b_1 \text{ and } b_2 = \text{slopes for } X_1 \text{ and } X_2, \text{ respectively.}$$

The mathematics of multiple regression becomes quite complex, especially when more than two independent variables are considered, so we leave formulas for a, b_1, and b_2 to more advanced texts. For now, let's assume that the new regression line, calculated by a computer, is:

$$\hat{Y} = a + b_1X_1 + b_2X_2$$
$$= 1.80 + .30X_1 - 5.0X_2$$

Further, we find the new coefficient of correlation is .96, implying the inclusion of the variable X_2, interest rates, adds even more strength to the linear relationship.

We can now estimate Triple A's sales from Equation 4-13 if we substitute in values for next year's payroll and interest rates. If Albany's payroll will be six hundred million dollars and interest rates will be .12 (12%), sales will be forecast as:

$$\text{Sales (\$100,000's)} = 1.80 + .30(6) - 5.0(.12)$$

the new forecast

$$= 1.80 + 1.80 - .60$$
$$= 3.00$$
$$\text{Sales} = \$300,000$$

Should interest rates drop to only .08, or 8%, can you see that the sales forecast would increase to $320,000?

Applicable Problem 4.25c

4.6 MONITORING AND CONTROLLING FORECASTS

Once a forecast has been completed, it is important that it not be forgotten. No manager wants to be reminded when his or her forecast is horribly inaccurate, but a firm needs to determine why the actual demand (or whatever variable is being examined) differed significantly from that projected.[5]

tracking signal

One way to monitor forecasts to ensure they are performing well is to employ a tracking signal. A *tracking signal* is a measurement of how well the forecast is predicting actual values. As forecasts are updated every week, month, or quarter, the newly available demand data are compared to the forecast values.

Transparency Master 4.5:
Measures of Accuracy and Error.

The tracking signal is computed as the *running sum of the forecast errors* (RSFE) divided by the mean absolute deviation.

$$\frac{\text{Tracking}}{\text{signal}} = \frac{\text{RSFE}}{\text{MAD}}$$

$$= \frac{\Sigma(\text{Actual demand in period } i - \text{Forecast demand in period } i)}{\text{MAD}}$$

(4-14)

where

$$\text{MAD} = \frac{\Sigma|\text{Forecast errors}|}{n}$$

as seen earlier in Equation 4-5.

Teaching Suggestion 4.7:
Wide Use of Adaptive Models. See the Instructor's Section for details.

Positive tracking signals indicate that demand is greater than the forecast. Negative signals mean that demand is less than forecast. A good tracking signal, that is, one with a low RSFE, has about as much positive error as it has negative error. In other words, small deviations are okay, but the positive and negative ones should balance one another so the tracking signal centers closely around zero.

Once tracking signals are calculated, they are compared to predetermined control limits. When a tracking signal exceeds an upper or lower limit, a signal is tripped. This means there is a problem with the forecasting method, and management may want to reevaluate the way it forecasts demand. Figure 4.9 shows the graph of a tracking signal that is exceeding the range of acceptable variation. If the model being used is exponential smoothing, perhaps the smoothing constant needs to be readjusted.

setting tracking limits

How do firms decide what the upper and lower tracking limits should be? There is no single answer, but they try to find reasonable values—in other words, limits not so low as to be triggered with every small forecast error and not so high as to allow bad forecasts to be regularly overlooked. George Plossl and Oliver Wight, two inventory control experts, suggested

---

[5] If the forecaster *is* accurate, that individual usually makes sure that everyone is aware of his or her talents. Very seldom does one read articles in *Fortune, Forbes,* or *The Wall Street Journal,* however, about money managers who are consistently off by 25% in their stock market forecasts.

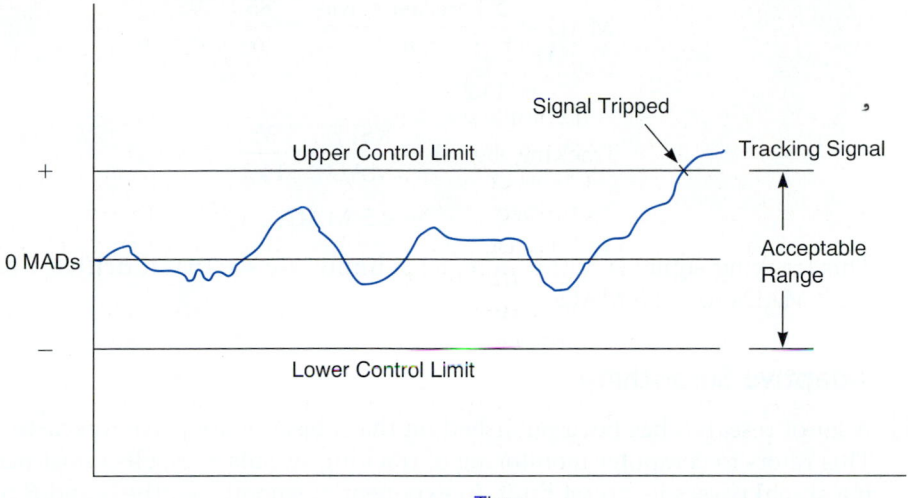

FIGURE 4.9
Plot of Tracking Signals

using maximums of ±4 MADs (for high-volume stock items) and ±8 MADs (for lower-volume items).[6] Other forecasters suggest slightly lower ranges. One MAD is equivalent to approximately .8 standard deviations, so that ±2 MADs = ±1.6 standard deviations, ±3 MADs = ±2.4 standard deviations, and ±4 MADs = ±3.2 standard deviations. This suggests that for a forecast to be "in control," 89% of the errors are expected to fall within ±2 MADs, 98% within ±3 MADs, or 99.9% within ±4 MADs.[7]

The following example shows how the tracking signal and RSFE can be computed. Kimball's Bakery's quarterly sales of croissants (in thousands), as well as forecast demand and error computations, are shown below. The objective is to compute the tracking signal and determine whether forecasts are performing adequately.

QUARTER	FORECAST DEMAND	ACTUAL DEMAND	ERROR	RSFE	FORECAST ERROR	CUMULATIVE ERROR	MAD	TRACKING SIGNAL
1	100	90	−10	−10	10	10	10.0	−1
2	100	95	−5	−15	5	15	7.5	−2
3	100	115	+15	0	15	30	10.0	0
4	110	100	−10	−10	10	40	10.0	−1
5	110	125	+15	+5	15	55	11.0	+0.5
6	110	140	+30	+35	30	85	14.2	+2.5

[6] See G.W. Plossl and O.W. Wight, *Production and Inventory Control*, Englewood Cliffs, NJ: Prentice-Hall, 1967.

[7] To prove these three percentages to yourself, just set up a normal curve for ±1.6 standard deviations (Z values). Using the Normal Table in Appendix A you find that the area under that curve is 0.89. This represents ±2 MADs. Likewise, ±3 MADs = ±2.4 standard deviations, encompasses 98% of the area, and so on for ±4 MADs.

Alternate Example 4.10

$$\text{MAD} = \frac{\Sigma \, \text{Forecast errors}}{n} = \frac{85}{6}$$

$$= 14.2$$

$$\text{Tracking signal} = \frac{\text{RSFE}}{\text{MAD}} = \frac{35}{14.2}$$

$$= 2.5 \text{ MADs}$$

This tracking signal is within acceptable limits. We see that it drifted from -2.0 MADs to $+2.5$ MADs.

Adaptive Smoothing

A lot of research has been published on the subject of adaptive forecasting. This refers to computer monitoring of tracking signals and self-adjustment if a signal passes its preset limit. In exponential smoothing, the α and β coefficients are first selected based on values that minimize error forecasts

---

APPLICATIONS OF QA

Flood Forecasting at NOAA

One of the major components of the National Oceanic and Atmospheric Administration (NOAA) is the national weather service (NWS). Saving lives and reducing property damage is one of the major objectives of the NWS. To accomplish this mission, an effective flood forecasting-response system is needed. The importance of an accurate and fast flood forecast cannot be overemphasized. Hundreds of lives and millions of dollars are at stake. In the United States, there are approximately 20,000 flood-prone areas. The NWS, at this time, develops approximately 3,000 flood warnings for specific areas or forecast points.

The flood forecast-response (FFR) system involves a number of steps. The first step is data collection. In this step, data from the field regarding potential floods are collected and sent to river forecast centers. The second step is the actual forecasting procedure. This includes a number of important mathematical models that transform rainfall, runoff, and a number of other factors into the actual flood forecasts. A flood forecast indicates the magnitude of the flood crest and the time of arrival of the flood crest at specific points along rivers. The third step is the dissemination of the information to the appropriate points. Radio, telephone, and television coverage are all used to inform both public and private organizations and individuals of the potential of floods according to the forecast. The fourth step is the decision procedure step. Formal decision models are used to help formulate responses to various flood conditions. This includes the specific type of protective action to be taken. The fifth step is the actual implementation of the specific actions to be taken both to prevent and to cope with flood type conditions.

In many forecast situations, like the flood forecast-response system described here, a lot more is involved than simply making the forecast. The appropriate data must be systematically collected, and the results must be carefully analyzed and disseminated so the appropriate decisions can be made. Robert Clark, director of the Office of Hydrology of the National Weather Service, stated that: "The work reported on has been of great value in examining the response of the entire flood forecast system including data collection, forecasting, dissemination, decisions by floodplain dwellers, and protective actions."

Source: Adapted from Roman Krzysztofowizz and Donald R. Davis, "Toward Improving Flood Forecast-Response Systems," *Interfaces* **14**, 3 (May–June 1984): 1–14.

and then adjusted accordingly whenever the computer notes an errant tracking signal. This is called *adaptive smoothing*.

4.7 USING THE COMPUTER TO FORECAST

Forecast calculations are seldom performed by hand in this day of computers. Numerous university and commercial packaged programs (such as SAS, SPSS, BIOMED, SYSTAB, and Minitab) are readily available to handle time series and causal projections. Even spreadsheet software, such as Lotus 1-2-3, can effectively manage small-to-medium forecasting problems.

Several mainframe-oriented packages, such as General Electric's Time Series Forecasting (called FCST1 and FCST2), are oriented toward organizations that need to perform large-scale regression and exponential smoothing projections. A large number of corporations use forecasting programs that also incorporate inventory control routines. Examples are IBM's IMPACT (Inventory Management Program and Control Technique) and COGS (Consumer Goods Program).

AB:QM Sample Computer Runs

In this section we'll look at the microcomputer forecasting software package AB:QM. AB:QM can project moving averages (both simple and weighted), do simple and trend-adjusted exponential smoothing, handle least squares trend projection, and solve linear regression (causal) problems.

To illustrate AB:QM, let's use the data in Table 4.13. We will forecast generator sales by moving averages, exponential smoothing, and then trend projection. Finally, linear regression will be used to attempt to establish a causal relationship between advertising budget and sales.

Programs 4.1 through 4.4 show AB:QM's four microcomputer forecasting options, with a sample run for each.

Program 4.1 is a simple moving average model using a three-year moving period. Its forecast for 1994 (period 8) is 123, with a MAD of 23.58.

Program 4.2 uses an alpha weight of .30 in an exponential smoothing model, where we select an initial forecast of 74, equal to 1987's actual sales figure. The result for 1994 (period 8) is a forecast of 110 (rounding upward) with a MAD of 16.94.

TABLE 4.13 Midwestern Manufacturing Data

YEAR	GENERATORS SOLD	ADVERTISING BUDGET ($)
1987	74	1,200
1988	79	1,500
1989	80	2,200
1990	90	2,000
1991	105	2,000
1992	142	2,500
1993	122	2,450

PROGRAM 4.1 Midwestern Manufacturing (Simple Moving Average)

```
Forecasting / Simple & Weighted Moving Average

Problem Title :  PROGRAM 4.1 MIDWESTERN MANUFACTURING
Number of Moving Periods        3           Weighted? (1=no/2=yes)    1
Number of Periods               7


              Data
Period  1      74
Period  2      79
Period  3      80
Period  4      90
Period  5     105
Period  6     142
Period  7     122



Help  New  Load  Save  Edit  Run  Print  Install  Directory  Esc


Program: Forecasting / Simple & Weighted Moving Average
Problem Title : PROGRAM 4.1 MIDWESTERN MANUFACTURING

***** Input Data *****

Number of Moving Periods :         3
Number of Periods        :         7
Weighted?                :        No

Input data are shown below.

***** Program Output *****

                             Forecast
Period      Data    Forecast   Error

   1       74.000
   2       79.000
   3       80.000
   4       90.000    77.667   -12.333
   5      105.000    83.000   -22.000
   6      142.000    91.667   -50.333
   7      122.000   112.333    -9.667
   8                123.000

Mean Absolute Deviation        :      23.5833
Mean Square Error              :     554.4082
Mean Forecast Error            :     -23.5833
Running Sum of Forecast Error  :      94.3333
Tracking Signal                :       4.0000

***** End of Output *****
```

PROGRAM 4.2 **Midwestern Manufacturing (Exponential Smoothing)**

```
Forecasting / Exponential Smoothing

Problem Title :  PROGRAM 4.2 MIDWESTERN MANUFACTURING
Alpha                         .30          Initial Estimated Forecast  74
Number of Periods             7

                Data
Period  1        74
Period  2        79
Period  3        80
Period  4        90
Period  5       105
Period  6       142
Period  7       122
```

```
Help   New   Load   Save   Edit   Run   Print   Install   Directory   Esc


Program: Forecasting / Exponential Smoothing

Problem Title : PROGRAM 4.2 MIDWESTERN MANUFACTURING

***** Input Data *****

Alpha                         :       0.300
Initial Estimated Forecast :       74.000
Number of Periods             :           7

Input data are shown below.

***** Program Output *****

                         Forecast
Period      Data      Forecast      Error

   1       74.000      74.000       0.000
   2       79.000      74.000      -5.000
   3       80.000      75.500      -4.500
   4       90.000      76.850     -13.150
   5      105.000      80.795     -24.205
   6      142.000      88.056     -53.944
   7      122.000     104.240     -17.760
   8                  109.568


Mean Absolute Deviation       :        16.9370
Mean Square Error             :       554.4082
Mean Forecast Error           :       -16.9370
Running Sum of Forecast Error :       118.5590
Tracking Signal               :         7.0000

***** End of Output *****
```

Program 4.3 employs least squares trend projection, and produces the model:

$$\text{Sales} = 56.71 + 10.54 \,(\text{Year})$$

If Year = 8, then the sales forecast will be 56.71 + 10.54(8) = 141 generators. The MAD is only 10.01.

PROGRAM 4.3 Midwestern Manufacturing (Least Squares Method)

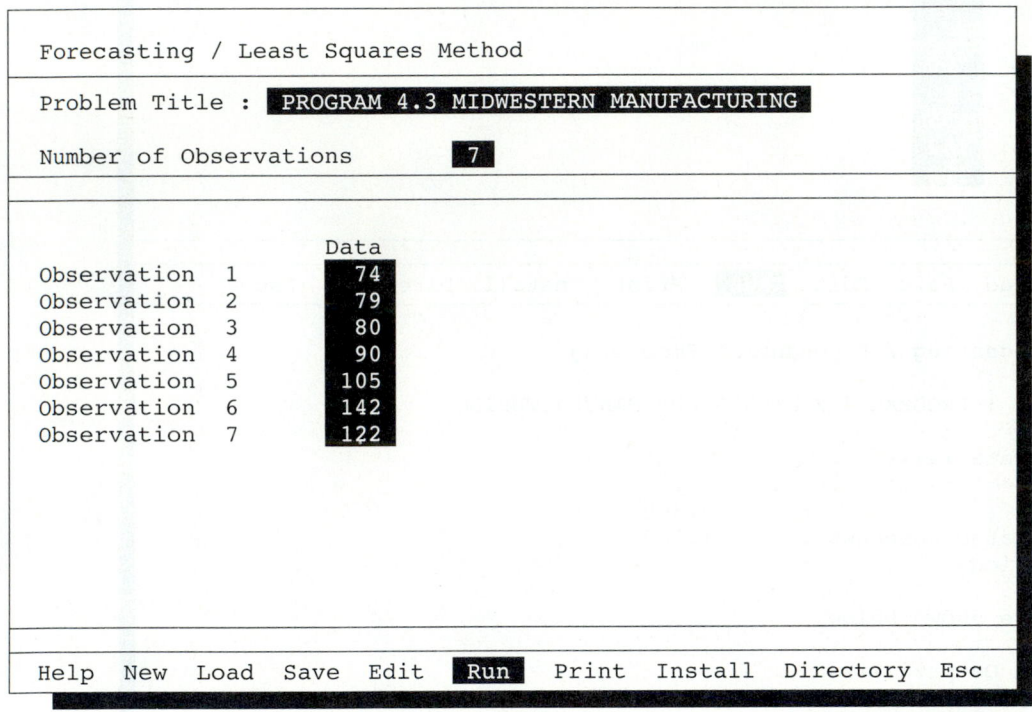

```
Forecasting / Least Squares Method

Problem Title :  PROGRAM 4.3 MIDWESTERN MANUFACTURING

Number of Observations        7


                        Data
Observation   1         74
Observation   2         79
Observation   3         80
Observation   4         90
Observation   5        105
Observation   6        142
Observation   7        122




 Help   New   Load   Save   Edit   Run   Print   Install   Directory   Esc
```

(continued)

PROGRAM 4.3 **Midwestern Manufacturing (Least Squares Method)** **(Continued)**

```
Program: Forecasting / Least Squares Method
Problem Title :  PROGRAM 4.3 MIDWESTERN MANUFACTURING
***** Input Data *****
```

Obs.	Data(Y)
1	74.000
2	79.000
3	80.000
4	90.000
5	105.000
6	142.000
7	122.000

```
***** Program Output *****
```

Parameter	Coefficient	SE B	t
Intercept	56.7143	10.5073	5.3976
b 1	10.5357	2.3495	4.4842

Coefficient of determination	:	0.8009
Correlation coefficient	:	0.8949
Standard Error	:	12.4324
Mean Absolute Deviation (MAD)	:	10.0119

ANOVA Table

Source of Variation	SS	df	MS
Regression	3108.036	1	3108.036
Residual	772.821	5	154.564
Total	3880.857	6	

```
F*  =      20.108

***** End of Output *****
```

Finally, Program 4.4 uses regression to examine the relationship between generator sales (Y) and advertising budget (X). The least squares model that results is:

$$\text{Sales} = 15.62 + .0421 \, (\text{Ad budget})$$

R^2 is .6291 and MAD is 12.64.

PROGRAM 4.4 Midwestern Manufacturing (Simple Regression)

```
Forecasting / Simple Regression

Problem Title :  PROGRAM 4.4 MIDWESTERN MANUFACTURING

Number of Observations        7


                            Y              X
Observation  1            74           1200
Observation  2            79           1500
Observation  3            80           2200
Observation  4            90           2000
Observation  5           105           2000
Observation  6           142           2500
Observation  7           122           2450




Help   New   Load   Save   Edit   Run   Print   Install   Directory   Esc
```

(continued)

PROGRAM 4.4 Midwestern Manufacturing (Simple Regression)
(Continued)

```
Program: Forecasting / Simple Regression

Problem Title :  PROGRAM 4.4 MIDWESTERN MANUFACTURING

***** Input Data *****
_____
Obs.        Y           X
_____
  1       74.000    1200.000
  2       79.000    1500.000
  3       80.000    2200.000
  4       90.000    2000.000
  5      105.000    2000.000
  6      142.000    2500.000
  7      122.000    2450.000
_____

***** Program Output *****
_____
Parameter     Coefficient        SE B            t
_____
Intercept       15.6157        29.2961        0.5330
   b 1            0.0421         0.0144        2.9120
_____


Coefficient of determination    :      0.6291
Correlation coefficient          :      0.7931
Standard Error                   :     16.9677


Prediction Error
_____
Obs.    Observed    Predicted           Residual
         Value        Value
_____
  1      74.000      66.102               7.898
  2      79.000      78.723               0.277
  3      80.000     108.173             -28.173
  4      90.000      99.759              -9.759
  5     105.000      99.759               5.241
  6     142.000     120.794              21.206
  7     122.000     118.691               3.309
_____


Mean Absolute Deviation (MAD)  :     12.6439


ANOVA Table
_____
Source of
Variation             SS           df           MS
_____
Regression         2441.347        1         2441.347
Residual           1439.510        5          287.902
_____
Total              3880.857        6
F*  =      8.480
_____

***** End of Output *****
```

4.8 SUMMARY

Forecasts are a critical part of a manager's function. Demand forecasts drive the production, capacity, and scheduling systems in a firm and affect the financial, marketing, and personnel planning functions.

This chapter introduced you to three types of forecasting models—time series, causal, and judgmental. Moving averages, exponential smoothing, and trend projection time series models were developed; a popular causal model, regression analysis, was illustrated; and four qualitative models were discussed. In addition, we explained the use of scatter diagrams, correlation coefficients, and the analysis of forecasting accuracy. In future chapters, you will see the usefulness of these techniques in determining values for the various decision-making models.

Table 4.14 compares seven forecasting approaches on a variety of scales, including time span, sophistication, computer needs, financial needs, inputs, and accuracy. It is excerpted from an excellent article on forecasting in the *Harvard Business Review* that we recommend you read.[8]

No forecasting method, as you can see in Table 4.14 and as we learned in this chapter, is perfect under all conditions. And even once management has found a satisfactory approach, it must still monitor and control its forecasts to make sure errors do not get out of hand. Forecasting can often be a very challenging, but rewarding, part of managing.

Transparency Master 4.6:
Forecasting Time Horizons.

[8] The article is by D. M. Georgoff and R. G. Murdick, "Manager's Guide to Forecasting," *Harvard Business Review* **64**, 1 (January–February 1986): 110–120.

TABLE 4.14 A Comparison of Forecasting Methods

			NAIVE EXTRAPOLATION	DELPHI TECHNIQUE	MOVING AVERAGES	EXPONENTIAL SMOOTHING	TIME SERIES EXTRAPOLATION	REGRESSION MODELS
Time	Span	Is the forecast period a: Present need, or Short-, Medium-, or Long-term projection?	Present need to Medium	Medium or Long	Short, Medium, or Long	Present need to Short or Medium	Short, Medium, or Long	Short, Medium, or Long
	Urgency	Is the forecast needed immediately?	Rapid results are a strong advantage of this technique. Devel. time Short Execution time Short	Urgency seriously compromises quality. Dev Moderate Ex Moderate to Long	Rapid results are a strong advantage of this technique. Dev Short Ex Short		Computation is quick if data are available; data gathering can cause delays. Dev Short to Moderate Ex Short	Model formulation takes time, but forecast computation is quick. Dev Moderate to Long Ex Short to Moderate
	Frequency	Are frequent forecast updates needed?	Can easily accommodate frequent updates.	Usually used for one-time forecasts, but they can be revised as new information becomes available.	Forecast can be systematically updated easily.			Forecast can be updated quickly if data are available.
Resource requirements	Mathematical sophistication	Are quantitative skills limited?	Minimal quantitative capabilities are required.					A fundamental competency level is required.
	Computer	Are computer capabilities limited?	Computer capabilities are not essential.		A computer is helpful for repetitive updating.		A computer is helpful for repetitive updating.	A computer is essential for most cases.
	Financial	Are only limited resources available?	Very inexpensive to implement and maintain.	Expense depends on makeup and affiliation of participants.	If data are readily available, out-of-pocket costs are minimal.		If data are readily available, out-of-pocket costs are minimal.	If data are on hand, development costs are moderate.
Input	Antecedent	Are only limited past data available?	Some past data are required, but extended history is not essential.		Past history is essential.	Only recent forecasts and current data are required once alpha is determined.		Past history is essential with detail required.
Output	Accuracy	Is a high level of accuracy critical?	Often provides a limited practical level of accuracy.	Not particularly accurate, but usually most accurate when horizons are extended and conditions are dynamic.	Accurate under stable conditions.	Generally rates high in accuracy for short-term forecasts.	Normally accurate for trends and stationary series.	Can be accurate if variable relationships are stable and the proportion of explained variance is high.

Source: D.M. Georgoff and R.G. Murdick, "Manager's Guide to Forecasting," *Harvard Business Review* **64,** 1 (January–February 1986): 110–20.

GLOSSARY

Time Series Models. Models that forecast using only historical data.

Causal Models. Models that forecast using variables and factors in addition to time.

Qualitative Models. Models that forecast using judgments, experience, and qualitative and subjective data.

Scatter Diagrams. Diagrams of the variable to be forecasted, plotted against another variable, such as time.

Moving Average. A forecasting technique that averages past values in computing the forecast.

Weighted Moving Average. A moving average forecasting method that places different weights on past values.

Exponential Smoothing. A forecasting method that is a combination of the last forecast and the last observed value.

Smoothing Constant. A value between 0 and 1 that is used in an exponential smoothing forecast. It is generally in the range from 0.1 to 0.3.

Mean Absolute Deviation (MAD). A technique for determining the accuracy of a forecasting model by taking the average of the absolute deviations.

Mean Squared Error (MSE). A technique for determining the accuracy of a forecasting model by taking the average of the squared error terms for a forecasting model.

Mean Absolute Percent Error (MAPE). A technique for determining the accuracy of a forecasting model by taking the average of the absolute errors as a percentage of the observed values.

Bias. A technique for determining the accuracy of a forecasting model by measuring the average total error and its direction.

Least Squares. A procedure used in trend projection and regression analysis to minimize the squared distances between the estimated straight line and the observed values.

Regression Analysis. A forecasting procedure that uses the least squares approach on one or more independent variables to develop a forecasting model.

Standard Error of the Estimate. A measure of the accuracy of regression estimates.

Correlation Coefficient. A measure of the strength of relationship between two variables.

Tracking Signal. A measure of how well the forecast is predicting actual values.

Delphi. A judgmental forecasting technique that uses decision makers, staff personnel, and respondents to determine a forecast.

Decision-Making Group. A group of experts in a Delphi technique that has the responsibility of making the forecast.

KEY EQUATIONS

(4-1) Moving average $= \dfrac{\sum_{i=1}^{n} \text{Demand in previous } n \text{ periods}}{n}$

An equation for computing a moving average forecast.

(4-2) Weighted moving average $= \dfrac{\Sigma \left(\begin{array}{c} \text{Weight for} \\ \text{period } n \end{array} \right) \left(\begin{array}{c} \text{Demand in} \\ \text{period } n \end{array} \right)}{\Sigma \text{ Weights}}$

An equation for computing a weighted moving average forecast.

(4-3) New forecast = Last period's forecast + α (Last period's actual demand − Last period's forecast)

An equation for computing an exponential smoothing forecast.

(4-4) $F_t = F_{t-1} + \alpha(A_{t-1} - F_{t-1})$

Equation 4-3 rewritten mathematically.

(4-5) $\text{MAD} = \dfrac{\Sigma|\text{Forecast errors}|}{n}$

A measure of overall forecast error called mean absolute deviation.

(4-6) $T_t = (1 - \beta)T_{t-1} + \beta(F_t - F_{t-1})$

Trend component of an exponential smoothing model.

(4-7) $\hat{Y} = a + bX$

A least squares straight line used in trend projection and regression analysis forecasting.

(4-8) $b = \dfrac{\Sigma XY - n\overline{X}\,\overline{Y}}{\Sigma X^2 - n\overline{X}^2}$

An equation used to compute the slope, b, of a regression line.

(4-9) $a = \overline{Y} - b\overline{X}$

An equation used to compute the Y-intercept, a, of a regression line.

(4-10) $S_{Y,X} = \sqrt{\dfrac{\Sigma(Y - Y_c)^2}{n - 2}}$

Standard error of the estimate.

(4-11) $S_{Y,X} = \sqrt{\dfrac{\Sigma Y^2 - a\Sigma Y - b\Sigma XY}{n - 2}}$

Another way to express Equation 4-10.

(4-12) $r = \dfrac{n\Sigma XY - \Sigma X \Sigma Y}{\sqrt{[n\Sigma X^2 - (\Sigma X)^2][n\Sigma Y^2 - (\Sigma Y)^2]}}$

Correlation coefficient.

(4-13) $\hat{Y} = a + b_1 X_1 + b_2 X_2$

The least squares line used in multiple regression.

(4-14) Tracking signal $= \dfrac{\text{RSFE}}{\text{MAD}} = \dfrac{\Sigma \left(\begin{array}{c} \text{Actual demand} \\ \text{in period } i \end{array} - \begin{array}{c} \text{Forecast demand} \\ \text{in period } i \end{array} \right)}{\text{MAD}}$

An equation for monitoring forecasts.

SOLVED PROBLEMS

Solved Problem 4-1

Demand for patient surgery at Washington General Hospital has increased steadily in the past few years, as seen in the following table.

YEAR	OUTPATIENT SURGERIES PERFORMED
1	45
2	50
3	52
4	56
5	58
6	

The director of medical services predicted six years ago that demand in year 1 would be 42 surgeries.

Using exponential smoothing with a weight of $\alpha = 0.20$, develop forecasts for years 2 through 6. What is the MAD?

Solution

YEAR	ACTUAL	FORECAST (SMOOTHED)	ERROR	|ERROR|
1	45	42	−3	3
2	50	42.6 = 42 + .2(45 − 42)	−7.4	7.4
3	52	44.1 = 42.6 + .2(50 − 42.6)	−7.9	7.9
4	56	45.7 = 44.1 + .2(52 − 44.1)	−10.3	10.3
5	58	47.7 = 45.7 + .2(56 − 45.7)	−10.3	10.3
6	—	49.8 = 47.7 + .2(58 − 47.7)		38.9

$$\text{MAD} = \frac{\Sigma |\text{Errors}|}{n} = \frac{38.9}{5} = 7.78$$

Solved Problem 4-2

Room registrations in the Toronto Towers Plaza Hotel have been recorded for the past nine years. Management would like to determine the mathematical trend of guest registration in order to project future occupancy. This estimate would help the hotel determine whether a future expansion will be needed. Given the following time series data, develop a regression equation relating registrations to time. Then forecast next year's registrations. Room registrations are in thousands:

Year 1: 17	Year 2: 16	Year 3: 16	Year 4: 21	Year 5: 20
Year 6: 20	Year 7: 23	Year 8: 25	Year 9: 24	

Solution

YEAR	REGISTRANTS Y (1,000's)	X^2	XY
1	17	1	17
2	16	4	32
3	16	9	48
4	21	16	84
5	20	25	100
6	20	36	120
7	23	49	161
8	25	64	200
9	24	81	216
$\Sigma X = 45$	$\Sigma Y = 182$	$\Sigma X^2 = 285$	$\Sigma XY = 978$

$$\overline{X} = \frac{45}{9} = 5, \qquad \overline{Y} = \frac{182}{9} = 20.22$$

$$b = \frac{\Sigma XY - n\overline{X}\,\overline{Y}}{\Sigma X^2 - n\overline{X}^2} = \frac{978 - (9)(5)(20.22)}{285 - (9)(25)} = \frac{978 - 909.9}{285 - 225} = \frac{68.1}{60} = 1.135$$

$$a = \overline{Y} - b\overline{X} = 20.22 - (1.135)(5) = 20.22 - 5.675 = 14.545$$

$$\hat{Y}\ (\text{registrations}) = 14.545 + 1.135X$$

The projection of registrations in year 11 is

$$\hat{Y} = 14.545 + (1.135)(11) = 27.03$$

or 27,030 guests in year 11.

Solved Problem 4-3

Quarterly demand for Jaguar XJ6s at a New York auto dealer is forecast with the equation:

$$\hat{Y} = 10 + 3X$$

where

$$X = \text{quarters: quarter I of last year} = 0,$$
$$\text{quarter II of last year} = 1,$$
$$\text{quarter III of last year} = 2,$$
$$\text{quarter IV of last year} = 3,$$
$$\text{quarter I of this year} = 4,$$
$$\text{and so on,}$$

and

$$\hat{Y} = \text{quarterly demand.}$$

The demand for sports sedans is seasonal and the indices for quarters I, II, III, and IV are .80, 1.00, 1.30, and .90, respectively. Forecast demand for each quarter of next year. Then seasonalize each forecast to adjust for quarterly variations.

Solution

Quarter II of this year is coded $X = 5$; quarter III of this year, $X = 6$; and quarter IV of this year, $X = 7$. Hence, quarter I of next year is coded $X = 8$; quarter II, $X = 9$; and so on.

$\hat{Y}$(next year quarter I) = $10 + 3(8) = 34$ Adjusted forecast = $(0.80)(34) = 27.2$
$\hat{Y}$(next year quarter II) = $10 + 3(9) = 37$ Adjusted forecast = $(1.00)(37) = 37$
$\hat{Y}$(next year quarter III) = $10 = 3(10) = 40$ Adjusted forecast = $(1.30(40) = 52$
$\hat{Y}$(next year quarter IV) = $10 + 3(11) = 43$ Adjusted forecast = $(0.90)(43) = 38.7$

DISCUSSION QUESTIONS AND PROBLEMS

Discussion Questions

4-1 Briefly describe the steps that are used to develop a forecasting system.

4-2 What is a time series forecasting model?

4-3 What is the difference between a causal model and a time series model?

4-4 What is a qualitative forecasting model, and when is it appropriate?

4-5 What is the meaning of least squares in a regression model?

4-6 What are some of the problems and drawbacks of the moving average forecasting model?

4-7 What effect does the value of the smoothing constant have on the weight given to the past forecast and the past observed value?

4-8 Briefly describe the Delphi technique.

4-9 What is MAD, and why is it important in the selection and use of forecasting models?

Problems

4-10 John Smith has developed the following forecasting model:

$$\hat{Y} = 36 + 4.3\ X1$$

where

$$\hat{Y} = \text{demand for K10 air conditioners, and}$$

$$X1 = \text{the outside temperature (°F).}$$

(a) Forecast demand for K10 when the temperature is 70°F.
(b) What is the demand for a temperature of 80°F?
(c) What is demand for a temperature of 90°F?

337
380
423

4-11 Develop a four-month moving average forecast for Wallace Garden Supply. A three-month moving average forecast was developed in the section on moving averages in Table 4.2.

4-12 Using MAD, determine whether the forecast in Problem 4-11 or the forecast in the section concerning Wallace Garden Supply is more accurate.

4-13 Data collected on the yearly demand for 50-lb. bags of fertilizer at Wallace Garden Supply are shown in the following table. Develop a three-year moving average to forecast sales. Then estimate demand again with a weighted moving average in which sales in the most recent year are given a weight of 2 and sales in the other two years are each given a weight of 1. Which method do you think is best?

YEAR	DEMAND FOR FERTILIZER (1,000'S OF BAGS)
1	4
2	6
3	4
4	5
5	10
6	8
7	7
8	9
9	12
10	14
11	15

4-14 Develop a two- and a four-year moving average for the demand for fertilizer in Problem 4-13.

4-15 In Problems 4-13 and 4-14, four different forecasts were developed for the demand for fertilizer. These four forecasts are a two-year moving average, a three-year moving average, a weighted moving average, and a four-year moving average. Which one would you use? Explain your answer.

4-16 Use exponential smoothing with a smoothing constant of .3 to forecast the demand for fertilizer given in Problem 4-13. Assume that last period's forecast for year 1 is 5,000 bags to begin the procedure. Would you prefer to use the exponential smoothing model or the weighted average model developed in Problem 4-13? Explain your answer.

4-17 Sales of Cool-Man air conditioners have grown steadily during the past five years.

YEAR	SALES
1	450
2	495
3	518
4	563
5	584
6	?

year 1 = 410.0; year 2 = 422.0; year 3 = 443.9; year 4 = 466.1; year 5 = 495.2; year 6 = 521.8

The sales manager had predicted, before the business started, that year 1's sales would be 410 air conditioners. Using exponential smoothing with an alpha weight of $\alpha = .30$, develop forecasts for years 2 through 6.

QA4-18
See Instructor's Section for details.

· **4-18** Using smoothing constants of .6 and .9, develop a forecast for the sales of Cool-Man air conditioners. See Problem 4-17.

QA4-19
$MAD_{\alpha=.3} 74.56;$
$MAD_{\alpha=.6} = 51.8;$
$MAD_{\alpha=.9} = 38.1$ (Best)

: **4-19** What effect did the smoothing constant have on the forecast for Cool-Man air conditioners? See Problems 4-17 and 4-18. Which smoothing constant gives the most accurate forecast?

QA4-20
487.667; 525.333; 555

· **4-20** Use a three-year moving average forecasting model to forecast the sales of Cool-Man air conditioners. See Problem 4-17.

QA4-21

$y = 522 + 33.6(X) = 622.8$

· **4-21** Using the trend projection method, develop a forecasting model for the sales of Cool-Man air conditioners. See Problem 4-17.

QA4-22
$MAD_{\alpha=.3} = 74.56;$
$MAD_{moving\ average} = 67;$
$MAD_{regression} = 5.6$ (Best)

: **4-22** Would you use exponential smoothing with a smoothing constant of .3, a three-year moving average, or trend to predict the sales of Cool-Man air conditioners? Refer to Problems 4-17, 4-20, and 4-21.

QA4-23

: **4-23** The operations manager of a musical instrument distributor feels that demand for bass drums may be related to the number of television appearances by the popular rock group Green Shades during the previous month. The manager has collected the data shown in the following table.

DEMAND FOR BASS DRUMS	GREEN SHADES TV APPEARANCES
3	3
6	4
7	7
5	6
10	8
8	5

See the Instructor's Section for the diagram.

$Y = 1.0 + 1.0X$

10

(a) Graph these data to see whether a linear equation might describe the relationship between the group's television shows and bass drum sales.
(b) Use the least squares regression method to derive a forecasting equation.
(c) What is your estimate for bass drum sales if the Green Shades performed on TV nine times last month?

QA4-24

: **4-24** Sales of industrial vacuum cleaners at R. Lowenthal Supply Co. over the past 13 months are shown below:

SALES (THOUSANDS)	MONTH	SALES (THOUSANDS)	MONTH
11	January	14	August
14	February	17	September
16	March	12	October
10	April	14	November
15	May	16	December
17	June	11	January
11	July		

See Instructor's Section for details.

(a) Using a moving average with three periods, determine the demand for vacuum cleaners for next February.
(b) Using a weighted moving average with three periods, determine the demand for vacuum cleaners for February. Use 3, 2, and 1 for the weights of the most recent, second most recent, and third most recent periods, respectively. For example, if you were forecasting the demand for February, November would have a weight of 1, December would have a weight of 2, and January would have a weight of 3.
(c) Evaluate the accuracy of each of these methods.
(d) What other factors might R. Lowenthal consider in forecasting sales?

MAD for Avg is 2.2.
MAD for Weighted Avg is 2.72.
Moving average forecast for February is 13.6667.
Weighted moving average forecast for February is 13.1667.

seasonality, causal variables such as advertising budget

: **4-25** Passenger miles flown on Northeast Airlines, a commuter firm serving the Boston hub, are shown below for the past 12 weeks.

QA4-25

WEEK	ACTUAL PASSENGER MILES (1,000'S)
1	17
2	21
3	19
4	23
5	18
6	16
7	20
8	18
9	22
10	20
11	15
12	22

(a) 17.00; 17.80; 18.04; 19.03; 18.83; 18.26; 18.61; 18.49; 19.19; 19.35; 18.48
(b) 2.60
(c) Consistently positive; track exceeds 5 MADs at week 10.

(a) Assuming an initial forecast for week 1 of 17,000 miles, use exponential smoothing to compute miles for weeks 2 through 12. Use $\alpha = .2$.
(b) What is the MAD for this model?
(c) Compute the RSFE and tracking signals. Are they within acceptable limits?

: **4-26** Emergency calls to Winter Park, Florida's 911 system for the past 24 weeks are shown below.

QA4-26

WEEK	CALLS	WEEK	CALLS
1	50	13	55
2	35	14	35
3	25	15	25
4	40	16	55
5	45	17	55
6	35	18	40
7	20	19	35
8	30	20	60
9	35	21	75
10	20	22	50
11	15	23	40
12	40	24	65

(a) Compute the exponentially smoothed forecast of calls for each week. Assume an initial forecast of 50 calls in the first week and use $\alpha = .1$. What is the forecast for the 25th week?

(b) Reforecast each period using $\alpha = .6$.

(c) Actual calls during the 25th week were 85. Which smoothing constant provides a superior forecast?

4-27 Using the 911 call data in Problem 4-26, forecast calls for weeks 2 through 25 with a trend-adjusted exponential smoothing model. Assume an initial forecast for 50 calls again for week 1 and an initial trend of 0. Use smoothing constants of $\alpha = .3$ and $\beta = .1$. Is this model better than that of Problem 4-26? What adjustment might be useful for further improvement? (Again, assume actual calls in week 25 were 85.)

4-28 Consulting income at Kate Walsh Associates for the period February–July has been as follows:

MONTH	INCOME ($1,000'S)
February	70.0
March	68.5
April	64.8
May	71.7
June	71.3
July	72.8

Use trend-adjusted exponential smoothing to forecst August's income. Assume that the initial forecast for February is $65,000 and the initial trend adjustment is 0. The smoothing constants selected are $\alpha = .1$ and $\beta = .2$.

4-29 Resolve Problem 4-28 with $\alpha = .1$ and $\beta = .8$. Using MAD, which smoothing constants provide a better forecast?

4-30 A study to determine the correlation between bank deposits and consumer price indices in Birmingham, Alabama, revealed the following (which was based on $n = 5$ years of data):

$$\Sigma X = 15$$

$$\Sigma X^2 = 55$$

$$\Sigma XY = 70$$

$$\Sigma Y = 20$$

$$\Sigma Y^2 = 130$$

Find the coefficient of correlation. What does it imply to you?

4-31 The accountant at O. H. Hall Coal Distributors, Inc., notes that the demand for coal seems to be tied to an index of weather severity developed by the U.S. Weather Bureau. That is, when weather was extremely cold in the United States over the past five years (and hence the index was high), coal sales were high. The accountant proposes that one good forecast of next year's coal demand could be made by developing a regression equation and then consulting the *Farmer's Almanac* to see how severe next year's winter will be.

(a) Derive a least squares regression and compute the coefficient of correlation for the data in the following table.

(b) Also compute the standard error of the estimate.

$\hat{Y} = 1 + 1x$; $r = .845$
$S_{yx} = 1.15$

COAL SALES (IN MILLIONS OF TONS) Y	WEATHER INDEX X
4	2
1	1
4	4
6	5
5	3

4-32 Bus and subway ridership in Washington, D.C., during the summer months is believed to be heavily tied to the number of tourists visiting the city. During the past 12 years, the following data have been obtained.

QA4-32

YEAR	NO. OF TOURISTS (MILLIONS)	RIDERSHIP (100,000'S)
1	7	15
2	2	10
3	6	13
4	4	15
5	14	25
6	15	27
7	16	24
8	12	20
9	14	27
10	20	44
11	15	34
12	7	17

See Instructor's Section for graph.
$y = 5.060 + 1.593x$

(a) Plot these data and decide if a linear model is reasonable.
(b) Develop a regression relationship.
(c) What is expected ridership if 10 million tourists visit the city?
(d) If there are no tourists at all, explain the predicted ridership.

2,099,000 people

506,000 people, but x = 0 is outside the range of observed values.

4-33 Accountants at the firm Walker and Walker believed that several traveling executives submit unusually high travel vouchers when they return from business trips. The accountants took a sample of 200 vouchers submitted from the past year; they then developed the following multiple regression equation relating expected travel cost ($\hat{Y}$) to number of days on the road (X_1) and distance traveled (X_2) in miles:

$$\hat{Y} = \$90.00 + \$48.50X_1 + \$0.40X_2$$

The coefficient of correlation computed was .68.

(a) If Thomas Williams returns from a 300-mile trip that took him out of town for five days, what is the expected amount he should claim as expenses?

$452.50

Question Thomas Williams about his expenses.

other variables should be included; r = .68

(b) Williams submitted a reimbursement request for $685; what should the accountant do?

(c) Comment on the validity of this model. Should any other variables be included? Which ones? Why?

QA4-34

year 11 → 65.8;
year 12 → 69.1;
year 13 → 72.4; r = 0.92

4-34 Dr. Jerilyn Ross, a New York City psychologist, specializes in treating patients who are phobic and afraid to leave their homes. The following table indicates how many patients Dr. Ross has seen each year for the past ten years. It also indicates what the robbery rate was in New York City during the same year.

YEAR	NUMBER OF PATIENTS	CRIME RATE (ROBBERIES PER 1,000 POPULATION)
1	36	58.3
2	33	61.6
3	40	73.4
4	41	75.7
5	40	81.1
6	55	89.0
7	60	101.1
8	54	94.8
9	58	103.3
10	61	116.2

Using trend analysis, how many patients do you think Dr. Ross will see in years 11, 12, and 13? How well does the model fit the data?

QA4-35

131.2 → 72.7 patients;
90.6 → 50.6 patients

4-35 Using the data in Problem 4-34, apply linear regression to study the relationship between the crime rate and Dr. Ross's patient load. If the robbery rate increases to 131.2 in year 11, how many phobic patients will Dr. Ross treat? If the crime rate drops to 90.6, what is the patient projection?

$\hat{y}_I = \$130,000$; $\hat{y}_{II} = \$108,000$; $\hat{y}_{III} = \$98,000$; $\hat{y}_{IV} = \$184,000$

4-36 Management of Davis's Department Store has used time series extrapolation to forecast retail sales for the next four quarters. The sales estimates are $100,000, $120,000, $140,000, and $160,000 for the respective quarters. Seasonal indices for the four quarters have been found to be 1.30, .90, .70, and 1.15, respectively. Compute a seasonalized or adjusted sales forecast.

Fall = 270; Winter = 390;
Spring = 189; Summer = 351

4-37 In the past, Judy Holmes's tire dealership sold an average of 1,000 radials each year. In the past two years 200 and 250, respectively, were sold in fall, 300 and 350 in winter, 150 and 165 in spring, and 300 and 285 in summer. With a major expansion planned, Ms. Holmes projects sales next year to increase to 1,200 radials. What will the demand be each season?

QA4-38

Y = 0.972 + 0.0035X;
r^2 = 0.479; X = 350; Y = 2.197; X = 800; Y = 3.77

4-38 Thirteen students entered the undergraduate business program at Rollins College two years ago. The following table indicates what their grade point averages (GPAs) were after being in the program for two years and what each student scored on the SAT exam when he or she was in high school. Is there a meaningful relationship between grades and SAT scores? If a student scores a 350 on the SAT, what do you think his or her GPA will be? What about a student who scores 800?

STUDENT	SAT SCORE	GPA
A	421	2.90
B	377	2.93
C	585	3.00
D	690	3.45
E	608	3.66
F	390	2.88
G	415	2.15
H	481	2.53
I	729	3.22
J	501	1.99
K	613	2.75
L	709	3.90
M	366	1.60

Data Set Problem

4-39 Smith Savings and Loan is proud of its long tradition in Apopka, Florida. Begun by Laurie Shader-Smith two years after World War II, the S&L has bucked the trend of financial and liquidity problems that have plagued the industry since 1985. Deposits have increased slowly but surely over the years, despite recessions in 1954, 1969, and 1981. Ms. Shader-Smith believes it necessary to have a long-range strategic plan for her firm, including a five-year forecast of deposits. She examines the past deposit data and also peruses Florida's Gross State Product (GSP) over the same 44 years. (GSP is analogous to Gross National Product, GNP, but on the state level.)

QA4-39

  (a) Using exponential smoothing, with $\alpha = .6$, then trend analysis, and finally, linear regression, discuss which forecasting model fits best for Shader-Smith's strategic plan. Justify why one model should be selected over another.

MAD for Exp Smooth. = 3.58
MAD for Trend = 10.83
MAD for Regression = 10.49

  (b) Carefully exmaine the data. Can you make a case for excluding a portion of the information? Why? Would that change your choice of model?

YEAR	DEPOSITS[1]	GSP[2]	YEAR	DEPOSITS[1]	GSP[2]	YEAR	DEPOSITS[1]	GSP[2]
1947	.25	.4	1962	2.3	1.6	1977	24.1	3.9
1948	.24	.4	1963	2.8	1.5	1978	25.6	3.8
1949	.24	.5	1964	2.8	1.6	1979	30.3	3.8
1950	.26	.7	1965	2.7	1.7	1980	36.0	3.7
1951	.25	.9	1966	3.9	1.9	1981	31.1	4.1
1952	.30	1.0	1967	4.9	1.9	1982	31.7	4.1
1953	.31	1.4	1968	5.3	2.3	1983	38.5	4.0
1954	.32	1.7	1969	6.2	2.5	1984	47.9	4.5
1955	.24	1.3	1970	4.1	2.8	1985	49.1	4.6
1956	.26	1.2	1971	4.5	2.9	1986	55.8	4.5
1957	.25	1.1	1972	6.1	3.4	1987	70.1	4.6
1958	.33	.9	1973	7.7	3.8	1988	70.9	4.6
1959	.50	1.2	1974	10.1	4.1	1989	79.1	4.7
1960	.95	1.2	1975	15.2	4.0	1990	94.0	5.0
1961	1.7	1.2	1976	18.1	4.0			

[1] In $ millions.
[2] In $ billions.

CASE STUDY

The North-South Airline*

In January 1988, Northern Airlines merged with Southeast Airlines to create the fourth largest U.S. carrier. The new North-South Airline inherited both an aging fleet of Boeing 727-200 aircraft and Stephen Ruth. Ruth was a tough former secretary of the navy who stepped in as new president and chairman of the board.

Ruth's first concern in creating a financially solid company was maintenance costs. It was commonly surmised in the airline industry that maintenance costs rise with the age of the aircraft. He quickly noticed that historically there had been a significant difference in the reported B727-200 maintenance costs (from ATA Form 41's) both in the airframe and engine areas between Northern Airlines and Southeast Airlines, with Southeast having the newer fleet.

On February 12, 1988, Peg Young, vice president for operations and maintenance, was called into Ruth's office and asked to study the issue. Specifically, Ruth wanted to know whether the average fleet age was correlated to direct airframe maintenance costs, and whether there was a relationship between average fleet age and direct engine maintenance costs. Young was to report back by February 26 with the answer, along with quantitative and graphical descriptions of the relationship.

Young's first step was to have her staff construct the average age of Northern and Southeastern B727-200 fleets, by quarter, since the introduction of that aircraft to service by each airline in late 1977 and early 1978. The average age of each fleet was calculated by first multiplying the total number of calendar days each aircraft had been in service at the pertinent point in time by the average daily utilization of the respective fleet to total fleet hours flown. The total fleet hours flown was then divided by the number of aircraft in service at that time, giving the age of the "average" aircraft in the fleet.

The average utilization was found by taking the actual total fleet hours flown at September 30, 1987, from Northern and Southeastern data, and dividing by the total days in service for all aircraft at that time. The average utilization for Southeast was 8.3 hours per day, and the average utilization for Northern was 8.7 hours per day. Since the available cost data were calculated for each yearly period ending at the end of the first quarter, average fleet age was calculated at the same points in time.

The fleet data are shown in the following table. Airframe cost data and engine cost data are both shown paired with fleet average age in that table.

Prepare Peg Young's response to Stephen Ruth.

Dates and names of airlines and individuals have been changed in this case to maintain confidentiality. The data and issues described here are actual.

North-South Airline Data for Boeing 727-200 Jets

	NORTHERN AIRLINE DATA			SOUTHEAST AIRLINE DATA		
YEAR	AIRFRAME COST PER AIRCRAFT	ENGINE COST PER AIRCRAFT	AVERAGE AGE (HOURS)	AIRFRAME COST PER AIRCRAFT	ENGINE COST PER AIRCRAFT	AVERAGE AGE (HOURS)
1981	$51.80	$43.49	6,512	$13.29	$18.86	5107
1982	54.92	38.58	8,404	25.15	31.55	8145
1983	69.70	51.48	11,077	32.18	40.43	7360
1984	68.90	58.72	11,717	31.78	22.10	5773
1985	63.72	45.47	13,275	25.34	19.69	7150
1986	84.73	50.26	15,215	32.78	32.58	9364
1987	78.74	79.60	18,390	35.56	38.07	8259

Kwik Lube

Dick Johnson, a successful textbook author and English professor at the University of Washington, retired from teaching in 1972, at age 40. His net worth was approximately a half-million dollars.

In 1979, during a trip to Los Angeles, he came across a very interesting type of new business. It was a very small gas station that specialized only in oil changes and lubrication jobs. The old gas station had been remodeled, the gas pumps had been removed, and the large sign above the small building read "OIL AND LUBE— $10 and 10 MINUTES." For two hours, Dick observed the converted gas station from a restaurant across the street.

During the next month, Dick made three trips to Los Angeles to talk to the owner, George, about how he got into the business and how the business worked. Dick paid George $1,000 for his advice and information and promised never to compete directly with George or ever to open or operate a similar type of business in the Los Angeles area.

After talking to his lawyer and accountant, Dick started to organize a new business—Kwik Lube. In March 1980, Dick had built his first Kwik Lube, and by the end of 1980, he had completed two additional Kwik Lubes in the Seattle area. The total gross revenues in 1980 from all three stations was $260,000.

Between 1980 and 1984, business picked up rapidly. Total gross sales in 1981 and 1982 were $680,000 and $750,000, respectively. In 1983, total gross sales for the three Kwik Lube stations was $750,000, and in 1984, total gross sales was $780,000. Dick was convinced that this sales increase was due to his not significantly increasing the price of his basic service, which was to change the oil, change the filter, and do a lube job. In 1980, the total price was $9.95. In 1983, the total price per job was $10.95, and by 1984, the total price was only $12.95.

In addition to running his three Kwik Lube stations in Seattle, Dick desired to franchise his idea in other cities in Washington and in other states such as Oregon, Idaho, and Montana. During the last three years, Dick had acquired considerable knowledge about this type of business. He was able to obtain the best possible prices for oil, lubricants, and filters. If he franchised Kwik Lube, he would even be able to make a profit from selling oil, filters, and lubricants.

Dick invested over $20,000 in lawyers' fees and another $2,000 in talking to other companies in the franchise business. He decided to set his franchise fee at $18,000, plus 6% of the gross sales of the stations. In addition, each new Kwik Lube station had to conform to exacting standards for the building and all of the equipment. Depending on the location, Dick could build and equip a Kwik Lube Station for under $200,000. Like his own Kwik Lube stations, these new stations would have two car or vehicle bays. In 1985, Dick sold his first franchise to T. A. Williams and another franchise to an investor in Eugene, Oregon. By 1988, Dick had sold a total of eleven franchises in Spokane, Washington; Eugene, Oregon; Portland, Oregon; Butte, Montana; and Boise, Idaho. In addition, Dick experienced a substantial growth rate for total gross sales for his three Kwik Lube stations in Seattle. In 1985, total gross sales were $990,000. In 1986, total gross sales were $1,040,000; in 1987, $1,200,000; and in 1988, $1,330,000.

Dick knew that it would only be a matter of time before someone else would start to compete directly with his Kwik Lube stations, but he never believed that the first competition would be in Seattle. Construction on the first two Speedy Lube Stations started in 1988, and both stations were in operation in early 1989. The two stores were almost identical to the Kwik Lube stations, but Speedy Lube was priced two dollars less than Kwik Lube's current price, which was now $19.95. Dick never dreamed that this new competition would cut so deeply into his total gross sales. Total gross sales for the three Kwik Lube stations in Seattle dropped to $1,110,000 for 1989, and the situation did not look any better for 1990. (Indeed, when 1990 figures became available, sales were again only $1,110,000.

Soon after the total gross sales figures came in for 1989, Dick got some startling information from one of his friends in Spokane. Over 50% of the stock in Speedy Lube, Inc., was owned by Richland, Inc., a holding company owned by T. A. Williams. Dick was outraged that one of the people who purchased a franchise from him was directly competing with his Kwik Lube stores and in direct violation of the franchise contract, which contained a noncompetition clause.

Dick had only two goals for the coming year: (1) to shut down the two Speedy Lube stations, and (2) to regain his lost sales for the two years from T. A. Williams. Both objectives were to be accomplished with a lawsuit.

Dick Johnson's lawyer strongly suggested that Dick employ a witness to testify on his behalf against Speedy Lube. While there seemed to be no question about who would win the case, Dick's lawyer believed that an expert witness could more accurately determine the damage. In addition, most juries place more importance on expert testimony. As a result, Dick decided to employ the services of Dr. Warren Gunn.

Dr. Gunn was a professor of marketing at Eastern Washington University, which was very close to Spokane. He had more than ten years' experience as an expert witness, and his specialty was determining damages for antitrust and franchise cases. His basic strategy was to find data about the same industry or a similar one in a location resembling the area in which the original problem occurred. In this case, Dr. Gunn needed data about the fast oil and lubrication business in a location similar to Seattle. Because Dick originally obtained his idea from a small station in Los Angeles and because Los Angeles had hundreds of these types of businesses by 1989, Dr. Gunn decided to collect data in the Los Angeles area. This would require the development and pilot testing of a questionnaire that could determine the total gross number of cars serviced for fast oil and lubrication businesses in the Los Angeles area between 1980 and 1990.

Although the questionnaire study would cost $20,000 to perform, Dr. Gunn and Dick both believed that it was the best approach. The data were collected in two weeks, and are summarized in Table 4.15. Both Dr. Gunn and Dick knew that if the results of the questionnaire were not favorable, they would not use it during the case.

TABLE 4.15 Analysis of Average Fast Oil and Lubrication. Total Gross Sales for Cars Serviced at Los Angeles Stations (Using Two Bays as a Basis for Comparison).

YEAR	AVERAGE TOTAL SALES	YEAR	AVERAGE TOTAL SALES
1980	$190,000	1986	$350,000
1981	220,000	1987	390,000
1982	250,000	1983	440,000
1983	240,000	1989	470,000
1984	260,000	1990	520,000
1985	330,000		

Discussion Questions

1. Using the data in Table 4.15, compute the loss for Kwik Lube stations during the last two years using regression. How accurate can the results claim to be?

2. Was it worth $20,000 to perform the marketing research?

3. What other factors might be introduced into the lawsuit?

Source: Adapted from B. Render, R. M. Stair, and I. Greenberg, *Cases and Readings in Management Science,* 2nd. ed. Boston: Allyn & Bacon, 1990.

BIBLIOGRAPHY

Ashley, R., and Guerard, J. "Applications of Time Series Analysis to Texas Financial Forecasting." *Interfaces* **13,** 4 (August 1983): 46–55.

Ashton, A. H., and Ashton, R. H. "Aggregating Subjective Forecasts." *Management Science* **31,** 12 (December 1985): 1499–1508.

Becker, B. C., and Sapienza, A. "Forecasting Hospital Reimbursement," *Hospital and Health Services Administration* **32,** (November 1987): 521–530.

Box, G. E. P., and Jenkins, G. *Time Series Analysis: Forecasting and Control.* San Francisco: Holden Day, 1970.

Brazziel, William F. "Forecasting Older Student Enrollment: A Cohort and Participation Rate Model." *Journal of Higher Education* **58,** 2 (March–April 1987): 222-231.

Brown, R. G. *Statistical Forecasting for Inventory Control.* New York: McGraw-Hill, 1959.

Bunn, D. W., and Seigal, J. P. "Forecasting the Effects of Television Programming upon Electricity Loads." *Journal of the Operational Research Society* **34,** (January 1983): 17–25.

Chambers, J. C., Satinder, C., Mullick, S. K., and Smith, D. D. "How to Choose the Right Forecasting Technique."

Harvard Business Review **49**, 4 (July–August 1971): 45–74.

Claycombe, W.W., and Sullivan, W.G. "Current Forecasting Techniques." *Journal of System Management* (September 1978): 18–20.

Gardner, E.S. "Exponential Smoothing: The State of the Art." *Journal of Forecasting* **4**, 1 (March 1985).

Georgoff, D.M., and Murdick, R.G. "Manager's Guide to Forecasting." *Harvard Business Review* **64**, 1 (January–February 1986): 110–120.

Gips, J., and Sullivan, B. "Sales Forecasting—Replacing Magic with Logic." *Production and Inventory Management Reveiw* **2**, 2 (February 1982).

Guerard, John, B., Jr., and Beidleman, Carl R. "Composite Earnings Forecasting Efficiency." *Interfaces* **17**, 5 (September–October 1987): 103–113.

Heizer, J., and Render, B. *Production and Operations Management.* 3rd edition. Boston: Allyn and Bacon, 1993.

Holz, B.W., and J.M. Wroth. "Improving Strength Forecasts: Support for Army Manpower Management." *Interfaces* **10**, 6 (December 1980): 31–52.

Lane, D., et al. "Forecasting Demand for Long Term Care Services." *Health Services Research* **20**, 4 (October 1985): 435–459.

Lee, D.R. "A Forecast of Lodging Supply and Demand." *The Cornell HRA Quarterly* (August 1984): 27–40.

Mabert, V.A., and Stocco, R.L. "Managing and Monitoring a Forecasting System: The Chemical Bank Experience." *Journal of Bank Research* (Autumn 1982): 195–201.

MacStravic, R.S. "An Early Warning Technique." *Hospital and Health Services Administration* **31**, 1 (January–Febrary 1986): 86–98.

Mahmoud, E. "Accuracy in Forecasting: A Summary." *Journal of Forecasting* (April–June 1984).

Makridakis, S., Wheelright, S.C., and McGee, V.E., *Forecasting Methods and Applications.* 2nd edition. New York: John Wiley and Sons, 1983.

Parker, G.C., and Segura, E.L., "How to Get a Better Forecast." *Harvard Business Review* (March–April 1971): 99–109.

Plossl, G.W., and Wight, O.W. *Production and Inventory Control.* Englewood Cliffs, N.J.: Prentice-Hall, 1967.

Render, B., Stair, R.M., and Greenberg, I. *Cases and Readings in Management Science,* 2nd edition. Boston: Allyn and Bacon, Inc., 1990.

Schnaars, S.P., and Bavuso, R.J. "Extrapolation Models on Very Short-term Forecasts." *Journal of Business Research* **14**, (1986): 27–36.

Van Dyke, D.T. "Why Economists Make Mistakes." *The Bankers Magazine* (May–June 1986): 69–75.

Weinberg, Charles B. "Arts Plan: Implementation, Evolution, and Usage." *Marketing Science* **5**, 2, (Spring 1986).

Appendix: Forecasting with Spreadsheets

Forecasting techniques that we have seen in this chapter are ideal vehicles for analysis by spreadsheet programs such as Lotus, Quattro, Excel, and others.

Exponential Smoothing

Exponential smoothing, using the Port of Baltimore data found in Table 4.4, is shown in Program 4.5. This symbolic spreadsheet shows the formulas and input data for an alpha value of 0.10, which appears in cell B3. Cells B6 through B13 contain actual tonnage loaded, while cell C6 contains the initial forecast for Quarter 1 of 175 tons. Cell D6 holds the formula for the exponentially weighted average of actual Quarter sales, the value of cell B6, and the tonnage forecast, which is the value of cell C6. $B$3 is an absolute reference to the value of alpha in cell B3. When we copy cell D6 to cells D7 through D13, the absolute reference to B3 stays the same, while the other cells change. For example, you can see that in copying the formula to D7 (rather than rekeying it from scratch), C6 and B6 change to C7 and B7, while B3, the alpha value, is absolute.

Cells E6 through E13 hold the formulas for computing the absolute differences of forecast tonnage in column C and actual in Column B. They are also rounded off. The @ sum and @avg commands in cells E14 and E15, respectively, total the absolute values and then provide their mean (the MAD).

PROGRAM 4.5 Using Spreadsheets to Compute the Port of Baltimore's Exponential Smoothing Forecast. The Symbolic Spreadsheet, Showing Formulas in Cells, Is Provided.

	A	B	C	D	E
1	Port of Baltimore Exponential Smoothing Forecast from Table 4.4				
2					
3	Alpha=	0.1			
4					
5	Quarter	Act.Tons	Frcst	$F_{t-1} + \alpha(A_{t-1} - F_{t-1})$	Abs. Error
6	1	180	175	+C6+$B$3*(B6−C6)	@ROUND(@ABS(B6−C6),0)
7	2	168	+D6	+C7+$B$3*(B7−C7)	@ROUND(@ABS(B7−C7),0)
8	3	159	+D7	+C8+$B$3*(B8−C8)	@ROUND(@ABS(B8−C8),0)
9	4	175	+D8	+C9+$B$3*(B9−C9)	@ROUND(@ABS(B9−C9),0)
10	5	190	+D9	+C10+$B$3*(B10−C10)	@ROUND(@ABS(B10−C10),0)
11	6	205	+D10	+C11+$B$3*(B11−C11)	@ROUND(@ABS(B11−C11),0)
12	7	180	+D11	+C12+$B$3*(B12−C12)	@ROUND(@ABS(B12−C12),0)
13	8	182	+D12	+C13+$B$3*(B13−C13)	@ROUND(@ABS(B13−C13),0)
14	Total				@SUM(E6..E13)
15	Average				@AVG(E6)..E13)

Spreadsheets now provide another useful feature. We can use the Data Table command to find the value of alpha that provides the lowest MAD. The other way, not very efficient, is to try one alpha after another in cell B3, until we finally locate one that yields the lowest mean error. Program 4.6 illustrates how the MAD for each value of alpha we wish to try is computed. Cell B19 contains the formula to compute the MADs, which will appear in cells B20 through B30, once the Data Table (DT) command is used. To start, we type /DT1, then enter the data table range (A19..B30). The input cell is B3. We conclude that an alpha = .2 gives the lowest MAD for the Port of Baltimore.

PROGRAM 4.6 Exponential Smoothing Evaluation of Alphas Using Data Table of MADs

	A	B	
19		@AVG(E6..E13)	
20	0	10.63	
21	0.1	10.50	
22	0.2	10.25	⟶ Lowest MAD
23	0.3	11.13	
24	0.4	11.63	
25	0.5	12.50	
26	0.6	12.63	
27	0.7	12.88	
28	0.8	12.63	
29	0.9	12.25	
30	1	12.38	

Regression Analysis

Using the Triple A Construction Company sales data from Table 4.11, we can also illustrate the use of spreadsheets in regression analysis and the /Data Regression command. As seen in Program 4.7, the dependent variable of sales is found in cells A5 through A10. Payroll, the independent variable, is placed in B5 through B10.

When we press /DR (for Data Regression), the following submenu appears:

   X-Range   Y-Range   Output-Range   Intercept   Reset   Go   Quit

We first use the *X-Range* option to select the independent variable(s). We specify B5..B10 (payroll) as our only independent variable. We then use the *Y-Range* option to specify the dependent variable of sales. We enter range A5..A10.

The *Output Range* option specifies where to display the regression results. This needs to be an unused area of the spreadsheet and must be at least nine rows long and two columns wider than the number of independent variables. We need only specify the upper left corner of the output range. Since we want the results to appear in the range A12..D20, we specify A12 at the prompt.

The Lotus default is to compute the Y-intercept, so we can proceed directly to the *Go* command. The constant output is the value of the Y-intercept. The X-coefficient is the coefficient (slope) of the independent variable chosen in the X-range option.

PROGRAM 4.7 **Regression Analysis with Spreadsheet Software and the /Data Regression Command**

```
        A              B              C           D        E       F
 1   Triple A Construction Regression Using Table 4.11 Data
 2
 3   Sales(Y)     Payroll(X)      Regression
 4   ($100,000) ($100,000,000)      Line
 5         2             1      +$C$19*$B5+$D$13
 6         3             3      +$C$19*$B6+$D$13
 7       2.5             4      +$C$19*$B7+$D$13
 8         2             2      +$C$19*$B8+$D$13
 9         2             1      +$C$19*$B9+$D$13
10       3.5             7      +$C$19*$B10+$D$13
11
12                Regression Output:
13   Constant                                   1.75
14   Std Err of Y Est                       0.306186
15   R Squared                                0.8125
16   No. Of Observations                           6
17   Degrees of Freedom                            4
18
19   X=coefficient(s)                 0.25
20   Std Err of Coef.       0.0600480577
```

We can also use the regression output to create a graph of the regression line. This is the constant, plus the X-coefficient times the value of the independent variable in each row of data. For Triple A, the formula would be $C$19 * $B$5 + $D$13. We will create a new range for the regression line in C5..C10 by copying that formula into that range.

To plot the original data plus our new regression line we enter the /Graph command, then select XY for the graph line. The range B5..B10 (the independent variable payroll) is our X data range. The range A5..A10 (dependent variable sales) is chosen for the A range. Finally, the range C5..C10 (the regression line) becomes the data range. The graph may now be viewed and saved.

Fundamentals of Decision Theory

CHAPTER OUTLINE

5.1 Introduction

5.2 The Six Steps in Decision Theory

5.3 Types of Decision-Making Environments

5.4 Decision Making under Risk

5.5 Decision Making under Uncertainty

5.6 Marginal Analysis with a Large Number of Alternatives and States of Nature

5.7 Using the Computer to Solve Decision Theory Problems

5.8 Summary

Glossary

Key Equations

Solved Problems

Discussion Questions and Problems

Case Study:
Starting Right Corporation

Bibliography

Appendix: Solving Decision Theory Theory Problems with Spreadsheets

5.1 INTRODUCTION

To a great extent, the successes or failures that a person experiences in life depend on the decisions he or she makes. The individual who managed the ill-fated space shuttle *Challenger* is no longer working for NASA. The person who designed the top-selling Mustang became president of Ford. Why and how did these people make their respective decisions? In general, what is involved in making good decisions? One decision may make the difference between a successful career and an unsuccessful one.

Decision theory is an analytic and systematic approach to studying decision making. In this and the next two chapters, we present the mathematical models useful in helping managers make the best possible decisions.

good versus bad decisions

What makes the difference between good and bad decisions? A good decision is one that is based on logic, considers all available data and possible alternatives, and applies the quantitative approach we are about to describe. Occasionally, a good decision results in an unexpected or unfavorable outcome. But if it is made properly, it is *still* a good decision. A bad decision is one that is not based on logic, does not use all available information, does not consider all alternatives, and does not employ appropriate quantitative techniques. If you make a bad decision, but are lucky and a favorable outcome occurs, you have *still* made a bad decision. Managers make many decisions. Although occasionally good decisions yield bad results, in the long run, using decision theory will result in successful outcomes.

5.2 THE SIX STEPS IN DECISION THEORY

Teaching Suggestion 5.1:
Using the Steps of the Decision Making Process. See the Instructor's Section for details.

Transparency Master 5.1:
Steps in Decision Theory.

Whether you are deciding about getting a haircut today, building a multi-million dollar plant, or buying a new camera, the steps in making a good decision are basically the same. These six steps are:

1. Clearly define the problem at hand.

2. List the possible alternatives.

3. Identify the possible outcomes.

4. List the payoff or profit of each combination of alternatives and outcomes.

5. Select one of the mathematical decision theory models.

6. Apply the model and make your decision.

We use the Thompson Lumber Company case as an example to illustrate these decision theory steps. John Thompson is the founder and president of Thompson Lumber Company, a profitable firm located in Portland, Oregon.

Step 1. The problem that John Thompson identifies is whether to expand his product line by manufacturing and marketing a new product—backyard storage sheds.

identify problem

Step 2. Thompson's second step is to generate the alternatives that are available to him. In decision theory, an *alternative* is defined as a course of action or a strategy that may be chosen by the decision maker. John decides that his alternatives are to construct: (1) a large new plant to manufacture the storage sheds, (2) a small plant, or (3) no plant at all (that is, he has the option of not developing the new product line.)

list alternatives

One of the biggest mistakes that decision makers make is to leave out some important alternatives. Although a particular alternative may seem to be inappropriate or of little value, it might turn out to be the best choice.

Teaching Suggestion 5.2: The Importance of Defining the Problem and Listing All Possible Alternatives. See the Instructor's Section for details.

Step 3. The third step involves identifying the possible outcomes of the various alternatives. The criteria for action are established at this time. Thompson determines that there are only two possible outcomes: the market for the storage sheds could be favorable, meaning there is a high demand for the product, or it could be unfavorable, meaning there is a low demand for the sheds.

identify possible outcomes

A common mistake is to forget about some of the possible outcomes. Optimistic decision makers tend to ignore bad outcomes, while pessimistic managers may discount a favorable outcome. If you don't consider all possibilities, you will not be making a logical decision and the results may be undesirable. If you do not think the worst can happen, you may design another Edsel automobile. In decision theory, those outcomes over which the decision maker has little or no control are called *states of nature*.

Step 4. Thompson's next step is to express the payoff resulting from each possible combination of alternatives and outcomes. Since in this case he wants to maximize his profits, he can use *profit* to evaluate each consequence. Not every decision, of course, can be based on money alone—any appropriate means of measuring benefit is acceptable. In decision theory, we call such payoffs or profits *conditional values*.

list payoffs

John Thompson has already evaluated the potential profits associated with the various outcomes. With a favorable market, he thinks a large facility would result in a net profit of $200,000 to his firm. This $200,000 is a *conditional value* because Thompson's receiving the money is conditional upon both his building a large factory and having a good market. The conditional value if the market is unfavorable would be a $180,000 net loss. A small plant would result in a net profit of $100,000 in a favorable market, but a net loss of $20,000 would occur if the market was unfavorable. Finally, doing nothing would result in a $0 profit in either market.

The easiest way to present these values is by constructing a *decision table*, sometimes called a *payoff table*. A decision table for Thompson's conditional values is shown in Table 5.1. All of the alternatives are listed down the left side of the table and all of the possible outcomes or states of nature are listed across the top. The body of the table contains the actual payoffs.

construct decision or payoff tables

Steps 5 and 6. The last two steps are to select a decision theory model and apply it to the data to help make the decision. Selecting the model depends on the environment in which you're operating and the amount of risk and uncertainty involved.

5.3 TYPES OF DECISION-MAKING ENVIRONMENTS

The types of decisions people make depend on how much knowledge or information they have about the situation. Three decision-making environments are defined and explained as follows.

Type 1. Decision Making under Certainty. In this environment, decision makers know with certainty the consequence of every alternative or decision choice. Naturally, they will choose the alternative that will maximize their well-being or will result in the best outcome. For example, let's say you have $1,000 to invest for a one-year period. One alternative is to open a savings account paying 6% interest and another is to invest in a government treasury bond paying 10% interest. If both investments are secure and guaranteed, then there is a certainty that the treasury bond will pay a higher return. The return after one year will be $100 in interest.

Type 2. Decision Making under Risk. Here the decision maker knows the probability of occurrence of each outcome. We know, for example, that the probability of being dealt a club is .25. The probability of rolling a 5 on a die is ⅙.

In decision making under risk, the decision maker attempts to maximize his or her expected well-being. Decision theory models for business problems in this environment typically employ two equivalent criteria—maximization of expected monetary value and minimization of expected loss.

Type 3. Decision Making under Uncertainty. In this category, the decision maker does not know the probabilities of the various outcomes. As an example, the probability that a Democrat will be president of the United States 25 years from now is not known. Sometimes it is impossible to assess the probability of success of a new undertaking or product. The criteria for decision making under uncertainty is explained in Section 5.5 of this chapter.

TABLE 5.1 Decision Table with Conditional Values for Thompson Lumber

	STATES OF NATURE	
ALTERNATIVES	FAVORABLE MARKET ($)	UNFAVORABLE MARKET ($)
Construct large plant	200,000	−180,000
Construct small plant	100,000	−20,000
Do nothing	0	0

Note: It is important to include all alternatives, including "Do nothing."

Let's see how decision making under certainty (the type 1 environment) could affect John Thompson. Here we assume that John knows exactly what will happen in the future. If it turns out he knows with certainty that the market for storage sheds will be favorable, what should he do? Look again at Thompson Lumber's conditional values in Table 5.1. Because the market is favorable, he should build the large plant, which has the highest profit of $200,000.

Few managers would be fortunate enough to have complete information and knowledge about the states of nature under consideration. Decision making under risk, discussed next, is a more realistic situation—and slightly more complicated.

Applicable Problems: 5-10, 5-11, 5-16, 5-18, 5-20, 5-21, 5-28

5.4 DECISION MAKING UNDER RISK

Decision making under risk is a probabilistic decision situation. Several possible states of nature may occur, each with a given probability. In this section, we consider one of the most popular methods of making decisions under risk, namely, selecting that alternative with the highest expected monetary value. We also look at the concepts of perfect information and opportunity loss.

probabilities are known

Transparency Master 5.3: Decision Making Under Risk.

Expected Monetary Value (EMV)

Given a decision table with conditional values (payoffs) and probability assessments for all states of nature, it is possible to determine the *expected monetary value* (EMV) for each alternative if the decision could be repeated a large number of times. The EMV for an alternative is just the sum of possible payoffs of the alternative, each weighted by the probability of that payoff occurring.

EMV

EMV (Alternative i) = (Payoff of first state of nature)

$\times$ (Probability of first state of nature)

+ (Payoff of second state of nature)

$\times$ (Probability of second state of nature)

+ $\cdots$ + (Payoff of last state of nature)

$\times$ (Probability of last state of nature)   (5-1)

Suppose John Thompson now believes that the probability of a favorable market is exactly the same as the probability of an unfavorable market; that is, each state of nature has a .50 probability. Which alternative would give the greatest expected monetary value? To determine this, John has expanded the decision table, as shown in Table 5.2. His calculations are:

Alternate Example 5-1

EMV (Large facility) = (.50)($200,000) + (.50)(−$180,000) = $10,000

EMV (Small facility) = (.50)($100,000) + (.50)(−$20,000) = $40,000

EMV (Do nothing) = (.50)($0) + (.50)($0) = $0

TABLE 5.2 Decision Table with Probabilities and EMVs for Thompson Lumber

| | STATES OF NATURE | | |
ALTERNATIVES	FAVORABLE MARKET ($)	UNFAVORABLE MARKET ($)	EMV COMPUTED ($)
Large facility	200,000	−180,000	10,000
Small facility	100,000	−20,000	40,000
Do nothing	0	0	0
Probabilities	.50	.50	

The largest expected value results from the second alternative, building a small factory. Thus, Thompson should proceed with the project and put up a small plant to manufacture storage sheds. The EMVs for the large plant and for doing nothing are $10,000 and $0, respectively.

Expected Value of Perfect Information

Teaching Suggestion 5.4: Starting the EVPI Concept. See the Instructor's Section for details.

John Thompson has been approached by Scientific Marketing, Inc., a firm that proposes to help John make the decision about whether or not to build the plant to produce storage sheds. Scientific Marketing claims that its technical analysis will tell John with certainty whether or not the market is favorable for his proposed product. In other words, it will change his environment from one of decision making under risk to one of decision making under certainty. This information could prevent John from making a very expensive mistake. Scientific Marketing would charge Thompson $65,000 for the information. What would you recommend to John? Should he hire the firm to make the marketing study? Even if the information from the study is perfectly accurate, is it worth $65,000? What would it be worth? Although some of these questions are difficult to answer, determining the value of such *perfect information* can be very useful. It places an upper bound on what you would be willing to spend on information such as that being sold by Scientific Marketing. In this section, two related terms are investigated: the *expected value of perfect information* (EVPI) and the *expected value with perfect information*. These techniques can help John make his decision about hiring the marketing firm.

KEY IDEA

The expected value *with* perfect information is the expected or average return, in the long run, if we have perfect information before a decision has to be made. In order to calculate this value, we choose the best alternative for each state of nature and multiply its payoff times the probability of occurrence of that state of nature.

Expected value *with* perfect information

> = (Best outcome or consequence for first state of nature)
> × (Probability of first state of nature)
> + (Best outcome for second state of nature)
> × (Probability of second state of nature)
> + ··· + (Best outcome for last state of nature)
> × (Probability of last state of nature)   **(5-2)**

The expected value of perfect information, EVPI, is the expected outcome *with* perfect information minus the expected outcome *without* perfect information, namely, the maximum EMV.

computing EVPI

EVPI = Expected value with perfect information
$$- \text{ maximum EMV} \quad (5\text{-}3)$$

By referring back to Table 5.2, Thompson can calculate the maximum that he would pay for information, that is, the expected value of perfect information, or EVPI. He follows a two-stage process. First of all, the expected value *with* perfect information is computed. Then, using this result, EVPI is calculated. The procedure is outlined as follows.

1. The best outcome for the state of nature "favorable market" is "build a large facility" with a payoff of $200,000. The best outcome for the state of nature "unfavorable market" is "do nothing" with a payoff of $0. Expected value with perfect information = ($200,000) (.50) + ($0) (.50) = $100,000. Thus, if we had perfect information, we would expect, on the average, $100,000 if the decision could be repeated many times.

2. The maximum EMV is $40,000, which is the expected outcome without perfect information.

EVPI = Expected value *with* perfect information

$$- \text{ Maximum EMV}$$

$$= \$100,000 - \$40,000 = \$60,000$$

Thus, the *most* Thompson would be willing to pay for perfect information is $60,000. This, of course, is again based on the assumption that the probability of each state of nature is .50.

Opportunity Loss

Applicable Problems
5-12, 5-17

An alternative approach to maximizing expected monetary value (EMV) is to minimize *expected opportunity loss* (EOL). Opportunity loss, sometimes called regret, refers to the difference between the optimal profit or payoff and the actual payoff received. In other words, it's the amount lost by not picking the best alternative.

cost of not picking best
solution

The minimum expected opportunity loss is found by constructing an opportunity loss table and computing EOL for each alternative. Let's see how the procedure works for the Thompson Lumber case.

Step 1. The first step is to create the opportunity loss table. This is done by determining the opportunity loss for not choosing the best alternative for each state of nature. Opportunity loss for any state of nature, or any column, is calculated by subtracting each outcome in the column from the *best* outcome in the same column. For a favorable market, the best outcome is $200,000 as a result of the first alternative, building a large facility. For an unfavorable market, the best outcome is $0 as a result of the third alternative, doing nothing. Table 5.3 illustrates these comparisons.

opportunity loss table

TABLE 5.3 Determining Opportunity Losses for Thompson Lumber

STATES OF NATURE	
FAVORABLE MARKET ($)	UNFAVORABLE MARKET ($)
200,000 − 200,000	0 − (−180,000)
200,000 − 100,000	0 − (−20,000)
200,000 − 0	0 − 0

Using Table 5.3, an opportunity loss table can be constructed. The values in Table 5.4 represent the opportunity loss for each state of nature for not choosing the best alternative.

Step 2. EOL is computed by multiplying the probability of each state of nature times the appropriate opportunity loss value.

$$\text{EOL (Building large facility)} = (.5)(\$0) + (.5)(\$180,000)$$

$$= \$90,000$$

$$\text{EOL (Building small facility)} = (.5)(\$100,000) + (.5)(\$20,000)$$

computing EOL

$$= \$60,000$$

$$\text{EOL (Do nothing)} = (.5)(\$200,000) + (.5)(\$0)$$

$$= \$100,000$$

Using minimum EOL as the decision criterion, the best decision would be the second alternative, build a small facility.

It is important to note that minimum EOL will *always* result in the same decision as maximum EMV, and that the following relationship always holds: EVPI = minimum EOL. Referring to the Thompson case, EVPI = $60,000 = minimum EOL.

Sensitivity Analysis

In the previous sections, we determined that the best decision for Thompson Lumber was to build the small facility with an expected value of $40,000. This conclusion depends on the values of the economic conse-

TABLE 5.4 Opportunity Loss Table for Thompson Lumber

	STATES OF NATURE	
ALTERNATIVES	FAVORABLE MARKET ($)	UNFAVORABLE MARKET ($)
Large facility	0	180,000
Small facility	100,000	20,000
Do nothing	200,000	0
Probabilities	.50	.50

quences and the two probability values of a favorable and unfavorable market. *Sensitivity analysis* investigates how our decision might change given a change in the problem data. In this section, we will investigate the impact that a change in the probability values would have on the decision facing Thompson Lumber. We first define the following variable:

Using sensitivity analysis

$$P = \text{the probability of a favorable market}$$

We can now express the expected monetary values (EMVs) in terms of P. This is done below. A graph of these EMV values is shown in Figure 5.1.

EMV (large facility) = $200,000P − $180,000(1 − P)

= $380,000P − $180,000

EMV (small facility) = $100,000P − $20,000(1 − P)

= $120,000P − $20,000

EMV (do nothing) = $0P + $0(1 − P) = $0

As you can see in Figure 5.1, the best decision is to do nothing as long as P is between 0 and Point 1, where the EMV for doing nothing is equal to the EMV for the small facility. When P is between Point 1 and Point 2, the best decision is to build the small facility. Point 2 is where the EMV for the small facility is equal to the EMV for the large facility. When P is greater

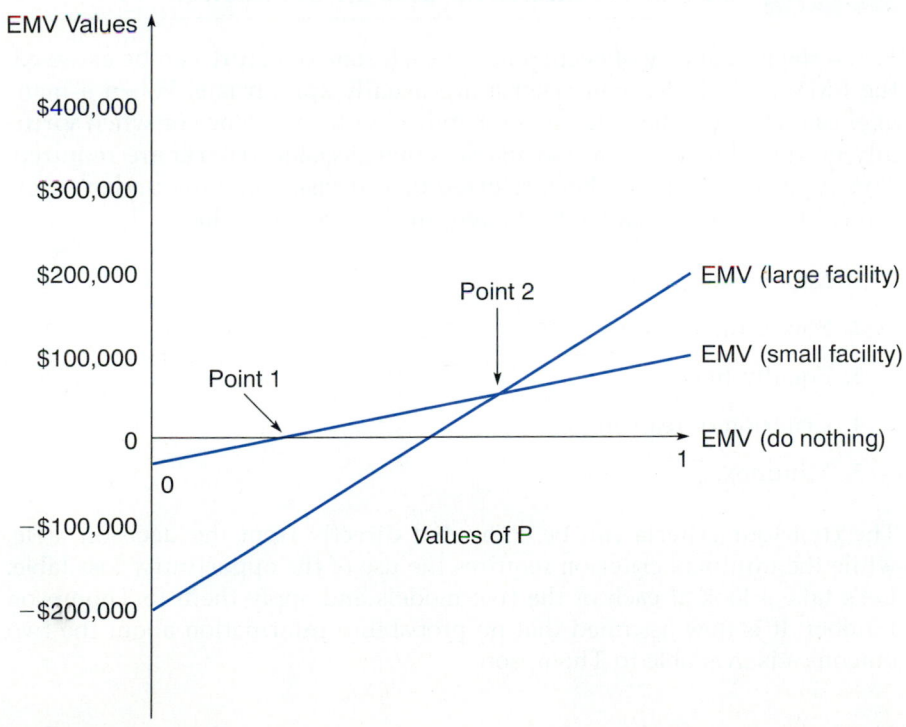

FIGURE 5.1
Sensitivity Analysis

than Point 2, the best decision is to build the large facility. Of course, this is what you would expect as P increases. Point 1 and Point 2 can be computed as follows:

Point 1: EMV (nothing) = EMV (small facility);

$$0 = \$120,000P - \$20,000; \qquad P = 20,000/120,000 = .167\,.$$

Point 2: EMV (small facility) = EMV (large facility);

$$\$120,000P - \$20,000 = \$380,000P - \$180,000;$$

$$260,000P = 160,000; \qquad P = 160,000/260,000 = .62\,.$$

The results of this sensitivity analysis are displayed in the following table.

ACTION	RANGE OF P VALUES
Do nothing	Less than .167
Build small facility	.167 − .62
Build large facility	Greater than .62

Teaching Suggestion 5.5:
Starting the Decision Making Under Uncertainty Material. See the Instructor's Section for details.

no probability data available

Transparency Master 5.4:
Decision Making Under Uncertainty.

Applicable Problems: 5-8, 5-9, 5-12, 5-13, 5-15, 5-17, 5-19, Start Right Case

5.5 DECISION MAKING UNDER UNCERTAINTY

When the probability of occurrence of each state of nature can be assessed, the EMV or EOL decision criteria are usually appropriate. When a manager *cannot* assess the outcome probability with confidence or when virtually no probability data are available, other decision criteria are required. This type of problem has been referred to as decision making under uncertainty. The criteria that we will cover in this section include:

1. Maximax.

2. Maximin.

3. Equally likely.

4. Criterion of realism.

5. Minimax.

The first four criteria can be computed directly from the decision table, while the minimax criterion requires the use of the opportunity loss table. Let's take a look at each of the five models and apply them to Thompson Lumber. It is now assumed that no probability information about the two outcomes is available to Thompson.

Maximax

Alternate Example 5.2

The maximax criterion finds the alternative that *max*imizes the *max*imum outcome or consequence for every alternative. You first locate the maxi-

TABLE 5.5 Thompson's Maximax Decision

	STATES OF NATURE		
ALTERNATIVES	FAVORABLE MARKET ($)	UNFAVORABLE MARKET ($)	MAXIMUM IN ROW ($)
Construct large plant	200,000	−180,000	200,000 Maximax
Construct small plant	100,000	−20,000	100,000
Do nothing	0	0	0

Transparency Master 5.5: Table 5.5 Thompson's Maximax Decision.

mum outcome within every alternative, and then pick that alternative with the maximum number. Since this decision criterion locates the alternative with the *highest* possible gain, it has been called an *optimistic decision criterion.*

In Table 5.5, we see that Thompson's maximax choice is the first alternative, to build a large facility. This is the maximum of the maximum number within each row or alternative.

maximax is an optimistic approach

Maximin

This criterion finds the alternative that *max*imizes the *min*imum outcome or consequence for every alternative. You first locate the minimum outcome within every alternative and then pick that alternative with the maximum number. Since this decision criterion locates the alternative that has the least possible *loss,* it has been called a *pessimistic decision criterion.*

Thompson's maximin choice, to do nothing, is shown in Table 5.6. This is the maximum of the minimum number within each row or alternative.

maximin is a pessimistic approach

Equally Likely (Laplace)

The equally likely, also called Laplace, decision criterion finds that alternative with the highest average outcome. You first calculate the average outcome for every alternative, which is the sum of all outcomes divided by the number of outcomes. Then pick that alternative with the maximum number. The equally likely approach assumes that all probabilities of occurrence for the states of nature are equal, and thus each state of nature is equally likely.

highest average outcome

TABLE 5.6 Thompson's Maximin Decision

	STATES OF NATURE		
ALTERNATIVES	FAVORABLE MARKET ($)	UNFAVORABLE MARKET ($)	MINIMUM IN ROW ($)
Construct large plant	200,000	−180,000	−180,000
Construct small plant	100,000	−20,000	−20,000
Do nothing	0	0	0 Maximin

Transparency Master 5.6: Table 5.6 Thompson's Maximin Decision

TABLE 5.7 Thompson's Equally Likely Decision

	STATES OF NATURE		
ALTERNATIVES	FAVORABLE MARKET ($)	UNFAVORABLE MARKET ($)	ROW AVERAGE ($)
Construct large plant	200,000	−180,000	10,000
Construct small plant	100,000	−20,000	40,000 *Equally likely*
Do nothing	0	0	0

The equally likely choice for Thompson Lumber is the second alternative, to build a small plant. This strategy, shown in Table 5.7, is the maximum of the average outcome of each alternative.

Criterion of Realism (Hurwicz Criterion)

Often called the weighted average, this criterion is a compromise between an optimistic and a pessimistic decision. To begin with, a coefficient of realism, α, is selected. This coefficient is between 0 and 1. When α is close to 1, the decision maker is optimistic about the future. When α is close to 0, the decision maker is pessimistic about the future. The advantage of this approach is that it allows the decision maker to build in personal feelings about relative optimism and pessimism. The formula is as follows:

Criterion of realism = α(Maximum in row) + $(1 - \alpha)$ (Minimum in row)

If we assume that John Thompson sets his coefficient of realism, α, to be .80, the best decision would be to build a large plant. As seen in Table 5.8, this alternative has the highest weighted average: $124,000 = (.80) (\$200,000) + (.20) (-\$180,000)$.

Minimax

The last decision criterion we discuss is based on opportunity loss. Minimax finds the alternative that *min*imizes the *max*imum opportunity loss

weighted average approach

minimax based on opportunity loss

TABLE 5.8 Thompson's Criterion of Realism Decision (also called Hurwicz Criterion)

	STATES OF NATURE		CRITERION OF REALISM OR WEIGHTED AVERAGE (α = .8) ($)
ALTERNATIVES	FAVORABLE MARKET ($)	UNFAVORABLE MARKET ($)	
Construct large plant	200,000	−180,000	124,000 *Realism*
Construct small plant	100,000	−20,000	76,000
Do nothing	0	0	0

Using Decision Theory in Forest Management

Prescribed fire is a modern forest management technique used to obtain a long-term healthy forest system. Although this technique is effective, there are many uncertainties involved with prescribed fire procedures. Heat and humidity factors, precipitation, and uncertainties about fire behavior can cause this forest management technique to be problematic. While prescribed fire can assist in eliminating forest residues and can enhance wildlife habitats, it also has the potential of destroying habitats due to uncontrolled or out-of-hand burning.

There are three major decision types or categories that must be carefully considered in the effective planning and execution of this policy. The first set of decisions deals with treatment selection—those areas that are to be treated with prescribed fire. These decisions can be made several months or even years before the actual burning process. Secondly, various planning decisions are made several weeks or months before the actual burn. These planning decisions consider the overall objectives of the burn, fuel and residue conditions, fire-fighting techniques to be em-

ployed, scheduling, and deployment of equipment. Thirdly, execution decisions are made a few days prior to the burn and during the burning process itself. Execution decisions look at daily and hourly weather conditions and forecasts. In addition, the decision to initiate or delay the burn is made. Should the burn continue, be modified, or be shut down? Is there a need for additional fire suppressing and retarding forces? These and related concerns are important executive decisions.

Decision tree analysis coupled with decision making under uncertainty have been used to assist in making effective prescribed fire decisions in areas of the Tahoe National Forest, the Prescott National Forest, and the Gifford Pinchot Natioanl Forest. Decision alternatives and possible states of nature were compared so total cost and potential losses could be reviewed. The result of decision analysis was a successful burning program for areas within these national forests.

Source: David Conch, Stephen Hass, David Radloff, and Richard Yanchik, "Using Fire in Forest Management: Decision Making Under Uncertainty," *Interfaces* **14**, 5 (September–October 1984): 8–19.

within each alternative. You first find the maximum opportunity loss within each alternative. Then pick that alternative with the minimum number.

Thompson's opportunity loss table is shown as Table 5.9. We can see that the minimax choice is the second alternative, build a small facility. Doing so minimizes the maximum opportunity loss.

TABLE 5.9 Thompson's MINIMAX Decision Using Opportunity Loss

| ALTERNATIVES | STATES OF NATURE | | |
	FAVORABLE MARKET ($)	UNFAVORABLE MARKET ($)	MAXIMUM IN ROW ($)
Construct large plant	0	180,000	180,000
Construct small plant	100,000	20,000	100,000 *Minimax*
Do nothing	200,000	0	200,000

Applicable Problems: 5-22 5-23, 5-24, 5-25, 5-26, 5-27

Applicable Problems: 5-22,
5-23, 5-24, 5-25, 5-26, 5-27

5.6 MARGINAL ANALYSIS WITH A LARGE NUMBER OF ALTERNATIVES AND STATES OF NATURE

So far, we have considered cases where there are only a few alternatives and states of nature. What happens when we have a large number of alternatives and states of nature? For example, a large restaurant might be able to stock from 0 to 100 cartons of doughnuts. Furthermore, demand could also range from 0 to 100 cartons per day. In this case, we will have to analyze 101 possible alternatives and states of nature. This would require a very large decision table if we used the decision theory approaches discussed so far in this chapter. When we can identify a marginal profit and loss, it is possible to use *marginal analysis* to obtain the best decision without using a large decision table.

marginal analysis

Teaching Suggestion 5.6:
The Use of Marginal
Analysis. See the Instructor's
Section for details.

Marginal analysis is a decision-making approach that can help select the optimal inventory level. It involves two new terms—marginal profit and marginal loss. Let's say you are a newspaper distributor; each daily paper costs you 19¢ and can be sold for 35¢. But if a paper is not sold at the end of the day, it is completely worthless (a 0¢ salvage value). In this case, the *marginal profit* (MP) is the profit made by selling each additional paper, namely, 16¢ (= 35¢ − 19¢). The *marginal loss* (ML) is the loss caused by stocking, but not selling, each additional newspaper—it would be 19¢ for every paper remaining at the end of the day.

marginal profit
marginal loss

When there are a manageable number of alternatives and states of nature, and we know the probabilities for each state of nature, then *marginal analysis with discrete distributions* can be used. When there are a very large number of possible alternatives and states of nature, and the probability distribution of the states of nature can be described with a normal distribution, then *marginal analysis with the normal distribution* is appropriate. Both of these techniques are discussed in the following sections.

Marginal Analysis with Discrete Distributions

KEY IDEA

Finding the best inventory level to stock is not difficult when we follow the marginal analysis procedure. Given any inventory level, we would only add an additional unit to our inventory level if its expected marginal profit equals or exceeds its expected marginal loss. This relationship is expressed symbolically below. First, we let

P = Probability that demand will be greater than or equal to a given supply (or the probability of selling at *least* one additional unit)

$1 - P$ = Probability that demand will be less than supply

expected marginal profit and loss

The expected marginal profit is then found by multiplying the probability that a given unit will be sold by the marginal profit, $P(MP)$. Likewise, the expected marginal loss is the probability of not selling the unit multiplied by the marginal loss, or $(1 - P)(ML)$.

The optimal decision rule is:

$$P(MP) \geq (1 - P)(ML)$$

With some basic mathematic manipulations, we can determine the level of P that will help solve marginal analysis problems:

$$P(MP) \geq ML - P(ML)$$

finding the optimal
probability level

or

$$P(MP) + P(ML) \geq ML$$

or

$$P(MP + ML) \geq ML$$

or

$$P \geq \frac{ML}{MP + ML} \tag{5-4}$$

In other words, as long as the probability of selling one more unit (P) is greater than or equal to ML/(MP + ML), we would stock the additional unit. An inventory example will illustrate the concept.

Café du Donut is a popular New Orleans dining spot on the edge of the French Quarter. Its specialty is coffee and doughnuts; it buys the dough-nuts fresh daily from a large industrial bakery. The café pays $4 for each carton (containing two dozen doughnuts) delivered each morning. Any cartons not sold at the end of the day are thrown away, for they would not be fresh enough to meet the café's standards. If a carton of doughnuts is sold, the total revenue is $6. Hence the marginal profit per carton of doughnuts is:

$$MP = \text{marginal profit} = \$6 - \$4 = \$2$$

The marginal loss is ML = $4, since the doughnuts cannot be returned or salvaged at day's end.

From past sales, the café's manager estimates that the daily sales will follow the probability distribution shown in Table 5.10. Management then follows three steps to find the optimal number of cartons of doughnuts to order each day.

TABLE 5.10 Café du Donut's Probability Distribution

Alternate Example 5.3

DAILY SALES (CARTONS OF DOUGHNUTS)	PROBABILITY SALES WILL BE AT THIS LEVEL
4	.05
5	.15
6	.15
7	.20
8	.25
9	.10
10	.10
Total	1.00

Step 1. Determine the value of P for the decision rule.

$$P \geq \frac{\text{ML}}{\text{ML} + \text{MP}} = \frac{\$4}{\$4 + \$2} = \frac{4}{6} = .66$$

$$P \geq .66$$

Step 2. Add a new column to the table to reflect the probability that doughnut sales will be at each level *or greater*. This is shown in the right column of Table 5.11.

For example, the probability sales will be four cartons or greater is 1.00 (= .05 + .15 + .15 + .20 + .25 + .10 + .10) since sales have always been between four and ten cartons per day. Likewise the probability sales will be eight cartons or greater is .45 (= .25 + .10 + .10), namely, the sum of probabilities for sales of eight, or nine, or ten cartons.

Step 3. Keep ordering additional cartons as long as the probability of selling at least one additional carton is greater than P, which is the indifference or break-even probability. If Café du Donut orders six cartons, marginal profits will still be greater than marginal loss.

$$P \text{ at 6 cartons} \geq \frac{\text{ML}}{\text{ML} + \text{MP}}$$

since .80 ≥ .66.

If seven cartons are ordered, however, the probability of selling seven or more cartons (.65) is *not* greater than .66. Thus, the expected marginal loss will be greater than the expected marginal profit if seven cartons are ordered. In other words, the café can expect to lose money on the seventh carton if it is puchased. The optimal decision is to order six cartons each day.

This problem *could* have been placed in a decision table and solved, but the table would require seven rows and seven columns (one for each sales level). Although marginal analysis with discrete distributions is very efficient compared to decision tables, where there are over 15 or 20 different alternatives and states of nature, marginal analysis with the normal distribution may be more appropriate.

TABLE 5.11 Marginal Analysis for Café du Donut

DAILY SALES (CARTONS OF DOUGHNUTS)	PROBABILITY SALES WILL BE AT THIS LEVEL	PROBABILITY SALES WILL BE AT THIS LEVEL OR GREATER
4	.05	1.00 ≥ .66
5	.15	.95 ≥ .66
6	.15	.80 ≥ .66
7	.20	.65
8	.25	.45
9	.10	.20
10	.10	.10
Total	1.00	

Marginal Analysis with the Normal Distribution

When product demand or sales follow a normal distribution, which is a common business situation, marginal analysis with the normal distribution can be applied. First we need to find four values:

1. The average or mean sales for the product, μ.

2. The standard deviation of sales, σ.

3. The marginal profit for the product, MP.

4. The marginal loss for the product, ML.

Once these quantities are known, the process of finding the best stocking policy is somewhat similar to marginal analysis with discrete distributions.

Step 1. Determine the value of P. With the normal distribution, P is equal to ML/(ML + MP).

$$P = \frac{ML}{ML + MP}$$

Step 2. Locate P on the normal distribution. For a given area under the curve, we can find Z from the standard normal table (Appendix A). Then, using the relationship

$$Z = \frac{X^* - \mu}{\sigma} \qquad (5\text{-}5)$$

we can solve for X^*, the optimal stocking policy.

An illustration will help explain. Demand for copies of the *Chicago Tribune* newspaper at Joe's Newsstand is normally distributed and has averaged 50 papers per day, with a standard deviation of 10 papers. With a marginal loss of 4¢ and a marginal profit of 6¢, what daily stocking policy should Joe follow?

Step 1. Joe should stock *Tribunes* until the probability of having a demand at a given level or greater is at least ML/(ML + MP).

$$P = \frac{ML}{ML + MP} = \frac{4¢}{4¢ + 6¢} = \frac{4}{10} = .40$$

Step 2. Figure 5.2 shows the normal distribution. Since the normal table has cumulative areas under the curve between the left side and any point, we look for .60 (= 1.0 − .40) in order to get the corresponding Z value.

$$Z = .25 \qquad \text{standard deviations from the mean}$$

In this problem, $\mu = 50$ and $\sigma = 10$, so

$$.25 = \frac{X^* - 50}{10}$$

Transparency Master 5.9:
Joe's Stocking Decision for *Chicago Tribunes.*

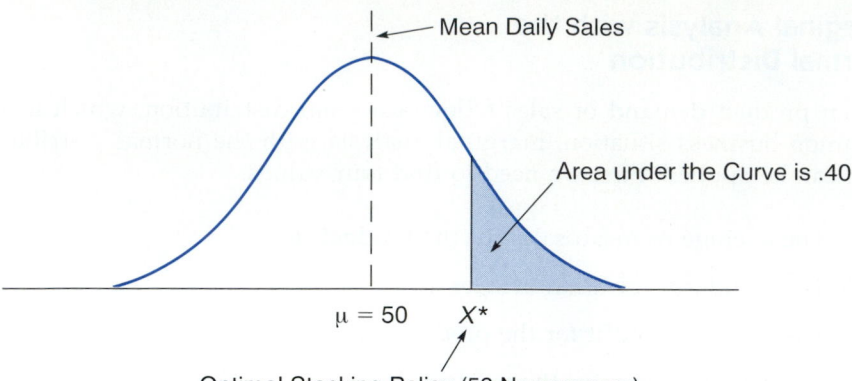

FIGURE 5.2
Joe's Stocking Decision for *Chicago Tribunes*

or

$$X^* = 10(.25) + 50 = 52.5, \quad \text{or} \quad 53 \text{ newspapers}$$

Thus, Joe should order 53 *Chicago Tribunes* daily.

This same procedure can be used when P is greater than .50. Let's say Joe's Newsstand also stocks the *Chicago Sun-Times* and its marginal loss is 8¢ and marginal profit is 2¢. The daily sales have averaged 100 *Sun-Times* with a standard deviation of 10 papers. The optimal stocking policy is as follows:

Step 1. $P = \dfrac{ML}{ML + MP} = \dfrac{8¢}{8¢ + 2¢} = \dfrac{8}{10} = .8$

Step 2. The normal curve is shown in Figure 5.3. Since the normal curve is symmetrical, we find Z for an area under the curve of .80 and multiply this number by -1.

$Z = -.84$ standard deviations from the mean for an area of .80

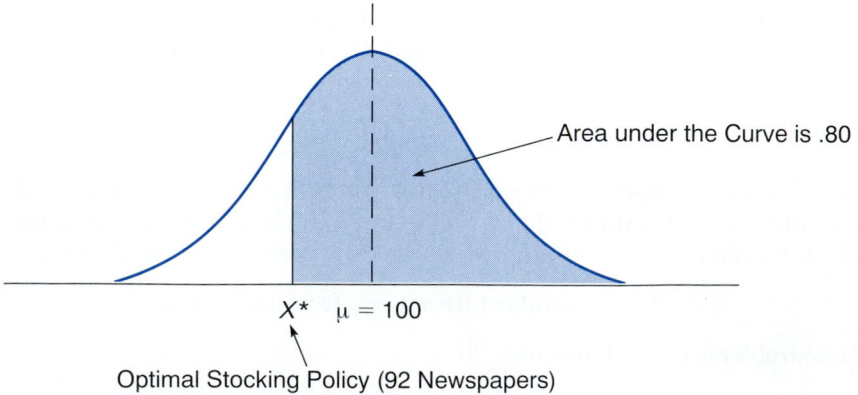

FIGURE 5.3
Joe's Stocking Decision for *Chicago Sun-Times*

With $\mu = 100$ and $\sigma = 10$,

$$-.84 = \frac{X^* - 100}{10}$$

or

$$X^* = -8.4 + 100 = 91.6, \quad \text{or} \quad 92 \text{ papers}$$

So Joe should order 92 *Sun-Times* every day.

The optimal stocking policies in these two examples are intuitively consistent. When marginal profit is *greater* than marginal loss, we would expect X^* to be *greater than* the average demand, μ, and when marginal profit is *less* than marginal loss, we would expect the optimal stocking policy, X^*, to be *less than* μ.

optimal stocking policies should be intuitively consistent

5.7 USING THE COMPUTER TO SOLVE DECISION THEORY PROBLEMS

Both AB:QM and STORM can be used to solve decision theory problems. The AB:QM software package will be fully explored in Chapter 6. In this chapter, we will give you an overview of AB:QM so you can solve simple EMV and decision making under uncertainty problems.

Like other AB:QM programs, we begin with the main menu. We then access a submenu with the following choices:

A	Decision Making Under Risk
B	Decision Making Under Uncertainty
C	Decision Tree Analysis
D	Bayes's Decision Rule

We can use both decision making under risk (menu selection A) and decision making under uncertainty (menu selection B) to solve some of the problems discussed in this chapter. Programs 5-1 and 5-2 show data input and output for typical problems. Refer to Chapter 6 for a complete discussion of how to use AB:QM in solving a wider variety of decision-making problems.

PROGRAM 5.1 Decision Making under Risk Using AB:QM

```
Program: Decision Theory / Decision Making Under Risk

Problem Title : Thompson

***** Input Data *****
```

(continued)

PROGRAM 5.1 **Decision Making under Risk Using AB:QM** (Continued)

```
Type of Problem : Profit Problem

                        Event 1            Event 2

Probability               0.500              0.500

Alternative 1       200000.000        -180000.000
Alternative 2       100000.000         -20000.000
Alternative 3            0.000              0.000

***** Program Output *****

Expected Profit Table

Alternative                      Expected Profit

     1                              10000.000
     2                              40000.000 <=
     3                                  0.000

<= indicate(s) the best alternative(s)

***** End of Output *****
```

PROGRAM 5.2 **Decision Making under Uncertainty Using AB:QM**

```
Program: Decision Theory / Decision Making Under Uncertainty

Problem Title : Thompson

***** Input Data *****

Type of Problem : Profit Problem

Hurwicz Alpha Coefficient:          0.800

                        Event 1            Event 2

Alternative 1       200000.000        -180000.000
Alternative 2       100000.000         -20000.000
Alternative 3            0.000              0.000

***** Program Output *****

Laplace

Alternative                      Expected Value

     1                              10000.000
     2                              40000.000 <=
     3                                  0.000
```

(continued)

PROGRAM 5.2 Decision Making under Uncertainty Using AB:QM (Continued)

```
Maximin
Alternative                      Expected Value

     1                            -180000.000
     2                             -20000.000
     3                                  0.000 <=


Maximax
Alternative                      Maximax Payoff

     1                             200000.000 <=
     2                             100000.000
     3                                  0.000


Hurwicz
Alternative                      Hurwicz Payoff

     1                             124000.000 <=
     2                              76000.000
     3                                  0.000


Minimax
Alternative                      Maximum Regret

     1                             180000.000
     2                             100000.000 <=
     3                             200000.000


<= indicate(s) the best alternative(s)

***** End of Output *****
```

5.8 SUMMARY

Decision theory is an analytic and systematic approach to studying decision making. Six steps are usually involved in making decisions in three environments—decision making under certainty, risk, and uncertainty. Such methods as determining expected monetary value (EMV), expected value of perfect information (EVPI), expected opportunity loss (EOL), and sensitivity analysis are used in decision making under risk. In decision making under uncertainty, decision tables are constructed to compute such criteria as maximax, maximin, equally likely, minimax, and criterion of realism. In solving problems with a large number of alternatives and states of nature, marginal analysis can be used. Software packages, such as AB:QM and STORM, are also used to solve decision theory problems.

GLOSSARY

Alternative. A course of action or a strategy that may be chosen by a decision maker.

State of Nature. An outcome or occurrence over which the decision maker has little or no control.

Conditional Value or Payoff. A consequence or outcome, normally expressed in a monetary value, that occurs as a result of a particular alternative and state of nature.

Decision Making under Certainty. A decision-making environment in which the future outcomes or states of nature are known.

Decision Making under Risk. A decision-making environment in which several outcomes or states of nature may occur as a result of a decision or alternative. The probabilities of the outcomes or states of nature are known.

Decision Making under Uncertainty. A decision-making environment in which several outcomes or states of nature may occur. The probabilities of these outcomes, however, are not known.

Expected Monetary Value (EMV). The average or expected monetary outcome of a decision if it can be repeated many times. This is determined by multiplying the monetary outcomes by their respective probabilities. The results are then added to arrive at EMV.

Expected Value with Perfect Information. The average or expected value of the decision if you knew what would happen ahead of time. You have perfect knowledge.

Expected Value of Perfect Information (EVPI). The average or expected value of information if it were completely accurate. The information is perfect.

Expected Opportunity Loss. The amount you would lose by not picking the best alternative. For any state of nature, this is the difference between the consequences of any alternative and the best possible alternative.

Maximax. An optimistic decision-making criterion. This is the alternative with the highest possible return.

Maximin. A pessimistic decision-making criterion. This alternative maximizes the minimum outcome. It is the best of the worst possible outcomes.

Equally Likely. A decision criterion that places an equal weight on all states of nature.

Coefficient of Realism (α). A number from 0 to 1. When the coefficient is close to one, the decision criterion is optimistic. When the coefficient is close to zero, the decision criterion is pessimistic.

Minimax. A criterion that minimizes the maximum opportunity loss.

Marginal Analysis. A decision-making technique that uses marginal profit and marginal loss in determining optimal decision policies. Marginal analysis is used when the number of alternatives and states of nature is large.

Marginal Profit. The additional profit that would be realized by stocking and selling one more unit.

Marginal Loss. The loss that would be incurred by stocking and not selling an additional unit.

KEY EQUATIONS

(5-1)   EMV (Alternative *i*) = (payoff of first state of nature) × (its probability) + (payoff of second state of nature) × (its probability) + ⋯ + (payoff of last state of nature) × (its probability)

This equation computes expected monetary values.

(5-2)   Expected value *with* perfect information = (best outcome for first state of nature) × (its probability) + (best outcome for second state of nature) × (its probability) + ⋯ + (best outcome for last state of nature) × (its probability)

(5-3)   EVPI = Expected value *with* perfect information − maximum EMV

This equation calculates the expected value of perfect information.

(5-4) $P \geqslant \dfrac{ML}{ML + MP}$

Equation used in marginal analysis to compute stocking policies.

(5-5) $Z = \dfrac{X^* - \mu}{\sigma}$

Equation used in marginal analysis to compute the optimal stocking policy, X^*, when demand follows a normal distribution.

SOLVED PROBLEMS

Solved Problem 5-1

Maria Rojas is considering the possibility of opening a small dress shop on Fairbanks Avenue, a few blocks from the university. She has located a good mall that attracts students. Her options are to open a small shop, a medium-sized shop, or no shop at all. The market for a dress shop can be good, average, or bad. The probabilities for these three possibilities are .2 for a good market, .5 for an average market, and .3 for a bad market. The net profit or loss for the medium-sized or small shops for the various market conditions are given below. Building no shop at all yields no loss and no gain. What do you recommend?

ALTERNATIVES	GOOD MARKET ($)	AVERAGE MARKET ($)	BAD MARKET ($)
Small shop	75,000	25,000	−40,000
Medium-sized shop	100,000	35,000	−60,000
No shop	0	0	0

Solution

The problem can be solved by developing a payoff table that contains all alternatives, states of nature, and probability values. The expected monetary value (EMV) for each alternative is also computed. See the following table.

	STATE OF NATURE			
ALTERNATIVES	GOOD MARKET ($)	AVERAGE MARKET ($)	BAD MARKET ($)	EMV ($)
Small shop	75,000	25,000	−40,000	15,500
Medium-sized shop	100,000	35,000	−60,000	19,500
No shop	0	0	0	0
Probabilities	.20	.50	.30	

$$\text{EMV (small shop)} = (.2)(\$75,000) + (.5)(\$25,000)$$
$$+ (.3)(-\$40,000) = \$15,500$$

$$\text{EMV (medium-sized shop)} = (.2)(\$100,000) + (.5)(\$35,000)$$
$$+ (.3)(-\$60,000) = \$19,500$$

$$\text{EMV (no shop)} = (.2)(\$0) + (.5)(\$0) + (.3)(\$0) = \$0$$

As can be seen, the best decision is to build the medium-sized shop. The EMV for this alternative is $19,500.

Solved Problem 5-2

Cal Bender and Becky Addison have known each other since high school. Two years ago, they entered the same university and today they are taking undergraduate courses in the business school. Both hope to graduate with degrees in finance. In an attempt to make extra money and to use some of the knowledge gained from their business courses, Cal and Becky have decided to look into the possibility of starting a small company that would provide typing services to students who needed term papers or other reports typed in a professional manner. Using a systems approach, Cal and Becky have identified three strategies. Strategy 1 is to invest in a fairly expensive microcomputer system with a high-quality laser printer. In a favorable market, they should be able to obtain a net profit of $10,000 over the next two years. If the market is unfavorable, they can lose $8,000. Strategy 2 is to purchase a less expensive system. With a favorable market, they could get a return during the next two years of $8,000. With an unfavorable market, they would incur a loss of $4,000. Their final strategy, strategy 3, is to do nothing. Cal is basically a risk taker, while Becky tries to avoid risk.

(a) What type of decision procedure should Cal use? What would Cal's decision be?

(b) What type of decision maker is Becky? What decision would Becky make?

(c) If Cal and Becky were indifferent to risk, what type of decision approach should they use? What would you recommend if this were the case?

Solution

The problem is one of decision making under uncertainty. Before answering the specific questions, a decision table should be developed showing the alternatives, states of nature, and related consequences.

ALTERNATIVES	FAVORABLE MARKET ($)	UNFAVORABLE MARKET ($)
Strategy 1	10,000	−8,000
Strategy 2	8,000	−4,000
Strategy 3	0	0

(a) Since Cal is a risk taker, he should use the maximax decision criteria. This approach selects the row that has the highest or maximum value. The $10,000 value, which is the maximum value from the table, is in row 1. Thus Cal's decision is to select strategy 1, which is an optimistic decision approach.

(b) Becky should use the maximin decision criteria. The minimum or worst outcome for each row, or strategy, is identified. These outcomes are −$8,000 for strategy 1, −$4,000 for strategy 2, and $0 for strategy 3. The maximum of these values is selected. Thus, Becky would select strategy 3, which reflects a pessimistic decision approach.

(c) If Cal and Becky are indifferent to risk, they should use the equally likely approach. This approach selects the alternative that maximizes the row averages. The row average for strategy 1 is $1,000 [$1,000 = ($10,000 − $8,000)/2]. The row average for strategy 2 is $2,000, and the row average for strategy 3 is $0. Thus, using the equally likely approach, the decision is to select strategy 2, which maximizes the row averages.

Solved Problem 5-3

Rick Miller has just opened a new bakery in Frisco, Colorado, called Morning Fresh. In performing an economic analysis, Rick has determined that the marginal cost or loss for each dozen doughnuts sold is $4. The marginal profit is estimated to be $2.75 per dozen doughnuts. At this time, Rick is considering stocking 10, 15, 20, 25, or 30 dozen doughnuts. The probability of selling 10 dozen doughnuts is 10%. The chance of selling 15 dozen doughnuts is 20%. There is a 30% chance that Morning Fresh will sell either 20 or 25 dozen doughnuts. Finally, there is a 10% chance of selling 30 dozen doughnuts, which is considered by Rick to be the most that Morning Fresh would be able to accommodate. What is your recommendation to Rick?

Solution

The problem facing Rick Miller involves the use of marginal analysis. First, we need to know the marginal loss and the marginal profit. This information was given in the problem: the marginal loss is $4, while the marginal profit is $2.75. Now we can compute the probability of selling one more unit (P):

$$P \geq \frac{\text{ML}}{\text{ML} + \text{MP}} = \frac{\$4}{\$4 + \$2.75} = .59$$

The probability of selling one more unit, which in this case is a dozen doughnuts, is .59. The next step is to develop a table showing the probability of selling doughnuts at a particular level or greater. The solution is to stock additional doughnuts as long as P is greater than or equal to .59. As seen in the table, the solution is to stock 20 dozen doughnuts.

DEMAND	PROBABILITY AT THIS LEVEL	PROBABILITY AT THIS LEVEL OR GREATER
10	.1	1.00
15	.2	.90
20	.3	.70 ←
25	.3	.40
30	.1	.10
Total	1.0	

DISCUSSION QUESTIONS AND PROBLEMS

Discussion Questions

5-1 Give an example of a good decision you made that resulted in a bad outcome. Also give an example of a bad decision you made that had a good outcome. Why was each decision good or bad?

5-2 Describe what is involved in the decision process.

5-3 What is an alternative? What is a state of nature?

5-4 Discuss the differences between decision making under certainty, decision making under risk, and decision making under uncertainty.

5-5 Mary Lillich is trying to decide whether to invest in real estate, stocks, or certificates of deposit. How well she does depends on whether the economy enters a period of recession or inflation. Develop a decision table (excluding the conditional values) to describe this situation.

5-6 Describe the meaning of EMV and EVPI.

5-7 What techniques are used to solve decision-making problems under uncertainty? Which technique results in an optimistic decision? Which technique results in a pessimistic decision?

Problems

5-8 Dr. Kenneth Brown is the principal owner of Brown Oil, Inc. After quitting his university teaching job, Ken has been able to increase his annual salary by a factor of over 100. At the present time, Ken is forced to consider purchasing some more equipment for Brown Oil because of competition. His alternatives are shown in the following table.

QA5-8

EQUIPMENT	FAVORABLE MARKET ($)	UNFAVORABLE MARKET ($)
SUB 100	300,000	−200,000
OILER J	250,000	−100,000
TEXAN	75,000	−18,000

For example, if Ken purchases a SUB 100, and if there is a favorable market, he will realize a profit of $300,000. On the other hand, if the market is unfavorable, Ken will suffer a loss of $200,000. But Ken has always been a very optimistic decision maker.

decision making under uncertainty; maximax criterion; SUB 100

(a) What type of decision is Ken facing?
(b) What decision criterion should he use?
(c) What alternative is best?

5-9 Although Ken Brown (discussed in Problem 5-8) is the principal owner of Brown Oil, his brother Bob is credited with making the company a financial success. Bob is vice president of finance. Bob attributes his success to his pessimistic attitude about business and the oil industry. Given the same information from Problem 5-8, it is likely that Bob will arrive at a different decision. What decision criterion should Bob use, and what alternative will he select?

QA5-9

maximin; TEXAN

5-10 The *Lubricant* is an expensive oil newsletter that many oil giants subscribe to, including Ken Brown. In the last issue, the letter described how the demand for oil products would be extremely high. Apparently, the American consumer will continue to use oil products even if the price of these products doubles. Indeed, one of the articles in the *Lubricant* states that the chances of a favorable market for oil products was 70%, while the chance of an unfavorable market was only 30%. Ken would like to use these probabilities in determining the best decision. (See Problem 5-8 for details.)

QA5-10

(a) What decision model should be used?
(b) What is the optimal decision?
(c) Ken believes that the $300,000 figure for the SUB 100 with a favorable market is too high. How much lower would this figure have to be for Ken to change his decision made in part (b) of this problem?

EMV
150,000 − SUB 100
292,857

5-11 Allen Young has always been proud of his personal investment strategies and has done very well over the last several years. He invests primarily in the stock market. Over the last several months, however, Allen has become very concerned about the stock market as a good investment. In some cases, it would have been better for Allen to have his money in a bank than in the market. During the next six months, Allen must decide whether to invest $10,000 in the stock market or in a six-month certificate of deposit (CD) at an interest rate of 9%. If the market is good, Allen believes that he could get a 14% return on his money. With a fair market, he expects to get an 8% return. If the market is bad, he will most likely get no return at all—in other words, the return

QA5-11

would be 0%. Allen estimates that the probability of a good market is .4, the probability of a fair market is .4, and the probability of a bad market is .2.

See Instructor's Section
Bank − $900 expected value

(a) Develop a decision table for this problem.
(b) What is the best decision?

QA5-12

: 5-12 Janet Kim, president of Kim Manufacturing, Inc., is considering whether or not to build more manufacturing plants in Wisconsin. Her decision is summarized in the following table.

ALTERNATIVES	FAVORABLE MARKET ($)	UNFAVORABLE MARKET ($)
Build large plant	400,000	−300,000
Build small plant	80,000	−10,000
Don't build	0	0
Market probabilities	.4	.6

See Instructor's Section;
$134,000 − Small Plant;
$134,000

(a) Construct an opportunity loss table.
(b) Determine EOL and the best strategy.
(c) What is the expected value of perfect information?

QA5-13

: 5-13 Helen Murvis, hospital administrator for Portland General Hospital, is trying to determine whether to build a large wing on to the existing hospital, build a small wing, or no wing at all. If the population of Portland continues to grow, a large wing could return $150,000 to the hospital each year. If the small wing were built, it would return $60,000 to the hospital each year if the population continues to grow. If the population of Portland remains the same, the hospital would encounter a loss of $85,000 if the large wing were built. Furthermore, a loss of $45,000 would be realized if the small wing were constructed and the population remains the same. Unfortunately, Helen does not have any information about the future population of Portland.

Decision Making Under
Uncertainty; See Instructor's
Section;
$32,500 − Large Wing

(a) What type of decision problem is this?
(b) Construct a decision table.
(c) Using the equally likely criterion, determine the best alternative.

: 5-14 In Problem 5-11, you helped Allen Young determine the best investment strategy. Now, Young is thinking about paying for a stock market newsletter. A friend of Young said that these types of letters could predict very accurately whether the market would be good, fair, or poor. Then, based on these predictions, Young could make better investment decisions.

$200

(a) What is the most that Young would be willing to pay for a newsletter?
(b) Young now believes that a good market will only give a return of 11% instead of 14%. Will this information change the amount that Young would be willing to pay for the newsletter? If your answer is yes, determine the most that Young would be willing to pay, given this new information.

Yes, $80

QA5-15

: 5-15 Hardie Lord, Helen Murvis's boss, is not convinced that Helen used the correct decision technique (refer to Problem 5-13). Hardie believes that Helen should use a coefficient of realism of .75 in determining the best alternative. Hardie thinks of himself as a realist.

See Instructor's Section;
$91,250 − Large Wing;

(a) Develop a decision table for this problem.
(b) Using the criterion of realism, what is the best decision?

(c) Did Hardie's decision technique result in a decision that was different from Helen's?

No

5-16 Brilliant Color is a small supplier of chemicals and equipment that are used by some photographic stores to process 35-mm film. One product that Brilliant Color supplies is BC-6. John Kubick, president of Brilliant Color, normally stocks 11, 12, or 13 cases of BC-6 each week. For each case that John sells he receives a profit of $35. Because BC-6, like many photographic chemicals, has a very short shelf life, if a case is not sold by the end of the week John must discard it. Since each case costs John $56, he loses $56 for every case that is not sold by the end of the week. There is a probability of .45 of selling 11 cases, a probability of .35 of selling 12 cases, and a probability of .2 of selling 13 cases.

QA5-16

(a) Construct a decision table for this problem. Include all conditional values and probabilities in the table.

(b) What is your recommended course of action?

(c) If John is able to develop BC-6 with an ingredient that stabilizes it so it no longer has to be discarded, how would this change your recommended course of action?

See Instructor's Section; Stock 11 Cases; Stock 13 cases

5-17 Today's Electronics specializes in manufacturing modern electronic components. It also builds the equipment that produces the components. Phyllis Weinberger, who is responsible for advising the president of Today's Electronics on electronic manufacturing equipment, has developed the following table concerning a proposed facility.

QA5-17

	PROFIT ($)		
	STRONG MARKET	FAIR MARKET	POOR MARKET
Large-sized facility	550,000	110,000	−310,000
Medium-sized facility	300,000	129,000	−100,000
Small-sized facility	200,000	100,000	−32,000
No facility	0	0	0

(a) Develop an opportunity loss table.

(b) What is the minimax decision?

See Instructor's Section; Medium facility $250,000

5-18 Megley Cheese Company is a small manufacturer of several different cheese products. One of the products is a cheese spread that is sold to retail outlets. Jason Megley must decide how many cases of cheese spread to manufacture each month. The probability that the demand will be six cases is .1, for 7 cases is .3, for 8 cases is .5, and for 9 cases is .1. The cost of every case is $45, and the price that Jason gets for each case is $95. Unfortunately, any cases not sold by the end of the month are of no value due to spoilage. How many cases of cheese should Jason manufacture each month?

QA5-18

8

5-19 Even though independent gasoline stations have been having a difficult time, Susan Solomon has been thinking about starting her own independent gasoline station. Susan's problem is to decide how large her station should be. The annual returns will depend on both the size of her station and a number of marketing factors related to the oil industry and demand for gasoline. After a careful analysis, Susan developed the following table.

QA5-19

SIZE OF FIRST STATION	GOOD MARKET ($)	FAIR MARKET ($)	POOR MARKET ($)
Small	50,000	20,000	−10,000
Medium	80,000	30,000	−20,000
Large	100,000	30,000	−40,000
Very large	300,000	25,000	−160,000

For example, if Susan constructs a small station and the market is good, she will realize a profit of $50,000.

See Instructor's Section;
Very large size;
Small size;
Very large size;
Very large size;
See Instructor's Section;
Very large size

(a) Develop a decision table for this decision.
(b) What is the maximax decision?
(c) What is the maximin decision?
(d) What is the equally likely decision?
(e) What is the criterion of realism decision? Use an α value of .8.
(f) Develop an opportunity loss table.
(g) What is the minimax decision?

QA5-20

5-20 Dorothy Stanyard has three major routes to take to work. She can take Tennessee Street the entire way, she can take several back streets to work, or she can use the expressway. The traffic patterns are very complex, however. Under good conditions, Tennessee Street is the fastest route. When Tennessee is congested, then one of the other routes is usually preferable. Over the last two months, Dorothy has tried each route several times under different traffic conditions. This information is summarized in minutes of travel time to work in the following table.

	NO TRAFFIC CONGESTION	MILD TRAFFIC CONGESTION	SEVERE TRAFFIC CONGESTION
Tennessee Street	15	30	45
Back roads	20	25	35
Expressway	30	30	30

In the past 60 days, Dorothy encountered severe traffic congestion 10 days and mild traffic congestion 20 days. Assume that the last 60 days are typical of traffic conditions.

See Instructor's Section;
Back roads;
3⅓ minutes

(a) Develop a decision table for this decision.
(b) What route should Dorothy take?
(c) Dorothy is about to buy a radio for her car that would tell her the exact traffic conditions before she started to work each morning. How much time in minutes on the average would Dorothy save by buying the radio?

QA5-21

5-21 Farm Grown, Inc., produces cases of perishable food products. Each case contains an assortment of vegetables and other farm products. Each case costs $5 and sells for $15. If there are any cases not sold by the end of the day, they are sold to a large food processing company for $3 a case. The probability that daily demand will be 100 cases is .3, the probability that daily demand will be 200 cases is .4, and the probability that daily demand will be 300 cases is .3. Farm Grown has a policy of always satisfying customer demands. If its own supply of cases is less than the demand, then they buy the necessary vegetables from a competitor. The estimated cost of doing this is $16 per case.

See Instructor's Section;
300 cases

(a) Draw a decision table for this problem.
(b) What do you recommend?

5-22 Teresa Granger is the manager of Chicago Cheese, which produces cheese spreads and other cheese-related products. E-Z Spread Cheese is a product that has always been popular. The probability of sales, in cases, is presented below:

DEMAND IN CASES	PROBABILITY
10	.2
11	.3
12	.2
13	.2
14	.1

A case of E-Z Spread Cheese sells for $100 and has a cost of $75. Any cheese that is not sold by the end of the week is sold to a local food processor for $50. Teresa never sells cheese that is more than a week old. How many cases of E-Z Spread Cheese should Teresa produce each week?

12 cases

5-23 Harry's Hardware does a brisk business during the year, but during Christmas, Harry's Hardware sells Christmas trees for a substantial profit. Unfortunately, any trees not sold at the end of the season are totally worthless. Thus, the number of trees that are stocked for a given season is a very important decision. The following table reveals the demand for Christmas trees.

DEMAND FOR CHRISTMAS TREES	PROBABILITY
50	.05
75	.1
100	.2
125	.3
150	.2
175	.1
200	.05

Harry sells trees for $15 each, but his cost is only $6.

(a) How many trees should Harry stock at his hardware store?

125

(b) If the cost increased to $12 per tree, how many trees should Harry stock?

100

(c) Harry is thinking about increasing the price to $18 per tree. Assume the cost per tree is $6. It is expected that the probability of selling 50, 75, 100, or 125 trees will be .25 each. Harry does not expect to sell more than 125 trees with this price increase. What do you recommend?

100

5-24 In addition to selling Christmas trees during the Christmas holidays, Harry's Hardware sells all of the ordinary hardware items. One of the most popular items is Great Glue HH, a glue that is made just for Harry's Hardware. The selling price is $2 per bottle, but unfortunately, the glue gets hard and unusable after one month. The cost of the glue is 75¢. During the past several months, the mean sales of glue have been 60 units, and the standard deviation is 7. How many bottles of glue should Harry's Hardware stock? Assume sales follow a normal distribution.

62

5-25 The marginal loss on Washington Reds, a brand of apples from the state of Washington, is $35 per case. The marginal profit is $15 per case. During the past year, the mean sales of Washington Reds in cases was 45,000 cases, and

42,686

the standard deviation was 4,450. How many cases of Washington Reds should be brought to market? Assume sales follow a normal distribution.

5-26 Linda Stanyon has been the production manager for Plano Produce for over eight years. Plano Produce is a small company located near Plano, Illinois. On the average, 400 cases of tomatoes are sold each day. In addition, 85% of the time the sales are between 350 and 450 cases. Each case sells for $3. All cases that are not sold must be discarded. A case costs approximately $2. How many cases of tomatoes should Linda stock?

385

5-27 Paula Shoemaker produces a weekly stock market report for an exclusive readership. She normally sells 3,000 reports per week, and 70% of the time her sales range from 2,990 to 3,010. The report costs Paula $15 to produce, but Paula is able to sell reports for $350 each. Of course, any reports not sold by the end of the week have no value. How many reports should Paula produce each week?

3016.50

Data Set Problem

QA5-28

5-28 Chris Dunphy, executive vice president for marketing and sales of Sumu Electronics, is considering the possibility of introducing a new line of inexpensive wristwatches, which would be oriented primarily toward young adults. The watch would have a plastic faceplate and wristband and a variety of features, including an alarm, a chronograph, and the ability to store and retrieve various split times. The watch has been designed to come in a variety of colors and styles. The retail price of the watch is expected to be $19. At this price, Chris feels that there is a substantial market for the watch. To help gain further information, Chris has hired a marketing research firm to study the market potential for this new venture.

The marketing research team conducted a survey and a pilot study to determine the potential market for the new watch being considered by Sumu. The team, realizing that there is market risk associated with any new product, looked at the potential market on a five-point scale. The number 1 represents the poorest or weakest market for the new product, while the number 5 represents the most optimistic market for the new watches. Using the five-point scale, the marketing research team looked at a variety of production, or stocking, policies related to each of the marketing segments. The stocking policies involve producing 100,000 to 500,000 watches.

The worst market scenario for Sumu was still expected to bring profitability through all stocking ranges. (Remember, the worst-case marketing scenario was assigned a value of 1 on the five-point scale.) The probability of having a 1-type market was estimated to be .10. A stocking policy of 100,000 units was expected to return a net profit of $100,000 for Sumu. A stocking policy of 150,000 units was expected to return only $90,000. Likewise, higher stocking policies for a market potential of 1 were expected to yield lower profits. A stocking policy of 200,000 was expected to return $85,000 in net profits. The stocking policies of 250,000, 300,000, 350,000, 400,000, 450,000, and 500,000 were expected to yield net profits of $80,000, $65,000, $50,000, $45,000, $30,000, and $20,000, respectively.

The next-best market scenario was categorized by the number 2. This market potential was categorized as below average, and the marketing research team estimated that the chance of getting a below average market was 20%. The net profit for the beginning stocking policy of 100,000 units was estimated to be $110,000. The net profit for stocking 150,000 units was $120,000. If

Sumu stocked 200,000 units, the net profit would be $110,000. A net profit of $120,000 would be realized if the stocking policy was 250,000 units. Stocking policies of 300,000, 350,000, 400,000, 450,000, and 500,000 would result in net profits of $100,000, $100,000, $95,000, $90,000, and $85,000, respectively.

The marketing research team estimated that the probability of an average market was 50%. This average market was coded with a 3 on the five-point scale. In general, profits were significantly higher for all stocking policies with this average market scenario. As before, profitability figures were estimated for all of the stocking policies ranging from 100,000 to 500,000 units. The net profitabilities for this range are $120,000, $140,000, $135,000, $155,000, $155,000, $160,000, $170,000, $165,000, and $160,000.

A good market potential for the watches was given a 4 on the five-point scale. The probability, however, of a good market was relatively low. It was estimated to be .1. Net profitability factors for stocking policies that range from 100,000 to 500,000 units were estimated to be $135,000, $155,000, $160,000, $170,000, $180,000, $190,000, $200,000, $230,000, and $270,000.

The probability of a very good market was estimated to be .1. This market received a 5 on the scale. Profitability factors for this market, in general, were higher. The profitability factors for stocking policies that range from 100,000 to 500,000 were $140,000, $170,000, $175,000, $180,000, $195,000, $210,000, $230,000, $245,000, and $295,000.

(a) Determine the expected monetary values for each of the stocking policy alternatives. Which stocking policy do you recommend?
(b) What is the expected value of perfect information for this situation?
(c) Chris has just received information that the original probability estimations were not accurate. Market 2 has a probability of .28, while market 5 has a probability of .02. Does this new information change any decisions?
(d) Chris has also received new information about stocking 500,000 watches. The return given a very good market is now estimated to be $340,000. What is the impact of the new probability values (given in c) and the new return for a very good market for stocking 500,000 units?

CASE STUDY

📖 Starting Right Corporation

After watching a movie about a young woman who quit a successful corporate career to start her own baby food company, Julia Day decided she wanted to do the same. In the movie, the baby food company was very successful.

Julia knew, however, that it is much easier to make a movie about a successful woman starting her own company than to actually do it. The product had to be of the highest quality, and Julia had to get the best people involved to launch the new company. Julia resigned from her job and launched her new company—Starting Right.

Julia decided to target the upper end of the baby food market by producing baby food that contained no preservatives but had a great taste. Although the price would be slightly higher than for existing baby food, Julia believed that parents would be willing to pay more for a high-quality baby food. Instead of putting baby food in jars, which would require preservatives to stabilize the food, Julia decided to try a new approach. The baby food would be frozen. This would allow for natural ingredients, no preservatives, and outstanding nutrition.

Getting good people to work for the new company was also important. Julia decided to find people with experience in finance, marketing, and production to get involved with Starting Right. With her enthusiasm and charisma, Julia was able to find such a group. Their first step was to develop prototypes of the new frozen baby food and to perform a small pilot test of the new product. The pilot test received rave reviews.

The final key to getting the young company off to a good start was to raise funds. Three options were considered—corporate bonds, preferred stock, and common stock. Julia decided that each investment should be in blocks of $30,000. Furthermore, each investor should have an annual income of at least $40,000 and a net worth of $100,000 to be eligible to invest in Starting Right. Corporate bonds would return 13% per year for the next five years. Julia furthermore guaranteed that investors in the corporate bonds would get at least $20,000 back at the end of five years. Investors in preferred stock should see their initial investment increase by a factor of 4 with a good market or have the investment worth only half of the initial investment with an unfavorable market. The common stock had the greatest potential. The initial investment was expected to increase by a factor of 8 with a good market, but investors would lose everything if the market was unfavorable. During the next five years, it was expected that inflation would increase by a factor of 4.5% each year.

(a) Sue Pansky, a retired grade-school teacher, is considering investing in Starting Right. She is very conservative and is a risk avoider. What do you recommend?

(b) Ray Cahn, who is currently a commodities broker, is also considering an investment, although he believes that there is only an 11% chance of success. What do you recommend?

(c) Lila Battle has decided to invest in Starting Right. While she believes that Julia has a good chance of being successful, Lila is a risk avoider and very conservative. What is your advice to Lila?

(d) George Yates believes that there is an equally likely chance for success. What is your recommendation?

(e) Peter Metarko is extremely optimistic about the market for the new baby food. What is your advice for Pete?

(f) Julia Day has been told that developing the legal documents for each fund-raising alternative is expensive. Julia would like to offer alternatives for both risk averse and risk seeking investors. Can Julia delete one of the financial alternatives and still offer investment choices for risk seekers and risk avoiders?

(a) Risk Avoider; (b) Do Nothing; (c) Corporate Bonds; (d) Common Stock; (e) Common Stock; (f) Yes, Delete Preferred Stock

BIBLIOGRAPHY

Brown, R. "Do Managers Find Decision Theory Useful?" *Harvard Business Review* (May–June 1970): 78–89.

Clarke, John R. "The Application of Decision Analysis to Clinical Medicine." *Interfaces* **17**, 2 (March–April 1987): 27–34.

Cohan, David, Stephen M. Hass, David L. Radloff, and F. Richard Yancik, "Using Fire in Forest Management: Decision Making Under Uncertainty." *Interfaces* **14**, 5 (September–October 1984): 8–19.

Fishburn, Peter C. "Multiattribute Nonlinear Utility Theory." *Management Science* **30**, 11 (November 1984): 1301–1310.

Flinn, R., and E. Turban. "Decision Tree Analysis for Industrial Research." *Research Management* **13**, 1 (January 1970): 27–34.

Hosseini, Jinoos. "Decision Analysis and Its Application in the Choice between Two Wildcat Oil Ventures." *Interfaces* **16**, 2 (March–April 1986): 75–85.

Janssen, C.T.L., and T.E. Daniel. "A Decision Theory Example in Football." *Decision Sciences* **15** (1984): 253–259.

Luce, R., and H. Raiffa. *Games and Decisions.* New York: John Wiley & Sons, Inc., 1957.

Luna, Robert E., Richard A. Reid. "Mortgage Selection Using a Decision Tree Approach." *Interfaces* **16**, 3 (May–June 1986): 73–81.

Mosler, K.S. "Stochastic Dominance Decision Rules When the Attributes Are Utility Dependent." *Management Science* **30**, 11 (November 1984): 1311–1322.

Pratt, J.W., H. Raiffa, and R. Schlaifer. *Introduction to Statistical Decision Theory.* New York: McGraw-Hill, 1965.

Raiffa, H. *Decision Analysis.* Reading, MA: Addison-Wesley Publishing Co., Inc., 1968.

Render, B., and R.M. Stair. *Cases and Readings in Quantitative Analysis.* Boston: Allyn and Bacon, Inc., 1982.

Schlaifer, R. *Analysis of Decisions Under Uncertainty.* New York: McGraw-Hill Book Company, 1969.

Sullivan, Gerald, and Kenneth Fordyce. "IBM Burlington's Logistics Management System," *Interfaces* **20**, 1 (January–February 1990): 43–64.

Ulvila, Jacob W. "Postal Automation (ZIP +4) Technology: A Decision Analysis." *Interfaces* **17**, 2 (March–April 1987): 1–12.

Weber, M. "A Method of Multiattribute Decision Making with Incomplete Information." *Management Science* **31**, 11 (November 1985): 1365–1371.

Winkler, R. *Introduction to Bayesian Inference and Decision.* New York: Holt, Rinehart and Winston, 1972.

Winkler, Robert L. "Research Decisions in Decision Making Under Uncertainty." *Decision Sciences* **14**, 4 (October 1982): 517–533.

Appendix: Solving Decision Theory Problems with Spreadsheets

Spreadsheets can be used to solve a number of decision theory problems, including decision making under uncertainty and risk problems.

Decision Making Under Risk

One of the most popular decision-making techniques is decision making under risk, which uses expected monetary value. Program 5.3 (a symbolic spreadsheet) reveals the use of a spreadsheet model to determine the expected monetary values for the Thompson Lumber decision table. (See Table 5.2.) The monetary values are entered in cells B8 through C10. These are the same values used in the chapter. Probability values are entered in cells B12 and C12.

Once these values are entered, the spreadsheet determines the EMV for each alternative, the maximum EMV, and a value for EVPI. The same formulas used in the book are used in the spreadsheet. For example, the formula +$B$12*B8 + $C$12*C8 is used to multiply the probability values times the monetary outcomes to get an EMV of $10,000 for the large facility in cell D8. Note the use of $, which creates an absolute cell. An absolute cell makes copying the general formula in cell D8 to cells D9 and D10 easier.

PROGRAM 5.3 Using a Spreadsheet to Compute EMV Values for Thompson Lumber

```
              A               B               C               D
 1   Expected Monetary Value
 2
 3           States      Favorable    Unfavorable           EMV
 4         of Nature        Market         Market      Computed
 5
 6     Alternatives
 7
 8   Large Facility        200000        -180000    +$B$12*B8+$C$12*C8
 9   Small Facility        100000         -20000    +$B$12*B9+$C$12*C9
10       Do Nothing             0              0    +$B$12*B10+$C$12*C10
11
12   Probabilities            0.5            0.5
13
14   Maximum EMV =                                  @MAX(D8..D10)
15          EVPI =                                  @MAX(B8..B10)*B12+@MAX(C8..C10)-D14
16
17
18
19
20
```

The $ and absolute cells will be used in spreadsheets throughout this chapter and the book. Cells D9 and D10 contain EMV values for the other alternatives. Cell D14 computes the maximum EMV with the formula @MAX(D8..D10) to be $40,000. Cell D15 computes a value for EVPI using the same type of approach discussed in the chapter. As with any spreadsheet, "what-if" analysis can be performed by making changes to the data and seeing the changes to the results—the EMV and EVPI values in this case.

Expected Opportunity Loss

Expected opportunity loss is computed using the spreadsheet shown in Program 5.4. Opportunity loss values are entered in cells B8 through C10. Probability values are entered in cells B12 and C12. The spreadsheet computes the EOL for each row by multiplying probability values times the opportunity loss values. For example, the formula used for the first alternative is +$B$12*B8 + $C$12*C8. Cell D14 computes the minimum EOL using the formula @MIN(D8..D10). This will determine the minimum value in the EOL computed column, which consists of cells D8 through D10.

Program 5.5 shows the use of a spreadsheet to compute the maximax, maximin, equally likely, and the criterion of realism for the Thompson Lumber problem presented in the chapter. The criterion of realism, which is .8 in this case, is entered in cell E2. The monetary values are entered in cells B9 through C11. Row maximums are computed in cells D9 through

PROGRAM 5.4 **Using a Spreadsheet to Compute Expected Opportunity Loss**

	A	B	C	D
1	Expected Opportunity Loss Table			
2				
3	States	Favorable	Unfavorable	EOL
4	of Nature	Market	Market	Computed
5				
6	Alternatives			
7				
8	Large Facility	0	180000	+$B$12*B8+$C$12*C8
9	Small Facility	100000	20000	+$B$12*B9+$C$12*C9
10	Do Nothing	200000	0	+$B$12*B10+$C$12*C10
11				
12	Probabilities	0.5	0.5	
13				
14	Minimum EOL =			@MIN(D8..D10)
15				
16				
17				
18				
19				
20				

D11 using the @MAX or maximum function. Row minimums are computed using the @MIN function. The row averages and realism criterion columns are computed by multiplying the monetary values times either .5 for the average or .8 and $(1 - .8)$ for criterion of realism. The procedures are the same as discussed in the chapter. The rows at the bottom of the table contain the final results. The maximax decision uses @MAX to find the maximax value—largest number in the row maximum column. The @MAX formula is also used to determine the maximin, equally likely, and criterion of realism values.

Minimax

The minimax criterion uses the opportunity loss table. (See Program 5.6.) The opportunity loss values are entered in cells B8 through C10. The maximums are computed using the @MAX function. For example, @MAX(B8..C8) is used to find the highest or maximum value in the first row, which is 180,000. Cell D13 computes the minimax value using the formula @MIN(D8..D10).

The spreadsheet models in this chapter were developed to solve the Thompson Lumber problems. The same spreadsheets could also be used to solve any decision table problem involving three alternatives and two states of nature. The spreadsheets could also be modified to handle larger problems. In addition, it would be possible to put these spreadsheets into a single spreadsheet or to link the spreadsheets together using linking formulas. This would allow data and results from one spreadsheet to be automatically transferred to other spreadsheets.

PROGRAM 5.5 Using a Spreadsheet to Solve Decision Making Under Uncertainty Problems

```
     A           B          C          D          E          F          G          H

 1
 2  Criterion of Realism Alpha Value      0.8
 3
 4                                        Row        Row        Row        Realism
 5    States                              Max        Min        Average    Criterion
      of Nature     1          2
 6
 7  Alternatives
 8
 9      1         200000     -180000   @MAX(B9..C9)    @MIN(B9..C9)    0.5*D9+0.5*E9    +$D$2*B9+(1-$D$2)*C9
10      2         100000     -20000    @MAX(B10..C1)   @MIN(B10..C10)  0.5*D10+0.5*E10  +$D$2*B10+(1-$D$2)*C10
11      3         0          0         @MAX(B11..C1)   @MIN(B11..C11)  0.5*D11+0.5*E11  +$D$2*B11+(1-$D$2)*C11
12
13  Maximax (The highest of the row maximums) =   @MAX(D9..D11)
14  Maximin (The highest of the row minimums) =   @MAX(E9..E11)
15  Equally Likely =                              @MAX(F9..F10)
16  Maximum Criterion of Realism =                @MAX(G9..G11)
17
18
19
20
```

PROGRAM 5.6 Using a Spreadsheet to Compute Minimax

```
           A              B               C              D
 1  Minimax Criterion
 2
 3            States    Favorable    Unfavorable        Maximum
 4         of Nature      Market        Market           in Row
 5
 6    Alternatives
 7
 8  Large Facility          0         180000        @MAX(B8..C8)
 9  Small Facility     100000          20000        @MAX(B9..C9)
10     Do Nothing      200000              0        @MAX(B10..C10)
11
12          Minimax
13  Minimum of Row Maximums                         @MIN(D8..D10)
14
15
16
17
18
19
20
```

6

Decision Trees and Utility Theory

CHAPTER OUTLINE

6.1 Introduction

6.2 Decision Trees

6.3 How Probability Values Are Estimated by Bayesian Analysis

6.4 Utility Theory

6.5 Use of AB:QM in Decision Theory

6.6 Summary

Glossary

Key Equations

Solved Problems

Discussion Questions and Problems

Case Studies:

Black Electronics

Sixty-Six-Year-Old Patient with a Hernia

Bibliography

Appendix: Using Spreadsheets to Solve Decision Tree and Bayesian Analysis Problems

Teaching Suggestion 6.1:
Decision Theory and Life-Time Decisions. See the Instructor's Section for details.

6.1   INTRODUCTION

In the last chapter we saw that problems with just a few alternatives and states of nature could be analyzed by using decision tables. This chapter moves us a step further in exploring decision theory by introducing the topics of decision trees, probability assessment, and utility theory.

Applicable Problems: 6-12, 6-13, 6-14, 6-15, 6-16, 6-18, 6-21, 6-22, 6-32, 6-33, 6-35, Blake Electronics Case, Sixty-Six-Year-Old Patient Case

Transparency Master 6.1:
Fundamentals of Decision Theory.

Teaching Suggestion 6.2:
The Popularity of Decision Trees among Business Executives. See the Instructor's Section for details.

symbols used in decision trees

Transparency Master 6.2:
Analyzing Problems with Decision Trees: The Five Steps.

6.2   DECISION TREES

Any problem that can be presented in a decision table can also be graphically illustrated in a *decision tree*. Let's take another look at the Thompson Lumber Company case first presented in Chapter 5. You may recall that John Thompson was trying to decide whether to expand his operation by building a new plant to produce storage sheds. A simple decision tree to represent John's decision is shown in Figure 6.1. Note that the tree presents the decision and outcomes in a sequential order. First, John decides whether to build a large plant, small plant, or no plant. Then, once that decision is made, the possible states of nature or outcomes (favorable or unfavorable market) will occur.

All decision trees are similar in that they contain *decision points* or *nodes* and *state of nature points* or *nodes*. These symbols are:

☐   A decision node from which one of several alternatives may be chosen.

○   A state of nature node out of which one state of nature will occur.

Analyzing problems with decision trees involves five steps:

1. Define the problem.
2. Structure or draw the decision tree.

Transparency Master 6.3:
Thompson's Decision Tree.

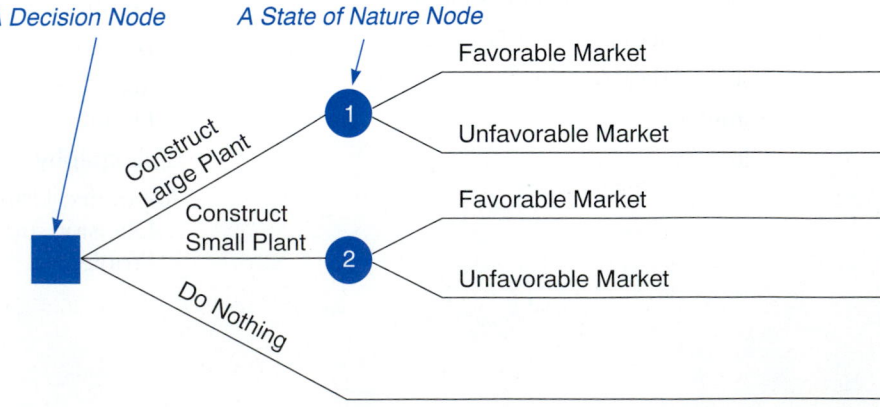

FIGURE 6.1
Thompson's Decision Tree

3. Assign probabilities to the states of nature.

4. Estimate payoffs for each possible combination of alternatives and states of nature.

5. Solve the problem by computing expected monetary values (EMVs) for each state of nature node. This is done by working backward, that is, starting at the right of the tree and working back to decision nodes on the left.

A completed and solved decision tree for Thompson Lumber is presented in Figure 6.2. Note that the payoffs are placed at the right side of each of the tree's branches. The probabilities (first used by Thompson in Chapter 5) are placed in parentheses next to each state of nature. The expected monetary values for each state of nature node are then calculated and placed by their respective nodes. The EMV of the first node is $10,000. This represents the branch from the decision node to construct a large plant. The EMV for node 2, to construct a small plant, is $40,000. Building no plant or doing nothing has, of course, a payoff of $0. The branch leaving the decision node leading to the state of nature node with the highest EMV should be chosen. In Thompson's case, a small plant should be built.

Teaching Suggestion 6.3:
The Importance of Accurate Tree Diagrams. See the Instructor's Section for details.

Alternate Example 6-1

A More Complex Decision for Thompson Lumber

When a *sequence* of decisions needs to be made, decision trees are much more powerful tools than decision tables. Let's say that John Thompson has two decisions to make, with the second decision dependent on the outcome of the first. Before deciding about building a new plant, John has the option

Teaching Suggestion 6.4:
Diagramming a Large Decision Problem Using Branches. See the Instructor's Section for details.

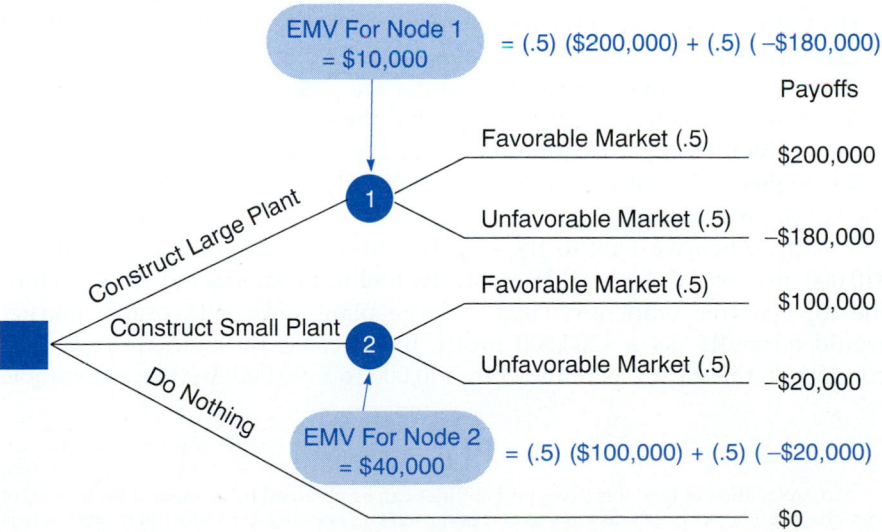

FIGURE 6.2
Completed and Solved Decision Tree for Thompson Lumber

**all outcomes and
alternatives must be
considered**

**first and second decision
points**

conditional probabilities

of conducting his own marketing research survey, at a cost of $10,000. The information from his survey could help him decide whether to build a large plant, a small plant, or not to build at all. John recognizes that such a market survey will not provide him with *perfect* information, but it may help quite a bit nevertheless.

John's new decision tree is represented in Figure 6.3. Let's take a careful look at this more complex tree. Note that *all possible outcomes and alternatives* are included in their logical sequence. This is one of the strengths of using decision trees in making decisions. The user is forced to examine all possible outcomes, including unfavorable ones. He or she is also forced to make decisions in a logical, sequential manner.

Examining the tree, we see that Thompson's first decision point is whether or not to conduct the $10,000 market survey. If he chooses not to do the study (the lower part of the tree), he can either build a large plant, a small plant, or no plant. This is John's second decision point. The market will either be favorable (.50 probability) or unfavorable (also .50 probability) if he builds. The payoffs for each of the possible consequences are listed along the right side. As a matter of fact, the lower portion of John's tree is *identical* to the simpler decision tree shown in Figure 6.2. Why is this so?

The upper part of Figure 6.3 reflects the decision to conduct the market survey. State of nature node number 1 has two branches coming out of it. There is a 45% chance that the survey results will indicate a favorable market for storage sheds. We also note that the probability is .55 that the survey results will be negative.[1]

The rest of the probabilities shown in parenthesis in Figure 6.3 are all *conditional probabilities*.[2] For example, .78 is the probability of a favorable market for the sheds given a favorable result from the market survey. Of course, you would expect to find a high probability of a favorable market given that the research indicated that the market was good. Don't forget, though, there is a chance that John's $10,000 market survey didn't result in perfect or even reliable information. Any market research study is subject to error. In this case, there's a 22% chance that the market for sheds will be unfavorable given that the survey results are positive.

We note that there is a 27% chance that the market for sheds will be favorable given that John's survey results are negative. The probability is much higher, .73, that the market will actually be unfavorable given that the survey was negative.

Finally, when we look to the payoff column in Figure 6.3, we see that $10,000, the cost of the marketing study, had to be subtracted from each of the top ten tree branches. Thus, a large plant with a favorable market would normally net a $200,000 profit. But because the market study was conducted, this figure is reduced by $10,000 to $190,000. In the unfavorable

---

[1]An explanation of how these two probabilities can be obtained is the topic of Section 6.3 of this chapter. For now, let's assume that Thompson's experience provides them and accept them as reasonable.

[2]The derivation of these probabilities (.78, .22, .27, and .73) is also discussed in the next section.

First Decision
Point

Second Decision
Point

Payoffs

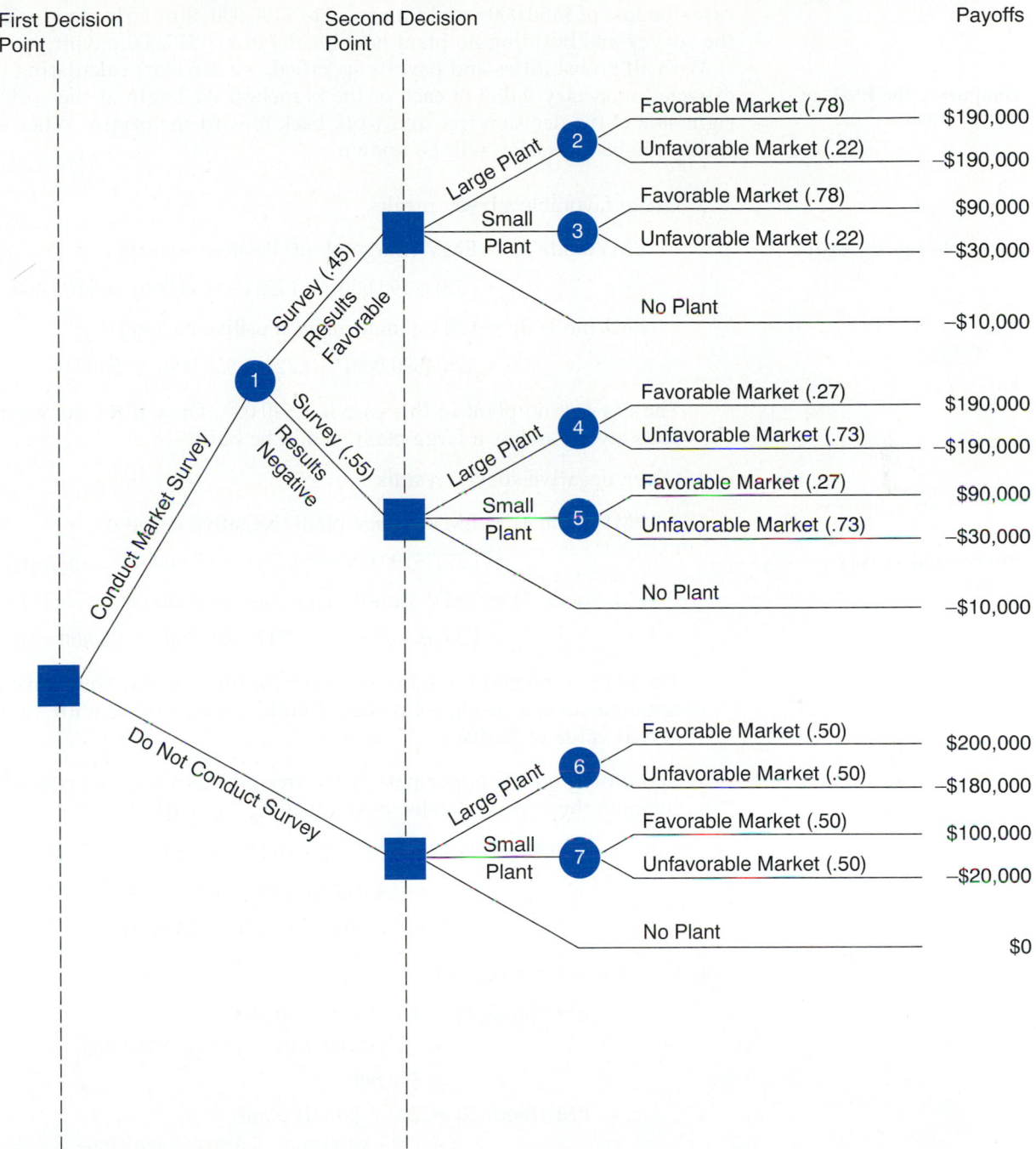

FIGURE 6.3
**Larger Decision Tree with Payoffs and Probabilities
for Thompson Lumber**

computing the EMV of each branch

case, the loss of $180,000 would increase to $190,000. Similarly, conducting the survey and building no plant now results in a −$10,000 payoff.

With all probabilities and payoffs specified, we can start calculating the expected monetary value of each of the branches. We begin at the end, or right side of the decision tree and work back toward the origin. When we finish, the best decision will be known.

1. Given favorable survey results,

favorable survey results

$$\text{EMV(node 2)} = \text{EMV (Large plant} | \text{Positive survey)}$$
$$= (.78)\ (\$190,000) + (.22)\ (-\$190,000) = \$106,400$$

$$\text{EMV(node 3)} = \text{EMV (Small plant} | \text{Positive survey)}$$
$$= (.78)\ (\$90,000) + (.22)\ (-\$30,000) = \$63,500$$

The EMV of no plant in this case is −$10,000. Thus, if the survey results are favorable, a large plant should be built.

2. Given negative survey results,

$$\text{EMV(node 4)} = \text{EMV (Large plant} | \text{Negative survey)}$$

unfavorable survey results

$$= (.27)\ (\$190,000) + (.73)\ (-\$190,000) = -\$87,400$$

$$\text{EMV(node 5)} = \text{EMV (Small plant} | \text{Negative survey)}$$
$$= (.27)\ (\$90,000) + (.73)\ (-\$30,000) = \$2,400$$

The EMV of no plant is again −$10,000 for this branch. Thus, given a negative survey result, John should build a small plant with an expected value of $2,400.

3. Continuing on the upper part of the tree and moving backward, we compute the expected value of conducting the market survey.

$$\text{EMV(node 1)} = \text{EMV (Conduct survey)}$$
$$= (.45)\ (\$106,400) + (.55)\ (\$2,400)$$
$$= \$47,880 + \$1,320 = \$49,200$$

4. If the market survey is *not* conducted,

$$\text{EMV(node 6)} = \text{EMV (Large plant)}$$
$$= (.50)\ (\$200,000) + (.50)\ (-\$180,000)$$
$$= \$10,000$$

$$\text{EMV(node 7)} = \text{EMV (Small plant)}$$
$$= (.50)\ (\$100,000) + (.50)\ (-\$20,000)$$
$$= \$40,000$$

The EMV of no plant is $0.

Thus, building a small plant is the best choice, given the marketing research is not performed.

5. Since the expected monetary value of conducting the survey is $49,200, versus an EMV of $40,000 for not conducting the study, the

best choice is to *seek* marketing information. If the survey results are favorable, John should build the large plant; but if the research is negative, John should build the small plant.

In Figure 6.4, these expected values are placed on the decision tree. Notice on the tree that a pair of slash lines // through a decision

Transparency Master 6.4:
Figure 6.4 A Decision Involving Conducting a Market Survey.

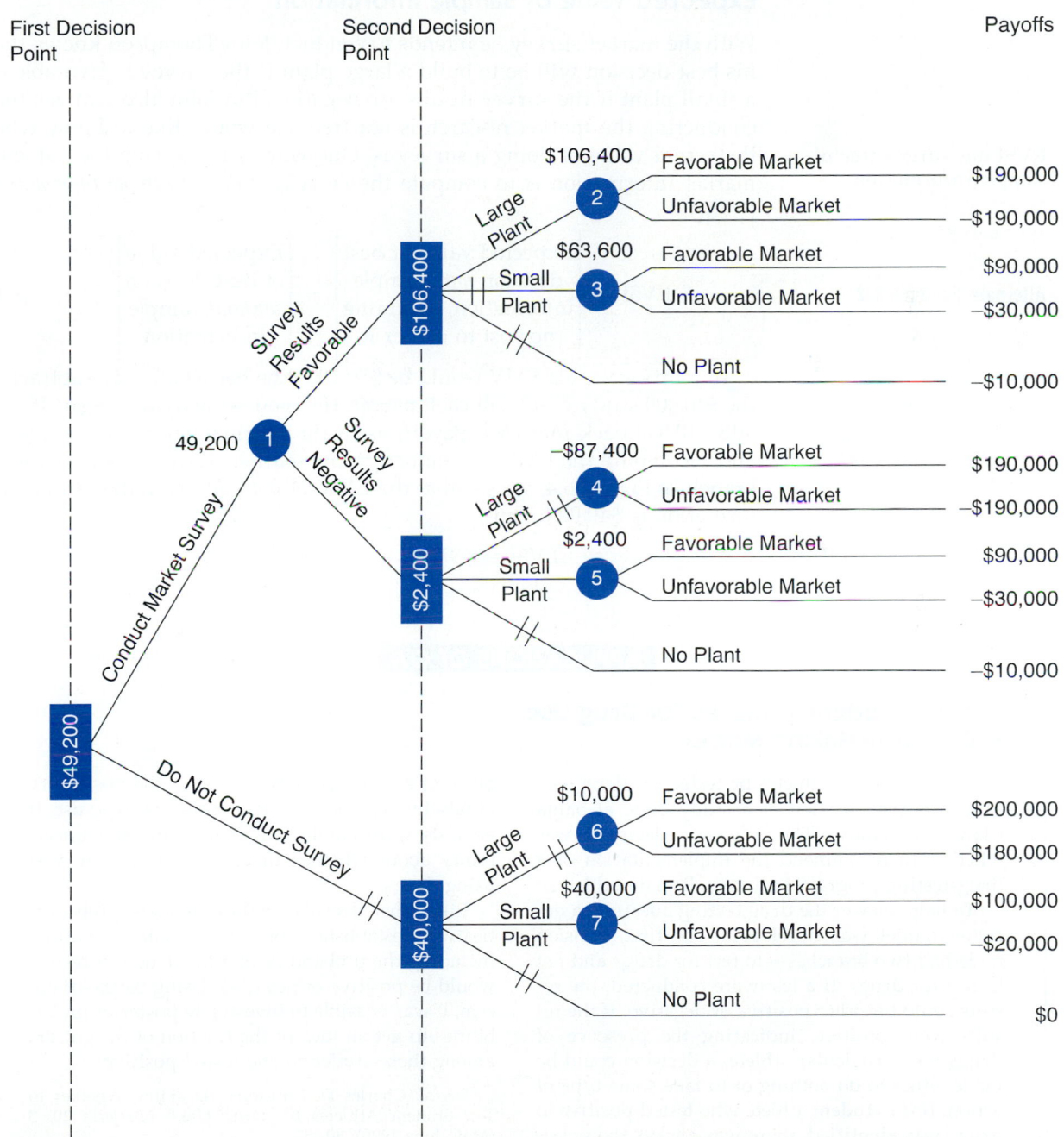

FIGURE 6.4
Thompson's Decision Tree with EMVs Shown

eliminating alternatives   branch indicates that a particular alternative is dropped from further consideration. This is because its EMV is lower than the best alternative. Once you have solved several decision tree problems, you may find it easier to do all of your computations on the tree diagram.

Expected Value of Sample Information

EVSI measures value of sample information

With the market survey he intends to conduct, John Thompson knows that his best decision will be to build a large plant if the survey is favorable or a small plant if the survey results are negative. But John also realizes that conducting the market research is not free. He would like to know what the actual value of doing a survey is. One way of measuring the value of market information is to compute the *expected value of sample information* (EVSI).

Alternate Example 6.2

$$\text{EVSI} = \begin{bmatrix} \text{Expected value of best} \\ \text{decision } with \text{ sample} \\ \text{information, assuming} \\ \text{no cost to gather it} \end{bmatrix} - \begin{bmatrix} \text{Expected value} \\ \text{of best decision} \\ without \text{ sample} \\ \text{information} \end{bmatrix} \qquad (6\text{-}1)$$

In John's case, his EMV would be $59,200 *if* he hadn't already subtracted the $10,000 study cost from each payoff. (Do you see why this is so? If not, add $10,000 back into each payoff, as in the original Thompson problem, and recompute the EMV of conducting the market study.) From the lower branch of Figure 6.4, we see that the EMV of *not* gathering the sample information is $40,000. Thus,

$$\text{EVSI} = \$59,200 - \$40,000 = \$19,200$$

APPLICATIONS OF QA

Testing Student Athletes for Drug Use: A Decision-Making Model

Should student athletes be tested for drug use? This was the question of a study done at Santa Clara University. The primary decision was whether to recommend the implementation of a drug-testing program for intercollegiate athletes.

To help answer the drug testing question, a decision model was developed. The first decision node had two branches—to test for drugs and not to test for drugs. If a test were conducted, the results could be either positive or negative. If the results were positive, indicating the presence of drugs for a particular athlete, a decision could be made either to do nothing or to take some type of action. If the student athlete who tested positive to drugs was identified, there was always the possi-

bility of a false accusation, that is, the possibility of falsely accusing a student athlete of drug use. If no tests were conducted, there remained uncertainty about whether the particular athlete was using drugs.

Like other decision-making models, probabilities were established for various states of nature, including the probability that the drug test results would be positive or negative. Using Bayes's theorem, it was possible to investigate posterior probabilities to get an idea of the fraction of drug users among those students who tested positive.

Source: Charles D. Feinstein, "Deciding Whether to Test Student Athletes for Drug Use," *Interfaces* **20**, 3 (May–June 1990): 80–87.

This means that John could have paid up to $19,200 for a market study and still come out ahead. Since it costs only $10,000, the survey is indeed worthwhile.

6.3 HOW PROBABILITY VALUES ARE ESTIMATED BY BAYESIAN ANALYSIS

Applicable Problems: 6-17, 6-19, 6-20, 6-22, 6-27, 6-33, Blake Electronic Case

There are many ways of getting probability data for a problem such as Thompson's. The numbers (such as .78, .22, .27, .73 in Figure 6.3) can be assessed by a manager based on experience and intuition. They can be derived from historical data, or they can be computed from other available data using Bayes's theorem. We discuss this last option in this section.

The Bayes's theorem approach recognizes that a decision maker does not know with certainty what state of nature will occur. It allows the manager to revise his or her initial or prior probability assessments. The revised probabilities are called *posterior probabilities*. (Before continuing, you may wish to review Bayes's theorem in Chapter 2.)

Teaching Suggestion 6.5: Using Tables to Perform Bayesian Analysis. See the Instructor's Section for details.

 KEY IDEA

Calculating Revised Probabilities

In the Thompson Lumber case solved in Section 6.2, we made the assumption that the following four conditional probabilities were known:

$$P(\text{Favorable market(FM)}|\text{Survey results positive}) = .78$$

$$P(\text{Unfavorable market(UM)}|\text{Survey results positive}) = .22$$

$$P(\text{Favorable market(FM)}|\text{Survey results negative}) = .27$$

$$P(\text{Unfavorable market(UM)}|\text{Survey results negative} = .73$$

We now show how John Thompson was able to derive these values with Bayes's theorem.

From discussions with market research specialists at the local university, John knows that special surveys such as his can either be positive (that is, predict a favorable market) or be negative (predict an unfavorable market). The experts have told John that, statistically, of all new *favorable market* (FM) products, market surveys were positive and correctly predicted success 70% of the time. Thirty percent of the time the surveys falsely predicted negative results or an *unfavorable market* (UM). On the other hand, when there was actually an unfavorable market for a new product, 80% of the surveys correctly predicted negative results. The surveys incorrectly predicted positive results the remaining 20% of the time. These conditional probabilities are summarized in Table 6.1. They are an indication of the accuracy of the survey that John is thinking of undertaking.

Recall that without any market survey information, John's best estimates of a favorable and unfavorable market are:

$$P(\text{FM}) = .50$$

$$P(\text{UM}) = .50$$

These are referred to as the prior probabilities.

Alternate Example 6.3

deriving conditional probabilities

TABLE 6.1 Market Survey Reliability in Predicting Actual States of Nature

	ACTUAL STATES OF NATURE	
RESULTS OF SURVEY	FAVORABLE MARKET (FM)	UNFAVORABLE MARKET (UM)
Positive (predicts favorable market for product)	P(Survey positive|FM) = .70	P(Survey positive|UM) = .20
Negative (predicts unfavorable market for product)	P(Survey negative|FM) = .30	P(Survey negative|UM) = .80

We are now ready to compute Thompson's revised or posterior probabilities. These desired probabilities are the reverse of the probabilities in Table 6.1. We need the probability of a favorable or unfavorable market given a positive or negative result from the market study. The general form of Bayes's theorem presented in Chapter 2 was:

$$P(A \mid B) = \frac{P(B \mid A) \cdot P(A)}{P(B \mid A) \cdot P(A) + P(B \mid \overline{A}) \cdot P(\overline{A})} \qquad \textbf{(6-2)}$$

where

$$A, B = \text{any two events, and}$$

$$\overline{A} = \text{the complement of } A.$$

Substituting the appropriate numbers into this equation, we obtain the conditional probabilities, given that the market survey is positive:

P(FM\|Survey positive)

$$= \frac{P(\text{Survey positive} \mid \text{FM}) \cdot P(\text{FM})}{P(\text{Survey positive} \mid \text{FM}) \cdot P(\text{FM}) + P(\text{Survey positive} \mid \text{UM}) \cdot P(\text{UM})}$$

$$= \frac{(.70)(.50)}{(.70)(.50) + (.20)(.50)} = \frac{.35}{.45} = .78$$

P(UM\|Survey positive)

$$= \frac{P(\text{Survey positive} \mid \text{UM}) \cdot P(\text{UM})}{P(\text{Survey positive} \mid \text{UM}) \cdot P(\text{UM}) + P(\text{Survey positive} \mid \text{FM}) \cdot P(\text{FM})}$$

$$= \frac{(.20)(.50)}{(.20)(.50) + (.70)(.50)} = \frac{.10}{.45} = .22$$

An alternative method for these calculations is to use a probability table as shown in Table 6.2.

The conditional probabilities, given the market survey is negative, are:

P(FM\|Survey negative)

$$= \frac{P(\text{Survey negative} \mid \text{FM}) \cdot P(\text{FM})}{P(\text{Survey negative} \mid \text{FM}) \cdot P(\text{FM}) + P(\text{Survey negative} \mid \text{UM}) \cdot P(\text{UM})}$$

$$= \frac{(.30)(.50)}{(.30)(.50) + (.80)(.50)} = \frac{.15}{.55} = .27$$

TABLE 6.2 Probability Revisions Given a Positive Survey

STATE OF NATURE	CONDITIONAL PROBABILITIES P(SURVEY POSITIVE | STATE OF NATURE)		PRIOR PROBABILITIES		JOINT PROBABILITIES		POSTERIOR PROBABILITIES $P\left(\dfrac{\text{STATE OF}}{\text{NATURE}} \middle\vert \dfrac{\text{SURVEY}}{\text{POSITIVE}}\right)$
FM	.70	×	.50	=	.35	$\dfrac{.35}{.45}$ =	.78
UM	.20	×	.50	=	.10	$\dfrac{.10}{.45}$ =	.22
		P(Survey results positive) =			.45		1.00

$P(\text{UM} \mid \text{Survey negative})$

$$= \frac{P(\text{Survey negative} \mid \text{UM}) \cdot P(\text{UM})}{P(\text{Survey negative} \mid \text{UM}) \cdot P(\text{UM}) + P(\text{Survey negative} \mid \text{FM}) \cdot P(\text{FM})}$$

$$= \frac{(.80)(.50)}{(.80)(.50) + (.30)(.50)} = \frac{.40}{.55} = .73$$

These computations could have been performed in a table instead, as in Table 6.3.

The posterior probabilities now provide John Thompson with estimates of each state of nature if the survey results are positive or negative. As you know, John's *prior probability* of success without a market survey was only .50. Now he is aware that the probability of successfully marketing storage sheds will be .78 if his survey shows positive results. His chances of success drop to 27% if the survey report is negative. This is valuable management information, as we saw in the earlier decision tree analysis.

new probabilities provide valuable information

A Potential Problem in Using Survey Results

In many decision-making problems, survey results or pilot studies are done before an actual decision (such as building a new plant or taking a particular course of action) is made. As discussed earlier in this section, Bayes's analysis is used to help determine the correct conditional probabilities that are needed to solve these types of decision theory problems. In computing these conditional probabilities, we need to have data about the

Transparency Master 6.5: Table 6.3 Probability Revisions Given a Negative Survey.

TABLE 6.3 Probability Revisions Given a Negative Survey

STATE OF NATURE	CONDITIONAL PROBABILITIES P(SURVEY NEGATIVE | STATE OF NATURE)		PRIOR PROBABILITIES		JOINT PROBABILITIES		POSTERIOR PROBABILITIES $P\left(\dfrac{\text{STATE OF}}{\text{NATURE}} \middle\vert \dfrac{\text{SURVEY}}{\text{NEGATIVE}}\right)$
FM	.30	×	.50	=	.15	$\dfrac{.15}{.55}$ =	.27
UM	.80	×	.50	=	.40	$\dfrac{.40}{.55}$ =	.73
		P(Survey results negative) =			.55		1.00

APPLICATIONS OF QA

Decision Trees in Selecting Drilling Sites

Where to drill for oil can make the difference between a successful wildcatter and one who goes into bankruptcy. This type of decision can be classified as a decision under uncertainty. In drilling decisions, there can be a large number of alternatives and a large number of possible consequences.

In order to be a successful wildcatter, a tremendous amount of investigation, detailed research, and paperwork has to be done. And perhaps a bit of luck is also needed. After the wildcatter first investigates the potential for oil, he or she must obtain an agreement from the landowner for drilling rights. Then the necessary steps required to place and operate a drilling rig on the land must be taken.

A number of variables must be considered in order to make a good decision. Both seismic and magnetic approaches are used to obtain important geographical information. The location of other oil wells or oil-producing areas is another important factor that must be taken into account. There are important economic and political factors as well—for example, oil prices, tax treatment for drilling for oil, potential inflation, competition, and operating costs.

Two lease areas in Kentucky—Blair East and Blair West—were investigated. Decision tree analysis was used to structure the possible deci-

sion alternatives as well as the states of nature that could result. In this case, the decision was whether or not to drill exploratory wells in either Blair East or Blair West. The decision included the analysis of 74 different possibilities or states of nature. The net present value of the various monetary contributions for the alternatives and possible states of nature were used in picking the best alternative. A contribution was defined as the net cash inflow minus operation expenses.

The decision analysis for this oil exploration decision provided the operator with a valuable decision tool. It allowed the quantification of important variables and a systematic approach to making the best decision. While no monetary savings were reported, the president of the oil company indicated that the use of decision tree analysis was a useful aid in the selection of drilling sites. The president further commented that decision tree analysis provided a systematic way of planning oil exploration decisions and clearer insight into the numerous and varied financial outcomes that are possible for any given alternative.

Source: Jinoos Hosseini, "Decision Analysis and Its Application in the Choice Between Two Wildcat Oil Ventures," *Interfaces* **16**, 2 (March–April 1986): 75–85.

---

surveys and their accuracies. If a decision to build a plant or to take another course of action is actually made, then we can determine the accuracy of our surveys. Unfortunately, we cannot get data about those situations where the decison was not to build a plant or not to take some course of action. Thus, when we use survey results, we are basing our probabilities only on those cases where a decision to build a plant or take some course of action is actually made. This means that conditional probability information is not quite as accurate as we would like. Even so, calculating conditional probabilities helps to refine the decision-making process and, in general, to make better decisions.

6.4   UTILITY THEORY

EMV not always the best approach

So far we have used EMV to make decisions. In practice, however, using EMV could lead to bad decisions in many cases. For example, suppose you are the lucky holder of a lottery ticket. Five minutes from now a fair coin could be flipped, and if it comes up tails, you would win $5 million. If it comes up heads, you would win nothing.

Just a moment ago a wealthy individual offered you $2 million for your ticket. Let's assume you have no doubts about the validity of the offer. The person will give you a certified check for the full amount, and you are absolutely sure the check would be good.

A decision tree is shown in Figure 6.5. EMV indicates you should hold on to your ticket, but what would you do? Just think, $2 million for *sure* instead of a 50% chance at nothing. Suppose you were greedy enough to hold on to the ticket, and then lost. How would you explain that to your friends? Wouldn't $2 million be enough to be comfortable for a while?

Most people would sell for $2 million. Most of us, in fact, would probably be willing to settle for a lot less. Just how low we would go is, of course, a matter of personal preference. People have different feelings about seeking or avoiding risk. EMV is not a good way to make these types of decisions.

One way to incorporate your own attitudes toward risk is through *utility theory*. The next section explores first how to measure utility and then how to use utility measures in decision making.

Measuring Utility and Constructing a Utility Curve

Utility assessment begins by assigning the worst outcome a utility of 0 and the best outcome a utility of 1. All other outcomes will have a utility value between 0 and 1. In determining the utilities of all outcomes, other than the best or worst outcome, a *standard gamble* is considered. This gamble is shown in Figure 6.6.

Applicable Problems: 6-23, 6-24, 6-25, 6-26, 6-28, 6-29, 6-30, 6-31, 6-34

KEY IDEA

determining utility using a standard gamble

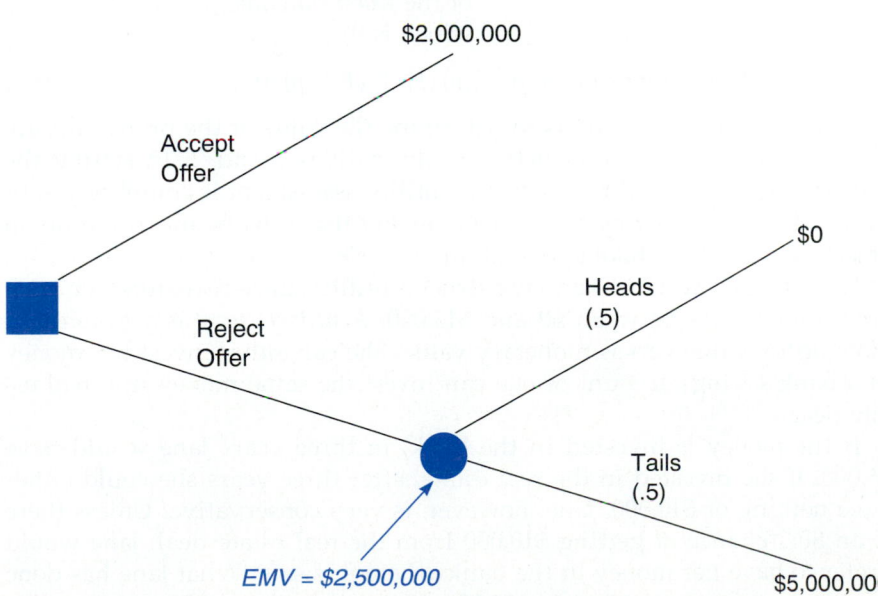

FIGURE 6.5
Your Decision Tree for the Lottery Ticket

Transparency Master 6.6:
Figure 6.6 and 6.7. Standard
Gamble and the Utility
of $5,000.

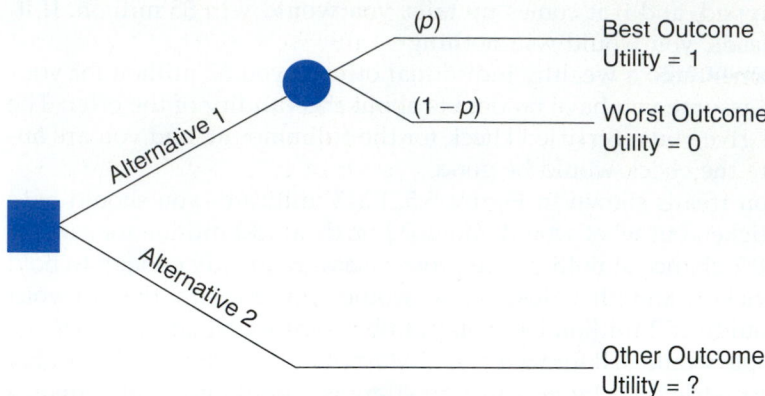

FIGURE 6.6
Standard Gamble for Utility Assessment

determining the
probability, *p*, that
makes you indifferent

In Figure 6.6, *p* is the probability of obtaining the best outcome, and
$(1 - p)$ is the probability of obtaining the worst outcome. Assessing the
utility of any other outcome involves determining the probability, *p*, that
makes you indifferent between alternative 1, which is the gamble between
the best and worst outcome, and alternative 2, which is obtaining the other
outcome for sure. When you are indifferent between alternative 1 and
alternative 2, then the expected utilities for these two alternatives must be
equal. This relationship is shown in Equation 6-3:

Expected utility of alternative 2 = Expected utility of alternative 1

Utility of other outcome = (*p*) (Utility of *best* outcome,
which is 1) + (1 − *p*) (Utility
of the *worst* outcome,
which is 0)

Utility of other outcome = $(p)(1) + (1 - p)(0) = p$　　　　**(6-3)**

Now, all you have to do is to determine the value of the probability (*p*)
that makes you indifferent between alternatives 1 and 2. In setting the
probability, you should be aware that utility assessment is completely subjective. It's a value set by the decision maker that can't be measured on an
objective scale. Let's take a look at an example.

Jane Dickson would like to construct a utility curve revealing her preference for money between $0 and $10,000. A *utility curve* is a graph that
plots utility value versus monetary value. She can either invest her money
in a bank savings account or she can invest the same money in a real estate deal.

If the money is invested in the bank, in three years Jane would have
$5,000. If she invested in the real estate, after three years she could either
have nothing or $10,000. Jane, however, is very conservative. Unless there
is an 80% chance of getting $10,000 from the real estate deal, Jane would
prefer to have her money in the bank where it is safe. What Jane has done
here is to assess her utility for $5,000. When there is an 80% chance (this
means that *p* is .8) of getting $10,000, Jane is indifferent between putting

her money in real estate or putting it in the bank. Jane's utility for $5,000 is thus equal to .8, which is the same as the value for p. This utility assessment is shown in Figure 6.7.

Other utility values can be assessed in the same way. For example, what is Jane's utility for $7,000? What value of p would make Jane indifferent between $7,000 and the gamble that would result in either $10,000 or $0? For Jane, there must be a 90% chance of getting the $10,000. Otherwise, she would prefer the $7,000 for sure. Thus, her utility for $7,000 is .90. Jane's utility for $3,000 can be determined in the same way. If there were a 50% chance of obtaining the $10,000, Jane would be indifferent between having $3,000 for sure and taking the gamble of either winning the $10,000 or getting nothing. Thus, the utility of $3,000 for Jane is .5. Of course, this process can be continued until Jane has assessed her utility for as many monetary values as she wants. These assessments, however, are enough to get an idea of Jane's feelings toward risk. In fact, we can plot these points in a *utility curve*, as was done in Figure 6.8. In the figure, the assessed utility points of $3,000, $5,000, and $7,000 are shown by dots, and the rest of the curve is eyeballed in.

Jane's utility curve is typical of a *risk avoider*. A risk avoider is a decision maker who gets less utility or pleasure from a greater risk and tends to avoid situations in which high losses might occur. As monetary value increases on her utility curve, the utility increases at a slower rate.

Figure 6.9 illustrates that an individual who is a *risk seeker* has an opposite shaped utility curve. This decision maker gets more utility from a greater risk and higher potential payoff. As monetary value increases on his or her utility curve, the utility increases at an increasing rate. A person who is *indifferent* to risk has a utility curve that is a straight line.

The shape of a person's utility curve depends on the specific decision being considered, the person's psychological frame of mind, and how the

determining other utility values

constructing a utility curve

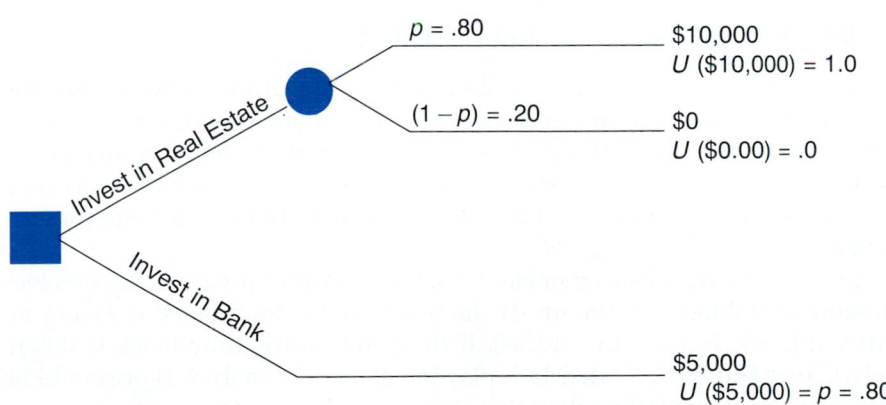

Utility for $5,000 $= U$ ($5,000) $= pU$ ($10,000) $+ (1 - p) U$ ($0) $= (.8)(1) + (.2)(0) = .8$

FIGURE 6.7
Utility of $5,000

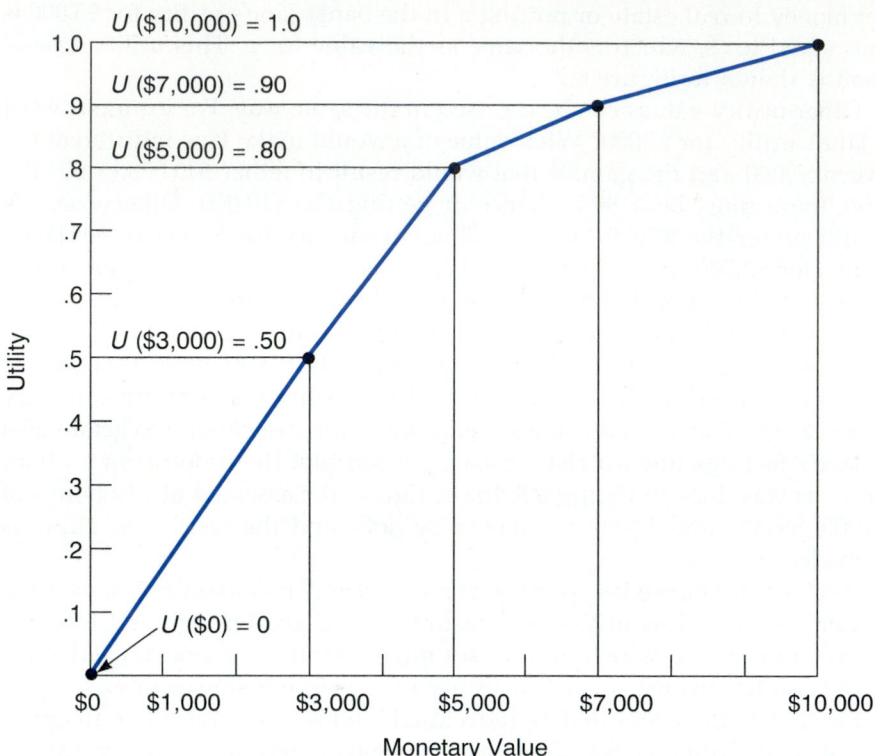

Transparency Master 6.7:
Figure 6.8 Utility Curve for
Jane Dickson.

FIGURE 6.8
Utility Curves for Jane Dickson

person feels about the future. It may well be that you have one utility curve for some situations you face and completely different curves for others.

Utility as a Decision-Making Criterion

utility values replacing monetary values

After a utility curve has been determined, the utility values from the curve are used in making decisions. Monetary outcomes or values are replaced with the appropriate utility values and then decision analysis is performed as usual. Let's take a look at an example in which a decision tree is used and expected utility values are computed in selecting the best alternative.

Alternate Example 6.4

Mark Simkin loves to gamble. He decides to play a game that involves tossing thumbtacks in the air. If the point on the thumbtack is facing up after it lands, Mark wins $10,000. If the point on the thumbtack is down, Mark loses $10,000. Should Mark play the game (alternative 1) or should he not play the game (alternative 2)?

Alternatives 1 and 2 are displayed in the tree shown in Figure 6.10. As can be seen, alternative 1 is to play the game. Mark believes that there is a 45% chance of winning $10,000 and a 55% chance of suffering the $10,000 loss. Alternative 2 is not to gamble. What should Mark do? Of course, this depends on Mark's utility for money. As previously stated, he likes to

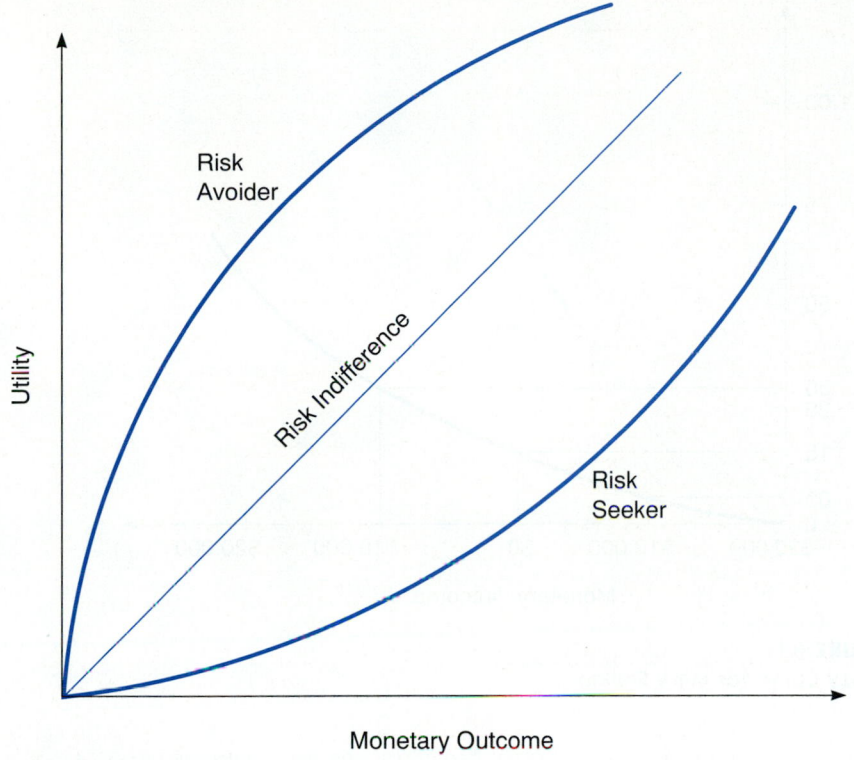

Transparency Master 6.8:
Figure 6.9 Preferences for Risk.

FIGURE 6.9
Preferences for Risk

gamble. Using the procedure just outlined, Mark was able to construct a utility curve showing his preference for money. This curve appears in Figure 6.11.

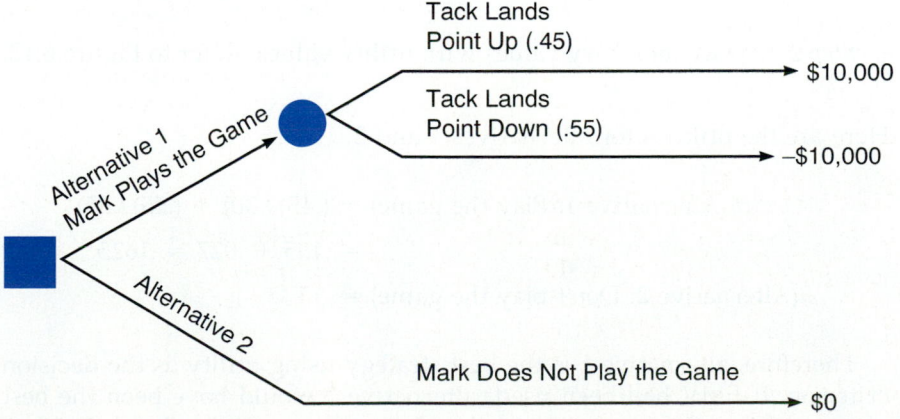

FIGURE 6.10
Decision Facing Mark Simkin

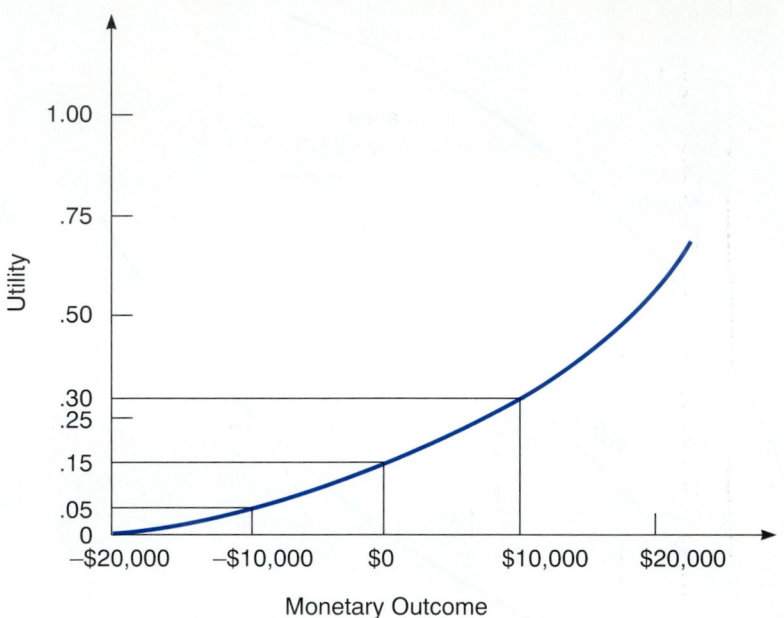

FIGURE 6.11
Utility Curve for Mark Simkin

We see that Mark's utility for −$10,000 is .05, his utility for not playing ($0) is .15, and his utility for $10,000 is .30. These values can now be used in the decision tree. Mark's objective is to maximize his expected utility, which can be done as follows:

Step 1.
$$U(-\$10{,}000) = .05$$
$$U(\$0) = .15$$
$$U(\$10{,}000) = .30$$

Step 2. Replace monetary values with utility values. Refer to Figure 6.12.

Here are the utilities for alternatives 1 and 2.

determining expected utility

$$E(\text{Alternative 1: Play the game}) = (.45)(.30) + (.55)(.05)$$
$$= .135 + .027 = .1625$$
$$E(\text{Alternative 2: Don't play the game}) = .15$$

Therefore, alternative 1 is the best strategy using utility as the decision criterion. If EMV had been used, alternative 2 would have been the best strategy. The utility curve is a risk-seeker utility curve, and the choice of playing the game certainly reflects this preference for risk.

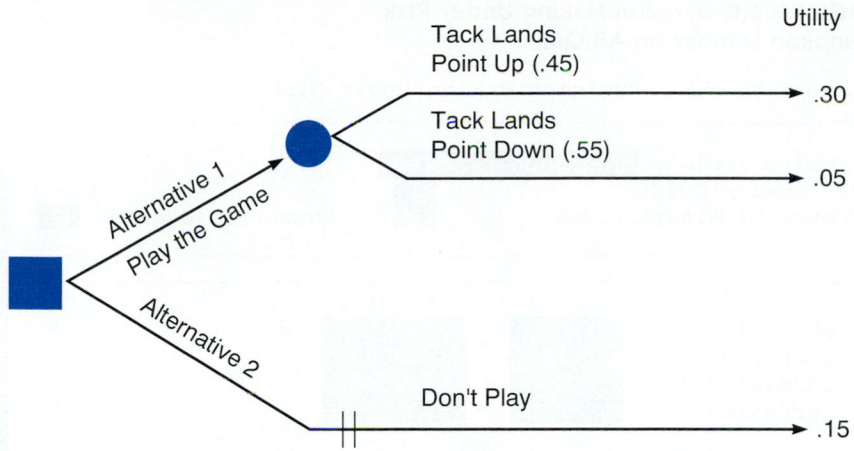

FIGURE 6.12
Using Expected Utilities in Decision Making

6.5 USE OF AB:QM IN DECISION THEORY

We briefly described the use of AB:QM software for decision theory problems in Chapter 5. Let us take a more detailed look at it now.

When the AB:QM decision theory programs start, a submenu will appear on the screen as shown in Program 6.1.

As you can see, we can perform decision making under risk, decision making under uncertainty, decision tree analysis, or analysis using Bayes's decision rule. We will start with decision making under risk. For this application, we can have up to 20 alternatives and 20 states of nature. The basic data entered for the Thompson Lumber Company problem are shown in Program 6.2. Notice that at the top of the screen there are three areas where overall problem data are added. Detailed data are added in the middle area of the screen. The commands discussed in Module F are listed at the bottom.

Once the data have been correctly entered, we can execute, or run, the program and obtain the desired output. Program output for Thompson Lumber is also shown in Program 6.2.

basic capabilities

decision making under risk

PROGRAM 6.1 Decision Theory Submenu for AB:QM

```
           Decision Theory
               Menu
 ┌────────────────────────────────────────┐
 │                                         │
 │    A    Decision Making Under Risk      │
 │    B    Decision Making Under Uncertainty│
 │    C    Decision Tree                   │
 │    D    Bayes's Decision Rule           │
 │  Esc   Back to Main Menu                │
 │                                         │
 └────────────────────────────────────────┘
```

PROGRAM 6.2 Decision Making Under Risk
Thompson Lumber on AB:QM

Decision Theory / Decision Making Under Risk

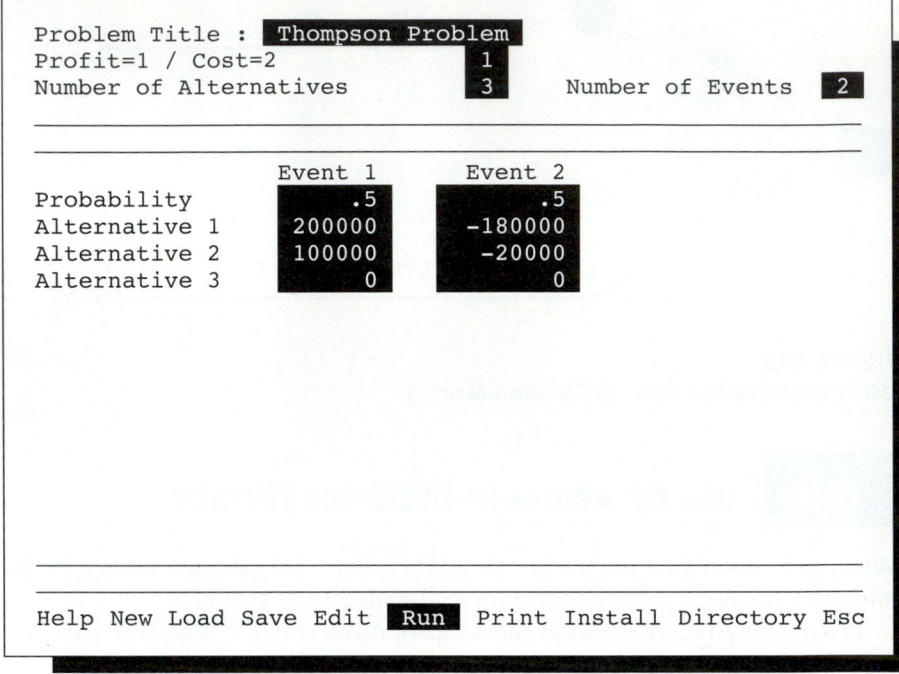

```
Problem Title :  Thompson Problem
Profit=1 / Cost=2                    1
Number of Alternatives              3        Number of Events    2
_____

                        Event 1            Event 2
Probability                 .5                 .5
Alternative 1           200000            -180000
Alternative 2           100000             -20000
Alternative 3                0                  0




_____

        Help New Load Save Edit  Run  Print Install Directory Esc
```

PROGRAM 6.2 output (continued)

Decision Theory / Decision Making Under Risk

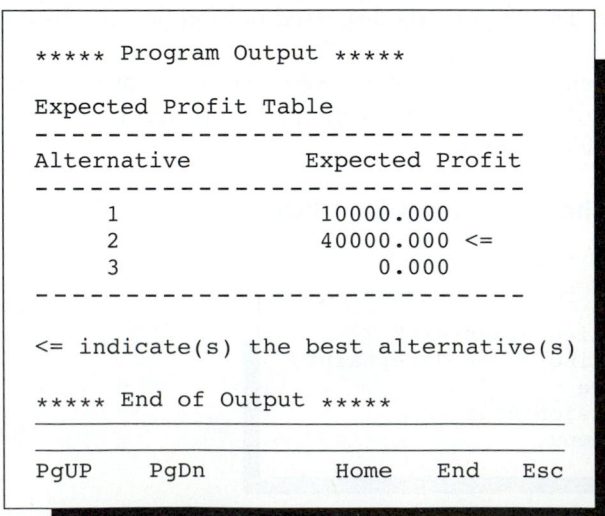

```
***** Program Output *****

Expected Profit Table
-------------------------
Alternative         Expected Profit
-------------------------
     1                  10000.000
     2                  40000.000 <=
     3                      0.000
-------------------------

<= indicate(s) the best alternative(s)

***** End of Output *****
_____

PgUP     PgDn          Home     End     Esc
```

Decision making under uncertainty problems can also be solved using AB:QM. For this decision model, there can be between 2 and 20 alternatives and events, or states of nature. The main difference between the input screen for decision making under risk and decision making under uncertainty is the lack of probability values for the decision making under uncertainty model. The output for the decision making under uncertainty model includes Laplace, maximin, maximax, and Hurwicz solutions. The Laplace solution is the equally likely solution that we discussed in Chapter 5. The Hurwicz solution is equivalent to the coefficient of realism, where a coefficient for α is entered. The input screen and the output for the decision making under uncertainty model are shown in Program 6.3.

decision making under uncertainty

The decision tree program of AB:QM can be used to solve a sequential decision problem. The program can handle between 2 and 50 different branches. In the Thompson Lumber decision problem, we considered a decision to conduct a survey followed by a decision to build or not to build a plant. The upper branch of the decision problem was to build a large plant, a small plant, or no plant at all (given a favorable result from the market survey). The expected monetary value for this situation, given a positive survey result, was $106,400. In this section we solve the same decision problem using AB:QM. The input screen for the upper branch of the decision tree and the output from the program are shown in Program 6.4.

decision tree problems

PROGRAM 6.3 **Decision Making Under Uncertainty Example Using AB:QM**

Decision Theory / Decision Making Under Uncertainty

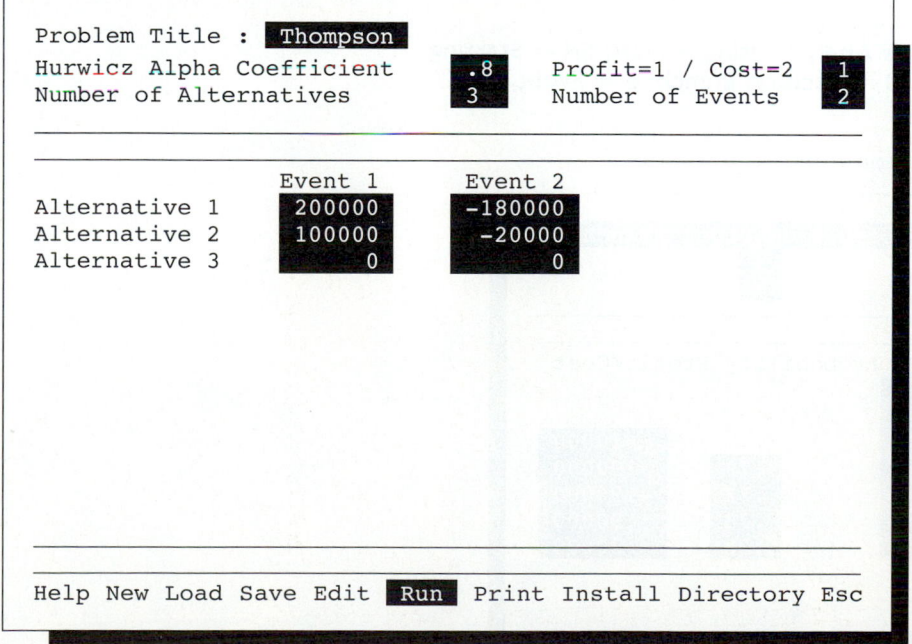

```
Problem Title :  Thompson
Hurwicz Alpha Coefficient      .8     Profit=1 / Cost=2    1
Number of Alternatives          3     Number of Events     2


                  Event 1        Event 2
Alternative 1      200000       -180000
Alternative 2      100000        -20000
Alternative 3           0             0








Help New Load Save Edit  Run  Print Install Directory Esc
```

PROGRAM 6.3 output (continued)

```
***** Program Output *****

Laplace                                  Hurwicz
-----------------------                  -----------------------
Alternative    Expected Value            Alternative    Hurwicz Payoff
-----------------------                  -----------------------
     1           10000.000                    1          12400.000 <=
     2           40000.000 <=                  2          76000.000
     3               0.000                     3              0.000
-----------------------                  -----------------------

Maximin                                  Minimax
-----------------------                  -----------------------
Alternative    Expected Value            Alternative    Maximum Regret
-----------------------                  -----------------------
     1         -180000.000                    1         180000.000
     2          -20000.000                    2         100000.000 <=
     3               0.000 <=                  3         200000.000
-----------------------                  -----------------------

Maximax                                  <= indicate(s) the best alternative(s)
-----------------------                  ***** End of Output *****
Alternative    Maximax Payoff
-----------------------
     1          200000.000 <=
     2          100000.000
     3               0.000
-----------------------
```

PROGRAM 6.4 Decision Tree Analysis Using AB:QM; SN = Starting Node; EN = Ending Node; d = Decision Branch; e = Event, or State-of-Nature Branch

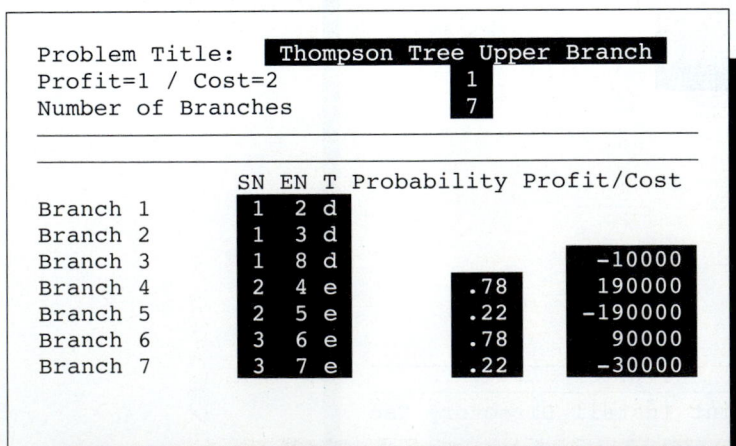

```
Decision Theory / Decision Tree
```

				Probability	Profit/Cost
Problem Title:	Thompson Tree Upper Branch				
Profit=1 / Cost=2	1				
Number of Branches	7				

	SN	EN	T	Probability	Profit/Cost
Branch 1	1	2	d		
Branch 2	1	3	d		
Branch 3	1	8	d		-10000
Branch 4	2	4	e	.78	190000
Branch 5	2	5	e	.22	-190000
Branch 6	3	6	e	.78	90000
Branch 7	3	7	e	.22	-30000

PROGRAM 6.4 output (continued)

```
***** Program Output *****

---------------------------------------------------------
  Nodes        Type      Probability   Payoff   Decision
---------------------------------------------------------
  1 ->  2    Decision      None     106400.000 <=  choice
  1 ->  3    Decision      None      63600.000
  1 ->  8    Decision      None     -10000.000
  2 ->  4    Event        0.780     148200.000
  2 ->  5    Event        0.220     -41800.000
  3 ->  6    Event        0.780      70200.000
  3 ->  7    Event        0.220      -6600.000
---------------------------------------------------------

The conditional payoff of solution :   106400.000

***** End of Output *****
```

Bayes's analysis can also be performed from the AB:QM decision theory submenu. In the Thompson Lumber decision problem, we computed conditional probabilities using Bayes's theorem. Now we make the same calculations using AB:QM, which can handle between 2 and 20 alternatives and events. The data input screen and output for Bayes's program are shown in Program 6.5.

Bayes's analysis

PROGRAM 6.5 The Use of Bayes's Theorem: AB:QM Software

Decision Theory / Bayes's Decision Rule

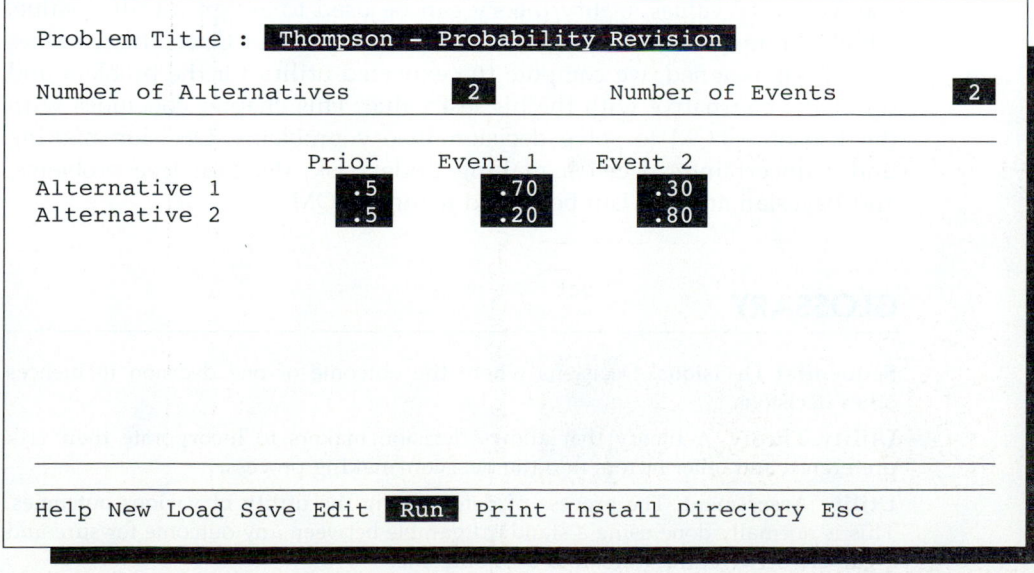

```
Problem Title :  Thompson - Probability Revision

Number of Alternatives        2          Number of Events         2

                      Prior    Event 1    Event 2
Alternative 1          .5        .70        .30
Alternative 2          .5        .20        .80




Help  New  Load  Save  Edit  Run  Print  Install  Directory  Esc
```

PROGRAM 6.5 output (continued)

```
***** Program Output *****

Bayes's Decision Rule
--------------------------------
                    Posterior Probability
--------------------------------
Alternative         Event 1    Event 2
--------------------------------
        1            0.778      0.273
        2            0.222      0.727
--------------------------------


***** End of Output *****
```

6.6   SUMMARY

In this chapter, we investigated a number of decision theory problems. Decision trees are used for larger decision problems, when one decision must be made before other decisions can be made. For example, a decision to take a sample or to perform market research is made before we decide to build a large, small, or no plant. In this case, we can also compute the expected value of sample information (EVSI). Bayesian analysis can be used to revise or update probability values. We can, for example, determine the probability of a favorable market given we have received positive survey results using Bayesian analysis. When it is impossible or inappropriate to use monetary values, utility theory can be used to assign a utility value, which can range from 0 to 1, to each decision outcome. Once utility values have been assigned, we compute the expected utility for the problem and select the alternative with the highest value. This chapter concludes with the use of AB:QM to solve decision theory problems. Decision making under uncertainty, decision making under risk, decision tree problems, and Bayesian analysis can be solved using AB:QM.

GLOSSARY

Sequential Decisions. Decisions where the outcome of one decision influences other decisions.

Utility Theory. A theory that allows decision makers to incorporate their risk preference and other factors into the decision-making process.

Utility Assessment. The process of determining the utility of various outcomes. This is normally done using a standard gamble between any outcome for sure and a gamble between the worst and best outcome.

Utility Curve. A graph or curve that reveals the relationship between utility and monetary values. Once this curve has been constructed, utility values from the curve can be used in the decision-making process.

Risk Avoider. An individual who avoids risk. On the utility curve, as the monetary value increases, the utility increases at a decreasing rate. This decision maker gets less utility for a greater risk and higher potential returns.

Risk Seeker. An individual who seeks risk. On the utility curve, as the monetary value increases, the utility increases at an increasing rate. This decision maker gets more pleasure for a greater risk and higher potential returns.

KEY EQUATIONS

(6-1) Expected value of sample information (EVSI) =

$$\begin{pmatrix} \text{Expected value of best} \\ \text{decision } \textit{with } \text{sample} \\ \text{information} \end{pmatrix} - \begin{pmatrix} \text{Expected value of best} \\ \text{decision } \textit{without} \\ \text{sample information} \end{pmatrix}$$

(6-2) $$P(A \mid B) = \frac{P(B \mid A) \cdot P(A)}{P(B \mid A) \cdot P(A) + P(B \mid \overline{A}) \cdot P(\overline{A})}$$

Bayes's theorem—it yields the conditional value of event A given that event B has occurred.

(6-3) Utility of other outcome $= (p)(1) + (1 - p)(0) = p$
The equation determining the utility of an intermediate outcome.

SOLVED PROBLEMS

Solved Problem 6-1

Monica Britt has enjoyed sailing small boats since she was seven years old when her mother first started sailing with her. Today, Monica is considering the possibility of starting a company to produce small sailboats for the recreational market. Unlike other mass-produced sailboats, however, these boats will be made specifically for children between the ages of 10 and 15. The boats will be of the highest quality, and extremely stable, and the sail size will be reduced to prevent problems of capsizing.

Because of the expense involved in developing the initial molds and acquiring the necessary equipment to produce fiberglass sailboats for young children, Monica has decided to conduct a pilot study to make sure that the market for the sailboats will be adequate. She estimates that the pilot study will cost her $10,000. Furthermore, the pilot study can be either successful or not successful. Her basic decisions are to build a large manufacturing facility, a small manufacturing facility, or no facility at all. With a favorable market, Monica can expect to make $90,000 from the large facility or $60,000 from the smaller facility. If the market is unfavorable, however, Monica estimates that she would lose $30,000 with a large facility, while she would only lose $20,000 with the small facility. Monica estimates that the probability of a favorable market given a successful pilot study is .8. The probability of an unfavorable market given an unsuccessful pilot study result is estimated to be .9. Monica feels that there is a 50-50 chance that the pilot study will be successful. Of course, Monica could bypass the pilot study and simply make the decision as to whether to build a large plant, small plant, or no facility at all. Without doing any testing in a pilot study, she estimates that the probability of a successful market is .6. What do you recommend?

Solution

Before Monica starts to solve this problem, she should develop a decision tree that shows all alternatives, states of nature, probability values, and economic consequences. This decision tree follows:

Once the decision tree has been developed, Monica can solve the problem by computing expected monetary values starting at the end points of

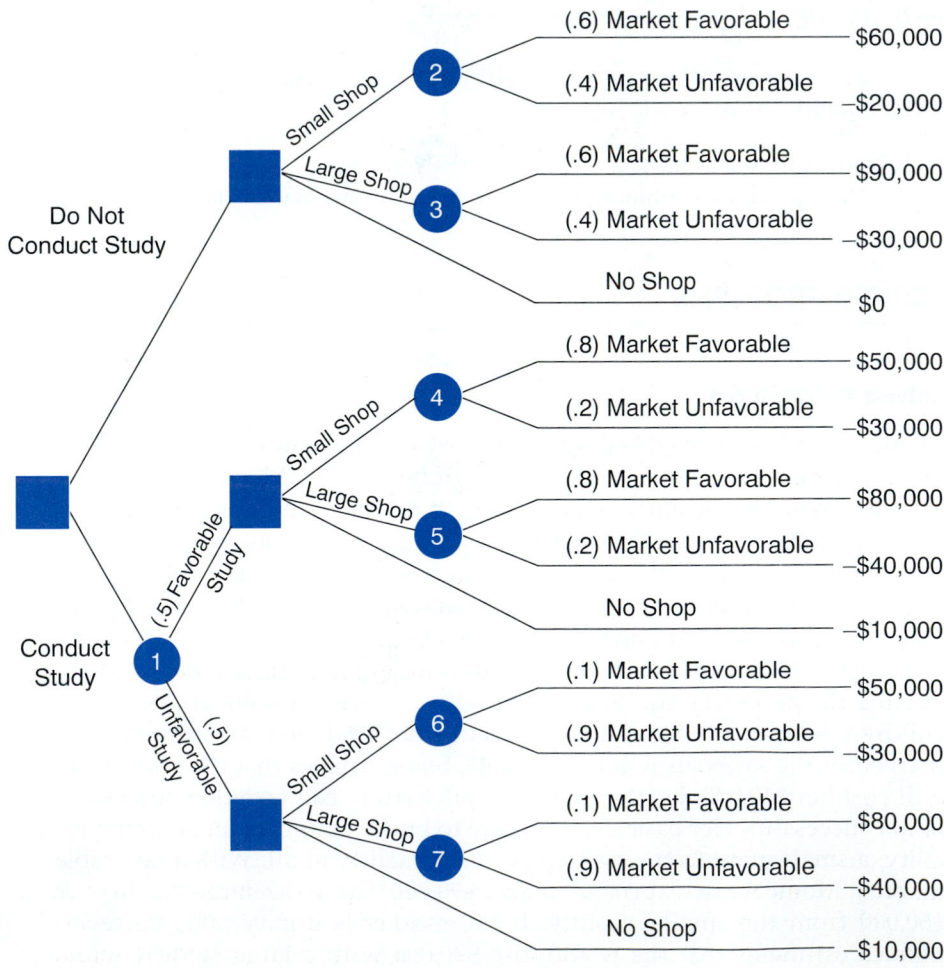

the decision tree. The final solution is shown on the revised decision tree, which follows. The optimal solution is to *not* conduct the study but to construct the large plant directly. The expected monetary value is $42,000.

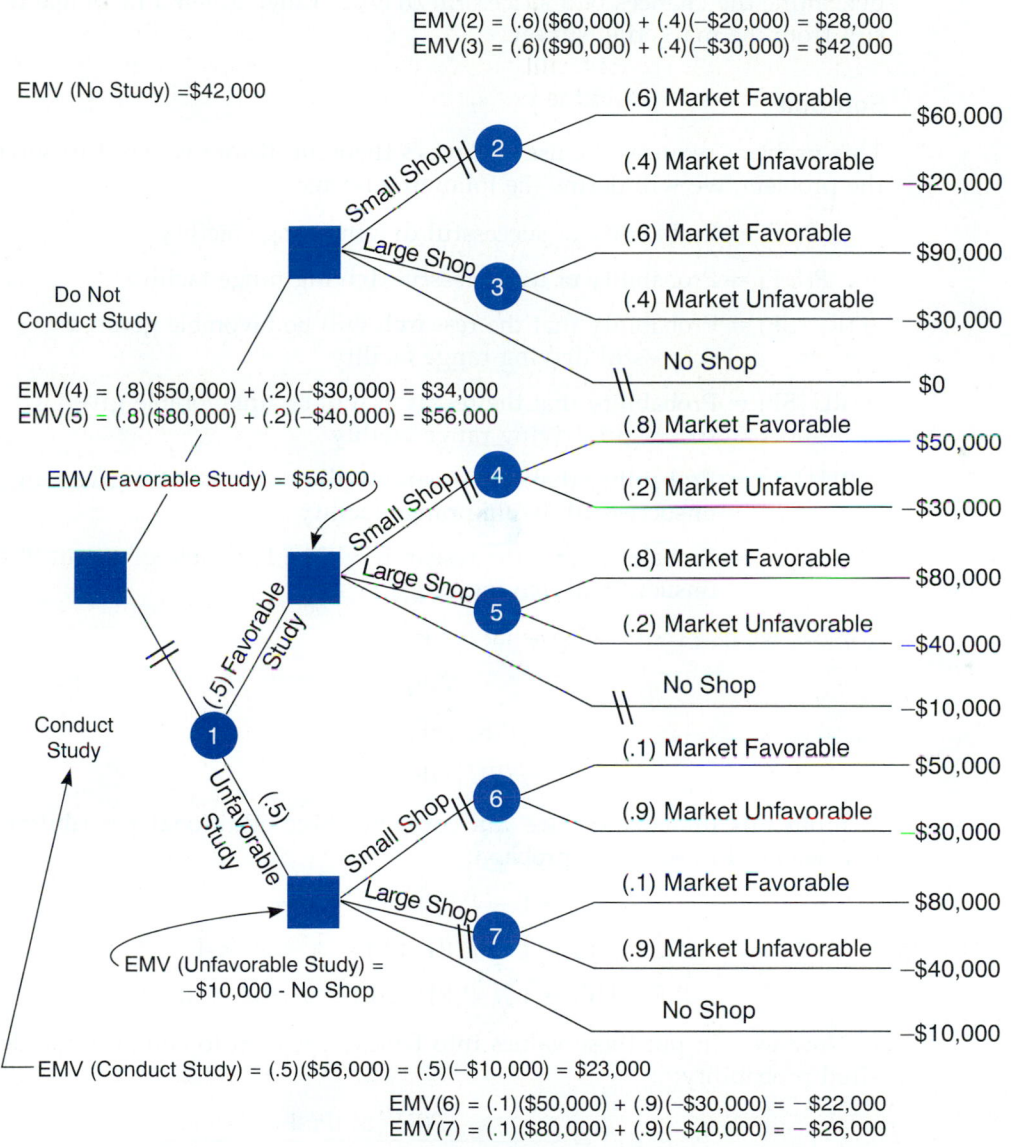

EMV(2) = (.6)($60,000) + (.4)(−$20,000) = $28,000
EMV(3) = (.6)($90,000) + (.4)(−$30,000) = $42,000

EMV (No Study) =$42,000

(.6) Market Favorable — $60,000

Small Shop ‖ ②

(.4) Market Unfavorable — −$20,000

Large Shop ③

(.6) Market Favorable — $90,000

(.4) Market Unfavorable — −$30,000

Do Not
Conduct Study

No Shop ‖ — $0

EMV(4) = (.8)($50,000) + (.2)(−$30,000) = $34,000
EMV(5) = (.8)($80,000) + (.2)(−$40,000) = $56,000

EMV (Favorable Study) = $56,000

Small Shop ‖ ④

(.8) Market Favorable — $50,000

(.2) Market Unfavorable — −$30,000

Large Shop ⑤

(.8) Market Favorable — $80,000

(.2) Market Unfavorable — −$40,000

No Shop ‖ — −$10,000

(.5) Favorable Study

① Conduct Study

(.5) Unfavorable Study

Small Shop ‖ ⑥

(.1) Market Favorable — $50,000

(.9) Market Unfavorable — −$30,000

Large Shop ⑦

(.1) Market Favorable — $80,000

(.9) Market Unfavorable — −$40,000

EMV (Unfavorable Study) =
−$10,000 - No Shop

No Shop — −$10,000

EMV (Conduct Study) = (.5)($56,000) = (.5)(−$10,000) = $23,000

EMV(6) = (.1)($50,000) + (.9)(−$30,000) = −$22,000
EMV(7) = (.1)($80,000) + (.9)(−$40,000) = −$26,000

Best Decision is No Study and Build the Large Plant. The EMV is $42,000

Solved Problem 6-2

Developing a small driving range for golfers of all abilities has long been a desire of John Jenkins. John, however, believes that the chance of a successful driving range is only about 40%. A friend of John's has suggested that he conduct a survey in the community to get a better feeling of the demand for such a facility. There is a .9 probability that the research will be favorable if the driving range facility will be successful. Furthermore, it is estimated that there is a .8 probability that the marketing research will be unfavorable if indeed the facility will be unsuccessful. John would like to determine the chances of a successful driving range given a favorable result from the marketing survey.

Solution

This problem requires the use of Bayes's theorem. Before we start to solve the problem, we will define the following terms:

$P(\text{SF})$ = Probability of successful driving range facility

$P(\text{UF})$ = Probability of unsuccessful driving range facility

$P(\text{RF}\,|\,\text{SF})$ = Probability that the research will be favorable given a successful driving range facility

$P(\text{RU}\,|\,\text{SF})$ = Probability that the research will be unfavorable given a successful driving range facility

$P(\text{RU}\,|\,\text{UF})$ = Probability that the research will be unfavorable given an unsuccessful driving range facility

$P(\text{RF}\,|\,\text{UF})$ = Probability that the research will be favorable given an unsuccessful driving range facility

Now, we can summarize what we know:

$$P(\text{SF}) = .4$$

$$P(\text{RF}\,|\,\text{SF}) = .9$$

$$P(\text{RU}\,|\,\text{UF}) = .8$$

From this information, we can compute three additional probabilities that we need to solve the problem:

$$P(\text{UF}) = 1 - P(\text{SF}) = 1 - .4 = .6$$

$$P(\text{RU}\,|\,\text{SF}) = 1 - P(\text{RF}\,|\,\text{SF}) = 1 - .9 = .1$$

$$P(\text{RF}\,|\,\text{UF}) = 1 - P(\text{RU}\,|\,\text{UF}) = 1 - .8 = .2$$

Now we can put these values into Bayes's theorem to compute the desired probability:

$$P(\text{SF}\,|\,\text{RF}) = \frac{P(\text{RF}\,|\,\text{SF})P(\text{SF})}{P(\text{RF}\,|\,\text{SF})P(\text{SF}) + P(\text{RF}\,|\,\text{UF})P(\text{UF})}$$

$$= \frac{(.9)\,(.4)}{(.9)\,(.4) + (.2)\,(.6)}$$

$$= .36/(.36 + .12) = .36/.48 = .75$$

In addition to using formulas to solve John's problem, it is possible to perform all calculations in a table:

Revised Probabilities Given a Favorable Research Result

STATE OF NATURE	CONDITIONAL PROBABILITY	PRIOR PROBABILITY	JOINT PROBABILITY	POSTERIOR PROBABILITY
Favorable market	.9	.4	.36	.36/.48 = .75
Unfavorable market	.2	.6	.12	.12/.48 = .25
			.48	

As you can see from the table, the results are the same. The probability of a successful driving range given a favorable research result is .36/.48 or .75.

Solved Problem 6-3

Like many students before her, Anne Martin is facing a difficult and important career decision. While at school, Anne worked for a local accounting firm. She did a good job and the firm has given her a standing offer to work for them for $20,000. She can take as much time as she wants to make her decision. There are, however, two other companies that are interested in her. Barnes Accounting has given her an offer of $22,000. Unfortunately, Barnes has given her only two weeks to make a decision. The company that Anne would really like to work for is Ketchum Accounting Services. This company, she feels, may make her an offer of $28,000. Unfortunately, Anne is quite uncertain about whether Ketchum will offer her the position. Thus, Anne has to make a difficult decision. Should she accept the offer from Barnes for $22,000, or should she wait and hope to get the offer from Ketchum? If she waits and doesn't get the offer from Ketchum, she can always go back to her old job for $20,000. The worst situation would be her old job, while the best situation would be the job with Ketchum. For Anne to be indifferent between taking the job with Barnes and the gamble of waiting and trying to get the job with Ketchum, the probability of landing the job at Ketchum would have to be .6. Given this information, what utility should Anne place on the three jobs?

Solution

The problem facing Anne Martin is one of determining utility values. We begin by assigning a utility value of 1 to the best situation, which is obtaining a job from Ketchum. We also assign a utility value of 0 to the worst outcome in this situation, which is keeping the old job. Furthermore, the problem states that the probability for Anne to be indifferent between taking the job with Barnes and taking the gamble of waiting and trying to get the job with Ketchum is .6. This indifference situation can be shown in the following diagram:

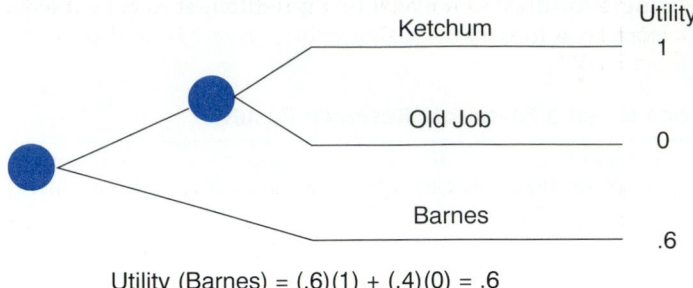

Utility (Barnes) = (.6)(1) + (.4)(0) = .6

Given the information and diagram, Anne can proceed to determine her indifference point. This point is where the utility (U) for getting the job with Barnes is equal to the gamble of getting the job with Ketchum, with a .6 probability, and her old job, with a .4 probability. The appropriate calculations are:

$$U\,(\text{Ketchum}) = 1.0$$

$$U\,(\text{Old Job}) = 0$$

$$U\,(\text{Barnes}) = (.6)U(\text{Ketchum}) + (.4)U(\text{Old Job})$$

$$= (.6)\,(1) + (.4)\,(0) = .6$$

DISCUSSION QUESTIONS AND PROBLEMS

Discussion Questions

6-1 Under what conditions is a decision tree preferable to a decision table?

6-2 What information should be placed on a decision tree?

6-3 Describe how you would determine the best decision using the EMV criterion with a decision tree.

6-4 What is the difference between prior and posterior probabilities?

6-5 What is the purpose of Bayesian analysis? Describe how you would use Bayesian analysis in the decision-making process.

6-6 Discuss some of the problems with using the EMV criterion. Give an example of a situation in which it would be inappropriate.

6-7 What is the overall purpose of utility theory?

6-8 Briefly discuss how a utility function can be assessed. What is a standard gamble, and how is it used in determining utility values?

6-9 How is a utility curve used in selecting the best decision for a particular problem?

6-10 What is a risk seeker? What is a risk avoider? How does the utility curve for these types of decision makers differ?

6-11 Draw a utility curve for a decision maker that is indifferent to risk. If a decision maker is indifferent to risk, will using utility values give a different decision than using EMV?

Problems

· **6-12** A group of medical professionals is considering the construction of a private clinic. If the medical demand is high (that is, there is a favorable market for the clinic), the doctors could realize a net profit of $100,000. If the market is not favorable, they could lose $40,000. Of course, they don't have to proceed at all, in which case there is no cost. In the absence of any market data, the best the doctors can guess is that there is a 50-50 chance the clinic will be successful.

Construct a decision tree to help analyze this problem. What should the medical professionals do?

$30,000 — Construct clinic.

: **6-13** The doctors in Problem 6-12 have been approached by a market research firm that offers to perform a study of the market, at a fee of $5,000. The market researchers claim their experience enables them to use Bayes's theorem to make the following statements of probability:

QA6-13

Probability of a favorable market given a favorable study = .82

Probability of an unfavorable market given a favorable study = .18

Probability of a favorable market given an unfavorable study = .11

Probability of an unfavorable market given an unfavorable study = .89

Probability of a favorable research study = .55

Probability of an unfavorable research study = .45

(a) Develop a new decision tree for the medical professionals to reflect the options now open with the market study.
(b) Use the EMV approach to recommend a strategy.
(c) What is the expected value of sample information? How much might the doctors be willing to pay for a market study?

See Instructor's Section.
$36,140 — Take survey
$11,140

: **6-14** Jerry Young is thinking about opening a bicycle shop in his hometown. Jerry loves to take his own bike on 50-mile trips with his friends, but he believes that any small business should be started only if there is a good chance of making a profit. Jerry can open a small shop, a large shop, or no shop at all. Because there will be a five-year lease on the building that Jerry is thinking about using, he wants to make sure that he makes the correct decision. Jerry is also thinking about hiring his old marketing professor to conduct a marketing research study. If the study is conducted, the results could be either favorable or unfavorable. Develop a decision tree for Jerry.

See Instructor's Section.

: **6-15** Jerry Young (of Problem 6-14) has done some analysis about the profitability of the bicycle shop. If Jerry builds the large bicycle shop, he will earn $60,000 if the market is favorable, but he will lose $40,000 if the market is unfavorable. The small shop will return a $30,000 profit in a favorable market and a $10,000 loss in an unfavorable market. At the present time, he believes that there is a 50-50 chance that the market will be favorable. His old marketing professor will charge him $5,000 for the marketing research. It is estimated that there is a .6 probability that the survey will be favorable. Furthermore, there is a .9

QA6-15

Conduct survey and build large shop if favorable or nothing if not.

probability that the market will be favorable given a favorable outcome from the study. However, the marketing professor has warned Jerry that there is only a probability of .12 of a favorable market if the marketing research results are not favorable. Jerry is confused. What should he do?

6-16 In Problem 6-15, Jerry Young determined whether or not he should seek marketing information from his marketing professor and whether or not he should open a bicycle shop. In this problem, Jerry's marketing professor estimated that there was a .6 probability that the marketing research would be favorable. Jerry, however, is not sure that this probability is correct. How sensitive is Jerry's decision, made in Problem 6-15, to this probability value? How far can this probability value deviate from .6 without causing Jerry to change his decision?

Deviation is −.3.

QA6-17

6-17 Karen Kimp would like to start a small dress shop, but she has decided that it would not work unless the probability of a successful shop (SS) is .6 or greater, or the probability of an unsuccessful shop (US) is .4 or less. At the present time, she believes that the chances of a successful or unsuccessful dress shop are about the same (50%). In today's local paper, there was an article that described a study done on the potential of retail stores, which Karen believed applied to her. She found out that the probability of a favorable study given a successful shop (Favorable study|SS) was .9, and the probability of an unfavorable study given a successful shop (Unfavorable study|SS) was .1. Furthermore, the probability of an unfavorable study given an unsuccessful shop (Unfavorable study|US) was .7, and the probability of a favorable study given an unsuccessful shop (Favorable study|US) was .3. Help Karen by revising the probability that the dress shop will be successful.

P(SS/Successful study) = .75
P(SS/Unsuccessful study = .25

QA6-18

6-18 Bill Holliday is not sure what he should do. He can either build a quadplex (that is, a building with four apartments), a duplex, gather additional information, or simply do nothing. If he gathers additional information, the results could be either favorable or unfavorable, but it would cost him $3,000 to gather the information. Bill believes that there is a 50-50 chance that the information will be favorable. If the rental market is favorable, Bill will earn $15,000 with the quadplex or $5,000 with the duplex. Bill doesn't have the financial resources to do both. With an unfavorable rental market, however, Bill could lose $20,000 with the quadplex or $10,000 with the duplex. Without gathering additional information, Bill estimates that the probability of a favorable rental market is .7. A favorable report from the study would increase the probability of a favorable rental market to .9. Furthermore, an unfavorable report from the additional information would decrease the probability of a favorable rental market to .4. Of course, Bill could forget all of these numbers and do nothing. What is your advice to Bill?

No information and build quadplex − $4,500

QA6-19

6-19 Before the marketing research was done, Peter Martin believed that there was a 50-50 chance that his brother's food store would be a success. The research team determined that there is a .8 probability that the marketing research will be favorable given a successful food store. Moreover, there is a .7 probability that the marketing research will be unfavorable given an unsuccessful food store. This information is based on past experience.

(a) If the marketing research is favorable, what is Peter's revised probability of a successful food store for his brother?

.73

(b) If the marketing research is unfavorable, what is Peter's revised probability of a successful food store for his brother?

.22

⌐ : **6-20** Mark Martinko has been a class A racquetball player for the last five years, and one of his biggest goals is to own and operate a racquetball facility. Unfortunately, Mark thinks that the chance of a successful racquetball facility is only 30%. Mark's lawyer has recommended that he employ one of the local marketing research groups to conduct a survey concerning the success or failure of a racquetball facility. There is a .8 probability that the research will be favorable given a successful racquetball facility. In addition, there is a .7 probability that the research will be unfavorable given an unsuccessful facility.

QA6-20

    (a) Compute revised probabilities of a successful racquetball facility given a favorable and an unfavorable survey using the equations presented in this chapter.

       .53 and .11

    (b) Compute revised probabilities of a successful racquetball facility given a favorable and an unfavorable survey using tables to make your computations.

       .53 and .11

⌐ : **6-21** Kuality Komponents buys on-off switches from two suppliers. The quality of the switches from the suppliers is indicated below:

QA6-21

PERCENT DEFECTIVE	PROBABILITY FOR SUPPLIER A	PROBABILITY FOR SUPPLIER B
1	.70	.30
3	.20	.40
5	.10	.30

For example, the probability of getting a batch of switches that are 1% defective from supplier A is .70. Since Kuality Komponents orders 10,000 switches per order, this would mean that there is a .7 probability of getting 100 defective switches out of the 10,000 switches if supplier A is used to fill the order. A defective switch can be repaired for 50¢. Although the quality of supplier B is lower, it will sell an order of 10,000 switches for $37 less than supplier A.

    (a) Develop a decision tree.
    (b) Which supplier should Kuality Komponents use?

       See Instructor's Section.
       Supplier A

    (c) For how much less would supplier B have to sell an order of 10,000 switches than supplier A for Kuality Komponents to be indifferent between the two suppliers?

       $60

⌐ : **6-22** Jim Sellers is thinking about producing a new type of electric razor for men. If the market were favorable, he would get a return of $100,000, but if the market for this new type of razor were unfavorable, he would lose $60,000. Since Ron Bush is a good friend of Jim Sellers, Jim is considering the possibility of using Bush Marketing Research to gather additional information about the market for the razor. Bush has suggested that Jim either use a survey or a pilot study to test the market. The survey would be a sophisticated questionnaire administered to a test market. It will cost $5,000. Another alternative is to actually run a pilot study. This would involve producing a limited number of the new razors and actually trying to sell them in two cities that are typical of American cities. The pilot study is more accurate, but is also more expensive. It will cost $20,000. Ron Bush has suggested that it would be a good idea for Jim to conduct either the survey or the pilot before Jim makes the decision concerning whether or not to produce

QA6-22

the new razor. But Jim is not sure if the value of the survey or the pilot is worth the cost.

Jim estimates that the probability of a successful market without performing a survey or pilot study is .5. Furthermore, the probability of a favorable survey result given a favorable market for razors is .7, and the probability of a favorable survey result given an unsuccessful market for razors is .2. In addition, the probability of an unfavorable pilot study given an unfavorable market is .9, and the probability of an unsuccessful pilot study result given a favorable market for razors is .2.

See Instructor's Section.

(a) Draw the decision tree for this problem without the probability values.
(b) Compute the revised probabilities needed to complete the decision, and place these values in the decision tree.

Conduct survey

(c) What is the best decision for Jim? Use expected monetary value as the decision criterion.

QA6-23

🖥 : **6-23** Jim Sellers has been able to estimate his utility for a number of different values. He would like to use these utility values in making the decision in Problem 6-22. The utility values are: $U(-\$80,000) = 0$, $U(-\$65,000) = .5$, $U(-\$60,000) = .55$, $U(-\$20,000) = .7$, $U(-\$5,000) = .8$, $U(\$0) = .81$, $U(\$80,000) = .9$, $U(\$95,000) = .95$, and $U(\$100,000) = 1$. Resolve Problem 6-22 using utility values. Is Jim a risk avoider?

Risk avoider.

QA6-24

🖥 : **6-24** In Problem 6-13, you helped the medical professionals analyze their decision using expected monetary value as the decision criterion. This group has also assessed their utility for money: $U(-\$45,000) = 0$, $U(-\$40,000) = .1$, $U(-\$5,000) = .7$, $U(\$0) = .9$, $U(\$95,000) = .99$, and $U(\$100,000) = 1$. Use expected utility as the decision criterion, and determine the best decision for the medical professionals. Are the medical professionals risk seekers or risk avoiders?

Do not conduct survey and do not construct clinic; risk avoiders.

· **6-25** Rhonda Radner has just been approached by her investment counselor, Charlie Armstrong. Charlie has an investment that would cost Rhonda $500. If the investment is a success, Rhonda could double her money, but if it is a failure, she could lose the initial investment. Charlie believes that there is a .6 probability that Rhonda will double her investment and get $1,000. Charlie reasons that the expected return of this investment is $600 ($600 = $0 × .4 + $1,000 × .6). Since the cost is only $500, Charlie has urged Rhonda to make the investment. Rhonda, however, does not agree with Charlie. She would only consider investing the $500 if the probability of getting $1,000 is .8. Rhonda believes that the investment with a .6 probability of getting $1,000 is only worth $300. Plot a utility curve for Rhonda. What is Rhonda's preference for risk?

See Instructor's Section; Risk avoider.

· **6-26** Charlie Armstrong cannot understand why Rhonda is not willing to make the investment. (See Problem 6-25.) Charlie believes that the investment is worth $600 with a probability of .6. Furthermore, Charlie believes that the investment is worth $800 if the probability of getting $1,000 is .8. Plot the utility curve for Charlie Armstrong. What is his preference for risk?

Indifferent to risk

QA6-27

🖥 : **6-27** In this chapter, a decision tree was developed for John Thompson. (See Figure 6.3 for the complete decision tree analysis.) After completing the analysis, John was not completely sure that he is indifferent to risk. After going through a number of standard gambles, John was able to assess his utility for money. Here are some of the utility assessments: $U(-\$190,000) = 0$,

$U(-\$180,000) = .05$, $U(-\$30,000) = .15$, $U(-\$20,000) = .1$, $U(-\$10,000) = .2$, $U(\$0) = .3$, $U(\$90,000) = .5$, $U(\$100,000) = .6$, $U(\$190,000) = .95$, and $U(\$200,000) = 1.0$. If John maximizes his expected utility, does his decision change?

Yes; He would not conduct the survey and build the large plant.

6-28 In the past few years, the traffic problems in Lynn McKell's hometown have gotten worse. Now, Broad Street is congested about half the time. The normal travel time to work for Lynn is only 15 minutes when Broad Street is used and there is no congestion. With congestion, however, it takes Lynn 40 minutes to get to work. If Lynn decides to take the expressway, it will take 30 minutes regardless of the traffic conditions. Lynn's utility for waiting is: $U(15$ minutes$) = .9$, $U(30$ minutes$) = .7$, and $U(40$ minutes$) = .2$.

    (a) Which route will minimize Lynn's expected travel time?
    (b) Which route will maximize Lynn's utility?
    (c) When it comes to travel time, is Lynn a risk seeker or a risk avoider?

Broad street − 27.5 minutes
Expressway
Risk avoider

6-29 Jack Belkin considers himself an expert when it comes to fine food and beverage, and Jack is proud to tell his out-of-town friends that the best restaurant that he has encountered, Old Tavern, is located in his hometown. Big Burger, a national franchise, is the worst restaurant he has ever been to. Unfortunately, Jack's kids love the french fries at Big Burger, and when his family is deciding where to eat, his kids always say "Let's flip a coin to see if we go to Big Burger or Old Tavern." Jack hates Big Burger, but his kids hate Old Tavern. Jack's wife always has a compromise. She wants to go to Ralph's Diner instead of flipping a coin. But Jack is totally indifferent to these two alternatives. Once when Jack and his wife were alone, his wife suggested that they flip a coin to see if they would go to Old Tavern or Ralph's Diner. (Jack's wife did not like the rich food at Old Tavern.) When Jack demurred at this gamble, his wife proposed that they simply go to the Vacation Inn Restaurant, which was slightly more expensive than Ralph's Diner. Again, Jack was totally indifferent to this choice. Determine Jack's utility for restaurants.

Old Tavern 1; Big Burger 0;
Ralph's Diner .5; Vacation
Inn .75

6-30 Jack Belkin's kids love to play games while riding in the car, and this outing was no exception. (See Problem 6-29 for some additional details.) The entire family was about 50 miles from home, and Jack was looking forward to eating at the Vacation Inn Restaurant, which was a compromise restaurant choice. His oldest kid said, "Let's make a bet. If we see three red Volkswagens between here and home, we will eat at Big Burger. Otherwise, we will go to Old Tavern." Jack believes that the probability of seeing three red Volkswagens is very low—about .20. Should Jack take his kids' bet, or should he tell them that they are eating at Vacation Inn Restaurant and that is final?

Accept kid's bet.

6-31 After driving down the road and seeing one red Volkswagen, Jack Belkin had second thoughts about his probability assessment. (Refer to Problem 6-30.) In Problem 6-30, Jack estimated that the probability of seeing three red Volkswagens before the family got home was .20. How sensitive is Jack's decision in Problem 6-30 to his probability assessment? What probability would make him indifferent between the bet his kid proposed and eating at Vacation Inn Restaurant?

.25

6-32 Coren Chemical Inc. develops industrial chemicals that are used by other manufacturers to produce photographic chemicals, preservatives, and lubricants. One of their products, K-1000, is used by several photographic companies to make a chemical that is used in the film developing process. To efficiently produce K-1000, Coren Chemical uses the batch approach, where a certain number of gallons is produced at one time. This reduces setup costs and allows Coren Chemical to produce K-1000 at a competitive price. Unfortunately, K-1000 has a very short shelf life of about one month.

Coren Chemical produces K-1000 in batches of 500 gallons, 1,000 gallons, 1,500 gallons and 2,000 gallons. Using historical data, David Coren was able to determine that the probability of selling 500 gallons of K-1000 is .2. The probabilities of selling 1,000, 1,500, and 2,000 gallons are .3, .4, and .1 respectively. The question facing David is how many gallons to produce of K-1000 in the next batch run. K-1000 sells for $20 per gallon. Manufacturing cost is $12 per gallon, and handling costs and warehousing costs are estimated to be $1 per gallon. In the past, David has allocated advertising costs to K-1000 at $3 per gallon. If K-1000 is not sold after the batch run, the chemical loses much of its important properties as a developer. It can, however, be sold at a salvage value of $13 per gallon. Furthermore, David has guaranteed to his suppliers that there will always be adequate supply of K-1000. If David does run out, he has agreed to purchase a comparable chemical from a competitor at $25 per gallon. Since David sells all of the chemical at $20 per gallon, his shortage means that David loses the $5 to buy the more expensive chemical.

See Instructor's Section.
Stock 1,500 gallons – $3,300
$1,500

(a) Develop a decision tree for this problem.
(b) What is the best solution?
(c) Determine the expected value of perfect information.

QA6-33   💻 : **6-33** The Jamis Corporation is involved with waste management. During the last ten years, it has become one of the largest waste disposal companies in the midwest, serving primarily Wisconsin, Illinois, and Michigan. Bob Jamis, president of the company, is considering the possibility of establishing a waste treatment plant in Mississippi. From past experience, Bob believes that a small plant in upper Mississippi would yield a $500,000 profit regardless of the market for the facility. The success of a medium-sized waste treatment plant would depend on the market. With a low demand for waste treatment, Bob expects a $200,000 return. A medium demand would yield a $700,000 return in Bob's estimation, and a high demand would return $800,000. While a large facility is much riskier, the potential return is much greater. With a high demand for waste treatment in Mississippi, the large facility should return a million dollars. With a medium demand, the large facility will only return $400,000. Bob estimates that the large facility would be a big loser if there is a low demand for waste treatment. He estimates that he would lose approximately $200,000 with a large treatment facility if demand was indeed low. Looking at the economic conditions for the upper part of the state of Mississippi and using his experience in the field, Bob estimates that the probability of a low demand for treatment plants is .15. The probability for a medium demand facility is approximately .40, and the probability of a high demand for a waste treatment facility is .45.

Because of the large potential investment and the possibility of a loss, Bob has decided to hire a market research team that is based in Jackson, Mississippi. This team will perform a survey to get a better feeling for the probability of a low, medium, or high demand for a waste treatment facility. The cost of the survey is $50,000. To help Bob determine whether or not to go ahead with the survey, the marketing research firm has provided Bob with the following information:

Do not conduct survey—
$670,000.

P(Survey results | Possible outcomes)

		SURVEY RESULTS		
		LOW SURVEY RESULTS	MEDIUM SURVEY RESULTS	HIGH SURVEY RESULTS
Possible Outcomes	Low demand	.7	.2	.1
	Medium demand	.4	.5	.1
	High demand	.1	.3	.6

As you see, the survey could result in three possible outcomes. Low survey results mean that a low demand is likely. In a likewise fashion, medium survey results or high survey results would mean a medium or a high demand, respectively. What should Bob do?

6-34 Monetary values are sometimes inappropriate in decision theory. In such cases, the concepts of utility theory can be used. Locate a friend or someone you know who has not worked Problem 6-33. Using a standard gamble for utility assessment, determine the utility values for all of the monetary outcomes for Problem 6-33. Then, construct a utility curve. In some cases, this may require several rounds of utility assessment to get an accurate and consistent utility curve. Then, using the utility values and the utility curve, resolve Problem 6-33. Is the friend or individual you know a risk taker or a risk avoider? Did you have any difficulties in assessing a utility curve? If so, explain. Discuss the usefulness as well as the potential problems in the use of utility theory in making decisions.

See Instructor's Section.

Data Set Problem

6-35 Lane Bailey must decide how many large Christmas trees to stock. To simplify the problem, he is looking at the possibility of stocking 100, 200, 300, 400, or 500 trees. These stocking options are summarized in the following table:

Basic Decisions

NODES	DECISION NUMBER	STOCKING POLICY (NUMBER OF TREES)
1 → 2	1	100
1 → 3	2	200
1 → 4	3	300
1 → 5	4	400
1 → 6	5	500

For each decision alternative, there are five possible states of nature representing possible demand values. These values, along with their probabilities and expected profits, are summarized in the following tables:

Stocking 100 Trees

NODES	DEMAND	PROBABILITY	PROFITS ($)
2 → 7	100	.10	1,000,000
2 → 8	200	.30	1,000,000
2 → 9	300	.40	1,000,000
2 → 10	400	.10	1,000,000
2 → 11	500	.10	1,000,000

Stocking 200 Trees

NODES	DEMAND	PROBABILITY	PROFITS ($)
3 → 12	100	.10	800,000
3 → 13	200	.30	900,000
3 → 14	300	.40	1,000,000
3 → 15	400	.10	1,100,000
3 → 16	500	.10	1,200,000

Stocking 300 Trees

NODES	DEMAND	PROBABILITY	PROFITS ($)
4 → 17	100	.10	700,000
4 → 18	200	.30	800,000
4 → 19	300	.40	1,000,000
4 → 20	400	.10	1,200,000
4 → 21	500	.10	1,300,000

Stocking 400 Trees

NODES	DEMAND	PROBABILITY	PROFITS ($)
5 → 22	100	.10	600,000
5 → 23	200	.30	800,000
5 → 24	300	.40	1,000,000
5 → 25	400	.10	1,100,000
5 → 26	500	.10	1,300,000

Stocking 500 Trees

NODES	DEMAND	PROBABILITY	PROFITS ($)
6 → 27	100	.10	500,000
6 → 28	200	.30	600,000
6 → 29	300	.40	1,000,000
6 → 30	400	.10	1,200,000
6 → 31	500	.10	1,300,000

(a) What is the best stocking policy given the information available?

Stock 100 $1,000

(b) Lane believes that he may be able to get a quantity discount for stocking 500 trees. This would increase his profits. He believes he may be able to make $100 more for each level of demand. Does this change the stocking decision?

Stock 100

(c) What if Lane receives $200 more for each level of demand for stocking 500 trees?

Stock 500 $1,080

(d) What if Lane receives $400 more for each level of demand for stocking 500 trees?

Stock 500 $1,280

Blake Electronics

In 1947, Steve Blake founded Blake Electronics in Long Beach, California, to manufacture resistors, capacitors, inductors, and other electronic components. During World War II, Steve was a radio operator, and it was during this time that he became proficient at repairing radios and other communications equipment. Steve viewed his four-year experience with the army with mixed feelings. He hated army life, but this experience gave him the confidence and the initiative to start his own electronics firm.

Over the years, Steve kept the business relatively unchanged. By 1960, total annual sales were in excess of $2 million. In 1964, Steve's son, Jim, joined the company after finishing high school and two years of courses in electronics at Long Beach Community College. Jim was always aggressive in high school athletics, and he became even more aggressive as general sales manager of Blake Electronics. This aggressiveness bothered Steve, who was more conservative. Jim would make deals to supply companies with electronic components before he bothered to find out if Blake Electronics had the ability or capacity to produce the components. On several occasions this behavior caused the company some embarrassing moments when Blake Electronics was unable to produce the electronic components for companies with which Jim had made deals.

In 1968, Jim started to go after government contracts for electronic components. By 1970, total annual sales had increased to over $10 million, and the number of employees exceeded 200. Many of these employees were electronic specialists and graduates of electrical engineering programs from top colleges and universities. But Jim's tendency to stretch Blake Electronics to contracts continued as well, and by 1975 Blake Electronics had a reputation with government agencies as a company that could not deliver what it promised. Almost overnight, government contracts stopped, and Blake Electronics was left with an idle work force and unused manufacturing equipment. This high overhead started to melt away profits, and in 1977, Blake Electronics was faced with the possibility of sustaining a loss for the first time in its history.

In 1978, Steve decided to look at the possibility of manufacturing electronic components for home use. Although this was a totally new market for Blake Electronics, Steve was convinced that this was the only way to keep Blake Electronics from dipping into the red. The research team at Blake Electronics was given the task of developing new electronic devices for home use. The first idea from the research team was the Master Control Center. The basic components for this system are shown in Figure 6.13.

The heart of the system is the master control box. This unit, which would have a retail price of $250, has two rows of five buttons. Each button controls one light or appliance, and can either be set as a switch or as a rheostat. When set as a switch, a light finger touch on the bottom either turns a light or appliance on or off. When set as a rheostat, a finger touching the bottom controls the intensity of the light. Leaving your finger on the button makes the light go through a complete cycle ranging from off to bright and back to off again.

In order to allow for maximum flexibility, each master control box is powered by two D-sized batteries that can last up to a year, depending on usage. In addition, the research team has developed three versions of the master control box—

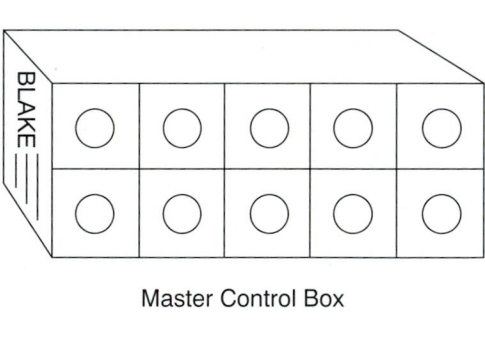

Master Control Box

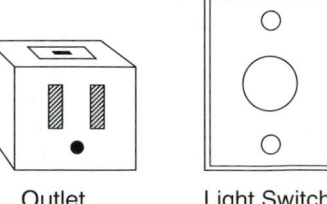

Outlet Adapter

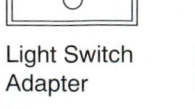

Light Switch Adapter

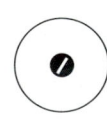

Light Bulb Disk

FIGURE 6.13
Master control center

versions A, B, and C. If a family wants to control more than ten lights or appliances, another master control box can be purchased.

The light bulb disk, which would have a retail price of $2.50, is controlled by the master control box and is used to control the intensity of any light. A different disk is available for each button position for all three master control boxes. By inserting the light bulb disk between the light bulb and the socket, the appropriate button on the master control box can completely control the intensity of the light. If a standard light switch is used, it must be on at all times for the master control box to work.

One disadvantage of using a standard light switch is that only the master control box can be used to control the particular light. To avoid this problem, the research team developed a special light switch adapter which would sell for $15. When this device is installed, either the master control box or the light switch adapter can be used to control the light.

When used to control appliances other than lights, the master control box must be used in conjunction with one or more outlet adapters. These adapters are plugged into a standard wall outlet, and the appliance is then plugged into the adapter. Each outlet adapter has a switch on top that allows the appliance to be controlled from the master control box or the outlet adapter. The price of each outlet adapter would be $25.

The research team estimated that it would cost $500,000 to develop the equipment and procedures needed to manufacture the master control box and accessories. If successful, this venture could increase sales by approximately $2 million. But will the master control boxes be a successful venture? With a 60 percent chance of success estimated by the research team, Steve had serious doubts about trying to market the master control boxes even though he liked the basic idea. Because of his reservations, Steve decided to send requests for proposals (RFPs) for additional marketing research to 30 marketing research companies in southern California.

The first RFP to come back was from a small company called Marketing Associates, Inc. (MAI), which would charge $100,000 for the survey. According to its proposal, MAI has been in business for about three years, and has conducted about 100 marketing research projects. MAI's major strengths appeared to be individual attention to each account, experienced staff, and fast work. Steve was particularly interested in one part of the proposal, which revealed MAI's success record with previous accounts. This is shown in Figure 6.14.

The only other proposal to be returned was by a branch office of Iverstine and Kinard, one of the largest marketing research firms in the country. The cost for a complete survey would be $300,000. While the proposal did not contain the same success record as MAI, the proposal from Iverstine and Kinard did contain some interesting information. The chance of getting a favorable survey result, given a successful venture, was 90 percent. On the other hand, the chance of getting an unfavorable survey result, given an unsuccessful venture, was 80 percent. Thus, it appeared to Steve that Iverstine and Kinard would be able to predict the success or failure of the master control boxes with a great amount of certainty.

Steve pondered the situation. Unfortunately, both marketing research teams gave different types of information in their proposals. Steve concluded that there would be no way that the two proposals could be compared unless he got additional information from Iverstine and Kinard. Furthermore, Steve wasn't sure what he would do with the information, and if it would be worth the expense of hiring one of the marketing research firms.

Discussion Questions

1. Does Steve need additional information from Iverstine and Kinard?

2. What would you recommend?

Outcome	Survey Results		
	Favorable	Unfavorable	Totals
Successful Venture	35	20	55
Unsuccessful Venture	15	30	45

FIGURE 6.14
Success figures for MAI

Sixty-Six-Year-Old Patient with a Hernia

A 66-year-old man has an inguinal hernia which he has asked a surgeon on your staff to repair by surgery.

Two years ago the patient had a heart attack which makes him face a higher-than-average risk of dying during surgery. He has had his hernia for a year. His internist said he should wear a truss that will hold the hernia in and thereby avoid the risk of operation. The patient has been wearing the truss. It is not uncomfortable or painful, but when he goes to his friend's swimming pool he is embarrassed by it. To avoid this embarrassment, he decided to be admitted for surgery.

The anesthesiologist explained the risks to him as follows: If he wears a truss, there is a 97% chance of living out the rest of his life without having the hernia strangulate (the intestinal bulge is pinched off, meaning loss of blood supply and emergency surgery). There is a 3% chance of strangulation. If strangulation occurs, there will be an emergency operation that has a 15% operative mortality. This patient is expected to live eight years. The emergency operative mortality would on the average be expected to shorten his life to four years. (This is because strangulation is assumed to occur halfway through his expected lifetime.)

If the patient chooses the elective surgery today, he faces a 5% operative mortality and a loss of eight years of life, and a 95% chance of surviving the operation and living out his remaining eight years. The elective surgery will cost about $1,500. Aware of these risks, he has chosen elective surgery now.

Discussion Questions

1. Do you think the patient *should* have the surgery now?

2. What other factors might be considered?

Source: Copyright © 1977 by the President and Fellows of Harvard College. Reproduced by permission. This case was prepared by Duncan Neuhauser.

BIBLIOGRAPHY

Chatterjee, R. "A Practical Bayesian Approach to Selection of Optimal Market Testing Strategies." *Journal of Marketing Research* **25** (November 1988): 363–375.

Currim, I.S. "Disaggregate Tree-Structured Modeling of Consumer Choice Data." *Journal of Marketing Research* **25** (August 1988): 253–265.

Dubois, R.W., and R.H. Brook. "Assessing Clinical Decision Making: Is the Ideal System Feasible?" *Inquiry* **25** (Spring 1988): 59–64.

Feinstein, Charles D. "Deciding Whether to Test Student Athletes for Drug Use," *Interfaces* **20**, 3 (May–June 1990): 80–87.

Freedman, J.S. "Decision-Tree Analysis: A Valuable Real Estate Investment Tool." *Pension World* **24** (November 1988): 20–22.

Fryar, E.O., and others. "Bayesian Evaluation of a Specific Hypothesis." *American Journal of Agricultural Economics* **70** (August 1988): 685–692.

Greer, O.L. "A Decision-Tree Approach to the Design and Implementation of Accounting and Information Systems for Small Businesses." *Journal of Small Business Management* **27** (January 1989): 8–16.

Heian, B.C., and J.R. Gale. "Mortgage Selection Using a Decision-Tree Approach: An Extension." *Interfaces* **18** (July–August 1988): 72–83.

Shyy, G. "Bullish or Bearish: A Bayesian Dichotomous Model to Forecast Turning Points in the Foreign Exchange Market." *Journal of Economics and Business* **41** (February 1989): 49–60.

Stone, Lawrence D. "Search for the SS *Central America:* Mathematical Treasure Hunting," *Interfaces* **21**, 1 (January–February 1992): 32–54.

Appendix: Using Spreadsheets to Solve Decision Tree and Bayesian Analysis Problems

The spreadsheets for this chapter perform decision tree analysis and revise probabilities using Bayesian analysis.

Decision Tree Analysis

In this chapter, we expanded the Thompson Lumber problem into a decision tree. (See Figure 6.4.) We now present a decision tree spreadsheet to handle the Thompson decision. Program 6.6 is a "value spreadsheet," that is, one showing the numbers used to solve the Thompson Lumber problem. As you can see, the indented format of the spreadsheet has been developed to approach the appearance of the decision tree presented in the chapter.

Program 6.7 is the "symbolic spreadsheet" that shows the formulas behind the values of Program 6.6. The economic consequences are entered in cells G1 through G18. Probability values are entered in cells F1 through F18 and in cells C2 and C8. The formulas in column D of the spreadsheet compute EMV values for the end branches. For example, the formula +F2*G2+F3*G3 computes EMV for the large facility given that the survey was conducted. Column B selects the highest EMV values using the @MAX function, and Column A computes EMV values for the survey and no-

PROGRAM 6.6 A Value Spreadsheet for the Thompson Lumber Decision Tree Problem

	A	B	C	D	E	F	G
1	Decision Tree Analysis						
2	Survey	Favorable	0.45	Large	Favorable	0.78	$190,000
3	$49,200	$106,400		$106,400	Unfavorable	0.22	($190,000)
4				Small	Favorable	0.78	$90,000
5				$63,600	Unfavorable	0.22	($30,000)
6				No Plant			($10,000)
7				($10,000)			
8		Negative	0.55	Large	Favorable	0.27	$190,000
9		$2,400		($87,400)	Unfavorable	0.73	($190,000)
10				Small	Favorable	0.27	$90,000
11				$2,400	Unfavorable	0.73	($30,000)
12				No Plant			($10,000)
13				($10,000)			
14	No Survey			Large	Unfavorable	0.5	$200,000
15	$40,000			$10,000	Favorable	0.5	($180,000)
16				Small	Unfavorable	0.5	$100,000
17				$40,000	Favorable	0.5	($20,000)
18				No Plant			$0
19				$0			
20	Maximum EMV =						$49,200

PROGRAM 6.7 **A Symbolic Spreadsheet for Thompson Lumber**

	A	B	C	D	E	F	G
1	Decision Tree Analysis						
2	Survey	Favorable	0.45	Large	Favorable	0.78	190000
3	+C2*B3+C8*B9	@MAX(D3..D7)		+F2*G2+F3*G3	Unfavorable	0.22	−190000
4				Small	Favorable	0.78	90000
5				+F4*G4+F5*G5	Unfavorable	0.22	−30000
6				No Plant			−10000
7				+G6			
8		Negative	0.55	Large	Favorable	0.27	190000
9		@MAX(D9..D13)		+F8*G8+F9*G9	Unfavorable	0.73	−190000
10				Small	Favorable	0.27	90000
11				+F10*G10+F11*G11	Unfavorable	0.73	−30000
12				No Plant			−10000
13				+G12			
14	No Survey			Large	Unfavorable	0.5	200000
15	@MAX(D15..D19)			+F14*G14+F15*G15	Favorable	0.5	−180000
16				Small	Unfavorable	0.5	100000
17				+F16*G16+F17*G17	Favorable	0.5	−20000
18				No Plant			0
19				+G18			
20	Maximum EMV =						@MAX(A2..A15)

survey alternatives. Cell G20 contains the maximum EMV for the problem. It also selects the highest EMV value using the @MAX function.

As with other spreadsheets, values can be changed to see the impact on the final decision. It should be noted that the spreadsheets shown in Program 6.6 and 6.7 can handle any decision tree problem with the same structure (same number of alternatives and states of nature) as the Thompson Lumber problem.

Bayesian Analysis

Tables 6.2 and 6.3 revealed the use of Bayesian analysis in updating or revising probability values. This analysis was used in determining probability values for the Thompson Lumber problem. Program 6.8 is a spreadsheet that performs the calculations shown in Tables 6.2 and 6.3. Conditional and prior probabilities are entered in cells B6, B7, C6, C7, B14, B15, C14, and C15. The formulas in the other cells are used to compute joint, marginal, and posterior probabilities. The overall approach is the same as discussed in the chapter.

PROGRAM 6.8 Bayesian Analysis

```
                                                                    READY

           A              B              C            D              E
 1  Bayesian Analysis
 2
 3  State of        Conditional        Prior   Joint          Posterior
 4  Nature          Probability    Probability Probability    Probability
 5
 6  FM                      0.7            0.5  +B6*C6         +D6/D9
 7  UM                      0.2            0.5  +B7*C7         +D7/D9
 8
 9                                      Total  +D6+D7
10
11  State of        Conditional        Prior   Joint          Posterior
12  Nature          Probability    Probability Probability    Probability
13
14  FM                      0.3            0.5  +B14*C14       +D14/D17
15  UM                      0.8            0.5  +B15*C15       +D15/D17
16
17                                      Total  +D14+D15
18
19
20
```

7

Statistical Quality Control

CHAPTER OUTLINE

7.1 Introduction
7.2 Defining and Measuring Quality
7.3 Total Quality Management (TQM)
7.4 Statistical Process Control (SPC)
7.5 Control Charts for Variables
7.6 Control Charts for Attributes

7.7 Summary
    Glossary
    Key Equations
    Solved Problems
    Discussion Questions and Problems
    Case Studies
        Bayfield Mud Company
        Morristown *Daily Tribune*
    Bibliography

Teaching Suggestion 7.1:
Student Opinions about
Quality. See the Instructor's
Section for details.

**Statistical process
control**

7.1 INTRODUCTION

For almost every product or service, there is more than one organization trying to make a sale. Price may be a major issue in whether a sale is made or lost, but another factor is quality. In fact, quality is often the major issue. And poor quality can be very expensive for both the producing firm and the customer.

Consequently, firms employ quality management tactics. Quality management, or as it is more commonly called, *quality control* (QC), is critical throughout the organization. One of the manager's major roles is to ensure that his or her firm can deliver a quality product at the right place, at the right time, and at the right price. Quality is not just of concern for manufactured products, either. It is also important in services, from banking to hospital care to education.

We begin this chapter with an attempt to define just what quality really is. We will look at the major dimensions of quality, why quality is important, and the evolution of quality as a major management issue. Then we will deal with the most important statistical methodology for quality management: statistical process control (SPC). SPC is the application of the statistical tools we discussed in Chapters 2 and 3 to the control of processes that result in products or services.

KEY IDEA

definition of quality

measuring quality

Transparency Master 7.2:
The Dimensions of Quality.

7.2 DEFINING AND MEASURING QUALITY

To some people, a high-quality product is one that is stronger, will last longer, is built heavier, and is, in general, more durable than other products. In some cases, this is a good definition of a quality product, but not always. A good circuit breaker, for example, is *not* one that lasts longer during periods of high current or voltage. So the *quality of a product or service* is the degree to which the product or service meets specifications. Increasingly, definitions of *quality* include an added emphasis on meeting the customer's needs. As you can see in Table 7.1, the first one is similar to our definition.

Measuring quality is not always as easy as it may seem. Not only are there quantitative dimensions such as specifications and performance ratings, but there are qualitative dimensions as well. In general, consumers view the quality of a good or service in terms of the following six dimensions:

1. *Operation.* The primary dimension many people consider is the performance or operation of the product. Does the auto accelerate and stop quickly? Does the insulation keep the house warm? Does the color TV have a clear picture?

TABLE 7.1 Several Definitions of Quality

"Quality is the degree to which a specific product conforms to a design or specification."
H. L. Gilmore, "Product Conformance Cost," *Quality Progress,* June 1974, p. 16.

"Quality is fitness for use."
J. M. Juran, ed., *Quality Control Handbook,* 3rd ed., New York: McGraw-Hill, 1974, p. 2.

"Quality's the totality of features and characteristics of a product or service that bear on its ability to satisfy stated or implied needs."
Ross Johnson and William O. Winchell, *Production and Quality,* Society of Quality Control, Milwaukee, Wisconsin, 1989, p. 2.

"Quality is defined by the customer; customers want products and services that, throughout their lives, meet customers' needs and expectations at a cost that represents value."
Ford's definition as presented in William W. Scherkenbach, *Deming's Road to Continual Improvement,* SPC Press, Knoxville, Tenn. 1991, p. 161.

"Even though quality cannot be defined, you know what it is."
R. M. Pirsig, *Zen and the Art of Motorcycle Maintenance,* New York: Bantam Books, 1974, p. 213.

Transparency Master 7.1:
Definitions of Quality.

Video—COMAP
Quality Control—Against All Odds: An Introduction to Control Charts and Look at Frito Lay's QC, with comments by Deming (6 minutes)

HISTORY

How Quality Control Has Evolved

In the early 1800s an individual skilled artisan started and finished a whole product. With the Industrial Revolution and the factory system, semi-skilled workers, each making a small portion of the final product, became common. With this, responsibility for the quality (and quantity) of the final product tended to shift to supervisors, and pride of workmanship declined.

As organizations became larger in the 1900s, inspection became more technical and organized. Inspectors were often grouped together; their job was to make sure that bad lots were not shipped to customers.

Starting in the 1920s, major statistical QC tools were developed. W. Shewhart introduced control charts in 1924, and in 1930 H. F. Dodge and H. G. Romig designed acceptance sampling tables. Also at that time the important role of quality control in all areas of the company's performance became recognized.

During and after World War II, the importance of quality grew, often with the encouragement of the U.S. government. Companies recognized that more than just inspection was needed to make a quality product. Quality needed to be built into the production process.

After World War II, an American named Dr. W. Edwards Deming went to Japan to teach statistical quality control concepts to the devastated Japanese manufacturing sector. A second pioneer, J. M. Juran, followed Deming to Japan, stressing top management support and involvement in the quality battle. In 1961, Professor A. V. Feigenbaum wrote his classic book *Total Quality Control,* which delivered a fundamental message: Make it right the first time! In 1979, Philip Crosby published *Quality Is Free,* stressing the need for management and employee commitment to the battle against poor quality.

In 1988 the U.S. presented its first awards for quality achievement. These are known as the Malcolm Baldrige National Quality Awards.

2. *Reliability and durability.* These reflect the probability of a product's failing or deteriorating. Does the auto always start on cold mornings? Do its tires last a long time? How often does one of the parking or tail lights burn out?

3. *Conformance.* Quality of conformance relates to the degree to which a product meets preestablished specifications. For example, are all doors for a particular model of auto within the acceptable range and tolerance of 32 inches $\pm$ 0.001 inch?

4. *Serviceability.* This dimension refers to the courtesy, speed, and accuracy of repairs. Mercedes Benz now promises 24-hour repair service in several states.

5. *Appearance.* Appearance and the next dimension, perceived quality, are more subjective. The product's appearance reflects personal feelings and includes such variables as looks, touch, sound, taste, and smell.

6. *Perceived quality.* Many products and services are judged by their brand names, images, or advertising. Sony TVs, Black & Decker drills, and Maytag washing machines have long conveyed an image of quality products, even to people who have never seen or used them.

7.3 TOTAL QUALITY MANAGEMENT (TQM)

Total quality management (TQM) refers to a quality emphasis that encompasses the entire organization, from supplier to customer. TQM emphasizes a commitment by management to have a company-wide drive toward excellence in all aspects of the products and services that are important to the customer.[1] TQM is a change from older, more traditional U.S. attitudes toward quality and closer to the more stringent Japanese position. Some of the issues differentiating the U.S. from Japan are cultural in nature; others are merely organizational and capable of being easily modified. Traditionally, in U.S. plants for example, the production department's job was to produce; a question about quality of products was referred to the QC department. In Japan, total responsibility for quality is in the production manager's hands. Similarly, quality efforts in U.S. companies have been more directed toward solving quality problems that have already arisen than toward developing and designing quality into products. The Japanese take just the opposite position.

---

[1]The term *company-wide quality control* (CWQC) is sometimes used to describe an organization's commitment to quality; see L. P. Sullivan, "The Seven Stages in Company-Wide Quality Control," *Quality Progress* (May 1986): 78.

7.4 STATISTICAL PROCESS CONTROL (SPC)

Statistical process control is concerned with establishing standards, monitoring standards, making measurements, and taking corrective action as a product or service is being produced. Samples of process outputs are examined; if they are within acceptable limits, the process is permitted to continue. If they fall outside certain specific ranges, the process is stopped and, typically, the assignable cause is located and removed.

SPC

Control charts are graphs that show upper and lower limits for the process we want to control. A **control chart** is a graphic presentation of data over time. Control charts are constructed in such a way that new data can be quickly compared to past performance. Upper and lower limits in a control chart can be in units of temperature, pressure, weight, length, and so on. We take samples of the process output and plot the average of these samples on a chart that has the limits on it.

control chart

APPLICATIONS OF QA

How Velcro Got Hooked on Quality

The phone call from Velcro's manager in Detroit came like a bolt out of the blue one morning. General Motors, a major customer, was dropping Velcro's supplier rating from a 1 (its highest score) to a 4 (its next to lowest). If a total quality control program at the Velcro plant was not in place in just three months, GM and the rest of the growing auto market could be lost.

On the day of the fateful call, Velcro had 23 quality control workers stationed around its New Hampshire factory. Quality was viewed by machine operators as the job of "those QC people." Inspections were based on random sampling and, if a part showed up bad, it was thrown out. With no pressure from GM or other customers to change, the process did not change.

"To assume that the production employees were causing the waste would have been a mistake," says Velcro's K.T. Krantz, "and to beat on them about it without giving them the tools to deal with the problems would have been a bigger mistake."

The company decided to pay more attention to operators, to machine repair and design, to measurement methods, communications, and responsibilities, and to invest more money in training.

First-line supervisors were a major barrier to making operators responsible for quality, and they had not pressed employees to change. Top managers would hear comments such as "My boss won't let me shut the machine down. We make junk on my shift, but he doesn't care."

Statistical quality control was a big step at Velcro in pinpointing where the production process needed the most improvement. Control charts put pressure on the people on the line who didn't believe that quality and quantity go hand in hand. As waste goes down, productivity goes up. Over time Velcro was able to pull half its quality control people out of the process, as defects continued to decline.

Source: Harvard Business Review, September–October 1989, pp. 34–40, and *The New York Times,* October 8, 1991, p. C15 and D22.

Figure 7.1 graphically reveals the useful information that can be portrayed in control charts. When the average of the samples falls within the upper and lower control limits and no discernible pattern is present, the process is said to be in control; otherwise, the process is out of control or out of adjustment.

Variability in the Process

Teaching Suggestion 7.4:
Four Interesting Quotes from QC Expert Philip Crosby. See the Instructor's Section for details.

All processes are subject to a certain degree of variability. Dr. Walter Shewhart of Bell Laboratories, while studying process data in the 1920s, made the distinction between the common and special causes of variation. The key is keeping variations under control. So we now look at how to build control charts that help managers and workers develop a process that is capable of producing within established limits.

Building Control Charts. When building control charts, averages of small samples (often of five items or parts) are used, as opposed to data on indi-

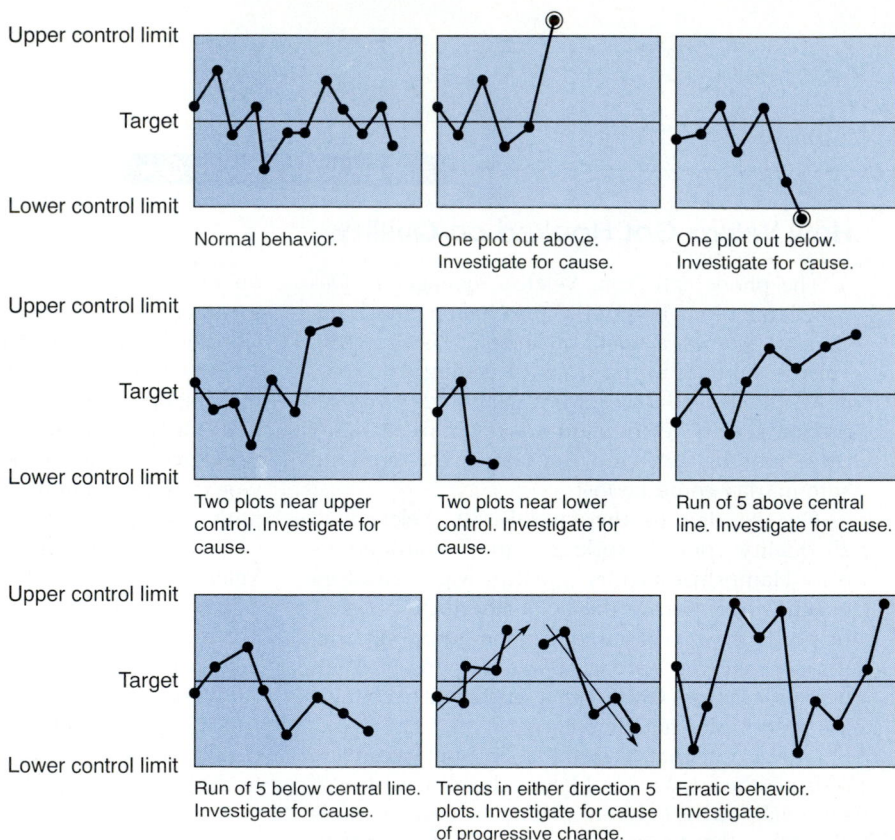

FIGURE 7.1

Patterns to look for on Control Charts.
(*Source:* Bertrand L. Hansen, *Quality Control: Theory and Applications,* © 1963, renewed 1991, p. 65. Reprinted by permission of Prentice-Hall, Englewood Cliffs, New Jersey.)

vidual parts. Individual pieces tend to be too erratic to make trends quickly visible. The purpose of control charts is to help distinguish between *natural variations* and *variations due to assignable causes.*

Natural Variations. Natural variations affect almost every production process and are to be expected. **Natural variations** are the many sources of variation within a process that is in statistical control. They behave like a constant system of chance causes. Although individual measured values are all different, as a group they form a pattern that can be described as a distribution. When these distributions are *normal,* they are characterized by two parameters. These parameters are:

- mean, μ (the measure of central tendency, in this case, the average value)

- standard deviation, σ (variation, the amount by which the smaller values differ from the larger ones)

As long as the distribution (output precision) remains within specified limits, the process is said to be "in control," and the modest variations are tolerated.

Assignable Variations. When a process is not in control, we must detect and eliminate special (assignable) causes of variation. Then its performance is predictable, and its ability to meet customer expectations can be assessed. The ability of a process to operate within statistical control is determined by the total variation that comes from natural causes—the minimum variation that can be achieved after all assignable causes have been eliminated. The objective of a process control system, then, is *to provide a statistical signal when assignable causes of variation are present.* Such a signal can quicken appropriate action to eliminate assignable causes.

Assignable variation in a process can be traced to a specific reason. Factors such as machine wear, misadjusted equipment, fatigued or untrained workers, or new batches of raw material are all potential sources of **assignable variations.** Control charts such as those illustrated in Figure 7.1 help the manager pinpont where a problem may lie.

7.5 CONTROL CHARTS FOR VARIABLES

Control charts for the mean, $\overline{x}$, and the range, R, are used to monitor processes that are measured in continuous units. The $\overline{x}$– **(x-bar) chart** tells us whether changes have occurred in the central tendency of a process. This might be due to such factors as tool wear, a gradual increase in temperature, a different method used on the second shift, or new and stronger materials. The **R-chart** values indicate that a gain or loss in uniformity has occurred. Such a change might be due to worn bearings, a loose tool part, an erratic flow of lubricants to a machine, or to sloppiness on the part of a

Teaching Suggestion 7.5:
Natural vs. Assignable Variations. See the Instructor's Section for details.

natural variation

the mean and standard deviation

assignable variations

$\overline{x}$-chart

R-chart

Teaching Suggestion 7.6:
Mean and Range Charts. See
the Instructor's Section for
details.

machine operator. The two types of charts go hand in hand when monitoring variables.

The Central Limit Theorem

central limit theorem

The statistical foundation for $\bar{x}$-charts is the **central limit theorem.** In general terms, this theorem states that, regardless of the distribution of the population of all parts or services, the distribution of $\bar{x}$'s (each of which is a mean of a sample drawn from the population) will tend to follow a normal curve as the sample size grows large. And fortunately, even if n is fairly small (say 4 or 5), the distributions of the averages will still roughly follow a normal curve. The theorem also states that (1) the mean of the distribution of the $\bar{x}$'s (called $\bar{\bar{x}}$) will equal the mean of the overall population (called μ); and (2) the standard deviation of the sampling distribution, $\sigma_{\bar{x}}$, will be the population deviation, σ_x, divided by the square root of the sample size, n. In other words,

$$\bar{\bar{x}} = \mu \quad \text{and} \quad \sigma_{\bar{x}} = \frac{\sigma_x}{\sqrt{n}}$$

Figure 7.2 shows three possible population distributions, each with its own mean, μ, and standard deviation σ_x. If a series of random samples, ($\bar{x}_1$, $\bar{x}_2$, $\bar{x}_3$, $\bar{x}_4$, and so on) each of size n is drawn from any one of these, the resulting distribution of $\bar{x}_i$'s will appear as in the bottom graph of that figure. Because this is a normal distribution (as discussed in Chapter 3), we can state that:

APPLICATIONS OF QA

Stalking Six Sigma at Motorola

Motorola's goal is expressed clearly: "Occasional failure is not inevitable. *All* errors are preventable." This means not only manufacturing flawless products, but eliminating defects everywhere in the firm. No mistyped letters, no late shipments, no poorly conceived policies. To describe its quest, Motorola uses the old engineering and statistics term, *six sigma.*

To clarify the concept, picture a plot of the heights of all male students in your class. The result would be a normal distribution with a mean of about 5'9". Let's say one standard deviation (a sigma) is 1". Then according to the normal distribution, plus or minus one sigma from the mean (i.e., from 5'8" to 5'10") includes 68.3% of all students; plus or minus two sigma includes 95.5% of everyone; and plus or minus three sigma (from

5'6" to 6'0") includes 99.73% of your classmates. Plus or minus six sigma includes a whopping 99.9999998% of all students.

Using parts produced at Motorola instead of students implies that plus or minus three sigma allows 2,700 errors per million parts to be output. (Since 99.73% are okay, 0.27% are not.) If a product has 1,200 parts in it, then the product can *average* 3.2 defects. This means that, on average, only 40 out of each 1,000 products is shipped with no defects.

Motorola's aim of plus or minus six sigma allows for only 3.4 defects per million. It is like being perfect 99.9999998% of the time.

Sources: Aviation Week and Space Technology, December 9, 1991, pp. 64–65; *ComputerWorld,* July 15, 1991, pp. 59–62; *Business Month,* January 1990, p. 42–46.

Some population distributions

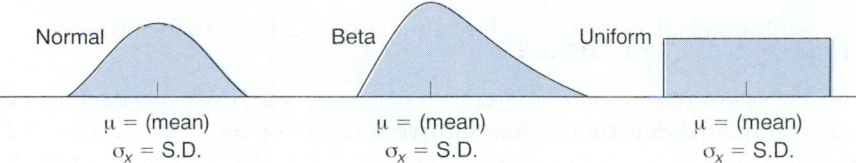

Sampling distribution of sample means (always normal)

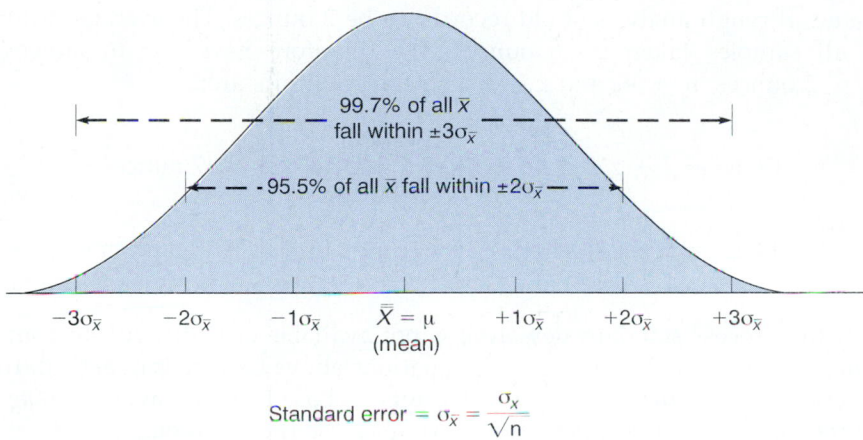

$$\text{Standard error} = \sigma_{\bar{x}} = \frac{\sigma_x}{\sqrt{n}}$$

FIGURE 7.2
Population and Sampling Distributions.

1. 99.7% of the time, the sample averages will fall within $\pm 3\sigma_{\bar{x}}$ if the process has only random variations; and

2. 95.5% of the time, the sample averages will fall within $\pm 2\sigma_{\bar{x}}$ if the process has only random variations.

If a point on the control chart falls outside the $\pm 3\sigma_{\bar{x}}$ control limits, then we are 99.7% sure the process has changed. This is the theory behind control charts.

Setting $\bar{x}$-Chart Limits

If we know, through historical data, the standard deviation of the process population, σ_x, we can set upper and lower control limits by these formulas:

$$\text{Upper control limit (UCL)} = \bar{\bar{x}} + z\sigma_{\bar{x}} \qquad (7\text{-}1)$$

$$\text{Lower control limit (LCL)} = \bar{\bar{x}} - z\sigma_{\bar{x}} \qquad (7\text{-}2)$$

Applicable Problems 7-6, 7-7, 7-8, 7-9, 7-10, 7-12, 7-13, Bayfield case

where

$$\bar{\bar{x}} = \text{Mean of the sample means}$$

z = Number of normal standard deviations (2 for 95.5% confidence, 3 for 99.7%)

$$\sigma_{\bar{x}} = \text{Standard deviation of the sample means} = \frac{\sigma_x}{\sqrt{n}}$$

Corn flakes example

Alternate Example 7.1

Box filling example. For example, let us say that a large production lot of boxes of corn flakes is sampled every hour. To set control limits that include 99.7% of the sample means, 36 boxes are randomly selected and weighed. The standard deviation of the overall population of boxes is estimated, through analysis of old records, to be 2 ounces. The average mean of all samples taken is 16 ounces. We therefore have $\bar{\bar{x}} = 16$ ounces, $\sigma_x = 2$ ounces, $n = 36$, and $z = 3$. The control limits are:

$$\text{UCL}_{\bar{x}} = \bar{\bar{x}} + z\sigma_{\bar{x}} = 16 + 3\left(\frac{2}{\sqrt{36}}\right) = 16 + 1 = 17 \text{ ounces}$$

$$\text{LCL}_{\bar{x}} = \bar{\bar{x}} - z\sigma_{\bar{x}} = 16 - 3\left(\frac{2}{\sqrt{36}}\right) = 16 - 1 = 15 \text{ ounces}$$

If the process standard deviation is not available or is difficult to compute, which is usually the case, the equations above become impractical. In practice, the calculation of control limits is based on the average *range* rather than on standard deviations. We may use the equations

using the range rather than the standard deviation

$$\text{UCL}_{\bar{x}} = \bar{\bar{x}} + A_2\bar{R} \tag{7-3}$$

and

$$\text{LCL}_{\bar{x}} = \bar{\bar{x}} - A_2\bar{R} \tag{7-4}$$

Alternate Example 7.2

where

$\bar{R}$ = Average range of the samples

A_2 = Value found in Table 7.2 (which assumes that $Z = 3$)

$\bar{\bar{x}}$ = Mean of the sample means

Here is an example.

Super Cola example

Super Cola bottles soft drinks labeled "net weight 16 ounce." An overall process average of 16.01 ounces has been found by taking several batches of samples, where each sample contained five bottles. The average range of the process is .25 ounce. We want to determine the upper and lower control limits for averages for this process.

Looking in Table 7.2 for a sample size of 5 in the mean factor A_2 column, we find the number .577. Thus the upper and lower control chart limits are:

$$\mathrm{UCL}_{\bar{x}} = \bar{\bar{x}} + A_2 \bar{R}$$
$$= 16.01 + (.577)(.25)$$
$$= 16.01 + .144$$
$$= 16.154$$
$$\mathrm{LCL}_{\bar{x}} = \bar{\bar{x}} - A_2 \bar{R}$$
$$= 16.01 - .144$$
$$= 15.866$$

The upper control limit is 16.154, and the lower control limit is 15.866.

Setting Range Chart Limits

We just determined the upper and lower control limits for the process *average*. In addition to being concerned with the process average, managers are interested in the *dispersion* or *variability*. Even though the process average is under control, the variability of the process may not be. For example, something may have worked itself loose in a piece of equipment. As a result, the average of the samples may remain the same, but the variation within the samples could be entirely too large. For this reason, it is very common to find a control chart for *ranges* in order to monitor the process

dispersion or variability

TABLE 7.2 Factors for Computing Control Chart Limits

SAMPLE SIZE, n	MEAN FACTOR, A_2	UPPER RANGE, D_4	LOWER RANGE, D_3
2	1.880	3.268	0
3	1.023	2.574	0
4	.729	2.282	0
5	.577	2.114	0
6	.483	2.004	0
7	.419	1.924	0.076
8	.373	1.864	0.136
9	.337	1.816	0.184
10	.308	1.777	0.223
12	.266	1.716	0.284
14	.235	1.671	0.329
16	.212	1.636	0.364
18	.194	1.608	0.392
20	.180	1.586	0.414
25	.153	1.541	0.459

Source: Reprinted by permission of American Society for Testing Materials, copyright. Taken from Special Technical Publication 15-C, "Quality Control of Materials," pp. 63 and 72, 1951.

variability. The theory behind the control charts for ranges is the same for the process average. Limits are established that contain ±3 standard deviations of the distribution for the average range $\overline{R}$. With a few simplifying assumptions, we can set the upper and lower control limits for ranges:

$$\text{UCL}_R = D_4 \overline{R} \tag{7-5}$$

$$\text{LCL}_R = D_3 \overline{R} \tag{7-6}$$

where

$$\text{UCL}_R = \text{Upper control chart limit for the range}$$

$$\text{LCL}_R = \text{Lower control chart limit for the range}$$

$$D_4 \text{ and } D_3 = \text{Values from Table 7.2}$$

Range example. As an example, consider a process in which the average *range* is 53 pounds. If the sample size is 5, we want to determine the upper and lower control chart limits.

Looking in Table 7.2 for a sample size of 5, we find that $D_4 = 2.114$ and $D_3 = 0$. The range control chart limits are

Alternate Example 7.3

$$\text{UCL}_R = D_4 \overline{R}$$
$$= (2.114)(53 \text{ pounds})$$
$$= 112.042 \text{ pounds}$$
$$\text{LCL}_R = D_3 \overline{R}$$
$$= (0)(53 \text{ pounds})$$
$$= 0$$

Steps to Follow in Using Control Charts. There are five steps that are generally followed in using $\overline{x}$- and R-charts:

Transparency Master 7.6:
Steps to Follow Using
Control Charts.

1. Collect 20 to 25 samples of $n = 4$ or $n = 5$ each and compute the mean and range of each.

2. Compute the overall means ($\overline{\overline{x}}$ and $\overline{R}$), set appropriate control limits, usually at the 99.7% level, and calculate the preliminary upper and lower control limits.

3. Graph the sample means and ranges on their respective control charts and determine whether they fall outside the acceptable limits.

4. Investigate points or patterns that indicate the process is out of control. Try to assign cases for the variation and then resume the process.

5. Collect additional samples and, if necessary, revalidate the control limits using the new data.

CONTROL CHARTS FOR ATTRIBUTES

Control charts for $\bar{x}$ and R do not apply when we are sampling *attributes*, which are typically classified as defective or nondefective. Measuring defectives involves counting them (for example, number of bad light bulbs in a given lot, or number of letters or data entry records typed with errors); whereas variables are usually measured for length or weight. There are two kinds of attribute control charts: (1) those that measure the percent defective in a sample—called *p*-charts, and (2) those that count the number of defects—called *c*-charts.

sampling attributes

P-Charts

P-charts are the principal means of controlling attributes. Although attributes that are either good or bad follow the binomial distribution, the normal distribution can be used to calculate *p*-chart limits when sample sizes are large. The procedure resembles the $\bar{x}$-chart approach, which was also based on the central limit theorem.

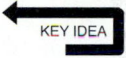
KEY IDEA

The formulas for *p*-chart upper and lower control limits follow:

p-chart limits

$$\text{UCL}_p = \bar{p} + z\sigma_p \qquad (7\text{-}7)$$

$$\text{LCL}_p = \bar{p} - z\sigma_p \qquad (7\text{-}8)$$

where

$\bar{p}$ = Mean fraction defective in the sample

z = Number of standard deviates
($z = 2$ for 95.5% limits; $z = 3$ for 99.7% limits)

σ_p = Standard deviation of the sampling distribution

σ_p is estimated by the formula:

$$\sigma_p = \sqrt{\frac{\bar{p}(1 - \bar{p})}{n}} \qquad (7\text{-}9)$$

where n = size of each sample.

ARCO *p* chart example. Using a popular database software package, data entry clerks at ARCO key in thousands of insurance records each day. Samples of the work of twenty clerks are shown on page 236. One hundred records entered by each clerk were carefully examined to make sure they contained no errors; the fraction defective in each sample was then computed.

Alternate Example 7.4

**Applicable Problems
7-11, 7-14, 7-15, 7-16,
Morristown case**

SAMPLE NUMBER	NUMBER OF ERRORS	FRACTION DEFECTIVE	SAMPLE NUMBER	NUMBER OF ERRORS	FRACTION DEFECTIVE
1	6	.06	11	6	.06
2	5	.05	12	1	.01
3	0	.00	13	8	.08
4	1	.01	14	7	.07
5	4	.04	15	5	.05
6	2	.02	16	4	.04
7	5	.05	17	11	.11
8	3	.03	18	3	.03
9	3	.03	19	0	.00
10	2	.02	20	4	.04
				80	

We want to set control limits that include 99.7% of the random variation in the entry process when it is in control. Thus, $Z = 3$.

$$\bar{p} = \frac{\text{Total number of errors}}{\text{Total number of records examined}} = \frac{80}{(100)(20)} = .04$$

$$\sigma_p = \sqrt{\frac{(.04)(1 - .04)}{(100)}} = .02$$

(Note: 100 is the size of each sample = n)

$$\text{UCL}_p = \bar{p} + z\sigma_p = .04 + 3(.02) = .10$$

$$\text{LCL}_p = \bar{p} - z\sigma_p = .04 - 3(.02) = 0$$

(since we cannot have a negative percent defective)

When we plot the control limits and the sample fraction defectives, we find that only one data entry clerk (number 17) is out of control. The firm may wish to examine that individual's work a bit more closely to see whether a serious problem exists (see Figure 7.3).

c-Charts

Applicable Problem 7-17

c-charts

In the ARCO example above, we counted the number of defective database records entered. A defective record was one that was not exactly correct. A bad record may contain more than one defect, however. We use **c-charts** to control the *number* of defects per unit of output (or per insurance record in the above case).

Control charts for defects are helpful for monitoring processes in which a large number of potential errors can occur but the actual number that do occur is relatively small. Defects may be mistyped words in a newspaper, blemishes on a table, or missing pickles on a fast-food hamburger.

The Poisson probability distribution, which has a variance equal to its mean, is the basis for c-charts. Since $\bar{c}$ is the mean number of defects per unit, the standard deviation is equal to $\sqrt{\bar{c}}$. To compute 99.7% control limits for $\bar{c}$, we use the formula:

$$\bar{c} \pm 3\sqrt{\bar{c}}$$

(7-10)

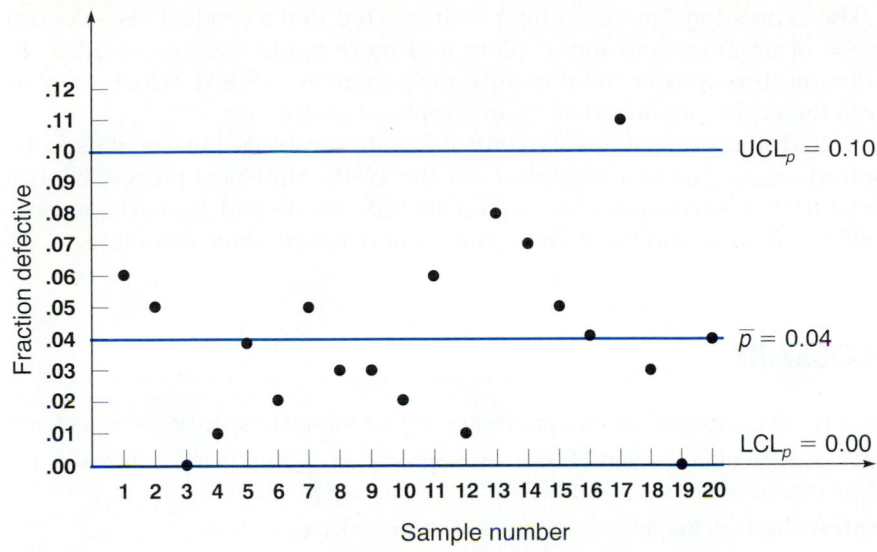

FIGURE 7.3
p-**Chart for Data Entry for ARCO**

Here is an example.

Red Top Cab Company *c*-chart example. Red Top Cab Company receives several complaints per day about the behavior of its drivers. Over a nine-day period (where days are the units of measure), the owner received the following numbers of calls from irate passengers: 3, 0, 8, 9, 6, 7, 4, 9, 8, for a total of 54 complaints.

Alternate Example 7.5

To compute 99.7% control limits, we take:

$$\bar{c} = \frac{54}{9} = 6 \text{ complaints per day}$$

Thus,

$$\text{UCL}_c = \bar{c} + 3\sqrt{\bar{c}} = 6 + 3\sqrt{6} = 6 + 3(2.45) = 13.35$$

$$\text{LCL}_c = \bar{c} - 3\sqrt{\bar{c}} = 6 - 3\sqrt{6} = 6 - 3(2.45) = 0$$
(since we cannot have a negative control limit)

After the owner plotted a control chart summarizing these data and posted it prominently in the drivers' locker room, the number of calls received dropped to an average of three per day. Can you explain why this may have occurred?

7.7 SUMMARY

Quality is a term that means different things to different people. But to the manager of a firm producing goods or services, quality is the degree to which the product meets specifications. Quality control has become one of the most important precepts of business.

The expression "quality cannot be inspected into a product" is a central theme of organizations today. More and more world-class companies are following the ideas of "total quality management" (TQM), which emphasizes the entire organization, from supplier to customer.

Statistical aspects of quality control date to the 1920s, but are of especial interest in our global marketplaces of the 1990s. Statistical process control (SPC) tools described in this chapter include the $\bar{x}$- and R-chart for variability sampling and the p-chart and c-chart for attribute sampling.

GLOSSARY

Quality. The degree to which a product or service meets the specifications set for it.

Total quality management (TQM). A emphasis on quality that encompasses the whole organization.

Control chart. A graphic presentation of process data over time.

Natural variations. Variabilities that affect almost every production process to some degree and are to be expected; also known as common causes.

Assignable variation. Variation in the production process that can be traced to specific causes.

$\bar{x}$- chart. A quality control chart for variables that indicates when changes occur in the central tendency of a production process.

r chart. A process control chart that tracks the "range" within a sample; indicates that a gain or loss of uniformity has occurred in a production process.

Central limit theorem. The theoretical foundation for $\bar{x}$-charts. It states that regardless of the distribution of the population of all parts or services, the distribution of $\bar{x}$'s will tend to follow a normal curve as the sample size grows.

p-chart. A quality control chart that is used to control attributes.

c-chart. A quality control chart that is used to control the number of defects per unit of output.

KEY EQUATIONS

(7-1)　Upper control limit (UCL) $= \bar{\bar{x}} + Z\sigma_{\bar{x}}$
　　　　The upper limit for an $\bar{x}$-chart using standard deviations.

(7-2)　Lower control limit (LCL) $= \bar{\bar{x}} - Z\sigma_{\bar{x}}$
　　　　The lower control limit for an x-chart using standard deviations.

(7-3)　$\text{UCL}_{\bar{x}} = \bar{\bar{x}} + A_2\bar{R}$
　　　　The upper control limit for an $\bar{x}$-chart using tabled values and ranges.

(7-4)　$\text{LCL}_{\bar{x}} = \bar{\bar{x}} - A_2\bar{R}$
　　　　The lower control limit for an $\bar{x}$-chart using tabled values and ranges.

(7-5)　$\text{UCL}_{R} = D_4\bar{R}$
　　　　Upper control limit for a range chart.

(7-6) $\mathrm{LCL}_R = D_3 \overline{R}$
Lower control limit for a range chart.

(7-7) $\mathrm{UCL}_p = \overline{p} + Z\sigma_p$
Upper control unit for a p-chart.

(7-8) $\mathrm{LCL}_p = \overline{p} - Z\sigma_p$
Lower control limit for a p-chart.

(7-9) $\sigma_p = \sqrt{\dfrac{\overline{p}(1 - \overline{p})}{n}}$
The standard deviation of a binomial distribution.

(7-10) $\overline{c} \pm 3\sqrt{\overline{c}}$
The upper and lower limits for a c-chart.

SOLVED PROBLEMS

Solved Problem 7-1

The manufacturer of precision parts for drill presses produces round shafts for use in the construction of drill presses. The average diameter of a shaft is .56 inch. The inspection samples contain six shafts each. The average range of these samples is .006 inch. Determine the upper and lower control chart limits.

Solution

The mean factor A_2 from Table 7.2 where the sample size is 6, is seen to be .483. With this factor, you can obtain the upper and lower control limits:

$$\mathrm{UCL} = .56 + (.483)(.006)$$
$$= .56 + .0029$$
$$= .5629$$
$$\mathrm{LCL} = .56 - .0029$$
$$= .5571$$

Solved Problem 7-2

Nocaf Drinks, Inc., a producer of decaffeinated coffee, bottles Nocaf. Each bottle should have a net weight of 4 ounces. The machine that fills the bottles with coffee is new, and the operations manager wants to make sure that it is properly adjusted. The operations manager takes a sample of $n = 8$ bottles and records the average and range in ounces for each sample. The data for several samples are in the following table. Note that every sample consists of 8 bottles.

SAMPLE	SAMPLE RANGE	SAMPLE AVERAGE	SAMPLE	SAMPLE RANGE	SAMPLE AVERAGE
A	.41	4.00	E	.56	4.17
B	.55	4.16	F	.62	3.93
C	.44	3.99	G	.54	3.98
D	.48	4.00	H	.44	4.01

Is the machine properly adjusted and in control?

Solution

We first find that $\bar{\bar{x}} = 4.03$ and $\bar{R} = .51$. Then, using Table 7.2, we find:

$$\text{UCL}_{\bar{x}} = \bar{\bar{x}} + A_2\bar{R} = 4.03 + (.373)(.51) = 4.22$$
$$\text{LCL}_{\bar{x}} = \bar{\bar{x}} - A_2\bar{R} = 4.03 - (.373)(.51) = 3.84$$
$$\text{UCL}_{\bar{R}} = D_4\bar{R} = (1.864)(.51) = .95$$
$$\text{LCL}_{\bar{R}} = D_3\bar{R} = (.136)(.51) = .07$$

It appears that the process average and range are both in control.

Solved Problem 7-3

Crabill Electronics, Inc., makes resistors, and, among the last 100 resistors inspected, the percent defective has been .05. Determine the upper and lower limits for this process for 99.7% confidence.

Solution

$$\text{UCL}_p = \bar{p} + 3\sqrt{\frac{\bar{p}(1-\bar{p})}{n}} = .05 + 3\sqrt{\frac{(.05)(1-.05)}{100}}$$

$$= .05 + 3(0.0218) = .1154$$

$$\text{LCL}_p = \bar{p} - 3\sqrt{\frac{\bar{p}(1-\bar{p})}{n}} = .05 - 3(.0218)$$

$$= .05 - .0654 = 0 \text{ (since percent defective cannot be negative)}$$

DISCUSSION QUESTIONS AND PROBLEMS

Discussion Questions

7-1 Why is the central limit theorem so important in statistical quality control?

7-2 Why are $\bar{x}$ and R-charts usually used hand in hand?

7-3 Explain the differences among the four types of control charts.

7-4 What might cause a process to be out of control?

7-5 Explain why a process can be out of control even though all the samples fall within the upper and lower control limits.

Problems

· **7-6** Shader Storage Technologies produces refrigeration units for food producers and retail food establishments. The overall average temperature that these units maintain is 46° Fahrenheit. The average range is 2° Fahrenheit. Samples of six are taken to monitor the process. Determine the upper and lower control chart limits for averages and ranges for these refrigeration units.

$UCL_x = 46.966$
$LCL_x = 45.034$
$UCL_R = 4.008$
$LCL_R = 0$

· **7-7** When set at the standard position, Autopitch can throw hard balls toward a batter at an average speed of 60 mph. Autopitch devices are made for both major- and minor-league teams to help them improve their batting averages. Autopitch executives take samples of ten Autopitch devices at a time to monitor these devices and to maintain the highest quality. The average range is 3 mph. Using control-chart techniques, determine control-chart limits for averages and ranges for Autopitch.

$UCL_x = 60.924$
$LCL_x = 59.076$
$UCL_R = 5.331$
$LCL_R = .669$

· **7-8** Zipper Products, Inc., produces granola cereal, granola bars, and other natural food products. Its natural granola cereal is sampled to ensure proper weight. Each sample contains eight boxes of cereal. The overall average for the samples is 17 ounces. The range is only 0.5 ounce. Determine the upper and lower control-chart limits for averages for the boxes of cereal.

$UCL_x = 17.187$
$LCL_x = 16.814$
$UCL_R = .932$
$LCL_R = .068$

: **7-9** Small boxes of NutraFlakes cereal are labeled "net weight 10 ounces." Each hour, random samples of size $n = 4$ boxes are weighed to check process control. Five hours of observations yielded the following:

$UCL_x = 10.42$
$LCL_x = 9.66$
$UCL_R = 1.187$
$LCL_R = 0$

WEIGHTS

Time	Box 1	Box 2	Box 3	Box 4
9 A.M.	9.8	10.4	9.9	10.3
10 A.M.	10.1	10.2	9.9	9.8
11 A.M.	9.9	10.5	10.3	10.1
Noon	9.7	9.8	10.3	10.2
1 A.M.	9.7	10.1	9.9	9.9

Using these data, construct limits for $\bar{x}$- and R-charts. Is the process in control? What other steps should the QC department follow at this point?

: **7-10** Sampling four pieces of precision-cut wire (to be used in computer assembly) every hour for the past 24 hours has produced the following results (refer to table):

HOUR	$\bar{x}$	R	HOUR	$\bar{x}$	R
1	3.25"	.71"	13	3.11"	.85"
2	3.10	1.18	14	2.83	1.31
3	3.22	1.43	15	3.12	1.06
4	3.39	1.26	16	2.84	.50
5	3.07	1.17	17	2.86	1.43
6	2.86	.32	18	2.74	1.29
7	3.05	.53	19	3.41	1.61
8	2.65	1.13	20	2.89	1.09
9	3.02	.71	21	2.65	1.08
10	2.85	1.33	22	3.28	.46
11	2.83	1.17	23	2.94	1.58
12	2.97	.40	24	2.64	.97

$UCL_x = 3.728$
$LCL_x = 2.236$
$UCL_R = 2.29$
$LCL_R = 0$
In control

Develop appropriate control limits and determine whether there is any cause for concern in the cutting process.

7-11 Due to the poor quality of various semiconductor products used in their manufacturing process, Microlaboratories has decided to develop a quality control program. Because the semiconductor parts they get from suppliers are either good or defective, Milton Fisher has decided to develop control charts for attributes. The total number of semiconductors in every sample is 200. Furthermore, Milton would like to determine the upper control chart limit and the lower control chart limit for various values of the fraction defective (p) in the sample taken. To allow more flexibility, he has decided to develop a table that lists value for p, UCL, and LCL. The values for p should range from .01 to 0.1, incrementing by .01 each time. What are the UCL's and the LCL's for 99.7% confidence?

7-12 For the last two months, Suzan Shader has been concerned about the number 5 machine at the West Factory. In order to make sure that the machine is operating correctly, samples are taken, and the average and range for each sample is computed. Each sample consists of 12 items produced from the machine. Recently 12 samples were taken, and for each, the sample range and average were computed. The sample range and sample average were 1.1 and 46 for the first sample, 1.31 and 45 for the second sample, .91 and 46 for the third sample, and 1.1 and 47 for the fourth sample. After the fourth sample, the sample averages increased. For the fifth sample, the range was 1.21 and the average was 48; for sample number 6 it was .82 and 47; for sample number 7, it was .86 and 50; and for the eighth sample, it was 1.11 and 49. After the eighth sample, the sample average continued to increase, never getting below 50. For sample number 9, the range and average were 1.12 and 51; for sample number 10, they were .99 and 52; for sample number 11, they were .86 and 50; and for sample number 12, they were 1.2 and 52.

While Suzan's boss wasn't overly concerned about the process, Suzan was. During installation, the supplier set a value of 47 for the process average with an average range of 1.0. It was Suzan's feeling that something was definitely wrong with machine number 5. Do you agree?

7-13 Kitty Products caters to the growing market for cat supplies, with a full line of products ranging from litter to toys to flea powder. One of its newer products, a tube of fluid that prevents hairballs in long-haired cats, is produced by an automated machine that is set to fill each tube with 63.5 grams of paste.

To keep this filling process under control, four tubes are pulled randomly from the assembly line every four hours. After several days, the data shown in the table below resulted. Set control limits for this process and graph the sample data for both the $\bar{x}$- and R-charts.

See Instructor's Section

$UCL_x = 48.86$
$LCL_x = 48.55$
$UCL_R = 1.8$
$LCL_R = .298$
The range is within the control limits
The mean is outside the control limits

$UCL_x = 64.54$
$LCL_x = 62.36$
$UCL_R = 3.423$
$LCL_R = 0$

SAMPLE NUMBER								
	$\bar{x}$	R		$\bar{x}$	R		$\bar{x}$	R
1	63.5	2.0	10	63.5	1.3	18	63.6	1.8
2	63.6	1.0	11	63.3	1.8	19	63.8	1.3
3	63.7	1.7	12	63.2	1.0	20	63.5	1.6
4	63.9	0.9	13	63.6	1.8	21	63.9	1.0
5	63.4	1.2	14	63.3	1.5	22	63.2	1.8
6	63.0	1.6	15	63.4	1.7	23	63.3	1.7
7	63.2	1.8	16	63.4	1.4	24	64.0	2.0
8	63.3	1.3	17	63.5	1.1	25	63.4	1.5
9	63.7	1.6						

· **7-14** The smallest defect in a computer chip will render the entire chip worthless. Therefore, tight quality-control measures must be established to monitor the chips. In the past, the percentage defective for these chips for a California-based company has been 1.1%. The sample size is 1,000. Determine upper and lower control chart limits for these computer chips. Use $z = 3$.

$UCL_p = .0208$
$LCL_p = .0011$

: **7-15** Barbara Schwartz's Office Supply Company manufactures paper clips and other office products. Although inexpensive, paper clips have provided Barbara with a high margin of profitability. The percentage defective for paper clips produced by Office Supply Company has been averaging 2.5%. Samples of 200 paper clips are taken. Establish upper and lower control chart limits for this process at 99.7% confidence.

$UCL_P = .0581$
$LCL_P = .0081$

: **7-16** Daily samples of 100 power drills are removed from Drill Master's assembly line and inspected for defects. Over the past 21 days, the following information has been gathered. Develop a 3 standard deviation (99.7% confidence) p chart and graph the samples. Is the process in control?

DAY	NUMBER OF DEFECTIVE DRILLS	DAY	NUMBER OF DEFECTIVE DRILLS
1	6	12	5
2	5	13	4
3	6	14	3
4	4	15	4
5	3	16	5
6	4	17	6
7	5	18	5
8	3	19	4
9	6	20	3
10	3	21	7
11	7		

$UCL_p = .11$; the process is in control

· **7-17** A random sample of 100 Modern Art dining room tables that came off the firm's assembly line is examined. Careful inspection reveals a total of 2,000 blemishes. What are the 99.7% upper and lower control limits for the number of blemishes? If one table had 42 blemishes, should any special action be taken?

$UCL_c = 33.4$
$LCL_c = 7$
Yes, 42 is above limit

Bayfield Mud Company

In November 1990, John Wells, a customer service representative of Bayfield Mud Company, was summoned to the Houston, Texas, warehouse of Wet-Land Drilling, Inc., to inspect three boxcars of mud-treating agents that Bayfield Mud Company had shipped to the Houston firm. (Bayfield's corporate offices and its largest plant are located in Orange, Texas, which is just west of the Louisiana–Texas border.) Wet-Land Drilling had filed a complaint that the 50-pound bags of treating agents that it had just received from Bayfield were short-weight by approximately 5%.

The light-weight bags were initially detected by one of Wet-Land's receiving clerks, who noticed that the railroad scale tickets indicated that the net weights were significantly less on all three of the boxcars than those of identical shipments received on October 25, 1990. Bayfield's traffic department was called to determine whether lighter-weight dunnage or pallets were used on the shipments. (This might explain the lighter net weights.) Bayfield indicated, however, that no changes had been made in the loading or palletizing procedures. Hence, Wet-Land randomly checked 50 of the bags and discovered that the average net weight was 47.51 pounds. They noted from past shipments that the bag net weights averaged exactly 50.0 pounds, with an acceptable standard deviation of 1.2 pounds. Consequently, they concluded that the sample indicated a significant short-weight. (The reader may wish to verify the above conclusion.) Bayfield was then contacted, and Wells was sent to investigate the complaint. Upon arrival, Wells verified the complaint and issued a 5% credit to Wet-Land.

Wet-Land's management, however, was not completely satisfied with only the issuance of credit for the short shipment. The charts followed by their mud engineers on the drilling platforms were based on 50-pound bags of treating agents. Lighter-weight bags might result in poor chemical control during the drilling operation and might adversely affect drilling efficiency. (Mud treating agents are used to control the pH and other chemical properties of the cone during drilling operation.)

This could cause severe economic consequences because of the extremely high cost of oil and natural gas well drilling operations. Consequently, special use instructions had to accompany the delivery of these shipments to the drilling platforms. Moreover, the light-weight shipments had to be isolated in Wet-Land's warehouse, causing extra handling and poor space utilization. Hence, Wells was informed that Wet-Land Drilling might seek a new supplier of mud treating agents if, in the future, it received bags that deviated significantly from 50 pounds.

The quality control department at Bayfield suspected that the light-weight bags may have resulted from "growing pains" at the Orange plant. Because of the earlier energy crisis, oil and natural gas exploration activity had greatly increased. This increased activity, in turn, created increased demand for products produced by related industries, including drilling muds. Consequently, Bayfield had to expand from a one-shift (6:00 A.M. to 2:00 P.M.) to a two-shift (6:00 A.M. to 10:00 P.M.) operation in mid-1988, and finally to a three-shift operation (24 hours per day) in the fall of 1990.

The additional night-shift bagging crew was staffed entirely by new employees. The most experienced foremen were temporarily assigned to supervise the night-shift employees. Most emphasis was placed on increasing the output of bags to meet the ever-increasing demand. It was suspected that only occasional reminders were made to double-check the bag weight-feeder. (A double-check is performed by systematically weighing a bag on a scale to determine whether the proper weight is being loaded by the weight-feeder. If there is significant deviation from 50 pounds, corrective adjustments are made to the weight-release mechanism.)

To verify this expectation, the quality control staff randomly sampled the bag output and prepared the following chart. Six bags were sampled and weighed each hour.

Source: Written by Dean Jerry Kindard (Francis Marion College).

| TIME | AVERAGE WEIGHT (POUNDS) | RANGE | | TIME | AVERAGE WEIGHT (POUNDS) | RANGE | |
		Smallest	Largest			Smallest	Largest
6:00 A.M.	49.6	48.7	50.7	6:00	46.8	41.0	51.2
7:00	50.2	49.1	51.2	7:00	50.0	46.2	51.7
8:00	50.6	49.6	51.4	8:00	47.4	44.0	48.7
9:00	50.8	50.2	51.8	9:00	47.0	44.2	48.9
10:00	49.9	49.2	52.3	10:00	47.2	46.6	50.2
11:00	50.3	48.6	51.7	11:00	48.6	47.0	50.0
12 Noon	48.6	46.2	50.4	12 Midnight	49.8	48.2	50.4
1:00 P.M.	49.0	46.4	50.0	1:00 A.M.	49.6	48.4	51.7
2:00	49.0	46.0	50.6	2:00	50.0	49.0	52.2
3:00	49.8	48.2	50.8	3:00	50.0	49.2	50.0
4:00	50.3	49.2	52.7	4:00	47.2	46.3	50.5
5:00	51.4	50.0	55.3	5:00	47.0	44.1	49.7
6:00	51.6	49.2	54.7	6:00	48.4	45.0	49.0
7:00	51.8	50.0	55.6	7:00	48.8	44.8	49.7
8:00	51.0	48.6	53.2	8:00	49.6	48.0	51.8
9:00	50.5	49.4	52.4	9:00	50.0	48.1	52.7
10:00	49.2	46.1	50.7	10:00	51.0	48.1	55.2
11:00	49.0	46.3	50.8	11:00	50.4	49.5	54.1
12 Midnight	48.4	45.4	50.2	12 Noon	50.0	48.7	50.9
1:00 A.M.	47.6	44.3	49.7	1:00 P.M.	48.9	47.6	51.2
2:00	47.4	44.1	49.6	2:00	49.8	48.4	51.0
3:00	48.2	45.2	49.0	3:00	49.8	48.8	50.8
4:00	48.0	45.5	49.1	4:00	50.0	49.1	50.6
5:00	48.4	47.1	49.6	5:00	47.8	45.2	51.2
6:00	48.6	47.4	52.0	6:00	46.4	44.0	49.7
7:00	50.0	49.2	52.2	7:00	46.4	44.4	50.0
8:00	49.8	49.0	52.4	8:00	47.2	46.6	48.9
9:00	50.3	49.4	51.7	9:00	48.4	47.2	49.5
10:00	50.2	49.6	51.8	10:00	49.2	48.1	50.7
11:00	50.0	49.0	52.3	11:00	48.4	47.0	50.8
12 Noon	50.0	48.8	52.4	12 Midnight	47.2	46.4	49.2
1:00 A.M.	50.1	49.4	53.6	1:00 A.M.	47.4	46.8	49.0
2:00	49.7	48.6	51.0	2:00	48.8	47.2	51.4
3:00	48.4	47.2	51.7	3:00	49.6	49.0	50.6
4:00	47.2	45.3	50.9	4:00	51.0	50.5	51.5
5:00	46.8	44.1	49.0	5:00	50.5	50.0	51.9

Discussion Questions

1. What is your analysis of the bag weight problem?

2. What procedures would you recommend to maintain proper quality control?

Process is definitely out of control in 2nd and 3rd shifts.

Morristown *Daily Tribune*

In July 1990, the Morristown *Daily Tribune* published its first newspaper in direct competition with two other newspapers—the Morristown *Daily Ledger* and the *Clarion Herald*, a weekly publication. Presently, the *Ledger* is the most widely read newspaper in the area, with a total circulation of 38,500. The *Tribune*, however, has made significant inroads into the readership market since its inception. Total circulation of the *Tribune* now exceeds 27,000.

Rita Bornstein, editor of the *Tribune*, attributes the success of the newspaper to the accuracy of its contents, a strong editorial section, and the proper blending of local, regional, national, and international news items. In addition, the paper has been successful in getting the accounts of several major retailers who advertise extensively in the display section. Finally, experienced reporters, photographers, copy writers, typesetters, editors, and other personnel have formed a "team" dedicated to

providing the most timely and accurate reporting of news in the area.

Of critical importance to quality newspaper printing is accurate typesetting. To assure quality in the final print, Ms. Bornstein has decided to develop a procedure for monitoring the performance of typesetters over a period of time. Such a procedure involves sampling output, establishing control limits, comparing the *Tribune*'s accuracy with that of the industry, and occasionally updating the information.

First, Ms. Bornstein randomly selected 30 newspapers published during the preceding 12 months. From each paper, 100 paragraphs were randomly chosen and were read for accuracy. The number of paragraphs with errors in each paper was recorded, and the fraction of paragraphs with errors in each sample was determined. The table below shows the results of the sampling.

SAMPLE	PARAGRAPHS WITH ERRORS IN THE SAMPLE	FRACTION OF PARAGRAPHS WITH ERRORS (PER 100)	SAMPLE	PARAGRAPHS WITH ERRORS IN THE SAMPLE	FRACTION OF PARAGRAPHS WITH ERRORS (PER 100)
1	2	.02	16	2	.02
2	4	.04	17	3	.03
3	10	.10	18	7	.07
4	4	.04	19	3	.03
5	1	.01	20	2	.02
6	1	.01	21	3	.03
7	13	.13	22	7	.07
8	9	.09	23	4	.04
9	11	.11	24	3	.03
10	0	.00	25	2	.02
11	3	.03	26	2	.02
12	4	.04	27	0	.00
13	2	.02	28	1	.01
14	2	.02	29	3	.03
15	8	.08	30	4	.04

Discussion Questions

1. Plot the overall fraction of errors $(\bar{p})$ and the upper and lower control limits on a control chart using a 95% confidence level.

2. Assume the industry upper and lower control limits are .1000 and .0400, respectively. Plot them on the control chart.

3. Plot the fraction of errors in each sample. Do all fall within the firm's control limits? When one falls outside the control limits, what should be done?

Source: Written by Dean Jerry Kinard (Francis Marion College).

$\bar{p} = .04$ $\sigma = 0.0196$ UCL $= .0784$ LCL $= .0018$ Upper control limits are exceeded.

BIBLIOGRAPHY

Besterfield, D. H. *Quality Control*, 2nd ed. Englewood Cliffs, NJ: Prentice-Hall, 1986.

Buffa, E.W. *Meeting the Competitive Challenge: Manufacturing Strategy for U.S. Companies.* Homewood, IL: Dow-Jones Irwin, 1984.

Crosby, P. B. *Quality Is Free.* New York: McGraw-Hill, 1979.

Deming, W. E. *Out of the Crisis.* Cambridge, MA: MIT Center for Advanced Engineering Study, 1986.

"Directory of Software for Quality Assurance and Quality Control." *Quality Progress* (March 1984): 33–53.

Duncalf, A. J., and B. G. Dale. "How British Industry Is Making Decisions on Product Quality." *Long Range Planning,* **8,** 5: 81–88.

Garvin, D. A. "Japanese Quality Management." *Columbia Journal of World Business,* **19,** 3 (Fall 1984): 3–12.

Gitlow, H. S., and P. T. Hertz. "Product Defects and Productivity." *Harvard Business Review,* **61,** 5 (September–October 1983): 131–141.

Gitlow, H. S., and S. Gitlow. *The Deming Guide to Achieving Quality and Competitive Position.* Englewood Cliffs, NJ: Prentice-Hall, 1987.

Grand, E. L., and R. S. Leavenworth. *Statistical Quality Control,* 6th ed. New York: McGraw-Hill, 1988.

Leonard, F. S., and E.W. Sasser, "The Incline of Quality." *Harvard Business Review,* **60,** 5 (September–October 1982): 163–171.

Messina, W. S. *Statistical Quality for Manufacturing Managers.* New York: John Wiley & Sons, 1987.

Reddy, J., and A. Berger. "Three Essentials of Product Quality." *Harvard Business Review,* **61,** 4 (July–August 1983): 153–159.

Saporito, B. "The Revolt Against Working Smarter." *Fortune* (July 21, 1986): 58–65.

Schonberger, R. J. *World Class Manufacturing.* New York: Free Press, 1986.

8

Inventory Control Models: I

CHAPTER OUTLINE

8.1 Introduction

8.2 Importance of Inventory Control

8.3 The Inventory Decision

8.4 Economic Order Quantity (EOQ): Determining How Much to Order

8.5 Reorder Point (ROP): Determining When to Order

8.6 Fixed Period Inventory Control System

8.7 Sensitivity Analysis

8.8 Summary

Glossary

Key Equations

Solved Problems

Discussion Questions and Problems

Case Studies:
    Sturdivant Sound Systems
    Western Ranchman Outfitters

Bibliography

Appendix:
    Determining EOQ with Calculus
    Using Spreadsheets to Solve
    Basic Inventory Problems

8.1   INTRODUCTION

inventory

Inventory is one of the most expensive and important assets to many companies, representing as much as 40% of total invested capital. Managers have long recognized that good inventory control is crucial. On one hand, a firm can try to reduce costs by reducing on-hand inventory levels. On the other hand, customers become dissatisfied when frequent inventory outages, called stockouts, occur. Thus, companies must make the balance between low and high inventory levels. As you would expect, cost minimization is the major factor in obtaining this delicate balance.

Inventory is any stored resource that is used to satisfy a current or a future need. Raw materials, work-in-process, and finished goods are examples of inventory. Inventory levels for finished goods are a direct function of demand. Once we determine the demand for completed clothes dryers, for example, it is possible to use this information to determine how much sheet metal, paint, electric motors, switches, and other raw materials and work-in-process are needed to produce the finished product.

All organizations have some type of inventory planning and control system. A bank has methods to control its inventory of cash. A hospital has methods used to control blood supplies and other important items. State and federal governments, schools, and, of course, virtually every manufacturing and production organization, are concerned with inventory planning and control.

Studying how organizations control their inventory is equivalent to studying how they achieve their objectives by supplying goods and services to their customers. Inventory is the common thread that ties all of the functions and departments of the organization together.

inventory planning

Figure 8.1 illustrates the basic components of an inventory planning and control system. The *planning* phase is primarily concerned with what inventory is to be stocked and how it is to be acquired (whether it is to be manufactured or purchased). This information is then used in *forecasting* demand for the inventory and in *controlling* inventory levels. The feedback

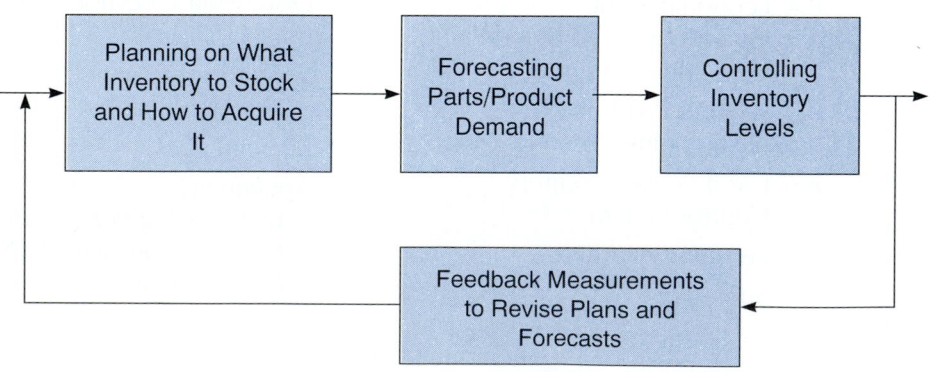

FIGURE 8.1
Inventory Planning and Control

loop in Figure 8.1 provides a way of revising the plan and forecast based on experiences and observation.

Through inventory planning, an organization determines what goods and/or services are to be produced. In cases of physical products, the organization must also determine whether or not to produce these goods, or purchase them from another manufacturer. Once this has been determined, the next step is to forecast the demand. As discussed in Chapter 4, there are many mathematical techniques that can be used in forecasting demand for a particular product. The emphasis in this chapter is on inventory control, that is, how to maintain adequate inventory levels within an organization.

Transparency Master 8.4:
The Inventory Process.

use of forecasting

8.2 IMPORTANCE OF INVENTORY CONTROL

Inventory control serves several important functions and adds a great deal of flexibility to the operation of the firm. Six uses of inventory are:

Teaching Suggestion 8.2:
Examples of the Functions of Inventory Control. See the Instructor's Section for details.

Transparency Master 8.5:
The Functions of Inventory.

1. The decoupling function.

2. Storing resources.

3. A hedge against inflation.

4. Irregular supply and demand.

5. Quantity discounts.

6. Avoiding stockouts and shortages.

The Decoupling Function

One of the major functions of inventory is to *decouple* manufacturing processes within the organization. If you did not store inventory, there could be many delays and inefficiencies. For example, when one manufacturing activity has to be completed before a second activity can be started, it could stop the entire process. If, however, you have some stored inventory between processes, it could act as a buffer.

inventory can act as a buffer

Storing Resources

Agricultural and seafood products often have definite seasons over which they can be harvested or caught, but the demand for these products is somewhat constant during the year. In these and similar cases, inventory can be used to store these resources.

In a manufacturing process, raw materials can be stored by themselves or in work-in-process or in the finished product. Thus, if your company makes lawn mowers, you might obtain lawn mower tires from another manufacturer. If you have 400 finished lawn mowers and 300 tires in inventory, you actually have 1,900 tires stored in inventory. Three hundred tires are

resources can be stored in work-in-process

stored by themselves, and 1,600 (1,600 = 4 tires per lawn mower ×
400 lawn mowers) tires are stored in the finished lawn mowers. In the
same sense, *labor* can be stored in inventory. If you have 500 subassemblies,
and it takes 50 hours of labor to produce each assembly, you actually have
25,000 labor hours stored in inventory in the subassemblies. In general, any
resource, physical or otherwise, can be stored in inventory.

A Hedge against Inflation

**increasing cost of
inventory**

Storing an organization's resources in inventory can be a hedge against inflation. If you place cash reserves in the bank, you might be able to get a 7%
return. On the other hand, some materials have increased in price by over
10% per year. Thus, it may be a better investment to keep your financial
reserves in inventory. Of course, you will have to consider the cost of holding or carrying the inventory, which will be discussed later in this chapter.

Irregular Supply and Demand

When the supply or demand for an inventory item is irregular, storing certain amounts in inventory can be important. If the greatest demand for
Diet-Delight beverage is during the summer, you will have to make sure
that there is enough supply to meet this irregular demand. This might
require that you produce more of the soft drink in the winter than is
actually needed to meet the winter demand. The inventory levels of Diet-
Delight will gradually build up over the winter, but this inventory will be
needed in the summer. The same is true for irregular *supplies*.

Quantity Discounts

Another use of inventory is to take advantage of quantity discounts. Many
suppliers offer discounts for large orders. For example, an electric jigsaw
might normally cost $10 per unit. If you order 300 or more saws in one or-
der, your supplier may lower the cost to only $8.75. Purchasing in larger
quantities can substantially reduce the cost of products. There are, however, some disadvantages of buying in larger quantities. You will have
higher storage costs and higher costs due to spoilage, damaged stock, theft,
insurance, and so on. Furthermore, by investing in more inventory, you
will have less cash to invest elsewhere.

Avoiding Stockouts and Shortages

Another important function of inventory is to avoid shortages or stockouts.
If you are repeatedly out of stock, customers are likely to go elsewhere to
satisfy their needs. Lost goodwill can be an expensive price to pay for not
having the right item at the right time.

APPLICATIONS OF QA

Using Expert Systems in Inventory Management and Logistics

Producing electronic chips and memory circuits is an interesting but often difficult process. Chip making begins with a silicon wafer and consists of approximately 200 complicated steps or procedures. Each silicon wafer, which is about eight inches in diameter, will eventually be converted into hundreds of memory or logic chips that will become the heart of a new computer.

IBM's logistics management system (LMS) is a real-time expert system that assists with the dispatching function, inventory control, and monitoring of the flow of materials through IBM's semiconductor facility, located near Burlington, Vermont. This particular plant produces a variety of memory and logic chips that are used in a number of computer systems produced by IBM. LMS has the ability to capture and manipulate all manufacturing- and materials-related transac-

tions and activities in a real-time mode. It also allows managers to quickly update various databases and models as required.

The success of LMS can be traced to its ability to quickly access, collect, organize, and deliver strategic data, knowledge, and model results in a real-time fashion. This allows various IBM Burlington employees, including line technicians, process operators, maintenance technicians, industrial engineers, and managers, to get the information they need to plan inventory control and scheduling functions. LMS is an example of a system that employs quantitative analysis to help in inventory control and management.

Source: Sullivan, Gerald, and Kenneth Fordyce, "IBM Burlington's Logistics Management System," *Interfaces,* **20**, 1 (January–February 1990): 43–64.

8.3   THE INVENTORY DECISION

Even though there are literally millions of different types of products produced in our society, there are only two fundamental decisions that you have to make when controlling inventory:

1. How much to order.
2. When to order.

The purpose of all inventory models and techniques is to determine rationally how much to order and when to order. As you know, inventory fulfills many important functions within the organization. But as the inventory levels go up to provide these functions, the cost of storing and holding inventory also increases. Thus, you must reach a fine balance in establishing inventory levels. A major objective in controlling inventory is to minimize total inventory costs. Some of the most significant inventory costs are:

1. Cost of the items.
2. Cost of ordering.
3. Cost of carrying, or holding, inventory.

Transparency Master 8.6: The Two Basic Questions.

minimizing inventory costs

4. Cost of safety stock.

5. Cost of stockouts.

**ordering costs and
carrying costs**

The inventory models discussed in *this* chapter assume that demand and the time it takes to receive an order are known and constant and that no quantity discounts are given. When this is the case, the most significant costs are the cost of placing an order and the cost of holding inventory items over a period of time (see Table 8.1 for a list of important factors making up these costs). Hence, in making inventory decisions, the overall objective is to minimize the sum of the carrying costs and the ordering costs. In Chapter 9 we will discuss several more sophisticated inventory models.

8.4 ECONOMIC ORDER QUANTITY (EOQ): DETERMINING HOW MUCH TO ORDER

Applicable Problems:
8-15, 8-17, 8-18, 8-19,
8-20, 8-22, 8-23, 8-24,
8-25, 8-26, 8-27, Sturdivant
Sound Case, Western
Ranchman Case

The *economic order quantity* (EOQ) is one of the oldest and most commonly known inventory control techniques. Research on its use dates back to a 1915 publication by Ford W. Harris. EOQ is still used by a large number of organizations today. This technique is relatively easy to use, but it does make a number of assumptions. Some of the more important assumptions are:

**assumptions of the EOQ
model**

1. Demand is known and constant.

2. The lead time, that is, the time between the placement of the order and the receipt of the order, is known and constant.

Teaching Suggestion 8.3:
The Importance of Basic
Inventory Assumptions. See
the Instructor's Section for
details.

3. The receipt of inventory is instantaneous. In other words, the inventory from an order arrives in one batch, at one point in time.

4. Quantity discounts are not possible.

Transparency Master 8.7:
Table 8.1 Inventory Cost
Factors.

TABLE 8.1 Inventory Cost Factors

ORDERING COST FACTORS	CARRYING COST FACTORS
1. Developing and sending purchase orders	1. Cost of capital
2. Processing and inspecting incoming inventory	2. Taxes
	3. Insurance
3. Bill paying	4. Spoilage
4. Inventory inquiries	5. Theft
5. Utilities, phone bills, and so forth, for the purchasing department	6. Obsolescence
6. Salaries and wages for purchasing department employees	7. Salaries and wages for warehouse employees
7. Supplies such as forms and paper for the purchasing department	8. Utilities and building costs for the warehouse
	9. Supplies such as forms and paper for the warehouse

Transparency Master 8.8:
Determining Inventory
Holding Costs.

5. The only variable costs are the cost of placing an order, *ordering cost,* and the cost of holding or storing inventory over time, *holding* or *carrying cost.*

6. If orders are placed at the right time, stockouts or shortages can be completely avoided.

With these assumptions, inventory usage has a sawtooth shape as in Figure 8.2. In Figure 8.2, Q represents the amount that is ordered. If this amount is 500 dresses, all 500 dresses arrive at one time when an order is received. Thus, the inventory level jumps from 0 to 500 dresses. In general, an inventory level increases from 0 to Q units when an order arrives.

Because demand is constant over time, inventory drops at a uniform rate over time. (Refer to the sloped line in Figure 8.2.) Another order is placed such that when the inventory level reaches 0, the new order is received and the inventory level again jumps to Q units, represented by the vertical lines. This process continues indefinitely over time.

inventory usage curve

Inventory Costs

The objective of most inventory models is to minimize the total costs. With the assumptions just given, the significant costs are the ordering cost and the carrying, or holding, cost. All other costs, such as the cost of the inventory itself, are constant. Thus, if we minimize the sum of the ordering and carrying costs, we are also minimizing the total costs. To help visualize this, Figure 8.3 graphs total costs as a function of the order quantity, Q. The optimal order size, Q^*, is the quantity that minimizes the total costs. As the quantity ordered increases, the total number of orders placed per year decreases. Thus, as the quantity ordered increases, the annual ordering cost decreases. But as the order quantity increases, the carrying cost increases due to larger average inventories that the firm has to maintain.

minimizing ordering and carrying cost

total cost as a function of the order quantity

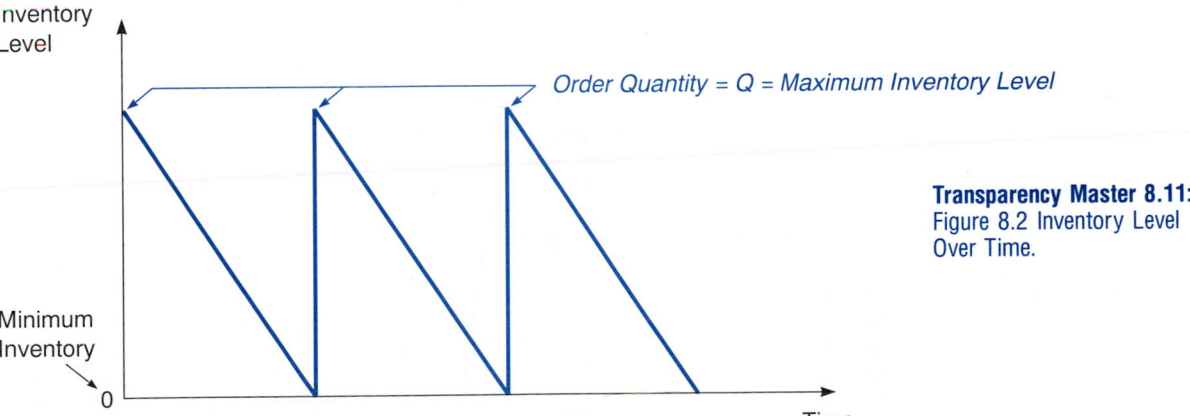

FIGURE 8.2
Inventory Usage over Time

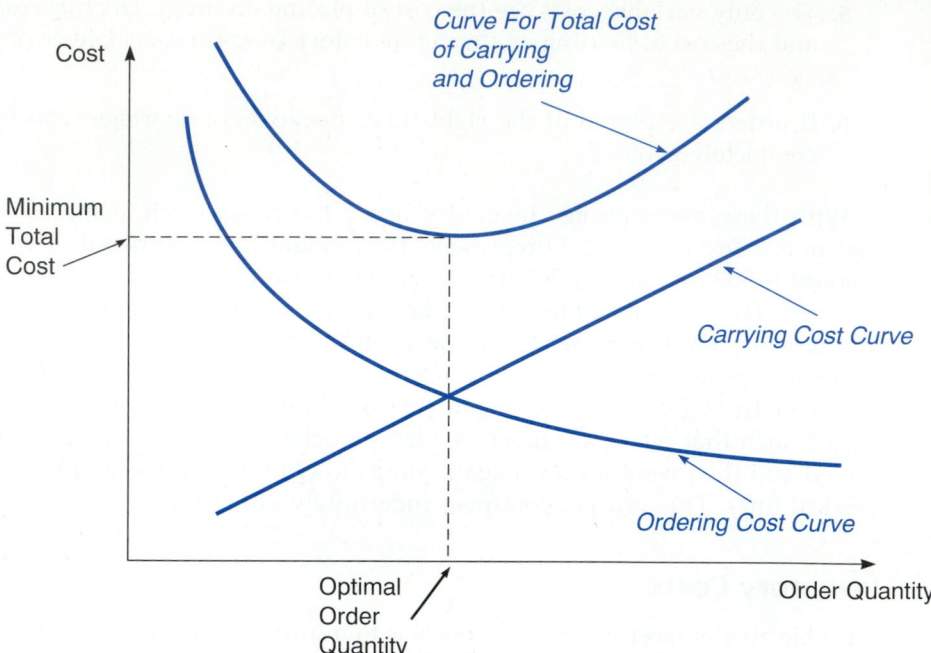

FIGURE 8.3
Total Cost as a Function of Order Quantity

Note in Figure 8.3 that the optimal order quantity occurred at the point where the ordering cost curve and the carrying cost curve intersected. This was not by chance. With the type of cost functions that we investigate in this chapter, the optimal quantity occurs at a point where the ordering cost is equal to the carrying cost. This is an important fact to remember.

Now that you have a better understanding of inventory costs, let's see how we can determine the optimal order quantity that minimizes these costs. In determining the *annual* carrying cost, it is convenient to use the average on-hand inventory level. We then multiply the average inventory level times a factor called *inventory carrying cost per unit per year* to determine the annual inventory cost. Table 8.2 illustrates how *average inventory*

TABLE 8.2 Computing Average Inventory

	INVENTORY LEVEL		
DAY	BEGINNING	ENDING	AVERAGE
April 1 (order received)	10	8	9
April 2	8	6	7
April 3	6	4	5
April 4	4	2	3
April 5	2	0	1

Maximum level April 1 = 10 units
Total of daily averages = 9 + 7 + 5 + 3 + 1 = 25
Number of days = 5
Average inventory level = $^{25}/_5$ = 5 units

can be calculated. It is important to note that the average inventory level for this problem is equal to one-half of the maximum level of 10. (This is due to a constant demand, coupled with the fact that ending inventory is 0.) This maximum level is equal to the order quantity. Thus, the average inventory in units is simply calculated as one-half of the order quantity.

determining annual carrying cost

$$\text{Average inventory level} = Q/2 \qquad \textbf{(8-1)}$$

Finding the Economic Order Quantity

We pointed out that the optimal order quantity is the point that minimizes the total cost, where total cost is the sum of ordering cost and carrying cost. We also indicated graphically that the optimal order quantity was at the point where the ordering cost was equal to the carrying cost. Now, let's develop equations that directly solve for the optimum. To accomplish this, the following steps need to be performed.[1]

determining Q^* by setting ordering cost equal to carrying cost

1. Develop an expression for ordering cost.

2. Develop an expression for carrying cost.

3. Set ordering cost equal to carrying cost.

4. Solve this equation for the desired optimum.

Teaching Suggestion 8.4: Setting Ordering Cost Equal to Carrying Cost Doesn't Always Work for More Complex Models. See the Instructor's Section for details.

Using the following variables, we can determine ordering cost, carrying cost, and Q^*, the economic order quantity:

Q = Number of pieces per order

Q^* = Optimal number of pieces per order

D = Annual demand in units, for the inventory item

C_o = Ordering cost for each order

C_h = Holding or carrying cost per unit per year

Here is the step-by-step procedure:

1. Annual ordering cost = (No. of orders placed per year)
   $\times$ (Order cost per order)

$$= \frac{\text{Annual demand}}{\text{No. of units in each order}} \times (\text{Order cost per order})$$

$$= \left(\frac{D}{Q}\right) \times (C_o) = \frac{D}{Q}(C_o)$$

---

[1]The use of calculus in determining Q^* is shown in the appendix to this chapter.

2. Annual holding or carrying cost = (Average inventory level)
$\times$ (Carrying cost per unit per year)

$$= \left(\frac{\text{Order quantity}}{2} \right) \times (\text{Carrying cost per unit per year})$$

$$= \left(\frac{Q}{2} \right) \times (C_h) = \frac{Q}{2} C_h$$

3. Optimal order quantity is found when ordering cost = carrying cost, namely:

$$\frac{D}{Q} C_o = \frac{Q}{2} C_h$$

4. To solve for Q^*, simply cross-multiply terms and isolate Q on the left of the equal sign:

$$Q = Q^* = \sqrt{\frac{2DC_o}{C_h}} \qquad \text{(8-2)}$$

KEY IDEA

determining optimal number of units per order

Now that the equation for the optimal order quantity, Q^*, has been derived, it is possible to solve inventory problems directly.

Sumco, a company that sells pump housings to other manufacturers, would like to reduce its inventory cost by determining the optimal number of pump housings to obtain per order. The annual demand is 1,000 units, the ordering cost is $10 per order, and the average carrying cost per unit per year is $.50. Using these figures, we can calculate the optimal number of units per order.

Alternate Example 8-1

$$Q^* = \sqrt{\frac{2DC_o}{C_h}}$$

$$Q^* = \sqrt{\frac{2(1,000)\,(10)}{.50}}$$

$$Q^* = \sqrt{40,000}$$

$$Q^* = 200 \text{ units}$$

The total annual inventory cost is the sum of the ordering costs and the carrying costs.

determining the total annual inventory cost

Total annual cost = Order cost + Holding cost

In terms of the variables in the model, total cost (TC) can now be expressed as:

$$\text{TC} = \frac{D}{Q} C_o + \frac{Q}{2} C_h \qquad \text{(8-3)}$$

The total annual inventory cost for Sumco is computed as follows:

$$TC = \frac{D}{C}C_o + \frac{Q}{2}C_h$$

$$= \frac{1000}{200}(10) + \frac{200}{2}(.5)$$

$$= \$50 + \$50 = \$100$$

As you might expect, the ordering cost is equal to the carrying cost. You may wish to try different values for Q, such as 100 or 300 pumps. You will find that the minimum total cost occurs when Q is 200 units. The economic order quantity, Q^*, is 200 pumps

Purchase Cost of Inventory Items

Sometimes the total inventory cost expression is written to include the actual cost of the material purchased. Purchase cost does not depend on the particular order policy found to be optimal, since regardless of how many orders are placed each year, we still incur the same annual purchase cost of $D \times P$, where P is the price per unit and D is the annual demand in units.[2]

It is useful to know how to calculate the average inventory level in dollar terms when the price per unit is given. This can be done as follows.

With the variable Q representing the quantity of units ordered, and assuming a unit price of P, we can determine the average dollar value of inventory.

$$\text{Average dollar level} = \frac{(PQ)}{2} \qquad \text{(8-4)}$$

This formula is analogous to Equation 8-1.

Inventory carrying costs for many businesses and industries are also often expressed as an annual percentage of the unit cost or price. When this is the case, a new variable is introduced.

Let I = annual inventory holding charge as a percent of unit price or cost. Then the cost of storing one unit of inventory for the year, C_h, is given by $C_h = IP$, where P is the unit price or cost of an inventory item. Q^* can be expressed, in this case, as:

annual carrying cost as a percentage of the cost per unit

$$Q^* = \sqrt{\frac{2DC_o}{IP}} \qquad \text{(8-5)}$$

---

[2]In Chapter 9 we will discuss the case in which price can affect order policy, that is, when quantity discounts are offered.

Applicable Problems:
8-16, 8-22, 8-25

8.5 | REORDER POINT (ROP): DETERMINING WHEN TO ORDER

Now that we have decided how much to order, we look at the second inventory question, when to order. In most simple inventory models, it is assumed that receipt of an order is instantaneous. That is, we assume that a firm waits until its inventory level for a particular item reaches 0, places an order, and receives the items in stock immediately

As we all know, however, the time between the placing and receipt of an order, called the lead time or delivery time, is often a few days or even a few weeks. Thus, the *when to order* decision is usually expressed in terms of a *reorder point*, the inventory level at which an order should be placed.

The reorder point, ROP, is given as:

KEY IDEA

$$ROP = (\text{Demand per day}) \times (\text{Lead time for a new order in days})$$
$$= d \times L \tag{8-6}$$

Figure 8.4 shows the reorder point graphically. The slope of the graph is the daily inventory usage. This is expressed in units demanded per day, d. The *lead time, L*, is the time that it takes to receive an order. Thus, if an order is placed when the inventory level reaches the ROP, the new inventory arrives at the same instant the inventory is reaching 0. Let's take a look at an example.

Transparency Master 8.13:
Figure 8.4 The Reorder Point
(ROP) Curve.

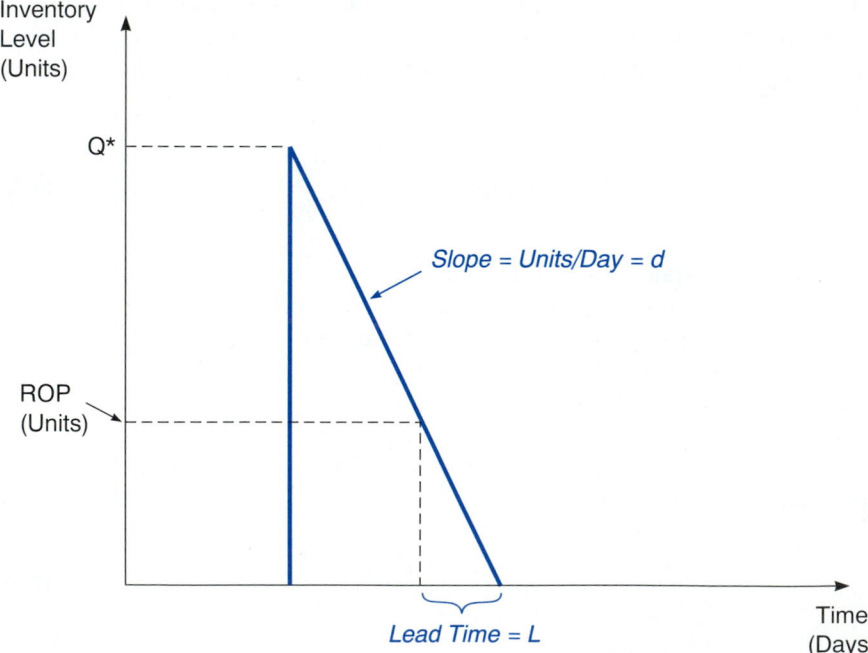

FIGURE 8.4
Reorder Point (ROP) Curve

Procomp's demand for computer chips is 8,000 per year. The firm has a daily demand of 40 units. On the average, delivery of an order takes three working days. The reorder point for chips is calculated as follows:

determining the reorder point (ROP)

$$ROP = \text{Reorder point} = d \times L = 40 \text{ units per day} \times 3 \text{ days}$$

$$ROP = 120 \text{ units}$$

Hence, when the inventory stock of chips drops to 120, an order should be placed. The order will arrive three days later, just as the firm's stock is depleted to 0. It should be mentioned that this calculation assumes that all of the assumptions listed previously are correct. When demand is not known with complete certainty, then these calculations have to be modified. This is discussed further in Chapter 9.

8.6 FIXED PERIOD INVENTORY CONTROL SYSTEM

Applicable Problems:
8-12, 8-13, 8-14, 8-22

Teaching Suggestion 8.5:
Other Ways of Looking at Inventory Problems. See the Instructor's Section for details.

The previous sections have discussed the derivation and use of the economic order quantity. This quantity determines *how much* is to be ordered. Since the approach results in a fixed number for the order quantity, it has been called the *fixed order system.* Another approach is to determine a fixed

---

APPLICATIONS OF QA

Inland Steel Uses Systems Contracts to Control Inventory Costs

Sound inventory control involves much more than computing the economic order quantity. In most cases, other practical and financial considerations must be taken into account to minimize total inventory costs and to provide tighter control on inventory levels. Both practical and financial considerations led Inland Steel to consider several inventory policies, including systems contracts.

Inland Steel produces approximately 5.5 million tons of steel each year. The steel mill has two blast furnaces that supply steel to four casting operations. Yet, steel inventory is not the company's only inventory concern. For many large corporations, office equipment such as typewriters, printers, and fax machines can represent a substantial investment. Furthermore, all steel-processing facilities are controlled through computers, which are considered office equipment by Inland Steel.

Tricia Wynn, a project buyer for Inland Steel, was concerned about high costs and a lack of stan-

dardization for office equipment. To overcome these problems, she developed a comprehensive inventory ordering system that took advantage of standardization and contract buying. The result was a contract ordering system that provided superior equipment at substantial savings. Most of the equipment was leased or rented. The new system provided low monthly rates for office equipment, free installation, and a 30-day free trial. Another advantage was a floating systems contract. With this type of contract, there is no termination date, which helps reduce the time and costs of maintaining leasing agreements. The bottom line is that a systems contract approach allowed Inland Steel to order quality office equipment for fewer dollars.

Source: K. Evans-Correia, "All Systems Go," *Purchasing,* March 23, 1989, pp. 106–107.

number that answers the *when to order* question. This is called the *fixed period inventory control system.* Although there are several quantities that can be computed with this type of system, the most commonly computed quantities are the optimal number of orders per year, Y^*, and the optimal number of days between orders, N^*. The optimal number of days between orders has also been called the optimal number of days' supply per order. As will be seen, these quantities result in an identical solution to the inventory control problem. They are simply looking at the same problem from a different point of view. We begin by investigating the optimal number of orders per year, Y^*.

optimal number of orders per year and optimal number of days between orders

Determining the Optimal Number of Orders per Year, *Y**

computing *Y** when *Q** is known

Determining Y^* tells us how many times per year an order should be placed. If annual demand is 100 and the economic order quantity is 50 units per order, how many orders must be placed every year? In order to meet demand, two orders of 50 units each must be placed to satisfy the annual demand of 100 units. This relationship is shown in Equation 8-7.

Transparency Master 8.14:
Fixed Period Models.

$$Y^* = \frac{D}{Q^*} \tag{8-7}$$

Sumco, in a previous example, determined that its economic order quantity was 200 pump housings and its annual demand was 1,000 pump housings. The optimal number of orders per year, Y^*, can be computed as follows:

$$Y^* = \frac{1,000}{200} = 5 \text{ orders per year}$$

In order to use this equation, it is necessary to determine the economic order quantity, Q^*, first. When you do not want to calculate the economic order quantity first, there is a way of directly solving for the optimal number of orders per year. This can be done as follows:

computing *Y** when *Q** is unknown

$$Y^* = \frac{D}{Q^*}$$

But we know that

$$Q^* = \sqrt{\frac{2DC_o}{C_h}}$$

Thus,

$$Y^* = \frac{D}{\sqrt{\frac{2DC_o}{C_h}}}$$

Rearranging terms and solving, we get:

$$Y^* = \sqrt{\frac{DC_h}{2C_o}} \tag{8-8}$$

Now, using Equation 8-8, we can solve for Y^* directly. Let's use Sumco to test the validity of Equation 8-8. As you recall, Sumco sells pump housings to other manufacturers. The annual demand, D, is 1,000 units; the ordering cost, C_o, is \$10; and the carrying cost, C_h, is \$.50. These numbers are placed in Equation 8-8 to solve for Y^*.

$$Y^* = \sqrt{\frac{DC_h}{2C_o}}$$

$$= \sqrt{\frac{(1,000)(.5)}{(2)(10)}} = \sqrt{\frac{500}{20}}$$

Alternate Example 8.2

$$= \sqrt{25} = 5 \text{ orders per year}$$

Determining the Optimal Number of Days between Orders, N*

Another approach is to determine the number of days between orders, N^*. This tells you how many days you will be able to operate after receiving an order without running out of inventory. In the case of Sumco, the optimal number of orders per year was 5. What is the number of days between any two orders? In other words, what is the number of days' supply per order? With 365 days in a year and 5 orders per year, each order will last 73 days (73 days = 365 days per year divided by 5 orders per year).[3]

This relationship is shown in Equation 8-9:

$$N^* = \frac{365}{Y^*} \qquad (8\text{-}9)$$

computing N* when Y* is known

But we know that

$$Y^* = \sqrt{\frac{DC_h}{2C_o}}$$

It is also possible to solve for N^* directly when we have not previously determined Y^*. This can be done as follows:

computing N* when Y* is unknown

$$N^* = \frac{365}{Y^*}$$

Thus,

$$N^* = \frac{365}{\sqrt{\dfrac{DC_h}{2C_o}}}$$

Rearranging terms, we get,

$$N^* = \sqrt{\frac{266,450C_o}{DC_h}} \qquad (8\text{-}10)$$

---

[3]If you use the number of working days in a year, such as 200 working days, then this number replaces 365 in the following equations.

Alternate Example 8.3

Using the data for Sumco, we can solve for N^* directly without knowing either Y^* or Q^*. With a demand of 1,000 units, a carrying cost of \$.50, and an ordering cost of \$10, we get the following:

$$N^* = \sqrt{\frac{266,450 C_o}{D C_h}}$$

$$= \sqrt{\frac{(266,450)\,(10)}{(1000)\,(.5)}} = \sqrt{\frac{2,664,500}{500}} = \sqrt{5329} = 73 \text{ days}$$

Y^* and N^* can also be determined by setting ordering cost equal to carrying cost or by using calculus

In this section, we have investigated the fixed period inventory control system. Once you determine when to order, you then order enough to satisfy demand until the next order. This is usually Q^*. For Sumco, this would still be 200 units. In addition, we have shown a simple way of determining Y^* if you already know Q^*, and we have shown a simple way of determining N^* if you already know Y^*. Furthermore, we have shown how these quantities can be determined directly from the annual demand, ordering cost, and carrying cost. These equations were derived by using straightforward algebraic manipulations. They could also be developed by setting ordering cost equal to carrying costs or by developing the total cost equations and using calculus. These approaches are explored further in the problems at the end of this chapter.

8.7 SENSITIVITY ANALYSIS

Applicable Problems:
8-21, 8-28

In the preceding examples we developed formulas that can be used to solve directly for Q^*, N^*, and Y^*. These formulas assume that all input values are known with certainty. What would happen, though, if one of the input values changed—for example, the cost of placing an order rises by \$5?

Teaching Suggestion 8.6:
Introducing Sensitivity
Analysis. See the Instructor's
Section for details.

The answer is that if any of the values used in one of the formulas changes, the optimal value changes also. Determining the effect of these changes is called *sensitivity analysis.* One approach to sensitivity analysis is to recalculate the optimal quantity when one of the inputs changes.

How would the order quantity be affected if Sumco's cost of placing an order were actually \$40 instead of \$10? Assume the annual demand for Sumco pump housings is still the same, namely, $D = 1,000$ units and that carrying cost is \$.50 per unit per year.

Alternate Example 8.4

$$Q^* = \sqrt{\frac{2DC_o}{C_h}} = \sqrt{\frac{2(1000)\,(40)}{.50}} = \sqrt{160,000}$$

$$Q^* = 400 \text{ units}$$

Thus, when the ordering cost *increases* by a *multiple of 4*, the optimal order quantity *doubles.*

KEY IDEA

In order to determine how sensitive the optimal solution is to a change in one of the variables in an equation, it is not always necessary to completely recalculate the order quantity Q^*. Usually, it is possible to determine the effect of a change in the optimal quantity by inspecting the basic EOQ formula.

Let us look at the formula for the optimal number of units to order equation derived previously. What effect would the following individual changes have on the value of Q^*?

1. Ordering cost increases by a factor of 4.

2. Carrying cost increases by a factor of 4.

3. The total number of pieces of inventory sold per year (or the annual demand) *decreases* by a factor of 9.

$$\text{The EOQ formula is given as } Q^* = \sqrt{\frac{2DC_o}{C_h}}$$

The following shortcuts can be used to test the effect of the changes listed.

1. The optimal order quantity will increase by a factor of 2 when C_o increases by a factor of 4. To see this we simply replace C_o in the formula by an ordering cost of 4 times that number, namely $(4)(C_o)$.

determining the new optimal order quantity

$$Q^* = \sqrt{\frac{2D(4)(C_o)}{C_h}}$$

Video 8.2 Blue Bell Trims Its Inventory

APPLICATIONS OF QA

Blue Bell Trims Its Inventory

Blue Bell is one of the world's largest apparel manufacturers, with annual sales totaling over one billion dollars. Headquartered in Greensboro, North Carolina, it employs over 27,000 people worldwide. Blue Bell has three major businesses, the largest of which is the Wrangler Group. Wrangler manufactures denim and corduroy jeans and several other product lines in sports and casual apparel. In basic styles of men's jeans, Wrangler makes 35 million pairs of jeans a year in 37 plants. There are over 10,000 individual stock keeping units (called SKUs) manufactured and stocked.

One task Blue Bell faced was to find a better balance of the cost of carrying inventory against the risk of shortages. Data analysis showed that inventory had not been well balanced at the SKU level. Some SKUs showed months of supply whereas others were out of stock. Thus, unless a systematic approach could be developed to consistently achieve a "balanced" inventory at the SKU level, it would be difficult for Blue Bell to attain a dramatic reduction in inventory.

When this effort began, the economic and competitive pressures that Blue Bell faced were severe.

The high cost of carrying inventory had become particularly acute. Short-term interest rates were hovering at 20 percent, and as a result, net interest expenses for Blue Bell had ballooned. Financing inventory had dramatically pushed up Blue Bell's cost of doing business.

Management science provided the means for senior executives and other managers to swiftly take effective action to turn the situation around. A new production planning process was designed, tested, and implemented that reduced inventories more than 31 percent (from $371 million to $256 million) without a decrease in sales or customer service. The new process also reduced manufacturing costs by approximately $1 million. The strong support of top management was a major factor in this achievement, and that support was communicated down the line so that employees at every level became enthusiastically involved.

Source: J. R. Edwards, H. M. Wagner, and W. P. Wood, *Interfaces,* **15,** 1 (January–February 1985): 34–52.

Bringing the number 4 outside the square root sign yields:

$$Q^* = 2\sqrt{\frac{2DC_o}{C_h}} = 2 \times \text{(Previous optimal order quantity)}$$

2. The optimal order quantity will decrease by a factor of ½ when C_h increases by a factor of 4.

$$Q^* = \sqrt{\frac{2DC_o}{(4)(C_h)}}$$

$$Q^* = \frac{1}{2}\sqrt{\frac{2DC_o}{C_h}} = \frac{1}{2} \times \text{(Previous optimal order quantity)}$$

3. The optimal order size will decrease by a factor of ⅓ (or become ⅓ of what it was before) when D decreases by a factor of 9.

$$Q^* = \sqrt{\frac{2(\frac{1}{9})(D)C_o}{C_h}}$$

$$Q^* = \frac{1}{3}\sqrt{\frac{2DC_o}{C_h}} = \frac{1}{3} \times \text{(Previous optimal order quantity)}$$

In each of these, we note that the optimal value of Q^* changes by the square root of the change in a variable used in the formula.

8.8   SUMMARY

In this chapter, we introduced the fundamentals of inventory control theory. We showed that the two most important questions are: (1) how much to order, and (2) when to order.

We investigated the economic order quantity, which determines how much to order, and the reorder point, which determines when to order. In addition, we discussed the fixed period inventory control system. Finally, we explored the use of sensitivity analysis. We use this analysis when we want to determine what happens to computations when one or more of the values used in one of the equations changes.

The inventory models presented in this chapter make a number of assumptions: (1) known and constant demand and lead times, (2) instantaneous receipt of inventory, (3) no quantity discounts, (4) no stockouts or shortages, and (5) the only variable costs are ordering costs and carrying costs. If these assumptions are valid, then the inventory models and techniques discussed in this chapter provide optimal solutions. On the other hand, if these assumptions do not hold, the analysis presented in this chapter may lead you to the wrong conclusions and decisions. In the next chapter, we relax and eliminate some of these assumptions. Although the inventory models in the next chapter are slightly more complex, they are preferable when the assumptions of this chapter do not apply.

GLOSSARY

EOQ. Economic order quantity. The amount of inventory ordered that will minimize the total inventory cost. It is also called the optimal order quantity, or Q^*.

Average Inventory. The average inventory on hand. In this chapter, the average inventory is $Q/2$.

Reorder Point (ROP). The number of units on hand when an order for more inventory is placed.

Lead Time. The time it takes to receive an order after it is placed (called L in the chapter).

Sensitivity Analysis. The process of determining how sensitive the optimal solution is to changes in the values used in the equations.

KEY EQUATIONS

(8-1) Average inventory level $= Q/2$

(8-2) $Q^* = \sqrt{\dfrac{2DC_o}{C_h}}$

The economic order quantity.

(8-3) $\text{TC} = \dfrac{D}{Q}C_o + \dfrac{Q}{2}C_h$

Total inventory cost.

(8-4) Average dollar level $= \dfrac{(PQ)}{2}$

(8-5) $Q^* = \sqrt{\dfrac{2DC_o}{IP}}$

The economic order quantity using the carrying cost, I, as a percentage of price, P.

(8-6) $\text{ROP} = d \times L$

The reorder point, where $d =$ daily demand and $L =$ lead time in days.

(8-7) $Y^* = \dfrac{D}{Q^*}$

Optimal number of orders per year.

(8-8) $Y^* = \sqrt{\dfrac{DC_h}{2C_o}}$

Optimal number of orders per year.

(8-9) $N^* = \dfrac{365}{Y^*}$

Optimal number of days between orders.

(8-10) $N^* = \sqrt{\dfrac{266{,}450C_o}{DC_h}}$

Optimal number of days between orders.

SOLVED PROBLEMS

Solved Problem 8-1

Patterson Electronics supplies microcomputer circuitry to a company that incorporates microprocessors into refrigerators and other home appliances. Currently, Patterson orders components from various suppliers. One of the components is ordered in batches of 150 units. It has been estimated that annual demand for these components is 250. Furthermore, carrying cost is estimated to be $1 per unit per year. For the order policy to be optimal, determine what the ordering cost would have to be.

Solution

The data for Patterson Electronics can be summarized as follows:

$$Q = 150 \text{ units}$$
$$D = 250 \text{ units}$$
$$C_h = \$1$$

Given an annual demand of 250, a carrying cost of $1, and an order quantity of 150, Patterson Electronics must determine what the ordering cost would have to be for the order policy of 150 units to be optimal. To find the answer to this problem, we must solve the traditional economic order quantity equation for the ordering cost. As you can see in the calculations that follow, an ordering cost of $45 is needed for the order quantity of 150 units to be optimal.

$$Q = \sqrt{\frac{2DC_o}{C_h}}$$

$$C_o = (Q^2)\left(\frac{C_h}{2D}\right)$$

$$= \frac{(150)^2(1)}{2(250)}$$

$$= \frac{22{,}500}{500} = \$45$$

Solved Problem 8-2

Annual demand for a popular speaker component for small stereo systems is 40,000. Dan Thesing estimates that the ordering cost is $15 per order. Furthermore, carrying cost is estimated to be $3 per unit per year. At this time, it takes 30 days between the time that Dan places an order and the time when the order is received. During this time, daily demand is 250 units. What is the optimal number of days between orders?

Solution

The data for the problem that Dan Thesing is facing is summarized as follows:

$$D = 40,000 \text{ units}$$

$$C_o = \$15$$

$$C_h = \$3$$

$$\text{Lead time} = 30 \text{ days}$$

$$\text{Daily demand} = 250 \text{ units}$$

In order to determine the optimal number of days between orders, we will determine the economic order quantity, Q^*, and the optimal number of orders per year, Y^*. As you can see from the calculations that follow, the optimal number of days between orders is approximately 6 days.

$$Q^* = \sqrt{\frac{2DC_o}{C_h}} = \sqrt{\frac{(2)(40,000)(15)}{3}}$$

$$= 632$$

$$Y^* = \frac{D}{Q^*} = \frac{40,000}{632} = 63.3$$

$$N^* = \frac{365}{Y^*} = \frac{365}{63.3} = 5.77$$

DISCUSSION QUESTIONS AND PROBLEMS

Discussion Questions

8-1 Why is inventory an important consideration for managers?

8-2 What is the purpose of inventory control?

8-3 Under what circumstances can inventory be used as a hedge against inflation?

8-4 Why wouldn't a company always store large quantities of inventory to eliminate shortages and stockouts?

8-5 Describe the major decisions that must be made in inventory control.

8-6 What are some of the assumptions made in using the economic order quantity?

8-7 Discuss the major inventory costs that are used in determining the economic order quantity.

8-8 What are some of the methods that are used in actually determining the equation for the economic order quantity?

8-9 What is the reorder point? How is it determined?

8-10 Describe some of the optimal quantities in fixed period inventory control systems.

8-11 What is the purpose of sensitivity analysis?

Problems

: 8-12 Develop the equation for the optimal number of orders per year. Use the symbols developed in this chapter. You should use the following steps:

(a) Determine the annual carrying cost.
(b) Determine the annual ordering cost.
(c) Set the annual ordering cost equal to the annual carrying cost.
(d) Solve for the optimal number of orders per year.

See Instructor's Section.

: 8-13 Develop the equation for the optimal number of days between orders. Use the same variables that are used in this chapter and the following steps:

(a) Determine the annual carrying cost.
(b) Determine the annual ordering cost.
(c) Set the annual carrying cost equal to the annual ordering cost.
(d) Solve for the optimal number of days between orders.

See Instructor's Section.

: 8-14 Using the variables presented in this chapter, develop the equations for the optimal number of orders per month and the optimal number of weeks between orders. Use the following procedure in obtaining both equations:

(a) Determine the annual ordering cost.
(b) Determine the annual carrying cost.
(c) Set the annual ordering cost equal to the annual carrying cost.
(d) Solve for the optimal quantity.

See Instructor's Section.

QA8-15

· 8-15 Lila Battle has determined that the annual demand for number 6 screws is 100,000 screws. Lila, who works in her brother's hardware store, is in charge of purchasing. She estimates that it costs $10 every time an order is placed. This cost includes her wages, the cost of the forms used in placing the order, and so on. Furthermore, she estimates that the cost of carrying one screw in inventory for a year is one-half of one cent. How many number 6 screws should Lila order at a time?

20,000

QA8-16

· 8-16 It takes approximately 8 working days for an order of number 6 screws to arrive once the order has been placed. (Refer to Problem 8-15.) The demand for number 6 screws is fairly constant, and on the average, Lila has observed that her brother's hardware store sells 500 of these screws each day. Since the demand is fairly constant, Lila believes that she can avoid stockouts completely if she only orders the number 6 screws at the correct time. What is the reorder point?

4,000

: 8-17 Lila's brother believes that she places too many orders for screws per year. He believes that an order should be placed only twice per year. If Lila follows her brother's policy, how much more would this cost every year over the ordering policy that she developed in Problem 8-15? If only two orders were placed each year, what effect would this have on the reorder point (ROP)?

$45 more
No effect

QA8-18

: 8-18 Barbara Bright is the purchasing agent for West Valve Co. West Valve sells industrial valves and fluid control devices. One of the most popular valves is the Western, which has an annual demand of 4,000 units. The cost of each valve is $90 and the inventory carrying cost is estimated to be 10% of the cost of each valve. Barbara has made a study of the costs involved in placing an order for any of the valves that West Valve stocks, and she has concluded that the average ordering cost is $25 per order. Furthermore, it takes about two weeks for an order to arrive from the supplier, and during this time the demand per week for West valves is approximately 80.

(a) What is the economic order quantity?   149

(b) What is the reorder point?   160

(c) What is the total annual inventory cost (carrying cost + ordering cost)? $1341

(d) What is the optimal number of orders per year?   27

(e) What is the optimal number of days between any two orders?   13.5

8-19 Ken Ramsing has been in the lumber business for most of his life. Ken's biggest competitor is Pacific Woods. Through many years of experience, Ken knows that the ordering cost for an order of plywood is $25 and that the carrying cost is 25% of the unit cost. Both Ken and Pacific Woods receive plywood in loads that cost $100 per load. Furthermore, Ken and Pacific Woods use the same supplier of plywood, and Ken was able to find out that Pacific Woods orders in quantities of 4,000 loads at a time. Ken also knows that 4,000 loads is the economic order quantity for Pacific Woods. What is the annual demand in loads of plywood for Pacific Woods?   8 million

8-20 Shoe Shine is a local retail shoe store located on the north side of Centerville. Annual demand for a popular sandal is 500 sandals, and John Dirk, the owner of Shoe Shine, has been in the habit of ordering 100 sandals at a time. John estimates that the ordering cost is $10 per order. The cost of the sandal is $5. For John's ordering policy to be correct, what would the carrying cost as a percentage of the unit cost have to be? If the carrying cost were 10% of the cost, what would the optimal order quantity be?   20%   141

8-21 In Problem 8-15 you helped Lila Battle determine the optimal order quantity for number 6 screws. She had estimated that the ordering cost was $10 per order. At this time, though, she believes that this estimate was too low. Although she does not know the exact ordering cost, she believes that it could be as high as $40 per order. How would the optimal order quantity change if the ordering cost were $20, $30, and $40?   20,000 for $C_o = \$10$; 28,284 for $C_o = \$20$; 34,641 for $C_o = \$30$; 40,000 for $C_o = \$40$

8-22 Annual demand for the Doll two-drawer filing cabinet is 50,000 units. Bill Doll, president of Doll Office Suppliers, controls one of the largest office supply stores in Nevada. He estimates that the ordering cost is $10 per order. The carrying cost is $4 per unit per year. It takes 25 days between the time that Bill places an order for the two-drawer filing cabinets and the time when they are received at his warehouse. During this time, the daily demand is estimated to be 250 units.   QA8-22

(a) What is the economic order quantity?   500

(b) What is the reorder point?   6250

(c) What is the optimal number of orders per year?   100

(d) What is the optimal number of days between orders?   3.65

(e) What is the optimal number of orders per month?   8.33

(f) What is the optimal number of weeks between orders?   .52

8-23 Pampered Pet, Inc., is a large pet store located in Eastwood Mall. Although the store specializes in dogs, it also sells fish, turtle, and bird supplies. Everlast Leader, which is a leather lead for dogs, costs Pampered Pet $7 each. There is an annual demand for 6,000 Everlast Leaders. The manager of Pampered Pet has determined that the ordering cost is $10 per order, and the carrying cost as a percent of the unit cost is 15%. Pampered Pet is now considering a new supplier of Everlast Leaders. Each lead would cost only $6.65, but in order to get this discount, Pampered Pet would have to buy shipments of 3,000 Everlast   QA8-23

Leaders at a time. Should Pampered Pet use the new supplier and take this discount for quantity buying?

Yes; Total cost = $41,416

QA8-24

🖥 : **8-24** Douglas Boats is a supplier of boating equipment for the states of Oregon and Washington. It sells 5,000 White Marine WM-4 diesel engines every year. These engines are shipped to Douglas in a shipping container that is 100 cubic feet, and Douglas Boats keeps the warehouse full of these WM-4 motors. The warehouse can hold 5,000 cubic feet of boating supplies. Douglas estimates that the ordering cost is $10 per order, and the carrying cost is estimated to be $10 per motor per year. Douglas Boats is considering the possibility of expanding the warehouse for the WM-4 motors. How much should Douglas Boats expand, and how much would it be worth for the company to make the expansion?

$250

QA8-25

🖥 : **8-25** Bill Doll (see Problem 8-22) now believes that the carrying cost may be as high as $16 per unit per year. Furthermore, Bill estimates that the lead time is 35 days instead of 25 days. Resolve Problem 8-22 using $16 for the carrying cost with a lead time of 35 days.

a. 250   b. 8750   c. 200
d. 1.83   e. 16.67   f. .26

: **8-26** Northern Distributors is a wholesale organization that supplies retail stores with lawn care and household products. One building is used to store Neverfail lawn mowers. The building is 25 feet wide by 40 feet deep by 8 feet high. Anna Young, manager of the warehouse, estimates that about 60% of the warehouse can be used to store the Neverfail lawn mowers. The remaining 40% is used for walkways and a small office. Each Neverfail lawn mower comes in a box that is 5 feet by 4 feet by 2 feet high. The annual demand for these lawn mowers is 12,000, and the ordering cost for Northern Distributors is $30 per order. It is estimated that it costs Northern $2 per lawn mower per year for storage. Northern Distributors is thinking about increasing the size of the warehouse. The company can only do this by making the warehouse deeper. At the present time, the warehouse is 40 feet deep. How many feet of depth should be added on to the warehouse to minimize the annual inventory costs? How much should the company be willing to pay for this addition? Remember that only 60% of the total area can be used to store Neverfail lawn mowers.

160 feet added
$1,920

QA8-27

🖥 : **8-27** Lisa Surowsky was asked to help in determining the best ordering policy for a new product. Currently, the demand for the new product has been projected to be about 1,000 units annually. In order to get a handle on the carrying and ordering costs, Lisa prepared a series of average inventory costs. Lisa thought that these costs would be appropriate for the new product. The results are summarized below. These data were compiled for 10,000 inventory items that were carried or held during the year and were ordered 100 times during the last year. Help Lisa determine the economic order quantity.

EOQ = 424.98

COST FACTOR	COST	COST FACTOR	COST
Taxes	$2,000	Inventory inquiries	$450
Processing and inspection	$1,500	Warehouse supplies	$280
New product development	$2,500	Research and development	$2,750
Bill paying	$500	Purchasing salaries	$3,000
Ordering supplies	$50	Warehouse salaries	$2,800
Inventory insurance	$600	Inventory theft	$800
Product advertising	$800	Purchase order supplies	$500
Spoilage	$750	Inventory obsolescence	$300
Sending purchasing orders	$800		

8-28 Melinda Sholer has spent the last few weeks determining inventory costs for Toco, a toy manufacturer located near Taos, New Mexico. She knows that annual demand will be 20,000 units per year and that carrying cost will be $.50 per unit per year. Ordering cost, on the other hand, can vary from $40 per order to $50 per order. During the last 486 working days, Melinda has observed the following frequency distribution for the ordering cost. Melinda's boss would like Melinda to determine an EOQ value for each possible ordering cost and to determine an EOQ value for the expected ordering cost.

QA8-28

ORDERING COST	FREQUENCY	ORDERING COST	FREQUENCY
$40	24	$46	64
$41	34	$47	45
$42	44	$48	44
$43	56	$49	23
$44	76	$50	10
$45	66		

See Instructor's Section.
EOQ = 1,890

CASE STUDY

Sturdivant Sound Systems

Sturdivant Sound Systems manufactures and sells stereo and CD sound systems in both console and component styles. All parts of the sound systems, with the exception of turntables, are produced in the Rochester, New York, plant. Turntables used in the assembly of Sturdivant's systems are purchased from Morris Electronics of Concord, New Hampshire.

Jason Pierce, purchasing agent for Sturdivant Sound Systems, submits a purchase requisition for the multispeed turntables once every four weeks. The company's annual requirements total 5,000 units (20 per working day), and the cost per unit is $60. (Sturdivant does not purchase in greater quantities because Morris Electronics, the supplier, does not offer quantity discounts.) Rarely does a shortage of turntables occur because Morris promises delivery within one week following receipt of a purchase requisition. (Total time between date of order and date of receipt is ten days.)

Associated with the purchase of each shipment are procurement costs. These costs, which amount

Source: Professor Jerry Kinard (Francis Marion College) and the late Professor Joe C. Iverstine. Used with permission of author.

to $20 per order, include the costs of preparing the requisition, inspecting and storing the delivered goods, updating inventory records, and issuing a voucher and a check for payment. In addition to procurement costs, Sturdivant Sound Systems incurs inventory carrying costs which include insurance, storage, handling, taxes, and so forth. These costs equal $6 per unit per year.

Beginning in August of this year, management of Sturdivant Sound Systems will embark on a company-wide cost control program in an attempt to improve its profits. One of the areas to be closely scrutinized for possible cost savings is inventory procurement.

Discussion Questions

1. Compute the optimal order quantity.

2. Determine the appropriate reorder point (in units).

3. Compute the cost savings which the company will realize if it implements the optimal inventory procurement decision.

4. Should procurement costs be considered a linear function of the number of orders?

Sturdivant 1. 183   2. 200   3. $354.55   4. No

CASE STUDY

Western Ranchman Outfitters

Western Ranchman Outfitters (WRO) is a family-owned and -operated mail order and retail store business in Cheyenne, Wyoming. It bills itself as "The Nation's Finest Western Store" and carries high-quality western apparel and riding supplies. Its catalog is mailed all over the world; the store and its president, John Veta, have appeared in a short article in *Fortune* magazine; and clothes from WRO were featured in an issue of *Mademoiselle*.

One of WRO's most staple items is the button front, shrink-to-fit blue jean made by Levi Strauss (model no. 501). This is the original riveted denim pant that cowboys shrank by sitting in a tub of hot water. It is the epitome of durability and fit and is still a popular jean. When Veta was asked his stock-out philosophy for this item, he answered, "Would you expect a drugstore to have aspirin?" Furthermore, Veta has had a pleasant relationship with Levi Strauss for all the years of his business career.

Don Randell, director of merchandising, takes a physical inventory of this item once a month. His records show annual usage, amount on hand, quantity ordered, and quantity received (which has been averaging 185 pairs per month, except in January–March when it averages 150 pairs per month), all dated by the month. The store attempts to keep a safety stock adequate for 60 days for two reasons: production problems of the supplier and a hedge against unusually large orders.

Randell described the problems of ordering: "The rag business," as it is known, "is made up of the most disorganized group of people I've ever had the opportunity to be associated with." The problems he cited include not specifying a delivery date, unexplained late deliveries, a general lack of productivity, and lead times of up to six months.

Randell contrasted this situation with his experience in the flexible packaging industry, where reliability was a hallmark and a delay of a single day warranted notification of the customer.

The most recent eight-month period is used to illustrate WRO's ordering difficulties. While the sample figures in the accompanying table may seem peculiar, they reflect WRO's philosophy of offering a full range of sizes and Randell's attempts to predict Levi Strauss' delivery pattern so that the store is close to obtaining the stock it

needs. For example, in the last eight months, no one bought a pair sized 27 × 36. Nevertheless, six were ordered and received so that should such a customer appear, he would be able to satisfy his needs. For size 27 × 34, 33 were ordered, but only 21 were received, which is very close to the 18 sold in the eight months of the previous year. The 27-inch and 28-inch waist sizes shown in the table are but two of the many available waist sizes, of course—waist sizes up to 60 inches are produced and sold.

Randell places an order for Levi blue jeans every month, doing his best to ensure an adequate supply for the business. Normally, WRO customers are not disappointed when requesting the Levi 501. However, in the past two months, the Wyoming Game and Fish Department has been requiring extra pairs of this jean, and WRO has not always had this exact jean in stock. Since there are at least four styles that satisfy the state requirements, the problem is usually overcome with other styles or brands.

Usage and Ordering of the Levi 501 for Selected Sizes

SIZE (IN INCHES) WAIST × LENGTH	USAGE	NUMBER ORDERED	NUMBER RECEIVED
27 × 28	11	—	—
27 × 29	1	—	—
27 × 30	6	—	—
27 × 31	0	—	—
27 × 32	4	—	—
27 × 33	—	—	—
27 × 34	18	33	21
27 × 36	—	6	6
28 × 28	—	—	—
28 × 29	—	—	—
28 × 30	—	—	—
28 × 31	—	3	3
28 × 32	4	—	—
28 × 33	7	—	—
28 × 34	8	21	12
28 × 36	27	30	18
	86	93	60*

* Approximately 65% of the number ordered were received.

Annual demand at WRO for the Levi 501 is 2,000 pair. The cost of placing an order is about $10, the carrying cost is 12%, and the cost of the Levi to WRO is $10.05 per pair.

Source: Barry Render, and others, *Cases and Readings in Management Science,* 2nd ed., Boston: Allyn and Bacon, Inc., 1990.

The model used is very close to the EOQ approach and is valid. See the Instructor's Section for details.

Discussion Questions

Evaluate Randell's ordering policy. How does it compare with formal mathematical approaches?

BIBLIOGRAPHY

Badinetti, Ralph D. "Optimal Safety Stock Investment Through Subjective Evaluation of Stockout Costs." *Management Science* **17**, 3 (1986): 312–328.

Banerjee, V. "Joint Economic Lot Size for Purchaser and Vendor." *Decision Sciences* **17**, 3 (Summer 1986): 292–311.

Chakravarty, Amiya K. "Joint Inventory Replenishment with Group Discounts Based on Invoice Value." *Management Science* **30**, 9 (September 1984): 1105–1112.

Mamer, John W., and Stephen H. Smith. "Job Completion Based Inventory Systems: Optimal Policies for Repair Kits and Spare Machines." *Management Science* **31**, 6 (June 1985): 703–718.

Mitra, A., and J. F. Cox. "EOQ Formula: Is it Valid Under Inflationary Conditions?" *Decision Sciences* **14**, 4 (1983): 360–374.

Noori, A. Hamid, and Gerald Keller. "Lot Size Reorder Point." *Decision Sciences* **17**, 3 (Summer 1986): 285–291.

Orlicky, J. *Material Requirements Planning.* New York: McGraw-Hill Book Co., 1975.

Roundy, Robin. "98% Effective Inter-Ration Lot-Sizing for One-Warehouse Multi-Retailer Systems." *Management Science* **31**, 11 (November 1985): 1416–1430.

Appendix: Determining EOQ with Calculus

In this appendix we investigate how the economic order quantity, Q*, can be determined using calculus. Although the other optimal quantities are not determined, the procedure is the same. The first step is to develop a total cost equation that is a function of the optimal quantity, in this case, Q. Then the first derivative is computed and set equal to 0. Finally, we solve for the optimal quantity. Here is how this is done with the economic order quantity.

1. Develop the equation for the total cost.

Total cost = Ordering cost + Carrying cost $TC = \dfrac{DC_o}{Q} + \dfrac{QC_h}{2}$

2. Take the first derivative and set it equal to 0.

$$\frac{dTC}{dQ} = 0 \qquad \frac{dTC}{dQ} = -\frac{DC_o}{Q^2} + \frac{C_h}{2} = 0$$

3. Solve for the optimal quantity.

$$-\frac{DC_o}{Q^2} + \frac{C_h}{2} = 0; \; \frac{C_h}{2} = \frac{DC_o}{Q^2}; \; \frac{Q^2 C_h}{2} = DC_o; \; Q^2 = \frac{2DC_o}{C_h}; \; Q = \sqrt{\frac{2DC_o}{C_h}}$$

In more complex inventory problems, setting ordering cost equal to carrying cost does not give the optimal solution. In these cases, it is necessary to use calculus to determine the best inventory policy.

Appendix: Using Spreadsheets to Solve Basic Inventory Problems

This chapter solved several basic inventory problems, including the economic order quantity, the reorder point, the optimal number of orders per year, and the optimal number of days between orders. These quantities can be easily determined using a spreadsheet. (See Program 8.1.) Note that this symbolic spreadsheet has input data and output results in different sections. All of the input data are entered in cells F5 through F10. The formulas are in cells F14 through F18. For example, the formula @SQRT(2*F7*F5/F6) computes the economic order quantity. The reorder point, optimal number of orders per year, and the optimal number of days between orders are computed using the formulas presented in the chapter.

PROGRAM 8.1 Using a Spreadsheet to Solve Basic Inventory Problems

```
        A         B         C         D      E         F
 1  Economic Order Quality
 2
 3  Inventory Input Data
 4
 5  Ordering Cost                                        10
 6  Carrying Cost                                       0.5
 7  Annual Demand                                      1000
 8
 9  Demand per Day Over Lead Time                        40
10  Lead Time in Days                                     3
11
12  Inventory Output Results
13
14  Economic Order Quantity in Units          @SQRT(2*F7*F5/F6)
15  Reorder Point in Units                    +F9*F10
16
17  Optimal Number of Orders per Year         +F7/F14
18  Optimal Number of Days Between Orders     365/F17
19
20
```

9

Inventory Control Models: II

CHAPTER OUTLINE

9.1 Introduction

9.2 EOQ Without the Instantaneous Receipt Assumption

9.3 Quantity Discount Models

9.4 Planned Shortages

9.5 Use of Safety Stock

9.6 ABC Analysis and Joint Ordering

9.7 Dependent Demand: The Case for Material Requirements Planning (MRP)

9.8 The Kanban System

9.9 Using the Computer to Solve Inventory Control Problems

9.10 Summary
    Glossary

Key Equations

Solved Problems

Discussion Questions and Problems

Case Study:
    Professional Video Management

Bibliography

Appendix: Solving the Planned Shortages (Back Order) Model with Calculus

Appendix: Using Spreadsheets to Solve Inventory Problems

9.1 INTRODUCTION

The fundamentals of inventory control were presented in Chapter 8. By making a number of assumptions, it was possible to develop some straightforward and easy-to-use inventory techniques that determine when to order and how much to order. However, the assumptions of Chapter 8 often do not apply. For example, in some production processes, inventory gradually builds up over time instead of being instantaneously received. In addition, discounts are often available when supplies are purchased in large quantities. Sometimes, shortages and stockouts cannot be avoided because demand is not known or constant.

Although the inventory models we look at in this chapter are more complex than the economic order quantity (EOQ) model seen earlier, the fundamental objectives are still the same. We are still trying to minimize total inventory cost. We begin this chapter by investigating how EOQ can be used in the production process.

9.2 EOQ WITHOUT THE INSTANTANEOUS RECEIPT ASSUMPTION

When a firm receives its inventory over a period of time, a new model is needed that does not require the *instantaneous inventory receipt* assumption of Chapter 8. This new model is applicable when inventory continuously flows or builds up over a period of time after an order has been placed or when units are produced and sold simultaneously. Under these circumstances, the daily demand rate must be taken into account. Figure 9.1 shows inventory levels as a function of time. Because this model is especially suited to the production environment, it is commonly called the *production run model*.

In the production process, instead of having an ordering cost, there will be a *setup cost*. This is the cost of setting up the production facility to

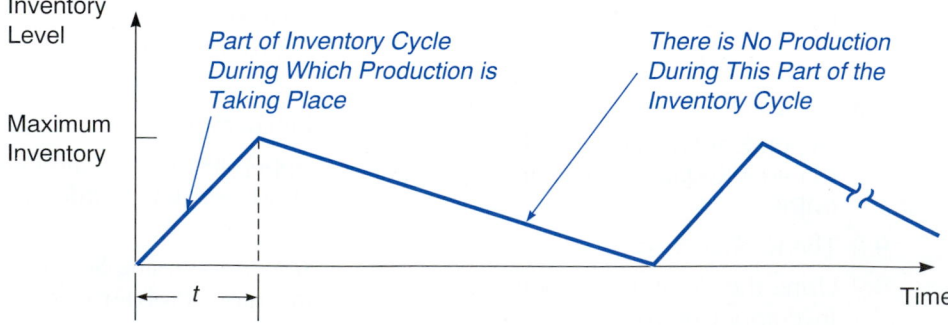

FIGURE 9.1
Inventory Control and the Production Process

manufacture the desired product. It normally includes the salaries and wages of employees who are responsible for setting up the equipment, engineering and design costs of making the setup, paperwork, supplies, utilities, and so on. The carrying cost per unit is composed of the same factors as the traditional EOQ model presented in the previous chapter, although the annual carrying cost equation changes.

The production run model can be derived by setting setup costs equal to holding or carrying costs and solving for the order quantity. Let's start by developing the expression for carrying cost. You should note, however, that making setup cost equal to carrying cost does not always guarantee optimal solutions for models more complex than the production run model.

solving the production run model

Determining the Annual Carrying Cost

Using the following variables, we can determine the expression for annual inventory carrying cost for the production run model:

Transparency Master 9.3: EOQ without the Instantaneous Receipt Assumption.

Q = Number of pieces per order or production run

C_h = Holding or carrying cost per unit per year

p = Daily product rate

d = Daily demand rate

t = Length of the production run in days

1. Annual inventory holding or carrying cost

   = (Average inventory level) × (Carrying cost per unit per year)

   = (Average inventory level) × C_h

2. Average inventory level = ½(Maximum inventory level)

3. Maximum inventory level

   $$= \begin{matrix} \text{(Total produced during} \\ \text{the production run)} \end{matrix} - \begin{matrix} \text{(Total used during} \\ \text{the production run)} \end{matrix}$$

   But Q = Total produced = pt, and thus $t = Q/p$. Therefore maximum inventory level = $p(Q/p) - d(Q/p) = Q - (d/p)Q = Q(1 - d/p)$.

4. Annual inventory carrying cost (or simply carrying cost)

   $$= \tfrac{1}{2}(\text{Maximum inventory level}) \times C_h \qquad \textbf{(9-1)}$$
   $$= \tfrac{1}{2} \times Q(1 - d/p) \times C_h$$

(*Note:* This is the same as the carrying cost developed in the EOQ model in the last chapter except that the factor $(1 - d/p)$ appears in the expression for carrying cost.)

Finding the Annual Setup Cost or the Annual Ordering Cost

When a product is being produced over time, setup cost replaces the ordering cost. Here is how *annual setup cost* and *annual ordering cost* can be determined.

1. Annual setup cost $= \left(\begin{array}{c}\text{Number of setups} \\ \text{per year}\end{array}\right)\left(\begin{array}{c}\text{Setup cost} \\ \text{per setup}\end{array}\right)$ (9-2)

$$= \frac{D}{Q_p}C_s$$

where

$$D = \text{annual demand in units,}$$

$$Q_p = \text{quantity produced in one batch, and}$$

$$C_s = \text{setup cost per setup.}$$

2. Annual ordering cost $= \dfrac{D}{Q}C_0$ (9-3)

(See Chapter 8.)

As you can see, the form of the equation for the annual setup cost is identical to the form of the equation for the annual ordering cost. In determining the optimal order quantity, we will use the variables presented in Equation 9-3 for the case where the inventory is ordered instead of produced. It should be noted, however, that the same optimal equation can be used in determining the optimal production quantity, Q_p^*, as well. Q_p and C_s would replace Q and C_o in the equation.

Determining the Optimal Order Quantity and Production Quantity

With this model, it is possible to determine the optimal quantity by setting the ordering cost equal to the carrying cost and solving for the desired quantity. Here is how this can be accomplished when the inventory is ordered.

1. Ordering cost $= \dfrac{D}{Q}C_o$.

2. Carrying cost $= \frac{1}{2}C_hQ\left(1 - \dfrac{d}{p}\right)$.

3. Set ordering cost equal to carrying cost.

$$\frac{D}{Q}C_o = \frac{1}{2}C_hQ\left(1 - \frac{d}{p}\right)$$

4. Solve for Q^*.

$$Q^2 = \frac{2DC_o}{C_h\left(1 - \dfrac{d}{p}\right)}$$

$$Q^* = \sqrt{\frac{2DC_o}{C_h\left(1 - \dfrac{d}{p}\right)}} \qquad \text{(9-4)} \qquad \text{optimal order quantity}$$

The same calculations can be made to determine the optimal production quantity, Q_p^*. The results of these calculations appear in Equation 9-5.

$$Q_p^* = \sqrt{\frac{2DC_s}{C_h\left(1 - \dfrac{d}{p}\right)}} \qquad \text{(9-5)} \qquad \text{optimal production quantity}$$

Brown Manufacturing Example

Brown Manufacturing produces commercial refrigeration units in batches. The firm's estimated demand for the year is 10,000 units. It costs about $100 to set up the manufacturing process, and the carrying cost is about 50¢ per unit per year. Once the production process has been set up, 80 refrigeration units can be manufactured daily. The demand during the production period has traditionally been 60 units each day. How many refrigeration units should Brown Manufacturing produce in each batch? How long should the production part of the cycle shown in Figure 9.1 last? Here is the solution:

Alternate Example 9-1

Annual demand $= D = 10,000$ units

Setup cost $= C_s = \$100$

Carrying cost $= C_h = \$.50$ per unit per year

Daily production rate $= p = 80$ units daily

Daily demand rate $= d = 60$ units daily

1. $Q_p^* = \sqrt{\dfrac{2DC_s}{C_h\left(1 - \dfrac{d}{p}\right)}}$

2. $Q_p^* = \sqrt{\dfrac{2 \times 10,000 \times 100}{.5\left(1 - \dfrac{60}{80}\right)}}$

$Q_p^* = \sqrt{\dfrac{2,000,000}{.5(¼)}} = \sqrt{16,000,000}$

$Q_p^* = 4,000$ units

If $Q_p^* = 4,000$ units and we know that 80 units can be produced daily, the length of each production cycle will be $Q/p = 4,000/80 = 50$ days. Thus, when Brown decides to produce refrigeration units, the equipment will be set up to manufacture the units for a 50-day time span.

We now turn to a model with different assumptions, the quantity discount model.

9.3 QUANTITY DISCOUNT MODELS

**Applicable Problems:
9-10, 9-23, 9-28,
Professional Video
Management Case**

To increase sales, many companies offer quantity discounts to their customers. A *quantity discount* is simply a reduced cost (*C*) for the item when it is purchased in larger quantities. It is not uncommon to have a discount schedule with several discounts for large orders. A typical quantity discount schedule appears in Table 9.1.

As can be seen in the table, the normal cost for the item is $5. When 1,000 to 1,999 units are ordered at one time, then the cost per unit drops to $4.80, and when the quantity ordered at one time is 2,000 units or more, the cost is $4.75 per unit. As always, management must decide when and how much to order. But with quantity discounts, how does the manager make these decisions?

→ KEY IDEA

As with other inventory models discussed so far, the overall objective will be to minimize the total cost. Since the unit cost for the third discount in Table 9.1 is lowest, you might be tempted to order 2,000 units or more to take advantage of the lower material cost. Placing an order for that quantity with the greatest discount cost, however, might not minimize the total inventory cost. As the discount quantity goes up, the material cost goes down, but the carrying cost increases because the orders are large. Thus, the major trade-off when considering quantity discounts is between the reduced material cost and the increased carrying cost. When we include the cost of the material, the equation for the total annual inventory cost becomes:

minimizing total cost

$$\text{Total cost} = \text{Material cost} + \text{Ordering cost} + \text{Carrying cost}$$

$$\text{Total cost} = DC + \frac{D}{Q} C_o + \frac{Q}{2} C_h \qquad (9\text{-}6)$$

TABLE 9.1 A Quantity Discount Schedule

DISCOUNT NUMBER	DISCOUNT QUANTITY	DISCOUNT (%)	DISCOUNT COST ($)
1	0 to 999	0	5.00
2	1,000 to 1,999	4	4.80
3	2,000 and over	5	4.75

where

$$D = \text{annual demand in units,}$$
$$C_o = \text{ordering cost per order,}$$
$$C = \text{cost per unit, and}$$
$$C_h = \text{holding cost per unit per year.}$$

Now, we have to determine the quantity that minimizes the total annual inventory cost. This process involves four steps:

1. For each discount, calculate a Q^* value using the following equation:

$$Q^* = \sqrt{\frac{2DC_o}{IC}}$$

Note that the carrying cost is IC instead of C_h. Because the cost of the item is a factor in annual carrying cost, we cannot assume that the carrying cost is a constant when the cost per unit changes for each quantity discount. Thus, it is common to express the carrying cost (I) as a percentage of unit cost (C) instead of as a constant cost per unit per year, C_h.

2. For any discount, if the order quantity is too low to qualify for the discount, adjust the order quantity upward to the lowest quantity that qualifies for the discount. For example, if Q^* for discount 2 in Table 9.1 were 500 units, you would adjust this value up to 1,000 units. Look at the second discount in Table 9.1. Order quantities between 1,000 and 1,999 qualify for the 4% discount. Thus, we adjust the order quantity up to be 1,000 units if Q^* is below 1,000 units.

    The reasoning for step 2 may not be obvious. If the order quantity is below the quantity range that qualifies for a discount, a quantity within this range may still result in the lowest total cost.

    As seen in Figure 9.2, the total cost curve is broken into three different total cost curves. There is a total cost curve for the first ($0 \le Q \le 999$), second ($1,000 \le Q \le 1,999$), and third ($Q \ge 2,000$) discount. Look at the total cost (TC) curve for discount 2. Q^* for discount 2 is less than the allowable discount range, which is from 1,000 to 1,999 units. As seen in the figure, the lowest allowable quantity in this range, which is 1,000 units, is the quantity that minimizes the total cost. Thus, the second step is needed to ensure that we do not discard an order quantity that may indeed produce the minimum cost. It should be noted that an order quantity computed in step 1 that is greater than the range that would qualify it for a discount may be discarded.

3. Using the total cost Equation 9-6, compute a total cost for every Q^* determined in steps 1 and 2. If you had to adjust Q^* upward because it was below the allowable quantity range, make sure to use the adjusted value for Q^*.

4. Select that Q^* that has the lowest total cost as computed in step 3. It will be the quantity that minimizes the total inventory cost.

Transparency Master 9.4: Quantity Discount Steps.

calculate Q^* values

I is used instead of C_h

Teaching Suggestion 9.3: Adjusting the Order Quantity Upward. See the Instructor's Section for details.

adjust the Q^* values

total cost curve is broken into parts

compute total cost

select Q^* with lowest total cost

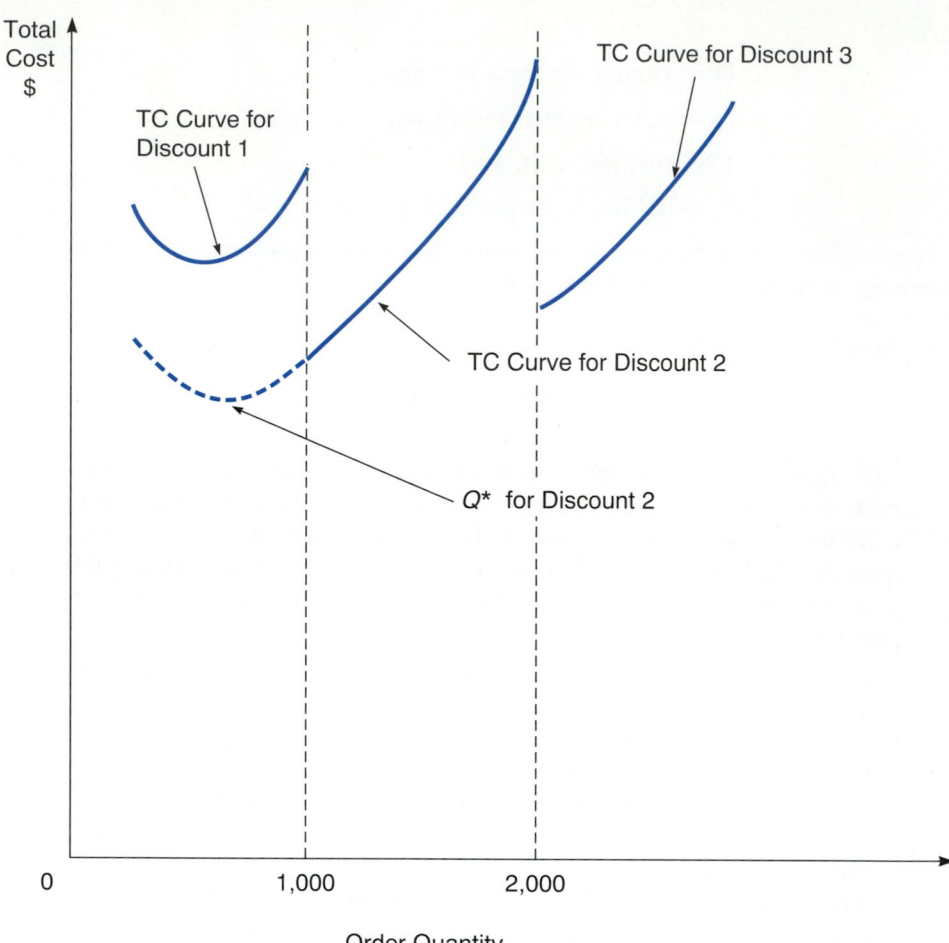

FIGURE 9.2
Total Cost Curve for the Quantity Discount Model

Brass Department store example

Let's see how this procedure can be applied by showing an example. Brass Department Store stocks toy race cars. Recently, the store was given a quantity discount schedule for the cars; this quantity schedule was shown in Table 9.1. Thus, the normal cost for the toy race cars is $5. For orders between 1,000 and 1,999 units, the unit cost is $4.80, and for orders of 2,000 or more units, the unit cost is $4.75. Furthermore, the ordering cost is $49 per order, the annual demand is 5,000 race cars, and the inventory carrying charge as a percentage of cost, I, is 20% or .2. What order quantity will minimize the total inventory cost?

The first step is to compute Q^* for every discount in Table 9.1. This is done as follows:

Alternate Example 9-2

$$Q_1^* = \sqrt{\frac{(2)(5{,}000)(49)}{(.2)(5.00)}} = 700 \text{ cars per order}$$

$$Q_2^* = \sqrt{\frac{(2)(5,000)(49)}{(.2)(4.80)}} = 714 \text{ cars per order}$$

Q* values are computed

$$Q_3^* = \sqrt{\frac{(2)(5,000)(49)}{(.2)(4.75)}} = 718 \text{ cars per order}$$

The second step is to adjust those values of Q^* that are below the allowable discount range. Since Q_1^* is between 0 and 999, it does not have to be adjusted. Q_2^* is below the allowable range of 1,000 to 1,999, and therefore, it must be adjusted to 1,000 units. The same is true for Q_3^*; it must be adjusted to 2,000 units. After this step, the following order quantities must be tested in the total cost equation:

Q* values are adjusted

$$Q_1^* = 700$$

$$Q_2^* = 1,000 \text{—adjusted}$$

$$Q_3^* = 2,000 \text{—adjusted}$$

The third step is to use the total cost Equation 9-6 and compute a total cost for each of the order quantities. This is accomplished with the aid of Table 9.2.

total cost is computed

The fourth step is to select that order quantity with the lowest total cost. Looking at Table 9.2, you can see that an order quantity of 1,000 toy race cars minimizes the total cost. It should be recognized, however, that the total cost for ordering 2,000 cars is only slightly greater than the total cost for ordering 1,000 cars. Thus, if the third discount cost is lowered to $4.65, for example, then this order quantity might be the one that minimizes the total inventory cost.

Q* is selected

9.4 PLANNED SHORTAGES

**Applicable Problems:
9-11, 9-16, 9-22, 9-26**

In previous inventory models, we have not allowed inventory shortages where there was not sufficient stock to meet current demand. There are many situations, however, that suggest that *planned shortages* or *stockouts* may be advisable. This is especially true with high inventory carrying costs for expensive items. Car dealerships and appliance stores rarely stock every model for this reason.

Teaching Suggestion 9.4:
The Planned Shortages
Model Is More Complex Than
Other Inventory Models. See
the Instructor's Section for
details.

In the following model, we assume that stockouts and back ordering are allowed. This model is called the *back order* or *planned shortages inventory model*. A back order is a situation in which a customer places an order,

TABLE 9.2 Total Cost Computations for Brass Department Store

DISCOUNT NUMBER	UNIT PRICE	ORDER QUANTITY	ANNUAL MATERIAL COST ($)	ANNUAL ORDERING COST ($)	ANNUAL CARRYING COST ($)	TOTAL ($)
1	$5.00	700	25,000	350	350	25,700
2	$4.80	1,000	24,000	245	480	24,725
3	$4.75	2,000	23,750	122.5	950	24,822.5

assumptions of the model

finds that the supplier is out of stock, and waits for the next shipment (the back order) to arrive. The model assumes that the customer's sale will not be lost due to the stockout. It also assumes that back orders will be satisfied before any new demand for the product. We use the following variables in the back order model:

$$Q = \text{Number of pieces per order}$$
$$D = \text{Annual demand in units}$$
$$C_h = \text{Carrying cost per unit per year}$$
$$C_o = \text{Ordering cost for each order}$$
$$C_b = \text{Back ordering cost per unit per year}$$
$$Q - S = \text{Remaining units after back order is satisfied}$$
$$S = \text{Amount back ordered}$$

back ordering cost

customer dissatisfaction cost

Two variables you have not seen before have been used. The first, C_b, is the *back ordering cost per unit per year.* As with regular orders, a back order is placed when a shortage occurs for the desired units or products. Thus, all of the costs of placing an ordinary order are involved in placing a back order. In addition, there is a cost that is due to customer dissatisfaction, or the loss of goodwill. For example, customers are not likely to keep buying from a supplier who is regularly out of stock and who regularly has to back order. Therefore, the back order cost includes a cost factor to account for the inconvenience of the back order to the customer. Since the back order cost depends upon how long the customer waits to receive an order, it is similar to the inventory carrying cost and is expressed in dollars per unit per year.

amount back ordered is S

The other new variable is S, which is the amount back ordered. $Q - S$ is the number of units remaining after the back order has been satisfied. Allowing back orders changes the inventory usage curve. When back orders are allowed, this curve has the appearance shown in Figure 9.3.

Finding Optimal Order and Back Order Levels

KEY IDEA

Teaching Suggestion 9.5:
The Difference Between the Planned Shortages Model and the Basic EOQ Model. See the Instructor's Section for details.

Given data for the preceding variables, we would like to determine optimal values for the order quantity, Q^*, and the optimal number of units that are actually back ordered, S^*. The previously used technique of setting ordering cost equal to carrying cost does not work because of the back ordering cost. Thus, it is necessary to develop a total cost equation. Then, calculus can be used to solve for the optimal quantities.

The total annual cost will be:

$$TC = \text{Ordering cost} + \text{Carrying cost} + \text{Back ordering cost}$$

ordering cost

The ordering cost is identical to the ordering cost developed for the traditional EOQ model. (See Chapter 8.)

$$\text{Ordering cost} = \frac{D}{Q} C_o$$

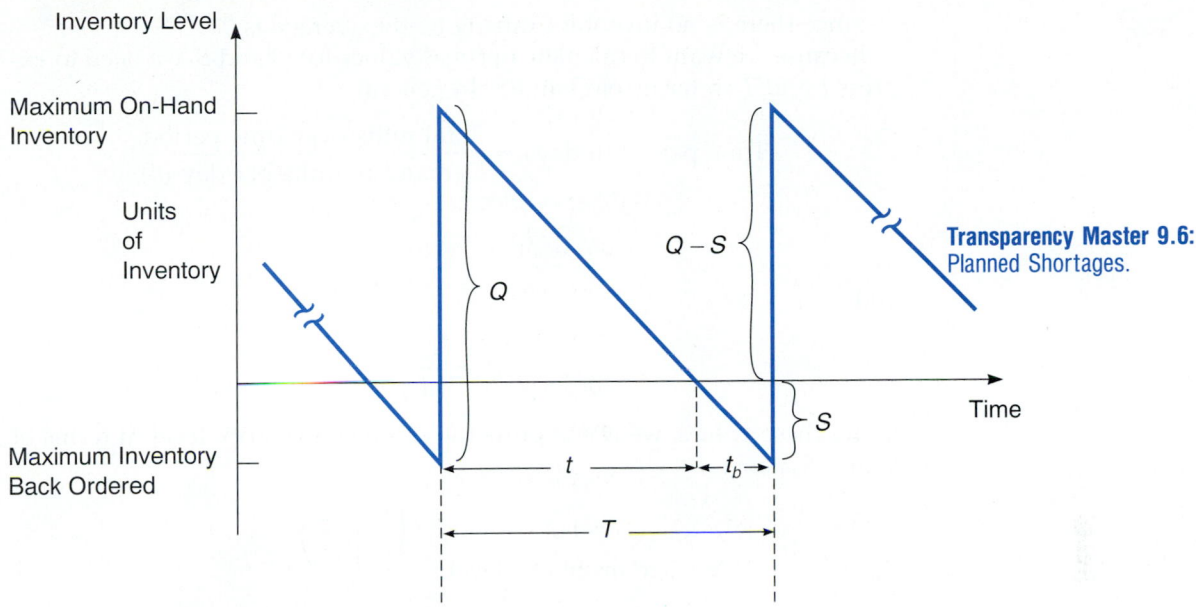

Transparency Master 9.6:
Planned Shortages.

FIGURE 9.3
Inventory Usage with Back Ordering

The carrying cost is the average inventory level times the holding or carrying cost per unit per year, C_h.

carrying cost

$$\text{Carrying cost} = (\text{Average inventory level})(C_h)$$

Now, the problem is to compute the average inventory level. In the past, this has been the maximum inventory level divided by 2. In this case, this would be $(Q - S)/2$. But this is the average inventory level during the period when we still have inventory, t, and not over the total time, T. Note that in Figure 9.3, important variables are:

$t =$ Time between the receipt of an order and when the inventory level drops to 0

$t_b =$ Time during which back order or stockouts will occur

$T =$ Total time: $T = t + t_b$

The average inventory level over the total time period is a weighted average.

$$\begin{aligned}
\text{Average} \atop \text{inventory} \atop \text{level} &= \frac{\left(\begin{array}{c}\text{Average level} \\ \text{over } t\end{array}\right)t + \left(\begin{array}{c}\text{Average level} \\ \text{over } t_b\end{array}\right)t_b}{T} \\[2em]
&= \frac{\left(\dfrac{Q - S}{2}\right)t + 0t_b}{T} \\[2em]
&= \frac{\left(\dfrac{Q - S}{2}\right)t}{T}
\end{aligned}$$

Since there is no inventory during t_b, the average is 0.

Because we want to calculate optimal values for Q and S, we need to express t and T in terms of Q and S. In general,

$$\text{Time period in days} = \frac{\text{Total units over time period}}{\text{Demand in units per day } (d)}$$

$$t = \frac{Q - S}{d}$$

and

$$T = \frac{Q}{d}$$

Using these values, we can express the average inventory level in terms of Q and S alone.

$$\text{Average inventory level} = \frac{\left(\dfrac{Q - S}{2}\right)t}{T}$$

$$= \frac{\left(\dfrac{Q - S}{2}\right)\left(\dfrac{Q - S}{d}\right)}{\dfrac{Q}{d}}$$

$$= \frac{(Q - S)^2}{2Q}$$

$$\text{Carrying cost} = \left(\begin{array}{c}\text{Average} \\ \text{inventory} \\ \text{level}\end{array}\right)C_h$$

$$= \frac{(Q - S)^2}{2Q}C_h$$

Back ordering cost must be computed in the same way. The average number of units on back order is:

$$\begin{array}{c}\text{Average number of} \\ \text{units on back order}\end{array} = \frac{0t + \left(\dfrac{S}{2}\right)t_b}{T}$$

$$= \frac{\left(\dfrac{S}{2}\right)t_b}{T}$$

Again, we must express t_b and T as a function of Q and S.

$$t_b = \frac{S}{d}$$

$$T = \frac{Q}{d}$$

Thus,

$$\text{Average number of units on back order} = \frac{\left(\dfrac{S}{2}\right)\left(\dfrac{S}{d}\right)}{\dfrac{Q}{d}} = \frac{S^2}{2Q}$$

$$\text{Back ordering cost} = \left(\text{Average number of units on back order}\right)C_b$$

$$= \frac{S^2}{2Q}C_b$$

Now we can write the expression for total annual cost.

total cost

$$\text{TC} = \underset{\text{cost}}{\text{Ordering}} + \underset{\text{cost}}{\text{Carrying}} + \underset{\text{cost}}{\text{Back ordering}} \qquad \text{(9-7)}$$

$$= \frac{D}{Q}C_o + \frac{(Q - S)^2}{2Q}C_h + \frac{S^2}{2Q}C_b$$

The optimal values for the order quantity, Q^*, and units back ordered, S^*, are found by using calculus. This is shown in the appendix to this chapter. The results are as follows:

$$Q^* = \sqrt{\frac{2DC_o}{C_h}\left(\frac{C_h + C_b}{C_b}\right)} \qquad \text{(9-8)}$$

optimal values for Q^* and S^*

$$S^* = Q^*\left(\frac{C_h}{C_h + C_b}\right) \qquad \text{(9-9)}$$

Butch Radner's Planned Shortages

Butch Radner, a supplier of ladies' garments, is trying to determine how many dresses to order for his fall collection. Because the number of different styles and sizes is extremely large, he has decided to have planned shortages. While customers are not happy with these shortages, back orders are very common because Butch is a charming man and his styles are beautiful. So far, no one has canceled an order because of the delay. The demand for a particular dress is 10,000 units. The carrying cost is $2 per dress per year, and the ordering cost is $7.50 per order. Butch estimates that his back ordering cost is $10 per dress per year. How many dresses should Butch order? How many garments will be back ordered each inventory cycle? The calculations are:

Alternate Example 9-3

$$D = 10{,}000 \text{ dresses}$$
$$C_h = \$2$$
$$C_o = \$7.50$$
$$C_b = \$10$$

$$Q^* = \sqrt{\frac{(2)\,(10{,}000)\,(7.5)}{2}\left(\frac{2+10}{10}\right)}$$

$$= \sqrt{75{,}000\left(\frac{12}{10}\right)} = 300 \text{ dresses per order}$$

$$S^* = Q^*\left(\frac{C_h}{C_h + C_b}\right)$$

$$= 300\left(\frac{2}{2+10}\right) = 50 \text{ back-ordered dresses per back order}$$

9.5   USE OF SAFETY STOCK

Applicable Problems:
9-12, 9-13, 9-17, 9-19, 9-27

Use of the back order inventory model assumes that a customer patiently waits until his or her order can be filled and that demand is certain. When management believes that these assumptions are not valid, it may turn to the use of *safety stock*.[1]

Safety stock is additional stock that is kept on hand. If, for example, safety stock for an item is 50 units, you are carrying an average of 50 units more of inventory during the year. When demand is unusually high, you dip into the safety stock instead of encountering a *stockout*. Thus, the main purpose of safety stock is to avoid stockouts when the demand is higher than expected. Its use is shown in Figure 9.4. Note that although stockouts can often be avoided by using safety stock there is still a chance that they may occur. The demand may be so high that all of the safety stock is used up, and thus there is still a stockout.

avoiding stockouts

safety stock and the reorder point

One of the best ways of maintaining a safety stock level is to use the re-order point, ROP. This can be accomplished by adding the number of units of safety stock as a buffer to the reorder point. As you recall,

$$\text{Reorder point} = \text{ROP} = d \times L$$

$$d = \text{Daily demand}$$

$$L = \text{Order lead time or the number}$$
$$\text{of working days it takes to}$$
$$\text{deliver an order}$$

With the inclusion of safety stock, the reorder point becomes

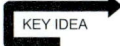
KEY IDEA

$$\text{ROP} = d \times L + \text{SS} \qquad\qquad \textbf{(9-10)}$$

$$\text{SS} = \text{Safety stock}$$

How to determine the correct amount of safety stock is the only remaining question. If cost data are available, the objective is to minimize total

---

[1] Safety stock is used only when demand is uncertain, and models under uncertainty are generally much harder to deal with than models under certainty.

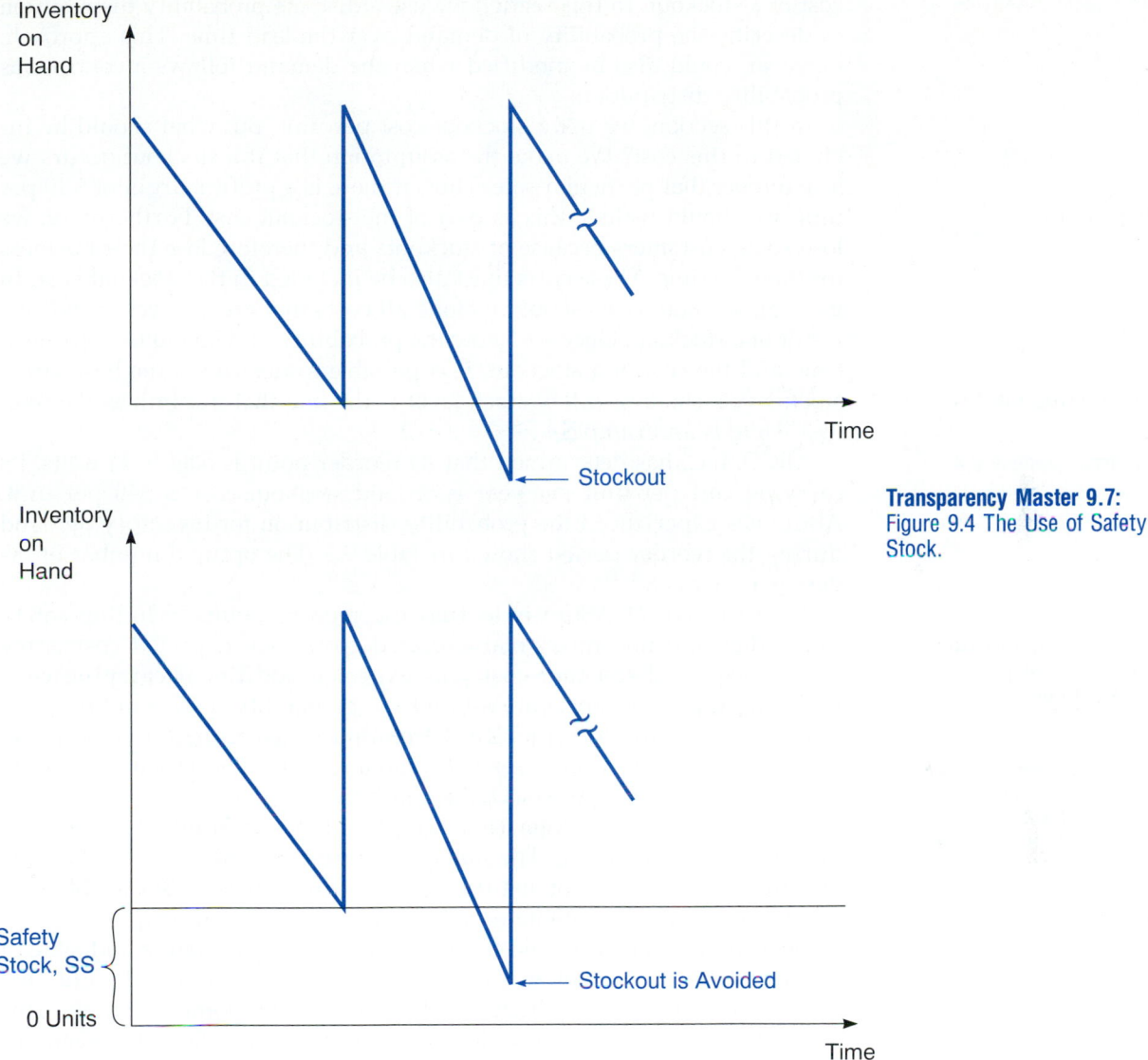

Transparency Master 9.7:
Figure 9.4 The Use of Safety
Stock.

FIGURE 9.4
Use of Safety Stock

cost. If cost data are not available, then it is necessary to establish a service level or policy.

Reorder Point with Known Stockout Costs

When the economic order quantity is fixed, and the reorder point is used to place orders, the only time that a stockout can occur is during the lead time. As you recall, the lead time is the time between when the order is placed and when it is received. In the techniques discussed here, it is necessary to know the probability of demand during the lead time and the

probability of demand

cost of a stockout. In this section we use a discrete probability distribution to describe the probability of demand over the lead time. This approach, however, could also be modified when the demand follows a continuous probability distribution.

In this section, we use a stockout cost per unit. But what should be included in this cost? We make the assumption that if a stockout occurs we lose forever that particular sale. Thus, if there is a profit margin of $.10 per unit, we should include this as part of the stockout cost. Furthermore, we lose some customers because of stockouts and therefore lose their business for their lifetime. These costs must also be included in the stockout cost. In general, stockout costs should include all costs that are a direct or indirect result of a stockout. Once we know the probability of demand over the lead time and the cost of a stockout, it is possible to determine the best safety stock level. The best safety stock level is the one that minimizes the total cost. Here is an example.

ABCO, Inc., has determined that its reorder point is 50($d \times L$) units. Its carrying cost per unit per year is $5 and stockout cost is $40 per unit. ABCO has experienced the probability distribution for inventory demand during the reorder period shown in Table 9.3. The optimal number of orders per year is 6.[2]

The objective of ABCO is to find the reorder point, including safety stock, that will minimize total expected cost. Total expected cost is the sum of **expected stockout cost** plus **expected additional carrying cost.** When we know the stockout cost and the probability of demand over the lead time, the inventory problem becomes a decision making under risk problem. (You may wish to refer to Chapter 5 for a discussion of decision making under risk.) For ABCO, the alternatives are to use a reorder point of 30 (Alternative 1), 40 (Alternative 2), 50 (Alternative 3), 60 (Alternative 4), or 70 units (Alternative 5). The states of nature are demand values 30 (State of nature 1), 40 (State of nature 2), 50 (State of nature 3), 60 (State of nature 4), and 70 units (State of nature 5) over the lead time.

Determining the economic consequence for any alternative and state of nature combination involves a careful analysis of stockout and additional carrying cost. Consider a situation where the reorder point is 30 units. This means that we will place an order for additional units when the inventory on hand reaches 30 units. If the demand over lead time is also 30 units,

margin notes (left column):

stockout cost

minimizing total cost

Alternate Example 9-4

minimizing additional carrying cost plus stockout cost

Teaching Suggestion 9.6: Stockout Cost Calculations May Be Difficult to Understand for Some. See the Instructor's Section for details.

TABLE 9.3 Probability of Demand for ABCO, Inc.

NUMBER OF UNITS		PROBABILITY
	30	.2
	40	.2
ROP ⟶	50	.3
	60	.2
	70	.1
		1.0

[2] We have assumed that we already know Q^* and ROP. If this assumption is not made, then Q^*, ROP, and safety stock would have to be determined simultaneously. This requires a more complex solution.

there will be no stockouts and no extra units on hand when the new order arrives. Thus, stockouts and additional carrying costs will be 0. When the reorder point equals the demand over lead time, total cost will be 0.

Total cost = 0: When reorder point equals demand over lead time.

Consider what happens when the reorder point is 30 units but the demand is 40 units. In this case, we will be 10 units short. The cost of this stockout situation is $2,400 ($2,400 = 10 units short × $40 per stockout × 6 orders per year). Note that we have to multiply the stockout cost per unit and the number of units short times the number of orders per year (6 in this case) to determine *annual* expected stockout cost. If the reorder point is 30 units and the demand over lead time is 50 units, the stockout cost will be $4,800 ($4,800 = 20 units short × $40 × 6). When the demand over lead time is 60 units, the stockout cost will be $7,200, and it will be $9,600 when demand over lead time is 70 units. In general, total cost is equal to stockout cost when the reorder point is less than demand over lead time.

Total cost = stockout cost = number of units short × stockout cost per unit × number of orders per year: When the reorder point is less than demand over lead time.

Now consider a reorder point of 70 units. As before, if demand over lead time is also 70, the total cost is 0. If the demand over lead time is 60 units, we will have 10 additional units on hand when the new inventory is received. If this situation continues during the year, we will have 10 additional units on hand on average. The additional carrying cost is $50 ($50 = 10 additional units × $5 carrying cost per unit per year). If the demand over lead time is 50 units, we will have 20 additional units on hand when the new inventory arrives (20 = 70 − 50). If this situation continues during the year, the additional annual carrying cost will be $100 ($100 = 20 additional units × $5 per unit per year). When the reorder point is greater than the demand over lead time, total costs will be equal to total additional carrying costs.

Total cost = total additional carrying cost = number of surplus units × the carrying cost: When the reorder point is greater than the expected demand over the lead time.

Using the above procedures, we can compute the economic consequence for every alternative and state of nature combination. The results are presented in the Table 9.4.

TABLE 9.4 ABCO's Stockout Costs: The Economic Consequences of Every Alternative and State of Nature

| | STATE OF NATURE | | | | |
ALTERNATIVE	30	40	50	60	70
30	$0	$2,400	$4,800	$7,200	$9,600
40	$50	$0	$2,400	$4,800	$7,200
50	$100	$50	$0	$2,400	$4,800
60	$150	$100	$50	$0	$2,400
70	$200	$150	$100	$50	$0

Using Table 9.4 and the probability of the demand value over lead time, we can use decision making under risk to determine the total expected cost of every alternative. The AB:QM solution is presented in Program 9.1. As you can see, the best alternative is to have a reorder point of 70 units. The total expected cost is $110. If the old reorder point is 50 units, this is equivalent to having a safety stock of 20 units.

Safety Stock with Unknown Stockout Costs

Teaching Suggestion 9.7:
The High Cost of a High
Service Level. See the
Instructor's Section for
details.

When stockout costs are not available or if they do not apply, then the preceding type of analysis cannot be used. Actually, there are many situations when stockout costs are unknown or extremely difficult to determine. For example, let's assume that you run a small bicycle shop that sells mopeds and bicycles with a one-year service warranty. Any adjustments made within the year are done at no charge to the customer. If the customer comes in for maintenance under the warranty, and you do not have the

PROGRAM 9.1 Solution to the ABCO Problem using AB:QM

```
Program: Decision Theory / Decision Making Under Risk

Problem Title : ABCO

***** Input Data *****

Type of Problem  : Cost  Problem


              Event  1      Event  2      Event  3      Event  4      Event  5

Prob          0.200         0.200         0.300         0.200         0.100

Alt 1         0.000      2400.000      4800.000      7200.000      9600.000
Alt 2        50.000         0.000      2400.000      4800.000      7200.000
Alt 3       100.000        50.000         0.000      2400.000      4800.000
Alt 4       150.000       100.000        50.000         0.000      2400.000
Alt 5       200.000       150.000       100.000        50.000         0.000


***** Program Output *****

Expected Cost Table


Alternative                Expected Cost

     1                        4320.000
     2                        2410.000
     3                         990.000
     4                         305.000
     5                         110.000 <=
```

necessary part, what is the stockout cost? It cannot be lost profit because the maintenance is done free of charge. Thus, the major stockout cost is the loss of goodwill. The customer may not buy another bicycle from your shop if you have a poor service record. In this situation, it could be very difficult to determine the stockout cost. In other cases, a stockout cost may simply not apply. What is the stockout cost for life-saving drugs in a hospital? The drug may only cost $10 per bottle. Is the stockout cost $10? Is it $100 or $10,000? Perhaps the stockout cost should be $1 million. What is the cost when a life may be lost as a result of not having the drug?

determining stockout costs may be difficult or impossible

An alternate approach to determining safety stock levels is to use a *service level*. In general, a service level is the percent of the time that you will *not* be out of stock of a particular item. Stated in other terms, the chance or probability of having a stockout is one minus the service level. This relationship is expressed as:

$$\text{Service level} = 1 - \text{Probability of a stockout}$$

or

$$\text{Probability of a stockout} = 1 - \text{Service level}$$

In order to determine the safety stock level, it is only necessary to know the probability of demand during the lead time and the desired service level. Here is an example of how the safety stock level can be determined when the probability of demand over the lead time follows a normal curve.

service level and the normal distribution

The Hinsdale Company carries an inventory item that has a normally distributed demand during the reorder period. The mean (average) demand is 350 units and the standard deviation is 10. Hinsdale wants to follow a policy that results in stockouts occurring only 5% of the time. How much safety stock should be maintained? Figure 9.5 may help you to visualize the example.

Hinsdale Company example

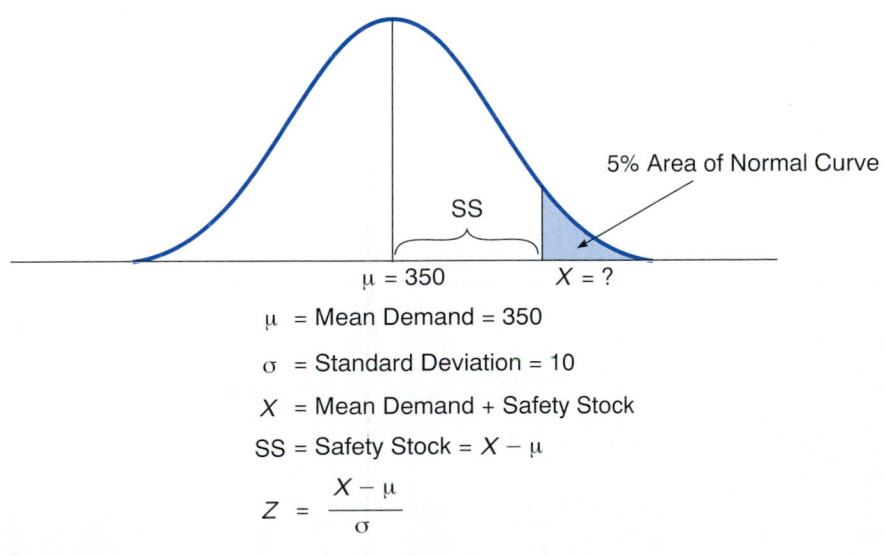

μ = Mean Demand = 350

σ = Standard Deviation = 10

X = Mean Demand + Safety Stock

SS = Safety Stock = $X - \mu$

$$Z = \frac{X - \mu}{\sigma}$$

FIGURE 9.5
Safety Stock and the Normal Distribution

We use the properties of a standardized normal curve to get a Z value for an area under the normal curve of .95 = (1 − .05). Using a normal table (see Appendix A), we find a Z value of 1.65.

$$Z = 1.65$$

$$Z \text{ is also equal to } \frac{X - \mu}{\sigma} = \frac{SS}{\mu}$$

$$Z = 1.65 = \frac{SS}{\sigma}$$

Solving for safety stock gives the following (since stock is usually in integer amounts):

$$SS = (1.65)(10) = 16.5 \text{ units, or } 17 \text{ units}$$

service levels, safety stock, and carrying costs

Different safety stock levels will be generated for different service levels. The relationship between service levels and safety stock, however, is not linear. As the service level increases, the safety stock increases at an increasing rate. Indeed, at service levels greater than 97%, the safety stock becomes very large. Of course, high levels of safety stock mean higher carrying costs. If you are using a service level, you should be aware of how much your service level is costing you in terms of carrying the safety stock in inventory. Let's assume that Hinsdale has a carrying cost of $1 per unit per year. What is the carrying cost for service levels that range from 90% to 99.99%? This cost information is summarized in Table 9.5.

Table 9.5 is developed by looking in the normal curve table for every service level. Finding the service level in the body of the table, we can obtain the Z value from the table in the standard way. Next, the Z values must be converted into the safety stock in units. As you recall, the standard deviation of sales during lead time for Hinsdale is 10. Therefore, the relationship between Z and the safety stock can be developed as follows:

1. We know that $Z = \dfrac{X - \mu}{\sigma}$

TABLE 9.5 Cost of Different Service Levels

SERVICE LEVEL (%)	Z VALUE FROM NORMAL CURVE TABLE	SAFETY STOCK (UNITS)	CARRYING COST ($)
90	1.28	12.8	12.80
91	1.34	13.4	13.40
92	1.41	14.1	14.10
93	1.48	14.8	14.80
94	1.55	15.5	15.50
95	1.65	16.5	16.50
96	1.75	17.5	17.50
97	1.88	18.8	18.80
98	2.05	20.5	20.50
99	2.32	23.2	23.20
99.99	3.72	37.2	37.20

2. And that SS $= X - \mu$

3. Thus we can rewrite Z as $Z = \dfrac{SS}{\sigma}$

4. Or by transposing terms

$$SS = Z\sigma = (Z)(10) \qquad\qquad \textbf{(9-11)}$$

Thus, the safety stock can be determined by multiplying the Z values by 10. Since the carrying cost is \$1 per unit per year, the carrying cost is the same numerically as the safety stock. A graph of the carrying cost as a function of service level is given in Figure 9.6.

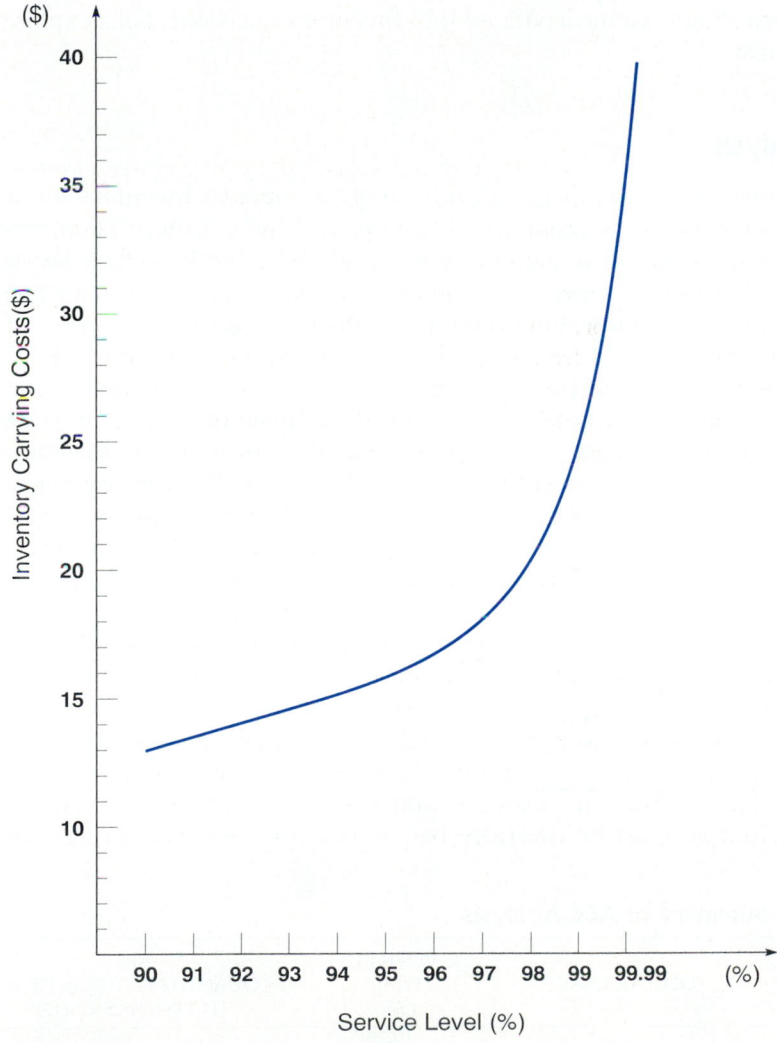

FIGURE 9.6
Service Level versus Annual Carrying Costs

As you can see from Figure 9.6, the carrying cost is increasing at an increasing rate. Moreover, the carrying cost gets extremely large when the service level is greater than 98%. Therefore, as you are setting service levels, you should be aware of the additional carrying cost that you will encounter. Although Figure 9.6 was developed for a specific case, the general shape of the curve is the same for all service level problems.

| 9.6 | ABC ANALYSIS AND JOINT ORDERING |

In the previous sections, we showed how to develop inventory policies using quantitative techniques. There are also some very *practical* considerations that should be incorporated into inventory decisions. Let's explore some of them.

ABC Analysis

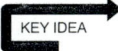
The purpose of *ABC analysis* is to divide all of a company's inventory items into three groups, the A group, the B group, and the C group. Then, depending on the group, it is necessary to decide how the inventory levels should be controlled in general. ABC analysis recognizes the fact that some inventory items are more important than others. A brief description of each group follows, with general guidelines as to which items are A, B, C.

The inventory items in the A group are critical to the functioning and operation of the organization. As a result, their inventory levels must be carefully monitored. These items typically make up over 70% of the company's *business in dollars*. Usually, they are only 10% of all inventory items. In other words, a *few inventory items are very important to the company*. As a result, the inventory control techniques discussed in Chapter 8 and in this chapter should be used where appropriate for every item in the A group. (Refer to Table 9.6.)

The items in the B group are important to the organization, but they are not critical. Thus, it may not be necessary to constantly monitor the levels of all of these items. B group items typically represent about 20% of the company's business and comprise about 20% of the items in inventory. The use of the quantitative inventory models should be used on only some of the items. The cost of implementing and using a quantitative inventory control technique must be carefully balanced with the benefits of better

TABLE 9.6 Summary of ABC Analysis

INVENTORY GROUP	DOLLAR USAGE (%)	INVENTORY ITEMS (%)	ARE QUANTITATIVE CONTROL TECHNIQUES USED?
A	70	10	Yes
B	20	20	In some cases
C	10	70	No

inventory control. Usually, less than half of B group items are carefully controlled through the use of quantitative inventory control techniques.

The items in the C group are not that important to the operation of the organization. These items represent perhaps only 10% of the company's business in dollars. They might, however, comprise 70% of the items in inventory. In other words, there are a large number of inventory items that represent a small amount of business. Group C could include inexpensive items such as bolts, washers, screws, and so forth. They are not controlled using quantitative inventory techniques, for the cost of implementing and using these techniques would exceed the value gained. Although complex quantitative models are not applied, group C items must be checked and ordered. One approach is to use joint ordering.

Joint Ordering

Joint ordering is the process of ordering two or more different inventory items on the same purchase order from the same supplier. When an order is placed for an item in the A or B group, the items in the C group can be checked and ordered if their quantities are low. Furthermore, it may be desirable to order some of the items in the A or B group even though they have not reached their reorder point.

As with other inventory strategies, joint ordering is done to lower total inventory cost. It can save a firm money by lowering ordering costs in several ways:

1. It is much less expensive to add another inventory item to the same order than place a second order by itself.

2. There may be savings in transportation costs by shipping several items together.

3. Unloading and receiving costs may be less.

4. There may be inspection-related cost savings, especially if a company has a rigorous quality control system that monitors incoming parts.

cost savings of joint ordering

Joint ordering can reduce total inventory cost, but how can it be carried out? When should items be joint ordered? How many units should be ordered using joint ordering?

Going back to the basics of inventory control, the only two decisions that can be made are when to order and how much to order. Since all of cost savings can be reflected in the annual ordering cost, the only quantity that is directly affected is order quantity. The reorder point, which answers the *when to order* question, is not a function of the ordering cost. Thus, joint ordering has a tendency to reduce the ordering cost, which changes the optimal order quantity. So we can actually have two optimal order quantities. Without joint ordering, we have the traditional order quantity. With joint ordering, we have the optimal order quantity for joint orders.

ordering decisions

Sumco example. In a Chapter 8 example, we determined that the optimal order quantity for Sumco was 200 pump housings. The annual demand was 1,000 units, the ordering cost was $10 per order, and the carrying cost was $.50 per unit per year. The total inventory cost (ordering + carrying cost) was $100. With joint ordering, it is expected that the ordering cost will be reduced to $7.50. Sumco believes that it can joint order pump housings with other items and thus reduce total inventory cost. If these items are joint ordered, what will be the optimal order quantity? What is the total cost with joint ordering?

$$Q^* \text{ Joint ordering} = \sqrt{\frac{2(1,000)(7.5)}{.50}}$$

$$= \sqrt{30000}$$

$$Q^* \text{ Joint ordering} = 173 \text{ units}$$

$$\text{TC with joint ordering} = \frac{1,000}{173} \times 7.5 + \frac{173}{2} \times .5$$

$$= \$43.30 + \$43.30$$

$$= \$86.60$$

Joint ordering has reduced the optimal order quantity from 200 to 173 units ordered. Moreover, it has resulted in a reduction of the total inventory cost from $100 per year to $86.60 per year, which is over a 15% cost savings.

In this example, we assumed that Sumco's pump housings are joint ordered all of the time. The total cost was reduced, the order quantity was reduced, and the number of orders per year was increased to meet the same annual demand. In most cases, though, you will not be able to place joint orders all of the time. Thus, the cost savings will not be quite as great as those just described. It might also be desirable to modify the reorder point from time to time. Let's say that you have two different types of electric drills, ¼-inch standard drills and ¼-inch reversible drills. Let's further assume that you have to order the standard drills because you have reached the reorder point. For the reversible drill, you may be only a few drills away from the reorder point as well. You now have a choice. Do you place a joint order for the reversible drills even though you have not reached the reorder point and will therefore incur an increased carrying cost? Or should you wait a few days or weeks until you have reached the reorder point for reversible drills and place an order for them alone? If you place a joint order, you will save on ordering cost, but you will have a higher carrying cost because you will have to hold larger inventories for a longer period of time. Thus, you have the same type of trade-off between ordering cost and carrying cost. As usual, you should make the decision on a total cost basis.

joint order decision is based on total cost

9.7 DEPENDENT DEMAND: THE CASE FOR MATERIAL REQUIREMENTS PLANNING (MRP)

Applicable Problems: 9-24, 9-25

Teaching Suggestion 9.9: The Practical Use of MRP. See the Instructor's Section for details.

In all of the inventory models we've discussed in Chapters 8 and 9, we assumed that the demand for one item was independent of the demand for other items. For example, the demand for refrigerators is usually independent of the demand for toaster ovens. Many inventory problems, however, are interrelated; the demand for one item is dependent on the demand for another item. Consider a manufacturer of small power lawn mowers. The demand for lawn mower wheels and spark plugs is dependent on the demand for lawn mowers. Four wheels and one spark plug are needed for each finished lawn mower. Usually when the demand for different items is dependent, the relationship between the items is known and constant. Thus, you should forecast the demand for the final products and compute the requirements for component parts.

KEY IDEA

As with the previously discussed inventory models, the major questions that must be answered are *how much to order* and *when to order*. But with dependent demand, inventory scheduling and planning can be very complex indeed. In these situations, *material requirements planning* (MRP) can be effectively employed. Some of the benefits of MRP are:

Transparency Master 9.12:
Benefits of MRP.

1. Increased customer service and satisfaction.

2. Reduced inventory costs.

3. Better inventory planning and scheduling.

4. Higher total sales.

5. Faster response to market changes and shifts.

6. Reduced inventory levels without reduced customer service.

benefits of MRP

Although most MRP systems are computerized, the analysis is straightforward and similar from one computerized system to the next. Here is the typical procedure.

The Material Structure Tree

Step one is to develop a material structure tree. Let's say that demand for product A is 50 units. Each unit of A requires 2 units of B and 3 units of C. Now, each unit of B requires 2 units of D and 3 units of E. Furthermore, each unit of C requires 1 unit of E and 2 units of F. Thus, the demand for B, C, D, E, and F is completely dependent on the demand for A. Given this information, a material structure tree can be developed for the related inventory items. See Figure 9.7.

material structure tree

The structure tree has three levels—0, 1, and 2. Items above any level are called *parents,* and items below any level are called *components*. There are three parents—A, B, and C. Each parent item has at least one level below it. Items B, C, D, E, and F are components because each item has at least one level above it. In this structure tree, B and C are both parents and components.

parents and components

Note that the number in the parentheses in Figure 9.7 indicates how many units of that particular item are needed to make the item immediately above it. Thus B(2) means that it takes 2 units of B for every unit of A, and F(2) means that it takes 2 units of F for every unit of C.

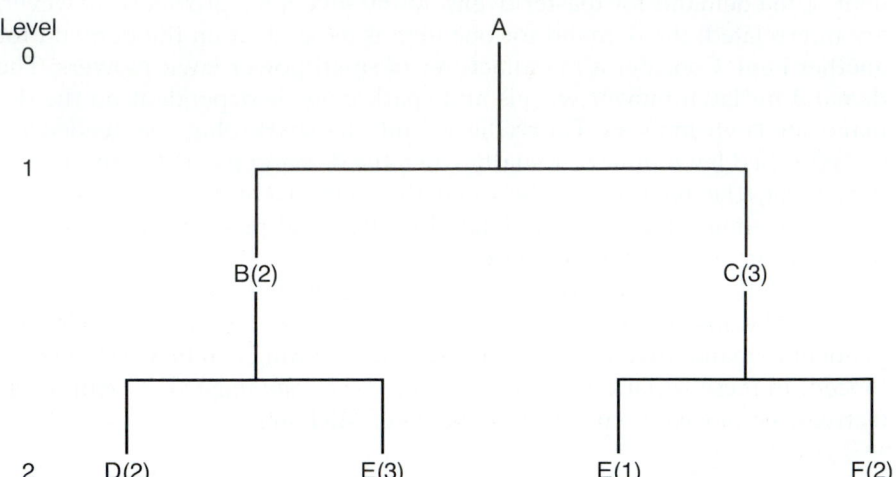

FIGURE 9.7
Material Structure Tree for Item A

**determining gross
requirements**

Once the material structure tree has been developed, the number of units of each item required to satisfy demand can be determined. This information can be displayed as follows:

Part B: $2 \times$ number of As $= 2 \times 50 = 100$

Part C: $3 \times$ number of As $= 3 \times 50 = 150$

Part D: $2 \times$ number of Bs $= 2 \times 100 = 200$

Part E: $3 \times$ number of Bs $+$

$1 \times$ number of Cs $= 3 \times 100 +$

$1 \times 150 = 450$

Part F: $2 \times$ number of Cs $= 2 \times 150 = 300$

Thus, for 50 units of A we need 100 units of B, 150 units of C, 200 units of D, 450 units of E, and 300 units of F. Of course, the numbers in this table could have been determined directly from the material structure tree by multiplying the numbers along the branches times the demand for A, which is 50 units for this problem. For example, the number of units of D needed is simply $2 \times 2 \times 50 = 200$ units.

Gross and Net Material Requirements Plan

**gross material
requirements plan**

The next step is to construct a gross material requirements plan. This is a time schedule that shows when an item must be ordered from suppliers when there is no inventory on hand, or when the production of an item must be started in order to satisfy the demand for the finished product at a particular date. Let's assume that all of the items are produced or manufactured by the same company. It takes one week to make A; two weeks to make B; one week to make C; one week to make D; two weeks to make E; and three weeks to make F. With this information, the gross material requirements plan can be constructed to reveal the production schedule needed to satisfy the demand of 50 units of A at a future date. Refer to Figure 9.8.

The interpretation of the material in Figure 9.8 is as follows: If you want 50 units of A at week 6, you must start the manufacturing process in week 5. Thus, in week 5 you need 100 units of B and 150 units of C. These two items take 2 weeks and 1 week to produce. (See the lead times.) Production of B should be started in week 3, and C should be started in week 4. (See the order release for these items.) Working backwards, the same computations can be made for all the other items. The material requirements plan graphically reveals when each item should be started and completed in order to have 50 units of A at week 6. Now, a net requirements plan can be developed given the on-hand inventory in Table 9.7; here is how it is done.

Week

		1	2	3	4	5	6	
A	Required Date						50	Lead Time = 1 Week
	Order Release					50		
B	Required Date					100		Lead Time = 2 Weeks
	Order Release			100				
C	Required Date					150		Lead Time = 1 Week
	Order Release				150			
D	Required Date			200				Lead Time = 1 Week
	Order Release		200					
E	Required Date			300	150			Lead Time = 2 Weeks
	Order Release	300	150					
F	Required Date				300			Lead Time = 3 Weeks
	Order Release	300						

FIGURE 9.8
Gross Material Requirements Plan for 50 Units of A

TABLE 9.7 On-Hand Inventory

ITEM	ON-HAND INVENTORY
A	10
B	15
C	20
D	10
E	10
F	5

net material requirements plan

Using these data, we can develop a net material requirements plan that includes gross requirements, on-hand inventory, net requirements, planned-order receipts, and planned-order releases for each item. It is developed by beginning with A and working backwards through the other items. Figure 9.9 shows a net material requirements plan for product A.

The net requirements plan is constructed like the gross requirements plan. Starting with item A, we work backwards determining net requirements for all items. These computations are done by constantly referring to the structure tree and lead times. The gross requirements for A are 50 units in week 6. Ten items are on hand, and thus, the net requirements and planned-order receipt are both 40 items in week 6. Because of the one-week lead time, the planned-order release is 40 items in week 5. (See the arrow connecting the order receipt and order release.) Look down column 5 and refer to the structure tree in Figure 9.7. Eighty (2 × 40) items of B and 120 = 3 × 40 items of C are required in week 5 in order to have a total of 50 items of A in week 6. The letter A in the upper-right corner for items B and C means that this demand for B and C was generated as a result of the demand for the parent, A. Now the same type of analysis is done for B and C to determine the net requirements for D, E, and F.

Two or More End Products

So far, we have only considered one end product. For most manufacturing companies, there are normally two or more end products that use some of the same parts or components. All of the end products must be incorporated into a single net material requirements plan.

In the MRP example just discussed, we developed a net material requirements plan for product A. Now, we'll show how to modify the net material requirements plan when a second end product is introduced. The second end product will be called AA. The material structure tree for product AA is shown below:

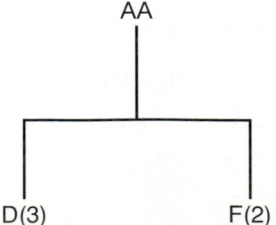

Item		Week 1	2	3	4	5	6	Lead Time
A	Gross						50	1
	On-Hand 10						10	
	Net						40	
	Order Receipt						40	
	Order Release					40		
B	Gross					80^A		2
	On-Hand 15					15		
	Net					65		
	Order Receipt					65		
	Order Release			65				
C	Gross					120^A		1
	On-Hand 20					20		
	Net					100		
	Order Receipt					100		
	Order Release				100			
D	Gross			130^B				1
	On-Hand 10			10				
	Net			120				
	Order Receipt			120				
	Order Release		120					
E	Gross			195^B	100^C			2
	On-Hand 10			10	0			
	Net			185	100			
	Order Receipt			185	100			
	Order Release	185	100					
F	Gross				200^C			3
	On-Hand 5				5			
	Net				195			
	Order Receipt				195			
	Order Release	195						

FIGURE 9.9
Net Material Requirements Plan

Let's assume that we need 10 units of AA. With this information, we can compute the gross requirements for AA:

Part D: 3 × number of AAs = 3 × 10 = 30

Part F: 2 × number of AAs = 2 × 10 = 20

Transparency Master 9.14:
Figure 9.10 Net Material
Requirements Plan, Including
AA.

In order to develop a net material requirements plan, we need to know the lead time for AA. Let's assume that it is one week. We also assume that we need 10 units of AA in week 6, and that we have no units of AA on hand.

Item	Inventory	Week 1	2	3	4	5	6	Lead Time
AA	Gross On-Hand: 0 Net Order Receipt Order Release					10	10 0 10 10	1 Week
A	Gross On-Hand: 10 Net Order Receipt Order Release					40	50 10 40 40	1 Week
B	Gross On-Hand: 15 Net Order Receipt Order Release			65		80 ^{A} 15 65 65		2 Weeks
C	Gross On-Hand: 20 Net Order Receipt Order Release				100	120 ^{A} 20 100 100		1 Week
D	Gross On-Hand: 10 Net Order Receipt Order Release		120	130 ^{B} 10 120 120	30	30 ^{AA} 0 30 30		1 Week
E	Gross On-Hand: 10 Net Order Receipt Order Release	185	100	195 ^{B} 10 185 185	100 ^{C} 0 100 100			2 Weeks
F	Gross On-Hand: 5 Net Order Receipt Order Release	195	20		200 ^{C} 5 195 195	20 ^{AA} 0 20 20		3 Weeks

FIGURE 9.10
Net Material Requirements Plan, Including AA

Now, we are in a position to modify the net material requirements plan for product A to include AA. This is done in Figure 9.10.

Look at the top row of Figure 9.10. As you can see, we have a gross requirement of 10 units of AA in week 6. Since we don't have any units of AA on hand, the net requirement is also 10 units of AA. Because it takes one week to make AA, the order release of 10 units of AA is in week 5. This means that we start making AA in week 5 and have the finished units in week 6.

Because we start making AA in week 5, we must have 30 units of D and 20 units of F in week 5. See the rows for D and F in Figure 9.10. The lead time for D is one week. Thus, we must give the order release in week 4 to have the finished units of D in week 5. Note that there was no inventory on hand for D in week 5. The original 10 units of inventory of D were used in week 5 to make B, which was subsequently used to make A. We also need to have 20 units of F in week 5 in order to produce 10 units of AA by week 6. Again, we have no on-hand inventory of F in week 5. The original 5 units were used in week 4 to make C, which was subsequently used to make A. The lead time for F is three weeks. Thus, the order release for 20 units of F must be in week 2. See the F row in Figure 9.10.

This example shows how the inventory requirements of two products can be reflected in the same net material requirements plan. Some manufacturing companies can have over 100 end products that must be coordinated in the same net material requirements plan. Although such a situation can be very complicated, the same principles we used in this example are employed. And remember that computer programs have been developed to handle large and complex manufacturing operations.

In addition to using MRP to handle end products and finished goods, MRP can also be used to handle spare parts and components. This is important because most manufacturing companies sell spare parts and components for maintenance. A net material requirements plan should also reflect these spare parts and components.

Transparency Master 9.15:
MRP Schedule.

Transparency Master 9.16:
MRP Planning Sheet.

9.8 THE KANBAN SYSTEM

Teaching Suggestion 9.10:
The Use of Kanban and JIT. See the Instructor's Section for details.

During the past decade, there has been a trend to make the manufacturing process more efficient. One objective is to have less in-process inventory on hand. This is known as *just-in-time* (JIT) inventory. With this approach, inventory arrives just in time to be used during the manufacturing process to produce subparts, assemblies, or finished goods. One technique of implementing JIT is a manual procedure called *Kanban*. *Kanban* in Japanese means "card." With a dual-card Kanban system, there is a conveyance Kanban, or C-Kanban, and a production Kanban, or P-Kanban. The Kanban system is very simple. Here is how it works.

Just-in-time (JIT) inventory

1. A user takes a container of parts or inventory along with its accompanying C-Kanban to his or her work area. When there are no more

---

APPLICATIONS OF QA

Using Just-in-Time (JIT) Principles to Improve Ecuador's Health Care Delivery System

The just-in-time control technique has helped reduce inventory levels and costs. The technique is especially appropriate when inventory systems are given a high priority, which was the situation in this case of the health care delivery in Ecuador.

Ecuador's medical supply system was experiencing poor planning and inadequate replenishment policies. The Ecuadorian Ministry of Public Health (MOH), along with several related organizations, considered several approaches to solving the problem of medical supply shortages. Like many other developing countries, Ecuador has a greater demand for health services than it can supply. In the past, the solution has been to develop highly visible facilities like hospitals. This approach, however, tends to centralize facilities and health care delivery, and the result is inferior health care delivery in rural or remote areas.

The medical delivery system is key to many health care systems. Unfortunately, the existing delivery system in Ecuador was inadequate and unable to meet health care demands for the most fundamental items (for example, aspirin, gauze,

cotton, eye ointment, and cough syrup). To help resolve the problem, six provinces representing diverse geographical areas were selected for study. Twenty-five percent of Ecuador's community health workers were within these provinces.

As a result of the study, procedures were initiated that allowed medical supplies to be received in one day in most cases. The major trade-off was between distance and number of supply sites. An algorithm was employed to minimize the number of facilities or sets of facilities needed to meet basic health supply needs. The new procedures called for community health workers to travel directly to the nearest MOH office and to personally place and receive orders for needed supplies. This approach mimics a JIT concept and has helped to improve the delivery of important medical supplies.

The implementation of the JIT concept in Ecuador helped provide an efficient, service-oriented health care delivery system.

Source: H. L. Smith, K. R. Mangelsdorf, J. C. Luna, and R. A. Reid, "Supplying Ecuador's Health Workers Just in Time," *Interfaces,* **19**, 3 (May–June 1989): 1–12.

---

parts or the container is empty, the user returns the empty container along with the C-Kanban to the producer area.

2. At the producer area, there is a full container of parts along with a P-Kanban. The user detaches the P-Kanban from the full container of parts. Then the user takes the full container of parts along with the original C-Kanban back to his or her area for immediate use.

3. The detached P-Kanban goes back to the producer area along with the empty container. The P-Kanban is a signal that new parts are to be manufactured or that new parts are to be placed into the container. When the container is filled, the P-Kanban is attached to the container.

4. This process repeats itself during the typical work day. The dual-card Kanban system is shown in Figure 9.11.

As seen in Figure 9.11, full containers along with their C-Kanban go from the storage area to a user area, typically on a manufacturing line. During the production process, parts in the container are used up. When the container is empty, the empty container along with the same C-Kanban

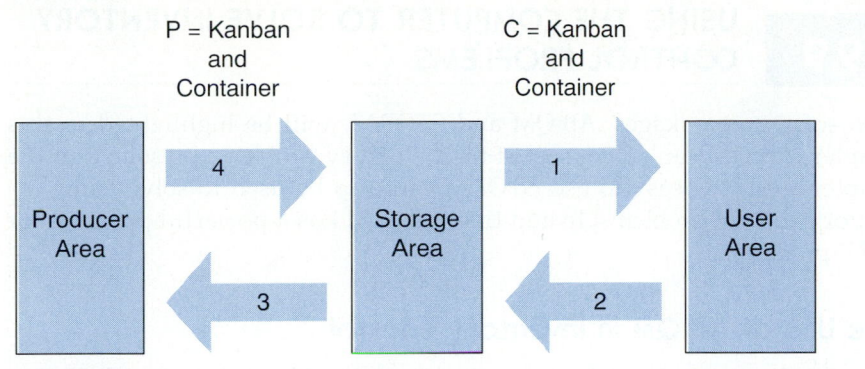

FIGURE 9.11
The Kanban System

goes back to the storage area. Here, the user picks up a new full container. The P-Kanban from the full container is removed and sent back to the production area along with the empty container to be refilled.

At a minimum, two containers are required using the Kanban system. One container is used at the user area, while another container is being refilled for future use. In reality, there are usually more than two containers. This is how inventory control is accomplished. Inventory managers can introduce additional containers and their associated P-Kanbans into the system. In a likewise fashion, the inventory manager can remove containers and the P-Kanbans to have tighter control over inventory buildups.

In addition to being a simple and easy-to-implement system, the Kanban system can also be very effective in controlling inventory costs and in uncovering production bottlenecks. Inventory arrives at the user area or on the manufacturing line just when it is needed. Inventory does not build up unnecessarily, cluttering the production line or adding to unnecessary inventory expense. The Kanban system reduces inventory levels and makes for a more effective operation. It is like putting the production line on an inventory diet. Like any diet, the inventory diet imposed by the Kanban system makes the production operation more streamlined. Furthermore, production bottlenecks and problems can be uncovered. Many production managers remove containers and their associated P-Kanban from the Kanban system in order to starve the production line to uncover bottlenecks and potential problems.

In implementing a Kanban system, a number of work rules or Kanban rules are normally implemented. One typical Kanban rule is that no containers are filled without the appropriate P-Kanban. Another rule is that each container must hold exactly the specified number of parts or inventory items. These and similar rules make the production process more efficient. Only those parts that are actually needed are produced. The production department does not produce inventory just to keep busy. It produces inventory or parts only when they are needed in the user area or on an actual manufacturing line.

controlling inventory costs and uncovering production bottlenecks

Kanban rules

9.9 | USING THE COMPUTER TO SOLVE INVENTORY CONTROL PROBLEMS

Two software packages, AB:QM and STORM, will be highlighted in this chapter. AB:QM can solve most of the inventory problems presented in the chapter, and it is easy to use. STORM can also be used to solve many inventory control problems. In addition, STORM has a powerful program for MRP problems.

AB:QM inventory models

The Use of AB:QM in Inventory Control

Once the inventory models are selected from the Main Menu of AB:QM, an inventory submenu consisting of five separate programs is shown (Program 9.2): ABC analysis, EOQ, economic lot size, planned shortages, and quantity discounts.

economic order quantity model

The first inventory model we will demonstrate is basic economic order quantity (EOQ). For our example we entered an annual demand of 1,000 units, a lead time of 3 days, an ordering cost of $10 per order, and a holding cost of $.50 per unit per year. We also entered the number of business days per year as 365. The data input screen along with the output for this example are shown in Program 9.3.

production run model

The second problem we will investigate is the production run model, which is called the economic lot size model in AB:QM. For this example, annual demand is 10,000 units. The daily demand rate is 60 units per day, and the daily production rate is 80 units. The lead time for the problem is 3 days, the setup cost is $100 per setup, and the holding cost is $.50 per unit per year. With these data, we can solve the production run model. The input screen and the results from running the program are shown in Program 9.4.

quantity discount model

A quantity discount problem in AB:QM can handle up to 50 price breaks. We will demonstrate the program with the model discussed in this chapter: it uses three price breaks. For quantities ranging from 0 units to 999 units—the first price break—the price per unit is $5. The second price break ranges from 1,000 to 1,999 units; unit price for this quantity is $4.80. Finally, the third price break starts at 2,000 units and is unlimited on the upper end; the unit price for this model is $4.75. The data input screen and program output are shown in Program 9.5.

PROGRAM 9.2 Inventory Submenu for AB:QM

```
_____ Menu _____

A    ABC Analysis
B    EOQ
C    Economic Lot Size (Production Run)
D    Planned Shortage (Back Order)
E    Quantity Discount
```

PROGRAM 9.3 Basic EOQ Model Using AB:QM

```
Inventory Models / EOQ

Problem Title :  Economic Order Quantity


Annual demand      (units/year)              1000
Business days      (days/year)                365
Lead time          (days)                       3
Ordering cost      ($/order)                   10
Holding cost       ($/unit/year)               .5



Help  New  Load  Save  Edit  Run   Print  Install  Directory  Esc

***** Program Output *****

Optimal order quantity   (units/order)   :   200.000
Number of orders         (orders/year)   :     5.000
Inventory cycle          (days)          :    73.000
Maximum inventory level  (units)         :   200.000
Average inventory level  (units)         :   100.000
Reorder point            (units)         :     8.219
Demand rate              (units/day)     :     2.740
Total holding cost       ($/year)        :    50.000
Total ordering cost      ($/year)        :    50.000
Total inventory cost     ($/year)        :   100.000

***** End of Output *****
```

PROGRAM 9.4 The Production Run Model Using AB:QM

```
Inventory Models / Economic Lot Size

Problem Title :  Production Run Model


Annual demand      (units/year)            10000
Demand rate        (units/day)                60
Lead time          (days)                      3
Setup cost         ($/setup)                 100
Holding cost       ($/unit/year)             .5
Production rate    (units/day)                80



Help  New  Load  Save  Edit  Run  Print  Install  Directory  Esc
```

(Continued)

PROGRAM 9.4 (Continued)

```
***** Program Output *****

Optimal order quantity    (units/order)   :    4000.000
Number of orders          (orders/year)   :       2.500
Production cycle          (days)          :      50.000
Maximum inventory level   (units)         :    1000.000
Average inventory level   (units)         :     500.000
Reorder point             (units)         :     180.000
Demand rate               (units/day)     :      60.000
Total holding cost        ($/year)        :     250.000
Total setup cost          ($/setup)       :     250.000
Total inventory cost      ($/year)        :     500.000


***** End of Output *****
```

PROGRAM 9.5 Quantity Discount Model Using AB:QM

```
Inventory Models / Quantity Discount

Problem Title  :  Quantity Discount
Method type(1:All/2:Increment)  1
Number of price breaks          3


                                        Lower           Upper
                                        Quantity        Quantity Unit Price
Annual demand (units/year)   5000       XXX      XXXXXXXXXX XXXXXXXXXX
Business days (days/year)     365        XXX      XXXXXXXXXX XXXXXXXXXX
Lead time     (days)           3         XXX      XXXXXXXXXX XXXXXXXXXX
Ordering cost ($/order)       49         XXX      XXXXXXXXXX XXXXXXXXXX
Holding cost as a fraction     2         XXX      XXXXXXXXXX XXXXXXXXXX
Price break   1                             0           999         5
Price break   2                          1000          1999      4.80
Price break   3                          2000       1000000      4.75


Help  New  Load  Save  Edit  Run  Print  Install  Directory  Esc

***** Program Output *****

ALL UNIT DISCOUNT

Optimal order price      :       4.800
Optimal order quantity   :    1000.000
Total inventory cost     :   24725.000
Reorder point            :      41.096

***** End of Output *****
```

The ABC analysis model in AB:QM will handle up to a maximum of 50 items. For every item, we enter the total demand and unit price. The output from the program includes the annual dollar volume, percentage of items, and percentage of cost. A sample input data screen and program output are shown in Program 9.6.

ABC analysis

The final AB:QM inventory program we will consider is the planned shortage model. This model requires values for the annual demand, the

planned shortage model

PROGRAM 9.6 ABC Analysis Using AB:QM

```
Inventory Models / ABC Analysis

Problem Title :  ABC Analysis Sample Problem

Number of Items          3


              Demand      Price
Item 1         7000        10
Item 2         2000        10
Item 3         1000        10


Help   New   Load   Save   Edit   Run   Print   Install   Directory   Esc

Program: Inventory Models / ABC Analysis

Problem Title : ABC Analysis

***** Input Data *****


                    Demand       Price

Item 1             7000.00       10.00
Item 2             2000.00       10.00
Item 3             1000.00       10.00


***** Program Output *****
```

Item Number	Annual demand	Unit cost	Annual $ volume	Percentage of items	Percentage of cost
1	7000.000	10.000	70000.000	70.000	70.000
2	2000.000	10.000	20000.000	90.000	90.000
3	1000.000	10.000	10000.000	100.000	100.000
Total			100000.000		

```
***** End of Output *****
```

number of business days, lead time, ordering cost, holding cost, and stock-out (or back order) cost. A sample input screen and output are shown in Program 9.7.

Use of STORM in Inventory Control

STORM programs for inventory management allow you to determine optimal order quantities and total inventory cost and to perform ABC and MRP analysis. The specific inventory functions supported by STORM include finding the standard economic order quantity as well as determination of order quantities for the production run model in which items are received or produced over time. STORM does not, however, have the ability to perform quantity discount analysis or to perform back order calculations. As with other STORM programs, the inventory control programs are menu driven. We will begin with a simple economic order quantity problem.

economic order quantity

After you select inventory management from the main menu, STORM shows you an opening screen that allows you to read an existing data file or to create a new data set. The opening screen and other screens needed to

PROGRAM 9.7 **Planned Shortage Model Using AB:QM**

```
Inventory Models / Planned Shortage

Problem Title :  Planned Shortage Sample Problem


    Annual demand (units/year)        10000
    Business days (days/year)           365
    Lead time     (days)                  3
    Ordering cost ($/order)             7.5
    Holding cost  ($/unit/year)           2
    Stockout cost ($/unit/year)          10



    Help  New  Load  Save  Edit  Run  Print  Install  Directory  Esc


***** Program Output *****

Optimal order quantity     (units/order)   :     300.000
Number of orders           (orders/year)   :      33.333
Inventory cycle            (days)          :      10.950
Maximum inventory level    (units)         :     250.000
Average inventory level    (units)         :     125.000
Reorder point              (units)         :      82.192
Demand rate                (units/day)     :      27.397
Total holding cost         ($/year)        :     208.333
Total ordering cost        ($/year)        :     250.000
Total inventory cost       ($/year)        :     500.000
Total shortage cost        ($/year)        :      41.667
Shortage backordered       (units)         :      50.000

***** End of Output *****
```

perform the Sumco problem, which was discussed in Chapter 8, are shown in Program 9.8.

PROGRAM 9.8 STORM Computer Run

```
                    INVENTORY MANAGEMENT : INPUT

              1)    Read an existing data file
              2)    Create a new data set

                    Select option  2


                  Press any key when ready
          STORM EDITOR : Inventory Management Module

  Title :  SUMCO
  Number of items        :        1  : Default order/setup cost :    10.
  Default carrying rate, % :      10.  : Time periods per year      :     1.
  Default service level, % :   99.999  :
                                        :

  R1  : C2      DEMAND/PD UNIT VALUE ORDR/SETUP CARRY RATE SIGMA(PD)  LEAD TIME
  ITEM   1        1000.        5.          .         .       0.        0.


                    INVENTORY MANAGEMENT : OUTPUT

          1)    Aggregate inventory values
          2)    Working stock exchange table
          3)    ABC classification of items
          4)    Order quantity for all items
          5)    Cost report for all items
          6)    Projected inventory status for all items
          7)    Detailed report for selected items

                    Select option  4


                            SUMCO
                     ORDERING INFORMATION
        Item          Item    Orders /    Order   Reorder  Max Orders
        Name          ID      Setups      Size    Point    Outstanding
        ITEM   1       1        5.0        200       0        1


                            SUMCO
                     ANNUAL COST INFORMATION
  Item          Item    Order   Working    Safety        Total
  Name          ID      Cost  Stock Cost Stock Cost       Cost
  ITEM   1       1      50.00    50.00      0.00         100.00
```

As you can see, we first selected number 2—create a new data set—from the main input menu. Once this is done, the STORM editor produces a screen that is used to enter the appropriate values. After entering the title SUMCO, we entered the other values. Because STORM does not have the ability to input carry cost in dollars per unit per year, it is necessary to enter the carrying cost rate as a percentage. As you can see, we entered 10%. We also entered a unit value of $5 to give us an equivalent carrying cost of $.50 per unit per year. Once the appropriate data have been entered, STORM produces the output menu, which gives us seven choices. We selected option 4 to display the order quantity for all items. The results are also shown in Program 9.8. As you can see, we obtained the same results we calculated in Chapter 8. The economic order quantity, or order size, is 200. The total cost is $100.

production run model   Another inventory problem that can be solved by STORM is the production run model. As in the previous problem, we start from the STORM editor where we are asked to enter the problem title along with other important information. The problem title we entered was BROWN (for the Brown Manufacturing example that was discussed earlier in this chapter). See Program 9.9, screen *a*. The carrying rate as a percentage of the inventory price is 10%. In addition, the time periods per year are 167, which we chose to make the problem characteristics similar to the problem discussed earlier. On occasion, it is necessary to enter values in such a way to make the problem characteristics reflective of the true situation or problem at hand. Next, we are presented with another screen (*b*), where the production rate per day or per period is entered. As you can see, we entered 80.

Once the basic data have been entered, the user is given a variety of process options (*c*): edit the current data set, save the current data set, print the current data set, and execute the module with the current data set. We

PROGRAM 9.9 **Production Run Inventory Model Using STORM**

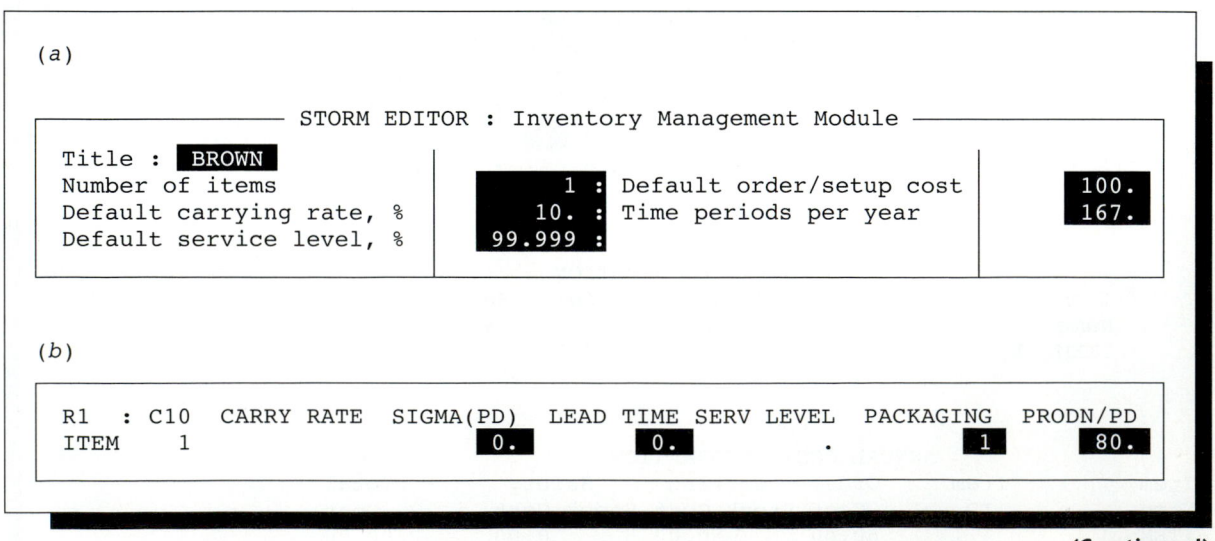

(*a*)

```
┌──────── STORM EDITOR : Inventory Management Module ────────┐
│  Title :  BROWN                                            │
│  Number of items             1 : Default order/setup cost   100.│
│  Default carrying rate, %   10. : Time periods per year     167.│
│  Default service level, % 99.999 :                          │
└────────────────────────────────────────────────────────────┘
```

(*b*)

```
R1  : C10  CARRY RATE  SIGMA(PD)  LEAD TIME SERV LEVEL  PACKAGING  PRODN/PD
ITEM    1                  0.         0.        .            1        80.
```

(Continued)

PROGRAM 9.9 (Continued)

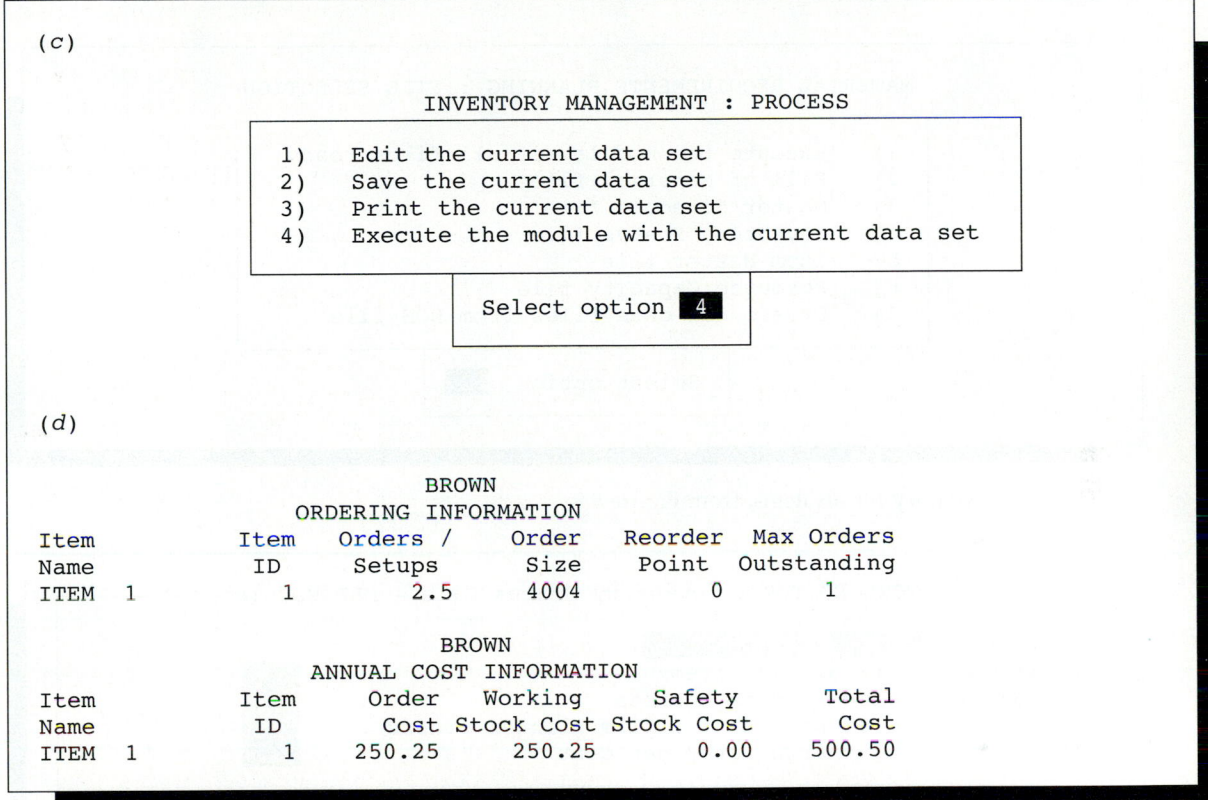

(c)

```
                    INVENTORY MANAGEMENT : PROCESS

        1)    Edit the current data set
        2)    Save the current data set
        3)    Print the current data set
        4)    Execute the module with the current data set


                Select option  4
```

(d)

```
                          BROWN
                   ORDERING INFORMATION
  Item         Item    Orders /    Order    Reorder  Max Orders
  Name          ID      Setups      Size     Point   Outstanding
  ITEM  1        1        2.5        4004       0          1

                          BROWN
                  ANNUAL COST INFORMATION
  Item         Item     Order   Working     Safety      Total
  Name          ID       Cost Stock Cost Stock Cost      Cost
  ITEM  1        1     250.25    250.25      0.00       500.50
```

selected option 4, which executes the module with the current data set. As a result, the computer displayed the beginning ordering information, all cost factors, and the economic order quantity (d).

The final application of STORM for this chapter is material requirements planning (MRP). Unlike other modules, the MRP requires that five data files be created before the program is run. Sample screens from the MRP problem discussed in this chapter are shown in Program 9.10, a through d.

MRP

PROGRAM 9.10 STORM's MRP Program

(*a*) Main STORM MRP Screen

```
         MATERIAL REQUIREMENTS PLANNING : FILE SELECTION

      ┌─────────────────────────────────────────────────────┐
      │  1)    Execute the module (if all files ready)       │
      │  2)    Bill of Material file                         │
      │  3)    Master Schedule file                          │
      │  4)    Inventory Status file                         │
      │  5)    Item Master file                              │
      │  6)    Resource Capacity file                        │
      │  7)    Create new data files from BOM file           │
      └─────────────────────────────────────────────────────┘
                              ┌──────────────────────────┐
                              │  Select option    2      │
                              └──────────────────────────┘
```

(*b*) On-hand: Inventory for all items, from Figure 9.9

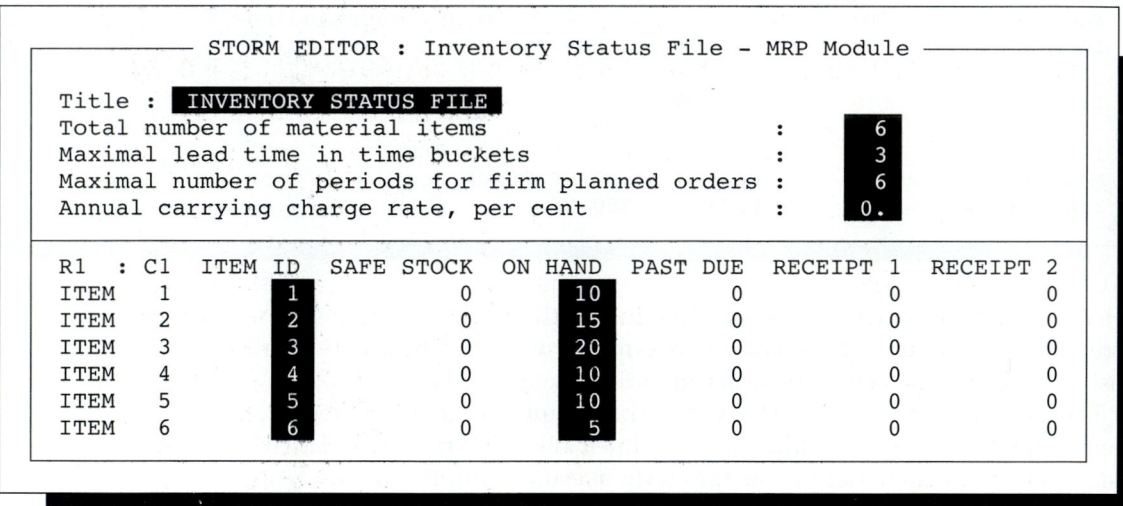

```
      ─── STORM EDITOR : Inventory Status File - MRP Module ───

   Title :  INVENTORY STATUS FILE
   Total number of material items                  :      6
   Maximal lead time in time buckets               :      3
   Maximal number of periods for firm planned orders :    6
   Annual carrying charge rate, per cent           :      0.

   R1  : C1   ITEM ID  SAFE STOCK   ON HAND   PAST DUE   RECEIPT 1   RECEIPT 2
   ITEM   1      1          0          10         0           0           0
   ITEM   2      2          0          15         0           0           0
   ITEM   3      3          0          20         0           0           0
   ITEM   4      4          0          10         0           0           0
   ITEM   5      5          0          10         0           0           0
   ITEM   6      6          0           5         0           0           0
```

(*c*) STORM's Main Output Menu

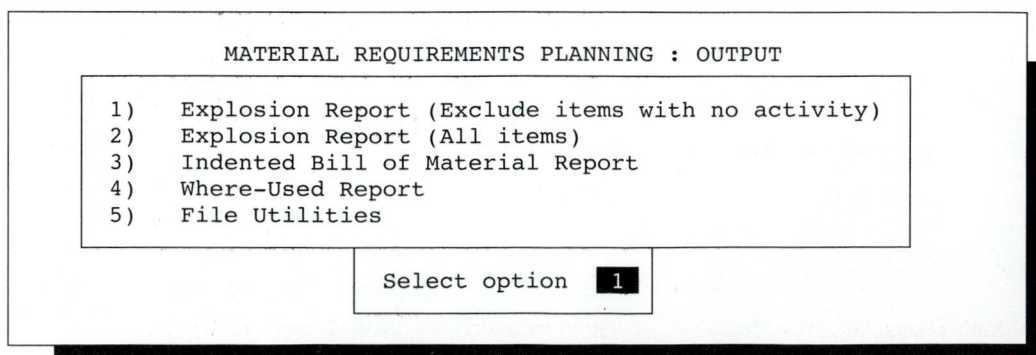

```
            MATERIAL REQUIREMENTS PLANNING : OUTPUT

      ┌─────────────────────────────────────────────────────────┐
      │  1)    Explosion Report (Exclude items with no activity) │
      │  2)    Explosion Report (All items)                      │
      │  3)    Indented Bill of Material Report                  │
      │  4)    Where-Used Report                                 │
      │  5)    File Utilities                                    │
      └─────────────────────────────────────────────────────────┘
                          ┌──────────────────────────┐
                          │  Select option    1      │
                          └──────────────────────────┘
```

PROGRAM 9.10 Continued

(*d*) This output table corresponds to Item A in Figure 9.9.

```
                        MASTER SCHEDULE FILE
                         EXPLOSION REPORT
   Planning        Gross    Sched'd   Projected    - Planned Orders -
   Period          Reqts    Receipts   On hand    Lot for Lot    Lot sized

   ITEM    1          1            Level 0      LT = 1      Lot size LFL
   Annual demand = 0             Scrap % = 0.00
   Order/Setup Cost = 0.00       Total order/setup cost = 0.00
   Unit Value = 0.00             Total carrying cost    = 0.00
   Safety stock = 0

                   GR         SR          OH           LFL          PO
   PAST DUE         0                     10
   PERIOD    1      0          0          10           0            0
   PERIOD    2      0          0          10           0            0
   PERIOD    3      0          0          10           0            0
   PERIOD    4      0          0          10           0            0
   PERIOD    5      0          0          10           40           40
   PERIOD    6     50          0           0           0            0
```

9.10 SUMMARY

You have been exposed to a number of different inventory control techniques in Chapters 8 and 9. We saw that there are many factors to consider: there may be quantity discounts, back orders may be allowed, inventory may not arrive in one large batch, or a firm may decide to employ the safety stock concept. There is also the possibility of joint ordering. In addition, demand may follow a complex probability distribution instead of being constant. In some cases, demand is *dependent* and a technique such as material requirements planning (MRP) is needed. The Kanban system can be used to make inventory control more efficient. Although it is beyond the scope of this book to develop one model to handle all of these factors, even the most sophisticated inventory model would make the same types of decisions we made. That is, the two major questions that all inventory models attempt to answer are *how much to order* and *when to order* in such a way that the total inventory cost is at a minimum. Knowing this makes it much easier to understand inventory models in general.

GLOSSARY

Instantaneous Inventory Receipt. A system in which inventory is received or obtained at one point in time and not over a period of time.

Production Run Model. An inventory model in which inventory is produced or manufactured instead of being ordered or purchased. This model eliminates the instantaneous receipt assumption.

Annual Setup Cost. The cost to set up the manufacturing or production process for the production run model.

Quantity Discount. The cost per unit when large orders of an inventory item are placed.

Planned Shortages. A situation where stockouts are planned.

Back Ordering Cost per Unit per Year (C_b). The cost of placing back orders for items that are not in stock.

Safety Stock. Extra inventory that is used to help avoid stockouts.

Stockout. A situation that occurs when there is no inventory on hand.

Safety Stock with Known Stockout Costs. An inventory model in which the probability of demand during lead time and the stockout cost per unit are known.

Safety Stock with Unknown Stockout Costs. An inventory model in which the probability of demand during lead time is known. The stockout cost is not known.

Service Level. The chance expressed as a percent, that there will not be a stockout. Service level = 1 − probability of a stockout.

ABC Analysis. An analysis that divides inventory into three groups. Group A is more important than group B, which is more important than group C.

Joint Ordering. Ordering two or more inventory items on the same order from the same supplier.

Material Requirements Planning. An inventory model that can handle dependent demand.

Just-in-Time (JIT) Inventory. An approach whereby inventory arrives just in time to be used in the manufacturing process.

Kanban. A manual JIT system developed by the Japanese. *Kanban* mans "card" in Japanese.

KEY EQUATIONS

(9-4) $Q^* = \sqrt{\dfrac{2DC_o}{C_h\left(1 - \dfrac{d}{p}\right)}}$

Order quantity when inventory is received over time.

(9-5) $Q_p^* = \sqrt{\dfrac{2DC_s}{C_h\left(1 - \dfrac{d}{p}\right)}}$

Optimal production quantity.

(9-6) $TC = DC + \dfrac{D}{Q}C_o + \dfrac{Q}{2}C_h$

Total inventory cost with quantity discounts.

(9-7) $\quad TC = \dfrac{D}{Q}C_o + \dfrac{(Q - S)^2}{2Q}C_h + \dfrac{S^2}{2Q}C_b$

Total inventory cost with planned shortages.

(9-8) $\quad Q^* = \sqrt{\dfrac{2DC_o}{C_h}\left(\dfrac{C_h + C_b}{C_b}\right)}$

Order quantity with planned shortages.

(9-9) $\quad S^* = Q^*\left(\dfrac{C_h}{C_h + C_b}\right)$

Amount back ordered.

(9-10) $\quad ROP = d \times L + SS$

Reorder point with safety stock.

(9-11) $\quad SS = Z\sigma$

Safety stock using the normal curve.

SOLVED PROBLEMS

Solved Problem 9-1

Flemming Accessories produces paper slicers used in offices and in art stores. The minislicer has been one of its most popular items: annual demand is 6,750 units. Kristen Flemming, owner of the firm, produces the minislicers in batches. On average, Kristen can manufacture 125 minislicers per day. Demand for these slicers during the production process is 30 per day. The setup cost for the equipment necessary to produce the minislicers is $150. Carrying costs are $1 per minislicer per year. How many minislicers should Kristen manufacture in each batch?

Solution

The data for Flemming Accessories is summarized as follows:

$$D = 6{,}750 \text{ units}$$
$$C_s = \$150$$
$$C_h = \$1$$
$$d = 30 \text{ units}$$
$$p = 125 \text{ units}$$

This is a production run problem that involves a daily production rate and a daily demand rate. The appropriate calculations are shown here:

$$Q_p^* = \sqrt{\frac{2DC_s}{C_h(1 - d/p)}}$$

$$Q_p^* = \sqrt{\frac{(2)(6{,}750)(150)}{1(1 - 30/125)}}$$

$$= 1{,}632$$

Solved Problem 9-2

Dorsey Distributors has an annual demand for a metal detector of 1,400. The cost of a typical detector to Dorsey is $400. Carrying cost is estimated to be 20% of the unit cost, and ordering cost is $25 per order. If Dorsey orders in quantities of 300 or more, it can get a 5% discount on the cost of the detectors. Should Dorsey take the quantity discount?

Solution

The solution to any quantity discount model involves determining the total cost of each alternative after quantities have been computed and adjusted for the original problem and every discount. We will start the analysis with no discount:

$$\text{EOQ (no discount)} = \sqrt{\frac{(2)(1{,}400)(25)}{(.2)(400)}}$$

$$= 29.6 \text{ units}$$

Total cost (no discount) = Material cost + Ordering cost + Carrying cost

$$= (\$400)(1{,}400) + (1{,}400)(25)/(29.6)$$
$$+ (29.6)(\$400)(.2)/2$$

$$= \$560{,}000 + \$1{,}182 + \$1{,}182 = \$562{,}400$$

The next step is to compute total cost for the discount:

$$\text{EOQ (with discount)} = \sqrt{\frac{(2)(1{,}400)(25)}{(.2)(\$380)}}$$

$$= 30.3 \text{ units}$$

$$\text{EOQ (Adjusted)} = 300 \text{ units}$$

Because this last economic order quantity is below the discounted price, we must adjust the order quantity to 300 units. The next step is to compute total cost.

Total cost (with discount)

$$= \text{Material cost} + \text{Ordering cost} + \text{Carrying cost}$$
$$= (\$380)(1{,}400) + (1{,}400)(25)/(300)$$
$$+ (300)(\$400)(.2)/2$$

$$= \$532{,}000 + \$117 + \$12{,}000 = \$544{,}117$$

The optimal strategy is to order 300 units at a total cost of $544,117.

Solved Problem 9-3

Mary Berger realizes that it is simply impossible to keep a supply of all types of fabric and sewing materials in her fabric store. The annual demand for one type of fabric Mary occasionally stocks is 4,000 bundles. The ordering cost is $40 per order, and the carrying cost is $3 per bundle of fabric per year. Further, Mary estimates that the total cost of using a back ordering policy is $100 per unit per year. If she uses the back ordering policy, how many bundles of this particular fabric should Mary order at one time? How many bundles of the fabric will be back ordered?

Solution

Berger's situation is a back ordering economic order quantity problem. The data for this problem are summarized as follows:

$$D = 4{,}000 \text{ units}$$
$$C_o = \$40$$
$$C_h = \$3$$
$$C_b = \$100$$

For Mary to solve this problem, she must use the appropriate back ordering equations for the economic order quantity and the number of bundles that will be back ordered. The calculations shown indicate that the optimal number of bundles to order at one time is 331 and that the number of bundles that will be back ordered is 9.65.

$$
\begin{aligned}
Q^* &= \sqrt{\frac{2DC_o}{C_h}\left(\frac{C_h + C_b}{C_b}\right)} \\
&= \sqrt{\frac{(2)(4{,}000)(40)}{3}\left(\frac{3 + 100}{100}\right)} \\
&= 331 \text{ units} \\
S^* &= Q^*\left(\frac{C_h}{C_h + C_b}\right) \\
&= 331\left(\frac{3}{3 + 100}\right) \\
&= 9.65 \text{ units per back order}
\end{aligned}
$$

DISCUSSION QUESTIONS AND PROBLEMS

Discussion Questions

9-1 What assumptions are made in the production run model?

9-2 What happens to the production run model when the daily production rate becomes very large?

9-3 In the quantity discount model, why is the carrying cost expressed as a percentage of the unit cost, I, instead of the cost per unit per year, C_h?

9-4 Briefly describe what is involved in solving a quantity discount model.

9-5 What assumptions are made in the planned shortages model?

9-6 Discuss the methods that are used in determining safety stock when the stockout cost is known and when the stockout cost is unknown.

9-7 Briefly describe what is meant by joint ordering and ABC analysis. What is the purpose of these inventory techniques?

Problems

QA9-8

9-8 Jan Gentry is the owner of a small company that produces electric scissors used to cut fabric. The annual demand is for 8,000 scissors, and Jan produces the scissors in batches. On the average, Jan can produce 150 scissors per day, and during the production process, demand for scissors has been about 40 scissors per day. The cost to set up the production process is $100, and it costs Jan 30¢ to carry one pair of scissors for one year. How many scissors should Jan produce in each batch?

2697

QA9-9

9-9 Jim Overstreet, inventory control manager for Itex, receives wheel bearings from Wheel-Rite, a small producer of metal parts. Unfortunately, Wheel-Rite can only produce 500 wheel bearings per day. Itex receives 10,000 wheel bearings from Wheel-Rite each year. Since Itex operates 200 working days each year, the average daily demand of wheel bearings by Itex is 50. The ordering cost for Itex is $40 per order, and the carrying cost is 60¢ per wheel bearing per year. How many wheel bearings should Itex order from Wheel-Rite at one time? Wheel-Rite has agreed to ship the maximum number of wheel bearings that it produces each day to Itex once an order has been received.

1217

QA9-10

Yes; Total cost = $49,913

9-10 North Manufacturing has a demand for 1,000 pumps each year. The cost of a pump is $50. It costs North Manufacturing $40 to place an order, and the carrying cost is 25% of the unit cost. If pumps are ordered in quantities of 200, North Manufacturing can get a 3% discount on the cost of the pumps. Should North Manufacturing order 200 pumps at a time and take the 3% discount?

QA9-11

9-11 Although Mary Henry never wants to be out of stock, it is simply impossible for her to keep a supply of every kitchen appliance from every manufacturer. Mary has an annual demand for Good Point, a popular range, of approximately 3,000 units. The ordering cost is $25, and the carrying cost is $4 per unit per year. Because Good Point is such a popular range, when customers ask for this range and Mary is out of stock, the customers always place a back order. Although Mary doesn't like disappointing customers, she knows that she will not lose sales when she doesn't have any Good Point ranges in stock. Mary estimates that the total cost of back ordering is $75 per unit per year. How many Good Point ranges should Mary order at one time? How many ranges will be back ordered?

199 backordered
10

9-12 Mr. Beautiful, an organization that sells weight training sets, has an ordering cost of $40 for the BB-1 set. (BB-1 stands for Body Beautiful Number 1.) The carrying cost for BB-1 is $5 per set per year. In order to meet demand, Mr. Beautiful orders large quantities of BB-1 seven times a year. The stockout cost for BB-1 is estimated to be $50 per set. Over the last several years, Mr. Beautiful has observed the following demand during the lead time for BB-1.

30

DEMAND DURING LEAD TIME	PROBABILITY
40	.1
50	.2
60	.2
70	.2
80	.2
90	.1

The reorder point for BB-1 is 60 units. What level of safety stock should be maintained for BB-1?

9-13 Linda Lechner is in charge of maintaining hospital supplies at General Hospital. During the past year, the mean lead time demand for bandage BX-5 was 60. Furthermore, the standard deviation for BX-5 was 7. Ms. Lechner would like to maintain a 90% service level. What safety stock level do you recommend for BX-5?

9

9-14 Ralph Janaro simply does not have time to analyze all of the items in his company's inventory. As a young manager, he has more important things to do. Below is a table of six items in inventory along with the unit cost and the demand in units.

QA9-14

33CP should be strictly controlled.

IDENTIFICATION CODE	UNIT COST	DEMAND IN UNITS
XX1	$ 5.84	1,200
B66	$ 5.40	1,110
3CPO	$ 1.12	896
33CP	$74.54	1,104
R2D2	$ 2.00	1,110
RMS	$ 2.08	961

Which item(s) should be carefully controlled using a quantitative inventory technique, and what item(s) should not be closely controlled?

9-15 In the past, George Wright always placed orders for wooden spice racks separately. The annual demand for spice racks is 3,000 units. The ordering cost is $35 per order, and the carrying cost is $1 per unit per year. George is now ordering several other products from the same supplier. If George orders the spice rack along with other products from the same supplier, he will be able to reduce the ordering cost to $25 per order.

   (a) What is the order quantity without joint ordering?
   (b) What is the order quantity with joint ordering?
   (c) What is the cost savings of using joint ordering?

458
387
$71

9-16 Dick Vidamann cannot believe the number of health food products available on the market. Dick's store, Do It Natural, is known for stocking many healthful food products. Dick's customers are also very loyal, and if Dick doesn't have a particular health food product, they will place an order and be content to wait until a new shipment arrives. Vitayum is not one of Dick's most popular food supplements, but Dick does order Vitayum on a regular basis. The annual demand for Vitayum is 500 bottles. The ordering cost is $4, holding cost is $0.50, and back ordering cost is $10.00.

QA9-16

89.44
91.65

30
4.36

(a) How many bottles of Vitayum should Dick order if he doesn't allow back ordering?
(b) How many bottles of Vitayum should he order with back ordering?
(c) If the lead time is 10 days and the daily demand is 3 bottles per day, what is the reorder point when back ordering is allowed?
(d) What is the amount back ordered?

: **9-17** The demand for barbecue grills has been fairly large in the past several years, and Home Supplies, Inc., usually orders new barbecue grills five times a year. It is estimated that the ordering cost is $60 per order. The carrying cost is $10 per grill per year. Furthermore, Home Supplies, Inc., has estimated that the stockout cost is $50 per unit. The reorder point is 650 units. Although the demand each year is high, it varies considerably. The demand during the lead time appears in the following table.

400

DEMAND DURING LEAD TIME	PROBABILITY
600	.3
650	.2
700	.1
750	.1
800	.05
850	.05
900	.05
950	.05
1000	.05
1050	.03
1100	.02
	1.00

The lead time is 12 working days. How much safety stock should Home Supplies, Inc., maintain?

: **9-18** Dillard Travey receives 5,000 tripods annually from Quality Suppliers to meet his annual demand. Dillard runs a large photographic outlet, and the tripods are used primarily with 35-mm cameras. The ordering cost is $15 per order, and the carrying cost is 50¢ per unit per year. Quality is starting a new option for its customers. When an order is placed, Quality will ship one-third of the order every week for three weeks instead of shipping the entire order at one time. Weekly demand over the lead time is 100 tripods.

547.7

717.9
Installment delivery; Total cost = $208.95

(a) What is the order quantity if Dillard has the entire order shipped at one time?
(b) What is the order quantity if Dillard has the order shipped over three weeks using the new option from Quality Suppliers, Inc.?
(c) Calculate the total cost for each option. What do you recommend?

: **9-19** Linda Lechner has just been severely chastised for her inventory policy. See Problem 9-13. Sue Surowski, her boss, believes that the service level should be either 95% or 98%. Compute the safety stock levels for a 95% and a 98% service level. Linda knows that the carrying cost of BX-5 is 50¢ per unit per year. Compute the carrying cost that is associated with a 90%, 95%, and a 98% service level.

$4.50 at 90%; $6.00 at 95%; $7.50 at 98%

: **9-20** Quality Suppliers, Inc., has decided to extend its shipping option. Refer to Problem 9-18 for details. Now, Quality Suppliers is offering to ship the amount ordered in five equal shipments once each week. It will take five weeks for this entire order to be received. What is the order quantity and total cost for this new shipping option?

Order quantity = 852; Total cost = $176

🖳 : **9-21** Xemex has collected the following inventory data for the six items that it stocks:

QA9-21

ITEM CODE	UNIT COST ($)	ANNUAL DEMAND IN UNITS	ORDERING COST ($)	CARRYING COST AS A PERCENTAGE OF UNIT COST (%)
1	10.60	600	40	20
2	11.00	450	30	25
3	2.25	500	50	15
4	150.00	560	40	15
5	4.00	540	35	16
6	4.10	490	40	17

Lynn Robinson, Xemex's inventory manager, does not feel that all of the items can be controlled.

What order quantities do you recommend for which inventory product(s)?

Order quantity of 45 units for Item 4.

🖳 : **9-22** The demand for Rocky Flier football dolls is 10,000 dolls per year. The ordering cost is $20 per order, and the carrying cost is $2 per doll per year.

QA9-22

(a) Compute the order quantity.

447.2

(b) Compute the order quantity when back ordering is allowed and the back ordering cost is $40 per doll per year.

458

(c) Compute the order quantity when back ordering is allowed and the back ordering cost is $100 per doll per year.

452

(d) Compute the order quantity when back ordering is allowed and the back ordering cost is $500 per doll per year.

448

(e) Compute the order quantity when back ordering is allowed and the back ordering cost is $1,000 per doll per year.

447.7

(f) What happens to the order quantity as the back ordering cost increases?

It increases.

(g) What assumptions are made with the back ordering model?

The same as EOQ, except back ordering is allowed.

🖳 : **9-23** Georgia Products offers the following discount schedule for its four-by-eight-foot sheets of quality plywood:

QA9-23

ORDER	UNIT COST ($)
9 sheets or less	18.00
10 to 50 sheets	17.50
More than 50 sheets	17.25

Order 51; Total cost = $1,901.22

Home Sweet Home Company orders plywood from Georgia Products. Home Sweet Home has an ordering cost of $45. The carrying cost is 20%, and the annual demand is 100 sheets. What do you recommend?

: **9-24** The demand for product S is 100 units. Each unit of S requires 1 unit of T and ½ unit of U. Each unit of T requires 1 unit of V, 2 units of W, and 1 unit of X. Finally, each unit of U requires ½ unit of Y and 3 units of Z. All items are manufactured by the same firm. It takes two weeks to make S; one week to make T; two weeks to make U; two weeks to make V; three weeks to make W; one week to make X; two weeks to make Y; and one week to make Z.

(a) Construct a material structure tree and a gross material requirements plan for the dependent inventory items.

(b) Identify all levels, parents, and components.

(c) Construct a net material requirements plan from the data and the following on-hand inventory:

ITEM	ON-HAND INVENTORY
S	20
T	20
U	10
V	30
W	30
X	25
Y	15
Z	10

9-25 Sunbright Citrus Products produces orange juice, grapefruit juice, and other citrus-related items. Sunbright obtains fruit concentrate from a cooperative in Orlando consisting of approximately 50 citrus growers. The cooperative will sell a minimum of 100 cans of fruit concentrate to citrus processors, such as Sunbright. The cost per can is $9.90.

Last year, a cooperative developed the Incentive Bonus Program (IBP) to give an incentive to their large customers to buy in quantity. Here is how the incentive bonus program works. If 200 cans of concentrate are purchased, 10 cans of free concentrate are included in the deal. In addition, the names of the companies purchasing the concentrate are added to a drawing for a new personal computer. The personal computer has a value of about $3,000, and currently there are about 1,000 companies that are eligible for this drawing. At 300 cans of concentrate, the cooperative will give away 30 free cans and will also place the company name in the drawing for the personal computer. When the quantity goes up to 400 cans of concentrate, 40 cans of concentrate will be given away free with the order. In addition, the company is also placed in a drawing for the personal computer and a free trip for two. The value of the trip for two is approximately $5,000. About 800 companies are expected to qualify and to be in the running for this trip. If the order quantity is 500 cans or greater, the cooperative will offer 50 cans of free concentrate. In addition, the company will be placed in a drawing for the computer, the trip, and a new car. The car has an estimated value of $10,000, and it is estimated that there are approximately 600 companies that will qualify to be in this particular drawing.

Sunbright estimates that its annual demand for fruit concentrate is 1,000 cans. In addition, the ordering cost is estimated to be $10.00, while the carrying cost is estimated to be 10%. The firm is intrigued with the incentive bonus plan. If the company decides that it will keep the car, the trip, or the computer if they are won, what should it do?

9-26 Conradi Pest Control is in the business of producing quality pesticides for commercial applications. Conradi is known for the free red hats that it gives out with Conradi's slogan on it, "Something bugging you—get Conradi Pest Control." Conradi develops the "bug be gone" formula and sells it in 5-gallon containers. These 5-gallon containers contain secret ingredients developed by the chemical engineers of Conradi Pest Control, in addition to 2 quarts of chemicals obtained from an outside supplier. Normally, Conradi sells 2,000 gallons of its pest control products every year. Billy Conradi, the fourth generation of Conradis to run the company, is very cost-conscious. His great-grandfather developed a successful company by watching his pennies, and the young Conradi is inclined to do the same. He estimates administrative costs to be approximately $1.00 per gallon of pesticide. Furthermore, overhead and advertising allocations are estimated to be $.50 and $.30 per gallon, respectively.

Sue Simon orders most of the products, including the 2 quarts that are needed from the outside company to produce the 5-gallon containers of pesticide. Ten dollars is allocated for Sue's work as a clerk for placing routine orders. If a special order is required because Conradi runs out of pesticides, a $15.00 charge is allocated. Furthermore, spoilage is estimated to be $1.00 per quart and shelving costs are estimated to be $1.50 per quart. Because of the outstanding job that "bug be gone" does, the younger Conradi knows that if he is temporarily out of stock, customers will come back another day to pick up their orders. Conradi keeps an adequate supply of the in-house chemicals to produce the pesticide. How many orders of the 2-quart material required from the outside supplier should Conradi make every year?

Orders per year is 20.7 at a total cost of $414.04.

9-27 George Grim used to be an accounting professor at a state university. Several years ago, he started to develop seminars and programs for the CPA review course. The CPA review course is a course to help accounting students and others interested in passing the CPA exam. In order to develop an effective seminar, George developed a number of books and other related materials to help. The main product was the CPA review manual developed by George. The manual was an instant success for his seminars and other seminars and courses across the country. Today, George spends most of his time refining and distributing this CPA review manual. The price of the manual is $45.95. George's total cost to manufacture and produce the manual is $32.90.

George wants to avoid stockouts or to develop a stockout policy that would be cost-effective. If there is a stockout on the CPA review manual, George loses the profit from the sale of the manual.

George has determined from past experience that the reorder point from his printer is 400 units, assuming no safety stock. The question that George must answer is how much safety stock he should have as a buffer. On the average, George places one order per year for the CPA review manual. The frequency of demand for the CPA review manuals during lead time is given below:

Safety stock level is 200 at a total cost of $993.

DEMAND	FREQUENCY	DEMAND	FREQUENCY
300	1	600	4
350	2	650	4
400	2	700	3
450	3	750	2
500	4	800	2
550	5		

George estimates that his carrying cost per unit per year is $7. What level of safety stock should George carry to minimize total inventory costs?

Data Set Problems

QA9-28

9-28 Rob Roller has been in charge of inventory policy at Cyclorama, a large retail bicycle shop in Orlando, Florida. He now orders Chrome-Moly frames from Frameco, a local frame supplier. Cyclorama builds each bike by adding different Shimano component groups to each frame. Currently, Cyclorama's annual demand for frames is 2,000 per year. The lead time is ten days, and the ordering cost per order is $50. Holding cost is estimated to be 25% of unit cost. Frameco offers the following discounts:

PRICE BREAK	LOWER QUANTITY UNITS	UPPER QUANTITY UNITS	UNIT PRICE ($)
1	0	10	220.00
2	11	20	219.99
3	21	30	219.98
4	31	40	219.97
5	41	50	219.96
6	51	60	219.95
7	61	70	219.94
8	71	80	219.93
9	81	90	219.92
10	91	100	219.91
11	101	110	219.90
12	111	120	219.89
13	121	130	219.88
14	131	140	219.87
15	141		219.86

a) Optimal order quantity is 61 at a total cost of $443,196.
b) Optimal order quantity is 81 at a total cost of $663,838.
c) Optimal order quantity is 91 at a total cost of $884,339.
d) Optimal order quantity increases and total inventory cost increases.

(a) What is the optimal order quantity and the total inventory cost for Cyclorama given the data?
(b) Rob is optimistic about future demand. If annual demand becomes 3,000 frames, what is the impact on the optimal order quantity?
(c) What is the impact if annual demand is 4,000 frames?
(d) In general, what happens to the order quantity and total inventory cost as demand increases?

9-29 Barry's Hardware store carries twenty different types of ladders. Some are used for industrial purposes and are quite expensive. Others are very inexpensive and intended for household use only. Barry has given each ladder an item number. The table below shows each ladder by item number, the demand in units for the year, and the average selling price for each ladder. Ordering cost is estimated to be $100 per order, and carrying cost is expected to be 7.5% of the selling price per year. Stockout cost is expected to be 200% of the price of the ladder, which includes the loss of current and future sales. What inventory policies do you recommend for the different types of ladders?

See Instructor's Section

A Items: 6, 8, and 11
B Items: 9, 4, 12, 1, and 18
C Items: all other items

ITEM NUMBER	DEMAND	PRICE	ITEM NUMBER	DEMAND	PRICE	ITEM NUMBER	DEMAND	PRICE
1	3200	$45	8	5400	$200	15	60	$145
2	5543	23	9	3456	50	16	230	60
3	123	200	10	456	100	17	1000	100
4	556	300	11	500	400	18	345	400
5	230	10	12	600	250	19	2000	10
6	5600	400	13	34	100	20	5600	20
7	450	30	14	450	20			

CASE STUDY

Professional Video Management

Ever since the introduction of the first home video systems for television, Steve Goodman has dreamed about manufacturing his own video system for professionals. During the early years of home video, Steve watched a lot of his favorite old movies on his home video and planned the eventual development of his own video system. He intended it to be used primarily by television stations, advertising agencies, and other individuals and groups that wanted the best in video systems. The overall configuration of this system is shown in the illustration.

The basic system includes a comprehensive control box, two separate video tape systems, a video disk, and a professional-quality television set. All these devices are fully integrated. In addition, the basic system comes with an elaborate remote control device. This device can operate both video systems, the video disk, and the TV system with ease. The remote control device works by sending infrared signals to the control box, which in turn controls the other devices in the system.

Steve's unique contribution to the video systems is the control box. The control box is an advanced microprocessor with the ability to coordinate the use and function of the other devices attached to it.

Steve's professional video system has numerous advantages over similar systems. To begin with, special effects can be introduced easily. Images from the video disk, one of the video systems, and the television system can easily be placed on the other video system. In addition, it is possible to connect the control box to several popular microcomputers, including the MacIntosh, the IBM Personal System/2, the Radio Shack Model 2000, and advanced Atari and Coleco computer systems. This makes it possible to develop attractive graphics on the microcomputer and to transfer them

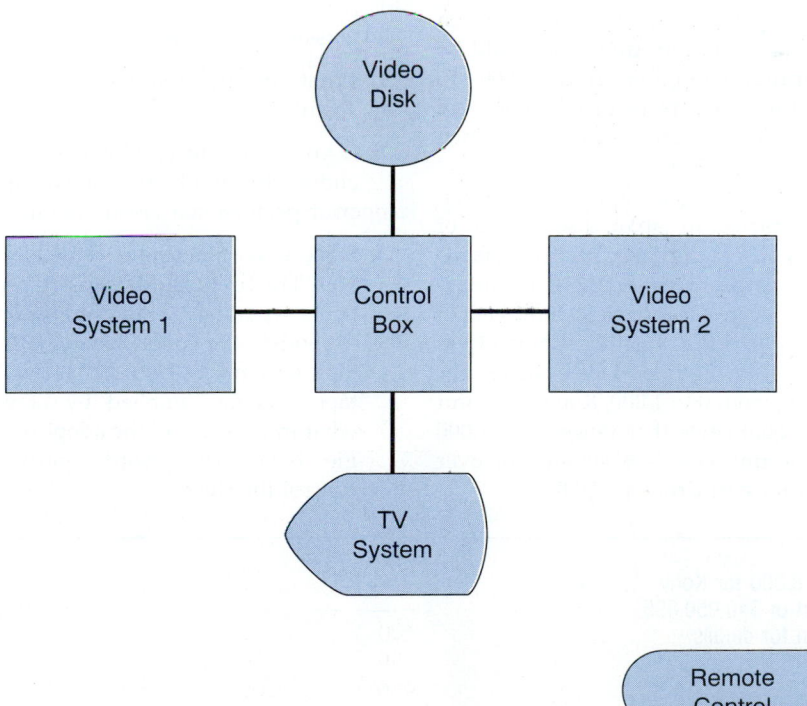

directly to the video system. It is also possible to hook a stereo system to the control box to integrate the highest quality stereo sound into the system and record it on one of the video systems.

The two video systems also offer remarkable flexibility in editing. Several special editing buttons were placed on the remote control station. It is possible to first record a program on one video system and then edit it by using the other video tape system to add and delete sections.

One of the best features of Steve's professional video system is the price. The basic system, including the control box, both video systems, the video disk, and the television system, has a retail price of $1,995.

Steve found manufacturers for the television system, the control box, and the video disk system in the United States. Because video tape systems are more popular, Steve had more choices. After extensive research, he was able to eliminate all of the potential suppliers but two. Both of these suppliers are Japanese companies. Toshiki is a new company located outside of Tokyo, Japan. Like other suppliers, Toshiki offers quantity discounts. For quantities ranging from 0 to 2,000 units, Toshiki would charge Steve a price of $250 per video system. For quantities that ranged between 2,000 and 8,000 units, the per unit cost would be $230. For quantities ranging from 8,000 to 20,000 units, the unit price drops to $220. For more than 20,000 units, the per unit price of the video systems would be only $210.

The other Japanese supplier is Kony. Although Kony originally started in Japan, also outside of Tokyo, it now has offices and manufacturing facilities around the world. One of these manufacturing facilities is located less than 100 miles north of Atlanta, Georgia. Like Toshiki, Kony offers quantity discounts for its video tape systems. For quantities ranging from 0 to 1,000, Kony's per unit cost is $250. For quantities that range from 1,000 to 5,000 units, the unit cost is $240; and for over 5,000 units, the unit cost drops to $220.

Because Kony has manufacturing facilities located in the United States, the cost to place an order and the delivery time are much more favorable than they are with Toshiki. The estimated per order cost from Kony is $40, and the expected delivery time is two weeks. On the other hand, the ordring cost is higher and delivery time is longer for Toshiki. The additional paper work and problems associated with ordering directly from Japan would increase Steve's cost to $90 per order. Furthermore, the delivery time for Toshiki is three months. Steve estimates that his carrying cost would be 30%. This is due primarily to storage and handling cost as well as the potential for technological obsolescence.

For the first year or so of operations, Steve decided to sell only the basic unit: the control box, the television set, the video disk, and the two video tape systems. The demand for the complete system was fairly constant during the past six months. For example, June sales were 7,970; July sales were 8,070; August sales were 7,950; and September sales were 8,010. This demand pattern is expected to continue for the next several months.

Discussion Questions

1. What are the reorder points for Kony and Toshiki?

2. If you were Steve, which company would you choose to supply the video tape systems for your professional video system?

3. Steve is considering several alternative strategies. The first would be to sell all of the components separately. The second strategy would be to modify the control box to allow other video tape systems to be used as well as the video tape systems supplied by Steve. In general, what impact would the adoption of these strategies have on the reorder point and inventory control for Steve?

48,000 for Toshiki and 8,000 for Kony
Toshiki with a total cost of $40,950,895
See Instructor's Section for details.

BIBLIOGRAPHY

Clifton, R. G. "JIT: Fad or Future Fact?" *Industrial Distribution* **78** (June 1989): 60.

LaForge, R. L., and C. W. McNichols. "An Integrative, Experiential Approach to Production Management Education." *Decision Sciences* **20** (Winter 1989): 198–207.

Mandel, M. J., and others. "Are Inventories Really Under Control." *Business Week* (July 31, 1989): 71.

Muller, E. J. "Harley's Got the Handle on Inbound." *Distribution* **88** (March 1989): 70+.

Mullins, P. J. "B-Line to Efficiency." *Automotive Industries* **169** (May 1989): 68–69.

Penlesky, R. J., and others. "Open Order Due Date Maintenance in MRP Systems." *Management Science* **35** (May 1989): 571–584.

Stokes, C. R. "JIT: Will Suppliers Embrace Their New Roles?" *Business* **39** (April–June 1989): 37–43.

Tatikonda, L. U., and R. J. Tatikonda. "What Are the Critical Success Factors of MRP?" *Management Accounting* **70** (May 1989): 34.

Teresko, J. "Decentralization Yields Solutions. *Industry Week* **238** (March 20, 1989): 51–53.

Appendix: Solving the Planned Shortages (Back Order) Model with Calculus

To solve for the optimal values of Q (order quantity) and S (units back ordered), we take partial derivatives of the total cost function with respect to each of the two variables, Q and S. Each partial derivative is set equal to 0, and the two resulting equations are solved simultaneously. The total cost, from Equation 9-7, was seen to be:

$$\text{TC} = \frac{D}{Q}C_o + \frac{(Q-S)^2}{2Q}C_h + \frac{S^2}{2Q}C_b \tag{1}$$

This can be rewritten as:

$$\text{TC} = \frac{D}{Q}C_o + \frac{Q^2 - 2QS + S^2}{2Q}C_h + \frac{S^2}{2Q}C_b$$

$$= \frac{D}{Q}C_o + \frac{Q}{2}C_h - SC_h + \frac{S^2}{2Q}(C_h + C_b) \tag{2}$$

The partial derivative with respect to Q is:

$$\frac{\partial \text{TC}}{\partial Q} = -\frac{D}{Q^2}C_o + \frac{C_h}{2} - \frac{S^2(C_h + C_b)}{2Q^2} = 0 \tag{3}$$

The partial derivative with respect to S is:

$$\frac{\partial \text{TC}}{\partial S} = \frac{C_h + C_b}{Q}S - C_h = 0 \tag{4}$$

Equation 4 can be solved for S:

$$S = Q\left[\frac{C_h}{C_h + C_b}\right] \tag{5}$$

Substituting this value for S into Equation 3 and solving for Q^* yields:

$$Q^* = \sqrt{\frac{2DC_o}{C_h}\left(\frac{C_h + C_b}{C_b}\right)} \tag{6}$$

Appendix: Using Spreadsheets to Solve Inventory Problems

This chapter contains a number of inventory problems, including the production run, quantity discount, planned shortages, and safety stock problems. These inventory problems can be solved using spreadsheets just as the basic EOQ model was illustrated in the Appendix to Chapter 8.

Production Run Model

Program 9.10 shows the use of a spreadsheet to solve production run problems. The input data are entered in cells E5 through E9. As you can see, the input data are those of the Brown Manufacturing example. The production run formula is in cell E13. This formula takes the square root of the appropriate quantities to determine the economic order or production run quantity.

Quantity Discount Model

A quantity discount problem solution by spreadsheet is illustrated in Program 9.11. This (symbolic) spreadsheet shows formulas. The major difference between this spreadsheet and the data for the Brass Department Store example is that minimum discount quantities are used in the spreadsheet instead of maximum discount quantities. This was done to make the formulas in the speadsheet easier to develop.

The formulas in cells B15, B16, and B17 transfer the unit price (or discount cost) values to the output results section, using the formulas +H7, +H8, and +H9. The order quantities are computed in column C using the @SQRT function. Column D adjusts the order quantities using the @IF function. These @IF functions use the minimum discount quantity values from the input section. If the order quantity is less than the minimum dis-

PROGRAM 9.10 The Production Run Model

```
           A          B          C                   D                E
  1    Economic Order Quantity:  Production Run Model
  2
  3    Inventory Input Data
  4
  5    Ordering Cost                                              100
  6    Carrying Cost                                              0.5
  7    Demand                                                   10000
  8    Daily Production Rate                                        80
  9    Daily Demand Rate                                           60
 10
 11    Inventory Output Results
 12
 13    Economic Prod Quantity       @SQRT(2*D7*D5/(D6*(1-D9/D8)))
 14
```

PROGRAM 9.11 Symbolic Spreadsheet for the Quantity Discount Problem

```
                                                              READY

          A         B             C               D          E          F
 1    Quantity Discount Model
 2    Input Data
 3
 4    Ordering Cost                   49                                    Minimum
 5    Carrying Cost %                 0.2           Discount       Discount
 6    Annual Demand                   5000          Number         Quantity
 7                                                     1                        0
 8                                                     2                     1000
 9                                                     3                     2000
10
11    Output Results
12                                          Adjusted       Annual    Annual
13    Discount    Unit     Order            Order          Material  Ordering
14     Number     Price    Quantity         Quantity       Cost      Cost
15        1       +H7      @SQRT(2*$C$6*$C$4/($C$5*H7))  @IF(C15<=F7,F7,C15)  +$C$6*H7  +$C$6/D15*$C$4
16        2       +H8      @SQRT(2*$C$6*$C$4/($C$5*H8))  @IF(C16<=F8,F8,C16)  +$C$6*H8  +$C$6/D16*$C$4
17        3       +H9      @SQRT(2*$C$6*$C$4/($C$5*H9))  @IF(C17<=F9,F9,C17)  +$C$6*H9  +$C$6/D17*$C$4
18
19                                                       Minimum Total Cost =
20

              G                   H

 5         Discount           Discount
 6         Percent            Percent
 7            0                   5
 8            4                  4.8
 9            5                 4.75
10
11
12      Annual
13      Ordering           Total
14       Cost              Cost
15    +D15/2*(B15*$C$5)    @SUM(E15..G15)
16    +D16/2*(B16*$C$5)    @SUM(E16..G16)
17    +D16/2*(B17*$C$5)    @SUM(E17..G17)
18
19                         @MIN(H15..H17)
20
```

count quantity, it is adjusted upward to the minimum discount quantity value. Columns E, F, and G compute the annual material, ordering, and carrying costs using the same formulas and procedures used in the chapter. Note that the $ symbol is used to create absolute cell references for some of the formulas to make it easier to copy them to other cells. The total cost is computed in column H using the @SUM function. The minimum total cost is displayed in cell H19 using the @MIN function.

Use of Safety Stock

Safety stock problems can be solved using a decision table as described in the chapter. Program 9.12 shows the use of a spreadsheet to solve ABCO's

PROGRAM 9.12 Using a Spreadsheet to Solve Safety Stock Problems. A symbolic spreadsheet is shown.

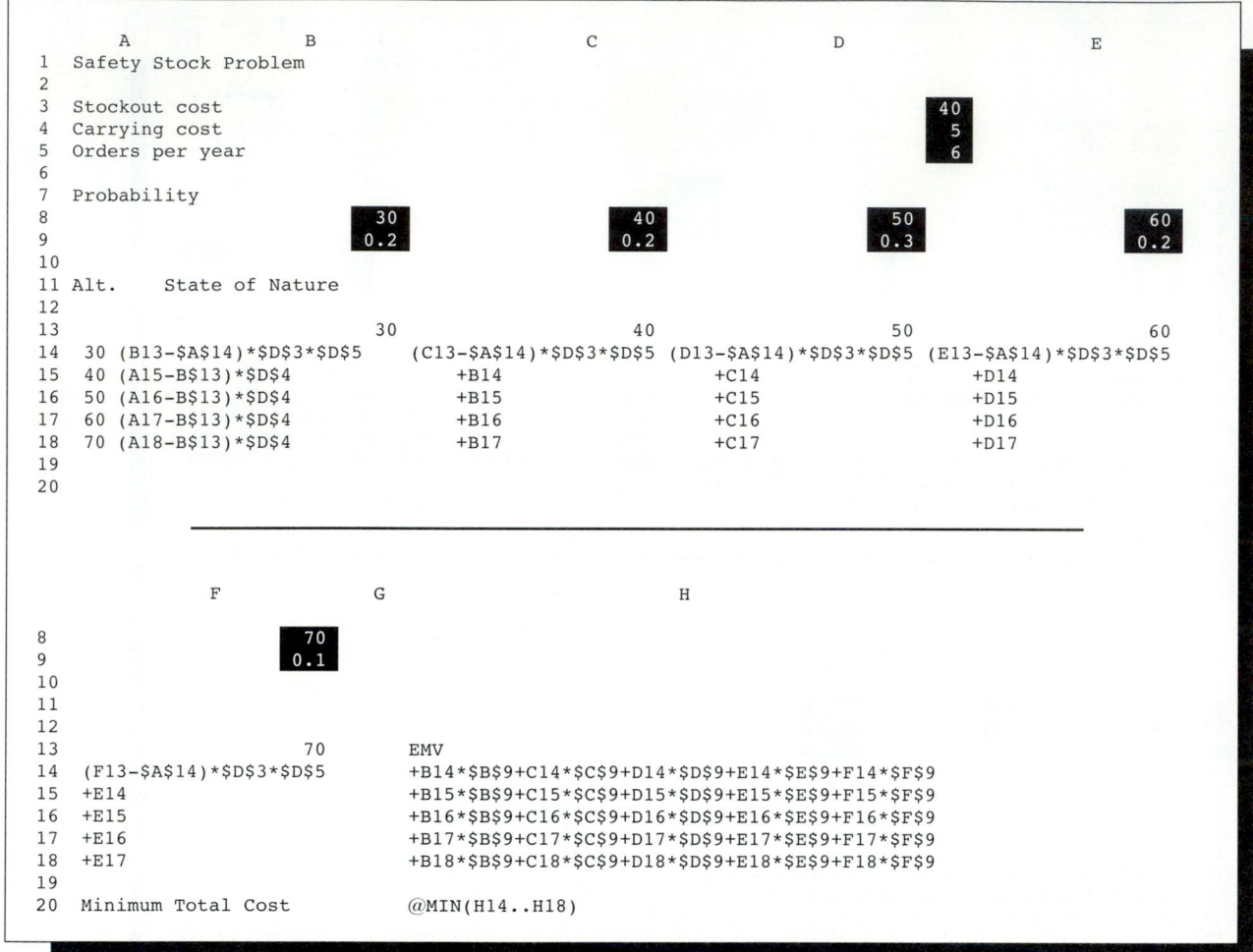

safety stock problem. Input data are at the top of the spreadsheet. The formulas are below row 13. These formulas use the same approach used in the book to compute the economic consequences or values. Note that a number of the formulas have been simplified. For example, cell C15 contains the same value (0 in this case) as cell B14. Thus, the formula in cell C15 is +B14. Of course, we could have computed cell C15 from scratch and gotten the same results. The economic monetary values are computed in column H. Because there are 5 possible states of nature and probability values, we have to multiply the five values for the states of nature times the probability values and sum the results to get the EMV value for each row.

10

Linear Programming: Graphical and Computer Methods

CHAPTER OUTLINE

10.1 Introduction

10.2 Requirements of a Linear Programming Problem

10.3 Formulating Linear Programming Problems

10.4 Graphical Solution to a Linear Programming Problem

10.5 Solving Flair Furniture's LP Problem by AB:QM, STORM, LINDO, and What's*BEST*!

10.6 An Introduction to Sensitivity Analysis

10.7 Solving Minimization Problems

10.8 Summary of the Graphical Solution Method

10.9 A Few Special Issues in Linear Programming

Glossary

Solved Problems

Discussion Questions and Problems

Case Study: Golding Landscaping and Plants, Inc.

Bibliography

Appendix: Linear Programming with Spreadsheet Software

10.1 INTRODUCTION

Transparency Master 10.1:
Outline: Linear Programming.

Transparency Master 10.2:
Examples of Successful LP Applications.

linear programming defined

Teaching Suggestion 10.1:
Linear Programming Relation to Computers. See the Instructor's Section for details.

properties of LP problems

Transparency Master 10.3:
Requirements of a Linear Programming Problem.

Many management decisions involve trying to make the most effective use of an organization's resources. Resources typically include machinery, labor, money, time, warehouse space, or raw materials. These resources may be used to produce products (such as machinery, furniture, food, or clothing) or services (such as schedules for shipping and production, advertising policies, or investment decisions). *Linear programming* (LP) is a widely used mathematical technique designed to help managers in planning and decision making relative to resource allocation. We shall devote this and the next three chapters to illustrating how and why linear programming works.

Despite its name, linear programming, and the more general category of techniques called *"mathematical" programming,* have very little to do with computer programming. In the world of management science, programming refers to modeling and solving a problem mathematically. Computer programming has, however, played an important role in the advancement and use of LP. Many real-life LP problems are too cumbersome to solve by hand or with a calculator. So, throughout the next four chapters we give examples of how valuable a computer program can be in solving a linear programming problem.

10.2 REQUIREMENTS OF A LINEAR PROGRAMMING PROBLEM

In the past 30 years, LP has been applied extensively to military, industrial, financial, marketing, accounting, and agricultural problems. Even though these applications are diverse, all LP problems have four properties in common.

1. First, all problems seek to *maximize* or *minimize* some quantity, usually profit or cost. We refer to this property as the *objective function* of an LP problem. The major objective of a typical manufacturer is to maximize dollar profits. In the case of a trucking or railroad distribution system, the objective might be to minimize shipping costs. In any event, this objective must be clearly stated and mathematically defined. It does not matter, by the way, whether profits and costs are measured in cents, dollars, or millions of dollars.

2. The second property that LP problems have in common is the presence of restrictions, or *constraints,* that limit the degree to which we can pursue our objective. For example, deciding how many units of each product in a firm's product line to manufacture is restricted by available personnel and machinery. Selection of an advertising policy or a financial portfolio is limited by the amount of money available to be spent or invested. We want, therefore, to maximize or minimize a quantity (the objective function) subject to limited resources (the constraints).

3. Third, there must be alternative courses of action to choose from. For example, if a company produces three different products, management may use LP to decide how to allocate among them its limited production resources (of personnel, machinery, and so on). Should it devote all manufacturing capacity to make only the first product; should it produce equal amounts of each product; or should it allocate the resources in some other ratio? If there were no alternatives to select from, we would not need LP.

4. Finally, the objective and constraints in linear programming problems must be expressed in terms of *linear* equations or inequalities. Linear mathematical relationships just mean that all terms used in the objective funciton and constraints are of the first degree (that is, not squared, or to the third or higher power, or appearing more than once). Hence, the equation $2A + 5B = 10$ is an acceptable linear function, while the equation $2A^2 + 5B^3 + 3AB = 10$ is not linear because the variable A is squared, the variable B is cubed, and the two variables appear again as a product of each other.

You will see the term *inequality* quite often when we discuss linear programming problems. By inequalities we mean that not all LP constraints need be of the form $A + B = C$. This particular relationship, called *an equation,* implies that the term A plus the term B are together exactly equal to the term C. In most LP problems, we see inequalities of the form $A + B \leq C$ or $A + B \geq C$. The first of these means that A plus B is less than or equal to C. The second means that A plus B is greater than or equal to C. This concept provides a lot of flexibility in defining problem limitations.

inequality

Basic Assumptions of LP

Technically, there are five additional requirements of an LP problem that you should be aware of:

1. We assume that conditions of *certainty* exist; that is, numbers in the objective and constraints are known with certainty and do not change during the period being studied.

certainty

2. We also assume that *proportionality* exists in the objective and constraints. This means that if production of 1 unit of a product uses 3 hours of a particular scarce resource, then making 10 units of that product uses 30 hours of the resource.

proportionality

3. The third technical assumption deals with *additivity,* meaning that the total of all activities equals the sum of the individual activities. For example, if an objective is to maximize profit = $8 per unit of first product made plus $3 per unit of second product made, and if one unit of each product is actually produced, then the profit contributions of $8 and $3 must add up to produce a sum of $11.

additivity

4. We make the *divisibility* assumption that solutions need not be in whole numbers (integers). Instead, they are divisible and may take

divisibility

How Linear Programming Started

Linear programming was conceptually developed before World War II by the outstanding Soviet mathematician, A. N. Kolmogorov. Another Russian, Leonid Kantorovich, won the Nobel prize in economics for advancing the concepts of optimal planning. An early application of linear programming, by Stigler in 1945, was in the area we today call "diet problems."

Major progress in the field, however, took place in 1947 and later when George D. Dantzig developed the solution procedure known as the simplex algorithm. Dantzig, then an Air Force mathematician, was assigned to work on logistics problems. He noticed that many problems involving limited resources and more than one demand could be set up in terms of a series of equations and inequalities. Although early LP applications were military in nature, industrial applications rapidly became apparent with the spread of business computers. In 1984, N. Karmarkar developed an algorithm that appears to be superior to the simplex method for many very large applications.

---

any fractional value. If a fraction of a product cannot be produced (like one-third of a submarine), an *integer programming problem* exists. Integer programming is discussed in more detail in Chapter 15.

nonnegativity

5. Finally, we assume that all answers or variables are *nonnegative*. Negative values of physical quantities are impossible: you simply cannot produce a negative number of chairs, shirts, lamps, or computers.

10.3 FORMULATING LINEAR PROGRAMMING PROBLEMS

product mix problem

Applicable Problems 10-24, 10-25

One of the most common linear programming applications is the *product mix problem*. Two or more products are usually produced using limited resources such as personnel, machines, raw materials, and so forth. The profit that the firm seeks to maximize is based on the profit contribution per unit of each product. (Profit contribution, you may recall, is just the selling price per unit minus the variable cost per unit.)[1] The company would like to determine how many units of each product it should produce so as to maximize overall profit given its limited resources.

The Flair Furniture Company

The Flair Furniture Company produces inexpensive tables and chairs. The production process for each is similar in that both require a certain number of hours of carpentry work and a certain number of labor hours in the painting and varnishing department. Each table takes 4 hours of carpentry and 2 hours in the painting and varnishing shop. Each chair requires

---

[1]Technically, we maximize total contribution margin, which is the difference between unit selling price and costs that vary in proportion to the quantity of the item produced. Depreciation, fixed general expense, and advertising are excluded from calculations. Problem 10-27, at the end of this chapter, deals with these issues.

3 hours in carpentry and 1 hour in painting and varnishing. During the current production period, 240 hours of carpentry time are available and 100 hours in painting and varnishing time are available. Each table sold yields a profit of $7; each chair produced is sold for a $5 profit.

Flair Furniture's problem is to determine the best possible combination of tables and chairs to manufacture in order to reach the maximum profit. The firm would like this production mix situation formulated as a linear programming problem.

We begin by summarizing the information needed to formulate and solve this problem (see Table 10.1). Further, let us introduce some simple notation for use in the objective function and constraints:

$$X_1 = \text{number of tables to be produced}$$

$$X_2 = \text{number of chairs to be produced}$$

Now we can create the LP objective function in terms of X_1 and X_2. The objective function is:

objective of the problem

$$\text{Maximize profit} = \$7X_1 + \$5X_2$$

Our next step is to develop mathematical relationships to describe the two constraints in this problem. One general relationship is that the amount of a resource *used* is to be less than or equal to ($\leq$) the amount of resource *available*.

In the case of the carpentry department, the total time used is:

(4 hours per table)(Number of tables produced)

$\quad\quad\quad$ + (3 hours per chair)(Number of chairs produced)

So the first constraint may be stated as follows: Carpentry time used is $\leq$ carpentry time available.

resource constraints

$$4X_1 + 3X_2 \leq 240 \quad \text{(hours of carpentry time)}$$

Similarly, the second constraint is: Painting and varnishing time used is $\leq$ painting and varnishing time available.

$$②X_1 + 1X_2 < 100 \quad \text{(hours of painting and varnishing time)}$$

(This means that each table produced takes two hours of the painting and varnishing resource.)

Both of these constraints represent production capacity restrictions and, of course, affect the total profit. For example, Flair Furniture cannot produce 70 tables during the production period because if $X_1 = 70$, both constraints

TABLE 10.1 Flair Furniture Company Problem Data

Transparency Master 10.4: Table 10.1 Flair Furniture Company Data.

DEPARTMENT	HOURS REQUIRED TO PRODUCE 1 UNIT		AVAILABLE HOURS THIS WEEK
	(X_1) TABLES	(X_2) CHAIRS	
Carpentry	4	3	240
Painting and varnishing	2	1	100
Profit per unit	$7	$5	

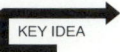

KEY IDEA

will be violated. It also cannot make $X_1 = 50$ tables and $X_2 = 10$ chairs. Why? Because this would violate the second constraint that no more than 100 hours of painting and varnishing time be allocated. Hence, we note one more important aspect of linear programming; that is, certain interactions will exist between variables. The more units of one product that a firm produces, the fewer it can make of other products. How this concept of interaction affects the optimal solution is seen as we now tackle the graphical solution approach.

10.4 GRAPHICAL SOLUTION TO A LINEAR PROGRAMMING PROBLEM

Applicable Problems 10-9, 10-10, 10-11, 10-12, 10-14, 10-16, 10-17, 10-20, 10-21, 10-23, 10-27

KEY IDEA

graphical method

The easiest way to solve a small LP problem such as that of the Flair Furniture Company is with the graphical solution approach. The graphical procedure is useful only when there are two decision variables (such as number of tables to produce, X_1, and number of chairs to produce, X_2) in the problem. When there are more than two variables, it is not possible to plot the solution on a two-dimensional graph and we must turn to more complex approaches—the topic of Chapter 12. But the graphical method is invaluable in providing us with insights into how other approaches work. For that reason alone, it is worthwhile to spend the rest of this chapter exploring graphical solutions as an intuitive basis for the chapters on mathematical programming that follow.

Graphical Representation of Constraints

Alternate Example 10.1

Teaching Suggestion 10.2:
Draw Constraints for a Graphical LP Solution. See the Instructor's Section for details.

nonnegativity constraints

In order to find the optimal solution to a linear programming problem, we must first identify a set, or region, of feasible solutions. The first step in doing so is to plot each of the problem's constraints on a graph.

The variable X_1 (tables, in our example) is usually plotted as the horizontal axis of the graph and the variable X_2 (chairs) is plotted as the vertical axis. In order to obtain meaningful solutions, the values for X_1 and X_2 must be nonnegative numbers. That is, all potential solutions must represent real tables and real chairs. Mathematically, this means that:

$X_1 \geq 0$ (*number of tables produced is greater than or equal to 0*)

$X_2 \geq 0$ (*number of chairs produced is greater than or equal to 0*)

Adding these *nonnegativity constraints* means that we are always working in the first (or northeast) quadrant of a graph. See Figure 10.1.

The complete problem may now be restated mathematically as:

mathematical statement of the LP problem

$$\text{Maximize profit} = \$7X_1 + \$5X_2$$

subject to the constraints:

$$4X_1 + 3X_2 \leq 240 \quad (\textit{carpentry constraint})$$
$$2X_1 + 1X_2 \leq 100 \quad (\textit{painting and varnishing constraint})$$
$$X_1 \geq 0 \quad (\textit{first nonnegativity constraint})$$
$$X_2 \geq 0 \quad (\textit{second nonnegativity constraint})$$

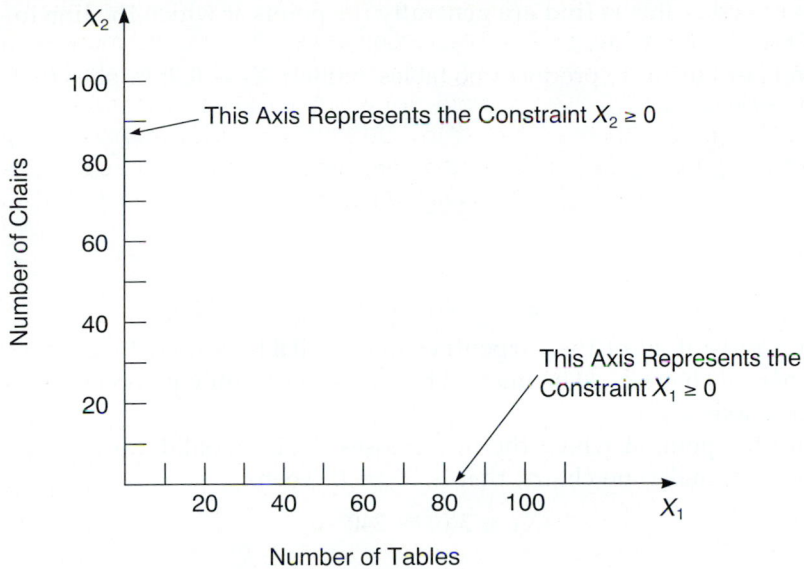

FIGURE 10.1
Quadrant Containing All Positive Values

To represent the first constraint graphically, $4X_1 + 3X_2 \leq 240$, we convert the inequality into an equality, more commonly called an equation, as follows:

$$4X_1 + 3X_2 = 240$$

As you may recall from elementary algebra, a linear equation in two variables is a straight line. The easiest way to plot the line is to find any two points that satisfy the equation, then draw the straight line through them.

Video 10.1: Management Science

APPLICATIONS OF QA

Linear Programming at New England Apple Products

Clothing fashions change every year—and so do food habits. As we shop in our supermarkets, new products appear and old ones disappear. A decade ago, for example, we drank fruit juices mostly at breakfast or when we were sick. Now we drink them anytime. One consequence of our increased consumption is that juice companies have created new blends to meet demand.

New England Apple Products, the manufacturer of the *Very Fine* beverage line, now has sixteen different juice beverages, ranging from apple-cherry

to cranapple to grapefruit. There are a large number of combinations of fruit juice possibilities, but New England Apple has only a limited supply of each juice as an ingredient. The firm uses linear programming to decide which combinations to market and how much of each to make. The bottom line question is: "What product mix will yield the best profit?" Although there are many ingredients listed on the side of a bottle of fruit juice blend, LP is one *hidden* ingredient.

The two easiest points to find are generally the points at which the line intersects the X_1 and X_2 axes.

plotting the first constraint

When Flair Furniture produces no tables, namely $X_1 = 0$, it implies that:

$$4(0) + 3X_2 = 240$$

or

$$3X_2 = 240$$

or

$$X_2 = 80$$

In other words, if *all* of the carpentry time available is used to produce chairs, then 80 chairs *could* be made. Thus, this constraint equation crosses the vertical axis at 80.

To find the point at which the line crosses the horizontal axis, we assume the firm makes no chairs, that is, $X_2 = 0$. Then,

$$4X_1 + 3(0) = 240$$

or

$$4X_1 = 240$$

or

$$X_1 = 60$$

Hence, when $X_2 = 0$, we se that $4X_1 = 240$, and that $X_1 = 60$.

The carpentry constraint is illustrated in Figure 10.2. It is bounded by the line running from point $A(X_1 = 0, X_2 = 80)$ to point $B(X_1 = 60, X_2 = 0)$.

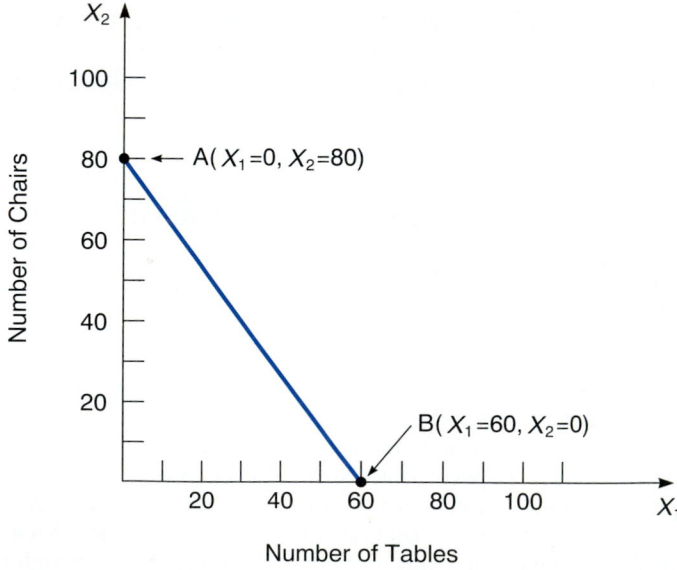

FIGURE 10.2
Graph of Carpentry Constraint Equation
$4X_1 + 3X_2 = 240$

Recall, however, that the actual carpentry constraint was the *inequality* $4X_1 + 3X_2 \leq 240$. How can we identify all of the solution points that satisfy this constraint? It turns out that there are three possibilities. First, we know that any point that lies on the line $4X_1 + 3X_2 = 240$ satisfies the constraint. Any combination of tables and chairs on the line will use up all 240 hours of carpentry time.[2] We see this by picking a point such as $X_1 = 30$ tables and $X_2 = 40$ chairs (see Figure 10.3). You should be able to see how exactly 240 hours of the carpentry resource are used.

The real question is, where are the problem points satisfying $4X_1 + 3X_2 \leq 240$? We can answer this question by checking two possible solution points, let's say ($X_1 = 30$, $X_2 = 20$) and ($X_1 = 70$, $X_2 = 40$). You see in Figure 10.3 that the first point is below the constraint line and that the second point lies above it. Let us examine the first solution more carefully. If we substitute the (X_1, X_2) values into the carpentry constraint, the result is:

$$4(X_1 = 30) + 3(X_2 = 20) = 4(30) + 3(20) = 120 + 60 = 180$$

Since 180 is less than the 240 hours available, the point (30, 20) satisfies the constraint. For the second solution point, we follow the same procedure.

$$4(X_1 = 70) + 3(X_2 = 40) = 4(70) + 3(40) = 280 + 120 = 400$$

Four hundred exceeds the carpentry time available and hence violates the constraint. So we now know that the point (70, 40) is an unacceptable production level. As a matter of fact, any point *above* the constraint line violates that restriction. (This is something you may wish to test for yourself

graphical representation of an inequality

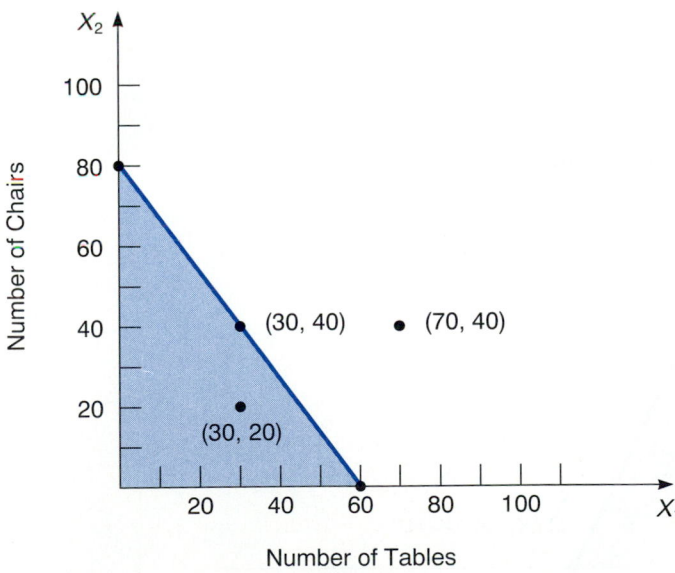

FIGURE 10.3
Region That Satisfies the Carpentry Constraint

[2]Thus, what we have done is to plot the constraint equation in its most binding position, that is, using all of the carpentry resource.

plotting the second constraint

with a few other points.) And any point *below* the line does not violate the constraint. In Figure 10.3 the shaded region represents all points that satisfy the original inequality constraint.

Next, let us identify the solution corresponding to the second constraint, which limits the time available in the painting and varnishing department. That constraint was given as $2X_1 + 1X_2 \leq 100$. As before, we start by changing the inequality to an equation:

$$2X_1 + 1X_2 = 100$$

Line *CD* in Figure 10.4 represents all combinations of tables and chairs that use exactly 100 hours of painting and varnishing department time. It is constructed in a fashion similar to the first constraint. When $X_1 = 0$, then,

$$2(0) + 1X_2 = 100$$

or

$$X_2 = 100$$

When $X_2 = 0$, then,

$$2X_1 + 1(0) = 100$$

or

$$2X_1 = 100$$

or

$$X_1 = 50$$

Transparency Master 10.5:
Flair Furniture Company Constraints.

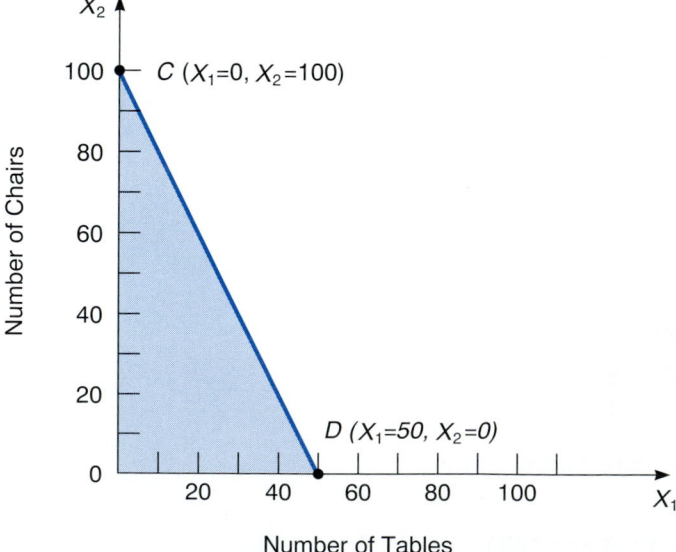

FIGURE 10.4
Region That Satisfies the Painting and Varnishing Constraint

The constraint is bounded by the line between $C(X_1 = 0, X_2 = 100)$ to $D(X_1 = 50, X_2 = 0)$ and the shaded area again contains all possible combinations that do not exceed 100 hours. Thus, the shaded area represents the original inequality $2X_1 + 1X_2 \leq 100$.

Now that each individual constraint has been plotted on a graph, it is time to move on to the next step. We recognize that in order to produce a chair or a table both the carpentry and painting and varnishing departments must be used. In an LP problem we need to find that set of solution points that satisfies *all* of the constraints *simultaneously*. Hence, the constraints should be redrawn on one graph (or superimposed one upon the other). This is shown in Figure 10.5.

The shaded region now represents the area of solutions that does not exceed either of the two Flair Furniture constraints. It is known by the term *area of feasible solutions* or, more simply, the *feasible region*. The feasible region in a linear programming problem must satisfy *all* conditions specified by the problem's constraints, and is thus the region where all constraints overlap. Any point in the region would be a *feasible solution* to the Flair Furniture problem; any point outside the shaded area would represent an *infeasible solution*. Hence, it would be feasible to manufacture 30 tables and 20 chairs ($X_1 = 30, X_2 = 20$) during a production period because both constraints are observed.

> *Carpentry constraint* $4X_1 + 3X_2 \leq 240$ hours available
>
> $4(30) + 3(20) = 180$ hours used $\checkmark$
>
> *Painting constraint* $2X_1 + 1X_2 \leq 100$ hours available
>
> $2(30) + 1(20) = 80$ hours used $\checkmark$

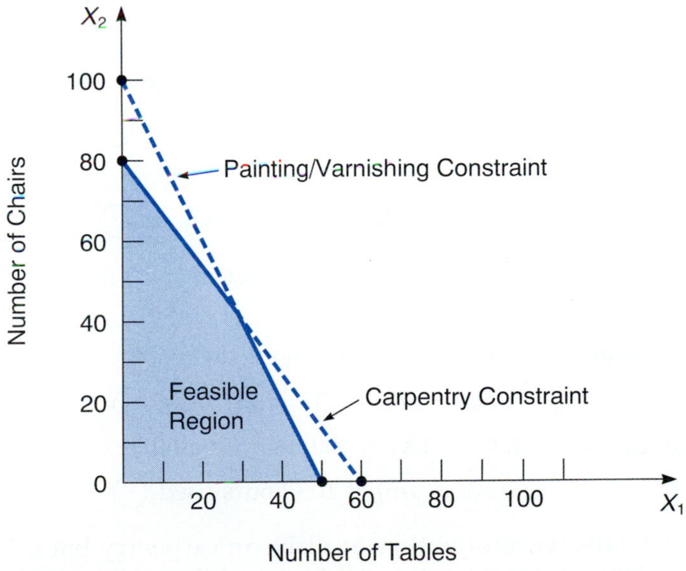

FIGURE 10.5
Feasible Solution Region for the Flair Furniture Company Problem

satisfying both
inequalities

feasible region

Teaching Suggestion 10.3:
Feasible Region is a Convex
Polygon. See the Instructor's
Section for details.

Transparency Master 10.6:
Flair Furniture Company
Feasible Region.

But it would violate both of the constraints to produce 70 tables and 40 chairs, as we see here mathematically:

$$\text{Carpentry constraint} \quad 4X_1 + 3X_2 \leq 240 \text{ hours available}$$
$$4(70) + 3(40) = 400 \text{ hours used } \otimes$$
$$\text{Painting constraint} \quad 2X_1 + 1X_2 \leq 100 \text{ hours available}$$
$$2(70) + 1(40) = 180 \text{ hours used } \otimes$$

Furthermore, it would also be infeasible to manufacture 50 tables and 5 chairs ($X_1 = 50$, $X_2 = 5$). Can you see why?

$$\text{Carpentry constraint} \quad 4X_1 + 3X_2 \leq 240 \text{ hours available}$$
$$4(50) + 3(5) = 215 \text{ hours used } \checkmark$$
$$\text{Painting constraint} \quad 2X_1 + 1X_2 \leq 100 \text{ hours available}$$
$$2(50) + 1(5) = 105 \text{ hours used } \otimes$$

This possible solution falls within the time available in carpentry but exceeds the time available in painting and varnishing and thus falls outside the feasible region.

Iso-Profit Line Solution Method

Now that the feasible region has been graphed, we may proceed to find the optimal solution to the problem. The optimal solution is the point lying in the feasible region that produces the highest profit. Yet there are many, many possible solution points in the region. How do we go about selecting the best one, the one yielding the highest profit?

There are a few different approaches that can be taken in solving for the optimal solution once the feasible region has been established graphically. The speediest one to apply is called the *iso-profit line method.*

We start the technique by letting profits equal some arbitrary, but small, dollar amount. For the Flair Furniture problem we may choose a profit of $210. This is a profit level that can easily be obtained without violating either of the two constraints. The objective function can be written as $210 = 7X_1 + 5X_2$.

This expression is just the equation of a line; we call it an *iso-profit line.* It represents all combinations of (X_1, X_2) that would yield a total profit of $210. To plot the profit line, we proceed exactly as we did to plot a constraint line. First, let $X_1 = 0$ and solve for the point at which the line crosses the X_2 axis.

$$\$210 = \$7(0) + \$5X_2$$

$$X_2 = 42 \text{ chairs}$$

Then, let $X_2 = 0$ and solve for X_1.

$$\$210 = \$7X_1 + \$5(0)$$

$$X_1 = 30 \text{ tables}$$

We can now connect these two points with a straight line. This profit line is illustrated in Figure 10.6. All points on the line represent feasible solutions that produce a profit of $210.[3]

Now, obviously, the iso-profit line for $210 does not produce the highest possible profit to the firm. In Figure 10.7, we try graphing two more lines, each yielding a higher profit. The middle equation, $280 = \$7X_1 + \$5X_2$, was plotted in the same fashion as the lower line. When $X_1 = 0$,

$$\$280 = \$7(0) + \$5X_2$$

$$X_2 = 56$$

When $X_2 = 0$,

$$\$280 = \$7X_1 + \$5(0)$$

$$X_1 = 40$$

Again, any combination of tables (X_1) and chairs (X_2) on this iso-profit line produces a total profit of $280.

Note that the third line generates a profit of $350, even more of an improvement. The farther we move from the 0 origin, the higher our profit

---

[3]*Iso* means "equal" or "similar." Thus an iso-profit line represents a line with all profits the same, in this case $210.

Teaching Suggestion 10.4:
Using the Iso-Profit Line Method. See the Instructor's Section for details.

iso-profit method

graphing parallel profit lines

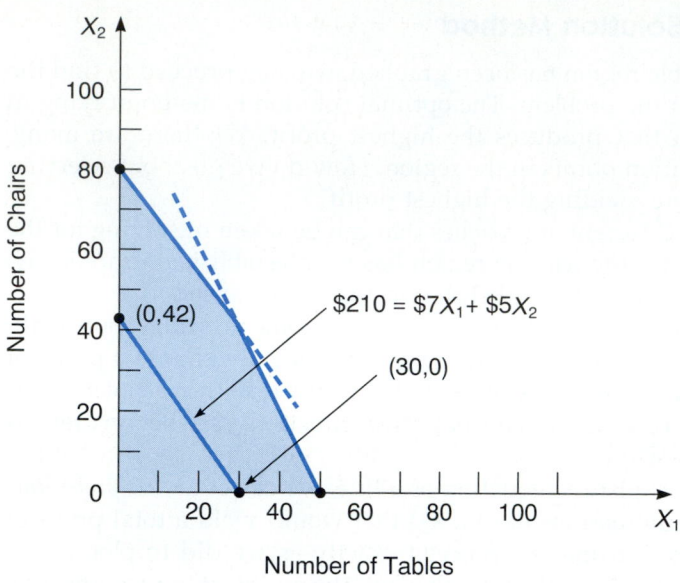

FIGURE 10.6
A Profit Line of $210 Plotted for the Flair Furniture Company

Transparency Master 10.7:
Flair Furniture Company
Iso-Profit Lines.

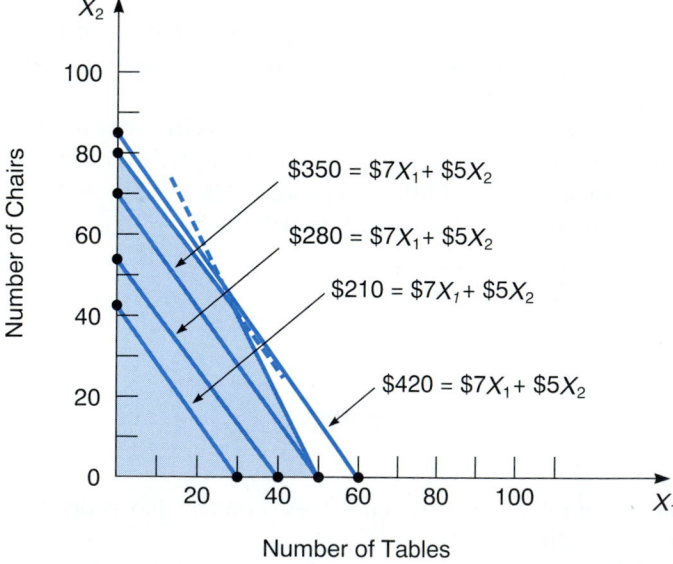

FIGURE 10.7
Four Iso-Profit Lines Plotted for the Flair Furniture Company

will be. Another important point to note is that these iso-profit lines are parallel. We now have two clues as to how to find the optimal solution to the original problem. We can draw a series of parallel lines (by carefully moving our ruler in a plane parallel to the first profit line). The highest profit line that still touches some point of the feasible region pinpoints the optimal solution. Notice that the fourth line ($420) is too high to be considered.

The highest possible iso-profit line is illustrated in Figure 10.8. It touches the tip of the feasible region at the corner point ($X_1 = 30$, $X_2 = 40$) and yields a profit of $410.

highest iso-profit line

The Corner Point Solution Method

A second approach to solving linear programming problems employs the *corner point method*. This technique is simpler, conceptually, than the iso-profit line approach, but it involves looking at the profit at every corner point of the feasible region.

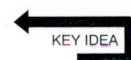

The mathematical theory behind linear programming states that an optimal solution to any problem (that is, the values of X_1, X_2 that yield the maximum profit) will lie at a *corner point*, or *extreme point,* of the feasible region. Hence, it is only necessary to find the values of the variables at each corner; the maximum profit or optimal solution will lie at one (or more) of them.

optimal solution at corner point

Once again we can see that the feasible region for the Flair Furniture Company problem is a four-sided polygon with four corner, or extreme, points (Figure 10.9). These points are labeled ①, ②, ③, and ④ on the

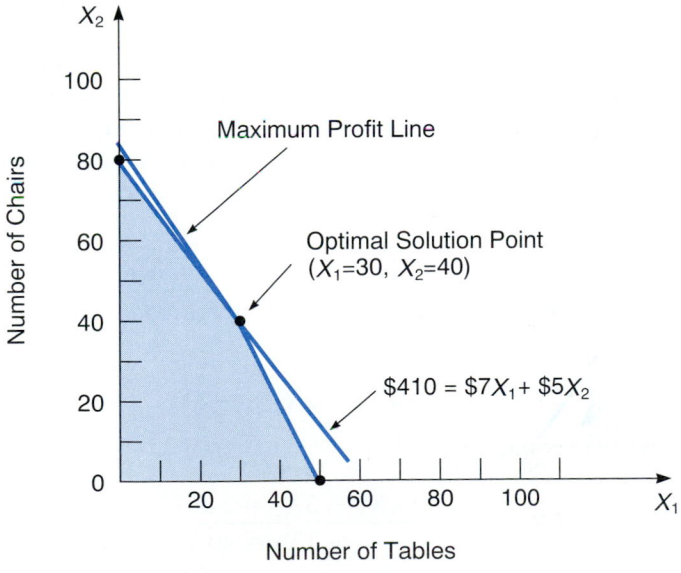

FIGURE 10.8
Optimal Solution to the Flair Furniture Problem

Transparency Master 10.8:
Flair Furniture Company Solution.

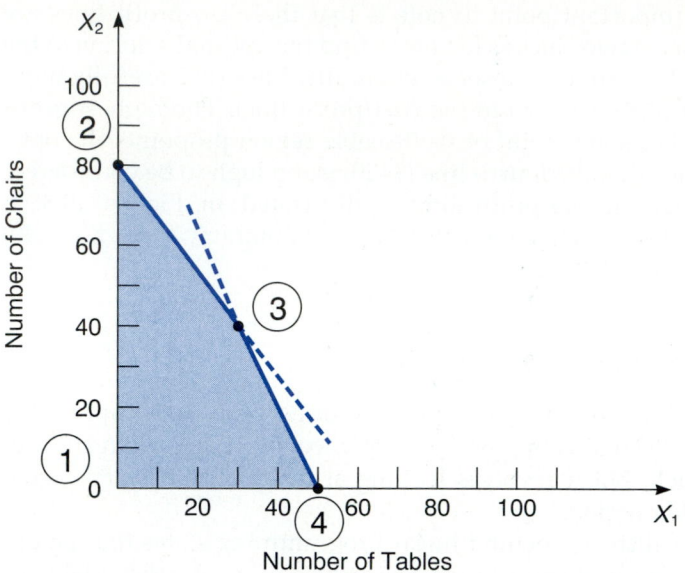

FIGURE 10.9
FIGURE 10.9
Four Corner Points of the Feasible Region

graph. To find the (X_1, X_2) values producing the maximum profit, we find

testing corner points ① ② and ④

out what the coordinates of each corner point are and test their profit levels.

Point ①: $(X_1 = 0,\ X_2 = 0)$ Profit $= \$7(0)\ + \$5(0)\ = \$0$

Point ②: $(X_1 = 0,\ X_2 = 80)$ Profit $= \$7(0)\ + \$5(80) = \$400$

Point ④: $(X_1 = 50, X_2 = 0)$ Profit $= \$7(50) + \$5(0)\ = \$350$

solving for corner point ③

We skipped corner point ③ momentarily because, in order to find its coordinates *accurately,* we have to solve for the intersection of the two constraint lines.[4] As you may recall from your last course in algebra, we can apply the method of *simultaneous equations* to the two constraint equations:

$$4X_1 + 3X_2 = 240 \quad \text{\textit{(carpentry line)}}$$
$$2X_1 + 1X_2 = 100 \quad \text{\textit{(painting line)}}$$

To solve these equations simultaneously, we multiply the second equation by -2.

$$-2(2X_1 + 1X_2 = 100) = -4X_1 - 2X_2 = -200$$

and then add it to the first equation:

$$\begin{aligned} +4X_1 + 3X_2 &= 240 \\ \hline + 1X_2 &= 40 \end{aligned}$$

---

[4]Of course, if a graph is perfectly drawn, you can always find point ③ by a careful examination of the intersection's coordinates. Otherwise, the algebraic method shown here provides more precision.

or

$$X_2 = 40$$

Doing this has enabled us to eliminate one variable, X_1, and to solve for X_2. We can now substitute 40 for X_2 in either of the original equations and solve for X_1. Let's use the first equation. When $X_2 = 40$, then,

$$4X_1 + 3(40) = 240$$

$$4X_1 + 120 = 240$$

or

$$4X_1 = 120$$

$$X_1 = 30$$

Thus point ③ has the coordinates ($X_1 = 30$, $X_2 = 40$); we can compute its profit level to complete the analysis.

　　Point ③:　($X_1 = 30, X_2 = 40$)　　Profit = $7(30) + $5(40) = $410

　Because point ③ produces the highest profit of any corner point, the product mix of $X_1 = 30$ tables and $X_2 = 40$ chairs is the optimal solution to Flair Furniture's problem. This solution yields a profit of $410 per production period, which is the same figure we obtained using the iso-profit line method.

10.5	**SOLVING FLAIR FURNITURE'S LP PROBLEM BY AB:QM, LINDO, STORM, AND WHAT'S*BEST!***

Almost every university, business, and government organization has access to computer programs that are capable of solving enormous linear programming problems. For example, organizations using General Electric Company computers may use a program called LINPRO. IBM mainframe users have Mathematical Program Systems (MPSX). Control Data's package is called Optima. Honeywell's is Advanced Linear Programming System (ALPS), and Grumman Data Systems has programs called LINPROG and SIMPLEX. In addition, universities provide students with variations of these and other LP programs with such names as LINDO or STORM.

Teaching Suggestion 10.5:
The Use of Software in Solving LP Problems. See the Instructor's Section for details.

　Although each computer program is slightly different, the approach each takes toward handling LP problems is basically the same. The format of the input data and the level of detail provided in output results may differ from program to program and computer to computer, but once you are experienced in dealing with computerized LP algorithms, you can easily adjust to minor changes.

　In this section we demonstrate our own microcomputer software, AB:QM, as well as three other popular commercial packages for microcomputers, all on the Flair Furniture Company problem data. As you can see in Programs 10.1, 10.2, 10.3, and 10.4, all are easy to run and understand. As we shall see in the next chapters, these programs are also capable of providing much more detailed output, including simplex tableaus (the topic of Chapter 12) and sensitivity analysis (the topic of Chapter 13). As with our printouts in this text, the information *we* input to the computer is shaded.

PROGRAM 10.1 Sample Linear Programming Computer Run Using AB:QM Microcomputer Software

```
Linear Programming
────────────────────────────────────────────────────────────────
Problem Title :  Flair Furniture Company
Type of Problem (Max=1/Min=2)  1         Tableau(All=1/Final=2/No=3)  3
Number of Constraints          2         Number of Variables          2
────────────────────────────────────────────────────────────────

              Tables            Chairs            Rhs
Obj.             7                 5      x   xxxxxxxxxx
Carpentry        4                 3      <        240
Painting         2                 1      <        100


────────────────────────────────────────────────────────────────

Help  New  Load  Save  Edit   Run   Print  Install  Directory  Esc
────────────────────────────────────────────────────────────────


Program: Linear Programming

Problem Title : Flair Furniture Company

***** Input Data *****

Max.  Z =  7 Tables + 5 Chairs

Subject to

Carpentry   4 Tables + 3 Chairs <= 240
Painting    2 Tables + 1 Chair  <= 100

***** Program Output *****


Final Optimal Solution

Z =    410.000


--------------------------------
Variable        Value      Reduced Cost
--------------------------------
 Tables        30.000         0.000
 Chairs        40.000         0.000
```

PROGRAM 10.2 **Flair Furniture Company Data Solved by STORM**

```
──────────── STORM EDITOR : Linear & Integer Programming Module ────────────

Title :  Flair Furniture Company
Number of variables      :          2
Number of constraints    :          2
Starting solution given  :         NO
Objective type (MAX/MIN) :        MAX
────────────────────────────────────────────────────────────────────────────
R1  : C1       VAR    1     VAR    2  CONST TYPE      R H S      RANGE
OBJ COEFF              7.           5.       XXXX       XXXX       XXXX
CONSTR    1            4.           3.       <=         240.        .
CONSTR    2            2.           1.       <=         100.        .
VARBL TYPE           POS          POS        XXXX       XXXX       XXXX
LOWR BOUND             .            .         XXXX       XXXX       XXXX
UPPR BOUND             .            .         XXXX       XXXX       XXXX
INIT SOLN            0.           0.          XXXX       XXXX       XXXX



────────────────────────────────────────────────────────────────────────────

F1 Block   F2 GoTo   F3 InsR   F4 DelR   F5 InsC   F6 DelC    F7 Done   F8 Help



                      Flair Furniture Company
          OPTIMAL SOLUTION - SUMMARY REPORT (NONZERO VARIABLES)
                   Variable        Value          Cost
              1    VAR   1        30.0000        7.0000
              2    VAR   2        40.0000        5.0000
          Objective Function Value = 410
```

PROGRAM 10.3 **Flair Furniture Company Data Solved by LINDO**

```
LINDO/PC

:  MAX 7X1 + 5X2
?  ST
?  4X1 + 3X2 < 240
?  2X1 + 1X2 < 100
?
:  LOOK
ROW :
ALL

MAX      7 X1 + 5 X2
SUBJECT TO
        2)    4 X1 + 3 X2 <=    240
        3)    2 X1 +   X2 <=    100
END
```

(Continued)

PROGRAM 10.3 (Continued)

```
: GO
LP OPTIMUM FOUND  AT STEP      2

              OBJECTIVE FUNCTION VALUE

  1)            410.000000

  VARIABLE            VALUE          REDUCED COST
        X1          30.000000            .000000
        X2          40.000000            .000000
```

PROGRAM 10.4 Flair Furniture Analysis with What's*Best!*

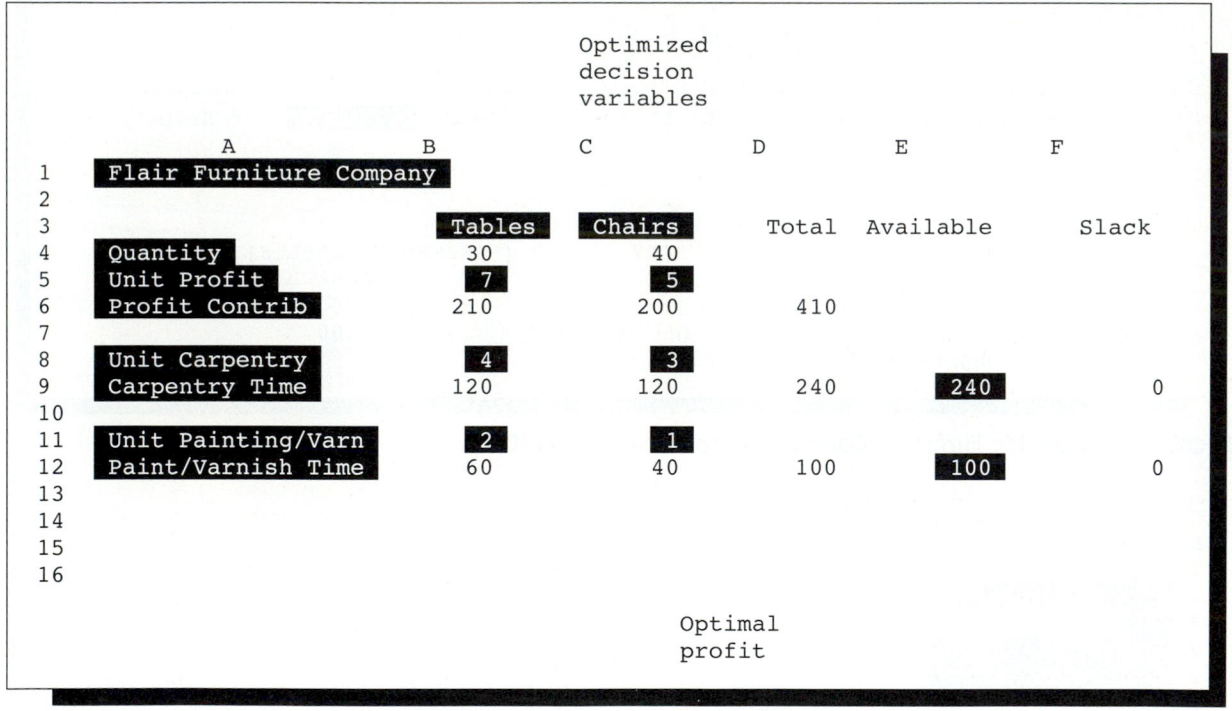

10.6 AN INTRODUCTION TO SENSITIVITY ANALYSIS

Programs 10.1 through 10.4, which solved the Flair Furniture Company problem using the AB:QM, LINDO, STORM, and What's*Best!* software packages, *can* provide more than just the answer to Flair's production mix decision. They all have the capability of also performing what is referred to as "sensitivity analysis." Sensitivity analysis tells us just how sensitive the final solution is to the data used to build the LP model. This is a very important part of LP, and we will treat the subject of "postoptimality analysis" or sensitivity analysis in depth in Chapter 13. We will see then how to analyze a solution both graphically and algebraically. But for now, let us take a quick overview of the topic, using Program 10.5 as our guide.

Program 10.5 illustrates two aspects of sensitivity analysis that almost every LP program is capable of generating. (This particular set of tables came from AB:QM). The upper rows provide information regarding the sensitivity of the objective function coefficients in the Flair Furniture problem. For example, the current values (probably provided by the accounting department) are that each table yields a profit contribution of $7 and each chair of $5. But how accurate are these figures? Should Flair still produce 30 tables and 40 chairs even if the real profit is only $6.50 per table? What if one chair actually yields a profit of $5.10, not $5?

The answers lie in the upper and lower limits provided by the LP software. We see that if the actual profit contribution per table is in the range from $6.67 to $10, Flair should *still* produce 30 tables and 40 chairs if all other data in the problem remain the same. Likewise, if the profit/chair is between $3.50 and $5.25, the current solution will remain optimal (again, with everything else remaining equal). The total profit will change, of course, but the product mix will remain the same.

PROGRAM 10.5 **Sensitivity Analysis on Flair Furniture Co. Final Solution**

```
Objective Coefficient Ranges
-----------------------------------------------------------------------
              Lower      Current      Upper     Allowable    Allowable
Variables     Limit      Values       Limit     Increase     Decrease
-----------------------------------------------------------------------
Tables        6.667      7.000        10.000    3.000        0.333
Chairs        3.500      5.000        5.250     0.250        1.500

Right-Hand-Side Ranges
-----------------------------------------------------------------------
              Lower      Current      Upper     Allowable    Allowable
Constraints   Limit      Values       Limit     Increase     Decrease
-----------------------------------------------------------------------
Carpentry     200.000    240.000      300.000   60.000       40.000
Painting      80.000     100.000      120.000   20.000       20.000


-----------------------------------------------------
Constraint   Slack/Surplus   Shadow Price
-----------------------------------------------------
Carpentry        0.000          1.500
Painting         0.000          0.500
-----------------------------------------------------
```

Now look to the bottom rows of program 10.5 which deal with "right-hand-side" ranges and shadow pricing.

The change in the value of the objective function for each unit increase in a right-hand side is called the "shadow price." Shadow pricing, goes hand in hand with right-hand-side ranging, which appears just above it. We see that Flair's carpentry constraint has a shadow price of $1.50. The shadow price is the additional amount of profit that Flair would make if one more hour of carpentry time becomes available. This means that management should be willing to pay up to $1.50 per hour for additional carpentry hours. The shadow prices shown here are valid over the right-hand-side ranges for their corresponding constraints. This means that as long as there are from 200 to 300 hours of carpentry time available, the shadow price of $1.50 is valid. For changes outside the range, the problem must be resolved and new shadow prices computed.

10.7   SOLVING MINIMIZATION PROBLEMS

Teaching Suggestion 10.6:
Applications of QA Boxes in the LP Chapters. See the Instructor's Section for details.

Many linear programming problems involve minimizing an objective such as cost instead of maximizing a profit function. A restaurant, for example, may wish to develop a work schedule to meet staffing needs while minimizing the total number of employees. A manufacturer may seek to distribute its products from several factories to its many regional warehouses in such a way as to minimize total shipping costs. A hospital may want to provide a daily meal plan for its patients that meets certain nutritional standards while at the same time minimizing food purchase costs.

Minimization problems can be solved graphically by first setting up the feasible solution region and then using either the corner point method or an iso-cost line approach (which is analogous to the iso-profit approach in maximization problems) to find the values of X_1 and X_2 that yield the minimum cost. Let's take a look at a common LP problem referred to as the diet problem. This situation is similar to the one that the hospital faces in feeding its patients at the least cost.

Applicable Problems 10-13 10-15, 10-19

The Holiday Meal Turkey Ranch

Alternate Example 10.2

The Holiday Meal Turkey Ranch is considering buying two different brands of turkey feed and blending them to provide a good, low-cost diet for its turkeys. Each feed contains, in varying proportions, some or all of the three nutritional ingredients essential for fattening turkeys. Each pound of brand 1 purchased, for example, contains 5 ounces of ingredient A, 4 ounces of ingredient B, and ½ ounce of ingredient C. Each pound of brand 2 contains 10 ounces of ingredient A, 3 ounces of ingredient B, but no ingredient C. The brand 1 feed costs the ranch 2¢ a pound, while the brand 2 feed costs 3¢ a pound. The owner of the ranch would like to use LP

APPLICATIONS OF QA

Manpower Planning at United Airlines with LP

In 1984, United Airlines started air service to cities in all of the 50 states, the only airline at that time to do so. The expansion required to achieve this growth created personnel scheduling problems but provided the potential for great cost savings. That year, United dramatically increased its operating profit to over $500 million from $160 million the year before. One major contributor to this increased profit was the ability to tightly control costs. In the past, United was not completely satisfied with the way it scheduled personnel. For example, 11 United reservation offices employed over 4,000 full-time or part-time sales representatives. Approximately 1,000 full-time or part-time customer service agents worked at the 10 largest airports United serviced.

As a result of the expansion, United Airlines had as a major objective the efficient and effective scheduling of personnel. In 1982, the Station Manpower Planning Project had been initiated. Its objectives were to determine the needs for personnel as a result of the expansion, to identify any excess personnel capacity, to produce a more timely and accurate schedule, and to reduce total scheduling costs while maintaining adequate customer service.

Before the personnel planning project, schedules were typically done by hand at the various reservation offices. Clearly, with the expansion, new and better planning approaches were needed.

The Station Manpower Planning System employs both linear and integer programming along with other techniques to perform the forecasting of personnel requirements as well as the actual scheduling of people. Used since 1983, it currently schedules work for approximately 4,000 employees on a regular basis, with plans to schedule 10,000 employees in the near future. In addition to being timely, the integer and linear programming approaches also resulted in cost savings. It has been estimated that over $6 million has been saved annually with the new system. In addition, the scheduled employees, the operating managers, and the upper-level managers are very pleased with the overall performance of their new personnel planning system.

Source: Thomas Hollorann and Judson Byrn, "United Airlines Stationed Manpower Planning System," *Interfaces* **16**, 1 (January–February 1986): 39–50.

Video 10.2: United Airlines Station Manpower Planning System

to determine the lowest-cost diet that meets the minimum monthly intake requirement for each nutritional ingredient.

Table 10.2 summarizes the relevant information. If we let

$$X_1 = \text{Number of pounds of brand 1 feed purchased}$$

$$X_2 = \text{Number of pounds of brand 2 feed purchased}$$

TABLE 10.2 Holiday Meal Turkey Ranch Data

INGREDIENT	COMPOSITION OF EACH POUND OF FEED (OZ.)		MINIMUM MONTHLY REQUIREMENT PER TURKEY (OZ.)
	BRAND 1 FEED	BRAND 2 FEED	
A	5	10	90
B	4	3	48
C	1/2	0	1 1/2
Cost per pound	2¢	3¢	

then we may proceed to formulate this linear programming problem as follows:

$$\text{Minimize cost (in cents)} = 2X_1 + 3X_2$$

subject to these constraints:

$$5X_1 + 10X_2 \geq 90 \text{ ounces} \quad (\textit{ingredient A constraint})$$
$$4X_1 + 3X_2 \geq 48 \text{ ounces} \quad (\textit{ingredient B constraint})$$
$$\tfrac{1}{2}X_1 \geq 1\tfrac{1}{2} \text{ ounces} \quad (\textit{ingredient C constraint})$$
$$X_1 \geq 0 \quad\quad\quad\quad (\textit{nonnegativity constraint})$$
$$X_2 \geq 0 \quad\quad\quad\quad (\textit{nonnegativity constraint})$$

Teaching Suggestion 10.7:
The Feasible Region for the Minimization Problem. See the Instructor's Section for details.

Before solving this problem, we want to be sure to note three features that affect its solution. First, you should be aware that the third constraint implies that the farmer *must* purchase enough brand 1 feed to meet the minimum standards for the C nutritional ingredient. Buying only brand 2 would not be feasible because it lacks C. Second, as the problem is formulated, we will be solving for the best blend of brands 1 and 2 to buy per turkey per month. If the ranch houses 5,000 turkeys in a given month, it need simply multiply the X_1 and X_2 quantities by 5,000 in order to decide how much feed to order overall. And third, we are now dealing with a series of greater-than-or-equal-to constraints. These cause the feasible solution area to be above the constraint lines, a common situation when handling minimization LP problems.

Using the Corner Point Method on a Minimization Problem

feasible solution region for the minimization problem

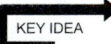

To solve the Holiday Meal Turkey Ranch problem, we first construct the feasible solution region. This is done by plotting each of the three constraint equations as in Figure 10.10. You may note that the third constraint, $\tfrac{1}{2}X_1 \geq 1\tfrac{1}{2}$, may be rewritten and plotted as $X_1 \geq 3$. (This involves multiplying both sides of the inequality by 2, but does not change the position of the constraint line in any way.) Minimization problems are often unbounded outward (that is, on the right side and on top), but this causes no difficulty in solving them. As long as they are bounded inward (on the left side and the bottom), corner points may be established. The optimal solution will lie at one of the corners as it would in a maximization problem.

solving for corner points algebraically

In this case, there are three corner points: *a, b,* and *c*. For point *a,* we find the coordinates at the intersection of the ingredient C and B constraints, that is, where the line $X_1 = 3$ crosses the line $4X_1 + 3X_2 = 48$. If we substitute $X_1 = 3$ into the B constraint equation, then the following sequence of computations may be performed:

$$4X_1 + 3X_2 = 48$$

or

$$4(3) + 3X_2 = 48$$

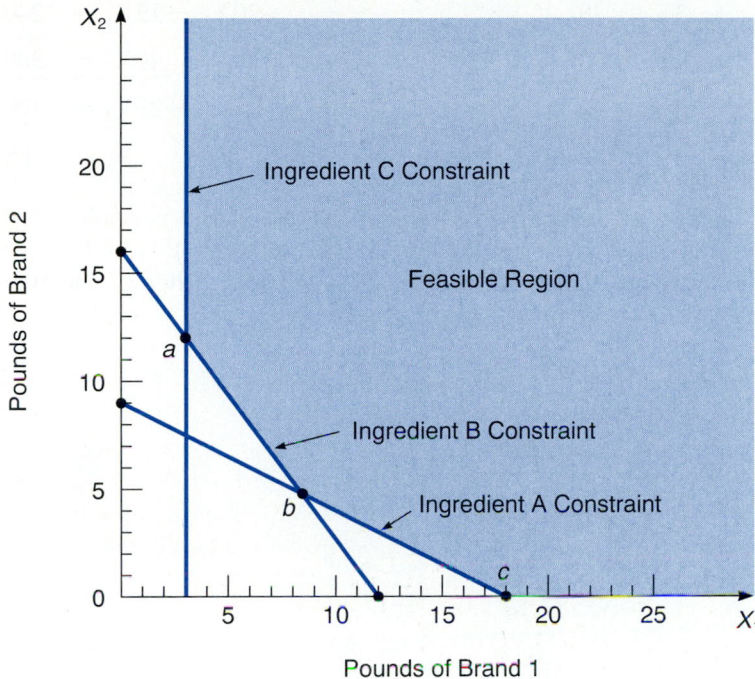

FIGURE 10.10
Feasible Region for the Holiday Meal Turkey Ranch Problem

or

$$12 + 3X_2 = 48$$

or

$$3X_2 = 36$$
$$X_2 = 12$$

Thus, point a has the coordinates ($X_1 = 3$, $X_2 = 12$) and a corresponding cost of:

$$\text{Cost at point } a = 2X_1 + 3X_2$$
$$= 2(3) + 3(12)$$
$$= 42¢$$

To find the values of point b algebraically we solve the equations $4X_1 + 3X_2 = 48$ and $5X_1 + 10X_2 = 90$ simultaneously. This can be done by (1) multiplying the first equation (representing the ingredient B constraint) by -5, then (2) multiplying the second equation (the ingredient A constraint line) by 4, and finally (3) adding the two new equations together.

1. $-5(4X_1 + 3X_2 = 48)$ $-20X_1 - 15X_2 = -240$

2. $4(5X_1 + 10X_2 = 90)$ $\underline{20X_1 + 40X_2 = 360}$

3. $ +25X_2 = 120$

$X_2 = 4.8$

The reason for this procedure was to eliminate one of the variables (X_1) from the equations, so that we could solve for the other (X_2). Now that we have a value for X_2, we may substitute $X_2 = 4.8$ into either of the two original equations to solve for X_1. Using the first equation:

$$4X_1 + 3(4.8) = 48$$

or

$$4X_1 + 14.4 = 48$$

or

$$4X_1 = 33.6$$

or

$$X_1 = 8.4$$

The cost at point b is now:

$$\text{Cost at point } b = 2X_1 + 3X_2$$
$$= 2(8.4) + 3(4.8)$$
$$= 31.2\textcent$$

Finally, the cost at point c must be computed. This is much easier, as it is evident that c has the coordinates $(X_1 = 18, X_2 = 0)$:

$$\text{Cost at point } c = 2X_1 + 3X_2$$
$$= 2(18) + 3(0)$$
$$= 36\textcent$$

Hence, the minimum cost solution is to purchase 8.4 pounds of brand 1 feed and 4.8 pounds of brand 2 feed per turkey per month. This will yield a cost of 31.2¢ per turkey.

Iso-Cost Line Approach

iso-cost line

As mentioned before, the *iso-cost line* approach may also be used to solve LP minimization problems such as that of the Holiday Meal Turkey Ranch. As with iso-profit lines, we need not compute the cost at each corner point, but instead draw a series of parallel cost lines. The lowest cost line (that is, the one closest in toward the origin) to touch the feasible region provides us with the optimal solution corner.

Applicable Problem 10-18

For example, we start in Figure 10.11 by drawing a 54¢ cost line, namely $54 = 2X_1 + 3X_2$. Obviously, there are many points in the feasible region that would yield a lower total cost. We proceed to move our iso-cost line

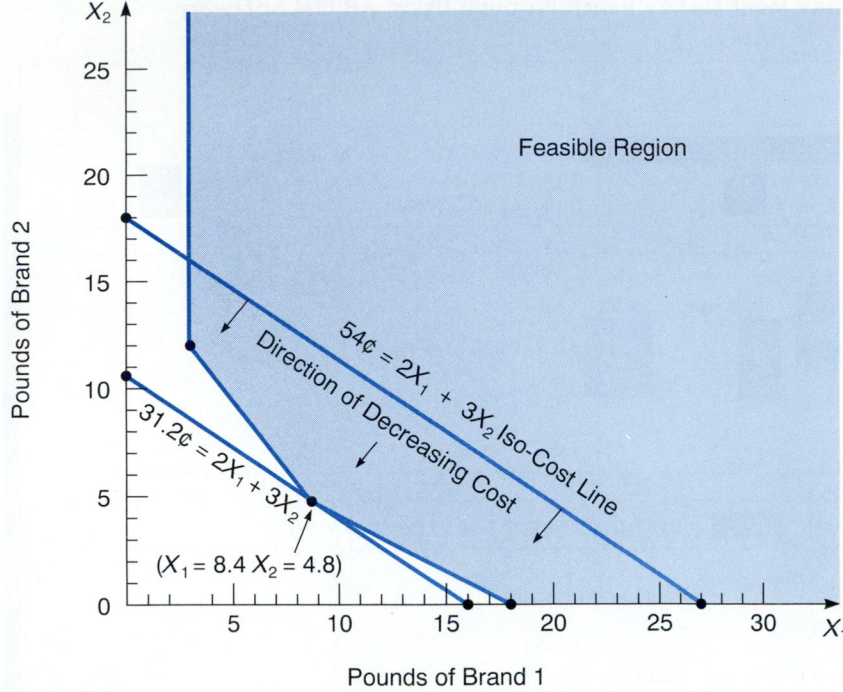

FIGURE 10.11
Graphical Solution to the Holiday Meal Turkey
Ranch Problem Using the Iso-Cost Line

toward the lower left, in a plane parallel to the 54¢ solution line. The last point we touch while still in contact with the feasible region is the same as corner point b of Figure 10.10. It has the coordinates ($X_1 = 8.4$, $X_2 = 4.8$) and an associated cost of 31.2¢.

Computer Approach

For the sake of completeness, we will also solve the Holiday Meal Turkey Ranch problem using our AB:QM software package. Program 10.6 illustrates the input (which is shaded) and output.

10.8 SUMMARY OF THE GRAPHICAL SOLUTION METHOD

As you saw in the cases of the Flair Furniture Company and the Holiday Meal Turkey Ranch, the graphical method of solving linear programming problems involves several steps. Let's review them briefly before moving on.

1. Formulate the problem in terms of a series of mathematical constraints and an objective function.

2. Graph each of the constraint equations.

graphical steps to solve LP problem

PROGRAM 10.6 Solving the Holiday Meal Turkey Ranch Problem Using AB:QM Software

```
Linear Programming

Problem Title : Holiday Meal Turkey Ranch
Type of Problem (Max=1/Min=2)  2        Tableau(All=1/Final=2/No=3)  3
Number of Constraints          3        Number of Variables          2


          X1          X2    T       Rhs
Obj.       2           3    x xxxxxxxxxx
C1         5          10    >        90
C2         4           3    >        48
C3        .5           >             1.5



Help  New  Load  Save  Edit  Run   Print  Install   Directory   Esc


Program: Linear Programming

Problem Title : Holiday Meal Turkey Ranch

***** Input Data *****


Min.  Z =  2x1 + 3x2

Subject to

C1    5x1 + 10x2 >= 90
C2    4x1 +  3x2 >= 48
C3    .5x1 >= 1.5

***** Program Output *****



Final Optimal Solution

Z =    31.200


------------------------------------
Variable        Value     Reduced Cost
------------------------------------
   x 1          8.400        0.000
   x 2          4.800        0.000
```

3. Identify the feasible solution region, that is, the area that satisfies all of the constraints simultaneously.

4. Select one of the two following graphical solution techniques and proceed to solve.

Corner Point Method	*Iso-Profit or Iso-Cost Method*
5. Identify each of the corner, or extreme, points of the feasible region by either visual inspection or the method of simultaneous equations.	5. Select a specific profit or cost line and graph it to reveal its slope or angle.
6. Compute the profit or cost at each corner point by substituting that point's coordinates into the objective function.	6. If you are dealing with a maximization problem, maintain the same slope, through a series of parallel lines, and move the line up and to the right until it touches the feasible region at only one point. If you have a minimization problem, move down and to the left until it touches only one point in the feasible region.
7. Identify the optimal solution as that corner point with the highest profit, in a maximization problem, or lowest cost, in a minimization problem.	7. Identify the optimal solution as the coordinates of that point on the feasible region touched by the highest possible iso-profit line or lowest possible iso-cost line.
	8. Read the optimal (X_1, X_2) coordinates from the graph, or compute their values by using the simultaneous equation method.
	9. Compute the profit or cost.

10.9 A FEW SPECIAL ISSUES IN LINEAR PROGRAMMING

Four special cases and difficulties arise at times when using the graphical approach to solving linear programming problems. They are called: (1) infeasibility, (2) unboundedness, (3) redundancy, and (4) alternate optimal solutions.

Transparency Master 10.9: Special Cases in LP.

Applicable Problem 10-22

Infeasibility

Infeasibility is a condition that arises when there is no solution to a linear programming problem that satisfies all of the constraints given. Graphically, it means that no feasible solution region exists—a situation that

lack of a feasible solution region

might occur if the problem was formulated with conflicting constraints. This, by the way, is a frequent occurrence in real-life, large-scale LP problems that involve hundreds of constraints. For example, if one constraint is supplied by the marketing manager who states that at least 300 tables must be produced (namely, $X_1 \geq 300$) to meet sales demand, and a second restriction is supplied by the production manager who insists that no more than 220 tables be produced (namely, $X_1 \leq 220$) because of a lumber shortage, then an infeasible solution region results. Once the operations research analyst coordinating the LP problem points out this conflict, one manager or the other must revise his or her inputs. Perhaps more raw materials could be procured from a new source, or perhaps sales demand could be lowered by substituting a different model table to customers.

As a further graphic illustration of infeasibility, let us consider the following three constraints:

$$X_1 + 2X_2 \leq 6$$
$$2X_1 + X_2 \leq 8$$
$$X_1 \geq 7$$

As seen in Figure 10.12, there is no feasible solution region for this LP problem because of the presence of conflicting constraints.

Unboundedness

Sometimes a linear program will not have a finite solution. This means that in a maximization problem, for example, one or more solution variables, and the profit, can be made infinitely large without violating any

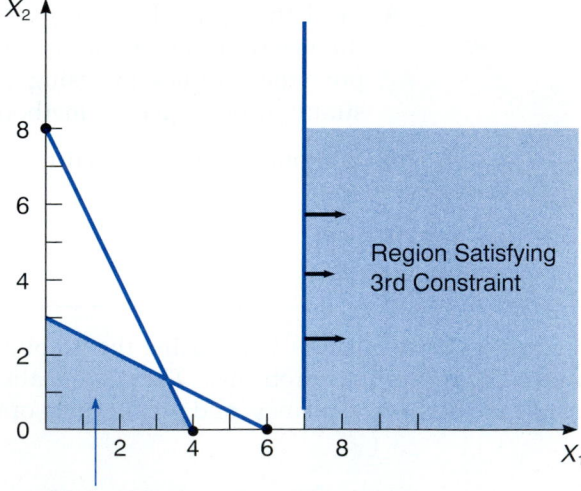

Region Satisfying
3rd Constraint

Region Satisfying First 2 Constraints

FIGURE 10.12
Problem with No Feasible Solution

constraints. If we try to solve such a problem graphically, we will note that the feasible region is open-ended.

Let us consider a simple example to illustrate the situation. A firm has formulated the following LP problem:

$$\text{Maximize profit} = \$3X_1 + \$5X_2$$

$$\text{Subject to:} \quad X_1 \quad\quad\quad \geqslant 5$$

$$X_2 \leqslant 10$$

$$X_1 + 2X_2 \geqslant 10$$

$$X_1, \quad X_2 \geqslant 0$$

As you see in Figure 10.13, since this is a maximization problem and the feasible region extends infinitely to the right, there is *unboundedness,* or an unbounded solution. This implies that the problem has been improperly formulated. It would indeed be wonderful for the company to be able to produce an infinite number of units of X_1 (at a profit of $3 each!), but obviously no firm has infinite resources available or infinite product demand.

Redundancy

The presence of redundant constraints is another common situation that occurs in large linear programming formulations. *Redundancy* causes no major difficulties in solving LP problems graphically, but you should be able to identify its occurrence. A redundant constraint is simply one that does not affect the feasible solution region. In other words, one constraint may be more binding or restrictive than another and thereby negate its need to be considered.

pager
redundant constraints

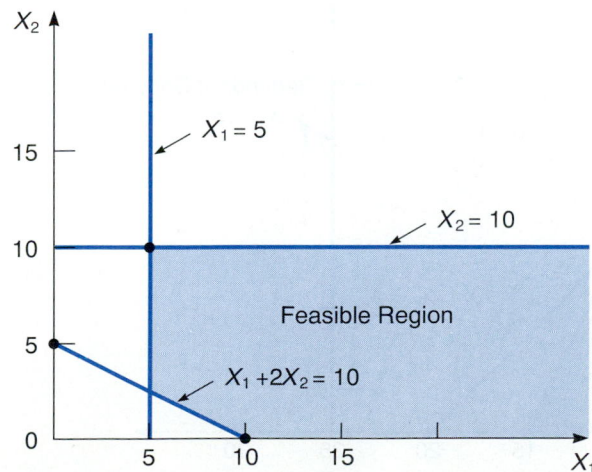

FIGURE 10.13
Solution Region That is Unbounded to the Right

Let's look at the following example of an LP problem with three constraints:

$$\text{Maximize profit} = \$1X_1 + \$2X_2$$

$$\text{Subject to:} \qquad X_1 + X_2 \leq 20$$

$$2X_1 + X_2 \leq 30$$

$$X_1 \qquad \leq 25$$

$$X_1, \ X_2 \geq 0$$

The third constraint, $X_1 \leq 25$, is redundant and unnecessary in the formulation and solution of the problem because it has no effect on the feasible region set from the first two more restrictive constraints. (See Figure 10.14.)

Alternate Optimal Solutions

multiple optimal solutions

A linear programming problem may, on occasion, have two or more *alternate optimal solutions*. Graphically, this is the case when the objective function's iso-profit or iso-cost line runs perfectly parallel to one of the problem's constraints—in other words, when they have the same slope.

Transparency Master 10.12:
A Problem with a Redundant Constraint.

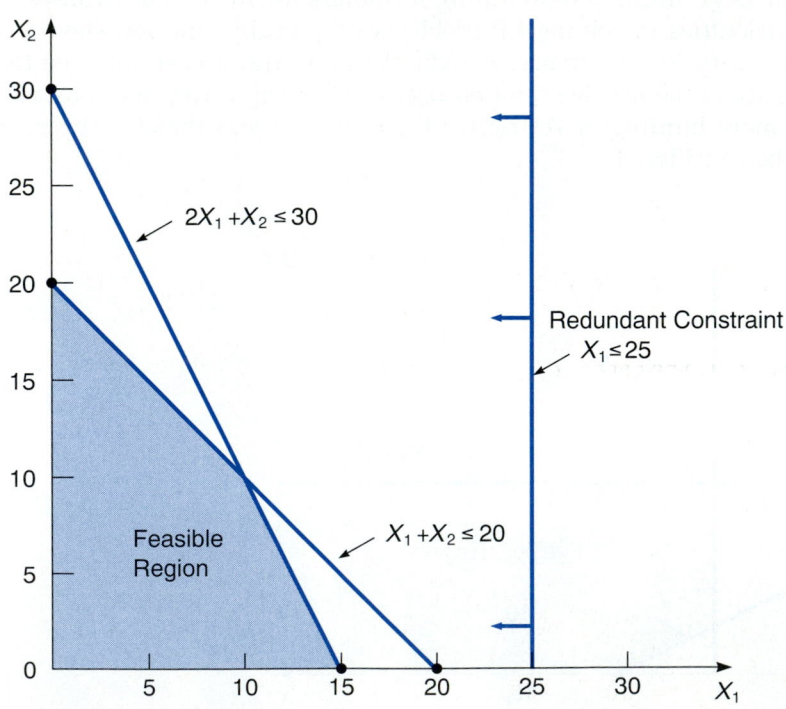

FIGURE 10.14
Problem with a Redundant Constraint

Management of a firm noticed the presence of more than one optimal solution when they formulated this simple LP problem:

$$\text{Maximize profit} = \$3X_1 + \$2X_2$$

$$\text{Subject to:} \qquad 6X_1 + 4X_2 \leq 24$$

$$X_1 \qquad\quad \leq 3$$

$$X_1, \ X_2 \geq 0$$

As we see in Figure 10.15, our first iso-profit line of $8 runs parallel to the constraint equation. At a profit level of $12, the iso-profit line will rest directly on top of the segment of the first constraint line. This means that any point along the line between A and B provides an optimal X_1 and X_2 combination. Far from causing problems, the existence of more than one optimal solution allows management great flexibility in deciding which combination to select. The profit remains the same at each alternate solution.

The graphical solution approaches of this chapter provide a conceptual basis for tackling larger, more complex problems, some of which are addressed in Chapter 11. To *solve* real-life linear programming problems with numerous variables and constraints, we need a solution procedure such as the simplex algorithm, the subject of Chapter 12. The simplex algorithm is the method that our computer software, AB:QM, uses to tackle LP problems.

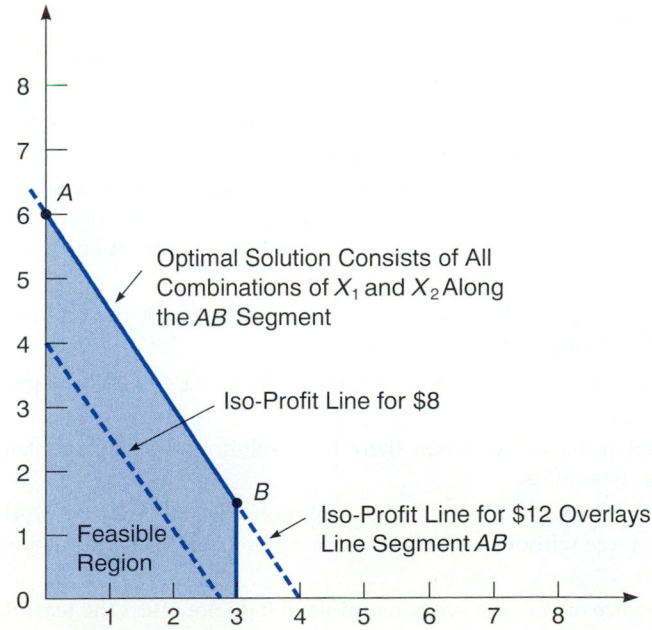

FIGURE 10.15
Example of Alternate Optimal Solutions

GLOSSARY

Linear Programming (LP). A mathematical technique used to help management decide how to make the most effective use of an organization's resources.

Mathematical Programming. The general category of mathematical modeling and solution techniques used to allocate resources while optimizing a measurable goal. LP is one type of programming model.

Objective Function. A mathematical statement of the goal of an organization, stated as an intent to maximize or to minimize some important quantity such as profits or costs.

Constraint. A restriction on the resources available to a firm (stated in the form of an inequality or an equation).

Inequality. A mathematical expression containing a greater-than-or-equal-to relation ($\geq$) or a less-than-or-equal-to relation ($\leq$) used to indicate that the total consumption of a resource must be $\geq$ or $\leq$ some limiting value.

Product Mix Problem. A common LP problem involving a decision as to which products a firm should produce, given that it faces limited resources.

Nonnegativity Constraints. A set of constraints that requires each decision variable to be nonnegative; that is, each X_i must be greater than or equal to 0.

Feasible Region. The area satisfying all of the problem's resource restrictions; that is, the region where all constraints overlap. All possible solutions to the problem lie in the feasible region.

Feasible Solution. A point lying in the feasible region. Basically, it is any point that satisfies all of the problem's constraints.

Infeasible Solution. Any point lying outside the feasible region. It violates one or more of the stated constraints.

Iso-Profit Line. A straight line representing all nonnegative combinations of X_1 and X_2 for a particular profit level.

Corner Point or Extreme Point. A point that lies on one of the corners of the feasible region. This means that it falls at the intersection of two constraint lines.

Corner Point Method. The method of finding the optimal solution to a linear programming problem by testing the profit or cost level at each corner point of the feasible region. The theory of LP states that the optimal solution must lie at one of the corner points.

Simultaneous Equation Method. The algebraic means of solving for the intersection point of two or more linear constraint equations.

Iso-Cost Line. A straight line representing all combinations of X_1 and X_2 for a particular cost level.

Infeasibility. A condition that arises when there is no solution to an LP problem that satisfies all of the constraints.

Unboundedness. A condition that exists when a solution variable and the profit can be made infinitely large without violating any of the problem's constraints in a maximization process.

Redundancy. The presence of one or more constraints that do not affect the feasible solution region.

Alternate Optimal Solution. A situation when more than one optimal solution is possible. It arises when the angle or slope of the objective function is the same as the slope of a constraint.

SOLVED PROBLEMS

Solved Problem 10-1

Personal Mini Warehouses is planning to expand its successful Orlando business into Tampa. In doing so, the company must determine how many storage rooms of each size to build. Its objective and constraints follow:

Maximize monthly earnings

$$= 50X_1 + 20X_2$$

Subject to:

$$2X_1 + 4X_2 \leqslant 400 \quad \textit{(advertising budget available)}$$

$$100X_1 + 50X_2 \leqslant 8{,}000 \quad \textit{(square footage required)}$$

$$X_1 \leqslant 60 \quad \textit{(rental limit expected)}$$

$$X_1, \quad X_2 \geqslant 0$$

where

$$X_1 = \text{number of large spaces developed, and}$$

$$X_2 = \text{number of small spaces developed.}$$

Solution

An evaluation of the five corner points of the accompanying graph indicates that corner point C produces the greatest earnings. Refer to the graph and table.

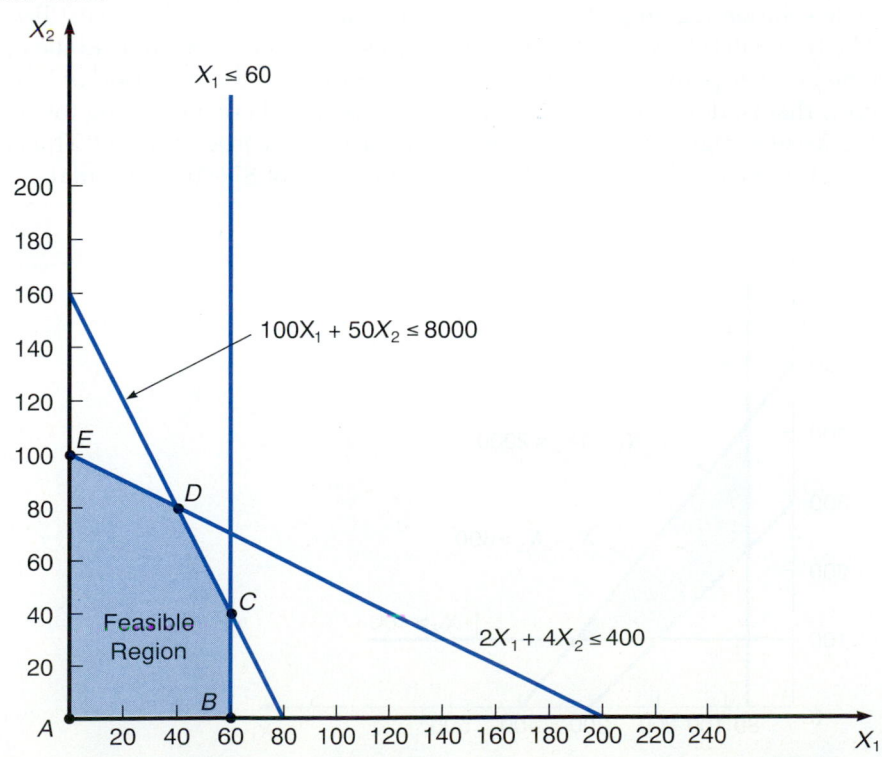

CORNER POINT	VALUES OF X_1, X_2	OBJECTIVE FUNCTION VALUE ($)
A	(0, 0)	0
B	(60, 0)	3,000
C	(60, 40)	3,800
D	(40, 80)	3,600
E	(0, 100)	2,000

Solved Problem 10-2

Solve the following LP formulation graphically, using the iso-cost line approach:

$$\text{Minimize costs} = 24X_1 + 28X_2$$

$$\text{Subject to:} \quad 5X_1 + 4X_2 \leq 2,000$$

$$X_1 \geq 80$$

$$X_1 + X_2 \geq 300$$

$$X_2 \geq 100$$

$$X_1, \quad X_2 \geq 0$$

Solution

A graph of the four constraints is shown below. The arrows indicate the direction of feasibility for each constraint. The next graph illustrates the feasible solution region and plots of two possible objective function cost lines. The first, $10,000, was selected arbitrarily as a starting point. To find the optimal corner point, we need to move the cost line in the direction of lower cost, that is, down and to the left. The last point where a cost line touches the feasible region as it moves toward the origin is corner point D. Thus D, which represents $X_1 = 200$, $X_2 = 100$, and a cost of $7,600, is optimal.

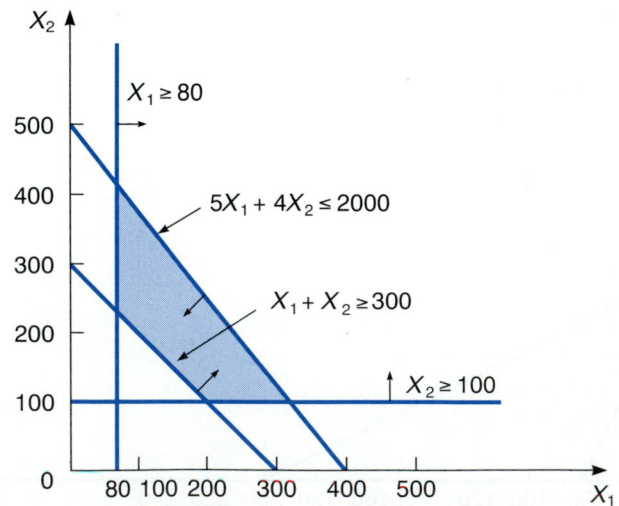

X_2 axis, $\$10,000 = 240X_1 + 280X_2$, points B (≈100, 410), A (≈100, 200), D (≈200, 100), C (≈330, 100), Feasible Region shaded. Optimal Solution, Optimal Cost Line $\$7,600 = 240X_1 + 280X_2$. X_1 axis.

Solved Problem 10-3

Solve the following problems given these constraints and objective function:

$$\text{Maximize profit} = 30X_1 + 40X_2$$

$$\text{Subject to:} \quad 4X_1 + 2X_2 \leq 16$$

$$2X_1 - X_2 \geq 2$$

$$X_2 \leq 2$$

$$X_1, \quad X_2 \geq 0$$

(a) Graph the feasible region.
(b) Evaluate the objective function at each corner point.
(c) Identify the optimal solution.

Solution

(a) The graph appears on page 374, with the feasible region shaded.

(b) CORNER POINT	COORDINATES	PROFIT ($)
A	$X_1 = 1, X_2 = 0$	30
B	$X_1 = 4, X_2 = 0$	120
C	$X_1 = 3, X_2 = 2$	170
D	$X_1 = 2, X_2 = 2$	140

(c) The optimal profit of $170 is at corner point C.

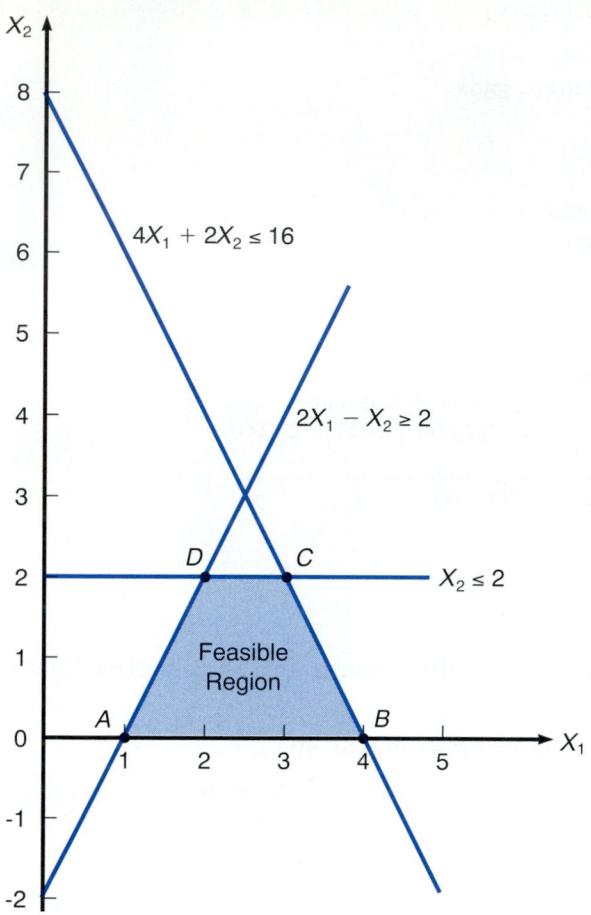

DISCUSSION QUESTIONS AND PROBLEMS

Discussion Questions

10-1 Discuss the similarities and differences between minimization and maximization problems using the graphical solution approaches of linear programming.

10-2 It is important to understand the assumptions underlying the use of any quantitative analysis model. What are the assumptions and requirements for a linear programming model to be formulated and used?

10-3 It has been said that each linear programming problem that has a feasible region has an infinite number of solutions. Explain.

10-4 You have just formulated a maximization linear programming problem and are preparing to solve it graphically. What criteria should you consider in deciding whether it would be easier to solve the problem by the corner point method or the iso-profit line approach?

10-5 Under what condition is it possible for an LP problem to have more than one optimal solution?

10-6 Develop your own individual set of constraint equations and inequalities and use them to illustrate graphically each of the following conditions:

(a) An unbounded problem.
(b) An infeasible problem.
(c) A problem containing redundant constraints.

10-7 The production manager of a large Cincinnati manufacturing firm once made the statement, "I would like to use linear programming, but it's a technique that operates under conditions of certainty. My plant doesn't have that certainty; it's a world of uncertainty. So LP can't be used here." Do you think this statement has any merit? Explain why the manager may have said it.

10-8 The mathematical relationships that follow were formulated by an operations research analyst at the Smith-Lawton Chemical Company. Which ones are invalid for use in a linear programming problem, and why?

$$\text{Maximize profit} = 4X_1 + 3X_1X_2 + 8X_2 + 5X_3$$

$$\text{Subject to:} \quad 2X_1 + X_2 + 2X_3 \leqslant 50$$

$$8X_1 - 4X_2 \geqslant 6$$

$$1.5X_1^2 + 6X_2 + 3X_3 \geqslant 21$$

$$19X_2 - \tfrac{1}{3}X_3 = 17$$

$$5X_1 + 4X_2 + 3\sqrt{X_3} \leqslant 80$$

$$-X_1 - X_2 + X_3 = 5$$

Problems

10-9 The Electrocomp Corporation manufactures two electrical products: air conditioners and large fans. The assembly process for each is similar in that both require a certain amount of wiring and drilling. Each air conditioner takes 3 hours of wiring and 2 hours of drilling. Each fan must go through 2 hours of wiring and 1 hour of drilling. During the next production period, 240 hours of wiring time are available and up to 140 hours of drilling time may be used. Each air conditioner sold yields a profit of $25. Each fan assembled may be sold for a $15 profit. Formulate and solve this LP production mix situation to find the best combination of air conditioners and fans that yields the highest profit. Use the corner point graphical approach.

QA 10-9

40 air conditioners and 60 fans: Profit will be $1,900.

10-10 Electrocomp's management realizes that it forgot to include two critical constraints (see Problem 10-9). In particular, management decides that, to ensure an adequate supply of air conditioners for a contract, at least 20 air conditioners should be manufactured. Since Electrocomp incurred an oversupply of fans the previous period, management also insists that no more than 80 fans be produced during this production period. Resolve this product mix problem to find the new optimal solution.

QA 10-10

Even though the shape of the feasible region changed from Problem 10-9, the optimal solution remains the same.

10-11 The Marriott Tub Company manufactures two lines of bathtubs, called model A and model B. Every tub requires blending a certain amount of steel and zinc; the company has available a total of 25,000 pounds of steel and 6,000 pounds of zinc. Each model A bathtub requires a mixture of 125 pounds of steel and 20 pounds of zinc, and each yields a profit to the firm of $90.

QA 10-11

$(X_1 = 200, X_2 = 0) =$
profit = $18,000

QA 10-12

$(X_1 = 262.5, X_2 = 25)$;
profit = $2,862.50

QA 10-13

40 undergraduate, 20 graduate, cost = $160,000

QA 10-14

10 Alpha 4's, 24 Beta 5's,
profit = $55,200

QA 10-15

30 lbs compost, 30 lbs sewage waste, cost = $2.70

QA 10-16

treasury notes = $150,000,
bonds = $100,000, ROI =
$21,000

Each model B tub produced can be sold for a profit of $70; it in turn requires 100 pounds of steel and 30 pounds of zinc. Find by graphical linear programming the best production mix of bathtubs.

□ · **10-12** The Outdoor Furniture Corporation manufactures two products, benches and picnic tables, for use in yards and parks. The firm has two main resources: its carpenters (labor force) and a supply of redwood for use in the furniture. During the next production cycle, 1,200 hours of manpower are available under a union agreement. The firm also has a stock of 3,500 feet of quality redwood. Each bench that Outdoor Furniture produces requires four labor hours and 10 feet of redwood; each picnic table takes six labor hours and 35 feet of redwood. Completed benches will yield a profit of $9 each, and tables will result in a profit of $20 each. How many benches and tables should Outdoor Furniture produce in order to obtain the largest possible profit? Use the graphical linear programming approach.

□ · **10-13** The dean of the Western College of Business must plan the school's course offerings for the fall semester. Student demands make it necessary to offer at least 30 undergraduate and 20 graduate courses in the term. Faculty contracts also dictate that at least 60 courses be offered in total. Each undergraduate course taught costs the college an average of $2,500 in faculty wages, while each graduate course costs $3,000. How many undergraduate and graduate courses should be taught in the fall so that total faculty salaries are kept to a minimum?

□ : **10-14** MSA Computer Corporation manufactures two models of minicomputers, the Alpha 4 and the Beta 5. The firm employs five technicians, working 160 hours each per month, on its assembly line. Management insists that full employment (that is, *all* 160 hours of time) be maintained for each worker during next month's operations. It requires 20 labor hours to assemble each Alpha 4 computer and 25 labor hours to assemble each Beta 5 model. MSA wants to see at least 10 Alpha 4s and at least 15 Beta 5s produced during the production period. Alpha 4s generate a $1,200 profit per unit, and Beta 5s yield $1,800 each. Determine the most profitable number of each model of minicomputer to produce during the coming month.

□ : **10-15** The Sweet Smell Fertilizer Company markets bags of manure labeled "not less than 60 pounds dry weight." The packaged manure is a combination of compost and sewage wastes. To provide a quality fertilizer, each bag should contain at least 30 pounds of compost, but no more than 40 pounds of sewage. Each pound of compost costs Sweet Smell 5¢ and each pound of sewage costs 4¢. Use a graphical linear programming method to determine the least cost blend of compost and sewage in each bag.

□ · **10-16** The National Credit Union has $250,000 available to invest in a 12-month commitment. The money can be placed in treasury notes yielding an 8% return or in municipal bonds at an average rate of return of 9%. Credit union regulations require diversification to the extent that at least 50% of the investment be placed in treasury notes. Because of defaults in such municipalities as Cleveland and New York, it is decided that no more than 40% of the investment be placed in bonds. How much should the National Credit Union invest in each security so as to maximize its return on investment?

: **10-17** Solve the following linear programming problem using the corner point graphical method:

QA 10-17

$$\text{Maximize profit} = 4X_1 + 4X_2$$

Subject to:
$$3X_1 + 5X_2 \leqslant 150$$
$$X_1 - 2X_2 \leqslant 10$$
$$5X_1 + 3X_2 \leqslant 150$$
$$X_1, X_2 \geqslant 0$$

$(X_1 = 18\frac{3}{4}, X_2 = 18\frac{3}{4},$
$\text{profit} = \$150)$

: **10-18** Consider this linear programming formulation:

QA 10-18

$$\text{Minimize cost} = \$1X_1 + \$2X_2$$

Subject to:
$$X_1 + 3X_2 \geqslant 90$$
$$8X_1 + 2X_2 \geqslant 160$$
$$3X_1 + 2X_2 \geqslant 120$$
$$X_2 \leqslant 70$$

Graphically illustrate the feasible region and apply the iso-cost line procedure to indicate which corner point produces the optimal solution. What is the cost of this solution?

$X_1 = 25.71; X_2 = 21.43;$
$\text{cost} = \$68.57$

: **10-19** The stock brokerage firm of Blank, Leibowitz, and Weinberger has analyzed and recommended two stocks to an investors' club of college professors. The professors were interested in factors such as short-term growth, intermediate growth, and dividend rates. These data on each stock are as follows:

QA 10-19

FACTORS	STOCK	
	LOUISIANA GAS AND POWER	TRIMEX INSULATION COMPANY
Short-term growth potential, per dollar invested	$ .36	$ .24
Intermediate growth potential (over next three years), per dollar invested	$1.67	$1.50
Dividend rate potential	4%	8%

Each member of the club has an investment goal of: (1) an appreciation of no less than $720 in the short term, (2) an appreciation of at least $5,000 in the next three years, and (3) a dividend income of at least $200 per year. What is the smallest investment that a professor can make in order to meet these three goals?

$ invested in Louisiana Gas and Power = $1,359;
$ invested in Trimex Insulation Co. = $1,818;
$3,179 optimal solution

: **10-20** The advertising agency promoting the new Breem dishwashing detergent wants to get the best exposure possible for the product within the $100,000 advertising budget ceiling placed upon it. To do so, the agency needs to decide how much of the budget to spend on each of its two most effective media: (1) television spots during the afternoon hours and (2) large ads in the city's Sunday newspaper. Each television spot costs $3,000; each Sunday

QA 10-20

newspaper ad costs $1,250. The expected exposure, based on industry ratings, is 35,000 viewers for each TV commercial and 20,000 readers for each newspaper advertisement. The agency director, Mavis Early, knows from experience that it is important to use both media in order to reach the broadest spectrum of potential Breem customers. She decides that at least 5 but no more than 25 television spots should be ordered; and that at least 10 newspaper ads should be contracted. How many times should each of the two media be used to obtain maximum exposure while staying within the budget? Use the graphical method to solve.

Number TV spots = 5; number of newspaper ads = 68; Exposure = 1,535,000

QA 10-21

🖥 : **10-21** The seasonal yield of olives in a Pireaus, Greece, vineyard is greatly influenced by a process of branch pruning. If olive trees are pruned every two weeks, output is increased. The pruning process, however, requires considerably more labor than permitting the olives to grow on their own and results in a smaller size olive. It also, though, permits olive trees to be spaced closer together. The yield of one barrel of olives by pruning requires 5 hours of labor and 1 acre of land. The production of a barrel of olives by the normal process requires only 2 labor hours, but takes 2 acres of land. An olive grower has 250 hours of labor available and a total of 150 acres for growing. Because of the olive size difference, a barrel of olives produced on pruned trees sells for $20, whereas a barrel of regular olives has a market price of $30. The grower has determined that because of uncertain demand, no more than 40 barrels of pruned olives should be produced. Use graphical linear programming to find:

Number of barrels of "pruned" olives = 25; number barrels of regular olives = 62.5; profit = $2,375

(a) The maximum possible profit.
(b) The best combination of barrels of pruned and regular olives.
(c) The number of acres that the olive grower should devote to each growing process.

QA 10-22

🖥 : **10-22** Consider the following four LP formulations. Using a graphical approach, determine:

Formulation 2
Formulation 3
Formulation 1
Formulation 4

(a) Which formulation has more than one optimal solution.
(b) Which formulation is unbounded.
(c) Which formulation is infeasible.
(d) Which formulation is correct as is.

Formulation 1

Maximize: $10X_1 + 10X_2$

Subject to: $2X_1 \leq 10$

$2X_1 + 4X_2 \leq 16$

$4X_2 \leq 8$

$X_1 \geq 6$

Formulation 2

Maximize: $X_1 + 2X_2$

Subject to: $X_1 \leq 1$

$2X_2 \leq 2$

$X_1 + 2X_2 \leq 2$

Formulation 3

Maximize: $3X_1 + 2X_2$

Subject to: $X_1 + X_2 \geq 5$

$X_1 \geq 2$

$2X_2 \geq 8$

Formulation 4

Maximize: $3X_1 + 3X_2$

Subject to: $4X_1 + 6X_2 \leq 48$

$4X_1 + 2X_2 \leq 12$

$3X_2 \geq 3$

$2X_1 \geq 2$

🖥 : **10-23 Serendipity***

QA 10-23

    The three princes of Serendip
Went on a little trip.
They could not carry too much weight;
More than 300 pounds made them hesitate.
They planned to the ounce. When they returned to Ceylon
They discovered that their supplies were just about gone
When, what to their joy, Prince William found
A pile of coconuts on the ground.
"Each will bring 60 rupees," said Prince Richard with a grin
As he almost tripped over a lion skin.
"Look out!" cried Prince Robert with glee
As he spied some more lion skins under a tree.
"These are worth even more—300 rupees each
If we can just carry them all down to the beach."
Each skin weighed fifteen pounds and each coconut, five,
But they carried them all and made it alive.
The boat back to the island was very small
15 cubic feet baggage capacity—that was all.
Each lion skin took up one cubic foot
While eight coconuts the same space took.
With everything stowed they headed to sea
And on the way calculated what their new wealth might be.
"Eureka!" cried Prince Robert, "Our worth is so great
That there's no other way we could return in this state.
Any other skins or nut which we might have brought
Would now have us poorer. And now I know what—
I'll write my friend Horace in England, for surely
Only he can appreciate our serendipity."

Number of coconuts carried = 24; number of skins carried = 12; P = 5,040 rupees

Formulate and *solve* Serendipity by graphical linear programming in order to calculate "what their new wealth might be."

Problems 10-24 and 10-25 test your ability to formulate linear programming problems that have more than two variables. They cannot be solved graphically, but will give you a chance to set up a larger problem.

🖥 : **10-24** The Feed 'N Ship Ranch fattens cattle for local farmers and ships them to meat markets in Kansas City and Omaha. The owners of the ranch seek to determine the amounts of cattle feed to buy so that minimum nutritional standards are satisfied, and at the same time total feed costs are minimized.

QA 10-24

    The feed mix used can be made up of the three grains that contain the following ingredients per pound of feed:

	FEED (OZ.)		
INGREDIENT	STOCK X	STOCK Y	STOCK Z
A	3	2	4
B	2	3	1
C	1	0	2
D	6	8	4

*The word *serendipity* was coined by the English writer Horace Walpole after a fairy tale entitled *The Three Princes of Serendip.* Source of problem is unknown.

$3X_1 + 2X_2 + 4X_3 \geqslant 64$
$2X_1 + 3X_2 + 1X_3 \geqslant 80$
$1X_1 + 0X_2 + 2X_3 \geqslant 16$
$6X_1 + 8X_2 + 4X_3 \geqslant 128$
$X_3 \leqslant 80$
Minimize Cost $= .02X_1 +$
$.04X_2 + .025X_3$

QA 10-25

The cost per pound of stocks X, Y, and Z are $.02, $.04, and $.025, respectively. The minimum requirement per cow per month is 4 lbs. of ingredient A, 5 lbs. of ingredient B, 1 lb. of ingredient C, and 8 lbs. of ingredient D.

The ranch faces one additional restriction: it can only obtain 500 lbs of stock Z per month from the feed supplier regardless of its need. Since there are usually 100 cows at the Feed 'N Ship Ranch at any given time, this means that no more than 5 lbs. of stock Z can be counted on for use in the feed of each cow per month.

Formulate this as a linear programming problem.

🖥 : **10-25** The Weinberger Electronics Corporation primarily manufactures four highly technical products that it supplies to aerospace firms that hold NASA contracts. Each of the products must pass through the following departments before they are shipped: wiring, drilling, assembly, and inspection. The time requirement in hours for each unit produced and its corresponding profit value are summarized in the following table.

PRODUCT	WIRING	DRILLING	ASSEMBLY	INSPECTION	UNIT PROFIT ($)
XJ201	.5	.3	.2	.5	9
XM897	1.5	1	4	1	12
TR29	1.5	2	1	.5	15
BR788	1	3	2	.5	11

10-25 is NOT feasible.
Here is formulation:

The production available in each department each month, and the minimum monthly production requirement to fulfill contracts, are as follows:

DEPARTMENT	CAPACITY IN HOURS	PRODUCT	MINIMUM PRODUCTION LEVEL
Wiring	15,000	XJ201	150
Drilling	17,000	XM897	100
Assembly	26,000	TR29	300
Inspection	12,000	BR788	400

Maximize profit $= 9X_1 +$
$12X_2 + 15X_3 + 11X_4$
Subject to:
$.5X_1 + 1.5X_2 + 1.5X_3 +$
$1X_4 \leqslant 15,000$
$.3X_1 + 1X_2 + 2X_3 +$
$3X_4 \leqslant 17,000$
$.2X_1 + 4X_2 + 1X_3 +$
$2X_4 \leqslant 26,000$
$.5X_1 + 1X_2 + .5X_3 +$
$.5X_4 \leqslant 12,000$
$X_1 \geqslant 150$
$X_2 \geqslant 100$
$X_3 \geqslant 300$
$X_4 \geqslant 400$

The production manager has the responsibility of specifying produciton levels for each product for the coming month. Help him by formulating (that is, setting up the constraints and objective function) Weinberger's problem using linear programming.

QA 10-26

🖥 : **10-26** Androgynous Bicycle Company (ABC) has the hottest new products on the upscale toy market—boys' and girls' bikes in bright fashion colors, with oversized hubs and axles, shell design safety tires, a strong padded frame, chrome-plated chains, brackets and valves, and a nonslip handlebar. Due to the seller's market for high-quality toys for the newest baby boomers, ABC can sell all the bicycles it manufactures at the following prices: boys' bikes—$220, girls' bikes—$175. This is the price payable to ABC at its Orlando plant.

The firm's accountant has determined that direct labor costs will be 45% of the price ABC receives for the boys' model and 40% of the price received for the girls' model. Production costs other than labor, but excluding painting and packaging, are $44 per boys' bicycle and $30 per girls' bicycle. Painting and packaging are $20 per bike, regardless of model.

$X_1 = 384, X_2 = 0$, profit $=$
$21,888
$X_1 = 0, X_2 = 390$, profit $=$
$21,450
$X_1 = 240, X_2 = 150$,
profit $= $21,930$
Sensitivity of the RHS and
optimal cost coefficient
are important.

The Orlando plant's overall production capacity is 390 bicycles per day. Each boy's bike requires 2.5 labor hours while each girl's model takes 2.4 hours to complete. ABC currently employs 120 workers, who each put in an 8-hour day. The firm has no desire to hire or fire to affect labor availability, for it believes its stable work force is one of its biggest assets.

Using a graphical approach, determine the best product mix for ABC.

10-27 Modem Corporation of America (MCA) is the world's largest producer of modem communication devices for microcomputers. Recognized by his computer peers as a brilliant entrepreneur, Hilliard Blank successfully carved out a small niche in the huge microcomputer industry by concentrating on only two devices: the MCA 300 Baud Modem and the MCA 1200 Baud Intelligent Modem. Both devices work on the same principle of modulation—demodulation, converting digital impulses to audio impulses and audio to digital. This process permits computers, which operate in digital signals, to "talk" to other computers via telephone lines, which use audio impulses. The MCA 1200 Baud Intelligent Modem is a high-speed device that has a microprocessor built into it to dial phone numbers automatically. The MCA 300 Baud Modem is slower (300 bits of data per second) and does not have its own microprocessor.

QA 10-27

MCA sold 9,000 of the 300 Baud model and 10,400 of the 1200 Baud model this September. Its income statement for the month is shown below. Costs presented are typical of prior months and are expected to remain at the same levels in the near future.

The firm is facing several constraints as it prepares its November production plan. First, it has experienced a tremendous demand and has been

MCA INCOME STATEMENT
MONTH ENDED SEPTEMBER 30

	REGULAR MODEMS	SMART MODEMS
Sales	$450,000	$640,000
Less: Discounts	10,000	15,000
Returns	12,000	9,500
Warranty replacements	4,000	2,500
Net Sales	$424,000	$613,000
Sales Costs		
Direct labor	60,000	76,800
Indirect labor	9,000	11,520
Materials cost	90,000	128,000
Depreciation	40,000	50,800
Cost of sales	$199,000	$267,120
Gross Profit	$225,000	$345,880
Selling and General Expenses		
General expenses—variable	30,000	35,000
General expenses—fixed	36,000	40,000
Advertising	28,000	25,000
Sales commissions	31,000	60,000
Total operating cost	$125,000	$160,000
Pre-tax income	$100,000	$185,880
Income taxes (25%)	25,000	46,470
Net income	$ 75,000	$139,410

X_1 = no. of MCA 300
Baud Modems
X_2 = no. of MCA 1200
Baud Modems
Maximize profit = $22.67 X_1$
+ $29.01 X_2$
$.555 X_1 + 1.0 X_2 \le 15,400$
$X_2 \le 8,000$

See Instructor's section for
graph. Optimal P = $629,000

Make all MCA 300 Baud
Modems (27,750 of them).

unable to keep any significant inventory in stock. This situation is not expected to change. Second, the firm is located in a small Iowa town from which additional labor is not readily available. Workers can be shifted from production of one modem to another, however. To produce the 9,000 300 Baud Modems in September required 5,000 direct labor hours. The 10,400 1200 Baud Intelligent Modems absorbed 10,400 direct labor hours. Third, MCA is experiencing a problem affecting the Intelligent Modems model. Its component supplier is able to guarantee only 8,000 microprocessors for November delivery. Each Intelligent Modem requires one of these specially made microprocessors. Alternative suppliers are not available on short notice.

Hilliard Blank wants to plan the optimal mix of the two modem models to produce in November to maximize profits for MCA.

(a) Formulate, using September's data, MCA's problem as a linear program.
(b) Solve the problem graphically.
(c) Discuss the implications of your recommended solution.

CASE STUDY

Golding Landscaping and Plants, Inc.

Kenneth and Patricia Golding spent a career as a husband-and-wife real estate investment partnership in Washington, D.C. When they finally retired to a 25-acre farm in northern Virginia's Fairfax County, they became ardent amateur gardeners. Kenneth Golding planted shrubs and fruit trees, while Patricia spent her hours potting all sizes of plants. When the volume of shrubs and plants reached the point where the Goldings began to think of their hobby in a serious vein, they built a greenhouse adjacent to their home and installed heating and watering systems in it.

Shortly thereafter, whenever a family member, friend, or neighbor of the Goldings was about to celebrate a birthday, anniversary, or seasonal holiday, it was quite likely that a plant or small decorative shrub would arrive as a gift. The Goldings' green thumbs even began to generate some demand for plants and shrubs that friends and neighbors were more than happy to pay for. By 1993, the Goldings realized their retirement from real estate had really led to a second career in the plant and shrub business, and they filed for a Virginia business license. Within a matter of months, they asked their attorney to file incorporation documents and formed the firm Golding Landscaping and Plants, Inc.

In addition to marketing potted plants to supermarkets and other retail stores, the Goldings received a series of small landscaping contracts. They designed and planted shrubs at banks, small shopping centers, gasoline stations, and a few apartment complexes.

Early in the new business's existence, Kenneth Golding recognized the need for a high-quality commercial fertilizer that he could blend himself, both for sale and for his own nursery. His goal was to keep his costs to a minimum while producing a top-notch product that was especially suited to the northern Virginia climate.

Working with chemists at Virginia Tech and George Washington Universities, Golding blended "Golding-Grow." It consists of four chemical compounds, C-30, C-92, D-21, and E-11. The cost per pound for each compound is indicated below.

CHEMICAL COMPOUND	COST PER POUND
C-30	$.12
C-92	.09
D-21	.11
E-11	.04

The specifications for Golding-Grow are established as:

a. Chemical E-11 must comprise at least 15% of the blend.

b. C-92 and C-30 must together constitute at least 45% of the blend.

c. D-21 and C-92 can together constitute no more than 30% of the blend.

d. Golding-Grow is packaged and sold in 50-pound bags.

Discussion Questions

1. Formulate an LP problem to determine what blend of the four chemicals will allow Golding to minimize the cost of a 50-pound bag of the fertilizer.

2. Solve by computer to find the best solution.

$X_1 = 7.5$ pounds of C-30
$X_2 = 15$ pounds of C-92
$X_3 = 0$ pounds of D-21
$X_4 = 27.5$ pounds of E-11
Cost = $3.35

BIBLIOGRAPHY

Anbil, R., et al. "Recent Advances in Crew-Pairing Optimization at American Airlines." *Interfaces* **21**, 1 (January–February 1991): 62–74.

Balbirer, Sheldon D., and David Shaw. "An Application of Linear Programming to Bank Financial Planning." *Interfaces* **11**, 5 (October 1981): 77–82.

Beare, G. C. "Linear Programming in Air Defense Modelling." *Journal of Operational Research Society* **38** (1987): 899–905.

Brosch, Lee C., Richard J. Buck, William H. Sparrow, and James R. White. "Boxcars, Linear Programming, and the Sleeping Kitten." *Interfaces* **10**, 6 (December 1980): 53–61.

Cabraal, R. Anil. "Production Planning in a Sri Lanka Coconut Mill Using Parametric Linear Programming." *Interfaces* **11**, 3 (June 1981): 16–21.

Ferris, M. C., and A. B. Philpott. "On the Performance of Karmarkar's Algorithm." *Journal of Operational Research Society* **39** (March 1988): 257–270.

Glen, J. J. "A Linear Programming Model for an Integrated Crop and Intensive Beef Production Enterprise." *Journal of Operational Research Society* **37** (May 1986): 487–494.

Gosselin, Karl, and Michel Truchon. "Allocation of Classrooms by Linear Programming." *Journal of Operational Research Society* **37** (1986): 561–569.

Hilal, Said S., and Warren Erikson. "Matching Supplies to Save Lives: Linear Programming the Production of Heart Valves." *Interfaces* **11**, 6 (December 1981): 48–56.

Holloran, Thomas, and Judson Byrn. "United Airlines Stationed Manpower Planning System." *Interfaces* **16**, 1 (January–February 1986): 39–50.

Jackson, Bruce L., and John M. Brown. "Using LP for Crude Oil Sales at Elk Hills." *Interfaces* **10**, 3 (June 1980): 65–70.

Lanzenauer, Christoph Haehling von. "RRSP Flood: LP to the Rescue." *Interfaces* **17**, 4 (July–August 1987): 27–33.

Leff, H. Stephen, Maqbool Dada, and Stephen C. Graves. "An LP Planning Model for a Mental Health Community Support System." *Management Science* **31**, 2 (February 1986): 139–155.

Marsten, Roy E., and Michael R. Muller. "A Mixed Integer Programming Approach to Air Cargo Fleet Planning." *Management Science* **26**, 11 (November 1980): 1096–1107.

McKay, A. C. "Linear Programming Applications on Microcomputers." *Journal of Operational Research Society* **36** (July 1985): 633–635.

Nauss, Robert M., and B. R. Keeler. "Minimizing Net Interest Cost in Municipal Bond Bidding." *Management Science* **27**, 4 (April 1981): 365–376.

Oliff, Michael, and Earl Burch. "Multiproduct Production Scheduling at Owens-Corning Fiberglass." *Interfaces* **15**, 5 (September–October 1985): 25–34.

Roy, Asim, Emma E. Defalomir, and Leon Lasdon. "An Optimization-Based Decision Support System for a Product Mix Problem." *Interfaces* **12**, 2 (April 1982): 26–33.

Sullivan, Robert, and Steven Secrist. "A Simple Optimization DSS for Production Planning at Dairyman's Cooperative Creamery." *Interfaces* **15**, 5 (September–October 1985)

Wild, W. G., Jr. "The Startling Discovery Bell Labs Kept in the Shadows." *Business Week* (September 21, 1987): 69+.

Appendix: Linear Programming with Spreadsheet Software

Earlier in Chapter 10 we presented Flair Furniture's computer solution using four popular software approaches: AB:QM (Program 10.1), STORM (Program 10.2), LINDO (Program 10.3), and What'sBest! (Program 10.4). The first three of these are interactive computer codes. To use them, you write out the formal LP model, then enter the data and let the computer try to solve it. If the model formulation was wrong (e.g., had conflicting constraints or was infeasible), you would debug it and retype the formulation into the computer. These "formal" LP models are easy to use and well documented. There are several reasons for using a "spreadsheet" optimizer, such as What'sBest!, however. In this appendix, we will show you how to develop the spreadsheet approach to LP modeling. This should help you understand the difference between Program 10.4 and the three other computer programs.

Symbolic Spreadsheet for Flair Furniture

A *symbolic spreadsheet* shows each of the formulas used to create the final output. Program 10.7, which we will now describe, contains all the formulas needed to compute the *value spreadsheet* shown in Program 10.4. So a value spreadsheet looks the same, except all the formulas have been computed and numbers appear in their cells.

We see that all the *labels* have been typed into the spreadsheet format in Program 10.7. They can be placed in any convenient location. For example, the words *Profit Contrib* were entered into Cell A6. Known, user-supplied,

PROGRAM 10.7 Symbolic Spreadsheet (with Formulas) for Flair Furniture's Tables and Chairs

```
                       Value for number of        Value for number of
                       tables to be supplied by user  chairs to be supplied by user

                 A           B         C          D          E         F
  1  Flair Furniture Company
  2
  3                        Tables   Chairs       Total    Available  Slack
  4  Quantity
  5  Unit Profit              7        5
  6  Profit Contrib        +B5*B4   +C5*C4    @SUM(B6..C6)
  7
  8  Unit Carpentry           4        3
  9  Carpentry Time        +B8*B4   +C8*C4    @SUM(B9..C9)    240   +E9-D9
 10
 11  Unit Painting/Varn.      2        1
 12  Paint/Varnish Time    +B11*B4  +C11*C4   @SUM(B12..C12)  100   +E12-D12
 13
 14
```

numbers are likewise placed in appropriate cells. We see the profit contributions per table ($7) and chairs ($5) in cells B5 and C5, respectively.

The empty boxes in cells B4 and C4 are highlighted to draw your attention to them. In a "what-if" analysis (which is a major strength of the spreadsheet approach to LP) the user supplies values to these cells. The user can then see what effect different numbers of tables and chairs have on total profit (cell D6), total resource usage (cells D9 and D12), and "slack" or unused resources (F9 and F12). Alternately, in a What'sBest! analysis, the computer finds the *optimal* values of tables and chairs for us, and places the answers in cells B4 and C4 as it did in Program 10.4. Even if you do not have an optimizing spreadsheet package such as What'sBest! available to you, you can still perform the what-if analysis in Lotus, or its equivalent, by simply entering a series of values into cells B4 and C4.

Now note the many *formulas* typed into cells in Program 10.7. The profit contribution from tables is found in cell B6, and is computed as +B5*B4 (which is just the contents of B5 times that of B4). So whatever value we enter, or What'sBest! computes, for tables in B4, the profit will be that number times $7, the unit profit in B5. Likewise the profit contribution for chairs is calculated in C6, and the total profit is placed in D6.

Slack is also an interesting concept and is computed by formulas in cells F9 and F12. The total carpentry time available to Flair Furniture was 240 hours (in cell E9). If all 240 hours were actually used (see cell D9), then there would be 0 slack, or unused, carpentry time available. This was the case in Program 10.4, when the optimal values of 30 tables and 40 chairs were computed by What'sBest!

An Example of a Value Spreadsheet

As an example of a spreadsheet where the user provides the values for tables and chairs (in cells B4 and C4), we turn to Program 10.8. Here we decide to see what happens if Flair produces 20 tables and 20 chairs. With these values entered, the spreadsheet computes all the formulas in Program 10.7, and replaces them with specific numeric values.

Now we see the results of the calculations. Cell D6 shows that the total profit is $240—$140 from tables and $100 from chairs. We have used a total of 140 carpentry hours, leaving 100 unused hours, and have used 60 painting hours, leaving 40 slack hours of that resource.

Why Use the Spreadsheet Approach?

We saw above that spreadsheets have one advantage over the formal LP programs, such as AB:QM, STORM, and LINDO, in that the user can perform numerous "what-if" analyses. There are two more reasons to consider the spreadsheet approach also. First, it provides a flexibility to handle *non-linear* relationships that formal models do not. For example, if total hours available in carpentry were not fixed at 240, but instead involved an exponential relationship to the number of carpenters scheduled to be on duty, the spreadsheet model could handle this complexity.

PROGRAM 10.8 Value Spreadsheet with Values of 20 Tables and 20 Chairs, for Flair Furniture. These User-Supplied Values Provide for "What-if" Analysis.

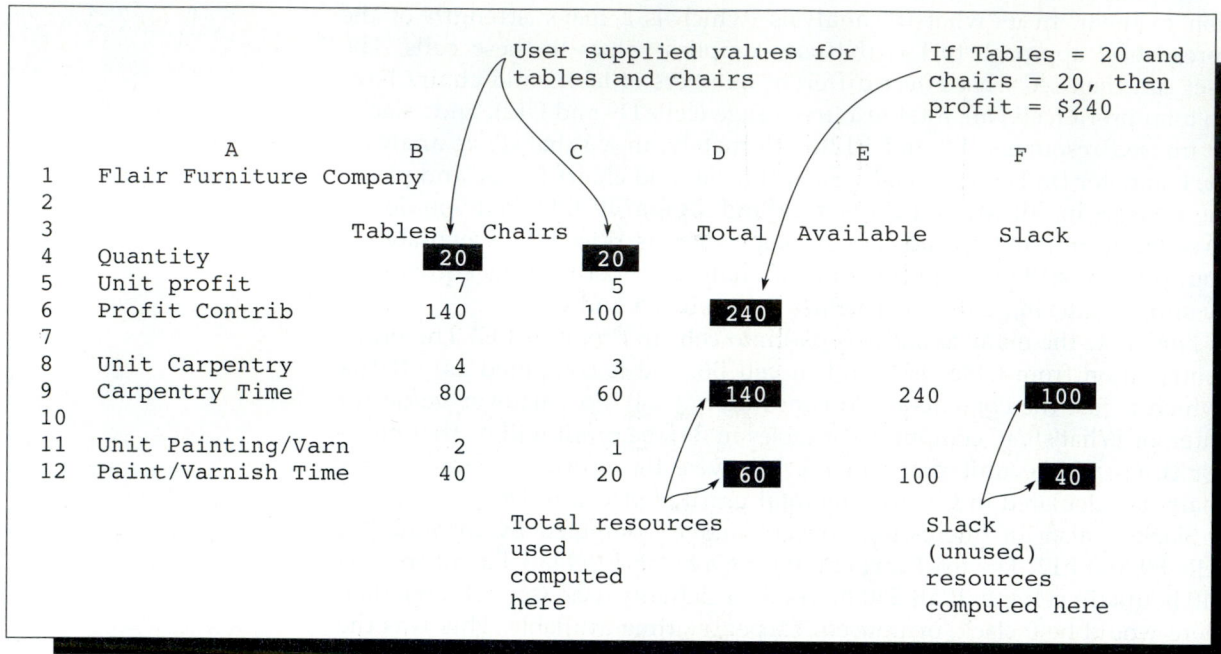

Second, and perhaps most important, the spreadsheet approach is a more understandable representation of LP than the formal model. Managers do not see what goes on inside the formal programs. But in a spreadsheet, every relationship is laid out in a way that makes understanding the LP model a good deal easier. This gives managers a more "hands-on" feel for LP. And when a user feels more comfortable with a quantitative analysis technique, that person is more likely to use, and *trust*, the results.

Linear Programming Applications: With Computer Analyses in AB:QM, STORM, LINDO, and What's*Best!*

CHAPTER OUTLINE

11.1 Introduction
11.2 Marketing Applications
11.3 Manufacturing Applications
11.4 Employee Scheduling Applications
11.5 Financial Applications

11.6 Transportation Applications
11.7 Ingredient Blending Applications
Problems
Case Study: Chase Manhattan Bank
Bibliography

11.1   INTRODUCTION

Teaching Suggestion 11.1:
The Importance of
Formulating Large LP
Problems. See the
Instructor's Section
for details.

The graphical method of linear programming discussed in Chapter 10 is useful for understanding how to formulate and solve small linear programming problems. The purpose of this chapter is to go one step further and show how a large number of real-life problems can be tackled using linear programming. We do this by presenting examples of applications in the areas of production mix, labor scheduling, job assignment, production scheduling, marketing research, media selection, shipping and transportation, ingredient mix, and financial portfolio selection.

Although some of these problems are relatively small numerically, the principles developed here are definitely applicable to larger problems. Moreover, this practice in "paraphrasing" LP model formulations should help develop your skills in applying the technique to other, less common applications.

11.2   MARKETING APPLICATIONS

Applicable Problems 11-6, 11-10

Media Selection

uses of media selection

Linear programming models have been used in the advertising field as a decision aid in selecting an effective media mix. Sometimes the technique is employed in allocating a fixed or limited budget across various media, which might include radio or television commercials, newspaper ads, direct mailings, magazine ads, and so on. In other applications, the objective is the maximization of audience exposure. Restrictions on the allowable media mix might arise through contract requirements, limited media availability, or company policy. An example follows.

The Win Big Gambling Club promotes gambling junkets from a large midwestern city to casinos in the Bahamas. The club has budgeted up to $8,000 per week for local advertising. The money is to be allocated among four promotional media: TV spots, newspaper ads, and two types of radio advertisements. Win Big's goal is to reach the largest possible high-potential audience through the various media. The following table presents the number of potential gamblers reached by making use of an advertisement in each of the four media. It also provides the cost per advertisement placed and the maximum number of ads that can be purchased per week.

MEDIUM	AUDIENCE REACHED PER AD	COST PER AD ($)	MAXIMUM ADS PER WEEK
TV spot (one minute)	5,000	800	12
Daily newspaper (full-page ad)	8,500	925	5
Radio spot (30 seconds, prime time)	2,400	290	25
Radio spot (one minute, afternoon)	2,800	380	20

Win Big's contractual arrangements require that at least five radio spots be placed each week. To ensure a broad-scoped promotional campaign, management also insists that no more than $1,800 be spent on radio advertising every week.

The problem can now be stated mathematically as follows. Let

X_1 = number of one-minute TV spots taken each week

X_2 = number of full-page daily newspaper ads taken each week

X_3 = number of 30-second prime-time radio spots taken each week

X_4 = number of one-minute afternoon radio spots taken each week

Objective:

Maximize audience coverage = $5{,}000X_1 + 8{,}500X_2 + 2{,}400X_3 + 2{,}800X_4$

Subject to: $X_1 \leqslant 12$ (*maximum TV spots/week*)

$X_2 \leqslant 5$ (*maximum newspaper ads/week*)

$X_3 \leqslant 25$ (*maximum 30-second radio spots/week*)

$X_4 \leqslant 20$ (*maximum one-minute radio spots/week*)

$800X_1 + 925X_2 + 290X_3 + 380X_4 \leqslant \$8{,}000$ (*weekly advertising budget*)

$X_3 + X_4 \geqslant 5$ (*minimum radio spots contracted*)

$290X_3 + 380X_4 \leqslant \$1{,}800$ (*maximum $ spent on radio*)

The solution to this LP formulation, using our AB:QM microcomputer software package (see Program 11.1), was found to be:

$X_1 = 1.97$ *TV spots*

$X_2 = 5$ *newspaper ads*

$X_3 = 6.2$ *30-second radio spots*

$X_4 = 0$ *one-minute radio spots*

This produces an audience exposure of 67,240 contacts. Since X_1 and X_3 are fractional, Win Big would probably round them to 2 and 6, respectively. Problems that demand all-integer solutions are discussed in detail in Chapter 15. An explanation of the meaning of shadow prices (the last portion of the output) is found in Chapter 13.

Marketing Research

Linear programming has also been applied to marketing research problems and the area of consumer research. The next example illustrates how statistical pollsters can reach strategy decisions with LP.

Management Sciences Associates (MSA) is a marketing and computer research firm based in Washington, D.C., that handles consumer surveys. One of their clients is a national press service that periodically conducts political polls on issues of widespread interest. In a survey for the press service, MSA determines that it must fulfill several requirements in order

marketing research applications

PROGRAM 11.1 Using AB:QM to Solve Win Big's LP Problem

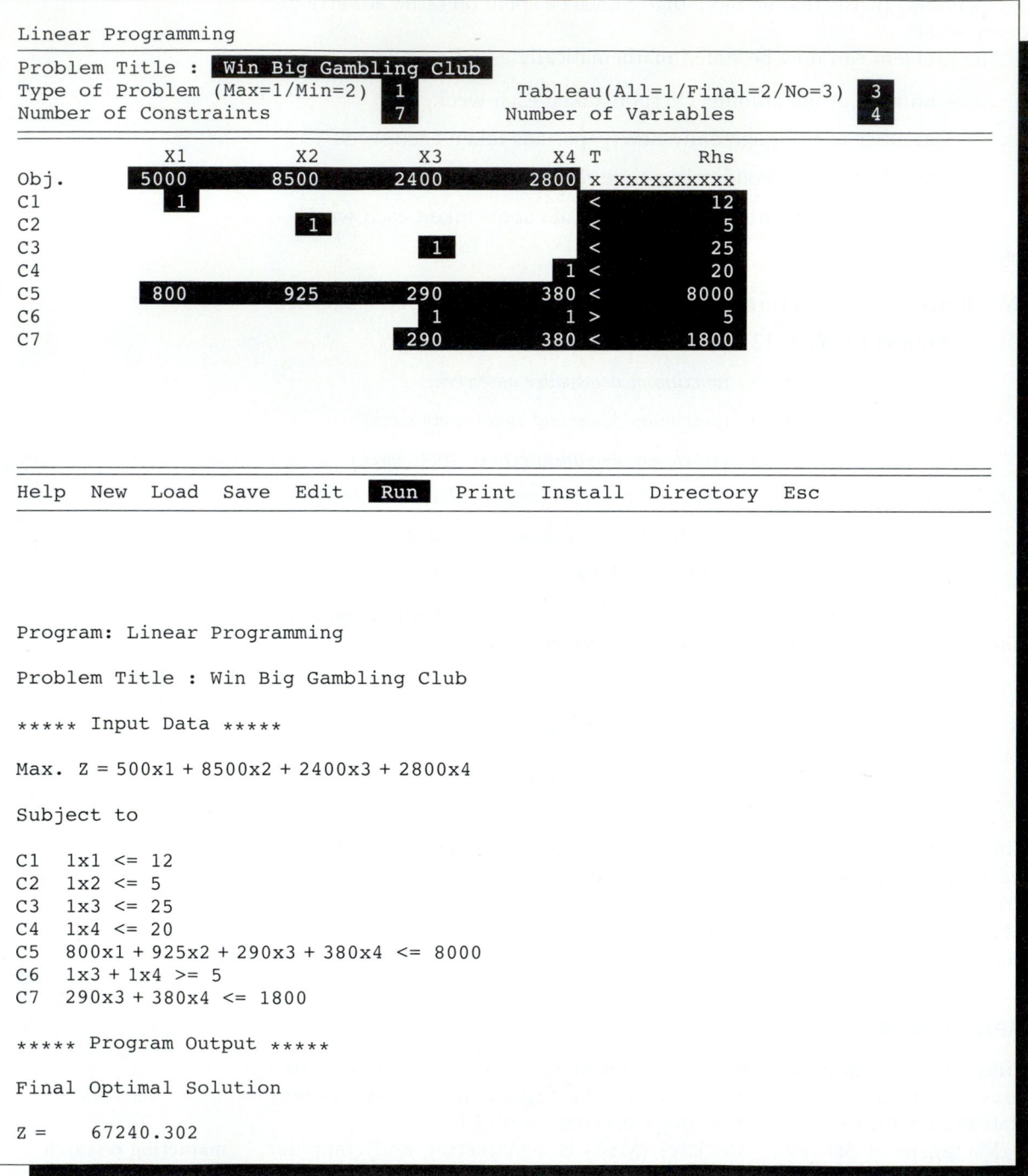

```
Linear Programming

Problem Title : Win Big Gambling Club
Type of Problem (Max=1/Min=2)    1        Tableau(All=1/Final=2/No=3)   3
Number of Constraints            7        Number of Variables          4

            X1          X2          X3          X4 T        Rhs
Obj.      5000        8500        2400        2800 x xxxxxxxxxx
C1           1                                     <         12
C2                       1                         <          5
C3                                   1             <         25
C4                                             1 <          20
C5         800         925         290         380 <       8000
C6                                   1         1 >          5
C7                                 290         380 <       1800




Help   New   Load   Save   Edit   Run   Print   Install   Directory   Esc




Program: Linear Programming

Problem Title : Win Big Gambling Club

***** Input Data *****

Max. Z = 500x1 + 8500x2 + 2400x3 + 2800x4

Subject to

C1   1x1 <= 12
C2   1x2 <= 5
C3   1x3 <= 25
C4   1x4 <= 20
C5   800x1 + 925x2 + 290x3 + 380x4 <= 8000
C6   1x3 + 1x4 >= 5
C7   290x3 + 380x4 <= 1800

***** Program Output *****

Final Optimal Solution

Z =    67240.302
```

(Continued)

PROGRAM 11.1 **Using AB:QM to Solve Win Big's LP Problem**
(Continued)

```
------------------------------------
Variable        Value      Reduced Cost
------------------------------------
    x 1         1.969          0.000
    x 2         5.000          0.000
    x 3         6.207          0.000
    x 4         0.000        344.828
------------------------------------
Constraint   Slack/Surplus   Shadow Price
------------------------------------
    C 1        10.031          0.000
    C 2         0.000       2718.750
    C 3        18.793          0.000
    C 4        20.000          0.000
    C 5         0.000          6.250
    C 6         1.207          0.000
    C 7         0.000          2.026
```

to draw statistically valid conclusions on the sensitive issue of new U.S.
immigration laws:

1. Survey at least 2,300 U.S. households in total.

2. Survey at least 1,000 households whose heads are 30 years of age or
   younger.

3. Survey at least 600 households whose heads are between 31 and
   50 years of age.

4. Ensure that at least 15% of those surveyed live in a state that borders
   on Mexico.

5. Ensure that no more than 20% of those surveyed who are 51 or over
   live in a state that borders on Mexico.

MSA decides that all surveys should be conducted in person. It estimates that the costs of reaching people in each age and region category are
as follows:

| | COST PER PERSON SURVEYED ($) | | |
REGION	AGE ≤ 30	AGE 31–50	AGE ≥ 51
State bordering Mexico	7.50	6.80	5.50
State not bordering Mexico	6.90	7.25	6.10

MSA's goal is to meet the five sampling requirements at the least possible cost.

We let

X_1 = number surveyed who are 30 or younger and live in a border state

X_2 = number surveyed who are 31–50 and live in a border state

X_3 = number surveyed who are 51 or older and live in a border state

X_4 = number surveyed who are 30 or younger and do not live in a border state

X_5 = number surveyed who are 31–50 and do not live in a border state

X_6 = number surveyed who are 51 or older and do not live in a border state

Objective function:

$$\text{Minimize total interview costs} = \$7.50X_1 + \$6.80X_2 + \$5.50X_3 \\ + \$6.90X_4 + \$7.25X_5 + \$6.10X_6$$

Constraints:

$$X_1 + X_2 + X_3 + X_4 + X_5 + X_6 \geq 2{,}300 \quad (total\ households)$$

$$X_1 \qquad\qquad + X_4 \qquad\qquad \geq 1{,}000 \quad (households\ 30\ or\ younger)$$

$$X_2 \qquad\qquad + X_5 \qquad \geq \ 600 \quad (households\ 31–50\ in\ age)$$

$$(X_1 + X_2 + X_3) \geq .15(X_1 + X_2 + X_3 + X_4 + X_5 + X_6) \quad (border\ states)$$

$$X_3 \leq .2(X_3 + X_6) \quad (limit\ on\ age\ group\ 51+\ who\ can \\ live\ in\ border\ state)$$

$$X_1, X_2, X_3, X_4, X_5, X_6 \geq 0$$

The solution to MSA's problem costs $15,166 and is presented in the following table and in Program 11.2, which again illustrates the input and output from AB:QM's LP module.

REGION	AGE ≤ 30	AGE 31–50	AGE ≤ 51
State bordering Mexico	0	600	140
State not bordering Mexico	1,000	0	560

Applicable Problems 11-1, 11-12, 11-14, 11-17, 11-18

11.3   MANUFACTURING APPLICATIONS

Production Mix

Alternate Example 11.1

A fertile field for the use of LP is in planning for the optimal mix of products to manufacture. A company must meet a myriad of constraints, ranging from financial concerns to sales demand to material contracts to union labor demands. Its primary goal is to generate the largest profit possible.

PROGRAM 11.2 MSA's Marketing Research Problem Solved with AB:QM

```
Linear Programming

Problem Title :  Management Sciences Associates
Type of Problem (Max=1/Min=2)   2        Tableau(All=1/Final=2/No=3)  3
Number of Constraints           5        Number of Variables          6

          X1        X2        X3        X4        X5       X6 T   Rhs
Obj.     7.5       6.8       5.5       6.9      7.25      6.1 x
C1         1         1         1         1         1        1 >  2300
C2         1                             1                    >  1000
C3                   1                             1          >   600
C4       .85       .85       .85      -.15      -.15     -.15 >     0
C5                            .8                          -.2 <     0


Help  New  Load  Save  Edit  Run   Print  Install  Directory  Esc


Program: Linear Programming

Problem Title : Management Sciences Associates

***** Input Data *****

Min. Z = 7.5x1 + 6.8x2 + 5.5x3 + 6.9x4 + 7.25x5 + 6.1x6

Subject to

C1   1x1 + 1x2 + 1x3 + 1x4 + 1x5 + 1x6 >= 2300
C2   1x1 + 1x4 >= 1000
C3   1x2 + 1x5 >= 600
C4   .85x1 + .85x2 + .85x3 - .15x4 - .15x5 - .15x6 >= 0
C5   .8x3 - .2x6 <= 0

***** Program Output *****

Final Optimal Solution

Z =   15166.000

--------------------------------------
Variable        Value        Reduced Cost
--------------------------------------
   x 1          0.000           0.600
   x 2        600.000           0.000
   x 3        140.000           0.000
   x 4       1000.000           0.000
   x 5          0.000           0.450
   x 6        560.000           0.000
```

Fifth Avenue Industries, a nationally known manufacturer of menswear, produces four varieties of ties. One is an expensive, all-silk tie, one is an all-polyester tie, and two are blends of polyester and cotton. The following table illustrates the cost and availability (per monthly production planning period) of the three materials used in the production process.

MATERIAL	COST PER YARD ($)	MATERIAL AVAILABLE PER MONTH (YARDS)
Silk	21	800
Polyester	6	3,000
Cotton	9	1,600

The firm has fixed contracts with several major department store chains to supply ties. The contracts require that Fifth Avenue Industries supply a minimum quantity of each tie, but allow for a larger demand if Fifth Avenue chooses to meet that demand. (Most of the ties are not shipped with the name Fifth Avenue on their label, incidentally, but with "private stock" labels supplied by the stores.) Table 11.1 summarizes the contract demand for each of the four styles of ties, the selling price per tie, and the fabric requirements of each variety.

Fifth Avenue's goal is to maximize its monthly profit. It must decide upon a policy for product mix. Let

X_1 = number of all-silk ties produced per month

X_2 = number of polyester ties

X_3 = number of blend #1 poly-cotton ties

X_4 = number of blend #2 poly-cotton ties

But first the firm must establish the profit per tie.

1. For all-silk ties (X_1), each requires .125 yard of silk, at a cost of $21 per yard. Therefore, the cost per tie is $2.62. The selling price per silk tie is $6.70, leaving a net profit of ($6.70 − $2.62 =) $4.08 per unit of X_1.

TABLE 11.1 Data for Fifth Avenue Industries

VARIETY OF TIE	SELLING PRICE PER TIE ($)	MONTHLY CONTRACT MINIMUM	MONTHLY DEMAND	MATERIAL REQUIRED PER TIE (YARDS)	MATERIAL REQUIREMENTS
All silk	6.70	6,000	7,000	.125	100% silk
All polyester	3.55	10,000	14,000	.08	100% polyester
Poly-cotton blend #1	4.31	13,000	16,000	.10	50% polyester 50% cotton
Poly-cotton blend #2	4.81	6,000	8,500	.10	30% polyester 70% cotton

2. For all-polyester ties (X_2), each requires .08 yard of polyester at a cost of $6 per yard. The cost per tie is, therefore, $.48. The net profit per unit of X_2 is ($3.55 − $.48 =) $3.07.

3. For poly-cotton blend #1 (X_3), each tie requires .05 yard of polyester at $6 per yard and .05 yard of cotton at $9 per yard, for a cost of $.30 + $.45 = $.75 per tie. The profit is $3.56.

4. Try to compute the net profit for blend #2. You should calculate a cost of $.81 per tie and a net profit of $4.

The objective function may now be stated as:

$$\text{Maximize profit} = \$4.08X_1 + \$3.07X_2 + \$3.56X_3 + \$4.00X_4$$

Subject to constraints:

$$
\begin{aligned}
.125X_1 & & & \leq & 800 & \quad \textit{(yards of silk)} \\
.08X_2 &+ .05X_3 &+ .03X_4 & \leq & 3{,}000 & \quad \textit{(yards of polyester)} \\
&.05X_3 &+ .07X_4 & \leq & 1{,}600 & \quad \textit{(yards of cotton)} \\
X_1 & & & \geq & 6{,}000 & \quad \textit{(contract minimum for all silk)} \\
X_1 & & & \leq & 7{,}000 & \quad \textit{(contract maximum)} \\
X_2 & & & \geq & 10{,}000 & \quad \textit{(contract minimum for all polyester)} \\
X_2 & & & \leq & 14{,}000 & \quad \textit{(contract maximum)} \\
X_3 & & & \geq & 13{,}000 & \quad \textit{(contract minimum for blend \#1)} \\
X_3 & & & \leq & 16{,}000 & \quad \textit{(contract maximum)} \\
X_4 & & & \geq & 6{,}000 & \quad \textit{(contract minimum for blend \#2)} \\
X_4 & & & \leq & 8{,}500 & \quad \textit{(contract maximum)} \\
\end{aligned}
$$

$$X_1, X_2, X_3, X_4 \geq 0$$

Using AB:QM, the computer-generated solution is to produce 6,400 all-silk ties each month; 14,000 all-polyester ties; 16,000 blend #1 poly-cotton ties; and 8,500 blend #2 poly-cotton ties. This produces a profit of $160,052 per production period. See Program 11.3 for details.

Production Scheduling

Setting a low-cost production schedule over a period of weeks or months is a difficult and important management problem in most plants. The production manager has to consider many factors: labor capacity, inventory and storage costs, space limitations, product demand, and labor relations. Since most companies produce more than one product, the scheduling process is often quite complex.

Basically, the problem resembles the product mix model for each period in the future. The objective is either to maximize profit or to minimize the total cost (production plus inventory) of carrying out the task.

Teaching Suggestion 11.2: Note on Production Scheduling Problems. See the Instructor's Section for details.

PROGRAM 11.3 AB:QM Solution to Fifth Avenue Industries Problem

```
Linear Programming

Problem Title :  Fifth Avenue Industries
Type of Problem (Max=1/Min=2)  1        Tableau(All=1/Final=2/No=3)  3
Number of Constraints         11        Number of Variables          4

          X1       X2       X3       X4 T      Rhs
Obj.     4.08     3.07     3.56     4.00 x xxxxxxxxxx
C1       .125                               <      800
C2                .08      .05      .03 <      3000
C3                         .05      .07 <      1600
C4         1                            >      6000
C5         1                            <      7000
C6                 1                     >     10000
C7                 1                     <     14000
C8                          1           >     13000
C9                          1           <     16000
C10                                 1 >        6000
C11                                 1 <        8500


Help   New   Load   Save   Edit   Run   Print   Install   Directory   Esc



Program: Linear Programming

Problem Title : Fifth Avenue Industries

***** Input Data *****

Min. Z = 4.08x1 + 3.07x2 + 3.56x3 + 4.00x4

Subject to

C1   .125x1 <= 800
C2   .08x2 + .05x3 + .03x4 <= 3000
C3   .05x3 + .07x4 <= 1600
C4   1x1 >= 6000
C5   1x1 <= 7000
C6   1x2 >= 10000
C7   1x2 <= 14000
C8   1x3 >= 13000
C9   1x3 <= 16000
C10  1x4 >= 6000
C11  1x4 <= 8500

***** Program Output *****

Final Optimal Solution

Z =    160052.000
```

(Continued)

PROGRAM 11.3 AB:QM Solution to Fifth Avenue Industries Problem (Continued)

```
---------------------------------
Variable        Value        Reduced Cost
---------------------------------
   x 1       6400.000         0.000
   x 2      14000.000         0.000
   x 3      16000.000         0.000
   x 4       8500.000         0.000
---------------------------------
Constraint   Slack/Surplus   Shadow Price
---------------------------------
   C 1          0.000         32.640
   C 2        825.000          0.000
   C 3        205.000          0.000
   C 4        400.000          0.000
   C 5        600.000          0.000
   C 6       4000.000          0.000
   C 7          0.000          3.070
   C 8       3000.000          0.000
   C 9          0.000          3.560
   C10       2500.000          0.000
   C11          0.000          4.000
```

Production scheduling is amenable to solution by LP because it is a problem that must be solved on a regular basis. Once the objective function and constraints for a firm are established, the inputs can easily be changed each month to provide an updated schedule.

Greenberg Motors, Inc., manufactures two different electrical motors for sale under contract to Drexel Corp., a well-known producer of small kitchen appliances. Its model GM3A is found in many Drexel food processors and its model GM3B is used in the assembly of blenders.

an example of production scheduling: Greenberg Motors

Three times each year, the procurement officer at Drexel contracts Irwin Greenberg, the founder of Greenberg Motors, to place a monthly order for each of the coming four months. Drexel's demand for motors varies each month based on its own sales forecasts, production capacity, and financial position. Greenberg has just received the January–April order and must begin his own four-month production plan. The demand for motors is shown in Table 11.2.

Production planning at Greenberg Motors must consider four factors:

1. The desirability of producing the same number of each motor each month. This simplifies planning and the scheduling of workers and machines.

TABLE 11.2 Four-Month Order Schedule for Electrical Motors

MODEL	JANUARY	FEBRUARY	MARCH	APRIL
GM3A	800	700	1,000	1,100
GM3B	1,000	1,200	1,400	1,400

2. The necessity to keep down inventory carrying, or holding, costs. This suggests producing in each month only what is needed in that month.

3. Warehouse limitations that cannot be exceeded without great additional storage costs.

4. The company's no-layoff policy, which has been effective in preventing a unionization of the shop. This suggests a minimum production capacity that should be used each month.

Although these four factors often conflict, Greenberg has found that linear programming is an effective tool in setting up a production schedule that will minimize his total costs of per unit production and monthly holding.

using double-subscripted variables

Double-subscripted variables can be used here to develop the LP model. We let

$$X_{A,i} = \text{number of model GM3A motors produced in month } i$$
$$(i = 1, 2, 3, 4 \text{ for January–April})$$

$$X_{B,i} = \text{number of model GM3B motors produced in month } i$$

Production costs are currently $10 per GM3A motor produced and $6 per GM3B unit. A labor agreement going into effect on March 1 will raise each figure by 10%, however. We can write the part of the objective function that deals with production cost as:

$$\text{Cost of production} = \$10X_{A1} + \$10X_{A2} + \$11X_{A3} + \$11X_{A4} + \$6X_{B1}$$
$$+ \$6X_{B2} + \$6.60X_{B3} + \$6.60X_{B4}$$

To include the inventory carrying costs in the model, we can introduce a second variable. Let

$$I_{A,i} = \text{level of on-hand inventory for GM3A motors at end of month } i$$
$$(i = 1, 2, 3, 4)$$

$$I_{B,i} = \text{level of on-hand inventory for GM3B motors at end of month } i$$

Each GM3A motor held in stock costs $.18 per month, while each GM3B has a carrying cost of $.13 per month. Greenberg's accountants allow monthly ending inventories as an acceptable approximation to the average inventory levels during the month. So the carrying cost part of the LP objective function is:

$$\text{Cost of carrying inventory} = \$.18I_{A1} + .18I_{A2} + .18I_{A3} + .18I_{A4}$$
$$+ .13I_{B1} + .13I_{B2} + .13I_{B3} + .13I_{B4}$$

The total objective function becomes:

$$\text{Minimize total costs} = 10X_{A1} + 10X_{A2} + 11X_{A3} + 11X_{A4} + 6X_{B1}$$
$$+ 6X_{B2} + 6.6X_{B3} + 6.6X_{B4} + .18I_{A1} + .18I_{A2}$$
$$+ .18I_{A3} + .18I_{A4} + .13I_{B1} + .13I_{B2} + .13I_{B3} + .13I_{B4}$$

In setting up the constraints, we must recognize the relationship between last month's ending inventory, the current month's production, and the sales to Drexel this month. The inventory at the end of a month is:

inventory constraints

$$\begin{pmatrix} \text{Inventory} \\ \text{at the} \\ \text{end of} \\ \text{this month} \end{pmatrix} = \begin{pmatrix} \text{Inventory} \\ \text{at the} \\ \text{end of} \\ \text{last month} \end{pmatrix} + \begin{pmatrix} \text{Current} \\ \text{month's} \\ \text{production} \end{pmatrix} - \begin{pmatrix} \text{Sales} \\ \text{to} \\ \text{Drexel} \\ \text{this month} \end{pmatrix}$$

KEY IDEA

Suppose Greenberg is starting the new four-month production cycle with a change in design specifications that left no old motors in stock on January 1. Then, recalling that January's demand for GM3As is 800 and for GM3Bs is 1,000, we can write:

$$I_{A1} = 0 + X_{A1} - 800$$
$$I_{B1} = 0 + X_{B1} - 1,000$$

Transposing all unknown variables to the left of the equal sign and multiplying all terms by a minus 1, these January constraints can be rewritten as:

$$X_{A1} - I_{A1} = 800$$
$$X_{B1} - I_{B1} = 1,000$$

The constraints on demand in February, March, and April follow:

$$X_{A2} + I_{A1} - I_{A2} = \quad 700 \quad \textit{February GM3A demand}$$
$$X_{B2} + I_{B1} - I_{B2} = 1,200 \quad \textit{February GM3B demand}$$
$$X_{A3} + I_{A2} - I_{A3} = 1,000 \quad \textit{March GM3A demand}$$
$$X_{B3} + I_{B2} - I_{B3} = 1,400 \quad \textit{March GM3B demand}$$
$$X_{A4} + I_{A3} - I_{A4} = 1,100 \quad \textit{April GM3A demand}$$
$$X_{B4} + I_{B3} - I_{B4} = 1,400 \quad \textit{April GM3B demand}$$

If Greenberg wants to also have on hand an additional 450 GM3As and 300 GM3Bs at the end of April, then we add the constraints:

$$I_{A4} = 450$$
$$I_{B4} = 300$$

The constraints discussed address demand; they do not, however, consider warehouse space or labor requirements. First, we note that the storage area for Greenberg Motors can hold a maximum of 3,300 motors of either type (they are similar in size) at any one time. Then

$$I_{A1} + I_{B1} \leq 3,300$$
$$I_{A2} + I_{B2} \leq 3,300$$
$$I_{A3} + I_{B3} \leq 3,300$$
$$I_{A4} + I_{B4} \leq 3,300$$

warehouse constraints

Second, we return to the issue of employment. So that no worker is ever laid off, Greenberg has a base employment level of 2,240 labor hours per month. In a busy period, though, the company can bring two skilled former employees on board (they are now retired) to increase capacity to 2,560 hours per month. Each GM3A motor produced requires 1.3 hours of labor, while each GM3B takes a worker .9 hour to assemble.

$$1.3X_{A1} + .9X_{B1} \geq 2,240 \quad \textit{(January minimum worker hours/month)}$$
$$1.3X_{A1} + .9X_{B1} \leq 2,560 \quad \textit{(January maximum labor available/month)}$$
$$1.3X_{A2} + .9X_{B2} \geq 2,240 \quad \textit{(February labor minimum)}$$
$$1.3X_{A2} + .9X_{B2} \leq 2,560 \quad \textit{(February labor maximum)}$$
$$1.3X_{A3} + .9X_{B3} \geq 2,240 \quad \textit{(March labor minimum)}$$
$$1.3X_{A3} + .9X_{B3} \leq 2,560 \quad \textit{(March labor maximum)}$$
$$1.3X_{A4} + .9X_{B4} \geq 2,240 \quad \textit{(April labor minimum)}$$
$$1.3X_{A4} + .9X_{B4} \leq 2,560 \quad \textit{(April labor maximum)}$$

employment constraints

The solution to the Greenberg Motors problem was found using LINDO and is shown in Table 11.3 and Program 11.4. The four-month total cost is $76,301.61.

This example illustrates a relatively simple production planning problem in that there were only two products being considered. The 16 variables and 22 constraints may not seem trivial, but the technique can also be successfully applied with dozens of products and hundreds of constraints.

Applicable Problems 11-3, 11-5, 11-7, 11-8, 11-13, Chase case

11.4 EMPLOYEE SCHEDULING APPLICATIONS

Assignment Problems

assigning people to jobs using LP

Assignment problems involve determining the most efficient assignment of people to jobs, machines to tasks, police cars to city sectors, salespeople to territories, and so on. The objective might be to minimize travel times or costs or to maximize assignment effectiveness. Assignments can be handled with their own special solution procedures (see Chapter 14). Assignment problems are unique because they not only have a coefficient of 1

Teaching Suggestion 11.3:
Solving Assignment Problems by LP. See the Instructor's Section for details.

TABLE 11.3 Solution to Greenberg Motor Problem

PRODUCTION SCHEDULE	JANUARY	FEBRUARY	MARCH	APRIL
Units of GM3A produced	1,277	1,138	842	792
Units of GM3B produced	1,000	1,200	1,400	1,700
Inventory of GM3A carried	477	915	758	450
Inventory of GM3B carried	0	0	0	300
Labor hours required	2,560	2,560	2,355	2,560

PROGRAM 11.4 Using LINDO to Solve the Greenberg Motors LP Problem

```
:   MIN 10XA1 + 10XA2 + 11XA3 + 11XA4 + 6XB1 + 6XB2 + 6.6XB3 +
?   6.6XB4 + .18IA1 + .18IA2 + .18IA3 + .18IA4 + .13IB1 + .13IB2 +
?   .13IB3 + .13IB4
?   ST
?   XA1 - IA1 = 800
?   XB1 - IB1 = 1000
?   XA2 + IA1 - IA2 = 700
?   XB2 + IB1 - IB2 = 1200
?   XA3 + IA2 - IA3 = 1000
?   XB3 + IB2 - IB3 = 1400
?   XA4 + IA3 - IA4 = 1100
?   XB4 + IB3 - IB4 = 1400
?   IA4 = 450
?   IB4 = 300
?   IA1 + IB1 < 3300
?   IA2 + IB2 < 3300
?   IA3 + IB3 < 3300
?   IA4 + IB4 < 3300
?   1.3XA1 + .9XB1 > 2240
?   1.3XA1 + .9XB1 < 2560
?   1.3XA2 + .9XB2 > 2240
?   1.3XA2 + .9XB2 < 2560
?   1.3XA3 + .9XB3 > 2240
?   1.3XA3 + .9XB3 < 2560

?
:   LOOK
ROW:
ALL

MIN     10 XA1 + 10 XA2 + 11 XA3 + 11 XA4 + 6 XB1 + 6 XB2 + 6.6 XB3
    + 6.6 XB4 + .18 IA2 + .18 IA1 + .13 IB1 + .13 IB2 + .18 IA3 + .13 IB3
    + .18 IA4 + .13 IB4
SUBJECT TO
        2)   XB1 - IB1 =       1000
        3)   XA2 - IA2 + IA1 =      700
        4)   XB2 + IB1 - IB2 =    1200
        5)   XA3 + IA2 - IA3 =    1000
        6)   XB3 + IB2 - IB3 =    1400
        7)   XA4 + IA3 - IA4 =    1100
        8)   XB4 + IB3 - IB4 =    1400
        9)   IA4 =      450
       10)   IB4 =      300
       11)   IA1 + IB1 <=     3300
       12)   IA2 + IB2 <=     3300
       13)   IA3 + IB3 <=     3300
       14)   IA4 + IB4 <=     3300
       15)   1.3 XA1 + .9 XB1 >=      2240
       16)   1.3 XA1 + .9 XB1 <=      2560
       17)   1.3 XA2 + .9 XB2 >=      2240
       18)   1.3 XA2 + .9 XB2 <=      2560
```

(Continued)

PROGRAM 11.4 Using LINDO to Solve the Greenberg Motors LP Problem (Continued)

```
    19)   1.3 XA3 + .9 XB3 >=      2240
    20)   1.3 XA3 + .9 XB3 <=      2560
    21)   1.3 XA4 + .9 XB4 >=      2240
    22)   1.3 XA4 + .9 XB4 <=      2560
    23)   XA1 - IA1 =      800
END

:

        OBJECTIVE FUNCTION VALUE

  1)        76301.6100

VARIABLE       VALUE          REDUCED COST
    XA1     1276.923000          .000000
    XA2     1138.462000          .000000
    XA3      842.307600          .000000
    XA4      792.307700          .000000
    XB1     1000.000000          .000000
    XB2     1200.000000          .000000
    XB3     1400.000000          .000000
    XB4     1700.000000          .000000
    IA2      915.384700          .000000
    IA1      476.923100          .000000
    IB1         .000000          .005384
    IB2         .000000          .097692
    IA3      757.692300          .000000
    IB3         .000000          .005384
    IA4      450.000000          .000000
    IB4      300.000000          .000000
```

associated with each variable in the LP constraints; the right-hand side of each constraint is also always equal to 1. The use of LP in solving assignment problems, as illustrated by the following case, yields solutions of either 0 or 1 for each variable in the formulation.

The law firm of Ivan and Ivan maintains a large staff of young attorneys who hold the title of junior partner. Ivan, concerned with the effective utilization of his personnel resources, seeks some objective means of making lawyer-to-client assignments.

On March 1, four new clients seeking legal assistance come to Ivan. While the current staff is overloaded, Ivan would like to accommodate the new clients. He reviews current case loads and identifies four junior partners who, although busy, could possibly be assigned to the cases. Each young lawyer can handle at most one new client. Furthermore, each lawyer differs in skills and specialty interests.

Seeking to maximize the overall effectiveness of the new client assignments, Ivan draws up the following table in which he rates the estimated effectiveness (on a scale of 1–9) of each lawyer on each new case.

	IVAN'S EFFECTIVENESS RATINGS		
	CLIENT'S CASE		
LAWYER	DIVORCE	CORPORATE MERGER	EMBEZZLEMENT	EXHIBITIONISM
Adams	6	2	8	5
Brooks	9	3	5	8
Carter	4	8	3	4
Darwin	6	7	6	4

To solve using LP, we again employ double-subscripted variables. Let

$$X_{ij} = \begin{cases} 1 & \text{if attorney } i \text{ is assigned to case } j \\ 0 & \text{otherwise} \end{cases}$$

where

$i = 1, 2, 3, 4$ stands for Adams, Brooks, Carter, and Darwin, respectively, and

$j = 1, 2, 3, 4$ stands for divorce, merger, embezzlement, and exhibitionism, respectively.

The LP formulation follows:

$$\text{Maximize effectiveness} = 6X_{11} + 2X_{12} + 8X_{13} + 5X_{14}$$
$$+ 9X_{21} + 3X_{22} + 5X_{23} + 8X_{24}$$
$$+ 4X_{31} + 8X_{32} + 3X_{33} + 4X_{34}$$
$$+ 6X_{41} + 7X_{42} + 6X_{43} + 4X_{44}$$

Subject to: $X_{11} + X_{21} + X_{31} + X_{41} = 1$ *(divorce case)*

$X_{12} + X_{22} + X_{32} + X_{42} = 1$ *(merger)*

$X_{13} + X_{23} + X_{33} + X_{43} = 1$ *(embezzlement)*

$X_{14} + X_{24} + X_{34} + X_{44} = 1$ *(exhibitionism)*

$X_{11} + X_{12} + X_{13} + X_{14} = 1$ *(Adams)*

$X_{21} + X_{22} + X_{23} + X_{24} = 1$ *(Brooks)*

$X_{31} + X_{32} + X_{33} + X_{34} = 1$ *(Carter)*

$X_{41} + X_{42} + X_{43} + X_{44} = 1$ *(Darwin)*

The law firm's problem is solved in Program 11.5 using LINDO. There is a total effectiveness rating of 30 by letting $X_{13} = 1$, $X_{24} = 1$, $X_{32} = 1$, and $X_{41} = 1$. All other variables are therefore equal to 0.

Labor Planning

Labor planning problems address staffing needs over a specific time period. They are especially useful when managers have some flexibility in

PROGRAM 11.5 Solving Ivan and Ivan's Assignment Scheduling LP Problem Using LINDO

```
LINDO/PC

COPYRIGHT(C) 1984 LINDO SYSTEMS, INC.

:  MAX 6X11 + 2X12 + 8X13 + 5X14 + 9X21 + 3X22 + 5X23 + 8X24 +
?  4X31 + 8X32 + 3X33 + 4X34 + 6X41 + 7X42 + 6X43 + 4X44
?  ST
?  X11 + X21 + X31 + X41 = 1
?  X12 + X22 + X32 + X42 = 1
?  X13 + X23 + X33 + X43 = 1
?  X14 + X24 + X34 + X44 = 1
?  X11 + X12 + X13 + X14 = 1
?  X21 + X22 + X23 + X24 = 1
?  X31 + X32 + X33 + X34 = 1
?  X41 + X42 + X43 + X44 = 1
?
:  LOOK
ROW:
ALL

MAX     6 X11 + 2 X12 + 8 X13 + 5 X14 + 9 X21 + 3 X22 + 5 X23 + 8 X24
    + 4 X31 + 8 X32 + 3 X33 + 4 X34 + 6 X41 + 7 X42 + 6 X43 + 4 X44
SUBJECT TO
        2)   X11 + X21 + X31 + X41 =      1
        3)   X12 + X22 + X32 + X42 =      1
        4)   X13 + X23 + X33 + X43 =      1
        5)   X14 + X24 + X34 + X44 =      1
        6)   X11 + X12 + X13 + X14 =      1
        7)   X21 + X22 + X23 + X24 =      1
        8)   X31 + X32 + X33 + X34 =      1
        9)   X41 + X42 + X43 + X44 =      1
END

:

        OBJECTIVE FUNCTION VALUE

1)      30.000000

VARIABLE        VALUE           REDUCED COST
    X11         .000000             .000000
    X12         .000000            7.000000
    X13        1.000000             .000000
    X14         .000000             .000000
    X21         .000000             .000000
    X22         .000000            9.000000
    X23         .000000            6.000000
    X24        1.000000             .000000
    X31         .000000            1.000000
    X32        1.000000             .000000
    X33         .000000            4.000000
    X34         .000000             .000000
    X41        1.000000             .000000
    X42         .000000            2.000000
    X43         .000000            2.000000
    X44         .000000            1.000000
```

assigning workers to jobs that require overlapping or interchangeable talents. Large banks frequently use LP to tackle their labor scheduling.

Arlington Bank of Commerce and Industry is a busy bank that has requirements for between 10 and 18 tellers depending on the time of day. The lunch time, from noon to 2 P.M., is usually heaviest. Table 11.4 indicates the workers needed at various hours that the bank is open.

The bank now employs 12 full-time tellers, but many people are on its roster of available part-time employees. A part-time employee must put in exactly four hours per day, but can start anytime between 9 A.M. and 1 P.M. Part-timers are a fairly inexpensive labor pool, since no retirement or lunch benefits are provided for them. Full-timers, on the other hand, work from 9 A.M.–5 P.M., but are allowed one hour for lunch. (Half of the full-timers eat at 11 A.M, the other half at noon.) Full-timers thus provide 35 hours per week of productive labor time.

By corporate policy, the bank limits part-time hours to a maximum of 50% of the day's total requirement.

Part-timers earn $4 per hour (or $16 per day) on the average, while full-timers earn $50 per day in salary and benefits, on the average. The bank would like to set a schedule that would minimize its total personnel costs. It will release one or more of its full-time tellers if it is profitable to do so.

We can let

Teaching Suggestion 11.4:
Labor Planning Problem—Arlington Bank. See the Instructor's Section for details.

F = full-time tellers

P_1 = part-timers starting at 9 A.M. (leaving at 1 P.M.)

P_2 = part-timers starting at 10 A.M. (leaving at 2 P.M.)

P_3 = part-timers starting at 11 A.M. (leaving at 3 P.M.)

P_4 = part-timers starting at noon (leaving at 4 P.M.)

P_5 = part-timers starting at 1 P.M. (leaving at 5 P.M.)

Objective function:

Minimize total daily personnel cost = $\$50F + \$16(P_1 + P_2 + P_3 + P_4 + P_5)$

TABLE 11.4 Arlington Bank of Commerce and Industry

TIME PERIOD	NUMBER OF TELLERS REQUIRED
9 A.M.–10 A.M.	10
10 A.M.–11 A.M.	12
11 A.M.–Noon	14
Noon–1 P.M.	16
1 P.M.–2 P.M.	18
2 P.M.–3 P.M.	17
3 P.M.–4 P.M.	15
4 P.M.–5 P.M.	10

APPLICATIONS OF QA

Crew Pairing Optimization at American Airlines

American Airlines (AA) employs more than 8,300 pilots and 16,200 flight attendants to fly one of the largest fleets in the U.S., with over 510 aircraft. Total crew cost, which includes salaries, benefits, and expenses, exceeds $1.3 billion every year and is second only to fuel cost. (Captains' salaries of $140,000 per year are typical.) But unlike fuel costs, a large part of crew costs are controllable. Therefore, a large priority at AA is to develop crew assignment plans that achieve a high level of crew utilization. To meet this goal, AA relies heavily on linear programming.

Clearly, every airline flight needs a full crew of pilots and flight attendants, but developing schedules that maintain a high level of crew utilization is a challenging logistics problem. Since crew members are people and not machines, scheduling their deployment is considerably more complicated than scheduling the use of aircraft, gates, or other equipment. The Federal Aviation Administration has established a complex set of limitations designed to ensure that crew members can fulfill their duties without significant risk of degradation of performance due to fatigue.

In addition, financial issues affect scheduling practices. At most major airlines, union contracts specify that flight crews will be guaranteed pay for some number of hours each day or each trip. Because of this, airline planners must try to build crew schedules that meet or exceed the crews' pay guarantees to the maximum extent possible. A trip containing one or more days with small amounts of flying time might be very expensive, because the crews would receive extra pay over and above the assigned flying time.

The Trip Reevaluation and Improvement Program (TRIP), fifteen labor-years in the making, uses LP to monthly assign crews in twelve different cities. The program spends about 500 hours of processing time each month on an IBM 3090 mainframe computer, but generates annual savings of over $20 million. Considered the best scheduling approach for problems of its type, AA has sold the program to ten other airlines and one railroad.

Source: R. Anbil et al. "Recent Advances in Crew Pairing Optimization at American Airlines." *Interfaces* **21**, 1 (Jan.–Feb. 1991): 62–74.

Video 11.1: Crew Pairing Optimization at American Airlines

Constraints:

For each hour, the available labor hours must be at least equal to the required labor hours.

$$F + P_1 \geq 10 \text{ (9 A.M.–10 A.M. needs)}$$

$$F + P_1 + P_2 \geq 12 \text{ (10 A.M.–11 A.M. needs)}$$

$$\tfrac{1}{2}F + P_1 + P_2 + P_3 \geq 14 \text{ (11 A.M.–noon needs)}$$

$$\tfrac{1}{2}F + P_1 + P_2 + P_3 + P_4 \geq 16 \text{ (noon–1 P.M. needs)}$$

$$F + P_2 + P_3 + P_4 + P_5 \geq 18 \text{ (1 P.M.–2 P.M. needs)}$$

$$F + P_3 + P_4 + P_5 \geq 17 \text{ (2 P.M.–3 P.M. needs)}$$

$$F + P_4 + P_5 \geq 15 \text{ (3 P.M.–4 P.M. needs)}$$

$$F + P_5 \geq 10 \text{ (4 P.M.–5 P.M. needs)}$$

Only 12 full-time tellers are available, so

$$F \leq 12$$

Part-time worker hours cannot exceed 50% of total hours required each day, which is the sum of the tellers needed each hour.

$$4(P_1 + P_2 + P_3 + P_4 + P_5) \le .50(10 + 12 + 14 + 16 + 18 + 17 + 15 + 10)$$

or

$$4P_1 + 4P_2 + 4P_3 + 4P_4 + 4P_5 \le .50(112)$$

$$F, P_1, P_2, P_3, P_4, P_5 \ge 0$$

There are several alternative optimal schedules that Arlington Bank can follow. The first is to employ only 10 full-time tellers ($F = 10$) and to start two part-timers at 10 A.M. ($P_2 = 2$), 7 part-timers at 11 A.M. ($P_3 = 7$) and 5 part-timers at noon ($P_4 = 5$). No part-timers would begin at 9 A.M. or 1 P.M.

alternate optimal solutions

The second solution also employs 10 full-time tellers, but starts 6 part-timers at 9 A.M. ($P_1 = 6$), 1 part-timer at 10 A.M. ($P_2 = 1$), 2 part-timers at 11 A.M. and 5 at noon ($P_3 = 2$ and $P_4 = 5$), and 0 part-timers at 1 P.M. ($P_5 = 0$). The cost of either of these two policies is \$724 per day. Program 11.6 illustrates the use of LINDO to reach the second solution.

PROGRAM 11.6 Use of LINDO at Arlington Bank

```
LINDO/PC
COPYRIGHT(C)  1984  LINDO  SYSTEMS,  INC.

:   MIN 50F + 16P1 + 16P2 + 16P3 + 16P4 + 16P5
?   ST
?   F + P1 > 10
?   F + P1 + P2 > 12
?   0.5F + P1 + P2 + P3 > 14
?   0.5F + P1 + P2 + P3 + P4 > 16
?   F + P2 + P3 + P4 + P5 > 18
?   F + P3 + P4 + P5 > 17
?   F + P4 + P5 > 15
?   F + P5 > 10
?   F < 12
?   4P1 + 4P2 + 4P3 + 4P4 + 4P5 < 56
?
:   LOOK
ROW:
ALL

MIN       50 F + 16 P1 + 16 P2 + 16 P3 + 16 P4 + 16 P5
SUBJECT TO
        2)    F + P1 >=    10
        3)    F + P1 + P2 >=    12
        4)    .5 F + P1 + P2 + P3 >=    14
        5)    .5 F + P1 + P2 + P3 + P4 >=    16
        6)    F + P2 + P3 + P4 + P5 >=    18
        7)    F + P3 + P4 + P5 >=    17
        8)    F + P4 + P5 >=    15
        9)    F + P5 >=    10
       10)    F <=    12
       11)    4 P1 + 4 P2 + 4 P3 + 4 P4 + 4 P5 <=    56
END
```

(Continued)

PROGRAM 11.6 Use of LINDO at Arlington Bank (Continued)

```
        OBJECTIVE FUNCTION VALUE

  1)         724.000000

  VARIABLE        VALUE          REDUCED COST
        F      10.000000             .000000
       P1       6.000000             .000000
       P2       1.000000             .000000
       P3       2.000000             .000000
       P4       5.000000             .000000
       P5        .000000             .000000
```

11.5   FINANCIAL APPLICATIONS

Applicable Problem 11-2

maximizing return on investment

Portfolio Selection

A problem frequently encountered by managers of banks, mutual funds, investment services, and insurance companies is the selection of specific investments from among a wide variety of alternatives. The manager's overall objective is usually to maximize expected return on investment, given a set of legal, policy, or risk restraints.

For example, the International City Trust (ICT) invests in short-term trade credits, corporate bonds, gold stocks, and construction loans. The board of directors has placed limits on the amount that can be committed to any one type of investment in order to encourage a diversified portfolio. ICT has $5 million available for immediate investment and wishes to do two things: (1) maximize the interest earned on the investments made over the next six months, and (2) satisfy the diversification requirements as set by the board of directors.

The specifics of the investment possibilities are:

INVESTMENT	INTEREST EARNED (%)	MAXIMUM INVESTMENT ($ MILLION)
Trade credit	7	1.0
Corporate bonds	11	2.5
Gold stocks	19	1.5
Construction loans	15	1.8

In addition, the board specifies that at least 55% of the funds invested must be in gold stocks and construction loans, and that no less than 15% be invested in trade credit.

To formulate ICT's investment decision as a linear programming problem, we let

$$X_1 = \$ \text{ invested in trade credit}$$

$$X_2 = \$ \text{ invested in corporate bonds}$$

$$X_3 = \$ \text{ invested in gold stocks}$$

$$X_4 = \$ \text{ invested in construction loans}$$

Objective:

Maximize dollars of interest earned $= .07X_1 + .11X_2 + .19X_3 + .15X_4$

Subject to:
$$X_1 \le 1{,}000{,}000$$
$$X_2 \le 2{,}500{,}000$$
$$X_3 \le 1{,}500{,}000$$
$$X_4 \le 1{,}800{,}000$$
$$X_3 + X_4 \ge .55(X_1 + X_2 + X_3 + X_4)$$
$$X_1 \ge .15(X_1 + X_2 + X_3 + X_4)$$
$$X_1 + X_2 + X_3 + X_4 \le 5{,}000{,}000$$

ICT maximizes its interest earned by making the following investment: Using STORM, we find that $X_1 = \$750{,}000$, $X_2 = \$950{,}000$, $X_3 = \$1{,}500{,}000$, and $X_4 = \$1{,}800{,}000$ and the total interest earned is $\$712{,}000$. See Program 11.7 for details.

11.6 TRANSPORTATION APPLICATIONS

Applicable Problems 11-19, 11-20

The Shipping Problem

The transportation or shipping problem involves determining the amount of goods or items to be transported from a number of origins to a number of destinations. The objective usually is to minimize total shipping costs or distances. Constraints in this type of problem deal with capacities at each origin and requirements at each destination. The transportation problem is a very specific case of linear programming and, in fact, a special algorithm has been developed to solve it. That solution procedure is one of the topics of Chapter 14.

transporting goods from several origins to several destinations efficiently

The Top Speed Bicycle Co. manufactures and markets a line of ten-speed bicycles nationwide. The firm has final assembly plants in two cities in which labor costs are low, New Orleans and Omaha. Its three major warehouses are located near the large market areas of New York, Chicago, and Los Angeles.

The sales requirements for the next year at the New York warehouse are 10,000 bicycles, at the Chicago warehouse 8,000 bicycles, and at the Los Angeles warehouse 15,000 bicycles. The factory capacity at each location is

PROGRAM 11.7 **Use of STORM to Solve the ICT LP Problem**

```
STORM EDITOR : Linear & Integer Programming Module

Title :  INTERNATIONAL CITY TRUST
Number of variables      :        4
Number of constraints    :        7
Starting solution given  :       NO
Objective type (MAX/MIN) :      MAX
─────────────────────────────────────────────────────────────────────
R1  : C1      VAR   1    VAR   2    VAR   3    VAR   4  CONST TYPE    R H S
OBJ COEFF       0.07       0.11       0.19       0.15   XXXX        XXXX
CONSTR   1      1.         0.         0.         0.        <= 1.0000E+06
CONSTR   2      0.         1.         0.         0.        <= 2.5000E+06
CONSTR   3      0.         0.         1.         0.        <= 1.5000E+06
CONSTR   4      0.         0.         0.         1.        <= 1.8000E+06
CONSTR   5      0.55       0.55      -0.45      -0.45      <=       0.
CONSTR   6     -0.85       0.15       .15        0.15      <=       0.
CONSTR   7      1.         1.         1.         1.        <= 5.0000E+06
VARBL TYPE      POS        POS        POS        POS     XXXX        XXXX
LOWR BOUND      .          .          .          .       XXXX        XXXX
UPPR BOUND      .          .          .          .       XXXX        XXXX
INIT SOLN    750000.    950000.  1.5000E+06 1.8000E+06   XXXX        XXXX

F1 Block   F2 GoTo   F3 InsR   F4 DelR   F5 InsC   F6 DelC   F7 Done  F8 Help KB:C

                   INTERNATIONAL CITY TRUST
         OPTIMAL SOLUTION - SUMMARY REPORT (NONZERO VARIABLES)
               Variable          Value           Cost
          1      VAR   1      750000.0000        0.0700
          2      VAR   2      950000.0000        0.1100
          3      VAR   3     1500000.0000        0.1900
          4      VAR   4     1800000.0000        0.1500

               Slack Variables
          5      CONSTR   1    250000.0000        0.0000
          6      CONSTR   2   1550000.0000        0.0000
          9      CONSTR   5    549999.9000        0.0000

          Objective Function Value = 712000
```

limited. New Orleans can assemble and ship 20,000 bicycles, while the Omaha plant can produce 15,000 bicycles per year.

The cost of shipping one bicycle from each factory to each warehouse differs, and these unit shipping costs are:

FROM \ TO	NEW YORK	CHICAGO	LOS ANGELES
NEW ORLEANS	$2	$3	$5
OMAHA	$3	$1	$4

The company wishes to develop a shipping schedule that will minimize its total annual transportation costs.

To formulate this problem using LP, we again employ the concept of double-subscripted variables. We let the first subscript represent the origin (factory) and the second subscript the destination (warehouse). Thus, in general, X_{ij} refers to the number of bicycles shipped from origin i to destination j. We could instead denote X_6 as the variable for origin 2 to destination 3, but we think you will find the double subscripts more descriptive and easier to use. So let

double-subscripted variables

X_{11} = number of bicycles shipped from New Orleans to New York

X_{12} = number of bicycles shipped from New Orleans to Chicago

X_{13} = number of bicycles shipped from New Orleans to Los Angeles

X_{21} = number of bicycles shipped from Omaha to New York

X_{22} = number of bicycles shipped from Omaha to Chicago

X_{23} = number of bicycles shipped from Omaha to Los Angeles

$$\text{Minimize total shipping costs} = 2X_{11} + 3X_{12} + 5X_{13} + 3X_{21} + 1X_{22} + 4X_{23}$$

Subject to:

$$X_{11} + X_{21} = 10{,}000 \quad \textit{(New York demand)}$$

$$X_{12} + X_{22} = 8{,}000 \quad \textit{(Chicago demand)}$$

$$X_{13} + X_{23} = 15{,}000 \quad \textit{(Los Angeles demand)}$$

$$X_{11} + X_{12} + X_{13} \leq 20{,}000 \quad \textit{(New Orleans factory supply)}$$

$$X_{21} + X_{22} + X_{23} \leq 15{,}000 \quad \textit{(Omaha factory supply)}$$

demand and supply constraints

Why are transportation problems a special class of linear programming problems? The answer is that every coefficient in front of a variable in the constraint equations is always equal to 1. This special trait is also seen in another special category of LP problems, the assignment problem discussed earlier.

Using LINDO, the computer-generated solution to Top Speed's problem is shown below and in Program 11.8. The total shipping cost is $96,000.

FROM	TO		
	NEW YORK	CHICAGO	LOS ANGELES
New Orleans	10,000	0	8,000
Omaha	0	8,000	7,000

The Truck Loading Problem

The truck loading problem involves deciding which items to load on a truck so as to maximize the value of a load shipped.

As an example, we consider Goodman Shipping, an Orlando firm owned by Steven Goodman. One of his trucks, with a capacity of

PROGRAM 11.8 **Top Speed Bicycle Solution Using LINDO**

```
LINDO/PC

COPYRIGHT(C)  1984  LINDO  SYSTEMS,  INC.

:  MIN 2X11 + 3X12 + 5X13 + 3X21 + 1X22 + 4X23
?  ST
?  X11 + X21 = 10000
?  X12 + X22 = 8000
?  X13 + X23 = 15000
?  X11 + X12 + X13 < 20000
?  X21 + X22 + X23 < 15000
?
:  LOOK
ROW:
ALL

MIN      2 X11 + 3 X12 + 5 X13 + 3 X21 + X22 + 4 X23
SUBJECT TO
        2)    X11 + X21 =       10000
        3)    X12 + X22 =       8000
        4)    X13 + X23 =       15000
        5)    X11 + X12 + X13 <=    20000
        6)    X21 + X22 + X23 <=    15000
END

:  GO



        OBJECTIVE FUNCTION VALUE

1)        96000.0000

VARIABLE       VALUE          REDUCED COST
    X11   10000.000000          .000000
    X12        .000000         1.000000
    X13    8000.000000          .000000
    X21        .000000         2.000000
    X22    8000.000000          .000000
    X23    7000.000000          .000000

    ROW    SLACK OR SURPLUS    DUAL PRICES
     2)         .000000        -2.000000
     3)         .000000        -2.000000
     4)         .000000        -5.000000
     5)    2000.000000          .000000
     6)         .000000         1.000000
```

10,000 pounds, is about to be loaded. Awaiting shipment are the items shown on the following page.[1]

---

[1]Adapted from an example in S. L. Savage, *What's Best!* General Optimization, Inc., and Holden-Day Inc., Oakland, CA: 1985.

DOLLAR VALUE AND WEIGHT FOR EACH ITEM		
ITEM	VALUE	WEIGHT
1	$22,500	7,500 lbs.
2	$24,000	7,500 lbs.
3	$ 8,000	3,000 lbs.
4	$ 9,500	3,500 lbs.
5	$11,500	4,000 lbs.
6	$ 9,750	3,500 lbs.

Each of these six items, we see, has an associated dollar value and weight.

The objective is to maximize the total value of the items loaded onto the truck without exceeding the truck's weight capacity. We let X_i = the proportion of each item i loaded on the truck.

$$\text{Maximize load value} = \$22,500X_1 + \$24,000X_2 + \$8,000X_3 + \$9,500X_4$$
$$+ \$11,500X_5 + \$9,750X_6$$

Subject to:

$$7,500X_1 + 7,500X_2 + 3,000X_3 + 3,500X_4 +$$

$$4,000X_5 + 3,500X_6 \le 10,000 \text{ lbs. capacity}$$

$$X_1 \le 1$$

$$X_2 \le 1$$

$$X_3 \le 1$$

$$X_4 \le 1$$

$$X_5 \le 1$$

$$X_6 \le 1$$

These final six constraints reflect the fact that at most one "unit" of an item can be loaded onto the truck. In effect, if Goodman can load a *portion* of an item (say item 1 is a batch of 1,000 folding chairs, not all of which need be shipped together), then the X_is will all be proportions ranging from 0 (nothing) to 1 (all of that item loaded).

To solve this problem, we turn to the popular spreadsheet software program What's*Best!* Program 11.9a shows Goodman's worksheet *before* optimization and Program 11.9b reflects the answer. The What's*Best!* solution recommends loading 33% of item 1, all of item 2, and none of the other items. This yields a total load value of $31,500.

This leads us to an interesting issue we will deal with in detail in Chapter 15. What does Goodman do if fractional values of items cannot be loaded? For example, if luxury cars were the items being loaded, we clearly cannot ship one-third of a Maserati.

If the proportion of item 1 was rounded up to 1.00, the weight of the load would increase to 15,000 pounds. This would violate the 10,000 pounds maximum weight constraint. Therefore, the fraction of item one must be rounded down to zero. This would drop the value of the load to 7,500 pounds, leaving 2,500 pounds of the load capacity unused. Since

PROGRAM 11.9 Using What's*Best!* to Solve Goodman Shipping's LP Problem

(a)

	A	B	C	D	E	F	G
1	TRUCK LOADING						
2						Maximum	
3		Load	Load	Proportion		Proportion	Proportion
4	Item	Value	Weight	Loaded		Loaded	Not Loaded
5							
6	1	$22,500	7,500	0.00	<	1	1
7							
8	2	$24,000	7,500	0.00	<	1	1
9							
10	3	$8,000	3,000	0.00	<	1	1
11							
12	4	$9,500	3,500	0.00	<	1	1
13							
14	5	$11,500	4,000	0.00	<	1	1
15							
16	6	$9,750	3,500	0.00	<	1	1
17							
18		Total Value		Total Weight		Maximum	
19		of Load:		of Load:		Load Weight	
20		$0		0	<	10,000	10,000

(b)

	A	B	C	D	E	F	G
1	TRUCK LOADING						
2						Maximum	
3		Load	Load	Proportion		Proportion	Proportion
4	Item	Value	Weight	Loaded		Loaded	Not Loaded
5							
6	1	$22,500	7,500	0.33	<	1	0.666666
7							
8	2	$24,000	7,500	1.00	<	1	0
9							
10	3	$8,000	3,000	0.00	<	1	1
11							
12	4	$9,500	3,500	0.00	<	1	1
13							
14	5	$11,500	4,000	0.00	<	1	1
15							
16	6	$9,750	3,500	0.00	<	1	1
17							
18		Total Value		Total Weight		Maximum	
19		of Load:		of Load:		Load Weight	
20		$31,500		10,000	<	10,000	-0.00007

no other item weighs less than 2,500 pounds, the truck cannot be filled up further.

Thus we see that by using regular linear programming and rounding the fractional weights, the truck would carry only item 2 for a load weight of 7,500 pounds and a load value of $24,000.

What's*Best!*, AB:QM, STORM, and LINDO are all capable of dealing with *integer programming* problems as well; that is, LP problems requiring integer solutions. Using What's*Best!*, the integer solution to Goodman's problem is to load items 3, 4, and 6 for a total weight of 10,000 pounds and load value of $27,250.

11.7 INGREDIENT BLENDING APPLICATIONS

Applicable Problems 11-4, 11-9, 11-11, 11-15, 11-16

Diet Problems

The diet problem, one of the earliest applications of linear programming, was originally used by hospitals to determine the most economical diet for patients. Known in agricultural applications as the feed mix problem, the diet problem involves specifying a food or feed ingredient combination that satisfies stated nutritional requirements at a minimum cost level.

Teaching Suggestion 11.5: Ingredient Blending Applications. See the Instructor's Section for details.

The Whole Food Nutrition Center uses three bulk grains to blend a natural cereal that it sells by the pound. The store advertises that each two-ounce serving of the cereal, when taken with 1/2 cup of whole milk, meets an average adult's minimum daily requirement for protein, riboflavin, phosphorus, and magnesium. The cost of each bulk grain and the protein, riboflavin, phosphorus, and magnesium units per pound of each are shown in Table 11.5.

blending different grains to make a brand of cereal

The minimum adult daily requirement (called the U.S. Recommended Daily Allowance, or USRDA) for protein is 3 units; for riboflavin, 2 units; for phosphorus, 1 unit; and for magnesium, .425 units. Whole Food wants to select the blend of grains that will meet the USRDA at a minimum cost.

Alternate Example 11.2

We let

$$X_A = \text{pounds of grain A in one 2-ounce serving of cereal}$$

$$X_B = \text{pounds of grain B in one 2-ounce serving of cereal}$$

$$X_C = \text{pounds of grain C in one 2-ounce serving of cereal}$$

Objective function:

Minimize total cost of mixing a 2-ounce serving
$$= \$.33X_A + \$.47X_B + \$.38X_C$$

TABLE 11.5 Whole Food's Natural Cereal Requirements

GRAIN	COST PER POUND (¢)	PROTEIN (UNITS/LB.)	RIBOFLAVIN (UNITS/LB.)	PHOSPHORUS (UNITS/LB.)	MAGNESIUM (UNITS/LB.)
A	33	22	16	8	5
B	47	28	14	7	0
C	38	21	25	9	6

Constraints:

$$22X_A + 28X_B + 21X_C \geqslant 3 \quad \text{(protein units)}$$

$$16X_A + 14X_B + 25X_C \geqslant 2 \quad \text{(riboflavin units)}$$

$$8X_A + 7X_8 + 9X_C \geqslant 1 \quad \text{(phosphorus units)}$$

$$5X_A + 0X_B + 6X_C \geqslant .425 \quad \text{(magnesium units)}$$

$$X_A + X_B + X_C = 1/8 \quad \text{(total mix is 2 ounces or 1/8 pound)}$$

$$X_A, X_B, X_C \geqslant 0$$

The solution to this problem requires mixing together .025 lb. of grain A, 0.50 lb. of grain B, and .050 lb. of grain C. Another way of stating the solution is in terms of the proportion of the 2-ounce serving of each grain, namely, 2/5 ounce of grain A, 4/5 ounce of grain B, and 4/5 ounce of grain C in each serving. The cost per serving is $.05075, a little over $.05 per serving. Program 11.10 illustrates this solution using our AB:QM software package. A discussion of shadow pricing is found in Chapter 13.

Ingredient Mix and Blending Problems

Diet and feed mix problems are actually special cases of a more general class of linear programming problems known as *ingredient* or *blending problems.* Blending problems arise when a decision must be made regarding the blending of two or more resources in order to produce one or more products. Resources, in this case, contain one or more essential ingredients that must be blended so that each final product contains specific percentages of each ingredient. The following example deals with an application frequently seen in the petroleum industry, the blending of crude oils to produce refinable gasoline.

blending crude oils to produce gasoline grades

The Low Knock Oil Company produces two grades of cut-rate gasoline for industrial distribution. The grades, regular and economy, are produced by refining a blend of two types of crude oil, Type X100 and Type X220. Each crude oil differs not only in cost per barrel, but in composition as well. The accompanying table indicates the percentage of crucial ingredients found in each of the crude oils and the cost per barrel for each.

CRUDE OIL TYPE	INGREDIENT A (%)	INGREDIENT B (%)	COST/ BARREL ($)
X100	35	55	30.00
X220	60	25	34.80

Weekly demand for the regular grade of Low Knock gasoline is at least 25,000 barrels, while demand for the economy is at least 32,000 barrels per week. *At least 45% of each barrel of regular must be ingredient A. At most 50% of each barrel of economy should contain ingredient B.*

PROGRAM 11.10 Using AB:QM to Solve Whole Food's LP Problem

```
Linear Programming

Problem Title :  WHOLE FOOD NUTRITION CENTER
Type of Problem (Max=1/Min=2)   2        Tableau(All=1/Final=2/No=3)   3
Number of Constraints           5        Number of Variables          3

            X1          X2          X3 T          Rhs
Obj.       .33         .47         .38 x xxxxxxxxxx
C1          22          28          21 >            3
C2          16          14          25 >            2
C3           8           7           9 >            1
C4           5           0           6 >         .425
C5           1           1           1 =         .125



Help   New   Load   Save   Edit   Run    Print   Install   Directory   Esc


Program: Linear Programming

Problem Title : WHOLE FOOD NUTRITION CENTER

***** Input Data *****

Max.   Z =    .33x1 + .47x2 + .38x3

Subject to

C1   22x1 + 28x2 + 21x3 >= 3
C2   16x1 + 14x2 + 25x3 >= 2
C3   8x1 + 7x2 + 9x3 >= 1
C4   5x1 + 6x3 >= .425
C5   1x1 + 1x2 + 1x3 = .125

***** Program Output *****

Final Optimal Solution

z =    0.051

-----------------------------------
Variable        Value      Reduced Cost
-----------------------------------
   x 1          0.025          0.000
   x 2          0.050          0.000
   x 3          0.050          0.000
-----------------------------------
Constraint   Slack/Surplus   Shadow Price
-----------------------------------
   C 1          0.000         -0.390
   C 2          0.350          0.000
   C 3          0.000          0.000
   C 4          0.000         -0.440
```

The Low Knock management must decide how many barrels of each type of crude oil to buy each week for blending in order to satisfy demand at minimum cost. To solve this as an LP problem, the firm lets

X_1 = barrels of crude X100 blended to produce the refined regular

X_2 = barrels of crude X100 blended to produce the refined economy

X_3 = barrels of crude X220 blended to produce the refined regular

X_4 = barrels of crude X220 blended to produce the refined economy

Objective:

$$\text{Minimize cost} = \$30X_1 + \$30X_2 + \$34.80X_3 + \$34.80X_4$$

Subject to:

$$X_1 + X_3 \geqslant 25{,}000 \quad \textit{(demand for regular)}$$
$$X_2 + X_4 \geqslant 32{,}000 \quad \textit{(demand for economy)}$$

At least 45% of each barrel of regular must be ingredient A.

$$(X_1 + X_3) = \text{total amount of crude blended to produce}$$
$$\text{the refined regular gasoline demand}$$

Thus

$$.45(X_1 + X_3) = \text{minimum amount of ingredient A required}$$

But

$$.35X_1 + .60X_3 = \text{amount of ingredient A in refined regular gas}$$

So

$$.35X_1 + .60X_3 \geqslant .45X_1 + .45X_3$$

or

$$-.10X_1 + .15X_3 \geqslant 0 \quad \textit{(ingredient A in regular constraint)}$$

Likewise, at most 50% of each barrel of economy should be ingredient B.

$$(X_2 + X_4) = \text{total amount of crude blended to produce}$$
$$\text{the refined economy gasoline demanded}$$

Thus

$$.50(X_2 + X_4) = \text{maximum amount of ingredient B allowed}$$

But

$$.55X_2 + .25X_4 = \text{amount of ingredient B in refined economy gas}$$

So

$$.55X_2 + .25X_4 \leqslant .50X_2 + .50X_4$$

or

$$.05X_2 - .25X_4 \leqslant 0 \quad \textit{(ingredient B in economy constraint)}$$

Here is the entire LP formulation:

$$\text{Minimize cost} = 30X_1 + 30X_2 + 34.80X_3 + 34.80X_4$$

$$\text{Subject to:} \quad X_1 + X_3 \geq 25{,}000$$

$$X_2 + X_4 \geq 32{,}000$$

$$-.10X_1 + .15X_3 \geq 0$$

$$.05X_2 - .25X_4 \leq 0$$

Using AB:QM, the solution to Low Knock Oil's formulation was found to be:

$$X_1 = 15{,}000 \text{ barrels of X100 into regular}$$

$$X_2 = 26{,}666\tfrac{2}{3} \text{ barrels of X100 into economy}$$

$$X_3 = 10{,}000 \text{ barrels of X220 into regular}$$

$$X_4 = 5{,}333\tfrac{1}{3} \text{ barrels of X220 into economy}$$

The cost of this mix is $1,783,600. Refer to Program 11.11 for details.

PROGRAM 11.11 Using AB:QM to Solve Low Knock Oil's LP Problem

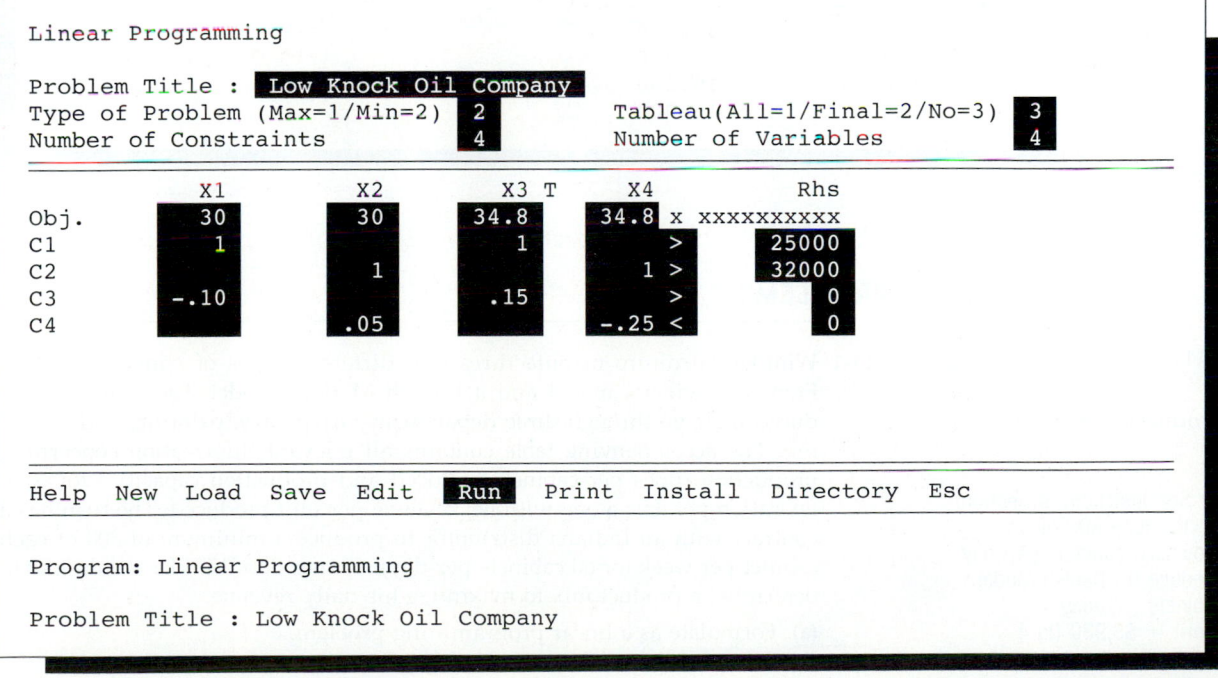

(Continued)

PROGRAM 11.11 **Using AB:QM to Solve Low Knock Oil's LP Problem (Continued)**

```
***** Input Data *****

Min.   Z =   30x1 + 30x2 + 34.8x3 + 34.8x4

Subject to

C1    1x1 + 1x3 >= 25000
C2    1x2 + 1x4 >= 32000
C3   -.10x1 + .15x3 >= 0
C4    .05x2 - .25x4 <= 0

***** Program Output *****

Final Optimal Solution

Z =  1783600.000

---------------------------------------
Variable          Value        Reduced Cost
---------------------------------------
   x 1         15000.000          0.000
   x 2         26666.667          0.000
   x 3         10000.000          0.000
   x 4          5333.333          0.000
---------------------------------------
Constraint   Slack/Surplus    Shadow Price
---------------------------------------
   C 1          0.000           -31.920
   C 2          0.000           -30.800
   C 3          0.000           -19.200
   C 4          0.000            16.000
```

PROBLEMS

QA11-1

production problem

(a) See Instructor's Section.
(b) Produce 60 French Provincial cabinets (X_1)/day
Produce 90 Danish Modern cabinets (X_2)/day
Profit = $3,930 (in 4 iterations)

11-1 Winkler Furniture manufactures two different types of china cabinets, a French Provincial model and a Danish Modern model. Each cabinet produced must go through three departments: carpentry, painting, and finishing. The accompanying table contains all relevant information concerning production times per cabinet produced and production capacities for each operation per day, along with net revenue per unit produced. The firm has a contract with an Indiana distributor to produce a minimum of 300 of each cabinet per week (or 60 cabinets per day). Owner Bob Winkler would like to determine a product mix to maximize his daily revenue.

(a) Formulate as a linear programming problem.
(b) Solve using a microcomputer LP software program.

CABINET STYLE	CARPENTRY (HRS./CABINET)	PAINTING (HRS./CABINET)	FINISHING (HRS./CABINET)	NET REVENUE/ CABINET ($)
French Provincial	3	$1\frac{1}{2}$	$\frac{3}{4}$	28
Danish Modern	2	1	$\frac{3}{4}$	25
Department capacity (hrs.)	360	200	125	

11-2 The Heinlein and Krampf Brokerage firm has just been instructed by one of its clients to invest $250,000 for her—money recently obtained through the sale of land holdings in Ohio. The client has a good deal of trust in the investment house, but she also has her own ideas about the distribution of the funds being invested. In particular, she requests that the firm select whatever stocks and bonds they believe are well rated, but within the following guidelines:

QA11-2

investment decision problem

1. Municipal bonds should comprise at least 20% of the investment.
2. At least 40% of the funds should be placed in a combination of electronics firms, aerospace firms, and drug manufacturers.
3. No more than 50% of the amount invested in municipal bonds should be placed in a high-risk, high-yield nursing home stock.

Subject to these restraints, the client's goal is to maximize projected return on investments. The analysts at Heinlein and Krampf, aware of these guidelines, prepare a list of quality stocks and bonds and their corresponding rates of return.

(a) See Instructor's Section.
(b) $50,000 invested in L.A. Municipal Bonds (X_1).
$0 invested in Thompson Electronics (X_2).
$0 invested in United Aerospace (X_3).
$175,000 invested in Palmer Drugs (X_4).
$25,000 invested in Happy Days (X_5).
This produces an annual return on investment of $20,300.

INVESTMENT	PROJECTED RATE OF RETURN (%)
Los Angeles Municipal Bonds	5.3
Thompson Electronics, Inc.	6.8
United Aerospace Corp.	4.9
Palmer Drugs	8.4
Happy Days Nursing Homes	11.8

(a) Formulate this portfolio selection problem using linear programming.
(b) Solve this problem.

11-3 The famous Y. S. Chang Restaurant is open 24 hours a day. Waiters and busboys report for duty at 3 A.M., 7 A.M., 11 A.M., 3 P.M., 7 P.M., or 11 P.M., and each works an eight-hour shift. The following table shows the minimum number of workers needed during the six periods into which the day is divided. Chang's scheduling problem is to determine how many waiters and busboys should report for work at the start of each time period in order to minimize the total staff required for one day's operation. (*Hint:* Let X_i equal the number of waiters and busboys beginning work in time period i, where $i = 1, 2, 3, 4, 5, 6$.)

QA11-3

restaurant work scheduling problem

Hire 30 workers
  16 begin at 7 A.M.
  9 begin at 3 P.M.
  2 begin at 7 P.M.
  3 begin at 11 P.M.

An alternate optimum is:
  3 begin at 3 A.M.
  9 begin at 7 A.M.
  7 begin at 11 A.M.
  2 begin at 3 P.M.
  9 begin at 7 P.M.
  0 begin at 11 P.M.

QA11-4

PERIOD	TIME	NUMBER OF WAITERS AND BUSBOYS REQUIRED
1	3 A.M.– 7 A.M.	3
2	7 A.M.–11 A.M.	12
3	11 A.M.– 3 P.M.	16
4	3 P.M.– 7 P.M.	9
5	7 P.M.–11 P.M.	11
6	11 P.M.– 3 A.M.	4

animal feed mix problem

11-4 The Battery Park Stable feeds and houses the horses used to pull tourist-filled carriages through the streets of Charleston's historic waterfront area. The stable owner, an ex-racehorse trainer, recognizes the need to set a nutritional diet for the horses in his care. At the same time, he would like to keep the overall daily cost of feed to a minimum.

The feed mixes available for the horses' diet are an oat product, a highly enriched grain, and a mineral product. Each of these mixes contains a certain amount of five ingredients needed daily to keep the average horse healthy. The accompanying table shows these minimum requirements, units of each ingredient per pound of feed mix, and costs for the three mixes.

Minimize Cost = $.09X_1 + .14X_2 + .17X_3$
$2X_1 + 3X_2 + 1X_3 \geq 6$
$\frac{1}{2}X_1 + 1X_2 + \frac{1}{2}X_3 \geq 2$
$3X_1 + 5X_2 + 6X_3 \geq 9$
$1X_1 + 1\frac{1}{2}X_2 + 2X_3 \geq 8$
$\frac{1}{2}X_1 + \frac{1}{2}X_2 + 1\frac{1}{2}X_3 \geq 5$
$X_1 + X_2 + X_3 \leq 6$

	FEED MIX			
DIET REQUIREMENT (INGREDIENTS)	OAT PRODUCT (UNITS/LB.)	ENRICHED GRAIN (UNITS/LB.)	MINERAL PRODUCT (UNITS/LB.)	MINIMUM DAILY REQUIREMENT (IN UNITS)
A	2	3	1	6
B	½	1	½	2
C	3	5	6	9
D	1	1½	2	8
E	½	½	1½	5
Cost/lb.	$.09	$.14	$.17	

$X_1 = 1\frac{1}{3}$, $X_2 = 0$, $X_3 = 3\frac{1}{3}$
Cost = .687

In addition, the stable owner is aware that an overfed horse is a sluggish worker. Consequently, he determines that six pounds of feed per day are the most any horse needs in order to function properly. Formulate this problem and solve for the optimal daily mix of the three feeds.

QA11-5

ballplayer selection problem

11-5 The Dubuque Sackers, a class D baseball team, face a tough four-game road trip against league rivals in Des Moines, Davenport, Omaha, and Peoria. Manager "Red" Revelle faces the task of scheduling his four starting pitchers for appropriate games. Since the games are to be played back to back in less than one week, Revelle cannot count on any pitcher to start in more than one game.

Revelle knows the strengths and weaknesses not only of his pitchers, but also of his opponents, and he is able to estimate the probability of winning each of the four games with each of the four starting pitchers. Those probabilities are listed in the following table.

STARTING PITCHER	OPPONENT			
	DES MOINES	DAVENPORT	OMAHA	PEORIA
"Dead-Arm" Jones	.60	.80	.50	.40
"Spitball" Baker	.70	.40	.80	.30
"Ace" Parker	.90	.80	.70	.80
"Gutter" Wilson	.50	.30	.40	.20

What pitching rotation should manager Revelle set to provide the highest winning probability (that is, the sum of the probabilities of winning each game) for the Sackers?

(a) Formulate this problem using linear programming.
(b) Solve the problem.

(a) Maximize Overall Probability $= .6X_{11} + .8X_{12} + .5X_{13} + .4X_{14} + .7X_{21} + .4X_{22} + 8X_{23} + .3X_{24} + .9X_{31} + .8X_{32} + .7X_{33} + .8X_{34} + .5X_{41} + .3X_{42} + .4X_{43} + .2X_{44}$

Subject to:
$X_{11} + X_{12} + X_{13} + X_{14} = 1$
$X_{21} + X_{22} + X_{23} + X_{24} = 1$
$X_{31} + X_{32} + X_{33} + X_{34} = 1$
$X_{41} + X_{42} + X_{43} + X_{44} = 1$
$X_{11} + X_{21} + X_{31} + X_{41} = 1$
$X_{12} + X_{22} + X_{32} + X_{42} = 1$
$X_{13} + X_{23} + X_{33} + X_{43} = 1$
$X_{14} + X_{24} + X_{34} + X_{44} = 1$
(b) See Instructor's Section.

QA11-6

11-6 The advertising director for Diversey Paint and Supply, a chain of four retail stores on Chicago's North Side, is considering two media possibilities. One plan is for a series of half-page ads in the Sunday *Chicago Tribune* newspaper, and the other is for advertising time on Chicago TV. The stores are expanding their lines of do-it-yourself tools, and the advertising director is interested in an exposure level of at least 40% within the city's neighborhoods and 60% in northwest suburban areas.

media selection problem

The TV viewing time under consideration has an exposure rating per spot of 5% in city homes and 3% in the northwest suburbs. The Sunday newspaper has corresponding exposure rates of 4% and 3% per ad. The cost of a half-page *Tribune* advertisement is \$925; a television spot costs \$2,000.

Diversey Paint would like to select the least costly advertising strategy that would meet desired exposure levels.

(a) Formulate using LP.
(b) Solve the problem.

(a) Minimize Cost $= \$925X_1 + \$2000X_2$
$.04X_1 + .05X_2 \geq .40$
$.03X_1 + .03X_2 \geq .60$
(b) Buy 20 Sunday newspaper ads (X_1); buy 0 TV ads; this has a cost of \$18,500.

QA11-7

11-7 Capitol Hill Construction Company (CHCC) must complete its current office building renovation as quickly as possible. The first portion of the project consists of six activities, some of which must be finished before others are started. The activities, their precedences, and their estimated times are shown in this table:

ACTIVITY		PRECEDENCE	TIME (IN DAYS)
Prepare financing options	(A)	—	2
Prepare preliminary sketches	(B)	—	3
Outline specifications	(C)	—	1
Prepare drawings	(D)	A	4
Write specifications	(E)	C and D	5
Run off prints	(F)	B	1

This network of tasks can be drawn as on the following page.

Let X_i represent the earliest completion of an activity where $i =$ A, B, C, D, E, F. Formulate and solve CHCC's problem as a linear program.

Minimize X_G (end of project)
$X_A \geq 2$
$X_B \geq 3$
$X_C \geq 1$
$X_D - X_A \geq 4$
$X_F - X_B \geq 1$
$X_E - X_C \geq 5$
$X_E - X_D \geq 5$
$X_G - X_E \geq 0$
$X_G - X_F \geq 0$

$z = 11$ days

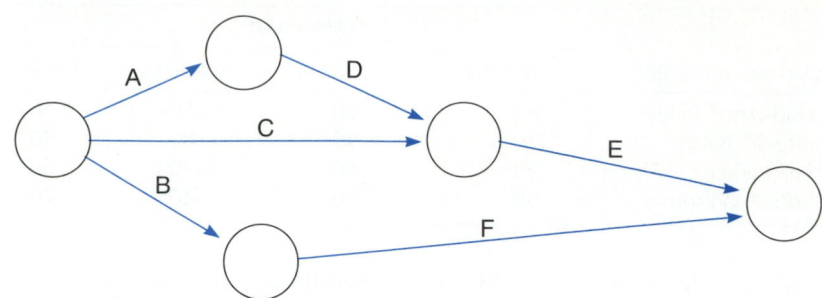

QA11-8

high school busing problem

Minimize Total Travel Miles
$= 5X_{AB} + 8X_{AC} + 6X_{AE}$
$\quad + 0X_{BB} + 4X_{BC} + 12X_{BE}$
$\quad + 4X_{CB} + 0X_{CC} + 7X_{CE}$
$\quad + 7X_{DB} + 2X_{DC} + 5X_{DE}$
$\quad + 12X_{EB} + 7X_{EC} + 0X_{EE}$
$X_{AB} + X_{AC} + X_{AE} = 700$
$X_{BB} + X_{BC} + X_{BE} = 500$
$X_{CB} + X_{CC} + X_{CE} = 100$
$X_{DB} + X_{DC} + X_{DE} = 800$
$X_{EB} + X_{EC} + X_{EE} = 400$
$X_{AB} + X_{BB} + X_{CB} + X_{DB}$
$\quad + X_{EB} \leq 900$
$X_{AC} + X_{BC} + X_{CC} + X_{DC}$
$\quad + X_{EC} \leq 900$
$X_{AE} + X_{BE} + X_{CE} + X_{DE} + X_{EE}$
≤ 900
Solution:
$X_{AB} = 400, X_{AE} = 300,$
$X_{BB} = 500, X_{CC} = 100,$
$X_{DC} = 800, X_{EE} = 400$

QA11-9

ingredient mix problem

11-8 The Arden County, Maryland, superintendent of education is responsible for assigning students to the *three* high schools in his county. He recognizes the need to bus a certain number of students, for several sectors of the county are beyond walking distance to a school. The superintendent partitions the county into *five* geographic sectors as he attempts to establish a plan that will minimize the total number of student miles traveled by bus. He also recognizes that if a student happens to live in a certain sector and is assigned to the high school in that sector, there is no need to bus him since he can walk to school. The three schools are located in sectors B, C, and E.

The accompanying table reflects the number of high-school-age students living in each sector and the distance in miles from each sector to each school.

	DISTANCE TO SCHOOL			
SECTOR	SCHOOL IN SECTOR B	SCHOOL IN SECTOR C	SCHOOL IN SECTOR E	NO. OF STUDENTS
A	5	8	6	700
B	0	4	12	500
C	4	0	7	100
D	7	2	5	800
E	12	7	0	400
			Total	2,500

Each high school has a capacity of 900 students. Set up the objective function and constraints of this problem using linear programming so that the total number of student miles traveled by bus is minimized. (Note the resemblance to the transportation problem illustrated earlier in this chapter.) Then solve the problem.

11-9 Bob Bell's fortieth birthday party promised to be the social event of the year in Cookeville. To prepare, Bob stocked up on the following liquors.

LIQUOR	AMOUNT ON HAND (OZ.)
Bourbon	52
Brandy	38
Vodka	64
Dry vermouth	24
Sweet vermouth	36

Bob decides to mix four drinks for the party: Chaunceys, Sweet Italians, bourbon on the rocks, and Russian martinis. A Chauncey consists of ¼ bourbon, ¼ vodka, ¼ brandy, and ¼ sweet vermouth. A Sweet Italian contains ¼ brandy, ½ sweet vermouth, and ¼ dry vermouth. Bourbon on the rocks contains only bourbon. Finally, a Russian martini consists of ⅓ dry vermouth and ⅔ vodka. Each drink contains 4 fluid ounces.

Bob's objective is to mix these ingredients in such a way as to make the largest possible number of drinks in advance.

(a) Formulate using linear programming.
(b) Solve using LP software.

26 Chaunceys (X_1)
5 Sweet Italians (X_2)
6½ Bourbon on the Rocks (X_3)
14¼ Russian Martinis (X_4)
Total of 51.75 drinks

11-10 The I. Kruger Paint and Wallpaper Store is a large retail distributor of the Supertrex brand of vinyl wallcoverings. Kruger will enhance its city-wide image in Miami if it can outsell other local stores in total number of rolls of Supertex next year. It is able to estimate the demand function as follows:

QA11-10

pricing and marketing strategy problem

Number of rolls of Supertrex sold = 20 × Dollars spent on advertising + 6.8 × Dollars spent on in-store displays + 12 × Dollars invested in on-hand wallpaper inventory − 65,000 × Percentage markup taken above wholesale cost of a roll.

The store budgets a total of $17,000 for advertising, in-store displays, and on-hand inventory of Supertrex for next year. It decides it must spend at least $3,000 on advertising; in addition, at least 5% of the amount invested in on-hand inventory should be devoted to displays. Markups on Supertrex seen at other local stores range from 20% to 45%. Kruger decides that its markup had best be in this range as well.

(a) Formulate as an LP problem.
(b) Solve the problem.
(c) What is the difficulty with the answer?
(d) What constraint would you add?

Spend $17,000 on advertising ($X_1$); spend nothing on displays or inventory (X_2 and X_3); take a 20% markup; store will sell 327,000 rolls.

11-11 Kathy Roniger, campus dietician for a small Idaho college, is responsible for formulating a nutritious meal plan for students. For an evening meal, she feels that the following five meal-content requirements should be met: (1) between 900 and 1,500 calories; (2) at least 4 milligrams of iron; (3) no more than 50 grams of fat; (4) at least 26 grams of protein; and (5) no more than 50 grams of carbohydrates. On a particular day, Roniger's food stock includes seven items that can be prepared and served for supper to meet these requirements. The cost per pound for each food item and its contribution to each of the five nutritional requirements are given in the accompanying table. What combination and amounts of food items will provide the nutrition Roniger requires at the least total food cost?

(a) Formulate as an LP problem.
(b) What is the cost per meal?
(c) Is this a well-balanced diet?

QA11-11

college meal selection problem

No milk ($X_1 = 0$)
.499 pound of ground meat (X_2)
.173 pound of chicken (X_3)
No fish ($X_4 = 0$)
No beans ($X_5 = 0$)
.105 pound of spinach (X_6)
.762 pound of white potatoes (X_7)
Each meal has a cost of $1.75.

TABLE OF FOOD VALUES* AND COSTS

FOOD ITEM	CALORIES/ POUND	IRON (MGS./LB.)	FAT (GMS./LB.)	PROTEIN (GMS./LB.)	CARBOHY- DRATES (GMS./LB.)	COST/ POUND ($)
Milk	295	.2	16	16	22	.60
Ground meat	1216	.2	96	81	0	2.35
Chicken	394	4.3	0	74	0	1.15
Fish	358	3.2	.5	83	0	2.25
Beans	128	3.2	.8	7	28	.58
Spinach	118	14.1	1.4	14	19	1.17
Potatoes	279	2.2	.5	8	63	.33

Source: Bowes and Church, *Food Values of Portions Commonly Used,* 12th ed. (Philadelphia: Lippincott, 1975).

QA11-12

high tech production problem

11-12 Quitmeyer Electronics Incorporated manufactures the following six microcomputer peripheral devices: internal modems, external modems, graphics circuit boards, floppy disk drives, winchester disk drives, and memory expansion boards. Each of these technical products requires time, in minutes, on three types of electronic testing equipment as shown below.

	DEVICE					
	INTER- NAL MODEM	EXTER- NAL MODEM	CIRCUIT BOARD	FLOPPY DISKS	WINCHESTER DISKS	MEMORY BOARDS
Test device #1	7	3	12	6	18	17
Test device #2	2	5	3	2	15	17
Test device #3	5	1	3	2	9	2

The first two test devices are available 120 hours per week. The third (device #3) requires more preventive maintenance and may be used only 100 hours each week. The market for all six computer components is vast and Quitmeyer Electronics believes it can sell as many units of each product as it can manufacture. The table that follows summarizes the revenues and material costs for each product.

DEVICE	REVENUE PER UNIT SOLD ($)	MATERIAL COST PER UNIT ($)
Internal modem	200	35
External modem	120	25
Graphics circuit board	180	40
Floppy disk drive	130	45
Winchester disk drive	430	170
Memory expansion board	260	60

$X_1 = 496.55$ internal modems
$X_2 = 1241.38$ external modems
X_3 through $X_6 = 0$
Profit = $195,504.80

In addition, variable labor costs are $15 per hour for test device #1, $12 per hour for test device #2, and $18 per hour for test device #3. Quitmeyer Electronics wants to maximize its profits.

(a) Formulate this problem as a linear programming model.

(b) Solve the problem by computer. What is the best product mix?

(c) What is the value of an additional hour of time per week on test device #1? Test device #2? Test device #3? Should Quitmeyer Electronics add more test device time? If so, on which equipment?

Values are $21.41, $5.75, and $0, respectively. See Chapters 10 and 13 for "shadow pricing" details.

11-13 South Central Utilities has just announced the August 1 opening of its second nuclear generator at its Baton Rouge, Louisiana, nuclear power plant. Its personnel department has been directed to determine how many nuclear technicians need to be hired and trained over the remainder of the year.

The plant currently employs 350 fully trained technicians and projects the following personnel needs:

QA11-13

nuclear plant staffing problem

MONTH	PERSONNEL NEEDED (HOURS)
August	40,000
September	45,000
October	35,000
November	50,000
December	45,000

By Louisiana law, a reactor employee can actually work no more than 130 hours per month. (Slightly over one hour per day is used for check-in and check-out, record keeping, and for daily radiation health scans.) Policy at South Central Utilities also dictates that layoffs are not acceptable in those months when the nuclear plant is overstaffed. So, if more trained employees are available than are needed in any month, each worker is still fully paid, even though he or she is not required to work the 130 hours.

Training new employees is an important and costly procedure. It takes one month of one-on-one classroom instruction before a new technician is permitted to work alone in the reactor facility. Therefore, South Central must hire trainees one month before they are actually needed. Each trainee teams up with a skilled nuclear technician and requires 90 hours of that employee's time, meaning that 90 hours less of the technician's time are available that month for actual reactor work.

Personnel department records indicate a turnover rate of trained technicians at 5% per month. In other words, about 5% of the skilled employees at the start of any month resign by the end of that month.

A trained technician earns an average monthly salary of $2,000 (regardless of the number of hours worked, as noted earlier). Trainees are paid $900 during their one month of instruction.

(a) Formulate this staffing problem using LP.

(b) Solve the problem. How many trainees must begin each month?

(a) Minimize total salaries paid
$= \$2,000X_1 + 2,000X_2 + 2,000X_3 + 2,000X_4 + 2,000X_5 + 900Y_1 + 900Y_2 + 900Y_3 + 900Y_4 + 900Y_5$
$130X_1 - 90Y_1 \geqslant 40,000$
$130X_2 - 90Y_2 \geqslant 45,000$
$130X_3 - 90Y_3 \geqslant 35,000$
$130X_4 - 90Y_4 \geqslant 50,000$
$130X_5 - 90Y_5 \geqslant 45,000$
$X_1 = 350$
$X_2 = X_1 + Y_1 - .05X_1$
$X_3 = X_2 + Y_2 - .05X_2$
$X_4 = X_3 + Y_3 - .05X_3$
$X_5 = X_4 + Y_4 - .05X_4$

(b) Month	Trainees beginning
Aug	13.7
Sept	0
Oct	72.2
Nov	0
Dec	0

11-14 Margaret Young's family owns five panels of farmland broken into a southeast sector, north sector, northwest sector, west sector, and southwest sector. Young is primarily involved in growing wheat, alfalfa, and barley crops and is currently preparing her production plan for next year. The Pennsylvania Water Authority has just announced its yearly water allotment, with the Young farm receiving 7,400 acre-feet. Each parcel can only tolerate a specified amount of irrigation per growing season, as specified below:

QA11-14

agricultural production planning problem

PARCEL	AREA (IN ACRES)	WATER IRRIGATION LIMIT (ACRE-FEET)
Southeast	2,000	3,200
North	2,300	3,400
Northwest	600	800
West	1,100	500
Southwest	500	600

Each of Young's crops needs a minimum amount of water per acre and there is a projected limit on sales of each crop. Crop data follow:

CROP	MAXIMUM SALES	WATER NEEDED PER ACRE (ACRE-FEET)
Wheat	110,000 bushels	1.6
Alfalfa	1,800 tons	2.9
Barley	2,200 tons	3.5

Young's best estimate is that she can sell wheat at a net profit of $2 per bushel, alfalfa at $40 per ton, and barley at $50 per ton. One acre of land yields an average of 1.5 tons of alfalfa and 2.2 tons of barley. The wheat yield is approximately 50 bushels per acre.

(a) Formulate Young's production plan.
(b) What should the crop plan be and what profit will it yield?
(c) The Water Authority informs Young that for a special fee of $6,000 this year, her farm will qualify for an additional allotment of 600 acre-feet of water. How should she respond?

See the Instructor's Section for problem formulation. The solution is to plant:
$X_{12} = 1,250$ acres of wheat in N parcel
$X_{13} = 500$ acres of wheat in NW parcel
$X_{14} = 312\frac{1}{2}$ acres of wheat in W parcel
$X_{15} = 137\frac{1}{2}$ acres of wheat in SW parcel
$X_{25} = 131$ acres of alfalfa in SW parcel
$X_{31} = 600$ acres of barley in SE parcel
$X_{32} = 400$ acres of barley in N parcel
Profit will be $337,862.10.

QA11-15

11-15 Amalgamated Products has just received a contract to construct steel body frames for automobiles that are to be produced at the new Japanese factory in Tennessee. The Japanese auto manufacturer has strict quality control standards for all of its component subcontractors and has informed Amalgamated that each frame must have the following steel content:

MATERIAL IN STEEL	MINIMUM PERCENT	MAXIMUM PERCENT
Manganese	2.1	2.3
Silicon	4.3	4.6
Carbon	5.05	5.35

Amalgamated mixes batches of eight different available materials to produce one ton of steel used in the body frames. The table that follows details these materials:

MATERIAL AVAILABLE	MANGANESE (%)	SILICON (%)	CARBON (%)	POUNDS AVAILABLE	COST PER POUND
Alloy 1	70.0	15.0	3.0	No limit	$.12
Alloy 2	55.0	30.0	1.0	300	$.13
Alloy 3	12.0	26.0	0	No limit	$.15
Iron 1	1.0	10.0	3.0	No limit	$.09
Iron 2	5.0	2.5	0	No limit	$.07
Carbide 1	0	24.0	18.0	50	$.10
Carbide 2	0	25.0	20.0	200	$.12
Carbide 3	0	23.0	25.0	100	$.09

Minimize cost = $.12x_1 + .13x_2 + .15x_3 + .09x_4 + .07x_5 + .10x_6 + .12x_7 + .09x_8$
Subject to:
$.70x_1 + .55x_2 + .12x_3 + .01x_4 + .05x_5 \geq 42$
$.70x_1 + .55x_2 + .12x_3 + .01x_4 + .05x_5 \leq 46$
$.15x_1 + .30x_2 + .26x_3 + .10x_4 + .025x_5 + .24x_6 + .25x_7 + .23x_8 \geq 86$
$.15x_1 + .30x_2 + .26x_3 + .10x_4 + .025x_5 + .24x_6 + .25x_7 + .23x_8 \leq 92$
$.03x_1 + .01x_2 + .03x_4 + .18x_6 + .20x_7 + .25x_8 \geq 101$
$.03x_1 + .01x_2 + .03x_4 + .18x_6 + .20x_7 + .25x_8 \leq 107$
$x_2 \leq 300 \quad x_6 \leq 50$
$x_7 \leq 200 \quad x_8 \leq 100$
$x_1 + x_2 + x_3 + x_4 + x_5 + x_6 + x_7 + x_8 = 2,000$
Solution: Problem Infeasible

Formulate and solve the linear programming model that will indicate how much each of the eight materials should be blended into a one-ton load of steel so that Amalgamated meets its requirements while minimizing costs.

11-16 Refer to Problem 11-15. Find the cause of the difficulty and recommend how to adjust it. Then solve the problem again.

See Instructor's Section. QA 11-16

11-17 Mt. Sinai Hospital in New Orleans is a large, private, 600-bed facility complete with laboratories, operating rooms, and X-ray equipment. In seeking to increase revenues, Mt. Sinai's administration has decided to make a 90-bed addition on a portion of adjacent land currently used for staff parking. The administrators feel that the labs, operating rooms, and X-ray department are not being fully utilized at present and do not need to be expanded to handle additional patients. The addition of 90 beds, however, involves deciding how many beds should be allocated to the medical staff for medical patients and how many to the surgical staff for surgical patients.

QA11-17

hospital expansion problem

The hospital's accounting medical records departments have provided the following pertinent information. The average hospital stay for a medical patient is eight days and the average medical patient generates $2,280 in revenues. The average surgical patient is in the hospital five days and receives a $1,515 bill. The laboratory is capable of handling 15,000 tests per year more than it was handling. The average medical patient requires 3.1 lab tests and the average surgical patient takes 2.6 lab tests. Furthermore, the average medical patient uses one X ray, while the average surgical patient requires two X rays. If the hospital were expanded by 90 beds, the X-ray department could handle up to 7,000 X rays without significant additional cost. Finally, the administration estimates that up to 2,800 additional operations could be performed in existing operating room facilities. Medical patients, of course, require no surgery, while each surgical patient generally has one surgery performed.

Maximize Revenue = $2,280X_1 + $1,515X_2$
$8X_1 + 5X_2 \leq 32,850$
$3.1X_1 + 2.6X_2 \leq 15,000$
$1X_1 + 2X_2 \leq 7,000$
$X_2 \leq 2,800$
$X_1 = 2,791$ medical patients;
$X_2 = 2,105$ surgical patients;
revenue = $9,551,659 per year.
This yields 61 medical beds and 29 surgical beds.

Formulate this problem so as to determine how many medical beds and how many surgical beds should be added in order to maximize revenues. Assume that the hospital is open 365 days a year. Then solve the problem.

11-18* Prepare a written report to the CEO of Mt. Sinai Hospital in Problem 11-17 on the expansion of the hospital. Round off your answers to the nearest *integer*. The format of presentation of results is important. The CEO is a busy person and wants to be able to find your optimal solution quickly in your report. Cover all the areas given below but do not mention any X's, slack or surplus variables, or shadow prices.

(a) What is the maximum revenue per year, how many medical patients/year are there, and how many surgical patients/year are there? How many medical beds and how many surgical beds of the 90-bed addition should be added?

a) 61 medical beds 29 surgical beds

(b) Are there any empty beds with this optimal solution? If so, how many empty beds are there? Discuss the effect of acquiring more beds if needed.

b) No empty beds

(c) Are the laboratories being used to their capacity? Is it possible to perform more lab tests/year? If so, how many more? Discuss the effect of acquiring more lab space if needed.

c) 876 unused tests

(d) Is the X-ray facility being used to its maximum? Is it possible to do more X rays/year? If so, how many more? Discuss the effect of acquiring more X-ray facilities if needed.

d) Used to maximum

Source: Professor C. Vertullo.

e) 695 available days

QA 11-19

Dubuque to 1 = 25
Dubuque to 3 = 125
Davenport to 3 = 175
Des Moines to 1 = 175
Des Moines to 2 = 100
Cost = $4,525

(e) Is the operating room being used to capacity? Is it possible to do more operations/year? If so, how many more? Discuss the effect of acquiring more operating room if needed.

⌨ : **11-19** Marc Smith's construction firm currently has three projects under way in various counties in Iowa. Each requires a specific supply of gravel. Three gravel pits are available in Iowa to provide for Smith's needs, but shipping costs differ from location to location. The table below summarizes the problem Smith faces. Determine the optimal shipping assignment so as to minimize total costs.

From ⟍ To	Job 1	Job 2	Job 3	Tonnage Allowance
Dubuque pit	$6	$8	$10	150
Davenport pit	$7	$11	$11	175
Des Moines pit	$4	$5	$12	275
Job requirements (in tons)	200	100	300	600

QA 11-20

⌨ : **11-20** Northwest General, a large hospital in Providence, Rhode Island, has initiated a new procedure to ensure that patients receive their meals while the food is still as hot as possible. The hospital will continue to prepare the food in its kitchen, but will now deliver it in bulk (not individual servings) to one of three new serving stations in the building. From there, the food will be reheated, meals will be placed on individual trays, loaded onto a cart, and distributed to the various floors and wings of the hospital.

The three new serving stations are as efficiently located as possible to reach the various hallways in the hospital. The number of trays that each station can serve are shown below:

LOCATION	CAPACITY (MEALS)
Station 5A	200
Station 3G	225
Station 1S	275

There are six wings to Northwest General that must be served. The number of patients in each follows:

WING	PATIENTS
1	80
2	120
3	150
4	210
5	60
6	80

The purpose of the new procedure is to increase the temperature of the hot meals that the patient receives. Therefore, the amount of time needed to deliver a tray from a serving station will determine the proper distribution of food from serving station to wing. The table below summarizes the time associated with each possible distribution channel.

What is your recommendation for handling the distribution of trays from the three serving stations?

				DISTRIBUTION TIME (minutes)			
FROM	TO	WING 1	WING 2	WING 3	WING 4	WING 5	WING 6
Station 5A		12	11	8	9	6	6
Station 3G		6	12	7	7	5	8
Station 1S		8	9	6	6	7	9

Source	Destination	Number of Trays
5A to	5	60
5A	6	80
5A	3	60
3G	1	80
3G	3	90
3G	4	55
1S	4	155
1S	2	120

Optimal cost: 4,825 minutes

CASE STUDY

Chase Manhattan Bank

The work load in many areas of bank operations has the characteristics of a nonuniform distribution with respect to time of day. For example, at Chase Manhattan Bank in New York, the number of domestic money transfer requests received from customers, if plotted against time of day, would appear to have the shape of an inverted U curve with the peak around 1 P.M. For efficient use of resources, the personnel available should, therefore, vary correspondingly. The accompanying illustration shows a typical work load curve and corresponding personnel requirements at different hours of the day.

A variable capacity can be achieved effectively by employing part-time personnel. Since part-timers are not entitled to all the fringe benefits,

they are often more economical than full-time employees. Other considerations, however, may limit the extent to which part-time people can be hired in a given department. The problem is to find an optimum work force schedule that would meet personnel requirements at any given time and also be economical.

Some of the factors affecting personnel assignment are listed here:

1. By corporate policy, part-time personnel hours are limited to a maximum of 40% of the day's total requirement.

2. Full-time employees work for eight hours (one hour for lunch included) per day. Thus, a full-timer's productive time is 35 hours per week.

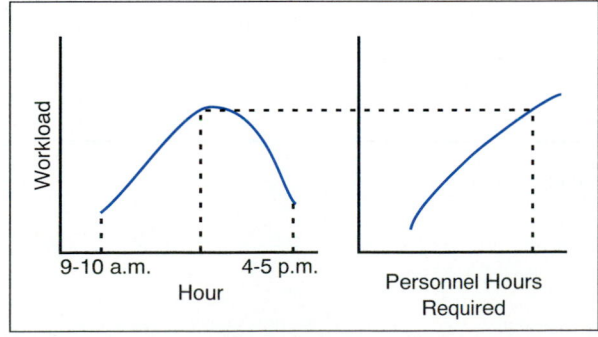

Work Load Curve

3. Part-timers work for at least four hours per day but less than eight hours and are not allowed a lunch break.

4. Fifty percent of the full-timers go to lunch between 11 A.M. and noon and the remaining 50% between noon and 1 P.M.

5. The shift starts at 9 A.M. and ends at 7 P.M. (that is, overtime is limited to two hours). Any work left over at 7 P.M. is considered holdover for the next day.

6. A full-time employee is not allowed to work more than five hours overtime per week. He or she is paid at the normal rate for overtime hours—*not* at one-and-a-half times the normal rate applicable to hours in excess of 40 per week. Fringe benefits are not applied to overtime hours.

In addition, the following costs are pertinent:

1. The average cost per full-time personnel hour (fringe benefits included) is $10.11.

2. The average cost per overtime personnel hour for full-timers (straight rate excluding fringe benefits) is $8.08.

3. The average cost per part-time personnel hour is $7.82.

The personnel hours required, by hour of day, are given in the table shown.

Source: Adapted by Barry Render from Shyam L. Moondra, "An L.P. Model for Work Force Scheduling for Banks," *Journal of Bank Research* Winter 1976.

Work Force Requirements

TIME PERIOD	NUMBER OF PERSONNEL REQUIRED
9–10 A.M.	14
10–11	25
11–12	26
12–1 P.M.	38
1–2	55
2–3	60
3–4	51
4–5	29
5–6	14
6–7	9

The bank's goal is to achieve the minimum possible personnel cost subject to meeting or exceeding the hourly work force requirements as well as the constraints on the workers listed earlier.

Discussion Questions

1. What is the minimum-cost schedule for the bank?

2. What are the limitations of the model used to answer the above question?

3. Costs might be reduced by relaxing the constraint that no more than 40% of the day's requirement be met by part-timers. Would changing the 40% to a higher value significantly reduce costs?

29 full-timers
11 part-timers starting at 11:00 A.M.

15 part-timers starting at noon
Cost = $3,476 per day
Alternate solutions exist.

BIBLIOGRAPHY

See Bibliography at end of Chapter 10.

12

Linear Programming: The Simplex Method

CHAPTER OUTLINE

12.1 Introduction

12.2 How to Set Up the Initial Simplex Solution

12.3 Simplex Solution Procedures

12.4 The Second Simplex Tableau

12.5 Developing the Third Tableau

12.6 Review of Procedures for Solving LP Maximization Problems

12.7 Surplus and Artificial Variables

12.8 Solving Minimization Problems

12.9 Review of Procedures for Solving LP Minimization Problems

12.10 Special Cases in Using the Simplex Method

12.11 Karmarkar's Algorithm

12.12 Summary

Glossary

Key Equation

Solved Problems

Discussion Questions and Problems

Case Study: Coastal States Chemicals and Fertilizers

Bibliography

12.1 INTRODUCTION

In Chapter 10 we looked at examples of linear programming problems that contained two decision variables. With only two variables it was possible to use a graphical approach. We plotted the feasible region and then searched for the optimal corner point and corresponding profit or cost. This approach provided a good way to understand the basic concepts of linear programming. Most real-life LP problems, however, have more than two variables and are thus too large for the simple graphical solution procedure. Problems faced in business and government can have dozens, hundreds, or even a thousand variables. We need a more powerful method than graphing—so in this chapter we turn to a procedure called the *simplex method*.

How does the simplex method work? The concept is simple, and similar to graphical LP in one important respect. In graphical linear programming we examined each of the corner points; LP theory told us that the optimal solution lies at one of them. In LP problems containing *several* variables, we may not be able to graph the feasible region, but the optimal solution will *still* lie at a corner point of the many-sided, many-dimensional figure (called an *n*-dimensional polyhedron) that represents the area of feasible solutions. The simplex method examines the corner points in a systematic fashion, using basic algebraic concepts. It does so in an *iterative* manner, that is, repeating the same set of procedures time after time until an optimal solution is reached. Each iteration brings a higher value for the objective function so that we are always moving closer to the optimal solution.

simplex as an iterative method

importance of simplex

Why should we study the simplex method? It is important to understand the ideas used to produce solutions. The simplex approach yields not only the optimal solution to the X_i variables and the maximum profit (or minimum cost), but valuable economic information as well.[1] To be able to use computers successfully and to interpret LP computer printouts, we need to know what the simplex method is doing and why.

In this chapter, we begin by solving a maximization problem using the simplex method. We then tackle a minimization problem and look at a few technical issues that are faced when employing the simplex procedure.

12.2 HOW TO SET UP THE INITIAL SIMPLEX SOLUTION

Transparency Master 12.1: Simplex Steps for Maximization.

Let us consider the case of the Flair Furniture Company from Chapter 10. Instead of the graphical solution we used in that chapter, we now demonstrate the simplex method. You may recall that we let

$$X_1 = \text{Number of tables produced}$$

Alternate Example 12.1

$$X_2 = \text{Number of chairs produced}$$

[1]The simplex method also applies for problems requiring integer solutions, as we see in Chapter 15.

and that the problem was formulated as:

Maximize profit $= \$7X_1 + \$5X_2$ *(objective function)*

Subject to: $2X_1 + 1X_2 \leq 100$ *(painting hours constraint)*

            $4X_1 + 3X_2 \leq 240$ *(carpentry hours constraint)*

            $X_1, \quad X_2 \geq 0$ *(nonnegativity constraints)*

Converting the Constraints to Equations

The first step of the simplex method requires that we convert each inequality constraint in an LP formulation into an equation.[2] Less-than-or-equal-to constraints ($\leq$) such as in the Flair problem are converted to equations by adding a *slack variable* to each constraint. Slack variables represent unused resources; these may be in the form of time on a machine, labor hours, money, warehouse space, or any number of such resources in various business problems.

In our case at hand, we can let

$S_1 =$ Slack variable representing unused hours
in the painting department

$S_2 =$ Slack variable representing unused hours
in the carpentry department

The constraints to the problem may now be written as:

$$2X_1 + 1X_2 + S_1 = 100$$

and

$$4X_1 + 3X_2 + S_2 = 240$$

Thus, if the production of tables (X_1) and chairs (X_2) uses less than 100 hours of painting time available, the unused time is the value of the slack variable, S_1. For example, if $X_1 = 0$ and $X_2 = 0$ (in other words, if nothing is produced), we have $S_1 = 100$ hours of slack time in the painting department. If Flair produces $X_1 = 40$ tables and $X_2 = 10$ chairs, then

$$2X_1 + 1X_2 + S_1 = 100$$
$$2(40) + 1(10) + S_1 = 100$$
$$S_1 = 10$$

and there will be 10 hours of slack, or unused, painting time available.

To include all variables in each equation, which is a requirement of the next simplex step, slack variables not appearing in an equation are added with a coefficient of 0. This means, in effect, that they have no influence on

slack variables

KEY IDEA

Teaching Suggestion 12.1:
The Meaning of Slack Variables. See the Instructor's Section for details.

---

[2]This is because the simplex is a matrix algebra method that requires all mathematical relationships to be equations, with each equation containing all of the variables.

the equations in which they are inserted; but it does allow us to keep tabs on all variables at all times. The equations now appear as:

$$2X_1 + 1X_2 + 1S_1 + 0S_2 = 100$$

$$4X_1 + 3X_2 + 0S_1 + 1S_2 = 240$$

$$X_1, X_2, S_1, S_2 \geqslant 0$$

Since slack variables yield no profit, they are added to the original objective function with 0 profit coefficients. The objective function becomes:

$$\text{Maximize profit} = \$7X_1 + \$5X_2 + \$0S_1 + \$0S_2$$

Finding an Initial Solution Algebraically

Let's take another look at the new constraint equations. We see that there are two equations and four variables. Think back to your last algebra course. When you have the same number of unknown variables as you have equations, it is possible to solve for unique values of the variables. But when there are four unknowns (X_1, X_2, S_1, and S_2, in this case) and only two equations, you can let two of the variables equal 0 and then solve for the other two. For example, if $X_1 = X_2 = 0$, then $S_1 = 100$ and $S_2 = 240$.

The simplex method begins with an initial feasible solution in which all real variables (such as X_1 and X_2) are set equal to 0. This trivial solution always produces a profit of $0, as well as slack variables equal to the constant (right-hand-side) terms in the constraint equations. It's not a very exciting solution in terms of economic returns, but it is one of the original corner point solutions (see Figure 12.1). As mentioned, the simplex method will start at this corner point (A), then move up or over to the corner point that yields the most improved profit (B or D). Finally, the technique will move to a new corner point (C), which happens to be the optimal solution to the Flair Furniture problem. The simplex method considers only feasible solutions and hence will touch no possible combinations other than the corner points of the shaded region in Figure 12.1.

simplex considers only corner points

The First Simplex Tableau

Applicable Problems 12-11, 12-12

To simplify handling the equations and objective function in an LP problem, we place all of the coefficients into a tabular form. The first *simplex tableau* is shown in Table 12.1. An explanation of its parts and how the tableau is derived follows.

Constraint Equations. We see that Flair Furniture's two constraint equations can be expressed as:

constraints in tabular form

SOLUTION MIX	X_1	X_2	S_1	S_2	QUANTITY (RIGHT-HAND SIDE)
S_1	2	1	1	0	100
S_2	4	3	0	1	240

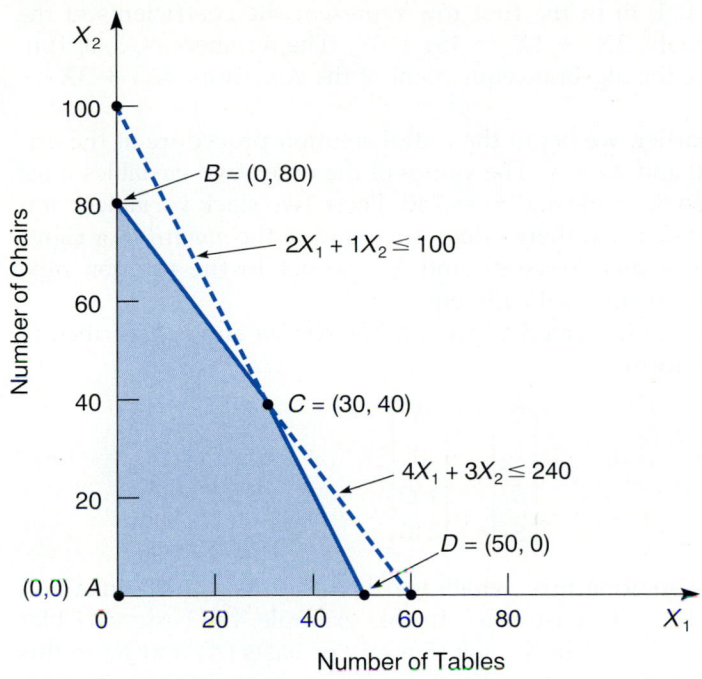

FIGURE 12.1

Corner Points of the Flair Furniture Company Problem

Transparency Master 12.2:
Flair Furniture Company's Feasible Region and Corner Points.

TABLE 12.1 Flair Furniture's Initial Simplex Tableau

		Profit per Unit Column →	Production Mix Column →	Real Variables Columns →		Slack Variables Columns →		Constant Column →	

$C_j \rightarrow$	Solution	$7	$5	$0	$0		Profit per
↓	Mix	X_1	X_2	S_1	S_2	Quantity	unit row
$0	S_1	2	1	1	0	100	Constraint
$0	S_2	4	3	0	1	240	equation rows
	Z_j	$0	$0	$0	$0	$0 ←	Gross profit row
	$C_j - Z_j$	$7	$5	$0	$0	$0 ←	Net profit row

Transparency Master 12.3:
Flair Furniture's Initial Simplex Tableau.

The numbers (2, 1, 1, 0) in the first row represent the coefficients of the first equation, namely, $2X_1 + 1X_2 + 1S_1 + 0S_2$. The numbers (4, 3, 0, 1) in the second row are the algebraic equivalent of the constraint $4X_1 + 3X_2 + 0S_1 + 1S_2$.

As suggested earlier, we begin the initial solution procedure at the origin, where $X_1 = 0$ and $X_2 = 0$. The values of the other two variables must then be nonzero, so $S_1 = 100$ and $S_2 = 240$. These two slack variables comprise the *initial solution mix;* their values are found in the *quantity* (or right-hand-side—RHS) *column.* Since X_1 and X_2 are not in the solution mix, their initial values are automatically equal to 0.

This initial solution is termed a *basic feasible solution* and is described in vector, or column, form as:

$$\begin{bmatrix} X_1 \\ X_2 \\ S_1 \\ S_2 \end{bmatrix} = \begin{bmatrix} 0 \\ 0 \\ 100 \\ 240 \end{bmatrix}$$

Variables in the solution mix, which is called the *basis* in LP terminology, are referred to as *basic variables.* In this example, the basic variables are S_1 and S_2. Variables not in the solution mix or basis (X_1 and X_2 in this case) are called *nonbasic variables.* Of course, if the optimal solution to this linear programming problem turned out to be $X_1 = 30$, $X_2 = 40$, $S_1 = 0$, and $S_2 = 0$, or

$$\begin{bmatrix} X_1 \\ X_2 \\ S_1 \\ S_2 \end{bmatrix} = \begin{bmatrix} 30 \\ 40 \\ 0 \\ 0 \end{bmatrix} \quad \text{in vector form,}$$

then X_1 and X_2 would be the final basic variables, while S_1 and S_2 would be the nonbasic variables.

Substitution Rates. Many students are unsure as to the actual meaning of the numbers in the columns under each variable. We know that the entries are the coefficients for that variable. Under X_1 are the coefficients $\binom{2}{4}$, under X_2 are $\binom{1}{3}$, under S_1 are $\binom{1}{0}$, and under S_2 are $\binom{0}{1}$. But what is their interpretation? The numbers in the body of the simplex tableau (see Table 12.1) may be thought of as *substitution rates.* For example, suppose we now wish to make X_1 larger than 0, that is, produce some tables. For every unit of the X_1 product introduced into the current solution, 2 units of S_1 and 4 units of S_2 must be removed from the solution. This is so because each table requires 2 hours of the currently unused painting department slack time, S_1. It also takes 4 hours of carpentry time; hence 4 units of variable S_2 must be removed from the solution for every unit of X_1 that enters. Likewise, the substitution rates for each unit of X_2 that enters the current solution are 1 unit of S_1 and 3 units of S_2.

initial solution mix

Teaching Suggestion 12.2:
Initial Solutions to LP Problems. See the Instructor's Section for details.

basic feasible solution

basic and nonbasic variables

Teaching Suggestion 12.3:
The Substitution Rates in a Simplex Table. See the Instructor's Section for details.

substitution rates

KEY IDEA

Another point that you are reminded of throughout this chapter is that for any variable ever to appear in the solution mix column, it must have the number 1 someplace in its column and 0s in every other place in that column. We see that column S_1 contains $\binom{1}{0}$, so variable S_1 is in the solution. Likewise, the S_2 column is $\binom{0}{1}$, so S_2 is also in the solution.[3]

Adding the Objective Function. We now continue to the next step in establishing the first simplex tableau. We add a row to reflect the objective function values for each variable. These contribution rates, called C_j, appear just above each respective variable as seen below:

$C_j \rightarrow$	SOLUTION MIX	$7 X_1	$5 X_2	$0 S_1	$0 S_2	QUANTITY
$0	S_1	2	1	1	0	100
$0	S_2	4	3	0	1	240

The unit profit rates are not just found in the top C_j row: in the left-most column, C_j indicates the unit profit for each variable *currently* in the solution mix. If S_1 were removed from the solution and replaced, for example, by X_2, then $5 would appear in the C_j column just to the left of the term X_2.

The Z_j and $C_j - Z_j$ Rows. We may complete the initial Flair Furniture simplex tableau by adding two final rows. These last two rows provide us with important economic information, including the total profit and the answer as to whether the current solution is optimal.

We compute the Z_j value for each column of the initial solution in Table 12.1 by multiplying the 0 contribution value of each number in the C_j column by each number in that row and the jth column, and summing. The Z_j value for the quantity column provides the total contribution (gross profit in this case) of the given solution.

adding the Z and $C - Z$ rows

Z_j (For gross profit) = (Profit per unit of S_1) $\times$ (Number of units of S_1)

$\qquad\qquad\qquad$ + (Profit per unit of S_2) $\times$ (Number of units of S_2)

$\qquad\qquad$ = $0 $\times$ 100 units + $0 $\times$ 240 units

$\qquad\qquad$ = $0 profit

---

[3]If there had been *three* less-than-or-equal-to constraints in the Flair Furniture problem, then there would be three slack variables, S_1, S_2 and S_3. The 1s and 0s would appear like this:

SOLUTION MIX	S_1	S_2	S_3
S_1	1	0	0
S_2	0	1	0
S_3	0	0	1

The Z_j values for the other columns (under the variables X_1, X_2, S_1, and S_2) represent the gross profit *given up* by adding one unit of this variable into the current solution. Their calculations are as follows:

$$Z_j \text{ (For column } X_1) = (\$0)(2) + (\$0)(4) = \$0$$

$$Z_j \text{ (For column } X_2) = (\$0)(1) + (\$0)(3) = \$0$$

$$Z_j \text{ (For column } S_1) = (\$0)(1) + (\$0)(0) = \$0$$

$$Z_j \text{ (For column } S_2) = (\$0)(0) + (\$0)(1) = \$0$$

We see that there is no profit *lost* by adding one unit of either X_1 (tables), X_2 (chairs), S_1, or S_2.

$C_j - Z_j$ is the net profit row

The $C_j - Z_j$ number in each column represents the net profit, that is, the profit gained minus the profit given up, that will result from introducing 1 unit of each product or variable into the solution. It is not calculated for the quantity column. To compute these numbers, simply subtract the Z_j total for each column from the C_j value at the very top of that variable's column. The calculations for the net profit per unit (the $C_j - Z_j$ row) in this example are:

	COLUMN			
	X_1	X_2	S_1	S_2
C_j for column	$7	$5	$0	$0
Z_j for column	$0	$0	$0	$0
$C_j - Z_j$ for column	$7	$5	$0	$0

reaching an optimal solution

It was obvious to us when we computed a profit of $0 that the initial solution was not optimal. By examining the numbers in the $C_j - Z_j$ row of Table 12.1, we see that the total profit can be increased by $7 for each unit of X_1 (tables) and by $5 for each unit of X_2 (chairs) added to the solution mix. A negative number in the $C_j - Z_j$ row would tell us that profits would *decrease* if the corresponding variable were added to the solution mix. An optimal solution is reached in the simplex method when the $C_j - Z_j$ row contains no positive numbers. Such is not the case in our initial tableau.

KEY IDEA

Applicable Problems 12-13, 12-14, 12-18, 12-23, 12-24, 12-25

12.3 SIMPLEX SOLUTION PROCEDURES

Once an initial tableau has been completed, we proceed through a series of five steps to compute all the numbers needed in the next tableau. The calculations are not difficult, but they are complex enough that even the smallest arithmetic error can produce a wrong answer.

five simplex steps

We first list the five steps and then carefully explain and apply them in completing the second and third tableaus for the Flair Furniture Company data.

variable entering

Step 1: Determine which variable to enter into the solution mix next. One way of doing this is by identifying the column, and hence, the variable, with the largest positive number in the $C_j - Z_j$ row of the previous tableau. This means that we will now be producing some of the product contributing the greatest additional profit per unit. The column identified in this step is called the *pivot column*.

Step 2: Determine which variable to replace. Since we have just chosen a new variable to enter the solution mix, we must decide which basic variable currently in the solution will have to leave to make room for it. Step 2 is accomplished by dividing each amount in the *quantity* column by the corresponding number in the column selected in step 1. The row with the *smallest nonnegative number* calculated in this fashion will be replaced in the next tableau. (This smallest number, by the way, gives the maximum number of units of the variable which may be placed in the solution.) This row is often referred to as the *pivot row*. The number at the intersection of the pivot row and pivot column is referred to as the *pivot number*.

Step 3: Compute new values for the pivot row. To do this, we simply divide every number in the row by the pivot number.

Step 4: Compute the new values for each remaining row. (In our Flair Furniture problem there are only two rows in the LP tableau, but most larger problems have many more rows.) All remaining row(s) are calculated as follows:

(New row numbers) = (Numbers in old row) −

$$\left[\left(\begin{array}{l} \text{Number above or below} \\ \text{pivot number} \end{array} \right) \times \left(\begin{array}{l} \text{Corresponding number in} \\ \text{the new row, that is, the} \\ \text{row replaced in step 3} \end{array} \right) \right] \quad \text{(12-1)}$$

Step 5: Compute the Z_j and $C_j - Z_j$ rows, as previously demonstrated in the initial tableau. If all numbers in the $C_j - Z_j$ row are 0 or negative, an optimal solution has been reached. If this is not the case, return to step 1.

(margin notes:) variable leaving · new pivot row · other new rows · Z_j and $C_j - Z_j$ rows

12.4   THE SECOND SIMPLEX TABLEAU

Now that we have listed the five steps needed to move from an initial solution to an improved solution, we apply them to the Flair Furniture problem. Our goal is to add a new variable to the solution mix, or basis, in order to raise the profit from its current tableau value of $0.

(margin note:) applying the five steps

Step 1: To decide which of the variables will enter the solution next (it must be either X_1 or X_2, since they are the only two nonbasic variables at this point), we select the one with the largest positive $C_j - Z_j$ value. Variable X_1, tables, has a $C_j - Z_j$ value of $7, implying that each unit of X_1 added into the solution mix will contribute $7 to the overall profit. Variable X_2, chairs, has a $C_j - Z_j$ value of only $5. The other two variables, S_1 and S_2, have 0 values, and can add nothing more to profit. Hence, we select X_1 as the variable to enter the solution mix, and identify its column (with an arrow) as the pivot column. This is shown in Table 12.2.

(margin note:) X_1 (tables) enters the solution mix

TABLE 12.2 Pivot Column Identified in the Initial Simplex Tableau

$C_j \rightarrow$	Solution Mix	$7 X_1	$5 X_2	$0 S_1	$0 S_2	Quantity (RHS)
$0	S_1	2	1	1	0	100
$0	S_2	4	3	0	1	240
	Z_j	$0	$0	$0	$0	$0
	$C_j - Z_j$	$7	$5	$0	$0	(total profit)

Pivot column

Step 2: Since X_1 is about to enter the solution mix, we must decide which variable is to be replaced. There can only be as many basic variables as there are constraints in any LP problem, so either S_1 or S_2 will have to leave to make room for the introduction of X_1, tables, into the basis. To identify the pivot row, each number in the quantity column is divided by the corresponding number in the X_1 column.

For the S_1 row:

$$\frac{100 \text{ (hours of painting time available)}}{2 \text{ (hours required per table)}} = 50 \text{ tables}$$

For the S_2 row:

$$\frac{240 \text{ (hours of carpentry time available)}}{4 \text{ (hours required per table)}} = 60 \text{ tables}$$

S_1 leaves the solution mix

The smaller of these two ratios, 50, indicates the maximum number of units of X_1 that can be produced without violating either of the original constraints. It also points out that the pivot row will be the first row. This means that S_1 will be the variable to be replaced at this iteration of the simplex method. The pivot row and the pivot number (the number at the intersection of the pivot row and pivot column) are identified in Table 12.3.

Step 3: Now that we have decided which variable is to enter the solution mix (X_1) and which is to leave (S_1), we begin to develop the second,

TABLE 12.3 Pivot Row and Pivot Number Identified in the Initial Simplex Tableau

Transparency Master 12.4: Pivot Row and Pivot Number Identified in the Initial Simplex Tableau.

$C_j \rightarrow$	Solution Mix	$7 X_1	$5 X_2	$0 S_1	$0 S_2	Quantity
$0	S_1	②	1	1	0	100 ← Pivot row
$0	S_2	4	3	0	1	240
	Z_j	$0	$0	$0	$0	$0
	$C_j - Z_j$	$7	$5	$0	$0	

Pivot number

Pivot column

improved simplex tableau. Step 3 involves computing a replacement for the pivot row. This is done by dividing every number in the pivot row by the pivot number:

$$\frac{2}{2} = 1 \qquad \frac{1}{2} = \frac{1}{2} \qquad \frac{1}{2} = \frac{1}{2} \qquad \frac{0}{2} = 0 \qquad \frac{100}{2} = 50$$

the new pivot row

The new version of the entire pivot row appears in the accompanying table. Note that X_1 is now in the solution mix and that 50 units of X_1 are being produced. The C_j value is listed as a \$7 contribution per unit of X_1 in the solution. This will definitely provide Flair Furniture with a more profitable solution than the \$0 generated in the initial tableau.

C_j	SOLUTION MIX	X_1	X_2	S_1	S_2	QUANTITY
\$7	X_1	1	$1/2$	$1/2$	0	50

Step 4: This step is intended to help us compute new values for the other row in the body of the tableau, that is, the S_2 row. It is slightly more complex than replacing the pivot row and uses the formula (Equation 12.1) shown earlier. The expression on the right side of the following equation is used to calculate the left side.

recomputing the S_2 row

$\begin{pmatrix} \text{NUMBER IN} \\ \text{NEW } S_2 \text{ ROW} \end{pmatrix}$	$=$	$\begin{pmatrix} \text{NUMBER IN} \\ \text{OLD } S_2 \text{ ROW} \end{pmatrix}$	$-$	$\left[\begin{pmatrix} \text{NUMBER BELOW} \\ \text{PIVOT NUMBER} \end{pmatrix} \right.$	$\times$	$\left. \begin{pmatrix} \text{CORRESPONDING NUMBER} \\ \text{IN THE NEW } X_1 \text{ ROW} \end{pmatrix} \right]$
0	$=$	4	$-$	(4)	$\times$	(1)
1	$=$	3	$-$	(4)	$\times$	($1/2$)
-2	$=$	0	$-$	(4)	$\times$	($1/2$)
1	$=$	1	$-$	(4)	$\times$	(0)
40	$=$	240	$-$	(4)	$\times$	(50)

This new S_2 row will appear in the second tableau in the following format:

C_j	SOLUTION MIX	X_1	X_2	S_1	S_2	QUANTITY
\$7	X_1	1	$1/2$	$1/2$	0	50
\$0	S_2	0	1	-2	1	40

Now that X_1 and S_2 are in the solution mix, take a look at the values of the coefficients in their respective columns. The X_1 column contains $\begin{pmatrix} 1 \\ 0 \end{pmatrix}$, a condition necessary for that variable to be in the solution. Likewise, the S_2 column has $\begin{pmatrix} 0 \\ 1 \end{pmatrix}$, that is, it contains a 1 and a 0. Basically, the algebraic manipulations we just went through in steps 3 and 4 were simply directed at producing 0s and 1s in the appropriate positions. In step 3 we divided every number in the pivot row by the pivot number; this guaranteed that

KEY IDEA

there would be a 1 in the X_1 column's top row. To derive the new second row, we multiplied the first row (each row is really an equation) by a constant (the number 4 here), and subtracted it from the second equation. The result was the new S_2 row with a 0 in the X_1 column.

Step 5: The final step of the second iteration is to introduce the effect of the objective function. This involves computing the Z_j and $C_j - Z_j$ rows. Recall that the Z_j entry for the quantity column gives us the gross profit for the current solution. The other Z_j values represent the gross profit given up by adding one unit of each variable into this new solution. The Z_j values are calculated as follows:

finding the new profit

$$Z_j \text{ (for } X_1 \text{ column)} = (\$7)(1) + (\$0)(0) = \$7$$

$$Z_j \text{ (for } X_2 \text{ column)} = (\$7)(\tfrac{1}{2}) + (\$0)(1) = \$\tfrac{7}{2}$$

$$Z_j \text{ (for } S_1 \text{ column)} = (\$7)(\tfrac{1}{2}) + (\$0)(-2) = \$\tfrac{7}{2}$$

$$Z_j \text{ (for } S_2 \text{ column)} = (\$7)(0) + (\$0)(1) = \$0$$

$$Z_j \text{ (for total profit)} = (\$7)(50) + (\$0)(40) = \$350$$

Note that the current profit is $350.

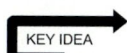

The $C_j - Z_j$ numbers represent the net profit that will result, given our present production mix, if we add one unit of each variable into the solution.

	COLUMN			
	X_1	X_2	S_1	S_2
C_j for column	$7	$5	$0	$0
Z_j for column	$7	$\tfrac{7}{2}$	$\tfrac{7}{2}$	$0
$C_j - Z_j$ for column	$0	$\tfrac{3}{2}$	$-\tfrac{7}{2}$	$0

The Z_j and $C_j - Z_j$ rows are inserted into the complete second tableau as shown in Table 12.4.

Interpreting the Second Tableau

Table 12.4 summarizes all of the information for the Flair Furniture Company's production mix decision as of the second iteration of the simplex method. Let's briefly look over a few important items.

TABLE 12.4 Completed Second Simplex Tableau for Flair Furniture

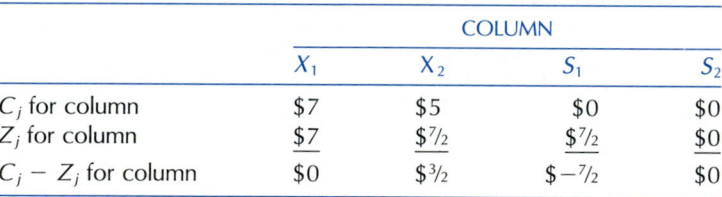

$C_j \rightarrow$ ↓	SOLUTION MIX	$7 X_1	$5 X_2	$0 S_1	$0 S_2	QUANTITY
$7	X_1	1	$\tfrac{1}{2}$	$\tfrac{1}{2}$	0	50
$0	S_2	0	1	-2	1	40
	Z_j	$7	$\tfrac{7}{2}$	$\tfrac{7}{2}$	$0	$350
	$C_j - Z_j$	$0	$\tfrac{3}{2}$	$-\tfrac{7}{2}$	$0	

Current Solution. At this point, the solution point of 50 tables and 0 chairs ($X_1 = 50$, $X_2 = 0$) generates a profit of $350. X_1 is a basic variable; X_2 is a nonbasic variable. Using a graphical LP approach, this corresponds to corner point D, as shown in Figure 12.2.

current solution as corner point in graphical method

Resource Information. We also see in Table 12.4 that slack variable S_2, representing the amount of unused time in the carpentry department, is in the basis. It has a value of 40, implying that 40 hours of carpentry time remain available. Slack variable S_1 is nonbasic, and has a value of 0 hours. There is no slack time in the painting department.

Substitution Rates. We mentioned earlier that the substitution rates are the coefficients in the heart of the tableau. Look at the X_2 column. If 1 unit of X_2 (1 chair) is added to the current solution, ½ unit of X_1 and 1 unit of S_2 must be given up. This is because the solution $X_1 = 50$ tables uses up all 100 hours of time in the painting department. (The original constraint, you may recall, was $2X_1 + 1X_2 + S_1 = 100$.) To capture the 1 painting hour needed to make 1 chair, ½ of a table *less* must be produced. This frees up 1 hour to be used in making 1 chair.

meaning of substitution rates

But why must 1 unit of S_2 (namely, 1 hour of carpentry time) be given up in order to produce 1 chair? The original constraint was $4X_1 + 3X_2 + S_2 = 240$ hours of carpentry time. Doesn't this indicate that 3 hours of carpentry time are required to produce 1 unit of X_2? The answer is that we are look-

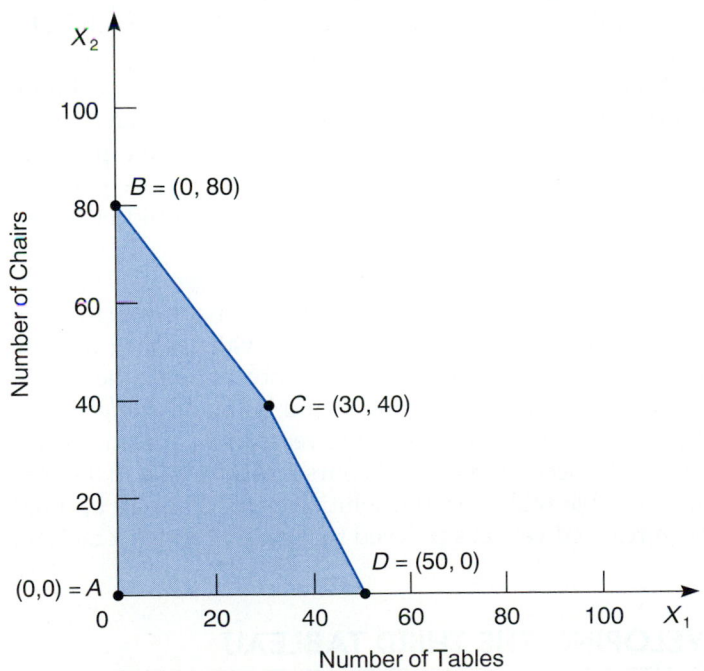

FIGURE 12.2
Flair Furniture Company's Feasible Region and Corner Points

ing at *marginal* rates of substitution. Adding 1 chair replaced ½ table. Since ½ table required (½ × 4 hours per table) = 2 hours of carpentry time, 2 units of S_2 are freed. Thus only 1 *more* unit of S_2 is needed to produce 1 chair.

Just to be sure you have this concept down pat, let's look at one more column, S_1, as well. The coefficients are $\begin{pmatrix} \frac{1}{2} \\ -2 \end{pmatrix}$. These substitution rate values mean that if 1 hour of slack painting time is added to the current solution, ½ of a table (X_1) *less* will be produced. However, note that if 1 unit of S_1 is added into the solution, 2 hours of carpentry time (S_2) will no longer be used. These will be *added* to the current 40 slack hours of carpentry time. Hence, a *negative* substitution rate means that if 1 unit of a column variable is added to the solution, the value of the corresponding solution (or row) variable will be increased. A *positive* substitution rate tells us that if 1 unit of the column variable is added to the solution, the row variable will decrease by the rate.

Can you interpret the rates in the X_1 and S_2 columns now?

is solution optimal?

Net Profit Row. The $C_j - Z_j$ row is important to us for two reasons. First, it indicates whether or not the current solution is optimal. When there are no positive numbers in the bottom row, an optimum solution to an LP maximization problem has been reached. In the case of Table 12.4, we see that $C_j - Z_j$ values for X_1, S_1, and S_2 are 0 or negative. The value for X_2 (³⁄₂) means that the net profit can be increased by $1.50 (= ³⁄₂) for each chair added into the current solution.

Because the $C_j - Z_j$ value for X_1 is 0, for every unit of X_1 added the total profit will remain unchanged, because we are already producing as many tables as possible. A negative number, such as the $-\frac{7}{2}$ in the S_1 column, implies that total profit will *decrease* by $3.50 if 1 unit of S_1 is added to the solution. In other words, making one slack hour available in the painting department ($S_1 = 0$ currently) means we would have to produce one half table less. Since each table results in a $7 contribution, we would be losing ½ × $7 = $⁷⁄₂, for a net loss of $3.50.

shadow prices

In Chapter 13, we discuss in detail the subject of *shadow prices*. These relate to $C_j - Z_j$ values in the slack variable columns. Shadow prices are simply another way of interpreting negative $C_j - Z_j$ values; they may be viewed as the potential *increase* in profit if one more hour of the scarce resource (such as painting or carpentry time) could be made *available*.

Teaching Suggestion 12.4:
The Importance of Shadow Prices. See the Instructor's Section for details.

We mentioned previously that there are two reasons to consider carefully the $C_j - Z_j$ row. The second reason, of course, is that we use the row to determine which variable will enter the solution next. Since an optimal solution has not been reached yet, let's proceed to the third simplex tableau.

12.5 DEVELOPING THE THIRD TABLEAU

Since not all numbers in the $C_j - Z_j$ row of the latest tableau are 0 or negative, the previous solution is not optimal, and we must repeat the five simplex steps.

Step 1: Variable X_2 will enter the solution next by virtue of the fact that its $C_j - Z_j$ value of $\frac{3}{2}$ is the largest (and only) positive number in the row. This means that for every unit of X_2 (chairs) we start to produce, the objective function will increase in value by $\$\frac{3}{2}$, or $\$1.50$. The X_2 column is the new pivot column.

Step 2: The next step involves identifying the pivot row. The question is, which variable currently in the solution (X_1 or S_2) will have to leave to make room for X_2 to enter? Again, each number in the quantity column is divided by its corresponding number in the X_2 column.

$$\text{For the } X_1 \text{ row: } \frac{50}{\frac{1}{2}} = 100 \text{ chairs}$$

$$\text{For the } S_2 \text{ row: } \frac{40}{1} = 40 \text{ chairs}$$

The S_2 row has the smallest ratio, meaning that variable S_2 will leave the basis and be replaced by X_2. The new pivot row, pivot column, and pivot number are all shown in Table 12.5.

Step 3: The pivot row is replaced by dividing every number in it by the (circled) pivot number. Since every number is divided by 1, there is no change.

$$\frac{0}{1} = 0 \quad \frac{1}{1} = 1 \quad \frac{-2}{1} = -2 \quad \frac{1}{1} = 1 \quad \frac{40}{1} = 40$$

The entire new X_2 row looks like this:

C_j	SOLUTION MIX	X_1	X_2	S_1	S_2	QUANTITY
$5	X_2	0	1	−2	1	40

It will be placed in the new simplex tableau in the same row position that S_2 was in before (see Table 12.6).

TABLE 12.5 Pivot Row, Pivot Column, and Pivot Number Identified in the Second Simplex Tableau

$C_j \rightarrow$ $\downarrow$	Solution Mix	$7 X_1	$5 X_2	$0 S_1	$0 S_2	Quantity
$7	X_1	1	$\frac{1}{2}$	$\frac{1}{2}$	0	50
$0	S_2	0	① Pivot number	−2	1	40 ← Pivot row
	Z_j	$7	$\frac{7}{2}$	$\frac{7}{2}$	$0	$350
	$C_j - Z_j$	$0	$\frac{3}{2}$	−$\frac{7}{2}$	$0	(Total Profit)
		Pivot column ↗				

(right margin notes)

X_2 (chairs) will be the next new variable

replacing a variable, S_2, in this case

pivot row for the third tableau

Transparency Master 12.6: Pivot Row, Pivot Column, and Pivot Number Identified in the Second Simplex Tableau.

Step 4: The new values for the X_1 row may now be computed.

$$\begin{pmatrix} \text{Number} \\ \text{in new} \\ X_1 \text{ row} \end{pmatrix} = \begin{pmatrix} \text{Number} \\ \text{in old} \\ X_1 \text{ row} \end{pmatrix} - \left[\begin{bmatrix} \text{Number} \\ \text{above} \\ \text{pivot} \\ \text{number} \end{bmatrix} \times \begin{pmatrix} \text{Corresponding} \\ \text{no. in new} \\ X_2 \text{ row} \end{pmatrix} \right]$$

the new X_1 row

1	=	1	−	(½)	×	(0)
0	=	½	−	(½)	×	(1)
³⁄₂	=	½	−	(½)	×	(−2)
−½	=	0	−	(½)	×	(1)
30	=	50	−	(½)	×	(40)

Hence, the new X_1 row will appear in the third tableau in the following position:

C_j	SOLUTION MIX	X_1	X_2	S_1	S_2	QUANTITY
$7	X_1	1	0	³⁄₂	−½	30
$5	X_2	0	1	−2	1	40

final step

Step 5: Finally, the Z_j and $C_j - Z_j$ rows for third tableau are calculated:

$$Z_j \text{ (for } X_1 \text{ column)} = (\$7)(1) + (\$5)(0) = \$7$$

$$Z_j \text{ (for } X_2 \text{ column)} = (\$7)(0) + (\$5)(1) = \$5$$

$$Z_j \text{ (for } S_1 \text{ column)} = (\$7)(³⁄₂) + (\$5)(-2) = \$½$$

$$Z_j \text{ (for } S_2 \text{ column)} = (\$7)(-½) + (\$5)(1) = \$³⁄₂$$

$$Z_j \text{ (for total profit)} = (\$7)(30) + (\$5)(40) = \$410$$

The net profit per unit row appears as follows:

	COLUMN			
	X_1	X_2	S_1	S_2
C_j for column	$7	$5	$0	$0
Z_j for column	$7	$5	$½	$³⁄₂
$C_j - Z_j$ for column	$0	$0	−$½	−$³⁄₂

TABLE 12.6 Final Simplex Tableau for the Flair Furniture Problem

$C_j \rightarrow$ $\downarrow$	SOLUTION MIX	$7 X_1	$5 X_2	$0 S_1	$0 S_2	QUANTITY
$7	X_1	1	0	³⁄₂	−½	30
$5	X_2	0	1	−2	1	40
	Z_j	$7	$5	$½	$³⁄₂	$410
	$C_j - Z_j$	$0	$0	−$½	−$³⁄₂	

All results for the third iteration of the simplex method are summarized in Table 12.6. Note that since every number in the tableau's $C_j - Z_j$ row is 0 or negative, an optimal solution has been reached.

That solution is:

optimal solution reached

final solution

$$X_1 = 30 \text{ tables} \qquad X_2 = 40 \text{ chairs}$$

$$S_1 = 0 \text{ slack hours in the painting department}$$

$$S_2 = 0 \text{ slack hours in the carpentry department}$$

$$\text{Profit} = \$410 \text{ for the optimal solution}$$

X_1 and X_2 are the final basic variables, while S_1 and S_2 are nonbasic (and thus automatically equal to 0). This solution corresponds to corner point C in Figure 12.2.

Since it's always possible to make an arithmetic error when you are going through the numerous simplex steps and iterations, it is a good idea to verify your final solution. This can be done in part by looking at the original Flair Furniture Company constraints and objective function.

verifying the solution

First constraint: $2X_1 + 1X_2 \leqslant 100$ painting department hours

$$2(30) + 1(40) \leqslant 100$$

$$100 \leqslant 100 \checkmark$$

Second constraint: $4X_1 + 3X_2 \leqslant 240$ carpentry department hours

$$4(30) + 3(40) \leqslant 240$$

$$240 \leqslant 240 \checkmark$$

Objective function: Profit $= \$7X_1 + \$5X_2$

$$= \$7(30) + \$5(40)$$

$$= \$410$$

12.6 REVIEW OF PROCEDURES FOR SOLVING LP MAXIMIZATION PROBLEMS

Before moving on to other issues concerning the simplex method, we briefly review what we've learned so far for LP maximization problems.

simplex steps reviewed

I. Formulate the LP problem's objective function and constraints.

II. Add slack variables to each less-than-or-equal-to constraint and to the problem's objective function.

III. Develop an initial simplex tableau with slack variables in the basis and their variables (the X_is) set equal to 0. Compute the Z_j and $C_j - Z_j$ values for this tableau.

IV. Follow these five steps until an optimal solution has been reached:

    A. Choose the variable with the greatest positive $C_j - Z_j$ to enter the solution. This is the pivot column.

Teaching Suggestion 12.5: Hand Calculations in a Simplex Table. See the Instructor's Section for details.

B. Determine the row to be replaced by selecting the one with the smallest (nonnegative) quantity-to-pivot column ratio. This is the pivot row.

C. Calculate the new values for the pivot row.

D. Calculate the new values for the other row(s).

E. Calculate the Z_j and $C_j - Z_j$ values for this tableau. If there are any $C_j - Z_j$ numbers greater than 0, return to step A. If there are no $C_j - Z_j$ numbers that are greater than 0, an optimal solution has been reached.

12.7   SURPLUS AND ARTIFICIAL VARIABLES

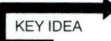
KEY IDEA

Up to this point in the chapter, all of the linear programming constraints you have seen were of the less-than-or-equal-to ($\leq$) variety. Just as common in real-life problems—especially in LP minimization problems—are greater-than-or-equal-to ($\geq$) constraints and equalities. To use the simplex method, each of these must be converted to a special form also. If they are not, the simplex technique is unable to set up an initial feasible solution in the first tableau.

Before moving on to the next section of this chapter which deals with solving LP minimization problems with the simplex method, we take a look at how to convert a few typical constraints.

$$\text{Constraint 1:}\quad 5X_1 + 10X_2 + 8X_3 \geq 210$$

$$\text{Constraint 2: } 25X_1 + 30X_2 = 900$$

Surplus Variables

subtracting surplus variables to form equalities

Greater-than-or-equal-to ($\geq$) constraints, such as constraint 1 as just described, require a different approach than do the less-than-or-equal-to ($\leq$) constraints we saw in the Flair Furniture problem. They involve the subtraction of a *surplus variable*, rather than the addition of a slack variable. The surplus variable tells us how much the solution exceeds the constraint resource. Because of its analogy to a slack variable, surplus is sometimes simply called *negative slack*. To convert the first constraint, we begin by subtracting a surplus variable, S_1, to create an equality.

$$\text{Constraint 1 rewritten: } 5X_1 + 10X_2 + 8X_3 - S_1 = 210$$

If, for example, a solution to an LP problem involving this constraint is $X_1 = 20$, $X_2 = 8$, $X_3 = 5$, then the amount of surplus, or unused resource, could be computed as follows:

$$5X_1 + 10X_2 + 8X_3 - S_1 = 210$$

$$5(20) + 10(8) + 8(5) - S_1 = 210$$

$$100 + 80 + 40 - S_1 = 210$$

$$-S_1 = 210 - 220$$

$$S_1 = 10 \text{ Surplus units of first resource}$$

There is one more step, however, in preparing a $\geq$ constraint for the simplex method.

Artificial Variables

There is one small problem in trying to use the first constraint (as it has just been rewritten) in setting up an initial simplex solution. Since all "real" variables such as X_1, X_2, and X_3 are set to 0 in the initial tableau, S_1 takes on a negative value.

$$5(0) + 10(0) + 8(0) - S_1 = 210$$
$$0 - S_1 = 210$$
$$S_1 = -210$$

All variables in LP problems, be they real, slack, or surplus, *must* be non-negative at all times. If $S_1 = -210$, this important condition is violated.

To resolve the situation, we introduce one last kind of variable, called an *artificial variable*. We simply add the artificial variable, A_1, to the constraint as follows:

artificial variables

Constraint 1 completed: $5X_1 + 10X_2 + 8X_3 - S_1 + A_1 = 210$

Now, not only the X_1, X_2, and X_3 variables may be set to 0 in the initial simplex solution, but the S_1 surplus variable as well. This leaves us with $A_1 = 210$.

Let's turn our attention to constraint 2 for a moment. This constraint is already an equality, so why worry about it? To be included in the initial simplex solution, it turns out, even an equality must have an artifical variable added to it.

Constraint 2 rewritten: $25X_1 + 30X_2 + A_2 = 900$

The reason for inserting an artificial variable into an equality constraint deals with the usual problem of finding an initial LP solution. In a simple constraint such as number 2, it's easy to guess that $X_1 = 0$, $X_2 = 30$ would yield an initial feasible solution. But what if our problem had ten equality constraints, each containing seven variables? It would be *extremely* difficult to sit down and "eyeball" a set of initial solutions. By adding artificial variables, such as A_2, we can provide an automatic initial solution. In this case, when X_1 and X_2 are set equal to 0, $A_2 = 900$.

Artificial variables have no meaning in a physical sense, and are nothing more than computational tools for generating initial LP solutions. Before the final simplex solution has been reached, all artificial variables must be gone from the solution mix. This matter is handled through the problem's objective function.

artificial variables have no physical meaning

Surplus and Artificial Variables in the Objective Function

Whenever an artificial or surplus variable is added to one of the constraints, it must also be included in the other equations and in the problem's objective function, just as was done for slack variables. Since artificial

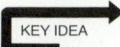
KEY IDEA

variables must be forced out of the solution, we can assign a very high C_j cost to each. In minimization problems, variables with *low* costs are the most desirable ones and the first to enter the solution. Variables with *high* costs leave the solution quickly, or never enter it at all. Rather than set an actual dollar figure of $10,000 or $1 million for each artificial variable, however, we simply use the letter M to represent a very large number.[4]

Surplus variables, like slack variables, carry a 0 cost.

If a problem we were about to solve had an objective function that read:

$$\text{Minimize cost} = \$5X_1 + \$9X_2 + \$7X_3$$

and constraints such as the two mentioned previously, then the completed objective function and constraints would appear as follows:

$$\text{Minimize cost} = \$5X_1 + \$9X_2 + \$7X_3 + \$0S_1 + \$MA_1 + \$MA_2$$

$$\text{Subject to:} \quad 5X_1 + 10X_2 + 8X_3 - 1S_1 + 1A_1 + 0A_2 = 210$$

$$25X_1 + 30X_2 + 0X_3 + 0S_1 + 0A_1 + 1A_2 = 900$$

12.8 SOLVING MINIMIZATION PROBLEMS

Applicable Problems 12-15, 12-20, 12-21, 12-22, 12-26

Now that we have learned how to deal with objective functions and constraints associated with minimization problems, let's see how to use the simplex method to solve a typical problem.

The Muddy River Chemical Corporation must produce exactly 1,000 pounds of a special mixture of phosphate and potassium for a customer. Phosphate costs $5 per pound and potassium costs $6 per pound. No more than 300 pounds of phosphate can be used, and at least 150 pounds of potassium must be used. The problem is to determine the least-cost blend of the two ingredients.

Alternate Example 12.2

This problem may be restated mathematically as:

mathematical formulation of the minimization problem

$$\text{Minimize cost} = \$5X_1 + \$6X_2$$

$$\text{Subject to:} \quad X_1 + X_2 = 1{,}000 \text{ lbs.}$$

$$X_1 \leq 300 \text{ lbs.}$$

$$X_2 \geq 150 \text{ lbs.}$$

$$X_1, \quad X_2 \geq 0$$

where

$$X_1 = \text{number of pounds of phosphate, and}$$

$$X_2 = \text{number of pounds of potassium.}$$

---

[4]A technical point: If an artificial variable is ever used in a *maximization* problem (an occasional event), it is assigned an objective function value of $-\$M$ to force it from the basis.

Note that there are three constraints, not counting the nonnegativity constraints: the first is an equality, the second a less-than-or-equal-to, and the third a greater-than-or-equal-to constraint.

Graphical Analysis

To have a better understanding of the problem, a brief graphical analysis may prove useful. There are only two decision variables, X_1 and X_2, so we are able to plot the constraints and feasible region. Since the first constraint, $X_1 + X_2 = 1,000$, is an equality, the solution must lie somewhere on the line ABC (see Figure 12.3). It must also lie between points A and B because of the constraint $X_1 \leq 300$. The third constraint, $X_2 \geq 150$, is actually redundant (or nonbinding) since X_2 will automatically be greater than 150 pounds if the first two constraints are observed. Hence, the feasible region consists of all points on the line segment AB. As you recall from Chapter 10, however, an optimal solution will always lie at a corner point of the feasible region (even if the region is only a straight line). The solution must therefore be either at point A or point B. A quick analysis reveals that the least-cost solution lies at corner B, namely $X_1 = 300$ pounds of phosphate, $X_2 = 700$ pounds of potassium. The total cost is $5,700.

looking at a graphical solution first

You don't need the simplex method to solve the Muddy River Chemical problem, of course. But we can guarantee you that few problems will be this simple. In general, you can expect to see several variables and many constraints. The purpose of this section is to illustrate the straightforward application of the simplex method to minimization problems.

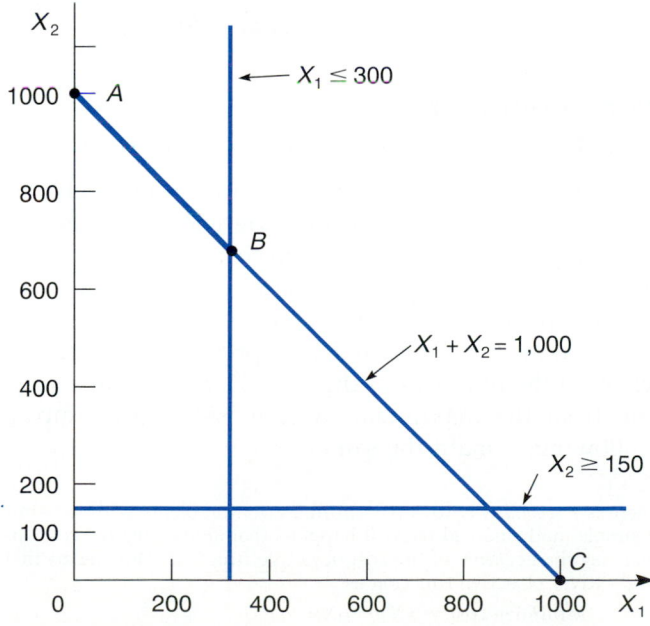

FIGURE 12.3
Muddy River Chemical Corporation's Feasible Region Graph

Converting the Constraints and Objective Function

insert slack, surplus, and artificial variables

The first step is to apply what we learned in the preceding section in order to convert the constraints and objective function into the proper form for the simplex method.

The equality constraint, $X_1 + X_2 = 1,000$, just involves adding an artificial variable, A_1.

$$X_1 + X_2 + A_1 = 1,000$$

The second constraint, $X_1 \leq 300$, requires the insertion of a slack variable—let's call it S_1.

$$X_1 + S_1 = 300$$

The last constraint is $X_2 \geq 150$, which is converted to an equality by subtracting a surplus variable, S_2, and adding an artificial variable, A_2.

$$X_2 - S_2 + A_2 = 150$$

Finally, the objective function, cost = $5X_1$ + $6X_2$, is rewritten as:

$$\text{Minimize cost} = \$5X_1 + \$6X_2 + \$0S_1 + \$0S_2 + \$MA_1 + \$MA_2$$

The complete set of constraints can now be expressed as follows:

$$1X_1 + 1X_2 + 0S_1 + 0S_2 + 1A_1 + 0A_2 = 1000$$
$$1X_1 + 0X_2 + 1S_1 + 0S_2 + 0A_1 + 0A_2 = 300$$
$$0X_1 + 1X_2 + 0S_1 - 1S_2 + 0A_1 + 1A_2 = 150$$
$$X_1, X_2, S_1, S_2, A_1, A_2 \geq 0$$

Rules of the Simplex Method for Minimization Problems

minimization rules are slightly different

Transparency Master 12.9: Simplex Steps for Minimization.

Minimization problems are quite similar to the maximization problems tackled earlier in this chapter. The significant difference involves the $C_j - Z_j$ row. Since our objective is now to minimize cost, the new variable to enter the solution in each tableau (the pivot column) will be the one with the *largest negative* number in the $C_j - Z_j$ row. Thus, we choose the variable that decreases costs the most. In minimization problems, an optimal solution is reached when all the numbers in the $C_j - Z_j$ row are 0 or *positive*—just the opposite from the maximization case.[5] All other simplex steps, as seen in the following, remain the same.

[5]We should note that there is a *second* way to solve minimization problems with the simplex method: it involves a simple mathematical trick. It happens that *minimizing* the cost objective is the same as *maximizing* the negative of the cost objective function. This means that instead of writing the Muddy River objective function as

$$\text{Minimize cost} = 5X_1 + 6X_2$$

we can instead write

$$\text{Maximize } (-\text{cost}) = -5X_1 - 6X_2$$

The solution that maximizes (−cost) also minimizes cost. It also means that the same simplex procedure shown earlier for maximization problems can be used if this trick is employed. The only change is that the objective function must be multiplied by (−1).

1. Choose the variable with the largest negative $C_j - Z_j$ to enter the solution. This is the pivot column.

2. Determine the row to be replaced by selecting the one with the smallest (nonnegative) quantity-to-pivot column ratio. This is the pivot row.

3. Calculate new values for the pivot row.

4. Calculate new values for the other rows.

5. Calculate the Z_j and $C_j - Z_j$ values for this tableau. If there are any $C_j - Z_j$ numbers less than 0, return to step 1.

First Simplex Tableau for the Muddy River Problem

Now we solve Muddy River Chemical Corporation's linear programming formulation using the simplex method. The initial tableau is set up just as in the earlier maximization example. Its first three rows are shown in the accompanying table. We note the presence of the M costs associated with artificial variables A_1 and A_2, but we treat them as if they were any large number. As noted earlier, they have the effect of forcing the artificial variables out of the solution quickly because of their large costs.

C_j	SOLUTION MIX	X_1	X_2	S_1	S_2	A_1	A_2	QUANTITY
$M	A_1	1	1	0	0	1	0	1,000
$0	S_1	1	0	1	0	0	0	300
$M	A_2	0	1	0	-1	0	1	150

The numbers in the Z_j row are computed by multiplying the C_j column on the far left of the tableau times the corresponding numbers in each other column. They are then entered into Table 12.7.

TABLE 12.7 Initial Simplex Tableau for the Muddy River Chemical Problem

$C_j \rightarrow$ $\downarrow$	Solution Mix	$5 X_1	$6 X_2	$0 S_1	$0 S_2	$M A_2	$M A_2	Quantity
$M	A_1	1	1	0	0	1	0	1,000
$0	S_1	1	0	1	0	0	0	300
$M	A_2	0	① Pivot number	0	-1	0	1	150 ← Pivot row
	Z_j	$M	$2M	0	$-M	$M	$M	$1,150M (Total cost)
	$C_j - Z_j$	$-M + 5	$-2M + 6 Pivot column	$0	$M	$0	$0	

$$
\begin{aligned}
Z_j \text{ (for } X_1 \text{ column)} &= \$M(1) &+ \$0(1) &+ \$M(0) &= \$M \\
Z_j \text{ (for } X_2 \text{ column)} &= \$M(1) &+ \$0(0) &+ \$M(1) &= \$2M \\
Z_j \text{ (for } S_1 \text{ column)} &= \$M(0) &+ \$0(1) &+ \$M(0) &= \$0 \\
Z_j \text{ (for } S_2 \text{ column)} &= \$M(0) &+ \$0(0) &+ \$M(-1) &= \$-M \\
Z_j \text{ (for } A_1 \text{ column)} &= \$M(1) &+ \$0(0) &+ \$M(0) &= \$M \\
Z_j \text{ (for } A_2 \text{ column)} &= \$M(0) &+ \$0(0) &+ \$M(1) &= \$M \\
Z_j \text{ (for total cost)} &= \$M(1{,}000) &+ \$0(300) &+ \$M(150) &= \$1{,}150M
\end{aligned}
$$

The $C_j - Z_j$ entries are determined as follows:

	COLUMN					
	X_1	X_2	S_1	S_2	A_1	A_2
C_j for column	$5	$6	$0	$0	$M	$M
Z_j for column	$M	$2M	$0	-$M	$M	$M
$C_j - Z_j$ for column	-$M + $5	-$2M + $6	$0	$M	$0	$0

initial simplex solution

This initial solution was obtained by letting each of the variables X_1, X_2, and S_2 assume a value of 0. The current basic variables are $A_1 = 1{,}000$, $S_1 = 300$, and $A_2 = 150$. This complete solution could be expressed in vector, or column, form as

$$
\begin{bmatrix} X_1 \\ X_2 \\ S_1 \\ S_2 \\ A_1 \\ A_2 \end{bmatrix} = \begin{bmatrix} 0 \\ 0 \\ 300 \\ 0 \\ 1{,}000 \\ 150 \end{bmatrix}
$$

An extremely high cost, $1,150M$, is associated with the above answer. We know this can be reduced significantly and now move on to the solution procedures.

Developing a Second Tableau

is current solution optimal?

In the $C_j - Z_j$ row of Table 12.7, we see that there are two entries with negative values, X_1 and X_2. In the simplex rules for minimization problems, this means that an optimal solution does not yet exist. The pivot column is the one with the *largest negative* entry in the $C_j - Z_j$ row—shown in Table 12.7 as the X_2 column, which means that X_2 will enter the solution next.

Which variable will leave the solution to make room for the new variable, X_2? To find out, we divide the elements of the quantity column by the respective pivot column values.

A_2 is pivot row

$$
\text{For the } A_1 \text{ row} = \frac{1{,}000}{1} = 1{,}000
$$

For the S_1 row $= \dfrac{300}{0}$ (This is an undefined ratio, so we ignore it.)

For the A_2 row $= \dfrac{150}{1} = 150$ Smallest quotient, indicating pivot row

Hence, the pivot row is the A_2 row, and the pivot number (circled) is at the intersection of the X_2 column and the A_2 row.

The entering row for the next simplex tableau is found by dividing each element in the pivot row by the pivot number, 1. This leaves the old pivot row unchanged, except that it now represents the solution variable X_2. The other two rows are altered one at a time by again applying the formula shown earlier in step 4.

(New row numbers) = (Numbers in old row)

$$-\left[\left(\frac{\text{Number above or below}}{\text{pivot number}} \right) \times \left(\begin{array}{c} \text{Corresponding number} \\ \text{in newly replaced row} \end{array} \right) \right]$$

A_1 Row		S_1 Row	
$1 =$	$1 - (1)(0)$	$1 =$	$1 - (0)(0)$
$0 =$	$1 - (1)(1)$	$0 =$	$0 - (0)(1)$
$0 =$	$0 - (1)(0)$	$1 =$	$1 - (0)(0)$
$1 =$	$0 - (1)(-1)$	$0 =$	$0 - (0)(-1)$
$1 =$	$1 - (1)(0)$	$0 =$	$0 - (0)(0)$
$-1 =$	$0 - (1)(1)$	$0 =$	$0 - (0)(1)$
$850 = 1{,}000 - (1)(150)$		$300 = 300 - (0)(150)$	

The Z_j and $C_j - Z_j$ rows are computed next.

$$Z_j \text{ (for } X_1) \quad = \$M(1) \quad + \$0(1) \quad + \$6(0) \quad = \$M$$
$$Z_j \text{ (for } X_2) \quad = \$M(0) \quad + \$0(0) \quad + \$6(1) \quad = \$6$$
$$Z_j \text{ (for } S_1) \quad = \$M(0) \quad + \$0(1) \quad + \$6(0) \quad = \$0$$
$$Z_j \text{ (for } S_2) \quad = \$M(1) \quad + \$0(0) \quad + \$6(-1) = \$M - 6$$
$$Z_j \text{ (for } A_1) \quad = \$M(1) \quad + \$0(0) \quad + \$6(0) \quad = \$M$$
$$Z_j \text{ (for } A_2) \quad = \$M(-1) + \$0(0) \quad + \$6(1) \quad = -\$M + 6$$
$$Z_j \text{ (for total cost)} = \$M(850) + \$0(300) + \$6(150) = \$850M + 900$$

	COLUMN					
	X_1	X_2	S_1	S_2	A_1	A_2
C_j for column	$\$5$	$\$6$	$\$0$	$\$0$	$\$M$	$\$M$
Z_j for column	$\$M$	$\$6$	$\$0$	$\$M - 6$	$\$M$	$-\$M + 6$
$C_j - Z_j$ for column	$-\$M + 5$	$\$0$	$\$0$	$-\$M + 6$	$\$0$	$\$2M - 6$

All of these computational results are presented in Table 12.8.

solution after second
tableau

The solution at the end of the second tableau is $A_1 = 850$, $S_1 = 300$, $X_2 = 150$. X_1, S_2, and A_2 are currently the nonbasic variables and have 0 value. The cost at this point is still quite high, $\$850M + \$900$. This answer is not optimal because not every number in the $C_j - Z_j$ row is 0 or positive.

Developing a Third Tableau

The new pivot column is the X_1 column. To determine which variable will leave the basis to make room for X_1, we check the quantity column-to-pivot column ratios again.

third tableau developed

$$\text{For the } A_1 \text{ row} = \frac{850}{1} = 850$$

$$\text{For the } S_1 \text{ row} = \frac{300}{1} = 300 \quad \textit{Smallest ratio}$$

$$\text{For the } X_2 \text{ row} = \frac{150}{0} = \text{Undefined}$$

Hence, variable S_1 will be replaced by X_1.[6] The pivot number, row, and column are labeled in Table 12.8.

To replace the pivot row, we divide each number in the S_1 row by 1 (the circled pivot number), leaving the row unchanged. The new X_1 row is shown in Table 12.9. The other computations for this third simplex tableau are shown following the table.

A_1 Row		X_2 Row	
$0 =$	$1 - (1)(1)$	$0 =$	$0 - (0)(1)$
$0 =$	$0 - (1)(0)$	$1 =$	$1 - (0)(0)$
$-1 =$	$0 - (1)(1)$	$0 =$	$0 - (0)(1)$
$1 =$	$1 - (1)(0)$	$-1 =$	$-1 - (0)(0)$
$1 =$	$1 - (1)(0)$	$0 =$	$0 - (0)(0)$
$-1 =$	$-1 - (1)(0)$	$1 =$	$1 - (0)(0)$
$550 =$	$850 - (1)(300)$	$150 =$	$150 - (0)(300)$

Z_j (for X_1) $\quad = \$M(0) \quad + \$5(1) \quad + \$6(0) \quad = \$5$

Z_j (for X_2) $\quad = \$M(0) \quad + \$5(0) \quad + \$6(1) \quad = \$6$

Z_j (for S_1) $\quad = \$M(-1) + \$5(1) \quad + \$6(0) \quad = -\$M + 5$

Z_j (for S_2) $\quad = \$M(1) \quad + \$5(0) \quad + \$6(-1) = \$M - 6$

Z_j (for A_1) $\quad = \$M(1) \quad + \$5(0) \quad + \$6(0) \quad = \$M$

Z_j (for A_2) $\quad = \$M(-1) + \$5(0) \quad + \$6(1) \quad = -\$M + 6$

Z_j (for total cost) $= \$M(550) + \$5(300) + \$6(150) = \$550M + \$2,400$

---

[6]At this point, it might appear to be more cost-effective to replace the A_1 row instead of the S_1 row. This would remove the last artificial variable, and its large $\$M$ cost, from the basis. The simplex method, however, does not always pick the most direct route to reaching the final solution. You may be assured, though, that it *will* lead us to the correct answer.

TABLE 12.8 Second Simplex Tableau for the Muddy River

$C_j \rightarrow$	Solution Mix	$5	$6	$0	$0	$M	$M	
$\downarrow$		X_1	X_2	S_1	S_2	A_1	A_2	Quantity
$M	A_1	1	0	0	1	1	−1	850
$0	S_1	①	0	1	0	0	0	300 ← Pivot row
		Pivot number						
$6	X_2	0	1	0	−1	0	1	150
	Z_j	$M	$6	$0	$M − 6	$M	−$M + 6	$850M + $900
	$C_j − Z_j$	−$M + 5·	$0	$0	−$M + 6	$0	$2M − 6	
		Pivot column						

	COLUMN					
	X_1	X_2	S_1	S_2	A_1	A_2
C_j for column	$5	$6	$0	$0	$M	$M
Z_j for column	$5	$6	−$M + 5	$M − 6	$M	−$M + 6
$C_j − Z_j$ for column	$0	$0	$M − 5	−$M + 6	$0	$2M − 6

The solution at the end of the three iterations is still not optimal because the S_2 column contains a $C_j − Z_j$ value that is negative. Note that the current total cost is nonetheless lower than at the end of the second tableau, which in turn is lower than the initial solution cost. We are headed in the right direction but have one more tableau to go!

third solution still not optimal

Fourth Tableau for the Muddy River Chemical Problem

The pivot column is now the S_2 column. The ratios that determine the row and variable to be replaced are computed as follows:

For the A_1 row: $\dfrac{550}{1} = 550$ *Row to be replaced*

For the X_1 row: $\dfrac{300}{0}$ *Undefined*

For the X_2 row: $\dfrac{150}{-1}$ *Not considered because it is negative*

TABLE 12.9 Third Simplex Tableau for the Muddy River Chemical Problem

$C_j \rightarrow$	Solution Mix	$5	$6	$0	$0	$M	$M	
$\downarrow$		X_1	X_2	S_1	S_2	A_1	A_2	Quantity
$M	A_1	0	0	−1	①	1	−1	550 ← Pivot row
					Pivot number			
$5	X_1	1	0	1	0	0	0	300
$6	X_2	0	1	0	−1	0	1	150
	Z_j	$5	$6	−$M + 5	$M − 6	$M	−$M + 6	$550M
	$C_j − Z_j$	$0	$0	$M − 5	−$M + 6	$0	$2M − 6	+2400
					Pivot column ↗			

computing fourth solution

Each number in the pivot row is divided by the pivot number (again 1, by coincidence). The other two rows are computed as follows and are shown in Table 12.10.

X_1 Row	X_2 Row
$1 = 1 - (0)(0)$	$0 = 0 - (-1)(0)$
$0 = 0 - (0)(0)$	$1 = 1 - (-1)(0)$
$1 = 1 - (0)(-1)$	$-1 = 0 - (-1)(-1)$
$0 = 0 - (0)(1)$	$0 = -1 - (-1)(1)$
$0 = 0 - (0)(1)$	$1 = 0 - (-1)(1)$
$0 = 0 - (0)(-1)$	$0 = 1 - (-1)(-1)$
$300 = 300 - (0)(550)$	$700 = 150 - (-1)(550)$

$$Z_j \text{ (for } X_1) \quad = \$0(0) \quad + \$5(1) + \$6(0) \quad = \$5$$
$$Z_j \text{ (for } X_2) \quad = \$0(0) \quad + \$5(0) + \$6(1) \quad = \$6$$
$$Z_j \text{ (for } S_1) \quad = \$0(-1) \quad + \$5(1) + \$6(-1) \quad = -\$1$$
$$Z_j \text{ (for } S_2) \quad = \$0(1) \quad + \$5(0) + \$6(0) \quad = \$0$$
$$Z_j \text{ (for } A_1) \quad = \$0(1) \quad + \$5(0) + \$6(1) \quad = \$6$$
$$Z_j \text{ (for } A_2) \quad = \$0(-1) \quad + \$5(0) + \$6(0) \quad = \$0$$
$$Z_j \text{ (for total cost)} = \$0(550) + \$5(300) + \$6(700) = \$5,700$$

	COLUMN					
	X_1	X_2	S_1	S_2	A_1	A_2
C_j for column	$\$5$	$\$6$	$\$0$	$\$0$	$\$M$	$\$M$
Z_j for column	$\$5$	$\$6$	$\$-1$	$\$0$	$\$6$	$\$0$
$C_j - Z_j$ for column	$\$0$	$\$0$	$\$1$	$\$0$	$\$M - 6$	$\$M$

optimal solution

On examining the $C_j - Z_j$ row in Table 12.10, only positive or 0 values are found. The fourth tableau therefore contains the optimum solution. That solution is $X_1 = 300$, $X_2 = 700$, $S_2 = 550$. The artificial variables are both

TABLE 12.10 Fourth and Optimal Solution to the Muddy River Chemical Problem

$C_j \rightarrow$ ↓	SOLUTION MIX	$\$5$ X_1	$\$6$ X_2	$\$0$ S_1	$\$0$ S_2	$\$M$ A_1	$\$M$ A_2	QUANTITY
$\$0$	S_2	0	0	-1	1	1	-1	550
$\$5$	X_1	1	0	1	0	0	0	300
$\$6$	X_2	0	1	-1	0	1	0	700
	Z_j	$\$5$	$\$6$	$\$-1$	$\$0$	$\$6$	$\$0$	$\$5,700$
	$C_j - Z_j$	$\$0$	$\$0$	$\$1$	$\$0$	$\$M - 6$	$\$M$	

equal to 0, as is S_1. Translated into management terms, the chemical company's decision should be to blend 300 pounds of phosphate (X_1) with 700 pounds of potassium (X_2). This provides a surplus (S_2) of 550 pounds of potassium more than required by the constraint $X_2 \geq 150$. The cost of this solution is $5,700. If you look back to Figure 12.3, you can see that this is identical to the answer found by the graphical approach.

Although small problems such as this can be solved graphically, more realistic product blending problems demand use of the simplex method, usually in computerized form.

12.9 REVIEW OF PROCEDURES FOR SOLVING LP MINIMIZATION PROBLEMS

Just as we summarized the steps for solving LP maximization problems with the simplex method in Section 12.6, let us do so for minimization problems here.

   I. Formulate the LP problem's objective function and constraints.

   II. Include slack variables in each less-than-or-equal-to constraint, surplus variables in each greater-than-or-equal-to constraint, and both surplus and artificial variables in each equality. Then add all of these variables to the problem's objective function.

   III. Develop an initial simplex tableau with artificial and slack variables in the basis and their variables (the X_i's) set equal to 0. Compute the Z_j and $C_j - Z_j$ values for this tableau.

   IV. Follow these five steps until an optimal solution has been reached:
   - **A.** Choose the variable with the greatest negative $C_j - Z_j$ to enter the solution. This is the pivot column.
   - **B.** Determine the row to be replaced by selecting the one with the smallest (nonnegative) quantity-to-pivot column ratio. This is the pivot row.
   - **C.** Calculate the new values for the pivot row.
   - **D.** Calculate the new values for the other row(s).
   - **E.** Calculate the Z_j and $C_j - Z_j$ values for the tableau. If there are any $C_j - Z_j$ numbers less than 0, return to step A. If there are no $C_j - Z_j$ numbers that are less than 0, an optimal solution has been reached.

12.10 SPECIAL CASES IN USING THE SIMPLEX METHOD

In Chapter 10 we addressed some special cases that may arise when solving LP problems graphically (see Section 8 of Chapter 10). Here we again describe these cases, this time as they refer to the simplex method.

Applicable Problems 12-16, 12-17, 12-18, 12-19

Infeasibility

**no feasible solution
exists**

Infeasibility, you may recall, comes about when there is no solution that satisfies all of the problem's constraints. In the simplex method, an infeasible solution is indicated by looking at the final tableau. In it, all $C_j - Z_j$ row entries will be of the proper sign to imply optimality, but an artificial variable (A_1) will still be in the solution mix.

Teaching Suggestion 12.6:
Infeasibility Is a Major
Problem in Large LP
Problems. See the
Instructor's Section for
details.

Table 12.11 illustrates the final simplex tableau for a hypothetical minimization type of linear programming problem. The table provides an example of an improperly formulated problem, probably containing conflicting constraints. No feasible solution is possible because an artificial variable, A_2, remains in the solution mix, even though all $C_j - Z_j$ are positive or 0 (the criterion for an optimal solution in a minimization case).

Unbounded Solutions

Unboundedness describes linear programs that do not have finite solutions. It occurs in maximization problems, for example, when a solution variable can be made infinitely large without violating a constraint (refer back to Figure 10.13). In the simplex method, the condition of unboundedness will be discovered prior to reaching the final tableau. We will note the problem when trying to decide which variable to remove from the solution mix. The procedure, as seen earlier in this chapter, is to divide each quantity column number by the corresponding pivot column number. The row with the smallest positive ratio is replaced. But if all the ratios turn out to be negative or undefined, it indicates that the problem is unbounded.

no finite solution exists

Table 12.12 illustrates the second tableau calculated for a particular LP maximization problem by the simplex method. It also points to the condition of unboundedness. The solution is not optimal because not all $C_j - Z_j$ entries are 0 or negative, as required in a maximization problem. The next variable to enter the solution should be X_1. To determine which variable will leave the solution, we examine the ratios of the quantity column numbers to their corresponding numbers in the X_1, or pivot, column.

Ratio for the X_2 row: $\dfrac{30}{-1}$

Ratio for the S_2 row: $\dfrac{10}{-2}$

Negative ratios unacceptable

TABLE 12.11 An Illustration of Infeasibility

$C_j \rightarrow$ $\downarrow$	SOLUTION MIX	$5 X_1	$8 X_2	$0 S_1	$0 S_2	$M A_1	$M A_2	QUANTITY
$5	X_1	1	0	-2	3	-1	0	200
$8	X_2	0	1	1	2	-2	0	100
$M	A_2	0	0	0	-1	-1	1	20
	Z_j	5	8	-2	$31 - M$	$-21 - M$	M	$1,800 + 20M$
	$C_j - Z_j$	$0	$0	$2	$M - 31$	$2M + 21$	$0	

TABLE 12.12 A Problem with an Unbounded Solution

$C_j \rightarrow$ $\downarrow$	Solution Mix	$6 X_1	$9 X_2	$0 S_1	$0 S_2	Quantity
$9	X_2	−1	1	2	0	30
$0	S_2	−2	0	−1	1	10
	Z_j	$−9	$9	$18	$0	$270
	$C_j − Z_j$	$15	$0	−$18	$0	

Pivot column

Since both pivot column numbers are negative, an unbounded solution is indicated.

Degeneracy

Degeneracy is another situation that can occur when solving an LP problem using the simplex method. It may develop when a problem contains a redundant constraint; that is, one or more of the constraints in the formulation makes another unnecessary. For example, if a problem has the three constraints $X_1 \leq 10$, $X_2 \leq 10$, and $X_1 + X_2 \leq 20$, the latter is unnecessary because the first two constraints make it redundant. Degeneracy arises when the ratio calculations are made. If there is a *tie* for the smallest ratio, this is a signal that degeneracy exists.

tied ratios

Table 12.13 provides an example of a degenerate problem. At this iteration of the given maximization LP problem, the next variable to enter the solution will be X_1, since it has the only positive $C_j − Z_j$ number.

The ratios are computed as follows:

$$\text{For the } X_2 \text{ row: } \frac{10}{\frac{1}{4}} = 40$$

$$\text{For the } S_2 \text{ row: } \frac{20}{4} = 5$$

$$\text{For the } S_3 \text{ row: } \frac{10}{2} = 5$$

Tie for the smallest ratio indicates degeneracy

TABLE 12.13 A Problem Illustrating Degeneracy

$C_j \rightarrow$ $\downarrow$	Solution Mix	$5 X_1	$8 X_2	$2 X_3	$0 S_1	$0 S_2	$0 S_3	Quantity
$8	X_2	$\frac{1}{4}$	1	1	−2	0	0	10
$0	S_2	4	0	$\frac{1}{3}$	−1	1	0	20
$0	S_3	2	0	2	$\frac{2}{5}$	0	1	10
	Z_j	$2	$8	$8	$16	$0	$0	$80
	$C_j − Z_j$	$3	$0	−$6	−$16	$0	$0	

Pivot column

cycling

Theoretically, degeneracy could lead to a situation known as *cycling*, in which the simplex algorithm alternates back and forth between the same nonoptimal solutions; that is, it puts a new variable in, then takes it out in the next tableau, puts it back in, and so on. One simple way of dealing with the issue is to select either row (S_2 or S_3 in this case) arbitrarily. If we are unlucky, and cycling does occur, we simply go back and select the other row.

Applicable Problem 12-18

alternative optimal solution

More Than One Optimal Solution

Multiple, or alternate, optimal solutions are spotted when the simplex method is being used by looking at the final tableau. If the $C_j - Z_j$ value is equal to 0 for a variable that is *not* in the solution mix, more than one optimal solution exists.

Let's take Table 12.14 as an example. Here is the last tableau of a maximization problem; each entry in the $C_j - Z_j$ row is 0 or negative, indicating that an optimal solution has been reached. That solution is read as $X_2 = 6$, $S_2 = 3$, profit = \$12. Note, however, that variable X_1 can be brought into the solution mix without increasing or decreasing profit. The new solution, with X_1 in the basis, would become $X_1 = 3$, $X_2 = \frac{3}{2}$, with profit still at \$12. Can you modify Table 12.14 to prove this? You might note, by the way, that this example of alternate optimal solution corresponds to the graphical solution shown in Figure 10.15.

12.11 KARMARKAR'S ALGORITHM

The biggest change to take place in the field of linear programming solution techniques in four decades has been the 1984 arrival of an alternative to the simplex algorithm. Developed by Narendra Karmarkar, the new method, called Karmarkar's algorithm, often takes significantly less computer time to solve very large scale LP problems.[7]

As we saw, the simplex algorithm finds a solution by moving from one adjacent corner point to the next, following the outside edges of the feasible

TABLE 12.14 A Problem with Alternate Optimal Solutions

$C_j \rightarrow$ ↓	SOLUTION MIX	\$3 X_1	\$2 X_2	\$0 S_1	\$0 S_2	QUANTITY
\$2	X_2	$\frac{3}{2}$	1	1	0	6
\$0	S_2	1	0	$\frac{1}{2}$	1	3
	Z_j	\$3	\$2	\$2	\$0	\$12
	$C_j - Z_j$	\$0	\$0	−\$2	\$0	

[7]For details, see Narendra Karmarkar, "A New Polynomial Time Algorithm for Linear Programming," *Combinatorica* Vol. 4, No. 4, 1984, pp. 373–395, or J. N. Hooker, "Karmarkar's Linear Programming Algorithm," *Interfaces* **16,** 4, July–August 1986, 75–90.

Finding Fast Algorithms Means Better Airline Service

Thomas Cook is President of American Airlines' Decision Technologies. Linear-programming techniques have a direct impact on the efficiency and profitability of major airlines, and Cook shares his ideas on why optimal solutions are essential to his business:

Finding an optimal solution means finding the best solution. Let's say you are trying to minimize a cost function of some kind. For example, we may want to minimize the excess costs related to scheduling crews, hotels, and other costs that are not associated with flight time. So we try to minimize that excess cost, subject to a lot of constraints, such as the amount of time a pilot can fly, how much rest time is needed, and so forth.

An optimal solution, then, is either a minimum-cost solution or a maximizing solution. For example, we might want to maximize the profit associated with assigning aircraft to the schedule; so we assign large aircraft to high-need segments and small aircraft to low-load segments. Whether it's a minimum or maximum solution depends on what function we are trying to optimize.

Finding fast solutions to linear-programming problems is also essential. If we can get an algorithm that's 50 to 100 times faster, we could do a lot of things that we can't do today. For example, some applications could be real-time applications, as opposed to batch applications. So instead of running a job overnight and getting an answer the next morning, we could actually key in the data or access the data base, generate the matrix, and come up with a solution that could be implemented a few minutes after keying in the data.

A good example of this kind of application is what we call a major weather disruption. If we get a major weather disruption at one of the hubs, such as Dallas or Chicago, then a lot of flights may get cancelled, which means we have a lot of crews and airplanes in the wrong places. What we need is a way to put that whole operation back together again, so that the crew and airplanes are in the right places. That way, we minimize the cost of the disruption and minimize the passenger inconvenience.

The simplex method, which was developed some 40 years ago by George Dantzig, has been very useful at American Airlines and, indeed, at a lot of large businesses. The difference between his solution and Karmarkar's is that if we can get an algorithm that comes up with basically the same optimal answer 50 to 100 times faster, then we can apply that technology to new problems, and even to problems that we wouldn't have tried using the simplex method. I think that's the primary reason for the excitement.

Source: Introduction to Contemporary Mathematics. New York: W. H. Freeman and Company, 1988, pp. 82–83.

region. In contrast, Karmarkar's method follows a path of points on the *inside* of the feasible region. Karmarkar's method is also unique in its ability to handle an *extremely* large number of constraints and variables, thereby giving LP users the capacity to solve previously unsolvable problems.

Although it is likely that the simplex method will continue to be used for many LP problems, a new generation of LP software built around Karmarkar's algorithm is already becoming popular. Delta Air Lines became the first commercial airline to use the Karmarkar program called KORBX, which was developed and is sold by AT&T. Delta found that the program streamlined the monthly scheduling of 7,000 pilots who fly more than 400 airplanes to 166 cities worldwide. With increased efficiency in allocating limited resources, Delta thinks it will save millions of dollars in crew time and related costs.

Video 12.1: Faster Algorithms at American Airlines

12.12 SUMMARY

simplex systematically
improves solution

In Chapter 10, we examined the use of graphical methods to solve linear programming problems that contained only two decision variables. This chapter moved us one giant step further by introducing the simplex method. The simplex method is an iterative procedure for reaching the optimal solution to LP problems of any dimension. It consists of a series of rules that, in effect, algebraically examine corner points in a systematic way. Each step moves us closer to the optimal solution by increasing profit or decreasing cost, while at the same time maintaining feasibility.

We saw the procedure for converting less-than-or-equal-to, greater-than-or-equal-to, and equality constraints into the simplex format. These conversions employed the inclusion of slack, surplus, and artificial variables. An initial simplex tableau was developed that portrayed the problem's original data formulations. It also contained a row providing profit or cost information and a net evaluation row. The latter, identified as the $C_j - Z_j$ row, was examined in determining whether an optimal solution had yet been reached. It also pointed out which variable would next enter the solution mix, or basis, if the current solution was nonoptimal.

The simplex method consists of five steps: (1) identifying the pivot column, (2) identifying the pivot row and number, (3) replacing the pivot row, (4) computing new values for each remaining row, and (5) computing the Z_j and $C_j - Z_j$ rows and examining for optimality. Each tableau of this iterative procedure was displayed and explained for a sample maximization and minimization problem.

Finally, a few special issues in linear programming that arise in using the simplex method were discussed. Examples of infeasibility, unbounded solutions, degeneracy, and multiple optimal solutions were presented.

Although large LP problems are seldom if ever solved by hand, the purpose of this chapter was to help you gain an understanding of how the simplex method works. Understanding the underlying principles will be of great help in interpreting and analyzing computerized linear programming solutions. It will also provide a foundation for another issue: answering questions about the problem after an optimal solution has been found, which is called postoptimality, or sensitivity, analysis.

GLOSSARY

Simplex Method. A matrix algebra method for solving linear programming problems.

Iterative Procedure. A process (algorithm) that repeats the same steps over and over.

Slack Variable. A variable added to less-than-or-equal-to constraints in order to create an equality for a simplex method. It represents a quantity of unused resource.

Simplex Tableau. A table for keeping track of calculations at each iteration of the simplex method.

Solution Mix. A column in the simplex tableau that contains all the variables in the solution.

Quantity Column. A column in the simplex tableau that gives the numeric value of each variable in the solution mix column.

Basic Feasible Solution. A solution to an LP problem that corresponds to a corner point of the feasible region.

Basis. The set of variables that are in the solution, have positive, nonzero values, and are listed in the solution mix column. They are also called basic variables.

Nonbasic Variables. Variables not in the solution mix or basis. Nonbasic variables are equal to 0.

Substitution Rates. The coefficients in the central body of each simplex table. They indicate the number of units of each basic variable that must be removed from the solution if a new variable (as represented at any column head) is entered.

Z_j **Row.** The row containing the figures for gross profit or loss given up by adding one unit of a variable into the solution.

$C_j - Z_j$ **Row.** The row containing the net profit or loss that will result from introducing one unit of the variable indicated in that column into the solution.

Pivot Column. The column with the largest positive number in the $C_j - Z_j$ row of a maximization problem, or the largest negative $C_j - Z_j$ value in a minimization problem. It indicates which variable will enter the solution next.

Pivot Row. The row corresponding to the variable that will leave the basis in order to make room for the variable entering (as indicated by the new pivot column). This is the smallest positive ratio found by dividing the quantity column values by the pivot column values for each row.

Pivot Number. The number at the intersection of the pivot row and pivot column.

Current Solution. The basic feasible solution that is the set of variables presently in the solution. It corresponds to a corner point of the feasible region.

Surplus Variable. A variable inserted in a greater-than-or-equal-to constraint to create an equality. It represents the amount of resource usage above the minimum required usage.

Artificial Variable. A variable that has no meaning in a physical sense but acts as a tool to help generate an initial LP solution.

Infeasibility. The situation in which there is no solution that satisfies all of a problem's constraints.

Unboundedness. A condition describing LP maximization problems having solutions that can become infinitely large without violating any stated constraints.

Degeneracy. A condition that arises when there is a tie in the values used to determine which variable will enter the solution next. It can lead to cycling back and forth between two nonoptimal solutions.

KEY EQUATION

(12-1) New row numbers = (Numbers in old row)

$$- \left[\begin{pmatrix} \text{Number in the intersection} \\ \text{of the pivot column and} \\ \text{the row to be replaced} \end{pmatrix} \times \begin{pmatrix} \text{Corresponding number} \\ \text{in new row, that is, new} \\ \text{values for pivot row} \end{pmatrix} \right]$$

Formula for computing new values for nonpivot rows in the simplex tableau (step 4 of the simplex procedure).

SOLVED PROBLEMS

Solved Problem 12-1

Convert the following constraints and objective function into the proper form for use in the simplex method.

$$\text{Minimize cost} = 4X_1 + 1X_2$$

$$\text{Subject to:} \quad 3X_1 + X_2 = 3$$

$$4X_1 + 3X_2 \geqslant 6$$

$$X_1 + 2X_2 \leqslant 3$$

Solution

$$\text{Minimize cost} = 4X_1 + 1X_2 + 0S_1 + 0S_2 + MA_1 + MA_2$$

$$\text{Subject to:} \quad 3X_1 + 1X_2 \qquad\qquad\quad + 1A_1 \qquad\quad = 3$$

$$4X_1 + 3X_2 - 1S_1 \qquad\qquad\quad + 1A_2 = 6$$

$$1X_1 + 2X_2 \qquad\quad + 1S_2 \qquad\qquad = 3$$

Solved Problem 12-2

Solve the following LP problem.

$$\text{Maximize profit} = \$9X_1 + \$7X_2$$

$$\text{Subject to:} \qquad 2X_1 + 1X_2 \leqslant 40$$

$$X_1 + 3X_2 \leqslant 30$$

Solution

We begin by adding slack variables and converting inequalities into equalities.

$$\text{Maximize profit} = 9X_1 + 7X_2 + 0S_1 + 0S_2$$

$$\text{Subject to:} \qquad 2X_1 + 1X_2 + 1S_1 + 0S_2 = 40$$

$$1X_1 + 3X_2 + 0S_1 + 1S_2 = 30$$

The initial tableau is then:

$C_j \rightarrow$		$\$9$	$\$7$	$\$0$	$\$0$	
$\downarrow$	SOLUTION MIX	X_1	X_2	S_1	S_2	QUANTITY
0	S_1	②	1	1	0	40
0	S_2	1	3	0	1	30
	Z_j	0	0	0	0	0
	$C_j - Z_j$	9	7	0	0	

The correct second tableau and third tableau and some of their calculations appear below. The optimal solutions, given in the third tableau, are: $X_1 = 18$, $X_2 = 4$, $S_1 = 0$, $S_2 = 0$, and profit = $190.

Steps 1 and 2. To go from the first to the second tableau, we note that the pivot column (in the first tableau) is X_1, which has the highest $C_j - Z_j$ value, $9. The pivot row is S_1 since 40/2 is less than 30/1, and the pivot number is 2.

Step 3. The new X_1 row is found by dividing each number in the old S_1 row by the pivot number, namely, 2/2 = 1, 1/2 = 1/2, 1/2 = 1/2, 0/2 = 0, and 40/2 = 20.

Step 4. The new values for the S_2 row are computed as follows:

$$\begin{pmatrix} \text{Number in} \\ \text{new } S_2 \text{ row} \end{pmatrix} = \begin{pmatrix} \text{Number in} \\ \text{old } S_2 \text{ row} \end{pmatrix} - \left[\begin{pmatrix} \text{Number} \\ \text{below pivot} \\ \text{number} \end{pmatrix} \times \begin{pmatrix} \text{Corresponding} \\ \text{number in} \\ \text{new } X_1 \text{ row} \end{pmatrix} \right]$$

0	=	1	−	[(1)	×	(1)]
5/2	=	3	−	[(1)	×	(1/2)]
−1/2	=	0	−	[(1)	×	(1/2)]
1	=	1	−	[(1)	×	(0)]
10	=	30	−	[(1)	×	(20)]

Step 5. The following new Z_j and $C_j - Z_j$ rows are formed:

Z_j (for X_1) = $9(1) + 0(0) = $9 $C_j - Z_j = $9 - $9 = 0

Z_j (for X_2) = $9(1/2) + 0(5/2) = $9/2 $C_j - Z_j = $7 - 9/2 = $5/2

Z_j (for S_1) = $9(1/2) + 0(-1/2) = $9/2 $C_j - Z_j = 0 - 9/2 = -$9/2

Z_j (for S_2) = $9(0) + 0(1) = $0 $C_j - Z_j = 0 - 0 = 0

Z_j (profit) = $9(20) + 0(10) = $180

$C_j \rightarrow$ $\downarrow$	SOLUTION MIX	$9 X_1	$7 X_2	$0 S_1	$0 S_2	QUANTITY
$9	X_1	1	1/2	1/2	0	20
0	S_2	0	⑤/2	−1/2	1	10 ← Pivot row
	Z_j	$9	$9/2	$9/2	0	$180
	$C_j - Z_j$	0	$5/2	−9/2	0	

↑
Pivot column

The above solution is not optimal and you must perform steps 1–5 again. The new pivot column is X_2, the new pivot row is S_2, and 5/2 (circled in the second tableau) is the new pivot number.

$C_j \rightarrow$		$9	$7	$0	$0	
$\downarrow$	SOLUTION MIX	X_1	X_2	S_1	S_2	QUANTITY
$9	X_1	1	0	3/5	−1/5	18
$7	X_2	0	1	−1/5	2/5	4
	Z_j	$9	$7	$4	$1	$190
	$C_j - Z_j$	0	0	−$4	−$1	

The final solution is $X_1 = 18$, $X_2 = 4$, profit $= \$190$.

DISCUSSION QUESTIONS AND PROBLEMS

Discussion Questions

12-1 Explain the purpose and procedures of the simplex method.

12-2 How do the graphical and simplex methods of solving linear programming problems differ? In what ways are they the same? Under what circumstances would you prefer to use the graphical approach?

12-3 What are slack, surplus, and artificial variables? When is each used, and why? What value does each carry in the objective function?

12-4 You have just formulated an LP problem with 12 decision variables and 8 constraints. How many basic variables will there always be? What is the difference between a basic and a nonbasic variable?

12-5 What are the simplex rules for selecting the pivot column? The pivot row? The pivot number?

12-6 How do maximization and minimization problems differ when applying the simplex method?

12-7 What is the reason behind the use of the minimum ratio test in selecting the pivot row? What might happen without it?

12-8 A particular linear programming problem has the following objective function:

$$\text{Maximize profit} = \$8X_1 + \$6X_2 + \$12X_3 - \$2X_4$$

Which variable should enter at the second simplex tableau? If the objective function was

$$\text{Minimize cost} = \$2.5X_1 + \$2.9X_2 + \$4.0X_3 + \$7.9X_4$$

which variable would be the best candidate to enter the second tableau?

12-9 What happens if an artificial variable is in the final optimal solution? What should the manager who formulated the LP problem do?

12-10 The great Romanian operations researcher, Dr. Ima Student, proposes that instead of selecting the variable with the largest positive $C_j - Z_j$ value (in a maximization LP problem) to enter the solution mix next, a different approach be used. She suggests that any variable with a positive $C_j - Z_j$ can be chosen, even if it isn't the largest. What will happen if we adopt this new rule for the simplex procedure? Will an optimal solution still be reached?

Problems

· **12-11** The Dreskin Development Company is building two apartment complexes. It must decide how many units to construct in each complex subject to labor and material constraints. The profit generated for each apartment in the first complex is estimated at $900, for each apartment in the second complex, $1,500. A partial initial simplex tableau for Dreskin is given in the accompanying table.

$C_j \rightarrow$		$900	$1,500	$0	$0	
$\downarrow$	SOLUTION MIX	X_1	X_2	S_1	S_2	QUANTITY
		14	4	1	0	3,360
		10	12	0	1	9,600
Z_j						
$C_j - Z_j$						

(a) Complete the initial tableau.
(b) Reconstruct the problem's original constraints (excluding slack variables).
(c) Write the problem's original objective function.
(d) What is the basis for the initial solution?
(e) Which variable should enter the solution at the next iteration?
(f) Which variable will leave the solution at the next iteration?
(g) How many units of the variable entering the solution next will be in the basis in the second tableau?

· **12-12** Consider the following linear programming problem:

$$\text{Maximize earnings} = \$.80X_1 + \$.40X_2 + \$1.20X_3 - \$.10X_4$$

$$\text{Subject to:} \quad X_1 + 2X_2 + X_3 + 5X_4 \leq 150$$

$$X_2 - 4X_3 + 8X_4 = 70$$

$$6X_1 + 7X_2 + 2X_3 - X_4 \geq 120$$

$$X_1, X_2, X_3, X_4 \geq 0$$

(a) Convert these constraints to equalities by adding the appropriate slack, surplus, or artificial variables. Also, add the new variables into the problem's objective function.
(b) Set up the complete initial simplex tableau for this problem. Do not attempt to solve.

· **12-13** Solve the following linear programming problem graphically. Then set up a simplex tableau and solve the problem using the simplex method. Indicate the corner points generated at each iteration by the simplex method on your graph.

$$\text{Maximize profit} = \$3X_1 + \$5X_2$$

$$\text{Subject to:} \qquad\qquad X_2 \leq 6$$

$$3X_1 + 2X_2 \leq 18$$

$$X_1, X_2 \geq 0$$

See the Instructor's Section for tableau.
$14X_1 + 4X_2 \leq 3,360$
$10X_1 + 12X_2 \leq 9,600$
$X_1, X_2 \geq 0$

Maximize Profit $= 900X_1 + 1,500X_2$
$S_1 = 3,360, S_2 = 9,600$
X_2
S_2
800 units of X_2

Max E $= .8X_1 + .4X_2 + 1.2X_3 - .1X_4 + 0S_1 + 0S_2 - MA_1 - MA_2$
Subject to:
$X_1 + 2X_2 + X_3 + 5X_4 + S_1 = 150$
$X_2 - 4X_3 + 8X_4 + A_1 = 70$
$6X_1 + 7X_2 + 2X_3 - X_4 - S_2 + A_2 = 120$

See Instructor's Section for table.

QA12-13

$X_1 = 2, X_2 = 6, S_1 = 0,$
$S_2 = 0,$ and profit $= \$36.$
See Instructor's Section for details.

QA12-14

12-14 Convert the following LP problem into the proper simplex form and solve by applying the simplex algorithm.

$$\text{Maximize profit} = 20X_1 + 10X_2$$

$$\text{Subject to:} \quad 5X_1 + 4X_2 \leqslant 250$$

$$2X_1 + 5X_2 \leqslant 150$$

$$X_1, X_2 \geqslant 0$$

$X_1 = 50$, $X_2 = 0$, and profit = \$1,000

Also solve the problem graphically and compare your answers.

QA12-15

12-15 Solve the following linear programming problem first graphically and then by the simplex algorithm.

Basis for 1st tableau:
$A_1 = 80$
$A_2 = 75$
Basis for 2nd tableau:
$A_1 = 55$
$X_1 = 25$
Basis for 3rd tableau:
$X_1 = 14$
$X_2 = 33$
Cost = 221 at optimal solution

$$\text{Minimize cost} = 4X_1 + 5X_2$$

$$\text{Subject to:} \quad X_1 + 2X_2 \geqslant 80$$

$$3X_1 + X_2 \geqslant 75$$

$$X_1, X_2 \geqslant 0$$

What are the values of the basic variables at each iteration? Which are the nonbasic variables at each iteration?

12-16 The final simplex tableau for an LP maximization problem is shown in the accompanying table.

This problem is infeasible. All $C_j - Z_j$ are 0 or negative, but an artificial variable remains in the basis.

$C_j \rightarrow$	SOLUTION MIX	3	5	0	0	$-M$	
$\downarrow$		X_1	X_2	S_1	S_2	A_1	QUANTITY
5	X_2	1	1	2	0	0	6
$-M$	A_1	-1	0	-2	-1	1	2
	Z_j	$5 + M$	5	$10 + 2M$	$+M$	$-M$	$30 - 2M$
	$C_j - Z_j$	$-2 - M$	0	$-10 - 2M$	$-M$	0	

Describe the situation encountered here.

QA12-17

12-17 Solve the following problem by the simplex method. What condition exists that prevents you from reaching an optimal solution?

Problem is UNBOUNDED: See Instructor's Section for details.

$$\text{Maximize profit} = 6X_1 + 3X_2$$

$$\text{Subject to:} \quad 2X_1 - 2X_2 \leqslant 2$$

$$-X_1 + X_2 \leqslant 1$$

$$X_1, X_2 \geqslant 0$$

QA12-18

12-18 Consider the following financial problem:

$$\text{Maximize return on investment} = \$2X_1 + \$3X_2$$

$$\text{Subject to:} \quad 6X_1 + 9X_2 \leqslant 18$$

$$9X_1 + 3X_2 \geqslant 9$$

$$X_1, X_2 \geqslant 0$$

$X_1 = 3$, $X_2 = 0$. ROI = \$6
X_2 has a $C_j - Z_j$ value of \$0

(a) Find the optimal solution using the simplex method.
(b) What evidence indicates that an alternate optimal solution exists?

(c) Find the alternate optimal solution.

(d) Solve this problem graphically as well, and illustrate the alternate optimal corner points.

$X_1 = 3/7 = .42; X_2 = 12/7$
$= 1.7;$ ROI $= \$6$

: **12-19** At the third iteration of a particular linear programming maximization problem, the following tableau is established.

$C_j \rightarrow$	SOLUTION MIX	$\$6$ X_1	$\$3$ X_2	$\$5$ X_3	0 S_1	0 S_2	0 S_3	QUANTITY
$\$5$	X_3	0	1	1	1	0	3	5
$\$6$	X_1	1	-3	0	0	0	1	12
$\$0$	S_2	0	2	0	1	1	-1	10
	Z_j	$\$6$	$-\$13$	$\$5$	$\$5$	$\$0$	$\$21$	$\$97$
	$C_j - Z_j$	$\$0$	$\$16$	$\$0$	$-\$5$	$\$0$	$-\$21$	

What special condition exists as you improve the profit and move to the next iteration? Proceed to solve the problem for the optimal solution.

The problem is degenerate. Variable X_2 should enter the solution next.
$X_1 = 27, X_2 = 5, X_3 = 0,$
Profit $= \$177$

: **12-20** A pharmaceutical firm is about to begin production of three new drugs. An objective function designed to minimize ingredient costs and three production constraints are shown below.

$$\text{Minimize cost} = 50X_1 + 10X_2 + 75X_3$$

$$\text{Subject to:} \quad X_1 - X_2 \qquad = 1,000$$
$$2X_2 + 2X_3 = 2,000$$
$$X_1 \qquad \leqslant 1,500$$
$$X_1, X_2, X_3 \geqslant 0$$

(a) Convert these constraints and objective function to the proper form for use in the simplex tableau.

(b) Solve the problem by the simplex method. What is the optimal solution and cost?

QA12-20

See the Instructor's Section.
$X_1 = 1500, X_2 = 500, X_3 = 500, C = \$117,500$

: **12-21** The S. Gillespie Corporation faces a blending decision in developing a new cat food called Yum-Mix. Two basic ingredients have been combined and tested, and the firm has determined that to each can of Yum-Mix at least 30 units of protein and at least 80 units of riboflavin must be added. These two nutrients are available in two competing brands of animal food supplements. The cost per kilogram of the brand A supplement is $9, while the cost per kilogram of brand B supplement is $15. A kilogram of brand A added to each production batch of Yum-Mix provides a supplement of 1 unit of protein and 1 unit of riboflavin to each can. A kilogram of brand B provides 2 units of protein and 4 units of riboflavin in each can. Gillespie must satisfy these minimum nutrient standards while keeping costs of supplements to a minimum.

(a) Formulate this problem to find the best combination of the two supplements to meet the minimum requirements at the least cost.

(b) Solve for the optimal solution by the simplex method.

QA12-21

Min Cost $= 9X_1 + 15X_2 + OS_1 + OS_2 + MA_1 + MA_2$
Subject to:
$X_1 + 2X_2 - S_1 + A_1 = 30$
$X_1 + 4X_2 - S_2 + A_2 = 80$
$X_1 = 0$ kg., $X_2 = 20$ kg.,
Cost $= \$300$

· **12-22** The Roniger Company produces two products: bed mattresses and box springs. A prior contract requires that the firm produce at least 30 mattresses or box springs, in any combination. In addition, union labor agreements

QA12-22

Min. Cost $= 20X_1 + 24X_2$
Subject to:
$X_1 + X_2 \geqslant 30$
$X_1 + 2X_2 \geqslant 40$
$X_1 = 20, X_2 = 10$, Cost $=$ 640

QA12-23

Max P $= 9X_1 + 12X_2$
Subject to:
$X_1 + X_2 \leqslant 10$
$X_1 + 2X_2 \leqslant 12$
$X_1 = 8, X_2 = 2$,
Profit $= 96

QA12-24

Max P $= 8X_1 + 6X_2 + 14X_3$
Subject to:
$2X_1 + X_2 + 3X_3 \leqslant 120$
$2X_1 + 6X_2 + 4X_3 = 240$
$X_1 = 0, X_2 = 17.14, X_3 =$ 34.29, P $= 582.86

QA12-25

demand that stitching machines be kept running at least 40 hours per week, which is one production period. Each box spring takes two hours of stitching time, while each mattress takes one hour on the machine. Each mattress produced costs $20, each box spring costs $24.

(a) Formulate this problem so as to minimize total production costs.
(b) Solve using the simplex method.

12-23 Each coffee table produced by Meising Designers nets the firm a profit of $9. Each bookcase yields a $12 profit. Meising's firm is small, and its resources limited. During any given production period of one week, 10 gallons of varnish and 12 lengths of high-quality redwood are available. Each coffee table requires approximately 1 gallon of varnish and 1 length of redwood. Each bookcase takes 1 gallon of varnish and 2 lengths of wood. Formulate Meising's production mix decision as a linear programming problem, and solve using the simplex method. How many tables and bookcases should be produced each week? What will the maximum profit be?

12-24 Bagwell Distributors packages and distributes industrial supplies. A standard shipment can be packaged in a class A container, a class K container, or a class T container. A single class A container yields a profit of $8; a class K container, a profit of $6; and a class T container, a profit of $14. Each shipment prepared requires a certain amount of packing material and a certain amount of time, as seen in the following table.

	RESOURCES NEEDED PER STANDARD SHIPMENT	
CLASS OF CONTAINER	PACKING MATERIAL (POUNDS)	PACKING TIME (HOURS)
A	2	2
K	1	6
T	3	4
Total amount of resource available each week	120 pounds	240 hours

Bill Bagwell, head of the firm, must decide the optimal number of each class of container to pack each week. He is bound by the previously mentioned resource restrictions, but he also decides that he must keep his six full-time packers employed all 240 hours (6 workers × 40 hours) each week. Formulate and solve this problem using the simplex method.

12-25 The Foggy Bottom Development Corporation has just purchased a small hotel for conversion to condominium apartments. The building, in a popular area of Washington, D.C., near the U.S. State Department, will be highly marketable, and each condominium sale is expected to yield a good profit. The conversion process, however, includes several options. Basically, four types of condominiums can be designed out of the former hotel rooms. They are: deluxe one-bedroom apartments, regular one-bedroom apartments, deluxe studios, and efficiency apartments. Each will yield a different profit, but each type also requires a different level of investment in carpeting, painting, appliances, and carpentry work. Bank loans dictate a limited budget that may be allocated to each of these needs. Profit and cost data, and cost of conversion requirements for each apartment are shown in the accompanying table.

RENOVATION REQUIREMENT	TYPE OF APARTMENT				TOTAL BUDGETED ($)
	Deluxe 1-Bedroom ($)	Regular 1-Bedroom ($)	Deluxe Studio ($)	Efficiency ($)	
New carpeting	1,100	1,000	600	500	35,000
Painting	700	600	400	300	28,000
New appliances	2,000	1,600	1,200	900	45,000
Carpentry work	1,000	400	900	200	19,000
Profit per unit	8,000	6,000	5,000	3,500	

Thus, we see that the cost of carpeting a deluxe one-bedroom unit will be $1,100, the cost of carpeting a regular one-bedroom unit is $1,000, and so on. A total of $35,000 is budgeted for all new carpeting in the building.

Zoning regulations dictate that the building contain no more than 50 condominiums when the conversion is completed—and no less than 25 units. The development company also decides that to have a good blend of owners, at least 40% but no more than 70% of the units should be one-bedroom apartments. Not all money budgeted in each category need be spent, although profit is not affected by cost savings. But since the money represents a bank loan, under no circumstances may it be exceeded or even shifted from one area, such as carpeting, to another, such as painting.

(a) Formulate Foggy Bottom Development Corporation's decision as a linear program to maximize profits.

(b) Convert your objective function and constraints to a form containing the appropriate slack, surplus, and artificial variables. Do not attempt to solve the problem.

> $\text{Max } P = 8,000X_1 + 6,000X_2 + 5,000X_3 + 3,500X_4$
> $1,100X_1 + 1,000X_2 + 600X_3 + 500X_4 \leq \$35,000$
> $700X_1 + 600X_2 + 400X_3 + 300X_4 \leq \$28,000$
> $2,000X_1 + 1,600X_2 + 1,200X_3 + 900X_4 \leq \$45,000$
> $1,000X_1 + 400X_2 + 900X_3 + 200X_4 \leq \$19,000$
> $X_1 + X_2 + X_3 + X_4 \leq 50$
> $X_1 + X_2 + X_3 + X_4 \geq 25$
> $.6X_1 + .6X_2 - .4X_3 - .4X_4 \geq 0$
> $.3X_1 + .3X_2 - .7X_3 - .7X_4 \leq 0$
>
> See the Instructor's Section for details.

12-26 The accompanying initial simplex tableau was developed by Tommy Gibbs, vice president of a large cotton spinning mill. Gibbs unfortunately quit before completing this important linear programming application. Stephanie Robbins, the newly hired replacement, was immediately given this task of using LP to determine what different kinds of yarn the mill should use to minimize costs. Her first need was to be certain that Gibbs correctly formulated the objective function and constraints. Since she could find no statement of the problem in the files, she decided to reconstruct the problem from the initial tableau.

(a) What is the correct formulation, using real decision variables (that is, X_is) only?

(b) Which variable will enter this current solution mix in the second tableau? Which basic variable will leave?

> QA12-26
> Minimize Cost = $12X_1 + 18X_2 + 10X_3 + 20X_4 + 7X_5 + 8X_8$
> Subject to:
> $X_1 - 3X_3 = 100$
> $25X_2 + X_3 + 2X_4 + 8X_5 \leq 900$
> $2X_1 + X_2 + 4X_4 + X_6 \geq 250$
> $18X_1 - 15X_2 - 2X_3 - X_4 + 15X_5 \geq 150$
> $25X_6 \leq 300$
> $2X_4 + 6X_5 \geq 70$
>
> Variable X_5 will enter the basis next: variable A_3 will leave the basis.

$C_j \rightarrow$ SOLUTION MIX	$12 X_1	$18 X_2	$10 X_3	$20 X_4	$7 X_5	$8 X_6	$0 S_1	$0 S_2	$0 S_3	$0 S_4	$0 S_5	M A_1	M A_2	M A_3	M A_4	QUANTITY
M A_1	1	0	−3	0	0	0	0	0	0	0	0	1	0	0	0	100
0 S_1	0	25	1	2	8	0	1	0	0	0	0	0	0	0	0	900
M A_2	2	1	0	4	0	1	0	−1	0	0	0	0	1	0	0	250
M A_3	18	−15	−2	−1	15	0	0	0	−1	0	0	0	0	1	0	150
0 S_4	0	0	0	0	0	25	0	0	0	1	0	0	0	0	0	300
M A_4	0	0	0	2	6	0	0	0	0	0	−1	0	0	0	1	70
Z_j	21M	−14M	−5M	5M	21M	M	0	0	−M	0	−M	M	M	M	M	570M
$C_j - Z_j$	12 − 21M	18 + 14M	10 + 5M	20 − 5M	7 − 21M	8 − M	0	0	M	0	M	0	0	0	0	

Coastal States Chemicals and Fertilizers

In December 1991, Bill Stock, general manager for the Louisiana Division of Coastal States Chemicals and Fertilizers, received a letter from Fred McNair of the Cajan Pipeline Company which notified Coastal States that priorities had been established for the allocation of natural gas. The letter stated that Cajan Pipeline, the primary supplier of natural gas to Coastal States, might be instructed to curtail natural gas supplies to its industrial and commercial customers by as much as 40% during the ensuing winter months. Moreover, Cajan Pipeline had the approval of the Federal Power Commission (FPC) to curtail such supplies.

Possible curtailment was attributed to the priorities established for the use of natural gas:

First priority: Residential and commercial heating

Second priority: Commercial and industrial users whereby natural gas is used as a source of raw material

Third priority: Commercial and industrial users whereby natural gas is used as boiler fuel

Almost all of Coastal State's uses of natural gas were in the second and third priorities. Hence, its plants were certainly subject to brown-outs, or natural gas curtailments. The occurrence and severity of the brown-outs depended on a number of complex factors. First of all, Cajan Pipeline was part of an interstate transmission network that delivered natural gas to residential and commercial buildings on the Atlantic Coast and in northeastern regions of the United States. Hence, the severity of the forthcoming winter in these regions would have a direct impact on the use of natural gas.

Secondly, the demand for natural gas was soaring because it was the cleanest and most efficient fuel. There were almost no environmental problems in burning natural gas. Moreover, maintenance problems due to fuel-fouling in fireboxes and boilers were negligible with natural gas systems. Also, burners were much easier to operate with natural gas as compared to the use of oil or the stoking operation when coal was used as fuel.

Finally, the supply of natural gas was dwindling. The traditionally depressed price of natural gas had discouraged new exploration for gas wells; hence, shortages appeared imminent.

Stock and his staff at Coastal States had been aware of the possibility of shortages of natural gas and had been investigating ways of converting to fuel oil or coal as a substitute for natural gas. Their plans, however, were still in the developmental stages. Coastal States required an immediate contingency plan to minimize the effect of a natural gas curtailment on its multiplant operations. The obvious question was, what operations should be curtailed and to what extent to minimize the adverse effect upon profits? Coastal States had the approval from the FPC and Cajan Pipeline to specify which of its plants would bear the burden of the curtailment if such cutbacks were necessary. McNair, of Cajan Pipeline, replied, "It's your 'pie': we don't care how you divide it if we make it smaller."

The Model

Six plants of Coastal States Louisiana Division were to share in the "pie." They were all located in the massive Baton Rouge-Geismar-Gramercy industrial complex along the Mississippi River between Baton Rouge and New Orleans. Products produced at those plants which required significant amounts of natural gas were phosphoric acid, urea, ammonium phosphate, ammonium nitrate, chlorine, caustic soda, vinyl chloride monomer, and hydrofluoric acid.

Stock called a meeting of members of his technical staff to discuss a contingency plan for allocation of natural gas among the products if a curtailment developed. The objective was to minimize the impact on profits. After detailed discussion, the meeting was adjourned. Two weeks later, the meeting reconvened. At this session, the data in the accompanying table were presented.

Coastal State's contract with Cajan Pipeline specified a maximum natural gas consumption of 36,000 cu ft $\times 10^3$ per day for all of the six member plants. With these data, the technical staff proceeded to develop a model that would specify changes in production rates in resposne to a natural gas curtailment. (Curtailments are based on contracted consumption and not current consumption.)

Contribution to Profit and Overhead

PRODUCT	$ PER TON	CAPACITY (TONS PER DAY)	MAXIMUM PRODUCTION RATE (PERCENT OF CAPACITY)	NATURAL GAS CONSUMPTION (1,000 CU FT PER TON)
Phosphoric acid	60	400	80	5.5
Urea	80	250	80	7.0
Ammonium phosphate	90	300	90	8.0
Ammonium nitrate	100	300	100	10.0
Chlorine	50	800	60	15.0
Caustic soda	50	1,000	60	16.0
Vinyl chloride monomer	65	500	60	12.0
Hydrofluoric acid	70	400	80	11.0

1. Develop a contingency model and specify the production rates for each product for:
   (a) a 20% natural gas curtailment and
   (b) a 40% natural gas curtailment.

2. Explain which of the products in the table should require the most emphasis with regard to energy conservation.

3. What problems do you foresee if production rates are not reduced in a planned and orderly manner?

4. What impact will the natural gas shortage have on company profits?

   Source: Dean Jerry Kinard (Francis Marion College).

Normal profit: $185,400/day
With 20 percent curtailment: $174,650/day
With 40 percent curtailment: $151,933/day

BIBLIOGRAPHY

See Bibliography at end of Chapter 10.

13

Linear Programming: Sensitivity Analysis and Duality

CHAPTER OUTLINE

13.1 Introduction

13.2 Sensitivity Analysis

13.3 The Dual in Linear Programming

13.4 The Role of Computer Software in Sensitivity Analysis: Looking at High Note Sound Company with AB:QM, STORM, LINDO, and What's*Best!*

13.5 Summary

Glossary

Solved Problem

Discussion Questions and Problems

Case Study: Red Brand Canners

Bibliography

13.1 INTRODUCTION

In Chapters 10, 11, and 12, we studied how to formulate linear programming problems and how to find optimal solutions by using the graphical
and simplex methods. As important as these subjects are, they do not complete our analysis of LP. For this chapter, we have saved two of the most
valuable aspects of linear programming from a managerial perspective.
The first, *sensitivity analysis,* recognizes that management operates in a dynamic environment. This means that costs and prices change, resources di-
minish or become more readily available, and technological advances
affecting production occur. And it means that a company using LP must
explore the sensitivity of an optimal LP solution to changes in the data
used to build the model. We very briefly introduced this topic in
Chapter 10.

sensitivity analysis

The second topic addressed in this chapter is the concept of the *dual,*
or duality. It turns out that all linear programming problems exist in
pairs. For every problem you have formulated so far in studying LP, a
sister dual problem could also have been designed. Its use in providing
economic information and in helping to reach a solution more quickly will
be discussed.

duality

13.2 SENSITIVITY ANALYSIS

Teaching Suggestion 13.1:
The Importance of Sensitivity
Analysis. See the Instructor's
Section for details.

Transparency Master 13.1:
Sensitivity Analysis.

Optimal solutions to linear programming problems have thus far been
found under what are called *deterministic assumptions.* This means that we
assume complete certainty in the data and relationships of a problem—
namely, prices are fixed, resources known, time needed to produce a unit
exactly set. But in the real world, conditions are dynamic and changing.
How can we handle this apparent discrepancy?

One way we can do so is by continuing to treat each particular LP problem as a deterministic situation. However, when an optimal solution is
found, we recognize the importance of seeing just how *sensitive* that solution is to model assumptions and data. For example, if a firm realizes that
profit per unit is not $5 as estimated, but instead closer to $5.50, how will
the final solution mix and total profit change? If additional resources, such
as ten labor hours or three hours of machine time, should become available,
will this change the problem's answer? Such analyses are used to examine
the effects of changes in three areas: (1) contribution rates (C_j's) for each
variable, (2) technological coefficients (the numbers in the constraint equations), and (3) available resources (the right-hand-side quantities in each
constraint). This task is alternately called *sensitivity analysis, postoptimality
analysis, parametric programming,* or *optimality analysis.*

**how sensitive is optimal
solution?**

**examining changes in
three areas**

The use of sensitivity analysis by management is also often centered
around a series of what-if questions. What if the profit on product 1 increases by 10%? What if less money is available in the advertising budget

constraint? What if workers each stay one hour longer every day at 1½-time pay to provide increased production capacity? What if new technology will allow a product to be wired in one-third the time it used to take? So we see that sensitivity analysis can be used to deal not only with errors in estimating input parameters to the LP model, but also with management's experiments with possible future changes in the firm that may affect profits.

There are two approaches to determining just how sensitive an optimal solution is to changes. The first is simply a trial-and-error approach. This approach usually involves resolving the entire problem, preferably by computer, each time one input data item or parameter is changed. It can take a long time to test a series of possible changes in this way.

The approach we prefer is the analytic postoptimality method. After an LP problem has been solved, we attempt to determine a range of changes in problem parameters that will not affect the optimal solution or change the variables in the basis. This is done without resolving the whole problem.

Let's investigate sensitivity analysis by developing a small production mix problem. Our goal will be to demonstrate graphically and through the simplex tableau how sensitivity analysis can be used to make linear programming concepts more realistic and insightful.

KEY IDEA

postoptimality analysis

The High Note Sound Company

The High Note Sound Company manufactures quality stereo record players and stereo receivers. Each of these products requires a certain amount of skilled craftsmanship, of which there is a limited weekly supply. The firm formulates the following linear programming problem in order to determine the best production mix of record players (X_1) and receivers (X_2):

Alternate Example 13.1

Maximize profit $= \$50X_1 + \$120X_2$

Subject to:

$2X_1 + 4X_2 \leq 80$ (*Hours of available electricians' time*)

$3X_1 + 1X_2 \leq 60$ (*Hours of audio technicians' time available*)

$X_1, \quad X_2 \geq 0$

The solution to this problem is illustrated graphically in Figure 13.1. Given this information and deterministic assumptions, the firm should produce only stereo receivers (20 of them) for a weekly profit of $2,400.

Changes in the Objective Function Coefficient

In real-life problems, contribution rates (usually profit or cost) in the objective functions fluctuate periodically, as do most of a firm's expenses. Graphically, this means that although the feasible solution region remains exactly the same, the slope of the iso-profit or iso-cost line will change. It is easy to see in Figure 13.2 that the High Note Sound Company's profit line is optimal at point *a*. But what if a technical breakthrough just occurred

**Applicable Problems
13-10, 13-12, 13-15a, b,
13-27g, 13-28e**

changes in contribution rates

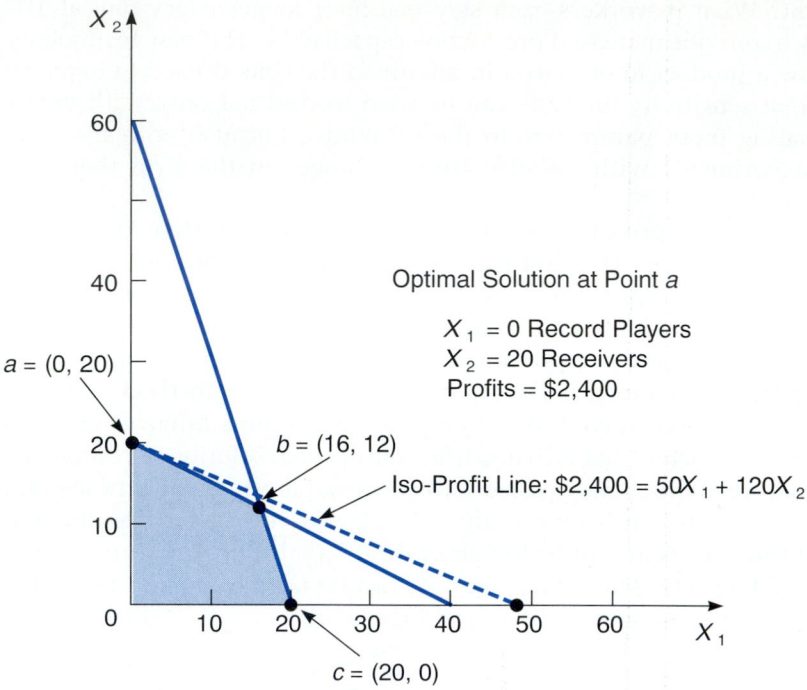

FIGURE 13.1
High Note Sound Company Graphical Solution

that raised the profit per stereo receiver (X_2) from $120 to $150? Is the solution still optimal? The answer is definitely *yes,* for in this case the slope of the profit line accentuates the profitability at point *a*. The new profit is $3,000 = 0($50) + 20($150).

On the other hand, if X_2's profit coefficient was overestimated and should only have been $80, the slope of the profit line changes enough to cause a new corner point (*b*) to become optimal. Here the profit is $1,760 = 16($50) + 12($80).

A second way of illustrating the sensitivity analysis of objective function coefficients is to consider the problem's final simplex tableau. For the High Note Sound Company, this tableau is shown in Table 13.1. The optimal solution is seen to be:

X_2 = 20 stereo receivers   } *Basic variables*

S_2 = 40 hours of slack time of audio technicians

X_1 = 0 record players   } *Nonbasic variables*

S_1 = 0 hours of slack time of electricians

Basic variables (those in the solution mix) and *nonbasic variables* (those set equal to 0) must be handled differently using sensitivity analysis. Let us first consider the case of a nonbasic variable.

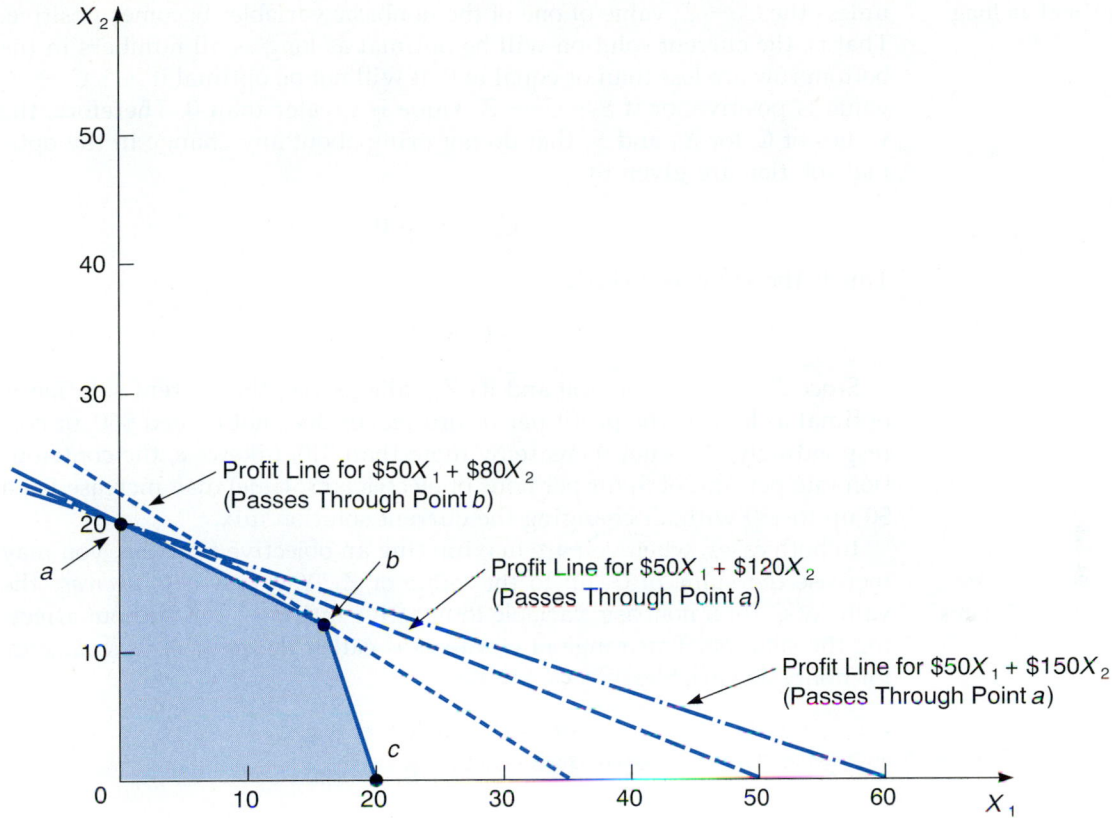

FIGURE 13.2
Changes in the Receiver Contribution Coefficients

Nonbasic Objective Function Coefficient. Our goal here is to find out how sensitive the problem's optimal solution is to changes in the contribution rates of variables not currently in the basis (X_1 and S_1). Just how much would the objective function coefficients have to change before X_1 or S_1 would enter the solution mix and replace one of the basic variables?

The answer lies in the $C_j - Z_j$ row of the final simplex tableau (as in Table 13.1). Since this is a maximization problem, the basis will not change

nonbasic variables

TABLE 13.1 Optimal Solution by the Simplex Method

$C_j \rightarrow$ $\downarrow$	SOLUTION MIX	$50 X_1	$120 X_2	$0 S_1	$0 S_2	QUANTITY
$120	X_2	$1/2$	1	$1/4$	0	20
$0	S_2	$5/2$	0	$-1/4$	1	40
	Z_j	60	120	30	0	$2,400
	$C_j - Z_j$	−10	0	−30	0	

solution optimal as long as all $C_j - Z_j \leq 0$

unless the $C_j - Z_j$ value of one of the nonbasic variables becomes positive. That is, the current solution will be optimal as long as all numbers in the bottom row are less than or equal to 0. It will not be optimal if X_1's $C_j - Z_j$ value is positive, or if S_1's $C_j - Z_j$ value is greater than 0. Therefore, the values of C_j for X_1 and S_1 that do not bring about any change in the optimal solution are given by:

$$C_j - Z_j \leq 0$$

This is the same as writing:

$$C_j \leq Z_j$$

Since X_1's C_j value is $50 and its Z_j value is $60, the current solution is optimal as long as the profit per record player does not exceed $60, or correspondingly, does not increase by more than $10. Likewise, the contribution rate per unit of S_1 (or per hour of electricians' time) may increase from $0 up to $30 without changing the current solution mix.

In both cases, when you are maximizing an objective function, you may increase the value of C_j up to the value of Z_j. You may also *decrease* the value of C_j for a nonbasic variable to negative infinity ($-\infty$) without affecting the solution. This range of C_j values is called the *range of insignificance* for nonbasic variables.

range over which C_j rates remain valid

$$-\infty \leq C_j \text{ (for } X_1) \leq \$60$$

$$-\infty \leq C_j \text{ (for } S_1) \leq \$30$$

Basic Objective Function Coefficient. Sensitivity analysis on objective function coefficients of variables that are in the basis or solution mix is slightly more complex. We saw that a change in the objective function coefficient for a nonbasic variable affects only the $C_j - Z_j$ value for that variable. But a change in the profit or cost of a basic variable can affect the $C_j - Z_j$ values of *all* nonbasic variables.

testing basic variables involves reworking final simplex tableau

Let us consider changing the profit contribution of stereo receivers in the High Note Sound Company problem. Currently, the objective function coefficient is $120. The change in this value can be denoted by the Greek letter Δ. We rework the final simplex tableau (first shown Table 13.1) and see our results in Table 13.2.

Notice the new $C_j - Z_j$ values for nonbasic variables X_1 and S_1. These were determined in exactly the same way as in Chapter 12. But wherever

TABLE 13.2 A Change in the Profit Contribution of Stereo Receivers

$C_j \rightarrow$ $\downarrow$	SOLUTION MIX	$50 X_1	$120 + \Delta$ X_2	$0 S_1	$0 S_2	QUANTITY
$120 + \Delta$	X_2	$1/2$	1	$1/4$	0	20
$0	S_2	$5/2$	0	$-1/4$	1	40
	Z_j	$60 + \frac{1}{2}\Delta$	$120 + \Delta$	$30 + \frac{1}{4}\Delta$	0	$2,400 + 20\Delta$
	$C_j - Z_j$	$-10 - \frac{1}{2}\Delta$	0	$-30 - \frac{1}{4}\Delta$	0	

the C_j value for X_2 of \$120 was seen in Table 13.1, a new value of $\$120 + \Delta$ is used in Table 13.2.

Once again, we recognize that the current optimal solution will change only if one or more of the $C_j - Z_j$ row values becomes greater than 0. The question is, how may the value of Δ vary so that all $C_j - Z_j$ entries remain positive? To find out, we solve for Δ in each column.

From the X_1 column:

$$-10 - \tfrac{1}{2}\Delta \leq 0$$
$$-10 \leq \tfrac{1}{2}\Delta$$
$$-20 \leq \Delta \qquad \text{or} \qquad \Delta \geq -20$$

This inequality means that the optimal solution will not change unless X_2's profit coefficient decreases by at least \$20, which is a change of $\Delta = \$-20$. Hence, variable X_1 will not enter the basis unless the profit per stereo receiver drops from \$120 to \$100 or less. This, interestingly, is exactly what we noticed graphically in Figure 13.2. When the profit per stereo dropped to \$80, the optimal solution changed from corner point a to corner point b.

Now we examine the S_1 column:

$$-30 - \tfrac{1}{4}\Delta \leq 0$$
$$-30 \leq \tfrac{1}{4}\Delta$$
$$-120 \leq \Delta \qquad \text{or} \qquad \Delta \geq -120$$

This inequality implies that S_1 is less sensitive to change than X_1. S_1 will not enter the basis unless the profit per unit of X_2 drops from \$120 all the way down to \$0.

Since the first inequality is more binding, we can say that the *range of optimality* for X_2's profit coefficient is:

range of optimality

$$\$100 \leq Cj \text{ (for } X_2) \leq \infty$$

As long as the profit per stereo receiver is greater than or equal to \$100, the current production mix of $X_2 = 20$ receivers and $X_1 = 0$ record players will be optimal.

In analyzing larger problems, we would use this procedure to test for the range of optimality of every real decision variable in the final solution mix. The procedure helps us avoid the time-consuming process of reformulating and resolving the entire linear programming problem each time a small change occurs. Within the bounds set, changes in profit coefficients would not force a firm to alter its prouct mix decision or change the number of units produced. Overall profits, of course, will change if a profit coefficient increases or decreases, but such computations are quick and easy to perform.

Changes in the Technological Coefficients

Applicable Problems 13-11, 13-13

Changes in what are called the *technological coefficients* often reflect changes in the state of technology. If fewer or more resources are needed to produce a product such as a record player or stereo receiver, coefficients in

changes in technological coefficients affect feasible solution region

the constraint equations will change. These changes will have no effect on the objective function of an LP problem, but they can produce a significant change in the shape of the feasible solution region, and hence in the optimal profit or cost. Sensitivity analysis of technological coefficients by the simplex method can become very detailed and is beyond the scope of this text. But a graphical demonstration should suit your needs at this time.

Figure 13.3 illustrates the original High Note Sound Company graphical solution as well as two separate changes in technological coefficients. In Figure 13.3a, we see that the optimal solution lies at point a, which represents $X_1 = 0$, $X_2 = 20$. You should be able to prove to yourself that point a remains optimal in Figure 13.3b despite a constraint change from $3X_1 + 1X_2 \leq 60$ to $2X_1 + 1X_2 \leq 60$. Such a change might take place when the firm discovers that it no longer demands three hours of audio technicians' time to produce a record player, but now only two hours.

In Figure 13.3c, however, a change in the other constraint changes the shape of the feasible region enough to cause a new corner point (g) to become optimal. Before moving on, see if you reach an objective function value of $1,954 profit at point g (versus a profit of $1,920 at point f).[1]

Changes in the Resources or Right-Hand-Side Values

The values on the right-hand-side of linear programming constraints can be considered to represent the reources available to the firm. These re-

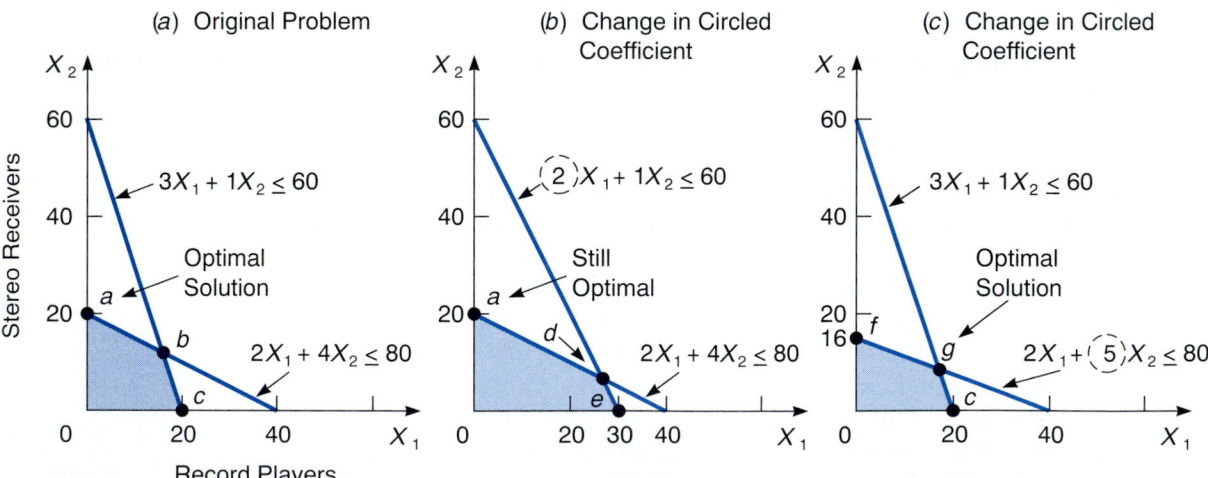

FIGURE 13.3
**Change in the Technological Coefficients for the
High Note Sound Company**

[1]Note that the values for X_1 and X_2 at point g are fractions. Although High Note Sound Company cannot produce ⅔, ¾, or ⁹⁄₁₀ of a record player or stereo, we can assume the firm can *begin* a unit one week and complete it the next. As long as the production process is fairly stable from week to week, this raises no major problems. If solutions *must* be whole numbers each period, refer to Chapter 15's discussion of integer programming to handle the situation.

sources may be labor hours or machine time available, or perhaps money or production materials available. In the High Note Sound Company example, the two resources are hours of available electricians' time and hours of audio technicians' time. Knowledge of how sensitive the optimal solution is to changes in resources such as these is important because of dynamic marketplace conditions.

Changes in the right-hand-side values result in changes in the feasible region and often in the optimal solution. Figure 13.4 illustrates two resource changes dealing with the number of hours of available electricians' time for each week's production process. An iso-profit line or corner point approach indicates in both Figure 13.4*a* and 13.4*b* that corner point *a* is

resource changes affect feasible region

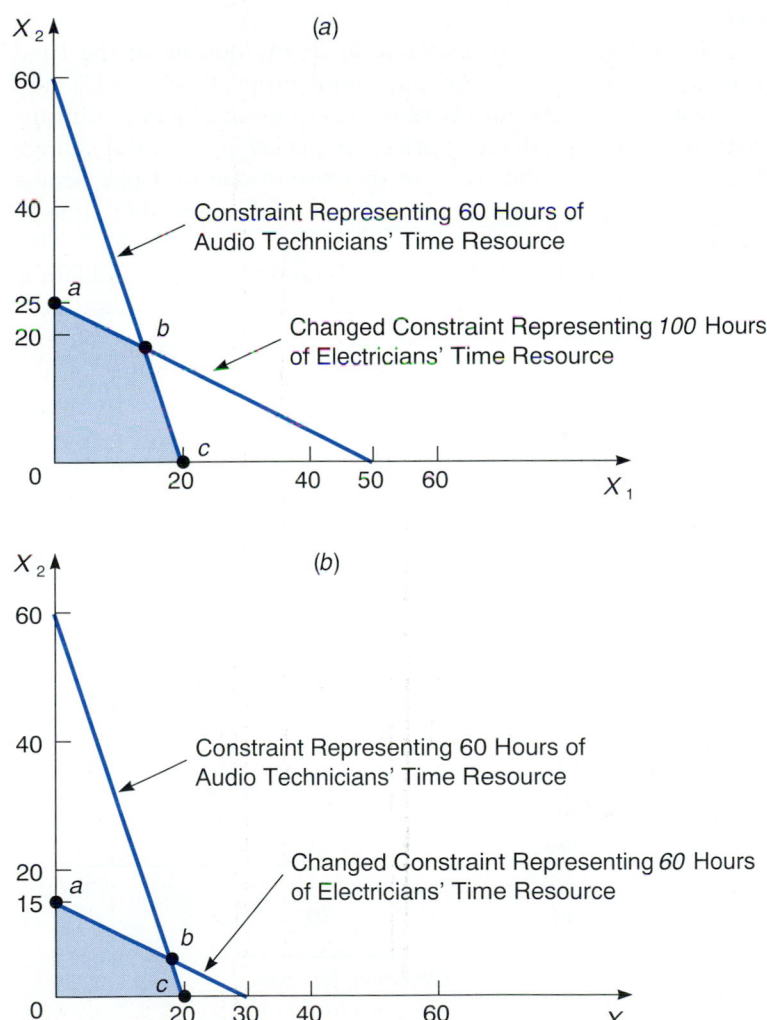

FIGURE 13.4
Changes in the Electricians' Time Resource for the High Note Sound Company

optimal. However, in Figure 13.4a, the new resource of 100 electricians' hours (as compared to 80 in the original problem) yields a solution of $X_1 = 0$ record players, $X_2 = 25$ receivers, and profit = $3,000. Reducing the available resource to only 60 hours (Figure 13.4b) alters the feasible region again. This time the optimal solution is to produce $X_1 = 0$ record players and $X_2 = 15$ receivers, for a profit of $1,800.

Transparency Master 13.3:
Shadow Prices.

value of additional resources

KEY IDEA

Applicable Problems 13-16, 13-17, 13-28b

Shadow Prices. This graphical example leads us to the important subject of *shadow prices.* Exactly how much should a firm be willing to pay to make additional resources available? Is one more hour of machine time worth $1 or $5 or $20? Is it worthwhile to pay workers an overtime rate to stay one extra hour each night in order to increase production output? Valuable management information could be provided if the worth of additional resources was known.

Fortunately, this information is available to us by looking at the final simplex tableau of an LP problem. An important property of the $C_j - Z_j$ row is that the negatives of the numbers in its slack variable(S_i) columns provide us with what we call shadow prices. A *shadow price* is the change in value of the objective function from an increase of one unit of a scarce resource (e.g., by making one more hour of machine time or labor time or other resource available).

The final simplex tableau for the High Note Sound Company problem is repeated as Table 13.3 (it was first shown as Table 13.1). The tableau indicates that the optimal solution is $X_1 = 0$, $X_2 = 20$, $S_1 = 0$, $S_2 = 40$, and that profit = $2,400. Recall that S_1 represents slack availability of the electricians' resource and S_2 the unused time in the audio technicians' department.

The firm is considering hiring an extra electrician on a part-time basis. Let's say it will cost $22 per hour in wages and benefits to bring the part-timer on board. Should the firm do this? The answer is *yes:* the shadow price of the electrician time resource is $30. Thus, the firm will *net* $8 (=$30 − $22) for every hour the new worker helps in the production process.

TABLE 13.3 Final Tableau for the High Note Sound Company

$C_j \rightarrow$ $\downarrow$	SOLUTION MIX	$50 X_1	$120 X_2	$0 S_1	$0 S_2	QUANTITY
$120	X_2	$1/2$	1	$1/4$	1	20
$0	S_2	$5/2$	0	$-1/4$	0	40
	Z_j	60	120	30	0	$2,400
	$C_j - Z_j$	−10	0	−30	0	

Objective function increases by $30 if 1 additional hour of electricians' time is made available

Should High Note also hire a part-time audio technician at a rate of $14 per hour? The answer is *no:* the shadow price is $0, implying no increase in the objective function by making more of this second resource available. Why? Because not all of the resource is currently being used—40 hours are still available. It would hardly pay to buy more of the resource.

Right-Hand-Side Ranging. Obviously we can't add an unlimited number of units of resource without eventually violating one of the problem's constraints. Once we understand and compute the shadow price for an additional hour of electricians' time ($30), we will want to determine how many hours we can actually use to increase profits. Should the new resource be added 1 hour per week, 2 hours, or 200 hours? In linear programming terms, this process involves finding the range over which shadow prices will stay valid. *Right-hand-side* (RHS) *ranging* tells us the number of hours High Note can add or remove from the electrician department and still have a shadow price of $30.

range over which shadow prices remain valid

Ranging is simple in that it resembles the simplex process we used in Chapter 12 to find the minium ratio for a new variable. The S_1 column and quantity column from Table 13.3 are repeated below; the ratios, both positive and negative, are also shown.

QUANTITY	S_1	RATIO		
20	$\frac{1}{4}$	$20/(\frac{1}{4})$	=	80
40	$-\frac{1}{4}$	$40/(-\frac{1}{4})$	=	-160

The smallest positive ratio (80 in this example) tells us by how many hours the electricians' time resource can be *reduced* without altering the current solution mix. Hence, we may decrease the right-hand-side resource by as much as 80 hours—basically from the current 80 hours all the way to 0 hours—without causing a basic variable to be pivoted out of the solution.

how to do RHS ranging

The smallest negative ratio (−160) tells us the number of hours that can be added to the resource before the solution mix changes. In this case, we may increase electricians' time by 160 hours, up to 240 (= 80 currently + 160 may be added) hours. We have now established the range of electricians' time over which the shadow price of $30 is valid. That range is from 0 to 240 hours.

The audio technician resource is slightly different in that all 60 hours of time originally available have not been used. (Note that $S_2 = 40$ hours in Table 13.3.) If we apply the ratio test, we see that we can reduce the number of audio technicians' hours by only 40 before a shortage occurs. But since we are not using all the hours currently available, we can increase them indefinitely without altering the problem's solution. Hence, the valid range for *this* shadow price would be from 20(= 60 − 40) hours to an unbounded upper limit.

Applicable Problems 13-20
13-21, 13-22, 13-23, 13-24
13-26

every LP primal has a dual

dual provides useful information

Teaching Suggestion 13.3:
Advantage of Duality and Its Role as an LP Topic. See the Instructor's Section for details.

Alternate Example 13.2

dual variables are potential value of resources

formulating the dual

13.3   THE DUAL IN LINEAR PROGRAMMING

Every linear programming problem has another LP problem associated with it, which is called its *dual*. The first way of stating a linear program is called the *primal* of the problem: we can view all of the problems formulated thus far as primals. The second way of stating the same problem is called the *dual*. The optimal solutions for the primal and the dual are equivalent, but they are derived through alternative procedures.

The dual contains economic information useful to management, and it may also be easier to solve, in terms of less computation, than the primal problem. Generally, if the LP primal involves maximizing a profit function subject to less-than-or-equal-to resource constraints, the dual will involve minimizing total opportunity costs subject to greater-than-or-equal-to product profit constraints. Formulating the dual problem from a given primal is not terribly complex, and once it is formulated, the solution procedure is exactly the same as for any LP problem.

Let's illustrate the *primal-dual relationship* with the High Note Sound Company data. As you recall, the primal problem is to determine the best production mix of record players (X_1) and stereo receivers (X_2) in order to maximize profit.

$$\text{Maximize profit} = \$50X_1 + \$120X_2$$

Subject to:

$$2X_1 + 4X_2 \leq 80 \quad \textit{(Hours of available electrician time)}$$

$$3X_1 + 1X_2 \leq 60 \quad \textit{(Hours of audio technician time available)}$$

The dual of this problem has the objective of minimizing the opportunity cost of not using the resources in an optimal manner. Let's call the variables that it will attempt to solve for U_1 and U_2. U_1 represents the potential hourly contribution or worth of electrician time, in other words the dual value of one hour of the electrician's resource. U_2 stands for the imputed worth of the audio technician's time, or the dual technician resource.

The right-hand-side quantities of the primal *constraints* become the dual's *objective function* coefficients. The total opportunity cost that is to be minimized will be represented by the funciton $80U_1 + 60U_2$, namely,

$$\text{Minimize opportunity cost} = 80U_1 + 60U_2$$

The corresponding dual constraints are formed from the transpose[2] of the primal constraints coefficients. Note that if the primal constraints are $\leq$, the dual constraints are $\geq$.

---

[2]For example, the transpose of the set of numbers $\begin{pmatrix} a & b \\ c & d \end{pmatrix}$ is $\begin{pmatrix} a & c \\ b & d \end{pmatrix}$. In the case of the transpose of the primal coefficients $\begin{pmatrix} 2 & 4 \\ 3 & 1 \end{pmatrix}$, the result is $\begin{pmatrix} 2 & 3 \\ 4 & 1 \end{pmatrix}$. Refer to Module A, dealing with matrices and determinants, for a review of the transpose concept.

$$2\,U_1 + 3\,U_2 \geq 50 \longrightarrow \text{\textit{Primal profit}}$$
$$\text{\textit{coefficients}}$$
$$4\,U_1 + 1\,U_2 \geq 120$$

→ *Coefficients from the second primal constraint*

Coefficients from the first primal constraint

Let's look at the meaning of these dual constraints. In the first inequality, the right-hand-side constant ($50) is the income from one record player. The coefficients of U_1 and U_2 are the amounts of each scarce resource (electrician time and audio technician time) that are required to produce a record player. That is, two hours of electricians' time and three hours of audio technicians' time are used up in making one record player. Each record player produced yields $50 of revenue to High Note Sound Company. This inequality states that the total imputed value or potential worth of the scarce resources needed to produce a record player must be at least equal to the profit derived from the product. The second constraint makes an analogous statement for the stereo receiver product.

APPLICATIONS OF QA

Linear Programming at Dairyman's Cooperative

In many cases, decision makers and managers need an interactive decision support system (DSS) to assist in analyzing data instead of an automated system that will replace traditional decision making.

The Dairyman's Cooperative Creamery Association (DCCA) needed a decision support system to help in its daily production planning. This cooperative, like other milk processing cooperatives, was concerned with the most efficient way of getting milk products through the processing plants. The DCCA is one of the largest single milk processing plants whose facilities are at one location in the United States. Approximately 5 million pounds of raw milk per day are received and stored in silos. The raw milk is then transferred to various stations for processing. From the raw milk, about 50 products are produced.

Daily production planning, inventory control, and forecasting are made difficult by all of the interactions between the various milk products. For any of the 50 products, a number of by-products are automatically produced. Many of these products can then be used as raw materials for other products. In the cheese-processing plant, for example, there are a number of by-products, including whey, scrap cheese, fines, and salty whey.

To help solve the problem, an interactive milk flow analysis program (MFAP) was developed. This program includes a preprocessor module and the actual solution module that uses a linear programming approach. The preprocessor asks the decision maker to enter various capacities, current inventory levels, supply and demand, and other related information. This information is then used by the second module, which is a linear programming module. The LP module automatically develops 36 linear programming constraints, including production conversion constraints, product flow and balancing constraints, and equipment and inventory capacity limitation constraints. These constraints are saved on a disk and can be used and modified. The objective function is to maximize the expected profit for the DCCA. Hardware and software cost amounted to only $15,000. It is estimated that the program will increase daily throughput at the plant, which should increase net profits by approximately $100,000 per year.

Source: Robert Sullivan and Steven Secrest, "A Simple Optimization DSS for Production Planning at Dairyman's Cooperative Creamery," *Interfaces* **15**, 5 (September–October 1985).

Dual Formulation Procedures

The mechanics of formulating a dual from the primal problem may be summarized as follows:

rules for formulating dual

1. If the primal is a maximization, the dual is a minimization, and vice versa.

2. The right-hand-side values of the primal constraints become the dual's objective function coefficients.

3. The primal objective function coefficients become the right-hand-side values of the dual constraints.

4. The transpose of the primal constraint coefficients become the dual constraint coefficients.

5. Constraint inequality signs are reversed.[3]

Solving the Dual of the High Note Sound Company Problem

The simplex algorithm, as we learned it in Chapter 12, is applied to solve the preceding dual problem. With appropriate surplus and artificial variables, it may be restated as:

Minimize opportunity cost $= 80U_1 + 60U_2 + 0S_1 + 0S_2 + MA_1 + MA_2$

Subject to:
$$2U_1 + 3U_2 - 1S_1 + 1A_1 \qquad = 50$$
$$4U_1 + 1U_2 - 1S_2 + 1A_2 = 120$$

The first and second tableaus are shown in Table 13.4. The third tableau, containing the optimal solution of $U_1 = 30$, $U_2 = 0$, $S_1 = 10$, $S_2 = 0$, opportunity cost $= \$2,400$, appears in Figure 13.5 along with the final tableau of the primal problem.

We mentioned earlier that the primal and dual lead to the same solution even though they are formulated differently. How can this be?

It turns out that in the final simplex tanbleau of a primal problem, the absolute values of the numbers in the $C_j - Z_j$ row under the slack variables

TABLE 13.4 First and Second Tableaus of the High Note Dual Problem

$C_j \rightarrow$	SOLUTION MIX	80	60	0	0	M	M	
$\downarrow$		U_1	U_2	S_1	S_2	A_1	A_2	QUANTITY
M	A_1	2	3	-1	0	1	0	50
M	A_2	4	1	0	-1	0	1	120
	Z_j	$6M$	$4M$	$-M$	$-M$	M	M	$170M$
	$C_j - Z_j$	$80 - 6M$	$60 - 4M$	M	M	0	0	

(Continued)

[3]If the jth primal constraint should be an equality, then the ith dual variable is unrestricted in sign. This technical issue is discussed on page 170 of *Methods and Applications of Linear Programming,* by L. Cooper and D. Steinberg (Saunders Co., 1974).

TABLE 13.4 First and Second Tableaus of the High Note Dual Problem (Continued)

$C_j \rightarrow$	SOLUTION MIX	80	60	0	0	M	M	
$\downarrow$		U_1	U_2	S_1	S_2	A_1	A_2	QUANTITY
80	U_1	1	3/2	-1/2	0	1/2	0	25
M	A_2	0	-5	2	-1	-2	1	20
	Z_j	80	$120 - 5M$	$-40 + 2M$	$-M$	$40 - 2M$	M	$2000 + 20M$
	$C_j - Z_j$	0	$5M - 60$	$-2M + 40$	M	$3M - 40$	0	

represent the solutions to the dual problem, that is, the optimal U_is. (See Figure 13.5.) In the preceding section on sensitivity analysis we termed these numbers in the columns of the slack variables *shadow prices*. Thus, the solution to the dual problem presents the marginal profits of each additional unit of resource.

dual solution yields shadow prices

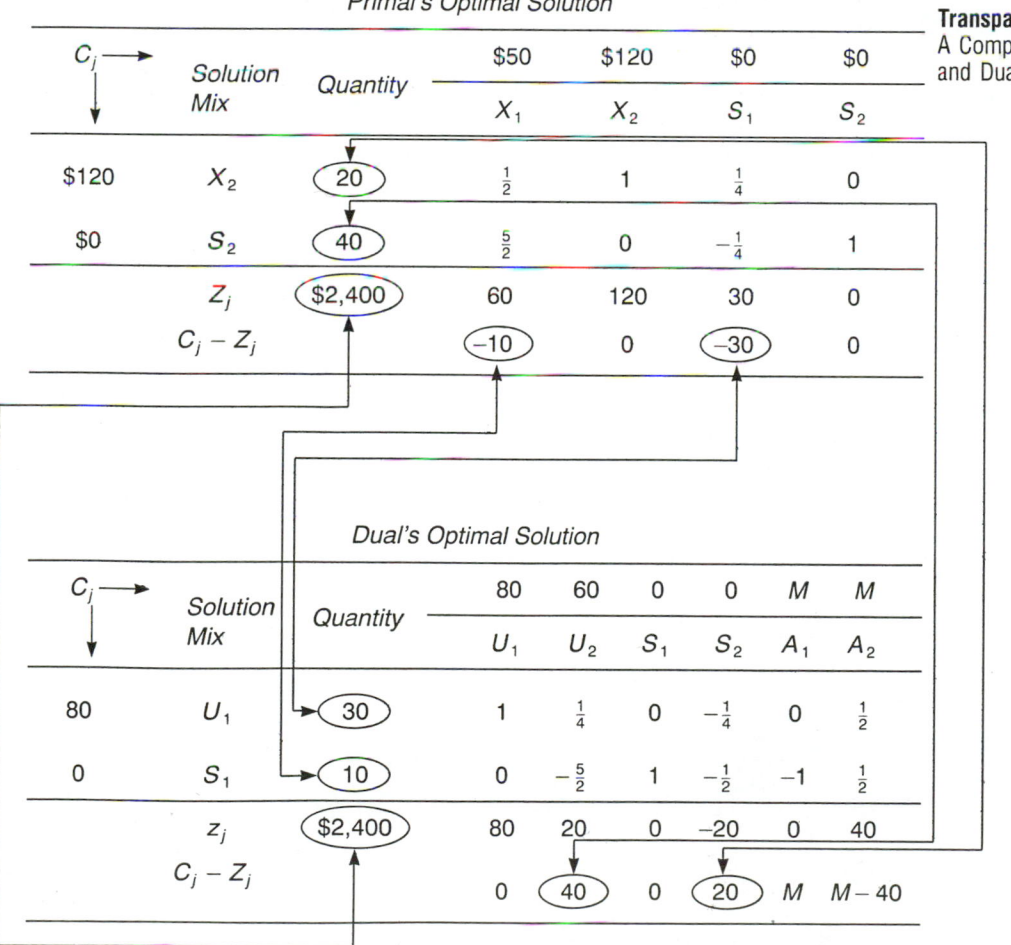

Primal's Optimal Solution

Dual's Optimal Solution

Transparency Master 13.4: A Comparison of the Primal and Dual Optimal Tableaus.

FIGURE 13.5
Comparison of the Primal and Dual Optimal Tableaus

It also happens that the absolute value of the $C_j - Z_j$ values of the slack variables in the optimal *dual* solution represent the optimal values of the *primal* X_1 and X_2 variables. The minimum opportunity cost derived in the dual must always equal the maximum profit derived in the primal.

Also note the other relationships between the primal and the dual that are indicated in Figure 13.5 by arrows. The columns A_1 and A_2 in the optimal dual tableau may be ignored because, as you recall, artificial variables have no physical meaning.

Computational Advantage of the Dual

solving the dual versus the primal

It was mentioned briefly at the beginning of this section on duality that sometimes it is computationally easier to solve the dual than the primal. Let's close the section with a quick example of how this can occur.

APPLICATIONS OF QA

Optimizing Wood Procurement in Cabinet Manufacturing

The Wellborn Cabinet Company in Alabama consists of a sawmill, four dry kilns, and a wood cabinet assembly plant that includes a rough mill for producing blanks (that is, cabinet components). The cabinet industry in the United States has been growing steadily and has been relatively profitable for the past 20 years because of a steady new housing market and an active replacement market. Manufacturers experience constant pressure to market quality products at competitive prices.

To produce blanks, Wellborn has been purchasing number 1 and number 2 grade hardwood logs as well as number 1 and number 2 common grade lumber (dry or green). Common grades of lumber are suitable for construction and general utility purposes; better quality is indicated by lower grade number.

Management is primarily concerned with the high cost of wood raw materials, which makes up about 45% of the total material cost of producing cabinets. Managers had no way of knowing what the least-cost combination of raw materials should be for processing blanks into cabinets and whether or not the sawmill and drying operations were cost effective. An LP model of the blank production system was developed; it was structured to minimize the total cost of producing blanks. Several data inputs were required for the model; they included the diameter and length measurements of randomly selected logs, a tally of the grades and sizes, the maximum weekly throughput, the delivered cost of logs and lumber, the costs of conversion and drying, and the weekly requirements of blanks.

Results from computer runs with the LP model indicate that Wellborn can minimize the total cost of producing blanks by purchasing only number 2 grade logs, which should have a small-end diameter of 9 to 15 inches, and number 2 common green lumber. By volume, about 88% of the dry lumber input requirements of the rough mill should come from number 2 grade logs and the rest should come from purchased number 2 common green lumber. By pursuing such a policy, the company can expect to save about $412,000 in raw material costs annually.

Source: Honorio F. Carino and Clinton H. LeNoir, Jr., *Interfaces* **18**, 2 (March–April 1988): 10–19.

The following primal problem could take seven or more simplex tableaus to reach an optimal solution:

$$\text{Maximize profit} = \$3X_1 + \$4X_2 + \$2X_3$$

Subject to:

$$
\begin{aligned}
X_1 + X_2 &\leqslant 8 \\
X_2 + X_3 &\leqslant 15 \\
8X_1 - 2X_2 &\leqslant 2 \\
X_1 + X_2 - X_3 &\leqslant 12 \\
2X_1 + 2X_2 + X_3 &\leqslant 22 \\
4X_1 + 3X_2 &\leqslant 21 \\
X_3 &\leqslant 3 \\
X_1, X_2, X_3 &\geqslant 0
\end{aligned}
$$

The dual will yield an equivalent solution. But because it contains only three constraints, it can reach an optimal solution in the fourth tableau, and hence save a great deal of computer time or time spent with a calculator by hand.[4]

$$\text{Minimize cost} = 8U_1 + 15U_2 + 2U_3 + 12U_4 + 22U_5 + 21U_6 + 3U_7$$

Subject to:

$$
\begin{aligned}
1U_1 + \quad\quad 8U_3 + 1U_4 + 2U_5 + 4U_6 \quad\quad &\geqslant 3 \\
1U_1 + 1U_2 - 2U_3 + 1U_4 + 2U_5 + 3U_6 \quad\quad &\geqslant 4 \\
1U_2 \quad\quad - 1U_4 + 1U_5 + \quad\quad 1U_7 &\geqslant 2
\end{aligned}
$$

THE ROLE OF COMPUTER SOFTWARE IN SENSITIVITY ANALYSIS: LOOKING AT HIGH NOTE SOUND COMPANY WITH AB:QM, STORM, LINDO, AND WHAT'S*Best!*

13.4

Virtually all of the LP computer programs have shadow pricing and sensitivity analyses as standard or optional outputs. To provide a side-by-side comparison of formats and features, and to help you review the section on sensitivity analysis, the AB:QM, STORM, LINDO, and What's*Best!* programs are run using the High Note Sound Company data. Much larger problems can, of course, be solved with each program.

Teaching Suggestion 13.4: Use of Software in Solving LP Problems. See the Instructor's Section for details.

13.5 SUMMARY

In this chapter we presented the important concept of sensitivity analysis. Sometimes referred to as postoptimality analysis, sensitivity analysis is

[4]For a more comprehensive analysis of duality, see Jay E. Strum, *Introduction to Linear Programming* (San Francisco: Holden-Day, 1972).

used by management to answer a series of what-if questions about LP model parameters. It also tests just how sensitive the optimal solution is to changes in profit or cost coefficients, technological coefficients, and right-hand-side resources. The value of additional resources was also analyzed through a discussion of shadow prices.

The relationship between a primal LP problem and its dual was explored. We illustrated how to derive the dual from a primal and how the solutions to the dual variables are actually the shadow prices.

Programs 13.1, 13.2, 13.3, and 13.4 helped to illustrate the role of the computer in shadow pricing and sensitivity analyses.

PROGRAM 13.1 Sample Linear Programming Computer Run Using AB:QM Microcomputer Software

```
Linear Programming

Problem Title : HIGH NOTE SOUND
Type of Problem (Max=1/Min=2)  1           Tableau(All=1/Final=2/No=3)  1
Number of Constraints          2                      Number of Variables   2

           X1        X2     T      Rhs
Obj.       50       120  x  xxxxxxxxxx
C1          2         4  <        80
C2          3         1  <        60



Help  New  Load  Save  Edit  Run   Print  Install  Directory  Esc

Program: Linear Programming

Problem Title : HIGH NOTE SOUND

***** Input Data *****

Max. Z = 50x1 + 120x2

Subject to

C1   2x1 + 4x2 <= 80
C2   3x1 + 1x2 <= 60

***** Program Output *****

Simplex Tableau :  0

         \Cj                   50.000     120.000     0.000      0.000
      Cb \     Basis     Bi       x  1       x  2      s  1       s  2

      0.000    s  1    80.000    2.000      4.000     1.000      0.000
      0.000    s  2    60.000    3.000      1.000     0.000      1.000

               Zj       0.000    0.000      0.000     0.000      0.000
               Cj-Zj            50.000    120.000     0.000      0.000
```

(Continued)

PROGRAM 13.1 Sample Linear Programming Computer Run Using AB:QM Microcomputer Software (Continued)

```
Simplex Tableau :  1

        \Cj                    50.000   120.000    0.000    0.000
     Cb \    Basis      Bi       x  1     x  2      s  1     s  2
```

Cb	Basis	Bi	x 1	x 2	s 1	s 2
120.000	x 2	20.000	0.500	1.000	0.250	0.000
0.000	s 2	40.000	2.500	0.000	-0.250	1.000
	Zj	2400.000	60.000	120.000	30.000	0.000
	Cj-Zj		-10.000	0.000	-30.000	0.000

Final Optimal Solution

Z =   2400.000

Variable	Value	Reduced Cost
x 1	0.000	10.000
x 2	20.000	0.000

Constraint	Slack/Surplus	Shadow Price
C 1	0.000	30.000
C 2	40.000	0.000

Objective Coefficient Ranges

Variables	Lower Limit	Current Values	Upper Limit	Allowable Increase	Allowable Decrease
x 1	No limit	50.000	60.000	10.000	No limit
x 2	100.000	120.000	No limit	No limit	20.000

Right-Hand-Side Ranges

Constraints	Lower Limit	Current Values	Upper Limit	Allowable Increase	Allowable Decrease
C 1	0.000	80.000	240.000	160.000	80.000
C 2	20.000	60.000	No limit	No limit	40.000

***** End of Output *****

PROGRAM 13.2 **High Note Sound Company Data Solved by STORM**

```
────────────── STORM EDITOR : Linear & Integer Programming Module ──────────────

 Title :  HIGH NOTE SOUND
 Number of variables          :      2
 Number of constraints        :      2
 Starting solution given      :     NO
 Objective type (MAX/MIN)     :    MAX
────────────────────────────────────────────────────────────────────────────────
 R4  : C2          VAR   1      VAR   2   CONST TYPE    R H S      RANGE
 OBJ COEFF           50.         120.      XXXX        XXXX       XXXX
 CONSTR  1            2.           4.       <=          80.         .
 CONSTR  2            3.           1.       <=          60.         .
 VARBL TYPE          POS          POS       XXXX        XXXX       XXXX
 LOWR BOUND           .            .        XXXX        XXXX       XXXX
 UPPR BOUND           .            .        XXXX        XXXX       XXXX
 INIT SOLN           0.           0.        XXXX        XXXX       XXXX

 F1 Block  F2 GoTo  F3 InsR  F4 DelR  F5 InsC  F6 DelC   F7 Done   F8 Help KB:C
```

```
                          HIGH NOTE SOUND
           OPTIMAL SOLUTION - SUMMARY REPORT (NONZERO VARIABLES)
                    Variable          Value           Cost

           2      VAR   2           20.0000        120.0000

           Slack Variables
           4   CONSTR   2           40.0000          0.0000

        Objective Function Value = 2400



                          HIGH NOTE SOUND
              SENSITIVITY ANALYSIS OF COST COEFFICIENTS
                              Current     Allowable    Allowable
                    Variable   Coeff.      Minimum      Maximum

           1        VAR   1    50.0000    -Infinity     60.0000
           2        VAR   2   120.0000    100.0000      Infinity

                          HIGH NOTE SOUND
            SENSITIVITY ANALYSIS OF RIGHT-HAND-SIDE VALUES
                                Current     Allowable    Allowable
              Constraint  Type    Value      Minimum      Maximum

           1   CONSTR  1   <=    80.0000      0.0000     240.0000
           2   CONSTR  2   <=    60.0000     20.0000      Infinity
```

PROGRAM 13.3 High Note Sound Company Data Solved by LINDO

```
LINDO/PC

COPYRIGHT © 1984 LINDO SYSTEMS, INC.

?
: MAX 50X1 + 120X2
? ST
? 2X1+4X2<80
? 3X1+1X2<60
?
: LOOK
ROW:
ALL


MAX   50 X1 + 120 X2
SUBJECT TO
   2) 2 X1 + 4 X2 <= 80
   3) 3 X1 + X2 <= 60
END

: GO
LP OPTIMUM FOUND AT STEP 1


           OBJECTIVE FUNCTION VALUE


1)        2400.00000

VARIABLE          VALUE          REDUCED COST
      X1          .000000          10.000000
      X2        20.000000            .000000


     ROW     SLACK OR SURPLUS     DUAL PRICES
     2)            .000000        30.000000
     3)          40.000000          .000000

NO. ITERATIONS = 1

DO RANGE (SENSITIVITY) ANALYSIS?
? YES
```

(Continued)

PROGRAM 13.3 High Note Sound Company Data Solved by LINDO (Continued)

```
RANGES IN WHICH THE BASIS IS UNCHANGED:

                                    OBJ COEFFICIENT RANGES
      VARIABLE          CURRENT       ALLOWABLE      ALLOWABLE
                          COEF         INCREASE       DECREASE
            X1         50.000000     10.000000      INFINITY
            X2        120.000000      INFINITY      20.000000

                                    RIGHT-HAND-SIDE RANGES
      ROW               CURRENT       ALLOWABLE      ALLOWABLE
                          RHS          INCREASE       DECREASE
             2          80.000000    160.000000     80.000000
             3          60.000000     INFINITY      40.000000
```

PROGRAM 13.4 High Note Sound Company Analyzed with What's*Best!* Software

	A	B	C	D	E	F
1	High Note Sound Company					
2						
3		Players	Receivers	Total	Available	Slack
4	Quantity	0	20			
5	Unit Profit	50	120			
6	Profit Contrib	0	2400	2400		
7						
8	Unit Electrician	2	4			
9	Electrician Time	0	80	80	80	0
10						
11	Unit Technician	3	1			
12	Technician Time	0	20	20	60	40
13						
14						
15						
16						

GLOSSARY

Sensitivity Analysis. The study of how sensitive an optimal solution is to model assumptions and to data changes. It is often referred to as postoptimality analysis.

Range of Insignificance. The range of values over which a nonbasic variable's coefficient can vary without causing a change in the optimal solution mix.

Range of Optimality. The range of values over which a basic variable's coefficient can change without causing a change in the optimal solution mix.

Technological Coefficients. Coefficients of the variables in the constraint equations. The coefficients represent the amount of resources needed to produce one unit of the variable.

Shadow prices. The coefficients of slack variables in the $C_j - Z_j$ row. They represent the value of one additional unit of a resource.

Right-Hand-Side Ranging. A method used to find the range over which shadow prices remain valid.

Primal-Dual Relationship. Alternative ways of stating a linear programming problem.

SOLVED PROBLEM

Solved Problem 13-1

Solve the following LP problem using LINDO and answer the questions regarding a firm that manufactures both lawn mowers and snowblowers.

Maximize profit = $30 Mower + $80 Blower

Subject to:

2 Mower + 4 Blower ≤ 1,000 labor hours available

6 Mower + 2 Blower ≤ 1,200 lbs. of steel available

1 Blower ≤ 200 snowblower engines available

(a) What is the best product mix? What is the optimal profit?
(b) What are the shadow prices? When the optimal solution has been reached, which resource has the highest marginal value?
(c) Over what range in each of the RHS values are these shadows valid?
(d) What are the ranges over which the objective function coefficients can vary for each of the two decision variables?
(e) State the dual to this problem. What is its solution?

Solution

(a) The best product mix is 100 lawn mowers and 200 snowblowers, yielding a profit (in row 1 of the output) of $19,000.
(b) The shadow prices are the "dual prices" in LINDO's printout. Each constraint (labeled rows 2, 3, and 4 for the three constraints) has one shadow price associated with it. For labor, the value of one additional hour over the existing 1,000 is $15. There is zero value to an additional pound of steel since the row 3 slack variable currently has a value of 200 pounds. In other words, with 200 unused pounds of steel, there is no point in paying for additional steel. Finally, there is a value of $20 for each additional snowblower engine made available. So snowblower engines have the highest marginal value at the optimal solution.
(c) The shadow price for labor hours is valid from 800 hours to 1,066.66 hours; that is, it can increase by 66⅔ (or 67) hours or decrease by as much as 200 hours. The shadow price for pounds of steel is valid from

PROGRAM 13.5 **LINDO Printout for Solved Problem 13-1**

```
LOOK ALL
MAX       30 MOWER + 80 BLOWER
SUBJECT TO
       2)    2 MOWER + 4 BLOWER <=     1000
       3)    6 MOWER + 2 BLOWER <=     1200
       4)    BLOWER <=    200


END

: GO
LP OPTIMUM Found  AT STEP       2

              OBJECTIVE FUNCTION VALUE

  1)         19000.0000

 VARIABLE           VALUE             REDUCED COST
   MOWER         100.000000               .000000
   BLOWER        200.000000               .000000

      ROW     SLACK OR SURPLUS        DUAL PRICES
       2)            .000000           15.000000
       3)         200.000000             .000000
       4)            .000000           20.000000

NO. ITERATIONS=         2

DO RANGE(SENSITIVITY) ANALYSIS?
? YES

RANGES IN WHICH THE BASIS IS UNCHANGED:

                         OBJ COEFFICIENT RANGES
VARIABLE          CURRENT          ALLOWABLE          ALLOWABLE
                  COEF             INCREASE           DECREASE
   MOWER          30.000000         10.000000          30.000000
   BLOWER         80.000000         INFINITY           20.000000

                      RIGHT-HAND-SIDE RANGES
   ROW            CURRENT          ALLOWABLE          ALLOWABLE
                  RHS              INCREASE           DECREASE
    2           1000.000000        66.666660         200.000000
    3           1200.000000        INFINITY          200.000000
    4            200.000000        50.000000          20.000000

: TABL

THE TABLEAU
   ROW   (BASIS)      MOWER      BLOWER      SLK2        SLK3       SLK4
    1 ART             .000        .000     15.000        .000     20.000  19000.000
    2     MOWER      1.000        .000       .500        .000     -2.000    100.000
    3 SLK     3       .000        .000     -3.000       1.000     10.000    200.000
    4     BLOWER      .000       1.000       .000        .000      1.000    200.000
```

1,000 pounds up to an infinite number of pounds. The shadow price for snowblower engines ranges from 180 engines up to 250 engines.
  (d) Without changing the current solution mix, the profit coefficient for the mowers can range from $0 to $40, while the coefficient for the blowers can range from $60 to infinity.
  (e) The dual can be written as:

$$\text{Minimize } 1{,}000 \quad U_1 + 1{,}200U_2 + 200U_3 \geq 30$$

$$\text{Subject to:} \quad 2U_1 + \quad 6U_2 + \quad 0U_3 \geq 30$$

$$4U_1 + \quad 2U_2 + \quad 1U_3 \geq 80$$

The solution to the dual will be the shadow prices in the primal. So, $U_1 = 15$, $U_2 = 0$, $U_3 = 20$. The dual solution provides the marginal profits of each additional unit of resource.

DISCUSSION QUESTIONS AND PROBLEMS

Discussion Questions

13-1 Discuss the role of sensitivity analysis in linear programming. Under what circumstances is it needed and under what conditions do you think it is not necessary?

13-2 Is sensitivity analysis a concept applied to linear programming only, or should it also be used when analyzing other techniques? Provide examples to prove your point.

13-3 What is a shadow price? How does the concept relate to the dual of an LP problem? How does it relate to the primal?

13-4 Develop your own original linear programming problem with two constraints and two real variables.
  (a) Explain the meaning of the numbers on the right-hand side of each of your constraints.
  (b) Explain the significance of the technological coefficients.
  (c) Solve your problem graphically to find the optimal solution.
  (d) Illustrate graphically the effect of increasing the contribution rate of your first variable (X_1) by 50% over the value you first assigned it. Does this change the optimal solution?

13-5 Explain how a change in a technological coefficient can affect a problem's optimal solution. How can a change in resource availability affect a solution?

13-6 If a primal problem has 12 constraints and 8 variables, how many constraints and variables will its corresponding dual have?

13-7 Explain the relationship between each number in a primal and corresponding numbers in the dual.

13-8 Create your own original LP maximization problem with two variables and three less-than-or-equal-to constraints. Now form the dual for this primal problem.

13-9 What is the value of the computer in solving linear programming problems today?

Problems

QA 13-10

💻 · **13-10** Graph the following LP problem and indicate the optimal solution point.

$$\text{Maximize profit} = \$3X_1 + \$2X_2$$
$$\text{Subject to:} \qquad 2X_1 + 1X_2 \leq 150$$
$$2X_1 + 3X_2 \leq 300$$

See the Instructor's Section
for graphs and details.
(a) Yes, it shifts to point *c*.
(b) Point *b* remains optimal.

(a) Does the optimal solution change if the profit per unit of X_1 changes to \$4.50?

(b) What happens if the profit function should have been $\$3X_1 + \$3X_2$?

QA 13-11

💻 · **13-11** Graphically analyze the following problem:

$$\text{Maximize profit} = \$4X_1 + \$6X_2$$
$$\text{Subject to:} \qquad 1X_1 + 2X_2 \leq 8$$
$$6X_1 + 4X_2 \leq 24$$

\$26 profit; $X_1 = 2$; $X_2 = 3$
See the Instructor's Section
for graph and details.

(a) What is the optimal solution?

(b) If the first constraint is altered to $1X_1 + 3X_2 \leq 8$, does the feasible region or optimal solution change?

QA 13-12

💻 · **13-12** Consider the following linear programming problem:

$$\text{Maximize profit} = \$1X_1 + \$1X_2$$
$$\text{Subject to:} \qquad 2X_1 + 1X_2 \leq 100$$
$$1X_1 + 2X_2 \leq 100$$

(a) Profit = \$66.67
($X_1 = 33\frac{1}{3}$, $X_2 = 33\frac{1}{3}$)
(b) ($X_1 = 50$, $X_2 = 0$),
P = \$150
(c) Solution in part (a) still
optimal

(a) What is the optimal solution to this problem? Solve it graphically.

(b) If a technical breakthrough occurred that raised the profit per unit of X_1 to \$3, would this affect the optimal solution?

(c) Instead of an increase in the profit coefficient X_1 to \$3, suppose profit was overestimated and should only have been \$1.25. Does this change the optimal solution?

QA 13-13

💻 · **13-13** Consider the LP formulation given in Problem 13-12. If the second constraint is changed from $1X_1 + 2X_2 \leq 100$ to $1X_1 + 4X_2 \leq 100$, what effect will this have on the optimal solution? (Use the same objective function, Profit $= 1X_1 + 1X_2$.)

($X_1 = 42\frac{6}{7}$, $X_2 = 14\frac{2}{7}$;
Profit = \$57½)

QA 13-14

💻 · **13-14** Examine the LP formulation in Problem 13-11. The problem's second constraint reads:

$$6X_1 + 4X_2 \leq 24 \text{ hours} \qquad \text{(time available on machine 2)}$$

The optimal solution mix
under the new constraint
yields a \$29 profit, or an
increase of \$3 over the
\$26 profit calculated.

If the firm decides that 36 hours of time can be made available on machine 2 (namely, an additional 12 hours) at an additional cost of \$10, should they add the hours?

: **13-15** Consider the following optimal tableau where S_1 and S_2 are slack variables added to the original problem.

$C_j \rightarrow$	SOLUTION MIX	$10	$30	$0	$0	
$\downarrow$		X_1	X_2	S_1	S_2	QUANTITY
$10	X_1	1	4	2	0	160
$0	S_2	0	6	−7	1	200
	Z_j	10	40	+20	0	$1,600
	$C_j - Z_j$	0	−10	−20	0	

(a) What is the range of optimality for the contribution rate of the variable X_1?

(b) What is the range of insignificance of the contribution rate of the variable X_2?

(c) How much would you be willing to pay for one more unit of the first resource, which is represented by slack variable S_1?

(d) What is the value of one more unit of the second resource? Why?

The *range of optimality* is
$7½ $\leq C_j$ (for X_2) $\leq \infty$
$-\infty \leq C_j$ (for X_2) $\leq $40

$20
$0 because there are still 200 unused units ($S_2 = 200$)

· **13-16** The following is the final simplex tableau of an LP problem that has three constraints and four variables.

$C_j \rightarrow$	SOLUTION MIX	$4	$6	$3	$1	$0	$0	$0	
$\downarrow$		X_1	X_2	X_3	X_4	S_1	S_2	S_3	QUANTITY
3	X_3	$1/20$	0	1	$1/2$	$3/10$	0	$-1/5$	125
0	S_2	$39/12$	0	0	$-1/2$	$-1/2$	1	0	425
6	X_2	$39/60$	1	0	$1/2$	$-1/10$	0	$3/5$	25
	Z_j	$81/20$	6	3	$9/2$	$3/10$	0	3	$525
	$C_j - Z_j$	$-1/20$	0	0	$-7/2$	$-3/10$	0	−3	

Value of *Reource* Adtl. Hr.
1st constraint (S_1) $.30
2nd constraint (S_2) $0
3rd constraint (S_3) $3.00

The second resource has a zero shadow price because not all of the resource is currently being used— 425 units are still available.

What are the values of each of the shadow prices? What meaning does a 0 shadow price have and how can it occur?

· **13-17** Clapper Electronics produces two models of telephone-answering devices, Model 102 (X_1) and Model H23 (X_2). Jim Clapper, vice president for production, formulates their constraints as:

$2X_1 + 1X_2 \leq 40$ (*Hours of time available on soldering machine*)

$1X_1 + 3X_2 \leq 30$ (*Hours of time available in inspection department*)

Clapper's objective function is:

     Maximize profit = $9X_1 + $7X_2

Solving this problem using the simplex method, he produces the following final tableau.

a) Produce of 18 of Model 102 and 4 of Model H23.
b) S_1 represents slack time on the soldering machine. S_2 represents available time in the inspection department.
c) Yes—the shadow price of the soldering machine time is $4.
d) Clapper will net $1.50 for every additional hour he rents.

$C_j \rightarrow$	SOLUTION MIX	$9	$7	$0	$0	
$\downarrow$		X_1	X_2	S_1	S_2	QUANTITY
$9	X_1	1	0	$3/5$	$-1/5$	18
$7	X_2	0	1	$-1/5$	$2/5$	4
	Z_j	$9	$7	$4	$1	$190
	$C_j - Z_j$	$0	$0	$-4	$-1	

(a) What is the optimal mix of Models 102 and H23 to produce?

(b) What do variables S_1 and S_2 represent?

(c) Clapper is considering renting a second soldering machine at a cost to the firm of $2.50 per hour. Should he do so?

No

(d) Clapper computes that he can hire a part-time inspector for only $1.75 per hour. Should he do so?

$S_1 = \$.50$; $S_2 = \$1.50$
The first shadow price represents the value of one more hour in the painting department. The second represents one additional hour in the carpentry department.
$6.67 to $10.00
$3.50 to $5.25
The range is from 80 hours to 120 hours.
The range is from 200 hours to 300 hours.

: **13-18** Refer to Table 12.6 in the previous chapter, which is the optimal tableau for the Flair Furniture Company problem.

(a) What are the values of the shadow prices?

(b) Interpret the physical meaning of each shadow price in the context of the furniture problem.

(c) What is the range over which the profit per table can vary without changing the optimal basis (solution mix)?

(d) What is the range of optimality for X_2 (number of chairs produced)?

(e) How many hours can Flair Furniture add to or remove from the first resource (painting department time) without changing the basis?

(f) Conduct right-hand-side ranging on the carpentry department resource to determine the range over which the shadow price remains valid.

For phosphate $X - \infty \leqslant$ 🖳
C_j (for X_1) $\leqslant \$6$
For potassium $\$5 \leqslant C_j$
(for X_2) $\leqslant \infty$
The limit can be raised to 850 pounds without changing the solution mix. However, the values of X_1, X_2, and S_2 would change. X_1 would now be 400, X_2 would be 600, and S_2 would be 450.

QA13-19

13-19 Consider the optimal solution to the Muddy River Chemical Corporation problem in Table 12.10 of Chapter 12.

(a) For each of the two chemical ingredients, phosphate and potassium, determine the range over which their cost may vary without affecting the basis.

(b) If the original constraint that "no more than 300 pounds of phosphate can be used" ($X_1 \leqslant 300$) were changed to $X_1 \leqslant 400$, would the basis change? Would the values of X_1, X_2, and S_2 change?

Minimize Cost $= 4U_1 + 8U_2$
Subject to:
$1U_1 + 2U_2 \geqslant 80$
$3U_1 + 5U_2 \geqslant 75$

· **13-20** Formulate the dual of this LP problem.

$$\text{Maximize profit} = 80X_1 + 75X_2$$

$$1X_1 + 3X_2 \leqslant 4$$

$$2X_1 + 5X_2 \leqslant 8$$

Find the dual of the problem's dual.

Maximize Profit $=$
$50U_1 + 4U_2$
Subject to:
$12U_1 + 1U_2 \leqslant 120$
$20U_1 + 3U_2 \leqslant 250$

· **13-21** What is the dual of the following LP problem?

$$\text{Primal: Minimize cost} = 120X_1 + 250X_2$$

$$\text{Subject to:} \quad 12X_1 + 20X_2 \geqslant 50$$

$$X_1 + 3X_2 \geqslant 4$$

· **13-22** The third, and final, simplex tableau for the LP problem stated here follows:

$$\text{Maximize profit} = 200X_1 + 200X_2$$

$$\text{Subject to:} \quad 2X_1 + X_2 \leqslant 8$$

$$X_1 + 3X_2 \leqslant 9$$

$U_1 = \$80$, $U_2 = \$40$,
Cost $= \$1000$

What are the solutions to the dual variables, U_1 and U_2? What is the optimal dual cost?

$C_j \rightarrow$	SOLUTION MIX	$200 X_1	$200 X_2	$0 S_1	$0 S_2	QUANTITY
$200	X_1	1	0	$3/5$	$-1/5$	3
$200	X_2	0	1	$-1/5$	$2/5$	2
	Z_j	200	200	80	40	$1,000
	$C_j - Z_j$	$0	$0	$-80	$-40	

13-23 The accompanying tableau provides the optimal solution to this dual:

$$\text{Minimize cost} = 120U_1 + 240U_2$$

$$\text{Subject to:} \quad 2U_1 + 2U_2 \geq .5$$
$$U_1 + 3U_2 \geq .4$$

Maximize Profit =
$.5X_1 + .4X_2$
$2X_1 + 1X_2 \leq 120$
$2X_1 + 3X_2 \leq 240$
Primal solution: $X_1 = 30$,
$X_2 = 60$, Profit = $39

$C_j \rightarrow$	SOLUTION MIX	120 U_1	240 U_2	0 S_1	0 S_2	M A_1	M A_2	QUANTITY
120	U_1	1	0	$-3/4$	$1/2$	$3/4$	$-1/2$	.175
240	U_2	0	1	$1/4$	$-1/2$	$-1/4$	$1/2$	.075
	Z_j	120	240	-30	-60	30	60	$39
	$C_j - Z_j$	0	0	30	60	$M - 30$	$M - 60$	

What does the corresponding primal problem look like, and what is its optimal solution?

13-24 Given the following dual formulation, reconstruct the original primal problem.

$$\text{Minimize cost} = 28U_1 + 53U_2 + 70U_3 + 18U_4$$

$$\text{Subject to:} \quad U_1 \qquad\qquad + U_4 \geq 10$$
$$U_1 + 2U_2 + U_3 \qquad \geq 5$$
$$-2U_2 \qquad + 5U_4 \geq 31$$
$$5U_3 \qquad \geq 28$$
$$12U_1 \qquad + 2U_3 - U_4 \geq 17$$
$$U_1, U_2, U_3, U_4 \geq 0$$

Maximize Profit = $10X_1 + 5X_2 + 31X_3 + 28X_4 + 17X_5$
Subject to:
$X_1 + X_2 + 12X_5 \leq 28$
$2X_2 - 2X_3 \leq 53$
$X_2 + 5X_4 + 2X_5 \leq 70$
$X_1 + 5X_3 - X_5 \leq 18$

13-25 A firm that makes three products, and has three machines available as resources, constructs the following LP problem.

$$\text{Maximize profit} = 4X_1 + 4X_2 + 7X_3$$

$$\text{Subject to:} \quad 1X_1 + 7X_2 + 4X_3 \leq 100 \text{ (hours on machine 1)}$$
$$2X_1 + 1X_2 + 7X_3 \leq 110 \text{ (hours on machine 2)}$$
$$8X_1 + 4X_2 + 1X_3 \leq 100 \text{ (hours on machine 3)}$$

QA 13-25
Machine number 3, as represented by slack variable S_3, still has 62 hours of unused time.
There is no unused time when the optimal solution is reached. All three slack variables have been removed

from the basis and have zero values.
An extra hour of time on machine number 3 is worth $0.26.
For *each* extra hour of time made available at no cost on machine number 2, profit will increase by $0.786. Thus, ten hours of time will be worth $7.86.

Solve this problem by computer and answer these questions:

(a) Before the third iteration of the simplex method, which machine still has unused time available?

(b) When the final solution is reached, is there any unused time available on any of the three machines?

(c) What would it be worth to the firm to make an additional hour of time available on the third machine?

(d) How much would the firm's profit increase if an extra 10 hours of time were made available on the second machine at no extra cost?

: **13-26** Management analysts at a Fresno laboratory have developed the following LP primal problem:

$$\text{Minimize cost} = 23X_1 + 18X_2$$

$$\text{Subject to:} \quad 8X_1 + 4X_2 \geqslant 120$$

$$4X_1 + 6X_2 \geqslant 115$$

$$9X_1 + 4X_2 \geqslant 116$$

This model represents a decision concerning number of hours spent by biochemists on certain laboratory experiments (X_1) and number of hours spent by biophysicists on the same series of experiments (X_2). A biochemist costs $23 per hour while a biophysicist's salary averages $18 per hour. Both types of scientists can be used on three needed laboratory operations: test 1, test 2, and test 3. The experiments and their times are:

LAB EXPERIMENT	SCIENTIST TYPE		MINIMUM TEST TIME NEEDED PER DAY
	BIOPHYSICIST	BIOCHEMIST	
Test 1	8	4	120
Test 2	4	6	115
Test 3	9	4	116

Maximize $Z = 120U_1 + 115U_2 + 116U_3$
$8U_1 + 4U_2 + 9U_3 \leqslant 23$
$4U_1 + 6U_2 + 4U_3 \leqslant 18$
$U_1, U_2, U_3 \geqslant 0$
$U_1 = \$2.07$ is the price of each test 1.
$U_2 = \$1.63$ is the price of each test 2.
$U_3 = \$0$ is the price of each test 3.

This means that a biophysicist can complete 8, 4, and 9 of tests 1, 2, and 3 per hour. Likewise, a biochemist can perform 4 of test 1, 6 of test 2, and 4 of test 3 per hour. The optimal solution to the lab's primal problem is:

$$X_1 = 8.12 \text{ hours and } X_2 = 13.75 \text{ hours}$$

$$\text{Total cost} = \$434.37 \text{ per day}$$

The optimal solution to the dual problem is:

$$U_1 = 2.07, U_2 = 1.63, U_3 = 0$$

(a) What is the dual of the above primal LP problem?

(b) Interpret the meaning of the dual and its solution.

QA13-27

: **13-27** The Flair Furniture Company first described in Chapter 10 manufactures inexpensive tables (X_1) and chairs (X_2). The firm's daily LP formulation is given as:

$$\text{Maximize profits} = \$7X_1 + \$5X_2$$

$$\text{Subject to:} \quad 4X_1 + 3X_2 \leqslant 240 \text{ hours of carpentry time available}$$

$$2X_1 + 1X_2 \leqslant 100 \text{ hours of painting time available}$$

In addition, Flair finds that three more constraints are in order. First, each table and chair must be inspected and may need rework. The following constraint describes the time required on the average for each:

$$\tfrac{1}{2}X_1 + \tfrac{3}{5}X_2 \leq 36 \text{ hours of inspection/}$$
$$\text{rework time available}$$

Second, Flair faces a resource constraint relating to the lumber needed for each table or chair and the amount available each day:

$$32X_1 + 10X_2 \leq 1{,}248 \text{ linear feet of lumber}$$
$$\text{available for production}$$

Finally, the demand for tables is found to be a maximum of 40 daily. There are no similar constraints regarding chairs.

$$X_1 \leq 40 \text{ maximum table production daily}$$

These data have been entered in the LP software program that is available with this book. The inputs and results are shown in the accompanying printout. Refer to the computer output in Program 13.6 in answering these questions.

a) $X_1 = 27.38$ tables, $X_2 = 37.18$ chairs daily, Profit = $377.58
b) Not all resources are used.
c) $0 value to making more carpentry and painting time available; 6.34 is the value of additional inspection/rework hours; $0.12 is the value of each additional foot of lumber made available.
d) More lumber *should* be purchased if it costs less than the $0.12 shadow price. More carpenters are not needed at any price. Flair has a slack (X_4) of 8.056 hours available daily in the painting department. It can spare this amount. Carpentry hours range: 221 to infinity.

PROGRAM 13.6 Computer Printout for Problem 13-27

```
Program: Linear Programming

Problem Title : REVISED FLAIR FURNITURE FOR PROBLEM 13.27

***** Input Data *****

Max. Z =   7x1 + 5x2

Subject to

C1   4x1 + 3x2 <= 240
C2   2x1 + 1x2 <= 100
C3   .5x1 + .6x2 <= 36
C4   32x1 + 10x2 <= 1248
C5   1x1 <= 40

***** Program Output *****

Simplex Tableau :   2
```

\Cj CB \	Basis	Bi	7.000 x 1	5.000 x 2	0.000 s 1	0.000 s 2
0.000	s 1	18.930	0.000	0.000	1.000	0.000
0.000	s 2	8.056	0.000	0.000	0.000	1.000
5.000	x 2	37.183	0.000	1.000	0.000	0.000
7.000	x 1	27.380	1.000	0.000	0.000	0.000
0.000	s 5	12.620	0.000	0.000	0.000	0.000
	Zj	377.577	7.000	5.000	0.000	0.000
	Cj-Zj		0.000	0.000	0.000	0.000

(Continued)

PROGRAM 13.6 **Computer Printout for Problem 13-27 (Continued)**

```
    \Cj                              0.000      0.000      0.000
  Cb \      Basis         Bi          s  3       s  4       s  5
  ─────────────────────────────────────────────────────────────
  0.000     s   1       18.930      -3.944     -0.063      0.000
  0.000     s   2        8.056      -0.845     -0.049      0.000
  5.000     x   2       37.183       2.254     -0.035      0.000
  7.000     x   1       27.380      -0.704      0.042      0.000
  0.000     x   5       12.620       0.704     -0.042      1.000
  ─────────────────────────────────────────────────────────────
            zj         377.577       6.338      0.120      0.000
          Cj-zj                     -6.338     -0.120      0.000
```

Final Optimal Solution

Z =   377.577

Variable	Value	Reduced Cost
x 1	27.380	0.000
x 2	37.183	0.000

Constraint	Slack/Surplus	Shadow Price
C 1	18.930	0.000
C 2	8.056	0.000
C 3	0.000	6.338
C 4	0.000	0.120
C 5	12.620	0.000

Objective Coefficient Ranges

Variables	Lower Limit	Current Values	Upper Limit	Allowable Increase	Allowable Decrease
X 1	4.167	7.000	16.000	9.000	2.833
X 2	2.188	5.000	8.400	3.400	2.813

Right-Hand-Side Ranges

Constraints	Lower Limit	Current Values	Upper Limit	Allowable Increase	Allowable Decrease
C 1	221.070	240.000	No limit	No limit	18.930
C 2	91.944	100.000	No limit	No limit	8.056
C 3	19.500	36.000	40.800	4.800	16.500
C 4	600.000	1248.000	1411.429	163.429	648.000
C 5	27.380	40.000	No limit	No limit	12.620

***** End of Output *****

(a) How many tables and chairs should Flair Furniture produce daily? What is the profit generated by this solution?

(b) Will Flair use all of its resources to their limits each day? Be specific in explaining your answer.

(c) Explain the physical meaning of each shadow price.

(d) Should Flair purchase more lumber if it is available at $.07 per linear foot? Should it hire more carpenters at $12.75 per hour?

(e) Flair's owner has been approached by a friend whose company would like to use several hours in the painting facility every day. Should Flair sell time to the other firm? If so, how much? Explain.

(f) What is the range within which the carpentry hours, painting hours, and inspection/rework hours can fluctuate before the optimal solution changes?

(g) Within what range for the current solution can the profit contribution of tables and chairs change?

e) Painting hours range: 92 to infinity. Inspection/rework hours range: 19½ to 41

f) Table profit range: $4.17 to $16.00

g) Chair profit range: $2.19 to $8.40

Data Set Problem

13-28 A Chicago manufacturer of office equipment is desperately attempting to control its profit and loss statement. The company currently manufactures 15 different products, each coded with a one-letter and three-digit designation.

QA 13-28
See Instructor's Section for printouts and details. Optimal solution of $9,683 Only the first product (A158) is not produced.

PRODUCT	STEEL ALLOY REQUIRED (LBS.)	PLASTIC REQUIRED (SQ. FT.)	WOOD REQUIRED (BD. FT.)	ALUMINUM REQUIRED (LBS.)	FORMICA REQUIRED (BD. FT.)	LABOR REQUIRED (HOURS)	MINIMUM MONTHLY DEMAND (UNITS)	CONTRIBUTION TO PROFIT
A158	—	.4	.7	5.8	10.9	3.1	—	$18.79
B179	4	.5	1.8	10.3	2.0	1.0	20	6.31
C023	6	—	1.5	1.1	2.3	1.2	10	8.19
D045	10	.4	2.0	—	—	4.8	10	45.88
E388	12	1.2	1.2	8.1	4.9	5.5	—	63.00
F422	—	1.4	1.5	7.1	10.0	.8	20	4.10
G366	10	1.4	7.0	6.2	11.1	9.1	10	81.15
H600	5	1.0	5.0	7.3	12.4	4.8	20	50.06
I701	1	.4	—	10.0	5.2	1.9	50	12.79
J802	1	.3	—	11.0	6.1	1.4	20	15.88
K900	—	.2	—	12.5	7.7	1.0	20	17.91
L901	2	1.8	1.5	13.1	5.0	5.1	10	49.99
M050	—	2.7	5.0	—	2.1	3.1	20	24.00
N150	10	1.1	5.8	—	—	7.7	10	88.88
P259	10	—	6.2	15.0	1.0	6.6	10	77.01
Availability per month	980	400	600	2,500	1,800	1,000		

(a) How many of each of the 15 products should be produced each month?

(b) Clearly explain the meaning of each shadow price.

(c) A number of workers interested in saving money for the holidays have offered to work overtime next month at a rate of $12.50 per hour. What should the response of management be?

(d) Two tons of steel alloy are available from an overstocked supplier at a total cost of $8,000. Should the steel be purchased? All or part of the supply?

(e) The accountants have just discovered that an error was made in the contribution to profit for product N150. The correct value is actually $8.88. What are the implications of this error?

(f) Management is considering the abandonment of five product lines (those beginning with the letters A through E). If no minimum monthly demand is established, what are the implications? Note that there already is no minimum for two of these products. Use the corrected value for N150.

The value of one more pound of steel, for example, is $2.71. There is no value to adding more workers, since all 1000 hours are not yet consumed. Two tons of steel at a total cost of $8,000 implies a cost per pound of $2.00. It should be purchased since the shadow price is $2.71. Profit declines to $8,865 with the change to $8.88. Profit drops to $9,380 and none of the products remain. Previously only A158 was *not* produced.

Red Brand Canners

On Monday, September 13, 1990, Mr. Mitchell Gordon, vice president of operations, asked the controller, the sales manager, and the production manager to meet with him to discuss the amount of tomato products to pack that season. The tomato crop, which had been purchased at planting, was beginning to arrive at the cannery, and packing operations would have to be started by the following Monday. Red Brand Canners is a medium-sized company that cans and distributes a variety of fruit and vegetable products under private brands in the western states.

William Cooper, the controller, and Charles Myers, the sales manager, were the first to arrive in Gordon's office. Dan Tucker, the production manager, came in a few minutes later and said that he had picked up Produce Inspection's latest estimate of the quality of the incoming tomatoes. According to the report, about 20% of the crop was grade A quality and the remaining portion of the 3-million-pound crop was grade B.

Gordon asked Myers about the demand for tomato products for the coming year. Myers replied that they could sell all of the whole canned tomatoes they could produce. The expected demand for tomato juice and tomato paste, on the other hand, was limited. The sales manager then passed around the latest demand forecast, which is shown in Table 1. He reminded the group that the selling prices had been set in light of the long-term marketing strategy of the company and that the potential sales had been forecast at these prices.

Bill Cooper, after looking at Myers' estimates of demand, said that it looked like the company "should do quite well [on the tomato crop] this year." With the new accounting system that had

been set up, he had been able to compute the contribution for each product, and according to his analysis the incremental profit on whole tomatoes was greater than the incremental profit on any other tomato product. In May, after Red Brand had signed contracts agreeing to purchase the grower's production at an average delivered price of 6 cents per pound, Cooper had computed the tomato products' contributions (see Table 2).

Dan Tucker brought to Cooper's attention that although there was ample production capacity, it was impossible to produce all whole tomatoes since too small a portion of the tomato crop was "grade A" quality. Red Brand used a numerical scale to record the quality of both raw produce and prepared products. This scale ran from 0 to 10—the higher number representing better quality. According to this scale, grade A tomatoes averaged nine points per pound and grade B tomatoes averaged five points per pound. Tucker noted that the minimum average input quality was eight points per pound for canned whole tomatoes and six points per pound for juice. Paste could be made entirely from grade B tomatoes. This meant that whole-tomato production was limited to 800,000 pounds.

Gordon stated that this was not a real limitation. He had been recently solicited to purchase 80,000 pounds of grade A tomatoes at 8½ cents per pound and at that time had turned down the offer. He felt, however, that the tomatoes were still available.

Myers, who had been doing some calculations, said that although he agreed that the company "should do quite well this year," it would not be by canning whole tomatoes. It seemed to him that the tomato cost should be allocated on the basis of

TABLE 1 Demand Forecasts

PRODUCT	SELLING PRICE PER CASE ($)	DEMAND FORECAST (CASES)
24—2½ whole tomatoes	4.00	800,000
24—2½ choice peach halves	5.40	10,000
24—2½ peach nectar	4.60	5,000
24—2½ tomato juice	4.50	50,000
24—2½ cooking apples	4.90	15,000
24—2½ tomato paste	3.80	80,000

TABLE 2 Product Item Profitability

PRODUCT	24—2½ WHOLE TOMATOES	24—2½ CHOICE PEACH HALVES	24—2½ PEACH NECTAR	24—2½ TOMATO JUICE	24—2½ COOKING APPLES	24—2½ TOMATO PASTE
Selling price	$4.00	$5.40	$4.60	$4.50	$4.90	$3.80
Variable costs:						
Direct labor	1.18	1.40	1.27	1.32	.70	.54
Variable overhead	.24	.32	.23	.36	.22	.26
Variable selling	.40	.30	.40	.85	.28	.38
Packaging material	.70	.56	.60	.65	.70	.77
Fruit*	1.08	1.80	1.70	1.20	.90	1.50
Total variable costs	$3.60	$4.38	$4.20	$4.38	$2.80	$3.45
Contribution	.40	1.02	.40	.12	1.10	.35
Less allocated overhead	.28	.70	.52	.21	.75	.23
Net profit	$ .12	$ .32	($ .12)	($ .09)	$ .35	$ .12

* Product usage is as given below:

Product	Pounds per Case
Whole tomatoes	18
Peach halves	18
Peach nectar	17
Tomato juice	20
Cooking apples	27
Tomato paste	25

quality and quantity rather than by quantity only, as Cooper had done. Therefore, he had recomputed the marginal profit on this basis (see Table 3), and from his results had concluded that Red Brand should use 2 million pounds of the grade B tomatoes for paste, and the remaining 400,000 pounds of grade B tomatoes and all of the grade A tomatoes for juice. If the demand expectations were realized, a contribution of $48,000 would be made on this year's tomato crop.

TABLE 3 Marginal Analysis of Tomato Products

Z = Cost per pound of grade A tomatoes in cents.

Y = Cost per pound of grade B tomatoes in cents.

$$(600,000 \text{ lb.} \times Z) + (2,400,000 \text{ lb.} \times Y) = (3,000,000 \text{ lb.} \times 6) \quad (1)$$

$$\frac{Z}{9} = \frac{Y}{5} \quad (2)$$

Z = 9.32 cents per pound

Y = 5.18 cents per pound

PRODUCT	CANNED WHOLE TOMATOES	TOMATO JUICE	TOMATO PASTE
Selling price	$4.00	$4.50	$3.80
Variable cost			
(excluding tomato cost)	2.52	3.18	1.95
	$1.48	$1.32	$1.85
Tomato cost	1.49	1.24	1.30
Marginal profit	($ .01)	$ .08	$ .55

Discussion Questions

1. Structure this problem verbally, including a written description of the constraints and objective. What are the decision variables?

Adopted from *Stanford Business Cases 1965, 1977,* with permission of the Publishers, Stanford University Graduate School of Business, © 1965 and 1977 by the Board of Trustees of the Leland Stanford Junior University.

2. Develop a *mathematical* formulation for Red Brand's objective function and constraints.

3. Solve the problem and discuss the results.

525,000 lbs. of Whole A
175,000 lbs. of Whole B
75,000 lbs. of Juice A
225,000 lbs. of Juice B
0 lbs. of Paste A
2,000,000 lbs. of Paste B

BIBLIOGRAPHY

See Bibliography at end of Chapter 10.

14

Transportation and Assignment Problems

CHAPTER OUTLINE

14.1 Introduction

14.2 Setting Up a Transportation Problem

14.3 Developing an Initial Solution: Northwest Corner Rule

14.4 Stepping-Stone Method: Finding a Least-Cost Solution

14.5 MODI Method

14.6 Vogel's Approximation Method: Another Way to Find an Initial Solution

14.7 Unbalanced Transportation Problems

14.8 Degeneracy in Transportation Problems

14.9 More than One Optimal Solution

14.10 Computer Solutions to the Transportation Problem

14.11 Facility Location Analysis

14.12 Approach of the Assignment Model

14.13 Dummy Rows and Dummy Columns

14.14 Maximization Assignment Problems

14.15 Using the Computer to Solve Assignment Problems

Glossary

Key Equations

Solved Problems

Discussion Questions and Problems

Case Studies:
   Custom Vans, Inc.
   Old Oregon Wood Store

Bibliography

14.1   INTRODUCTION

In this chapter, we explore two special linear programming models. Because of their structure, these models—called the transportation and assignment models—can be solved using more efficient computational procedures than the simplex method.

Both transportation and assignment problems are members of a category of linear programming techniques called *network flow problems.* Networks, described in detail in Chapter 18, consist of nodes (or points) and arcs (or lines) that join the modes together. Roadways, telephone systems, and citywide water systems are all examples of networks.

Transportation Model

The first model we will examine, the *transportation problem,* deals with the distribution of goods from several points of supply (sources) to a number of points of demand (destinations). Usually, we have a given capacity of goods at each source and a given requirement for the goods at each destination. An example of this is shown in Figure 14.1. The objective of such a problem is to schedule shipments from sources to destinations so that total transportation and production costs are minimized.

Transportation models can also be used when a firm is trying to decide where to locate a new facility. Before opening a new warehouse, factory, or sales office, it is good practice to consider a number of alternative sites. Good financial decisions concerning facility location also attempt to minimize total transportation and production costs for the entire system.

Assignment Model

The assignment problem refers to the class of linear programming problems that involve determining the most efficient assignment of people to

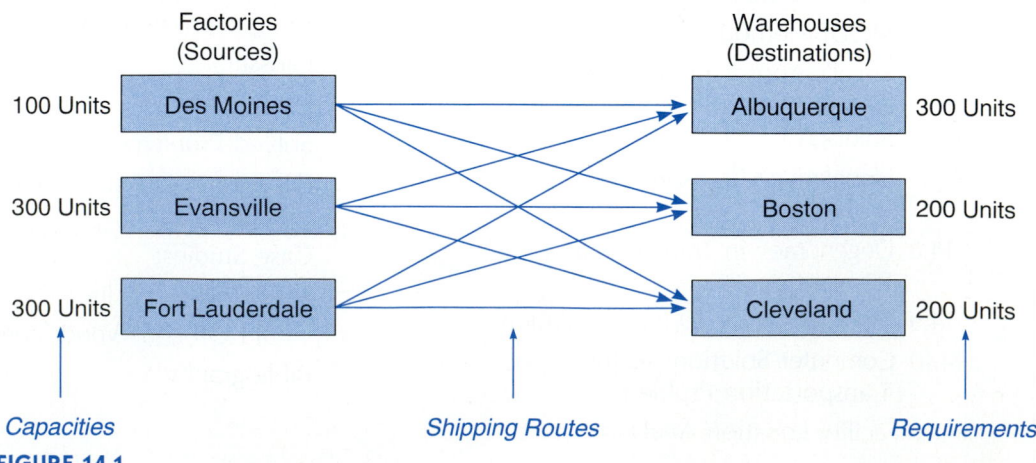

FIGURE 14.1
Example of a Transportation Problem

HISTORY

How Transportation Methods Started

The use of transportation models to minimize the cost of shipping from a number of sources to a number of destinations was first proposed in 1941. This study, called "The Distribution of a Product from Several Sources to Numerous Localities," was written by F. L. Hitchcock. Six years later, T. C. Koopmans independently produced the sec-ond major contribution, a report entitled "Opti-mum Utilization of the Transportation System." In 1953, A. Charnes and W.W. Cooper developed the stepping-stone method, an algorithm discussed in detail in this chapter. The modified-distribution (MODI) method, a quicker computational ap-proach, came about in 1955.

projects, salespeople to territories, contracts to bidders, jobs to machines, and so on. The objective is most often to minimize total costs or total time of performing the tasks at hand. One important characteristic of assign-ment problems is that only one job or worker is assigned to one machine or project.

Special Purpose Algorithms

Although linear programming can be used to solve these types of problems (as seen in Chapter 11), more efficient special-purpose algorithms have been developed for the transportation and assignment applications. As in the simplex algorithm, they involve finding an initial feasible solution and then making step-by-step improvements until an optimal solution is reached. Unlike the simplex method, the transportation and assignment methods are fairly simple in terms of computation.

more efficient than using LP

Streamlined versions of the simplex method are important for three reasons:

1. Their computation times are generally 100 times faster than the sim-plex algorithm.

2. They require less computer memory (and hence can permit larger problems to be solved).

3. They produce integer solutions, which is important because it is hard to ship one-half of a car from a factory or to assign one-third of an astronaut to a shuttle flight.

In the first half of this chapter, we take a look at the makeup of a typical transportation problem. Several solution techniques—the northwest corner rule, the stepping-stone method, the modified distribution (MODI) method and Vogel's approximation method—are discussed. Complications that commonly arise, such as the situation where demand is not exactly equal to supply or the case of a degenerate solution, are also examined. We then look at how the computer can be used to help solve transportation problems.

In the second half of the chapter, we introduce a solution procedure for assignment problems alternately called the *Hungarian method, Flood's*

Teaching Suggestion 14.1:
Transportation Models in the Chapter. See the Instructor's Section for details.

Transparency Master 14.1:
Transportation Solution Techniques.

technique, or the *reduced matrix method.* We also illustrate the use of our microcomputer software package to solve this category of problem.

14.2 SETTING UP A TRANSPORTATION PROBLEM

Transparency Master 14.2:
Transportation Problem.

Alternate Example 14.1

Let us begin with an example dealing with the Executive Furniture Corporation, which manufactures office desks at three locations: Des Moines, Evansville, and Fort Lauderdale. The firm distributes the desks through regional warehouses located in Albuquerque, Boston, and Cleveland (see Figure 14.2).

An estimate of the monthly production capacity at each factory and an estimate of the number of desks that are needed each month at each of the three warehouses is shown as Figure 14.1.

The firm has found that production costs per desk are identical at each factory, and hence the only relevant costs are those of shipping from each *source* to each *destination*. These costs are shown in Table 14.1. They are as-

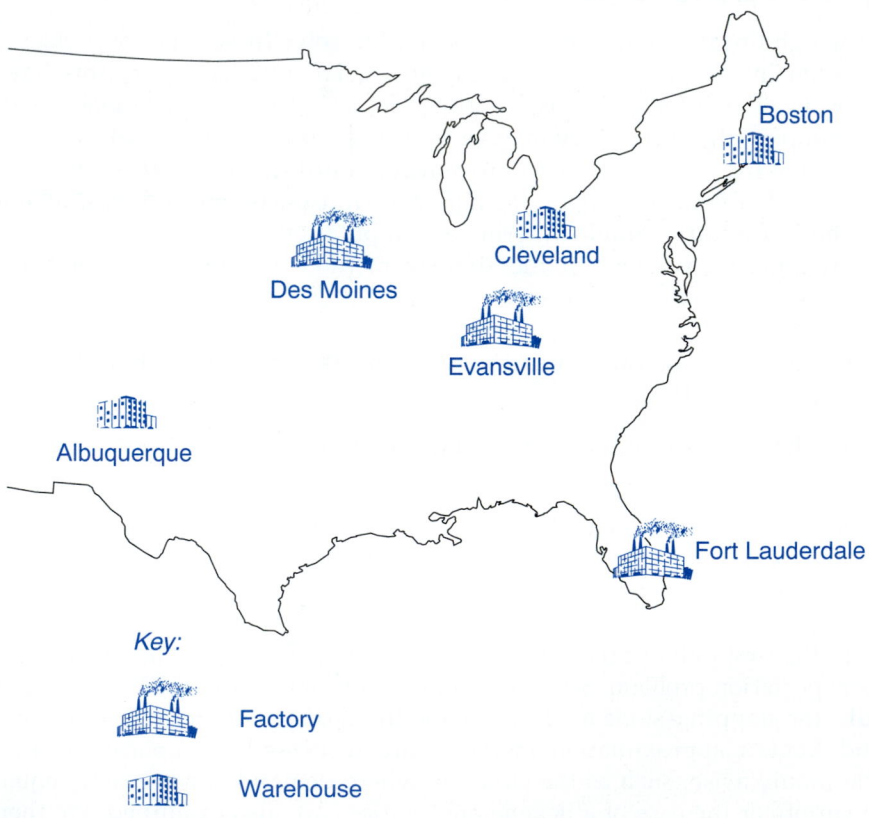

FIGURE 14.2
Geographical Locations of Executive Furniture's Factories and Warehouses

TABLE 14.1 Transportation Costs per Desk for Executive Furniture Corp.

FROM \ TO	ALBUQUERQUE	BOSTON	CLEVELAND
Des Moines	$5	$4	$3
Evansville	$8	$4	$3
Fort Lauderdale	$9	$7	$5

Transparency Master 14.3:
Transportation Costs.

sumed to be constant regardless of the volume shipped.[1] The transportation problem may now be described as *how to select the shipping routes to be used and the number of desks shipped on each route so as to minimize total transportation cost.* This, of course, must be done while observing the restrictions regarding factory capacities and warehouse requirements.

minimizing total
transportation cost

The first step at this point is setting up a *transportation table;* its purpose is to summarize conveniently and concisely all relevant data and to keep track of algorithm computations. (In this respect, it serves the same role as the simplex tableau did for linear programming problems.) Using the information for the Executive Furniture Corporation displayed in Figure 14.1 and Table 14.1, we proceed to construct a transportation table and to label its various components in Table 14.2.

transportation table

Transparency Master 14.4:
Transportation Table.

Transparency Master 14.5:
Transportation Table.

TABLE 14.2 Transportation Table for Executive Furniture Corp.

Transparency Master 14.6:
Transportation Table.

FROM \ TO	Warehouse at Albuquerque	Warehouse at Boston	Warehouse at Cleveland	Factory Capacity
Des Moines Factory	$5	$4	$3	100
Evansville Factory	$8	$4	$3	300
Fort Lauderdale Factory	$9	$7	$5	300
Warehouse Requirements	300	200	200	700

Des Moines
capacity constraint

Cell representing a
source-to-destination
(Evansville to Cleveland)
shipping assignment that
could be made

Cleveland
warehouse demand

Total demand and total supply

Cost of shipping 1 unit from Fort Lauderdale
factory to Boston warehouse

[1]The other assumptions that held for linear programming problems (see Chapter 10) are still applicable to transportation problems.

balanced supply and demand

We see in Table 14.2 that the total factory supply available is exactly equal to the total warehouse demand. When this situation of equal demand and supply occurs (something that is rather unusual in real life) a *balanced problem* is said to exist. Later in this chapter, we take a look at how to deal with unbalanced problems, namely, those where destination requirements may be greater than or less than origin capacities.

Applicable Problems 14-11a, 14-12a, 14-13, 14-14, 14-16, 14-19

Teaching Suggestion 14.2:
Using the Northwest Corner Rule. See the Instructor's Section for details.

14.3	**DEVELOPING AN INITIAL SOLUTION: NORTHWEST CORNER RULE**

Once the data have been arranged in tabular form, we must establish an initial feasible solution to the problem. One systematic procedure, known as the *northwest corner rule,* requires that we start in the upper left-hand cell (or northwest corner) of the table and allocate units to shipping routes as follows:

Transparency Master 14.7:
Initial Solution Using the Northwest Corner Rule.

1. Exhaust the supply (factory capacity) at each row before moving down to the next row.

2. Exhaust the (warehouse) requirements of each column before moving to the right to the next column.

3. Check that all supply and demands are met.

We can now use the northwest corner rule to find an initial feasible solution to the Executive Furniture Corporation problem shown in Table 14.2.

It takes five steps in this example to make the initial shipping assignments (see Table 14.3):

explanation of steps

1. Beginning in the upper left-hand corner, we assign 100 units from Des Moines to Albuquerque. This exhausts the capacity or supply at the Des Moines factory. But it still leaves the warehouse at Albuquerque 200 desks short. Move down to the second row in the same column.

2. Assign 200 units from Evansville to Albuquerque. This meets Albuquerque's demand for a total of 300 desks. Since the Evansville factory has 100 units remaining, we move to the right to the next column of the second row.

3. Assign 100 units from Evansville to Boston. The Evansville supply has now been exhausted, but Boston's warehouse is still short by 100 desks. At this point, we move down vertically in the Boston column to the next row.

4. Assign 100 units from Fort Lauderdale to Boston. This shipment will fulfill Boston's demand for a total of 200 units. We note, though, that the Fort Lauderdale factory still has 200 units available that have not been shipped.

5. Assign 200 units from Fort Lauderdale to Cleveland. This final move exhausts Cleveland's demand *and* Fort Lauderdale's supply. This always happens with a balanced problem. The initial shipment schedule is now complete.

TABLE 14.3 Initial Solution to Executive Furniture Problem Using the Northwest Corner Method

FROM \ TO	Albuquerque (A)	Boston (B)	Cleveland (C)	Factory Capacity
Des Moines (D)	$5 100	$4	$3	100
Evansville (E)	$8 200	$4 100	$3	300
Fort Lauderdale (F)	$9	$7 (100)	$5 200	300
Warehouse Requirements	300	200	200	700

Means that the firm is shipping 100 units along the Fort Lauderdale to Boston route

Transparency Master 14.8: Transportation Table.

We can easily compute the cost of this shipping assignment.

TOTAL COST OF INITIAL SOLUTION				
ROUTE FROM	TO	UNITS SHIPPED	× PER UNIT COST ($)	= TOTAL COST ($)
D	A	100	5	500
E	A	200	8	1,600
E	B	100	4	400
F	B	100	7	700
F	C	200	5	1,000
			Total	4,200

This solution is feasible since demand and supply constraints are all satisfied. It was also very quick and easy to reach. However, we would be very lucky if this solution yielded the optimal transportation cost for the problem, because this route-loading method totally ignored the costs of shipping over each of the routes.

feasible solution

Applicable Problems 14-11b, 14-13, 14-14

Transparency Master 14.9: The Stepping-Stone Method.

14.4 STEPPING-STONE METHOD: FINDING A LEAST-COST SOLUTION

The *stepping-stone method* is an iterative technique for moving from an initial feasible solution to an optimal feasible solution. In order for the stepping-stone method to be applied to a transportation problem, one rule about the number of shipping routes being used must first be observed. The rule is this: *the number of occupied routes (or squares) must always be equal to one less than the sum of the number of rows plus the number of columns*. In the Executive Furniture problem, this means that the initial solution must have $3 + 3 - 1 = 5$ squares used. Thus,

$$\text{Occupied shipping routes (squares)} = \text{Number of rows}$$
$$+ \text{ Number of columns} - 1$$
$$5 = 3 + 3 - 1$$

Teaching Suggestion 14.3: Using the Stepping-Stone Method. See the Instructor's Section for details.

When the number of occupied routes is less than this, the solution is called *degenerate*. Later in this chapter, we talk about what to do if the number of used squares is less than the number of rows plus the number of columns minus 1.

Testing the Solution for Possible Improvement

How does the stepping-stone method work? Its approach is to evaluate the cost-effectiveness of shipping goods via transportation routes *not* currently in the solution. Each unused shipping route (or square) in the transportation table is tested by asking the following question: "What would happen to total shipping costs if *one* unit of our product (in our example, one desk) were tentatively shipped on an unused route?"

testing each unused route

This testing of each unused square is conducted by the following five steps:

1. Select an unused square to be evaluated.

2. Beginning at this square, trace a closed path back to the original square via squares that are currently being used and moving with only horizontal and vertical moves.

3. Beginning with a plus (+) sign at the unused square, place alternate minus (−) signs and plus signs on each corner square of the closed path just traced.

4. Calculate an *improvement index* by adding together the unit cost figures found in each square containing a plus sign and then subtracting the unit costs in each square containing a minus sign.

5. Repeat steps 1–4 until an improvement index has been calculated for all unused squares. If all indices computed are greater than or equal to 0, an optimal solution has been reached. If not, it is possible to improve the current solution and decrease total shipping costs.

To see how the stepping-stone method works, let us apply these steps to the Executive Furniture Corporation data in Table 14.3 to evaluate unused shipping routes. The four currently unassigned routes are: Des Moines to Boston, Des Moines to Cleveland, Evansville to Cleveland, and Fort Lauderdale to Albuquerque.

Steps 1 and 2. Beginning with the Des Moines–Boston route, we first trace a closed path using only currently occupied squares (see Table 14.4), and then place alternate plus signs and minus signs in the corners of this path. To indicate more clearly the meaning of a *closed path*, we see that only squares currently used for shipping can be used in turning the corners of the route being traced. Hence, the path Des Moines–Boston to Des Moines–Albuquerque to Fort Lauderdale–Albuquerque to Fort Lauderdale–Boston to Des Moines–Boston would not be acceptable since the Fort Lauderdale–Albuquerque square is currently empty. It turns out that *only one* closed route is possible for each square we wish to test.

closed paths

Step 3. How do we decide which squares are given plus signs and which minus signs? The answer is simple. Since we are testing the cost-effectiveness of the Des Moines-to-Boston shipping route, we pretend as if we are shipping one desk from Des Moines to Boston. This is one more unit

how to assign + and − signs

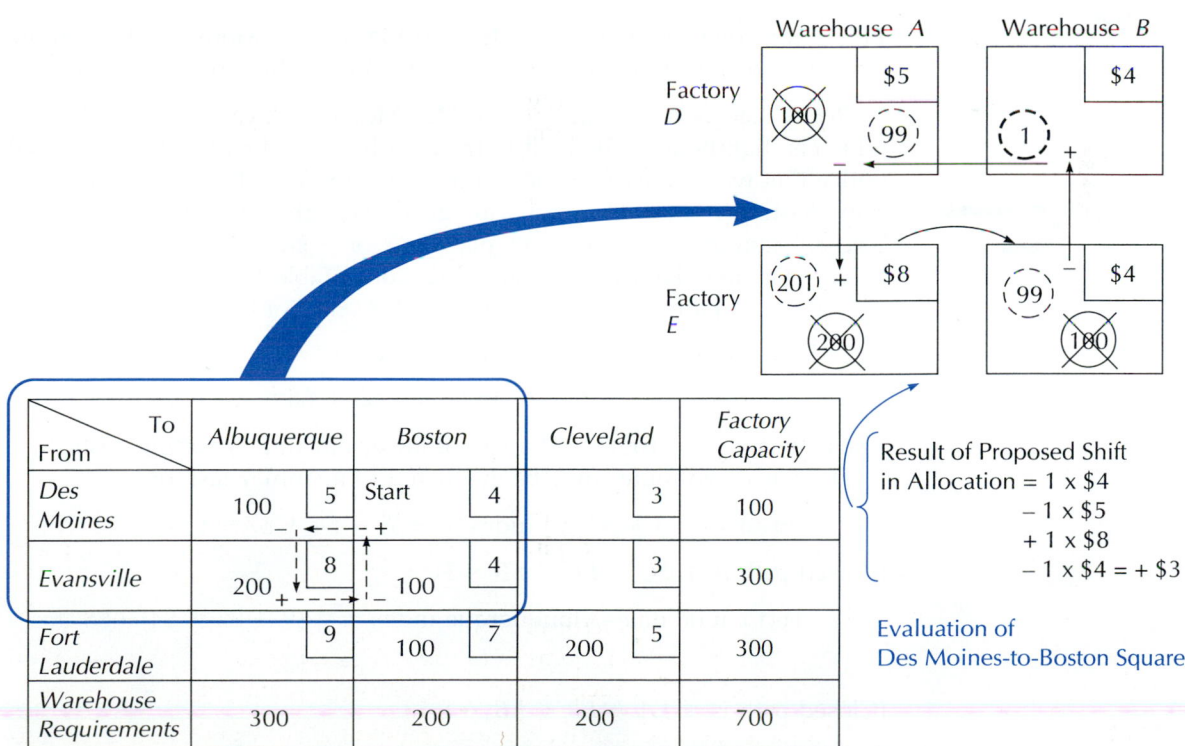

TABLE 14.4 Evaluating the Unused Des Moines–Boston Shipping Route

than we *were* sending between the two cities, so we place a plus sign in the box. But, if we ship one *more* unit than before from Des Moines to Boston, we end up sending 101 desks out of the Des Moines factory.

That factory's capacity is only 100 units, hence we must ship one desk *less* from Des Moines to Albuquerque—this change is made to avoid violating the factory capacity constraint. To indicate that the Des Moines-to-Albuquerque shipment has been reduced, we place a minus sign in its box. Continuing along the closed path, we notice that we are no longer meeting the Albuquerque warehouse requirement for 300 units. In fact, if the Des Moines-to-Albuquerque shipment is reduced to 99 units, the Evansville-to-Albuquerque load has to be increased by 1 unit, to 201 desks. Therefore, we place a plus sign in that box to indicate the increase. Finally, we note that if the Evansville-to-Albuquerque route is assigned 201 desks, then the Evansville-to-Boston route must be reduced by 1 unit, to 99 desks, in order to maintain the Evansville factory capacity constraint of 300 units. Thus, a minus sign is placed in the Evansville-to-Boston box. We observe in Table 14.4 that all four routes on the closed path are hereby balanced in terms of demand-and-supply limitations.

Step 4. An improvement index for the Des Moines–Boston route is now computed by adding unit costs in squares with plus signs and subtracting costs in squares with minus signs. Hence,

improvement index computation

$$\text{Des Moines–Boston index} = +\$4 - \$5 + \$8 - \$4 = +\$3$$

This means that for every desk shipped via the Des Moines–Boston route, total transportation costs will *increase* by \$3 over their current level.

Step 5. Let us now examine the Des Moines–Cleveland unused route, which is slightly more difficult to trace with a closed path. Again, you will notice that we turn each corner along the path only at squares that represent existing routes. The path can go *through* the Evansville–Cleveland box, but cannot turn a corner or place a + or − sign there. Only an occupied square may be used as a stepping stone (Table 14.5).

The closed path we use is $+ DC - DA + EA - EB + FB - FC$.

Des Moines–Cleveland improvement index

$$= +\$3 - \$5 + \$8 - \$4 + \$7 - \$5 = +\$4$$

Thus, opening this route will also not lower our total shipping costs.

The other two routes may be evaluated in a similar fashion:

$$\text{Evansville–Cleveland index} = +\$3 - \$4 + \$7 - \$5 = +\$1$$

(Closed path is $+ EC - EB + FB - FC$.)

$$\text{Fort Lauderdale–Albuquerque index} = +\$9 - \$7 + \$4 - \$8$$
$$= -\$2$$

(Closed path is $+ FA - FB + EB - EA$.)

Because this last improvement index is negative, a cost savings may be attained by making use of the (currently unused) Fort Lauderdale–Albuquerque route.

TABLE 14.5 Evaluating the Des Moines–Cleveland (D–C) Shipping Route

FROM \ TO	A	B	C	FACTORY CAPACITY
D	$5 100 ←	$4	$3 start +	100
E	$8 + 200	$4 – 100	$3	300
F	$9	$7 + 100	$5 – 200	300
WAREHOUSE REQUIREMENTS	300	200	200	700

Transparency Master 14.10: Stepping-Stone Method: Tracing a Closed Path for the Des Moines to Cleveland Route.

Obtaining an Improved Solution

Each negative index computed by the stepping-stone method represents the amount by which total transportation costs could be decreased if 1 unit or product were shipped on that route. We found only one negative index in the Executive Furniture problem, that being −$2 on the Fort Lauderdale-factory-to-Albuquerque-warehouse route. If, however, there were more than one negative improvement index, our strategy would be to choose the route (unused square) with the *largest* negative index.

selecting route with largest negative index

The next step, then, is to ship the maximum allowable number of units (or desks, in our case) on the new route (Fort Lauderdale to Albuquerque). What is the maximum quantity that can be shipped on the money-saving route? That quantity is found by referring to the closed path of plus signs and minus signs drawn for the route and selecting the *smallest number* found in those squares containing *minus signs*.

To obtain a new solution, that number is added to all squares on the closed path with plus signs, and subtracted from all squares on the path assigned minus signs.

changing the shipping route

Let us see how this process can help improve Executive Furniture's solution. We repeat the transportation table (Table 14.6) for the problem. Note that the stepping-stone route for Fort Lauderdale to Albuquerque (*F* to *A*) is drawn in.

The maximum quantity that can be shipped on the newly opened route (*F–A*) is the smallest number found in squares containing minus signs—in this case, 100 units. Why 100 units? Since the total cost decreases by $2 per unit shipped, we know we would like to ship the maximum possible number of units. Table 14.6 indicates that each unit shipped over the *F–A* route results in an increase of 1 unit shipped from *E* to *B* and a decrease of 1 unit

TABLE 14.6 Stepping-Stone Path Used to Evaluate Route F–A

FROM \ TO	A	B	C	FACTORY
D	$5 100	$4	$3	100
E	$8 − 200	$4 + 100	$3	300
F	$9 +	$7 − 100	$5 200	300
WAREHOUSE	300	200	200	700

in both the amounts shipped from F to B (now 100 units) and from E to A (now 200 units). Hence, the maximum we can ship over the F–A route is 100. This results in 0 units being shipped from F to B.

We add 100 units to the 0 now being shipped on route F–A; then proceed to subtract 100 from route F–B, leaving 0 in that square (but still balancing the row total for F); then add 100 to route E–B, yielding 200; and finally, subtract 100 from route E–A, leaving 100 units shipped. Note that the new numbers still produce the correct row and column totals as required.

The new solution is shown in Table 14.7.

TABLE 14.7 Second Solution to the Executive Furniture Problem

FROM \ TO	A	B	C	FACTORY
D	$5 100	$4	$3	100
E	$8 100	$4 200	$3	300
F	$9 100	$7	$5 200	300
WAREHOUSE	300	200	200	700

Total shipping cost has been reduced by (100 units) × ($2 saved per unit) = $200, and is now $4,000. This cost figure can, of course, also be derived by multiplying each unit shipping cost times the number of units transported on its route, namely, (100 × $5) + (100 × $8) + (200 × $4) + (100 × $9) + (200 × $5) = $4,000.

The solution shown in Table 14.7 may or may not be optimal. To determine whether further improvement is possible, we return to the first five steps given earlier to test each square that is *now* unused. The four improvement indices—each representing an available shipping route—are as follows:

improvement indices

$$D \text{ to } B = +\$4 - \$5 + \$8 - \$4 = +\$3$$

$$(\textit{closed path}: +DB - DA + EA - EB)$$

$$D \text{ to } C = +\$3 - \$5 + \$9 - \$5 = +\$2$$

$$(\textit{closed path}: +DC - DA + FA - FC)$$

$$E \text{ to } C = +\$3 - \$8 + \$9 - \$5 = -\$1$$

$$(\textit{closed path}: +EC - EA + FA - FC)$$

$$F \text{ to } B = +\$7 - \$4 + \$8 - \$9 = +\$2$$

$$(\textit{closed path}: +FB - EB + EA - FA)$$

Hence, an improvement can be made by shipping the maximum allowable number of units from *E* to *C* (see Table 14.8). Only the squares *E–A* and *F–C* have minus signs in the closed path; since the smallest number in these two squares is 100, we add 100 units to *E–C* and *F–A* and subtract 100 units from *E–A* and *F–C*. The new cost for this third solution of $3,900 is computed below.

TABLE 14.8 Path to Evaluate the E–C Route

FROM \ TO	A	B	C	FACTORY
D	100 $5	$4	$3	100
E	100 − $8	200 $4	Start + $3	300
F	100 + $9	$7	200 − $5	300
WAREHOUSE	300	200	200	700

ROUTE		DESKS		PER UNIT		TOTAL
FROM	TO	SHIPPED	×	COST ($)	=	COST ($)
D	A	100		5		500
E	B	200		4		800
E	C	100		3		300
F	A	200		9		1,800
F	C	100		5		500
					Total	3,900

TOTAL COST OF THIRD SOLUTION

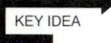

Table 14.9 contains the optimal shipping assignments because each improvement index that can be computed at this point is greater than or equal to zero as shown in the following equations. Improvement indices for the table are:

D to B = +\$4 − \$5 + \$9 − \$5 + \$3 − \$4

$$= \underline{+\$2} \quad (path: +DB - DA + FA - FC + EC - EB)$$

D to C = +\$3 − \$5 + \$9 − \$5 = $\underline{+\$2}$ (path: +DC − DA + FA − FC)

E to A = +\$8 − \$9 + \$5 − \$3 = $\underline{+\$1}$ (path: +EA − FA + FC − EC)

F to B = +\$7 − \$5 + \$3 − \$4 = $\underline{+\$1}$ (path: +FB − FC + EC − EB)

The hardest part in solving problems like this is identifying every stepping-stone path so that we may compute the improvement indices. An easier way to find the optimal solution to transportation problems, especially larger ones with more sources and destinations, is called the MODI method.

TABLE 14.9 Third and Optimal Solution

FROM \ TO	A	B	C	FACTORY
D	$5 100	$4	$3	100
E	$8	$4 200	$3 100	300
F	$9 200	$7	$5 100	300
WAREHOUSE	300	200	200	700

Transportation Problem for Irish Pharmaceutical Distributor

The Cahill May Roberts company (CMR), one of Ireland's largest wholesale distributors of pharmaceuticals, faced a major *transportation problem*. The firm had its head office and three warehouses in the Dublin area, with five more warehouses scattered about Ireland. CMR supplied 400 customers (mainly retail druggists) in the Dublin area and over 800 customers in 300 outlying towns and villages. Customers were supplied by a fleet of delivery vans, with a drop-off frequency varying from twice per day to once per week.

Prior to the transportation problem analysis, no coherent distribution plan for the whole company

Source: H. Harrison, "A Planning System for Facilities and Resources in Distribution Networks," *Interfaces* **9**, (February 1979): 6–22.

had been formulated. It was even common for customers to receive their supplies from more than one warehouse. The illogical transportation system meant that delivery patterns were not very efficient in satisfying druggists' demands.

According to the director of finance, the transportation planning model yielded the following results:

1. A 27% reduction in delivery and transportation costs.

2. A $765,000 savings in overhead.

3. A reduction of $125,000 in capital investments, with more savings anticipated.

4. A 60% increase in customer service leading to a sales increase of $2,457,000.

14.5 MODI METHOD

Applicable Problems 14-15, 14-16, 14-18

MODI versus stepping-stone method

The MODI (*modified distribution*) method allows us to compute improvement indices quickly for each unused square without drawing all of the closed paths. Because of this, it can often provide considerable time savings over the stepping-stone method for solving transportation problems.

MODI provides a new means of finding the unused route with the largest negative improvement index. Once the largest index is identified, we are required to trace only one closed path. Just as with the stepping-stone approach, this path helps determine the maximum number of units that can be shipped via the best unused route.

How to Use the MODI Approach

In applying the MODI method, we begin with an initial solution obtained by using the northwest corner rule.[2] But now, we must compute a value for each row (call the values R_1, R_2, R_3 if there are three rows) and for each column (K_1, K_2, K_3) in the transportation table. In general, we let

R_i = value assigned to row i

K_j = value assigned to column j

C_{ij} = cost in square ij (cost of shipping from source i to destination j)

Transparency Master 14.11: MODI Method: 5 Steps.

[2]Note that any initial feasible solution will do: northwest corner rule, Vogel's approximation method solution, or any arbitrary assignment.

MODI steps

The MODI method then requires five steps.

1. To compute the values for each row and column, set

$$R_i + K_j = C_{ij} \qquad (14\text{-}1)$$

but *only for those squares that are currently used or occupied.* For example, if the square at the intersection of row 2 and column 1 is occupied, we set $R_2 + K_1 = C_{21}$.

2. After all equations have been written, set $R_1 = 0$.

3. Solve the system of equations for all R and K values.

4. Compute the improvement index for each unused square by the formula:

$$\text{Improvement index} = C_{ij} - R_i - K_j \qquad (14\text{-}2)$$

5. Select the largest negative index and proceed to solve the problem as you did using the stepping-stone method.

Solving the Executive Furniture Problem with MODI

Let us try out these rules on the Executive Furniture Corporation problem. The initial northwest corner solution is repeated in Table 14.10. MODI will be used to compute an improvement index for each unused square. Note that the only change in the transportation table is the border labeling the R_is (rows) and K_js (columns).

TABLE 14.10 Initial Solution to Executive Furniture Problem in the MODI Format

	K_j	K_1	K_2	K_3	
R_i	TO FROM	ALBUQUERQUE	BOSTON	CLEVELAND	FACTORY CAPACITY
R_1	DES MOINES	5 / 100	4	3	100
R_2	EVANSVILLE	8 / 200	4 / 100	3	300
R_3	FORT LAUDERDALE	9	7 / 100	5 / 200	300
	WAREHOUSE REQUIREMENTS	300	200	200	700

We first set up an equation for each occupied square:

solving for R and K
values

(1) $R_1 + K_1 = 5$

(2) $R_2 + K_1 = 8$

(3) $R_2 + K_2 = 4$

(4) $R_3 + K_2 = 7$

(5) $R_3 + K_3 = 5$

Letting $R_1 = 0$, we can easily solve, step by step, for K_1, R_2, K_2, R_3, and K_3.

(1) $R_1 + K_1 = 5$

     $0 + K_1 = 5$ $K_1 = 5$

(2) $R_2 + K_1 = 8$

     $R_2 + 5 = 8$ $R_2 = 3$

(3) $R_2 + K_2 = 4$

     $3 + K_2 = 4$ $K_2 = 1$

(4) $R_3 + K_2 = 7$

     $R_3 + 1 = 7$ $R_3 = 6$

(5) $R_3 + K_3 = 5$

     $6 + K_3 = 5$ $K_3 = -1$

You can observe that these R and K values will not always be positive; it is common for 0 and negative values to occur as well. We also think that after solving for the Rs and Ks in a few practice problems, you may become so proficient that the calculations can be done in your head instead of by writing the equations out.

The next step is to compute the improvement index for each unused cell. That formula, again, is: Improvement index $= C_{ij} - R_i - K_j$.

Des Moines–Boston index $= C_{12} - R_1 - K_2 = 4 - 0 - 1$

         $= +\$3$

Des Moines–Cleveland index $= C_{13} - R_1 - K_3 = 3 - 0 - (-1)$

         $= +\$4$

Evansville–Cleveland index $= C_{23} - R_2 - K_3 = 3 - 3 - (-1)$

         $= +\$1$

Fort Lauderdale–Albuquerque index $= C_{31} - R_3 - K_1 = 9 - 6 - 5$

         $= -\$2$

Note that these indices are exactly the same as the ones calculated when we used the stepping-stone approach (see Tables 14.4 and 14.5). Since one of the indices is negative, the current solution is not optimal. But now it is necessary to trace only the one closed path, for Fort Lauderdale–

KEY IDEA

Albuquerque, in order to proceed with the solution procedures as used in the stepping-stone method.

improving the solution

For your convenience, the steps we follow to develop an improved solution after the improvement indices have been computed are briefly outlined:

1. Beginning at the square with the best improvement index (Fort Lauderdale–Albuquerque), trace a closed path back to the original square via squares that are currently being used.

2. Beginning with a plus (+) sign at the unused square, place alternate minus (−) signs and plus signs on each corner square of the closed path just traced.

3. Select the smallest quantity found in those squares containing minus signs. *Add* that number to all squares on the closed path with plus signs; *subtract* the number from all squares assigned minus signs.

4. Compute new improvement indices for this new solution using the MODI method.

Following this procedure, the second and third solutions to the Executive Furniture Corporation problem can be found. In tabular form, the result of your MODI computations will look identical to Tables 14.7 (second solution using stepping-stone) and 14.9 (optimal solution). With each new MODI solution, we must recalculate the R and K values. These values then are used to compute new improvement indices in order to determine whether further shipping cost reduction is possible.

Applicable Problems 14-17, 14-18

14.6 VOGEL'S APPROXIMATION METHOD: ANOTHER WAY TO FIND AN INITIAL SOLUTION

In addition to the northwest corner method of setting an initial solution to transportation problems, we talk about one other important technique—*Vogel's approximation method* (VAM). VAM is not quite as simple as the northwest corner approach, but it facilitates a very good initial solution—as a matter of fact, one that is often the *optimal* solution.

Vogel's approximation method tackles the problem of finding a good initial solution by taking into account the costs associated with each route alternative. This is something that the northwest corner rule did not do. To apply the VAM, we first compute for each row and column the penalty faced if we should ship over the *second best* route instead of the *least-cost* route.

The six steps involved in determining an initial VAM solution are illustrated on our now familiar Executive Furniture Corporation data. (We begin with the same layout originally shown in Table 14.2.)

steps of VAM

VAM Step 1. For each row and column of the transportation table, find the difference between the two lowest unit shipping costs. These numbers represent the difference between the distribution cost on the *best* route in the row or column and the *second best* route in the row or column. (This is the *opportunity* cost of not using the best route.)

Step 1 has been done in Table 14.11. The numbers at the heads of the columns and to the right of the rows represent these differences.

For example, in row *E* the three transportation costs are $8, $4, and $3. Since the two lowest costs are $4 and $3, their difference is $1.

VAM Step 2. Identify the row or column with the greatest opportunity cost, or difference. In case of Table 14.11, the row or column selected is column *A*, with a difference of 3.

VAM Step 3. Assign as many units as possible to the lowest-cost square in the row or column selected.

Step 3 has been done in Table 14.12. Under column *A*, the lowest cost route is *D–A* (with a cost of $5) and 100 units have been assigned to that square. No more were placed in the square because doing so would exceed *D*'s availability.

VAM Step 4. Eliminate any row or column that has just been completely satisfied by the assignment just made. This can be done by placing X's in each appropriate square.

Step 4 has been done in Table 14.12's *D* row. No future assignments will be made to the *D–B* or *D–C* routes.

assignment based on penalty costs

TABLE 14.11 Transportation Table with VAM Row and Column Differences Shown

FROM \ TO	ALBUQUERQUE A	BOSTON B	CLEVELAND C	TOTAL AVAILABLE	
	3	0	0		
DES MOINES D	5	4	3	100	1
EVANSVILLE E	8	4	3	300	1
FORT LAUDERDALE F	9	7	5	300	2
TOTAL REQUIRED	300	200	200	700	

TABLE 14.12 VAM Assignment with D's Requirements Satisfied

FROM \ TO	A ~~3~~ 1	B ~~0~~ 3	C ~~0~~ 2	TOTAL AVAILABLE	
D	5 100	4 X	3 X	100	~~X~~
E	8	4	3	300	1
F	9	7	5	300	2
TOTAL REQUIRED	300	200	200	700	

VAM Step 5. Recompute the cost differences for the transportation table, omitting rows or columns crossed out in the preceding step.

This is also shown in Table 14.12. A's, B's, and C's differences each change. D's row is eliminated, and E's and F's differences remain the same as in Table 14.11.

VAM Step 6. Return to step 2 and repeat the steps until an initial feasible solution has been obtained.

In our case, column B now has the greatest difference, which is 3. We assign 200 units to the lowest-cost square in column B that has not been crossed out. This is seen to be E–B. Since B's requirements have now been met, we place an X in the F–B square to eliminate it. Differences are once again recomputed. This process is summarized in Table 14.13.

The greatest difference is now in row E. Hence, we shall assign as many units as possible to the lowest-cost square in row E, that is, E–C with a cost of $3. The maximum assignment of 100 units depletes the remaining availability at E. The square E–A may therefore be crossed out. This is illustrated in Table 14.14.

The final two allocations, at F–A and F–C, may be made by inspecting supply restrictions (in the rows) and demand requirements (in the columns). We see that an assignment of 200 units to F–A and 100 units to F–C completes the table (see Table 14.15).

The cost of this VAM assignment is = (100 units × $5) + (200 units × $4) + (100 units × $3) + (200 units × $9) + (100 units × $5) = $3,900.

VAM may yield optimal solution

It is worth noting that the use of Vogel's approximation method on the Executive Furniture Corporation data produces the optimal solution to this

TABLE 14.13 Second VAM Assignment with B's Requirements Satisfied

FROM \ TO	~~3~~ 1 A	~~Ø~~ ~~3~~ B	~~Ø~~ 2 C	TOTAL AVAILABLE	
D	5 / 100	4 / X	3 / X	100	~~X~~
E	8 /	4 / 200	3 /	300	~~X~~ 5
F	9 /	7 / X	5 /	300	~~2~~ 4
TOTAL REQUIRED	300	200	200	700	

problem. Even though VAM takes many more calculations to find an initial solution than does the northwest corner rule, it almost always produces a much better initial solution. Hence, VAM tends to minimize the total number of computations needed to reach an optimal solution.

TABLE 14.14 Third VAM Assignment with C's Requirements Satisfied

FROM \ TO	A	B	C	TOTAL AVAILABLE
D	5 / 100	4 / X	3 / X	100
E	8 / X	4 / 200	3 / 100	300
F	9 /	7 / X	5 /	300
TOTAL REQUIRED	300	200	200	700

TABLE 14.15 Final Assignments to Balance Column and Row Requirements

FROM \ TO	A	B	C	TOTAL AVAILABLE
D	100 [5]	X [4]	X [3]	100
E	X [8]	200 [4]	100 [3]	300
F	200 [9]	X [7]	100 [5]	300
TOTAL REQUIRED	300	200	200	700

Transparency Master 14.12:
Special Problems in
Transportation Method.

KEY IDEA

**dummy sources or
destinations**

Teaching Suggestion 14.4:
Dummy Rows and Columns.
See the Instructor's Section
for details.

14.7 UNBALANCED TRANSPORTATION PROBLEMS

A situation occurring quite frequently in real-life problems is the case where total demand is not equal to total supply. These *unbalanced problems* can be handled easily by the preceding solution procedures if we first introduce *dummy sources* or *dummy destinations*. In the event that total supply is greater than total demand, a dummy destination (warehouse), with demand exactly equal to the surplus, is created. If total demand is greater than total supply, we introduce a dummy source (factory) with a supply equal to the excess of demand over supply. In either case, shipping cost coefficients of zero are assigned to each dummy location or route because no shipments will actually be made from a dummy factory or to a dummy warehouse.

Demand Less Than Supply

Considering the original Executive Furniture Corporation problem, suppose that the Des Moines factory increases its rate of production to 250 desks. (That factory's capacity used to be 100 desks per production period.) The firm is now able to supply a total of 850 desks each period. Warehouse requirements, however, remain the same (at 700 desks), so the row and column totals do not balance.

To balance this type of problem, we simply add a dummy column which will represent a fake warehouse requiring 150 desks. This is somewhat analogous to adding a slack variable in solving a linear programming problem. And just as slack variables were assigned a value of 0 dollars in the LP objective function, the shipping costs to this dummy warehouse are all set equal to 0.

The northwest corner rule is used once again, in Table 14.16, to find an initial solution to this modified Executive Furniture problem. As you can see, expanding capacity at Des Moines has decreased total cost. If you wanted to complete this task and find an optimal solution, either stepping-stone or MODI methods would now be employed.

Note that the 150 units from Fort Lauderdale to the dummy warehouse represent 150 units that are *not* shipped from Fort Lauderdale.

Demand Greater Than Supply

The second type of unbalanced condition occurs when total demand is greater than total supply. This means that customers or warehouses require more of a product than the firm's factories can provide. In this case, we need to add a dummy row representing a fake factory. The new factory will have a supply exactly equal to the difference between total demand and total real supply. The shipping costs from the dummy factory to each destination will be 0.

Alternate Example 14.2

Let us set up such an unbalanced problem for the Happy Sound Stereo Company. Happy Sound assembles high-fidelity stereophonic systems at three plants and distributes through three regional warehouses. The production capacities at each plant, demand at each warehouse, and unit shipping costs are presented in Table 14.17.

TABLE 14.16 Initial Solution to an Unbalanced Problem Where Demand Is Less Than Supply

FROM \ TO	ALBUQUER- QUE A		BOSTON B		CLEVELAND C		DUMMY WAREHOUSE		FACTORY CAPACITY
DES MOINES D		5		4		3		0	
	250								250
EVANSVILLE E		8		4		3		0	
	50		200		50				300
FORT LAUDERDALE F		9		7		5		0	
					150		150		300
WAREHOUSE REQUIRE- MENTS	300		200		200		150		850

New Des Moines capacity

Total cost = 250($5) + 50($8) + 200($4) + 50($3) + 150($5) + 150($0) = $3,350

Moving Sand with the Transportation Approach

Most large construction and civil engineering projects require the transportation of gravel, rock, sand, and other materials from one location to another. The modification of the Brisbane International Airport in Australia posed such a problem. Sand from nearby bay areas was to be moved to various parts of the airport site and used as a fill. This became a classic transportation problem involving the shipment of sand, in this case, from various sources to various destinations.

The estimated quantity of sand to be moved in total was approximately 1.8 million cubic meters.

Source: Mervyn Lawrence and Chad Perry, "Earthmoving On Construction Projects: A Postscript," *Interfaces* **14**, 2 (March–April 1984): 84–86.

There were about 26 sources or sites and about 35 final fill destinations that were identified. In addition to cost and distance factors, there was also a time factor. Sand could not be removed from the initial reclaimed areas or sites until one year after it was placed at the sites. Final dates for sand removal were also set by the construction program and the construction schedule. As a result of some of these time constraints, an approach called the out-of-kilter algorithm (OKA) was used to solve this transportation problem. It was estimated that using this algorithm and this transportation approach saved approximately $802,044, which represented about 27% of the total hauling component for the project.

TABLE 14.17 Unbalanced Transportation Table for Happy Sound Stereo Company

FROM \ TO	WAREHOUSE A	WAREHOUSE B	WAREHOUSE C	PLANT SUPPLY
PLANT W	$6	$4	$9	200
PLANT X	$10	$5	$8	175
PLANT Y	$12	$7	$6	75
WAREHOUSE DEMAND	250	100	150	500 / 450

Totals do not balance

TABLE 14.18 Initial Solution to an Unbalanced Problem Where Demand Is Greater Than Supply

TO / FROM	WAREHOUSE A	WAREHOUSE B	WAREHOUSE C	PLANT SUPPLY
PLANT W	6 / 200	4	9	200
PLANT X	10 / 50	5 / 100	8 / 25	175
PLANT Y	12	7	6 / 75	75
DUMMY	0	0	0 / 50	50
WAREHOUSE DEMAND	250	100	150	500

Total cost of initial solution = 200($6) + 50($10) + 100($5) + 25($8) + 75($6) + 50($0)
= $2,850

As can be seen in Table 14.18, a dummy plant adds an extra row, balances the problem, and allows us to apply the northwest corner rule to find the initial solution shown. This initial solution shows 50 units being shipped from the dummy plant to warehouse C. This means that warehouse C will be 50 units short of its requirements. In general, any units shipped from a dummy source represent unmet demand at the respective destination.

14.8 DEGENERACY IN TRANSPORTATION PROBLEMS

Applicable Problem 14-19

We briefly mentioned the subject of *degeneracy* earlier in this chapter. Degeneracy occurs when the number of occupied squares or routes in a transportation table solution is less than the number of rows plus the number of columns minus 1. Such a situation may arise in the initial solution or in any subsequent solution. Degeneracy requires a special procedure in order to correct the problem. Without enough occupied squares to trace a closed

Teaching Suggestion 14.5:
Handling Degeneracy in
Transportation Problems.
See the Instructor's Section
for details.

path for each unused route, it would be impossible to apply the stepping-stone method or to calculate the *R* and *K* values needed for the MODI technique. You might recall that no problem discussed in Chapter 14 thus far has been degenerate.

To handle degenerate problems, we create an artificially occupied cell—that is, we place a 0 (representing a fake shipment) in one of the unused squares and then treat that square as if it were occupied. The square chosen must be in such a position as to allow *all* stepping-stone paths to be closed, although there is usually a good deal of flexibility in selecting the unused square that will receive the 0.

Degeneracy in an Initial Solution

Degeneracy can occur in our application of the northwest corner rule to find an initial solution, as we see in the case of the Martin Shipping Company. Martin has three warehouses from which to supply its three major retail customers in San Jose. Martin's shipping costs, warehouse supplies, and customer demands are presented in Table 14.19. Note that origins in this problem are warehouses and destinations are retail stores. Initial shipping assignments are made in the table by application of the northwest corner rule.

This initial solution is degenerate because it violates the rule that the number of used squares must be equal to the number of rows plus the number of columns minus 1 (namely, $3 + 3 - 1 = 5$ is greater than the number of occupied boxes). In this particular problem, degeneracy arose because both a column and a row requirement (that being column 1

TABLE 14.19 Initial Solution of a Degenerate Problem

FROM \ TO	CUSTOMER 1	CUSTOMER 2	CUSTOMER 3	WAREHOUSE SUPPLY
WAREHOUSE 1	100 _(8)_	_(2)_	_(6)_	100
WAREHOUSE 2	_(10)_	100 _(9)_	20 _(9)_	120
WAREHOUSE 3	_(7)_	_(10)_	80 _(7)_	80
CUSTOMER DEMAND	100	100	100	300

and row 1) were satisfied simultaneously. This broke the stair-step pattern we usually see with northwest corner solutions.

To correct the problem, we may place a 0 in an unused square. In this case, those squares representing either the shipping route from warehouse 1 to customer 2 or from warehouse 2 to customer 1 will do. If you treat the new 0 square just like any other occupied square, any of the regular solution methods can be used.

Degeneracy During Later Solution Stages

A transportation problem can become degenerate *after* the initial solution stage if adding an unused square results in the elimination of two previously occupied routes, instead of eliminating the usual *one.* Such a problem occurs when two squares assigned minus signs on a closed path both have the same lowest quantity.

After one iteration of the stepping-stone method, cost analysts at Bagwell Paint produced the following transportation table (see Table 14.20). We observe that the solution in Table 14.20 is not degenerate, but it is also not optimal.

The improvement indices for the four currently unused squares are:

Factory A − Warehouse 2 index = + 2

Factory A − Warehouse 3 index = + 1

Factory B − Warehouse 3 index = −15 ← *Only route with a negative index*

Factory C − Warehouse 2 index = +11

TABLE 14.20 Bagwell Paint Transportation Table

FROM \ TO	WAREHOUSE 1		WAREHOUSE 2		WAREHOUSE 3		FACTORY CAPACITY
FACTORY A	70	8		5		16	70
FACTORY B	50	15	80	10		7	130
FACTORY C	30	3		9	50	10	80
WAREHOUSE REQUIREMENT	150		80		50		280

Total shipping cost = $2,700

TABLE 14.21 Tracing a Closed Path for the Factory B–Warehouse 3 Route

TO FROM	WAREHOUSE 1	WAREHOUSE 3
FACTORY B	15 50 — ←─────	7 +
FACTORY C	3 30 + ─ ─ ─ →	10 ─ 50

Hence, an improved solution may be obtained by opening the route from factory *B* to warehouse 3. Let us go through the stepping-stone procedure for finding the next solution to Bagwell Paint's problem. We begin by drawing a closed path for the unused square representing factory *B*–warehouse 3. This is shown in Table 14.21, which is an abbreviated version of Table 14.20 and contains only the factories and warehouses necessary to close the path.

Since the smallest quantity in a square containing a minus sign is 50, we assign 50 units to the factory *B*–warehouse 3 and factory *C*–warehouse 1 routes, and subtract 50 units from the two squares containing minus signs. However, this act causes both formerly occupied squares to drop to 0. It also means that there are not enough occupied squares in the new solution and that it will be degenerate. We will have to place an artificial 0 in one of the squares (generally, the one with the lowest shipping cost) in order to handle the degeneracy problem.

Applicable Problems 14-11c, 14-12b

KEY IDEA

14.9 MORE THAN ONE OPTIMAL SOLUTION

Just as with linear programming problems, it is possible for a transportation problem to have multiple optimal solutions. Such a situation is indicated when one or more of the improvement indices that we calculate for each unused square is 0 in the optimal solution. This means that it is possible to design alternate shipping routings with the same total shipping cost. The alternate optimal solution can be found by shipping the most to this unused square. Practically speaking, multiple optimal solutions provide management with greater flexibility in selecting and using resources.

Applicable Problems 14-20, 14-21, 14-22, 14-37

14.10 COMPUTER SOLUTIONS TO THE TRANSPORTATION PROBLEM

Computer programs exist to solve not only linear programming problems, but the less complicated transportation problems as well. In this section, we illustrate how both our AB:QM microcomputer software program (see Program 14.1) and STORM (see Program 14.2) handle transportation problems. Note that the problem need not be balanced before the data are entered. The computer programs are demonstrated on a small problem involving allocation of shipments from three factories to three warehouses. All appropriate costs and shipment data are summarized in Table 14.22 (on p. 542).

PROGRAM 14.1 Sample Transportation Model Computer Run Using AB:QM

```
Transportation

Problem Title :  SAMPLE TRANSPORTATION RUN, TABLE 14.22
Type of Problem (Max=1/Min=2)   2      Initial (NW=1/MC=2/VAM=3)   1
Number of Sources               3      Number of Destinations      3


            D1          D2          D3        Sources
S1         200         600         300           8
S2         400         200         700          11
S3         500         800         300          12
Des.        10          12           9          31
```

```
 Help   New   Load   Save   Edit   Run   Print   Install   Directory   Esc
```

```
Program: Transportation

Problem Title : SAMPLE TRANSPORTATION RUN, TABLE 14.22

***** Input Data *****

Minimization Problem:

        |      1       2       3|   Supply
--------------------------------------------
    1   |   200.0   600.0   300.0|      8.0
    2   |   400.0   200.0   700.0|     11.0
    3   |   500.0   800.0   300.0|     12.0
--------------------------------------------
Demand|     10.0    12.0     9.0|     31.0
```

(Continued)

```
***** Program Output *****


Initial Solution by Northwest Corner Method
       |      1        2        3|   Supply
-----------------------------------------
   1   |      8.0      0.0      0.0|      8.0
   2   |      2.0      9.0      0.0|     11.0
   3   |      0.0      3.0      9.0|     12.0
-----------------------------------------
Demand|     10.0     12.0      9.0|     31.0

Initial Solution  :        9300.0


Optimal Solution by MODI
       |      1        2        3|   Supply
-----------------------------------------
   1   |      8.0      0.0      0.0|      8.0
   2   |      0.0     11.0      0.0|     11.0
   3   |      2.0      1.0      9.0|     12.0
-----------------------------------------
Demand|     10.0     12.0      9.0|     31.0

Optimal Solution :        8300.0



***** End of Output *****
```

TABLE 14.22 Sample Data for Computer Program

FROM \ TO	WAREHOUSE 1	WAREHOUSE 2	WAREHOUSE 3	AMOUNT AVAILABLE
FACTORY 1	200	600	300	8
FACTORY 2	400	200	700	11
FACTORY 3	500	800	300	12
AMOUNT NEEDED	10	12	9	31

PROGRAM 14.2 **STORM Program Output on Table 14.22**

```
_____ STORM EDITOR : Transportation Module _____

  Title :  SAMPLE RUN OF STORM ON TABLE 14.22 DATA

  Capacitated (CAP/UNCP)    :    UNCP    Number of rows          :      3
  Number of columns         :      3     Objective type (MAX/MIN) :    MIN
  Bounds(ROW/COL/BOTH/NONE) :    NONE

  R2  : C1  COLUMN   1 COLUMN   2 COLUMN   3     DUMMY      SUPPLY
  ROW    1     200.       600.       300.                    |       8
  ROW    2     400.       200.       700.                    |      11
  ROW    3     500.       800.       300.                    |      12
  DUMMY       ----       ----       ----       ----    |    ----
  DEMAND        10         12          9                |    XXXX

  F1 Block   F2 GoTo   F3 InsR   F4 DelR   F5 InsC   F6 DelC   F7 Done   F8 Help KB:C
```

```
                SAMPLE RUN OF STORM ON TABLE 14.22 DATA
          TRANSPORTATION - OPTIMAL SOLUTION - TABLEAU OUTPUT

                   COLUMN 1 COLUMN 2 COLUMN 3 U(I)\SUPPLY
                 +--------+--------+--------+
         ROW 1   |200.000 |600.000 |300.000 |0.000
                 |       8| 100.000| 300.000|      8
                 +--------+--------+--------+
         ROW 2   |400.000 |200.000 |700.000 |-300.000
                 | 500.000|      11|1000.000|     11
                 +--------+--------+--------+
         ROW 3   |500.000 |800.000 |300.000 |300.000
                 |       2|       1|       9|     12
                 +--------+--------+--------+
         V(J)     200.000  500.000   0.000
         DEMAND        10       12        9

                     Total Cost = 8300.0000

                SAMPLE RUN OF STORM ON TABLE 14.22 DATA
          TRANSPORTATION - OPTIMAL SOLUTION - SUMMARY REPORT
          ------- Cell -------              Unit        Cell
          Row          Column    Amount     Cost        Cost

          ROW   1   COLUMN  1        8    200.0000   1600.0000
          ROW   1 Subtotal = 1600.0000

          ROW   2   COLUMN  2       11    200.0000   2200.0000
          ROW   2 Subtotal = 2200.0000

          ROW   3   COLUMN  1        2    500.0000   1000.0000
          ROW   3   COLUMN  2        1    800.0000    800.0000
          ROW   3   COLUMN  3        9    300.0000   2700.0000
          ROW   3 Subtotal = 4500.0000

          Total Cost = 8300.0000
          Number of iterations = 1
```

Applicable Problems 14-23, 14-24, 14-25, 14-26, Custom Vans Case

locating a new facility

Teaching Suggestion 14.6: Facility Location Problems. See the Instructor's Section for details.

Alternate Example 14.3

14.11 FACILITY LOCATION ANALYSIS

The transportation method has proved to be especially useful in helping a firm decide where to locate a new factory or warehouse. Since a new location is an issue of major financial importance to a company, several alternative locations must ordinarily be considered and evaluated. Even though a wide variety of subjective factors are considered, including quality of labor supply, presence of labor unions, community attitude and appearance, utilities, and recreational and educational facilities for employees, a final decision also involves minimizing total shipping and production costs. This means that each alternative facility location should be analyzed within the framework of one *overall* distribution system. The new location that will yield the *minimum cost* for the *entire system* will be the one recommended. Let us consider the case of the Hardgrave Machine Company.

Locating a New Factory for Hardgrave Machine Company

The Hardgrave Machine Company produces computer components at its plants in Cincinnati, Salt Lake City, and Pittsburgh. These plants have not been able to keep up with demand for orders at Hardgrave's four warehouses in Detroit, Dallas, New York, and Los Angeles. As a result, the firm has decided to build a new plant to expand its productive capacity. The two sites being considered are Seattle and Birmingham, Alabama; both cities are attractive in terms of labor supply, municipal services, and ease of factory financing.

Table 14.23 presents the production costs and output requirements for each of the three existing plants, demand at each of the four warehouses, and estimated production costs of the new proposed plants.

Transportation costs from each plant to each warehouse are summarized in Table 14.24.

TABLE 14.23 Hardgrave's Demand and Supply Data

WAREHOUSE	MONTHLY DEMAND (UNITS)	PRODUCTION PLANT	MONTHLY SUPPLY	COST TO PRODUCE ONE UNIT ($)
Detroit	10,000	Cincinnati	15,000	48
Dallas	12,000	Salt Lake	6,000	50
New York	15,000	Pittsburgh	14,000	52
Los Angeles	9,000		35,000	
	46,000			

Supply needed from new plant = 46,000 − 35,000 = 11,000 units per month

ESTIMATED PRODUCTION COST PER UNIT AT PROPOSED PLANTS	
Seattle	$53
Birmingham	$49

TABLE 14.24 Hardgrave's Shipping Costs

FROM \ TO	DETROIT	DALLAS	NEW YORK	LOS ANGELES
CINCINNATI	$25	$55	$40	$60
SALT LAKE	35	30	50	40
PITTSBURGH	36	45	26	66
SEATTLE	60	38	65	27
BIRMINGHAM	35	30	41	50

The important question that Hardgrave now faces is "which of the new locations will yield the lowest cost for the firm in combination with the existing plants and warehouses?" Note that the cost of each individual plant-to-warehouse route is found by adding the shipping costs (in the body of Table 14.24) to the respective unit production costs (from Table 14.23). Thus, the total production plus shipping cost of one computer component from Cincinnati to Detroit is $73 ($25 for shipping plus $48 for production).

To determine which new plant (Seattle or Birmingham) shows the lowest total systemwide cost of distribution and production, we solve two transportation problems—one for each of the two possible combinations. Tables 14.25 and 14.26 show the resulting two optimum solutions with the total cost for each. (We used the computer program to solve each problem.) It appears that Seattle should be selected as the new plant site: its total cost of $3,704,000 is less than the $3,741,000 cost at Birmingham.

new plant with lowest system cost

14.12 APPROACH OF THE ASSIGNMENT MODEL

Transparency Master 14.13: The Assignment Method Algorithm.

assignment table

The second special purpose LP algorithm to be discussed in this chapter is the assignment method. Each assignment problem has a table, or matrix, associated with it. Generally, the rows contain the objects or people we wish to assign, and the columns comprise the tasks or things we want them assigned to. The numbers in the table are the costs associated with each particular assignment.

As an illustration of the assignment method, let us consider the case of the Fix-It Shop, which has just received three new rush projects to repair:

TABLE 14.25 Birmingham Plant Optimal Solution: Total Hardgrave Cost is $3,741,000

FROM \ TO	DETROIT	DALLAS	NEW YORK	LOS ANGELES	MONTHLY SUPPLY
CINCINNATI	73 — 10,000	103	88 — 1,000	108 — 4,000	15,000
SALT LAKE	85	80 — 1,000	100	90 — 5,000	6,000
PITTSBURGH	88	97	78 — 14,000	118	14,000
BIRMINGHAM	84	79 — 11,000	90	99	11,000
MONTHLY DEMAND	10,000	12,000	15,000	9,000	46,000

Alternate Example 14.4

(1) a radio, (2) a toaster oven, and (3) a broken coffee table. Three repairmen, each with different talents and abilities, are available to do the jobs. The Fix-It Shop owner estimates what it will cost in wages to assign each of the workers to each of the three projects. The costs, which are shown in Table 14.27, differ because the owner believes each worker will differ in speed and skill on these quite varied jobs.

KEY IDEA →

The owner's objective is to assign the three projects to the workers in a way that will result in the lowest total cost to the shop. Note that the assignment of people to projects must be on a one-to-one basis; each project will be assigned exclusively to one worker only. Hence, the number of rows must always equal the number of columns in an assignment problem's cost table.

enumeration of solutions

Since the Fix-It Shop problem only consists of three workers and three projects, one easy way to find the best solution is to list all possible assignments and their respective costs. For example, if Adams is assigned to project 1, Brown to project 2, and Cooper to project 3, the total cost will be $11 + $10 + $7 = $28. Table 14.28 summarizes all six assignment options.

The table also shows that the least-cost solution would be to assign Cooper to project 1, Brown to project 2, and Adams to project 3, at a total cost of $25.

TABLE 14.26 Seattle Plant Optimal Solution: Total Hardgrave Cost Is $3,704,000

FROM \ TO	DETROIT	DALLAS	NEW YORK	LOS ANGELES	MONTHLY SUPPLY
CINCINNATI	73 / 10,000	103 / 4,000	88 / 1,000	108 /	15,000
SALT LAKE	85 /	80 / 6,000	100 /	90 /	6,000
PITTSBURGH	88 /	97 /	78 / 14,000	118 /	14,000
SEATTLE	113 /	91 / 2,000	118 /	80 / 9,000	11,000
MONTHLY DEMAND	10,000	12,000	15,000	9,000	46,000

TABLE 14.27 Estimated Project Repair Costs for the Fix-It Shop Assignment Problem

	PROJECT		
PERSON	1	2	3
Adams	$11	$14	$ 6
Brown	8	10	11
Cooper	9	12	7

TABLE 14.28 Summary of Fix-It Shop Assignment Alternatives and Costs

PROJECT ASSIGNMENTS			LABOR COSTS ($)	TOTAL COSTS $
1	2	3		
Adams	Brown	Cooper	11 + 10 + 7	28
Adams	Cooper	Brown	11 + 12 + 11	34
Brown	Adams	Cooper	8 + 14 + 7	29
Brown	Cooper	Adams	8 + 12 + 6	26
Cooper	Adams	Brown	9 + 14 + 11	34
Cooper	Brown	Adams	9 + 10 + 6	25

Obtaining solutions by enumeration works well for small problems, but quickly becomes inefficient as assignment problems become larger. For example, a problem involving the assignment of four workers to four projects requires that we consider 4! (= $4 \times 3 \times 2 \times 1$) or 24 alternatives. A problem with eight workers and eight tasks, which actually is not that large in a realistic situation, yields 8! (= $8 \times 7 \times 6 \times 5 \times 4 \times 3 \times 2 \times 1$) or 40,320 possible solutions! Since it would clearly be impractical to compare so many alternatives, a more efficient solution method is needed.

The Hungarian Method (Flood's Technique)

Applicable Problems 14-27, 14-28, 14-29, 14-30, 14-32, 14-34, 14-35, 14-36, Old Oregon Case

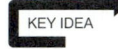

opportunity costs

The Hungarian method of assignment provides us with an efficient means of finding the optimal solution without having to make a direct comparison of every option. It operates on a principle of *matrix reduction*, which means that by subtracting and adding appropriate numbers in the cost table or matrix, we can reduce the problem to a matrix of *opportunity costs*. Opportunity costs show the relative penalties associated with assigning *any* person to a project as opposed to making the *best* or least-cost assignment. If we can reduce the matrix to the point where there is one 0 element in each row and column, it will then be possible to make optimal assignments, that is, assignments in which all of the opportunity costs are 0.

There are basically three steps in the assignment method.[3]

steps of assignment method

1. *Find the opportunity cost table* by

    (a) Subtracting the smallest number in each row of the original cost table or matrix from every number in that row, and

    (b) Then subtracting the smallest number in each column of the table obtained in part a from every number in that column.

Teaching Suggestion 14.7: Sensitivity Analysis on the Assignment Problem. See the Instructor's Section for details.

2. *Test the table resulting from step 1 to see whether an optimal assignment can be made.* The procedure is to draw the minimum number of vertical and horizontal straight lines necessary to cover all zeros in the table. If the number of lines equals either the number of rows or columns in the table, then an optimal assignment can be made. If the number of lines is less than the number of rows or columns, we proceed to step 3.

3. *Revise the present opportunity cost table.* This is done by subtracting the smallest number not covered by a line from every other uncovered number. This same smallest number is also added to any number(s) lying at the intersection of horizontal and vertical lines. We then return to step 2 and continue the cycle until an optimal assignment is possible.

assignment method easier than LP

This assignment "algorithm" is not nearly as difficult to apply as the linear programming algorithm we discussed in Chapters 10–13, or even as

---

[3]The steps apply if we can assume the matrix is balanced, that is, the number of rows in the matrix equals the number of columns. In Section 14.13 we discuss how to handle unbalanced problems.

complex as the transportation procedures we saw earlier in this chapter. All it requires is some careful addition and subtraction and close attention to the three preceding steps. These steps are charted for your convenience in Figure 14.3. Let us now apply them.

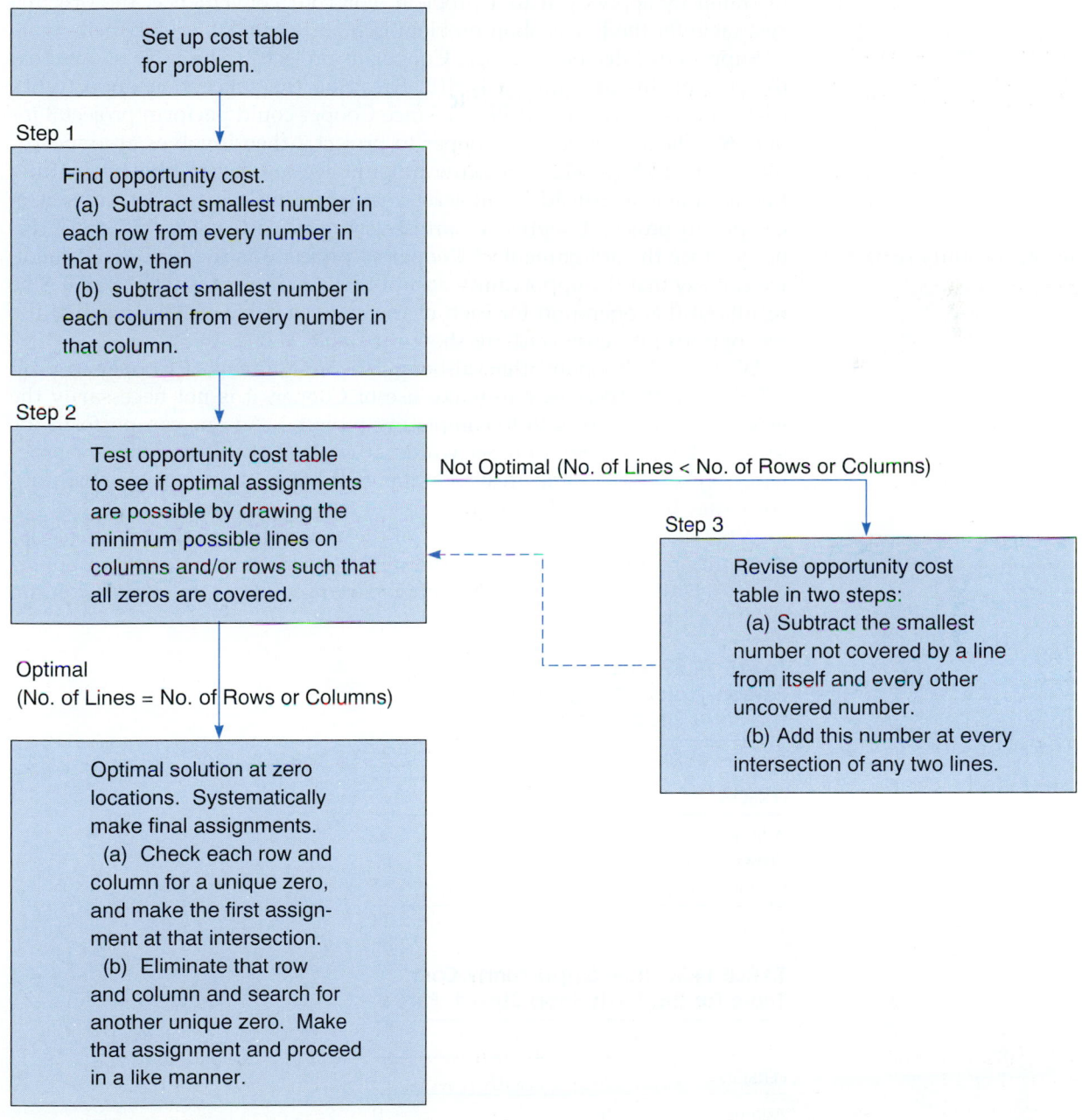

FIGURE 14.3
Steps in the Assignment Method

Step 1: Find the Opportunity Cost Table. As we mentioned earlier, the opportunity cost of any decision we make in life consists of the opportunities that are sacrificed in making that decision. For example, the opportunity cost of the unpaid time a person spends starting a new business is the salary that person would earn for those hours he or she could have worked on another job. This important concept in the assignment method is best illustrated by applying it to a problem. For your convenience, the original cost table for the Fix-It Shop problem is repeated in Table 14.29 below.

Suppose we decide to assign Cooper to project 2. The table shows that the cost of this assignment is $12. Based on the concept of opportunity costs, this is not the best decision, since Cooper could perform project 3 for only $7. The assignment of Cooper to project 2 then involves an opportunity cost of $5 (= $12 − $7), the amount we are sacrificing by making this assignment instead of the least-cost one. Similarly, an assignment of Cooper to project 1 represents an opportunity cost of $9 − $7 = $2. Finally, since the assignment of Cooper to project 3 is the best assignment, we can say that the opportunity cost of this assignment is 0 ($7 − $7). The results of this operation for each of the rows in Table 14.29 are called the *row* opportunity costs and are shown in Table 14.30.

row opportunity costs

We note at this point that, although the assignment of Cooper to project 3 is the cheapest way to make use of Cooper, it is not necessarily the least-expensive approach to completing project 3. Adams can perform the same task for only $6. In other words, if we look at this assignment problem from a project angle, instead of a people angle, the *column* opportunity costs may be completely different.

column opportunity costs

What we need to complete step 1 of the assignment method is a *total* opportunity cost table, that is, one that reflects both row and column opportunity costs. This involves following part b of step 1 to derive column

total opportunity costs

TABLE 14.29 Cost of Each Person-Project Assignment for the Fix-It Shop Problem

PERSON	PROJECT		
	1	2	3
Adams	$11	$14	$ 6
Brown	8	10	11
Cooper	9	12	7

TABLE 14.30 Row Opportunity Cost Table for the Fix-It Shop Step 1, Part a

PERSON	PROJECT		
	1	2	3
Adams	5	8	0
Brown	0	2	3
Cooper	2	5	0

opportunity costs.[4] We simply take the costs in Table 14.30 and subtract the smallest number in each column from each number in that column. The resulting total opportunity costs are given in Table 14.31.

You might note that the numbers in columns 1 and 3 are the same as those in Table 14.30, since the smallest column entry in each case was 0. Thus, it may turn out that the assignment of Cooper to project 3 is part of the optimal solution because of the relative nature of opportunity costs. What we are trying to measure are the relative efficiencies for the entire cost table and to find what assignments are best for the overall solution.

Step 2: Test for an Optimal Assignment. The objective of the Fix-It Shop owner is to assign the three workers to the repair projects in such a way that total labor costs are kept at a minimum. When translated to making assignments using our total opportunity cost table, this means that we would like to have a total assigned opportunity cost of 0. In other words, an optimal solution has 0 opportunity costs for all of the assignments.

Looking at Table 14.31, we see that there are four possible 0 opportunity cost assignments. We could assign Adams to project 3 and Brown to either project 1 or project 2. But this leaves Cooper without a 0 opportunity cost assignment. Recall that two workers cannot be given the same task; each must do one and only one repair project, and each project must be assigned to only one person. Hence, even though four 0s appear in this cost table, it is not yet possible to make an assignment yielding a total opportunity cost of 0.

A simple test has been designed to help us determine whether an optimal assignment can be made. The method consists of finding the *minimum* number of straight lines (vertical and horizontal) necessary to cover all 0s in the cost table. (Each line is drawn so that it covers as many 0s as possible at one time.) If the number of lines equals the number of rows or columns in the table, then an optimal assignment can be made. If, on the other hand, the number of lines is less than the number of rows or columns, an optimal assignment cannot be made. In this latter case, we must proceed to step 3 and develop a new total opportunity cost table.

Table 14.32 illustrates that it is possible to cover all four 0 entries in Table 14.31 with only two lines. Because there are three rows, an optimal assignment may not yet be made.

optimal solution at 0 opportunity costs

line test to see if solution is optimal

TABLE 14.31 Total Opportunity Cost Table for the Fix-It Shop Step 1, Part b

PERSON	PROJECT		
	1	2	3
Adams	5	6	0
Brown	0	0	3
Cooper	2	3	0

[4]Can you think of a situation in which part b of step 1 would not be required? See if you can design a cost table in which an optimal solution is possible after part a of step 1 is completed.

TABLE 14.32 Test for Optimal Solution to Fix-It Shop Problem

PERSON	PROJECT		
	1	2	3
Adams	5	6	0
Brown	0	0	3	→ Covering line 1
Cooper	2	3	0

Covering line 2

Step 3: Revise the Opportunity-Cost Table. An optimal solution is seldom obtained from the initial opportunity cost table. Often, we need to revise the table in order to shift one (or more) of the 0 costs from its present location (covered by lines) to a new uncovered location in the table. Intuitively, we would want this uncovered location to emerge with a new 0 opportunity cost.

This is accomplished by *subtracting* the smallest number not covered by a line from all numbers not covered by a straight line. This same smallest number is then added to every number (including 0s) lying at the intersection of any two lines.

The smallest uncovered number in Table 14.32 is 2, so this value is subtracted from each of the four uncovered numbers. A 2 is also added to the number that is covered by the intersecting horizontal and vertical lines. The results of step 3 are shown in Table 14.33.

To test now for an optimal assignment, we return to step 2 and find the minimum number of lines necessary to cover all 0s in the revised opportunity cost table. Since it requires three lines to cover the zeros (see Table 14.34), an optimal assignment can be made.

TABLE 14.33 Revised Opportunity Cost Table for the Fix-It Shop Problem

PERSON	PROJECT		
	1	2	3
Adams	3	4	0
Brown	0	0	5
Cooper	0	1	0

TABLE 14.34 Optimality Test on the Revised Fix-It Shop Opportunity Cost Table

PERSON	PROJECT		
	1	2	3
Adams	3	4	0
Brown	0	0	5	→ Covering line 2
Cooper	0	1	0

Covering line 1   *Covering line 3*

Making the Final Assignment

It is apparent that the Fix-It Shop problem's optimal assignment is Adams to project 3, Brown to project 2, and Cooper to project 1. In solving larger problems, however, it is best to rely on a more systematic approach to making valid assignments. One such way is to first select a row or column that contains only one 0 cell. Such a situation is found in the first row, Adams's row, in which the only 0 is in the project 3 column. An assignment can be made to that cell, and then lines drawn through its row and column (see Table 14.35). From the uncovered rows and columns, we again choose a row or column in which there is only one 0 cell. We make that assignment and continue the procedure until each person is assigned to one task.

making an optimal assignment

The total labor costs of this assignment are computed from the original cost table (see Table 14.29). They are as follows:

ASSIGNMENT	COST ($)
Adams to project 3	6
Brown to project 2	10
Cooper to project 1	9
Total cost	25

14.13   DUMMY ROWS AND DUMMY COLUMNS

The solution procedure to assignment problems just discussed requires that the number of rows in the table equal the number of columns. Often, however, the number of people or objects to be assigned does not equal the number of tasks or clients or machines listed in the columns. When this occurs and we have more rows than columns, we simply add a *dummy column* or task (similar to how we handled unbalanced transportation problems earlier in this chapter). If the number of tasks that need to be done exceeds the number of people available, we add a *dummy row*. This creates a table of equal dimensions and allows us to solve the problem as before. Since the dummy task or person is really nonexistent, it is reasonable to enter zeroes in its row or column as the cost or time estimate.

Suppose the owner of the Fix-It Shop realizes that a fourth worker, Davis, is also available to work on one of the three rush jobs that just came

TABLE 14.35 Making the Final Fix-It Shop Assignments

(A) FIRST ASSIGNMENT			(B) SECOND ASSIGNMENT			(C) THIRD ASSIGNMENT		
1	2	3	1	2	3	1	2	3
Adams	3	4	[0]	Adams	3	4	0	Adams	3	4	0
Brown	0	0	5	Brown	0	0	5	Brown	0	[0]	5
Cooper	0	1	0	Cooper	[0]	1	0	Cooper	0	1	0

in. Davis can do the first project for $10, the second for $13, and the third project for $8. The shop's owner still faces the same basic problem, that is, which worker to assign to which project in order to minimize total labor costs. Since we do not have a fourth project, however, we simply add a dummy column or dummy project. The initial cost table is shown in Table 14.36. One of the four workers, you should realize, will be assigned to the dummy project; in other words, the worker will not really be assigned any of the tasks. Problem 14-35 at the end of the chapter asks you to find the optimal solution for the data in Table 14.36.

TABLE 14.36 Estimated Project Repair Costs for Fix-It Shop with Davis Included

	PROJECT			
PERSON	1	2	3	DUMMY
Adams	$11	$14	$ 6	$0
Brown	8	10	11	0
Cooper	9	12	7	0
Davis	10	13	8	0

APPLICATIONS OF QA

Scheduling American League Umpires with the Assignment Model

Scheduling umpires in professional baseball is a complex problem that must include a number of criteria. The American Baseball League, like most professional, collegiate, and high school athletic organizations has a supervisor of officials whose major responsibilities include selecting, training, and evaluating officials as well as assigning them to games. In assigning officials to games, one objective typically is to minimize total travel cost while satisfying a set of frequency-oriented constraints such as limiting the number of times an official or crew is exposed to each team, balancing home and away game exposures, balancing exposures to teams over the course of a season, and so on. These constraints complicate the problem to such an extent that, except for the most trivial cases, the use of a computer-based system is essential.

The American League is composed of 14 professional baseball teams organized into Western and Eastern divisions. The Western Division is comprised of Seattle, Oaland, California, Texas, Kansas City, Minnesota, and Chicago. The Eastern Division is comprised of Milwaukee, Detroit, Cleveland, Toronto, Baltimore, New York, and Boston. The game schedule, constructed each winter prior to the start of the baseball season, is a difficult scheduling problem in itself. Consideration must be given to such factors as the number of games played against other teams both within and outside a division, the split between home games and road trips, travel time, and possible conflicts in cities that have teams in the National League.

The objective of balancing crew assignments relatively evenly and minimizing travel costs are by nature conflicting. Attempting to balance crew assignments necessitates considerable airline travel and equipment moves, and hence increased travel costs.

Using an assignment model as part of a microcomputer-based decision support system, the American League was able to reduce travel mileage by about 4% during the first year of use. This not only saved the league $30,000 but improved the crew exposure balance.

Source: James R. Evans, "Scheduling American League Umpires: A Microcomputer-Based DSS," *Proceedings of the Annual Meeting of the Decision Sciences Institute,* Honolulu, 1986, pp. 914–16. The Annual Meeting Proceedings are published by the Decision Sciences Institute located at Georgia State University in Atlanta, Ga.

14.14 MAXIMIZATION ASSIGNMENT PROBLEMS

Applicable Problems 14-31, 14-33, 14-38

Some assignment problems are phrased in terms of maximizing the payoff, profit, or effectiveness of an assignment instead of minimizing costs. It is easy to obtain an equivalent minimization problem by converting all numbers in the table to opportunity costs. This is brought about by subtracting every number in the original payoff table from the largest single number in that table. The transformed entries represent opportunity costs; it turns out that minimizing opportunity costs produces the same assignment as the original maximization problem. Once the optimal assignment for this transformed problem has been computed, the total payoff or profit is found by adding the original payoffs of those cells that are in the optimal assignment.

Let us consider the following example. The British navy wishes to assign four ships to patrol four sectors of the North Sea. Since in some areas ships are to be on the outlook for illegal fishing boats, and in other sectors to watch for enemy submarines, the commander rates each ship in terms of its probable efficiency in each of the sectors. These relative efficiencies are illustrated in Table 14.37. On the basis of the ratings shown, the commander wants to determine the patrol assignments producing the greatest overall efficiencies.

Step by step, the solution procedure is as follows. We first convert the maximizing efficiency table into a minimizing opportunity cost table. This is done by subtracting each rating from 100, the largest rating in the whole table. The resulting opportunity costs are given in Table 14.38.

We now follow steps 1 and 2 of the assignment algorithm. The smallest number in each row is subtracted from every number in that row (see

Teaching Suggestion 14.8: Maximizing Assignment Problems. See the Instructor's Section for details.

KEY IDEA

subtract each rating from largest in table

TABLE 14.37 Efficiencies of British Ships in Patrol Sectors

SHIP	SECTOR			
	A	B	C	D
1	20	60	50	55
2	60	30	80	75
3	80	100	90	80
4	65	80	75	70

TABLE 14.38 Opportunity Costs of British Ships

SHIP	SECTOR			
	A	B	C	D
1	80	40	50	45
2	40	70	20	25
3	20	0	10	20
4	35	20	25	30

Table 14.39); and then the smallest number in each column is subtracted from every number in that column (as shown in Table 14.40).

The minimum number of straight lines needed to cover all 0s in this total opportunity cost table is four. Hence, an optimal assignment can be made already. You should be able by now to spot the best solution, namely, ship 1 to sector *D*, ship 2 to sector *C*, ship 3 to sector *B*, and ship 4 to sector *A*.

The overall efficiency, computed from the original efficiency data in Table 14.37, can now be shown:

ASSIGNMENT	EFFICIENCY
Ship 1 to sector D	55
Ship 2 to sector C	80
Ship 3 to sector B	100
Ship 4 to sector A	65
Total efficiency	300

14.15 USING THE COMPUTER TO SOLVE ASSIGNMENT PROBLEMS

computer program for assignment problems

Computer programs designed to solve the standard assignment problem are as commonly available as are computerized linear programming and transportation problem programs. They are quick and efficient, especially for large assignments. Printouts illustrating both the microcomputer software that accompanies this text (AB:QM) and STORM are provided in Programs 14.3 and 14.4.

TABLE 14.39 Row Opportunity Costs for the British Navy Problem

row subtractions

	SECTOR			
SHIP	A	B	C	D
1	40	0	10	5
2	20	50	0	5
3	20	0	10	20
4	15	0	5	10

column subtractions

TABLE 14.40 Total Opportunity Costs for the British Navy Problem

	SECTOR			
SHIP	A	B	C	D
1	25	0	10	0
2	5	50	0	0
3	5	0	10	15
4	0	0	5	5

TABLE 14.41 Cost Data for Carhart Machine Tool Company

JOB	DRILLING MACHINE		
	1	2	3
1	$100	$60	$80
2	124	80	76
3	140	96	68

These programs are very flexible and capable of handling unbalanced as well as balanced problems. They can also solve both maximization and minimization problems.

Let us consider the following problem for a computerized assignment. The Carhart Machine Tool Company has three drilling jobs that can each be completed on any of three available drilling machines. The cost of each assignment differs according to job specifications and the age of each machine. Costs are estimated in Table 14.41.

See Program 14.3 for the AB:QM sample run and Program 14.4 for the STORM package output.

PROGRAM 14.3 Computer Solution to the Carhart Machine Tool Problem Using AB:QM

```
Assignment

Problem Title :  CARHART MACHINE TOOL
Type of Problem (Max=1/Min=2)  2
Number of Rows              3          Number of Columns        3


            C1        C2        C3
R1         100        60        80
R2         124        80        76
R3         140        96        68


Help   New   Load   Save   Edit   Run   Print   Install   Directory   Esc


Program: Assignment

Problem Title : CARHART MACHINE TOOL

***** Input Data *****

Minimization Problem :

      |     1      2      3
  ----------------------------
   1  |  100.0   60.0   80.0
   2  |  124.0   80.0   76.0
   3  |  140.0   96.0   68.0
  ----------------------------
```

(Continued)

PROGRAM 14.3 **Computer Solution to the Carhart Machine Tool Problem Using AB:QM (Continued)**

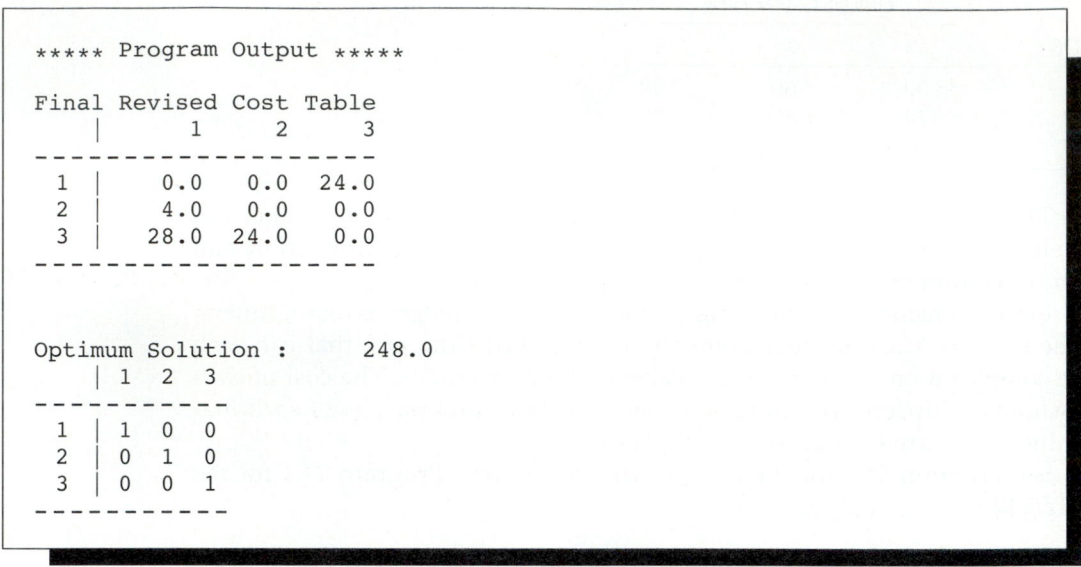

```
***** Program Output *****

Final Revised Cost Table
    |     1     2     3
-------------------
  1 |    0.0   0.0  24.0
  2 |    4.0   0.0   0.0
  3 |   28.0  24.0   0.0
-------------------


Optimum Solution :      248.0
    | 1  2  3
-----------
  1 | 1  0  0
  2 | 0  1  0
  3 | 0  0  1
-----------
```

PROGRAM 14.4 **STORM Solution to Carhart Machine Tool Problem**

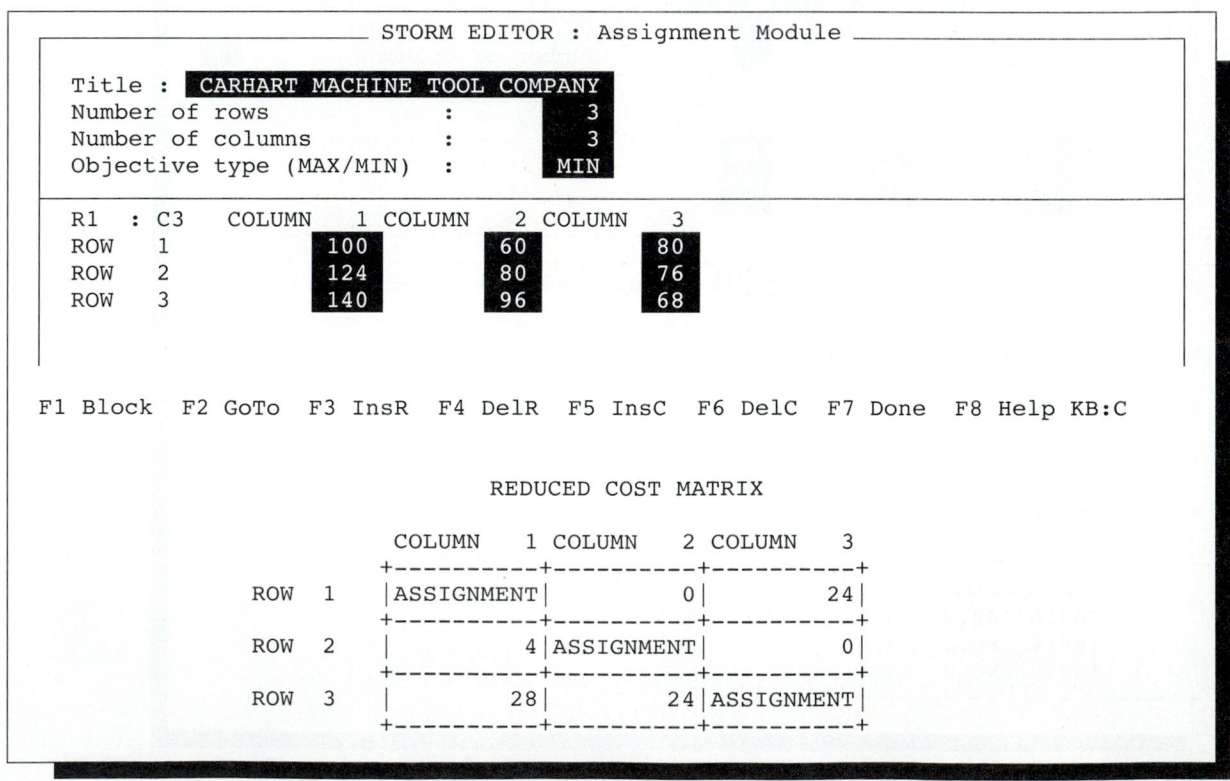

```
_____ STORM EDITOR : Assignment Module _____

   Title : CARHART MACHINE TOOL COMPANY
   Number of rows         :        3
   Number of columns      :        3
   Objective type (MAX/MIN) :     MIN

   R1  : C3   COLUMN    1 COLUMN    2 COLUMN    3
   ROW   1           100          60          80
   ROW   2           124          80          76
   ROW   3           140          96          68



F1 Block  F2 GoTo  F3 InsR  F4 DelR  F5 InsC  F6 DelC  F7 Done  F8 Help KB:C


                      REDUCED COST MATRIX

                 COLUMN   1 COLUMN   2 COLUMN   3
                 +----------+----------+----------+
         ROW  1  |ASSIGNMENT|        0|       24|
                 +----------+----------+----------+
         ROW  2  |        4|ASSIGNMENT|        0|
                 +----------+----------+----------+
         ROW  3  |       28|       24|ASSIGNMENT|
                 +----------+----------+----------+
```

(Continued)

PROGRAM 14.4 STORM Solution to Carhart Machine Tool Problem (Continued)

```
              CARHART MACHINE TOOL COMPANY
                    OPTIMAL SOLUTION
        Row              Column            Cost

        ROW   1       COLUMN   1             100
        ROW   2       COLUMN   2              80
        ROW   3       COLUMN   3              68

        Total Cost = 248
        Number of Iterations = 2
```

GLOSSARY

Transportation Problem. A specific case of linear programming concerned with scheduling shipments from sources to destinations so that total transportation costs are minimized.

Source. An origin or supply location in a transportation problem.

Destination. A demand location in a transportation problem.

Transportation Table. A table summarizing all transportation data to help keep track of all algorithm computations. It stores information on demands, supplies, shipping costs, units shipped, origins, and destinations.

Northwest Corner Rule. A systematic procedure for establishing an initial feasible solution to the transportation problem.

Stepping-Stone Method. An iterative technique for moving from an initial feasible solution to an optimal solution in transportation problems.

Improvement Index. The net cost of shipping one unit on a route not used in the current transportation problem solution.

Modified Distribution (MODI) Method. Another algorithm for finding the optimal solution to a transportation problem. It can be used in place of the stepping-stone method.

Vogel's Approximation Method (VAM). An algorithm used to find a relatively efficient initial feasible solution to a transportation problem. This initial solution is often the optimal solution.

Balanced Problem. The condition under which total demand (at all destinations) is equal to total supply (at all sources).

Unbalanced Problem. A situation in which total demand is not equal to total supply.

Dummy Source. An artificial source added when total demand is greater than total supply. The supply at the dummy source is set so that total demand and supply are equal. The transportation cost for dummy source cells is zero.

Dummy Destination. An artificial destination added when total supply is greater than total demand. The demand at the dummy destination is set so that total supply and demand are equal. The transportation cost for dummy destination cells is zero.

Degeneracy. A condition that occurs when the number of occupied squares in any solution is less than the number of rows plus the number of columns minus 1 in a transportation table.

Facility Location Analysis. An application of the transportation method to help a firm decide where to locate a new factory or warehouse.

Matrix Reduction. The approach of the assignment method which reduces the original assignment costs to a table of opportunity costs.

Opportunity Costs. The costs associated with a sacrificed opportunity in order to make a particular decision.

Dummy Rows or Columns. Extra rows or columns added in order to "balance" an assignment problem so that the number of rows equals the number of columns.

KEY EQUATIONS

(14-1) $R_i + K_j = C_{ij}$
An equation used to compute the MODI cost values (R_i, K_j) for each column and row intersection for squares in the solution.

(14-2) Improvement index $= C_{ij} - R_i - K_j$
The equation used to compute the improvement index for each unused square by the MODI method. If all improvement indices are greater than or equal to 0, an optimal solution has been reached.

SOLVED PROBLEMS

Solved Problem 14.1

Don Yale, president of Hardrock Concrete Company, has plants in three locations and is currently working on three major construction projects, located at different sites. The shipping cost per truckload of concrete, plant capacities, and project requirements are provided in the accompanying table.

(a) Formulate an initial feasible solution to Hardrock's transportation problem using the northwest corner rule.
(b) Then evaluate each unused shipping route (each empty cell) by applying the stepping-stone method and computing all improvement indices. Remember to:

1. Check that supply and demand are equal.
2. Load the table via the northwest corner method.
3. Check that there are the proper number of occupied cells for a "normal" solution, namely, number of rows + number of columns − 1 = number of occupied cells.
4. Find a closed path to each empty cell.
5. Determine the improvement index for each unused cell.
6. Move as many units as possible to the cell that provides the most improvement (if there is one).
7. Repeat steps 3 through 6 until no further improvement can be found.

FROM \ TO	PROJECT A	PROJECT B	PROJECT C	PLANT CAPACITY
PLANT 1	$10	$ 4	$11	70
PLANT 2	$12	$ 5	$ 8	50
PLANT 3	$ 9	$ 7	$ 6	30
PROJECT REQUIRE-MENTS	40	50	60	150

Solution

(a) Northwest Corner Solution

Initial cost = 40($10) + 30($4) + 20($5) + 30($8) + 30($6) = $1,040

FROM \ TO	PROJECT A	PROJECT B	PROJECT C	PLANT CAPACITIES
PLANT 1	40 | $10	30 | $4	| $11	70
PLANT 2	| $12	20 | $5	30 | $8	50
PLANT 3	| $9	| $7	30 | $6	30
PROJECT REQUIREMENTS	40	50	60	150

(d) Using the stepping-stone method, the following improvement indices are computed:

Path: Plant 1 to project C = $11 − $4 + $5 − $8 = +$4
(Closed path = 1C to 1B to 2B to 2C)

Path: plant 1 to project C

FROM \ TO	PROJECT A	PROJECT B	PROJECT C	PLANT CAPACITIES
PLANT 1	| 10	| 4	| 11	70
PLANT 2	| 12	| 5	| 8	50
PLANT 3	| 9	| 7	| 6	30
PROJECT REQUIREMENTS	40	50	60	150

Path: Plant 2 to project $A = \$12 - \$5 + \$4 - \$10 = +\$1$
(Closed path $= 2A$ to $2B$ to $1B$ to $1A$)

FROM \ TO	PROJECT A	PROJECT B	PROJECT C	PLANT CAPACITIES
PLANT 1	10	4	11	70
PLANT 2	12	5	8	50
PLANT 3	9	7	6	30
PROJECT REQUIREMENTS	40	50	60	150

Path: plant 2 to project A

Path: Plant 3 to project $A = \$9 - \$6 + \$8 - \$5 + \$4 - \$10 = \$0$
(Closed path $= 3A$ to $3C$ to $2C$ to $2B$ to $1B$ to $1A$)

FROM \ TO	PROJECT A	PROJECT B	PROJECT C	PLANT CAPACITY
PLANT 1	10	4	11	70
PLANT 2	12	5	8	50
PLANT 3	9	7	6	30
PROJECT REQUIREMENTS	40	50	60	150

Path: plant 3 to project A

Path: Plant 3 to project $B = \$7 - \$6 + \$8 - \$5 = +\$4$
(Closed path $= 3B$ to $3C$ to $2C$ to $2B$)

FROM \ TO	PROJECT A	PROJECT B	PROJECT C	PLANT CAPACITY
PLANT 1	10	4	11	70
PLANT 2	12	5	8	50
PLANT 3	9	7	6	30
PROJECT REQUIREMENTS	40	50	60	150

Path: plant 3 to project B

Since all indices are greater than or equal to zero (all are positive or 0), this initial solution provides the optimal transportation schedule, namely, 40 units from 1 to A, 30 units from 1 to B, 20 units from 2 to B, 30 units from 2 to C, and 30 units from 3 to C.

Had we found a path that allowed improvement, we would move all units possible to that cell and then check every empty cell again.

Solved Problem 14.2

Use a software package such as LINDO to solve the Hardgrave Machine Company facility location problem seen in Table 14.26 on page 549 with a linear programming formulation.

Teaching Suggestion 14.9:
Using LINDO to Solve a Transportation Problem. See the Instructor's Section for details.

Solution

First we shall formulate this transportation problem as an LP model by introducing double-subscripted decision variables. We let X_{11} denote the number of units shipped from origin 1 (Cincinnati) to destination 1 (Detroit), X_{12} denote shipments from origin 1 (Cincinnati) to destination 2 (Dallas), and so on. In general, the decision variables for a transportation problem having m origins and n destinations are written as:

X_{ij} = number of units shipped from origin i to destination j

where $i = 1, 2, \ldots, m$ and $j = 1, 2, \ldots, n$

Since the objective of the transportation model is to minimize total transportation costs, we develop the following cost expression:

$$\text{Minimize} = 73X_{11} + 103X_{12} + 88X_{13} + 108X_{14}$$
$$+ 85X_{21} + 80X_{22} + 100X_{23} + 90X_{24}$$
$$+ 88X_{31} + 97X_{32} + 78X_{33} + 118X_{34}$$
$$+ 113X_{41} + 91X_{42} + 118X_{43} + 80X_{44}$$

Now we establish supply constraints for each of the four plants:

$$X_{11} + X_{12} + X_{13} + X_{14} \leq 15,000 \; (Cincinnati\ supply)$$
$$X_{21} + X_{22} + X_{23} + X_{24} \leq 6,000 \; (Salt\ Lake\ supply)$$
$$X_{31} + X_{32} + X_{33} + X_{34} \leq 14,000 \; (Pittsburgh\ supply)$$
$$X_{41} + X_{42} + X_{43} + X_{44} \leq 11,000 \; (Seattle\ supply)$$

With four warehouses as the destinations, we need the following four demand constraints:

$$X_{11} + X_{21} + X_{31} + X_{41} = 10,000 \; (Detroit\ demand)$$
$$X_{12} + X_{22} + X_{32} + X_{42} = 12,000 \; (Dallas\ demand)$$
$$X_{13} + X_{23} + X_{33} + X_{43} = 15,000 \; (New\ York\ demand)$$
$$X_{14} + X_{24} + X_{34} + X_{44} = 9,000 \; (Los\ Angeles\ demand)$$

In Chapters 10, 11, and 13, we saw how LINDO can be used to solve LP problems. We now see that the same program can handle transportation problems as well.

The computer solution in the accompanying program confirms that total shipping costs will be $3,704,000. With $X_{11} = 10,000$ we see that 10,000 units should be shipped from Cincinnati to Detroit. With $X_{44} = 9,000$, we also see that 9,000 units should be sent from Seattle to Los Angeles. Other answers likewise match with findings in Table 14.26.

PROGRAM 14.5 LINDO LP Solution to a Facility Location Problem

```
:  LOOK ALL

MIN      73 X11 + 103 X12 + 88 X13 + 108 X14 + 85 X21 + 80 X22 + 100 X23
       + 90 X24 + 88 X31 + 97 X32 + 78 X33 + 118 X34 + 113 X41 + 91 X42
       + 118 X43 + 80 X44
SUBJECT TO
        2)   X11 + X12 + X13 + X14 <=     15000
        3)   X21 + X22 + X23 + X24 <=     6000
        4)   X31 + X32 + X33 + X34 <=     14000
        5)   X41 + X42 + X43 + X44 <=     11000
        6)   X11 + X21 + X31 + X41 =      10000
        7)   X12 + X22 + X32 + X42 =      12000
        8)   X13 + X23 + X33 + X43 =      15000
        9)   X14 + X24 + X34 + X44 =      9000



:  GO
LP OPTIMUM FOUND  AT STEP     10

             OBJECTIVE FUNCTION VALUE

1)         3704000.00

VARIABLE           VALUE          REDUCED COST
      X11       10000.000000          .000000
      X12        4000.000000          .000000
      X13        1000.000000          .000000
      X14          .000000         16.000000
      X21          .000000         35.000000
      X22        6000.000000          .000000
      X23          .000000         35.000000
      X24          .000000         21.000000
      X31          .000000         25.000000
      X32          .000000          4.000000
      X33       14000.000000          .000000
      X42        2000.000000          .000000
      X34          .000000         36.000000
      X41          .000000         52.000000
      X43          .000000         42.000000
      X44        9000.000000          .000000


      ROW      SLACK OR SURPLUS      DUAL PRICES
--More--
        2)          .000000            .000000
        3)          .000000          23.000000
        4)          .000000          10.000000
        5)          .000000          12.000000
        6)          .000000         -73.000000
        7)          .000000        -103.000000
        8)          .000000         -88.000000
        9)          .000000         -92.000000

NO. ITERATIONS=        10
```

Although linear programming codes such as LINDO can indeed be used on transportation problems, the special codes of AB:QM and STORM, illustrated earlier in Programs 14.1 and 14.2, tend to be easier to input, run, and interpret.

Solved Problem 14.3

Allyn and Bacon, Inc., a publisher headquartered in Boston, wants to assign three recently hired college graduates, Jones, Smith, and Wilson to regional sales districts in Omaha, Dallas, and Miami. But the firm also has an opening in New York and would send one of the three there if it were more economical than a move to Omaha, Dallas, or Miami. It will cost $1,000 to relocate Jones to New York, $800 to relocate Smith there, and $1,500 to move Wilson. What is the optimal assignment of personnel to offices?

HIREE \ OFFICE	OMAHA	MIAMI	DALLAS
JONES	$800	$1,100	$1,200
SMITH	$500	$1,600	$1,300
WILSON	$500	$1,000	$2,300

Solution

(a) The cost table has a fourth column to represent New York. To balance the problem, we add a dummy row (person) with a zero relocation cost to each city.

HIREE \ OFFICE	OMAHA	MIAMI	DALLAS	NEW YORK
JONES	$800	$1,100	$1,200	$1,000
SMITH	$500	$1,600	$1,300	$ 800
WILSON	$500	$1,000	$2,300	$1,500
DUMMY	0	0	0	0

(b) Subtract smallest number in each row and cover zeros (column subtraction will give the same numbers and therefore is not necessary).

HIREE \ OFFICE	OMAHA	MIAMI	DALLAS	NEW YORK
JONES	0	300	400	200
SMITH	0	1,100	800	300
WILSON	0	500	1,800	1,000
DUMMY	0	0	0	0

(c) Subtract smallest uncovered number (200), add it to each square where two lines intersect, and cover all zeros.

HIREE \ OFFICE	OMAHA	MIAMI	DALLAS	NEW YORK
JONES	0	100	200	0
SMITH	0	900	600	100
WILSON	0	300	1,600	800
DUMMY	200	0	0	0

(d) Subtract smallest uncovered number (100), add it to each square where two lines intersect, and cover all zeros.

HIREE \ OFFICE	OMAHA	MIAMI	DALLAS	NEW YORK
JONES	0	0	100	0
SMITH	0	800	500	100
WILSON	0	200	1,500	800
DUMMY	300	0	0	100

(e) Subtract smallest uncovered number (100), add it to squares where two lines intersect, and cover all zeros.

HIREE \ OFFICE	OMAHA	MIAMI	DALLAS	NEW YORK
JONES	100	0	100	0
SMITH	0	700	400	0
WILSON	0	100	1,400	700
DUMMY	400	0	0	100

(f) Since it takes four lines to cover all zeros, an optimal assignment can be made at zero squares. We assign:

Dummy (no one) to Dallas

Wilson to Omaha

Smith to New York

Jones to Miami

Cost = $0 + $500 + $800 + $1,100

= $2,400

DISCUSSION QUESTIONS AND PROBLEMS

Discussion Questions

14-1 Is the transportation model an example of decision making under certainty or decision making under uncertainty? Why?

14-2 Why does Vogel's approximation method provide a good initial feasible solution? Could the northwest corner rule ever provide an initial solution with as low a cost?

14-3 What is a *balanced* transportation problem? Describe the approach you would use to solve an *unbalanced* problem.

14-4 How do the MODI and stepping-stone methods differ?

14-5 Develop a *northeast* corner rule and explain how it would work. Set up an initial solution to the Executive Furniture Corporation problem shown in Table 14.2 using your new approach. What comment might you make about this initial solution?

14-6 Explain what happens when the solution to a transportation problem does not have $m + n - 1$ occupied squares (where m = number of rows in the table and n = number of columns in the table).

14-7 What is the enumeration approach to solving assignment problems? Is it a practical way to solve a 5 row $\times$ 5 column problem? A 7×7 problem? Why?

14-8 Think back to the transportation problem in the beginning of this chapter. How could an assignment problem be solved using the transportation approach? Set up the Fix-It Shop problem (shown in Table 14.27) using the transportation approach. What condition will make the solution of this problem difficult?

14-9 You are the plant supervisor and are responsible for scheduling workers to jobs on hand. After estimating the cost of assigning each of five available workers in your plant to five projects that must be completed immediately, you solve the problem using the Hungarian method. The following solution is reached and you post these job assignments:

> Jones to project A
>
> Smith to project B
>
> Thomas to project C
>
> Gibbs to project D
>
> Heldman to project E

The optimal cost was found to be $492 for these assignments.

The plant general manager inspects your original cost estimates and informs you that increased employee benefits mean that each of the 25 numbers in your cost table is too low by $5. He suggests that you immediately rework the problem and post the new assignments.

Is this necessary? Why? What will the new optimal cost be?

14-10 Sue Simmons's marketing research firm has local representatives in all but five states. She decides to expand to cover the whole United States by transferring five experienced volunteers from their current locations to new offices in each of the five states. Simmons's goal is to relocate the five representatives at the least total cost. Consequently, she sets up a 5 × 5 relocation cost table and prepares to solve it for the best assignment by use of the Hungarian method. At the last moment, Simmons recalls that, although the first four volunteers did not pose any objections to being placed in any of the five new cities, the fifth volunteer *did* make one restriction. That person absolutely refused to be assigned to the new office in Tallahassee, Florida—fear of Southern roaches, the representative claimed! How should Sue Simmons alter the cost matrix to assure that this assignment is not included in the optimal solution?

Problems

QA14-11

14-11 The management of the Executive Furniture Corporation decided to expand the production capacity at its Des Moines factory and to cut back production at its other factories. It also recognizes a shifting market for its desks and revises the requirements at its three warehouses.

NEW WAREHOUSE REQUIREMENTS		NEW FACTORY CAPACITIES	
Albuquerque (A)	200 desks	Des Moines (D)	300 desks
Boston (B)	200 desks	Evansville (E)	150 desks
Cleveland (C)	300 desks	Fort Lauderdale (F)	250 desks

D–A = 200
D–B = 100
E–B = 100
E–C = 50
F–C = 250
Cost = $3,200

FROM \ TO	ALBUQUERQUE	BOSTON	CLEVELAND
DES MOINES	5	4	3
EVANSVILLE	8	4	3
FORT LAUDERDALE	9	7	5

D–C index path = $0
E–A index path = $3
F–A index path = +$2
F–B index path = +$1
Presence of multiple optimal solutions
Total cost of alternate optimal solution = $3,200

(a) Use the northwest corner rule to establish an initial feasible shipping schedule and calculate its cost.
(b) Use the stepping-stone method to test whether an improved solution is possible.
(c) Explain the meaning and implications of an improvement index that is equal to 0. What decisions might management make with this information? Exactly how is the final solution affected?

QA14-12

14-12 The Hardrock Concrete Company has plants in three locations and is currently working on three major construction projects, each located at a different site. The shipping cost per truckload of concrete, daily plant capacities, and daily project requirements are provided in the accompanying table.

TO FROM	PROJECT A	PROJECT B	PROJECT C	PLANT CAPACITY
PLANT 1	$10	$ 4	$11	70
PLANT 2	12	5	8	50
PLANT 3	9	7	6	30
PROJECT REQUIREMENTS	40	50	60	150

(a) Formulate an initial feasible solution to Hardrock's transportation problem using the northwest corner rule. Then evaluate each unused shipping route by computing all improvement indices. Is this solution optimal? Why?

(b) Is there more than one optimal solution to this problem? Why?

14-13 Hardrock Concrete's owner has decided to increase the capacity at his smallest plant (see Problem 14.12). Instead of producing 30 loads of concrete per day at plant 3, that plant's capacity is doubled to 60 loads.

Find the new optimal solution using the northwest corner rule and stepping-stone method. How has changing the third plant's capacity altered the optimal shipping assignment? Discuss the concepts of degeneracy and multiple optimal solutions with regard to this problem.

14-14 The Saussy Lumber Company ships pine flooring to three building supply houses from its mills in Pineville, Oak Ridge, and Mapletown. Determine the best transportation schedule for the data given in the accompanying table. Use the northwest corner rule and the stepping-stone method.

TO FROM	SUPPLY HOUSE 1	SUPPLY HOUSE 2	SUPPLY HOUSE 3	MILL CAPACITY (TONS)
PINEVILLE	$3	$3	$2	25
OAK RIDGE	4	2	3	40
MAPLETOWN	3	2	3	30
SUPPLY HOUSE DEMAND (TONS)	30	30	35	95

14-15 Using the same Saussy Lumber Company data and the same initial solution you found with the northwest corner rule, resolve Problem 14-14 using the MODI method.

14-16 The Krampf Lines Railway Company specializes in coal handling. On Friday, April 13, Krampf had empty cars at the following towns in the quantities indicated.

See the Instructor's Section for the initial solution. Since all indices are greater than or equal to zero, this initial solution provides the optimal transportation schedule. There is an alternate optimal solution.

QA14-13

See the Instructor's Section for details.

QA14-14

See the Instructor's Section for details.
Initial cost = $260
The improved solution is $255.
The cost of the final solution is $230.

See the Instructor's Section for details.

QA14-16

TOWN	SUPPLY OF CARS
Morgantown	35
Youngstown	60
Pittsburgh	25

By Monday, April 16, the following towns will need coal cars as follows:

TOWN	DEMAND FOR CARS
Coal Valley	30
Coaltown	45
Coal Junction	25
Coalsburg	20

Using a railway city-to-city distance chart, the dispatcher constructs a mileage table for the preceding towns. The result is:

	TO			
FROM	*Coal Valley*	*Coaltown*	*Coal Junction*	*Coalsburg*
Morgantown	50	30	60	70
Youngstown	20	80	10	90
Pittsburgh	100	40	80	30

Minimizing total miles over which cars are moved to new locations, compute the best shipment of coal cars. Use the northwest corner rule and the MODI method.

See the Instructor's Section for details.
Initial solution's total cost = 6,050 car-miles
Second Kramp R.R. Solution: Cost = 5,500 miles
Third and optimal Krampf Railway solution: Cost = 3,100 miles

QA14-17   🖳 : **14-17** The Jessie Cohen Clothing Group owns factories in three towns (*W*, *Y*, and *Z*) which distribute to three Cohen retail dress shops (in *A*, *B*, and *C*). Factory availabilities, projected store demands, and unit shipping costs are summarized in the table that follows.

FROM \ TO	A		B		C		FACTORY AVAILABILITY
W		4		3		3	35
X		6		7		6	50
Y		8		2		5	50
STORE DEMAND	30		65		40		135

See the Instructor's Section for details.
Total cost = $505

Use Vogel's approximation method to find an initial feasible solution to this transportation problem. Is your VAM solution optimal?

QA14-18   🖳 : **14-18** The state of Missouri has three major power-generating companies (*A*, *B*, and *C*). During the months of peak demand, the Missouri Power Authority authorizes these companies to pool their excess supply and to distribute it to smaller independent power companies that do not have generators large enough to handle the demand.

Excess supply is distributed on the basis of cost per kilowatt-hour transmitted. The accompanying table shows the demand and supply in millions of kilowatt-hours and the costs per kilowatt-hour of transmitting electric power to four small companies in cities W, X, Y, and Z.

FROM \ TO	W	X	Y	Z	EXCESS SUPPLY
A	12¢	4¢	9¢	5¢	55
B	8¢	1¢	6¢	6¢	45
C	1¢	12¢	4¢	7¢	30
UNFILLED POWER DEMAND	40	20	50	20	

Use Vogel's approximation method to find an initial transmission assignment of the excess power supply. Then apply the MODI technique to find the least cost distribution system.

See the Instructor's Section for details.
Total VAM cost = 635. This is also optimal.

14-19 Consider the following transportation problem.

QA14-19

FROM \ TO	DESTINATION A	DESTINATION B	DESTINATION C	SUPPLY
SOURCE 1	8	9	4	72
SOURCE 2	5	6	8	38
SOURCE 3	7	9	6	46
SOURCE 4	5	3	7	19
DEMAND	110	34	31	175

Find an initial solution using the northwest corner rule. What special condition exists? Explain how you will proceed to solve the problem.

Degeneracy exists.
Optimal cost = $1036
See the Instructor's Section for details.

14-20 The three blood banks in Franklin County are coordinated through a central office which facilitates blood delivery to four hospitals in the region. The cost to ship a standard container of blood from each bank to each hospital is shown in the next table. Also given are the biweekly number of containers available at each bank and the biweekly number of containers of blood needed at each hospital.

How many shipments should be made biweekly from each blood bank to each hospital so that total shipment costs are minimized?

QA14-20

Bank 1 — Hosp. 1 = 50
Bank 2 — Hosp. 1 = 10
Bank 2 — Hosp. 2 = 70
Bank 3 — Hosp. 1 = 30
Bank 3 — Hosp. 3 = 40
Bank 3 — Hosp. 4 = 50
Cost = $2,020

FROM / TO	HOSPITAL 1	HOSPITAL 2	HOSPITAL 3	HOSPITAL 4	SUPPLY
BANK 1	8	9	11	16	50
BANK 2	12	7	5	8	80
BANK 3	14	10	6	7	120
DEMAND	90	70	40	50	250

QA14-21

14-21 The B. Hall Real Estate Investment Corporation has identified four small apartment buildings in which it would like to invest. Mrs. Hall has approached three savings and loan companies regarding financing. Because Hall has been a good client in the past and has maintained a high credit rating in the community, each savings and loan company is willing to consider providing all or part of the mortgage loan needed on each property. Each loan officer has set differing interest rates on each property (rates are affected by the neighborhood of the apartment building, condition of the property, and desire by the individual savings and loan to finance various size buildings), *and* each loan company has placed a maximum credit ceiling on how much it will lend Hall in total. This information is summarized in the accompanying table.

SAVINGS AND LOAN COMPANY	PROPERTY (INTEREST RATES) (%)				MAXIMUM CREDIT LINE ($)
	HILL ST.	BANKS ST.	PARK AVE.	DRURY LANE	
First Homestead	8	8	10	11	80,000
Commonwealth	9	10	12	10	100,000
Washington Federal	9	11	10	9	120,000
Loan Required to Purchase Building	$60,000	$40,000	$130,000	$70,000	

Each apartment building is equally attractive as an investment to Hall, so she has decided to purchase all buildings possible at the lowest total payment of interest. From which savings and loan companies should she borrow to purchase which buildings? More than one savings and loan can finance the same property.

Interest cost would be $28,300, an average rate of 9.43%. An alternate optimal solution exists.

QA14-22

14-22 The J. Mehta Company's production manager is planning for a series of one-month production periods for stainless steel sinks. The demand for the next four months is as follows:

MONTH	DEMAND FOR STAINLESS STEEL SINKS
1	120
2	160
3	240
4	100

The Mehta firm can normally produce 100 stainless steel sinks in a month. This is done during regular production hours at a cost of $100 per sink. If demand in any one month cannot be satisfied by regular production, the production manager has three other choices: (1) he can produce up to 50 more sinks per month in overtime, but at a cost of $130 per sink; (2) he can purchase a limited number of sinks from a friendly competitor for resale (the maximum number of outside purchases over the four-month period is 450 sinks, at a cost of $150 each); or (3) he can fill the demand from his on-hand inventory. The inventory carrying cost is $10 per sink per month. Back orders are not permitted.

Inventory on hand at the beginning of month 1 is 40 sinks.

Set up this "production smoothing" problem as a transportation problem to minimize cost. Use the northwest corner rule to find an initial level for production and outside purchases over the four-month period.

See the Instructor's Section for details.

14-23 Ashley's Auto Top Carriers currently maintains plants in Atlanta and Tulsa
QA14-23 which supply major distribution centers in Los Angeles and New York. Because of an expanding demand, Ashley has decided to open a third plant and has narrowed the choice to one of two cities—New Orleans or Houston. The pertinent production and distribution costs, as well as the plant capacities and distribution demands, are shown in the accompanying table.

Upon comparing total costs for the Houston option ($19,500) to those for the New Orleans option ($20,000), we would recommend to Ashley that, all factors being equal, the Houston site should be selected. See the Instructor's Section for details.

FROM PLANTS	TO DISTRIBUTION CENTERS / LOS ANGELES	NEW YORK	NORMAL PRODUCTION	UNIT PRODUCTION COST ($)	
Existing plants ATLANTA	$8	$5	600	6	
TULSA	$4	$7	900	5	
Proposed locations NEW ORLEANS	$5	$6	500	4	(anticipated)
HOUSTON	$4	$6	500	3	(anticipated)
FORECAST DEMAND	800	1,200	2,000		

Indicates distribution cost (shipping, handling, storage) will be $6 per carrier if sent from Houston to New York

Which of the new possible plants should be opened?

14-24 Marc Smith, vice president for operations of HHN, Inc., a manufacturer of cabinets for telephone switches, is constrained from meeting the five-year forecast by limited capacity at the existing three plants. These three plants are Waterloo, Pusan, and Bogota. You, as his able assistant, have been told that because of existing capacity constraints and the expanding world market for HHN cabinets, a new plant is to be added to the existing three plants. The real estate department has advised Mr. Smith that two sites seem particularly good because of a stable political situation and tolerable exchange rate. These two acceptable locations are Dublin, Ireland, and Fontainebleau, France. Mr. Smith suggests that you should be able to take the data below and determine where the fourth plant should be located on the basis of production costs and transportation costs. *Note:* This problem is degenerate with the data for both locations.

Fontainbleau cost =
$1,530,000, which is $5,000
less than Dublin

MARKET AREA	PLANT LOCATION				
	Waterloo	Pusan	Bogota	Fontainebleau	Dublin
Canada					
Demand 4,000					
Production cost	50	30	40	50	45
Transportation cost	10	25	20	25	25
South America					
Demand 5,000					
Production cost	50	30	40	50	45
Transportation cost	20	25	10	30	30
Pacific Rim					
Demand 10,000					
Production cost	50	30	40	50	45
Transportation cost	25	10	25	40	40
Europe					
Demand 5,000					
Production cost	50	30	40	50	45
Transportation cost	25	40	30	10	20
Capacity	8000	2000	5000	9000	9000

QA14-25

$17,400 with East St. Louis;
$17,250 with St. Louis

14-25 Don Levine Corporation is considering adding an additional plant to their three existing facilities in Decatur, Minneapolis, and Carbondale. Both St. Louis and East St. Louis are being considered. Evaluating only the transportation costs per unit as shown in the table, which site is best?

TO	FROM EXISTING PLANTS			
	Decatur	Minneapolis	Carbondale	Demand
Blue Earth	$20	$17	$21	250
Ciro	25	27	20	200
Des Moines	22	25	22	350
Capacity	300	200	150	

TO	FROM PROPOSED PLANTS	
	East St. Louis	St. Louis
Blue Earth	$29	$27
Ciro	30	28
Des Moines	30	31
Capacity	150	150

QA14-26
$60,900 with East St. Louis;
$62,250 with St. Louis

14-26 Using the data from Problem 14-25 plus the unit production costs shown below, which locations yield the lowest cost?

LOCATION	PRODUCTION COSTS
Decatur	$50
Minneapolis	60
Carbondale	70
East St. Louis	40
St. Louis	50

14-27 In a job shop operation, four jobs may be performed on any of four machines. The hours required for each job on each machine are presented in the accompanying table. The plant supervisor would like to assign jobs so that total time is minimized. Use the assignment method to find the best solution.

	MACHINE			
JOB	W	X	Y	Z
A12	10	14	16	13
A15	12	13	15	12
B 2	9	12	12	11
B 9	14	16	18	16

QA14-27

Job A12 to Machine W
Job A15 to Machine Z
Job B2 to Machine Y
Job B9 to Machine X
Time = 10 + 12 + 12 + 16 = 50 hours

14-28 The personnel director of Dollar Finance Corp. must assign three recently hired college graduates to three regional offices. The three new loan officers are equally well qualified, so the decision will be based on the costs of relocating the graduates' families. Cost data are presented in the accompanying table.

OFFICER \ OFFICE	OMAHA	MIAMI	DALLAS
Jones	$800	$1,100	$1,200
Smith	$500	$1,600	$1,300
Wilson	$500	$1,000	$2,300

Use the assignment algorithm to solve this problem.

QA14-28

Optimal assignment
Jones to Dallas
Smith to Omaha
Wilson to Miami
Cost = $1,200 + $500 + $1,000 = $2,700

14-29 The Orange Top Cab Company has a taxi waiting at each of four cab stands in Evanston, Illinois. Four customers have called and requested service. The distances, in miles, from the waiting taxis to the customers are given in the accompanying table. Find the optimal assignment of taxis to customers so as to minimize total driving distances to the customers.

	CUSTOMER			
CAB SITE	A	B	C	D
Stand 1	7	3	4	8
Stand 2	5	4	6	5
Stand 3	6	7	9	6
Stand 4	8	6	7	4

QA14-29

Taxi at Post 1 to Customer C
Taxi at Post 2 to Customer B
Taxi at Post 3 to Customer A
Taxi at Post 4 to Customer D
4 + 4 + 6 + 4 = 18 miles

14-30 The Burlington Police Department has five detective squads available for assignment to five open crime cases. The chief of detectives wishes to assign the squads so that the total time to conclude the cases is minimized. The average number of days, based on past performance, for each squad to complete each case is as follows:

	CASE				
SQUAD	A	B	C	D	E
1	14	7	3	7	27
2	20	7	12	6	30
3	10	3	4	5	21
4	8	12	7	12	21
5	13	25	24	26	8

QA14-30

Squad 1 to Case C
Squad 2 to Case D
Squad 3 to Case B
Squad 4 to Case A
Squad 5 to Case E
Total person days projected using this assignment = 3 + 6 + 3 + 8 + 8 = 28 days

Each squad is composed of different types of specialists and, as noted, whereas one squad may be very effective in certain types of cases, they may be almost useless in others. Solve the problem by using the assignment method.

QA14-31

⌨ : **14-31** Roscoe Davis, chairman of a college's business department, has decided to apply the Hungarian method in assigning professors to courses next semester. As a criterion for judging who should teach each course, Professor Davis reviews the past two years' teaching evaluations (which were filled out by students). Since each of the four professors taught each of the four courses at one time or another during the two-year period, Davis is able to record a course rating for each instructor. These ratings are shown in the accompanying table. Find the best assignment of professors to courses to maximize the overall teaching rating.

Assignment
Anderson—Finance
Sweeney—Economics
Williams—Statistics
McKinney—Management
Rating
95
75
85
80
‾‾‾‾
335 = Total Rating

PROFESSOR	COURSE			
	Statistics	*Management*	*Finance*	*Economics*
Anderson	90	65	95	40
Sweeney	70	60	80	75
Williams	85	40	80	60
McKinney	55	80	65	55

QA14-32

⌨ : **14-32** The hospital administrator at St. Charles General must appoint head nurses to four newly established departments: urology, cardiology, orthopedics, and obstetrics. In anticipation of this staffing problem, she had hired four nurses: Hawkins, Condriac, Bardot, and Hoolihan. Believing in the quantitative analysis approach to problem solving, the administrator has interviewed each nurse, considered her background, personality, and talents, and developed a cost scale ranging from 0 to 100 to be used in the assignment. A 0 for Nurse Bardot being assigned to the cardiology unit implies that she would be perfectly suited to that task. A value close to 100, on the other hand, would imply that she is not at all suited to head that unit. The accompanying table gives the complete set of cost figures that the hospital administrator felt represented all possible assignments. Which nurse should be assigned to which unit?

Assignment
Hawkins to Cardiology
Condriac to Urology
Bardot to Orthopedics
Hoolihan to Obstetrics
Rating
18
32
24
12
‾‾‾‾
86 = Total "Cost Scale"

NURSE	DEPARTMENT			
	Urology	*Cardiology*	*Orthopedics*	*Obstetrics*
Hawkins	28	18	15	75
Condriac	32	48	23	38
Bardot	51	36	24	36
Hoolihan	25	38	55	12

QA14-33

⌨ : **14-33** The Gleaming Company has just developed a new dishwashing liquid and is preparing for a national television promotional campaign. The firm has decided to schedule a series of one-minute commercials during the peak home-maker audience viewing hours of 1–5 P.M. To reach the widest possible audience, Gleaming wants to schedule one commercial on each of four networks and to have one commercial appear during each of the four one-hour time blocks. The exposure ratings for each hour, which represent the number of viewers per $1,000 spent, are presented in the accompanying table. Which network should be scheduled each hour in order to provide the maximum audience exposure?

	NETWORKS			
VIEWING HOURS	A	B	C	Independent
1–2 P.M.	27.1	18.1	11.3	9.5
2–3 P.M.	18.9	15.5	17.1	10.6
3–4 P.M.	19.2	18.5	9.9	7.7
4–5 P.M.	11.5	21.4	16.8	12.8

14-34 The G. Saussy Manufacturing Company is putting out four new electronic components. Each of Saussy's four plants has the capacity to add one more product to its current line of electronic parts. The unit manufacturing costs for producing the different parts at the four plants are shown in the accompanying table. How should Saussy assign the new products to the plants in order to minimize manufacturing costs?

ELECTRONIC COMPONENTS	PLANTS			
	1	2	3	4
C53	$.10	$.12	$.13	$.11
C81	.05	.06	.04	.08
D5	.32	.40	.31	.30
D44	.17	.14	.19	.15

14-35 As mentioned in Section 14.13 of this chapter, the Fix-It Shop has added a fourth repairman, Davis. Solve the accompanying cost table for the new optimal assignment of workers to projects. Why did this solution occur?

WORKER	PROJECT			
	1	2	3	Dummy
Adams	$11	$14	$ 6	$ 0
Brown	8	10	11	0
Cooper	9	12	7	0
Davis	10	13	8	0

14-36 The Patricia Garcia Company is producing seven new medical products. Each of Garcia's eight plants can add one more product to its current line of medical devices. The unit manufacturing costs for producing the different parts at the eight plants are shown below. How should Garcia assign the new products to the plants in order to minimize manufacturing costs?

ELECTRONIC COMPONENTS	PLANTS							
	1	2	3	4	5	6	7	8
C53	$.10	$.12	$.13	$.11	$.10	$.06	$.16	$.12
C81	.05	.06	.04	.08	.04	.09	.06	.06
D5	.32	.40	.31	.30	.42	.35	.36	.49
D44	.17	.14	.19	.15	.10	.16	.19	.12
E2	.06	.07	.10	.05	.08	.10	.11	.05
E35	.08	.10	.12	.08	.09	.10	.09	.06
G99	.55	.62	.61	.70	.62	.63	.65	.59

Assignment
1-2 P.M. on A
2-3 P.M. on C
3-4 P.M. on B
4-5 P.M. on Indpt.
Rating
27.1
17.1
18.5
12.8
75.5 = Overall Rating

QA14-34
Assignment
C53 at Plant 1
C81 at Plant 3
D5 at Plant 4
D44 at Plant 2
Rating
10¢
4¢
30¢
14¢
58¢ = Total Manufacturing Cost

QA14-35

Adams to 3, Brown to 2, Cooper to 1, Davis to Dummy, $25
No change in optimal solution.

QA14-36
Assignments
Component C53 to Plant 6
Component D5 to Plant 4
Component D44 to Plant 5
Component E35 to Plant 8
Component G99 to Plant 1
Component E2 to Plant 2
Component C81 to Plant 3
Cost
0.06
0.30
0.10
0.06
0.55
0.07
0.04
Total Cost: $1.18

Data Set Problem

14-37 Haifa Instruments, an Israeli producer of portable kidney dialysis units and other medical products, develops an eight-month aggregate plan. Demand and capacity (in units) are forecast as follows:

CAPACITY SOURCE	JAN.	FEB.	MAR.	APR.	MAY	JUNE	JULY	AUG.
Labor								
Regular Time	235	255	290	300	300	290	300	290
Overtime	20	24	26	24	30	28	30	30
Subcontract	12	15	15	17	17	19	19	20
Demand	255	294	321	301	330	320	345	340

The cost of producing each dialysis unit is $1,000 on regular time, $1,300 on overtime, and $1,500 on a subcontract. Inventory carrying cost is $100 per unit per month. There is no beginning or ending inventory in stock.

(a) Set up a production plan, using the transportation model, that minimizes cost. What is this plan's cost?

(b) Through better planning, regular time production can be set at exactly the same value, 275, per month. Does this alter the solution?

(c) If overtime costs rise from $1,300 to $1,400, does this change your answer to part a? What if they fall to $1,200?

Data Set Problem

14-38 NASA's astronaut crew currently includes 10 mission specialists who hold a Ph.D. in either astrophysics or astromedicine. One of these specialists will be assigned to each of the 10 flights scheduled for the upcoming nine months. Mission specialists are responsible for carrying out scientific and medical experiments in space or for launching, retrieving, or repairing satellites. The chief of astronaut personnel, himself a former crew member with three missions under his belt, must decide who should be assigned and trained for each of the very different missions. Clearly, astronauts with medical educations are more suited to missions involving biological or medical experiments, while those with engineering- or physics-oriented degrees are best suited to other types of missions. The chief assigns each astronaut a rating on a scale of 1 to 10 for each possible mission, with a 10 being a perfect match for the task at hand and a 1 being a mismatch. Only one specialist is assigned to each flight, and none is reassigned until all others have flown at least once.

(a) Who should be assigned to which flight?

(b) We have just been notified that Anderson is getting married in February and has been granted a highly sought publicity tour in Europe that month. (He intends to take his wife and let the trip double as a honeymoon.) How does this change the final schedule?

(c) Certo has complained that he was misrated on his January mission. Both ratings should be 10s, he claims to the chief, who agrees and recomputes the schedule. Do any changes occur over the schedule set in part b?

(d) What are the strengths and weaknesses of this approach to scheduling?

ASTRONAUT	MISSION									
	Jan. 12	Jan. 27	Feb. 5	Feb. 26	Mar. 26	Apr. 12	May 1	Jun. 9	Aug. 20	Sep. 19
Vincze	9	7	2	1	10	9	8	9	2	6
Veit	8	8	3	4	7	9	7	7	4	4
Anderson	2	1	10	10	1	4	7	6	6	7
Herbert	4	4	10	9	9	9	1	2	3	4
Schatz	10	10	9	9	8	9	1	1	1	1
Plane	1	3	5	7	9	7	10	10	9	2
Certo	9	9	8	8	9	1	1	2	2	9
Moses	3	2	7	6	4	3	9	7	7	9
Brandon	5	4	5	9	10	10	5	4	9	8
Drtina	10	10	9	7	6	7	5	4	8	8

CASE STUDY

Custom Vans, Inc.

Custom Vans, Inc., specializes in converting standard vans into campers. Depending on the amount of work and customizing to be done, the customizing could cost less than $1,000 to over $5,000. In less than four years, Tony Rizzo was able to expand his small operation in Gary, Indiana, to other major outlets in Chicago, Milwaukee, Minneapolis, and Detroit.

Innovation was the major factor in Tony's success in converting a small van shop into one of the largest and most profitable custom van operations in the Midwest. Tony seemed to have a special ability to design and develop unique features and devices that were always in high demand by van owners. An example was Shower-Rific, which was developed by Tony only six months after Custom Vans, Inc. was started. These small showers were completely self-contained, and they could be placed in almost any type of van and in a number of different locations within a van. Shower-Rific was made of fiberglass, and contained towel racks, built-in soap and shampoo holders, and a unique plastic door. Each Shower-Rific took 2 gallons of fiberglass and 3 hours of labor to manufacture.

Most of the Shower-Rifics were manufactured in Gary in the same warehouse where Custom Vans, Inc. was founded. The manufacturing plant in Gary could produce 300 Shower-Rifics in a month, but this capacity never seemed to be enough. Custom Van shops in all locations were complaining about not getting enough Shower-Rifics, and because Minneapolis was farther away from Gary than the other locations, Tony was always inclined to ship Shower-Rifics to the other locations before Minneapolis. This infuriated the manager of Custom Vans at Minneapolis, and after many heated discussions, Tony decided to start another manufacturing plant for Shower-Rifics at Fort Wayne, Indiana. The manufacturing plant at Fort Wayne could produce 150 Shower-Rifics per month.

The manufacturing plant at Fort Wayne was still not able to meet current demand for Shower-Rifics, and Tony knew that the demand for his unique camper shower would grow rapidly in the next year. After consulting with his lawyer and banker, Tony concluded that he should open two new manufacturing plants as soon as possible. Each plant would have the same capacity as the Fort Wayne manufacturing plant. An initial investigation into possible manufacturing locations was made, and Tony decided that the two new plants should be located in Detroit, Michigan; Rockford, Illinois; or Madison, Wisconsin. Tony knew that selecting the best location for the two new manufacturing plants would be difficult. Transportation costs and demands for the various locations should be important considerations.

The Chicago shop was managed by Bill Burch. This Custom Van shop was one of the first established by Tony, and it continued to outperform the other locations. The manufacturing plant at Gary was supplying 200 Shower-Rifics each month, although Bill knew that the demand for the showers in Chicago was 300 units. The transportation cost per unit from Gary was $10, and although the transportation cost from Fort Wayne was double that amount, Bill was always pleading with Tony to get an additional 50 units from the Fort Wayne manufacturer. The two additional manufacturing plants would certainly be able to supply Bill with the additional 100 showers he needed. The transportation costs would, of course, vary, depending on which two locations Tony picked. The transportation cost per shower would be $30 from Detroit, $5 from Rockford, and $10 from Madison.

Wilma Jackson, manager of the Custom Van shop in Milwaukee, was the most upset about not getting an adequate supply of showers. She had a demand for 100 units, and at the present time, she was only getting half of this demand from the Fort Wayne manufacturing plant. She could not understand why Tony didn't ship her all 100 units from Gary. The transportation cost per unit from Gary was only $20, while the transportation cost from Fort Wayne was $30. Wilma was hoping that Tony would select Madison for one of the manufacturing locations. She would be able to get all of the showers needed, and the transportation cost per unit would only be $5. If not Madison, a new plant in Rockford would be able to supply her total needs, but the transportation cost per unit would be twice as much as it would be from Madison. Because the transportation cost per unit from Detroit would be $40, Wilma speculated that even if Detroit became one of the new plants, she would not be getting any units from Detroit.

Custom Vans, Inc., of Minneapolis was managed by Tom Poanski. He was getting 100 showers from the Gary plant. Demand was 150 units. Tom faced the highest transportation costs of all locations. The transportation cost from Gary was $40 per unit. It would cost $10 more if showers were sent from the Fort Wayne location. Tom was hoping that Detroit would not be one of the new plants, as the transportation cost would be $60 per unit. Rockford and Madison would have a cost of $30 and $25, respectively, to ship one shower to Minneapolis.

The Detroit shop's position was similar to Milwaukee's—only getting half of the demand each month. The 100 units that Detroit did receive came directly from the Fort Wayne plant. The transportation cost was only $15 per unit from Fort Wayne, while it was $25 from Gary. Dick Lopez, manager of Custom Vans, Inc., of Detroit, placed the probability of having one of the new plants in Detroit

fairly high. The factory would be located across town, and the transportation cost would be only $2 per unit. He could get 150 showers from the new plant in Detroit and the other 50 showers from Fort Wayne. Even if Detroit was not selected, the other two locations were not intolerable. Rockford had a transportation cost per unit of $35, and Madison had a transportation cost of $40.

Tony pondered the dilemma of locating the two new plants for several weeks before deciding to call a meeting of all the managers of the van shops. The decision was complicated, but the objective was clear—to minimize total costs. The meeting was held in Gary, and everyone was present except Wilma.

Tony: Thank you for coming. As you know, I have decided to open up two new plants at Rockford, Madison, or Detroit. The two locations, of course, will change our shipping practices, and I sincerely hope that they will supply you with the Shower-Rifics that you have been wanting. I know you could have sold more units, and I want you to know that I am sorry for this situation.

Dick: Tony, I have given this situation a lot of consideration, and I feel strongly that at least one of the new plants should be located in Detroit. As you know, I am now only getting half of the showers that I need. My brother, Leon, is very interested in running the plant, and I know he would do a good job.

Tom: Dick, I am sure that Leon could do a good job, and I know how difficult it has been since the recent layoffs by the auto industry. Nevertheless, we should be considering total costs and not personalities. I believe that the new plants should be located in Madison and Rockford. I am farther away from the other plants than any other shop, and these locations would significantly reduce transportation costs.

Dick: That may be true, but there are other factors. Detroit has one of the largest suppliers of fiberglass, and I have checked prices. A new plant in Detroit would be able to purchase fiberglass for $2 less than any of the other existing or proposed plants.

Tom: At Madison, we have an excellent labor force. This is primarily due to the large number of students attending the University of Madison. These students are hard workers, and they will work for $1 less per hour than the other locations that we are considering.

Bill: Calm down, you two. It is obvious that we will not be able to satisfy everyone in locating the new plants. Therefore I would

like to suggest that we vote on the two best locations.

Tony: I don't think that voting would be a good idea. Wilma was not able to attend, and we should be looking at all of these factors together in some type of logical fashion.

Where would you locate the two new plants?

New plants in Detroit and Madison for a total cost of $10,200

Old Oregon Wood Store

In 1975, George Brown started the Old Oregon Wood Store to manufacture Old Oregon tables. Each table is carefully constructed by hand using the highest quality oak. Old Oregon tables can support over 500 pounds, and since the start of the Old Oregon Wood Store, not one table has been returned because of faulty workmanship or structural problems. In addition to being rugged, each table is beautifully finished using a urethane varnish that George developed over 20 years of working with wood-finishing materials.

The manufacturing process consists of four steps: preparation, assembly, finishing, and packaging. Each step is performed by one person. In addition to overseeing the entire operation, George does all of the finishing. Tom Surowski performs the preparation step, which involves cutting and forming the basic components of the tables. Leon Davis is in charge of the assembly, and Cathy Stark performs the packaging.

While each person is responsible for only one step in the manufacturing process, everyone can perform any one of the steps. It is George's policy that occasionally everyone should complete several tables on his or her own without any help or assistance. A small competition is used to see who can complete an entire table in the least amount of time. George maintains average total and intermediate completion times. The data are shown in Figure 1 on next page.

It takes Cathy longer than the other employees to construct an Old Oregon table. In addition to being slower than the other employees, Cathy is also unhappy about her current responsibility of packaging, which leaves her idle most of the day. Her first preference is finishing, and her second preference is preparation.

In addition to quality, George is concerned with costs and efficiency. When one of the employees

misses a day, it causes major scheduling problems. In some cases, George assigns another employee overtime to complete the necessary work. At other times, George simply waits until the employee returns to work to complete his or her step in the manufacturing process. Both solutions cause problems. Overtime is expensive, and waiting causes delays and sometimes stops the entire manufacturing process.

To overcome some of these problems, Randy Lane was hired. Randy's major duties are to perform miscellaneous jobs and to help out if one of the employees is absent. George has given Randy training in all phases of the manufacturing process, and he is pleased with the speed at which Randy has been able to learn how to completely assemble Old Oregon tables. Total and intermediate completion times are given in Figure 2.

Discussion Questions

1. What is the fastest way to manufacture Old Oregon tables using the original crew? How many could be made per day?

2. Would production rates and quantities change significantly if George would allow Randy to perform one of the four functions and make one of the original crew the backup person?

3. What is the fastest time to manufacture a table with the original crew if Cathy is moved to either preparation or finishing?

4. Whoever performs the packaging function is severely underutilized. Can you find a better way of utilizing the four- or five-person crew than either giving each a single job or allowing each to manufacture an entire table? How many tables could be manufactured per day with this scheme?

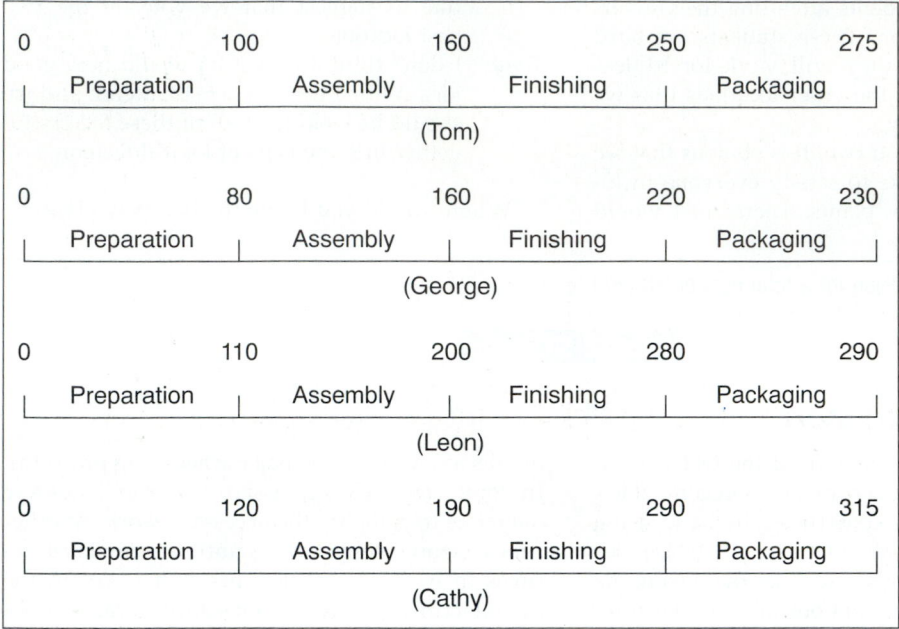

FIGURE 1

Manufacturing Time in Minutes

0	110	190	290	300
	Preparation	Assembly	Finishing	Packaging

FIGURE 2

1. Tom—Preparation; Cathy—Assembly; George—Finishing; Leon—Packaging. 240 minutes
2. 10 minutes times saving with Cathy becoming backup.
3. 250 minutes

BIBLIOGRAPHY

Aarvik, O., and P. Randolph. "The Application of Linear Programming to the Determination of Transmission Fees in an Electrical Power Network." *Interfaces* **6**, (Nov. 1975).

Bowman, E. "Production Scheduling by the Transportation Method of Linear Programming." *Operations Research* **4** (1956).

Breslaw, J. A. "A Linear Programming Solution to the Faculty Assignment Problem." *Socio-Economic Planning Sciences* **10**, 6 (1976).

Choypeng, P., P. Puakpong, and Richard E. Rosenthal. "Optimal Ship Routing and Personnel Assignment for Naval Recruitment in Thailand." *Interfaces* **16**, 4 (July–Aug. 1986): 49–52.

Evans, James R., John E. Hebert, and Richard F. Deckro. "Play Ball! The Scheduling of Sports Officials." *Perspectives in Computing* **4**, 1 (Spring 1984): 18–29.

Glassey, C. Roger, and Michael Mizrach. "A Decision Support System for Assigning Classes to Rooms." *Interfaces* **16**, 5 (September–October 1986): 92–100.

Harrison, H. "A Planning System for Facilities and Resources in Distribution Networks." *Interfaces* **9**, 2, Part 2 (February 1979).

Holladay, J. "Some Transportation Problems and Techniques for Solving Them." *Naval Research Logistics Quarterly* **11**, (1974).

McKeown, P., and B. Workman. "A Study in Using Linear Programming to Assign Students to Schools." *Interfaces* **6**, 4 (August 1976).

Render, B., R. M. Stair, and I. Greenberg. *Cases and Readings in Management Science,* 2nd ed. Boston: Allyn and Bacon, Inc., 1990.

Ross, G. T., and R. M. Soland. "Modeling Facility Location Problems as Generalized Assignment Problems." *Management Science* **24**, 3 (1977).

Integer Programming, Goal Programming, and the Branch and Bound Method

CHAPTER OUTLINE

15.1 Introduction
15.2 Integer Programming
15.3 The Branch and Bound Method
15.4 Goal Programming
15.5 Nonlinear Programming
15.6 Summary
 Glossary

Solved Problems
Discussion Questions and Problems
Case Studies: Schank Marketing
 Research
 The Oakton River
 Bridge
 The Puyallup Mall
Bibliography

15.1 INTRODUCTION

Transparency Master 15.1:
Mathematical Programming
Extensions.

Teaching Suggestion 15.1:
The Topics in This Chapter.
See the Instructor's Section
for details.

integer programming

goal programming

nonlinear programming

We have just seen two special types of linear programming models—the transportation and assignment models—that were handled by making certain modifications to the general LP approach. This chapter presents a series of other important mathematical programming models that arise when some of the basic assumptions of LP are made more or less restrictive.

For example, one assumption of linear programming is that decision variables can take on fractional values such as $X_1 = .33$, $X_2 = 1.57$, or $X_3 = 109.4$. Yet a large number of business problems can be solved only if variables have *integer* values. When an airline decides how many Boeing 757s or Boeing 767s to purchase, it can't place an order for 5.38 aircraft; it must order 4, 5, 6, 7 or some other integer amount. In Section 15.2, we present the subject of *integer programming*. We show you how to solve integer programming problems both graphically and by use of an algorithm called the *branch and bound method.*

A major limitation of linear programming is that it forces the decision maker to state one objective only. But what if a business has several objectives? Management may indeed want to maximize profit, but also maximize market share, maintain full employment, and minimize costs. Many of these goals can be conflicting and difficult to quantify. South States Power and Light, for example, wants to build a nuclear power plant in Taft, Louisiana. Its objectives are to maximize power generated, reliability, and safety, and to minimize cost of operating the system and the environmental effects on the community. *Goal programming* is an extension to linear programming that can permit multiple objectives such as these.

Linear programming can, of course, by applied only to cases in which the constraints and objective function are linear. Yet in many situations this is not the case. The price of various products, for example, may be a function of the number of units produced. As more are made, the price per unit decreases. Hence, an objective function may read:

$$\text{Maximize profit} = 25X_1 - .4X_1^2 + 30X_2 - .5X_2^2$$

Because of the squared terms, this is a nonlinear programming problem.

Let's examine each of these extensions of LP—integer, goal, and nonlinear programming—one at a time.

15.2 INTEGER PROGRAMMING

Applicable Problems 15-14, 15-15, 15-32, Oakton case

solution values must be whole numbers

An integer programming model is a model that has constraints and an objective function identical to that formulated by linear programming. The only difference is that one or more of the decision variables has to take on an integer value in the final solution. Let's look at a simple example of an integer programming problem and see how to solve it.

The Harrison Electric Company Example of Integer Programming

The Harrison Electric Company, located in Chicago's Old Town area, produces two products popular with home renovators: old-fashioned chandeliers and ceiling fans. Both the chandeliers and fans require a two-step production process involving wiring and assembly. It takes about 2 hours to wire each chandelier, and 3 hours to wire a ceiling fan. Final assembly of the chandeliers and fans requires 6 and 5 hours, respectively. The production capability is such that only 12 hours of wiring time and 30 hours of assembly time are available. If each chandelier produced nets the firm $7 and each fan $6, Harrison's production mix decision can be formulated using linear programming as follows:

$$\text{Maximize profit} = \$7X_1 + \$6X_2$$

$$\text{Subject to:} \qquad 2X_1 + 3X_2 \leq 12 \quad \textit{(wiring hours)}$$

$$6X_1 + 5X_2 \leq 30 \quad \textit{(assembly hours)}$$

$$X_1, X_2 \geq 0$$

where

$$X_1 = \text{number of chandeliers produced, and}$$

$$X_2 = \text{number of ceiling fans produced.}$$

With only two variables and two constraints, Harrison's production planner, Wes Wellace, employed the graphical linear programming approach (see Figure 15.1) to generate the optimal solution of $X_1 = 3.75$ chandeliers and $X_2 = 1.5$ ceiling fans during the production cycle. Recognizing that the company could not produce and sell a fraction of a product, Wes decided that he was dealing with an integer programming problem.

It seemed to Wes that the simplest approach was to round off the optimal fractional solutions for X_1 and X_2 to integer values of $X_1 = 4$ chandeliers and $X_2 = 2$ ceiling fans. Unfortunately, rounding can produce two problems. First, the new integer solution may not be in the feasible region and thus is not a practical answer. This is the case if we round to $X_1 = 4$, **rounding off** $X_2 = 2$. Second, even if we round off to a feasible solution, such as $X_1 = 4$, $X_2 = 1$, it may not be the *optimal* feasible integer solution. Table 15.1 lists the entire set of integer-valued solutions to the Harrison Electric problem. By inspecting the right-hand column, we see that the optimal *integer* solution is:

$$X_1 = 5 \text{ chandeliers,} \quad X_2 = 0 \text{ ceiling fans with a profit} = \$35$$

Note that this integer restriction results in a lower profit level than the original optimal linear programming solution. As a matter of fact, an integer programming solution can *never* produce a greater profit than the LP solution to the same problem; *usually* it means a lesser value.

KEY IDEA

Applicable Problems 15-13, 15-16

Transparency Master 15.2: Integer Programming Techniques.

method for solving integer programs

adding Gomory cuts

The Cutting Plane Method

Although it is possible to solve simple integer programming problems like Harrison Electric's by inspection or enumeration, several more complicated methods are available to handle larger, more complex problems. Gomory's *cutting plane method* is one such integer programming algorithm.

In applying the cutting plane algorithm, integer requirements are first ignored, and the linear programming problem is solved in the usual way, usually with the simplex method. If the solution has all integer values, then the current answer is also the integer programming answer and no further steps are needed. But if the solution does *not* have integer values, we must add one or more new constraints to the problem. These new constraints, called *Gomory cuts,* construct a new, smaller area covering all integer values of the feasible region. They exclude the original optimal *noninteger* solution and allow us to converge on the integer solution.

Transparency Master 15.3: Harrison Electric Problem.

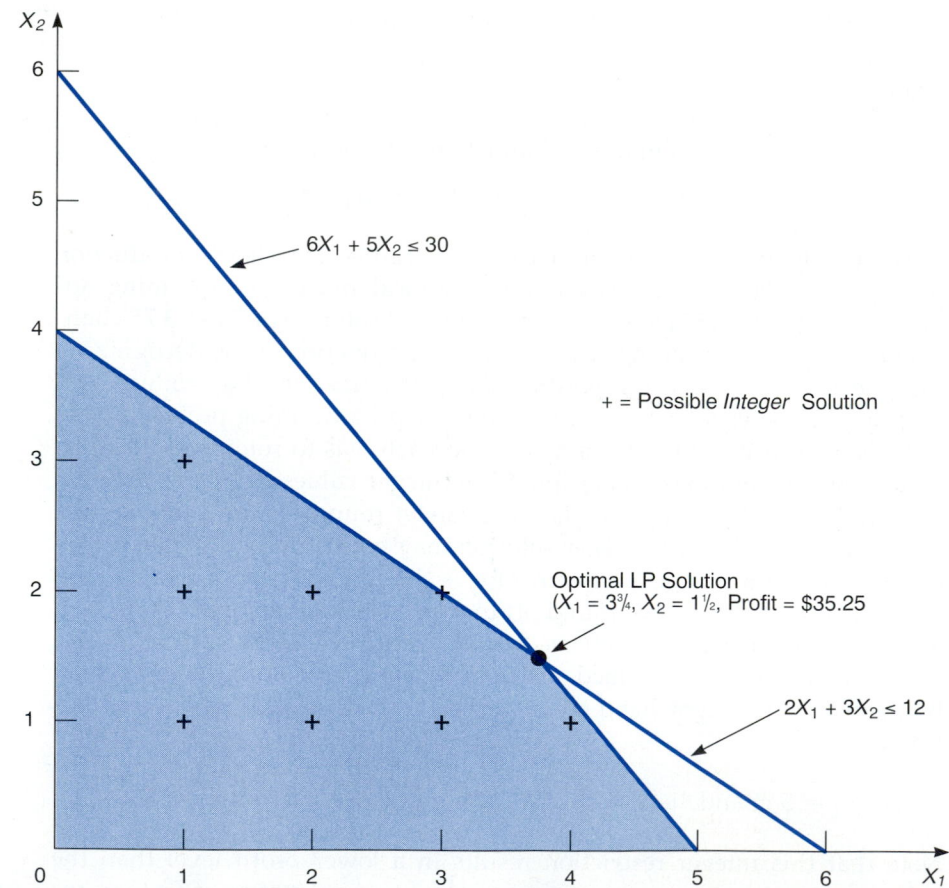

FIGURE 15.1
Harrison Electric Problem

TABLE 15.1 Integer Solutions to the Harrison Electric Company Problem

CHANDELIERS (X_1)	CEILING FANS (X_2)	PROFIT ($\$7X_1 + \$6X_2$)	
0	0	$ 0	
1	0	7	
2	0	14	
3	0	21	
4	0	28	
5	0	35	← Optimal solution to integer programming problem
0	1	6	
1	1	13	
2	1	20	
3	1	27	
4	1	34	← Solution if rounding off is used
0	2	12	
1	2	19	
2	2	26	
3	2	33	
0	3	18	
1	3	25	
0	4	24	

Figure 15.2 illustrates the addition of a first cut, the constraint $X_1 + X_2 \leq 5$. This equation was selected as a first cut by observation.[1] It goes through a series of integer points without excluding any that were in the original feasible region. If you look carefully, you will also see it is the *only* constraint that could be added to cut the size of the feasible region without excluding any integer points.

The cut creates a new feasible region *ABCD*. Once the cut is made, the revised problem can be solved by the simplex method, or graphically. If an integer solution is reached now, we are done. If not, we continue to add Gomory cuts, one at a time. Sooner or later, the optimal integer solution will be found.

Teaching Suggestion 15.2:
The Cutting Plane Method. See the Instructor's Section for details.

Types of Integer Programming Problems

The Harrison Electric production decision is an example of one of the three types of integer programming problems:

1. *Pure integer programming* problems, such as Harrison Electric's, are cases in which *all* decision variables must have integer solutions.

2. *Mixed-integer programming* problems are cases in which *some,* but not all, of the decision variables are required to have integer values.

3. *Zero-one integer programming* problems are special cases in which all decision variables must have integer solution values of 0 or 1.

We now look at application examples of the latter two problems.

Transparency Master 15.5:
Types of Integer Programming Problems.

pure integer programming, mixed-integer programming, zero-one integer programming

[1]An algorithm also exists for the simplex method to do the cuts.

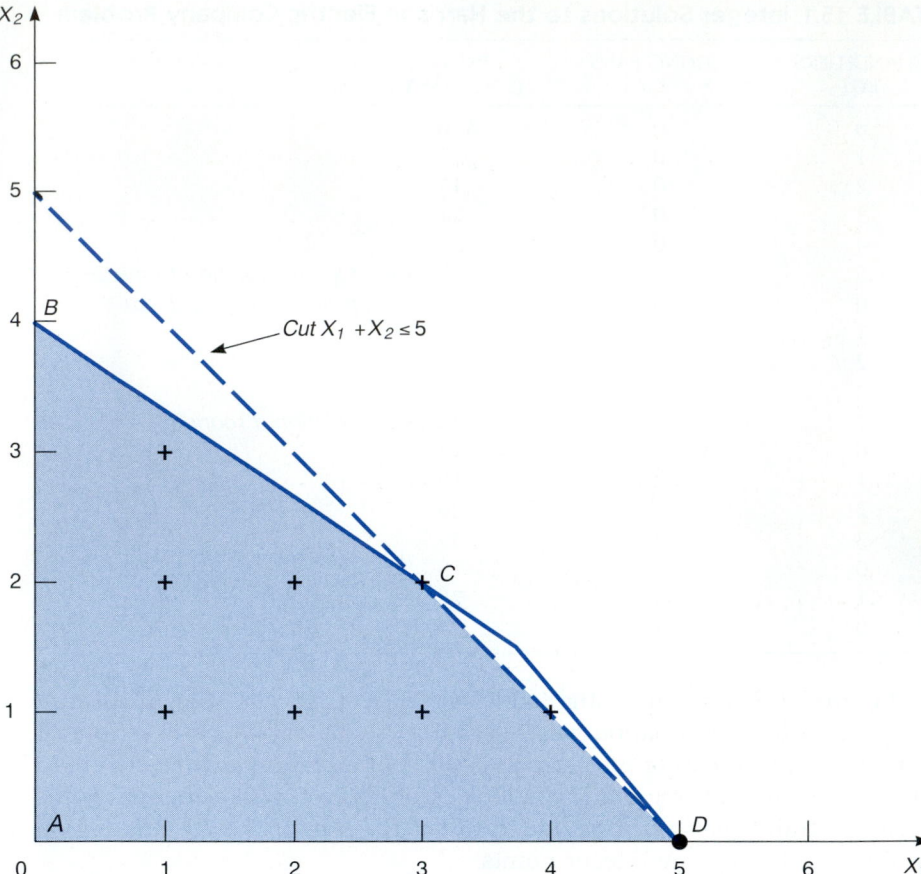

Transparency Master 15.4:
Harrison Electric Problem.

FIGURE 15.2
**Harrison Electric Problem with Cut $X_1 + X_2 \leq 5$
Added**

A Mixed-Integer Programming
Problem Example

Bagwell Chemical Company, in Jackson, Mississippi, produces two industrial chemicals. The first product, xyline, must be produced in 50-pound bags; the second, hexall, is sold by the pound in dry bulk and hence can be produced in any quantity. Both xyline and hexall are composed of three ingredients, A, B, and C, as follows:

AMOUNT PER 50-POUND BAG OF XYLINE (lbs.)	AMOUNT PER POUND OF HEXALL (lbs.)	AMOUNT OF INGREDIENTS AVAILABLE
30	0.5	2,000 lbs.—ingredient A
18	0.4	800 lbs.—ingredient B
2	0.1	200 lbs.—ingredient C

APPLICATIONS OF QA

Selling Seats at American Airlines Using Integer Programming

American Airlines (AA) describes *yield management* as "selling the right seats to the right customers at the right prices." The role of yield management at AA is like inventory control for a manufacturer. Planning departments determine the airline's flight schedule and fares. The combination of schedule and fares defines the products to be offered to the public. Yield management then determines how much of each product to put on the shelf (make available for sale). American's "store front" is the computerized reservations system, SABRE (semi-automated business research environment).

To increase the responsiveness and effectiveness of yield-management strategies and to coordinate reservations inventory decisions with SABRE, American has continually supported the development of automated decision tools. The AA yield-managment problem is a mixed-integer program that requires data, such as passenger demand, cancellations, and other estimates of passenger behavior that are subject to frequent changes. To solve the system-wide yield-management problem would require approximately 250 million decision variables.

To bring this problem down to a manageable size, AA developed a model, called DINAMO, that creates three smaller and easier subproblems. The airline looks at:

1. Overbooking, which is the practice of intentionally selling more reservations for a flight than there are actual seats on the aircraft.

2. Discount allocation, which is the process of determining the number of discount fares to offer on a flight. Airlines offer discount fares to stimulate demand and fill seats that would otherwise be empty.

3. Traffic management, which is the process of controlling reservations by passenger origin and destination to provide the mix of markets (multiple-flight connecting markets versus single-flight markets) that maximizes revenue.

R. L. Crandall, president of AA, speaking of the benefits of DINAMO, states, "We estimate that yield management has generated $1.4 billion in incremental revenue in the last three years alone. The development of AA's system has been long and sometimes difficult, but this investment has paid off."

Source: Barry Smith, John Leimkuhler, and Ross Darrow, "Yield Management at American Airlines." *Interfaces,* **22,** 1 (Jan.–Feb. 1992): 8–31.

Bagwell sells 50-pound bags of xyline for $85 and hexall in any weight for $1.50 per pound.

If we let X_1 = number of 50-pound bags of xyline produced and X_2 = number of pounds of hexall (in dry bulk) mixed, Bagwell's problem can be described with mixed integer programming:

$$\text{Maximize profit} = \$85X_1 + \$1.50X_2$$

$$\text{Subject to:} \qquad 30X_1 + 0.5X_2 \leq 2{,}000$$

$$18X_1 + 0.4X_2 \leq 800$$

$$2X_1 + 0.1X_2 \leq 200$$

with $X_1, X_2 \geq 0$ and X_1 integer.

Note that X_2 represents bulk weight of hexall and is not required to be integer valued.

Teaching Suggestion 15.3:
Using the Computer to Solve
Mixed-Integer Programming
Problems. See the
Instructor's Section for
details.

STORM, the software package first demonstrated in Chapter 10, is also capable of handling mixed-integer programming problems such as the Bagwell case. Program 15.1 illustrates the input data and solution computed by STORM. The optimal value of $3,770 is obtained when 44 bags of xyline and 20 pounds of hexall are produced.

PROGRAM 15.1 STORM Analysis of Bagwell's Mixed-Integer Program

```
┌────────── STORM EDITOR : Linear & Integer Programming Module ──────────┐
│                                                                         │
│   Title : BAGWELL CHEMICAL COMPANY                                      │
│   Number of variables      :        2                                   │
│   Number of constraints    :        3                                   │
│   Starting solution given  :       NO                                   │
│   Objective type (MAX/MIN) :      MAX                                    │
│ ─────────────────────────────────────────────────────────────────────── │
│   R1  : C1         XYLINE      HEXALL  CONST TYPE      R H S      RANGE   │
│   OBJ COEFF          85.          1.5    XXXX    XXXX    XXXX            │
│   CONSTR    1        30.          0.5     <=    2000.       .            │
│   CONSTR    2        18.          0.4     <=     800.       .            │
│   CONSTR    3         2.          0.1     <=     200.       .            │
│   VARBL TYPE        IPOS          POS    XXXX    XXXX    XXXX            │
│   LOWR BOUND          .            .     XXXX    XXXX    XXXX            │
│   UPPR BOUND          .            .     XXXX    XXXX    XXXX            │
│   INIT SOLN           .            .     XXXX    XXXX    XXXX            │
│                                                                         │
│                                                                         │
│ ─────────────────────────────────────────────────────────────────────── │
│   F1 Block   F2 GoTo   F3 InsR   F4 DelR   F5 InsC   F6 DelC   F7 Done   F8 Help KB:CN │
│ ─────────────────────────────────────────────────────────────────────── │
│                                                                         │
│                                                                         │
│                        BAGWELL CHEMICAL COMPANY                         │
│                  OPTIMAL SOLUTION - DETAILED REPORT                      │
│             Variable        Value        Cost     Red. cost   Status     │
│        1    XYLINE         44.0000     85.0000     17.5000 Upper bound    │
│        2    HEXALL         20.0000      1.5000      0.0000    Basic       │
│                                                                         │
│        Slack Variables                                                   │
│        3    CONSTR   1    670.0000      0.0000      0.0000    Basic       │
│        4    CONSTR   2      0.0000      0.0000     -3.7500 Lower bound    │
│        5    CONSTR   3    110.0000      0.0000      0.0000    Basic       │
│                                                                         │
│        Objective Function Value = 3770                                   │
└─────────────────────────────────────────────────────────────────────────┘
```

Zero-One Integer Programming Problem Example

Applicable Problems
15-17, 15-18

Alternate Example 15.1

The Houston-based investment firm of Simkin, Simkin, and Steinberg specializes in recommending oil stock portfolios for wealthy clients. One such client has made the following specifications: (1) at least two Texas oil firms must be in the portfolio, (2) no more than one investment can be made in foreign oil companies, (3) one of the two California oil stocks must be purchased. The client has up to $3 million available for investments and insists on purchasing large blocks of shares of each company that he invests in. Table 15.2 describes various stocks that Simkin considers. The objective is to maximize annual return on investment subject to the constraints.

stock portfolio analysis
with zero-one
programming

TABLE 15.2 Oil Investment Opportunities

STOCK	COMPANY NAME	EXPECTED ANNUAL RETURN (in $1,000's)	COST FOR BLOCK OF SHARES (in $1,000's)
1	Trans-Texas Oil	50	480
2	British Petroleum	80	540
3	Dutch Shell	90	680
4	Houston Drilling	120	1,000
5	Texas Petroleum	110	700
6	San Diego Oil	40	510
7	California Petro	75	900

To formulate this as a 0-1 integer programming problem, Simkin lets X_i be a 0-1 integer variable, where $X_i = 1$ if stock i is purchased and $X_i = 0$ if stock i is not purchased.

$$\text{Maximize return} = 50X_1 + 80X_2 + 90X_3 + 120X_4 + 110X_5 + 40X_6 + 75X_7$$

Subject to: $X_1 + X_4 + X_5 \geq 2$ (*Texas constraint*)

$X_2 + X_3 \leq 1$ (*foreign oil constraint*)

$X_6 + X_7 = 1$ (*California constraint*)

$480X_1 + 540X_2 + 680X_3 + 1,000X_4 + 700X_5 + 510X_6 + 900X_7 \leq \$3,000$ (*$3 million limit*)

All variables must be 0 or 1 in value.

To solve this problem by computer, you may run the software with this text (AB:QM), LINDO, STORM, or What's*Best!* Program 15.2 illustrates the AB:QM input and output, while Program 15.3 shows the LINDO approach.

AB:QM and LINDO first solve the general LP problem, then apply a technique called the branch and bound method (our next topic in this chapter) to find the best integer answer. As we see in the printouts, X_3, X_4, X_5, and X_6 are all equal to 1 in the all-integer solution, while X_1, X_2, and X_7 are 0. This means Simkin should invest in Dutch Shell, Houston Drilling, Texas Petroleum, and San Diego Oil, and not in the other three oil firms. The expected return is $360,000.

PROGRAM 15.2 AB:QM Solution to Simkins 0-1 Programming Problem

```
Program: Zero One Programming

Problem Title : SIMKIN INVESTMENT

***** Input Data *****

Max.  Z =  50x1 + 80x2 + 90x3 + 120x4 + 110x5 + 40x6 + 75x7

Subject to

C1   1x1 + 1x4 + 1x5 >= 2
C2   1x2 + 1x3 <= 1
C3   1x6 + 1x7 = 1
C4   480x1 + 540x2 + 680x3 + 1000x4 + 700x5 + 510x6 + 900x7 <= 3000

***** Program Output *****


Final Optimal Solution

Z =   360.000

- - - - - - - - - - - - - - - - - -
Variable          Value
- - - - - - - - - - - - - - - - - -
  x 1               0
  x 2               0
  x 3               1
  x 4               1
  x 5               1
  x 6               1
  x 7               0
- - - - - - - - - - - - - - - - - -

***** End of Output *****
```

PROGRAM 15.3 Use of LINDO to Solve the 0-1 Integer Programming
Problem for Simkin

```
:   MAX 50X1+80X2+90X3+120X4+110X5+40X6+75X7
?   ST
?   X1+X4+X5>2
?   X2+X3<1
?   X6+X7=1
?   480X1+540X2+680X3+1000X4+700X5+510X6+900X7<3000
?   END
```

(Continued)

```
:  INTEGER X1
:  INTEGER X2
:  INTEGER X3
:  INTEGER X4
:  INTEGER X5
:  INTEGER X6
:  INTEGER X7
:  GO
```

LP OPTIMUM FOUND AT STEP   10

            OBJECTIVE FUNCTION VALUE

  1)   376.041700

VARIABLE   VALUE   REDUCED COST
    X1   .520833   .000000
    X2   1.000000   -4.583328
    X3   .000000   .000000
    X4   1.000000   -15.833340
    X5   1.000000   -37.083340
    X6   1.000000   -5.625000
    X7   .000000   .000000

    ROW   SLACK OR SURPLUS   DUAL PRICES
    2)   .520833   .000000
    3)   .000000   19.166670
    4)   .000000   -18.750000
    5)   .000000   .104167

NO. ITERATIONS=   10
BRANCHES=   0 DETERM= -4.800E 2
SET   X1 TO 0 AT   1 BND=   372.43590 TWIN=   372.40000
SET   X7 TO 0 AT   2 BND=   360.00000 TWIN=   372.43590

NEW INTEGER SOLUTION OF   360.000   AT BRANCH   2 PIVOT   16

            OBJECTIVE FUNCTION VALUE

  1)   360.000000

VARIABLE   VALUE   REDUCED COST
    X1   .000000   -50.000000
    X2   .000000   10.000000
    X3   1.000000   .000000
    X4   1.000000   -120.000000
    X5   1.000000   -110.000000
    X6   1.000000   .000000
    X7   .000000   -35.000000

    ROW   SLACK OR SURPLUS   DUAL PRICES
    2)   .000000   .000000
    3)   .000000   90.000000
    4)   .000000   40.000000
    5)   110.000000   .000000
```
```

You might also recall that assignment problems solved by linear programming, in Chapter 11, are also actually 0-1 integer programs. All assignments of people to jobs, for example, are presented by either a 1 (person gets job) or a 0 (person not assigned to particular job).

Applicable Problems 15-19, 15-20, 15-21, 15-22

Teaching Suggestion 15.4: How the Branch and Bound Method Can Help. See the Instructor's Section for details.

15.3 THE BRANCH AND BOUND METHOD

The *branch and bound method* is an algorithm that can be used to solve all-integer and mixed-integer linear programs. It searches for an optimal solution by examining only a small part of the total number of possible solutions. This is especially useful when enumeration becomes economically impractical or impossible because there are a large number of feasible solutions.

subproblems

Branch and bound works by breaking the area of feasible solutions into smaller and smaller parts (subproblems) until the optimal solution is reached. It introduces the concept of feasible and infeasible bounds. Each subproblem that we examine with a total cost or profit worse than the current feasible bound will be discarded, and we will only examine the remaining subproblems. At the point where no more subproblems can be created, we will find an optimal solution.

An Assignment Problem Example

In the previous chapter, we faced the problem of trying to make the best assignment of three workers to three projects. Table 15.3 shows the costs associated with assigning each employee in the Fix-It Shop to a project. For example, it costs the firm $14 for Adams to complete project number 2. The firm's objective is to minimize the total cost of doing all three jobs. We demonstrate the use of the branch and bound method to solve this problem in three steps.

Step 1. First, the lowest possible total-cost bound is found. This is the assignment which yields the lowest cost; it does *not* have to be a feasible solution. This means we are allowed to assign more than one worker to the same project. We are "bounding" total cost on the low side, saying that no possible assignment of people to projects can cost less.

lower bound on total cost

The easiest way to set the lower bound is to select the smallest cost from each row. We assign Adams to project 3 (*A*3), Brown to 1 (*B*1) and Cooper to 3 (*C*3) for a total cost of $6 + $8 + $7 = $21.

TABLE 15.3 Cost of Each Person-Project Assignment

PERSON	PROJECT		
	1	2	3
Adams (A)	$11	$14	$ 6
Brown (B)	8	10	11
Cooper (C)	9	12	7

APPLICATIONS OF QA

An Integer Programming System for Assigning Classes to Rooms

The University of California at Berkeley enrolls about 30,000 students who are distributed among 80 academic departments. Responsibility for assigning 4,000 classes to about 250 classrooms falls on a scheduling office. A decade ago, this office consisted of three schedulers (one for each academic quarter) plus a supervisor. The manual assignment strategy they used was "don't rock the boat"; that is, they began with the schedule for the corresponding quarter of the previous year and made the minimum necessary modifications to accommodate changes in departmental requests.

In the mid-1980s, Berkeley converted from a quarter to a semester calendar. The list of courses offered was so unlike the previous fall quarter that the old schedule was not a particularly useful starting point. The change to semesters forced the university to take a fresh look at the room assignment process and presented an opportunity to program a new system. The problem of assigning classes to rooms is part of a larger scheduling problem, often referred to as the timetabling problem, in which the time each class is offered and the professor are also decision variables. A large *zero-one integer program* is solved as part of a decision system for assigning classes to rooms.

From the professor's point of view, a room close to the office is more desirable than one on the other side of the campus. A room with fewer seats than students is, of course, undesirable, as is one that is too large. Some courses require special equipment such as TV monitors, slide projectors, and so forth. Students prefer consecutive classes close together, but that is an objective difficult to address directly. However, if professorial travel is minimized, then at least students who take consecutive classes in the same department will not have far to travel.

A rough calculation indicates how large this program for Berkeley would be. Since an activity is defined for each feasible assignment of a class to a room, about half a million variables are needed, assuming that on average half of the rooms are feasible for a randomly selected class. There are at least 26,500 constraints. There is only a limited opportunity to reduce the size of the problem by grouping rooms of similar size (as was done), because rooms in different buildings must be kept separate if distance is to be an objective.

With the aid of the new system, the scheduling office is able to accomplish its part of the cycle several weeks faster than it was with the entirely manual method. The system is a success and it is still being used.

Source: C. Glassey and M. Mizrach, *Interfaces* **16**, 5 (September–October 1986): 92–100.

Teaching Suggestion 15.5:
Applications Box on Assigning Classes. See the Instructor's Section for details.

LOWER BOUND ASSIGNMENT	COST ($)
A3	6
B1	8
C3	7
Total	21

Because two people were assigned the same project (both *A* and *C* are assigned to 3), this solution is infeasible. If it had been feasible, incidentally, it would also be the optimal solution and we would be done. Since it was not, we begin with this *lower bound* and proceed to find the lowest-cost feasible solution.

creating new subproblems

Step 2. We now do our first branching and divide the problem to search for solutions. We can change any one assignment in the current infeasible solution of A3, B1, C3 and create three new problems. Suppose we consecutively assign A, B, and C to project 2 and observe each of the outcomes.

First A is assigned to project 2; the other original assignments of B1 and C3 remain unchanged. This solution is feasible with a cost of $29:

A assigned to project 2

ASSIGNMENT	COST ($)
A2	14
B1	8
C3	7
Total	29

Second, B is assigned to project 2; A's and C's original assignments of A3 and C3 are kept. This solution is *infeasible,* with a cost of $23:

B assigned to project 2

ASSIGNMENT	COST ($)
A3	6
B2	10
C3	7
Total	23

Finally, C is assigned to project 2; the original assignment of A3 and B1 are kept. This solution is also feasible and has a $26 cost:

C assigned to project 2

ASSIGNMENT	COST ($)
A3	6
B1	8
C2	12
Total	26

As we can see in Figure 15.3, the original problem has now been partitioned into three new problems. The *best* solution, which is still infeasible, is now $23; this becomes the *new lower bound* and replaces the previous problem's lower bound of $21. Why is $23 best? Because it's the smallest of the three new costs. Notice that the new lower bound is closer to the feasible region than the previous one. Of the two feasible solutions, the one with the lowest value, $26, is the best one. It is set as an *upper feasible bound.* The optimal solution to this assignment problem must lie between the upper bound of $26 and the lower bound of $23. Solution branch A2 is dropped from further consideration because it is above the upper bound.

We can see at this point that branch and bound method evaluates only a portion of the possible solutions, while not eliminating any possible optimal solutions.

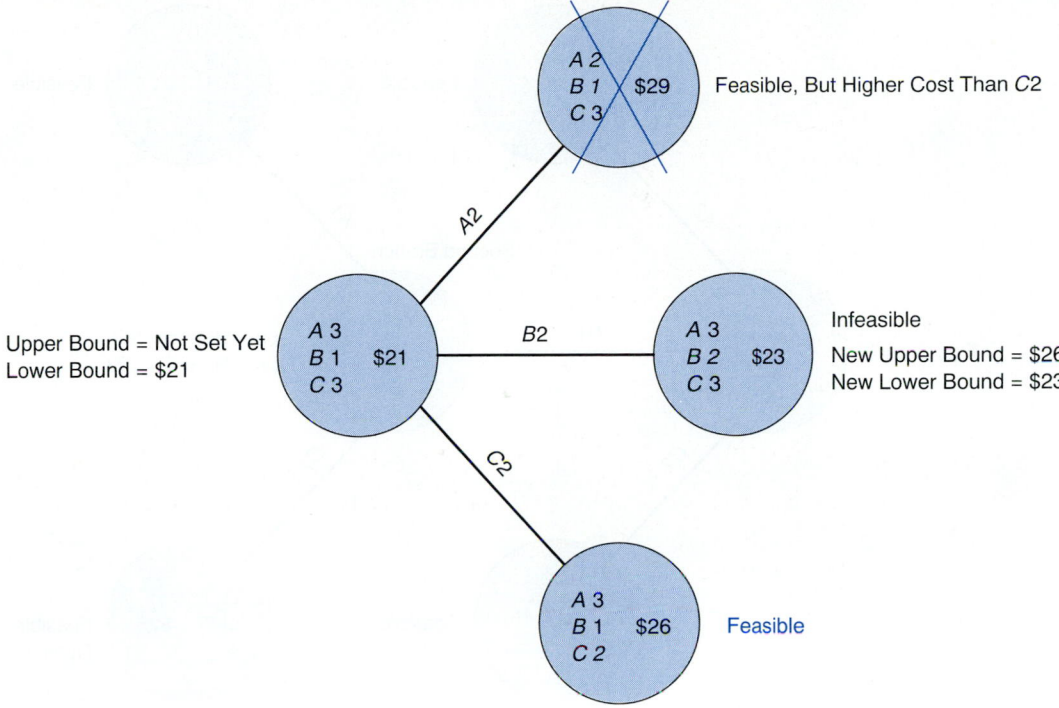

FIGURE 15.3
First Branching: Steps 1 and 2 of Branch and Bound Method

Step 3. In the second branching, we start from *B*2 because this is currently the best solution that is infeasible. Even though the $23 cost of *B*2 is not feasible, other higher-cost solutions on this branch *may* be feasible.

This time there are only *two* possible branches from *A*3, *B*2, and *C*3 because *B*2 is already set and we can only change one assignment. Either *A*3 can become *A*1, or *C*3 can become *C*1. Branches *A*1 and *C*1 are shown in Figure 15.4.

Branch *A*1 is dropped because its cost of assigning *A*1, *B*2, and *C*3 is ($11 + 10 + 7 =) $28, which is greater than the current upper bound of $26. Because both alternatives in step 3 are feasible, and feasible solutions are not partitioned, we see that branch *C*1 provides the optimal solution of $25. The assignment is:

OPTIMAL ASSIGNMENT	COST ($)
A to 3	6
B to 2	10
C to 1	9
Total	25

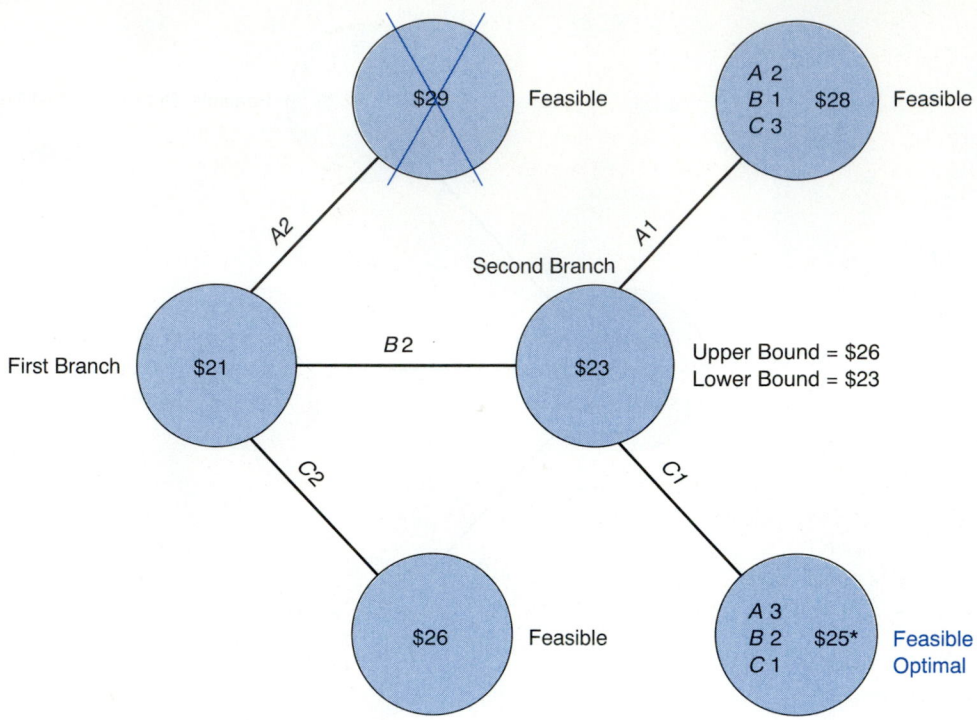

FIGURE 15.4
Second Branching: Steps 1, 2, and 3 of Branch and Bound Method

The branch and bound procedure we followed is very flexible in that we could have looked at the problem from a perspective of column assignment instead of row assignment. This means that we could have selected the smallest number in each column at step 1 and still reached the same answer.

maximization problems   Branch and bound can also be used in maximization problems, of course. We need only rephrase the three steps slightly.

Step 1. Find the maximum possible profit assignment, row by row, disregarding the infeasibility of the assignment. (If the solution is feasible, it means we have found the optimal solution.)

Step 2. Change any one assignment in this newly established infeasible solution. This partitions the problem into a series of new subproblems—three if there are three people or machines, four if there are four people, and so on. The *new upper bound* is the infeasible solution closer to the lower feasible area value than the previous upper bound was. Of the proposed feasible solutions, the one with the highest value is chosen as the best, and labeled the *new lower (feasible) bound.*

Step 3. We continue branching, if necessary, from the current best feasible solution until no further branches are possible.

Solving an Integer Programming Problem with Branch and Bound

Let us now turn to the familiar Harrison Electric Company integer programming problem again, using the branch and bound method to solve it this time. The approach entails six steps when dealing with a maximization problem[2]:

Step 1. Solve the original problem using LP. If the answer satisfies the integer constraints, we are done. If not, this value provides an initial upper bound.

Step 2. Find any feasible solution that meets the integer constraints for use as a lower bound. Usually rounding down each variable will accomplish this.

Step 3. Branch on one variable from step 1 that does not have an integer value. Split the problem into two subproblems based on integer values that are immediately above and below the noninteger value. For example, if $X_2 = 3.75$ was in the final LP solution, introduce the constraint $X_2 \geq 4$ in the first subproblem and $X_2 \leq 3$ in the second subproblem.

Step 4. Create nodes at the top of these new branches by solving the new problems.

Step 5. a. If a branch yields a solution to the LP problem that is *not feasible*, terminate the branch.
b. If a branch yields a solution to the LP problem that is feasible, but not an integer solution, go to step 6.
c. If the branch yields a *feasible integer* solution, examine the value of the objective function. If this value equals the upper bound, an optimal solution has been reached. If it is not equal to the upper bound, but exceeds the lower bound, set it as the new lower bound and go to step 6. Finally, if it is less than the lower bound, terminate this branch.

Step 6. Examine both branches again and set the upper bound equal to the maximum value of the objective function at all final nodes. If the upper bound equals the lower bound, stop. If not, go back to step 3.

Harrison Electric Company Revisited

We recall from earlier in this chapter that the Harrison Electric Company's integer programming formulation was:

Alternate Example 15.2

$$\text{Maximize profit} = \$7X_1 + \$6X_2$$

$$\text{Subject to:} \quad 2X_1 + 3X_2 \leq 12$$

$$6X_1 + 5X_2 \leq 30$$

and both X_1 and X_2 must be nonnegative integers,

[2]Minimization problems involve reversing the roles of the upper and lower bounds.

where

$$X_1 = \text{number of chandeliers produced, and}$$

$$X_2 = \text{number of ceiling fans produced.}$$

Figure 15.1 illustrated graphically that the optimal, noninteger solution is:

$$X_1 = 3.75 \text{ chandeliers}$$

$$X_2 = 1.5 \text{ ceiling fans}$$

$$\text{Profit} = \$35.25$$

Since X_1 and X_2 are not integers, this solution is not valid. The profit value of $35.25 will serve as an initial *upper bound*. We note that rounding down gives $X_1 = 3$, $X_2 = 1$, profit = $27, which is feasible and can be used as a *lower bound*.

subproblems A and B   The problem is now divided into two subproblems, A and B. We can consider branching on either variable that does not have an integer solution; let us pick X_1 this time.

Subproblem A	*Subproblem B*
Maximize profit = $7X_1 + \$6X_2$	Maximize profit = $7X_1 + \$6X_2$
Subject to:	Subject to:
$2X_1 + 3X_2 \leqslant 12$	$2X_1 + 3X_2 \leqslant 12$
$6X_1 + 5X_2 \leqslant 30$	$6X_1 + 5X_2 \leqslant 30$
$X_1 \qquad \geqslant 4$	$X_1 \qquad \leqslant 3$

If you solve both subproblems graphically, you will observe the solutions:

Subproblem A's optimal solution = [$X_1 = 4$, $X_2 = 1.2$, Profit = $35.20]

Subproblem B's optimal solution = [$X_1 = 3$, $X_2 = 2$, Profit = $33.00]

This information is presented in branch form in Figure 15.5. We have completed steps 1–4 of the branch and bound method.

We may stop the search of the subproblem B branch since it has an all-integer feasible solution (see step 5c). The profit value of $33 becomes the new *lower bound*. Subproblem A's branch is searched further since it has a noninteger solution. The second *upper bound* takes on the value $35.20, replacing $35.25 from the first node.

subproblems C and D   Subproblem A is now branched into two new subproblems: C and D. Subproblem C has the additional constraint of $X_2 \geqslant 2$. Subproblem D adds the constraint $X_2 \leqslant 1$. The logic for developing these subproblems is that, since subproblem A's optimal solution of $X_2 = 1.2$ is not feasible, the integer feasible answer must lie either in the region $X_2 \geqslant 2$ or in the region $X_2 \leqslant 1$.

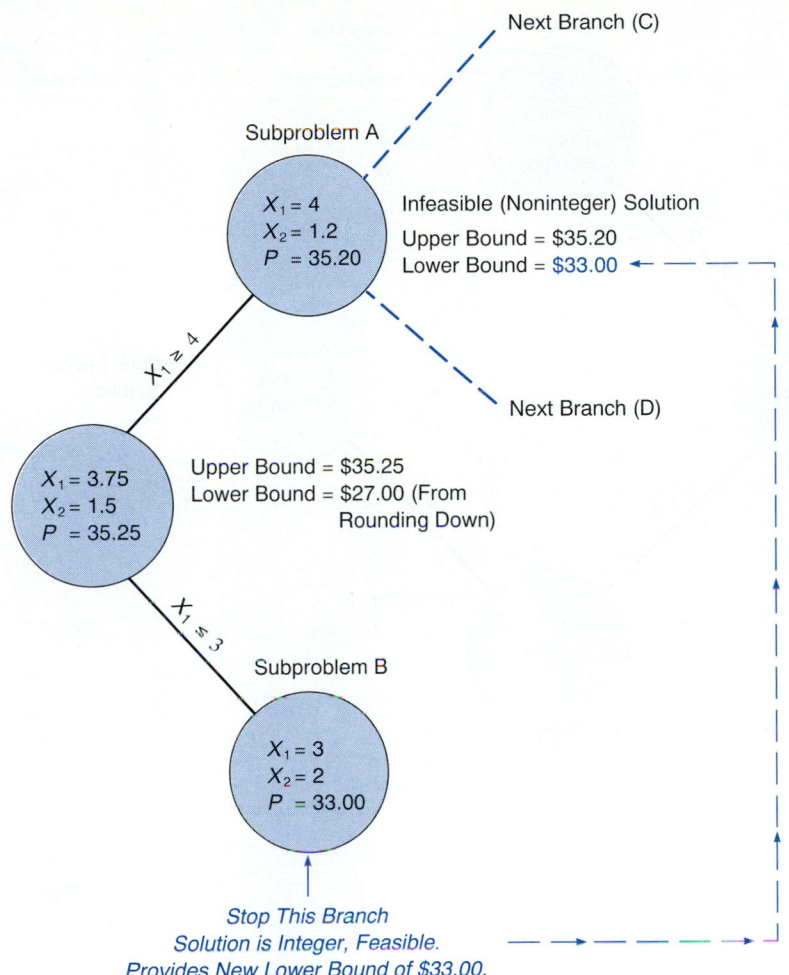

Next Branch (C)

Subproblem A

$X_1 = 4$
$X_2 = 1.2$
$P = 35.20$

Infeasible (Noninteger) Solution
Upper Bound = $35.20
Lower Bound = $33.00

$X_1 \geq 4$

$X_1 = 3.75$
$X_2 = 1.5$
$P = 35.25$

Upper Bound = $35.25
Lower Bound = $27.00 (From
            Rounding Down)

Next Branch (D)

$X_1 \leq 3$

Subproblem B

$X_1 = 3$
$X_2 = 2$
$P = 33.00$

Stop This Branch
Solution is Integer, Feasible.
Provides New Lower Bound of $33.00.

FIGURE 15.5
**Harrison Electric's First Branching: Subproblems *A*
and *B***

Subproblem C	Subproblem D
Maximize profit = $7X_1 + $6X_2$	Maximize profit = $7X_1 + $6X_2$
Subject to:	Subject to:
$2X_1 + 3X_2 \leq 12$	$2X_1 + 3X_2 \leq 12$
$6X_1 + 5X_2 \leq 30$	$6X_1 + 5X_2 \leq 30$
$X_1 \geq 4$	$X_1 \geq 4$
$X_2 \geq 2$	$X_2 \leq 1$

Subproblem C has no feasible solution whatsoever because the first two constraints are violated if the $X_1 \geq 4$ and $X_2 \geq 2$ constraints are observed. We terminate this branch and do not consider its solution.

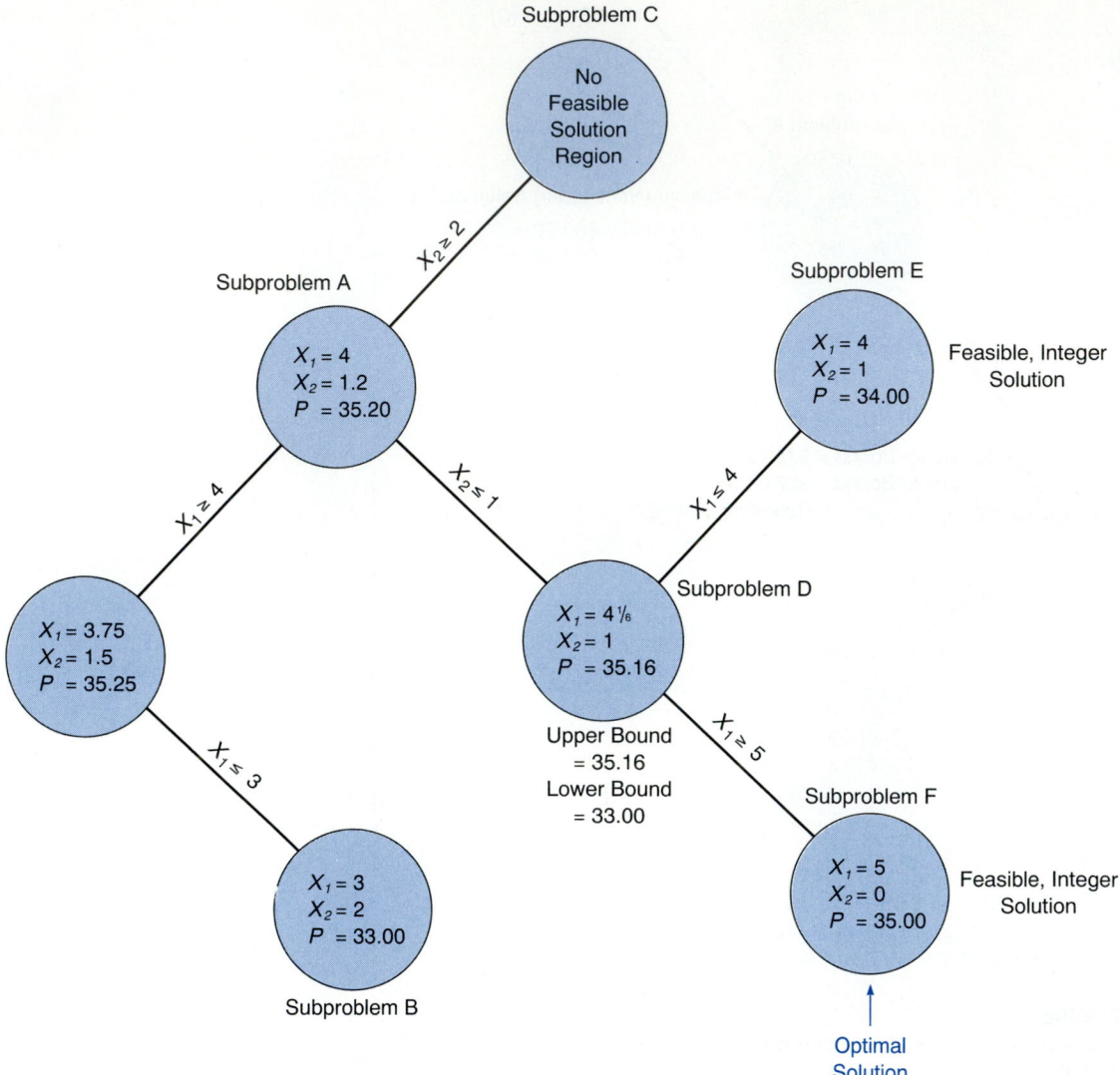

FIGURE 15.6
Harrison Electric's Full Branch and Bound Solution

Subproblem D's optimal solution $= [X_1 = 4\frac{1}{6}, X_2 = 1, \text{Profit} = \$35.16]$. This noninteger solution yields a *new upper bound* of \$35.16, replacing \$35.20. Subproblems C and D, as well as the final branches for the problem, are shown in Figure 15.6.

Finally, we create subproblems E and F and solve for X_1 and X_2 with the added constraints $X_1 \leq 4$ and $X_1 \geq 5$. The subproblems and their solutions are:

Subproblem E	*Subproblem F*

Subproblem E

Maximize profit $= \$7X_1 + \$6X_2$

Subject to:

$$2X_1 + 3X_2 \leqslant 12$$
$$6X_1 + 5X_2 \leqslant 30$$
$$X_1 \geqslant 4$$
$$X_1 \leqslant 4$$
$$X_2 \leqslant 1$$

Optimal solution to E:

$$X_1 = 4, X_2 = 1, \text{Profit} = \$34$$

Subproblem F

Maximize profit $= \$7X_1 + \$6X_2$

Subject to:

$$2X_1 + 3X_2 \leqslant 12$$
$$6X_1 + 5X_2 \leqslant 30$$
$$X_1 \geqslant 4$$
$$X_1 \geqslant 5$$
$$X_2 \leqslant 1$$

Optimal solution to F:

$$X_1 = 5, X_2 = 0, \text{Profit} = \$35$$

The stopping rule for the branching process is that we continue until the new upper bound is less than or equal to the lower bound *or* no further branching is possible. The latter is the case here since both branches yielded feasible integer solutions. The optimal solution is at subproblem F's node: $X_1 = 5$, $X_2 = 0$, Profit $= \$35$. You can, of course, confirm this by looking back to Table 15.1.

The branch and bound method has been computerized and does a good job of solving problems with a small to medium number of integer variables. On especially large problems, the analyst must sometimes settle for a near-optimal answer. Much research has been conducted on this subject and new algorithms that increase the computer's efficiency are constantly under study.

15.4 GOAL PROGRAMMING

In today's business environment, profit maximization or cost minimization are not always the only objectives that a firm sets forth. Often maximizing total profit is just one of several goals, including such contradictory objectives as maximizing market share, maintaining full employment, providing quality ecological management, minimizing noise level in the neighborhood, and meeting numerous other noneconomic goals.

Mathematical programming techniques such as linear and integer programming have the shortcoming that their objective function is measured in one dimension only. It's not possible for linear programming to have *multiple goals* unless they are all measured in the same units (such as dollars), a highly unusual situation. An important technique that has been developed to supplement linear programming is called *goal programming*.

Goal programming is capable of handling decision problems involving multiple goals. A relatively new concept, it began with the work of

Transparency Master 15.6:
Goal Programming (vs. LP).

firms usually have more than one goal

Teaching Suggestion 15.6:
Multiple Goals. See the Instructor's Section for details.

goal programming permits multiple goals

APPLICATIONS OF QA

Branch and Bound Technique for Establishing Insurance Sales Territories

Breaking up any territory or geographical area into distinct sales territories is an important decision for an organization since good sales territory decisions can result in substantial savings. This type of decision can be complex when obstacles such as mountains, rivers, and/or roads must be taken into account.

The Variable Annuity Life Insurance Company (VALIC), located in Houston, faced just this problem. VALIC offers annuity and insurance products to employees of nonprofit organizations and various governmental agencies and organizations. With approximately 346 employees and 16 distinct regions, VALIC had to determine various sales territories.

This problem was tackled by the branch and bound technique, which involves splitting a decision into branches and then binding these decisions or eliminating ones that are not feasible or don't need to be considered further. The problem involved minimizing both variable costs and fixed costs of potential alternatives. As a result of the branch and bound technique, VALIC was able to obtain a cost savings of $8,833,000.

Source: Betsy Gelb and Basheer Khumawala, "Reconfiguration of an Insurance Company's Sales Regions." *Interfaces* **14**, 6 (November–December 1984)

Charnes and Cooper in 1961 and has been refined and extended by Lee in the 1970s (see Bibliography).

In typical decision-making situations, the goals set by management can be achieved only at the expense of other goals. It is necessary to establish a hierarchy of importance among these goals so that lower-priority goals are tackled only after higher-priority ones are satisfied. Since it is not always possible to achieve every goal to the extent the decision maker desires, goal programming attempts to reach a satisfactory level of multiple objectives. This, of course, differs from linear programming which tries to find the best possible outcome for a *single* objective. Nobel laureate Herbert A. Simon, of Carnegie-Mellon University, states that modern managers may not be able to optimize, but may instead have to "*satisfice*" or "come as close as possible" to reaching goals. This is the case with models such as goal programming.

How, specifically, does goal programming differ from linear programming? The objective function is the main difference. Instead of trying to maximize or minimize the objective function directly, with goal programming we try to minimize *deviations* between set goals and what we can actually achieve within the given constraints. In the LP simplex approach, such deviations are called *slack variables* and they are used only as dummy variables. In goal programming, these slack terms are either positive or negative, and not only are they real variables, but they are also the only terms in the objective function. The objective is to minimize these *deviational variables.*

Once the goal programming model is formulated, the computational algorithm is almost the same as a minimization problem solved by the simplex method.

goal programming "satisfices"

KEY IDEA

deviational variables

An Example of Goal Programming: Harrison Electric Revisited

Applicable Problems 15-23, 15-25, 15-27, 15-30, Schank case

To illustrate the formulation of a goal programming problem, let's look back at the Harrison Electric Company case presented earlier in this chapter as an integer programming problem. That problem's LP formulation, you recall, was:

$$\text{Maximize profit} = \$7X_1 + \$6X_2$$

$$\text{Subject to:} \quad 2X_1 + 3X_2 \leq 12 \quad \text{(wiring hours)}$$

$$6X_1 + 5X_2 \leq 30 \quad \text{(assembly hours)}$$

$$X_1, X_2 \geq 0$$

where

$$X_1 = \text{number of chandeliers produced, and}$$

$$X_2 = \text{number of ceiling fans produced.}$$

We saw that if Harrison's management had a single goal, say profit, linear programming could be used to find the optimal solution. But let's assume that the firm is moving to a new location during a particular production period and feels that maximizing profit is not a realistic goal. Management sets a profit level, which would be satisfactory during the adjustment period, of $30. We now have a goal programming problem in which we want to find the production mix that achieves this goal as closely as possible, given the production time constraints. This simple case will provide a good starting point for tackling more complicated goal programs.

We first define two deviational variables:

$$d_1^- = \text{the underachievement of the profit target}$$

$$d_1^+ = \text{the overachievement of the profit target}$$

Teaching Suggestion 15.7: Deviational Variables Are the Key in Goal Programming. See the Instructor's Section for details.

Now we can state the Harrison Electric problem as a *single-goal* programming model.

$$\text{Minimize under- or overachievement of profit target} = d_1^- + d_1^+$$

$$\text{Subject to:} \ \$7X_1 + \$6X_2 + d_1^- - d_1^+ = \$30 \quad \text{(profit goal constraint)}$$

$$2X_1 + 3X_2 \leq 12 \quad \text{(wiring hours constraint)}$$

$$6X_1 + 5X_2 \leq 30 \quad \text{(assembly hours constraint)}$$

$$X_1, X_2, d_1^-, d_1^+ \geq 0$$

Note that the first constraint states that the profit made, $7X_1 + $6X_2$, plus any underachievement of profit minus any overachievement of profit has to equal the target of $30. For example, if $X_1 = 3$ chandeliers and $X_2 = 2$ ceiling fans, then $33 profit has been made. This exceeds $30 by $3, so d_1^+ must be equal to 3. Since the profit goal constraint was *overachieved*,

deviational variables are 0 if goal completely obtained

Harrison did not underachieve and d_1^- will clearly be equal to 0. This problem is now ready for solution by a goal programming algorithm.

If the target profit of \$30 is exactly achieved, we see that both d_1^+ and d_1^- are equal to 0. The objective function will also be minimized at 0. If Harrison's management was only concerned with *underachievement* of the target goal, how would the objective function change? It would be: minimize underachievement $= d_1^-$. This is also a reasonable goal since the firm would probably not be upset with an overachievement of its target.

In general, once all goals and constraints are identified in a problem, management should analyze each goal to see if underachievement or overachievement of that goal is an acceptable situation. If overachievement is acceptable, the appropriate d^+ variable can be eliminated from the objective function. If underachievement is okay, the d^- variable should be dropped. If management seeks to attain a goal exactly, both d^- and d^+ must appear in the objective function.

An Extension to Equally Important Multiple Goals

Let's now look at the situation in which Harrison's management wants to achieve several goals, each equal in priority.

Goal 1. To produce as much profit above \$30 as possible during the production period.

Goal 2. To fully utilize the available wiring department hours.

Goal 3. To avoid overtime in the assembly department.

Goal 4. To meet a contract requirement to produce at least seven ceiling fans.

The deviational variables can be defined as follows:

definition of deviational variables

$d_1^- =$ underachievement of the profit target

$d_1^+ =$ overachievement of the profit target

$d_2^- =$ idle time in the wiring department (underutilization)

$d_2^+ =$ overtime in the wiring department (overutilization)

$d_3^- =$ idle time in the assembly department (underutilization)

Alternate Example 15.3

$d_3^+ =$ overtime in the assembly department (overutilization)

$d_4^- =$ underachievement of the ceiling fan goal

$d_4^+ =$ overachievement of the ceiling fan goal

Management is unconcerned about whether there is overachievement of the profit goal, overtime in the wiring department, idle time in the assembly department, or whether more than seven ceiling fans are produced: hence, d_1^+, d_2^+, d_3^-, and d_4^+ may be omitted from the objective function. The new objective function and constraints are:

$$\text{Minimize total deviation} = d_1^- + d_2^- + d_3^+ + d_4^-$$

Subject to: $\quad 7X_1 + 6X_2 + d_1^- - d_1^+ = 30 \quad$ (*profit constraint*)

$$2X_1 + 3X_2 + d_2^- - d_2^+ = 12 \quad \text{(\textit{wiring hours constraint})}$$

$$6X_1 + 5X_2 + d_3^- - d_3^+ = 30 \quad \text{(\textit{assembly constraint})}$$

$$X_2 + d_4^- - d_4^+ = 7 \quad \text{(\textit{ceiling fan constraint})}$$

All X_i, d_i variables ≥ 0.

Ranking Goals

In most goal programming problems, one goal will be more important than another, which in turn will be more important than a third. The idea is that goals can be ranked with respect to their importance in management's eyes. Lower-order goals are considered only after higher-order goals are met. Priorities (P_i's) are assigned to each deviational variable— with the ranking that P_1 is the most important goal, P_2 the next most important, then P_3 and so on.

assigning priorities

Let's say Harrison Electric sets the priorities shown in the accompanying table.

GOAL	PRIORITY
Reach a profit as much above $30 as possible	P_1
Fully use wiring department hours available	P_2
Avoid assembly department overtime	P_3
Produce at least seven ceiling fans	P_4

This means, in effect, that the priority of meeting the profit goal (P_1) is infinitely more important than the wiring goal (P_2), which is, in turn, infinitely more important than the assembly goal (P_3), which is infinitely more important than producing at least seven ceiling fans (P_4).

With ranking of goals considered, the new objective function becomes:

$$\text{Minimize total deviation} = P_1d_1^- + P_2d_2^- + P_3d_3^+ + P_4d_4^-$$

The constraints remain identical to the previous ones.

Solving Goal Programming Problems Graphically

Applicable Problems 15-24, 15-26

Just as we solved linear programming problems graphically in Chapter 10, we can analyze goal programming problems graphically. First, we must be aware of three characteristics of goal programming problems: (1) goal programming models are all minimization problems; (2) there is no single objective, but multiple goals to be attained; and (3) the deviation from a high-priority goal must be minimized to the greatest extent possible before the next-highest-priority goal is considered.

Alternate Example 15.3

Let us use the Harrison Electric Company goal programming problem as an example. The model was formulated as:

$$\text{Minimize total deviation} = P_1 d_1^- + P_2 d_2^- + P_3 d_3^+ + P_4 d_4^-$$

$$\text{Subject to: } 7X_1 + 6X_2 + d_1^- - d_1^+ = 30 \quad \textit{(profit)}$$

$$2X_1 + 3X_2 + d_2^- - d_2^+ = 12 \quad \textit{(wiring)}$$

$$6X_1 + 5X_2 + d_3^- - d_3^+ = 30 \quad \textit{(assembly)}$$

$$X_2 + d_4^- - d_4^+ = 7 \quad \textit{(ceiling fans)}$$

$$X_1, X_2, d_i^-, d_i^+ \geq 0 \quad \textit{(nonnegativity)}$$

where

$$X_1 = \text{number of chandeliers produced, and}$$

$$X_2 = \text{number of ceiling fans produced.}$$

To solve this problem, we graph one constraint at a time, starting with the one that has the highest-priority deviational variables. This is the profit constraint, since d_1^- has priority P_1 in the objective function. Figure 15.7

graphical constraints

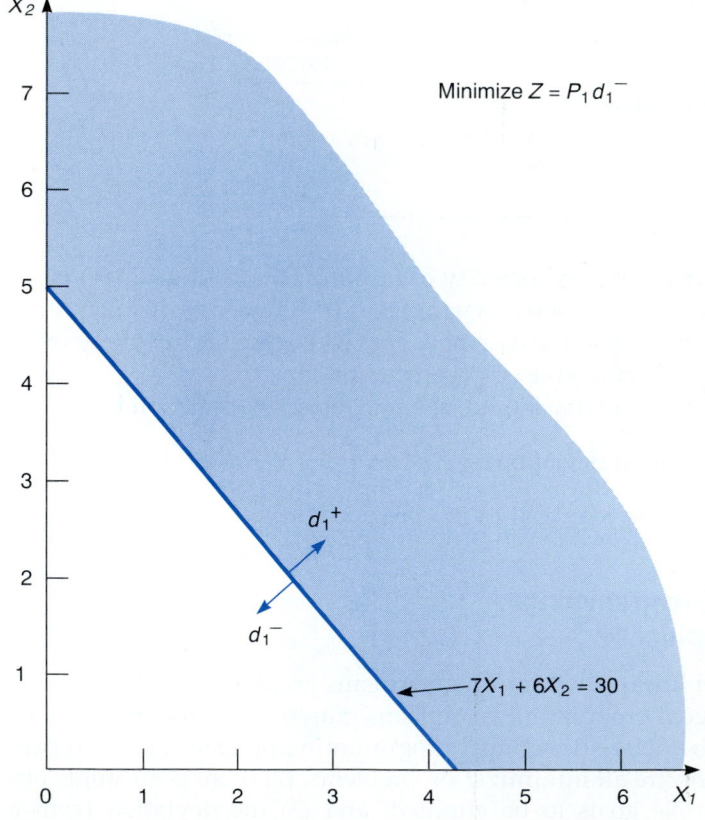

FIGURE 15.7
Analysis of First Goal

shows the profit constraint line. Note that in graphing the line, the deviational variables d_1^- and d_1^+ are ignored. To minimize d_1^- (the underachievement of \$30 profit), the feasible area is the shaded region. Any point in the shaded region satisfies the first goal because profit exceeds \$30.

Figure 15.8 includes the second priority goal of minimizing d_2^-. The region below the constraint line $2X_1 + 3X_2 = 12$ represents the values for d_2^-, while the region above the line stands for d_2^+. To avoid underutilizing wiring department hours, the area below the line is eliminated. But this goal must be attained within the feasible area already defined by satisfying the first goal.

The third goal is to avoid overtime in the assembly department, which means we want d_3^+ to be as close to 0 as possible. As we can see in Figure 15.9, this goal can also be fully attained. The area that contains solution points that will satisfy the first three priority goals is bounded by the points A, B, C, D. Inside this narrow strip, any solution will meet the three most critical goals.

The fourth goal is to produce at least seven ceiling fans, and hence to minimize d_4^-. To achieve this final goal, the area below the constraint line $X_2 = 7$ must be eliminated. But we cannot do this without violating one of

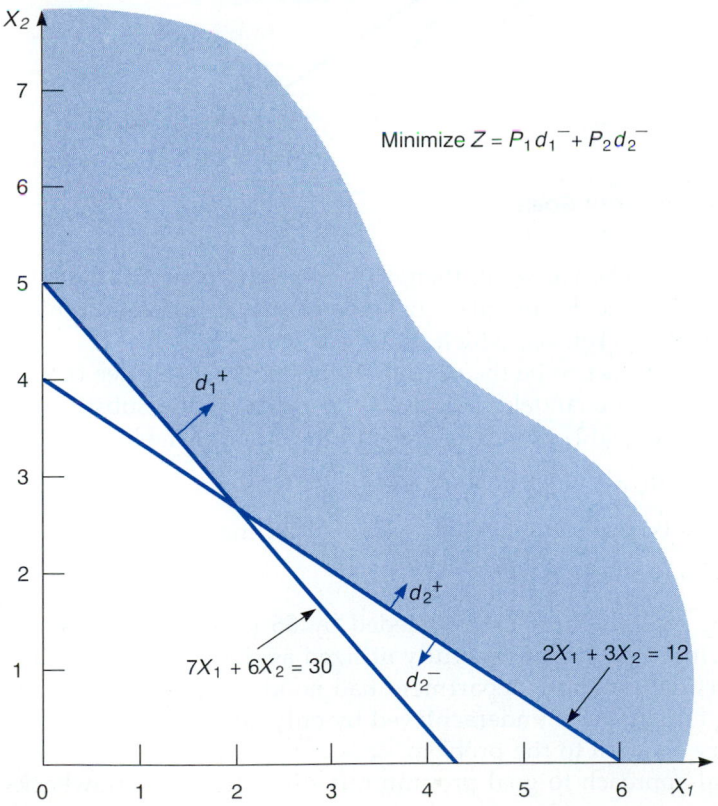

FIGURE 15.8
Analysis of First and Second Goals

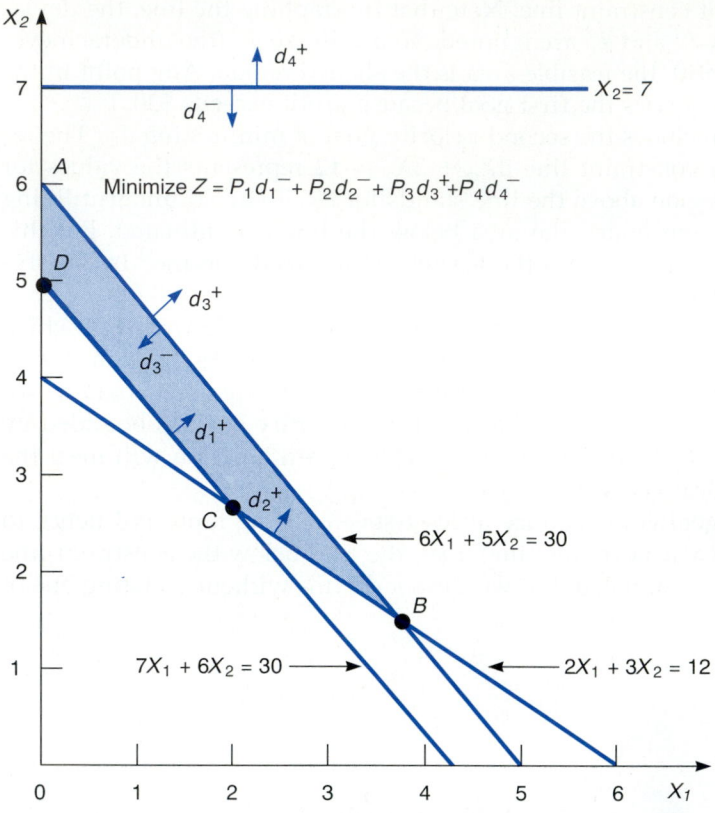

FIGURE 15.9
Analysis of All Four Priority Goals

the higher-priority goals. We want, then, to find a solution point that still satisfies the first three goals, and also comes as close as possible to achieving the fourth goal. Do you see which point this would be?

solution   Corner point A appears to be the optimal solution. We easily see that its coordinates are $X_1 = 0$ chandeliers and $X_2 = 6$ ceiling fans. Substituting these values into the goal constraints, we find the other variables are:

$$d_1^- = \$0, \; d_1^+ = \$6, \; d_2^- = 0 \text{ hours}, \; d_2^+ = 6 \text{ hours},$$

$$d_3^- = 0 \text{ hours}, \; d_3^+ = 0 \text{ hours}, \; d_4^- = 1 \text{ ceiling fan},$$

$$d_4^+ = 0 \text{ ceiling fans}$$

Thus, the profit goal was met and exceeded by $6 (a $36 profit was attained), the wiring department was fully utilized as six hours of overtime were used there, the assembly department had no idle time (or overtime), and the ceiling fan goal was underachieved by only one fan. This was the most satisfactory solution to the problem.

The graphical approach to goal programming has the same drawbacks as it did to linear programming, namely, it can only handle problems with two real variables. By modifying the simplex method of LP, a more general solution to goal programming problems can be found.

A Modified Simplex Method for Goal Programming

**Applicable Problems
15-28, 15-29**

To demonstrate how the modified simplex method can be used to solve a goal programming problem, we again turn to the Harrison Electric Company example.

Alternate Example 15.4

$$\text{Minimize} = P_1 d_1^- + P_2 d_2^- + P_3 d_3^+ + P_4 d_4^-$$

$$\text{Subject to:} \quad 7X_1 + 6X_2 + d_1^- - d_1^+ = 30$$

$$2X_1 + 3X_2 + d_2^- - d_2^+ = 12$$

$$6X_1 + 5X_2 + d_3^- - d_3^+ = 30$$

$$X_2 + d_4^- - d_4^+ = 7$$

$$X_1, X_2, d_i^-, d_i^+ \geq 0$$

Table 15.4 presents the initial simplex tableau for this problem. We should point out four features of this tableau that differ from the simplex tableaus we saw in Chapter 12:

1. The variables in the problem are listed at the top, with the decision variables (X_1 and X_2) first, then the negative deviational variables, and finally the positive deviational variables. The priority level of each variable is assigned on the very top row.

differences between LP simplex tableau and GP tableau

2. The negative deviational variables for each constraint provide the initial basic feasible solution. This is analogous to the LP simplex tableau

TABLE 15.4 Initial Goal Programming Tableau

$C_j \rightarrow$ ↓	SOLUTION MIX	0 X_1	0 X_2	P_1 d_1^-	P_2 d_2^-	0 d_3^-	P_4 d_4^-	0 d_1^+	0 d_2^+	P_3 d_3^+	0 d_4^+	QUANTITY
P_1	d_1^-	7	6	1	0	0	0	−1	0	0	0	30
P_2	d_2^-	2	3	0	1	0	0	0	−1	0	0	12
0	d_3^-	6	5	0	0	1	0	0	0	−1	0	30
P_4	d_4^-	0	1	0	0	0	1	0	0	0	−1	7
P_4 {	Z_j	0	1	0	0	0	1	0	0	0	−1	7
	$C_j - Z_j$	0	−1	0	0	0	0	0	0	0	+1	
P_3 {	Z_j	0	0	0	0	0	0	0	0	0	0	0
	$C_j - Z_j$	0	0	0	0	0	0	0	0	1	0	
P_2 {	Z_j	2	3	0	1	0	0	0	−1	0	0	12
	$C_j - Z_j$	−2	−3	0	0	0	0	0	1	0	0	
P_1 {	Z_j	7	6	1	0	0	0	−1	0	0	0	30
	$C_j - Z_j$	−7	−6	0	0	0	0	1	0	0	0	

↑
Pivot column

Transparency Master 15.10:
The Initial Goal Programming Tableau.

Teaching Suggestion 15.9:
Using the Goal Programming Simplex Method. See the Instructor's Section for details.

in which slack variables provide the initial solution. (Thus, we see that $d_1^- = 30$, $d_2^- = 12$, $d_3^- = 30$, and $d_4^- = 7$.) The priority level of each variable in the current solution mix is entered in the C_j column on the far left. Note that the coefficients in the body of the tableau are set up exactly as they were in the regular simplex approach.

3. There is a separate Z_j and $C_j - Z_j$ row for each of the P_i priorities. Since profit goals, department hour goals, and production goals are each measured in different units, the four separate priority rows are needed. In goal programming, the bottom row of the simplex tableau contains the highest ranked (P_1) goal, the next row up has the P_2 goal, and so on. The rows are computed exactly as in the regular simplex method, but they are done for each priority level. In Table 15.4, the $C_j - Z_j$ value for column X_1, for example, is read as $-7P_1 - 2P_2 + 0P_3 + 0P_4$.

4. In selecting the variable to enter the solution mix, we start with the highest-priority row, P_1, and select the most negative $C_j - Z_j$ value in it. (The pivot column is X_1 in Table 15.4.) If there was no negative number in the $C_j - Z_j$ row for P_1, we would move up to priority P_2's $C_j - Z_j$ row and select the largest negative number there. A negative $C_j - Z_j$ that has a positive number in a P row underneath it, however, is ignored. This means that deviations from a more important goal (one in a lower row) would be *increased* if that variable were brought into the solution.

After we set up the initial modified simplex tableau, we move toward the optimal solution just as with the regular minimization simplex procedures described in detail in Chapter 12. Keeping in mind the four features just listed, the next step in moving from Table 15.4 to Table 15.5 is to find the pivot row. We do this by dividing the quantity values by their corresponding pivot column (X_1) values and picking the one with the smallest positive ratio. Thus d_1^- leaves the basis in the second tableau and is replaced by X_1.

The new rows of the tableau are computed exactly as they are in the regular simplex method. You may recall that this means first computing a new pivot row, then using the formula in Section 3 of Chapter 12 to find the other new rows.

We see in the new $C_j - Z_j$ row for priority P_1, in Table 15.5, that there are no negative values. Thus, the first priority's goal has been reached. Priority 2 is the next objective, and we find two negative entries in its $C_j - Z_j$ row. Again, the largest one is selected as the pivot column and X_2 will become the next variable to enter the solution mix.

Let us skip two tableaus and go directly to Table 15.6, which contains the most satisfactory solution to the problem. (One of the homework problems gives you the chance to work through to this final tableau.)

Notice in the final solution that the first, second, and third goals have been totally achieved: there are no negative $C_j - Z_j$ entries in their rows. A negative value appears (in the d_3^+ column) in the priority 4 row, however, indicating that it has not been fully attained. Indeed, d_4^- is equal to 1,

TABLE 15.5 Second Goal Programming Tableau

$C_j \rightarrow$ ↓ SOLUTION MIX	0 X_1	0 X_2	P_1 d_1^-	P_2 d_2^-	0 d_3^-	P_4 d_4^-	0 d_1^+	0 d_2^+	P_3 d_3^+	0 d_4^+	QUANTITY
0 X_1	1	6/7	1/7	0	0	0	−1/7	0	0	0	30/7
P_2 d_2^-	0	9/7	−2/7	1	0	0	2/7	−1	0	0	24/7
0 d_3^-	0	−1/7	−6/7	0	1	0	6/7	0	−1	0	30/7
P_4 d_4^-	0	1	0	0	0	1	0	0	0	−1	7
P_4 Z_j	0	1	0	0	0	1	0	0	0	−1	7
P_4 $C_j - Z_j$	0	−1	0	0	0	0	0	0	0	+1	
P_3 Z_j	0	0	0	0	0	0	0	0	0	0	0
P_3 $C_j - Z_j$	0	0	0	0	0	0	0	0	1	0	
P_2 Z_j	0	9/7	−2/7	1	0	0	2/7	−1	0	0	24/7
P_2 $C_j - Z_j$	0	−9/7	+2/7	0	0	0	−2/7	+1	0	0	
P_1 Z_j	0	0	0	0	0	0	0	0	0	0	0
P_1 $C_j - Z_j$	0	0	1	0	0	0	1	0	0	0	

↑ Pivot column

Transparency Master 15.11: The Second Goal Programming Tableau.

meaning we have underachieved the ceiling fan goal by one fan. But there is a positive number (see the shaded "1") in the d_3^+ column at the P_3 priority level, and thus at a higher-priority level. If we try to force d_3^+ into the solution mix to attain the P_4 goal, it will be at the expense of a more important

TABLE 15.6 Final Solution to Harrison Electrical's Goal Program

$C_j \rightarrow$ ↓ SOLUTION MIX	0 X_1	0 X_2	P_1 d_1^-	P_2 d_2^-	0 d_3^-	P_4 d_4^-	0 d_1^+	0 d_2^+	P_3 d_3^+	0 d_4^+	QUANTITY
0 d_2^+	8/5	0	0	−1	3/5	0	0	1	−3/5	0	6
0 X_2	6/5	1	0	0	1/5	0	0	0	−1/5	0	6
0 d_1^+	1/5	0	−1	0	6/5	0	1	0	−6/5	0	6
P_4 d_4^-	−6/5	0	0	0	−1/5	1	0	0	1/5	−1	1
P_4 Z_j	−6/5	0	0	0	−1/5	1	0	0	1/5	−1	1
P_4 $C_j - Z_j$	6/5	0	0	0	1/5	0	0	0	−1/5	+1	
P_3 Z_j	0	0	0	0	0	0	0	0	0	0	0
P_3 $C_j - Z_j$	0	0	0	0	0	0	0	0	**1**	0	
P_2 Z_j	0	0	0	0	0	0	0	0	0	0	0
P_2 $C_j - Z_j$	0	0	0	1	0	0	0	0	0	0	
P_1 Z_j	0	0	0	0	0	0	0	0	0	0	0
P_1 $C_j - Z_j$	0	0	1	0	0	0	0	0	0	0	

Transparency Master 15.12: The Final Solution to Harrison Electrical's Goal Program.

goal (P_3) which has already been satisfied. We do not want to sacrifice the P_3 goal, so this will be the best possible goal programming solution. The answer is:

$$X_1 = 0 \text{ chandeliers produced}$$

$$X_2 = 6 \text{ ceiling fans produced}$$

$$d_1^+ = \$6 \text{ over the profit goal}$$

$$d_2^+ = 6 \text{ wiring hours over the minimum set}$$

$$d_4^- = 1 \text{ fan less than desired}$$

Our microcomputer software program, AB:QM, has a goal programming module which is illustrated in Program 15.4. The input screen appears first, followed by the final tableau, which is identical in content to Table 15.6. Program 15.4 also provides analyses of deviations and goal achievement and has a final section on goal conflicts. Note again that, in the analysis of deviations section, the first two constraints have deviational variables equal to +6 and the fourth constraint has a negative deviation of 1.

15.5   NONLINEAR PROGRAMMING

Applicable Problem 15-31

Linear, integer, and goal programming all assume that a problem's objective function and constraints are linear. That means that they contain no nonlinear terms such as X_1^3, $1/X_2$, $\log X_3$, or $5X_1X_2$. Yet in many mathematical programming problems, the objective function and/or one or more of the constraints are nonlinear.

A Nonlinear Objective Function

nonlinear objective function

The Great Western Appliance Company sells two models of toaster ovens, the Microtoaster (X_1) and the Self-Clean Toaster Oven (X_2). The firm earns a profit of $28 for each Microtoaster regardless of the number sold. Profits for the Self-Clean model, however, increase as more units are sold because of fixed overhead. Profit on this model may be expressed as $21X_2 + .25X_2^2$.

Hence, the firm's objective function is nonlinear:

$$\text{Maximum profit} = 28X_1 + 21X_2 + .25X_2^2$$

Great Western's profit is subject to two linear constraints on production capacity and sales time available.

$$X_1 + X_2 \leq 1{,}000 \quad \textit{(units of production capacity)}$$

$$.5X_1 + .4X_2 \leq 500 \quad \textit{(hours of sales time available)}$$

$$X_1, X_2 \geq 0$$

When an objective function contains squared terms (such as $.25X_2^2$) and the problem's constraints are linear, it is called a *quadratic programming* problem. A number of useful problems in the field of portfolio selection fall into this category. Quadratic programs can be solved by a modified method of the simplex method. Such work is outside the scope of this text but can be found in sources listed in the Bibliography.

quadratic programming

PROGRAM 15.4 Harrison Electric's Goal Programming Analysis Using AB:QM

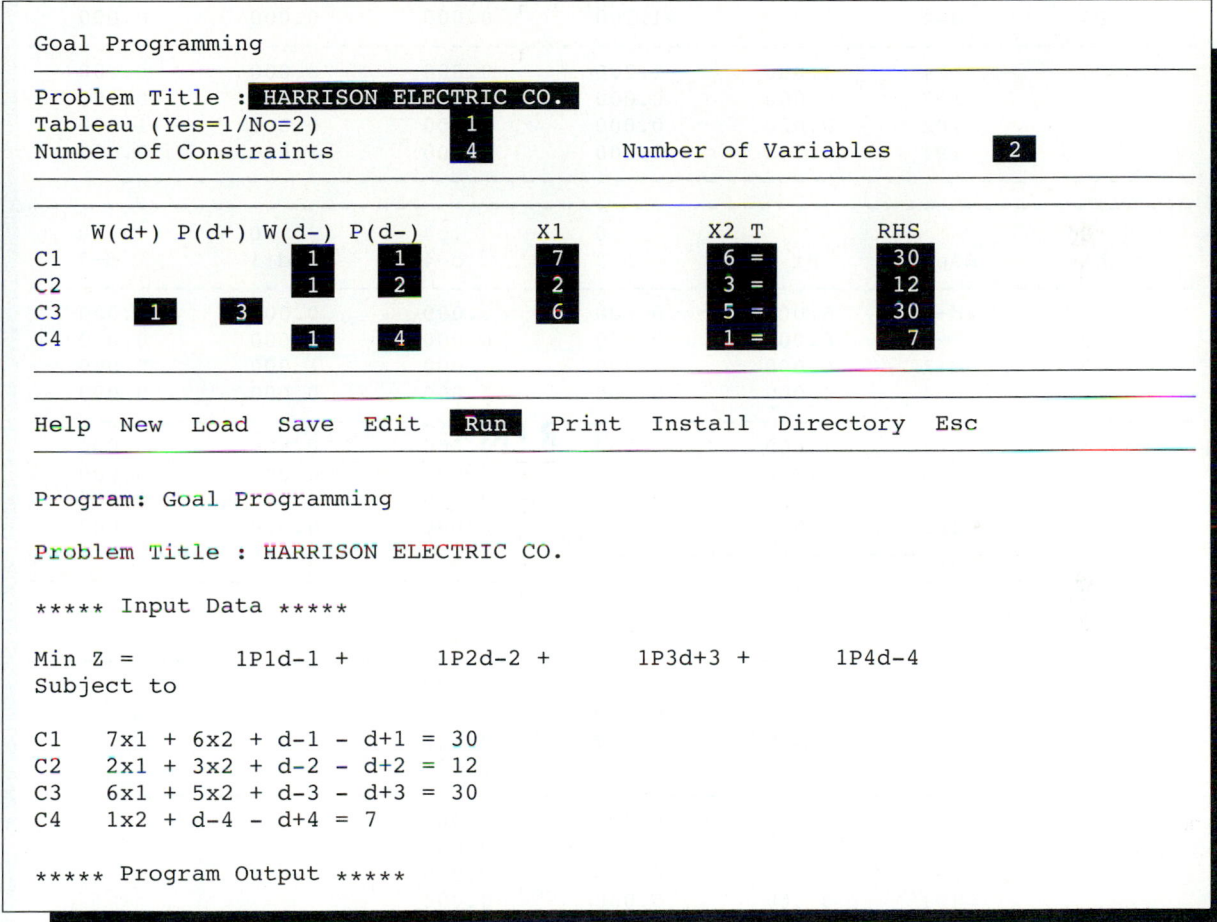

```
Goal Programming
_____
Problem Title : HARRISON ELECTRIC CO.
Tableau (Yes=1/No=2)          1
Number of Constraints         4        Number of Variables        2
_____

     W(d+) P(d+) W(d-) P(d-)        X1          X2 T          RHS
C1                 1     1          7           6 =           30
C2                 1     2          2           3 =           12
C3     1     3                      6           5 =           30
C4                 1     4                      1 =            7
_____

Help  New  Load  Save  Edit   Run   Print  Install  Directory  Esc
_____

Program: Goal Programming

Problem Title : HARRISON ELECTRIC CO.

***** Input Data *****

Min Z =        1P1d-1 +       1P2d-2 +      1P3d+3 +      1P4d-4
Subject to

C1    7x1 + 6x2 + d-1 - d+1 = 30
C2    2x1 + 3x2 + d-2 - d+2 = 12
C3    6x1 + 5x2 + d-3 - d+3 = 30
C4    1x2 + d-4 - d+4 = 7

***** Program Output *****
```

(Continued)

PROGRAM 15.4 Harrison Electric's Goal Programming Analysis Using AB:QM (Continued)

```
Final Solution Tableau at Iteration   4
------------------------------------------------------------------------
     \Cj                            0         0        1P1       1P2
     Cb\       Basis     Bi         x1        x2       d-1       d-2
------------------------------------------------------------------------
      0        d+2      6.000      1.600     0.000     0.000    -1.000
      0        x2       6.000      1.200     1.000     0.000     0.000
      0        d+1      6.000      0.200     0.000    -1.000     0.000
     1P4       d-4      1.000     -1.200     0.000     0.000     0.000
------------------------------------------------------------------------
    Zj-Cj      1P4      1.000     -1.200     0.000     0.000     0.000
               1P3      0.000      0.000     0.000     0.000     0.000
               1P2      0.000      0.000     0.000     0.000    -1.000
               1P1      0.000      0.000     0.000    -1.000     0.000
------------------------------------------------------------------------
------------------------------------------------------------------------
     \Cj                            0        1p4        0         0
     Cb\       Basis     Bi         d-3       d-4       d+1       d+2
------------------------------------------------------------------------
      0        d+2      6.000      0.600     0.000     0.000     1.000
      0        x2       6.000      0.200     0.000     0.000     0.000
      0        d+1      6.000      1.200     0.000     1.000     0.000
     1P4       d-4      1.000     -0.200     1.000     0.000     0.000
------------------------------------------------------------------------
    Zj-Cj      1P4      1.000     -0.200     0.000     0.000     0.000
               1P3      0.000      0.000     0.000     0.000     0.000
               1P2      0.000      0.000     0.000     0.000     0.000
               1P1      0.000      0.000     0.000     0.000     0.000
------------------------------------------------------------------------
------------------------------------------------------------------------
     \Cj                           1P3        0
     Cb\       Basis     Bi         d+3       d+4
------------------------------------------------------------------------
      0        d+2      6.000     -0.600     0.000
      0        x2       6.000     -0.200     0.000
      0        d+1      6.000     -1.200     0.000
     1P4       d-4      1.000      0.200    -1.000
------------------------------------------------------------------------
    Zj-Cj      1P4      1.000      0.200    -1.000
               1P3      0.000     -1.000     0.000
               1P2      0.000      0.000     0.000
               1P1      0.000      0.000     0.000
------------------------------------------------------------------------
Analysis of deviations
-------------------------------------------------
Constraint RHS Value    d+        d-
-------------------------------------------------
    C1        30.000    6.000     0.000
    C2        12.000    6.000     0.000
    C3        30.000    0.000     0.000
    C4         7.000    0.000     1.000
-------------------------------------------------
```

(Continued)

PROGRAM 15.4 Harrison Electric's Goal Programming Analysis Using AB:QM (Continued)

```
Analysis of decision variables
----------------------------
Variable        Solution value
----------------------------
   X1                   0.000
   X2                   6.000
----------------------------

Analysis of the objective function
----------------------------------
Priority             Nonachievement
----------------------------------
   P1                     0.000
   P2                     0.000
   P3                     0.000
   P4                     1.000
----------------------------------

Analysis of Goal Conflicts
-------------------------------------------------------------------------
                                                              Marginal
Goal            Relevant      Relevant     Allowable    Allowable   Substitution
Conflict        Variable      Column       Increase     Decrease      Rate
-------------------------------------------------------------------------
Priority4        (d-4)                        1.00                     0.20
Priority3        (d+3)        (d+3)                       5.00         1.00
-------------------------------------------------------------------------

***** End of Output *****
```

Other Nonlinear Problems

Two more types of *nonlinear programming* problems are possible. Case 1 is a situation with nonlinear constraints, but a linear objective function, and case 2 has both a nonlinear objective and constraints.

Case 1.   Minimize cost $= 5X_1 + 7X_2$ **nonlinear constraints**

Subject to: $3X_1 + .25X_1^2 + 4X_2 + .3X_2^2 \geq 125$

$13X_1 + X_1^3 \geq 80$

$.7X_1 + X_2 \geq 17$

Case 2.   Maximize revenue $= 13X_1 + 6X_1X_2 + 5X_2 + 1/X_2$ **objective and constraints both nonlinear**

Subject to: $2X_1^2 + 4X_2 \leq 90$

$X_1 + X_2^3 \leq 75$

$8X_1 - 2X_2 \leq 61$

APPLICATIONS OF QA

A Goal Programming Model for Prison Expenditures in Virginia

This study demonstrates the applicability of goal programming to the capital allocation problem faced by the department of corrections of Virginia. As is the case in most states, correctional institutions are overcrowded and there is need for immediate expansion of prison capacity and replacement or renovation of obsolete facilities.

The expenditure items considered by the Virginia corrections department include new and renovated maximum, medium, and minimum security facilities; community diversion programs; and personnel increases. The integer goal programming technique forces all prison projects to be completely accepted or rejected. Personnel increases are considered in integer increments only.

The goal programming model encompasses two types of model variables. The variables define the construction, renovation, or establishment of a particular type of correctional facility for a specific location or purpose. The variables also indicate the number of personnel required by the facilities and programs determined in the model. The goal constraints in this model fall into five categories: additional inmate capacity created by new and renovated correctional facilities;

operating and personnel costs associated with each expenditure item; the impact of facility construction and renovation on imprisonment, sentence length, and early releases and parole; the mix of different facility types required by the system; and the personnel requirements resulting from the various capital expenditures for correctional facilities.

For Virginia, the solution results are as follows: one new maximum security facility for drug, alcohol, and psychiatric treatment activities; one new minimum security facility for youthful offenders; two new regular minimum security facilities; one new community diversion program in urban area 1; one new community diversion program in urban area 2; one renovation of an existing medium security facility; one renovation of an existing minimum security facility; 250 new correctional officers; four new administrators; 46 new treatment specialist/counselors; and six new medical personnel.

Source: R. Russell, B. Taylor III, and A. Keown, *Computer Environmental Urban Systems,* Vol. 11, No. 4, 1986, pp. 135–146.

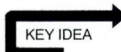

gradient method

separable programming

Unlike linear programming methods, computational procedures to solve many nonlinear problems do not always yield an optimal solution in a finite number of steps. In addition, there is no general method for solving all nonlinear problems. *Classical optimization* techniques, based on calculus, can handle some special cases, usually simpler types of problems. The *gradient method,* sometimes called the *steepest ascent method,* is an iterative procedure that moves from one feasible solution to the next in improving the value of the objective function. It has been computerized and can handle problems with both nonlinear constraints and objectives. But perhaps the best way to deal with nonlinear problems is to try to reduce them into a form that is linear or almost linear. *Separable programming* deals with a class of problems in which the objective and constraints are approximated by linear functions. In this way, the powerful simplex algorithm may again be applied. In general, work in the area of nonlinear programming is the least charted and most difficult of all the quantitative analysis models.

15.6   SUMMARY

This chapter addressed three special types of linear programming problems. The first, integer programming, examines LP problems that cannot have fractional answers. We saw how to tackle such problems graphically, with the cutting plane method. We also noted that there are three types of integer programming problems: (1) pure, or all, integer programs, (2) mixed problems, where *some* solutions variables need not be integer, and (3) 0-1 problems, where all solutions are either 0 or 1. STORM, AB:QM, and LINDO were used to illustrate computer approaches to these problems. The branch and bound method, a popular algorithm for solving all-integer and mixed-integer linear problems, was also described.

The latter part of the chapter dealt with goal programming. This extension of LP allows problems to have multiple goals. We saw how to solve such a problem both graphically and by use of a modified method of the simplex algorithm. Again, software such as AB:QM is a powerful tool in solving this offshoot of linear programming. Finally, the advanced topic of non-linear programming was introduced as a special mathematical programming problem.

GLOSSARY

Integer Programming. A mathematical programming technique that produces integer solutions to linear programming problems.

Cutting Plane Method. A means of adding one or more constraints to linear programming problems to help produce an optimum integer solution.

Zero-One Integer Programming. Problems in which all decision variables must have integer values of 0 or 1.

Branch and Bound Method. An algorithm for solving all-integer and mixed-integer linear programs and assignment problems. It divides the set of feasible solutions into subsets that are systematically examined.

Goal Programming. A mathematical programming technique that permits decision makers to set and prioritize multiple objective functions.

Satisficing. The process of coming as close as possible to reaching your set of objectives.

Deviational Variables. Terms that are minimized in a goal programming problem. Like slack variables in LP, they are real. They are the only terms in the objective function.

Nonlinear Programming. A category of mathematical programming techniques that allow the objective function and/or constraints to be nonlinear.

SOLVED PROBLEMS

Solved Problem 15.1

Consider the 0-1 integer programming problem that follows:

$$\text{Maximize} \quad 50X_1 + 45X_2 + 48X_3$$

$$\text{Subject to:} \quad 19X_1 + 27X_2 + 34X_3 \leq 80$$

$$22X_1 + 13X_2 + 12X_3 \leq 40$$

$$X_2, X_2, X_3 \text{ must be either 0 or 1}$$

Now reformulate this problem with additional constraints so that no more than two of the three variables can take on a value equal to 1 in the solution. Further, make sure that if $X_1 = 1$, then $X_2 = 1$ also. Then solve the new problem using LINDO's IP coding.

Solution

The LINDO program can handle all-integer, mixed-integer, and 0-1 integer problems. Program 15.5 shows two new constraints to handle the reformulated problem. It also illustrates the Integer n command in LINDO which specifies that the first n variables in the problem must be 0-1. The optimal solution is $X_1 = 1$, $X_2 = 1$, $X_3 = 0$, with an objective function value of 95.

Solved Problem 15.2

Recall the Harrison Electrical Company goal programming problem seen in Section 15.4 of this chapter. Its LP formulation was:

$$\text{Maximize profit} = \$7X_1 + \$6X_2$$

$$\text{Subject to:} \quad 2X_1 + 3X_2 \leq 12 \ \textit{(wiring hours)}$$

$$6X_1 + 5X_2 \leq 30 \ \textit{(assembly hours)}$$

$$X_1, X_2 \geq 0$$

where X_1 = number of chandeliers produced, and

X_2 = number of ceiling fans produced.

Reformulate Harrison Electrical as a goal programming model with the following goals:

Priority 1: Produce at least 4 chandeliers and 3 ceiling fans.

Priority 2: Maximize profit.

Priority 3: Limit overtime in the assembly department to 10 hours and in the wiring department to 6 hours.

PROGRAM 15.5 LINDO Output for Solved Problem 15.1

```
:    MAX 50X1+45X2+48X3
?    ST
?    19X1+27X2+34X3<80
?    22X1+13X2+12X3<40
?    X1+X2+X3<2
?    X1-X2=0

?    END

:    INTEGER 3
:    GO
```

OBJECTIVE FUNCTION VALUE

1)   95.0000000

VARIABLE	VALUE	REDUCED COST
X1	1.000000	-50.000000
X2	1.000000	-45.000000
X3	.000000	-48.000000
INTEGER	.000000	.000000

ROW	SLACK OR SURPLUS	DUAL PRICES
2)	34.000000	.000000
3)	5.000000	.000000
4)	.000000	.000000
5)	.000000	.000000
6)	.000000	.000000

Solution

$$\text{Minimize} = P_1(d_1^- + d_2^-) + P_2 d_3^- + P_3(d_4^+ + d_5^+)$$

Subject to:

$$X_1 + d_1^- - d_1^+ = 4 \qquad \left.\begin{array}{l} \\ \\ \end{array}\right\} \quad \textit{Priority 1}$$
$$X_2 + d_2^- - d_2^+ = 3$$

$$7X_1 + 6X_2 + d_3^- - d_3^+ = 99{,}999 \qquad \} \quad \textit{Priority 2}$$

$$2X_1 + 3X_2 + d_4^- - d_4^+ = 18 \qquad \left.\begin{array}{l} \\ \\ \end{array}\right\} \quad \textit{Priority 3}$$
$$6X_1 + 5X_2 + d_5^- - d_5^+ = 40$$

In the priority 2 goal constraint, the 99,999 represents an unrealistically high profit. It is just a mathematical trick to use as a target so we can get as close as possible to the maximum profit.

DISCUSSION QUESTIONS AND PROBLEMS

Discussion Questions

15-1 Compare the similarities and differences between linear and goal programming.

15-2 Provide your own examples of five applications of integer programming.

15-3 List the advantages and disadvantages of solving integer programming problems by (a) rounding off, (b) enumeration, (c) the cutting plane method, and (d) the branch and bound method.

15-4 Explain in your own words how the cutting plane method works.

15-5 What is the difference between the three types of integer programming problems? Which do you think is most common and why?

15-6 What is the meaning and role of the lower bound and upper bound in the branch and bound method?

15-7 What is meant by "satisficing," and why is the term often used in conjunction with goal programming?

15-8 What are deviational variables? How do they differ from decision variables in traditional linear programming problems?

15-9 If you were the president of the college you are attending and were employing goal programming to assist in decision making, what might your goals be? What kinds of constraints would you include in your model?

15-10 What does it mean to rank goals in goal programming? How does this affect the problem's solution?

15-11 How does the solution of goal programming problems with the modified simplex method differ from the use of the regular simplex approach for LP problems?

15-12 Which of the following are nonlinear programming problems, and why?

(a) Maximize profit $= 3X_1 + 5X_2 + 99X_3$

Subject to: $X_1 \geqslant 10$

  $X_2 \leqslant 5$

  $X_3 \geqslant 18$

(b) Minimize cost $= 25X_1 + 30 X_2 + 8X_1X_2$

Subject to: $X_1 \geqslant 8$

  $X_1 + X_2 \geqslant 12$

  $.0005X_1 - X_2 = 11$

(c) Minimize $Z = P_1d_1^- + P_2d_2^+ + P_3d_3^+$

Subject to: $X_1 + X_2 + d_1^- - d_1^+ = 300$

  $X_2 + d_2^- - d_2^+ = 200$

  $X_1 \qquad + d_3^- - d_3^+ = 100$

(d) Maximize profit $= 3X_1 + 4X_2$

Subject to: $\qquad X_1^2 - 5X_2 \geqslant 8$

$\qquad\qquad\quad 3X_1 + 4X_2 \geqslant 12$

(e) Minimize cost $= 18X_1 + 5X_2 + X_2^2$

Subject to: $\qquad 4X_1 - 3X_2 \geqslant 8$

$\qquad\qquad\quad X_1 + \ X_2 \geqslant 18$

Are any of these quadratic programming problems?

Problems

15-13 Use the cutting plane method to solve the following pure-integer programming problem.

$$\text{Maximize profit} = \ 8X_1 + 6X_2$$

$$\text{Subject to:} \qquad 4X_1 + 6X_2 \leqslant 16$$

$$15X_1 + 3X_2 \leqslant 27$$

$$X_1, X_2 \text{ integers} \geqslant 0$$

QA15-13

First cut is $X_1 \leqslant 1$, optimal solution is at $X_1 = 1$, $X_2 = 2$, profit $= \$20$.

15-14 Student Enterprises sells two sizes of wall posters, a large 3- by 4-foot poster and a smaller 2- by 3-foot poster. The profit earned from the sale of each large poster is \$3; each smaller poster earns \$2. The firm, although profitable, is not large; it consists of one art student, Jan Meising, at the University of Kentucky. Because of her classroom schedule, Jan has the following weekly constraints: (1) up to three large posters can be sold, (2) up to five smaller posters can be sold, (3) up to 10 hours can be spent on posters during the week, with each large poster requiring 2 hours of work, and each small one taking 1 hour. With the semester almost over, Jan plans on taking a three-month summer vacation to England and doesn't want to leave any unfinished posters behind. Find the integer solution that will maximize her profit.

QA15-14

$(x_1 = 3, x_2 = 4,$ Profit $= \$17)$

15-15 An airline owns an aging fleet of Boeing 727 jet airplanes. It is considering a major purchase of up to 17 new Boeing model 757 and 767 jets. The decision must take into account numerous cost and capability factors, including the following: (1) the airline can finance up to \$400 million in purchases; (2) each Boeing 757 will cost \$35 million, while each Boeing 767 will cost \$22 million; (3) at least one-third of the planes purchased should be the longer-ranged 757; (4) the annual maintenance budget is to be no more than \$8 million; (5) the annual maintenance cost per 757 is estimated to be \$800,000, it is \$500,000 for each 767 purchased; and finally (6), each 757 can carry 125,000 passengers per year, while each 767 can fly 81,000 passengers annually. Formulate this as an integer programming problem to maximize the annual passenger-carrying capability. What category of integer programming problem is this?

QA15-15

Maximize: $125{,}000x_1 +$ $81{,}000x_2$
$35x_1 + 22x_2 \leqslant 400$
$2/3x_1 - 1/3x_2 \geqslant 0$
$800{,}000x_1 + 500{,}000x_2 =$ \$8,000,000
$x_1 + x_2 \leqslant 17$
$x_1 = 5, x_2 = 8$
$Z = 1{,}273{,}000$ passengers
Pure integer program

15-16 Solve Problem 15-15 by the cutting plane method.

15-17 Innis Construction Company specializes in building moderately priced homes in Cincinnati, Ohio. Tom Innis has identified eight potential locations to construct new single family dwellings, but he cannot put up homes on all of the sites because he has only \$300,000 to invest in all projects. The accompanying table shows the cost of constructing homes in each area, and the

QA15-17

expected profit to be made from the sale of each home. Note that the home-building costs differ considerably due to lot costs, site preparation, and differences in the models to be built. Note also that a fraction of a home cannot be built.

LOCATION	COST OF BUILDING AT THIS SITE ($)	EXPECTED PROFIT ($)
1. Clifton	60,000	5,000
2. Mt. Auburn	50,000	6,000
3. Mt. Adams	82,000	10,000
4. Amberly	103,000	12,000
5. Norwood	50,000	8,000
6. Covington	41,000	3,000
7. Roselawn	80,000	9,000
8. Eden Park	69,000	10,000

Formulate Innis's problem using 0-1 integer programming.

Maximize profit =
$5,000x_1 + 6,000x_2 + 10,000x_3 + 12,000x_4 + 8,000x_5 + 3,000x_6 + 9,000x_7 + 10,000x_8$
Subject to:
$60,000x_1 + 50,000x_2 + 82,000x_3 + 103,000x_4 + 50,000x_5 + 41,000x_6 + 80,000x_7 + 69,000x_8 \leq 300,000$

QA15-18

15-18 Stockbroker Anna Lundberg has made the following recommendations to her client:

TYPE OF INVESTMENT	COST ($)	EXPECTED RETURN ($)
Hanover Municipal bonds	500	50
Hamilton City bonds	1,000	100
S.E. Power & Light Co.	350	30
Nebraska Electric Service	490	45
Southern Gas and Electric	700	65
Samuels Products Co.	270	20
Nation Builder Paint Co.	800	90
Hammer Head Hotels Co.	400	35

See the Instructor's Section for details.

The client agrees to this list, but provides several conditions: (1) no more than $3,000 can be invested, and (2) the money is to be spread among at least five investments, (3) no more than one type of bond can be purchased, (4) at least two utility stocks and at least two regular stocks must be purchased. Formulate this as a 0-1 integer programming problem for Ms. Lundberg to maximize expected return.

$x_1 = 1, x_2 = 2,$
$P = \$20.00$

15-19 Solve Problem 15-13 using the branch and bound method.

15-20 Solve Problem 15-15 using the branch and bound method.

$x_1 = 5, x_2 = 8,$
$Z = 1,273,000$

15-21 Four incoming jobs at Golding Manufacturing must be assigned to any of four available machines. The cost of doing each job on each machine is shown below:

JOBS	MACHINES #1	#2	#3	#4
A	$85	$70	$60	$10
B	6	15	90	76
C	50	80	5	75
D	75	84	82	25

Use the branch and bound method to generate the least-total-cost assignment of performing the four jobs.

: **15-22** Solve the following integer programming problem using the branch and bound approach.

$$\text{Maximize profit} = \$2X_1 + \$3X_2$$

$$\text{Subject to:} \quad X_1 + 3X_2 \le 9$$

$$3X_1 + X_2 \le 7$$

$$X_1 - X_2 \le 1$$

where both X_1 and X_2 must be nonnegative integer values.

15-23 Geraldine Shawhan is president of Shawhan File Works, a firm that manufactures two types of metal file cabinets. The demand for her two-drawer model is up to 600 cabinets per week; demand for a three-drawer cabinet is limited to 400 per week. Shawhan File Works has a weekly operating capacity of 1,300 hours, with the two-drawer cabinet taking one hour to produce and the three-drawer cabinet requiring two hours. Each two-drawer model sold yields a $10 profit, while the profit for the large model is $15. Shawhan has listed the following goals in order of importance:

1. Attain a profit as close to $11,000 as possible each week.
2. Avoid underutilization of the firm's production capacity.
3. Sell as many two-drawer and three-drawer cabinets as the demand indicates.

Set this up as a goal programming problem.

: **15-24** Solve Problem 15-23 graphically. Are any goals unachieved in this solution? Explain.

15-25 Harris Segal, marketing director for North-Central Power and Light, is about to begin an advertising campaign promoting energy conservation. In trying to budget between television and newspaper advertisements, he sets the following goals in order of importance:

1. The total advertising budget of $120,000 should not be exceeded.
2. There should be a mix of TV and newspaper ads, with at least 10 TV spots (costing $5,000 each) and at least 20 newspaper ads (costing $2,000 each).
3. The total number of people to read or hear the advertisements should be at least 9 million.

Each television spot reaches approximately 300,000 people. A newspaper advertisement is read by about 150,000 persons. Formulate Segal's goal programming problem to find out how many of each type of ad to place.

: **15-26** Solve Problem 15-25 graphically. How many people, in total, will read or hear the advertisements?

15-27 Hilliard Electronics produces specially coded computer chips for laser surgery in 64K, 256K, and 512K sizes. (1K means the chip holds 1,024 bits of information—thus a 64K chip contains 65,536 bits.) To produce a 64K chip requires 8 hours of labor, a 256K chip takes 13 hours, and a 512K chip requires 16 hours. Hilliard's monthly production capacity is 1,200 hours. Mr. Blank, the firm's sales manager, estimates that the maximum monthly sales of the

---

Answer column (right margin):

A4, B1, C3, D2, *or* A4, B2, C3, D1 for a cost of $105

$x_1 = 0$, $x_2 = 3$, Profit = $9.00

QA15-23

Minimize deviations =
$P_1 d_1^- + P_2 d_1^+ + P_2 d_2^- + P_3 d_3^- + P_3 d_4^-$
$10x_1 + 15x_2 + d_1^- - d_1^+ = \$11,000$
$1x_1 + 2x_2 + d_2^- = 1,300$ hours
$1x_1 + d_3^- = 600$ cabinets
$x_2 + d_4^- = 400$ cabinets

$x_1 = 500$, $x_2 = 400$, $d_3^- = 100$

QA15-25

Minimize deviations =
$P_1 d_1^+ + P_2 d_2^- + P_2 d_3^- + P_3 d_4^-$
$5,000x_1 + 2,000x_2 - d_1^+ = \$120,000$
$x_1 + d_2^- = 10$
$x_2 + d_3^- = 20$
$300,000x_1 + 150,000x_2 + d_4^- = 9,000,000$

$x_1 = 10$ TV spots
$x_2 = 35$ newspaper ads
Total exposure = 8,250,000 people $d_4^- = 750,000$

QA15-27

Minimize deviations $=$
$P_1 d_1^- + P_1 d_2^- + P_2 d_3^- + P_2 d_4^- + P_2 d_5^- + P_3 d_6^-$
$x_1 + d_1^- - d_1^+ = 30$
$x_2 + d_2^- - d_2^+ = 35$
$x_1 + d_3^- - d_3^+ = 40$
$x_2 + d_4^- - d_4^+ = 50$
$x_3 + d_5^- - d_5^+ = 60$
$8x_1 + 13x_2 + 16x_3 + d_6^-$
$= 1200$

See the Instructor's Section
for the two tableaus.

64K, 256K, and 512K chips are 40, 50, and 60 respectively. The company has the following goals (ranked in order from most important to least important):

1. Fill an order from the best customer for thirty 64K chips and thirty-five 256K chips.
2. Provide sufficient chips to at least equal the sales estimates set by Mr. Blank.
3. Avoid underutilization of the production capacity.

Formulate this problem using goal programming.

: **15-28** The modified simplex method was presented for the Harrison Electrical Company example in Tables 15.4, 15.5, and 15.6 in this chapter. Two iterations of the method were skipped between the second tableau in Table 15.5 and the final tableau in Table 15.6. Apply the method to provide the missing third and fourth tableaus. Which corner points (*A*, *B*, *C*, or *D*) in Figure 15.9 does each of these tableaus correspond to?

QA15-29

: **15-29** An Oklahoma manufacturer produces two products: speaker telephones (X_1) and push-button telephones (X_2). The following goal programming model has been formulated to find the number of each to produce each day to meet the firm's goals.

$$\text{Minimize} \quad P_1 d_1^- + P_2 d_2^- + P_3 d_3^+ + P_4 d_1^+$$

$$\text{Subject to:} \quad 2X_1 + 4X_2 + d_1^- - d_1^+ = 80$$

$$8X_1 + 10X_2 + d_2^- - d_2^+ = 320$$

$$8X_1 + 6X_2 + d_3^- - d_3^+ = 240$$

$$\text{All} \quad X_i, d_i \geq 0$$

See the Instructor's Section
for the tableau.
$x_1 = 15$
$x_2 = 20$
$d_1^+ = 30$

(a) Set up the complete initial goal programming tableau for this problem.
(b) Find the optimal solution using the modified simplex method.

QA15-30

: **15-30** Major Bill Bligh, director of the Army War College's new six-month attaché training program, is concerned about how the 20 officers taking the course spend their precious time while in his charge. Major Bligh recognizes that there are 168 hours per week and thinks his students have been using them rather inefficiently. Bligh lets

$X_1 =$ number of hours of sleep needed per week

$X_2 =$ number of personal hours (eating, personal hygiene, handling laundry, and so on)

$X_3 =$ number of hours of class and studying

$X_4 =$ number of hours of social time off base (dating, sports, family visits, and so on)

Minimize $= P_1 d_1^- +$
$P_1 d_1^+ + P_2 d_2^+ + P_3 d_3^-$
$1X_1 + 1X_2 + 1X_3 + 1X_4 \leq 168$
$1X_3 + d_1^- - d_1^+ = 30$
$1X_1 - d_2^+ = 49$
$1X_4 + d_3^- = 20$

He thinks that 30 hours per week should be enough study/class time for student to absorb the material, and that this is his most important goal. Bligh feels that students need at most 7 hours sleep per night on average and that this goal is number 2. He believes that goal number 3 is to provide at least 20 hours per week of social time. Formulate this as a goal programming problem.

: **15-31** Hinkel Rotary Engine, Ltd., produces four- and six-cylinder models of automobile engines. The firm's profit for each four-cylinder engine sold during its quarterly production cycle is $1,800 - $50X_1$, where X_1 is the number sold. Hinkel makes $\$2,400 - \$70X_2$ for each of the larger engines sold, with X_2 equal to the number of six-cylinder engines sold. There are 5,000 hours of production time available during each production cycle. A four-cylinder engine requires 100 hours of production time, whereas six-cylinder engines take 130 hours to manufacture. Formulate but do not solve this production planning problem for Hinkel.

Maximize profit $= 1800x_1 - 50x_1^2 + 2400x_2 - 70x_2^2$
Subject to:
$100x_1 + 130x_2 \leq 5000$ hours

Data Set Problem

□ : **15-32** The following integer programming problem has been developed to help First National Bank decide where, out of 10 possible sites, to locate four new branch offices:

Maximize expected returns $=$

$$120X_1 + 100X_2 + 110X_3 + 140X_4 + 155X_5 + 128X_6$$
$$+ 145X_7 + 190X_8 + 170X_9 + 150X_{10}$$

such that

$$20X_1 + 30X_2 + 20X_3 + 25X_4 + 30X_5 + 30X_6 + 25X_7$$
$$+ 20X_8 + 25X_9 + 30X_{10} \leq 110$$
$$15X_1 + 5X_2 + 20X_3 + 20X_4 + 5X_5 + 5X_6$$
$$+ 10X_7 + 20X_8 + 5X_9 + 20X_{10} \leq 50$$
$$X_2 + X_6 + X_7 + X_9 + X_{10} \leq 3$$
$$X_2 + X_3 + X_5 + X_8 + X_9 \geq 2$$
$$X_1 + X_3 + X_{10} \geq 1$$
$$\Sigma X_i \leq 4$$
$$\text{All } X_i = 0 \text{ or } 1$$

where $X_i =$ Winter Park, Maitland, Osceola, Downtown, South Orlando, Airport, Winter Garden, Apopka, Lake Mary, Cocoa Beach for i equals 1 to 10 respectively.

(a) Where should the four new sites be located and what will be the expected return?

(b) If at least one new branch *must* be opened in Maitland or Osceola, will this change the answers? Add the new constraint and rerun.

(c) The expected return at Apopka was overestimated. The correct value is $\$160,000$ per year (that is, 160). Does your answer to part a change?

S. Orlando, Apopka, Lake Mary, and Cocoa Beach, $665,000

The expected return drops to $625,000. Osceola opens and Cocoa Beach closes.

Apopka corrected, the new solution has a return of $635,000, but the same locations as part a.

■ **CASE STUDY** ■

Schank Marketing Research

Schank Marketing Research has just signed contracts to conduct studies for four clients. At present, three project managers are free for assignment to the tasks. Although all are capable of handling each assignment, the times and costs to complete the studies depend on the experience and knowledge of each manager. Using his judgment, John Schank, the president, has been able to establish a cost for each possible assignment. These costs, which are really the salaries each manager would draw on each task, are summarized below.

PROJECT MANAGER	CLIENT			
	Hines Corp.	NASA	General Foundry	CBT Television
Gardener	$3,200	$3,000	$2,800	$2,900
Ruth	2,700	3,200	3,000	3,100
Hardgraves	1,900	2,100	3,300	2,100

Schank is very hesitant about neglecting NASA, which has been an important customer in the past. (NASA has employed the firm to study the public's attitude toward the Space Shuttle and proposed Space Station.) In addition, Schank has promised to try to provide Ruth a salary of at least

$3,000 on his next assignment. From previous contracts, Schank also knows that Gardener does not get along well with the management at CBT Television so he hopes to avoid assigning her to CBT. Finally, as Hines Corporation is also an old and valued client, Schank feels it is twice as important to immediately assign a project manager to Hines's task as it is to provide one to General Foundry, a brand-new client. Schank wants to minimize the total costs of all projects while considering each of these goals. He feels that all of these goals are important, but if he had to rank them, he would put his concern about NASA first, his worry about Gardener second, his need to keep Hines Corporation happy third, his promise to Ruth fourth, and his concern about minimizing all costs last.

Each project manager can handle, at most, one new client.

1. If Schank were not concerned about noncost goals, how would he formulate this problem so that it could be solved quantitatively?

2. Develop a formulation that will incorporate all five objectives.

■ **CASE STUDY** ■

The Oakton River Bridge

The Oakton River had long been considered an impediment to the development of a certain medium-sized metropolitan area in the southeast. Lying to the east of the city, the river made it difficult for people living on its eastern bank to commute to jobs in and around the city and to take advantage of the shopping and cultural attractions that the city had to offer. Similarly, the river inhibited those on its western bank from access to the ocean resorts lying one hour to the east. The bridge over the Oakton River had been built prior to World War II and was grossly inadequate to handle the existing traffic, much less the increased traffic that would accompany the forecasted growth in the area. A congressional delegation from the state prevailed upon the federal

government to fund a major portion of a new toll bridge over the Oakton River and the state legislature appropriated the rest of the needed monies for the project.

Progress in construction of the bridge has been in accordance with what was anticipated at the start of construction. The state highway commission, which will have operational jurisdiction over the bridge, has concluded that opening of the bridge for traffic is likely to take place at the beginning of the next summer, as scheduled. A personnel task force has been established to recruit, train, and schedule the workers needed to operate the toll facility.

The personnel task force is well aware of the budgetary problems facing the state. They have taken as part of their mandate the requirement that personnel costs be kept as low as possible. One particular area of concern is the number of toll collectors that will be needed. The bridge is scheduling three shifts of collectors: shift A from midnight to 8 A.M., shift B from 8 A.M. to 4 P.M., and shift C from 4 P.M. to midnight. Recently, the state employees union negotiated a contract with the state which requires that all toll collectors be permanent, full-time employees. In addition, all collectors must work a five-on, two-off schedule on the same shift. Thus, for example, a worker could be assigned to work Tuesday, Wednesday, Thursday, Friday, and Saturday on shift A, followed by Sunday and Monday off. An employee could not be scheduled to work, say, Tuesday on shift A followed by Wednesday, Thursday, Friday, and Saturday on shift B or on any other mixture of shifts during a five-day block. The employees would choose their assignments in order of their seniority.

The task force has received projections of traffic flow on the bridge by day and hour. These projections are based on extrapolations of existing traffic patterns—the pattern of commuting, shopping, and beach traffic currently experienced with growth projections factored in. Standards data from other state-operated toll facilities have allowed the task force to convert these traffic flows into toll collector requirements, that is, the minimum number of collectors required per shift, per day, to handle the anticipated traffic load. These toll collector requirements are summarized in the accompanying table.

Minimum Number of Toll Collectors Required Per Shift

SHIFT	SUN.	MON.	TUE.	WED.	THU.	FRI.	SAT.
A	8	13	12	12	13	13	15
B	10	10	10	10	10	13	15
C	15	13	13	12	12	13	8

The numbers in the table include one or two extra collectors per shift to fill in for collectors who call in sick and to provide relief for collectors on their scheduled breaks. Note that each of the eight collectors needed for shift A on Sunday, for example, could have come from any of the A shifts scheduled to begin on Wednesday, Thursday, Friday, Saturday, or Sunday.

Discussion Questions

1. Determine the minimum number of toll collectors that would have to be hired to meet the requirements expressed in the table.

2. The union had indicated that it might lift its opposition to the mixing of shifts in a five-day block in exchange for additional compensation and benefits. By how much could the numbers of toll collectors required be reduced if this is done?

Source: Adopted from B. Render, R. Stair, and I. Greenberg, *Cases and Readings in Management Science,* 2nd ed., Boston: Allyn and Bacon, 1990.

CASE STUDY

The Puyallup Mall

Jane Rodney, president of the Rodney Development Company, was trying to decide what types of stores to include in her new shopping center at Puyallup Mall. She had already contracted for a supermarket, a drug store, and a few other stores that she considered essential. However, she had available an additional 16,000 square feet of floor space yet to allocate. She drew up a list of the 15 types of stores she might consider (see Table) including the floor space required by each. Rodney did not think she would have any trouble finding occupants for any type of store.

The lease agreements Rodney used in her developments included two types of payment. The store had to pay a certain annual rent, depending on the size and type of store. In addition, Rodney was to receive a small percentage of the store's sales, if the sales exceeded a specified minimum amount. The amount of annual rent from each store is shown in the second column of the table. In order to estimate the profitability of each type of store, Rodney calculated the present value of all future rent and sales percentage payments. These are given in the third column. Rodney wants to achieve the highest total *present value* over the set of stores she selects. However, she could not simply pick those stores with the highest present values, for there were several restrictions. The first, of course, was that she has available only 16,000 square feet.

In addition, a condition on the financing of the project required that the total annual rent should be at least as much as the annual fixed costs (taxes, management fees, debt service, and so forth). These annual costs were $150,000 for this part of the project. Finally, the total funds available for construction of this part of the project were $700,000, and each type of store required different construction costs depending on the size and type of store (fourth column in the table).

In addition, Rodney had certain requirements in terms of the mix of stores that she considered best. She wanted at least one store from each of the clothing, hardgoods, and miscellaneous groups, and at least two from the restaurant category. She wanted no more than two from the clothing group. Furthermore, the number of stores in the miscellaneous group should not exceed the total number of stores in the clothing and hardgoods groups combined.

Discussion Question

Which tenants should be selected for the mall?

Adapted from H. Bierman, C. P. Bonini, and W. H. Hausman, *Quantitative Analysis,* 7th edition, Irwin Publishing, pp. 467–468, Copyright 1986.

TABLE Characteristics of possible leases, Puyallap Mall shopping center

TYPE OF STORE	SIZE OF STORE (000 OF SQ. FT.)	ANNUAL RENT ($000)	PRESENT VALUE ($000)	CONSTRUCTION COST ($000)
Clothing				
1. Men's	1.0	$ 4.4	$ 28.1	$24.6
2. Women's	1.6	6.1	34.6	32.0
3. Variety (both)	2.0	8.3	50.0	41.4
Restaurants				
4. Fancy restaurant	3.2	24.0	162.0	124.4
5. Lunch room	1.8	19.5	77.8	64.8
6. Cocktail lounge	2.1	20.7	100.4	79.8
7. Candy and ice cream shop	1.2	7.7	45.2	38.6
Hardgoods				
8. Hardware store	2.4	19.4	80.2	66.8
9. Cutlery and variety	1.6	11.7	51.4	45.1
10. Luggage and leather	2.0	15.2	62.5	54.3
Miscellaneous				
11. Travel agency	0.6	3.9	18.0	15.0
12. Tobacco shop	0.5	3.2	11.6	13.4
13. Camera store	1.4	11.3	50.4	42.0
14. Toys	2.0	16.0	73.6	63.7
15. Beauty parlor	1.0	9.6	51.2	40.0

BIBLIOGRAPHY

Anderson, A. M., and M. D. Earle. "Diet Planning in the Third World by Linear and Goal Programming." *Journal of Operations Research Society* **34** (1983): 9–16.

Bean, James C., Charles E. Noon, Sarah M. Ryan, and Gary J. Salton. "Selecting Tenants in a Shopping Mall." *Interfaces* **18**, 2 (March–April 1988): 1–9.

Boot, J. C. G. *Quadratic Programming.* Chicago: Rand McNally, 1964.

Bres, E. S., D. Burns, A. Charnes, and W. W. Cooper. "A Goal Programming Model for Planning Officer Accessions." *Management Science* **26**, 8 (August 1980): 773–781.

Buffa, Frank P., and Wade M. Jackson. "A Goal Programming Model for Purchasing Planning." *Journal of Purchasing and Material Management* Fall (1983): 27–34.

DeKluyver, Cornelis A., and Herbert Moskowitz. "Assessing Scenario Probabilities Via Interactive Goal Programming." *Management Science* **30**, 3 (March 1984): 273–278.

Gass, S. I. "A Process for Determining Priorities and Weights for Large-Scale Linear Goal Programs." *Journal of Operational Research Society* **37** (August 1986): 779–785.

Ignizio, J. P. *Goal Programming and Extensions.* Lexington, Mass.: D. C. Heath and Co., 1976.

Jones, Lawrence, and N. K. Kwak. "A Goal Programming Model for Allocating Human Resources for the Good Laboratory Practice Regulations." *Decision Sciences* **13**, 1 (1982): pp. 156–166.

Lee, S. M. *Goal Programming for Decision Analysis.* Philadelphia: Auerbach Publishers, Inc., 1972.

Lee, Sang M., and Marc J. Schniederjans. "A Multicriterial Assignment Problem: A Goal Programming Approach." *Interfaces* **13**, 4 (August 1983): 75–79.

Nauss, Robert M., and Robert E. Markland. "Theory and Application of an Optimizing Procedure for Lock Box Location Analysis." *Managment Science* **27**, 8 (August 1981): 855–865.

Russell, Roberta S., Bernard W. Taylor III, and Art J. Keown. "An Integer Goal Programming Model for Determining Capital Expenditures for Correctional Facilities." *Computer Environment Urban Systems* **11**, 4 (1986): 135–146.

Ruth, R. Jean. "A Mixed Integer Programming Model for Regional Planning of a Hospital Inpatient Service." *Management Science* **27**, 5 (May 1981): 521–533.

Schniederjans, Marc J., N. K. Kwak, and Mark C. Helmer. "An Application of Goal Programming to Resolve a Site Location Problem." *Interfaces* **12**, 3 (June 1982): 65–72.

Schniederjans, Marc J., and Gyu Chan Kim. "A Goal Programming Model to Optimize Departmental Preference in Course Assignments." *Computer Operations Research* **14**, 2 (1987): 87–96.

Stafford, E. F. "On the Development of a Mixed-Integer Linear Programming Model for the Flowshop Sequencing Problem." *Journal of Operational Research Society* **39** (December 1988): 1163–1174.

Stowe, J. D. "An Integer Programming Solution for the Optimal Credit Investigation/Credit Granting Sequence." *Financial Management* **14** (Summer 1985): 66–76.

Taylor, B. W., and others, "An Integer Nonlinear Goal Programming Model for the Deployment of State Highway Patrol Units." *Management Science* **31**, 11 (November 1985): 1335–1347.

Tingley, Kim M., and Judith S. Liebmen. "A Goal Programming Example in Public Health Resource Allocation." *Management Science* **30**, 3 (March 1984): 279–289.

Zangwill, W. I. *Nonlinear Programming: A Unified Approach.* Englewood Cliffs, NJ: Prentice Hall, 1969.

16

Waiting Lines: Queuing Theory

CHAPTER OUTLINE

16.1 Introduction

16.2 Waiting Line Costs

16.3 Characteristics of a Queuing System

16.4 Single-Channel Queuing Model with Poisson Arrivals and Exponential Service Times

16.5 Multiple-Channel Queuing Model with Poisson Arrivals and Exponential Service Times

16.6 Constant Service Time Model

16.7 Finite Population Model

16.8 More Complex Queuing Models and the Use of Simulation

16.9 Summary

Glossary

Key Equations

Solved Problems

Discussion Questions and Problems

Case Studies:

The Shader Lane Hotel

New England Castings

Bibliography

Appendix: Queuing Analysis with Spreadsheets

Transparency Master 16.1:
Outline: Waiting Line Models.

Teaching Suggestion 16.1:
The Topic of Queuing. See
the Instructor's Section for
details.

16.1   INTRODUCTION

The study of *waiting lines*, called *queuing theory*, is one of the oldest and most widely used quantitative analysis techniques. Waiting lines are an everyday occurrence, affecting people shopping for groceries, buying gasoline, making a bank deposit, or waiting on the telephone for the first available airline reservationist to answer. Queues,[1] another term for waiting lines, may also take the form of machines waiting to be repaired, trucks in line to be unloaded, or airplanes lined up on a runway waiting for permission to take off. The three basic components of a queuing process are arrivals, service facilities, and the actual waiting line.

In this chapter we discuss how analytical models of waiting lines can help managers evaluate the cost and effectiveness of service systems. We begin with a look at waiting line costs, then describe the characteristics of waiting lines and the underlying mathematical assumptions used to develop queuing models. We also provide the equations needed to compute the operating characteristics of a service system and show examples of how they are used. Later in the chapter, you will see how to save computational time by applying queuing tables and by running waiting line computer programs.

16.2   WAITING LINE COSTS

Applicable Problem 16-10

**finding the best level
of service**

Most waiting line problems are centered about the question of finding the ideal level of services that a firm should provide. Supermarkets must decide how many cash register checkout positions should be opened. Gasoline stations must decide how many pumps should be opened and how many attendants should be on duty. Manufacturing plants must determine the optimal number of mechanics to have on duty each shift to repair machines that break down. Banks must decide how many teller windows to keep open to serve customers during various hours of the day. In most cases, this level of service is an option over which management has control. An extra teller, for example, can be borrowed from another chore or can be quickly hired and trained if demand warrants it. This may not always be the case, though. A plant may not be able to locate or hire skilled mechanics to repair sophisticated electronic machinery. And a gas station owner with 10 pumps may have a gasoline allotment large enough to open only 5 or 6 pumps.

When an organization *does* have control, its objective is usually to find a happy medium between two extremes. On the one hand, a firm can retain a large staff and provide *many* service facilities. This may result in excellent customer service, with seldom more than one or two customers in a queue. Customers are kept happy with the quick response and appreciate the convenience. This, however, can become expensive.

---

[1]The word *queue* is pronounced like the letter Q, that is, "kew."

How Queuing Models Began

Queuing theory had its beginning in the research work of a Danish engineer named A. K. Erlang. In 1909 Erlang experimented with fluctuating demand in telephone traffic. Eight years later he published a report addressing the delays in automatic dialing equipment. At the end of World War II, Erlang's early work was extended to more general problems and to business applications of waiting lines.

The other extreme is to have the *minimum* possible number of checkout lines, gas pumps, or teller windows open. This keeps the *service cost* down, but may result in customer dissatisfaction. How many times would you return to a large discount department store that had only one cash register open during the day you shop? As the average length of the queue increases and poor service results, customers and goodwill may be lost.

Most managers recognize the trade-off that must take place between the cost of providing good service and the cost of customer waiting time. They want queues that are short enough so that customers don't become unhappy and either storm out without buying or buy but never return. But they are willing to allow some waiting in line if it is balanced by a significant savings in service costs.

One means of evaluating a service facility is thus to look at a *total expected cost*, a concept illustrated in Figure 16.1. Total expected cost is the sum of expected *service costs* plus expected *waiting costs*.

Service costs are seen to increase as a firm attempts to raise its level of service. For example, if three teams of stevedores, instead of two, are

KEY IDEA

total expected cost

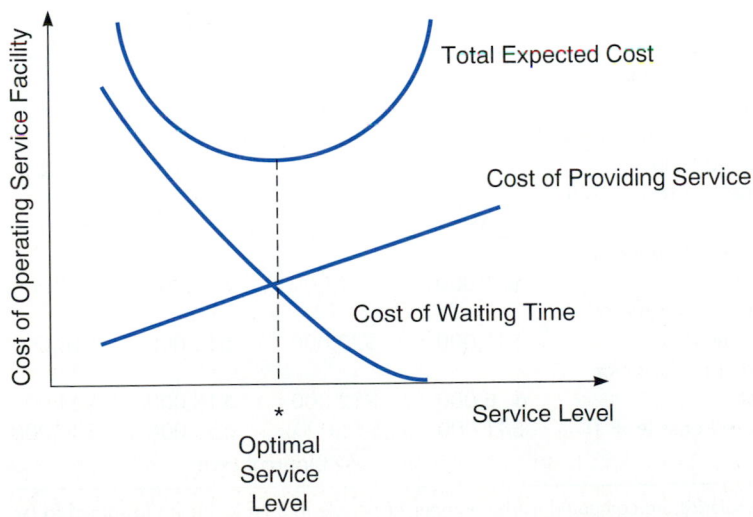

FIGURE 16.1
Queuing Costs and Service Levels

Transparency Master 16.2:
Queuing Costs and Service
Levels.

Teaching Suggestion 16.2:
Cost of Waiting Time From
an Organizational Perspective.
See the Instructor's Section
for details.

employed to unload a cargo ship, service costs are increased by the additional price of wages. As service improves in speed, however, the cost of time spent waiting in lines decreases. This waiting cost may reflect lost productivity of workers while their tools or machines are awaiting repairs, or may simply be an estimate of the costs of customers lost because of poor service and long queues.

As an illustration, let's look at the case of the Three Rivers Shipping Company. Three Rivers runs a huge docking facility located on the Ohio River near Pittsburgh. Approximately five ships arrive to unload their cargoes of steel and ore during every 12-hour work shift. Each hour that a ship sits idle in line waiting to be unloaded costs the firm a great deal of money, about $1,000 per hour. From experience, management estimates that if one team of stevedores is on duty to handle the unloading work, each ship will wait an average of 7 hours to be unloaded. If two teams are working, the average waiting time drops to 4 hours; for three teams, it's 3 hours; and for four teams of stevedores, only 2 hours. But each additional team of stevedores is also an expensive proposition, due to union contracts.

minimum total expected cost

Three River's superintendent would like to determine the optimal number of teams of stevedores to have on duty each shift. The objective is to minimize total expected costs. This analysis is summarized in Table 16.1.

In order to minimize the sum of service costs and waiting costs, the firm makes the decision to employ two teams of stevedores each shift.

TABLE 16.1 Three Rivers Shipping Company Waiting Line Cost Analysis

	NUMBER OF TEAMS OF STEVEDORES WORKING			
	1	2	3	4
(a) Average number of ships arriving per shift	5	5	5	5
(b) Average time each ship waits to be unloaded (hours)	7	4	3	2
(c) Total ship hours lost per shift (a × b)	35	20	15	10
(d) Estimated cost per hour of idle ship time	$ 1,000	$ 1,000	$ 1,000	$ 1,000
(e) Value of ship's lost time or waiting cost (c × d)	$35,000	$20,000	$15,000	$10,000
(f) Stevedore team salary,* or service cost	$ 6,000	$12,000	$18,000	$24,000
(g) Total expected cost (e + f)	$41,000	($32,000)	$33,000	$34,000
		↳Optimal cost		

*Stevedore team salaries are computed as the number of people in a typical team (assumed to be 50), times the number of hours each person works per day (12 hours), times an hourly salary of $10 per hour. If two teams are employed the rate is just doubled.

Transparency Master 16.3:
Characteristics of a Waiting
Line System.

16.3   CHARACTERISTICS OF A QUEUING SYSTEM

In this section, we take a look at the three parts of a queuing system: (1) the arrivals or inputs to the system (sometimes referred to as the *calling population*), (2) the queue or the waiting line itself, and (3) the service facility. These three components have certain characteristics that must be examined before mathematical queuing models can be developed.

Arrival Characteristics

The input source that generates arrivals or customers for the service system has three major characteristics. It is important to consider the *size* of the calling population, the *pattern* of arrivals at the queuing system, and the *behavior* of the arrivals.

Size of the Calling Population. Population sizes are considered to be either *unlimited* (essentially *infinite*) or *limited* (*finite*). When the number of customers or arrivals on hand at any given moment is just a small portion of potential arrivals, the calling population is considered unlimited. For practical purposes, examples of unlimited populations include cars arriving at a highway toll both, shoppers arriving at a supermarket, or students arriving to register for classes at a large university. Most queuing models assume such an infinite calling population. When this is not the case, modeling becomes much more complex. An example of a finite population is a shop with only eight machines that might break down and require service.

**unlimited versus limited
calling populations**

Pattern of Arrivals at the System. Customers either arrive at a service facility according to some known schedule (for example, one patient every 15 minutes or one student for advising every half hour) or else they arrive *randomly*. Arrivals are considered random when they are independent of one another and their occurrence cannot be predicted exactly. Frequently in queuing problems, the number of arrivals per unit of time can be estimated by a probability distribution known as the *Poisson distribution*. For any given arrival rate, such as two customers per hour, or four trucks per minute, a discrete Poisson distribution can be established by using the following formula.

random arrivals

Teaching Suggestion 16.3:
The Use of Poisson and
Exponential Probability
Distributions to Describe
Arrival and Service Rates.
See the Instructor's Section
for details.

$$P(X) = \frac{e^{-\lambda}\lambda^{X}}{X!} \qquad \text{for } X = 0, 1, 2, 3, 4, \ldots \qquad (16\text{-}1)$$

where

$P(X) =$ probability of X arrivals,

$X =$ number of arrivals per unit of time,

$\lambda =$ average arrival rate, and

$e = 2.7183.$

**Poisson probability
distribution**

With the help of the table in Appendix D, these values are easy to compute. Figure 16.2 illustrates the Poisson distribution for $\lambda = 2$ and $\lambda = 4$. This means that if the average arrival rate is $\lambda = 2$ customers per hour, the probability of 0 customers arriving in any random hour is about 13%, probability of 1 customer is about 27%, 2 customers about 27%, 3 customers about 18%, 4 customers about 9%, and so on. The chances that 9 or more will arrive are virtually nil. Arrivals, of course, are not always Poisson (they may follow some other distribution) and should be examined to make certain that they are well approximated by Poisson before that distribution is applied. This usually involves observing arrivals, plotting the data, and applying statistical measures of goodness-of-fit, a topic discussed in more advanced texts.

Behavior of the Arrivals. Most queuing models assume that an arriving customer is a patient customer. Patient customers are people or machines that wait in the queue until they are served and do not switch between lines. Unfortunately, life and quantitative analysis are complicated by the fact that people have been known to *balk* or *renege*. Balking refers to customers who refuse to join the waiting line because it is too long to suit their needs or interests. Reneging customers are those who enter the queue, but then become impatient and leave without completing their transaction. Actually, both of these situations just serve to accentuate the need for queuing theory and waiting line analysis. How many times have you seen a shopper with a basket full of groceries, including perishables such as milk,

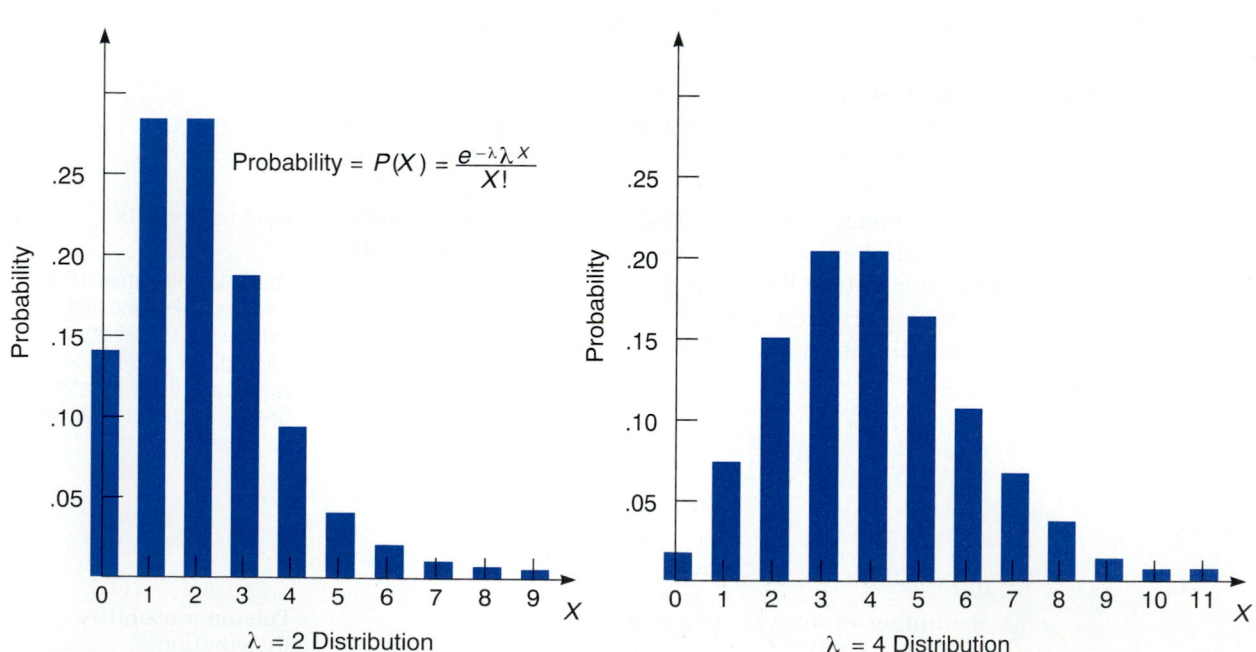

$$\text{Probability} = P(X) = \frac{e^{-\lambda}\lambda^X}{X!}$$

$\lambda = 2$ Distribution

$\lambda = 4$ Distribution

FIGURE 16.2
Two Examples of the Poisson Distribution for Arrival Times

frozen food, or meats, simply abandon the shopping cart before checking out because the line was too long? This expensive occurrence for the store makes managers acutely aware of the importance of service level decisions.

Waiting Line Characteristics

The waiting line itself is the second component of a queuing system. The length of a line can be either *limited* or *unlimited*. A queue is limited when it cannot, by law of physical restrictions, increase to an infinite length. This may be the case in a small restaurant that has only 10 tables and can serve no more than 50 diners an evening. Analytic queuing models are treated in this chapter under an assumption of *unlimited* queue length. A queue is unlimited when its size is unrestricted, as in the case of the toll booth serving arriving automobiles.

limited and unlimited lines

A second waiting line characteristic deals with *queue discipline*. This refers to the rule by which customers in the line are to receive service. Most systems use a queue discipline known as the *first-in, first-out rule* (FIFO). In a hospital emergency room or an express checkout line at a supermarket, however, various assigned priorities may preempt FIFO. Patients who are critically injured will move ahead in treatment priority over patients with broken fingers or noses. Shoppers with fewer than 10 items may be allowed to enter the express checkout queue but are *then* treated as first come, first served. Computer programming runs are another example of queuing systems that operate under priority scheduling. In most large companies, when computer-produced paychecks are due out on a specific date, the payroll program has highest priority over other runs.[2]

first-in, first-out rule

Service Facility Characteristics

The third part of any queuing system is the service facility. It is important to examine two basic properties: (1) the configuration of the service system and (2) the pattern of service times.

Basic Queuing System Configurations. Service systems are usually classified in terms of their number of channels, or number of servers, and number of phases, or number of service stops, that must be made. A *single-channel system*, with one server, is typified by the drive-in bank that has only one open teller, or by the type of drive-through fast-food restaurant that has become increasingly popular in the United States. If, on the other hand, the bank had several tellers on duty, and each customer waited in one common line for the first available teller, then we would have a *multiple-channel system* at work. Many banks today are multichannel service systems, as are most large barber shops and many airline ticket counters.

number of service channels

A *single-phase system* is one in which the customer receives service from only one station and then exits the system. A fast-food restaurant in which

single-phase versus multiphase systems

---

[2]The term *FIFS* (first in first served) is often used in place of FIFO. Another discipline, LIFS (last in, first served), is common when material is stacked or piled and the items on top are used first.

APPLICATIONS OF QA

Queuing Theory at Eastman Kodak

In some cases, inventory control is so complex that traditional inventory control models are not appropriate. This was the case with Eastman Kodak, a multi-item manufacturer. In many situations at Eastman, a particular job would spend only 10% to 15% of its time in actual processing. The other time was wasted waiting in line or in queues at particular processing centers before processing actually began. When this occurred, both the lead time, or waiting time, before processing and the size of batches that are to be processed were of concern. In order to analyze the lot-sizing and lead-time performance, the firm employed simulation and queuing techniques.

Using queuing theory, a formula was developed to determine the time spent in the system by a given batch. Time was a function of the total work to be done, the processing rate or service rate, the batch size, and the setup time per batch.

Furthermore, the queuing theory approach was used to help validate the simulation models that were used. It was shown that the queuing and simulation approaches were close, but that the queuing theory had a 20% advantage in terms of cost. As a result of the analysis, John C. Barnes, the manager of planning at the US Apparatus Division of the Eastman Kodak Company stated: "We are now planning to establish lot sizes using the analytical model instead of the traditional EOQ approach. The confidence gained has allowed us to commit the manufacturing operation to accomplish a very substantial reduction in planned lead time and, therefore, inventory level."

Source: Uday Karmarkar, Sham Kekre, Sunder Kekre, Susan Freeman, "Lot-Sizing and Lead-Time Performance in a Manufacturing Cell." *Interfaces* **15,** 2 (March–April 1985): 1–9.

Transparency Master 16.5: Basic Queuing System Configurations.

the person who takes your order also brings you the food and takes your money is a single-phase system. So is a driver's license agency in which the person taking your application also grades your test and collects the license fee. But if the restaurant requires you to place your order at one station, pay at a second, and pick up the food at a third service stop, it becomes a *multiphase system.* Likewise, if the driver's license agency is large or busy, you will probably have to wait in a line to complete the application (the first service stop), then queue again to have the test graded (the second service stop), and finally go to a third service counter to pay the fee. To help you relate the concepts of channels and phases, Figure 16.3 presents four possible configurations.

service times often follow negative exponential distribution

Service Time Distribution. Service patterns are like arrival patterns in that they may be either constant or random. If service time is constant, it takes the same amount of time to take care of each customer. This is the case in a machine-performed service operation such as an automatic car wash. More often, service times are randomly distributed. In many cases, it can be assumed that random service times are described by the *negative exponential probability distribution.* This is a mathematically convenient assumption if arrival rates are Poisson distributed.

Figure 16.4 illustrates that if service times follow an exponential distribution, the probability of any very long service time is low. For example, when an average service time is 20 minutes, seldom if ever will a customer require more than 90 minutes in the service facility. If the mean service

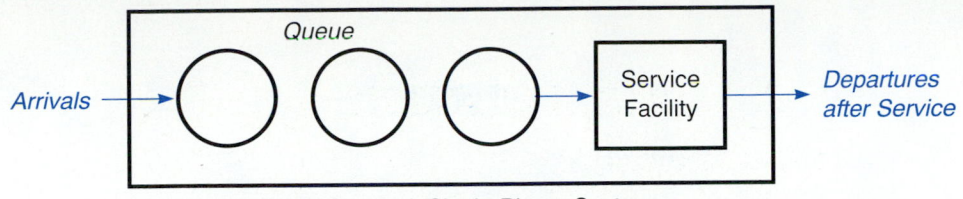

Single-Channel, Single-Phase System

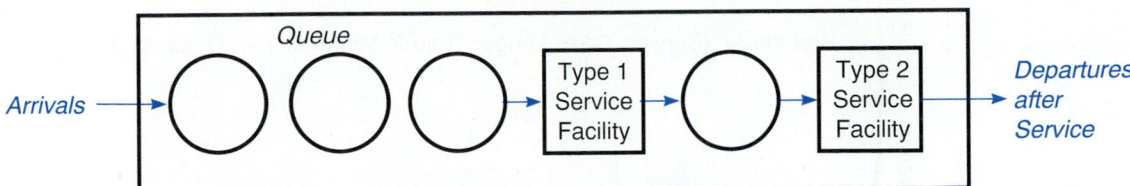

Single-Channel, Multiphase System

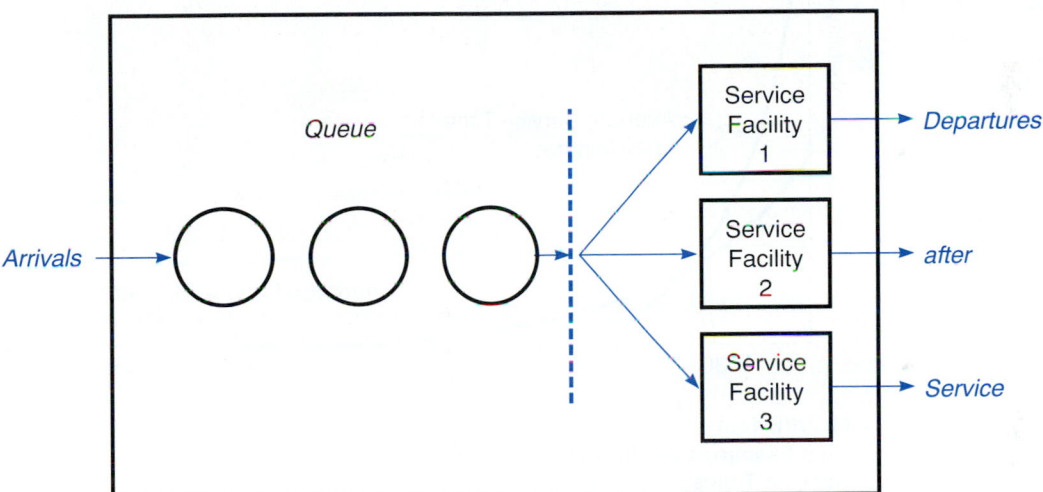

Multichannel, Single-Phase System

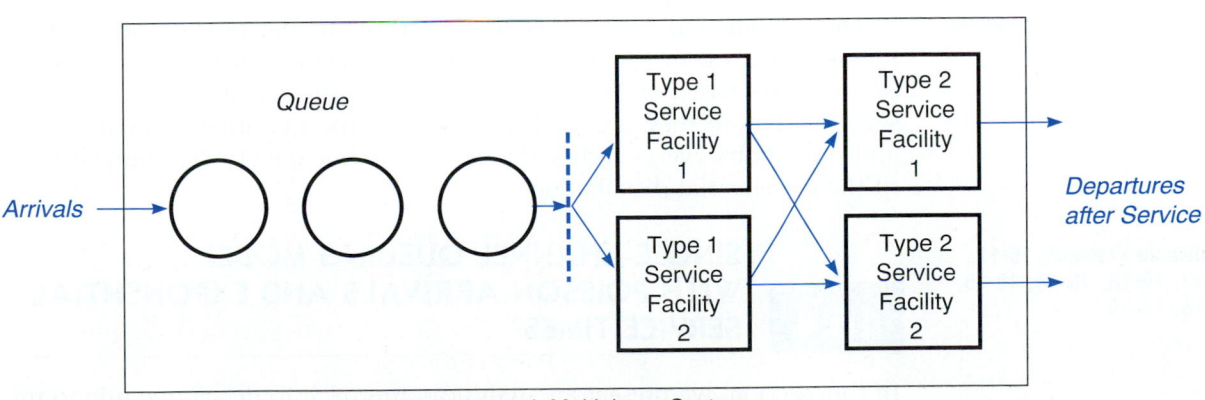

Multichannel, Multiphase System

FIGURE 16.3
Four Basic Queuing System Configurations

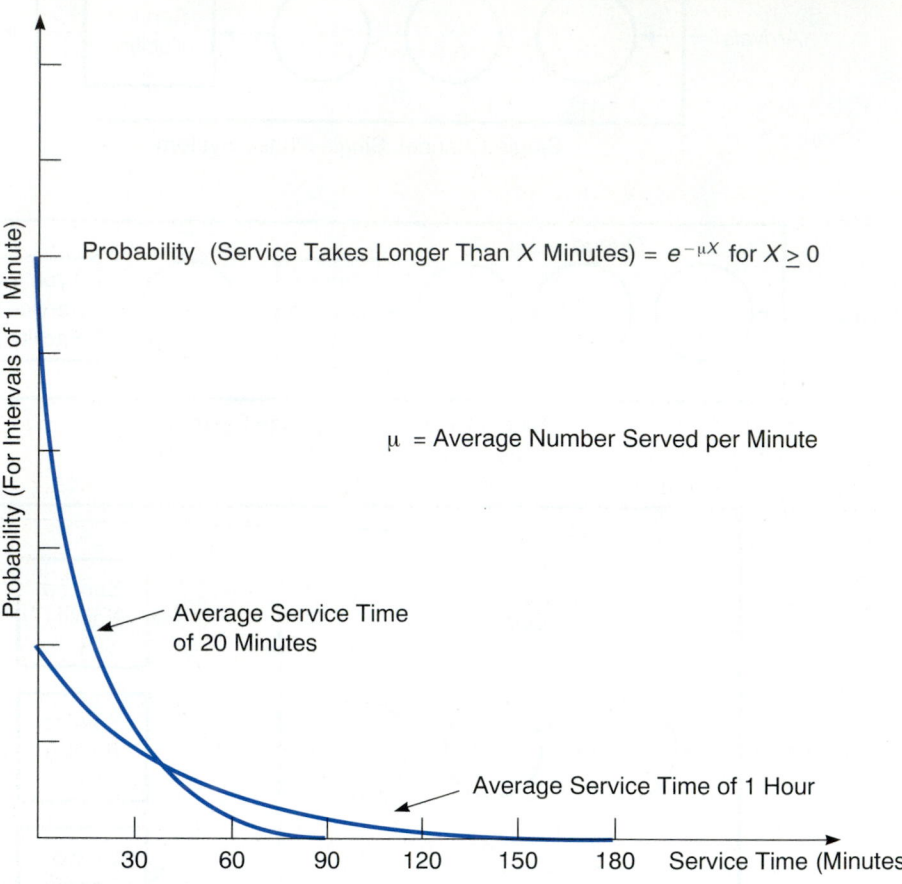

Transparency Master 16.6:
Two Examples of the
Exponential Distribution for
Service Times.

FIGURE 16.4
**Two Examples of the Exponential Distribution for
Service Times**

time is one hour, the probability of spending more than 180 minutes in service is virtually zero.

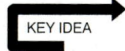

The exponential distribution is important to the process of building mathematical queuing models since many of the models' theoretical underpinnings are based on the assumption of Poisson arrivals and exponential services. Before they are applied, however, the quantitative analyst can and should observe, collect, and plot service time data to determine if they fit the exponential distribution.

**Applicable Problems 16-11,
16-12, 16-13, 16-14, 16-15,
16-16, 16-19**

16.4 SINGLE-CHANNEL QUEUING MODEL WITH POISSON ARRIVALS AND EXPONENTIAL SERVICE TIMES[3]

In this section, we present an analytical approach to determine important measures of performance in a typical service system. Once these numeric

---

[3]In the technical terminology of the operations research world, this model is also referred to as the M/M/1 queuing model.

Queuing up Customers on L. L. Bean's Phone Network

L. L. Bean, the widely known retailer of high-quality outdoor goods and apparel, handles more than 85 percent of its sales volume through mail orders and telephone orders via 800-service. While 15% of the $600 million in 1989 sales was conducted through store transactions and 20% was mail-ordered, about 65% of the total annual sales volume was generated through orders taken at two telemarketing centers located in Maine.

The firm faced severe problems, however. During the peak selling season in 1988, service level provided to incoming calls was unacceptable: during certain periods, 80% of the calls received a busy signal, and those that did not often had to wait up to 10 minutes before speaking with a sales agent. L. L. Bean estimated it lost $10 million in profit because of the way it allocated telemarketing resources. Keeping customers waiting "in line" (on the phone) was costing $25,000 per day; on exceptionally busy days, the total orders lost because of queue problems approached $500,000 in gross revenues.

Here is the concept behind the L. L. Bean phone network: (1) An arriving call seizes one of the phone trunk lines if one is available; otherwise, it is routed to a busy signal. (2) The call arrives at an L. L. Bean switch; the switch checks the queue length; if the queue is full, the call is routed to a busy signal, freeing the trunk line; otherwise the call enters the queue, taking up a queue position. (3) Callers may "renege" (hang up) while waiting for an agent, freeing the trunk and queue position. (4) When one of the Bean agents is available, the call is serviced, freeing a queue position. (5) When the call is completed, a trunk line and an agent are freed.

Developing queuing models similar to those in this chapter, L. L. Bean was able to optimally set the number of phone lines and the number of agents to have on duty for each half-hour of every day of the season. By 1989, use of the model resulted in 24% more calls answered, 17% more orders taken, and 16% more revenues. It also meant 81% fewer abandoned callers, and 84% faster answering time. The percent of calls spending less than 20 seconds in the queue increased from 25% to 77%. Queuing theory changed the way L. L. Bean thinks about telecommunications.

Source: Phil Quinn, Bruce Andrews, and Henry Parsons, "Allocating Telecommunications Resources at L. L. Bean, Inc." *Interfaces* **21**, 1 (Jan.–Feb. 1991): 75–91.

---

measures have been computed, it will be possible to add in cost data and begin to make decisions that balance desirable service levels with waiting line service costs.

Assumptions of the Model

The single-channel, single-phase model considered here is one of the most widely used and simplest queuing models. It assumes that seven conditions exist:

1. Arrivals are served on a first-in, first-out (FIFO) basis.

2. Every arrival waits to be served regardless of the length of the line; that is, there is no balking or reneging.

3. Arrivals are independent of preceding arrivals, but the average number of arrivals (the arrival rate) does not change over time.

4. Arrivals are described by a Poisson probability distribution and come from an infinite or very large population.

Video 16.1: Queuing up Customers on L. L. Bean's Phone Network

KEY IDEA

Transparency Master 16.7: Assumptions of the Basic Queuing Model.

5. Service times also vary from one customer to the next and are independent of one another, but their average rate is known.

6. Service times occur according to the negative exponential probability distribution.

7. The average service rate is greater than the average arrival rate.

When these seven conditions are met, we can develop a series of equations that define the queue's *operating characteristics*. The mathematics used to derive each equation is rather complex and outside the scope of this text, so we will just present the resulting formulas here.

Queuing Equations

We let

λ = mean number of arrivals per time period (for example, per hour)

μ = mean number of people or items served per time period

The queuing equations follow.

**queuing equations for
the single-channel,
single-phase model**

1. The average number of customers or units in the system, L; that is, the number in line plus the number being served:

$$L = \frac{\lambda}{\mu - \lambda} \qquad (16\text{-}2)$$

2. The average time a customer spends in the system, W; that is, the time spent in line plus the time spent being served:

$$W = \frac{1}{\mu - \lambda} \qquad (16\text{-}3)$$

3. The average number of customers in the queue, L_q:

$$L_q = \frac{\lambda^2}{\mu(\mu - \lambda)} \qquad (16\text{-}4)$$

4. The average time a customer spends waiting in the queue, W_q:

$$W_q = \frac{\lambda}{\mu(\mu - \lambda)} \qquad (16\text{-}5)$$

5. The utilization factor for the system, ρ; that is, the probability that the service facility is being used:

$$\rho = \frac{\lambda}{\mu} \qquad (\rho \text{ is the Greek letter rho}) \qquad (16\text{-}6)$$

6. The percent idle time, P_0; that is, the probability that no one is in the system:

$$P_0 = 1 - \frac{\lambda}{\mu} \qquad (16\text{-}7)$$

7. The probability that the number of customers in the system is greater than k, $P_{n>k}$:

$$P_{n>k} = \left(\frac{\lambda}{\mu}\right)^{k+1} \tag{16-8}$$

Arnold's Muffler Shop Case

We now apply these formulas to the case of Arnold's Muffler Shop in New Orleans. Arnold's mechanic, Reid Blank, is able to install new mufflers at an average rate of 3 per hour, or about 1 every 20 minutes. Customers needing this service arrive at the shop on the average of 2 per hour. Larry Arnold, the shop owner, studied queuing models in an MBA program and feels that all seven of the conditions for a single-channel model are met. He proceeds to calculate the numerical values of the preceding operating characteristics.

Alternate Example 16-1

$\lambda = 2$ cars arriving per hour

$\mu = 3$ cars serviced per hour

$L = \dfrac{\lambda}{\mu - \lambda} = \dfrac{2}{3 - 2} = \dfrac{2}{1} = 2$ cars in the system on the average

$W = \dfrac{1}{\mu - \lambda} = \dfrac{1}{3 - 2} = 1$ hour that an average car spends in the system

$L_q = \dfrac{\lambda^2}{\mu(\mu - \lambda)} = \dfrac{2^2}{3(3 - 2)} = \dfrac{4}{3(1)} = \dfrac{4}{3} = 1.33$ cars waiting in line on the average

$W_q = \dfrac{\lambda}{\mu(\mu - \lambda)} = \dfrac{2}{3(3 - 2)} = \dfrac{2}{3}$ hour $= 40$ minutes $=$ Average waiting time per car

$\rho = \dfrac{\lambda}{\mu} = \dfrac{2}{3} = .67 =$ Percent of time mechanic is busy, or the probability that the server is busy

$P_0 = 1 - \dfrac{\lambda}{\mu} = 1 - \dfrac{2}{3} = .33 =$ Probability there are 0 cars in the system

Probability of More than k Cars in the System

k	$P_{n>k} = (2/3)^{k+1}$	
0	.667	⟵ Note that this is equal to $1 - P_0 = 1 - 0.33 = 0.667$.
1	.444	
2	.296	
3	.198	⟵ Implies that there is a 19.8% chance that more than 3 cars are in the system.
4	.132	
5	.088	
6	.058	
7	.039	

Teaching Suggestion 16.5:
Use of Queuing Software.
See the Instructor's Section
for details.

conducting an economic analysis

Teaching Suggestion 16.6:
Importance of L_q and W_q in
Economic Analysis. See the
Instructor's Section for
details.

customer waiting time

service cost and total cost

Program 16.1 illustrates the ease of use of AB:QM in dealing with queuing problems. The only required inputs to this program were a title, the average arrival rate (2 cars per hour), and the service rate (3 cars per hour).

Now that the characteristics of the queuing system have been computed, Arnold decides to do an economic analysis of their impact. The waiting line model was valuable in predicting potential waiting times, queue lengths, idle times, and so on. But it did not identify optimal decisions or consider cost factors. As stated earlier, the solution to a queuing problem may require management to make a trade-off between the increased cost of providing better service and the decreased waiting costs derived from providing that service.

Arnold estimates that the cost of customer waiting time, in terms of customer dissatisfaction and lost goodwill, is $10 per hour of time spent *waiting* in line. (Once customers' cars are actually being serviced on the rack, they don't seem to mind waiting.) Since on the average a car has a ⅔ hour wait and there are approximately 16 cars serviced per day (2 per hour times 8 working hours per day), the total number of hours that customers spend waiting for mufflers to be installed each day is ⅔ × 16 = ³²⁄₃, or 10⅔ hours. Hence, in this case,

Customer waiting cost = ($10/hour) × (10⅔ hours/day) = $106 per day

The only other major cost that Larry Arnold can identify in the queuing situation is the salary of Reid Blank, the mechanic. Blank is paid $7 per hour, or $56 per day. Total anticipated costs, then, are $106 + $56 = $162 per day.

PROGRAM 16.1 Sample Computer Run Using AB:QM

```
Program: Queuing Theory / M/M/1

Problem Title : ARNOLD MUFFLER SINGLE CHANNEL MODEL

***** Input Data *****

Mean Arrival Rate                         :      2.000
Mean Service Rate                         :      3.000


***** Program Output *****

Mean Number of Units in the System        :      2.000
Mean Number of Units in the Queue         :      1.333
Mean Time in the System                   :      1.000
Mean Time in the Queue                    :      0.667
Service Facility Utilization Factor       :      0.667
Probability of No Units in System         :      0.333

***** End of Outuput *****
```

Now comes a decision. Arnold finds out through the muffler business grapevine that The Rusty Muffler, a crosstown competitor, employs a mechanic named Jimmy Smith who can efficiently install new mufflers at the rate of 4 per hour. Larry Arnold contacts Smith and inquires as to his interest in switching employers. Smith says he would consider leaving The Rusty Muffler, but only if he were paid a $9 per hour salary. Arnold, being a crafty businessman, decides that it may be worthwhile to fire Blank and replace him with the speedier but more expensive Smith.

Alternate Example 16.2

He first recomputes all the operating characteristics using a new service rate of 4 mufflers per hour.

$\lambda = 2$ cars arriving per hour

$\mu = 4$ cars serviced per hour

$L = \dfrac{\lambda}{\mu - \lambda} = \dfrac{2}{4 - 2} = 1$ car in the system on the average

$W = \dfrac{1}{\mu - \lambda} = \dfrac{1}{4 - 2} = \dfrac{1}{2}$ hour in the system on the average

$L_q = \dfrac{\lambda^2}{\mu(\mu - \lambda)} = \dfrac{2^2}{4(4 - 2)} = \dfrac{4}{8} = \dfrac{1}{2}$ cars waiting in line on the average

$W_q = \dfrac{\lambda}{\mu(\mu - \lambda)} = \dfrac{2}{4(4 - 2)} = \dfrac{2}{8} = \dfrac{1}{4}$ hour = 15 minutes average waiting time per car in the queue

$\rho = \dfrac{\lambda}{\mu} = \dfrac{2}{4} = .5 =$ Percent of time mechanic is busy

$P_0 = 1 - \dfrac{\lambda}{\mu} = 1 - .5 = .5 =$ Probability there are 0 cars in the system

Probability of More than k Cars in the System

k	$P_{n>k} = (^2/_4)^{k+1}$
0	.5
1	.25
2	.125
3	.062
4	.031
5	.016
6	.008
7	.004

It is quite evident that Smith's speed will result in considerably shorter queues and waiting times. For example, a customer would now spend an average of ½ hour in the system and ¼ hour waiting in the queue, as opposed to one hour in the system and ⅔ hour in the queue with Blank as mechanic.

**recompute total cost and
decide**

Total hours customers spend *waiting* if Smith is on duty = (16 cars/day) × (¼ hour/car) = 4 hours.

Customer waiting cost = $10/hour × 4 hours = $40 per day

Service cost of Smith = 8 hours/day × $9/hour = $72 per day

Total expected cost = Waiting cost + Service cost = $40 + $72

= $112 per day

Since the total daily expected cost with Blank as mechanic was $162, Arnold may very well decide to hire Smith and reduce costs by $162 − $112 = $50 per day.

**Applicable Problems 16-14f,
16-16c, 16-17, 16-18,
16-20, 16-21, 16-22, 16-24,
16-27**

16.5 MULTIPLE-CHANNEL QUEUING MODEL WITH POISSON ARRIVALS AND EXPONENTIAL SERVICE TIMES[4]

The next logical step is to look at a multiple-channel queuing system, in which two or more servers or channels are available to handle arriving customers. Let us still assume that customers awaiting service form one single line and then proceed to the first available server. An example of such a multichannel, single-phase waiting line is found in many banks today. A common line is formed and the customer at the head of the line proceeds to the first free teller. (Refer back to Figure 16.3 for a typical multichannel configuration.)

The multiple channel system presented here again assumes that arrivals follow a Poisson probability distribution and that service times are exponentially distributed. Service is first come, first served, and all servers are assumed to perform at the same rate. Other assumptions listed earlier for the single-channel model apply as well.

**assumptions of the
model**

Equations for the Multichannel Queuing Model

If we let M equal the number of channels open, then the following formulas may be used in the waiting line analysis.

$$\lambda = \text{average arrival rate}$$

$$\mu = \text{average service rate at each channel}$$

queuing equations

The probability that there are 0 customers or units in the system:

$$P_0 = \frac{1}{\left[\sum_{n=0}^{n=M-1} \frac{1}{n!}\left(\frac{\lambda}{\mu}\right)^n\right] + \frac{1}{M!}\left(\frac{\lambda}{\mu}\right)^M \frac{M\mu}{M\mu - \lambda}} \quad \text{for } M\mu > \lambda \quad (16\text{-}9)$$

[4]This model is also known by the technical name of the M/M/m model.

The average number of customers or units in the system:

$$L = \frac{\lambda\mu(\lambda/\mu)^M}{(M-1)!(M\mu - \lambda)^2}P_0 + \frac{\lambda}{\mu}$$ (16-10)

The average time a unit spends in the waiting line or being serviced (namely, in the system):

$$W = \frac{\mu(\lambda/\mu)^M}{(M-1)!(M\mu - \lambda)^2}P_0 + \frac{1}{\mu} = \frac{L}{\lambda}$$ (16-11)

The average number of customers or units in line waiting for service:

$$L_q = L - \frac{\lambda}{\mu}$$ (16-12)

The average time a customer or unit spends in the queue waiting for service:

$$W_q = W - \frac{1}{\mu} = \frac{L_q}{\lambda}$$ (16-13)

Utilization rate:

$$\rho = \frac{\lambda}{M\mu}$$ (16-14)

These equations are obviously more complex than the ones used in the single-channel model, yet they are used in exactly the same fashion and provide the same type of information as did the simpler model.

Arnold's Muffler Shop Revisited

Alternate Example 16.3

For an application of the multichannel queuing model, let's return to the case of Arnold's Muffler Shop. Larry Arnold previously examined two options. He could retain his current mechanic, Reid Blank, at a total expected cost of $162 per day. Or he could fire Blank and hire a slightly more expensive but faster worker named Jimmy Smith. With Smith on board, service system costs could be reduced to $112 per day.

A third option is now explored. Arnold finds that at minimal after-tax cost he can open a *second* garage bay in which mufflers can be installed. Instead of firing his first mechanic, Blank, he would hire a second worker. The new mechanic would be expected to install mufflers at the same rate as Blank—about $\mu = 3$ per hour. Customers, who would still arrive at the rate of $\lambda = 2$ per hour, would wait in a single line until one of the two mechanics is free. To find out how this option compares to the old single-channel waiting line system, Arnold computes several operating characteristics for the $M = 2$ channel system.

opening a second muffler service channel

$$P_0 = \cfrac{1}{\left[\sum_{n=0}^{1} \cfrac{1}{n!}\left(\cfrac{2}{3}\right)^n\right] + \cfrac{1}{2!}\left(\cfrac{2}{3}\right)^2 \left(\cfrac{2(3)}{2(3) - 2}\right)}$$

$$= \cfrac{1}{1 + \cfrac{2}{3} + \cfrac{1}{2}\left(\cfrac{4}{9}\right)\left(\cfrac{6}{6 - 2}\right)} = \cfrac{1}{1 + \cfrac{2}{3} + \cfrac{1}{3}} = \cfrac{1}{2} = .5$$

= Probability of 0 cars in the system

$$L = \left(\cfrac{(2)(3)(2/3)^2}{1![2(3) - 2]^2}\right)\left(\cfrac{1}{2}\right) + \cfrac{2}{3} = \cfrac{8/3}{16}\left(\cfrac{1}{2}\right) + \cfrac{2}{3} = \cfrac{3}{4} = .75$$

= Average number of cars in the system

$$W = \cfrac{L}{\lambda} = \cfrac{3/4}{2} = \cfrac{3}{8} \text{ hours} = 22\tfrac{1}{2} \text{ minutes}$$

= Average time a car spends in the system

$$L_q = L - \cfrac{\lambda}{\mu} = \cfrac{3}{4} - \cfrac{2}{3} = \cfrac{1}{12} = .083 = \text{Average number of cars in the}$$
$$\text{queue}$$

$$W_q = \cfrac{L_q}{\lambda} = \cfrac{.083}{2} = .0415 \text{ hours} = 2\tfrac{1}{2} \text{ minutes}$$

= Average time a car spends in the queue

Program 16.2 confirms these computations. The only difference between this run and that of Program 16.1 is that the number of servers has been entered as 2.

PROGRAM 16.2 AB:QM Output for Arnold's Muffler Shop with Two Servers

```
Program: Queuing Theory / M/M/m

Problem Title : ARNOLD

***** Input Data *****

Mean Arrival Rate                          :        2.000
Mean Service Rate                          :        3.000
Number of Servers                          :        2.000


***** Program Output *****

Mean Number of Units in the System         :        0.750
Mean Number of Units in the Queue          :        0.083
Mean Time in the System                    :        0.375
Mean Time in the Queue                     :        0.042
Service Facility Utilization Factor        :        0.333
Probability of No Units in System          :        0.500

***** End of Output *****
```

These data are compared to earlier operating characteristics in Table 16.2. The increased service from opening a second channel has a dramatic effect on almost all characteristics. In particular, time spent waiting in line drops from 40 minutes with one mechanic (Blank) or 15 minutes with Smith down to only 2½ minutes! Likewise, the average number of cars in the queue falls to .083 (about ¹⁄₁₂ of a car).[5] But does this mean that a second bay should be opened?

lower waiting time results from second bay

To complete his economic analysis, Arnold assumes that the second mechanic would be paid the same as the current one, Blank, namely, $7 per hour. Total time customers will now spend waiting will be = (16 cars per day) × (0.0415 hours per car) = .664 hours.

cost analysis

$$\text{Customer waiting cost} = \$10/\text{hour} \times .664 \text{ hours} = \$6.64 \text{ per day}$$

$$\text{Service cost of 2 mechanics} = 2 \times 8 \text{ hours each/day} \times \$7/\text{hour} = \$112 \text{ per day}$$

$$\text{Total expected cost} = \text{Waiting cost} + \text{Service cost}$$

$$= \quad \$6.64 \quad + \$112.00 \quad = \$118.64 \text{ per day}$$

As you recall, total cost with just Blank as mechanic was found to be $162 per day. Cost with just Smith was just $112. Although opening a second channel would be likely to have a positive effect on customer goodwill and hence lower the cost of waiting time, it means an increase in the cost of providing service. Look back to Figure 16.1 and you will see that such trade-offs are the basis of queuing theory. Arnold's decision is to replace his present worker with the speedier Smith, and *not* to open a second service bay.

Use of Waiting Line Tables

Imagine the work a manager would face in dealing with $M = 3, 4,$ or 5 channel waiting line models if he or she did not have a computer readily

TABLE 16.2 Effect of Service Level on Arnold's Operating Characteristics

	LEVEL OF SERVICE		
OPERATING CHARACTERISTIC	One Mechanic (Reid Blank) $\mu = 3$	Two Mechanics $\mu = 3$ for Each	One Fast Mechanic (Jimmy Smith) $\mu = 4$
Probability the system is empty (P_o)	.33	.50	.50
Average number of cars in the system (L)	2 cars	.75 cars	1 car
Average time spent in the system (W)	60 min.	22.5 min.	30 min.
Average number of cars in the queue (L_q)	1.33 cars	.083 cars	.50 cars
Average time spent in the queue (W_q)	40 min.	2.5 min.	15 min.

[5]You might note that adding a second mechanic does not cut queue waiting time and length just in half, but makes it even smaller. This is because of the *random* arrival and service processes. When there is only one mechanic and two customers arrive within a minute of each other, the second will have a long wait. The fact that the mechanic may have been idle for 30 to 40 minutes before they both arrive does not change this average waiting time. Thus, single-channel models often have high wait times relative to multichannel models.

available. The arithmetic becomes increasingly troublesome. Fortunately, much of the burden of manually examining multiple channel queues can be avoided by turning to tables such as Table 16.3. This table, the result of hundreds of computations, represents the relationship between three things: (1) service facility utilization factor, ρ (which is simple to find—it's

TABLE 16.3 Values of L_q for $M = 1$–5 Service Channels and Various Values of $\rho = \lambda/\mu$*

	POISSON ARRIVALS, EXPONENTIAL SERVICE TIMES				
	NUMBER OF SERVICE CHANNELS, M				
ρ	1	2	3	4	5
.10	.0111				
.15	.0264	.0008			
.20	.0500	.0020			
.25	.0833	.0039			
.30	.1285	.0069			
.35	.1884	.0110			
.40	.2666	.0166			
.45	.3681	.0239	.0019		
.50	.5000	.0333	.0030		
.55	.6722	.0449	.0043		
.60	.9000	.0593	.0061		
.65	1.2071	.0767	.0084		
.70	1.6333	.0976	.0112		
.75	2.2500	.1227	.0147		
.80	3.2000	.1523	.0189		
.85	4.8166	.1873	.0239	.0031	
.90	8.1000	.2285	.0300	.0041	
.95	18.0500	.2767	.0371	.0053	
1.0		.3333	.0454	.0067	
1.2		.6748	.0904	.0158	
1.4		1.3449	.1778	.0324	.0059
1.6		2.8444	.3128	.0604	.0121
1.8		7.6734	.5320	.1051	.0227
2.0			.8888	.1739	.0398
2.2			1.4907	.2770	.0659
2.4			2.1261	.4305	.1047
2.6			4.9322	.6581	.1609
2.8			12.2724	1.0000	.2411
3.0				1.5282	.3541
3.2				2.3856	.5128
3.4				3.9060	.7365
3.6				7.0893	1.0550
3.8				16.9366	1.5184
4.0					2.2164
4.2					3.3269
4.4					5.2675
4.6					9.2885
4.8					21.6384

*Reprinted by permission of John Wiley & Sons, Inc., from Elwood S. Buffa, *Modern Production Management: Managing the Operations Function,* 5th edition, 1977.

just λ/μ), (2) number of service channels open, and (3) the average number of customers in the queue, L_q (which is what we'd like to find). For any combination of utilization rate (ρ) and $M = 1, 2, 3, 4,$ or 5 open service channels, you can quickly look in the body of the table to read off the appropriate value for L_q.

Let's say, for example, that a bank is trying to decide how many drive-in teller windows to open on a busy Saturday. It estimates that customers arrive at a rate of about $\lambda = 18$ per hour, and that each teller can service about $\mu = 20$ customers per hour. Then the utilization rate is $\rho = \lambda/\mu = {}^{18}\!/_{20} = .90$. Turning to Table 16.3, under $\rho = .90$, we see that if only $M = 1$ service window is open, the average number of customers in line will be 8.1. If two windows are open, L_q drops to .2285 customers, to .03 for $M = 3$ tellers, and to .0041 for $M = 4$ tellers. Adding more open windows at this point will result in an average queue length of 0.

It is also a simple matter to compute the average waiting time in the queue, W_q, since $W_q = L_q/\lambda$. When one channel is open, $W_q = 8.1$ customers/(18 customers per hour) = .45 hours = 27 minutes waiting time; when two tellers are open, $W_q = .2285$ customers/(18 customers per hour) = .0126 hours = ¾ minute; and so on. Perhaps you might check Larry Arnold's computations against tabled values just to practice their use. Don't forget to interpolate if your exact ρ value is not found in the first column.

Other common operating characteristics besides L_q have been published in table form and are often found in production management books and manuals.

Teaching Suggestion 16.7: Waiting Line Tables and Nomographs. See the Instructor's Section for details.

16.6 CONSTANT SERVICE TIME MODEL[6]

Applicable Problem 16-23

Some service systems have constant service times instead of exponentially distributed times. When customers or equipment are processed according to a fixed cycle, as in the case of an automatic car wash or an amusement park ride, constant service rates are appropriate. Because constant rates are certain, the values for L_q, W_q, L, and W are always less than they would be in the models we have just discussed, which have variable service times. As a matter of fact, both the average queue length and the average waiting time in the queue are halved with the constant service rate model.

constant service rates speed the process

Equations for the Constant Service Time Model

Constant service model formulas follow:

1. Average length of the queue: $L_q = \dfrac{\lambda^2}{2\mu(\mu - \lambda)}$ (16-15)

2. Average waiting time in the queue: $W_q = \dfrac{\lambda}{2\mu(\mu - \lambda)}$ (16-16)

[6]In the operations research literature, this is also referred to as the M/D/1 model.

3. Average number of customers in the system: $L = L_q + \dfrac{\lambda}{\mu}$ **(16-17)**

4. Average waiting time in the system: $W = W_q + \dfrac{1}{\mu}$ **(16-18)**

Garcia-Golding Recycling Inc.

Alternate Example 16.4

Garcia-Golding Recycling, Inc., collects and compacts aluminum cans and glass bottles in New York City. Their truck drivers, who arrive to unload these materials for recycling, currently wait an average of 15 minutes before emptying their loads. The cost of the driver and truck time wasted while in queue is valued at $60 per hour. A new automated compactor can be purchased that will process truck loads at a constant rate of 12 trucks per hour (that is, 5 minutes per truck). Trucks arrive according to a Poisson distribution at an average rate of 8 per hour. If the new compactor is put in use, its cost will be amortized at a rate of $3 per truck unloaded. A summer intern from a local college did the following analysis to evaluate the costs versus benefits of the purchase.

Current waiting cost/trip = (¼ hr. waiting now) ($60/hr. cost) = $15/trip

New system: $\lambda = 8$ trucks/hr. arriving $\mu = 12$ trucks/hr. served

Average waiting time in queue = $W_q = \dfrac{\lambda}{2\mu(\mu - \lambda)} = \dfrac{8}{2(12)(12 - 8)} = \dfrac{1}{12}$ hr.

Waiting cost/trip with new compactor = (¹⁄₁₂ hr. wait) ($60/hr. cost) = $5/trip

Savings with new equipment = $15 (current system) − $5 (new system) = $10/trip

Cost of new equipment amortized = $3/trip

Net savings = $7/trip

The complete analysis for this problem using AB:QM is seen in Program 16.3. (Note that ¹⁄₁₂ of an hour = .083 hour average/mean waiting time in queue.)

16.7   FINITE POPULATION MODEL

Applicable Problems 16-25, 16-26

When there is a limited population of potential customers for a service facility, we need to consider a different queuing model. This model would be used, for example, if you were considering equipment repairs in a factory that has five machines, if you were in charge of maintenance for a fleet of 10 commuter airplanes, or if you ran a hospital ward that has 20 beds. The limited population model permits any number of repair people (servers) to be considered.

The reason this model differs from the three earlier queuing models is that there is now a *dependent* relationship between the length of the queue and the arrival rate. To illustrate the extreme situation, if your factory had five machines and all were broken and awaiting repair, the ar-

PROGRAM 16.3 Computer Run Using AB:QM for Garcia-Golding's Constant Service Time Problem

```
Program: Queuing Theory / M/D/1

Problem Title : GARCIA-GOLDING RECYCLING INC.

***** Input Data *****

Mean Arrival Rate                        :        8.000
Constant Service Rate                    :       12.000


***** Program Output *****

Mean Number of Units in the System       :        1.333
Mean Number of Units in the Queue        :        0.667
Mean Time in the System                  :        0.167
Mean Time in the Queue                   :        0.083
Service Facility Utilization Factor      :        0.667
Probability of No Units in System        :        0.333

***** End of Output *****
```

rival rate would drop to zero. In general, as the waiting line becomes longer in the limited population model, the arrival rate of customers or machines drops lower.

In this section, we will describe a finite calling population model that has the following assumptions:

1. There is only one server.[7]

2. The population of units seeking service is finite.[8]

3. Arrivals follow a Poisson distribution, while service times are exponentially distributed.

4. Customers are served on a first-come, first-served basis.

Equations for the Finite Population Model

Using λ = mean arrival rate, μ = mean service rate, and N = size of the population, here are the operating characteristics for the finite population model with a single channel, or server on duty:

[7]In the operations research literature, this is called the M/M/1 finite source model.

[8]Although there is no definite number that we can use to divide finite from infinite populations, the general rule of thumb is this: if the number in the queue is a significant proportion of the calling population, use a finite queuing model. *Finite Queuing Tables*, by Peck and Hazelwood (John Wiley & Sons, 1958), eliminates much of the mathematics involved in computing the operating characteristics for such a model.

1. Probability the system is empty:

$$P_0 = \frac{1}{\displaystyle\sum_{n=0}^{N} \frac{N!}{(N-n)!}\left(\frac{\lambda}{\mu}\right)^n} \qquad (16\text{-}19)$$

2. Average length of the queue:

$$L_q = N - \left(\frac{\lambda + \mu}{\lambda}\right)(1 - P_0) \qquad (16\text{-}20)$$

3. Average number of customers (units) in the system:

$$L = L_q + (1 - P_0) \qquad (16\text{-}21)$$

4. Average waiting time in the queue:

$$W_q = \frac{L_q}{(N - L)\lambda} \qquad (16\text{-}22)$$

5. Average waiting time in the system:

$$W = W_q + \frac{1}{\mu} \qquad (16\text{-}23)$$

6. Probability of n units in the system:

$$P_n = \frac{N!}{(N-n)!}\left(\frac{\lambda}{\mu}\right)^n P_0 \qquad for \ n = 0, 1, \dots, N \qquad (16\text{-}24)$$

Department of Commerce Example

Past records indicate that each of the five high-speed "page" printers at the U.S. Department of Commerce, in Washington, D.C., needs repair after about 20 hours of use. Breakdowns have been determined to be Poisson distributed. The one technician on duty can service a printer in an average of two hours, following an exponential distribution.

To compute the system's operation characteristics we first note that the mean arrival rate is $\lambda = \frac{1}{20} = 0.05$ printers per hour. The mean service rate is $\mu = \frac{1}{2} = 0.50$ printers per hour. Then,

1. $P_0 = \dfrac{1}{\displaystyle\sum_{n=0}^{5} \frac{5!}{(5-n)!}\left(\frac{.05}{.5}\right)^n} = .564$ (We leave these calculations for you to confirm)

2. $L_q = 5 - \left(\dfrac{.05 + .5}{.05}\right)(1 - P_0) = 5 - (11)(1 - .564) = 5 - 4.8$

   $= .2$ printers

3. $L = .2 + (1 - .564) = .64$ printers

4. $W_q = \dfrac{.2}{(5 - .64)(.05)} = \dfrac{.2}{.22} = .91$ hours

5. $W = .91 + \dfrac{1}{.50} = 2.91$ hours

If printer downtime costs \$120 per hour and the technician is paid \$25 per hour, we can also compute the total cost per hour.

Total hourly cost = (Average no. of printers down)(Cost per downtime hour)
+ cost per technician hour = (.64)(\$120) + \$25 = \$76.80 + \$25.00 = \$101.80

16.8 MORE COMPLEX QUEUING MODELS AND THE USE OF SIMULATION

Many practical waiting line problems that occur in production and operations service systems have characteristics like those of Arnold's Muffler Shop, Garcia-Golding Recycling Inc., or the Department of Commerce. This is true when the situation calls for single- or multiple-channel waiting lines, with Poisson arrivals and exponential or constant service times, an infinite calling population, and first-in, first-out service.

Often, however, *variations* of this specific case are present in an analysis. Service times in an automobile repair shop, for example, tend to follow the normal probability distribution instead of the exponential. A college registration system in which seniors have first choice of courses and hours over all other students is an example of a first-come, first-served model with a preemptive priority queue discipline. A physical examination for military recruits is an example of a multiphase system—one that differs from the single-phase models discussed in this chapter. A recruit first lines up to have blood drawn at one station, then waits to take an eye exam at the next station, talks to a psychiatrist at the third, and is examined by a doctor for medical problems at the fourth. At each phase, the recruit must enter another queue and wait his or her turn.

models exist to handle variations of basic assumptions

Models to handle these cases have been developed by operations researchers. The computations for the resulting mathematical formulations are somewhat more complex than the ones covered in this chapter.[9] And many real-world queuing applications are too complex to be modeled analytically at all. When this happens, quantitative analysts usually turn to *computer simulation.*

KEY IDEA

Simulation, the topic of Chapter 17, is a technique in which random numbers are used to draw inferences about probability distributions (such as arrivals and services). Using this approach, many hours, days, or months of data can be developed by a computer in a few seconds. This allows analysis of controllable factors, such as adding another service channel, without actually doing so physically. Basically, whenever a standard

simulation defined

---

[9]Often the *qualitative* results of queuing models are as useful as the quantitative results. Results show that it is inherently more efficient to pool resources, use central dispatching, and provide single multiple-server systems rather than multiple single-server systems.

analytical queuing model provides only a poor approximation of the actual service system, it is wise to develop a simulation model instead.

16.9 SUMMARY

assumptions recalled

Waiting lines and service systems are important parts of the business world. In this chapter, we described several common queuing situations and presented mathematical models for analyzing waiting lines following certain assumptions. Those assumptions were that: (1) arrivals come from an infinite, or very large, population; (2) arrivals are Poisson distributed; (3) arrivals are treated on a first-in, first-out basis and do not balk or renege; (4) service times follow the negative exponential distribution or are constant; and (5) the average service rate is faster than the average arrival rate.

The models illustrated in this chapter were for single-channel, single-phase and multiple-channel, single-phase problems. After a series of operating characteristics were computed, total expected costs were studied. As shown graphically in Figure 16.1, total cost is the sum of the cost of providing service plus the cost of waiting time.

key system characteristics

Key operating characteristics for a system were shown to be: (1) utilization rate, (2) percent idle time, (3) average time spent waiting in the system and in the queue, (4) average number of customers in the system and in the queue, and (5) probabilities of various numbers of customers in the system.

It was emphasized that a variety of queuing models exist that do not meet all of the assumptions of the traditional models. In these cases, we use more complex mathematical models or turn to a technique called computer simulation. The application of simulation to problems of queuing systems, inventory control, machine breakdown, and other quantitative analysis situations is our next topic, as you will see in Chapter 17.

GLOSSARY

Waiting Line. One or more customers or objects waiting to be served.

Queuing Theory. The mathematical study of waiting lines or queues.

Service Cost. The cost of providing a particular level of service.

Waiting Cost. The cost to the firm of having customers or objects waiting in line to be serviced.

Calling Population. The population of items from which arrivals at the queuing system come.

Unlimited or Infinite Population. A calling population that is very large relative to the number of customers currently in the system.

Limited or Finite Population. A case in which the number of customers in the system is a significant proportion of the calling population.

Poisson Distribution. A probability distribution that is often used to describe random arrivals in a queue.

Balking. The case in which arriving customers refuse to join the waiting line.

Reneging. The case in which customers enter a queue but then leave before being serviced.

Limited Queue Length. A waiting line that cannot increase beyond a specific size.

Unlimited Queue Length. A queue that can increase to an infinite size.

Queue Discipline. The rule by which customers in a line receive service.

FIFO. A queue discipline (meaning first-in, first-out) in which the customers are served in the strict order of arrival.

Operating Characteristics. Descriptive characteristics of a queuing system, including the average number of customers in a line and in the system, the average waiting times in a line and in the system, and percent idle time.

Single-Channel Queuing System. A system with one service facility fed by one queue.

Multiple-Channel Queuing System. A system that has more than one service facility, all fed by the same single queue.

Single-Phase System. A queuing system in which service is received at only one station.

Multiphase System. A system in which service is received from more than one station, one after the other.

Negative Exponential Distribution. A probability distribution that is often used to describe random service times in a service system.

M/M/1. Another name for the single-channel model with Poisson arrivals and exponential service times.

Utilization Factor (ρ). The proportion of the time service facilities are in use.

M/M/m. A technical name for the multichannel queuing model (with m servers) and Poisson arrivals and exponential service times.

M/D/1. A technical name for the constant service time model.

Waiting Line Tables. Tabled values that help in determining the operating characteristics of large or complex queuing systems.

Simulation. A technique for representing queuing models that are complex and difficult to model analytically.

KEY EQUATIONS

λ = Mean number of arrivals per time period

μ = Mean number of people or items served per time period

(16-1) $\quad P(X) = \dfrac{e^{-\lambda}\lambda^X}{X!}$

Poisson probability distribution used in describing arrivals.

Equations 16-2 through 16-8 describe operating characteristics in the single-channel model that has Poisson arrival and exponential service rates.

(16-2) $\quad L$ = Average number of units (customers) in the system

$\qquad = \dfrac{\lambda}{\mu - \lambda}$

(16-3) W = Average time a unit spends in the system (Waiting time + Service time) $= \dfrac{1}{\mu - \lambda}$

(16-4) L_q = Average number of units in the queue $= \dfrac{\lambda^2}{\mu(\mu - \lambda)}$

(16-5) W_q = Average time a unit spends waiting in the queue $= \dfrac{\lambda}{\mu(\mu - \lambda)}$

(16-6) ρ = Utilization factor for the system $= \dfrac{\lambda}{\mu}$

(16-7) P_0 = Probability of 0 units in the system (that is, the service unit is idle)
$$= 1 - \dfrac{\lambda}{\mu}$$

(16-8) $P_{n>k}$ = Probability of more than k units in the system $= \left(\dfrac{\lambda}{\mu}\right)^{k+1}$

Equations 16-9 through 16-14 describe operating characteristics in multiple-channel models that have Poisson arrival and exponential service rates, where M = the number of open channels.

(16-9) $P_0 = \dfrac{1}{\left[\displaystyle\sum_{n=0}^{n=M-1} \dfrac{1}{n!}\left(\dfrac{\lambda}{\mu}\right)^n\right] + \dfrac{1}{M!}\left(\dfrac{\lambda}{\mu}\right)^M \dfrac{M\mu}{M\mu - \lambda}}$ for $M\mu > \lambda$

The probability that there are 0 people or units in the system.

(16-10) $L = \dfrac{\lambda\mu(\lambda/\mu)^M}{(M-1)!(M\mu - \lambda)^2}P_0 + \dfrac{\lambda}{\mu}$

The average number of people or units in the system.

(16-11) $W = \dfrac{\mu(\lambda/\mu)^M}{(M-1)!(M\mu - \lambda)^2}P_0 + \dfrac{1}{\mu} = \dfrac{L}{\lambda}$

The average time a unit spends in the waiting line or being serviced (namely, in the system).

(16-12) $L_q = L - \dfrac{\lambda}{\mu}$

The average number of people or units in line waiting for service.

(16-13) $W_q = W - \dfrac{1}{\mu} = \dfrac{L_q}{\lambda}$

The average time a person or unit spends in the queue waiting for service.

(16-14) $\rho = \dfrac{\lambda}{M\mu}$

Utilization rate.

Equations 16-15 through 16-18 describe operating characteristics in single-channel models that have Poisson arrivals and constant service rates.

(16-15) $L_q = \dfrac{\lambda^2}{2\mu(\mu - \lambda)}$

The average length of the queue.

(16-16) $W_q = \dfrac{\lambda}{2\mu(\mu - \lambda)}$

The average waiting time in the queue.

(16-17) $L = L_q + \dfrac{\lambda}{\mu}$

The average number of customers in the system.

(16-18) $W = W_q + \dfrac{1}{\mu}$

The average waiting time in the system.

Equations 16-19 through 16-24 describe operating characteristics in single-channel models that have Poisson arrivals and exponential service rates and a finite calling population.

(16-19) $P_0 = \dfrac{1}{\displaystyle\sum_{n=0}^{N} \dfrac{n!}{(N-n)!}\left(\dfrac{\lambda}{\mu}\right)^n}$

The probability the system is empty.

(16-20) $L_q = N - \left(\dfrac{\lambda + \mu}{\lambda}\right)(1 - P_0)$

Average length of the queue.

(16-21) $L = L_q + (1 - P_0)$

Average number of units in the system.

(16-22) $W_q = \dfrac{L_q}{(N - L)\lambda}$

Average time in the queue.

(16-23) $W = W_q + \dfrac{1}{\mu}$

Average time in the system.

(16-24) $P_n = \dfrac{N!}{(N-n)!}\left(\dfrac{\lambda}{\mu}\right)^n P_0 \text{ for } n = 0, 1, \dots, N$

Probability of n units in the system.

SOLVED PROBLEMS

Solved Problem 16-1

The Maitland Furniture store gets an average of 50 customers per shift. The manager of Maitland wants to calculate whether she should hire 1, 2, 3, or

4 salespeople. She has determined that average waiting times will be 7 minutes with one salesperson, 4 minutes with two salespeople, 3 minutes with three salespeople, and 2 minutes with four salespeople. She has estimated the cost per minute that customers wait at $1. The cost per salesperson per shift (including fringe benefits) is $70.

How many salespeople should be hired?

Solution

The manager's calculations are as follows:

	NUMBER OF SALESPEOPLE			
	1	2	3	4
(a) Average number of customers per shift	50	50	50	50
(b) Average waiting time per customer (minutes)	7	4	3	2
(c) Total waiting time per shift (a × b) (minutes)	350	200	150	100
(d) Cost per minute of waiting time (estimated)	$1.00	$1.00	$1.00	$1.00
(e) Value of lost time (c × d) per shift	$350	$200	$150	$100
(f) Salary cost per shift	$ 70	$140	$210	$280
(g) Total cost per shift	$420	$340	$360	$380

Since the minimum total cost per shift relates to two salespeople, the manager's optimum strategy is to hire two salespeople.

Solved Problem 16-2

Marty Schatz owns and manages a chili dog and soft drink store near the campus. While Marty can service 30 customers per hour on the average (μ), he only gets 20 customers per hour (λ). Since Marty could wait on 50% more customers than actually visit his store, it doesn't make sense to him that he should have any waiting lines.

Marty hires you to examine the situation and to determine some characteristics of his queue. After looking into the problem, you make the seven assumptions listed in Section 16.4. What are your findings?

Solution

$$L = \frac{\lambda}{\mu - \lambda} = \frac{20}{30 - 20} = 2 \text{ customers in the system on the average}$$

$$W = \frac{1}{\mu - \lambda} = \frac{1}{30 - 20} = .1 \text{ hours (6 minutes) that the average customer spends in the total system}$$

$$L_q = \frac{\lambda^2}{\mu(\mu - \lambda)} = \frac{20^2}{30(30 - 20)} = 1.33 \text{ customers waiting for service in line on the average}$$

$$W_q = \frac{\lambda}{\mu(\mu - \lambda)} = \frac{20}{30(30 - 20)} = 1/15 \text{ hour} = (4 \text{ minutes}) = \text{Average}$$

waiting time of a customer
in the queue awaiting service

$$\rho = \frac{\lambda}{\mu} = \frac{20}{30} = .67 = \text{Percent of the time Marty is busy waiting}$$

on customers

$$P_0 = 1 - \frac{\lambda}{\mu} = 1 - \rho = .33 = \text{Probability that there are no customers}$$

in the system (being waited on or
waiting in the queue) at any given time

Probability of k or More Customers Waiting in Line and/or Being Waited On:

k	$P_{(n>k)} = \left(\frac{\lambda}{\mu}\right)^{k+1}$
0	.667
1	.444
2	.296
3	.198

Solved Problem 16-3

Refer to the preceding solved problem. Marty agreed that these figures seemed to represent his approximate business situation. You are quite surprised at the length of the lines and elicit from him an estimated value of the customer's waiting time (in the queue, not being waited on) at 10¢ per minute. During the 12 hours that he is open he gets $(12 \times 20) = 240$ customers. The average customer is in a queue 4 minutes, so the total customers waiting time is $(240 \times 4 \text{ minutes}) = 960$ minutes. The value of 960 minutes is $(\$.10)(960 \text{ minutes}) = \$96$. You tell Marty that not only is 10¢ per minute quite conservative, but he could probably save most of that $96 of customer ill-will if he hired another salesclerk. After much haggling, Mary agrees to provide you with all the chili dogs you can eat during a week-long period in exchange for your analysis of the results of having two clerks wait on the customers.

Assuming that Marty hires one additional salesclerk whose service rate equals Marty's rate, complete the analysis.

Solution

With two cash registers open, the system becomes two-channel, or $M = 2$. The computations yield:

$$L = \left[\frac{(20)(30)(20/30)^2}{(2 - 1)![(2)(30) - 20]^2}\right].5 + \frac{20}{30} = .75 \text{ customers in the system}$$

on the average

$$W = \frac{L}{\lambda} = \frac{3/4}{20} = \frac{3}{80} \text{ hours} = 2.25 \text{ minutes that the average}$$
customer spends in the total system

$$L_q = L - \frac{\lambda}{\mu} = \frac{3}{4} - \frac{20}{30} = \frac{1}{12} = .083 \text{ customers waiting for service}$$
in line on the average

$$W_q = \frac{L_q}{\lambda} = \frac{1/12}{20} = \frac{1}{240} \text{ hour} = \frac{1}{4} \text{ minute} = \text{Average waiting time}$$
of a customer in the queue
itself (not being serviced)

$$\rho = \frac{\lambda}{M\mu} = \frac{20}{2(30)} = \frac{1}{3} = .33 = \text{Utilization rate}$$

$$P_0 = \frac{1}{\left[\sum_{n=0}^{n=M-1} \frac{1}{n!} \left[\frac{20}{30}\right]^n\right] + \frac{1}{2!} \left[\frac{20}{30}\right]^2 \left[\frac{2(30)}{(2)(30) - 20}\right]}$$

$$= \frac{1}{(1)(2/3)^0 + (1)(2/3)^1 + (1/2)(4/9)(6/4)} = .5$$

= Probability of no customers in the system

You now have (240 customers) × (1/240 hours) = 1 hour total customer waiting time per day.

Total cost of 60 minutes of customer waiting time is (60 minutes) ($.10 per minute) = $6.

Now you are ready to point out to Marty that the hiring of one additional clerk will save $96 − $6 = $90 of customer ill will per 12-hour shift. Marty responds that the hiring should also reduce the number of people who look at the line and leave as well as those who get tired of waiting in line and leave. You tell Marty that you are ready for two chili dogs, extra hot.

DISCUSSION QUESTIONS AND PROBLEMS

Discussion Questions

16-1 What is the waiting line problem? What are the components in a waiting line system?

16-2 What are the assumptions underlying common queuing models?

16-3 Describe the important operating characteristics of a queuing system.

16-4 Why must the service rate be greater than the arrival rate in a single-channel queuing system?

16-5 Briefly describe three situations in which the first-in, first-out (FIFO) discipline rule is not applicable in queuing analysis.

16-6 Provide examples of four situations in which there is a limited, or finite, waiting line.

16-7 What are the components of the following systems? Draw and explain the configuration of each.

(a) Barber shop.
(b) Car wash.
(c) Laudromat.
(d) Small grocery store.

16-8 Do doctor's offices generally have random arrival rates for patients? Are service times random? Under what circumstances might service times be constant?

16-9 Do you think the Poisson distribution, which assumes independent arrivals, is a good estimation of arrival rates in the following queuing systems? Defend your position in each case.

(a) Cafeteria in your school.
(b) Barbershop.
(c) Hardware store.
(d) Dentist's office.
(e) College class.
(f) Movie theater.

Problems

: **16-10** The Golding Discount Department Store has approximately 300 customers shopping in its store between 9 A.M. and 5 P.M. on Saturdays. In deciding how many cash registers to keep open each Saturday, Golding's manager considers two factors: customer waiting time (and the associated waiting cost) and the service costs of employing additional checkout clerks. Checkout clerks are paid an averge of $4 per hour. When only one is on duty, the waiting time per customer is about 10 minutes (or $\frac{1}{6}$ of an hour); when two clerks are on duty, the average checkout time is 6 minutes per person; 4 minutes when three clerks are working; and 3 minutes when four clerks are on duty.

Golding's managment has conducted customer satisfaction surveys and has been able to estimate that the store suffers approximately $5 in lost sales and goodwill for every *hour* of customer time spent waiting in checkout lines. Using the information provided, determine the optimal number of clerks to have on duty each Saturday in order to minimize the store's total expected cost.

Optimal number of checkout clerks on duty = 3, $196

16-11 The Rockwell Electronics Corporation retains a service crew to repair machine breakdowns that occur on an average of $\lambda = 3$ per day (approximately Poisson in nature). The crew can service an average of $\mu = 8$ machines per day, with a repair time distribution that resembles the exponential distribution.

QA16-11

(a) What is the utilization rate of this service system?
(b) What is the average downtime for a machine that is broken?
(c) How many machines are waiting to be serviced at any given time?
(d) What is the probability that more than one machine is in the system? Probability that more than two are broken and waiting to be repaired or being serviced? More than three? More than four?

.375
1.6 hours
.225

.141, .053, .020, .007

16-12 Harry's Car Wash is open six days a week, but its heaviest day of business is always on Saturday. From historical data, Harry estimates that dirty cars arrive at the rate of 20 per hour all day Saturday. With a full crew working the

QA16-12

wash line, he figures that cars can be cleaned at the rate of one every two minutes. One car at a time is cleaned in this example of a single-channel waiting line.

Assuming Poisson arrivals and exponential service times, find the

1.33
4 minutes
6 minutes
.6667
.333

(a) Average number of cars in line.
(b) Average time a car waits before it is washed.
(c) Average time a car spends in the service system.
(d) Utilization rate of the car wash.
(e) Probability no cars are in the system.

QA16-13

🖳 · **16-13** Mike Dreskin manages a large Los Angeles movie theater complex called Cinema I, II, III, and IV. Each of the four auditoriums plays a different film; the schedule is set so that starting times are staggered to avoid the large crowds that would occur if all four movies started at the same time. The theater has a single ticket booth and a cashier who can maintain an average service rate of 280 movie patrons per hour. Service times are assumed to follow an exponential distribution. Arrivals on a normally active day are Poisson distributed and average 210 per hour.

In order to determine the efficiency of the current ticket operation, Mike wishes to examine several queue operating characteristics.

2.25
.75
.857 minutes

.64 minutes

42%, 32%, 24%

(a) Find the average number of moviegoers waiting in line to purchase a ticket.
(b) What percentage of the time is the cashier busy?
(c) What is the average time a customer spends in the system?
(d) What is the average time spent waiting in line to get to the ticket window?
(e) What is the probability that there are more than two people in the system? More than three people? More than four?

QA16-14

🖳 : **16-14** A university cafeteria line in the student center is a self-serve facility in which students select the food items they want, then form a single line to pay the cashier. Students arrive at a rate of about four per minute according to a Poisson distribution. The single cashier ringing up sales takes about 12 seconds per customer, following an exponential distribution.

51.2%, 41.0%, 32.8%
.20

.80 minutes
3.2
4
$P_0 = .429$, $W_q = .0380$ minutes, $L_q = .1523$, $L = .9523$

(a) What is the probability there are more than two students in the system? More than three students? More than four?
(b) What is the probability that the system is empty?
(c) How long will the average student have to wait before reaching the cashier?
(d) What is the expected number of students in the queue?
(e) What is the average number in the system?
(f) If a second cashier is added (who works at the same pace), how will the operating characteristics computed in (b), (c), (d), and (e) change? Assume customers wait in a single line and go to the first available cashier.

QA16-15

🖳 : **16-15** The wheat harvesting season in the American Midwest is short, and most farmers deliver their truckloads of wheat to a giant central storage bin within a two-week span. Because of this, wheat-filled trucks waiting to unload and return to the fields have been known to back up for a block at the receiving bin. The central bin is owned cooperatively, and it is to every farmer's benefit to make the unloading/storage process as efficient as possible. The cost of grain deterioration caused by unloading delays and the cost of truck rental and idle driver time are significant concerns to the cooperative members. Although farmers have difficulty quantifying crop damage, it is easy to assign a waiting and unloading cost for truck and driver of $18 per hour. The storage bin is open and operated 16 hours per day and 7 days per week during the harvest season and is capable of unloading 35 trucks per hour according to an exponential distribution. Full trucks arrive all day long (during the hours the bin is open) at a rate of about 30 per hour, following a Poisson pattern.

To help the cooperative get a handle on the problem of lost time while trucks are waiting in line or unloading at the bin, find the

(a) Average number of trucks in the unloading system.

(b) Average time per truck in the system.

(c) Utilization rate for the bin area.

(d) Probability that there are more than three trucks in the system at any given time.

(e) Total daily cost to the farmers of having their trucks tied up in the unloading process.

(f) The cooperative, as mentioned, uses the storage bin only two weeks per year. Farmers estimate that enlarging the bin would cut unloading costs by 50% next year. It will cost $9,000 to do so during the off-season. Would it be worth the cooperative's while to enlarge the storage area?

> 6 trucks
> 12 minutes
> .857143
>
> 54%
>
> $1,728/day
>
> Yes, save $3,096.

16-16 Ashley's Department Store in Kansas City maintains a successful catalogue sales department in which a clerk takes orders by telephone. If the clerk is occupied on one line, incoming phone calls to the catalogue department are answered automatically by a recording machine and asked to wait. As soon as the clerk is free, the party that has waited the longest is transferred and answered first. Calls come in at a rate of about 12 per hour. The clerk is capable of taking an order in an average of four minutes. Calls tend to follow a Poisson distribution, and service times tend to be exponential.

The clerk is paid $5 per hour, but because of lost goodwill and sales, Ashley's loses about $25 per hour of customer time spent waiting for the clerk to take an order.

(a) What is the average time that catalogue customers must wait before their calls are transferred to the order clerk?

(b) What is the average number of callers waiting to place an order?

(c) Ashley is considering adding a second clerk to take calls. The store would pay that person the same $5 per hour. Should it hire another clerk? Explain.

> QA16-16
>
> 16 minutes
> 3.20 callers
> A second order clerk should definitely be added. The cost saving is $85 − $13.81 = $71.19/hour.

16-17 Sal's International Barber Shop is a popular haircutting and styling salon near the campus of the University of New Orleans. Four barbers work full-time and spend an average of 15 minutes on each customer. Customers arrive all day long at an averge rate of 12 per hour. When they enter, they take a number to wait for the first available barber. Arrivals tend to follow the Poisson distribution, while service times are exponentially distributed.

(a) What is the probability that the shop is empty?

(b) What is the average number of customers in the barber shop?

(c) What is the average time spent in the shop?

(d) What is the average time that a customer spends waiting to be called to the barber chair?

(e) What is the average number waiting to be served?

(f) What is the shop's utilization factor?

(g) Sal's is thinking of adding a fifth barber. How will this affect the utilization rate?

> QA16-17
>
> 3.8%
> 4.528
> 22.6 minutes
>
> 7.6 minutes
> 1.5282
> 75%
>
> 60%

QA16-18

3,2,4 MDs respectively

💻 : **16-18** The medical director of a large emergency clinic faces a problem of providing treatment for patients who arrive at different rates during the day. There are four doctors available to treat patients when needed. If not needed, they can be assigned to other responsibilities (for example, lab tests, reports, x-ray diagnoses) or else rescheduled to work at other hours.

It is important to provide quick and responsive treatment, and the medical director feels that, on the average, patients should not have to sit in the waiting area for more than five minutes before being seen by a doctor. Patients are treated on a first-come, first-served basis and see the first available doctor after waiting in the queue. The arrival pattern for a typical day is:

TIME	ARRIVAL RATE
9 A.M.–3 P.M.	6 patients/hour
3 P.M.–8 P.M.	4 patients/hour
8 P.M.–Midnight	12 patients/hour

These arrivals follow a Poisson distribution, and treatment times, 12 minutes on the average, follow the exponential pattern.

How many doctors should be on duty during each period in order to maintain the level of patient care expected?

QA16-19

$L = 3$, $W = 1$ hr., $L_q = 2.25$, $W_q = \frac{3}{4}$ hr., $P_0 = .25$

💻 · **16-19** Juhn and Sons Wholesale Fruit Distributors employ one worker whose job it is to load fruit on outgoing company trucks. Trucks arrive at the loading gate at an average of 24 per day, or 3 per hour, according to a Poisson distribution. The worker loads them at a rate of 4 per hour, following approximately the exponential distribution in service times.

Determine the operating characteristics of this loading gate problem. What is the probability that there will be more than three trucks either being loaded or waiting? Discuss the result of your queuing model computation.

QA16-20

$L = .6$, $W = .2$ hr, $L_q = .225$, $W_q = .075$ hr, $P_0 = .625$

💻 : **16-20** Juhn believes that adding a second fruit loader will substantially improve the firm's efficiency. He estimates that a two-person crew, still acting like a single-server system, at the loading gate will double the loading rate from 4 trucks per hour to 8 trucks per hour. Analyze the effect on the queue of such a change and compare the results to those found in Problem 16-19.

QA16-21

Save $18 per hour.

💻 · **16-21** Truck drivers working for Juhn and Sons (see Problems 16-19, 16-20) are paid a salary of $10 per hour on the average. Fruit loaders receive about $6 per hour. Truck drivers waiting in the queue or at the loading gate are drawing a salary, but are productively idle and unable to generate revenue during that time. What would be the *hourly* cost savings to the firm associated with employing two loaders instead of one?

QA16-22

$P_0 = 0.454$, $L = 0.873$, $W = 0.291$, $L_q = 0.123$, $W_q = 0.041$

💻 : **16-22** Juhn and Sons Wholesale Fruit Distributors (of Problem 16-19) are considering building a second platform or gate to speed the process of loading their fruit trucks. This, they think, will be even more efficient than simply hiring another loader to help out the first platform (as in Problem 16-20).

Assume that workers at each platform will be able to load 4 trucks per hour each and that trucks will continue to arrive at the rate of 3 per hour. Then apply the preceding equations to find the waiting line's new operating conditions. Is this new approach indeed speedier than the other two considered?

QA16-23

💻 · **16-23** Customers arrive at an automated coffee vending machine at a rate of four per minute, following a Poisson distribution. The coffee machine dispenses a cup of coffee at a constant rate of 10 seconds.

(a) What is the average number of people waiting in line?

(b) What is the average number in the system?

(c) How long does the average person wait in line before receiving service?

.666, 1.333, 10 seconds

: **16-24** The average number of customers in the system in the single-channel, single-phase model described in Section 16.4 is:

$$L = \frac{\lambda}{\mu - \lambda}$$

Show that for $M = 1$ server, the multichannel queuing model in Section 16.5, shown as follows,

$$L = \frac{\lambda\mu\left(\dfrac{\lambda}{\mu}\right)^{M}}{(M-1)!(M\mu - \lambda)^{2}} P_0 + \frac{\lambda}{\mu}$$

is identical to the single-channel system. Note that the formula for P_0 (Equation 16-9) must be utilized in this highly algebraic exercise.

See the Instructor's Section for details.

: **16-25** One mechanic services five drilling machines for a steel plate manufacturer. Machines break down on an average of once every six working days, and breakdowns tend to follow a Poisson distribution. The mechanic can handle an average of one repair job per day. Repairs follow an exponential distribution.

QA 16-25

(a) How many machines are waiting for service, on the average?

(b) How many are currently being served?

(c) How many drills are in running order, on the average?

(d) What is the average waiting time in the queue?

(e) What is the average wait in the system?

.52
1.16
3.84
.82 days
1.82 days

: **16-26** A technician monitors a group of five computers that run an automated manufacturing facility. It takes an average of 15 minutes (exponentially distributed) to adjust a computer that develops a problem. The computers run for an average of 85 minutes (Poisson distributed) without requiring adjustments. What is the:

QA 16-26

(a) average number of computers waiting for adjustment?

(b) average number of computers not in working order?

(c) probability the system is empty?

(d) average time in the queue?

(e) average time in the system?

.576
1.24
.34
.217 hrs.
.467 hrs.

: **16-27** The typical subway station in Washington, D.C., has six turnstiles, each of which can be controlled by the station manager to be used for either entrance or exit control—but never for both. The manager must decide at different times of the day just how many turnstiles to use for entering passengers and how many to be set up to allow exiting passengers.

At the Washington College Station, passengers enter the station at a rate of about 84 per minute between the hours of 7 and 9 A.M. Passengers exiting trains at the stop reach the exit turnstile area at a rate of about 48 per minute during the same morning rush hours. Each turnstile can allow an average of 30 passengers per minute to enter or exit. Arrival and service times have been thought to follow Poisson and exponential distributions, respectively. Assume riders from a common queue at both entry and exit turnstile areas and proceed to the first empty turnstile.

QA 16-27

The Washington College Station manager does not want the average passenger at his station to have to wait in a turnstile line for more than six seconds nor more than eight people in any queue at any average time.

4 entrance plus 2 exit turnstiles

(a) How many turnstiles should be opened in each direction every morning?

(b) Discuss the assumptions underlying the solution of this problem using queuing theory.

1. 30 minutes
2. a) For 30% diverted, overall average = 28.3 minutes

b) For 5 clerks, 7.6 minutes

c) ATM option, overall 13.1 minutes

CASE STUDY

🖥 The Shader Lane Hotel

Productivity at a hotel front desk is largely dependent on the flow of customers. The desk is at its greatest efficiency when it has a steady flow of guests at all stations. Weighing against the hotel's desire for efficiency is the guest's desire for prompt service. Adding employees to speed up service will ultimately decrease efficiency, because some clerks will inevitably be idle from time to time. And when all waiting guests have been served, employee productivity drops to nothing. Management's task is to schedule enough employees so that customers are served promptly, but not so many employees that some stand idle.

For the customer with a confirmed reservation at a hotel there is little alternative to waiting in the queue, since hotel policy is generally to charge the customer for the room whether it is used or not. Even if the guest is not liable for room charges, he or she might be slow to balk or renege, given the likelihood that the next inn might be full or that the lines would be as long. That the guest remains in the line, however, does not indicate great satisfaction.

Some hotels have established a form of dedicated channel, known as concierge or executive check-in, for frequent-guest program participants, but few hotels have applied queuing theory to the extent that other service industries have. No queuing system predominates at hotel front desks.

Donna Shader, the manager of the Shader Lane Hotel, is considering how to restructure the front desk to reach an optimum level of staff efficiency and guest service. At present, the hotel has five clerks on duty, each with a separate waiting line, during peak check-in time of 3:00 P.M. to 5:00 P.M. Observation of arrivals during this time shows that an average of 90 guests arrive each hour (although there is no upward limit on the number that could arrive at any given time). It takes an average of three minutes for the front-desk clerk to register each guest.

Ms. Shader is considering three plans for improving guest service by reducing the length of time guests spend waiting in line. The first proposal would designate one employee as a quick-service clerk for guests registering under corporate accounts, a market segment that fills about 30% of all occupied rooms. Since corporate guests are preregistered, their registration takes just two minutes. With these guests separated from the rest of the clientele, the average time for registering a typical guest would climb to 3.4 minutes. Under plan one, noncorporate guests would choose any of the remaining four lines.

The second plan is to implement a single-line system. All guests could form a single waiting line to be served by whichever of five clerks became available. This option would require sufficient lobby space for what could be a substantial queue.

The use of an automatic "teller" machine (ATM) for check-in is the basis of the third proposal. Given that initial use of this new technology might be minimal, Shader estimated that 20% of customers, primarily frequent guests, would be willing to use the machines. (This might be a conservative estimate if the guests perceive direct benefits from using the ATM, as bank customers do. Citibank reports that some 80% of its Manhattan customers use its ATMs). Ms. Shader would set up a single queue for customers who prefer human check-in clerks. This would be served by the five clerks, although Shader is hopeful that the machine will allow a reduction to four.

Discussion Questions

1. Determine the average amount of time that a guest spends checking in.

2. How would this change under each of the stated options?

CASE STUDY

💻 New England Castings

For over 75 years, New England Castings, Inc., has manufactured wood stoves for home use. In recent years, with increasing energy prices, George Mathison, president of New England Castings, has seen sales triple. This dramatic increase in sales has made it even more difficult for George to maintain quality in all of the wood stoves and related products.

Unlike other companies manufacturing wood stoves, New England Castings is *only* in the business of making stoves and stove-related products. Their major products are the Warmglo I, the Warmglo II, the Warmglo III, and the Warmglo IV. The Warmglo I is the smallest wood stove, with a heat output of 30,000 BTUs, while the Warmglo IV is the largest, with a heat output of 60,000 BTUs. In addition, New England Castings, Inc., produces a large array of products that have been designed to be used with one of their four stoves. These products include warming shelves, surface thermometers, stovepipes, adaptors, stove gloves, trivets, mitten racks, andirons, chimneys, and heat shields. New England Castings also publishes a newsletter and several paperback books on stove installation, stove operation, stove maintenance, and wood sources. It is George's belief that their wide assortment of products was a major contributor to the sales increases.

The Warmglo III outsells all of the other stoves by a wide margin. The heat output and available accessories are ideal for the typical home. The Warmglo III also has a number of outstanding features that make it one of the most attractive and heat-efficient stoves on the market. Each Warmglo III has a thermostatically controlled primary air intake valve that allows the stove to adjust itself automatically to produce the correct heat output for varying weather conditions. A secondary air opening is used to increase the heat output in case of very cold weather. The internal stove parts produce a horizontal flame path for more efficient burning, and the output gases are forced to take an S-shaped path through the stove. The S-shaped path allows more complete combustion of the gases and better heat transfer from the fire and gases through the cast iron to the area to be heated. These features, along with the accessories, resulted in expanding sales and prompted George to build a new factory to manufacture Warmglo III stoves. An overview diagram of the factory is shown in Figure 1.

The new foundry uses the latest equipment, including a new Disamatic that helps in manufacturing stove parts. Regardless of new equipment or procedures, casting operations have remained basically unchanged for hundreds of years. To begin with, a wooden pattern is made for every cast iron piece in the stove. The wooden pattern is an exact duplication of the cast iron piece that is to be manufactured. New England Castings has all of its patterns made by Precision Patterns, Inc., and these patterns are stored in the pattern shop and maintenance room. Then, a specially formulated sand is molded around the wooden pattern. There can be two or more sand molds for each pattern. Mixing the sand and making the molds are done in the molding room. When the wooden pattern is removed, the resulting sand molds form a negative image of the desired casting. Next, the molds are transported to the casting room, where molten iron is poured into the molds and allowed to cool. When the iron has solidified, the molds are moved into the cleaning, grinding, and preparation room. The molds are dumped into large vibrators that shake most of the sand from the casting. The rough castings are then subjected to both sandblasting to remove the rest of the sand and grinding to finish some of the surfaces of the castings.

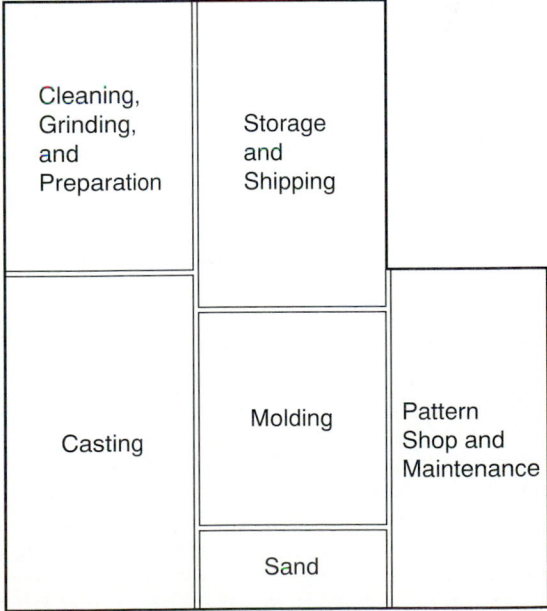

FIGURE 1
Overview of Factory

The castings are then painted with a special heat-resistant paint, assembled into workable stoves, and inspected for manufacturing defects that may have gone undetected thus far. Finally, the finished stoves are moved to storage and shipping, where they are packaged and shipped to the appropriate locations.

At present, the pattern shop and the maintenance department are located in the same room. One large counter is used by both maintenance personnel to get tools and parts and by sand molders that need various patterns for the molding operation. Pete Nawler and Bob Bryan, who work behind the counter, are able to service a total of 10 people per hour (or about 5 per hour each). On the average, 4 people from maintenance and 3 people from the molding department arrive at the counter per hour. People from the molding department and from maintenance arrive randomly, and to be served they form a single line. Pete and Bob have always had a policy of first come, first served. Because of the location of the pattern shop and maintenance department, it takes about three minutes for an individual from the maintenance department to walk to the pattern and maintenance room, and it takes about one minute for an individual to walk from the molding department to the pattern and maintenance room.

After observing the operation of the pattern shop and maintenance room for several weeks, George decided to make some changes to the layout of the factory. An overview of these changes appears in Figure 2.

Separating the maintenance shop from the pattern shop had a number of advantages. It would take people from the maintenance department only one minute instead of three to get to the new maintenance department. Using time and motion studies, George was also able to determine that

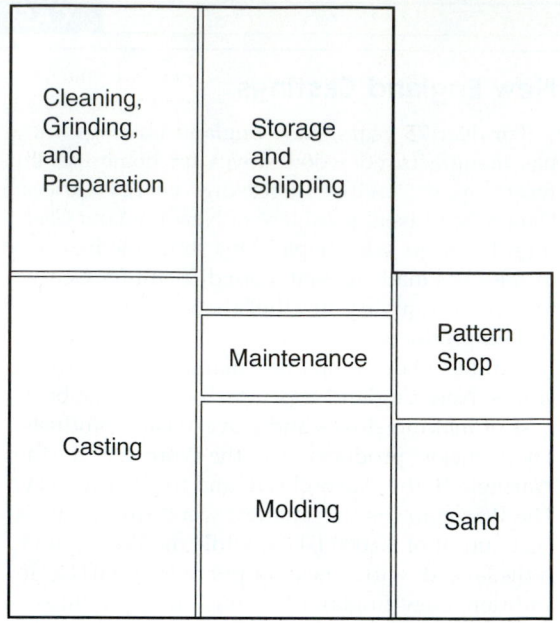

FIGURE 2
Overview of Factory after Changes

improving the layout of the maintenance department would allow Bob to serve 6 people from the maintenance department per hour, and improving the layout of the pattern department would allow Pete to serve 7 people from the molding shop per hour.

Discussion Questions

1. How much time would the new layout save?

2. If maintenance personnel were paid $9.50 per hour and molding personnel were paid $11.75 per hour, how much could be saved per hour with the new factory layout?

1. Maintenance: increase of 2¼ min. per trip.
   Molding: decrease of 8¾ min. per trip.
2. Savings of $1.35 per trip.

BIBLIOGRAPHY

Albin, Susan L. "Delays for Customers from Different Arrival Streams to a Queue." *Management Science* **32**, 3 (March 1986): 329–340.

Byrd, J. "The Value of Queuing Theory." *Interfaces* **8**, 3 (May 1978): 22–26.

Corkindale, D.R. "Queuing Theory in the Solution of a Transport Evaluation Problem." *Operational Research Quarterly* **26**, 2: 259.

Cooper, R.B. *Introduction to Queuing Theory*, 2nd Edition. New York: Elsevier-North Holland, 1980.

Cox, D.R. and W.L. Smith, *Queues*. New York: John Wiley & Sons, 1965.

Edmond, E.D., and R.P. Maggs. "How Useful Are Queue Models in Port Investment Decisions for Container Berths." *Journal of the Operations Research Society* **29**, 8.

Erikson, W. "Management Science and the Gas Shortage." *Interfaces* **4**, 4 (August 1974): 47–51.

Eschcoli, A.Z., and I. Adiri. "Single-Lane Budget Serving Two-Lane Traffic." *Naval Research Logistics Quarterly* **24**, 1 (March 1977): 113–25.

Foote, B.L. "Queuing Case Study of Drive-In Banking." *Interfaces* **6**, 4 (August 1976).

Gostl, J., and I. Greenberg. "An Application of Queuing Theory to the Design of a Message-Switching Computer System." *Communications of the ACM* **28**, 5 (May 1985): 500–505.

Graff, G. "Simple Queuing Theory Saves Unnecessary Equipment." *Industrial Engineering* **3** (February 1971): 15–18.

Grassmann, Winfried, K. "Finding the Right Number of Servers in Real-World Queueing Systems." *Interfaces* **18**, 2, March–April 1988, 94–104.

Green, L., and P. Kolesar. "The Feasibility of One-Officer Patrol in New York City." *Management Science* **30**, 8 (August 1974): 964–981.

Kaplan, Edward H. "A Public Housing Queue with Reneging and Task-Specific Servers." *Decision Sciences* **19** (1988): 383–391.

Larson, Richard C. "Travel-Time Analysis of New York City Police Patrol Cars." *Interfaces* **17**, 2 (March–April 1987): 15–20.

Lawless, Michael W. "Institutionalization of a Management Science Innovation in Police Departments." *Management Science* **33**, 2 (February 1987): 244–252.

Morse, Philip M. *Queues, Inventories and Maintenance*. New York: John Wiley & Sons, 1958.

Panico, J.A. *Queuing Theory: A Study of Waiting Lines for Business, Economics and Sciences*. Englewood Cliffs, N.J.: Prentice-Hall, 1969.

Paul, R.J., and Stevens, R.E. "Staffing Service Activities with Waiting Line Models." *Decision Sciences* **2** (April 1971): 206–218.

Sze, D. "A Queuing Model for Telephone Operator Staffing." *Operations Research* **32**, 2 (March–April 1984): 229–249.

Worthington, D.J. "Queuing Models for Hospital Waiting Lists." *Journal of the Operational Research Society* **38**, 5: 413–422.

Appendix: Queuing Analysis with Spreadsheets

The four queuing models developed in this chapter can be analyzed by spreadsheet as well as with structured software such as AB:QM. Program 16.4 provides an example of a single channel (M/M/1) analysis using the data from Arnold's Muffler Shop.

This "symbolic spreadsheet" shows the formulas and the input data for an arrival rate of 2 (in cell B4) and service rate of 3 (in cell B5). Cells D4 through D9 contain the output parameters such as average time and average number of people or items in the system, average number and time in the queue, utilization, and idle percent. Cells D12 through D20 provide the probabilities of more than 0, 1, 2, 3, 4, 5, 6, 7, and 8 customers in the system.

PROGRAM 16.4 Using Spreadsheets to Develop Queuing Parameters. The Symbolic Spreadsheet, Showing Formulas in Cells, Is Provided

```
              A           B         C                  D               E
 1  Arnold's Muffler Shop Queuing With M/M/1   Single Channel Model
 2
 3                  Inputs                     Outputs
 4  Arrival rate(lambda)  2  Av.#system(L)     +B4/(B5-B4)
 5  Service rate(mu)      3  Av. time sys(W)   1/(B5-B4)
 6                           Av.#queue(Lq)     +B4^2/B5*(B5-B4)
 7                           Av.time queue(Wq) +B4/B5*(B5-B4)
 8                           Util.factor(rho)  +B4-B5
 9                           Percent idle(Po)  1-B4/B5
10
11                                             K  P(n>k) cust in system
12                                             0  ($B$4/$B$5)^(C12+1)
13                                             1  ($B$4/$B$5)^(C13+1)
14                                             2  ($B$4/$B$5)^(C14+1)
15                                             3  ($B$4/$B$5)^(C15+1)
16                                             4  ($B$4/$B$5)^(C16+1)
17                                             5  ($B$4/$B$5)^(C17+1)
18                                             6  ($B$4/$B$5)^(C18+1)
19                                             7  ($B$4/$B$5)^(C19+1)
20                                             8  ($B$4/$B$5)^(C20+1)
```

17

Simulation

CHAPTER OUTLINE

17.1 Introduction

17.2 Advantages and Disadvantages of Simulation

17.3 Monte Carlo Simulation

17.4 Simulation and Inventory Analysis

17.5 Simulation of a Queuing Problem

17.6 Simulation Model for a Maintenance Policy

17.7 Two Other Types of Simulation Models

17.8 Role of Computers in Simulation

17.9 Summary

Glossary

Solved Problems

Discussion Questions and Problems

Case Studies: Biales Waste Disposal, GmbH

Abjar Transport Company

Bibliography

Appendix: Conducting a Simulation with Spreadsheets

Transparency Master 17.1:
Outline: Simulation.

We are all aware to some extent of the importance of simulation models in our world. The Boeing, McDonnell Douglas, and Lockheed companies, for example, commonly build simulation models of their proposed jet aircraft and then test the aerodynamic properties of the models. Your local civil defense organization may carry out rescue and evacuation practices as it simulates the natural disaster conditions of a hurricane or tornado. The U.S. Army simulates enemy attacks and defense strategies in war games played on a computer. Business students take courses that use management games to simulate realistic competitive business situations. And thousands of business, government, and service organizations develop simulation models to assist in making decisions concerning inventory control, maintenance scheduling, plant layout, investments, and sales forecasting.

As a matter of fact, simulation is one of the most widely used quantitative analysis tools. Various surveys of the largest U.S. corporations revealed that 25% to 30% use simulation in corporate planning.

Simulation sounds like it may be the solution to all management problems. This is, unfortunately, by no means true. Yet we think you may find it one of the most flexible and fascinating of the quantitative techniques in your studies. Let's begin our discussion of simulation with a simple definition.

Teaching Suggestion 17.1:
There Are Many Kinds of Simulations. See the Instructor's Section for details.

To *simulate* is to try to duplicate the features, appearance, and characteristics of a real system. In this chapter, we show how to simulate a business or management system by building a *mathematical model* that comes as close as possible to representing the reality of the system. We won't build any *physical* models, as might be used in airplane wind tunnel simulation tests. But just as physical model airplanes are tested and modified under experimental conditions, so our mathematical models are experimented with to estimate the effects of various actions. The idea behind simulation is to imitate a real-world situation mathematically, then to study its properties and operating characteristics, and finally to draw conclusions and make action decisions based on the results of the simulation. In this way, the real-life system is not touched until the advantages and disadvantages of what may be a major policy decision are first measured on the system's model.

KEY IDEA

steps of simulation

Using simulation, a manager should: (1) define a problem; (2) introduce the variables associated with the problem; (3) construct a numerical model; (4) set up possible courses of action for testing; (5) run the experiment; (6) consider the results (possibly deciding to modify the model or change data inputs); and (7) decide what course of action to take. These steps are illustrated in Figure 17.1.

The problems tackled by simulation may range from very simple to extremely complex, from bank teller lines to an analysis of the U.S. economy. Although very small simulations may be conducted by hand, effective use of this technique requires some automated means of calculation, namely, a computer. Even large-scale models, simulating perhaps years of business

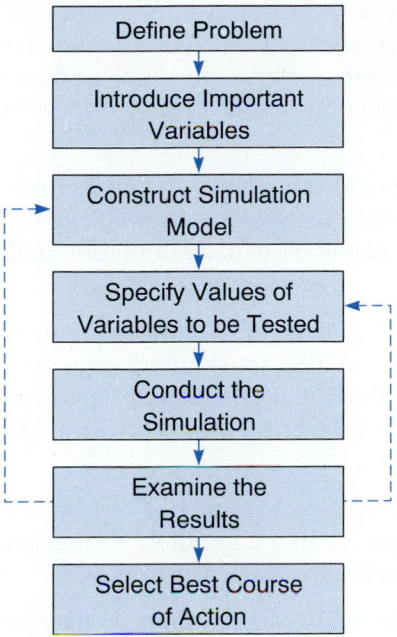

FIGURE 17.1
Process of Simulation

Transparency Master 17.2:
The Process of Simulation.

decisions, can be handled in a reasonable amount of time by computer. Though simulation is one of the oldest quantitative analysis tools (see the "History" box on page 681), it was not until the introduction of computers in the mid-1940s and early 1950s that it became a practical means of solving management and military problems.

    We begin this chapter with a presentation of the advantages and disadvantages of simulation. An explanation of the Monte Carlo method of simulation follows. Three sample simulations, in the areas of inventory control, queuing, and maintenance planning, are presented. Other simulation models besides the Monte Carlo approach are also briefly discussed. And finally, the important role of computers in simulation is illustrated.

computers and simulation

17.2   ADVANTAGES AND DISADVANTAGES OF SIMULATION

Simulation is a tool that has become widely accepted by managers for several reasons.

Teaching Suggestion 17.2:
Examples of Advantages of Simulation. See the Instructor's Section for details.

1. It is relatively straightforward and flexible.

advantages of simulation

2. It can be used to analyze large and complex real-world situations that can't be solved by conventional quantitative analysis models. For example, it may not be possible to build and solve a mathematical

Transparency Master 17.3:
Advantages of Simulation.

model of a city government system that incorporates important economic, social, environmental, and political factors. Simulation has been successfully used to model urban systems, hospitals, educational systems, national and state economies, and even world food systems.

3. Sometimes simulation is the only method available. When the National Aeronautics and Space Administration (NASA) is unable to observe the actual environment on the planet Saturn, a simulation may be needed.

4. Simulation models are built for management problems and require management input. The quantitative analyst must interface extensively with the manager. This means that the user is usually involved in the modeling process, has a stake in its success, and is not afraid to use it.

5. Simulation allows what-if types of questions. Managers like to know in advance what options are attractive. With a computer, a manager can try out several policy decisions within a matter of minutes.

6. Simulations do not interfere with the real-world system. It may be too disruptive, for example, to actually experiment with new policies or ideas in a hospital, school, or manufacturing plant. With simulation, experiments are done with the model, not on the system itself.

7. Simulation allows us to study the interactive effect of individual components or variables in order to determine which ones are important.

8. "Time compression" is possible with simulation. The effect of ordering, advertising, or other policies over many months or years can be obtained by computer simulation in a short time.

9. Simulation allows for the inclusion of real-world complications that most quantitative analysis models cannot permit. For example, some queuing models require exponential or Poisson distributions; some inventory and network models require normality. But simulation can use *any* probability distribution that the user defines; it does not require standard distributions.

The main disadvantages of simulation are:

disadvantages of simulation

1. Good simulation models can be very expensive. It is often a long, complicated process to develop a model. A corporate planning model, for example, may take years to develop.

Transparency Master 17.4:
Disadvantages of Simulation.

2. Simulation does not generate optimal solutions to problems as do other quantitative analysis techniques such as EOQ, linear programming, or PERT. It is a trial and error approach that may produce different solutions in repeated runs.

3. Managers must generate all of the conditions and constraints for solutions that they want to examine. The simulation model doesn't produce answers by itself.

Simulation

The history of simulation goes back 5,000 years to Chinese war games, called *weich'i*, and continues through 1780, when the Prussians used the games to help train their army. Since then, all major military powers have used war games to test out military strategies under simulated environments.

From military or operational gaming, a new concept, *Monte Carlo simulation*, was developed as a quantitative technique by the great mathematician John Von Neumann during World War II. Working with neutrons at the Los Alamos Scientific Laboratory, Von Neumann used simulation to solve physics problems that were too complex or expensive to analyze by hand or by physical

model. The random nature of the neutrons suggested the use of a roulette wheel in dealing with probabilities. Because of the gaming nature, Von Neumann called it the Monte Carlo model of studying laws of chance.

With the advent and common use of business computers in the 1950s, simulation grew as a management tool. Specialized computer languages were developed in the 1960s (GPSS and SIMSCRIPT) to handle large-scale problems more effectively. In the 1980s, prewritten simulation programs to handle situations ranging from queuing to inventory were developed. They have such names as Xcell, SLAM, Witness, and MAP/1.

4. Each simulation model is unique. Its solutions and inferences are not usually transferable to other problems.

17.3 MONTE CARLO SIMULATION

Applicable Problems 17-20, 17-21, 17-24, 17-26

When a system contains elements that exhibit chance in their behavior, the *Monte Carlo method* of simulation may be applied. The basis of Monte Carlo simulation is experimentation on the chance (or *probabilistic*) elements through random sampling.

The technique breaks down into five simple steps:

1. Setting up a probability distribution for important variables.

2. Building a cumulative probability distribution for each variable in step 1.

3. Establishing an interval of random numbers for each variable.

4. Generating random numbers.

5. Actually simulating a series of trials.

Transparency Master 17.5: The Monte Carlo Simulation Technique.

This section examines each of these steps in turn.

Step 1: Establishing Probability Distributions. The basic idea in Monte Carlo simulation is to generate values for the variables making up the model being studied. There are a lot of variables in real-world systems that are probabilistic in nature and that we might want to simulate. A few of these variables are:

1. Inventory demand on a daily or weekly basis.

2. Lead time for inventory orders to arrive.

variables we may want to simulate

3. Times between machine breakdowns.

4. Times between arrivals at a service facility.

5. Service times.

6. Times to complete project activities.

7. Number of employees absent from work each day.

Alternate Example 17.1

Applicable Problems 17-12, 17-13, 17-14

establish a probability distribution for tires

One common way to establish a *probability distribution* for a given variable is to examine historical outcomes. The probability, or relative frequency, for each possible outcome of a variable is found by dividing the frequency of observation by the total number of observations.

The daily demand for radial tires, for example, at Harry's Auto Tire over the past 200 days is shown in Table 17.1. We can convert these data to a probability distribution, if we assume that past arrival rates will hold in the future, by dividing each demand frequency by the total demand, 200. This is illustrated in Table 17.2.

Probability distributions, we should note, need not be based solely on historical observations. Often, managerial estimates based on judgment and experience are used to create a distribution. Sometimes, a sample of sales, machine breakdowns, or service rates is used to create probabilities for those variables. And the distributions themselves can be either empirical, as in Table 17.1, or based on the commonly known normal, binomial, Poisson, or exponential patterns.

Teaching Suggestion 17.3:
Use of the Cumulative Probability Distribution in Setting Random Number Intervals. See the Instructor's Section for details.

cumulative probabilities

Step 2: Building a Cumulative Probability Distribution for Each Variable. The conversion from a regular probability distribution, such as in the right-hand column of Table 17.2, to a *cumulative distribution* is an easy job. In Table 17.3, we see that the cumulative probability for each level of demand is the sum of the number in the probability column (middle column) added to the previous cumulative probability (right-most column). The cumulative probability, graphed in Figure 17.2, is used in step 3 to help assign random numbers.

Step 3: Setting Random Number Intervals. Once we have established a cumulative probability distribution for each variable included in the simu-

TABLE 17.1 Historical Daily Demand for Radial Tires at Harry's Auto Tire

DEMAND FOR TIRES	FREQUENCY (DAYS)
0	10
1	20
2	40
3	60
4	40
5	30
	200

TABLE 17.2 Probability of Demand for Radial Tires

DEMAND VARIABLE	PROBABILITY OF OCCURRENCE
0	$^{10}/_{200} =$ .05
1	$^{20}/_{200} =$ .10
2	$^{40}/_{200} =$ .20
3	$^{60}/_{200} =$ .30
4	$^{40}/_{200} =$ .20
5	$^{30}/_{200} =$ .15
	$^{200}/_{200} =$ 1.00

TABLE 17.3 Cumulative Probabilities for Radial Tires

DAILY DEMAND	PROBABILITY	CUMULATIVE PROBABILITY
0	.05	.05
1	.10	.15
2	.20	.35
3	.30	.65
4	.20	.85
5	.15	1.00

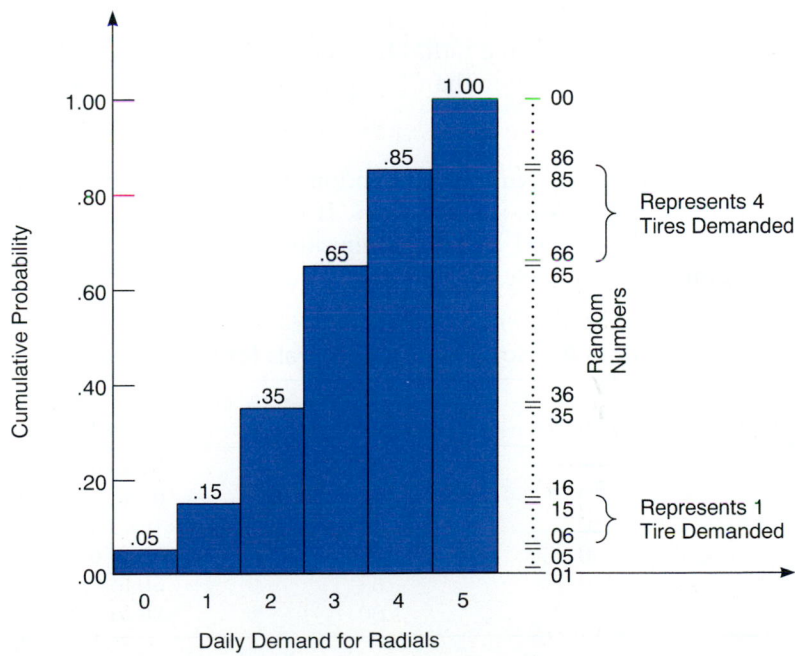

Transparency Master 17.6: Graphical Representation of the Cumulative Probability Distribution for Radial Tires.

FIGURE 17.2

Graphical Representation of the Cumulative Probability Distribution for Radial Tires

lation, we must assign a set of numbers to represent each possible value or outcome. These are referred to as *random number intervals*. Random numbers are discussed in detail in step 4. Basically, a *random number* is a series of digits (say two digits from $01, 02, \ldots, 98, 99, 00$) that have been selected by a totally random process.

If there is a 5% chance that demand for a product (such as Harry's radial tires) is 0 units per day, then we want 5% of the random numbers available to correspond to a demand of 0 units. If a total of 100 two-digit numbers is used in the simulation (think of them as being numbered chips in a bowl), we could assign a demand of 0 units to the first 5 random numbers: 01, 02, 03, 04, and 05.[1] Then a simulated demand for 0 units would be created every time one of the numbers 01 to 05 was drawn. If there is also a 10% chance that demand for the same product is one unit per day, we could let the next 10 random numbers (06, 07, 08, 09, 10, 11, 12, 13, 14, and 15) represent that demand—and so on for other demand levels.

In general, using the cumulative probability distribution computed and graphed in step 2, we can set the interval of random numbers for each level of demand in a very simple fashion. You will note in Table 17.4 that the interval selected to represent each possible daily demand is very closely related to the cumulative probability on its left. The top end of each interval is always equal to the cumulative probability percentage.

Similarly, we can see in Figure 17.2 and in Table 17.4 that the length of each interval on the right corresponds to the probability of one of each of the possible daily demands. Hence, in assigning random numbers to the daily demand for three radial tires, the range of the random number interval (36 to 65) corresponds *exactly* to the probability (or proportion) of that outcome. A daily demand for three radial tires occurs 30% of the time. Any of the 30 random numbers greater than 35 up to and including 65 are assigned to that event.

Step 4: Generating Random Numbers. Random numbers may be generated for simulation problems in several ways. If the problem is very large and the process being studied involves thousands of simulation trials, computer programs are available to generate the random numbers needed.

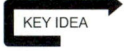
TABLE 17.4 Assignment of Random Number Intervals for Harry's Auto Tire

DAILY DEMAND	PROBABILITY	CUMULATIVE PROBABILITY	INTERVAL OF RANDOM NUMBERS
0	.05	.05	01 to 05
1	.10	.15	06 to 15
2	.20	.35	16 to 35
3	.30	.65	36 to 65
4	.20	.85	66 to 85
5	.15	1.00	86 to 00

[1]Alternatively, we could have assigned the random numbers 00, 01, 02, 03, 04 to represent a demand of 0 units. The two digits 00 can be thought of as either 0 or 100. As long as 5 numbers out of 100 are assigned to the 0 demand, it doesn't make any difference which 5 they are.

If the simulation is being done by hand, as in this book, the numbers may be selected by the spin of a roulette wheel that has 100 slots, by blindly grabbing numbered chips out of an urn, or by any method that allows you to make a random selection.[2] The most commonly used means is to choose numbers from a table of random digits such as Table 17.5.

Table 17.5 was itself generated by a computer program. It has the characteristic that every digit or number in it has an equal chance of occurring. In a very large random number table, 10% of digits would be 1s, 10 percent 2s, 10 percent 3s, and so on. Because *everything* is random, we can select numbers from anywhere in the table to use in our simulation procedures in step 5.

Step 5: Simulating the Experiment. We may simulate outcomes of an experiment by simply selecting random numbers from Table 17.5. Beginning

TABLE 17.5 Table of Random Numbers

52	06	50	88	53	30	10	47	99	37	66	91	35	32	00	84	57	07
37	63	28	02	74	35	24	03	29	60	74	85	90	73	59	55	17	60
82	57	68	28	05	94	03	11	27	79	90	87	92	41	09	25	36	77
69	02	36	49	71	99	32	10	75	21	95	90	94	38	97	71	72	49
98	94	90	36	06	78	23	67	89	85	29	21	25	73	69	34	85	76
96	52	62	87	49	56	59	23	78	71	72	90	57	01	98	57	31	95
33	69	27	21	11	60	95	89	68	48	17	89	34	09	93	50	44	51
50	33	50	95	13	44	34	62	64	39	55	29	30	64	49	44	30	16
88	32	18	50	62	57	34	56	62	31	15	40	90	34	51	95	26	14
90	30	36	24	69	82	51	74	30	35	36	85	01	55	92	64	09	85
50	48	61	18	85	23	08	54	17	12	80	69	24	84	92	16	49	59
27	88	21	62	69	64	48	31	12	73	02	68	00	16	16	46	13	85
45	14	46	32	13	49	66	62	74	41	86	98	92	98	84	54	33	40
81	02	01	78	82	74	97	37	45	31	94	99	42	49	27	64	89	42
66	83	14	74	27	76	03	33	11	97	59	81	72	00	64	61	13	52
74	05	81	82	93	09	96	33	52	78	13	06	28	30	94	23	37	39
30	34	87	01	74	11	46	82	59	94	25	34	32	23	17	01	58	73
59	55	72	33	62	13	74	68	22	44	42	09	32	46	71	79	45	89
67	09	80	98	99	25	77	50	03	32	36	63	65	75	94	19	95	88
60	77	46	63	71	69	44	22	03	85	14	48	69	13	30	50	33	24
60	08	19	29	36	72	30	27	50	64	85	72	75	29	87	05	75	01
80	45	86	99	02	34	87	08	86	84	49	76	24	08	01	86	29	11
53	84	49	63	26	65	72	84	85	63	26	02	75	26	92	62	40	67
69	84	12	94	51	36	17	02	15	29	16	52	56	43	26	22	08	62
37	77	13	10	02	18	31	19	32	85	31	94	81	43	31	58	33	51

Source: Excerpted from *A Million Random Digits with 100,000 Normal Deviates,* The Free Press, 1955, p. 7, with permission of the Rand Corporation.

Transparency Master 17.7:
Table of Random Numbers.

[2]One more method of generating random numbers is called the Von Neumann midsquare method, developed in the 1940s. Here's how it works: (1) select any arbitrary number with n digits (for example, $n = 4$ digits), (2) square the number, (3) extract the middle n digits as the next random number. As an example of a 4-digit arbitrary number, use 3,614. The square of 3,614 is 13,060,996. The middle four digits of this new number are 0609. Thus 0609 is the next random number and steps 2 and 3 are repeated. The midsquare method is simple and easily programmed, but sometimes the numbers repeat quickly and are *not* random. For example, try using the method starting with 6,100 as your first arbitrary number!

TABLE 17.6 Ten-Day Simulation of Demand for Radial Tires

DAY NUMBER	RANDOM NUMBER	SIMULATED DAILY DEMAND
1	52	3
2	37	3
3	82	4
4	69	4
5	98	5
6	96	5
7	33	2
8	50	3
9	88	5
10	90	5

39   Total 10-day demand

3.9 = Average daily demand for tires

anywhere in the table, we note the interval in Table 17.4 or Figure 17.2 into which each number falls. For example, if the random number chosen is 81 and the interval 65 to 85 represents a daily demand for four tires, then we select a demand of four tires.

sample simulation

We now illustrate the concept further by simulating 10 days of demand for radial tires at Harry's Auto Tire (see Table 17.6). We select the random numbers needed from Table 17.5, starting in the upper left-hand corner and continuing down the first column.

simulated versus analytical results

It is interesting to note that the average demand of 3.9 tires in this 10-day simulation differs significantly from the *expected* daily demand, which we may compute from the data in Table 17.2.

Teaching Suggestion 17.6: Use of Computers for Speedy Simulations. See the Instructor's Section for details.

$$\text{Expected daily demand} = \sum_{i=0}^{5} (\text{Probability of } i \text{ tires}) \times (\text{Demand of } i \text{ tires})$$

$$= (.05)(0) + (.10)(1) + (.20)(2) + (.30)(3)$$

$$+ (.20)(4) + (.15)(5)$$

$$= 2.95 \text{ tires}$$

If this simulation were repeated hundreds or thousands of times, it is much more likely that the average *simulated* demand would be nearly the same as the *expected* demand.

Naturally, it would be risky to draw any hard and fast conclusions regarding the operation of a firm from only a short simulation. It is also unlikely that anyone would actually want to go to the effort of simulating such a simple model containing only one variable. Simulating by hand does, however, demonstrate the important principles involved and *may* be useful in small-scale studies. As you might expect, the computer can be a very helpful tool in carrying out the tedious work in larger simulation undertakings.

Program 17.1 is a Monte Carlo Simulation using our accompanying software package, AB:QM. It reveals that after 250 runs the average daily de-

PROGRAM 17.1 Monte Carlo Computer Simulation Using AB:QM

```
Simulation / Monte Carlo Simulation


Problem Title :  HARRY'S AUTO TIRE
Number of Runs Desired      250
Number of Categories        6


              Value    Probability
Category 1      0          .05
Category 2      1          .10
Category 3      2          .20
Category 4      3          .30
Category 5      4          .20
Category 6      5          .15



Help  New  Load  Save  Edit   Run    Print  Install  Directory  Esc


        Program: Simulation / Monte Carlo Simulation

        Problem Title : HARRY'S AUTO TIRE

        ***** Program Output *****

        - - - - - - - - - - - - - - - - - - - - - - - - - -
                                    Cumulative
                        Value     Probability
        - - - - - - - - - - - - - - - - - - - - - - - - - -
        Cateogry 1      0.000        0.050
        Category 2      1.000        0.150
        Category 3      2.000        0.350
        Category 4      3.000        0.650
        Category 5      4.000        0.850
        Category 6      5.000        1.000
        - - - - - - - - - - - - - - - - - - - - - - - - - -

        Number of Runs     250
        Average Value      2.968

        ***** End of Output *****
```

mand is 2.968 tires. If even more repetitions occurred, we would clearly come closer to the expected value of 2.95 tires.

Applicable Problems 17-16, 17-23, 17-27, 17-28, 17-29

17.4 SIMULATION AND INVENTORY ANALYSIS

Teaching Suggestion 17.7: Relating Simulation Back to the Inventory Chapter. See the Instructor's Section for details.

In Chapter 8 we introduced the subject of deterministic inventory models. These commonly used models are based on the assumption that both prod-

simulation useful when
demand and lead time
are probabilistic

uct demand and reorder lead time are known, constant values. In many real-world inventory situations, though, demand and lead time are variables, and accurate analysis becomes extremely difficult to handle by any means other than simulation.

In this section we present an inventory problem with two decision variables and two probabilistic components. The owner of the hardware store we are about to describe would like to establish *order quantity* and *reorder point* decisions for a particular product that has probabilistic (uncertain) daily demand and reorder lead time. He wants to make a series of simulation runs, trying out various order quantities and reorder points, in order to minimize his total inventory cost for the item. Inventory costs in this case include an ordering, holding, and stockout cost.

Simkin's Hardware Store

Alternate Example 17.2

Simkin's Hardware sells the Ace model electric drill. Daily demand for the drill is relatively low but subject to some variability. Over the past 300 days, Simkin has observed the sales shown in column 2 of Table 17.7. He converts this historical frequency data into a probability distribution for the variable daily demand (column 3). A cumulative probability distribution is formed in column 4. Finally, Simkin establishes an interval of random numbers to represent each possible daily demand (column 5).

When Simkin places an order to replenish his inventory of Ace electric drills, there is a delivery lag of from one to three days. This means that lead time may also be considered a probabilistic variable. The number of days it took to receive the past 50 orders is presented in Table 17.8. In a fashion similar to that for the demand variable, Simkin establishes a probability distribution for the lead time variable (column 3 of Table 17.8), computes the cumulative distribution (column 4), and assigns random number intervals for each possible time (column 5).

The first inventory policy that Simkin's Hardware wants to simulate is an order quantity of 10 with a reorder point of 5. That is, every time the on-hand inventory level at the end of the day is 5 or less, Simkin will call his supplier and place an order for 10 more drills. If the lead time is one day, by the way, the order will not arrive the next morning, but rather at the beginning of the following working day.

TABLE 17.7 Probabilities and Random Number Intervals for Daily Ace Drill Demand

(1) DEMAND FOR ACE DRILL	(2) FREQUENCY (DAYS)	(3) PROBABILITY	(4) CUMULATIVE PROBABILITY	(5) INTERVAL OF RANDOM NUMBERS
0	15	.05	.05	01 to 05
1	30	.10	.15	06 to 15
2	60	.20	.35	16 to 35
3	120	.40	.75	36 to 75
4	45	.15	.90	76 to 90
5	30	.10	1.00	91 to 00
	300	1.00		

TABLE 17.8 Probabilities and Random Number Intervals for Reorder Lead Time

(1) LEAD TIME (DAYS)	(2) FREQUENCY (ORDERS)	(3) PROBABILITY	(4) CUMULATIVE PROBABILITY	(5) RANDOM NUMBER INTERVAL
1	10	.20	.20	01 to 20
2	25	.50	.70	21 to 70
3	15	.30	1.00	71 to 00
	50	1.00		

The logic of the simulation process is presented in Figure 17.3. Such a *flow diagram* or *flowchart* is useful in the logical coding procedures for programming this simulation process.

The entire process is simulated for a 10-day period in Table 17.9. We can assume that beginning inventory is 10 units on day 1. (Actually, it makes little difference in a long simulation what the initial inventory level is. Since we would tend in real life to simulate hundreds or thousands of days, the beginning values will tend to be averaged out.) Random numbers for Simkin's inventory problem are selected from the second column of Table 17.5.

Table 17.9 is filled in by proceeding one day (or line) at a time, working from left to right. It is a four-step process:

1. Begin each simulated day by checking whether any ordered inventory has just arrived (column 2). If it has, increase the current inventory (in column 3) by the quantity ordered (10 units, in this case).

2. Generate a daily demand from the demand probability distribution in Table 17.7 by selecting a random number. This random number is recorded in column 4. The demand simulated is recorded in column 5.

3. Compute the ending inventory every day and record it in column 6. Ending inventory equals beginning inventory minus demand. If on-hand inventory is insufficient to meet the day's demand, satisfy as much as possible and note the number of lost sales (in column 7).

4. Determine whether the day's ending inventory has reached the re-order point (5 units). If it has, and if there are no outstanding orders, place an order (column 8). Lead time for a new order is simulated by first choosing a random number from Table 17.5 and recording it in column 9. (We may continue down the same string of the random number table that we were using to generate numbers for the demand variable.) Finally, we convert this random number into a lead time by using the distribution set in Table 17.8.

Analyzing Simkin's Inventory Costs

Simkin's first inventory simulation yields some interesting results. The average daily ending inventory is:

$$\text{Average ending inventory} = \frac{41 \text{ total units}}{10 \text{ days}} = 4.1 \text{ units per day}$$

Transparency Master 17.8:
Flow Diagram for Simkin's
Inventory Example.

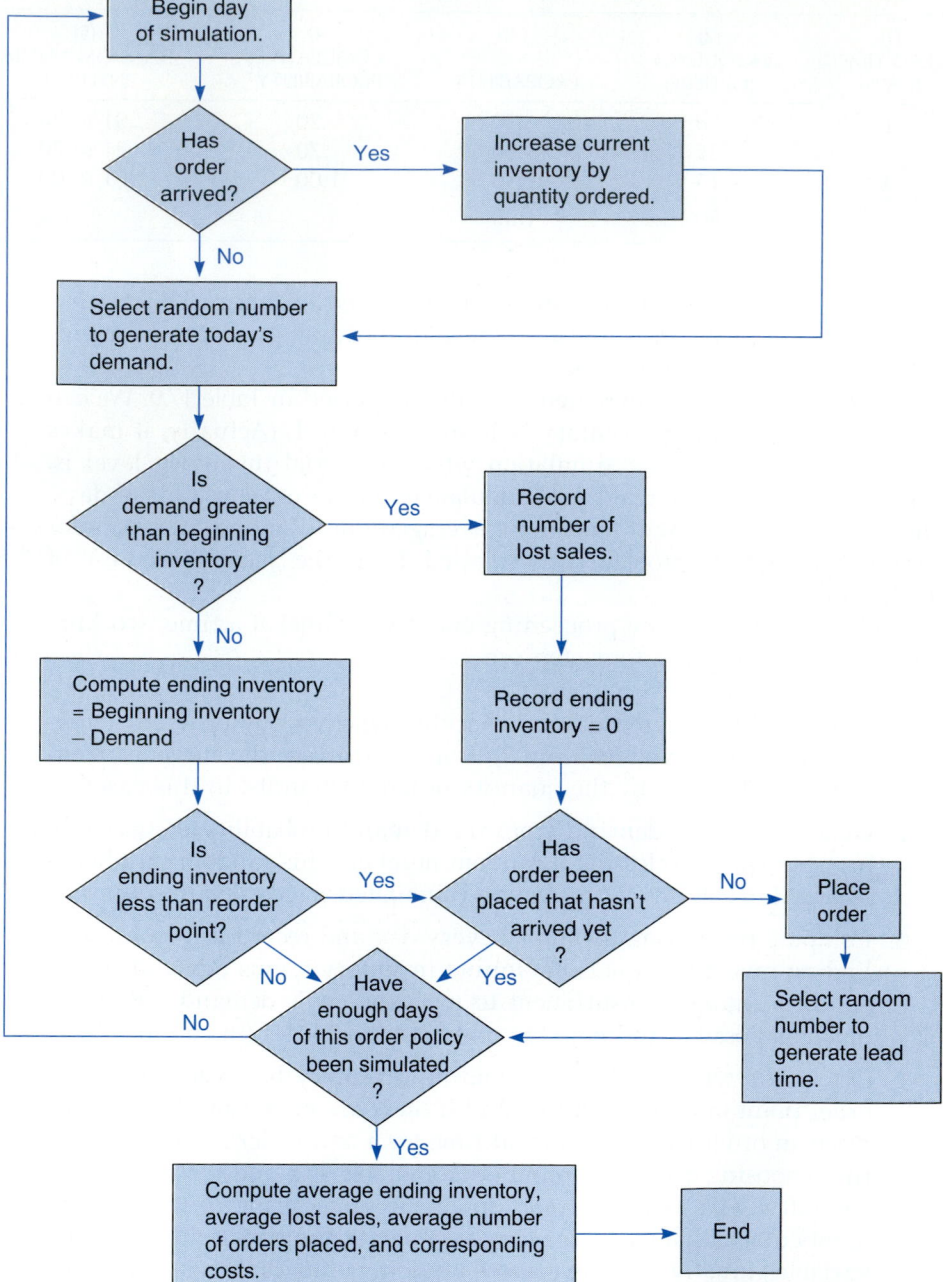

FIGURE 17.3
Flow Diagram for Simkin's Inventory Example

We also note the average lost sales and number of orders placed per day:

$$\text{Average lost sales} = \frac{2 \text{ sales lost}}{10 \text{ days}} = .2 \text{ units per day}$$

$$\text{Average number of orders placed} = \frac{3 \text{ orders}}{10 \text{ days}} = .3 \text{ orders per day}$$

TABLE 17.9 Simkin Hardware's First Inventory Simulation

(1) DAY	(2) UNITS RECEIVED	(3) BEGINNING INVENTORY	ORDER QUANTITY = 10 UNITS (4) RANDOM NUMBER	(5) DEMAND	REORDER POINT = 5 UNITS (6) ENDING INVENTORY	(7) LOST SALES	(8) ORDER?	(9) RANDOM NUMBER	(10) LEAD TIME
1	...	10	06	1	9	0	No		
2	0	9	63	3	6	0	No		
3	0	6	57	3	③[1]	0	Yes	⑩②[2]	1
4	0	3	㊈④[3]	5	0	2	No[4]		
5	⑩[5]	10	52	3	7	0	No		
6	0	7	69	3	4	0	Yes	33	2
7	0	4	32	2	2	0	No		
8	0	2	30	2	0	0	No		
9	⑩[6]	10	48	3	7	0	No		
10	0	7	88	4	3	0	Yes	14	1
				Totals	41	2			

[1]This is the first time inventory dropped to the reorder point of 5 drills. Since no prior order was outstanding, an order is placed.
[2]The random number 02 is generated to represent the first lead time. It was drawn from column 2 of Table 17.5 as the next number in the list being used. A separate column could have been used to draw lead time random numbers from if we had wanted to do so, but in this example we did not do so.
[3]Again, notice that the random digits 02 were used for lead time (see footnote 2). So the next number in the column is 94.
[4]No order is placed on day 4 because there is one outstanding from the previous day that has not yet arrived.
[5]The lead time for the first order placed is one day, but as noted in the text, an order does not arrive the next morning, but rather the beginning of the following working day. Thus, the first order arrives at the start of day 5.
[6]This is the arrival of the order placed at the close of business of day 6. Fortunately for Simkin, no lost sales occurred during the two-day lead time until the order arrived.

These data are useful in studying the inventory costs of the policy being simulated.

Simkin's store is open for business 200 days per year. He estimates that the cost of placing each order for Ace drills is $10. The cost of holding a drill in stock is $6 per drill per year, which can also be viewed as 3¢ per drill per day (over a 200-day year). Finally, Simkin estimates that the cost of each shortage, or lost sale, is $8. What is Simkin's total daily inventory cost for the ordering policy of order quantity, $Q = 10$ and reorder point, $ROP = 5$?

Let us examine the three cost components:

Daily order cost = (Cost of placing one order) × (Number of orders placed per day)

= $10 per order × .3 orders per day = $3

Daily holding cost = (Cost of holding one unit for one day) × (Average ending inventory)

= $.03 per unit per day × 4.1 units per day

= $0.12

Daily stockout cost = (Cost per lost sale) × (Average number of lost sales per day)

= $8 per lost sale × .2 lost sales per day

= $1.60

Total daily inventory cost = Daily order cost + Daily holding cost + Daily stockout cost = $4.72

KEY IDEA

Thus, the total daily inventory cost for this simulation is $4.72. Annualizing this daily figure to a 200-day working year suggests that this inventory policy's cost is approximately $1,330.

Now once again we want to emphasize something very important. This simulation should be extended many more days before we draw any conclusions as to the cost of the inventory policy being tested. If a hand simulation is being conducted, 100 days would provide a better representation. If a computer is doing the calculations, 1,000 days would be helpful in reaching accurate cost estimates.

Let's say that Simkin *does* complete a 1,000-day simulation of the policy that order quantity = 10 drills, reorder point = 5 drills. Does this complete his analysis? The answer is *no*—this is just the beginning! Simkin must now compare *this* potential strategy to other possibilities. For example, what about $Q = 10$, ROP = 4; or $Q = 12$, ROP = 6; or $Q = 14$, ROP = 5? Perhaps every combination of values of Q from 6 to 20 drills and ROP from 3 to 10 should be simulated. After simulating all reasonable combinations of order quantities and reorder points, Simkin would likely select the pair yielding the lowest total inventory cost.

A Computer Simulation to Help Simkin

AB:QM, the software package that accompanies this text, contains an inventory simulation module in addition to the Monte Carlo module illustrated in Program 17.1. This inventory simulation, shown in Program 17.2, examines a range of Q and ROP values of our choosing. It conducts a number of simulations on each combination of Q and ROP and then shows the costs for ordering, holding, shortage, and the total. In Program 17.2, for example, we selected Qs ranging from a minimum order quantity of 9 to a maximum order quantity of 11 and ROPs ranging from a minimum reorder point of 4 to a maximum reorder point of 6. After entering the appropriate demand and lead time distributions and responding to cost data requests, we receive a printout analyzing all 9 combinations of Q and ROP. After 25 simulation runs, this particular printout indicates we should order $Q = 10$ drills per order with a ROP = 6 drills as the reorder point. Even with 25 runs, we should note, however, that randomness exists. Simulating 100, 200, or 1,000 runs can lead to different conclusions.

Computer simulation may not provide an exact conclusion, but it does permit some interesting sensitivity analyses. For example, we can quickly rerun the program with a shortage cost of $10 or with a holding cost of $7 to inspect the impact of small (or large) changes on the conclusions.

Applicable Problems 17-15, 17-17, 17-22, 17-25

17.5   SIMULATION OF A QUEUING PROBLEM

An important area of simulation application has been in the analysis of waiting line problems. As mentioned earlier, the assumptions required for solving queuing problems analytically are quite restrictive. For most realistic queuing systems, simulation may actually be the only approach available.

PROGRAM 17.2 Computer Inventory Simulation Using AB:QM

```
Program: Simulation / Inventory Simulation

Problem Title :  SIMKIN'S HARDWARE

***** Input Data *****

Ordering cost          ($/order)       10.00
Holding cost           ($/units)        6.00
Shortage cost          ($/units)        8.00
Business days          (/year)        200.00
Min order quantity     (units)          9.00
Max order quantity     (units)         11.00
Min reorder point      (units)          4.00
Max reorder point      (units)          6.00
Initial inventory      (units)         10.00
```

Demand	Probability	Cumulative Probability		Lead Time	Probability	Cumulative Probability
0.00	0.050	0.050		1.00	0.200	0.200
1.00	0.100	0.150		2.00	0.500	0.700
2.00	0.200	0.350		3.00	0.300	1.000
3.00	0.400	0.750				
4.00	0.150	0.900				
5.00	0.100	1.000				

```
***** Program Output *****

Annual Inventory cost after 25 simulation runs
```

Order Quantity	Reorder Quantity	Ordering Cost	Holding Cost	Shortage Cost	Total Cost
9	4	480.000	3936.000	832.000	5248.000
	5	560.000	912.000	8064.000	9536.000
	6	640.000	2928.000	1152.000	4720.000
10	4	480.000	3648.000	960.000	5088.000
	5	480.000	4032.000	640.000	5152.000
	6	560.000	1728.000	1920.000	4208.000
11	4	480.000	3600.000	896.000	4976.000
	5	480.000	5712.000	128.000	6320.000
	6	480.000	3840.000	512.000	4832.000

(Continued)

PROGRAM 17.2 Computer Inventory Simulation Using AB:QM (Continued)

```
Annual total inventory cost for various Q and R combinations

------------------------------------------------------------------------
(Q\R)         4             5             6
------------------------------------------------------------------------
    9      5248.000      9536.000      4720.000
   10      5088.000      5152.000      4208.000
   11      4976.000      6320.000      4832.000
------------------------------------------------------------------------

Minimum Annual Total Inventory Cost   :    4208.000
Minimum Order Quantity                :          10
Minimum Reorder Point                 :           6

***** End of Output *****
```

This section illustrates the simulation at a large unloading dock and its associated queue. Arrivals of barges at the dock are not Poisson distributed, and unloading rates (service times) are not exponential or constant. As such, the mathematical waiting line models of Chapter 16 cannot be used.

Port of New Orleans

Alternate Example 17.3

barge arrivals are probabilistic

Fully loaded barges arrive at night in New Orleans following their long trips down the Mississippi River from industrial midwestern cities. The number of barges docking on any given night ranges from 0 to 5. The probability of 0, 1, 2, 3, 4, or 5 arrivals is displayed in Table 17.10. In the same table, we establish cumulative probabilities and corresponding random number intervals for each possible value.

A study by the dock superintendent reveals that because of the nature of their cargo, the number of barges unloaded also tends to vary from day to day. The superintendent provides information from which we can create a probability distribution for the variable *daily unloading rate* (see Table 17.11). As we just did for the arrival variable, we can set up an interval of random numbers for the unloading rates.

unloading rates vary

TABLE 17.10 Overnight Barge Arrival Rates and Random Number Intervals

NUMBER OF ARRIVALS	PROBABILITY	CUMULATIVE PROBABILITY	RANDOM NUMBER INTERVAL
0	.13	.13	01 to 13
1	.17	.30	14 to 30
2	.15	.45	31 to 45
3	.25	.70	46 to 70
4	.20	.90	71 to 90
5	.10	1.00	91 to 00

TABLE 17.11 Unloading Rates and Random Number Intervals

DAILY UNLOADING RATE	PROBABILITY	CUMULATIVE PROBABILITY	RANDOM NUMBER INTERVAL
1	.05	.05	01 to 05
2	.15	.20	06 to 20
3	.50	.70	21 to 70
4	.20	.90	71 to 90
5	.10	1.00	91 to 00
	1.00		

Barges are unloaded on a first-in, first-out basis. Any barges that are not unloaded the day of arrival must wait until the following day. Tying up a barge in dock is an expensive proposition, and the superintendent cannot ignore the angry phone calls from barge line owners reminding him that "time is money!" He decides that, before going to the Port of New Orleans's controller to request additional unloading crews, a simulation study of arrivals, unloadings, and delays should be conducted. A 100-day simulation would be ideal, but for purposes of illustration, the superintendent begins with a shorter 15-day analysis. Random numbers are drawn from the top row of Table 17.5 to generate daily arrival rates. They are drawn from the second row of Table 17.5 to create daily unloading rates. Table 17.12 shows the day-by-day port simulation.

TABLE 17.12 Queuing Simulation of Port of New Orleans Barge Unloadings

(1) DAY	(2) NUMBER DELAYED FROM PREVIOUS DAY	(3) RANDOM NUMBER	(4) NUMBER NIGHTLY ARRIVALS	(5) TOTAL TO BE UNLOADED	(6) RANDOM NUMBER	(7) NUMBER UNLOADED
1	—[1]	52	3	3	37	3
2	0	06	0	0	63	0[2]
3	0	50	3	3	28	3
4	0	88	4	4	02	1
5	3	53	3	6	74	4
6	2	30	1	3	35	3
7	0	10	0	0	24	0[3]
8	0	47	3	3	03	1
9	2	99	5	7	29	3
10	4	37	2	6	60	3
11	3	66	3	6	74	4
12	2	91	5	7	85	4
13	3	35	2	5	90	4
14	1	32	2	3	73	3[4]
15	0	00	5	5	59	3
	20		41			39
	Total delays		Total arrivals			Total unloadings

[1]We can begin with no delays from the previous day. In a long simulation, even if we started with 5 overnight delays, that initial condition would be averaged out.
[2]Three barges *could* have been unloaded on day 2. But because there were no arrivals and no backlog existed, zero unloadings took place.
[3]The same situation as noted in footnote 2 takes place.
[4]This time 4 barges could have been unloaded, but since only 3 were in queue, the number unloaded is recorded as 3.

The superintendent will likely be interested in at least three useful and important pieces of information:

simulation results

Average number of barges delayed to the next day

$$= \frac{20 \text{ delays}}{15 \text{ days}} = 1.33 \text{ barges delayed per day}$$

$$\text{Average number of nightly arrivals} = \frac{41 \text{ arrivals}}{15 \text{ days}} = 2.73 \text{ arrivals}$$

$$\text{Average number of barges unloaded each day} = \frac{39 \text{ unloadings}}{15 \text{ days}}$$

$$= 2.60 \text{ unloadings}$$

When these data are analyzed in the context of delay costs, idle labor costs, and the cost of hiring extra unloading crews, it will be possible for the dock superintendent and port controller to make a better staffing decision. They may even elect to resimulate the process assuming different unloading rates that would correspond to increased crew sizes. Although simulation is a tool that cannot guarantee an optimal solution to problems such as this, it can be helpful in recreating a process and identifying good decision alternatives.

Applicable Problems 17-18, 17-19

17.6 SIMULATION MODEL FOR A MAINTENANCE POLICY

maintenance problems

Simulation is a valuable technique for analyzing various maintenance policies before actually implementing them. A firm can decide whether to add additional maintenance staff based on machine downtime costs and costs of additional labor. It can simulate replacing parts that have not yet failed in exploring ways to prevent future breakdowns. Many companies use computerized simulation models to decide if and when to shut down a whole plant for maintenance activities. This section provides an example of the value of simulation in setting maintenance policy.

Three Hills Power Company

The Three Hills Power Company provides electricity to a large metropolitan area through a series of almost 200 hydroelectric generators. Management recognizes that even a well-maintained generator will have periodic failures or breakdowns. Energy demands over the past three years have been consistently high, and the company is concerned over downtime of generators. It currently employs four highly skilled and highly paid ($30 per hour) repairpersons. Each works every fourth 8-hour shift. In this way there is a repairperson on duty 24 hours a day, seven days a week.

generator breakdowns

As expensive as the maintenance staff salaries are, breakdown expenses are even more costly. For each hour that one of its generators is down, Three Hills loses approximately $75. This amount is the charge for re-

APPLICATIONS OF QA

Simulating Canadian National Railways Line Capacity

The Canadian National Railway is one of the largest and oldest companies owned by the federal government of Canada. Geographically, the Canadian National Railway operates in areas that range all the way from Thunder Bay, Ontario, to Prince Rupert, in British Columbia. Included in this stretch are the beautiful Rocky Mountains that go through such areas as Jasper and Blue River. The railway originally started in 1923 from a collection of Canadian railways that were near bankruptcy. Since then, many changes have been made. In the 1970s, estimates were made that traffic and volume over Canada's National Railway would double. Any significant increase in traffic requires a lot of planning and a large investment in new equipment, tracks, and so forth.

In order to handle this new traffic, very large amounts of capital were needed to improve railway service, equipment, and manpower. These costs were projected to be approximately 3.5 billion Canadian dollars between 1985 and 1989. This represented a projected increase of traffic ranging from 60 to 75 million gross tons by 1990, up from 40 to 50 million gross tons in 1980.

In order to plan for this expansion, a number of simulation models were developed and used. The Signal Wake model was used to determine the minimum train headway that should be established for a given fleet or number of trains that are following each other. Another simulation model, the Route Capacity Model, investigated such important variables as train delay and overall efficiency as a function of specified track maintenance activities.

Using simulation, a number of initial studies and investigations were made and were subsequently refined. The overall result was a proposal for future capacity expansion. Using computer simulation, Canadian National Railway was able to defer spending approximately 350 million Canadian dollars.

Source: Norma Welch and James Gusso, "Expansion of Canadian National Railways Line Capacity." *Interfaces* **16,** 1 (January–February 1986): 51–64.

serve power that Three Hills must "borrow" from the neighboring utility company.

Stephanie Robbins has been assigned to conduct a management analysis of the breakdown problem. She determines that simulation is a viable tool because of the probabilistic nature of two important maintenance system components.

First, the time between successive generator breakdowns varies historically from as little as one-half hour to as much as three hours. For the past 100 breakdowns Robbins tabulates the frequency of various times between machine failures (see Table 17.13). She also creates a probability distribution and assigns random number intervals to each expected time range.

Robbins then notes that the people who do repairs log their maintenance time in one-hour time blocks. Because of the time it takes to reach a broken generator, repair times are generally rounded to one, two, or three hours. In Table 17.14 she performs a statistical analysis of past repair times, similar to that conducted for breakdown times.

Robbins's objective is to determine: (1) the service maintenance cost, (2) the simulated machine breakdown cost, and (3) the total simulated maintenance cost of the current system. She does this by selecting a series of random numbers to generate simulated times between generator breakdowns and a second series to simulate repair times required. A simulation

TABLE 17.13 Time between Generator Breakdowns at Three Hills Power

TIME BETWEEN RECORDED MACHINE FAILURES (hours)	NUMBER OF TIMES OBSERVED	PROBABILITY	CUMULATIVE PROBABILITY	RANDOM NUMBER INTERVAL
½	5	.05	.05	01 to 05
1	6	.06	.11	06 to 11
1½	16	.16	.27	12 to 27
2	33	.33	.60	28 to 60
2½	21	.21	.81	61 to 81
3	19	.19	1.00	82 to 00
	100	1.00		

of 15 machine failures is presented in Table 17.15. We now examine the elements in the table, one column at a time.

Column 1, Breakdown Number. This is just the count of breakdowns as they occur, going from 1 to 15.

Column 2, Random Number for Breakdowns. This is a number used to simulate time between breakdowns. The numbers in this column have been selected from Table 17.5, from the second column from the right.

Column 3, Time between Breakdowns. This number is generated from column 2 random numbers and the random number intervals defined in Table 17.13. The first random number, 57, falls in the interval 28 to 60, implying a time of 2 hours since the prior breakdown.

Column 4, Time of Breakdown. This converts the data in column 3 into an actual time of day for each breakdown. This simulation assumes that the first day begins at midnight (00:00 hours). Since the time between zero breakdowns and the first breakdown is 2 hours, the first recorded machine failure is at 02:00 on the clock. The second breakdown, you note, occurs 1½ hours later, at a calculated clock time of 03:30 (or 3:30 A.M.).

Column 5, Time Repairperson Is Free to Begin Repair. This is 02:00 hours for the first breakdown if we assume that the repairperson began work at 00:00 hours and was not tied up from a previous generator failure. Before recording this time on the second and all subsequent lines, however, we

TABLE 17.14 Generator Repair Times Required

REPAIR TIME REQUIRED (hours)	NUMBER OF TIMES OBSERVED	PROBABILITY	CUMULATIVE PROBABILITY	RANDOM NUMBER INTERVAL
1	28	.28	.28	01 to 28
2	52	.52	.80	29 to 80
3	20	.20	1.00	81 to 00
	100	1.00		

TABLE 17.15 Simulation of Generator Breakdowns and Repairs

(1) BREAKDOWN NUMBER	(2) RANDOM NUMBER FOR BREAKDOWNS	(3) TIME BETWEEN BREAKDOWNS	(4) TIME OF BREAKDOWN	(5) TIME REPAIRPERSON IS FREE TO BEGIN THIS REPAIR	(6) RANDOM NUMBER FOR REPAIR TIME	(7) REPAIR TIME REQUIRED	(8) TIME REPAIR ENDS	(9) NUMBER OF HOURS MACHINE DOWN
1	57	2	02:00	02:00	07	1	03:00	1
2	17	1½	03:30	03:30	60	2	05:30	2
3	36	2	05:30	05:30	77	2	07:30	2
4	72	2½	08:00	08:00	49	2	10:00	2
5	85	3	11:00	11:00	76	2	13:00	2
6	31	2	13:00	13:00	95	3	16:00	3
7	44	2	15:00	16:00	51	2	18:00	3
8	30	2	17:00	18:00	16	1	19:00	2
9	26	1½	18:30	19:00	14	1	20:00	1½
10	09	1	19:30	20:00	85	3	23:00	3½
11	49	2	21:30	23:00	59	2	01:00	3½
12	13	1½	23:00	01:00	85	3	04:00	5
13	33	2	01:00	04:00	40	2	06:00	5
14	89	3	04:00	06:00	42	2	08:00	4
15	13	1½	05:30	08:00	52	2	10:00	4½
								Total 44

must check column 8 to see what time the repairperson finishes the previous job. Look, for example, at the seventh breakdown. The breakdown occurs at 15:00 hours (or 3:00 P.M.). But the repairperson does not complete the previous job, the sixth breakdown, until 16:00 hours. Hence the entry in column 5 is 16:00 hours.

One further assumption is made in order to handle the fact that each repairperson works only an 8-hour shift. It is that when each person is replaced by the next shift, he or she simply hands the tools over to the new worker. The new repairperson continues working on the same broken generator until the job is completed. There is no lost time and no overlap of workers. Hence, labor costs for each 24-hour day are exactly 24 hours × $30 per hour = $720.

Column 6, Random Number for Repair Time. This is a number selected from the right-most column of Table 17.5. It helps simulate repair times.

Column 7, Repair Time Required. This is generated from column 6's random numbers and Table 17.14's repair time distribution. The first random number, 07, represents a repair time of 1 hour since it falls in the random number interval 01 to 28.

Column 8, Time Repair Ends. This is the sum of the entry in column 5 (time repairperson is free to begin) plus the required repair time from column 7. Since the first repair begins at 02:00 and takes one hour to complete, the time repair ends is recorded in column 8 as 03:00.

Column 9, Number of Hours the Machine Is Down. This is the difference between column 4 (time of breakdown) and column 8 (time repair ends). In the case of the first breakdown, that difference is 1 hour (03:00 minus 02:00). In the case of the tenth breakdown, the difference is 23:00 hours minus 19:30 hours, or 3½ hours.

Cost Analysis of the Simulation

The simulation of 15 generator breakdowns in Table 17.15 spans a time of 34 hours of operation. The clock began at 00:00 hours of day 1 and ran until the final repair at 10:00 hours of day 2.

The critical factor that interests Robbins is the total number of hours that generators are out of service (from column 9). This is computed to be 44 hours. She also notes that toward the end of the simulation period, a backlog is beginning to appear. The thirteenth breakdown occurred at 01:00 hours, but could not be worked on until 04:00 hours. The fourteenth and fifteenth breakdowns experienced similar delays. Robbins is determined to write a computer program to carry out a few hundred more simulated breakdowns, but first wants to analyze the data she has collected thus far.

Video 17.2: Simulating Automation at the U.S. Postal Service

APPLICATIONS OF QA

Simulating Automation at the U.S. Postal Service

No public agency, perhaps with the exception of the IRS, touches the lives of the American public as closely as the United States Postal Service (USPS). For two centuries it has played a key role in the lives of all citizens.

Today the U.S. Postal Service delivers over 500 million pieces of mail each day, or 166 billion pieces a year, to over 100 million delivery locations. It handles 40% of the world's volume at a unit cost that is the lowest in the world. With approximately 750,000 career employees, it is the nation's largest civilian employer. Faced with both rising mail volumes and escalating costs, the postal service has sought ways to improve on its mail-processing methods.

In 1988, the USPS released its corporate automation plan, an ambitious program that includes a capital investment of $12 billion and labor savings of $4 billion by 1995. The backbone of the analysis leading to the plan was performed with a comprehensive simulation model called META (model for evaluating technology alternatives). META has spawned a family of systems for use at both head-

quarters and field levels of the USPS, accelerating and enhancing the use of quantitative analysis throughout the organization.

META's job is to quantify the impacts of changes in mail processing and delivery operations. Managers input the type and quantity of mail to be processed, the methods (equipment and people) used to sort mail, the flow of mail through the postal network of sorting operations, and unit costs. META models how the entire nationwide mail processing system would function given these inputs, and it produces figures for capacity utilization, total pieces handled, and the work hours and costs required.

Extrapolation of the results achieved to date shows total annual savings of one million work years of mail carrier labor, which will allow the USPS to maintain its lowest cost status and to continue to keep postage rate increases in the United States lower than inflation.

Source: M. E. Debry, A. H. DeSilva, and F. J. DiLisio, "Management Science in Automating Postal Operations." *Interfaces* **22**, 1 (Jan.–Feb. 1992): 110–130.

She measures her objectives as follows:

Service maintenance cost = 34 hours of worker service time

$$\times \ \$30 \text{ per hour}$$

$$= \$1,020$$

Simulated machine breakdown cost = 44 total hours of breakdown

$$\times \ \$75 \text{ lost per hour of downtime}$$

$$= \$3,300$$

Total simulated maintenance
cost of the current system = Service cost + Breakdown cost

$$= \$1,020 + \$3,300$$

$$= \$4,320$$

A total cost of $4,320 is reasonable only when compared to other more attractive or less attractive maintenance options. Should, for example, the Three Hills Power Company add a second full-time repairperson to each shift? Should it add just one more worker, and let him or her come on duty every fourth shift to help catch up on any backlogs? These are two alternatives that Robbins may choose to consider through simulation. You may help by solving Problem 17-19 at the end of this chapter.

As mentioned at the outset of this section, simulation can also be used in other maintenance problems, including the analysis of *preventive mainte-nance*. Perhaps the Three Hills Power Company should consider strategies for replacing generator motors, valves, wiring, switches, and other miscellaneous parts that typically fail. It could: (1) replace all parts of a certain type when one fails on any generator, or (2) repair or replace all parts after a certain length of service based on an estimated average service life. This would again be done by setting probability distributions for failure rates, selecting random numbers, and simulating past failures and their associated costs.

preventive maintenance

17.7   TWO OTHER TYPES OF SIMULATION MODELS

Simulation models are often broken into three categories. The first, the Monte Carlo method just discussed, uses the concepts of probability distribution and random numbers to evaluate system responses to various policies. The two other categories are called operational gaming and systems simulation. Although in theory the three methods are distinctly different, the growth of computerized simulation has tended to create a common basis in procedures and blur these differences.[3]

---

[3]Theoretically, random numbers are used only in Monte Carlo simulation. However, in some complex gaming or systems simulation problems in which all relationships cannot be defined exactly, it may be necessary to use the probability concepts of the Monte Carlo method.

Operational Gaming

Operational gaming refers to simulation involving two or more competing players. The best examples are military games and business games. Both allow participants to match their management and decision-making skills in hypothetical situations of conflict.

military games

Military games are used worldwide to train a nation's top military officers, to test offensive and defensive strategies, and to examine the effectiveness of equipment and armies.

business games

Business games, first developed by the firm Booz, Allen and Hamilton in the 1950s, are popular with both executives and business students. They provide an opportunity to test business skills and decision-making ability in a competitive environment. The person or team that performs best in the simulated environment is rewarded by knowing that his or her company has been most successful in earning the largest profit, grabbing a high market share, or perhaps increasing the firm's trading value on the stock exchange.

Teaching Suggestion 17.8: Gaming in Business Courses. See the Instructor's Section for details

computer outputs for a business game

During each period of competition, be it a week, month, or quarter, teams respond to market conditions by coding their latest management decisions with respect to inventory, production, financing, investment, marketing, and research. The competitive business environment is simulated by computer, and a new printout summarizing current market conditions is presented to players. This allows teams to simulate years of operating conditions in a matter of days, weeks, or a semester.

Systems Simulation

Systems simulation is similar to business gaming in that it allows users to test various managerial policies and decisions to evaluate their effect on the operating environment. This variation of simulation models the dynamics of large *systems*. Such systems include corporate operations,[4] the national economy, a hospital, or a city government system.

corporate operating systems

In a *corporate operating system,* sales, production levels, marketing policies, investments, union contracts, utility rates, financing, and other factors are all related in a series of mathematical equations that are examined by simulation. In a simulation of an *urban government,* systems simulation may be employed to evaluate the impact of tax increases, capital expenditures for roads and buildings, housing availability, new garbage routes, in-migration and out-migration, locations of new schools or senior citizen centers, birth and death rates, and many more vital issues. Simulations of *economic systems,* often called econometric models, are used by government agencies, bankers, and large organizations to predict inflation rates, domestic and foreign money supplies, and unemployment levels. Inputs and outputs of a typical economic system simulation are illustrated in Figure 17.4.

economic systems

---

[4]This is sometimes referred to as *industrial dynamics,* a term coined by Jay Forrester. Forrester's goal was to find a way "to show how policies, decisions, structure, and delays are interrelated to influence growth and stability" in industrial systems. See J.W. Forrester, *Industrial Dynamics* (Cambridge, Mass.: The M.I.T. Press, 1961).

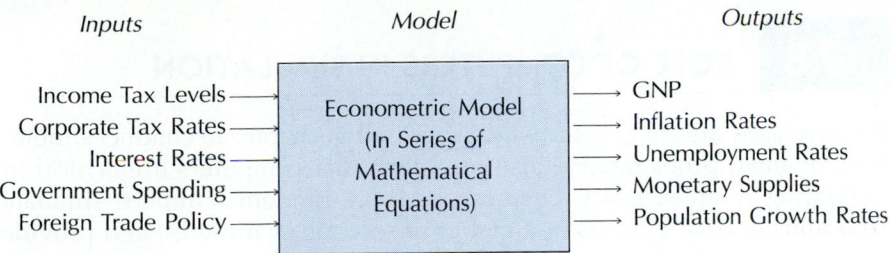

FIGURE 17.4
Inputs and Outputs of a Typical Economic System Simulation

The value of systems simulation lies in its allowance of what-if questions to test the effects of various policies. A corporate planning group, for example, can change the value of any input, such as an advertising budget, and examine the impact on sales, market share, or short-term costs. Simulation can also be used to evaluate different research and development projects or to determine long-range planning horizons.

allows what-if questions

Video 17.3: The Integration of Simulation and Other Models for Netherlands Water Planning

---

APPLICATIONS OF QA

The Integration of Simulation and Other Models for Netherlands Water Planning

Because of a severe drought, the Netherlands had approximately $2.5 billion in agricultural losses. This represented about 4 percent of the gross domestic product. To state the problem simply, during this period, the Dutch faced a problem of too little fresh water and too much pollution in existing water systems.

One of the main water systems for the Netherlands is the Rhine River, referred to by many as the "Sewer of Europe," because of its use as an industrial dumping ground. It is a major water source for agricultural purposes, and also a major river for shipping and general transportation.

In order to clean up the water pollution and to supply a higher quality and more abundant source of fresh water, the PAWN project (standing for "Policy Analysis for the Water Management of the Netherlands") was initiated.

The tactics considered by PAWN included additions and modifications to the current water distribution system, changes in managerial structure and policies, the use of taxes and other charges on water use, discharge, pollution, and various regu-

lations and legal restrictions on the use of water or the discharge of materials into the water system.

In order to develop an effective decision-making approach, PAWN produced 50 integrated models. These included environmental models, power plant models, shipping and locks models, industrial and agricultural models, and various water uses and distribution models. The water uses and distribution models included lakes, external water supplies, ground water storage, and a water distribution system. The models included 12 computer simulations.

It was estimated that the new national water management policy developed from these models saved hundreds of millions of dollars in investment expenditures and resulted in the reduction of agriculturally related problems. It was also estimated that the agricultural damage was reduced by approximately $15 million per year.

Source: Bruce Goeller and the PAWN Team, "Planning the Netherlands Water Resources." *Interfaces* **15**, 1 (January–February 1985): 3–33.

17.8 ROLE OF COMPUTERS IN SIMULATION

We have used the *AB:QM* software twice in this chapter to conduct simulations of small problems. We also recognize that computers are critical in simulating complex tasks. They can generate random numbers, simulate thousands of time periods in a matter of seconds or minutes, and provide management with reports that make decision making easier. As a matter of fact, a computer approach is almost a necessity in order for us to draw valid conclusions from a simulation. Since we require a very large number of simulations, it would be a real burden to rely on pencil and paper alone.

general purpose programming languages

Two types of computer programming languages are available to help the simulation process. The first type, *general purpose languages,* includes FORTRAN, BASIC, COBOL, PL/1, Pascal, and Ada. If you have taken an introductory computer course you may have been exposed to one or more of these.

special simulation languages

Let's look at the second type of programming languages available: *special purpose simulation languages.* These languages have been specially developed to handle simulation problems and have three advantages: (1) they require less programming time for large simulations, (2) they are usually more efficient and easier to check for errors, and (3) they have random number generators already built in as subroutines. The major special purpose languages are: GPSS (General Purpose System Simulator, developed by IBM), SIMSCRIPT (created by the Rand Corporation), DYNAMO (developed at MIT), and GASP (General Activity Simulation Package, also

PROGRAM 17.3 GPSS Language Sample Simulation for a Bank
(*Source:* Minuteman Software, P.O. Box 171, Stowe, MA 01775)

```
 ;    GPSS/PC Program file TEST24.GPS
20             GENERATE    300,100,,,300          ;Create next customer.
30             QUEUE       TELLER                 ;Begin queue time.
40             SEIZE       TELLER                 ;Own or wait for teller.
50             DEPART      TELLER                 ;End queue time.
60             ADVANCE     400,200                ;Bank deposit takes a few minutes.
65             TABULATE    LINETABLE              ;Record waiting line in histogram.
70             RELEASE     TELLER                 ;Deposit done. Give up the teller.
71             ASSIGN      LINESIZE,Q$TELLER      ;Remember the size of the queue
72             SAVEVALUE   CLOCKSAVE,C1           ;Save the clock
73             LOGIC S     SWITCH1                ;Set the switch
75             JOIN        DEPOSITS,1995          ;Record the deposit
76             JOIN        CUSTOMERS              ;Join the group of customers
77             LINK        TAXILINE,FIFO,EXITDOOR  ;
79 EXITDOOR    ENTER       MOTORPOOL              ;Get a taxi.
86             ADVANCE     2000                   ;Go home.
88             UNLINK      TAXILINE,EXITDOOR,1,BACK    ;Leave the taxi queue
89             LEAVE       MOTORPOOL              ;Give up the taxi.
90             SPLIT       1,DESTINATION          ;Create a new transaction.
95             BUFFER
100            TERMINATE   1                      ;Customer leaves the simulation.
```

by IBM). A detailed discussion of the logic and technique of these languages is beyond the scope of this book, but you might wish to read the reference manuals that exist for each.

A sample of a microcomputer-based GPSS program is provided in Program 17.3. It represents a queuing simulation in which customers arrive at a bank according to a known arrival pattern. If a teller is free, the deposit is made; if the teller is busy, the customer enters a queue. When the transaction is completed, the customer "gives up" the teller, takes a taxi home, and departs the simulation. Quite similar GPSS programs can be written to handle such diverse queuing analyses as waiting at a barber-shop, buying a ticket at a theater, or receiving service at a repair facility.

sample GPSS queuing simulation

Simulation has proven so popular that commercial, easy-to-use prewritten simulation programs are also available. Some are generalized to handle a wide variety of situations ranging from queuing to inventory. The names of a few such programs are: Witness (by Istel Incorporated, Chicago), Xcell, MAP/1, and Slam (by Pritsker and Associates, Inc., West Lafayette, Indiana).

17.9   SUMMARY

The purpose of this chapter was to discuss the concept and approach of simulation as a problem-solving tool. Simulation involves building a mathematical model that attempts to describe a real-world situation. The model's goal is to incorporate important variables and their interrelationships in such a way that we can study the impact of managerial changes upon the total system. The approach has many advantages over other quantitative analysis techniques and is especially useful when a problem is too complex or difficult to solve by other means.

Teaching Suggestion 17.9: Outside Research Articles. See the Instructor's Section for details.

The Monte Carlo method of simulation is developed through the use of probability distributions and random numbers. Random number intervals are established to represent possible outcomes for each probabilistic variable in the model. Random numbers are then either selected from a random number table or generated by computer to simulate variable outcomes. The simulation procedure is conducted for many time periods in order to evaluate the long-term impact of each policy value being studied. Monte Carlo simulation was illustrated by hand on problems of inventory control, queuing, and machine maintenance.

Operational gaming and systems simulation, two other categories of simulation, were also presented in this chapter. We concluded with a discussion of the important role of the computer in the simulation process.

GLOSSARY

Simulation. A quantitative analysis technique that involves building a mathematical model that represents a real-world situation. The model is then experimented with to estimate the effects of various actions and decisions.

Monte Carlo Simulation. Simulations that experiment with probabilistic elements of a system by generating random numbers to create values for those elements.

Random Number. A number whose digits are selected completely at random.

Random Number Interval. A range of random numbers assigned to represent a possible simulation outcome.

Flow Diagram or Flowchart. A graphical means of presenting the logic of a simulation model. It is a tool that helps in writing a simulation computer program.

Operational Gaming. The use of simulation in competitive situations such as military games and business or management games.

Systems Simulation. Simulation models dealing with the dynamics of large organizational or governmental systems.

General Purpose Languages. Computer programming languages, such as FORTRAN, BASIC, or COBOL, that are used to simulate a problem.

Special Purpose Simulation Languages. Programming languages especially designed to be efficient in handling simulation problems. The category includes GPSS, SIMSCRIPT, GASP, DYNAMO, Xcell, MAP/1, and SLAM.

SOLVED PROBLEMS

Solved Problem 17.1

Higgins Plumbing and Heating maintains a stock of 30-gallon hot water heaters that it sells to homeowners and installs for them. Owner Jerry Higgins likes the idea of having a large supply on hand to meet customer demand, but he also recognizes that it is expensive to do so. He examines hot water heater sales over the past 50 weeks and notes the following:

HOT WATER HEATER SALES PER WEEK	NUMBER OF WEEKS THIS NUMBER WAS SOLD
4	6
5	5
6	9
7	12
8	8
9	7
10	3
	50

(a) If Higgins maintains a constant supply of 8 hot water heaters in any given week, how many times will he be out of stock during a 20-week simulation? We use random numbers from the seventh column of Table 17.5, beginning with the random digits 10.

(b) What is the average number of sales per week (including stockouts) over the 20-week period?

(c) Using an analytic nonsimulation technique, what is the expected number of sales per week? How does this compare to the answer in b?

Solution

HEATER SALES	PROBABILITY	RANDOM NUMBER INTERVALS
4	.12	01 to 12
5	.10	13 to 22
6	.18	23 to 40
7	.24	41 to 64
8	.16	65 to 80
9	.14	81 to 94
10	.06	95 to 00
	1.00	

(a)

WEEK	RANDOM NUMBER	SIMULATED SALES	WEEK	RANDOM NUMBER	SIMULATED SALES
1	10	4	11	08	4
2	24	6	12	48	7
3	03	4	13	66	8
4	32	6	14	97	10
5	23	6	15	03	4
6	59	7	16	96	10
7	95	10	17	46	7
8	34	6	18	74	8
9	34	6	19	77	8
10	51	7	20	44	7

With a supply of 8 heaters, Higgins will be out of stock three times during the 20-week period (in weeks 7, 14, and 16).

(b) Average sales by simulation = total sales/20 weeks = $\dfrac{135}{20}$ = 6.75 per week.

(c) Using expected values,

$$E(\text{sales}) = .12 \ (4 \text{ heaters}) + .10(5)$$
$$+ \ .18(6) + .24(7) + .16(8)$$
$$+ \ .14(9) + .06(10) = 6.88 \text{ heaters}$$

With a longer simulation, these two approaches will lead to even closer values.

Solved Problem 17.2

The manager of Denton Savings and Loan is attempting to determine how many tellers are needed at the drive-in window during peak times. As a general policy, the manager wishes to offer service such that average customer waiting time does not exceed 2 minutes. Given the existing service level, as shown in the data below, does the drive-in window meet this criteria?

DATA FOR SERVICE TIME

SERVICE TIME (MINUTES)	PROBABILITY (FREQUENCY)	CUMULATIVE PROBABILITY	RANDOM NUMBER INTERVAL
0	.00	.00	(impossible)
1.0	.25	.25	01 to 25
2.0	.20	.45	26 to 45
3.0	.40	.85	46 to 85
4.0	.15	1.00	86 to 00

DATA FOR CUSTOMER ARRIVALS

TIME BETWEEN SUCCESSIVE CUSTOMER ARRIVALS	PROBABILITY (FREQUENCY)	CUMULATIVE PROBABILITY	RANDOM NUMBER INTERVAL
0	.10	.10	01 to 10
1.0	.35	.45	11 to 45
2.0	.25	.70	46 to 70
3.0	.15	.85	71 to 85
4.0	.10	.95	86 to 95
5.0	.05	1.00	96 to 00

Solution

(1) CUSTOMER NUMBER	(2) RANDOM NUMBER	(3) INTERVAL TO ARRIVAL	(4) TIME OF ARRIVAL	(5) RANDOM NUMBER	(6) SERVICE TIME	(7) START SERVICE	(8) END SERVICE	(9) WAIT TIME	(10) IDLE TIME
1	50	2	9:02	52	3	9:02	9:05	0	2
2	28	1	9:03	37	2	9:05	9:07	2	0
3	68	2	9:05	82	3	9:07	9:10	2	0
4	36	1	9:06	69	3	9.10	9:13	4	0
5	90	4	9:10	98	4	9:13	9:17	3	0
6	62	2	9:12	96	4	9:17	9:21	5	0
7	27	1	9:13	33	2	9:21	9:23	8	0
8	50	2	9:15	50	3	9:23	9:26	8	0
9	18	1	9:16	88	4	9:26	9:30	10	0
10	36	1	9:17	90	4	9:30	9:34	13	0
11	61	2	9:19	50	3	9:34	9:37	15	0
12	21	1	9:20	27	2	9:37	9:39	17	0
13	46	2	9:22	45	2	9:39	9:41	17	0
14	01	0	9:22	81	3	9:41	9:44	19	0
15	14	1	9:23	66	3	9:44	9:47	21	0

Read the data as in the following example for the first row:
 Column 1: Number of customer.
 Column 2: From third column of random number Table 17.5
 Column 3: Time interval corresponding to random number (random number of 50 implies a 2-minute interval).
 Column 4: Starting at 9 A.M. the first arrival is at 9:02.
 Column 5: From the first column of the random number Table 17.5.
 Column 6: Teller time corresponding to random number 52 is 3 minutes.
 Column 7: Teller is available and can start at 9:02.
 Column 8: Teller completes work at 9:05 (9:02 + :03).
 Column 9: Wait time for customer is 0 as the teller was available.
 Column 10: Idle time for the teller was 2 minutes (9:00 to 9:02).

The drive-in window clearly does not meet the manager's criteria for an average wait time of 2 minutes. As a matter of fact, we can observe an increasing queue buildup after only a few customer simulations. This observation can be confirmed by expected value calculations on both arrival and service rates.

DISCUSSION QUESTIONS AND PROBLEMS

Discussion Questions

17-1 What are the advantages and limitations of simulation models?

17-2 Why might a manager be forced to use simulation instead of an analytical model in dealing with a problem of:

(a) Inventory ordering policy.
(b) Ships docking in a port to unload.
(c) Bank teller service windows.
(d) The U.S. economy.

17-3 What types of management problems can be solved more easily by quantitative analysis techniques other than simulation?

17-4 What are the major steps in the simulation process?

17-5 What is Monte Carlo simulation? What principles underlie its use, and what steps are followed in applying it?

17-6 List three ways in which random numbers may be generated for use in a simulation.

17-7 In the simulation of an order policy for drills at Simkin's Hardware, would the results (Table 17.9) change significantly if a longer period were simulated? Why is the 10-day simulation valid or invalid?

17-8 Why is a computer necessary in conducting a real-world simulation?

17-9 What is operational gaming? What is systems simulation? Give examples of how each may be applied.

17-10 Do you think the application of simulation will increase strongly in the next 10 years? Why or why not?

17-11 Why would an analyst ever prefer a general purpose language such as FORTRAN or BASIC in a simulation when there are advantages to using special purpose languages such as GPSS or SIMSCRIPT?

Problems

The problems that follow involve simulations that are to be done by hand. You are aware that in order to obtain accurate and meaningful results, long periods must be simulated. This is usually handled by computer. If you are able to program some of the problems in a language you are familiar with, we suggest you try to do so. If not, the hand simulations will still help you in understanding the simulation process.

17-12 Clark Property Management is responsible for the maintenance, rental, and day-to-day operation of a large apartment complex on the east side of New Orleans. George Clark is especially concerned about the cost projections for replacing air conditioner compressors. He would like to simulate the number of compressor failures each year over the next 20 years. Using data from a similar apartment building he manages in a New Orleans suburb, Clark establishes a table of relative frequency of failures during a year as shown on page 710.

QA17-12

NUMBER OF A.C. COMPRESSOR FAILURES	PROBABILITY (RELATIVE FREQUENCY)
0	.06
1	.13
2	.25
3	.28
4	.20
5	.07
6	.01

He decides to simulate the 20-year period by selecting two-digit random numbers from the third column of Table 17.5, starting with the random number 50.

Conduct the simulation for Clark. Is it common to have three or more consecutive years of operation with two or less compressor failures per year?

No, it's not common.

QA17-13

· **17-13** The number of cars arriving at Lundberg's Car Wash during the past 200 hours of operation is observed to be the following:

NUMBER OF CARS ARRIVING	FREQUENCY
3 or less	0
4	20
5	30
6	50
7	60
8	40
9 or more	0
	200

(a) Set up a probability and cumulative probability distribution for the variable of car arrivals.
(b) Establish random number intervals for the variable.
(c) Simulate 15 hours of car arrivals and compute the average number of arrivals per hour. Select the random numbers needed from the first column, Table 17.5, beginning with the digits 52.

See the Instructor's Section for details.

QA17-14

· **17.14** Refer to the data in Solved Problem 17.1, which deals with Higgins Plumbing and Heating. Higgins has now collected 100 weeks of data and finds the following distribution for sales.

HOT WATER HEATER SALES PER WEEK	NUMBER OF WEEKS THIS NUMBER WAS SOLD	HOT WATER HEATER SALES PER WEEK	NUMBER OF WEEKS THIS NUMBER WAS SOLD
3	2	8	12
4	9	9	12
5	10	10	10
6	15	11	5
7	25		

(a) Resimulate the number of stockouts incurred over a 20-week period (assuming Higgins maintains a constant supply of 8 heaters).

5 times

(b) Conduct this 20-week simulation two more times and compare your answers with those in part a. Did they change significantly? Why or why not?

(c) What is the new expected number of sales per week?

6.95 times, yes
7.16 heaters

17-15 An increase in the size of the barge unloading crew at the Port of New Orleans (see Section 5) has resulted in a new probability distribution for daily unloading rates. In particular, Table 17.11 may be revised as shown here.

DAILY UNLOADING RATE	PROBABILITY
1	.03
2	.12
3	.40
4	.28
5	.12
6	.05

See the Instructor's Section.
Average number delayed =
$\frac{6}{15} = .40$
Average number arrivals =
2.07
Average number unloaded =
2.07

(a) Resimulate 15 days of barge unloadings and compute the average number of barges delayed, average number of nightly arrivals, and average number of barges unloaded each day. Draw random numbers from the bottom row of Table 17.5 to generate daily arrivals and from the second-from-the-bottom row to generate daily unloading rates.

(b) How do these simulated results compare to those in the chapter?

17-16 Simkin's Hardware Store simulated an inventory ordering policy for Ace electric drills that involved an order quantity of 10 drills with a reorder point of 5. The first attempt to develop a cost-effective ordering strategy was illustrated in Table 17.9 of Section 4. The brief simulation resulted in a total daily inventory cost of $4.72.

Simkin would now like to compare this strategy to one in which he orders 12 drills, with a reorder point of 6. Conduct a 10-day simulation for him and discuss the cost implications.

Results will differ from student to student.

17-17 Draw a flow diagram to represent the logic and steps of simulating barge arrivals and unloadings at the Port of New Orleans (see Section 5). For a refresher in flowcharts see Figure 17.3.

See the flowchart in the Instructor's Section.

17-18 Draw a flow diagram for the simulation of generator maintenance by the Three Hills Power Company (Section 6 of this chapter).

See the flowchart in the Instructor's Section.

17-19 Stephanie Robbins is the Three Hills Power Company management analyst assigned to simulate maintenance costs. Section 6 described the simulation of 15 generator breakdowns and the repair times required when one repairperson is on duty per shift. The total simulated maintenance cost of the current system was $4,320.

Robbins would now like to examine the relative cost-effectiveness of adding one more worker per shift. The new repairperson would be paid $30 per hour, the same rate as the first is paid. The cost per breakdown hour is still $75. Robbins makes one vital assumption as she begins—that repair times with two workers will be exactly one-half the times required with only one repairperson on duty per shift. Table 17.14 can then be restated as:

REPAIR TIME REQUIRED (HOURS)	PROBABILITY
$\frac{1}{2}$	.28
1	.52
$1\frac{1}{2}$	.20
	1.00

See the Instructor's Section for the simulation.
It is cheaper to hire the second worker each shift.
Total cost with only one repairperson was $4320.

(a) Simulate this proposed maintenance system change over a 15-generator breakdown period. Select the random numbers needed for time between breakdowns from the second-from-the-bottom row of Table 17.5 (beginning with the digits 69). Select random numbers for generator repair times from the last row of the table (beginning with 37).

(b) Should Three Hills add a second repairperson each shift?

17-20 Vincent Maruggi, an MBA student at Northern Massachusetts University, has been having problems balancing his checkbook. His monthly income is derived from a graduate research assistantship; however, he also makes extra money in most months by tutoring undergraduates in their quantitative analysis course. His chances of various income levels are shown here.

MONTHLY INCOME* ($)	PROBABILITY
350	.40
400	.20
450	.30
500	.10

*Assume this income is received at the beginning of each month.

Maruggi's expenditures also vary from month to month, and he estimates that they will follow this distribution:

MONTHLY EXPENSES ($)	PROBABILITY
300	.10
400	.45
500	.30
600	.15

See the Instructor's Section.

He begins his final year with $600 in his checking account. Simulate the entire year (12 months) and discuss Maruggi's financial picture.

17-21 The Brennan Aircraft Division of TLN Enterprises operates a large number of computerized plotting machines. For the most part, the plotting devices are used to create line drawings of complex wing airfoils and fuselage part dimensions. The engineers operating the automated plotters are called loft lines engineers.

The computerized plotters consist of a minicomputer system connected to a 4- by 5-foot flat table with a series of ink pens suspended above it. When a sheet of clear plastic or paper is properly placed on the table, the computer directs a series of horizontal and vertical pen movements until the desired figure is drawn.

The plotting machines are highly reliable, with the exception of the four sophisticated ink pens that are built in. The pens constantly clog and jam in a raised or lowered position. When this occurs, the plotter is unusable.

Currently, Brennan Aircraft replaces each pen as it fails. The service manager has, however, proposed replacing all four pens every time one fails. This should cut down the frequency of plotter failures. At present, it takes one hour to replace one pen. All four pens could be replaced in two hours. The total cost of a plotter being unusable is $50 per hour. Each pen costs $8.

If only one pen is replaced each time a clog or jam occurs, the following breakdown data are thought to be valid:

HOURS BETWEEN PLOTTER FAILURES IF ONE PEN IS REPLACED DURING A REPAIR	PROBABILITY
10	.05
20	.15
30	.15
40	.20
50	.20
60	.15
70	.10

Based on the service manager's estimates, if all four pens are replaced each time one pen fails, the probability distribution between failures is:

HOURS BETWEEN PLOTTER FAILURES IF ALL FOUR PENS ARE REPLACED DURING A REPAIR	PROBABILITY
100	.15
110	.25
120	.35
130	.20
140	.05

(a) Simulate Brennan Aircraft's problem and determine the best policy. Should the firm replace one pen or all four pens on a plotter each time a failure occurs?

(b) Develop a second approach to solving this problem, this time without simulation. Compare the results. How does it affect Brennan's policy decision using simulation?

Based on sample simulations replacing all 4 pens is generally preferable. Expected cost/hour of replacing one pen = $1.38/hour Expected cost/hour for 4 pens = $1.12/hour

17-22 Dr. Mark Greenberg practices dentistry in Topeka, Kansas. Greenberg tries hard to schedule appointments so that patients do not have to wait beyond their appointment time. His October 20 schedule is shown in the accompanying table.

SCHEDULED APPOINTMENT AND TIME		EXPECTED TIME NEEDED
Adams	9:30 A.M.	15
Brown	9.45 A.M.	20
Crawford	10:15 A.M.	15
Dannon	10:30 A.M.	10
Erving	10:45 A.M.	30
Fink	11:15 A.M.	15
Graham	11:30 A.M.	20
Hinkel	11:45 A.M.	15

Unfortunately, not every patient arrives exactly on schedule, and expected times to examine patients are just that, *expected.* Some examinations take longer than expected, while some take less time.

Greenberg's experience dictates the following:

(a) 20% of the patients will be 20 minutes early.
(b) 10% of the patients will be 10 minutes early.
(c) 40% of the patients will be on time.
(d) 25% of the patients will be 10 minutes late.
(e) 5% of the patients will be 20 minutes late.

He further estimates that:

(a) 15% of the time he will finish in 20% less time than expected.
(b) 50% of the time he will finish in the expected time.
(c) 25% of the time he will finish in 20% more time than expected.
(d) 10% of the time he will finish in 40% more time than expected.

In one simulation (see the Instructor's Section), he's only 1 minute late—will probably catch flight. But must repeat this simulation several times and take average schedule.

Dr. Greenberg has to leave at 12:15 P.M. on October 20 in order to catch a flight to a dental convention in New York. Assuming he is ready to start his workday at 9:30 A.M., and that patients are treated in order of their scheduled exam (even if one late patient arrives after an early one), will he be able to make the flight? Comment on this simulation.

: **17-23** The Pelnor Corporation is the nation's largest manufacturer of industrial-size washing machines. A main ingredient in the production process is 8- by 10-foot sheets of stainless steel. The steel is used for both interior washer drums and outer casings.

Steel is purchased weekly on a contractual basis from the Smith-Layton Foundry which, because of limited availability and lot sizing, can ship either 8,000 or 11,000 square feet of stainless steel each week. When Pelnor's weekly order is placed, there is a 45% chance that 8,000 square feet will arrive and a 55% chance of receiving the larger size order.

Pelnor uses the stainless steel on a stochastic (nonconstant) basis. The probabilities of demand each week are shown on page 715

STEEL NEEDED PER WEEK (SQ. FT.)	PROBABILITY
6,000	.05
7,000	.15
8,000	.20
9,000	.30
10,000	.20
11,000	.10

Pelnor has a capacity to store no more than 25,000 square feet of steel at any time. Because of the contract, orders *must* be placed each week regardless of the on-hand supply.

(a) Simulate stainless steel order arrivals and use for 20 weeks. (Begin the first week with a starting inventory of 0 stainless steel.) If an end-of-week inventory is ever negative, assume that back orders are permitted and fill the demand from the next arriving order.

(b) Should Pelnor add more storage area? If so, how much? If not, comment on the system.

See the Instructor's Section. The expected supply is = .45(8,000) + .55(11,000) = 9,650 sq. ft. The expected demand = 8,150 sq. ft. Over the long run the on-hand supply will grow to an infinite level.

17-24 Milwaukee's General Hospital has an emergency room that is divided into six departments: (1) the initial exam station to treat minor problems or make diagnoses; (2) an X-ray department; (3) an operating room; (4) a cast-fitting room; (5) an observation room for recovery and general observation before final diagnoses or release; and (6) an out-processing department where clerks check patients out and arrange for payment or insurance forms.

The probabilities that a patient will go from one department to another are presented in the accompanying table.

FROM	TO	PROBABILITY
Initial exam at emergency room entrance	X-ray department	.45
	Operating room	.15
	Observation room	.10
	Out-processing clerk	.30
X-ray department	Operating room	.10
	Cast-fitting room	.25
	Observation room	.35
	Out-processing clerk	.30
Operating room	Cast-fitting room	.25
	Observation room	.70
	Out-processing clerk	.05
Cast-fitting room	Observation room	.55
	X-ray department	.05
	Out-processing clerk	.40
Observation room	Operating room	.15
	X-ray department	.15
	Out-processing clerk	.70

(a) Simulate the trail followed by 10 emergency room patients. Proceed one patient at a time from each one's entry at the initial exam station until he or she leaves through out-processing. You should be aware that a patient can enter the same department more than once.

(b) Using your simulation data, what are the chances that a patient enters the X-ray department twice?

See the Instructor's Section.

17-25 Management of the First Syracuse Bank is concerned over a loss of customers at its main office downtown. One solution that has been proposed is to add one or more drive-through teller stations to make it easier for customers in cars to obtain quick service without parking. Chris Carlson, the bank president, thinks the bank should only risk the cost of installing one drive-through. He is informed by his staff that the cost (amortized over a 20-year period) of building a drive-through is $12,000 per year. It also costs $16,000 per year in wages and benefits to staff each new teller window.

The director of management analysis, Anita Greenberg, believes that the following two factors encourage the immediate construction of two drive-through stations, however. According to a recent article in *Banking Research* magazine, customers who wait in long lines for drive-through teller service will cost banks an average of $1 per minute in loss of goodwill. Also, adding a second drive-through will cost an additional $16,000 in staffing, but amortized construction costs can be cut to a total of $20,000 per year if two drive-throughs are installed together, instead of one at a time. To complete her analysis, Greenberg collected one month's arrival and service rates at a competing downtown bank's drive-through stations. These data are shown as Observation Analysis 1 and 2 below.

(a) Simulate a one-hour time period, from 1 to 2 P.M., for a single-teller drive-through.

(b) Simulate a one-hour time period, from 1 to 2 P.M., for a two-teller system.

See the Instructor's Section.

(c) Conduct a cost analysis of the two options. Assume the bank is open 7 hours per day and 200 days per year.

OBSERVATION ANALYSIS 1—INTERARRIVAL TIMES FOR 1,000 OBSERVATIONS		OBSERVATION ANALYSIS 2—CUSTOMER SERVICE TIME FOR 1,000 CUSTOMERS	
TIME BETWEEN ARRIVALS (MINUTES)	NUMBER OF OCCURRENCES	SERVICE TIME (MINUTES)	NUMBER OF OCCURRENCES
1	200	1	100
2	250	2	150
3	300	3	350
4	150	4	150
5	100	5	150
		6	100

17-26 The Alfredo Fragrance Company produces only one product, a perfume called Hint of Elegance. Hint of Elegance consists of two secret ingredients blended into an exclusive fragrance which is marketed in Zurich. An economic expression referred to as the Cobb-Douglas function describes the production of Hint of Elegance, as follows:

$$X = \sqrt{(\text{Ingredient 1})(\text{Ingredient 2})}$$

where X is the amount of perfume produced.

The company operates at a level where ingredient 1 is set daily at 25 units and ingredient 2 at 36 units. Although the price Alfredo pays for ingredient 1 is fixed at $50 per unit, the cost of ingredient 2 and the selling price for the final perfume are both probabilistic. The sales price for Hint of Elegance follows this distribution:

SALES PRICE ($)	PROBABILITY
300	.2
350	.5
400	.3

The cost for ingredient 2 is:

INGREDIENT 2 COST ($)	PROBABILITY
35	.1
40	.6
45	.3

(a) What is the profit equation for Alfredo Fragrance Company?
(b) What is the expected profit to the firm?
(c) Simulate the firm's profit for a period of nine days, using these random numbers from Table 17.5: 52, 06, 50, 88, 53, 30, 10, 47, 99, 37, 66, 91, 35, 32, 00, 84, 57, 07.
(d) What is the expected daily profit as simulated in part c?

Profit = 30 (Sales Price) − $1,250 − 36 (Ingredient 2 Cost)
$7,924/day
See the Instructor's Section.
$7,810.00 per day expected profit from simulation

: **17-27** Julia Walters owns and operates one of the largest Mercedes-Benz auto dealerships in Washington, D.C. In the past 36 months her sales of this luxury car have ranged from a low of 6 new cars to a high of 12 new cars, as reflected in the following table:

SALES OF NEW CARS PER MONTH	FREQUENCY
6	3
7	4
8	6
9	12
10	9
11	1
12	1
	36 months

Walters believes that sales will continue during the next 24 months at about the same historical rates and that delivery times will also continue to follow this pace (stated in probability form):

DELIVERY TIME (MONTHS)	PROBABILITY
1	.44
2	.33
3	.16
4	.07
	1.00

See the Instructor's Section for a sample 2-year simulation. Average demand is about 8.75, average lead time is 1.86, average end inventory = 6.50, average lost sales = 4.04.

For a sample simulation, total cost = $520,110 or $21,671 per month.

Average end inventory = 8.90; average lost sales = 3.41; total cost = $488,568 or $20,357/month. This new policy seems preferable.

Walters's current policy is to order 14 cars at a time (two full truckloads, with 7 autos on each truck) and to place a new order whenever the stock on hand reaches 12 autos. What are the results of this policy when simulated over the next two years?

· **17-28** Referring to problem 17-27, Julia Walters establishes the following relevant costs: (1) the carrying cost per Mercedes per month is $600; (2) the cost of a lost sale averages $4,350; and (3) the cost of placing an order is $570. What is the total inventory cost of the policy simulated ($Q = 14$, ROP = 12) in problem 17-27?

: **17-29** Julia Walters (see problems 17-27 and 17-28) wishes to try a new simulated policy, ordering 21 cars per order, with a reorder point of 10 autos. Which policy is better, this one or the one formulated in problems 17-27 and 17-28?

CASE STUDY

Biales Waste Disposal, GmbH

Biales Waste Disposal, GmbH, headquartered in the industrial city of Dusseldorf, Germany, operates seven specially constructed semitrailers and cabs for commercial long-distance hauling of radioactive waste materials. Each truck averages one completed load per week, picking up the radioactive containers from chemical companies and other manufacturers in central Europe. The loads are carefully driven to a government site near Dresden, which until the reunification was a manufacturing center in East Germany. Currently, pickups are made in eight countries: Italy, Germany, Austria, France, Belgium, Netherlands, Denmark, and Poland.

Biales maintains an office in each country's capitol. Staffing includes not only a manager and a secretary at each national office, but a part-time lobbyist/attorney to assist in the many political, cross-cultural, border, and legal issues that arise in the nuclear waste disposal industry.

Sybil Biales, owner of the firm, is seriously considering dropping Italy as source of business. Last year, only 25 truckloads of wastes were handled there. Since textile manufacturers in northern Italy are the primary source of trucking for Biales, the size and revenues from their shipments will determine if it is profitable to retain an office and do business in that country.

To analyze the Italian market, Biales gathers data on last year's shipments and revenues. Each of the 25 trucks that were loaded in Italy last year carried between 26 and 50 barrels of waste. The income generated per barrel differed significantly (ranging from 50 to 80 German marks, or Dmarks)

based on the type of radioactive material being loaded and the weight of the barrels to be shipped. (See the accompanying table for details.)

Biales decided that if she were to simulate 25 truckloads out of Italy she could determine if it would be profitable to continue to operate there next year. She estimates that each shipment to the Dresden dump site costs 900 Dmarks, including driver, gasoline, and truck expenses; other cargo and loading and unloading costs average 120 Dmarks per shipment. In addition, it costs 41,000 Dmarks per year to operate the Italian office, including salaries and indirect overhead costs from the home office in Dusseldorf.

Discussion Question

1. Will the shipments in Italy next year generate enough revenues to cover Biales' costs there?

Biales' Italian Data

NUMBER OF 55-GALLON BARRELS OF WASTE LOADED	NUMBER OF TIMES TRUCK CARRIED THIS SIZE LOAD LAST YEAR	REVENUE PER BARREL (Dmarks)	NUMBER OF TRIPS AT THIS REVENUE
26–30	3	50	5
31–35	4	60	11
36–40	6	70	7
41–45	9	80	2
46–50	3	—	—
	25		25

Based on one short simulation, in the Instructor's Section, money will be lost by continuing in Italy.

CASE STUDY

Abjar Transport Company

In 1988, Samir Khaldoun, after receiving an MBA degree from a leading university in the United States, returned to Jeddah, Saudi Arabia, where his family has extensive business holdings. Samir's first assignment was to stabilize and develop a newly formed, family-owned transport company—Abjar Transport.

An immediate problem facing Samir was the determination of the number of trucks needed to handle the forecasted freight volume. Heretofore, trucks were added to the fleet on an "as needed" basis without comprehensive capacity planning. This approach created problems of driver recruitment, truck service and maintenance, and excessive demurrage because of delays at unloading docks and retention of cargo containers.

Samir forecasts that Abjar's freight volume should average 160,000 tons per month with a standard deviation of 30,000 tons. Freight is unloaded on a uniform basis throughout the month. Based on past experience, the amount handled per month is assumed to be normally distributed, as seen in the table below:

LESS THAN (TONS)	PROBABILITY
100,000	0.02
130,000	0.16
160,000	0.50
190,000	0.84
220,000	0.98

After extensive investigation, Samir concluded that the fleet should be standardized to 40-foot Mercedes 2624 2 × 4 tractor-trailer rigs, which are suitable for carrying two 20-foot containers, one 30-foot container, or one 40-foot container. Cargo capacity is approximately 60 tons per rig. Each tractor-trailer unit is estimated to cost 240,000 riyals. Moreover, they must meet Saudi Arabian specifications—double cooling fans, oversized radiators, and special high-temperature tires. Historical evidence suggests that these Mercedes rigs will operate 96 percent of the time.

Approximately 25 percent of the freight handled by these tractor-trailer rigs is containerized in container lengths of 20, 30, and 40 feet. (The balance of the freight—75 percent—is not containerized.) The 20-foot containers hold approximately 20 tons of cargo; the 30-foot containers hold 45 tons; and the 40-foot containers hold 60 tons of freight. Approximately 60 percent of the containerized freight is shipped in 40-foot units; 20 percent is shipped in 30-foot units; and 20 percent is transported in 20-foot units.

Abjar Transport picks up freight at the dock and delivers it directly to customers, or warehouses it for later delivery. Based on his study of truck routing and scheduling patterns, Samir concluded that each rig should pick up freight at the dock three times each day.

Discussion Question

1. How many tractor-trailer rigs should make up the Abjar Transport fleet?

Source: Adapted from *Cases and Readings in Management Science,* 2nd ed., by B. Render, R. Stair, and I. Greenberg, Allyn & Bacon, Boston, 1990.

Solution: See Instructor's Section—daily truck requirements range from 15 to 27.

BIBLIOGRAPHY

Dileepan, Parthasarati, and Louis M. Johnson, Jr. "Planning Academic Microcomputer Laboratory Resources: A Simulation Approach." *Journal of Education for Business* (February 1988): 210–214.

Easa, Said M. "Assessing Future Management Strategies in the Port of Thunder Bay." *Transportation Research* **20A**, 3 (1986): pp. 185–195.

Eyrl, A.D. "Modelling the Emergency Service in North Eastern Gas." *Journal of the Operational Research Society* **37**, 8 (1986): 769–778.

Ginter, P.M., and A.C. Ricks. "Strategic Models and Simulations: An Emerging Decision-Making Aid." *Journal of Systems Management* **35** (June 1984): 12–16.

Hamzawi, Salah G. "Management and Planning of Airport Gate Capacity: A Microcomputer-Based Gate Assignment Simulation Model." *Transportation Planning and Technology* **11** (1986): 189–202.

Hannan, Edward L., and Christopher J. Gimbrone. "Predicting the Impact of Instituting a Priority Readmission Policy in Nursing Homes." *Computers and Operations*

Research **14**, 6 (1987): 493–505.

Harris, Carl M., Karla L. Hoffman, and Patsy B. Saunders. "Modeling the IRS Telephone Taxpayer Information System." *Operations Research* **35**, 4 (July–August 1987): pp. 504–522.

Kaplan, A., and S. Frazza. "Empirical Inventory Simulation: A Case Study." *Decision Sciences* **14** (January 1983): 62–75.

Keating, Barry. "Simulations: Put the Real World in Your Computer." *Creative Computing* **11** (November 1985): 56–62.

Lambo, E. "The Use of Simulation Models to Improve Health Institutions in Nigeria." *Interfaces* **13** (June 1983): 29.

Lev, Benjamin, and Eugene Kwatny. "Simulation of a Regional Scheduling Problem." *Interfaces* **18**, 2 (March–April 1988): 28–37.

Main, Linda. "Computer Simulation and Library Management." *Journal of Information Science* **13** (1987): 285–296.

Parkan, Celik. "Simulation of a Fast-Food Operation Where Dissatisfied Customers Renege." *Journal of Operational Research Society* **38**, 2 (1987): 137–148.

Riccio, Lucius J., and Ann Litke. "Making a Clean Sweep: Simulating the Effects of Illegally Parked Cars on New York City's Mechanical Street-Cleaning Efforts." *Operations Research* **34**, 5 (September–October 1986): 661–666.

Romanin-Jacur, Giorgio, and Paola Faccin. "Optimal Planning of a Pediatric Semi-Intensive Care Unit via Simulation." *European Journal of Operational Research* **29** (1987): 192–198.

Russell, Robert A., and Regina Hickel. "Simulation of a CD Portfolio." *Interfaces* **16**, 3 (May–June 1986): 49–54.

Solomon, S. L. *Simulation of Waiting Lines*. Englewood Cliffs, NJ: Prentice-Hall, 1983.

Stein, K. J. "Simulation Techniques Converging to Meet Military, Commercial Needs." *Aviation Week & Space Technology* (March 18, 1985): 239.

Watson, H. J. *Computer Simulation in Business*. New York: John Wiley & Sons, 1981.

Welch, Norma, and James Gussow. "Expansion of Canadian National Railway's Line Capacity." *Interfaces* **16**, 1 (January–February 1986): 51–64.

Wright, M. B. "The Application of a Surgical Bed Simulation Model." *European Journal of Operational Research* **32** (1987): 26–32.

Appendix: Conducting a Simulation with Spreadsheets

Spreadsheet software, such as Lotus, has two features that make it a useful tool for conducting simulation analysis: (1) built-in random number functions and generators (through the @ RAND command), and (2) lookup tables that easily permit us to match a simulated random number to a specific event (through the @ VLOOKUP command).

Program 17.4 illustrates these concepts on the Harry's Auto Tire example shown at the beginning of this chapter. This "symbolic spreadsheet" shows formulas (as opposed to values) in each appropriate cell. For example, the @ RAND function is placed in each row of column C (from C15 through C24) for the 10 days of the radial tire simulation. The @ RAND function returns a random number between 0 and 1, all values being equally likely. This is an example of a "continuous uniform distribution" in which each random number may take on any fractional value. The actual simulated demand is in cells D15 through D24 and employs the @ VLOOKUP function.

PROGRAM 17.4 A Spreadsheet Simulation for Harry's Auto Tire Seen in Table 17.4.
A Symbolic Spreadsheet, Using Formulas, Is Shown Here.

	A	B	C	D
1	Note: This is a slightly restructured table (differing from Table 17.4)			
2		needed to accommodate the @VLOOKUP command		
3	Prob-	Cumulative	Demand for	
4	ability	Probability	Tires	
5	0.05	0	0	
6	0.1	0.05	1	
7	0.2	0.15	2	
8	0.3	0.35	3	
9	0.2	0.65	4	
10	0.15	0.85	5	
11				
12	Ten-day simulation of demand for radial tires (as in Table 17.6)			
13		Day	Random	Simulated Daily
14		Number	Number	Demand
15		1	@RAND	@VLOOKUP(C15,$B$5..$C$10,1)
16		2	@RAND	@VLOOKUP(C16,$B$5..$C$10,1)
17		3	@RAND	@VLOOKUP(C17,$B$5..$C$10,1)
18		4	@RAND	@VLOOKUP(C18,$B$5..$C$10,1)
19		5	@RAND	@VLOOKUP(C19,$B$5..$C$10,1)
20		6	@RAND	@VLOOKUP(C20,$B$5..$C$10,1)
21		7	@RAND	@VLOOKUP(C21,$B$5..$C$10,1)
22		8	@RAND	@VLOOKUP(C22,$B$5..$C$10,1)
23		9	@RAND	@VLOOKUP(C23,$B$5..$C$10,1)
24		10	@RAND	@VLOOKUP(C24,$B$5..$C$10,1)
25			Total	@SUM(D15..D24)
26			Aver.	+D25/10
27				
28	Press F9 to recalculate the numbers.			
29				

Here is how the lookup concept works. To simulate the first day's demand for tires, the @ VLOOKUP in cell D15 looks first to the random number just generated in C15. It then takes that number and moves to the small table of probabilities for demand just above it. Cells B5 through C10 comprise the "value lookup" table. These random variables for demand have one of several discrete values (0–5 in our case). Cumulative probabilities always start at zero. If the random number generated is between 0 and .05, a demand of 0 tires results. If the random number falls between .05 and .15, the lookup table indicates a demand for one tire, and so on. The "1" in the @ VLOOKUP command, by the way, means that demand is "looked up" in the first column to the right of the cumulative probability.

The F9 function key permits the entire simulation to be redone, with all new random numbers, each time it is pressed.

18

Network Models

CHAPTER OUTLINE

18.1 Introduction

18.2 PERT

18.3 PERT/Cost

18.4 Critical Path Method

18.5 Minimal-Spanning Tree Technique

18.6 Maximal-Flow Technique

18.7 Shortest-Route Technique

18.8 Using the Computer to Solve Network Problems

18.9 Summary

Glossary

Key Equations

Solved Problems

Discussion Questions and Problems

Case Studies:

Haygood Brothers Construction Company

Bay Community Hospital

The Ranch Development Project

Bibliography

Appendix: Using Spreadsheets to Solve Network Problems

Teaching Suggestion 18.1:
Chapter Coverage. See the
Instructor's Section for
details.

Transparency Master 18.1:
Network Models.

**managing complex
projects**

Transparency Master 18.2:
Questions Which May Be
Addressed by PERT and CPM.

Transparency Master 18.3:
Project Planning, Scheduling,
and Controlling.

Teaching Suggestion 18.2:
The Importance of PERT. See
the Instructor's Section for
details.

Transparency Master 18.4:
The Six Steps Common to
PERT and CPM.

18.1 INTRODUCTION

Most realistic projects that organizations undertake are large and complex. A builder putting up an office building, for example, must complete thousands of activities costing millions of dollars. NASA must inspect countless components before it launches a rocket. Avondale Shipyards in New Orleans requires tens of thousands of steps in constructing an ocean-going tugboat. Almost every industry worries about how to manage similar large-scale, complicated projects effectively.

It is a difficult problem, and the stakes are high. Millions of dollars in cost overruns have been wasted due to poor planning of projects. Unnecessary delays have occurred due to poor scheduling. How can such problems be solved?

Program Evaluation and Review Technique (PERT) and the *Critical Path Method* (CPM) are two popular quantitative analysis techniques that help managers plan, schedule, monitor, and control large and complex projects. They were developed because there was a critical need for a better way to manage (see the "History" box).

Framework of PERT and CPM

There are six steps common to both PERT and CPM. The procedure is as follows:

1. Define the project and *all* of its significant activities or tasks.

2. Develop the relationships among the activities. Decide which activities must precede and follow others.

3. Draw the network connecting all of the activities.

4. Assign time and/or cost estimates to each activity.

5. Compute the longest time path through the network; this is called the *critical path.*

6. Use the network to help plan, schedule, monitor, and control the project.

critical path

PERT versus CPM

Finding the critical path is a major part of controlling a project. The activities on the critical path represent tasks that will delay the entire project if they are delayed. Managers derive flexibility by identifying noncritical activities and replanning, rescheduling, and reallocating resources such as personnel and finances.

Although PERT and CPM are similar in their basic approach, they do differ in the way activity times are estimated. For every PERT activity, three time estimates are combined to determine the expected activity completion time and its variance. Thus, PERT is a *probabilistic* technique: it allows us to find the probability the entire project will be completed by any given date. CPM, on the other hand, is called a *deterministic* approach. It

How PERT and CPM Started

Managers have been planning, scheduling, monitoring, and controlling large-scale projects for hundreds of years, but it has only been in the last 50 years that QA techniques have been applied to major projects. One of the earliest techniques was the *Gantt chart.* This type of chart shows the start and finish time of one or more activities as seen in the accompanying figure.

In 1958, the Special Projects Office of the U.S. Navy developed Program Evaluation and Review Technique (PERT) to plan and control the Polaris missile program. This project involved the coordination of thousands of contractors. Today PERT is still used to monitor numerous government contract schedules. At about the same time (1957), Critical Path method (CPM) was developed by J. E. Kelly of Remington Rand and M. R. Walker of du Pont. Originally, CPM was used to assist in the building and maintenance of chemical plants at du Pont.

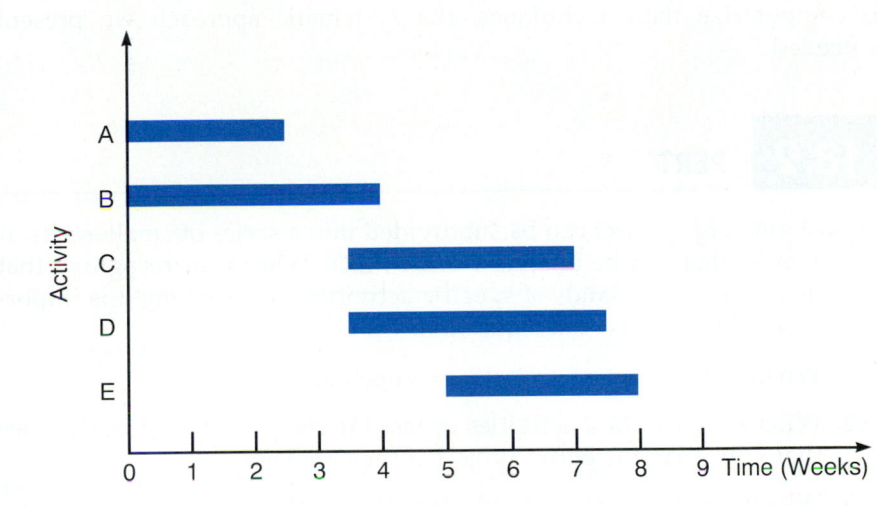

uses two time estimates, the *normal time* and the *crash time* for each activity. The normal completion time is the time we estimate it will take under normal conditions to complete the activity. The crash completion time is the shortest time it would take to finish an activity if additional funds and resources were allocated to the task.

In this chapter we investigate not only PERT and CPM, but also a technique called PERT/Cost that combines the benefits of both PERT and CPM.

Video 18–1: Trains, Planes, and Critical Path

Other Network Techniques

In addition to PERT and CPM, several other network techniques will be covered in this chapter. The *minimal-spanning tree technique* determines the path through the network that connects all the points while minimizing total distance. When the points represent houses in a subdivision, the minimal-spanning tree technique can be used to determine the best way to connect all of the houses to electrical power, water systems, and so on, in a way that minimizes the total distance or length of power lines or water pipes. The *maximal-flow technique* finds the maximum flow of any quantity or substance through a network. This technique can determine, for example, the maximum number of vehicles (cars, trucks, and so forth), that can go through a network of roads from one location to another. Finally, the *shortest-route technique* can find the shortest path through a network. For example, this technique can find the shortest route from one city to another through a network of roads.

All of the examples used to describe the various network techniques in this chapter are small and simple compared to real problems. This is done to make it easier for you to understand the techniques. In many cases, these smaller network problems can be solved by inspection or intuition. For larger problems, however, finding a solution can be very difficult and it becomes necessary to use these powerful network techniques. Larger problems may require hundreds, or even thousands, of iterations. In order to computerize these techniques, the systematic approach we present is needed.

18.2   PERT

Applicable Problems 18-12, 18-13, 18-14, 18-15, 18-16, 18-17, 18-18, 18-19, 18-20, 18-28, 18-29, 18-30, 18-31, Haygood Brothers Case

Teaching Suggestion 18.3: Getting Students Involved with PERT. See the Instructor's Section for details.

Transparency Master 18.5: Advantages of PERT/CPM.

Transparency Master 18.6: Limitations of PERT/CPM.

Almost any large project can be subdivided into a series of smaller activities or tasks that can be analyzed with PERT. When you recognize that projects can have thousands of specific activities, you see why it is important to be able to answer such questions as:

1. When will the entire project be competed?

2. What are the *critical* activities or tasks in the project, that is, the ones that will delay the entire project if they are late?

3. Which are the *noncritical* activities, that is, the ones that can run late without delaying the whole project's completion?

4. What is the probability that the project will be completed by a specific date?

5. At any particular date, is the project on schedule, behind schedule, or ahead of schedule?

6. On any given date, is the money spent equal to, less than, or greater than the budgeted amount?

7. Are there enough resources available to finish the project on time?

8. If the project is to be finished in a shorter amount of time, what is the best way to accomplish this at the least cost?

PERT (or PERT/Cost) can help answer each of these questions.

General Foundry Example of PERT

Alternate Example 18-1

General Foundry, Inc., a metalworks plant in Milwaukee, has long been trying to avoid the expense of installing air pollution control equipment. The local environmental protection group has recently given the foundry

16 weeks to install a complex air filter system on its main smokestack. General Foundry was warned that it will be forced to close unless the device is installed in the allotted period. Lester Harky, the managing partner, wants to make sure the installation of the filtering system progresses smoothly and on time.

When the project begins, the building of the internal components for the device (activity A) and the modifications that are necessary for the floor and roof (activity B) can be started. The construction of the collection stack (activity C) can begin once the internal components are completed, and the pouring of the new concrete floor and installation of the frame (activity D) can be completed as soon as the roof and floor have been modified. Once the collection stack has been constructed, the high-temperature burner can be built (activity E), and the installation of the pollution control system (activity F) can begin. The air pollution device can be installed (activity G) after the high-temperature burner has been built, the concrete floor has been poured, and the frame has been installed. Finally, after the control system and pollution device have been installed, the system can be inspected and tested (activity H).

All of these activities seem rather confusing and complex until they are placed in a network. First, all of the activities must be listed. This information is shown in Table 18.1.

We see in the table that before the collection stack can be constructed (activity C), the internal components must be built (activity A). Thus, activity A is the immediate predecessor to activity C. Likewise, both activities D and E must be performed just prior to installation of the air pollution device (activity G).

project activities

predecessors

Drawing the PERT Network

Once the activities have all been specified (step 1 of the PERT procedure) and management has decided which activities must precede and follow others (step 2), the network can be drawn (step 3).

An *activity* carries the arrow symbol, →. This represents a task or subproject that uses time or resources. The only other piece needed to create a network is called an *event*. An event marks the start or completion of a particular activity. It is denoted by the symbol ◯, which contains a

Teaching Suggestion 18.4: Constructing a Network. See the Instructor's Section for details.

activities and events

TABLE 18.1 Activities and Immediate Predecessors for General Foundry, Inc.

ACTIVITY	DESCRIPTION	IMMEDIATE PREDECESSORS
A	Build internal components	
B	Modify roof and floor	
C	Construct collection stack	A
D	Pour concrete and install frame	B
E	Build high-temperature burner	C
F	Install control system	C
G	Install air pollution device	D, E
H	Inspection and testing	F, G

number that helps identify its location. For example, activity A can be drawn as follows:

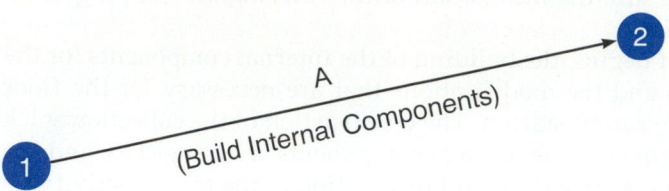

It begins with event 1 and ends with event 2. Activity C's only *immediate predecessor* is activity A, so it can be drawn like this:

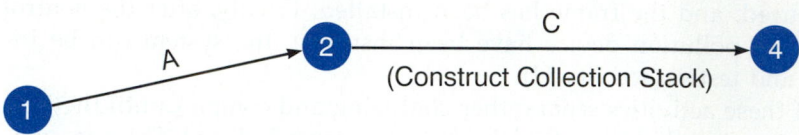

The number inside the event is used to identify the beginning or ending of an activity more easily.

Now we are ready to draw the whole *network* for General Foundry. This is shown in Figure 18.1.

You should note that drawing a PERT network takes some time and experience. You start with the beginning node, node 1. You then draw the activities from this node that do not have any immediate predecessor activities (in this case, A and B). Successive nodes and activities are drawn, making sure that the appropriate relationships between activities and nodes

Transparency Master 18.7:
Figure 18.1 Network for General Foundry, Inc.

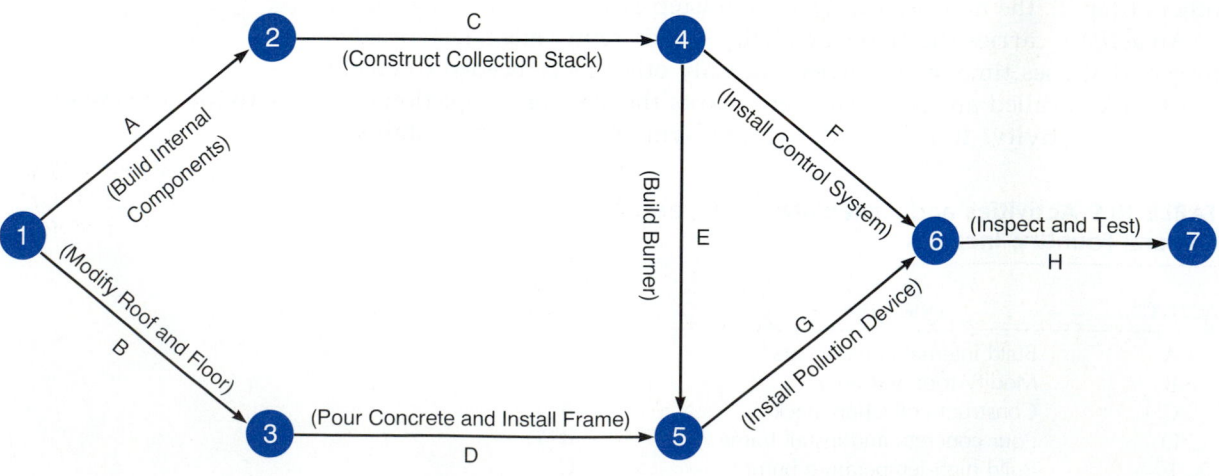

FIGURE 18.1
Network for General Foundry, Inc.

are maintained. You must take care that all immediate predecessor activities are appropriately reflected in the network. When you first draw the network, it is usually impossible to draw all the activities as straight lines. It is good to first get a rough draft version of the network, making sure that all of the appropriate relationships are intact. Then, you can redraw the network to make all of the activity lines straight.

Activity Times

The next step in the PERT procedure is to assign estimates of the time required to complete each activity. Time is usually given in units of weeks.

For one-of-a-kind projects or for new jobs, providing *activity time estimates* is not always an easy task. Without solid historical data, managers are often uncertain as to activity times. For this reason, the developers of PERT employed a probability distribution based on three time estimates for each activity.

The three estimates are:

Optimistic time (a) = Time an activity will take if everything goes as well as possible. There should be only a small probability (say, $\frac{1}{100}$) of this occurring.

Most likely time (m) = Most realistic time estimate to complete the activity.

Pessimistic time (b) = Time an activity would take assuming very unfavorable conditions. There should also be only a small probability that the activity will really take this long.

PERT often assumes time estimates follow the *beta probability distribution* (see Figure 18.2). This continuous distribution has been found to be appro-

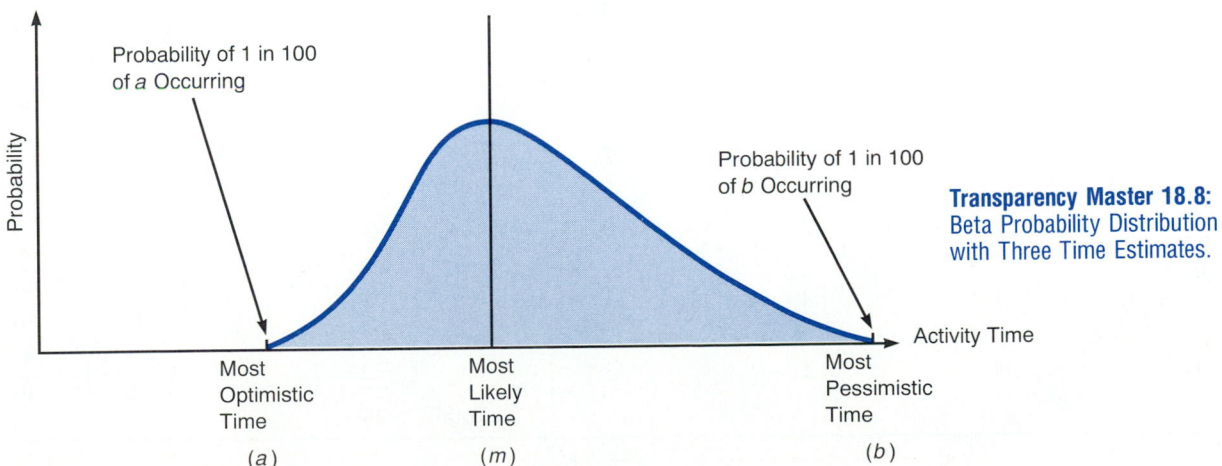

FIGURE 18.2
Beta Probability Distribution with Three Time Estimates

priate, in many cases, for determining an expected value and variance for activity completion times.

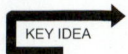
KEY IDEA

To find the expected time (t) for an activity, the beta distribution weights the estimates as follows:

$$t = \frac{a + 4m + b}{6}$$

(18-1)

To compute the dispersion or variance of this expected time estimate, we use the formula.[1]

$$\text{Variance} = \left(\frac{b - a}{6}\right)^2$$

(18-2)

Table 18.2 shows General Foundry's optimistic, most likely, and pessimistic time estimates for each activity. It also reveals the expected time (t) and variance for each of the activities, as computed with Equations 18-1 and 18-2.

Teaching Suggestion 18.6:
Finding the Critical Path. See the Instructor's Section for details.

How to Find the Critical Path

Transparency Master 18.9:
Time Estimates (in weeks) for General Foundry, Inc.

Once the expected completion time for each activity has been determined, we accept it as the actual time of that task. Variability in times will be considered later.

TABLE 18.2 Time Estimates (in weeks) for General Foundry, Inc.

ACTIVITY	OPTIMISTIC a	MOST PROBABLE m	PESSIMISTIC b	EXPECTED TIME $t = [(a + 4m + b)/6]$	VARIANCE $[(b - a)/6]^2$
A	1	2	3	2	$\left(\frac{3 - 1}{6}\right)^2 = \frac{4}{36}$
B	2	3	4	3	$\left(\frac{4 - 2}{6}\right)^2 = \frac{4}{36}$
C	1	2	3	2	$\left(\frac{3 - 1}{6}\right)^2 = \frac{4}{36}$
D	2	4	6	4	$\left(\frac{6 - 2}{6}\right)^2 = \frac{16}{36}$
E	1	4	7	4	$\left(\frac{7 - 1}{6}\right)^2 = \frac{36}{36}$
F	1	2	9	3	$\left(\frac{9 - 1}{6}\right)^2 = \frac{64}{36}$
G	3	4	11	5	$\left(\frac{11 - 3}{6}\right)^2 = \frac{64}{36}$
H	1	2	3	$\frac{2}{}$	$\left(\frac{3 - 1}{6}\right)^2 = \frac{4}{36}$
				Total 25	

[1]This formula (18-2) is based on the statistical concept that from one end of the beta distribution to the other is 6 standard deviations (± 3 standard deviations from the mean). Since $b - a$ is 6 standard deviations, one standard deviation is $(b - a)/6$. Thus, the variance is $[(b - a)/6]^2$.

Although Table 18.2 indicates that the total expected time for all eight of General Foundry's activities is 25 weeks, it is obvious in Figure 18.3 that several of the tasks can be taking place simultaneously. To find out just how long the project will take, we perform the critical path analysis for the network.

The *critical path* is the longest time path route through the network. If Lester Harky wants to reduce the total project time for General Foundry, he will have to reduce the length of some activity on the critical path. Conversely, any delay of an activity on the critical path will delay completion of the entire project.

KEY IDEA

To find the critical path we need to determine the following quantities for each activity in the network.

1. *Earliest start time* (ES). This is the earliest time an activity can begin without violation of immediate predecessor requirements.

2. *Earliest finish time* (EF). This is the earliest time at which an activity can end.

3. *Latest start time* (LS). This is the latest time an activity can begin without delaying the entire project.

4. *Latest finish time* (LF). This is the latest time an activity can end without delaying the entire project.

We begin at the network's origin, event 1, to compute the earliest start time (ES) and earliest finish time (EF) for each activity. For the first event, the starting time is always set equal to 0. Since activity A has an expected time of 2 weeks, its earliest finish time is 2, as seen on the next page.

computing earliest start and finish

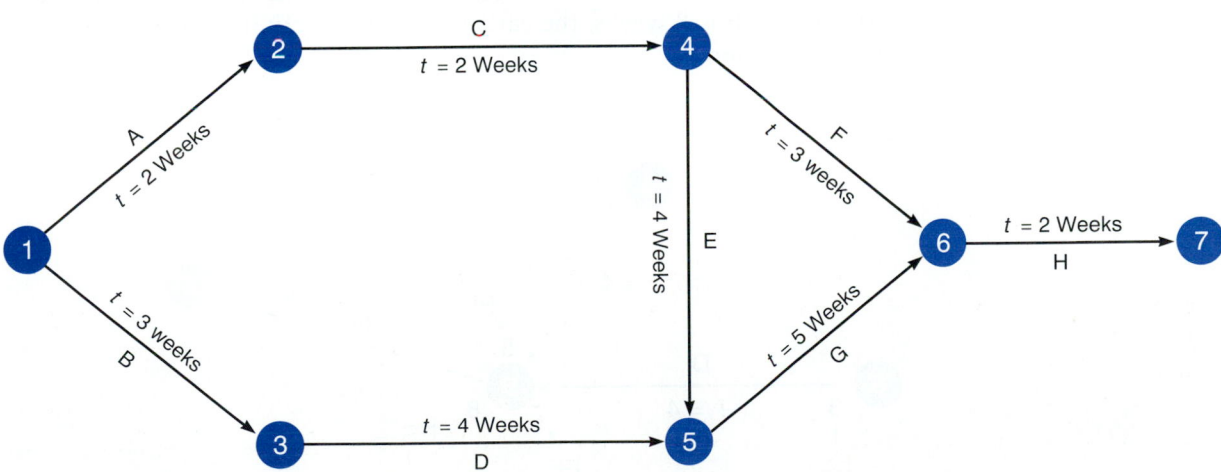

FIGURE 18.3
General Foundry's Network with Expected Activity Times

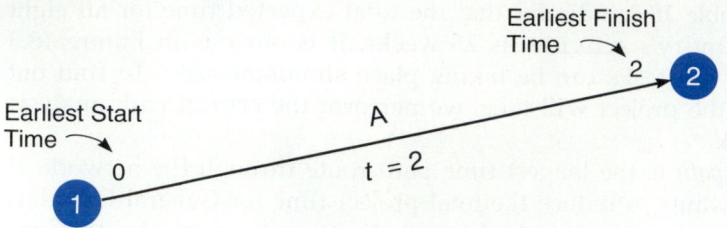

The earliest finish time can be computed by:

Earliest finish time = Earliest start time + Expected activity time

$$EF = ES + t$$

(18-3)

Earliest Start Time Rule. There is one basic rule to follow as you find ES and EF for all activities in the network. Before any activity can be started, *all* of its predecessor activities must be completed. In other words, we search for the *longest* path to an activity in determining ES. For example, we see that ES for activity C is 2 weeks. Its only predecessor activity is A which has an EF of 2 weeks.

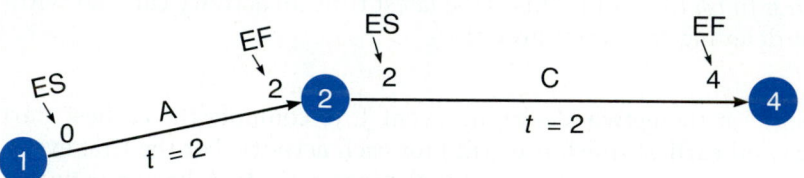

Earliest start time for activity G, however, is 8 weeks. It has 2 predecessor activities, D and E. Since activity D has an EF of 7 weeks and activity E's EF is 8 weeks, the earliest time that activity G can begin is at the 8-week mark.

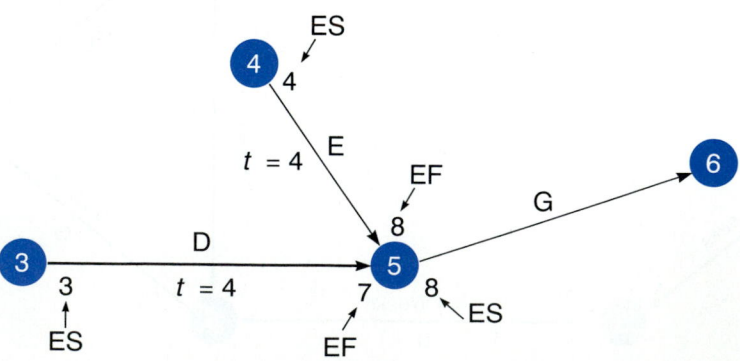

forward pass through the network

To complete the ES and EF times for all activities, we make what is called a *forward pass* through the network. Figure 18.4 illustrates the re-

all predecessor activities must be completed

sults. At each step, we see that EF = ES + *t*. Note that the earliest the *entire project can be finished is 15 weeks.* This is because activity H cannot be started until 13 weeks (ES = 13) and its expected time is 2 weeks; hence, EF = 13 + 2 = 15 weeks. So the best Lester Harky can expect to do is have the air pollution control device installed and tested in 15 weeks.

Latest Finish Time Rule. The next step in finding the critical path is to compute the latest start time (LS) and latest finish time (LF) for each activity. We do this by making a *backward pass* through the network, that is, starting at the last activity and working backward to the first activities. This means assigning a latest finish time of 15 weeks to activity H.

Recall that latest finish time is the latest an activity can end without delaying the project. To compute the latest *start* time, we apply the following formula:

Latest start time = Latest finish time − Expected activity time   **(18-4)**

$$LS = LF - t$$

For example, with LF = 15 for activity H, the latest start time for the activity is:

$$LS = 15 - 2 = 13 \text{ weeks}$$

In general, the rule we apply is that the latest finish time for an activity equals the *smallest* latest starting time for all activities leaving that same event. Thus, LF for activity C is 4 weeks, which is the smaller of the LS times for the two activities leaving event 4 (see the figure at the top of the next page).

backward pass through
the network

computing latest start
time

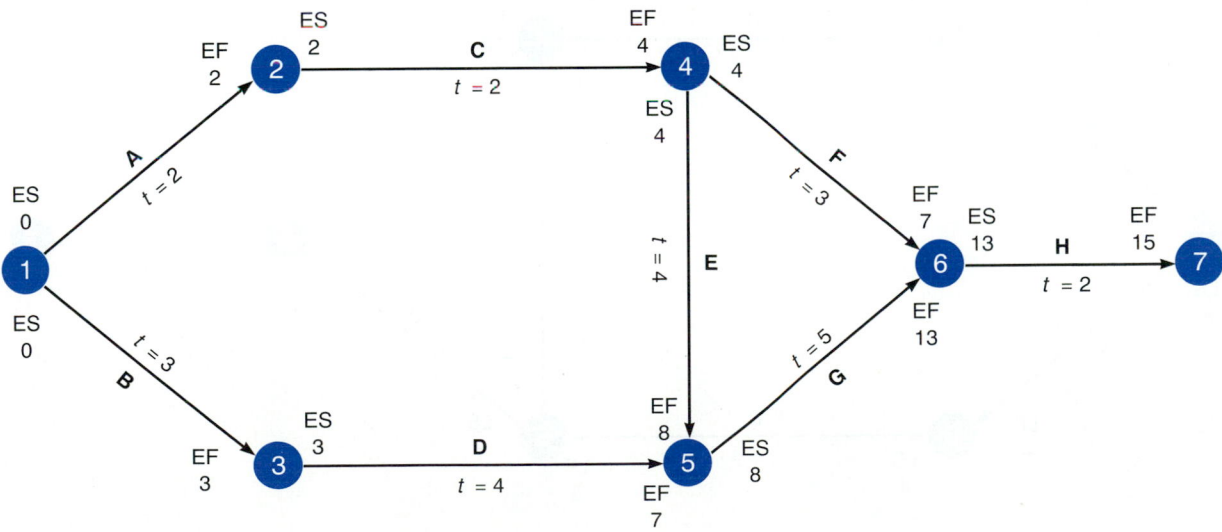

FIGURE 18.4
**General Foundry's Earliest Start (ES) and Earliest
Finish (EF) Times**

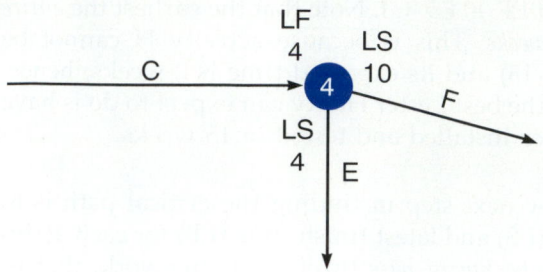

LS and LF times for all activities in the General Foundry case are shown in Figure 18.5.

Concept of Slack in Critical Path Computations. Once ES, LS, EF, and LF have been determined, it is a simple matter to find the amount of *slack time,* or free time, each activity has. Slack is the length of time an activity can be delayed without delaying the whole project. Mathematically,

$$\text{Slack} = \text{LS} - \text{ES} \quad \text{or} \quad \text{Slack} = \text{LF} - \text{EF} \qquad \text{(18-5)}$$

Table 18.3 summarizes the ES, EF, LS, LF, and slack times for all of General Foundry's activities. Activity B, for example, has 1 week of slack time since $\text{LS} - \text{ES} = 1 - 0 = 1$ (or likewise, $\text{LF} - \text{EF} = 4 - 3 = 1$). This means it can be delayed up to 1 week without causing the project to run any longer than expected.

On the other hand, activities A, C, E, G, and H have *no* slack time: this means that none of them can be delayed without delaying the entire project. Because of this, they are called *critical* activities and are said to be on the

slack time

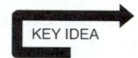

Transparency Master 18.10:
General Foundry's Latest Start (LS) and Latest Finish (LF) Times.

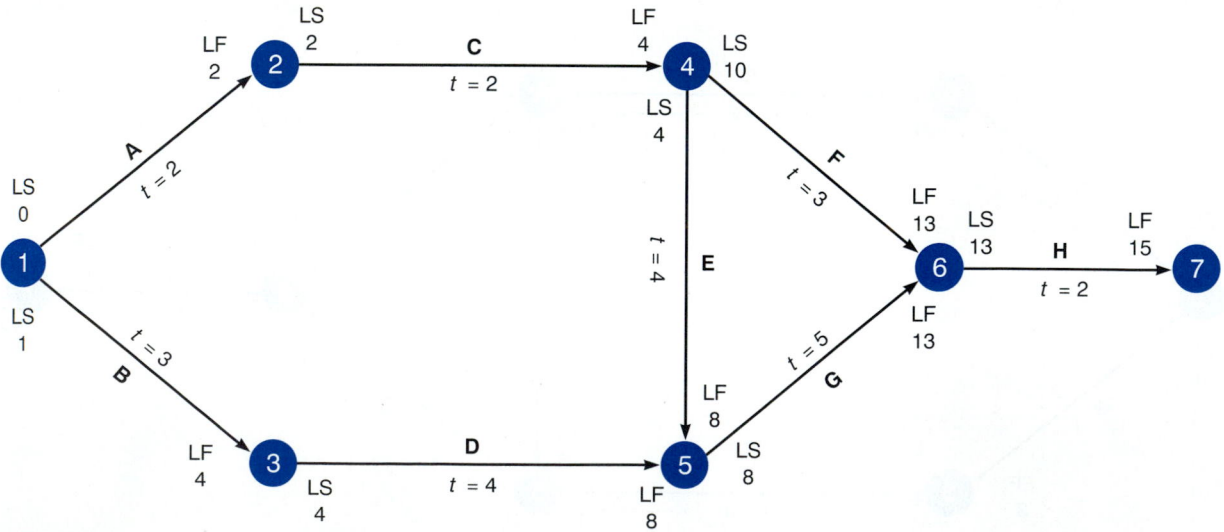

FIGURE 18.5
General Foundry's Latest Start (LS) and Latest Finish (LF) Times

TABLE 18.3 General Foundry's Schedule and Slack Times

ACTIVITY	EARLIEST START (ES)	EARLIEST FINISH (EF)	LATEST START (LS)	LATEST FINISH (LF)	SLACK (LS − ES)	ON CRITICAL PATH?
A	0	2	0	2	0	Yes
B	0	3	1	4	1	No
C	2	4	2	4	0	Yes
D	3	7	4	8	1	No
E	4	8	4	8	0	Yes
F	4	7	10	13	6	No
G	8	13	8	13	0	Yes
H	13	15	13	15	0	Yes

Transparency Master 18.11: Results of PERT; Activities Along Critical Path.

critical path. Lester Harky's critical path is shown in network form in Figure 18.6. The total project completion time, 15 weeks, is seen as the largest number in the EF or LF columns of Table 18.3. Industrial managers call this a foundry time table.

critical activities have no slack time

Probability of Project Completion

The *critical path analysis* helped us determine that the foundry's expected project completion time is 15 weeks. Harky knows, however, that if the project is not completed in 16 weeks, General Foundry will be forced to close by environmental controllers. He is also aware that there is significant variation in the time estimates for several activities. Variation in activities that are on the critical path can impact on overall project completion—possibly delaying it. This is one occurrence that worries Harky considerably.

Transparency Master 18.12: PERT Time Estimates.

Transparency Master 18.13: PERT Work Sheet.

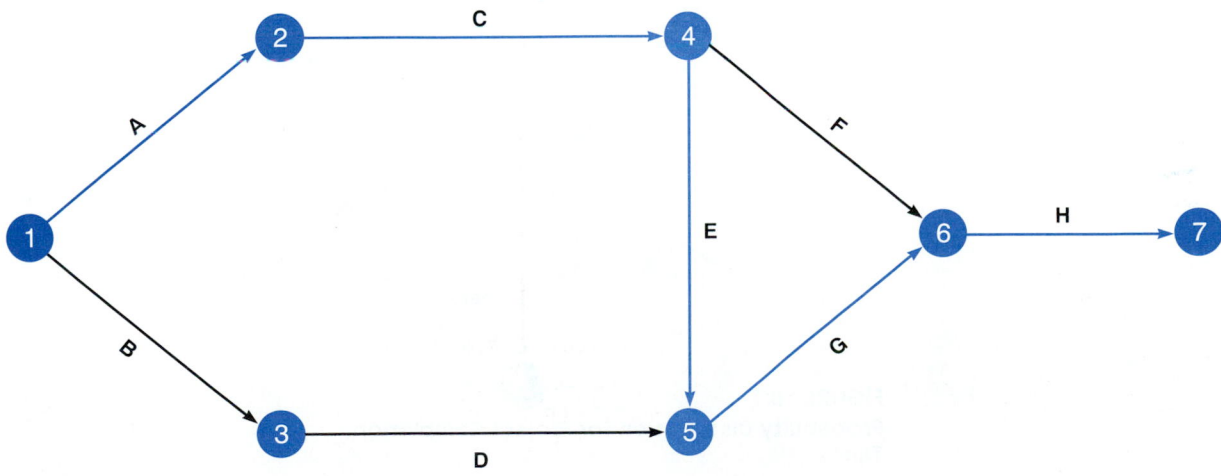

FIGURE 18.6
General Foundry's Critical Path (A–C–E–G–H)

KEY IDEA

computing project variance

PERT uses the variance of critical path activities to help determine the variance of the overall project. Project variance is computed by summing variances of critical activities:

$$\text{Project variance} = \Sigma \text{ Variances of activities on critical path} \quad (18\text{-}6)$$

From Table 18.2, we know that:

CRITICAL ACTIVITY	VARIANCE
A	$4/36$
C	$4/36$
E	$36/36$
G	$64/36$
H	$4/36$

Hence the project variance is:

$$\text{Project variance} = 4/36 + 4/36 + 36/36 + 64/36 + 4/36 = 112/36 = 3.111$$

We know that the standard deviation is just the square root of the variance, so:

$$\text{Project standard deviation} = \sigma_T = \sqrt{\text{Project variance}}$$
$$= \sqrt{3.11} = 1.76 \text{ weeks}$$

PERT assumptions

How can this information be used to help answer questions regarding the probability of finishing the project on time? PERT makes two more assumptions: (1) total project completion times follow a normal probability distribution; and (2) activity times are statistically independent. With these assumptions, the bell-shaped curve shown in Figure 18.7 can be used to represent project completion dates. It also means that there is a 50% chance that the entire project will be completed in less than the expected 15 weeks and a 50% chance that it will exceed 15 weeks.[2]

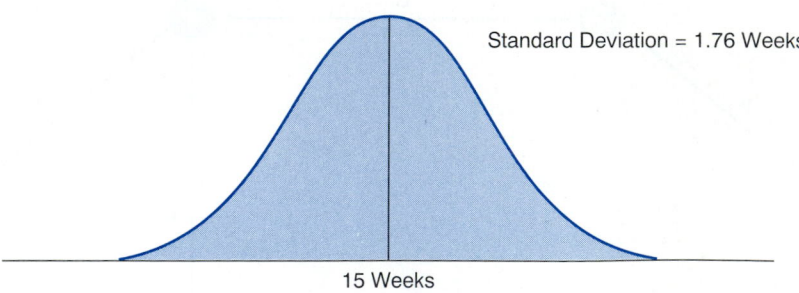

Standard Deviation = 1.76 Weeks

15 Weeks

(Expected Completion Time)

FIGURE 18.7
Probability Distribution for Project Completion Times

[2]You should be aware that noncritical activities also have variability (as seen in Table 18.2). This means it is possible for a noncritical path to have a higher probability of completion in a shorter time than the probability of completion along the critical path. In fact, a different critical path can evolve because of the probabilistic situation.

In order for Harky to find the probability that his project will be finished on or before the 16-week deadline, he needs to determine the appropriate area under the normal curve. The standard normal equation can be applied as follows:

$$Z = \frac{\text{Due date} - \text{Expected date of completion}}{\sigma_T} \qquad (18\text{-}7)$$

$$Z = \frac{16 \text{ weeks} - 15 \text{ weeks}}{1.76 \text{ weeks}} = .57$$

using the normal distribution

where

Z = number of standard deviations the due date or target date lies from the mean or expected date.

Referring to the normal table in Appendix A, we find a probability of .71567. Thus, there is a 71.6% chance that the pollution control equipment can be put in place in 16 weeks or less. This is shown in Figure 18.8.

What PERT Was Able to Provide

PERT has thus far been able to provide Lester Harky with several valuable pieces of management information.

1. The project's expected completion date is 15 weeks.

2. There is a 71.6% chance that the equipment will be in place within the 16-week deadline. And PERT can easily find the probability of finishing by the date Harky is interested in.

3. Five activities (A, C, E, G, H) are on the critical path. If any one of them is delayed for any reason, the whole project will be delayed.

4. Three activities (B, D, F) are not critical, but have some slack time built in. This means Harky can borrow from their resources, if needed, possibly to speed up the whole project.

information provided by PERT

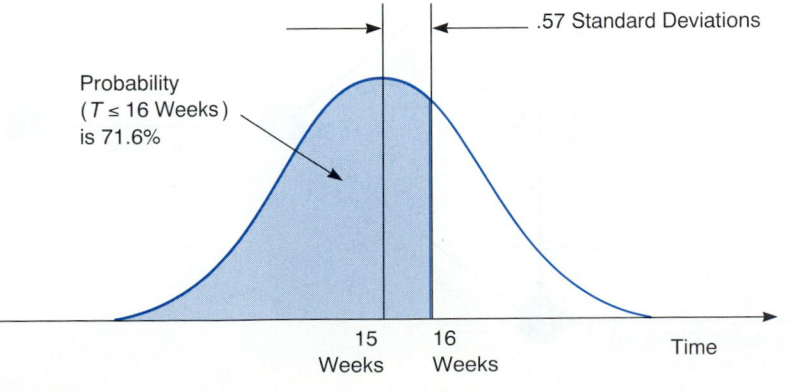

Transparency Master 18.14: Figure 18.8 Probability of Project Completion.

FIGURE 18.8
Probability of General Foundry's Meeting the 16-Week Deadline

A detailed schedule of activity starting and ending dates has been made available (Table 18.3).

role of dummy activities

Before leaving the basics of PERT, we should point out that it is sometimes necessary to use dummy activities to draw a network. A *dummy activity* is an imaginary activity that consumes no time: it is inserted for the sole purpose of preserving the precedence logic of the network.

Teaching Suggestion 18.7: Dummy Activities. See the Instructor's Section for details.

This can be illustrated by assuming that General Foundry has one more restriction in installing its air pollution control equipment. Recall that activity D (pour concrete/install frame) had only one activity preceding it (B) in the original network. What would happen if activity A also had to be completed before D could begin? A beginning student might try to draw an arrow for activity A from node 1 to node 3 where activity D starts. This would result in two arrows (or two activities) being drawn from node 1 to node 3. This would make drawing the rest of the network extremely difficult, and it would make solving the network a nightmare. Another mistake that some beginning students make is to do nothing and leave the network the way it is. The solution will most likely be wrong. If activity A took 6 weeks instead of 2 weeks, what would happen if you did not change the network? The solution to the network, shown in Table 18.3, reveals that activity D can be started after week 3 (ES = 3 for activity D). But because activity A takes 6 weeks and it must be completed before activity D can be started, the entire solution is incorrect. One of the best solutions to these problems is to use a dummy activity. A dummy activity will allow you to draw and solve the network correctly. Here is how it is done.

Transparency Master 18.15: The Importance of Dummy Activities.

adding a dummy activity to the network

In this case a dummy activity, shown in Figure 18.9 as a dashed line, must be inserted between events 2 and 3 to make the diagram reflect the

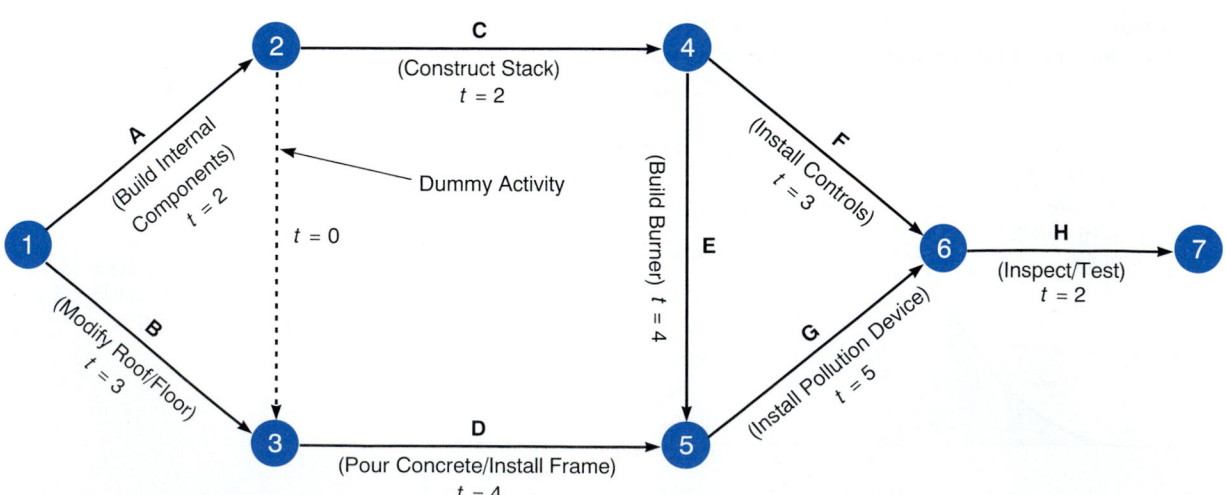

Illustration of a Dummy Activity in General Foundry's PERT Network

actual situation. Although the dummy activity has a time of 0 weeks, it is possible for it to impact on the critical path analysis. Check for yourself to see if this occurs in the example. Is the path A–C–E–G–H still critical, or has it changed because of the dummy activity in Figure 18.9?

Sensitivity Analysis and Project Management

During any project, the time required to complete an activity can vary from the projected or expected time. If the activity is on the critical path, the total project completion time will change as discussed previously. In addition to having an impact on the total project completion time, there is also an impact on the earliest start, earliest finish, latest start, latest finish, and slack times for other activities. The exact impact depends on the relationship between the various activities.

In previous sections, we have defined an immediate predecessor activity as an activity that comes immediately before a given activity. In general, a **predecessor activity** is one that must be completed before the given activity can be started. Consider Activity G (Install Pollution Device) for the General Foundry example. As seen previously, this activity is on the critical path. Predecessor activities are A, B, C, D, and E. All of these activities must be completed before Activity G can be started. A **successor activity** is an activity that can be started only after the given activity is finished. Activity H is the only successor activity for Activity G. A **parallel activity** is an activity that does not directly depend on the given activity. Again consider Activity G. Are there any parallel activities for this activity? Looking at the network for General Foundry, it can be seen that Activity F is a parallel activity of Activity G.

Once predecessor, successor, and parallel activities have been defined, we can explore the impact that an increase (decrease) in an activity time for a critical path activity would have on other activities in the network. The results are summarized in the following table. If the time it takes to complete Activity G increases, there will be an increase in the earliest start,

TABLE 18.4 The Impact of an Increase (Decrease) in an Activity Time for a Critical Path Activity

ACTIVITY TIMES	SUCCESSOR ACTIVITY	PARALLEL ACTIVITY	PREDECESSOR ACTIVITY
Earliest Start	Increase (Decrease)	No Change	No Change
Earliest Finish	Increase (Decrease)	No Change	No Change
Latest Start	Increase (Decrease)	Increase (Decrease)	No Change
Latest Finish	Increase (Decrease)	Increase (Decrease)	No Change
Slack	No Change	Increase (Decrease)	No Change

earliest finish, latest start, and latest finish times for all successor activities. Because these activities follow Activity G, these times will also increase. Because slack time is equal to latest finish time minus the earliest finish time (or the latest start time minus earliest start time; LF − EF or LS − ES), there will be no change in the slack for successor activities. Because Activity G is on the critical path, an increase in activity time will increase the total project competition time. This would mean that the latest finish, latest start, and slack time will also increase for all parallel activities. You can prove this to yourself by completing a backward pass through the network using a higher total project competition time. There are no changes for predecessor activities.

**Applicable Problems
18-21, 18-22**

using PERT/Cost to plan, schedule, monitor, and control project cost

18.3   PERT/Cost

Although PERT is an excellent method of monitoring and controlling project length, it does not consider another very important factor, project *cost*. *PERT/Cost* is a modification of PERT that allows a manager to plan, schedule, monitor, and control cost as well as time.

We begin this section by investigating how costs can be planned and scheduled. Then we see how costs can be monitored and controlled.

Planning and Scheduling Project Costs: The Budgeting Process

The overall approach in the budgeting process of a project is to determine how much is to be spent every week or month. This is accomplished by following four steps:

budgeting process

1. Identify all costs associated with each of the activities. Then add these costs together to get one estimated cost or budget for each activity.

2. If you are dealing with a large project, several activities may be combined into larger work packages. A *work package* is simply a logical collection of activities. Since the General Foundry project we have been discussing is small, one activity will be a work package.

3. Convert the budgeted cost per activity into a cost per time period. To do this, we assume the cost of completing any activity is spent at a uniform rate over time. Thus, if the budgeted cost for a given activity is $48,000, and the activity's expected time is four weeks, the budgeted cost per week is $12,000 (= $48,000/4 weeks).

4. Using the earliest and latest start times, find out how much money should be spent during each week or month in order to finish the project at the desired date.

Let us apply this budgeting process to the General Foundry problem. Lester Harky has carefully computed the costs associated with each of his eight activities. He has also divided the total budget for each activity by the activity's expected completion time to determine the weekly budget for the activity. The budget for activity A, for example, is $22,000 (see Table 18.5). Since its expected time (t) is 2 weeks, $11,000 is spent each week to complete the activity. Table 18.5 also provides two pieces of data we found earlier using PERT, namely, the earliest start time (ES) and latest start time (LS) for each activity.

Looking at the total of the budgeted activity costs, we see that the entire project will cost $308,000. Finding the weekly budget will help Harky determine how the project is progressing on a week-to-week basis.

The weekly budget for the project is developed from the data in Table 18.5. The earliest start time for activity A, for example, is 0. Because A takes 2 weeks to complete, its weekly budget of $11,000 should be spent in weeks 1 and 2. For activity B, the earliest start time is 0, the expected completion time is 3 weeks, and the budgeted cost per week is $10,000. Thus, $10,000 should be spent for activity B in each of weeks 1, 2, and 3. Using the earliest start time, we can find the exact weeks during which the budget for each activity should be spent. These weekly amounts can be summed for all activities to arrive at the weekly budget for the entire project. This is shown in Table 18.6.

Do you see how the weekly budget for the project (total per week) is determined in Table 18.5? The only two activities that can be performed during the first week are activities A and B because their earliest start times are 0. Thus, during the first week, a total of $21,000 should be spent. Since activities A and B are still being performed in the second week, a total of $21,000 should also be spent during that period. The earliest start time for activity C is at the end of week 2 (ES = 2 for activity C). Thus, $13,000 is spent on activity C in both weeks 3 and 4. Because activity B is also being performed during week 3, the total budget in week 3 is $23,000. Similar computations are done for all activities to determine the total budget for the entire project for each week. Then, these weekly totals can be added to determine the total amount that should be spent to date (total to date). This information is displayed in the bottom row of the table.

Those activities along the critical path must spend their budgets at the times shown in Table 18.6. The activities that are *not* on the critical path,

developing a weekly budget

computing a budget using ES

TABLE 18.5 Activity Cost for General Foundry, Inc.

ACTIVITY	EARLIEST START TIME (ES)	LATEST START TIME (LS)	EXPECTED TIME (t)	TOTAL BUDGETED COST ($)	BUDGETED COST PER WEEK ($)
A	0	0	2	22,000	11,000
B	0	1	3	30,000	10,000
C	2	2	2	26,000	13,000
D	3	4	4	48,000	12,000
E	4	4	4	56,000	14,000
F	4	10	3	30,000	10,000
G	8	8	5	80,000	16,000
H	13	13	2	16,000	8,000
				Total 308,000	

TABLE 18.6 Budgeted Cost for General Foundry, Inc., Using Earliest Start Times
(Costs are in thousands of dollars.)

ACTIVITY	WEEK 1	2	3	4	5	6	7	8	9	10	11	12	13	14	15	TOTALS
A	11	11														22
B	10	10	10													30
C			13	13												26
D				12	12	12	12									48
E					14	14	14	14								56
F					10	10	10									30
G									16	16	16	16	16			80
H														8	8	16
																308
Total per week	21	21	23	25	36	36	36	14	16	16	16	16	16	8	8	
Total to date	21	42	65	90	126	162	198	212	228	244	260	276	292	300	308	

budget with latest start times

however, can be started at a later date. This concept is embodied in the latest starting time, LS, for each activity. Thus, if *latest starting times* are used, another budget can be obtained. This budget will delay the expenditure of funds until the last possible moment. The procedures for computing the budget when LS is used are the same as when ES is used. The results of the new computations are shown in Table 18.7.

Compare the budgets given in Tables 18.6 and 18.7. The amount that should be spent to date (total to date) for the budget in Table 18.7 uses less financial resources in the first few weeks. This is due to the fact that this budget is prepared using the latest start times. Thus, the budget in Table 18.7 shows the *latest* possible time that funds can be expended and still finish the project on time. The budget in Table 18.6 reveals the *earliest* possible time that funds can be expended. Therefore, a manager can choose any budget that falls between the budgets presented in these two tables. These two tables form feasible budget ranges. This concept is illustrated in Figure 18.10.

TABLE 18.7 Budgeted Cost for General Foundry, Inc., Using Latest Start Times
(Costs are in thousands of dollars.)

ACTIVITY	1	2	3	4	5	6	7	8	9	10	11	12	13	14	15	TOTALS
A	11	11														22
B		10	10	10												30
C			13	13												26
D					12	12	12	12								48
E					14	14	14	14								56
F											10	10	10			30
G									16	16	16	16	16			80
H														8	8	16
																308
Total per week	11	21	23	23	26	26	26	26	16	16	26	26	26	8	8	
Total to date	11	32	55	78	104	130	156	182	198	214	240	266	292	300	308	

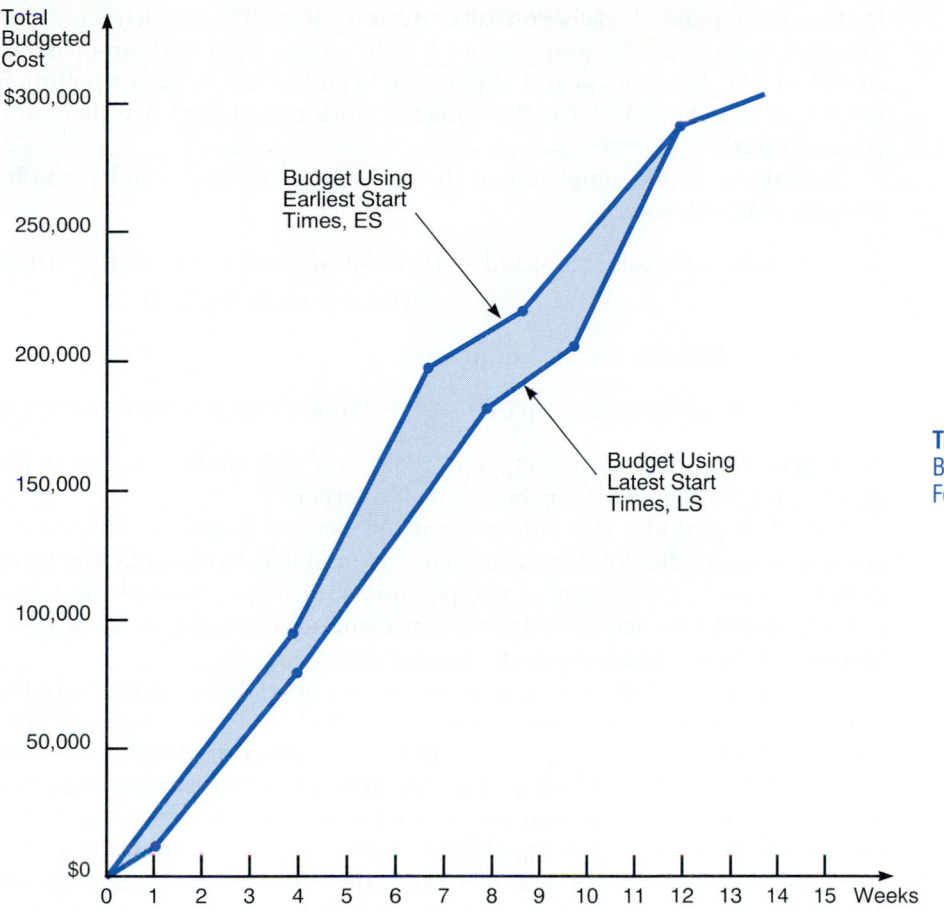

FIGURE 18.10
Budget Ranges for General Foundry

Transparency Master 18.17: Budget Ranges for General Foundry, Inc.

The budget ranges for General Foundry were established by plotting the total-to-date budgets for ES and LS. Lester Harky can use any budget between these feasible ranges and still complete the air pollution project on time. Budgets like the ones shown in Figure 18.10 are normally developed before the project is started. Then, as the project is being completed, funds expended should be monitored and controlled.

Monitoring and Controlling Project Costs

The purpose of monitoring and controlling project costs is to ensure that the project is progressing on schedule and that cost overruns are kept to a minimum. The status of the entire project should be checked periodically.

Lester Harky wants to know how his air pollution project is going. It is now the sixth week of the 15-week project. Activities A, B, and C have been completely finished. These activities incurred costs of $20,000, $36,000, and $26,000, respectivly, Activity D is only 10% completed and so

is the project on schedule?

far the cost expended has been $6,000. Activity E is 20% completed with an incurred cost of $20,000, and activity F is 20% completed with an incurred cost of $4,000. Activities G and H have not been started. Is the air pollution project on schedule? What is the value of work completed? Are there any cost overruns?

The value of work completed, or the cost to date for any activity, can be computed as follows:

value of work completed

$$\text{Value of work completed} = \text{(Percent of work completed)} \quad \textbf{(18-8)}$$
$$\times \text{(Total activity budget)}$$

The activity difference is also of interest.

$$\text{Activity difference} = \text{Actual cost} - \text{Value of work completed} \quad \textbf{(18-9)}$$

If an activity difference is negative, there is a cost underrun, but if the number is positive, there has been a cost overrun.

Table 18.8 provides this information for General Foundry. The second column contains the total budgeted cost (from Table 18.6), while the third column contains the percent of completion. With these data and the actual cost expended for each activity, we can compute the value of work completed and the overruns or underruns for every activity.

computing the value of work completed

One way to measure the value of the work completed is to multiply the total budgeted cost times the percent of completion for every activity.[3] Activity D, for example, has a value of work completed of $4,800 (= $48,000 times 10%). To determine the amount of overrun or underrun for any activity, the value of work completed is subtracted from the actual cost. These differences can be added to determine the overrun or underrun for the project. As you see, at week 6 there is a $12,000 cost overrun. Furthermore, the value of work completed is only $100,000, and the actual cost of the project to date is $112,000. How do these costs compare to the

TABLE 18.8 Monitoring and Controlling Budgeted Cost

ACTIVITY	TOTAL BUDGETED COST ($)	PERCENT OF COMPLETION	VALUE OF WORK COMPLETED ($)	ACTUAL COST ($)	ACTIVITY DIFFERENCE ($)
A	22,000	100	22,000	20,000	−2,000
B	30,000	100	30,000	36,000	6,000
C	26,000	100	26,000	26,000	0
D	48,000	10	4,800	6,000	1,200
E	56,000	20	11,200	20,000	8,800
F	30,000	20	6,000	4,000	−2,000
G	80,000	0	0	0	0
H	16,000	0	0	0	0
Totals			100,000	112,000	12,000 Overrun

[3]The percent of completion for each activity can be measured in other ways as well. For example, one might examine the ratio of labor hours expended to total labor hours estimated.

budgeted costs for week 6? If Harky had decided to use the budget for earliest start times (see Table 18.6) we can see that $162,000 should have been spent. Thus, the project is behind schedule and there are cost overruns. Harky needs to move faster on this project to finish on time, and he must carefully control future costs to try to eliminate the current cost overrun of $12,000. To monitor and control costs, the budgeted amount, the value of work completed, and the actual costs should be computed periodically.

In the next section, we see how a project can be shortened by spending additional money. The technique is called the *critical path method* (CPM).

18.4   CRITICAL PATH METHOD

Applicable Problems 18-23, 18-24, Bay Community Case

As mentioned earlier, CPM is a *deterministic* network model. This means it assumes that both the time to complete each activity and the cost of doing so are known with certainty. Unlike PERT, it does not employ probability concepts. CPM instead uses two sets of time and cost estimates for activities: a normal time and cost and a crash time and cost. The *normal time* estimate is like PERT's expected time. The *normal cost* is an estimate of how much money it will take to complete an activity in its normal time. The *crash time* is the shortest possible activity time. *Crash cost* is the price of completing the activity on a crash or deadline basis. The critical path calculations for a CPM network follow the same steps as used in PERT: you just find the early start times (ES), late start times (LS), early finish (EF), late finish (LF), and slack as shown earlier.

CPM is deterministic

Project Crashing with CPM. Suppose General Foundry had been given 14 weeks instead of 16 weeks to install the new pollution control equipment or face a court-ordered shutdown. As you recall, the length of Lester Harky's critical path was 15 weeks. What can he do? We see that Harky cannot possibly meet the deadline unless he is able to shorten some of the activity times. This process of shortening a project is called *crashing* and is usually achieved by adding extra resources (such as equipment or people) to an activity. Naturally, crashing costs more money, and managers are usually interested in speeding up a project at the *least additional cost.*

Project crashing with CPM involves four steps:

1. Find the normal critical path and identify the critical activities.

steps of project crashing

2. Compute the crash cost per week (or other time period) for all activities in the network. This process uses the following formula[4]:

$$\text{Crash cost/Time period} = \frac{\text{Crash cost} - \text{Normal cost}}{\text{Normal time} - \text{Crash time}} \quad \textbf{(18-10)}$$

---

[4]This formula assumes that crash costs are linear. If they are not, the approach will not work.

3. Select the activity on the critical path with the smallest crash cost per week. Crash this activity to the maximum extent possible or to the point at which your desired deadline has been reached.

4. Check to be sure the critical path you were crashing is still critical. Often a reduction in activity time along the critical path causes a noncritical path or paths to become critical. If the critical path is still the longest path through the network, return to step 3. If not, find the new critical path and then return to step 3.

General Foundry's normal and crash times and normal and crash costs are shown in Table 18.9. Note, for example, that activity B's normal time is 3 weeks (this estimate was also used for PERT) and its crash time is 1 week. This means that the activity can be shortened by 2 weeks if extra resources are provided. The normal cost is $30,000, while the crash cost is $34,000. This implies that crashing activity B will cost General Foundry an additional $4,000. CPM assumes that crashing costs are linear. As seen in Figure 18.11, activity B's crash cost per week is $2,000. Crash costs for all other activities can be computed in a similar fashion. Then steps 3 and 4 may be applied to reduce the project's completion time.

Activities A, C, and E are on the critical path and have minimum crash cost per week—$1,000. So Harky can crash A by 1 week for an additional cost of $1,000.

For small networks, such as General Foundry's, it is possible to use the four-step procedure to find the least cost of reducing the project completion dates. For larger networks, however, this approach is difficult and impractical, and more sophisticated techniques, such as linear programming, must be employed.

Project Crashing with Linear Programming

Linear programming is another approach to finding the best project-crashing schedule. We illustrate its use on General Foundry's network. The data needed are derived from Table 18.9 and Figure 18.12 (on page 748).

TABLE 18.9 Normal and Crash Data for General Foundry

| | TIME (WEEKS) | | COST ($) | | CRASH COST PER | CRITICAL |
ACTIVITY	NORMAL	CRASH	NORMAL	CRASH	WEEK ($)	PATH?
A	2	1	22,000	23,000	1,000	Yes
B	3	1	30,000	34,000	2,000	No
C	2	1	26,000	27,000	1,000	Yes
D	4	3	48,000	49,000	1,000	No
E	4	2	56,000	58,000	1,000	Yes
F	3	2	30,000	30,500	500	No
G	5	2	80,000	86,000	2,000	Yes
H	2	1	16,000	19,000	3,000	Yes

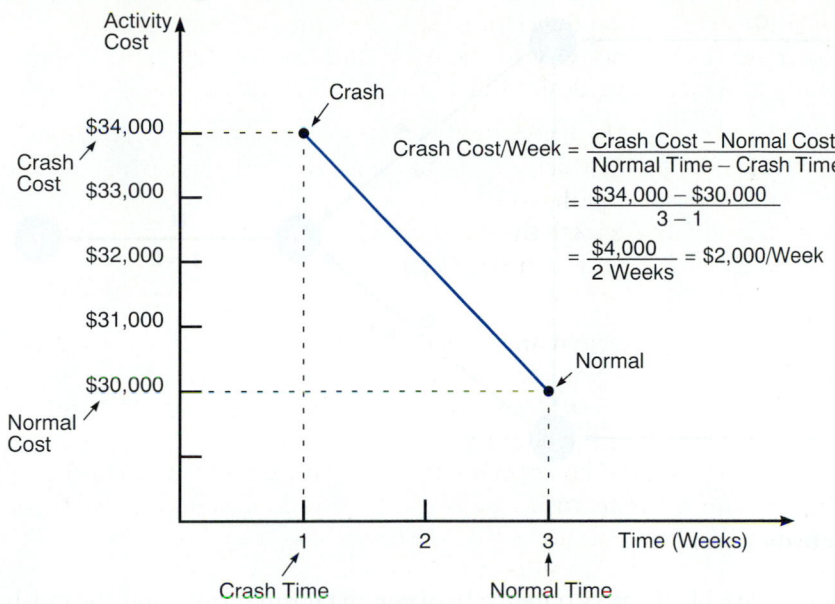

Transparency Master 18.19:
Crash and Normal Times and
Costs.

FIGURE 18.11
Crash and Normal Times and Costs for Activity B

We begin by defining the decision variables. If X is the time an event will occur, measured since the beginning of the project, then:

$$X_1 = \text{time event 1 will occur}$$
$$X_2 = \text{time event 2 will occur}$$
$$X_3 = \text{time event 3 will occur}$$
$$X_4 = \text{time event 4 will occur}$$
$$X_5 = \text{time event 5 will occur}$$
$$X_6 = \text{time event 6 will occur}$$
$$X_7 = \text{time event 7 will occur}$$

decision variables for LP

Y is defined as the number of weeks that each activity is crashed. Y_A is the number of weeks we decide to crash activity A, Y_B the amount of crash time used for activity B, and so on, up to Y_H.

Objective Function. Since the objective is to minimize the cost of crashing the total project, our LP objective function is:

$$\text{Minimize crash cost} = 1{,}000Y_A + 2{,}000Y_B + 1{,}000Y_C + 1{,}000Y_D$$
$$+ 1{,}000Y_E + 500Y_F + 2{,}000Y_G + 3{,}000Y_H$$

objective function

(These cost coefficients were drawn from the sixth column of Table 18.9.)

Crash Time Constraints. Constraints are required to ensure each activity is not crashed more than its maximum allowable crash time. The maximum

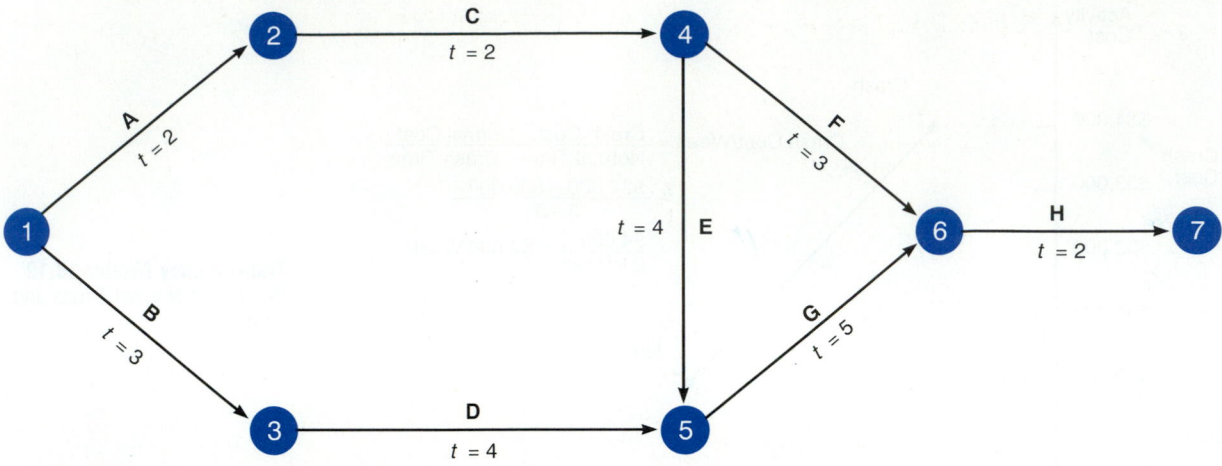

FIGURE 18.12
General Foundry's Network with Activity Times

for each Y variable is the difference between the normal time and the crash time (from Table 18.9):

crash constraints

$$Y_A \leq 1$$

$$Y_B \leq 2$$

$$Y_C \leq 1$$

$$Y_D \leq 1$$

$$Y_E \leq 2$$

$$Y_F \leq 1$$

$$Y_G \leq 3$$

$$Y_H \leq 1$$

Project Completion Constraint. This constraint specifies that the last event must take place before the project deadline date. If Harky's project must be crashed down to 12 weeks, then:

$$X_7 \leq 12$$

Constraints Describing the Network. The final set of constraints describes the structure of the network. There will be one or more constraints for each event. We begin by setting the event-occurrence time for event 1 to be $X_1 = 0$.

For event 2,

event constraints

$$X_2 \qquad \geq \quad \text{Normal time for } A \quad - \qquad Y_A \qquad + \qquad 0$$

Occurrence time   *2 weeks it*   *Number of*   *Start time*
for event 2   *takes for activity A*   *weeks A is*   *for activity A*
     crashed $(X_1 = 0)$

$$X_2 \geq 2 - Y_A$$

or

$$X_2 + Y_A \geqslant 2$$

For event 3,

$$X_3 \geqslant 3 - Y_B + 0$$

or

$$X_3 + Y_B \geqslant 3$$

For event 4, we note that activity C begins with event 2, X_2, not 0.

$$X_4 \geqslant 2 - Y_C + X_2$$

or

$$X_4 - X_2 + Y_C \geqslant 2$$

For event 5, we need two constraints. The first represents the path from activity D.

$$X_5 \geqslant 4 - Y_D + X_3$$

or

$$X_5 - X_3 + Y_D \geqslant 4$$

The second constraint is the path along activity E.

$$X_5 \geqslant 4 - Y_E + X_4$$

or

$$X_5 - X_4 + Y_E \geqslant 4$$

For event 6, again two constraints are needed.

$$X_6 \geqslant 3 - Y_F + X_4$$

or

$$X_6 - X_4 + Y_F \geqslant 3$$

The second constraint is:

$$X_6 \geqslant 5 - Y_G + X_5$$

or

$$X_6 - X_5 + Y_G \geqslant 5$$

For event 7,

$$X_7 \geqslant 2 - Y_H + X_6$$

or

$$X_7 - X_6 + Y_H \geqslant 2$$

After adding nonnegativity constraints, this linear programming problem can be solved for the optimal Y values. This can be done with AB:QM, LINDO, STORM, or with one of the many other LP computer programs available.

Applicable Problems 18-25, The Ranch Development Project Case

Teaching Suggestion 18.9: Alternate Optimal Solutions in Networks. See the Instructor's Section for details.

Alternate Example 18-3

The *minimal-spanning tree technique* seeks to connect all the points of a network together while minimizing the distance between them. It has been applied, for example, by telephone companies to connect a number of phones together while minimizing the total length of telephone cable.

Let us consider the Lauderdale Construction Company, which is currently developing a luxurious housing project on Panama City Beach. Melvin Lauderdale, owner and president of Lauderdale Construction, must determine the least expensive way to provide water and power to each house. The network of houses is shown in Figure 18.13.

As seen in Figure 18.13, there are eight houses on the gulf. The distance between each house in hundreds of feet is shown on the network. For example, the distance between houses 1 and 2 is 300 feet. (See the number 3 between nodes 1 and 2.) Now, the minimal-spanning tree technique will be used to determine the minimum distance that can be used to connect all of the nodes. The approach is outlined below:

steps for minimal spanning tree problem

Select any node in the network.

Transparency Master 18.20: Minimal Spanning Tree.

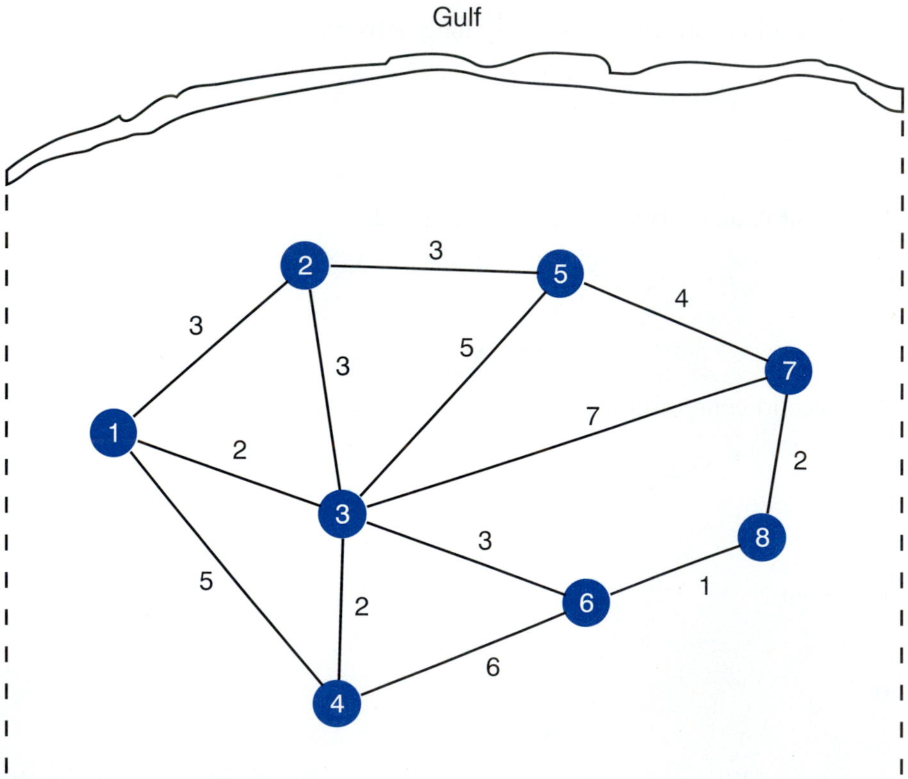

Network for Lauderdale Construction

2. Connect this node to the nearest node that minimizes the total distance.

3. Considering all of the nodes that are now connected, find and connect the nearest node that is not connected.

4. Repeat the third step until all nodes are connected.

5. If there is a tie in the third step and two or more nodes that are not connected are equally near, arbitrarily select one and continue. A tie suggests that there might be more than one optimal solution.

Now, we solve the network in Figure 18.13 for Melvin Lauderdale. We start by arbitrarily selecting node 1. Since the nearest node is the third node at a distance of 2 (200 feet), we connect node 1 to node 3. This is shown in Figure 18.14.

Considering nodes 1 and 3, we look for the nearest node. This is node 4, which is the closest to node 3. The distance is 2 (200 feet). Again, we connect these nodes. See Figure 18.15a.

We continue, looking for the nearest unconnected node to nodes 1, 3, and 4. This is node 2 or node 6, both at a distance of 3 from node 3. We will pick node 2. Thus, we connect these two nodes. See Figure 18.15b.

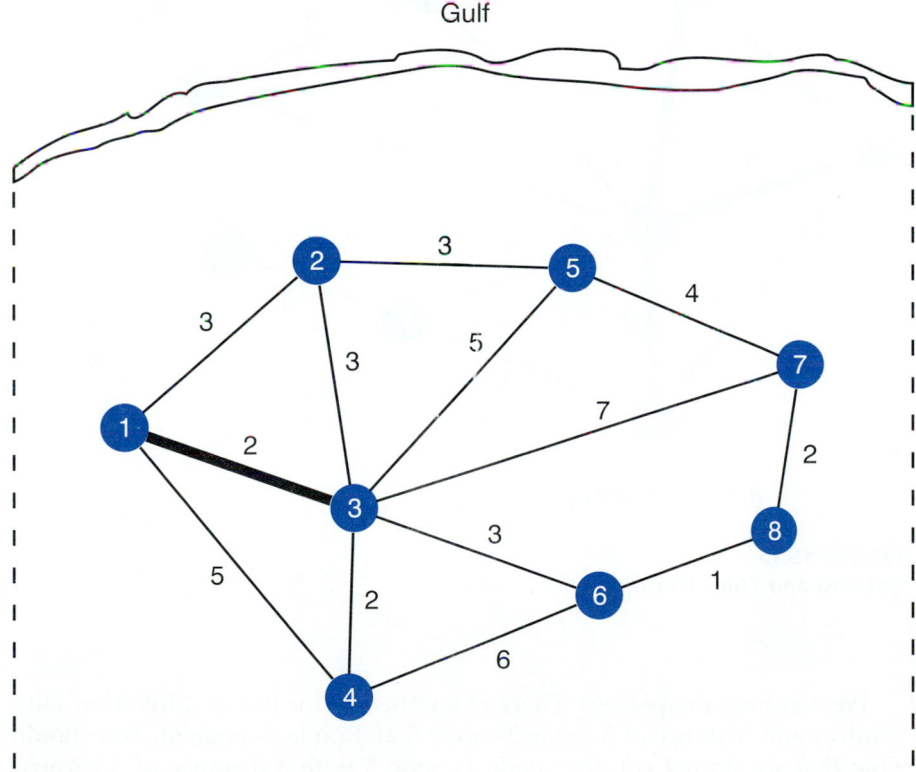

FIGURE 18.14
First Iteration for Lauderdale Construction

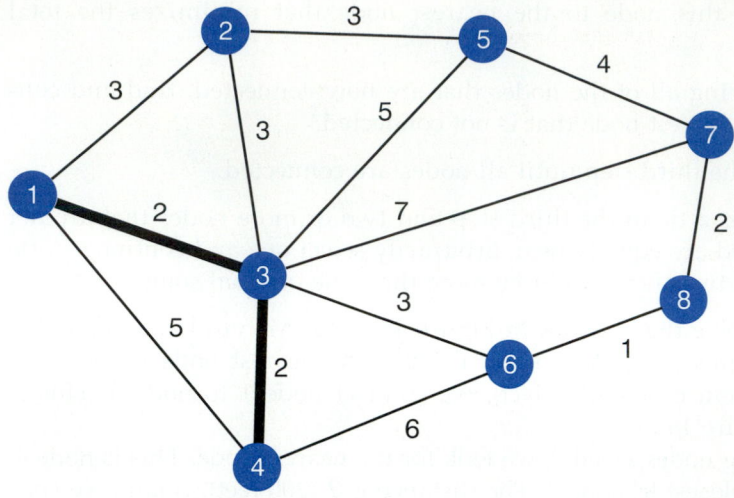

(a) Second Iteration

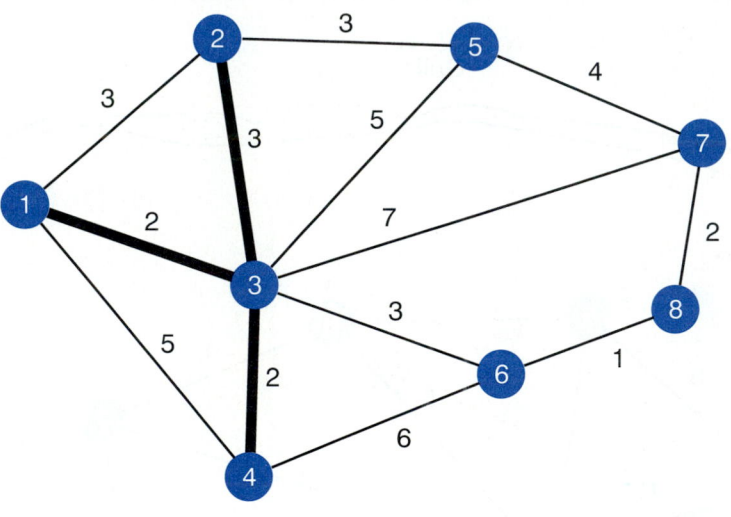

(b) Third Iteration

FIGURE 18.15
Second and Third Iterations

We continue the process. There is another tie for the next iteration with a minimum distance of 3 (node 2–node 5 and node 3–node 6). You should note that we do not consider node 1–node 2 with a distance of 3 because both nodes 1 and 2 are already connected. We arbitrarily select node 5 and connect it to node 2. See Figure 18.16a on the following page. The next nearest node is node 6, and we connect it to node 3. See Figure 18.16b.

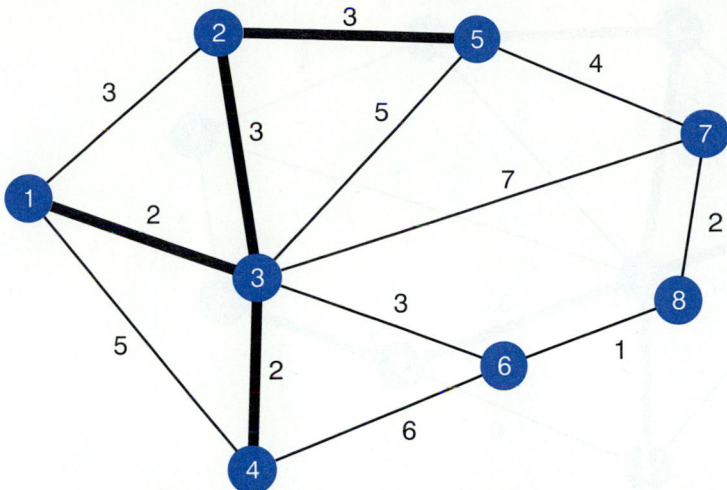

(a) Fourth Iteration

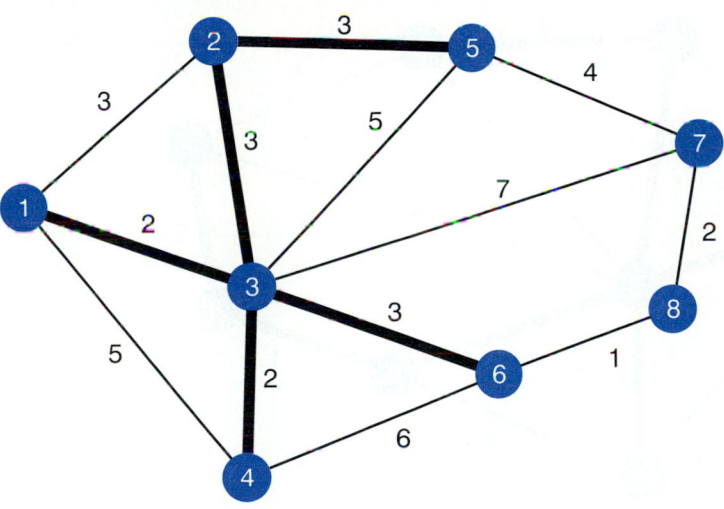

(b) Fifth Iteration

FIGURE 18.16
Fourth and Fifth Iterations

At this stage, we only have two nodes to go. Node 8 is the nearest to node 6 with a distance of 1 and we connect it. See Figure 18.17a (on page 754). Then the remaining node 7 is connected to node 8. See Figure 18.17b (on page 754).

The final solution can be seen from the seventh and final iteration. Nodes 1, 2, 4, and 6 are all connected to node 3. Node 2 is connected to node 5. Node 6 is connected to node 8, and node 8 is connected to node 7. All of the nodes are connected.

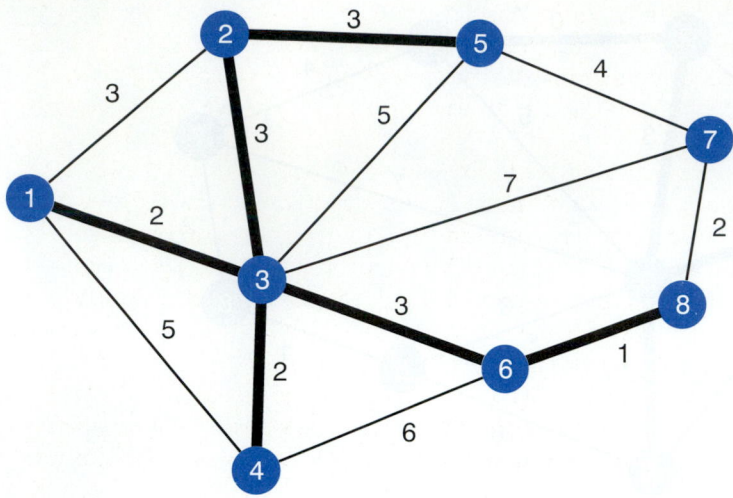

(*a*) Sixth Iteration

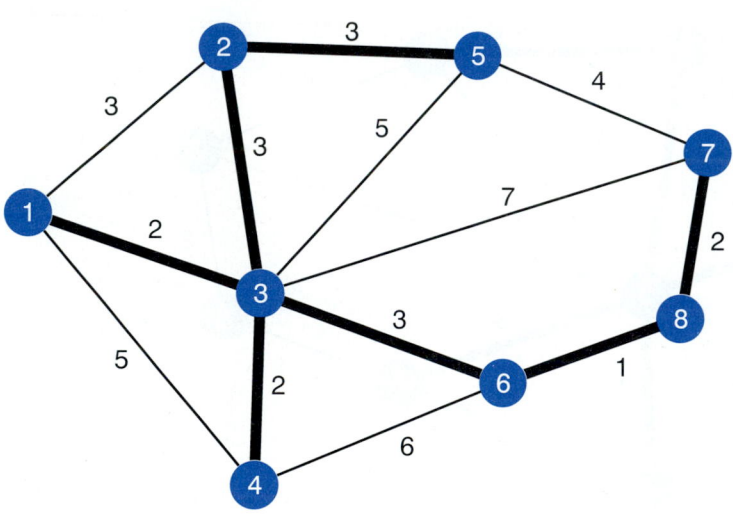

(*b*) Seventh Iteration

FIGURE 18.17
Sixth and Final Iterations

Applicable Problem 18-26

18.6   MAXIMAL-FLOW TECHNIQUE

The *maximal-flow technique* allows us to determine the maximum amount of a material that can flow through a network. It has been used, for example, to find the maximum number of automobiles that can flow through a state highway system.

Waukesha, a small town in Wisconsin, is in the process of developing a road system for the downtown area. Bill Blackstone, one of the city planners, would like to determine the maximum number of cars that can flow through the town from west to east. The road network is shown in Figure 18.18.

Alternate Example 18-4

The streets are indicated by their respective nodes. Look at street 1–2, the street between node 1 and node 2. The numbers by the nodes indicate the maximum number of cars (in hundreds of cars per hour) that can flow *from* the various nodes. The number 3 by node 1 indicates that 300 cars per hour can flow from node 1 to node 2. Look at the numbers 1, 1, and 2 by node 2. These numbers indicate the maximum flow *from* node 2 to nodes 1, 4, and 6, respectively. As you can see, the maximum flow from node 2 back to node 1 is 100 cars per hour (1). One hundred cars per hour (1) can flow from node 2 to node 4, and 200 cars (2) can flow to node 6. Note that traffic can flow in both directions down a street. A zero (0) means no flow or a one-way street.

The maximal-flow technique is not too difficult. It involves the following steps.

1. Pick any path (streets from west to east) with some flow.

2. Increase the flow (number of cars) as much as possible.

3. Adjust the flow capacity numbers on the path (streets).

4. Repeat the above steps until an increase in flow is no longer possible.

maximal-flow technique steps

We start by arbitrarily picking the path 1–2–6, which is at the top of the network. What is the maximum flow from west to east? It is 2 because only

Transparency Master 18.21: Maximal Flow.

Capacity in Hundreds
of Cars per Hour

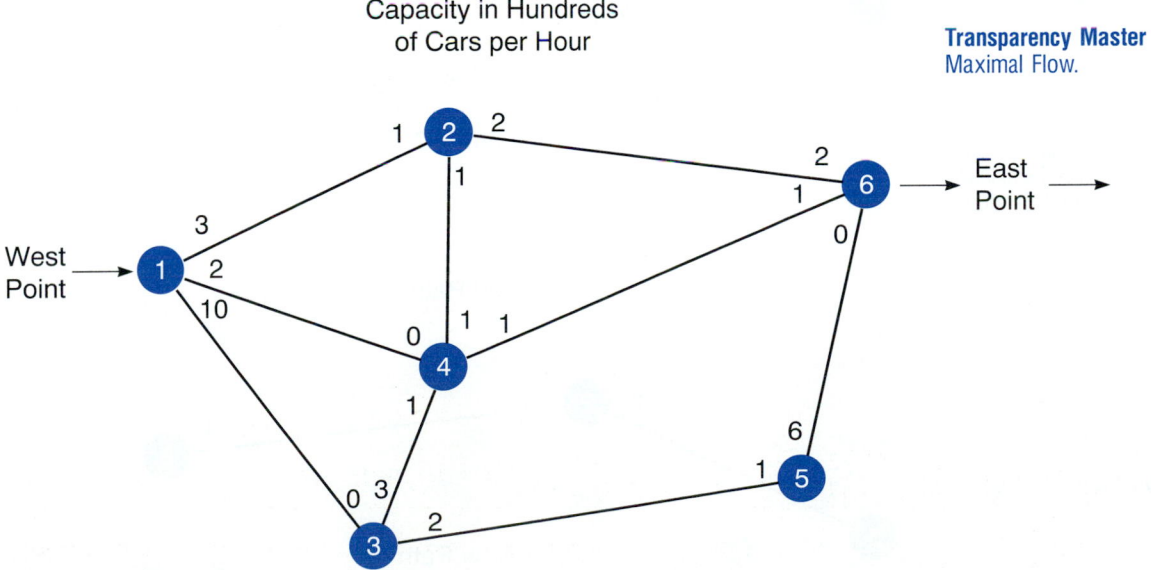

FIGURE 18.18
Road Network for Waukesha

**arbitrarily picking a
path and adjusting the
flow**

2 units (200 cars) can flow from node 2 to node 6. Now we adjust the flow
capacities. Refer to Figure 18.19. As you can see in the figure, we subtracted the maximum flow of 2 along the path 1–2–6 in the direction of the
flow (west to east) and added 2 to the path in the direction against the flow
(east to west). The result is the new path in Figure 18.19.

It is important to note that the new path in Figure 18.19 reflects the new
relative capacity at this stage. The flow number by any node represents
two factors. One factor is the flow that can come *from* that node. The second factor is flow that can be *reduced* coming *into* the node. First, consider
the flow from west to east. Look at the path that goes from node 1 to
node 2. The number 1 by node 1 tells us that 100 cars can flow *from* node 1
to node 2. Looking at the path from node 2 to node 6, we can see that
number 0 by node 2 tells us that 0 cars can flow *from* node 2 to node 6.
Now, consider the flow from east to west shown in the new path in
Figure 18.19. First, consider the path from node 6 to node 2. The number 4
by node 6 tells us that we can reduce the flow *into* node 6 by 2 (or 200 cars)
and that there is a capacity of 2 (or 200 cars) that can come *from* node 6.

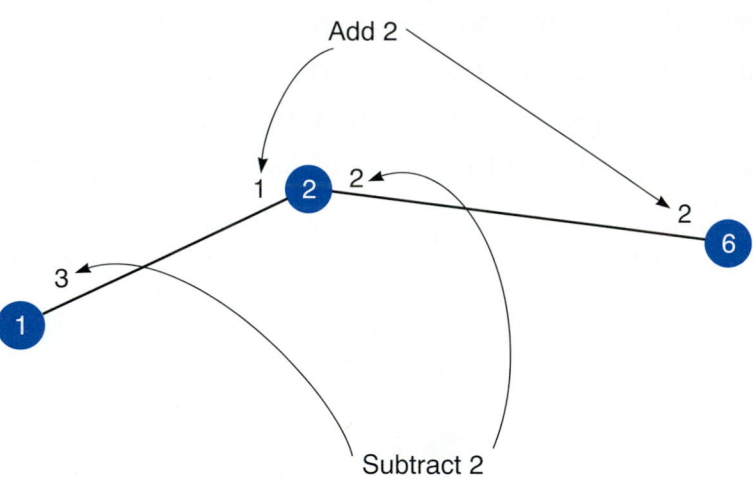

Teaching Suggestion 18-10:
The Maximal-Flow Technique.
See the Instructor's Section
for details.

Old Path

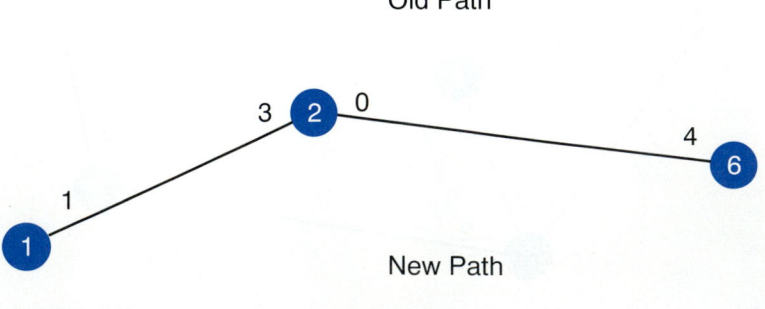

New Path

FIGURE 18.19
Capacity Adjustment for Path 1–2–6 Iteration 1

These two factors total 4. Looking at the path from node 2 to node 1, we see the number 3 by node 2. This tells us that we can reduce the flow *into* node 2 by 2 (or 200 cars) and that we have a capacity of 1 (or 100 cars) *from* node 2 to node 1. At this stage, we have a flow of 200 cars through the network from node 1 to node 2 to node 6. We have also reflected the new relative capacity as seen in the new path in Figure 18.19.

Now we repeat the process by picking another path with existing capacity. We will arbitrarily pick path 1–2–4–6. The maximum capacity along this path is 1. In fact, the capacity at every node along this path (1–2–4–6) going from west to east is 1. Remember, the capacity of branch 1–2 is now 1 because 2 units (200 cars per hour) are now flowing through the network.

repeating the process

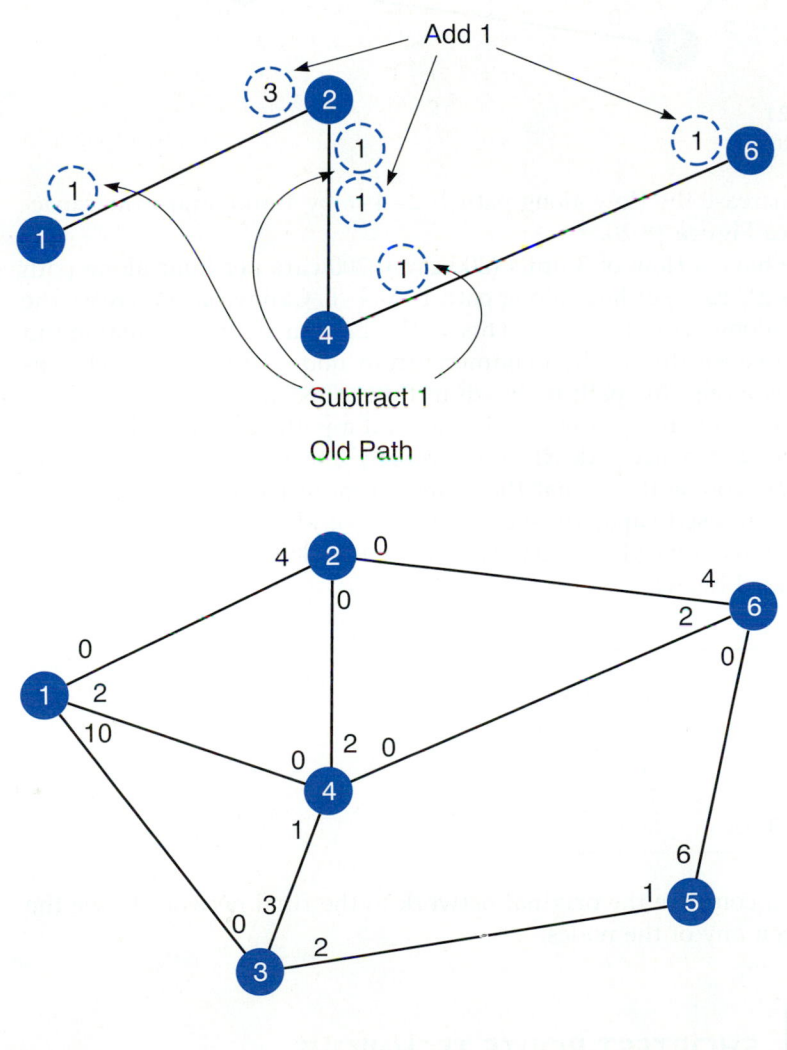

Old Path

New Network

FIGURE 18.20
Second Iteration

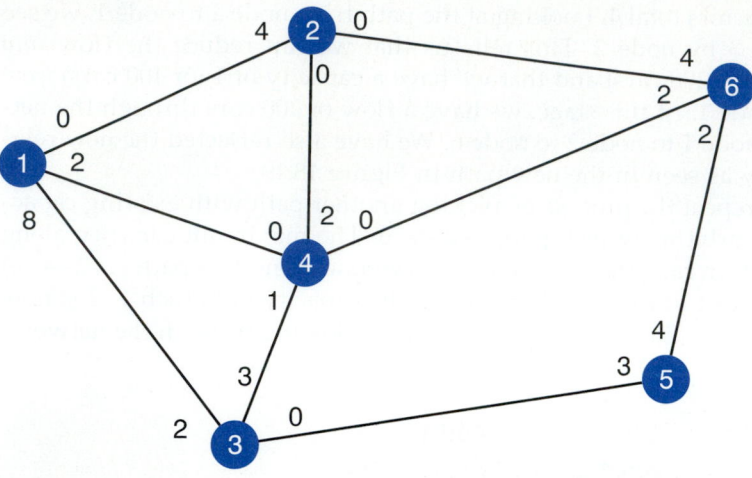

FIGURE 18.21
Third Iteration

Thus, we increase the flow along path 1–2–4–6 by 1 and adjust the capacity flow. See Figure 18.20.

Now we have a flow of 3 units (300 cars): 200 cars per hour along path 1–2–6 plus 100 cars per hour along path 1–2–4–6. Can we still increase the flow? Yes, along path 1–3–5–6. This is the bottom path. The maximum flow is 2 because this is the maximum from node 3 to node 5. The increased flow along this path is shown in Figure 18.21.

no more paths with unused capacity

Again we repeat the process, trying to find a path with any unused capacity through the network. If you carefully check the last iteration in Figure 18.21, you will see that there are no more paths from node 1 to node 6 with unused capacity, even though several other branches in the network do have unused capacity. The maximum flow of 500 cars per hour is summarized below:

PATH	FLOW (CARS PER HOUR)
1–2–6	200
1–2–4–6	100
1–3–5–6	200
Total	500

You can also compare the original network to the final network to see the flow between any of the nodes.

Applicable Problem 18-27

18.7 SHORTEST-ROUTE TECHNIQUE

The *shortest-route technique* finds how a person or item can travel from one location to another while minimizing the total distance traveled. In other words, it finds the shortest route to a series of destinations.

Every day, Ray Design, Inc., must transport beds, chairs, and other furniture items from the factory to the warehouse. This involves going through several cities. Ray would like to find the route with the shortest distance. The road network is shown in Figure 18.22.

The shortest-route technique can be used to minimize total distance from any starting node to a final node. The technique is summarized in the following steps.

1. Find the nearest node to the origin (plant). Put the distance in a box by the node.

2. Find the next nearest node to the origin (plant), and put the distance in a box by the node. In some cases, several paths will have to be checked to find the nearest node.

3. Repeat this process until you have gone through the entire network. The last distance at the ending node will be the distance of the shortest route. You should note that the distances placed in the boxes by each node are the shortest route to this node. These distances are used as intermediate results in finding the next nearest node.

Looking at Figure 18.22, we can see that the nearest node to the plant is node 2, with a distance of 100 miles. Thus, we will connect these two nodes. This first iteration is shown in Figure 18.23.

Now we look for the next nearest node to the origin. We check nodes 3, 4, and 5. Node 3 is the nearest, but there are two possible paths. Path 1–2–3 is nearest to the origin with a total distance of 150 miles. See Figure 18.24.

We repeat the process. The next nearest node is either node 4 or node 5. Node 4 is 200 miles from node 2, and node 2 is 100 miles from node 1. Thus, node 4 is 300 miles from the origin. There are two paths for node 5, 2–5 and 3–5, to the origin. Note that we don't have to go all the way back to the origin because we already know the shortest route from node 2 and node 3 to the origin. The minimum distances are placed in boxes by these nodes. Path 2–5 is 100 miles, and node 2 is 100 miles from the origin. Thus,

Alternate Example 18-5

shortest-route technique steps

looking for the nearest node to the origin

repeating the process

Transparency Master 18.22: Shortest Route.

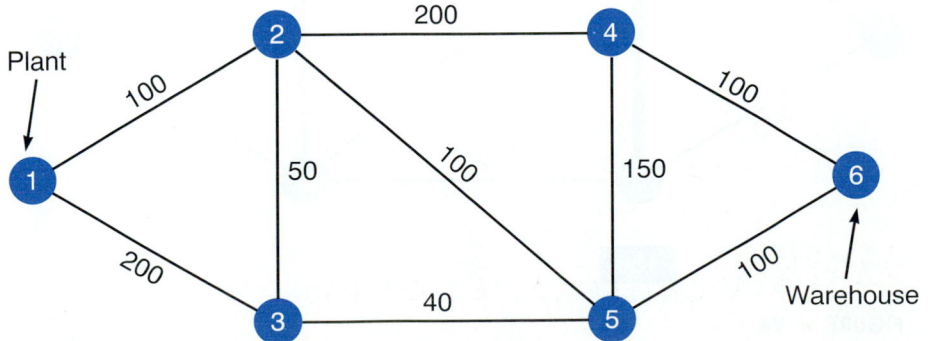

FIGURE 18.22
Roads from Ray's Plant to Warehouse

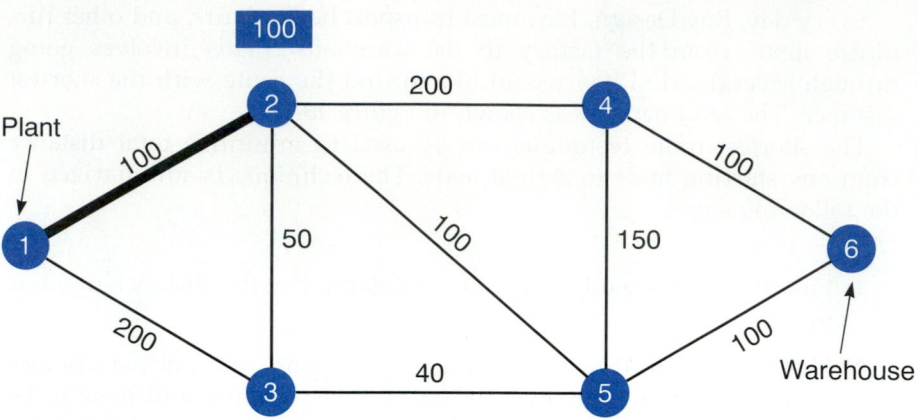

FIGURE 18.23
First Iteration

the total distance is 200 miles. In a similar fashion, we can determine that the path from node 5 to the origin through node 3 is 190 (40 miles between node 5 and 3 plus 150 miles from node 3 to the origin). Thus, we pick node 5 going through node 3 to the origin. See Figure 18.25.

The next nearest node will be either node 4 or node 6, the last remaining nodes. Node 4 is 300 miles from the origin (300 = 200 from node 4 to node 2 plus 100 from node 2 to the origin). Node 6 is 290 miles from the origin (290 = 100 + 190). Node 6 has the minimum distance, and because it is the ending node, we are done. Refer to Figure 18.26. The shortest route is path 1–2–3–5–6 with a minimum distance of 290 miles.

finding the minimum distance

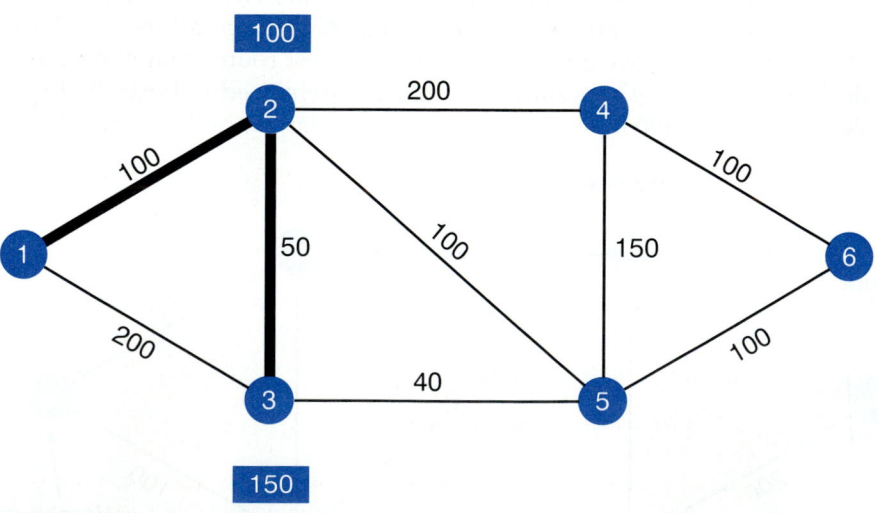

FIGURE 18.24
Second Iteration

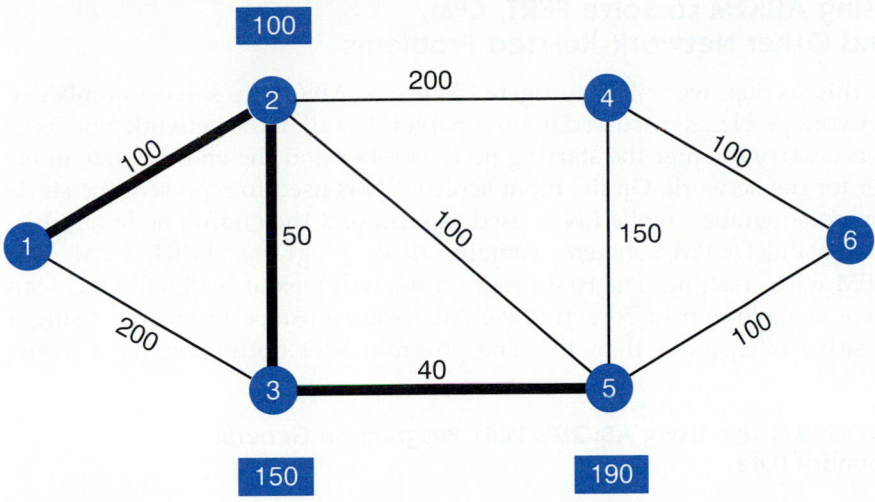

FIGURE 18.25
Third Iteration

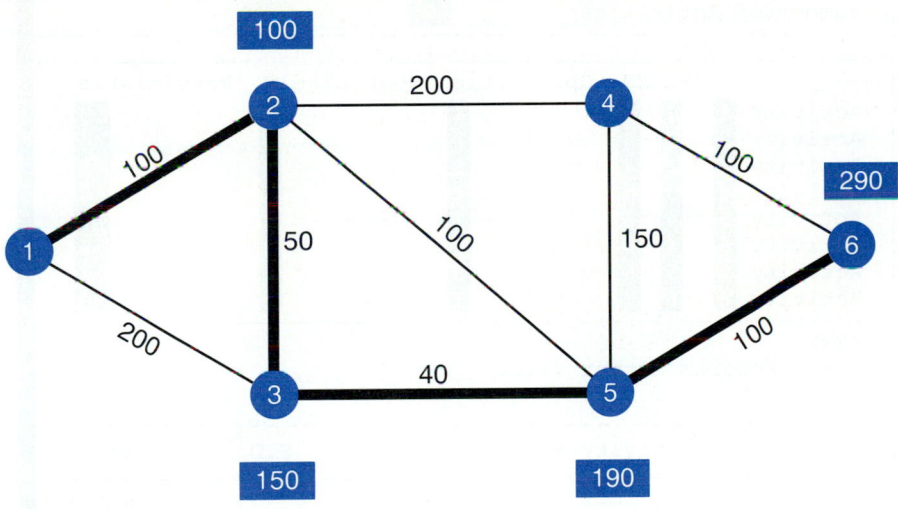

FIGURE 18.26
Fourth and Final Iteration

18.8 USING THE COMPUTER TO SOLVE NETWORK PROBLEMS

AB:QM and STORM can be used to solve network-related problems. Both packages can assist in solving PERT and CPM problems along with other network problems—minimal-spanning tree, maximal flow, and shortest route. We will begin with the AB:QM package.

Using AB:QM to Solve PERT, CPM, and Other Network-Related Problems

In this section, we will investigate the use of AB:QM to solve a number of network problems discussed in this chapter. For all of the network models, it is necessary to enter the starting node number and the ending node number for the network. On the input screen, SN is used to represent the starting node number, while EN is used to represent the ending node number.

using PERT

The PERT/CPM submenu contains three programs: PERT, CPM, and CPM with crashing. The first program we will look at is PERT, which can have a maximum of 50 activities. All nodes must be numbered using a positive integer less than 101. The program uses optimistic, most likely,

PROGRAM 18.1 Using AB:QM's PERT Program on General Foundry Data

```
CPM/PERT / PERT

Problem Title :  General Foundry

Number of Activities          8

               SN EN  Optimistic  Most Likely  Pessimistic
Activity 1     1  2        1           2            3
Activity 2     1  3        2           3            4
Activity 3     2  4        1           2            3
Activity 4     3  5        2           4            6
Activity 5     4  5        1           4            7
Activity 6     4  6        1           2            9
Activity 7     5  6        3           4           11
Activity 8     6  7        1           2            3

PERT
***** Program Output *****

------------------------------------------------
Activity      Activity Nodes    Mean    S.D.   Variance
------------------------------------------------
   1 *         1  -->  2       2.000   0.333    0.111
   2           1  -->  3       3.000   0.333    0.111
   3 *         2  -->  4       2.000   0.333    0.111
   4           3  -->  5       4.000   0.667    0.444
   5 *         4  -->  5       4.000   1.000    1.000
   6           4  -->  6       3.000   1.333    1.778
   7 *         5  -->  6       5.000   1.333    1.778
   8 *         6  -->  7       2.000   0.333    0.111
------------------------------------------------
(* : Critical Path Activities)

Expected Completion Time :      15.000

***** End of Output *****
```

and pessimistic time estimates for each activity. Output includes the mean, standard deviation, and variance for each activity; expected completion time is also given. The input data screen and the program output for the General Foundry problem are shown in Program 18.1.

The CPM program is similar to PERT, but three time estimates are *not* needed for each activity. Unlike the PERT program, however, the CPM program does compute early times, late times, and slack values for all activities. Since the input and output from this program are so similar to PERT, we do not provide a sample printout for CPM.

using CPM

The third program under the submenu is CPM with crashing. For this application, you enter the normal time, the crash time, the normal cost, and the crash cost for your particular network. The computer then determines the maximum crash time along with the total crash cost. This program allows you to specify how many days, weeks, or time periods you want the network to be crashed. This is called the expected project time.

using CPM with crashing

The program computes the crash cost, the activity time, and the activity cost for all activities. The normal completion time and expected crash completion time are also given. The input screen and the program output are shown in Program 18.2.

Using AB:QM to Solve Other Network Models

The shortest-route, minimum-spanning tree, and maximal-flow problems can also be solved using AB:QM. The first problem we will illustrate is the minimum-spanning tree case illustrated by the Lauderdale Construction problem we saw earlier in this chapter. The program determines the best way to connect all points in a network while minimizing the distance between them. It can handle between 3 and 50 nodes and 3 and 50 branches. The input screen and program output for the Lauderdale Construction problem are given in Program 18.3.

minimum-spanning tree problem

The maximum-flow program can be used to determine the maximum number of cars or vehicles going through a road system given the flows on each road or branch. It can handle between 3 and 50 nodes and between 3 and 50 branches. The input screen and output are shown in Program 18.4. You should note that "Value" is used to enter the flow in one direction along the network, while "Inv.Value" is used to show the flow in the opposite direction. (Inv.Value stands for *inverse value* or capacity on the branch.)

maximal-flow technique

The final network program, the shortest-route technique, determines the shortest route through a network from one point to the other. Like the other two network models, this one can handle between 3 and 50 branches and between 3 and 50 nodes. The input data resemble that for the minimum spanning tree program, so they are not illustrated here.

shortest-route technique

Using STORM for Project Management

STORM provides a project management module, which can be initiated by choosing selection 6 from the main STORM menu shown in Chapter 1. This

PROGRAM 18.2 AB:QM's Program for CPM with Crashing

```
CPM/PERT / CPM With Crashing

Problem Title :  General Foundry
Expected Project Time            7
Number of Activities             8


             SN EN  Normal Time  Crashed Time  Normal Cost  Crashed Cost
Activity 1   1  2        2            1           22000        23000
Activity 2   1  3        3            1           30000        34000
Activity 3   2  4        2            1           26000        27000
Activity 4   3  5        4            3           48000        49000
Activity 5   4  5        4            2           56000        58000
Activity 6   4  6        3            2           30000        30500
Activity 7   5  6        5            2           80000        86000
Activity 8   6  7        2            1           16000        19000




Help   New   Load   Save   Edit   Run   Print   Install   Directory   Esc
```

```
CPM With Crashing

***** Program Output *****

------------------------------------------------------------------
                                    Crashing   Activity   Activity
Activity   Activity Nodes  Crash by   Cost       Time       Cost
------------------------------------------------------------------
  1 *   1  -->  2        1.000    1000.000     1.000    23000.000
  2 *   1  -->  3        2.000    4000.000     1.000    34000.000
  3 *   2  -->  4        1.000    1000.000     1.000    27000.000
  4 *   3  -->  5        1.000    1000.000     3.000    49000.000
  5 *   4  -->  5        2.000    2000.000     2.000    58000.000
  6     4  -->  6        0.000       0.000     3.000    30000.000
  7 *   5  -->  6        3.000    6000.000     2.000    86000.000
  8 *   6  -->  7        1.000    3000.000     1.000    19000.000
------------------------------------------------------------------
(* : Critical Path Activities)        18000.00            326000.000

Expected Normal Completion Time  :    15.000
Expected Crashed Completion Time :     7.000

***** End of Output *****
```

PROGRAM 18.3 AB:QM's Minimum-Spanning Tree Program on Lauderdale Construction Company Data

```
Network Models / Minimum Spanning Tree

Problem Title :   Lauderdale Construction
Number of Nodes            8
Number of Branches        13


              SN    EN      Value
Branch   1    1     2         3
Branch   2    1     3         2
Branch   3    1     4         5
Branch   4    2     3         3
Branch   5    2     5         3
Branch   6    3     4         2
Branch   7    3     5         5
Branch   8    3     6         3
Branch   9    3     7         7
Branch  10    4     6         6
Branch  11    5     7         4
Branch  12    6     8         1
Branch  13    7     8         2


Help   New   Load   Save   Edit   Run   Print   Install   Directory   Esc


Program: Network Models / Minimum Spanning Tree

***** Program Output *****

- - - - - - - - - - - - - - - - - - - -
   SN      EN          Value
- - - - - - - - - - - - - - - - - - - -
   1 <---> 2           3.00
   1 <---> 3           2.00
   2 <---> 5           3.00
   3 <---> 6           3.00
   3 <---> 4           2.00
   6 <---> 8           1.00
   7 <---> 8           2.00
- - - - - - - - - - - - - - - - - - - -

Total Minimum Spanning Tree Lengths  :      16.00

***** End of Output *****
```

PROGRAM 18.4 AB:QM's Maximum-Flow Program on Waukesha Data

```
Network Models / Maximum Flow

Problem Title :   Waukesha
Number of Nodes                    6
Number of Branches                 9


              SN    EN        Value        Inv. Value
Branch   1    1     2            3              1
Branch   2    1     3           10              0
Branch   3    1     4            2              0
Branch   4    2     4            1              1
Branch   5    2     6            2              2
Branch   6    3     4            3              1
Branch   7    3     5            2              1
Branch   8    4     6            1              1
Branch   9    5     6            6              0



Program: Network Models / Maximum Flow

***** Program Output *****

- - - - - - - - - - - - - - - - - - - - -
  SN        EN              Flow
- - - - - - - - - - - - - - - - - - - - -
  1 ----> 2               2.00
  1 ----> 3               2.00
  1 ----> 4               1.00
  2 ----> 6               2.00
  3 ----> 5               2.00
  4 ----> 6               1.00
  5 ----> 6               2.00
- - - - - - - - - - - - - - - - - - - - -

Total Maximum Flow    :         5.00

***** End of Output *****
```

begins the PERT/CPM module; the module will be used to solve the General Foundry problem discussed in this chapter. The results are shown in Program 18.5.

project management

As with other STORM modules, the opening module (Program 18.5a) for the project management program allows the user to read an existing data file or to create a new data set. We select option 2 to create a new data set. Next, we are given a beginning data screen **(b).** Here, we enter the problem title, the number of activities, whether or not the activity times are probabilistic or deterministic, whether the activity representation is *arc* or *node,* and the number of predecessor columns. As you can see, for the General

(a)

```
        PROJECT MANAGEMENT (PERT/CPM) : INPUT

        ┌──────────────────────────────────────┐
        │  1)   Read an existing data file      │
        │  2)   Create a new data set           │
        └──────────────────────────────────────┘
            ┌──────────────────────────────┐
            │   Select option      2        │
            └──────────────────────────────┘
```

(b)

```
  ──── STORM EDITOR : Project Management Module ────
  ┌─────────────────────────────────────────────────────┐
  │  Title :  GENERAL FOUNDRY                            │
  │  Number of activities                         8      │
  │  Activity time option (DET/PROB)           PROB      │
  │  Activity representation option (ARC/NODE)  ARC      │
  │  Number of predecessor columns (NODE only)    0      │
  └─────────────────────────────────────────────────────┘
```

(c)

R8 : C6	SYMBOL	OPTIMISTIC	LIKELY	PESSIMISTIC	START NODE	END NODE
ACT 1	A	1.	2.	3.	1	2
ACT 2	B	2.	3.	4.	1	3
ACT 3	C	1.	2.	3.	2	4
ACT 4	D	2.	4.	6.	3	5
ACT 5	E	1.	4.	7.	4	5
ACT 6	F	1.	2.	9.	4	6
ACT 7	G	3.	4.	11.	5	6
ACT 8	H	1.	2.	3.	6	7

(d)

```
            PROJECT MANAGEMENT : PROCESS

  ┌────────────────────────────────────────────────┐
  │  1)   Edit the current data set                 │
  │  2)   Save the current data set                 │
  │  3)   Print the current data set                │
  │  4)   Execute the module with the curent data set│
  └────────────────────────────────────────────────┘
          ┌──────────────────────────────┐
          │   Select option      4        │
          └──────────────────────────────┘
```

(e)

GENERAL FOUNDRY
ACTIVITIES IN THE ORDER AS ENTERED

Activity Name	Symb	Mean Time /Std Dev	Earliest Start/Fin	Latest Start/Fin	Slack
ACT 1	A	2.0000	0.0000	0.0000	0.0000 c
		0.3333	2.0000	2.0000	
ACT 2	B	3.0000	0.0000	1.0000	1.0000
		0.3333	3.0000	4.0000	
ACT 3	C	2.0000	2.0000	2.0000	0.0000 c
		0.3333	4.0000	4.0000	
ACT 4	D	4.0000	3.0000	4.0000	1.0000
		0.6667	7.0000	8.0000	
ACT 5	E	4.0000	4.0000	4.0000	0.0000 c
		1.0000	8.0000	8.0000	
ACT 6	F	3.0000	4.0000	10.0000	6.0000
		1.3333	7.0000	13.0000	
ACT 7	G	5.0000	8.0000	8.0000	0.0000 c
		1.3333	13.0000	13.0000	
ACT 8	H	2.0000	13.0000	13.0000	0.0000 c
		0.3333	15.0000	15.0000	

(Continued)

PROGRAM 18.5 STORM's Project Management Program on General
Foundry Data (Continued)

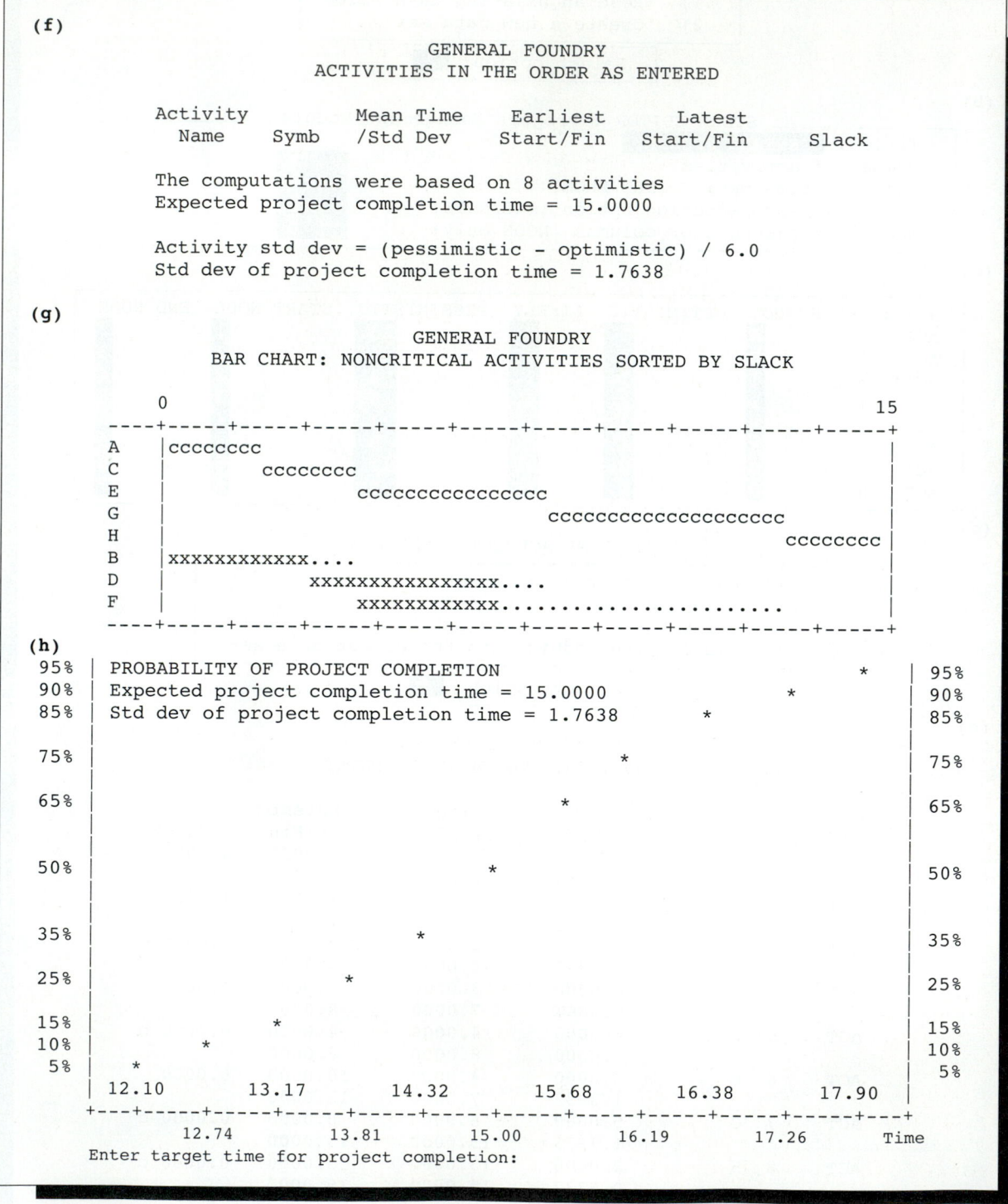

```
(f)
                        GENERAL FOUNDRY
                 ACTIVITIES IN THE ORDER AS ENTERED

        Activity            Mean Time    Earliest      Latest
         Name     Symb      /Std Dev    Start/Fin    Start/Fin      Slack

        The computations were based on 8 activities
        Expected project completion time = 15.0000

        Activity std dev = (pessimistic - optimistic) / 6.0
        Std dev of project completion time = 1.7638

(g)
                        GENERAL FOUNDRY
              BAR CHART: NONCRITICAL ACTIVITIES SORTED BY SLACK

        0                                                         15
    ----+-----+-----+-----+-----+-----+-----+-----+-----+-----+-----+
    A   |ccccccccc
    C   |        ccccccccc
    E   |               cccccccccccccccc
    G   |                              cccccccccccccccccccc
    H   |                                                  ccccccccc
    B   |xxxxxxxxxxxx....
    D   |         xxxxxxxxxxxxxxxxx....
    F   |              xxxxxxxxxxxx.......................
    ----+-----+-----+-----+-----+-----+-----+-----+-----+-----+-----+
```

```
(h)
   95% | PROBABILITY OF PROJECT COMPLETION                       *   | 95%
   90% | Expected project completion time = 15.0000          *      | 90%
   85% | Std dev of project completion time = 1.7638      *         | 85%
       |
   75% |                                          *                 | 75%
       |
   65% |                                      *                     | 65%
       |
       |
   50% |                              *                             | 50%
       |
       |
   35% |                        *                                   | 35%
       |
   25% |                  *                                         | 25%
       |
   15% |            *                                               | 15%
   10% |        *                                                   | 10%
    5% |    *                                                       | 5%
       | 12.10        13.17        14.32        15.68        16.38        17.90 |
       +---+-----+-----+-----+-----+-----+-----+-----+-----+-----+-----+---+
            12.74        13.81        15.00        16.19        17.26      Time
       Enter target time for project completion:
```

Foundry problem there are eight activities. We will use probabilistic time estimates and *arc* notation. Arc representation was used throughout this chapter. We do not require predecessor columns because we are not using the *node* representation. Once we enter this beginning data, STORM provides us another screen to enter the appropriate data **(c)**. In this screen, we enter the likely, optimistic, and pessimistic time estimates for all eight of the activities. We also indicate the starting node numbers and ending node numbers as well. Once these data have been entered, STORM gives us a processing menu **(d)**, which is the same processing menu shown with other applications. As before, the processing menu allows us to edit the current data set, save the current data set, print the current data set, or execute the existing module. We select option 4, which executes the module.

The first output screen **(e)** gives the average, or mean, times and the standard deviations for all activities. In addition, the earliest and latest start and finished times are given. Slack times for all activities are also presented. Note that the letter c beside an activity represents an activity that is on the critical path. The next screen **(f)** summarizes the calculations by giving the average (mean) completion time and the standard deviation of project completion time.

Once this basic information is presented, other outputs can also be displayed. STORM allows us to obtain bar charts **(g)** for completion times for the various activities. The bar chart shows us which activities are critical and which are not. The c in the charts again indicates critical activities. We are also given a graph of the probability of project completion **(h)**. This shows us the probability of completing the project in a range of time from about 12 periods to 18 periods.

Using STORM's Distance Network Module

STORM has two different subprograms, or modules, that are used to handle the other network techniques discussed in this chapter. Distance networks, which is selection 4 from the STORM main menu, allows us to perform the shortest-route technique and the maximal-flow technique. The flow networks module, which is selection 5 from the main menu, allows us to perform the minimal-spanning tree technique. We illustrate STORM's features by looking at applications for the distance network module.

Shortest-route problems can be solved using the distance networks module. First we are given a screen (Program 18.6a) that allows us to read an existing data file or to create a new data set. We will create a new data set. Next, STORM allows us to enter the appropriate data, including the problem title, the number of nodes, and the network type **(b)**.

As you can see, we have entered the title Ray Design. The number of nodes is 6 and this will be an asymmetrical matrix. Next, we are given a screen **(c)** showing the various network algorithms. Selection 1 is the shortest-path alternative, and thus we will select this alternative to solve the Ray Design problem. Now we are allowed to enter data and to make various selections **(d)**. Once this is done, the shortest path from node 1 is determined and displayed by the computer **(e)**.

shortest-route technique

PROGRAM 18.6 STORM's Shortest-Route Program on Ray Design Data

(a)

```
            DISTANCE NETWORKS (PATHS, TOURS, TREES) : INPUT

                    1)    Read an existing data file
                    2)    Create a new data set

                        Select option    2
```

(b)

```
                   STORM EDITOR : Distance Networks Module
         Title :  RAY DESIGN
         Number of nodes                    :        6
         Distance matrix type (SYM/ASYM)    :      ASYM


       C1   NODE 1   NODE 2   NODE 3   NODE 4   NODE 5   NODE 6
DIST 1   .     100.     200.      .        .        .
DIST 2   .       .       50.     200.     100.       .
DIST 3   .       .        .        .       40.       .
DIST 4   .       .        .        .      150.      100.
DIST 5   .       .        .        .        .       100.
DIST 6   .       .        .        .        .        .
```

(c)

```
                        NETWORK ALGORITHMS

                    1)    Shortest paths
                    2)    Longest paths
                    3)    Traveling salesperson's tour
                    4)    Minimal spanning tree
                    5)    Maximal spanning tree

                        Select option    1
```

(d)

```
           SELECTION OF DESTINATION NODES              CANDIDATES

       Select destination nodes to which paths     *  NODE 2
            from NODE 1 are to be computed          *  NODE 3
                                                    *  NODE 4
       Note : * marks nodes of interest             *  NODE 5
                                                    *  NODE 6
```

(e)

```
                        RAY DESIGN
                  SHORTEST PATHS FROM NODE 1

       Destination    Distance    Path
       NODE 2         100.0000    NODE 2

       NODE 3         150.0000    NODE 2--NODE 3

       NODE 4         300.0000    NODE 2--NODE 4

       NODE 5         190.0000    NODE 2--NODE 3--NODE 5

       NODE 6         290.0000    NODE 2--NODE 3--NODE 5--NODE 6
```

PROGRAM 18.7 Sample PERT Chart Using Harvard Total Project Manager Software

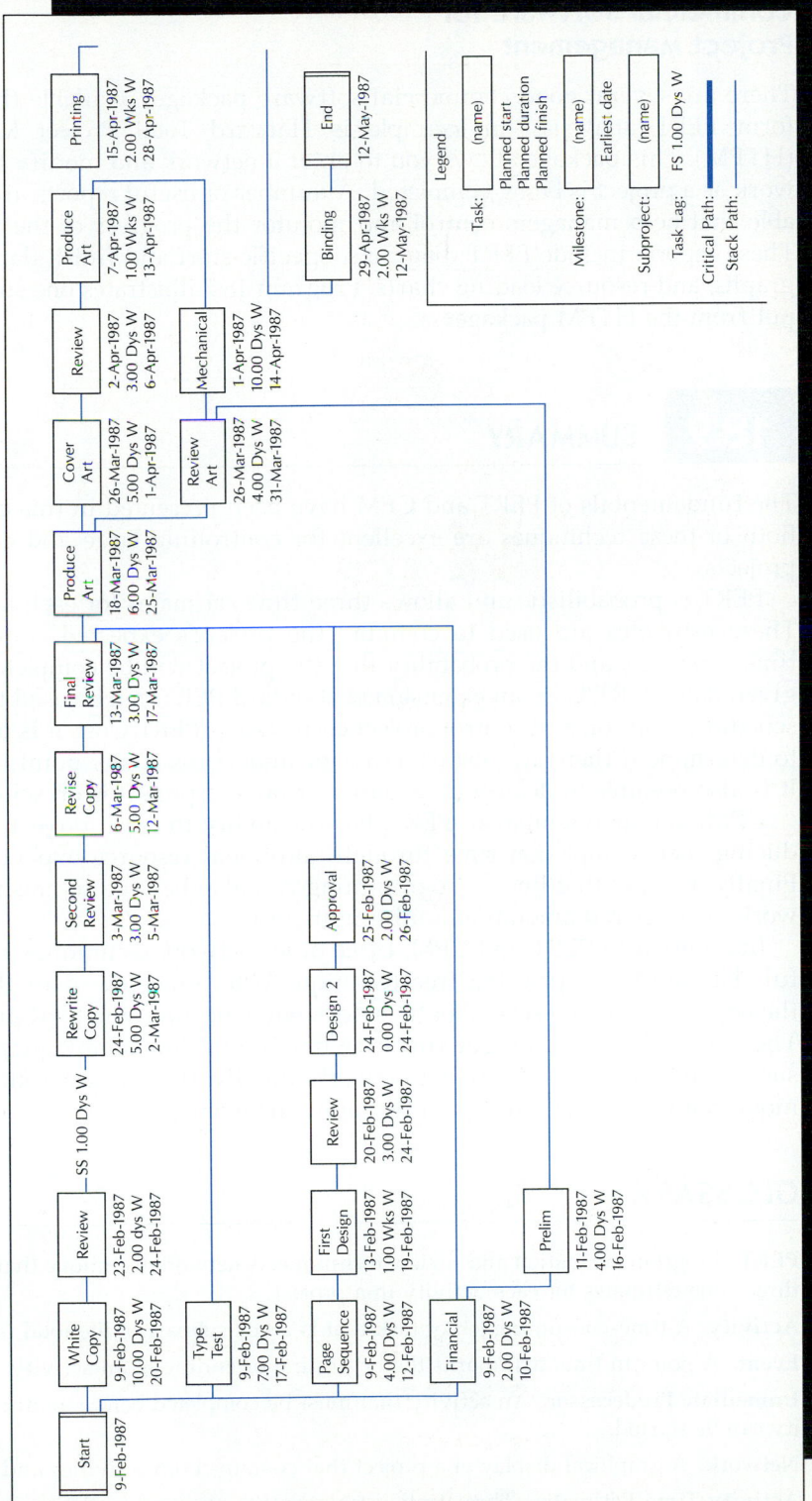

Commercial Software for Project Management

There are several good commercial software packages available that perform PERT analysis. An example is Harvard Total Project Manager (HTPM). This package allows you to enter a network and modify the network as a project is being completed. A number of useful reports are available that help managers control and monitor the progress of the project. These reports include PERT diagrams, specific start and finish dates, cost graphs, and resource loading charts. Program 18.7 illustrates one such output from the HTPM package.

18.9 SUMMARY

The fundamentals of PERT and CPM have been presented in this chapter. Both of these techniques are excellent for controlling large and complex projects.

PERT is probabilistic and allows three time estimates for each activity. These estimates are used to compute the project's expected completion time, variance, and the probability that the project will be completed by a given date. PERT/Cost, an extension of standard PERT, can be used to plan, schedule, monitor, and control project costs. Using PERT/Cost, it is possible to determine if there are cost overruns or underruns at any point in time. It is also possible to determine whether or not the project is on schedule.

CPM, although similar to PERT, has the ability to crash projects by reducing their completion time through additional resource expenditures. Finally, we saw that linear programming can also be used to crash a network by a desired amount at a minimum cost.

In addition to PERT and CPM, three other network techniques are useful. The minimal-spanning tree technique determines the path through the network that connects all of the nodes while minimizing total distance. The maximal-flow technique finds the maximum flow of any quantity or substance that can go through a network. Finally, the shortest-route technique can find the shortest path through a network.

GLOSSARY

PERT. Program evaluation and review technique. A network technique that allows three time estimates for each activity in a project.

Activity. A time-consuming job or task that is a key subpart of the total project.

Event. A point in time that marks the beginning or ending of an activity.

Immediate Predecessor. An activity that must be completed before another activity can be started.

Network. A graphical display of a project that contains both activities and events.

Activity Time Estimates. Three time estimates that are used in determining the expected completion time and variance for an activity in a PERT network.

Optimistic Time (a). The shortest amount of time that could be required to complete the activity.

Pessimistic Time (b). The greatest amount of time that could be required to complete the activity.

Most Likely Time (m). The amount of time that you would expect it would take to complete the activity.

Beta Distribution. A probability distribution that is often used in computing the expected activity completion times and variances in networks.

Earliest Start Time (ES). The earliest time that an activity can start without violation of precedence requirements.

Latest Start Time (LS). The latest time that an activity can be started without delaying the entire project.

Earliest Finish Time (EF). The earliest time that an activity can be finished without violation of precedence requirements.

Latest Finish Time (LF). The latest time that an activity can be finished without delaying the entire project.

Forward Pass. A procedure that moves from the beginning of a network to the end of the network. It is used in determining earliest activity start times and earliest finish times.

Backward Pass. A procedure that moves from the end of the network to the beginning of the network. It is used in determining the latest finish and start times.

Slack. The amount of time that an activity can be delayed without delaying the entire project. Slack is equal to the latest start time minus the earliest start time, or the latest finish time minus the earliest finish time.

Critical Path. The series of activities that have a zero slack. It is the longest time path through the network. A delay for any activity that is on the critical path will delay the completion of the entire project.

Critical Path Analysis. An analysis that determines the total project completion time, the critical path for the project, slack, ES, EF, LS, and LF for every activity.

Expected Activity Time. The average time that it should take to complete an activity. $t = (a + 4m + b)/6$.

Variance of Activity Completion Time. A measure of dispersion of the activity completion time. Variance $= [(b - a)/6]^2$.

Dummy Activity. A fictitious activity that consumes no time and is inserted into a network to make the network display the proper predecessor relationships between activities.

PERT/Cost. A technique that allows a decision maker to plan, schedule, monitor, and control project *cost* as well as project time.

CPM. Critical path method. A deterministic network technique that is similar to PERT, but allows for project crashing.

Crashing. The process of reducing the total time that it takes to complete a project by expending additional funds.

Minimal-Spanning Tree Technique. Determines the path through the network that connects all of the nodes while minimizing total distance.

Maximal-Flow Technique. Finds the maximum flow of any quantity or substance through a network.

Shortest-Route Technique. Determines the shortest path through a network.

KEY EQUATIONS

(18-1) $t = \dfrac{a + 4m + b}{6}$
Expected activity completion time.

(18-2) $\text{Variance} = \left(\dfrac{b - a}{6}\right)^2$
Activity variance.

(18-3) $\text{EF} = \text{ES} + t$
Earliest finish time.

(18-4) $\text{LS} = \text{LF} - t$
Latest start time.

(18-5) $\text{Slack} = \text{LS} - \text{ES}$ or $\text{Slack} = \text{LF} - \text{EF}$
Slack time in an activity.

(18-6) Project variance = Σ Variances of activities on critical path.

(18-7) $Z = \dfrac{\text{Due date} - \text{Expected date of completion}}{\sigma_T}$
Number of standard deviations the target date lies from the expected date, using the normal distribution.

(18-8) Value of work completed = (Percent of work completed) $\times$ (Total activity budget)

(18-9) Activity difference = Actual cost − Value of work completed

(18-10) $\text{Crash cost/time period} = \dfrac{\text{Crash cost} - \text{Normal cost}}{\text{Normal time} - \text{Crash time}}$
The cost in CPM of reducing an activity's length per time period.

SOLVED PROBLEMS

Solved Problem 18-1

In order to complete the wing assembly for an experimental aircraft, Scott DeWitte has laid out the major steps and seven activities involved. These activities have been labeled A through G in the following table, which also shows their estimated completion times and immediate predecessors. Determine the expected time and variance for each activity.

ACTIVITY	a	m	b	IMMEDIATE PREDECESSORS
A	1	2	2	—
B	2	3	3	—
C	4	5	6	A
D	8	9	11	B
E	2	5	5	C, D
F	3	5	6	B
G	1	2	3	E

Solution

Although not required for this problem, a diagram showing all of the activities can be useful. A PERT diagram for the wing assembly follows:

Expected times and variances can be computed using the formulas presented in the chapter. The results are summarized in the accompanying table.

PERT Diagram for Scott DeWitte (Solved Problem 18.1)

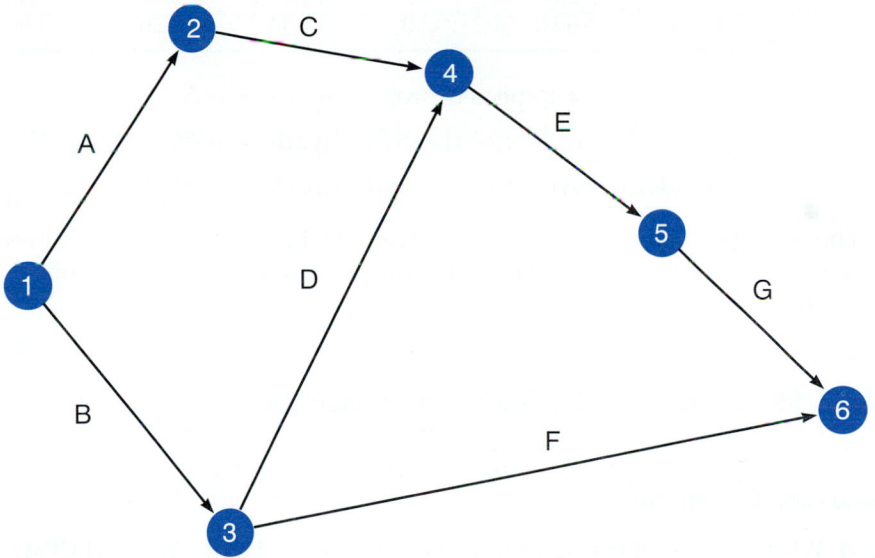

ACTIVITY	NODES	EXPECTED TIME	EXPECTED VARIANCE
A	1 → 2	1.83	0.028
B	1 → 3	2.83	0.028
C	2 → 4	5.00	0.111
D	3 → 4	9.17	0.250
E	4 → 5	4.50	0.250
F	3 → 6	4.83	0.250
G	5 → 6	2.00	0.111

Solved Problem 18-2

Now Scott would like to determine the critical path for the entire wing assembly project as well as expected completion time for the total project. In addition, he would like to determine the earliest and latest start and finish times for all activities.

Solution

The critical path, earliest start times, earliest finish times, latest start times, and latest finish times can be determined using the procedures outlined in the chapter. The results are summarized in the following table.

ACTIVITY	NODES	ACTIVITY TIMES				SLACK
		ES	EF	LS	LF	
A	1 → 2	0.00	1.83	5.17	7.00	5.17
B	1 → 3	0.00	2.83	0.00	2.83	0.00
C	2 → 4	1.83	6.83	7.00	12.00	5.17
D	3 → 4	2.83	12.00	2.83	12.00	0.00
E	4 → 5	12.00	16.50	12.00	16.50	0.00
F	3 → 6	2.83	7.67	13.67	18.50	10.83
G	5 → 6	16.50	18.50	16.50	18.50	0.00

Expected project length = 18.5

Variance of the critical path = .6388

Standard deviation of the critical path = .7993

The activities along the critical path are B, D, E, and G. These activities have 0 slack, as seen in the table. The expected project completion time is 18.5. The earliest and latest start and finish times are shown in the table.

DISCUSSION QUESTIONS AND PROBLEMS

Discussion Questions

18-1 What are some of the questions that can be answer with PERT and CPM?

18-2 What are the major differences between PERT and CPM?

18-3 What is an activity? What is an event? What is an immediate predecessor?

18-4 Describe how expected activity times and variances can be computed in a PERT network.

18-5 Briefly discuss what is meant by critical path analysis. What are critical path activities and why are they important?

18-6 What are the earliest activity start time and latest activity start time? How are they computed?

18-7 Describe the meaning of slack and discuss how it can be determined.

18-8 How can we determine the probability that a project will be completed by a certain date? What assumptions are made in this computation?

18-9 Briefly describe PERT/Cost and how it is used.

18-10 What is crashing and how is it done by hand?

18-11 Why is linear programming useful in CPM crashing?

Problems

18-12 Sid Davidson is the personnel director of Babson and Willcount, a company that specializes in consulting and research. One of the training programs that Sid is considering for the middle-level managers of Babson and Willcount is leadership training. Sid has listed a number of activities that must be completed before a training program of this nature could be conducted. The activities and immediate predecessors appear in the accompanying table.

ACTIVITY	IMMEDIATE PREDECESSOR
A	
B	
C	
D	B
E	A, D
F	C
G	E, F

Develop a network for this problem.

See Instructor's Section.

18-13 Sid Davidson was able to determine the activity times for the leadership training program. He would like to determine the total project completion time and the critical path. The activity times appear in the accompanying table. (See Problem 8-12.)

QA18-13

26 days; Critical path is 1–2–3–5–6.

ACTIVITY	TIME (DAYS)
A	2
B	5
C	1
D	10
E	3
F	6
G	8
Total	35

18-14 Monohan Machinery specializes in developing weed-harvesting equipment that is used to clear small lakes of weeds. George Monohan, president of Monohan Machinery, is convinced that harvesting weeds is far better than using chemicals to kill weeds. Chemicals cause pollution, and the weeds seem to grow faster after chemicals have been used. George is contemplating the construction of a machine that would harvest weeds on narrow rivers and waterways. The activities that are necessary to build one of these experimental weed-harvesting machines are listed in the accompanying table. Construct a network for these activities.

See Instructor's Section.

ACTIVITIES	IMMEDIATE PREDECESSORS
A	
B	
C	A
D	A
E	B
F	B
G	C, E
H	D, F

QA 18-15

See Instructor's Section; completion time is 19; there are two critical paths— A–C–G and B–E–G.

⌨ : **18-15** After consulting with Butch Radner, George Monohan was able to determine the activity times for constructing the weed-harvesting machine to be used on narrow rivers. George would like to determine ES, EF, LS, LF, and slack for each activity. The total project completion time and the critical path should also be determined. See Problem 18-14 for details. Here are the activity times.

ACTIVITY	TIME (WEEKS)
A	6
B	5
C	3
D	2
E	4
F	6
G	10
H	7

QA18-16

See Instructor's Section.

⌨ : **18-16** Zuckerman Wiring and Electric is a company that installs wiring and electrical fixtures in residential construction. John Zuckerman has been concerned with the amount of time that it takes to complete wiring jobs. Some of his workers are very unreliable. A list of activities and their optimistic, their pessimistic, and their most likely completion times in days are given in the accompanying table.

ACTIVITY	a	m	b	IMMEDIATE PREDECESSORS
A	3	6	8	
B	2	4	4	
C	1	2	3	
D	6	7	8	C
E	2	4	6	B, D
F	6	10	14	A, E
G	1	2	4	A, E
H	3	6	9	F
I	10	11	12	G
J	14	16	20	C
K	2	8	10	H, I

Determine the expected completion time and variance for each activity.

: **18-17** John Zuckerman would like to determine the total project completion time and the critical path for installing electrical wiring and equipment in residential houses. See Problem 18-16 for details. In addition, determine ES, EF, LS, LF, and slack for each activity.

QA18-17

36.33 days; Critical path is C–D–E–F–H–K.

· **18-18** What is the probability that Zuckerman will finish the project described in Problem 18-16 and 18-17 in 40 days or less?

.9463

: **18-19** Tom Schriber, director of personnel of Management Resources, Inc., is in the process of designing a program that their customers can use in the job-finding process. Some of the activities include preparing resumes, writing letters, making appointments to see prospective employers, researching companies and industries, and so on. Some of the information on the activities appears in the accompanying table.

QA18-19

ACTIVITY	a	(DAYS) m	b	IMMEDIATE PREDECESSORS
A	8	10	12	
B	6	7	9	
C	3	3	4	
D	10	20	30	A
E	6	7	8	C
F	9	10	11	B, D, E
G	6	7	10	B, D, E
H	14	15	16	F
I	10	11	13	F
J	6	7	8	G, H
K	4	7	8	I, J
L	1	2	4	G, H

(a) Construct a network for this problem.
(b) Determine the expected times and variances for each activity.
(c) Determine ES, EF, LS, LF, and slack for each activity.
(d) Determine the critical path and project completion time.
(e) Determine the probability that the project will be finished in 70 days.
(f) Determine the probability that the project will be finished in 80 days.
(g) Determine the probability that the project will be finished in 90 days.

See Instructor's Section.
68.7 days; Critical path is A–D–F–H–J–K.
.644
.9994
.9999

· **18-20** Using PERT, Ed Rose was able to determine that the expected project completion time for the construction of a pleasure yacht is 21 months, and the project variance is 4 months.

(a) What is the probability that the project will be completed in 17 months?
(b) What is the probability that the project will be completed in 20 months?
(c) What is the probability that the project will be completed in 23 months?
(d) What is the probability that the project will be completed in 25 months?

.0228
.3085
.8413
.9772

: **18-21** The air pollution project discussed in the chapter has progressed over the last several weeks and it is now week 8. Lester Harky would like to know the value of the work completed, the amount of any cost overruns or underruns for the project, and the extent to which the project is ahead of schedule or behind schedule by developing a table like Table 18.7. The revised cost figures appear in the accompanying table.

$181,600; Cost underrun = $9,600; behind schedule

ACTIVITY	PERCENT OF COMPLETION	ACTUAL COST ($)
A	100	20,000
B	100	36,000
C	100	26,000
D	100	44,000
E	50	25,000
F	60	15,000
G	10	5,000
H	10	1,000

18-22 Fred Ridgeway has been given the responsibility of managing a training and development program. He knows the earliest start time, the latest start time, and the total costs for each activity. This information is given in the accompanying table.

ACTIVITY	ES	LS	t	TOTAL COST ($1,000's)
A	0	0	6	10
B	1	4	2	14
C	3	3	7	5
D	4	9	3	6
E	6	6	10	14
F	14	15	11	13
G	12	18	2	4
H	14	14	11	6
I	18	21	6	18
J	18	19	4	12
K	22	22	14	10
L	22	23	8	16
M	18	24	6	18

(a) Using earliest start times, determine Fred's total monthly budget.
(b) Using latest start times, determine Fred's total monthly budget.

See Instructor's Section.
QA 18-23

18-23 General Foundry's project crashing data were shown in Table 18.8. Crash this project to 13 weeks using CPM. What are the final times for each activity after crashing?

See Instructor's Section.
QA18-24

18-24 Bowman Builders manufactures steel storage sheds for commercial use. Joe Bowman, president of Bowman Builders, is contemplating producing sheds for home use. The activities necessary to build an experimental model and related data are given in the accompanying table.

ACTIVITY	NORMAL TIME	CRASH TIME	NORMAL COST ($)	CRASH COST ($)	IMMEDIATE PREDECESSORS
A	3	2	1,000	1,600	
B	2	1	2,000	2,700	
C	1	1	300	300	
D	7	3	1,300	1,600	A
E	6	3	850	1,000	B
F	2	1	4,000	5,000	C
G	4	2	1,500	2,000	D, E

(a) What is the project completion date?

(b) Formulate a linear programming problem to crash this project to 10 weeks.

14

See Instructor's Section.

□ : **18-25** Bechtold Construction is in the process of installing power lines to a large housing development. Steve Bechtold wants to minimize the total length of wire used, which will minimize his costs. The housing development is shown as a network in the following illustration. Each house has been numbered, and the distances between houses is given in hundreds of feet. What do you recommend?

QA18-25

One solution is 1–2, 1–3, 1–4, 3–6, 4–5, 6–7, 7–9, 9–8, 9–10, 9–12, 10–11, 11–13, 12–14.

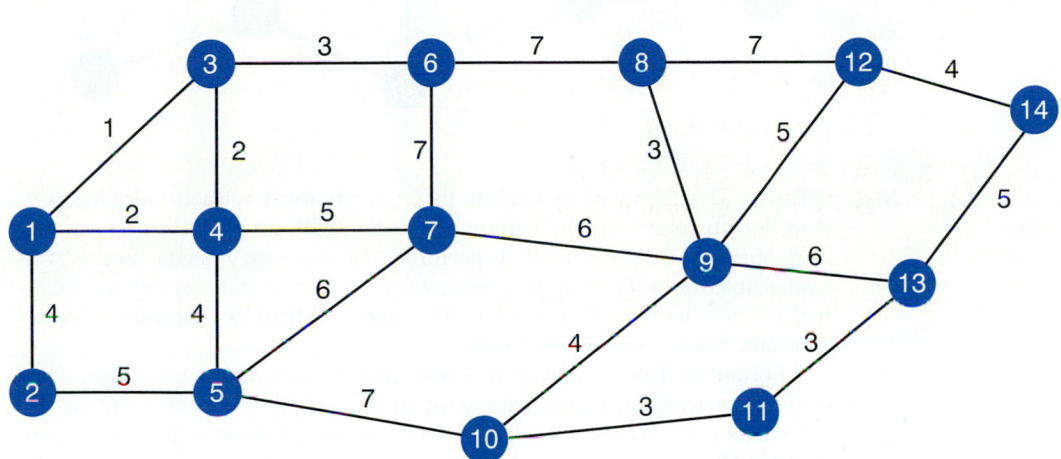

□ : **18-26** The city of New Berlin is considering making several of its streets one way. What is the maximum number of cars per hour that can travel from east to west? The network is shown in the following illustration.

QA18-26

500

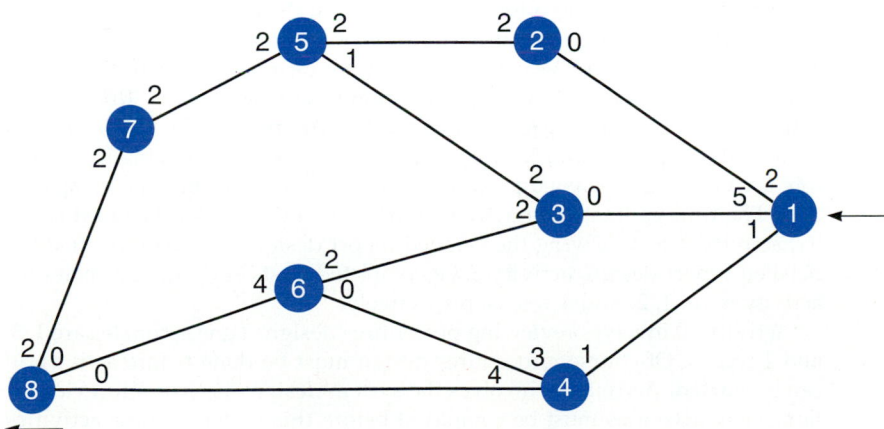

□ : **18-27** Transworld Moving has been hired to move the office furniture and equipment of Cohen Properties to their new headquarters. What route do you recommend? The network of roads is shown in the next diagram.

QA18-27
1–3–5–7–10–13; distance is 430 miles.

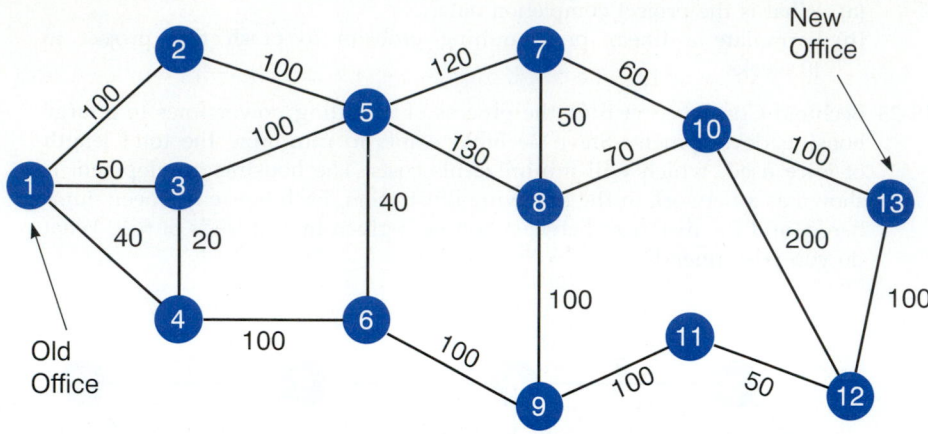

QA18-28

:   **18-28** Software Development Specialists (SDS) is involved with developing software for customers in the banking industry. SDS breaks a large programming project into teams that perform the necessary steps. Team A is responsible for going from general systems design all the way through to actual systems testing. This involves 18 separate activities. Team B is then responsible for the final installation.

In order to determine cost and time factors, optimistic, most likely, and pessimistic time estimates have been made for all of the 18 activities involved for team A. The first step that this team performs is general systems design. The optimistic, most likely, and pessimistic times are 3 weeks, 4 weeks, and 5 weeks. Following this, a number of activities can begin. Activity 2 is involved with procedures design. Optimistic, most likely, and pessimistic times for completing this activity are 4, 5, and 7 weeks. Activity 3 is developing detailed report designs. Optimistic, most likely, and pessimistic time estimates are 6, 8, and 9 weeks. Activity 4, detailed forms design, has optimistic, most likely, and pessimistic time estimates of 2, 3, and 5 weeks.

The fifth and sixth activities involve writing detailed program specifications and developing file specifications. The three time estimates for activity 5 are 6, 7, and 9 weeks, and the 3 time estimates for activity 6 are 3, 4, and 5 weeks. Activity 7 is to specify system test data. Before this is done, activity 6 involving file specifications must be completed. The time estimates for activity 7 are 2, 4, and 5 weeks. Activity 8 involves reviewing forms. Before activity 8 can be conducted, detailed forms design must be completed first. The time estimates for activity 8 are 3, 4, and 6 weeks. The next activity, activity 9, is reviewing the detailed report design. This requires that the detailed report design, activity 3, be completed first. The time estimates for activity 9 are 1, 2, and 4 weeks, respectively.

Activity 10 involves reviewing procedures design. Time estimates are 1, 3, and 4 weeks. Of course, procedures design must be done before activity 10 can be started. Activity 11 involves the system design check-point review. A number of activities must be completed before this is done. These activities include reviewing the forms, reviewing the detailed report design, reviewing the procedures design, writing detailed program specs, and specifying system test data. The optimistic, most likely, and pessimistic time estimates for activity 11 are 3, 4, and 6 weeks. Performing program logic design is activity 12. This can only be started after the system design check-point review is completed. The time estimates for activity 12 are 4, 6, and 7 weeks.

Activity 13, coding the programs, is done only after the program logic design is completed. The time estimates for this activity are 6, 8, and 10 weeks. Activity 14 is involved in developing test programs. Activity 13 is the immediate predecessor. Time estimates for activity 14 are 3, 4, and 6 weeks. Developing a system test plan is activity 15. A number of activities must be completed before activity 15 can be started. These activities include specifying system test data, writing detailed program specifications, and reviewing procedure designs, the detailed report design, and forms.

The time estimates for activity 15 are 3, 4, and 5 weeks. Activity 16, creating system test data, has time estimates of 2, 4, and 6 weeks. Activity 15 must be done before activity 16 can be started. Activity 17 is reviewing program test results. The immediate predecessor to activity 17 is to test the programs (activity 14). The three time estimates for activity 17 are 2, 3, and 4 weeks. The final activity is conducting system tests. This is activity 18. Before activity 18 can be started, activities 16 and 17 must be complete. The three time estimates for conducting these system tests are 3, 5, and 6 weeks.

How long will it take for team A to complete their programming assignment? What would happen if activity 5, writing detailed program specifications, had larger time estimates? Assume these time estimates are 12, 14, and 15.

44 weeks; completion time increases to 47.8 weeks.

18-29 The Bender Construction Co. is involved in constructing municipal buildings and other structures that are used primarily by city and state municipalities. This requires developing legal documents, drafting feasibility studies, obtaining bond ratings, and so forth. Recently, Bender was given a request to submit a proposal for the construction of a municipal building. The first step is to develop legal documents and to perform all necessary steps before the construction contract is signed. This requires over 20 separate activities that must be completed. These activities, their immediate predecessors, and time requirements are given in the following table.

QA18-29

ACTIVITY	a	TIME REQUIRED (WEEKS) m	b	DESCRIPTION OF ACTIVITY	IMMEDIATE PREDECESSOR(S)
1	1	4	5	Drafting legal documents	—
2	2	3	4	Preparation of financial statements	—
3	3	4	5	Draft of history	—
4	7	8	9	Draft demand portion of feasibility study	—
5	4	4	5	Review and approval of legal documents	1
6	1	2	4	Review and approval of history	3
7	4	5	6	Review feasibility study	4
8	1	2	4	Draft final financial portion of feasibility study	7
9	3	4	4	Draft facts relevant to the bond transaction	5
10	1	1	2	Review and approval of financial statements	2

(Continued)

ACTIVITY	TIME REQUIRED (WEEKS)			DESCRIPTION OF ACTIVITY	IMMEDIATE PREDECESSOR(S)
	a	m	b		
11	18	20	26	Firm price received of project	—
12	1	2	3	Review and completion of financial portion of feasibility study	8
13	1	1	2	Draft statement completed	6, 9, 10, 11, 12
14	.10	.14	.16	All material sent to bond rating services	13
15	.2	.3	.4	Statement printed and distributed to all interested parties	14
16	1	1	2	Presentation to bond rating services	14
17	1	2	3	Bond rating received	16
18	3	5	7	Marketing of bonds	15, 17
19	.1	.1	.2	Purchase contract executed	18
20	.1	.14	.16	Final statement authorized and completed	19
21	2	3	6	Purchase contract	19
22	.1	.1	.2	Bond proceeds available	20
23	.0	.2	.2	Sign construction contract	21, 22

34 weeks; critical path activities are 11, 13, 14, 16, 17, 18, 19, 21, and 23.

As you can see, optimistic (a), most likely (m), and pessimistic (b) time estimates have been given for all of the activities described in the table. Using the data, determine the total project completion time for this preliminary step, the critical path, and slack time for all activities involved.

18-30 Getting a degree from a college or university can be a long and difficult task. Certain courses must be completed before other courses may be taken. Develop a network diagram, where every activity is a particular course that must be taken for a given degree program. The immediate predecessors will be course prerequisites. Don't forget to include all university, college, and departmental course requirements. Then try to group these courses into semesters or quarters for your particular school. How long do you think it will take you to graduate? Which courses, if not taken in the proper sequence, could delay your graduation?

Class Discussion

Data Set Problem

QA18-31

18-31 Sager Products has been in the business of manufacturing and marketing toys for toddlers for the past two decades. Jim Sager, president of the firm, is considering the development of a new manufacturing line to allow it to produce high-quality plastic toys at reasonable prices. The development process is long and complex. Jim estimates that there are five phases involved and multiple activities for each phase.

Phase 1 of the development process involves the completion of four activities. These activities have no immediate predecessors. Activity A has an optimistic completion time of 2 weeks, a probable completion time of 3 weeks, and a pessimistic completion time of 4 weeks. Activity B has estimated completion times of 5, 6, and 8 weeks; these represent optimistic, probable, and pessimistic time estimates. Similarly, activity C has estimated completion times of 1 week, 1 week, and 2 weeks; and activity D has expected completion times of 8 weeks, 9 weeks, and 11 weeks.

Phase 2 involves six separate activities. Activity E has activity A as an immediate predecessor. Time estimates are 1 week, 1 week, and 4 weeks. Activity F and activity G both have activity B as their immediate predecessor. For activity F, the time estimates are 3 weeks, 3 weeks, and 4 weeks. For activity G, the time estimates are 1 week, 2 weeks, and 2 weeks. The only immediate predecessor for activity H is activity C. Time estimates for activity H are 5 weeks, 5 weeks, and 6 weeks. Activity D must be performed before activity I and activity J can be started. Activity I has estimated completion times of 9 weeks, 10 weeks, and 11 weeks. Activity J has estimated completion times of 1 week, 2 weeks, and 2 weeks.

Phase 3 is the most difficult and complex of the entire development project. It also consists of six separate activities. Activity K has three time estimates of 2 weeks, 2 weeks, and 3 weeks. The immediate predecessor for this activity is activity E. The immediate predecessor for activity L is activity F. The time estimates for activity L are 3 weeks, 4 weeks, and 6 weeks. Activity M has 2 weeks, 2 weeks, and 4 weeks for the estimates of the optimistic, probable, and pessimistic time estimates. The immediate predecessor for activity M is activity G. Activities N and O both have activity I as their immediate predecessor. Activity M has 8 weeks, 9 weeks, and 11 weeks for its three time estimates. Activity O has 1 week, 1 week, and 3 weeks as its time estimates. Activity O has 1 week, 1 week, and 3 weeks as its time estimates. Finally, activity P has time estimates of 4 weeks, 4 weeks, and 8 weeks. Activity J is its only immediate predecessor.

Phase 4 involves five activities. Activity Q requires activity K to be completed before it can be started. The three time estimates for activity Q are 6 weeks, 6 weeks, and 7 weeks. Activity R requires that both activity L and activity M be completed first. The three time estimates for activity R are 1, 2, and 4 weeks. Activity S requires activity N to be completed first. Its time estimates are 6 weeks, 6 weeks, and 7 weeks. Activity T requires that activity O be completed. The time estimates for activity T are 3 weeks, 3 weeks, and 4 weeks. The final activity for phase 4 is activity U. The time estimates for this activity are 1 week, 2 weeks, and 3 weeks. Activity P must be completed before activity U can be started.

Phase 5 is the final phase of the development project. It consists of only two activities. Activity V requires that activity Q and activity R be completed before it can be started. Time estimates for this activity are 9 weeks, 10 weeks, and 11 weeks. Activity W is the final activity of the process. It requires three activities to be completed before it can be started. These are activities S, T, and U. The estimated completion times for activity W are 2 weeks, 4 weeks, and 5 weeks.

(a) Given this information, determine the expected completion time for the entire process. Also determine those activities along the critical path. Jim hopes that the total project will take less than 40 weeks. Is this likely to occur?

(b) Jim has just determined that activity D has already been completed and no additional work is required. What is the impact of this change on the activities along the critical path?

(c) What is the impact on the critical path and the total project completion time if both activity D and activity I have been completed?

(d) What would happen if the immediate predecessor activity changed? For example, activity F may have an immediate predecessor of activity A instead of activity B. Is it possible to handle this type of change with AB:QM?

Project completion time is 38 weeks.

Activity D is still on critical path; project completion time is 29.

Completion time is 26.

Completion time is 23.

Haygood Brothers Construction Company

George and Harry Haygood are building contractors who specialize in the construction of private home dwellings, storage warehouses, and small businesses (less than 20,000 sq. ft. of floor space). Both George and Harry entered a carpenter union's apprenticeship program in the early 1980s and, upon completion of the apprenticeship, became skilled craftsmen in 1986. Before going into business for themselves, they worked for several local building contractors in the Detroit area.

Typically, the Haygood Brothers submit competitive bids for the construction of proposed dwellings. Whenever their bids are accepted, various aspects of the construction (electrical wiring, plumbing, brick laying, painting, and so forth) are subcontracted. George and Harry, however, perform all carpentry work. In addition, they plan and schedule all construction operations, frequently arrange interim financing, and supervise all construction activities.

The philosophy under which the Haygood Brothers have always operated can be simply stated—"Time is money." Delays in construction increase the costs of interim financing and postpone the initiation of their building projects. Consequently, they deal with all bottlenecks promptly and avoid all delays whenever possible. To minimize the time consumed in a construction project, the Haygood Brothers use PERT.

First, all construction activities and events are itemized and properly arranged (in parallel and sequential combinations) in a network. Then, time estimates for each activity are made; the expected time for completing each activity is determined; and the critical (longest) path is calculated. Finally, earliest times, latest times, and slack values are computed. Having made these calculations, George and Harry can place their resources in the critical areas in order to minimize the time of completing the project.

The following are the activities that constitute an upcoming project (home dwelling) of the Haygood Brothers:

1. Arrange financing (1–2).

2. Let subcontracts (2–3).

3. Set and pour foundations (3–4).

4. Plumbing (3–5).

5. Framing (4–6).

6. Roofing (6–7).

7. Electrical wiring (6–8).

8. Installation of windows and doors (6–9).

9. Duct work and insulation (including heating and cooling units) (6–10).

10. Sheet rock, paneling, and paper hanging (10–11).

11. Installation of cabinets (11–12).

12. Bricking (11–13).

13. Outside trim (13–14).

14. Inside trim (including fixtures) (12–15).

15. Painting (15–16).

16. Flooring (16–17).

The PERT diagram (see page 787), together with the optimistic (*a*), most likely (*m*), and pessimistic (*b*) time estimates, are as follows:

ACTIVITY	*a*	*m*	*b*
1–2	4	5	6
2–3	2	5	8
3–4	5	7	9
3–5	4	5	6
4–6	2	4	6
6–7	3	5	9
6–8	4	5	6
6–9	3	4	7
6–10	5	7	9
10–11	10	11	12
11–12	4	6	8
11–13	7	8	9
13–14	4	5	10
12–15	5	7	9
15–16	5	6	7
16–17	2	3	4

1. What is the time length of the critical path? What is the significance of the critical path?

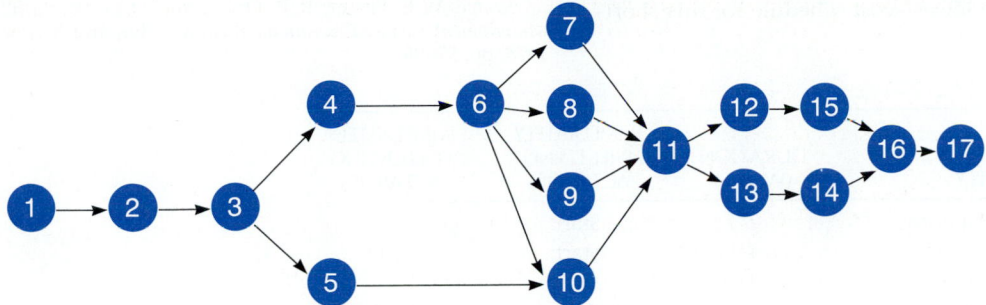

2. Compute the amount of time that the completion of each event can be delayed without affecting the overall project.

3. The project was begun August 1. What is the probability that his project can be completed by September 30? (*Note:* Scheduled completion time = 60 days.)

Source: Jerry Kinard (Francis Marion College) and Joe C. Iverstine (deceased). Used with permission of author.

Haygood Bros. 1. 61 days
2. A delay of an equal amount of time 3. 30.15%

CASE STUDY

Bay Community Hospital

The staff of the Bay Community Hospital had committed itself to introduce a new diagnostic procedure in the clinic. This procedure required the acquisition, installation, and introduction of a new medical instrument. Dr. Ed Windsor was assigned the responsibility for assuring that the introduction be performed as quickly and smoothly as possible.

Dr. Windsor created a list of activities that would have to be completed before the new service could begin. Initially, three individual steps had to be taken: (1) write instructions and procedures, (2) select techniques to operate the equipment, and (3) procure the equipment. The instructions and selection of the operators had to be completed before the training could commence. Dr. Windsor also believed it was necessary to choose the operators and evaluate their qualifications before formally announcing the new service to the local medical community. Upon arrival and installation of the equipment and completion of the operators' training, Dr. Windsor wanted to spend a period checking the procedures, operators, and equipment before declaring the project was successfully completed. The activities and times are listed in the table on page 788.

Jack Worth, a member of the Bay Community Hospital staff, reported that it would be possible to save time on the project by paying some premiums to complete certain activities faster than the normal schedule listed in the table. Specifically, if the equipment were shipped by express truck, 1 week could be saved. Air freight would save 2 weeks. However, a premium of $200 would be paid for the express truck shipment and $750 would be paid for air shipment. The operator training period could also be reduced by 1 week if the trainees worked overtime. However, this would cost the hospital an additional $600. The time required to complete the instructions could be reduced by 1 week with the additional expenditure of $400. However, $300 could be saved if this activity was allowed to take 3 weeks.

Discussion Questions

1. What is the shortest time period in which the project can be completed using the expected times listed in the table?

2. What is the shortest time in which the project can be completed?

3. What is the lowest-cost schedule for this shortest time?

Source: W. E. Sasser, R. P. Olsen, and D. D. Wyckoff, *Management Service Operations,* Boston: Allyn and Bacon, 1978, pp. 97–98.

ACTIVITY	DURATION (WEEKS)	IMMEDIATELY PRECEDING ACTIVITIES	IMMEDIATELY FOLLOWING ACTIVITIES
A: Write instructions	2	Start	C
B: Select operators	4	Start	C, D
C: Train operators	3	A, B	F
D: Announce new service	4	B	End
E: Purchase, ship, and receive equipment	8	Start	F
F: Test new operators on equipment	2	C, E	End

Bay Community Hospital. See Instructor's Section.

CASE STUDY

The Ranch Development Project

One hundred years ago, a high plains area near the continental divide in Colorado was used as a working ranch. The views were majestic, although the winters could be harsh. As a result of the boom in skiing, snowmobiling, and other winter sports, the area quickly became a major tourist attraction. The result was a higher population base to support tourism and increased property values. During the late 1960s and 1970s, the area experienced dramatic growth. Many people from states such as Oklahoma and Texas vacationed here, and so purchased land, houses, or condominiums. Many property developers who finished their projects before the mid-1980s and early 1990s did very well financially. The success of other developers led to the organization of the Ranch Development Project.

The Ranch Development Project was undertaken by two real estate companies in the Colorado high country and several investors from Oklahoma. The idea was to convert the working ranch into a luxury single-family development. The project became known as The Ranch. The average home price was $475,000, and it was not uncommon to have homes valued at over $1 million. The center of the development was a first-class 18-hole golf course. Greens fees could approach $100 per day depending on services required. Some have claimed that the course is one of the best in Colorado. The Ranch also had a 4-star restaurant located in a beautiful and spacious log cabin, which included a fireplace big enough for a 6-foot-tall person to walk into without hitting his head. Other amenities included a heated pool, lighted tennis courts, and a complete workout center. Free shuttle service was provided to the ski slopes a few miles away.

To preserve the beauty of the area and to enhance property values, each home site varied from 1/2 acre to over 20 acres. There were numerous building restrictions. Every home and structure had to be completely approved by The Ranch Development Board. Approval required developing a scale model of all buildings on the property and a complete set of blueprints. The average cost of preparing the necessary plans was $25,000. The concept of a footprint was also used. A *footprint* is a relatively small circular area on each plot of land. Homes and all structures had to be placed inside the footprint. While the homeowner held title to the entire property, all structures had to be placed in the footprint, unless special permission was given by The Ranch Development Board (a rare occurrence).

Each homeowner had to pay monthly fees, depending on the location and value of the land. The fees could vary from $450 to over $1,250 per month. These fees included water, sewer, cable TV, and access to the pool, tennis courts, and exercise facility. Golf and restaurant fees were additional.

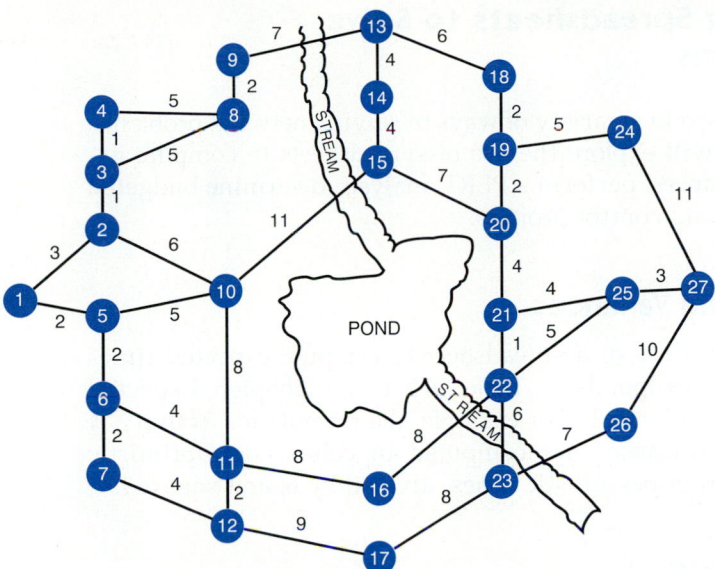

One of the developments in The Ranch is outlined in the preceding network. The development was not as close to the golf course as some of the others, but it had a beautiful trout stream and pond in the center. The footprints are shown in the network. Distances between footprints are given in hundreds of feet.

1. What is the least expensive way to connect all homes with water and sewer lines? Assume that minimizing total distance will also minimize total costs.

2. The Ranch Development Board is considering the possibility of expanding the pond area. This would allow for boating, including sailing and water skiing. This would increase property values, but some distances would change. The distance for path 11–16 would be 9, and the distance for path 16–22 would be 12. What impact would this have on the plan for the water and sewer system?

See Instructor's Section.

BIBLIOGRAPHY

Badiru, A. B. "Towards the Standardization of Performance Measures For Project Scheduling Heuristics." *IEEE Transaction on Engineering Management* **35** (May 1988): 82–89.

Berman, O., and B. Jewkes. "Optimal M/G/I Server Location on a Network Having a Fixed Facility." *Journal of Operational Research Society* **39** (December 1988): 1137–1146.

Chan, K. H. "Decision Support Systems for Human Resource Management." *Journal of Systems Management* **23** (April 1984): 17–25.

Current, J. "The Minimum-Covering/Shortest Path Problem." *Decision Sciences* **19** (Summer 1988): 490–503.

Golenko, Ginzburg D. "On the Distribution of Activity Time in PERT." *Journal of Operational Research Society* **39** (August 1988): 767–771.

Jain, A., and J.W. Mamer. "Approximations for the Random Minimal Spanning Tree with Application to Network Provisioning." *Operations Research* **36** (July–August 1988): 575–584.

Render, B., and R. M. Stair, *Cases and Readings in Managment Science,* 2nd ed. Boston: Allyn and Bacon, 1990.

Sancho, N. G. F. "On the Maximum Expected Flow in a Network." *Journal of Operational Research Society* **39** (May 1988): 481–485.

Shelmerdine, E. K. "Planning for Project Management." *Journal of Systems Management* **40** (January 1989): 16–20.

Vemuganti, R. R., and others. "Network Models for Fleet Management." *Decision Sciences* **20** (Winter 1989): 182–197.

Appendix: Using Spreadsheets to Solve Network Problems

Spreadsheets can be used in a variety of ways in solving network problems. In this appendix, we will explore the use of spreadsheets to compute expected times and variances, perform a PERT analysis, determine budgeted costs, and to monitor and control projects.

Expected Times and Variances

Program 18.8 shows the use of a spreadsheet to compute expected times and variances. This corresponds to Table 18.2 in the chapter. Expected times are computed in column E. For example, the formula for Activity A is (B6+4*C6+D6)/6. Variances are computed in column F. Optimistic times are subtracted from pessimistic times, divided by 6, and squared.

Performing PERT Analysis

Table 18.3 summarized the PERT analysis done for the General Foundry problem. Program 18.7 performs the same analysis. Input data (activity times) are entered in the first 10 rows. PERT analysis is done from row 11 through row 20. The spreadsheet performs like the example in the chapter. ES values for Activities A and B are 0. EF values for Activities A and B are 2 and 3. These values are computed from the formulas +B3 and +B4 in cells C13 and C14. ES for Activity C is equal to ES for Activity A or +C13. EF for Activity C is ES for Activity C plus the activity time or +B15+B5. Note Activities G and H in column A. The @MAX function is used to make sure that *all* activities are completed before these activities are started. Computing ES and EF completes the forward pass through the network.

PROGRAM 18.8 Using a Spreadsheet to Compute Expected Times and Variances

	A	B	C	D	E	F
1	Expected Times and Variances					
2						
3			Most		Expected	
4	Act.	Opt.	Prob.	Pess.	Time	Variance
5						
6	A	1	2	3	(B6+4*C6+D6)/6	((D6-B6)/6)^2
7	B	2	3	4	(B7+4*C7+D7)/6	((D7-B7)/6)^2
8	C	1	2	3	(B8+4*C8+D8)/6	((D8-B8)/6)^2
9	D	2	4	6	(B9+4*C9+D9)/6	((D9-B9)/6)^2
10	E	1	4	7	(B10+4*C10+D10)/6	((D10-B10)/6)^2
11	F	1	2	9	(B11+4*C11+D11)/6	((D11-B11)/6)^2
12	G	3	4	11	(B12+4*C12+D12)/6	((D12-B12)/6)^2
13	H	1	2	3	(B13+4*C13+D13)/6	((D13-B13)/6)^2

PROGRAM 18.9 Using a Spreadsheet to Perform PERT Analysis

	A	B	C	D	E	F
1	Input Data					
2	Activity	Times				
3	A	2				
4	B	3				
5	C	2				
6	D	4				
7	E	4				
8	F	3				
9	G	5				
10	H	2				
11	Output Results					
12	Activity		ES	EF	LS	LF	Slack
13	A		0	+B3	+E13−B3	+D15	+E13−C13
14	B		0	+B4	+E14−B4	+D16	+E14−C14
15	C		+C13	+B15+B5	+E15−B5	@MIN(D17..D18)	+E15−C15
16	D		+C14	+B16+B6	+E16−B6	+D19	+E16−C16
17	E		+C15	+B17+B7	+E17−B7	+D19	+E17−C17
18	F		+C15	+B18+B8	+E18−B8	+D20	+E18−C18
19	G		@MAX(C16..C17)	+B19+B9	+E19−B9	+D20	+E19−C19
20	H		@MAX(C18..C19)	+B20+B10	+E20−B10	+C20	+E20−C20

The backward pass starts with the last activity—Activity H. The LF value for Activity H is the same as EF for this activity (15 or +C20). The LS value is computed by subtracting the activity time from the LF value. For Activity H, this is +E20−B10. The same calculations are then made for the other activities starting with G and proceeding to Activity A. Note the use of @MIN for Activity C. This is needed because there are two paths between Activity C and the end of the network. After the backward pass has been completed, slack values are determined. This is done in column F. Slack is equal to LF minus EF. For example, the slack for Activity A is computed with the formula +E13−C13.

PERT/Cost

Table 18.6 and Figure 18.10 can be used to develop tables to monitor project costs. Program 18.10 performs this analysis. Weekly cost data are entered in cells A5 through I19. Column J computes the total costs for each week, and column K computes the overall or cumulative total. These columns correspond to the last two rows of Table 18.6.

Monitoring and Controlling Cost

Managers often have a need to monitor and control budget costs for a project and each activity in the project. Table 18.8 in the chapter was used to determine the value of work completed and cost differences between the budget and actual expenditures. Program 18.9 can be used to perform this type of analysis. The total budget, percent of completion, and actual costs for each activity are entered in columns B, C, and E. The

PROGRAM 18.10 **Using a Spreadsheet to Compute Budgeted Cost**

```
    A     B  C  D  E  F  G  H  I        J          K
 1        Budgeted Cost Using Latest Start Weekly   Overall
 2        Activity A  B  C  D  E  F  G  H  Total    Total
 3        Week
 4
 5        1  11                          @SUM(B5..I5)    +J5
 6        2  11 10                       @SUM(B6..I6)    +K5+J6
 7        3     10 13                    @SUM(B7..I7)    +K6+J7
 8        4     10 13                    @SUM(B8..I8)    +K7+J8
 9        5           12 14              @SUM(B9..I9)    +K8+J9
10        6           12 14              @SUM(B10..I10)  +K9+J10
11        7           12 14              @SUM(B11..I11)  +K10+J11
12        8           12 14              @SUM(B12..I12)  +K11+J12
13        9                 16           @SUM(B13..I13)  +K12+J13
14       10                 16           @SUM(B14..I14)  +K13+J14
15       11              10 16           @SUM(B15..I15)  +K14+J15
16       12              10 16           @SUM(B16..I16)  +K15+J16
17       13              10 16           @SUM(B17..I17)  +K16+J17
18       14                    8         @SUM(B18..I18)  +K17+J18
19       15                    8         @SUM(B19..I19)  +K18+J19
20 Type /GV to View the Graph and the Space Bar and Q to Return
```

spreadsheet computes the value of work completed in column D and the activity differences in column F. The procedures are the same as discussed in the chapter.

PROGRAM 18.11 **Monitoring and Controlling Budgeted Cost**

```
         A            B          C          D          E         F
 1 Monitoring and Controlling Budgeted Cost
 2
 3
 4                  Total    Percent    Value of
 5                  Budgeted    of       Work     Actual   Activity
 6    Activity      Cost  Completion  Completed   Cost    Difference
 7
 8      A           22000       1     +B8*C8      20000   +E8-D8
 9      B           30000       1     +B9*C9      36000   +E9-D9
10      C           26000       1     +B10*C10    26000   +E10-D10
11      D           48000     0.1     +B11*C11     6000   +E11-D11
12      E           56000     0.2     +B12*C12    20000   +E12-D12
13      F           30000     0.2     +B13*C13     4000   +E13-D13
14      G           80000       0     +B14*C14        0   +E14-D14
15      H           16000       0     +B15*C15        0   +E15-D15
16
17 Type /GV to View the Graph and the Space Bar and Q to Return
18
19
20
```

19

Markov Analysis

CHAPTER OUTLINE

19.1 Introduction

19.2 States and State Probabilities: A Grocery Store Example

19.3 Matrix of Transition Probabilities

19.4 Predicting Future Market Shares

19.5 Markov Analysis of Machine Operations

19.6 Equilibrium Conditions

19.7 Absorbing States and the Fundamental Matrix: An Accounts Receivable Application

19.8 Solving Markov Analysis Problems by Computer

19.9 Summary

Glossary

Key Equations

Solved Problems

Discussion Questions and Problems

Case Study: Rentall Trucks

Bibliography

Appendix: Using Spreadsheets to Solve Markov Analysis Problems

use of Markov analysis

Markov analysis is a technique that deals with the probabilities of future occurrences by analyzing presently known probabilities.[1] The technique has numerous applications in business, including market share analysis, bad debt prediction, university enrollment predictions, and determining whether a machine will break down in the future.

Teaching Suggestion 19.1: The Use of Matrix Algebra. See the Instructor's Section for details.

Markov analysis makes the assumption that the system starts in an initial state or condition. For example, two competing manufacturers might have 40% and 60% of the market sales, respectively, as initial states. Perhaps in two months the market shares for the two companies will change to 45% and 55% of the market, respectively. Predicting these future states involves knowing the system's likelihood or probability of changing from one state to another. For a particular problem, these probabilities can be collected and placed in a matrix or table. This *matrix of transition probabilities* reveals the likelihood that the system will change from one time period to the next. This is the Markov process, and it enables us to predict future states or conditions.

Transparency Master 19.1: Assumptions of Markov Analysis.

matrix of transition probabilities

Like many other quantitative techniques, Markov analysis can be studied at any level of depth and sophistication. Fortunately, the major mathematical requirements are just that you know how to perform basic matrix manipulations and solve several equations with several unknowns. If you are not familiar with these techniques, you may wish to review Module A, which covers matrices and other useful mathematical tools, before you begin this chapter.

Transparency Master 19.2: The Markov Process.

Since the level of this course prohibits a detailed study of Markov mathematics, we limit our discussion to Markov processes that follow four assumptions:

assumptions of Markov analysis

1. There is a limited or finite number of possible states.

2. The probability of changing states remains the same over time.

3. We can predict any future state from the previous state and the matrix of transition probabilities.

4. The size and makeup of the system (for example, the total number of manufacturers and customers) do not change during the analysis.

examples of states

States are used to identify all possible conditions of a process or a system. For example, a machine can be in one of two states at any point in time. It can be either functioning correctly or not functioning correctly. We can call the proper operation of the machine the first state, and we can call the

---

[1] The founder of the concept was A. A. Markov, whose 1905 studies of the sequence of experiments connected in a chain were used to describe the principle of Brownian motion.

incorrect functioning the second state. Indeed, it is possible to identify specific states for many processes or systems. If there are only three grocery stores in a small town, a resident can be a customer of any one of the three at any point in time. Therefore, there are three states corresponding to the three grocery stores. If students can take one of three specialties in the management area (let's say management science, management information systems, or general management), then each of these areas can be considered a state.

In Markov analysis, we also assume that the states are both *collectively exhaustive* and *mutually exclusive*. Collectively exhaustive means that we can list all of the possible states of a system or process. Our discussion of Markov analysis assumes that there is a finite number of states for any system. Mutually exclusive means that a system can be in only one state at any point in time. A student can be in only one of the three management specialty areas and *not* in two or more areas at the same time. It also means that a person can only be a customer of *one* of the three grocery stores at any point in time.

collectively exhaustive and mutually exclusive states

Once the states have been identified, the next step is to determine the probability that the system is in this state. Such information is then placed into a *vector of state probabilities*.

$$\pi(i) = \text{vector of state probabilities for period } i$$

$$\pi(i) = (\pi_1, \pi_2, \pi_3, \ldots, \pi_n) \tag{19-1}$$

where

$$n = \text{the number of states, and}$$

$$\pi_1, \pi_2, \ldots, \pi_n = \text{probability of being in state 1, state 2, \ldots, state } n.$$

In some cases, where we are only dealing with one item, such as one machine, it is possible to know with complete certainty what state this item is in. For example, if we are investigating only one machine, we may know that at this point in time the machine is functioning correctly. Then, the vector of states can be represented as follows:

states of a machine

$$\pi(1) = (1, 0)$$

where

$$\pi(1) = \text{vector of states for the machine in period 1,}$$

$$\pi_1 = 1 = \text{probability of being in the first state, and}$$

$$\pi_2 = 0 = \text{probability of being in the second state.}$$

This shows that the probability the machine is functioning correctly, state 1, is 1, and the probability that the machine is functioning incorrectly, state 2, is 0 for the first period. In most cases, however, we are dealing with more than one item.

Let's look at the vector of states for people in the small town with the three grocery stores. There could be a total of 100,000 people that shop at the three grocery stores during any given month. Forty thousand people may be shopping at American Food Store, which will be called state 1. Thirty thousand people may be shopping at Food Mart, which will be called state 2, and 30,000 people may be shopping at Atlas Foods, which will be called state 3. The probability that a person will be shopping at one of these three grocery stores is as follows:

State 1—American Food Store: 40,000/100,000 = .40 = 40%

State 2—Food Mart   : 30,000/100,000 = .30 = 30%

State 3—Atlas Foods   : 30,000/100,000 = .30 = 30%

These probabilities can be placed in the vector of state probabilities shown below:

$$\pi(1) = (.4, .3, .3)$$

where

$\pi(1)$ = vector of state probabilities for the three grocery stores for period 1,

$\pi_1 = .4$ = probability that a person will shop at American Food, state 1,

$\pi_2 = .3$ = probability that a person will shop at Food Mart, state 2, and

$\pi_3 = .3$ = probability that a person will shop at Atlas Foods, state 3.

using market shares

You should also notice that the probabilities in the vector of states for the three grocery stores represent the *market shares* for these three stores for the first period. Thus, American Food has 40% of the market, Food Mart has 30%, and Atlas Foods has 30% of the market in period 1. When we are dealing with market shares, the market shares can be used in place of probability values.

Once the initial states and state probabilities have been determined, the next step is to find the matrix of transition probabilities. This matrix is used along with the state probabilities in predicting the future.

19.3   MATRIX OF TRANSITION PROBABILITIES

Teaching Suggestion 19.2:
The Matrix of Transition. See the Instructor's Section for details.

The concept that allows us to get from a current state, such as market shares, to a future state is the *matrix of transition probabilities.* This is a matrix of conditional probabilities of being in a future state given a current state. The following definition is helpful:

Let P_{ij} = conditional probability of being in state j in the future given the current state of i

Transparency Master 19.3:
Predicting Future States.

For example, P_{12} is the probability of being in state 2 in the future given the event was in state 1 in the period before.

Let P = matrix of transition probabilities

$$P = \begin{bmatrix} P_{11} & P_{12} & P_{13} & \cdots & P_{1n} \\ P_{21} & P_{22} & P_{23} & \cdots & P_{2n} \\ \cdot & & & & \\ \cdot & & & & \\ \cdot & & & & \\ P_{m1} & & \cdots & & P_{mn} \end{bmatrix}$$

(19-2)

Individual P_{ij} values are usually determined empirically. For example, if we have observed over time that 10% of the people currently shopping at store 1 (or state 1) will be shopping at store 2 (state 2) next period, then we know that $P_{12} = .1$ or 10%.

Transition Probabilities for the Three Grocery Stores

Let's say we can determine the matrix of transition probabilities for the three grocery stores by using historical data. The results of our analysis appear in the following matrix:

$$P = \begin{bmatrix} .8 & .1 & .1 \\ .1 & .7 & .2 \\ .2 & .2 & .6 \end{bmatrix}$$

Recall that American Food represents state 1, Food Mart is state 2, and Atlas Foods is state 3. The meaning of these probabilities can be expressed in terms of the various states, as follows.

Row 1
.8 = P_{11} = Probability of being in state 1 after being in state 1 the previous period

.1 = P_{12} = Probability of being in state 2 after being in state 1 the previous period

.1 = P_{13} = Probability of being in state 3 after being in state 1 the previous period

Row 2
.1 = P_{21} = Probability of being in state 1 after being in state 2 the previous period

.7 = P_{22} = Probability of being in state 2 after being in state 2 the previous period

.2 = P_{23} = Probability of being in state 3 after being in state 2 the previous period

Row 3
.2 = P_{31} = Probability of being in state 1 after being in state 3 the previous period

.2 = P_{32} = Probability of being in state 2 after being in state 3 the previous period

.6 = P_{33} = Probability of being in state 3 after being in state 3 the previous period

Note that the three probabilities in the top row sum to 1. The probabilities for any row in a matrix of transition probabilities will also sum to 1.

Once the state probabilities have been determined along with the matrix of transition probabilities, it is possible to predict future state probabilities.

KEY IDEA

Applicable Problems 19-7, 19-8, 19-9, 19-11, 19-12, 19-14, 19-20, 19-21, 19-22, 19-23, Rentall Trucks Csae

Teaching Suggestion 19.3: The Application of Markov Analysis. See the Instructor's Section for details.

19.4 PREDICTING FUTURE MARKET SHARES

One of the purposes of Markov analysis is to predict the future. Given the vector of state probabilities and the matrix of transition probabilities, it is not very difficult to determine the state probabilities at a future date. With this type of analysis, we are able to compute the probability that a person will be shopping at one of the grocery stores in the future. Because this probability is equivalent to market share, it is possible to determine future market shares for American Food, Food Mart, and Atlas Foods. When the current period is 1, calculating the state probabilities for the next period (period 2) can be accomplished as follows:

$$\pi(2) = \pi(1)P \qquad (19\text{-}3)$$

Furthermore, if we are in any period n, we can compute the state probabilities for period $n + 1$ as follows:

$$\pi(n + 1) = \pi(n)P \qquad (19\text{-}4)$$

future state

Equation 19-3 can be used to answer the question of next period's market shares for the grocery stores. The computations are:

$$\pi(2) = \pi(1)P$$

$$\pi(2) = (.4, .3, .3) \begin{bmatrix} .8 & .1 & .1 \\ .1 & .7 & .2 \\ .2 & .2 & .6 \end{bmatrix}$$

$$\pi(2) = [(.4)(.8) + (.3)(.1) + (.3)(.2), (.4)(.1) + (.3)(.7) \\ + (.3)(.2), (.4)(.1) + (.3)(.2) + (.3)(.6)]$$

$$\pi(2) = (.41, .31, .28)$$

Teaching Suggestion 19.4: Sensitivity Analysis and Markov Analysis. See the Instructor's Section for details.

As you can see, the market share for American Food and Food Mart has increased, while the market share for Atlas Foods has decreased. Will this trend continue in the future? Will Atlas eventually lose all of its market share? Or will a stable condition be reached for all three grocery stores? Questions such as these can be answered with a discussion of equilibrium conditions. To help introduce the concept of equilibrium, we present a second application of Markov analysis—machine breakdowns.

19.5 MARKOV ANALYSIS OF MACHINE OPERATIONS

Alternate Example 19-1

machine matrix of transition probabilities

Paul Tolsky, owner of Tolsky Works, has recorded the operation of his milling machine for several years. Over the past two years, 80% of the time the milling machine functioned correctly during the current month if it had functioned correctly in the previous month. This also means that only 20% of the time did the machine not function correctly for a given month when it was functioning correctly during the previous month. In addition, it has been observed that 90% of the time the machine remained incorrectly adjusted for any given month if it was incorrectly adjusted the previous month. Only 10% of the time did the machine operate correctly in a given month when it did *not* operate correctly during the last month. In other words, this machine *can* correct itself when it has not been functioning correctly in the past, and this happens 10% of the time. These values can now be used to construct the matrix of transition probabilities. Again, state 1 is a situation where the machine is functioning correctly, and state 2 is a situation where the machine is not functioning correctly. The matrix of transition probabilities for this machine is:

$$P = \begin{bmatrix} .8 & .2 \\ .1 & .9 \end{bmatrix}$$

where

$P_{11} = .8 =$ Probability that the machine will be *correctly* functioning this month given it was *correctly* functioning last month.

$P_{12} = .2 =$ Probability that the machine will *not* be correctly functioning this month given it was *correctly* functioning last month.

$P_{21} = .1 =$ Probability that the machine will be functioning *correctly* this month given it was *not* correctly functioning last month, and

$P_{22} = .9 =$ Probability that the machine will *not* be correctly functioning this month given that it was *not* correctly functioning last month.

Look at this matrix for the machine. The two probabilities in the top row are the probabilities of functioning correctly and not functioning correctly, given that the machine was functioning correctly in the last period. Because these are mutually exclusive and collectively exhaustive, the row probabilities again sum to 1.

What is the probability that Tolsky's machine will be functioning correctly one month from now? What is the probability that the machine will be functioning correctly in two months? To answer these questions, we again apply Equation 19-3:

$$\pi(2) = \pi(1)P$$

$$\pi(2) = (1,0) \begin{bmatrix} .8 & .2 \\ .1 & .9 \end{bmatrix}$$

$$\pi(2) = [(1)(.8) + (0)(.1), (1)(.2) + (0)(.9)]$$

$$\pi(2) = (.8, .2)$$

Therefore, the probability that the machine will be functioning correctly one month from now, given that it is now functioning correctly, is .80. The probability that it will *not* be functioning correctly in one month is .20. Now we can use these results to determine the probability that the machine will be functioning correctly two months from now. The analysis is exactly the same:

$$\pi(3) = \pi(2)P$$

$$\pi(3) = (.8, .2) \begin{bmatrix} .8 & .2 \\ .1 & .9 \end{bmatrix}$$

$$\pi(3) = [(.8)(.8) + (.2)(.1), (.8)(.2) + (.2)(.9)]$$

$$\pi(3) = (.66, .34)$$

This means that in the third period, or month, there is a probability of .66 that the machine will still be functioning correctly. The probability that the machine will not be functioning correctly is .34. Of course, we could continue this analysis as many times as we want in computing state probabilities for future months.

Applicable Problems: 19-8, 19-13, 19-15, 19-16, 19-17, 19-20, 19-21, 19-22

19.6 EQUILIBRIUM CONDITIONS

Looking at the Tolsky machine example, it is easy to think that eventually all market shares or state probabilities will be either 0 or 1. This is usually not the case. *Equilibrium share* of the market values or probabilities are normally encountered.

Teaching Suggestion 19.5:
Equilibrium Conditions and the Beginning State or Condition. See the Instructor's Section for details.

One way to compute the equilibrium share of the market, or equilibrium state probabilities, is to use Markov analysis for a large number of periods. It is possible to see if the future values are approaching a stable value. For example, it is possible to repeat Markov analysis for 15 periods for Tolsky's machine. This is not too difficult to do by hand. The results for this computation appear in Table 19.1.

computing equilibrium share of market

TABLE 19.1 State Probabilities for the Machine Example for 15 Periods

PERIOD	STATE 1	STATE 2
1	1.0	.0
2	.8	.2
3	.66	.34
4	.562	.438
5	.4934	.5066
6	.44538	.55462
7	.411766	.588234
8	.388236	.611763
9	.371765	.628234
10	.360235	.639754
11	.352165	.647834
12	.346515	.653484
13	.342560	.657439
14	.339792	.660207
15	.337854	.662145

Transparency Master 19.5:
Number of Periods to Reach Equilibrium.

The machine starts off functioning correctly (in state 1) in the first period. In period 5, there is only a .4934 probability that the machine is still functioning correctly, and by period 10, this probability is only .360235. In period 15, the probability that the machine is still functioning correctly is about .34. The probability that the machine will be functioning correctly at a future period is decreasing—but it is decreasing at a decreasing rate. What would you expect in the long run? If we made these calculations for 100 periods, what would happen? Would there be an equilibrium in this case? If the answer is *yes*, what would it be? Looking at Table 19.1, it appears that there will be an equilibrium at .333333 or ⅓. But how can we be sure?

By definition, an *equilibrium condition* exists if the state probabilities or market shares do not change after a large number of periods. Thus, at equilibrium, the state probabilities for a future period must be the same as the state probabilities for the current period. This fact is the key to solving for the equilibrium state probabilities. This relationship can be expressed as follows:

At equilibrium,

$$\pi(\text{next period}) = \pi(\text{this period})P$$

or

$$\pi = \pi P \qquad (19\text{-}5)$$

Equation 19-5 states that, at equilibrium, the state probabilities for the *next* period are the same as the state probabilities for the *current* period. For Tolsky's machine, this can be expressed as follows:

$$\pi = \pi P$$

$$(\pi_1, \pi_2) = (\pi_1, \pi_2) \begin{bmatrix} .8 & .2 \\ .1 & .9 \end{bmatrix}$$

Using matrix multiplication we get:

$$(\pi_1, \pi_2) = [(\pi_1)(.8) + (\pi_2)(.1), (\pi_1)(.2) + (\pi_2)(.9)]$$

The *first term* on the left-hand side, π_1, is equal to the *first term* on the right-hand side, $(\pi_1)(.8) + (\pi_2)(.1)$. In addition, the *second term* on the left-hand side, π_2, is equal to the *second term* on the right-hand side, $(\pi_1)(.2) + (\pi_2)(.9)$. This gives us the following:

$$\pi_1 = .8\pi_1 + .1\pi_2 \qquad (19\text{-}6)$$

$$\pi_2 = .2\pi_1 + .9\pi_2 \qquad (19\text{-}7)$$

We also know that the state probabilities, π_1 and π_2 in this case, must sum to 1. (Looking at Table 19.1, you note that π_1 and π_2 sum to 1 for all 15 periods.) We can express this property as follows:

$$\pi_1 + \pi_2 + \cdots + \pi_n = 1 \qquad (19\text{-}8)$$

For Tolsky's machine, we have:

$$\pi_1 + \pi_2 = 1 \qquad (19\text{-}9)$$

determining equilibrium conditions

 KEY IDEA

Transparency Master 19.4: Equilibrium Conditions.

equilibrium computations

Alternate Example 19-2

Now, we have three equations for the machine (19-6, 19-7, and 19-9). We know that Equation 19-9 must hold. Thus, we can drop either Equation 19-6 or 19-7 and solve the remaining two equations for π_1 and π_2. It is necessary to drop one of the equations so that we end up with two unknowns and two equations. If we were solving for equilibrium conditions that involved three states, we would end up with four equations. Again, it would be necessary to drop one of the equations so that we end up with three equations and three unknowns. In general, when solving for equilibrium conditions, it will always be necessary to drop one of the equations such that the total number of equations is the same as the total number of variables that we are solving for. The reason that we can drop one of the equations is that they are mathematically interrelated. In other words, one of the equations is redundant in specifying the relationships between the various equilibrium equations.

Let us arbitrarily drop Equation 19-6. Thus, we will be solving the following two equations:

$$\pi_2 = .2\pi_1 + .9\pi_2$$

$$\pi_1 + \pi_2 = 1$$

Rearranging the first equation, we get

$$.1\pi_2 = .2\pi_1$$

or

$$\pi_2 = 2\pi_1$$

Substituting this into Equation 19-9, we have:

$$\pi_1 + \pi_2 = 1$$

or

$$\pi_1 + 2\pi_1 = 1$$

or

$$3\pi_1 = 1$$

$$\pi_1 = \tfrac{1}{3} = .33333333$$

Thus,

$$\pi_2 = \tfrac{2}{3} = .66666667$$

Compare these results with Table 19.1. As you can see, the equilibrium state probability for state 1 is .33333333, and the equilibrium state probability for state 2 is .66666667. These values are what you would expect by looking at the tabled results. This analysis indicates that it is only necessary to know the matrix of transition in determining the equilibrium market shares. The initial values for the state probabilities or the market shares do not influence the equilibrium state probabilities. The analysis for determining equilibrium state probabilities or market shares is the same when there are more states. If there are three states (as in the grocery store ex-

ample), we have to solve three equations for the three equilibrium states; if there are four states, we have to solve four simultaneous equations for the four unknown equilibrium values, and so on.

You may wish to prove to yourself that the equilibrium states we have just computed are, in fact, equilibrium states. This can be done by multiplying the equilibrium states times the original matrix of transition. The results will be the same equilibrium states. Performing this analysis is also an excellent way to check your answers to end-of-chapter problems or examination questions.

<table><tr><td>**19.7**</td><td>**ABSORBING STATES AND THE FUNDAMENTAL MATRIX: AN ACCOUNTS RECEIVABLE APPLICATION**</td></tr></table>

Applicable Problems 19-18, 19-19

Teaching Suggestion 19.6: Absorbing State Analysis and Matrix Algebra. See the Instructor's Section for details.

absorbing states

In the examples discussed thus far, we assumed that it is possible for the process or system to go from one state to any other state between any two periods. In some cases, however, if you are in a state, you cannot go to another state in the future. In other words, once you are in a given state, you are "absorbed" by it, and you will remain in that state. Any state that has this property is called an *absorbing state.* An example of this is the accounts receivable application.

An accounts receivable system normally places debts or receivables from its customers into one of several categories or states depending on how overdue the oldest unpaid bill is. Of course, the exact categories or states depend on the policy set by each company. Four typical states or categories for an accounts receivable application are shown below.

State 1 (π_1): Paid, all bills.

State 2 (π_2): Bad debt, overdue more than three months.

State 3 (π_3): Overdue less than one month.

State 4 (π_4): Overdue between one and three months.

At any given period, in this case one month, a customer can be in one of these four states.[2] For this example, it will be assumed that if the oldest unpaid bill is over three months due, it is automatically placed in the bad debt category. Therefore, a customer can be paid in full (state 1), have the oldest unpaid bill overdue less than one month (state 3), have the oldest unpaid bill overdue between one and three months inclusive (state 4), or have the

---

[2] You should also be aware that the four states can be placed in any order you choose. For example, it might seem more natural to order this problem with the states:

1. Paid.
2. Overdue less than one month.
3. Overdue one to three months.
4. Overdue more than three months; bad debt.

This is perfectly legitimate and the only reason this ordering is not used is to facilitate some matrix manipulations you will see shortly.

matrix of transition
probabilities

probabilities for
absorbing states

probabilities of being in
various states

oldest unpaid bill overdue more than three months, which is a bad debt (state 2).

Like any other Markov process, we can set up a matrix of transition probabilities for these four states. This matrix will reflect the propensity of customers to move among the four accounts receivable categories from one month to the next. The probability of being in the paid category for any item or bill in a future month, given that a customer is in the paid category for a purchased item this month, is 100% or 1.0. It is impossible for a customer to completely pay for a product one month and to owe money on it in a future month. Another absorbing state is the bad debts state. If a bill is not paid in three months, we are assuming that the company will completely write it off and not try to collect it in the future. Thus, once a person is in the bad debt category, that person will remain in that category forever. For any absorbing state, the probability that a customer will be in this state in the future is 1, and the probability that a customer will be in any other state is 0.

These values will be placed in the matrix of transition probabilities. But before we construct this matrix, we need to know the probabilities for the other two states—a debt of less than one month and a debt that is between one and three months old. For a person in the less than one month category, there is a .60 probability of being in the paid category, a 0 probability of being in the bad debt category, a .20 probability of remaining in the less than one month category, and a probability of .20 of being in the one to three month category in the next month. Note that there is a 0 probability of being in the bad debt category the next month because it is impossible to get from state 3, less than one month, to state 2, more than three months overdue, in just one month. For a person in the one to three month category, there is a .40 probability of being in the paid category, a .10 probability of being in the bad debt category, a .30 probability of being in the less than one month category, and a .20 probability of remaining in the one to three month category in the next month.

How can we get a probability of .30 of being in the one to three month category for one month, and in the one month or less category in the next month? Because these categories are determined by the oldest unpaid bill, it is possible to pay one bill which is one to three months old and still have another bill that is one month or less old. In other words, any customer may have more than one outstanding bill at any point in time. With this information, it is possible to construct the matrix of transition probabilities of the problem.

	THE NEXT MONTH			
THIS MONTH	PAID	BAD DEBT	< 1 MONTH	1 TO 3 MONTHS
Paid	1	0	0	0
Bad debit	0	1	0	0
Less than 1 month	.6	0	.2	.2
1 to 3 months	.4	.1	.3	.2

Thus,

$$P = \begin{bmatrix} 1 & 0 & 0 & 0 \\ 0 & 1 & 0 & 0 \\ .6 & 0 & .2 & .2 \\ .4 & .1 & .3 & .2 \end{bmatrix}$$

If we know the fraction of the people in each of the four categories or states for any given period, we can determine the fraction of the people in these four states or categories for any future period. These fractions are placed in a vector of state probabilities and multiplied times the matrix of transition probabilities. This procedure was described in Section 4 of this chapter.

Even more interesting are the equilibrium conditions. Of course, in the long run, everyone will be either in the paid or bad debt category. This is because the categories are absorbing states. But how many people, or how much money, will be in each of these categories? Knowing the total amount of money that will be in either the paid or bad debt category will help a company manage its bad debts and cash flow. This analysis requires the use of the *fundamental matrix*.

determining equilibrium conditions

In order to obtain the fundamental matrix, it is necessary to *partition* the matrix of transition, P. This can be done as follows:

fundamental matrix

$$P = \begin{array}{c} \overset{I}{\downarrow} \qquad\qquad \overset{0}{\downarrow} \\ \left[\begin{array}{cc|cc} 1 & 0 & 0 & 0 \\ 0 & 1 & 0 & 0 \\ \hline .6 & 0 & .2 & .2 \\ .4 & .1 & .3 & .2 \end{array}\right] \\ \quad\uparrow \qquad\qquad \uparrow \\ \quad A \qquad\qquad B \end{array} \qquad\text{(19-10)}$$

$$I = \begin{bmatrix} 1 & 0 \\ 0 & 1 \end{bmatrix} \qquad 0 = \begin{bmatrix} 0 & 0 \\ 0 & 0 \end{bmatrix}$$

$$A = \begin{bmatrix} .6 & 0 \\ .4 & .1 \end{bmatrix} \qquad B = \begin{bmatrix} .2 & .2 \\ .3 & .2 \end{bmatrix}$$

where

I = an identity matrix (that is, a matrix with 1s on the diagonal and 0s everyplace else), and

0 = a matrix with all zeros.

The fundamental matrix can be computed as follows:

$$F = (I - B)^{-1} \qquad\text{(19-11)}$$

In Equation 19-11, $(I - B)$ means that we subtract matrix B from matrix I. The superscript -1 means that we take the inverse of the result of

$(I - B)$. Here is how we can compute the fundamental matrix for the accounts receivable application:

$$F = (I - B)^{-1}$$

or

$$F = \left(\begin{bmatrix} 1 & 0 \\ 0 & 1 \end{bmatrix} - \begin{bmatrix} .2 & .2 \\ .3 & .2 \end{bmatrix} \right)^{-1}$$

Subtracting B from I, we get

$$F = \begin{bmatrix} .8 & -.2 \\ -.3 & .8 \end{bmatrix}^{-1}$$

Taking the inverse, -1, involves several steps, described in Module A. The results of these steps are:

$$F = \begin{bmatrix} 1.38 & .34 \\ .52 & 1.38 \end{bmatrix}$$

Now we are in a position to use the fundamental matrix in computing the amount of bad debts that we could expect in the long run. First we need to multiply the fundamental matrix, F, times the matrix A. This is accomplished as follows:

$$FA = \begin{bmatrix} 1.38 & .34 \\ .52 & 1.38 \end{bmatrix} \cdot \begin{bmatrix} .6 & 0 \\ .4 & .1 \end{bmatrix}$$

or

$$FA = \begin{bmatrix} .97 & .03 \\ .86 & .14 \end{bmatrix}$$

meaning of the *FA* matrix

The new *FA* matrix has an important meaning. It indicates the probability that an amount in one of the nonabsorbing states will end up in one of the absorbing states. The top row of this matrix indicates the probabilities that an amount in the less than one month category will end up in the paid and the bad debt category. The probability that an amount that is less than one month overdue will be paid is .97, and the probability that an amount that is less than one month overdue will end up as a bad debt is .03. The second row has a similar interpretation for the other nonabsorbing state, which is the one to three month category. Therefore, .86 is the probability that an amount that is one to three months overdue will eventually be paid, and .14 is the probability that an amount that is one to three months overdue will never be paid, but will become a bad debt.

matrix *M*

This matrix can be used in a number of ways. If we know the amount of the less than one month category and the one to three month category, we can determine the amount of money that will be paid and the amount of money that will become bad debts. We let the matrix M represent the amount of money that is in each of the nonabsorbing states as follows:

$$M = (M_1, M_2, M_3, \ldots, M_n)$$

APPLICATIONS OF QA

Using Markov Analysis to Forecast Long-Term Care

Long-term care of elderly patients has become more important and more expensive in the past several years. Programs on television and in-depth articles in newspapers and magazines have described how dramatic increases in life expectancy have been realized. Unfortunately, the quality of life and general health of the aged has not followed suit. Many individuals who are living longer need expensive long-term care.

In order to forecast long-term care in British Columbia, Canada, a Markov model was used. This model investigated changes in traditional modes of health care and analyzed the nature and extent of required services. More than 9,000 clients, members of British Columbia's long-term care (LTC) program, were studied through data collected between 1978 and 1983. The Markov approach was able to trace movement between the following levels of health care treatment:

Source: Health Services Researcher **22** (December 1987): 671–707.

1. Personal care at home or at facility.

2. Intermediate care 1 at home or at facility.

3. Intermediate care 2 at home or at facility.

4. Intermediate care 3 at home or at facility.

5. Extended care at home or at facility.

In addition to these five levels, two absorbing or inactive states were considered—one that represented a patient being discharged and one that represented a dead patient. Aggregated client data were studied.

One of the most important measures of success of health care treatment programs is adequate patient care. A key aspect of long-term health for elderly patients is forecasting health-related needs. A good forecasting procedure can be the heart of long-term planning and effective delivery of needed health care. In British Columbia's LTC program, Markov analysis was used to determine important projections of future health care needs. It is expected that this type of forecasting will provide superior health care at a reasonable cost.

---

where

$$n = \text{number of nonabsorbing states,}$$

$$M_1 = \text{amount in the first state or category,}$$

$$M_2 = \text{amount in the second state or category, and}$$

$$M_n = \text{amount in the } n\text{th state or category.}$$

Assume that there is $2,000 in the less than one month category and $5,000 in the one to three month category. Then M would be represented as follows:

$$M = (2000, 5000)$$

The amount of money that will end up as being paid and the amount that will end up as bad debts can be computed by multiplying the matrix M times the FA matrix that was computed previously. Here are the computations:

determining amount paid and bad debts

Amount paid and amount in bad debts $= MFA$

$$= (2000, 5000) \begin{bmatrix} .97 & .03 \\ .86 & .14 \end{bmatrix}$$

$$= (6240, 760)$$

Thus, out of the total of $7,000 ($2,000 in the less than one month category and $5,000 in the one to three month category), $6,240 will be eventually paid, and $760 will end up as bad debts.

19.8	SOLVING MARKOV ANALYSIS PROBLEMS BY COMPUTER

AB:QM's Markov analysis program allows for a maximum of 200 periods and 20 states. In this chapter, we discussed a problem involving three food stores. The input screen and the computer output for the problem are shown in Program 19.1.

PROGRAM 19.1 Using AB:QM's Markov Analysis Program

```
Markov Analysis

Problem Title :  Market Share
Number of Periods              5
Number of ''From'' States (Row)  3          Number of ''To'' States (Col)  3


            Initial Value    State 1    State 2    State 3
State 1          .4            .8          .1          .1
State 2          .3            .1          .7          .2
State 3          .3            .2          .2          .6


Help   New   Load   Save   Edit   Run   Print   Install   Directory   Esc

***** Program Output *****

<<Transition Matrix for Each Period>>

<Initial Matrix>
--------------------------------------------------
From\To      Value    State 1    State 2    State 3
--------------------------------------------------
State 1      0.40     0.80000    0.10000    0.10000
State 2      0.30     0.10000    0.70000    0.20000
State 3      0.30     0.20000    0.20000    0.60000
--------------------------------------------------


< Period 1 >
--------------------------------------------------
From\To      Value    State 1    State 2    State 3
--------------------------------------------------
State 1      0.41     0.80000    0.10000    0.10000
State 2      0.31     0.10000    0.70000    0.20000
State 3      0.28     0.20000    0.20000    0.60000
--------------------------------------------------
```

(Continued)

PROGRAM 19.1 Using AB:QM's Markov Analysis Program (Continued)

```
< Period 2 >
------------------------------------------------
From\To     Value    State 1    State 2    State 3
------------------------------------------------
State 1     0.41    0.67000    0.17000    0.16000
State 2     0.31    0.19000    0.54000    0.27000
State 3     0.27    0.30000    0.28000    0.42000
------------------------------------------------

< Period 3 >
------------------------------------------------
From\To     Value    State 1    State 2    State 3
------------------------------------------------
State 1     0.42    0.58500    0.21800    0.19700
State 2     0.32    0.26000    0.45100    0.28900
State 3     0.27    0.35200    0.31000    0.33800
------------------------------------------------

< Period 4 >
------------------------------------------------
From\To     Value    State 1    State 2    State 3
------------------------------------------------
State 1     0.42    0.52920    0.25050    0.22030
State 2     0.32    0.31090    0.39950    0.28960
State 3     0.26    0.38020    0.31980    0.30000
------------------------------------------------

<<Transition Matrix for Final Period>>

< Period 5 >
------------------------------------------------
From\To     Value    State 1    State 2    State 3
------------------------------------------------
State 1     0.42    0.49247    0.27233    0.23520
State 2     0.32    0.34659    0.36866    0.28475
State 3     0.26    0.39614    0.32188    0.28198
------------------------------------------------

<<Steady State>>

------------------------------------------------
States          Probability          Value
------------------------------------------------
   1              0.42105             0.42
   2              0.31579             0.32
   3              0.26316             0.26
------------------------------------------------

***** End of Output *****
```

19.9 SUMMARY

With the assumptions discussed in this chapter, it was possible to use Markov analysis to predict future states and to determine equilibrium conditions. We also explored a special case of Markov analysis where there were one or more absorbing states. This involved using the fundamental matrix to determine equilibrium conditions.

In this chapter only three applications of Markov analysis were explored. We investigated Tolsky's machine, the market shares for three grocery stores, and an accounts receivable system. The applications of the method are far reaching, and any dynamic system that meets the model's assumptions can be analyzed by the Markov approach.

GLOSSARY

Markov Analysis. A type of analysis that allows us to predict the future by using the state probabilities and the matrix of transition probabilities.

State Probability. The probability of an event occurring at a point in time. Examples include the probability that a person will be shopping at a given grocery store during a given month.

Vector of State Probabilities. A collection or vector of all state probabilities for a given system or process. The vector of state probabilities could be the initial state or future state.

Market Share. The fraction of the population that shops at a particular store or market. When expressed as a fraction, market shares can be used in place of state probabilities.

Transition Probability. The conditional probability that we will be in a future state given a current or existing state.

Matrix of Transition Probabilities. A matrix containing all transition probabilities for a certain process or system.

Equilibrium Condition. A condition that exists when the state probabilities for a future period are the same as the state probabilities for a previous period.

Absorbing State. A state that, once entered, cannot be left. The probability of going from an absorbing state to any other state is 0.

Fundamental Matrix. A matrix that is the inverse of the I minus B matrix. It is needed to compute equilibrium conditions when absorbing states are involved.

KEY EQUATIONS

(19-1) $\pi(i) = (\pi_1, \pi_2, \pi_3, \ldots, \pi_n)$
The vector of state probabilities for period i.

$$(19\text{-}2) \quad P = \begin{bmatrix} P_{11} & P_{12} & P_{13} & \cdots & P_{1n} \\ P_{21} & P_{22} & P_{23} & \cdots & P_{2n} \\ \cdot & & & & \cdot \\ \cdot & & & & \cdot \\ \cdot & & & & \cdot \\ P_{m1} & P_{m2} & P_{m3} & & P_{mn} \end{bmatrix}$$

The matrix of transition probabilities, that is, the probability of going from one state into another.

$$(19\text{-}3) \quad \pi(2) = \pi(1)P$$

Formula for calculating the state 2 probabilities, given state 1 data.

$$(19\text{-}4) \quad \pi(n + 1) = \pi(n)P$$

Formula for calculating the state probabilities for the period $n + 1$ if we are in period n.

$$(19\text{-}5) \quad \pi = \pi P \text{ at equilibrium}$$

The equilibrium state equation used to derive equilibrium probabilities.

$$(19\text{-}10) \quad P = \begin{bmatrix} I & | & 0 \\ \hline A & | & B \end{bmatrix}$$

The partition of the matrix of transition for absorbing state analysis.

$$(19\text{-}11) \quad F = (I - B)^{-1}$$

The fundamental matrix, used in computing probabilities of ending up in an absorbing state.

SOLVED PROBLEMS

Solved Problem 19-1

George Walls, president of Bradley School, is concerned about declining enrollments. Bradley School is a technical college that specializes in training computer programmers and computer operators. Over the years, there has been a lot of competition among Bradley School, International Technology, and Career Academy. The three schools compete in providing education in the areas of programming, computer operations, and basic secretarial skills.

In order to gain a better understanding of which of these schools is emerging as a leader, George decided to conduct a survey. His survey looked at the number of students who transferred from one school to the other during their academic careers. On the average, Bradley School was able to retain 65% of those students it originally enrolled. Twenty percent of the students originally enrolled transferred to Career Academy and 15% transferred to International Technology. Career Academy had the highest retention rate: 90% of its students remained at Career Academy for their full academic program. George estimated that about half the students who left Career Academy went to Bradley School, while the other half went to

International Technology. International Technology was able to retain 80% of its students, once they enrolled. Ten percent of the originally enrolled students transferred to Career Academy and the other 10% percent enrolled in Bradley School.

Currently, Bradley School has 40% of the market. Career Academy, a much newer school, has 35% of the market. The remaining market share—25%—consists of students attending International Technology. George would like to determine the market share for Bradley for the next year. What are the equilibrium market shares for Bradley School, International Technology, and Career Academy?

Solution

The data for this problem are summarized below:

State 1 initial share = .40—Bradley School

State 2 initial share = .35—Career Academy

State 3 initial share = .25—International Technology

The transition matrix values are:

	TO		
FROM	1 BRADLEY	2 CAREER	3 INTERNATIONAL
1 Bradley	.65	.20	.15
2 Career	.05	.90	.05
3 International	.10	.10	.80

In order for George to determine market share for Bradley School for next year, he has to multiply the current market shares times the matrix of transition probability. Here is the overall structure of these calculations.

$$(.40 \quad .35 \quad .25) \begin{bmatrix} .65 & .20 & .15 \\ .05 & .90 & .05 \\ .10 & .10 & .80 \end{bmatrix}$$

Thus, the market shares for Bradley School, International Technology, and Career Academy can be computed by multiplying the current market shares times the matrix of transition probabilities as shown. The result will be a new matrix with three numbers, each representing the market share for one of the schools. The detailed matrix computations follow:

Market share for Bradley School = $(.40)(.65) + (.35)(.05) + (.25)(.10)$

$= .303$

Market share for Career Academy = $(.40)(.20) + (.35)(.90) + (.25)(.10)$

$= .420$

Market share for International Technology $= (.40)(.15) + (.35)(.05) + (.25)(.80)$

$= .278$

Now George would like to compute the equilibrium market shares for the three schools. At equilibrium conditions, the future market share is equal to the existing or current market share times the matrix of transition probabilities. By letting the variable X represent various market shares for these three schools, it is possible to develop a general relationship that will allow us to compute equilibrium market shares:

Let X_1 = Market share for Bradley School

X_2 = Market share for Career Academy

X_3 = Market share for International Technology

At equilibrium,

$$(X_1, X_2, X_3) = (X_1, \quad X_2, \quad X_3) \begin{bmatrix} .65 & .20 & .15 \\ .05 & .90 & .05 \\ .10 & .10 & .80 \end{bmatrix}$$

The next step is to make the appropriate multiplications on the right-hand side of the equation. Doing this will allow us to obtain three equations with the three unknown X values. In addition, we also know that the sum of the market shares for any particular period must equal 1. Thus, we are able to generate four equations, which are now summarized:

$$X_1 = .65X_1 + .05X_2 + .10X_3$$

$$X_2 = .20X_1 + .90X_2 + .10X_3$$

$$X_3 = .15X_1 + .05X_2 + .80X_3$$

$$1 = X_1 + X_2 + X_3$$

Since we have four equations and only three unknowns, we are able to delete one of the top three equations, which will give us three equations and three unknowns. These equations can then be solved using standard algebraic procedures to obtain the equilibrium market share values for Bradley School, International Technology, and Career Academy. The results of these calculations are shown in the following table:

SCHOOL	MARKET SHARE
X_1 (Bradley)	.158
X_2 (Career)	.579
X_3 (International)	.263

Solved Problem 19-2

Central State University administers computer competency examinations every year. These exams allow students to "test out" of the introductory computer class held at the university. Results of the exams can be placed in one of the following four states:

State 1 = Pass all of the computer exams and be exempt from the course

State 2 = Do not pass all of the computer exams on the third attempt and be required to take the course

State 3 = Fail the computer exams on the first attempt

State 4 = Fail the computer exams on the second attempt

The course coordinator for the exams has noticed the following matrix of transition probabilities:

$$\begin{bmatrix} 1 & 0 & 0 & 0 \\ 0 & 1 & 0 & 0 \\ .8 & 0 & .1 & .1 \\ .2 & .2 & .4 & .2 \end{bmatrix}$$

Currently, there are 200 students who did not pass all of the exams on the first attempt. In addition, there are 50 students who did not pass on the second attempt. In the long run, how many students will be exempted from the course by passing the exams? How many of the 250 students will be required to take the computer course?

Solution

The transition matrix values are summarized below:

FROM	1	2	3	4
		TO		
1	1.00	.00	.00	.00
2	.00	1.00	.00	.00
3	.80	.00	.10	.10
4	.20	.20	.40	.20

The first step in determining how many students will be required to take the course and how many will be exempt from it is to partition the transition matrix into four matrices. These are the I, 0, A, and B matrices:

$$I = \begin{bmatrix} 1 & 0 \\ 0 & 1 \end{bmatrix}$$

$$0 = \begin{bmatrix} 0 & 0 \\ 0 & 0 \end{bmatrix}$$

$$A = \begin{bmatrix} .8 & 0 \\ .2 & .2 \end{bmatrix}$$

$$B = \begin{bmatrix} .1 & .1 \\ .4 & .2 \end{bmatrix}$$

The next step is to compute the fundamental matrix, which is represented by the letter F. This matrix is determined by subtracting the B matrix from the I matrix and taking the inverse of the result:

$$F = (I - B)^{-1}$$

$$F = \begin{bmatrix} 1.176 & 0.147 \\ .588 & 1.324 \end{bmatrix}$$

Now multiply the *F* matrix by the *A* matrix. This step is needed to determine how many students will be exempt from the course and how many will be required to take it. Multiplying the *F* matrix times the *A* matrix is fairly straightforward:

$$FA = \begin{bmatrix} 1.176 & .147 \\ .588 & 1.324 \end{bmatrix} \begin{bmatrix} .8 & 0 \\ .2 & .2 \end{bmatrix}$$

$$FA = \begin{bmatrix} .971 & .029 \\ .735 & .265 \end{bmatrix}$$

The final step is to multiply the results from the *FA* matrix by the M matrix, as shown below:

$$MFA = (200 \quad 50) \begin{bmatrix} .971 & .029 \\ .735 & .265 \end{bmatrix}$$

$$= (231 \quad 19)$$

As you can see, the *MFA* matrix consists of two numbers. The number of students who will be exempt from the course is 231. The number of students who will eventually have to take the course is 19.

DISCUSSION QUESTIONS AND PROBLEMS

Discussion Questions

19-1 List the assumptions that are made in Markov analysis.

19-2 What are the vector of state probabilities and the matrix of transition probabilities and how can they be determined?

19-3 Describe how we can use Markov analysis to make future predictions.

19-4 What is an equilibrium condition? How do we know that we have an equilibrium condition, and how can we compute equilibrium conditions given the matrix of transition probabilities?

19-5 What is an absorbing state? Give several examples of absorbing states.

19-6 What is the fundamental matrix, and how is it used in determining equilibrium conditions?

Problems

19-7 Ray Cahnman is the proud owner of a 1955 sports car. On any given day, Ray never knows whether or not his car will start. Ninety percent of the time it will start if it started the previous morning, and 70% of the time it will not start if it did not start the previous morning.

(a) Construct the matrix of transition probabilities.
(b) What is the probability that it will start tomorrow if it started today?
(c) What is the probability that it will start tomorrow it it did *not* start today?

QA19-7

See Instructor's Section.
.90
.30

QA19-8

.23

.308

.75

💻 · **19-8** Alan Resnik, a friend of Ray Cahnman, bet Ray five dollars that Ray's car would not start five days from now. (See Problem 19-7.)

(a) What is the probability that it will not start five days from now if it started today?

(b) What is the probability that it will not start five days from now if it did not start today?

(c) What is the probability that it will start in the long run if the matrix of transition probabilities does not change?

QA19-9

$^4/_{15}$, $^5/_{15}$, and $^6/_{15}$; 19.52%, 32.52%, and 47.96%

💻 : **19-9** Over any given month, Dress-Rite loses 10% of its customers to Fashion, Inc., and 20% of its market to Luxury Living. But Fashion, Inc., loses 5% of its market to Dress-Rite and 10% of its market to Luxury Living each month; and Luxury Living loses 5% of its market to Fashion, Inc., and 5% of its market to Dress-Rite. At the present time, each of these clothing stores has an equal share of the market. What do you think the market shares will be next month? What will they be in three months?

QA19-10

💻 : **19-10** Goodeating Dog Chow Company produces a variety of brands of dog chow. One of their best values is the 50-pound bag of Goodeating Dog Chow. George Hamilton, president of Goodeating, uses a very old machine to automatically load 50 pounds of Goodeating Chow into each bag. Unfortunately, because the machine is old, it occasionally over or under fills the bags. When the machine is *correctly* placing 50 pounds of dog chow into each bag, there is a .10 probability that the machine will only put 49 pounds in each bag the following day, and there is a .20 probability that 51 pounds will be placed in each bag the next day. If the machine is currently placing 49 pounds of dog chow in each bag, there is a .30 probability that it will put 50 pounds in each bag tomorrow and a .20 probability that it will put 51 pounds in each bag tomorrow. In addition, if the machine is placing 51 pounds in each bag today, there is a .40 probability it will place 50 pounds in each bag tomorrow and a .10 probability it will place 49 pounds in each bag tomorrow.

70%

30%

40%

(a) If the machine is loading 50 pounds in each bag today, what is the probability that it will be placing 50 pounds in each bag tomorrow?

(b) Resolve part **a** when the machine is only placing 49 pounds in each bag today.

(c) Resolve part **a** when the machine is placing 51 pounds in each bag today.

QA19-11

💻 : **19-11** The University of South Wisconsin has had steady enrollments over the past five years. The school has its own bookstore, called University Book Store, but there are also three private bookstores in town: Bill's Book Store, College Book Store, and Battle's Book Store. The university is concerned about the large number of students who are switching to one of the private stores. As a result, South Wisconsin's president, Andy Lange, has decided to give a student three hours of university credit to look into the problem. The following matrix of transition probabilities was obtained.

18.75%, 26.25%, 30%, and 25% for University, Bill's, College, and Battle's

	UNIVERSITY	BILL's	COLLEGE	BATTLE's
University	.6	.2	.1	.1
Bill's	0	.7	.2	.1
College	.1	.1	.8	0
Battle's	.05	.05	.1	.8

At the present time, each of the four book stores has an equal share of the market. What will the market shares be for the next period?

⌐ : **19-12** Resolve Problem 19-10 (Goodeating Dog Chow) for five periods.

⌐ : **19-13** Andy Lange, president of the University of South Wisconsin, is concerned with the declining business at the University Book Store. (See Problem 19-11 for details.) The students tell him that the prices are simply too high. Andy, however, has decided not to lower the prices. If the same conditions exist, what long-run market shares can Andy expect for the four book stores?

⌐ : **19-14** During the day, the traffic on North Monroe Street in Quincy is fairly steady, but the traffic conditions can vary considerably from one hour to the next due to slow drivers and traffic accidents. As one driver said, "The traffic conditions on Monroe can be either fair, tolerable, or miserable." If the traffic conditions are fair in one hour, there is a 20% chance that they will be tolerable in the next hour and a 10% chance that they will be miserable. If the traffic conditions are tolerable, there is a 20% chance that they will be fair in the next hour and a 5% chance that they will be miserable. In addition, if the traffic conditions are miserable, there is a 60% chance that they will remain that way and a 30% chance that they will be fair in the next hour. If the traffic conditions are miserable at this time, what is the probability that they will be fair in two hours? What is the probability that they will be tolerable in two hours?

⌐ : **19-15** Greg Cracker, mayor of Quincy, is alarmed about the traffic conditions on Monroe Street. (See Problem 19-14.) In the long run, what percent of the time will traffic conditions be fair, tolerable, and miserable on Monroe Street?

⌐ : **19-16** The tiger minnow, which can be found in Lake Jackson and in Lake Bradford, is a small meat-eating fish. At the present time, there are 900 tiger minnows in Lake Jackson and 100 tiger minnows in Lake Bradford, but a new 10-foot-wide canal between these two lakes will soon change these numbers. Since tiger minnows eat other fish and themselves, the total population remains about the same. Bob Brite, an Eagle Scout from Troop B, has done nothing but watch the tiger minnows going through the canal. During the past month Bob has observed 90 tiger minnows go from Lake Jackson to Lake Bradford, and he has observed 5 tiger minnows go from Lake Bradford to Lake Jackson. Assuming that these migration patterns will remain the same, how many tiger minnows will be in each lake in the long run?

: **19-17** The residents of Lake Bradford are angry about the canal between Lake Bradford and Lake Jackson. This canal has allowed too many tiger minnows into Lake Bradford, and, as a result, the value of the lake property on Lake Bradford has gone down considerably. One solution would be to place a one-way dam in the canal. This would only reduce the fraction of the tiger minnows migrating from Lake Jackson to Lake Bradford. (See Problem 19-16 for details.) In other words, the dam would have the effect of reducing the probability of a tiger minnow migrating from Lake Jackson to Lake Bradford. What would this probability have to be to restore the original number of tiger minnows in each lake?

QA19-12 55%, 53.98%, 54.75%
QA19-13

12.90%, 25.81%, 41.94%, and 19.35%

QA19-14

41% for fair and 19.5% for tolerable

QA19-15
fair 43.18%, tolerable 40.91%, and 15.9% miserable

QA19-16

333 in Lake Jackson and 667 in Lake Bradford

Probability is .005556.

19-18 In Section 7 of this chapter, we investigated an accounts receivable problem. How would the paid category and the bad debt category change with the following matrix of transition probabilities?

$$P = \begin{bmatrix} 1 & 0 & 0 & 0 \\ 0 & 1 & 0 & 0 \\ .7 & 0 & .2 & .1 \\ .4 & .2 & .2 & .2 \end{bmatrix}$$

$5,645.16 paid and
$1,354.84 bad debt

19-19 Professor Green gives two-month computer programming courses during the summer term. Students must pass a number of exams to pass the course, and each student is given three chances to take the exams. The following states describe the possible situations that could occur.

1. State 1: Pass all of the exams and pass the course.

2. State 2: Do not pass all of the exams by the third attempt and flunk the course.

3. State 3: Fail an exam in the first attempt.

4. State 4: Fail an exam in the second attempt.

After observing several classes, Professor Green was able to obtain the following matrix of transition probabilities:

$$P = \begin{bmatrix} 1 & 0 & 0 & 0 \\ 0 & 1 & 0 & 0 \\ .6 & 0 & .1 & .3 \\ .3 & .3 & .2 & .2 \end{bmatrix}$$

At the present time there are 50 students who did not pass all exams on the first attempt, and there are 30 students who did not pass all remaining exams on the second attempt. How many students in these two groups will pass the course and how many will fail the course?

61 will pass and 19 will fail.

19-20 Hicourt Industries is a commercial printing outfit in a medium-sized town in Central Florida. Its only competitors are the Printing House and Gandy Printers. Last month, Hicourt Industries had approximately 30% of the market for the printing business in the area. The Printing House had 50% of the market, and Gandy Printers had 20% of the market. The association of printers, a locally run association, had recently determined how these three printers and smaller printing operations not involved in the commercial market were able to retain their customer base. Hicourt was the most successful in keeping its customers. Eighty percent of its customers for any one month remained customers for the next month. The Printing House, on the other hand, had only a 70% retention rate. Gandy Printers was in the worst condition. Only 60% of the customers for any one month remained with the firm. In one month, the market share had significantly changed. This was very exciting to George Hicourt, president of Hicourt Industries. This month Hicourt Industries was able to obtain a 38% market share. The Printing House, on the other hand, lost market share. This month, it only had 42% of the market share. Gandy Printers remained the same; it kept its 20% of the market. Just looking at market share, George concluded that he was able to take 8% per month away from the Printing House. George estimated that in a few short months, he could basically run the Printing House out of business. His hope was to capture 80% of the total market, representing his original 30% along with the 50% share that the Printing House started off with. Will George be able to reach his goal? What market share can George expect next month? What do you think the long-term market shares will be for these three commercial printing operations? Will Hicourt Industries be able to completely run the Printing House out of business?

No. Printing House will have 30%, Hicourt will have 50% of the market.

19-21 John Jones of Bayside Laundry has been providing cleaning and linen service for rental condominiums on the gulf coast for over 10 years. Currently, John is servicing 26 condominium developments. John's two major competitors are Cleanco, which currently services 15 condominium developments, and Beach Services, which performs laundry and cleaning services for 11 condominium developments.

Recently, John contacted Bay Bank about a loan to expand his business operations. In order to justify the loan, John has kept detailed records of his customers and the customers that he received from his two major competitors. During the last year, he was able to keep 18 of his original 26 customers. During the same period, he was able to get 1 new customer from Cleanco and 2 new customers from Beach Services. Unfortunately, John lost 6 of his original customers to Cleanco and 2 of his original customers to Beach Services during the same year. John has also learned that Cleanco has kept 80% of its current customers. He also knows that Beach Services will keep at least 50% of its customers. In order for John to get the loan from Bay Bank, he needs to show the loan officer that he will maintain an adequate share of the market. The officers of Bay Bank are concerned about the recent trends for market share, and they have decided not to give John a loan unless he will keep at least 35% of the market share in the long run. What types of equilibrium market shares can John expect? If you were an officer of Bay Bank, would you give John a loan?

No. John will not be able to retain 35% or more of the market.

Data Set Problems

19-22 Sandy Sprunger is part-owner in one of the largest quick oil change operations for a medium-sized city in the Midwest. Currently, the firm has 60% of the market. There are a total of 10 quick lubrication shops in the area. After performing some basic marketing research, Sandy has been able to capture the initial probabilities, or market shares, along with the matrix of transition, which represents probabilities that customers will switch from one quick lubrication shop to another. These values are shown in the following table:

QA19-22

See Instructor's Section.

FROM	1	2	3	4	5	6	7	8	9	10
1	.60	.10	.10	.10	.05	.01	.01	.01	.01	.01
2	.01	.80	.01	.01	.01	.10	.01	.01	.01	.03
3	.01	.01	.70	.01	.01	.10	.01	.05	.05	.05
4	.01	.01	.01	.90	.01	.01	.01	.01	.01	.02
5	.01	.01	.01	.10	.80	.01	.03	.01	.01	.01
6	.01	.01	.01	.01	.01	.91	.01	.01	.01	.01
7	.01	.01	.01	.01	.01	.10	.70	.01	.10	.04
8	.01	.01	.01	.01	.01	.10	.03	.80	.01	.01
9	.01	.01	.01	.01	.01	.10	.01	.10	.70	.04
10	.01	.01	.01	.01	.01	.10	.10	.05	.00	.70

(TO) — column headers 1–10 span under "TO"

Initial probabilities, or market share, for shops 1 through 10 are .6, .1, .1, .1, .05, .01, .01, .01, .01 and .01.

(a) Given these data, determine market shares for the next period for each of the 10 shops.

(b) What are the equilibrium market shares?

(c) Sandy believes that the original estimates for market shares were wrong. She believes that shop 1 has 40% of the market, while shop 2 has 30%. All other values are the same. If this is the case, what is the impact on market shares for next-period and equilibrium shares?

(d) A marketing consultant believes that shop 1 has tremendous appeal. She believes that this shop will retain 99% of its current market share; 1% may switch to shop 2. If the consultant is correct, will shop 1 have 90% of the market in the long run?

QA19-23

19-23 During a recent trip to her favorite restaurant, Sandy (Owner of Shop 1) met Chris Talley (Owner of Shop 7). (See Problem 19-22.) After an enjoyable lunch, Sandy and Chris had a heated discussion about market share for the quick oil change operations in their city. Here is their conversation:

Sandy: My operation is so superior that after someone changes oil at one of my shops, they will never do business with anyone else. On second thought, maybe 1 person out of 100 will try your shop after visiting one of my shops. In a month, I will have 99% of the market and you will have 1% of the market.

Chris: You have it completely reversed. In a month, I will have 99% of the market and you will only have 1% of the market. In fact, I will treat you to a meal at a restaurant of your choice if you are right. If I am right, you will treat me to one of those big steaks at David's Steak House. Do we have a deal?

Sandy: Yes! Get your checkbook or your credit card. You will have the privilege of paying for two very expensive meals at Anthony's Seafood Restaurant.

See Instructor's Section.

(a) Assume Sandy is correct about customers visiting one of her quick oil change shops. Will she win the bet with Chris?

See Instructor's Section.

(b) Assume Chris is correct about customers visiting one of his quick oil change shops. Will he win the bet?

See Instructor's Section.

(c) Describe what would happen if both Sandy and Chris are correct about customers visiting their quick oil change operations.

Rentall Trucks

Jim Fox, an executive for Rentall Trucks, could not believe it. He had hired one of the town's best law firms, Folley, Smith, and Christensen. Their fee for drawing up the legal contracts was over $50,000. Folley, Smith, and Christensen had made one important omission from the contracts, and this blunder would more than likely cost Rentall Trucks millions of dollars. For the hundredth time, Jim carefully reconstructed the situation and pondered the inevitable.

Rentall Trucks was started by Robert (Bob) Renton over ten years ago. It specialized in renting trucks to businesses and private individuals. The company prospered, and Bob increased his net worth by millions of dollars. Bob was a legend in the rental business and was known all over the world for his keen business abilities.

Only a year and a half ago some of the executives of Rentall and some additional outside investors offered to buy Rentall from Bob. Bob was close to retirement, and the offer was unbelievable. His children and their children would be able to live in high style off the proceeds of the sale. Folley, Smith, and Christensen developed the contracts for the executives of Rentall and other investors, and the sale was made.

Being a perfectionist, it was only a matter of time until Bob was marching down to the Rentall headquarters, telling everyone the mistakes that Rentall was making and how to solve some of their problems. Pete Rosen, president of Rentall, became extremely angry about Bob's constant interference, and in a brief ten-minute meeting, Pete told Bob never to enter the Rentall offices again. It was at this time that Bob decided to reread the contracts, and it was also at this time that Bob and his lawyer discovered that there was no clause in the contracts that prevented Bob from competing directly with Rentall.

The brief ten-minute meeting with Pete Rosen was the beginning of Rentran. In less than six months, Bob Renton had lured some of the key executives away from Rentall and into his new business, Rentran, which would compete directly with Rentall Trucks in every way. After a few months of operation, Bob estimated that Rentran had about 5 percent of the total national market for truck rentals. Rentall had about 80 percent of the market, and another company, National Rentals, had the remaining 15 percent of the market.

Rentall's Jim Fox was in total shock. In a few months, Rentran had already captured 5 percent of the total market. At this rate, Rentran might completely dominate the market in a few short years. Pete Rosen even wondered if Rentall could maintain 50 percent of the market in the long run. As a result of these concerns, Pete hired a marketing research firm that analyzed a random sample of truck rental customers. The sample consisted of 1,000 existing or potential customers. The marketing research firm was very careful to make sure that the sample represented the true market conditions. The sample, taken in August, consisted of 800 customers of Rentall, 60 customers of Rentran, and the remainder National customers. The same sample was then analyzed the next month concerning the customers' propensity to switch companies. Of the original Rentall customers, 200 switched to Rentran, and 80 switched to National. Rentran was able to retain 51 of their original customers. Three customers switched to Rentall, and 6 customers switched to National. Finally, 14 customers switched from National to Rentall, and 35 customers switched from National to Rentran.

The board of directors meeting was only two weeks away, and there would be some difficult questions to answer—what happened and what can be done about Rentran? In Jim Fox's opinion, nothing could be done about the costly omission made by Folley, Smith, and Christensen. The only solution was to take immediate corrective action that would curb Rentran's ability to lure customers away from Rentall.

After a careful analysis of Rentran, Rentall, and the truck rental business in general, Jim concluded that immediate changes would be needed in three areas: rental policy, advertising, and product line. Regarding rental policy, a number of changes were needed to make truck rental both easier and faster. Rentall could implement many of the techniques used by Hertz and other car rental agencies. In addition, changes in the product line were needed. Rentall's smaller trucks had to be more comfortable and easier to drive. Automatic transmission, comfortable bucket seats, air conditioners, quality radio and tape stereo systems, and cruise control should be included. Although expensive and difficult to maintain, these items could make a significant difference in market shares. Finally, Jim knew that additional advertising was needed.

The advertising had to be immediate and aggressive. Television and journal advertising had to be increased, and a good advertising company was needed. If these new changes were implemented now, there would be a good chance that Rentall would be able to maintain close to its 80 percent of the market. In order to confirm Jim's perceptions, the same marketing research firm was employed to analyze the effect of these changes, using the same sample of 1,000 customers.

The marketing research firm, Meyers Marketing Research, Inc., performed a pilot test on the sample of 1,000 customers. The results of the analysis revealed that Rentall would only lose 100 of its original customers to Rentran and 20 to National if the new policies were implemented. In addition, Rentall would pick up customers from both Rentran and National. It was estimated that Rentall would now get 9 customers from Rentran and 28 customers from National.

Discussion Questions

1. What will the market shares be in one month if these changes are made? If no changes are made?

2. What will the market shares be in three months with the changes?

3. If market conditions remain the same, what market share would Rentall have in the long run? How does this compare with the market share that would result if the changes were not made?

1. (.718, .175, .107) with changes; (.54, .28, .18) no changes. 2. (.615, .292, .093) with changes; 3. 52% with changes vs. 15% without.

BIBLIOGRAPHY

Butt, Abbas A., Mohamed Y. Shahin, Kieran J. Feighan, and R. Blumenthal. *Markov Process and Potential Theory.* New York: Academic Press, Inc., 1968.

Carpenter, Samuel H. "Pavement Performance Prediction Model Using the Markov Process." *Transportation Research Record* **1123** (November 1986): 12–19.

Derman, C. *Finite State Markov Decision Process.* New York: Academic Press, Inc., 1970.

Freedman, D. *Markov Chains.* San Francisco: Holden-Day, Inc., 1971.

Hipp, S. K., and U. D. Holzbaur. "Decision Processes with Monotone Hysteretic Policies." *Operations Research* **36** (July–Aug. 1988): 585–588.

Lal, R., and U. N. Bhat. "Reduced Systems Algorithms for Markov Chain." *Management Science* **34** (October 1988): 1202–1220.

Martin, J. *Bayesian Decision Problems and Markov Chains.* New York: John Wiley & Sons, Inc., 1967.

Render, B., R. M. Stair, and Irwin Greenberg. *Cases and Readings in Quantitative Analysis,* Second Edition. Boston: Allyn and Bacon, Inc., 1990.

Szpankowski, W. "Stability Conditions for Multidimensional Queueing Systems with Computer Applications." *Operations Research* **36** (November–December 1988): 944–957.

White, Douglas John. "Real Applications to Markov Decision Processes." *Interfaces* **15** (November–December 1985): 73–83.

Wort, Donald H., and J. Kenton Zumwalt. "The Trade Discount Decision: A Markov Chain Approach." *Decision Sciences* **16,** 1 (Winter 1985): 43–56.

Appendix: Using Spreadsheets to Solve Markov Analysis Problems

Spreadsheets can be used to perform Markov analysis, including absorbing state problems.

Markov Analysis

Given the matrix of transition and the initial state conditions, it is possible to determine the equilibrium conditions and market shares for future periods. In the Tolsky Works example, equilibrium conditions were determined and state probabilities for 15 periods were computed. (See Table 19.1.) Program 19.2 shows how these calculations can be made using a spreadsheet. The data for the matrix of transition are entered in cells B3 through D4. The initial conditions are entered in D3 and D4 as 1 and 0, as discussed in the chapter. The formulas for the equilibrium shares are in cells A9 and B9. Note that cell B9 is 1-A9. Once we know the probability for State 1, we can subtract this value from 1 to get the probability for State 2. State probabilities for 15 periods are computed in columns D and E. Note that row values for column E are equal to 1 minus the values in column D. As with other spreadsheets, a graph can be constructed to plot how the state probabilities change over the 15 periods.

PROGRAM 19.2 Equilibrium Conditions and State Probabilities for 15 Periods

	A	B	C	D	E
1	Input Data:	Matrix of Transition			Initial Condition
2		State 1	State 2		
3	State 1	0.8	0.2	1	State 1
4	State 2	0.1	0.9	0	State 2
5	Output Results		Period	State 1	State 2
6			1	+D3	+D4
7	Equilibrium		2	+D6*$B$3+E6*$B$4	1-D7
8	State 1	State 2	3	+D7*$B$3+E7*$B$4	1-D8
9	+B4/(1-B3+B4)	1-A9	4	+D8*$B$3+E8*$B$4	1-D9
10			5	+D9*$B$3+E9*$B$4	1-D10
11			6	+D10*$B$3+E10*$B$4	1-D11
12			7	+D11*$B$3+E11*$B$4	1-D12
13			8	+D12*$B$3+E12*$B$4	1-D13
14			9	+D13*$B$3+E13*$B$4	1-D14
15			10	+D14*$B$3+E14*$B$4	1-D15
16			11	+D15*$B$3+E15*$B$4	1-D16
17			12	+D16*$B$3+E16*$B$4	1-D17
18			13	+D17*$B$3+E17*$B$4	1-D18
19			14	+D18*$B$3+E18*$B$4	1-D19
20			15	+D19*$B$3+E19*$B$4	1-D20

Absorbing State Analysis

This chapter covers how absorbing state analysis can be used to determine the amount of paid bills and bad debt over time for the accounts receivables example. Program 19.3 is a spreadsheet that performs the necessary calculations. The matrix of transition is entered in cells B5 through E8. The initial M matrix values of 2,000 and 5,000 are entered in cells F5 and F6 (Note: These cells are not displayed in Program 19.3). The output results appear from row 10 to row 19. The I-B matrix is computed in cells A13 through B14 as was done in the chapter. In order to compute the F matrix, we have to get the inverse of the (I-B) matrix. This is done by using the inverse command in Lotus. We start by typing /D for the data command. Then we type *M* for matrix operations and *I* for inverse. Now we must enter an input range, which is the location of the (I-B) matrix. Thus, we enter cells A13..B14. Next, Lotus asks us to enter the output range, which is where the new inverse matrix will appear. This must be an empty area on the spreadsheet. We enter cells C13..D14. Once this is done, Lotus computes the inverse and puts the values in cells C13 through D14. Next, the spreadsheet computes the FA matrix. This is done in cells A17 through B18. The formulas in these cells are straightforward matrix multiplication formulas. Finally, the spreadsheet multiplies M times FA. This is done in cells D17 and D19. These cells correspond to the amount of the loan that will be paid and the amount that will end up as bad debt.

PROGRAM 19.3 Absorbing State Analysis

```
            A                 B               C              D             E
 1  Absorbing State Analysis
 2
 3  Input Data:  Matrix of Transition
 4                            State 1    State 2       State 3        State 4
 5           State 1             1          0             0              0
 6           State 2             0          1             0              0
 7           State 3            0.6         0            0.2            0.2
 8           State 4            0.4        0.1           0.3            0.2
 9
10   Output Results                      F = (I-B) Inverse
11                                       To Get the Inverse, Do the Following
12            (I-B)                      Type /DMI and press the return key twice
13  1-D7              0-E7               1.37931034    0.3448275862
14  0-D8              1-E8               0.51724137    1.3793103448
15
16              FA                                              MFA
17  +C13*B7+D13*B8    +C13*C7+D13*C8          +F5*A17+F6*A18
18  +C14*B7+D14*B8    +C14*C7+D14*C8
19                                                +F5*B17+F6*B18
20
```

Mathematical Tools: Determinants and Matrices

MODULE OUTLINE

A.1 Introduction

A.2 Determinants

A.3 Matrices

A.4 Summary

Glossary

Problems

Bibliography

A.1 INTRODUCTION

Two new mathematical concepts, determinants and matrices, are introduced in this module. These tools are especially useful in Chapter 19 and Module B, which deal with Markov analysis and game theory, but they are also handy computational aids for many other quantitative analysis problems, including linear programming, the topic of Chapters 10, 11, 12, and 13.

A.2 DETERMINANTS

A *determinant* is simply a square array of numbers arranged in rows and columns. Every determinant has a unique numerical value for which we can solve. As a mathematical tool, determinants are of value in helping to solve a series of simultaneous equations.

A 2-row by 2-column (2×2) determinant will have the following form, where a, b, c, and d are numbers.

$$\begin{vmatrix} a & b \\ c & d \end{vmatrix}$$

Similarly, a 3×3 determinant has 9 entries.

$$\begin{vmatrix} a & b & c \\ d & e & f \\ g & h & i \end{vmatrix}$$

One common procedure for finding the numerical value of a 2×2 or 3×3 determinant is to draw its primary and secondary diagonals. In the case of a 2×2 determinant, the value is found by multiplying the numbers on the primary diagonal and subtracting from that product the product of the numbers on the secondary diagonal:

$$\text{Value} = (a)(d) - (c)(b)$$

Primary diagonal → $\begin{vmatrix} a & b \\ c & d \end{vmatrix}$ ← *Secondary diagonal*

For a 3×3 determinant, we redraw the first two columns to help visualize all diagonals and follow a similar procedure.

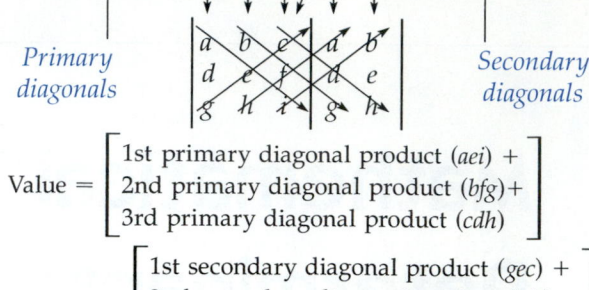

Primary diagonals   *Secondary diagonals*

$$\text{Value} = \begin{bmatrix} \text{1st primary diagonal product } (aei) + \\ \text{2nd primary diagonal product } (bfg) + \\ \text{3rd primary diagonal product } (cdh) \end{bmatrix}$$
$$- \begin{bmatrix} \text{1st secondary diagonal product } (gec) + \\ \text{2nd secondary diagonal product } (hfa) + \\ \text{3rd secondary diagonal product } (idb) \end{bmatrix}$$
$$= aei + bfg + cdh - gec - hfa - idb$$

Let's use this approach to find the numerical values of the following 2×2 and 3×3 determinants:

(a) $\begin{vmatrix} 2 & 5 \\ 1 & 8 \end{vmatrix}$ (b) $\begin{vmatrix} 3 & 1 & 2 \\ 2 & 5 & 1 \\ 4 & -2 & -1 \end{vmatrix}$

(a) $\begin{vmatrix} 2 & 5 \\ 1 & 8 \end{vmatrix}$ Value $= (2)(8) - (1)(5) = 11$

(b) $\begin{vmatrix} 3 & 1 & 2 & 3 & 1 \\ 2 & 5 & 1 & 2 & 5 \\ 4 & -2 & -1 & 4 & -2 \end{vmatrix}$

$$\text{Value} = (3)(5)(-1) + (1)(1)(4) + (2)(2)(-2)$$
$$- (4)(5)(2) - (-2)(1)(3) - (-1)(2)(1)$$
$$= -15 + 4 - 8 - 40 + 6 + 2 = -51$$

A set of *simultaneous equations* may be solved through the use of determinants by setting up a ratio of two special determinants for each unknown variable. This fairly easy procedure is best illustrated with an example.

Given the three simultaneous equations

$$2X + 3Y + 1Z = 10$$
$$4X - 1Y - 2Z = 8$$
$$5X + 2Y - 3Z = 6$$

we may structure determinants to help solve for unknown quantities X, Y, and Z.

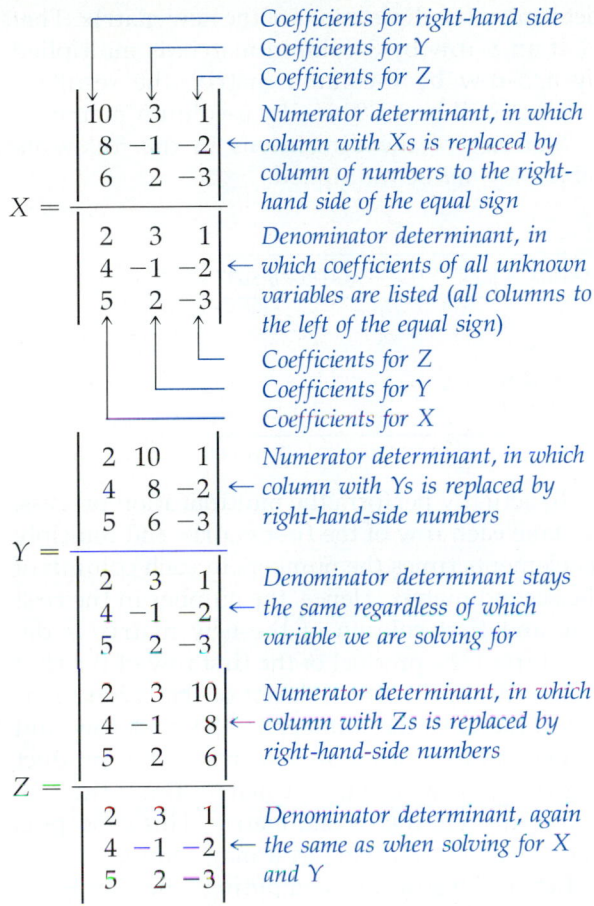

$$X = \cfrac{\begin{vmatrix} 10 & 3 & 1 \\ 8 & -1 & -2 \\ 6 & 2 & -3 \end{vmatrix}}{\begin{vmatrix} 2 & 3 & 1 \\ 4 & -1 & -2 \\ 5 & 2 & -3 \end{vmatrix}}$$

Coefficients for right-hand side
Coefficients for Y
Coefficients for Z

← *Numerator determinant, in which column with Xs is replaced by column of numbers to the right-hand side of the equal sign*

← *Denominator determinant, in which coefficients of all unknown variables are listed (all columns to the left of the equal sign)*

Coefficients for Z
Coefficients for Y
Coefficients for X

$$Y = \cfrac{\begin{vmatrix} 2 & 10 & 1 \\ 4 & 8 & -2 \\ 5 & 6 & -3 \end{vmatrix}}{\begin{vmatrix} 2 & 3 & 1 \\ 4 & -1 & -2 \\ 5 & 2 & -3 \end{vmatrix}}$$

← *Numerator determinant, in which column with Ys is replaced by right-hand-side numbers*

← *Denominator determinant stays the same regardless of which variable we are solving for*

$$Z = \cfrac{\begin{vmatrix} 2 & 3 & 10 \\ 4 & -1 & 8 \\ 5 & 2 & 6 \end{vmatrix}}{\begin{vmatrix} 2 & 3 & 1 \\ 4 & -1 & -2 \\ 5 & 2 & -3 \end{vmatrix}}$$

← *Numerator determinant, in which column with Zs is replaced by right-hand-side numbers*

← *Denominator determinant, again the same as when solving for X and Y*

Determining the values of X, Y, and Z now involves finding the numerical values of the four separate determinants using the method shown earlier in this module.

$$X = \frac{\text{Numerical value of numerator determinant}}{\text{Numerical value of denominator determinant}}$$

$$= \frac{128}{33} = 3.88$$

$$Y = \frac{-20}{33} = -.61$$

$$Z = \frac{134}{33} = 4.06$$

To verify that $X = 3.88$, $Y = -.61$, and $Z = 4.06$, we may choose any one of the original three simultaneous equations and insert these numbers. For example,

$$2X + 3Y + 1Z = 10$$

$$2(3.88) + 3(-.61) + 1(4.06) = 7.76 -$$
$$1.83 + 4.06 = 10$$

A.3 MATRICES

A *matrix*, like a determinant, can also be defined as an array of numbers arranged in rows and columns. Matrices, which are usually enclosed in parentheses or brackets, have no numerical value as do determinants, but are used as an effective means of presenting or summarizing business data.

The following 2-row by 3-column (2×3) matrix, for example, might be used by television station executives to describe the channel switching behavior of their 5 o'clock TV news audience.

The number in the first row and first column indicates that there is a .80 probability that someone currently watching the Channel 6 news will continue to do so next month. Likewise, 15% of Channel 6's viewers are expected to switch to Channel 8 next month (row 1, column 2), 5% will not be watching the 5 o'clock news at all (row 1, column 3), and so on for the second row.

The remainder of this module deals with the numerous mathematical operations that can be performed on matrices. These include matrix addition, subtraction and multiplication, transposing a matrix, finding its cofactors and adjoint, and matrix inversion.

AUDIENCE SWITCHING PROBABILITIES, NEXT MONTH'S ACTIVITY			
CURRENT STATION	CHANNEL 6	CHANNEL 8	STOP VIEWING
Channel 6	.80	.15	.05
Channel 8	.20	.70	.10

2 × 3 matrix

Matrix Addition and Subtraction

Matrix addition and *subtraction* are the easiest operations. Matrices of the same dimensions, that is, the same number of rows and columns, can be added or subtracted by adding or subtracting the numbers in the same row and column of each matrix. Here are two small matrices:

$$\text{matrix } A = \begin{pmatrix} 5 & 7 \\ 2 & 1 \end{pmatrix}$$

$$\text{matrix } B = \begin{pmatrix} 3 & 6 \\ 3 & 8 \end{pmatrix}$$

To find the sum of these 2×2 matrices, we add corresponding elements to create a new matrix.

matrix C = matrix A + matrix B

$$= \begin{pmatrix} 5 & 7 \\ 2 & 1 \end{pmatrix} + \begin{pmatrix} 3 & 6 \\ 3 & 8 \end{pmatrix} = \begin{pmatrix} 8 & 13 \\ 5 & 9 \end{pmatrix}$$

To subtract matrix B from matrix A, we simply subtract the corresponding elements in each position.

matrix C = matrix A − matrix B

$$= \begin{pmatrix} 5 & 7 \\ 2 & 1 \end{pmatrix} - \begin{pmatrix} 3 & 6 \\ 3 & 8 \end{pmatrix} = \begin{pmatrix} 2 & 1 \\ -1 & -7 \end{pmatrix}$$

Matrix Multiplication

Matrix multiplication is an operation that may take place *only* if the number of columns in the first matrix equals the number of rows in the second matrix. Thus, matrices of the dimensions in the table below may be multiplied.

MATRIX A SIZE	MATRIX B SIZE	SIZE OF A × B RESULTING
3 × 3	3 × 3	3 × 3
3 × 1	1 × 3	3 × 3
3 × 1	1 × 1	3 × 1
2 × 4	4 × 3	2 × 3
6 × 9	9 × 2	6 × 2
8 × 3	3 × 6	8 × 6

We also note, in the far right column in the table, that the outer two numbers in the matrix sizes determine the dimensions of the new matrix. That is, if an 8-row by 3-column matrix is multiplied by a 3-row by 6-column matrix, the resultant product will be an 8-row by 6-column matrix.

Matrices of the dimensions in the following table may *not* be multiplied.

MATRIX A SIZE	MATRIX B SIZE
3 × 4	3 × 3
1 × 2	1 × 2
6 × 9	8 × 9
2 × 2	3 × 3

To actually perform the multiplication process, we take each row of the first matrix and multiply its elements times the numbers in each column of the second matrix. Hence, the number in the first row and first column of the new matrix is derived from the product of the first row of the first matrix times the first column of the second matrix. Likewise, the number in the first row and second column of the new matrix is the product of the first row of the first matrix times the second column of the second matrix. This concept is not nearly as confusing as it may sound.

Let us begin by computing the value of matrix C, which is the product of matrix A times matrix B.

$$\text{matrix } A = \begin{pmatrix} 5 \\ 2 \\ 3 \end{pmatrix} \qquad \text{matrix } B = (4 \quad 6)$$

This is a legitimate task since matrix A is 3×1 and matrix B is 1×2. The product, matrix C, will have 3 rows and 2 columns (3×2).

Symbolically, the operation is matrix $A \times$ matrix B = matrix C

$$\begin{pmatrix} a \\ b \\ c \end{pmatrix} \times (d \quad e) = \begin{pmatrix} ad & ae \\ bd & be \\ cd & ce \end{pmatrix} \tag{A-1}$$

Using the actual numbers, we have

$$\begin{pmatrix} 5 \\ 2 \\ 3 \end{pmatrix} \times (4 \quad 6) = \begin{pmatrix} 20 & 30 \\ 8 & 12 \\ 12 & 18 \end{pmatrix} = \text{matrix } C$$

As a second example, let matrix R be (6 2 5) and matrix S be

$$\begin{pmatrix} 3 \\ 1 \\ 2 \end{pmatrix}$$

Then the product, matrix T = matrix R × matrix S, will be of dimension 1×1 since we are multiplying a 1×3 matrix by a 3×1 matrix.

matrix R × matrix S = matrix T
(1 × 3)   (3 × 1)   (1 × 1)

$$(a \quad b \quad c) \times \begin{pmatrix} d \\ e \\ f \end{pmatrix} = (ad + be + cf)$$

$$(6 \quad 2 \quad 5) \times \begin{pmatrix} 3 \\ 1 \\ 2 \end{pmatrix} = \begin{array}{l} ((6)(3) + (2)(1) + (5)(2)) \\ = (30) \end{array}$$

To multiply any larger-sized matrices, we combine the approaches of the preceding examples.

$$\text{matrix } U = \begin{pmatrix} 6 & 2 \\ 7 & 1 \end{pmatrix} \quad \text{matrix } V = \begin{pmatrix} 3 & 4 \\ 5 & 8 \end{pmatrix}$$

matrix U × matrix V =   matrix Y

(2 × 2) × (2 × 2)   (2 × 2)   **(A-2)**

$$\begin{pmatrix} a & b \\ c & d \end{pmatrix} \times \begin{pmatrix} e & f \\ g & h \end{pmatrix} = \begin{pmatrix} ae + bg & af + bh \\ ce + dg & cf + dh \end{pmatrix}$$

$$\begin{pmatrix} 6 & 2 \\ 7 & 1 \end{pmatrix} \times \begin{pmatrix} 3 & 4 \\ 5 & 8 \end{pmatrix} = \begin{pmatrix} 18 + 10 & 24 + 16 \\ 21 + 5 & 28 + 8 \end{pmatrix}$$

$$= \begin{pmatrix} 28 & 40 \\ 26 & 36 \end{pmatrix}$$

To introduce a special type of matrix, called the *identity matrix*, let's try a final multiplication example.

$$\text{matrix } H = \begin{pmatrix} 4 & 7 \\ 2 & 3 \end{pmatrix} \quad \text{matrix } I = \begin{pmatrix} 1 & 0 \\ 0 & 1 \end{pmatrix}$$

matrix H × matrix I =   matrix J

$$\begin{pmatrix} 4 & 7 \\ 2 & 3 \end{pmatrix} \times \begin{pmatrix} 1 & 0 \\ 0 & 1 \end{pmatrix} = \begin{pmatrix} 4 + 0 & 0 + 7 \\ 2 + 0 & 0 + 3 \end{pmatrix}$$

$$= \begin{pmatrix} 4 & 7 \\ 2 & 3 \end{pmatrix}$$

Matrix I is called an identity matrix. An identity matrix has 1s on its diagonal and 0s in all other positions. When multiplied by any matrix of the same square dimensions, it yields the original matrix. So in this case, matrix J = matrix H.

Matrix multiplication can also be useful in performing business computations.

Blank Plumbing and Heating is about to bid on three contract jobs—to install plumbing fixtures in a new university dormitory, an office building, and an apartment complex.

The number of toilets, sinks, and bathtubs needed at each project is summarized in matrix notation as follows. The cost per plumbing fixture is also given. Matrix multiplication may be used to provide an estimate of total cost of fixtures at each job.

PROJECT	DEMAND			COST/UNIT	
	Toilets	Sinks	Bathtubs		
Dormitory	5	10	2	Toilet	$40
Office	20	20	0	Sink	$25
Apartments	15	30	15	Bathtub	$50

Job demand matrix × Fixture cost matrix =   Job cost matrix

(3 × 3)   (3 × 1)   (3 × 1)

$$\begin{pmatrix} 5 & 10 & 2 \\ 20 & 20 & 0 \\ 15 & 30 & 15 \end{pmatrix} \times \begin{pmatrix} \$40 \\ \$25 \\ \$50 \end{pmatrix} = \begin{pmatrix} \$200 + 250 + 100 \\ \$800 + 500 + 0 \\ \$600 + 750 + 750 \end{pmatrix} = \begin{pmatrix} \$\ 550 \\ \$1,300 \\ \$2,100 \end{pmatrix}$$

Hence, Blank Plumbing can expect to spend $550 on fixtures at the dormitory project, $1,300 at the office building, and $2,100 at the apartment complex.

Matrix Transpose

The *transpose* of a matrix is a means of presenting data in different form. To create the transpose of a given matrix, we simply interchange the rows with the columns. Hence, the first row of a matrix becomes its first column, the second row becomes the second column, and so on.

Two matrices are transposed here:

$$\text{matrix } A = \begin{pmatrix} 5 & 2 & 6 \\ 3 & 0 & 9 \\ 1 & 4 & 8 \end{pmatrix}$$

$$\text{Transpose of matrix } A = \begin{pmatrix} 5 & 3 & 1 \\ 2 & 0 & 4 \\ 6 & 9 & 8 \end{pmatrix}$$

$$\text{matrix } B = \begin{pmatrix} 2 & 7 & 0 & 3 \\ 8 & 5 & 6 & 4 \end{pmatrix}$$

$$\text{Transpose of matrix } B = \begin{vmatrix} 2 & 8 \\ 7 & 5 \\ 0 & 6 \\ 3 & 4 \end{vmatrix}$$

Matrix of Cofactors and Adjoint

Two more useful concepts in the mathematics of matrices are the *matrix of cofactors* and the *adjoint* of a matrix. A *cofactor* is defined as the set of numbers that remains after a given row and column have been taken out of a matrix. An *adjoint* is simply the transpose of the matrix of cofactors. The real value of the two concepts lies in their usefulness in forming the inverse of a matrix—something that we investigate in the next section.

In order to compute the matrix of cofactors for a particular matrix, we proceed as follows.

1. Select an element in the original matrix.

2. Draw a line through the row and column of the element selected. The numbers uncovered represent the cofactor for that element.

3. Calculate the value of the determinant of the cofactor.

4. Add together the location numbers of the row and column crossed out in step 2. If the sum is even, the sign of the determinant's value (from step 3) does not change. If the sum is an odd number, change the sign of the determinant's value.

5. The number just computed becomes an entry in the matrix of cofactors; it is located in the same position as the element selected in step 1.

6. Return to step 1 and continue until all elements in the original matrix have been replaced by their cofactor values.

Let's compute the matrix of cofactors, and then the adjoint, for the following matrix.

$$\begin{pmatrix} 3 & 7 & 5 \\ 2 & 0 & 3 \\ 4 & 1 & 8 \end{pmatrix}$$

$$\text{Matrix of cofactors} = \begin{pmatrix} -3 & -4 & 2 \\ -51 & 4 & 25 \\ 21 & 1 & -14 \end{pmatrix}$$

$$\text{Adjoint of the matrix} = \begin{pmatrix} -3 & -51 & 21 \\ -4 & 4 & 1 \\ 2 & 25 & -14 \end{pmatrix}$$

(from Table A.1)

Finding the Inverse of a Matrix

The *inverse* of a matrix is a unique matrix of the same dimensions which, when multiplied by the original matrix, produces a *unit* or *identity* matrix. For example, if A is any 2×2 matrix, and its inverse is denoted A^{-1}, then

$$A \times A^{-1} = \begin{pmatrix} 1 & 0 \\ 0 & 1 \end{pmatrix} = \text{Identity matrix} \qquad \textbf{(A-3)}$$

The adjoint of a matrix is extremely helpful in forming the inverse of the original matrix. We simply compute the value of the determinant of the original matrix and divide each term of the adjoint by this value.

To find the inverse of the matrix just presented, we need to know the adjoint (already computed) and the value of the determinant of the original matrix.

TABLE A.1 Matrix of Cofactor Calculations

ELEMENT REMOVED	COFACTORS	DETERMINANT OF COFACTORS	VALUE OF COFACTOR
Row 1, Column 1	$\begin{pmatrix} 0 & 3 \\ 1 & 8 \end{pmatrix}$	$\begin{vmatrix} 0 & 3 \\ 1 & 8 \end{vmatrix} = -3$	−3 (sign not changed)
Row 1, Column 2	$\begin{pmatrix} 2 & 3 \\ 4 & 8 \end{pmatrix}$	$\begin{vmatrix} 2 & 3 \\ 4 & 8 \end{vmatrix} = 4$	−4 (sign changed)
Row 1, Column 3	$\begin{pmatrix} 2 & 0 \\ 4 & 1 \end{pmatrix}$	$\begin{vmatrix} 2 & 0 \\ 4 & 1 \end{vmatrix} = 2$	2 (sign not changed)
Row 2, Column 1	$\begin{pmatrix} 7 & 5 \\ 1 & 8 \end{pmatrix}$	$\begin{vmatrix} 7 & 5 \\ 1 & 8 \end{vmatrix} = 51$	−51 (sign changed)
Row 2, Column 2	$\begin{pmatrix} 3 & 5 \\ 4 & 8 \end{pmatrix}$	$\begin{vmatrix} 3 & 5 \\ 4 & 8 \end{vmatrix} = 4$	4 (sign not changed)
Row 2, Column 3	$\begin{pmatrix} 3 & 7 \\ 4 & 1 \end{pmatrix}$	$\begin{vmatrix} 3 & 7 \\ 4 & 1 \end{vmatrix} = -25$	25 (sign changed)
Row 3, Column 1	$\begin{pmatrix} 7 & 5 \\ 0 & 3 \end{pmatrix}$	$\begin{vmatrix} 7 & 5 \\ 0 & 3 \end{vmatrix} = 21$	21 (sign not changed)
Row 3, Column 2	$\begin{pmatrix} 3 & 5 \\ 2 & 3 \end{pmatrix}$	$\begin{vmatrix} 3 & 5 \\ 2 & 3 \end{vmatrix} = -1$	1 (sign changed)
Row 3, Column 3	$\begin{pmatrix} 3 & 7 \\ 2 & 0 \end{pmatrix}$	$\begin{vmatrix} 3 & 7 \\ 2 & 0 \end{vmatrix} = -14$	−14 (sign not changed)

$$\begin{pmatrix} 3 & 7 & 5 \\ 2 & 0 & 3 \\ 4 & 1 & 8 \end{pmatrix} = \text{Original matrix}$$

Value of determinant

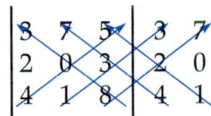

Value $= 0 + 84 + 10 - 0 - 9 - 112 = -27$

The inverse is found by dividing each element in the adjoint by -27.

$$\text{Inverse} = \begin{pmatrix} -3/-27 & -51/-27 & 21/-27 \\ -4/-27 & 4/-27 & 1/-27 \\ 2/-27 & 25/-27 & -14/-27 \end{pmatrix}$$

$$= \begin{pmatrix} 3/27 & 51/27 & -21/27 \\ 4/27 & -4/27 & -1/27 \\ -2/27 & -25/27 & 14/27 \end{pmatrix}$$

We may verify that this is indeed the correct inverse of the original matrix by multiplying the original matrix times the inverse.

Original matrix $\times$ Inverse $=$ Identity matrix

$$\begin{pmatrix} 3 & 7 & 5 \\ 2 & 0 & 3 \\ 4 & 1 & 8 \end{pmatrix} \times \begin{pmatrix} 3/27 & 51/27 & -21/27 \\ 4/27 & -4/27 & -1/27 \\ -2/27 & -25/27 & 14/27 \end{pmatrix} = \begin{pmatrix} 1 & 0 & 0 \\ 0 & 1 & 0 \\ 0 & 0 & 1 \end{pmatrix}$$

A.4   SUMMARY

This module contained a brief presentation of determinants and matrices, two mathematical tools often used in quantitative analysis. Determinants are useful in solving a series of simultaneous equations. Matrices are the basis for the simplex method of linear programming. The module's discussion included matrix addition, subtraction, multiplication, transposition, cofactors, adjoints, and inverses.

GLOSSARY

Determinant. A square array of numbers arranged in rows and columns. Every determinant has a unique numerical value.

Simultaneous Equations. A series of equations that must be solved at the same time.

Matrix. An array of numbers that can be used to present or summarize business data.

Identity Matrix. A square matrix with 1s on its diagonal and 0s in all other positions.

Transpose. The interchange of rows and columns in a matrix.

Matrix of cofactors. The determinants of the numbers remaining in a matrix after a given row and column have been removed.

Adjoint. The transpose of a matrix of cofactors.

Inverse. A unique matrix that may be multiplied by the original matrix to create an identity matrix.

Problems

A-1 Find the numerical values of the following determinants.

(a) $\begin{vmatrix} 6 & 3 \\ -5 & 2 \end{vmatrix}$ (b) $\begin{vmatrix} 3 & 7 & -6 \\ 1 & -1 & 2 \\ 4 & 3 & -2 \end{vmatrix}$

A-2 Use determinants to solve the following set of simultaneous equations.

$$5X + 2Y + 3Z = 4$$
$$2X + 3Y + 1Z = 2$$
$$3X + 1Y + 2Z = 3$$

A-3 Perform the following operations.

(a) Add matrix A to matrix B.
(b) Subtract matrix A from matrix B.
(c) Add matrix C to matrix D.
(d) Add matrix C to matrix A.

$$\text{matrix } A = \begin{pmatrix} 2 & 4 & 1 \\ 3 & 8 & 7 \end{pmatrix} \qquad \text{matrix } C = \begin{pmatrix} 3 & 6 & 9 \\ 7 & 8 & 1 \\ 9 & 2 & 4 \end{pmatrix}$$

$$\text{matrix } B = \begin{pmatrix} 7 & 6 & 5 \\ 0 & 1 & 2 \end{pmatrix} \qquad \text{matrix } D = \begin{pmatrix} 5 & 1 & 6 \\ 4 & 0 & 6 \\ 3 & 1 & 5 \end{pmatrix}$$

A-4 Perform the following matrix multiplications.

(a) matrix C = matrix A × matrix B
(b) matrix G = matrix E × matrix F
(c) matrix T = matrix R × matrix S
(d) matrix Z = matrix W × matrix Y

$$\text{matrix } A = \begin{pmatrix} 2 \\ 1 \end{pmatrix} \qquad \text{matrix } B = (3 \quad 4 \quad 5)$$

$$\text{matrix } E = (5 \quad 2 \quad 6 \quad 1) \qquad \text{matrix } F = \begin{pmatrix} 4 \\ 3 \\ 2 \\ 0 \end{pmatrix}$$

$$\text{matrix } R = \begin{pmatrix} 2 & 3 \\ 1 & 4 \end{pmatrix} \qquad \text{matrix } S = \begin{pmatrix} 1 & 0 \\ 0 & 1 \end{pmatrix}$$

$$\text{matrix } W = \begin{pmatrix} 3 & 5 \\ 2 & 1 \\ 4 & 4 \end{pmatrix} \qquad \text{matrix } Y = \begin{pmatrix} 1 & 4 & 5 & 1 \\ 2 & 3 & 6 & 5 \end{pmatrix}$$

A-5 RLB Electrical Contracting, Inc., bids on the same three jobs as Blank Plumbing (Section 3 of this module). RLB must supply wiring, conduits, electrical wall fixtures, and lighting fixtures. The following are needed supplies and their costs per unit.

	DEMAND			
PROJECT	WIRING (ROLLS)	CONDUITS	WALL FIXTURES	LIGHTING FIXTURES
Dormitory	50	100	10	20
Office	70	80	20	30
Apartments	20	50	30	10

ITEM	COST/UNIT ($)
Wiring	1.00
Conduits	2.00
Wall fixtures	3.00
Lighting fixtures	5.00

Use matrix multiplication to compute the cost of materials at each job site.

A-6 Transpose matrices R and S.

$$\text{matrix } R = \begin{bmatrix} 6 & 8 & 2 & 2 \\ 1 & 0 & 5 & 7 \\ 6 & 4 & 3 & 1 \\ 3 & 1 & 2 & 7 \end{bmatrix}$$

$$\text{matrix } S = \begin{pmatrix} 3 & 1 \\ 2 & 2 \\ 5 & 4 \end{pmatrix}$$

A-7 Find the matrix of cofactors and adjoint of this matrix.

$$\begin{pmatrix} 1 & 4 & 7 \\ 2 & 0 & 8 \\ 3 & 6 & 9 \end{pmatrix}$$

A-8 Find the inverse of original matrix of Problem A-7 and verify its correctness.

BIBLIOGRAPHY

Childress, R. L. *Sets, Matrices, and Linear Programming.* Englewood Cliffs, N.J.: Prentice-Hall, Inc., 1974.

Reiner, I. *Introduction to Matrix Theory and Linear Algebra.* New York: Holt, Rinehart and Winston, Inc., 1971.

B

Game Theory

MODULE OUTLINE

B.1 Introduction
B.2 Language of Games
B.3 Pure Strategy Games
B.4 Minimax Criterion
B.5 Mixed Strategy Games
B.6 Dominance
B.7 Games Larger Than 2 × 2

B.8 Using the Computer to Solve Game Theory Problems
B.9 Summary
Glossary
Discussion Questions and Problems
Bibliography

B.1 INTRODUCTION

This module deals with the fascinating subject of game theory. A *game* is a contest involving two or more decision makers, each of whom wants to win. *Game theory* is the study of how optimal strategies are formulated in conflict.

The subject dates back to 1944, the year in which John Von Neumann and Oscar Morgenstern published their classic book, *Theory of Games and Economic Behavior*. Since then, game theory has been used by army generals to plan war strategies, by union negotiators and managers in collective bargaining sessions, and by poker and chess players trying to win their games. Game models are classified by the *number of players*, the *sum of all payoffs*, and the *number of strategies* employed. Owing to the mathematical complexity of game theory, we limit the analysis in this module to games that are two person and zero sum. A *two-person game* is one where only two parties can play—as in the case of a union and a company in a bargaining session. For simplicity, X and Y represent the two game players. *Zero sum* means that the sum of losses for one player must equal the sum of gains for the other player. Thus, if X wins 20 points or dollars, Y loses 20 points or dollars. With any zero sum game, the sum of the gains for one player is always equal to the sum of the losses for the other player. When you sum the gains and losses for both players, the result is zero. This is why these games are called zero sum games.

B.2 LANGUAGE OF GAMES

To introduce you to the notation used in game theory, let us consider a simple game. Suppose there are only two lighting fixture stores, X and Y, in Urbana, Illinois (this is called a duopoly). The respective market shares have been stable up until now, but the situation may change. The daughter of the owner of store X has just completed her MBA and has developed two distinct advertising strategies, one using radio spots and the other newspaper ads. Upon hearing this, the owner of store Y also proceeds to prepare radio and newspaper ads.

The 2×2 payoff matrix in Table B.1 shows what will happen to current market shares if both stores begin advertising. By convention, payoffs are shown only for the first game player, X, in this case. Y's payoffs will just be the negative of each number. For this game, there are only two strategies being used by each player. If store Y had a third strategy, a situation illustrated in Section 7 of this module, we would be dealing with a 2×3 payoff matrix.

A positive number in Table B.1 means that X wins and Y loses.

A negative number means that Y wins and X loses.

Look at Table B.1. It is obvious that the game favors competitor X, since all values are positive except one. If the game had favored player Y, the values in the table would have been negative. In other words, the game in Table B.1 is biased

TABLE B.1 Store *X*'s Payoff Matrix

		GAME PLAYER *Y*'S STRATEGIES	
		Y_1 (Use radio)	Y_2 (Use newspaper)
GAME PLAYER *X*'S	X_1 (Use radio)	2	7
STRATEGIES	X_2 (Use newspaper)	6	−4

against Y. However, since Y must play the game, he or she will play to minimize total losses.

Game Outcomes

STORE X'S STRATEGY	STORE Y'S STRATEGY	OUTCOME (IN % CHANGE IN MARKET SHARE)
X_1 (use radio)	Y_1 (use radio)	X wins 2, and Y loses 2
X_1 (use radio)	Y_2 (use newspaper)	X wins 7, and Y loses 7
X_2 (use newspaper)	Y_1 (use radio)	X wins 6, and Y loses 6
X_2 (use newspaper)	Y_2 (use newspaper)	X loses 4, and Y wins 4

B.3 PURE STRATEGY GAMES

In some games, the strategies each player follows will always be the same regardless of the other player's strategy. This is called a *pure strategy*. A *saddle point* is a situation where both players are facing pure strategies. Strategies for *saddle point games* can be determined without performing any calculations.

Consider the following game. Does it have a saddle point?

		SECOND PLAYER'S (Y) STRATEGIES	
		Y_1	Y_2
FIRST PLAYER'S	X_1	3	5
(X) STRATEGIES	X_2	1	-2

The answer is *yes*. Here is how we can determine the strategies for X and Y.

1. X will always play strategy X_1. The worst outcome for X playing strategy X_1 is $+3$ points. The best outcome for X playing X_2 is $+1$.

2. Knowing that X will always play strategy X_1, Y will always play strategy Y_1. Y will lose three points by playing Y_1. If Y_2 is played, Y will lose five points.

3. Both players have a dominant or pure strategy, and therefore the game has a saddle point. The numerical value of the saddle point is the game outcome. For this example, the saddle point is 3.

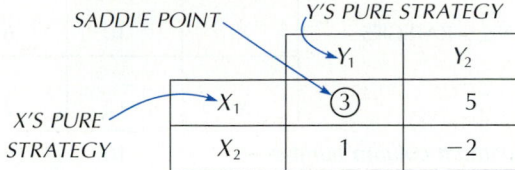

Why do we have a saddle point for this situation? Looking at the payoffs, we can see that X will always play strategy X_1. The lowest, or worst, outcome for playing this strategy is better than the best outcome for playing the other strategy, X_2. Thus, player X will always play strategy X_1. Knowing this, Y will always play strategy Y_1 to minimize losses. The loss for playing strategy Y_1 is 3, while the loss for playing Y_2 is 5.

In reality, players X and Y may not see the saddle point at first. After the game is played for some time, however, each player will realize that there is only one strategy that should be played. From then on, these players will play only one strategy, which corresponds to the saddle point.

The *value of the game* is the average or expected game outcome if the game is played an infinite number of times. The value of the game for this example is 3. If a game has a saddle point, the value of the game is equal to its numerical value.

You will note that the saddle point in this example, 3, is the largest number in its column and the smallest number in its row. This is true of all saddle points. There is a convenient way of determining whether or not a game has a saddle point. A saddle point exists if both of the following conditions exist for a number in the table: if it is the largest number in its column, and if it is the smallest number in its row.

B.4 MINIMAX CRITERION

In Chapter 5 it was shown that a pessimistic decision maker would want to maximize his or her minimum gains. This is called the *maximin deci-*

TABLE B.2 Example of the Minimax Criterion

		PLAYER Y'S STRATEGIES		Minimum row number ↓
		Y_1	Y_2	
PLAYER X'S STRATEGIES	X_1	10	6	⑥ ← Lower value
	X_2	−12	2	−12
Maximum column number →		10	⑥	

Upper value

sion criteria. Minimizing one's maximum losses is identical to maximizing one's minimum gains. In game theory, this is the so-called *minimax criterion.* This criterion is one approach to selecting strategies that will minimize losses for each player.

The minimax procedure is accomplished as follows. Find the smallest number in each row. Pick the largest of these numbers. This number is called the *lower value* of the game, and the row is X's maximin strategy.

Next, find the largest number in each column. Pick the smallest of these numbers. This number is called the *higher value* of the game, and the column is Y's minimax strategy.

If the upper value and lower value of the game are the same, there is a saddle point which is equal to the upper or lower value. This is an alternate method of determining whether or not a saddle point exists. Table B.2 above illustrates how we can determine if there is a saddle point using the minimax criterion. Since the upper value equals the lower value of the game, the saddle point is 6. X's strategy is to play X_1, and Y's strategy is to play Y_2.

B.5 MIXED STRATEGY GAMES

When there is no saddle point, then players will play each strategy for a certain percentage of the time. This is called a *mixed strategy game,* and the rest of this module investigates ways to determine the percentage of the time each strategy will be played.

For 2×2 games (where both players have only two possible strategies), an algebraic approach can be used to solve for the percentage of the time each strategy is played. The following diagram can be helpful:

	P	1 − P
Q		
1 − Q		

where

$Q, 1 - Q$ = fraction of the time X plays strategies X_1 and X_2, respectively, and

$P, 1 - P$ = fraction of the time Y plays strategies Y_1 and Y_2, respectively.

The overall objective of each player is to determine the fraction of the time each strategy is to be played to maximize winnings. Each player desires a strategy that will result in the most winnings no matter what the other player's strategy happens to be.

The solution to the mixed strategy 2×2 game may be found by equating a player's expected winnings for one of the opponent's strategies with his expected winnings for the opponent's other strategy. With this approach, X wants to divide its plays between the two rows in such a way that the expected winnings from playing the first row will be exactly equal to the expected winnings from playing the second row despite what Y does. In other words, X wants to determine the best possible strategy that is independent of the strategy that player Y will adopt. Thus, it is necessary to equate the expected winnings of strategy X_1, which is row 1, and strategy X_2, which is row 2.

The same approach used to determine X's strategy can be used to determine Y's strategy. Y will want to divide its time between the columns in such a way that no matter what X does, Y will minimize its losses or maximize its winnings.

1. To find X's best strategy, multiply Q and $1 - Q$ times the appropriate game outcome numbers and solve for Q and $1 - Q$ by setting column 1 equal to column 2 in the game.

2. To find Y's best strategy, multiply P and $1 - P$ times the appropriate game outcome numbers and solve for P and $1 - P$ by setting row 1 equal to row 2 in the game.

Here is how you would determine the optimal strategies for X and Y in the following game.

Y'S STRATEGIES

X'S STRATEGIES		Y_1	Y_2
	X_1	4	2
	X_2	1	10

Step 1.

	P	$1 - P$
Q	4	2
$1 - Q$	1	10

Step 2. X's optimal strategy:
  (a) Column 1 is $4Q + 1(1 - Q)$.
  (b) Column 2 is $2Q + 10(1 - Q)$.
  (c) Equating column 1 and column 2 gives: $4Q + 1(1 - Q) = 2Q + 10(1 - Q)$.
  (d) Solving for Q and $1 - Q$ yields the following: $4Q - Q - 2Q + 10Q = -1 + 10$. $Q = \frac{9}{11}$, and thus $1 - Q = 1 - \frac{9}{11} = \frac{2}{11}$.
  (e) $\frac{9}{11}$ and $\frac{2}{11}$ represent the fraction of the time X should play X_1 and X_2, respectively.

Step 3. Y's optimal strategy:
  (a) Row 1 is $4(P) + 2(1 - P)$.
  (b) Row 2 is $1(P) + 10(1 - P)$.
  (c) Equating row 1 and row 2 gives: $4(P) + 2(1 - P) = 1(P) + 10(1 - P)$.
  (d) Solving for P and $1 - P$ yields the following: $4P - 2P - P + 10P = -2 + 10$. $P = \frac{8}{11}$; $1 - P = \frac{3}{11}$.
  (e) $\frac{8}{11}$ and $\frac{3}{11}$ represent the fraction of the time Y should play Y_1 and Y_2, respectively.

Once this procedure is understood, it is possible to write the appropriate equations directly from the game. This is shown in the following example game:

	Y_1	Y_2
X_1	−6	−1
X_2	−2	−8

Step 1.

	P	$1 - P$
Q	−6	−1
$1 - Q$	−2	−8

Step 2. The equation for X's strategy is:
$-6Q - 2(1 - Q) = -1Q - 8(1 - Q)$
$-6Q + 2Q + Q - 8Q = 2 - 8$
$Q = \frac{6}{11}$; $1 - Q = \frac{5}{11}$

Step 3. The equation for Y's strategy is:
$-6P - 1(1 - P) = -2P - 8(1 - P)$
$-6P + P + 2P - 8P = +1 - 8$
$P = \frac{7}{11}$; $1 - P = \frac{4}{11}$

Once player strategies have been determined, the value of the game can be calculated. The value of the game is the average or expected game outcome after a large number of plays. It can be computed by multiplying each game outcome times the P and Q factors of respective strategies. The results are then added up to obtain the value of the game. The following example shows how the exact calculations are performed:

	Y_1	Y_2
X_1	4	2
X_2	1	10

$$Q = \tfrac{9}{11}$$
$$1 - Q = \tfrac{2}{11}$$
$$P = \tfrac{8}{11}$$
$$1 - P = \tfrac{3}{11}$$

The next diagram is usually helpful:

	$P = \tfrac{8}{11}$	$1 - P = \tfrac{3}{11}$
$Q = \tfrac{9}{11}$	4	2
$1 - Q = \tfrac{2}{11}$	1	10

To get a game outcome of 4, strategies X_1 and Y_1 must be played. The P and Q factors are $\tfrac{9}{11}$ and $\tfrac{8}{11}$. Therefore, we multiply 4 times $\tfrac{9}{11}$ times $\tfrac{8}{11}$. We do the same for all game outcomes and add the results. The calculations are displayed in the accompanying table.

GAME OUTCOME	P FACTOR		Q FACTOR	
4	×	$\tfrac{9}{11}$	×	$\tfrac{8}{11} = 2.38$
2	×	$\tfrac{9}{11}$	×	$\tfrac{3}{11} = .45$
1	×	$\tfrac{2}{11}$	×	$\tfrac{8}{11} = .13$
10	×	$\tfrac{2}{11}$	×	$\tfrac{3}{11} = .50$
				Value of the game = 3.46

Thus, on the average, X will win 3.46 points and Y will lose 3.46 points per game if the game is played many times.

Although this procedure will give the expected value of the game, a shortcut method does exist. Since optimal strategies are obtained by equating expected gains of both strategies for each player, the value of the game may be computed by multiplying game outcomes times their probabilities of occurrence for any row or column. The following illustration reveals the computational procedures.

		COLUMN 1 $P = \tfrac{8}{11}$	COLUMN 2 $1 - P = \tfrac{3}{11}$
ROW 1	$Q = \tfrac{9}{11}$	4	2
ROW 2	$1 - Q = \tfrac{2}{11}$	1	10

Row 1: Value of the game =
$$(4)\left(\tfrac{8}{11}\right) + (2)\left(\tfrac{3}{11}\right) = \tfrac{38}{11}$$
Row 2: Value of the game =
$$(1)\left(\tfrac{8}{11}\right) + (10)\left(\tfrac{3}{11}\right) = \tfrac{38}{11}$$
Column 1: Value of the game =
$$(4)\left(\tfrac{9}{11}\right) + (1)\left(\tfrac{2}{11}\right) = \tfrac{38}{11}$$
Column 2: Value of the game =
$$(2)\left(\tfrac{9}{11}\right) + (10)\left(\tfrac{2}{11}\right) = \tfrac{38}{11}$$

Thus, the value of the game can be computed using any row or column. The value of this game, which was computed to be 3.46, is $\tfrac{38}{11}$.

B.6 DOMINANCE

The principle of *dominance* can be used to reduce the size of games by eliminating strategies that would never be played. A strategy for a player can be eliminated if the player can always do as well or better playing another strategy. In other words, a strategy can be eliminated if all its game's outcomes are the same or worse than the corresponding game outcomes of another strategy.

Using the principle of dominance, we reduce the size of the following game:

	Y_1	Y_2
X_1	4	3
X_2	2	20
X_3	1	1

In this game, X_3 will never be played because X can always do better by playing X_1 or X_2. The new game is:

	Y_1	Y_2
X_1	4	3
X_2	2	20

Here is another example:

	Y_1	Y_2	Y_3	Y_4
X_1	−5	4	6	−3
X_2	−2	6	2	−20

In this game, Y would never play Y_2 and Y_3 because Y could *always* do better playing Y_1 or Y_4. The new game is:

	Y_1	Y_4
X_1	−5	−3
X_2	−2	−20

B.7 GAMES LARGER THAN 2 × 2

It is not always possible to reduce a large game to a 2 × 2 game. There are several techniques, including solution by *subgames* and the graphical approach that may be used to solve 2 × m and m × 2 games where m is a number larger than 2. The procedure used to solve 2 × 2 games can also be expanded to solve larger games. One final technique is discussed, however, that is appropriate for any game. This approach is linear programming. Figure B.1 (page 842) shows when linear programming should be used. There are several advantages in using linear programming:

1. It is appropriate for 2 × 2 or larger games.

2. Linear programming computer programs are usually available, making the process of solution much easier.

3. Most linear programming computer programs have postoptimality techniques that allow the decision maker to analyze what effect changes in the game will have on optimal strategies.

Before we begin, several terms should be defined. Let

V = Optimal value of the game

$\hat{X}_i$ = Fraction of time X plays strategy X_i

$\hat{Y}_i$ = Fraction of time Y plays strategy Y_i

To illustrate the use of linear programming, consider the following game.

		Y'S STRATEGIES		
		Y_1	Y_2	Y_3
X'S STRATEGIES	X_1	3	2	1
	X_2	1	4	6

Since this is not a pure strategy game, each strategy will be played a certain fraction of the time. It will be our objective to find V and every $\hat{X}_i$ and $\hat{Y}_i$.

X wants to maximize the value of the game, but if X plays only one strategy, the value of the game will be less than or equal to the optimal value of the game, V. For example, if X plays only X_1, then the value of this game, which is $3\hat{Y}_1 + 2\hat{Y}_2 + 1\hat{Y}_3$, will be less than or equal to the optimal value of the game, which is V. Stating this algebraically we get:

$$3\hat{Y}_1 + 2\hat{Y}_2 + 1\hat{Y}_3 \leq V$$

Using the same reasoning for X_2, we get:

$$1\hat{Y}_1 + 4\hat{Y}_2 + 6\hat{Y}_3 \leq V$$

These inequalities become linear programming constraints.

We also know that all of Y's fractions must add up to 1.

$$\hat{Y}_1 + \hat{Y}_2 + \hat{Y}_3 = 1$$

This equation is used to construct the objective function. Now, to obtain our linear programming formulation, we divide each of these equations by

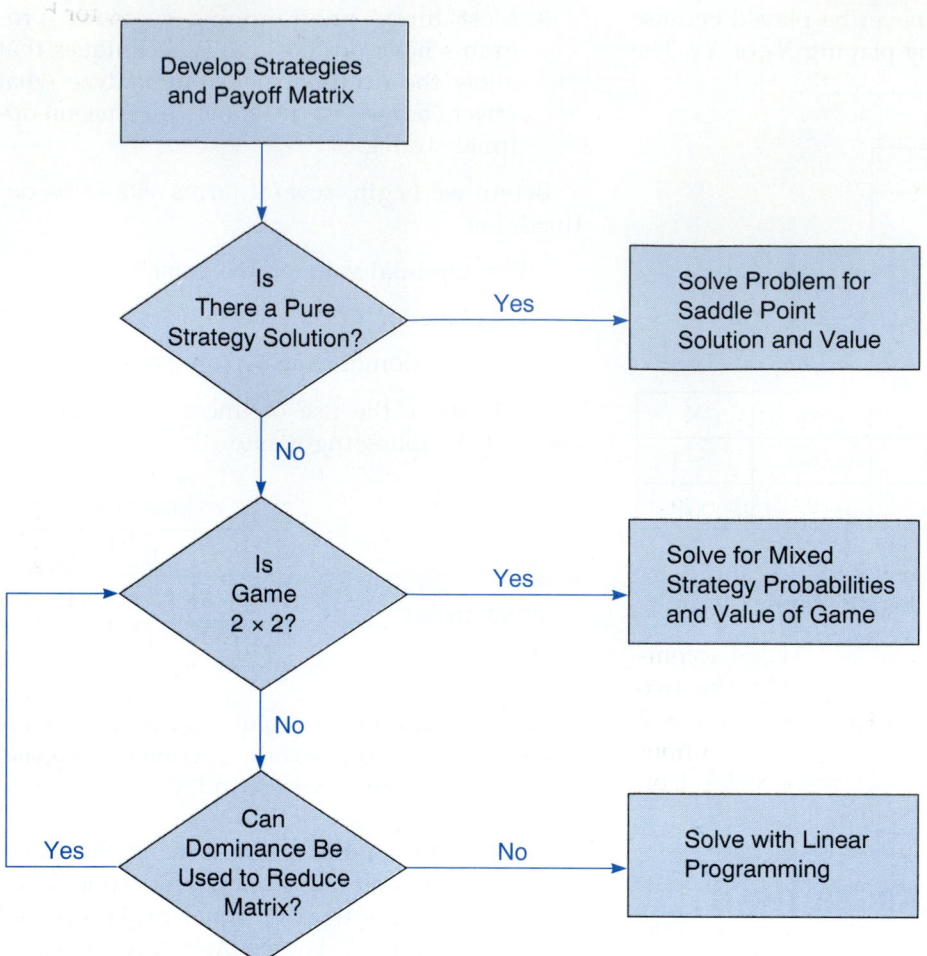

FIGURE B.1
Procedure for Solving Two-Person, Zero Sum Games

V, and note that Y wants to minimize V, or maximize $1/V$.

$$\frac{\hat{Y}_1}{V} + \frac{\hat{Y}_2}{V} + \frac{\hat{Y}_3}{V} = \frac{1}{V}$$

$$\frac{3\hat{Y}_1}{V} + \frac{2\hat{Y}_2}{V} + \frac{1\hat{Y}_3}{V} \le 1$$

$$\frac{1\hat{Y}_1}{V} + \frac{4\hat{Y}_2}{V} + \frac{6\hat{Y}_3}{V} \le 1$$

Y will want to maximize $\frac{1}{V}$ subject to these constraints

If we define $\overline{Y}_i = \dfrac{\hat{Y}_i}{V}$ the linear programming formulation is:

Maximize: $\overline{Y}_1 + \overline{Y}_2 + \overline{Y}_3$

Subject to: $3\overline{Y}_1 + 2\overline{Y}_2 + 1\overline{Y}_3 \le 1$

$\qquad\qquad 1\overline{Y}_1 + 4\overline{Y}_2 + 6\overline{Y}_3 \le 1$

With experience, a linear programming formulation for Y's strategies and the value of the game can be made directly from a game. Here is an example.

	Y_1	Y_2	Y_3
X_1	3	2	3
X_2	1	4	4
X_3	5	6	1

The solution is:

Maximize: $\overline{Y}_1 + \overline{Y}_2 + \overline{Y}_3$

Subject to: $3\overline{Y}_1 + 2\overline{Y}_2 + 3\overline{Y}_3 \leq 1$

$1\overline{Y}_1 + 4\overline{Y}_2 + 4\overline{Y}_3 \leq 1$

$5\overline{Y}_1 + 6\overline{Y}_2 + 1\overline{Y}_3 \leq 1$

B.8 USING THE COMPUTER TO SOLVE GAME THEORY PROBLEMS

The game theory program for AB:QM can accommodate up to 50 strategies for each of the two players. In this module, we discussed a 2×2 game theory problem. That problem's input screen and output are shown in Program B.1 on page 844.

B.9 SUMMARY

Game theory is the study of how optimal strategies are formulated in conflict. Because of the mathematical complexities of game theory, this module was limited to two-person and zero sum games. A two-person game allows only two individuals or groups to be involved in the game. Zero sum means that the sum of the losses for one player must equal the sum of the gains for the other player. The overall sum of the losses and gains for both players, in other words, must be zero.

Depending on the actual payoffs in the game and the size of the game, a number of solution techniques can be used. In a pure strategy game, strategies for the players can be obtained without making any calculations. When there is *not* a pure strategy, also called a saddle point, for both players, it is necessary to use other techniques, such as the mixed strategy approach, dominance, and linear programming for games larger than 2×2.

GLOSSARY

Two-Person Game. A game that has only two players.

Zero Sum Game. A game where the losses for one player equal the gains for the other player.

Pure Strategy. A game where both players will always play just one strategy.

Saddle Point Game. A game that has a pure strategy.

Value of the Game. The expected winnings of the game if the game is played a large number of times.

Minimax Criterion. A criterion that minimizes one's maximum losses. This is another way of solving a pure strategy game.

Mixed Strategy Game. A game where the optimal strategy for both players involves playing more than one strategy over time. Each strategy is played a given percentage of the time.

Dominance. A procedure that is used to reduce the size of the game.

Games Larger than 2×2. A game that involves more than two strategies for one or both players. One way of solving this type of game is to use linear programming.

DISCUSSION QUESTIONS AND PROBLEMS

Discussion Questions

B-1 What is a two-person, zero sum game?

B-2 How do you compute the value of the game?

B-3 What is a pure strategy and how is dominance used?

B-4 What is a mixed game, and how is it solved?

B-5 How is linear programming used to solve games that are larger than 2×2?

PROGRAM B.1 AB:QM's Game Theory Program

```
Game Theory

Problem Title :  Game1

No. of A's Strategies (Row)      2     No. of B's Strategies (Col)   2

              Strategy  1  Strategy  2
Strategy  1              4            2
Strategy  2              1           10

Help  New  Load  Save  Edit   Run   Print  Install  Directory  Esc


Game Theory

***** Program Output *****

- - - - - - - - - -
Mixed Strategy
- - - - - - - - - -

For Player A:

Probability of Strategy   1       0.818
Probability of Strategy   2       0.182

For Player B:

Probability of Strategy   1       0.727
Probability of Strategy   2       0.273

Value for this game is        3.45

***** End of Output *****
```

Problems

B-6 Determine the strategies for X and Y given the following game. What is the value of the game?

	Y_1	Y_2
X_1	2	-4
X_2	6	10

B-7 What is the value of the following game and the strategies for A and B?

	B_1	B_2
A_1	19	20
A_2	5	-4

B-8 Determine each player's strategy and the value of the game given the following table.

	Y_1	Y_2
X_1	86	42
X_2	36	106

B-9 What is the value of the following game?

	S_1	S_2
R_1	21	116
R_2	89	3

B-10 Player A has a one-dollar bill and a twenty-dollar bill, while player B has a five-dollar bill and a ten-dollar bill. Each player will select a bill from the other player without knowing what bill the other player selected. If the total of the bills selected is odd, player A gets both bills, but if the total is even, player B gets both bills.

(a) Develop a payoff table for this game.
(b) What are the best strategies for each player?
(c) What is the value of the game? Which player would you like to be?

B-11 Resolve Problem B-10. If the total of the bills is even, player A gets both bills, but if the total is odd, player B gets both bills.

B-12 Solve the following game.

	Y_1	Y_2
X_1	−5	−10
X_2	12	8
X_3	4	12
X_4	−40	−5

B-13 Shoe Town and Fancy Foot are both vying for more share of the market. If Shoe Town does no advertising, it will not lose any share of the market if Fancy Foot does nothing. It will lose 2% of the market if Fancy Foot invests $10,000 in advertising, and it will lose 5% of the market if Fancy Foot invests $20,000 in advertising. On the other hand, if Shoe Town invests $15,000 in advertising, it will gain 3% of the market if Fancy Foot does nothing; it will gain 1% of the market if Fancy Foot invests $10,000 in advertising; and

it will lose 1% if Fancy Foot invests $20,000 in advertising.

(a) Develop a payoff table for this problem.
(b) How would you determine the various strategies using linear programming?
(c) How would you determine the value of the game?

B-14 Assume that a 1% increase in the market means a profit of $1,000. Resolve Problem B-13 using monetary value instead of market share.

B-15 Solve for the optimal strategies and the value of the following game.

A \\ B	STRATEGY 1	STRATEGY 2	STRATEGY 3
Strategy 1	−10	5	15
Strategy 2	20	2	−20
Strategy 3	6	2	6
Strategy 4	−13	−10	44
Strategy 5	−30	0	45
Strategy 6	16	−20	6

Data Set Problem

B-16 Petroleum Research, Inc., and Extraction International, Inc., have both developed a new extraction procedure that will remove metal and other contaminants from used automotive engine oil. The equipment is expensive, the extraction process is complex, but the approach allows for an economical way to recycle used engine oil. Both companies have developed unique technical procedures. Both companies also believe that advertising and promotion are critical to their success. Petroleum Research, with the help of an advertising firm, has developed 15 possible strategies. Extraction International has developed 5 possible advertising strategies. The economic outcome in millions of dollars is shown in the following table. What strategy do you recommend for Petroleum Research? How much money can they expect from their approach? (See page 846.)

Extraction International, Inc. (B)

A \ B	STRATEGY 1	STRATEGY 2	STRATEGY 3	STRATEGY 4	STRATEGY 5
Petroleum Research, Inc. (A)					
Strategy 1	1	2	2	1	4
Strategy 2	−1	3	−6	7	5
Strategy 3	10	−3	−5	−20	12
Strategy 4	6	−8	5	2	2
Strategy 5	−5	3	3	7	5
Strategy 6	−1	−1	−3	4	−2
Strategy 7	−1	0	0	0	−1
Strategy 8	3	6	−6	8	3
Strategy 9	2	6	−5	4	−7
Strategy 10	0	0	0	−5	7
Strategy 11	4	8	−5	3	3
Strategy 12	−3	−3	0	3	3
Strategy 13	1	0	0	−2	2
Strategy 14	4	3	3	5	7
Strategy 15	4	−4	4	−5	5

BIBLIOGRAPHY

Bowen, Kenneth Credson, with contributions by Janet I. Harris. *Research Games: An Approach to the Study of Decision Process.* New York: Halstead Press, 1978.

Davis, M. *Game Theory: A Nontechnical Introduction.* New York: Basic Books, Inc., 1970.

Ichiishi, Tatsuro. *Game Theory for Economic Analysis.* New York: Academic Press, 1983.

Karnani, Aneel. "The Value of Market Share and the Product Life Cycle—A Game Theoretic Model." *Management Science* 30 (June 1984): 696–712.

Klein, J.H. "The Level of Interpretation of Games." *Journal of Operational Research Society* 39 (June 1988): 527–535.

Lucas, W. "An Overview of the Mathematical Theory of Games." *Management Science* 8, 5, Part II (January 1972): 3–19.

Luce, R.D., and H. Raiffa. *Games and Decisions.* New York: John Wiley and Sons, 1957.

Matthews, S.A. "Veto Threats: Rhetoric in a Bargaining Game." *Quarterly Journal of Economics* 104 (May 1989): 347–369.

Shubik, M. *The Uses and Methods of Game Theory.* New York: American Elsevier, 1957.

Sterman, J.D. "Modeling Managerial Behavior: Misperceptions of Feedback in a Dynamic Decision Making Experiment." *Management Science* 35 (March 1989): 321–339.

Troutt, M.D. "A Purchase Timing Model for Life Insurance Decision Support Systems." *Journal of Risk and Insurance* 55 (December 1988): 628–643.

Von, Neumann, J., and O. Morgenstern. *Theory of Games and Economic Behavior.* Princeton, N.J.: Princeton University Press, 1944.

Williams, J.D. *The Compleat Strategyst,* Revised Edition. New York: McGraw-Hill Book Company, 1966.

Dynamic Programming

MODULE OUTLINE

C.1 Introduction

C.2 A Shortest-Route Problem Solved by Dynamic Programming

C.3 Dynamic Programming Terminology

C.4 Using the Computer to Solve Dynamic Programming Problems

Glossary

Discussion Questions and Problems

Bibliography

C.1 INTRODUCTION

Dynamic programming is a quantitative analysis technique that has been widely applied to large, complex problems that have a sequence of decisions to be made. Dynamic programming divides problems into a number of *decision stages,* where the outcome of a decision at one stage affects the decision at each of the next stages. The technique is useful in a large number of multiperiod business problems, such as smoothing production employment, allocating capital funds, allocating salespeople to marketing areas, and evaluating investment opportunities.

Dynamic programming differs from linear programming in two ways. First, there is no algorithm (like the simplex method) that can be programmed to solve all problems. Dynamic programming is instead a technique that allows us to break up difficult problems into a sequence of easier subproblems, which are then evaluated by stages. Second, linear programming is a method that gives *single-stage* (one time period) solutions. Dynamic programming has the power to determine the optimal solution over a one-year time horizon by breaking the problem into 12 smaller one-month time horizon problems and to solve each of these optimally. Hence, it uses a *multistage* approach.

Solving problems with dynamic programming involves four steps.

1. Divide the original problem into subproblems called stages.

2. Solve the last stage of the problem for all possible conditions or states.

3. Working backwards from the last stage, solve each intermediate stage. This is done by determining optimal policies from that stage to the end of the problem (last stage).

4. Obtain the optimal solution for the original problem by solving all stages sequentially.

In this brief module, we show how to solve one typical dynamic programming problem as an illustration of the approach. The problem is commonly referred to as a shortest-route problem.

C.2 A SHORTEST-ROUTE PROBLEM SOLVED BY DYNAMIC PROGRAMMING

George Yates is about to make a trip from Rice, Georgia (1) to Dixieville, Georgia (7). George would like to find the shortest route. Unfortunately, there are a number of small towns between Rice and Dixieville. His road map is shown in Figure C.1 on page 849.

The circles on the map, called *nodes,* represent cities such as Rice, Dixieville, Brown, and so on. The arrows, called *arcs,* represent highways between the cities. Distances in miles are indicated along each arc.

This problem can, of course, be solved by inspection. But seeing how dynamic programming can be used on this simple problem will teach you how to solve larger and more complex problems.

Step 1. The first step is to divide the problem into subproblems or stages. Figure C.2 (p. 850) reveals the stages of this problem. In dynamic programming, we usually start with the last part of the problem, stage 1, and work backwards to the beginning of the problem or network, which is stage 3 in this problem. Table C.1 summarizes the arcs and arc distances for each stage.

Step 2. We next solve stage 1, the last part of the network. Usually this is trivial. We find the shortest path to the end of the network, node 7 in this problem. At stage 1, the shortest paths from node 5 and node 6 to node 7 are the *only* paths.

TABLE C.1 Distance Along Each Arc

STAGE	ARC	ARC DISTANCE
1	5–7	14
	6–7	2
2	4–5	10
	3–5	12
	3–6	6
	2–5	4
	2–6	10
3	1–4	4
	1–3	5
	1–2	2

APPLICATIONS OF QA

Dynamic Programming at Weyerhaeuser

Weyerhaeuser is a very large company involved with forest products located primarily in the northwest. Its annual revenues are in the billions of dollars. Weyerhaeuser uses a number of mills and other production facilities to produce plywood, paper products, lumber, and even wood fuel from logs and other tree-related products. The firm processes a staggering volume of over one billion cubic feet of lumber products every year.

One of the most difficult and critical decisions is to find the most effective and profitable use of its raw materials, logs and other wood products. Depending on how the logs are cut and subsequently used to produce final products, Weyerhaeuser can have a profound impact on its own profits. But with logs of different sizes and shapes and a large variety of end products, how is it pos-

sible to determine the best use of a particular log or a set of logs to produce the best results? To assist Weyerhaeuser's managers in making important raw material decisions, a decision simulator called VISION was developed.

One of the main purposes of the VISION decision simulator is to help determine the best overall use of raw materials coming into Weyerhaeuser's plants. First designed in 1984, VISION uses dynamic programming to allocate resources to various production operations which produce the final products. In the past several years, this program has gone through several changes resulting in a number of improvements.

What has been the impact of the decision simulator? It has been estimated that benefits so far have increased by approximately $1 million. Using dynamic programming and the VISION decision simulator, Weyerhaeuser has been able to significantly improve the use of its major raw material, incoming logs, to produce the most profitable mix of finished products.

Source: Mark Lembersky and Uli Chi, "Weyerhaeuser Decision Simulator Improves Timber Products," *Interfaces* **16**, 1 (January–February, 1986).

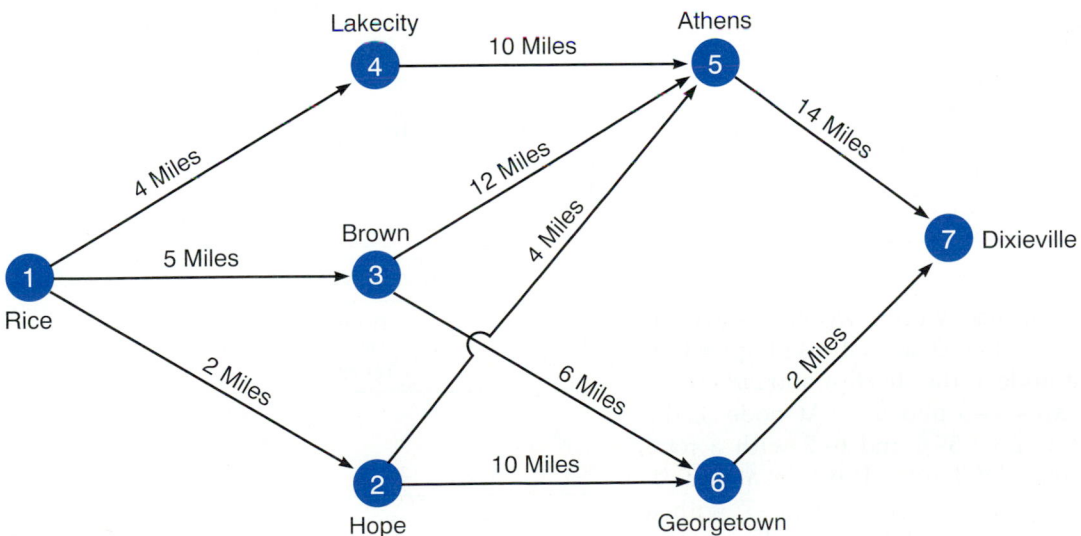

FIGURE C.1
Highway Map Between Rice and Dixieville

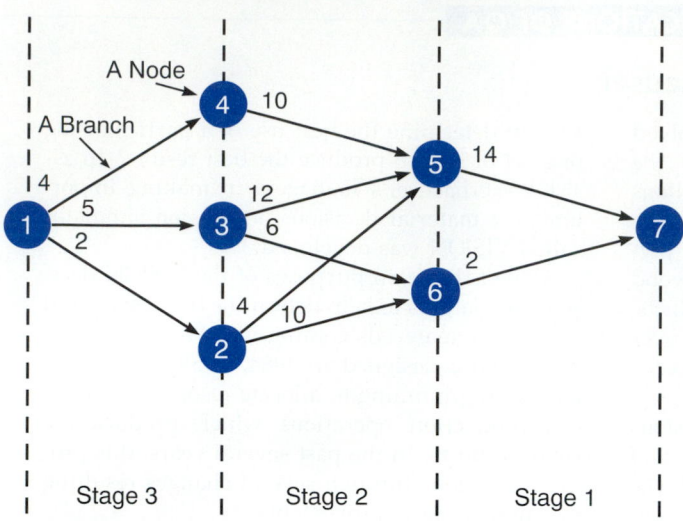

FIGURE C.2
Three Stages to George Yates's Problem

You may also note in Figure C.3 (p. 851) that the minimum distances are enclosed in boxes by the entering nodes to stage 1, node 5 and node 6. The objective is to find the shortest distance to node 7. The table that follows summarizes this procedure for stage 1. As previously mentioned, the shortest distance is the only distance at stage 1.

TABLE FOR STAGE 1		
BEGINNING NODE	SHORTEST DISTANCE TO NODE 7	ARCS ALONG THIS PATH
5	14	5–7
6	2	6–7

Step 3. Moving backwards, we now solve for stages 2 and 3. At stage 2 we will use Figure C.4.

If we are at node 4, the shortest and *only* route to node 7 is arcs 4–5 and 5–7. At node 3, the shortest route is arcs 3–6 and 6–7 with a total minimum distance of 8 miles. If we are at node 2, the shortest route is arcs 2–6 and 6–7 with a minimum total distance of 12 miles. This information is summarized in the stage 2 table.

TABLE FOR STAGE 2		
BEGINNING NODE	SHORTEST DISTANCE TO NODE 7	ARCS ALONG THIS PATH
4	24	4–5 5–7
3	8	3–6 6–7
2	12	2–6 6–7

The solution to stage 3 can be completed using the table for stage 3 below and the network in Figure C.5 on page 852.

TABLE FOR STAGE 3		
BEGINNING NODE	SHORTEST DISTANCE TO NODE 7	ARCS ALONG THIS PATH
1	13	1–3 3–6 6–7

To obtain the optimal solution at any stage, all we consider are the arcs to the next stage and the

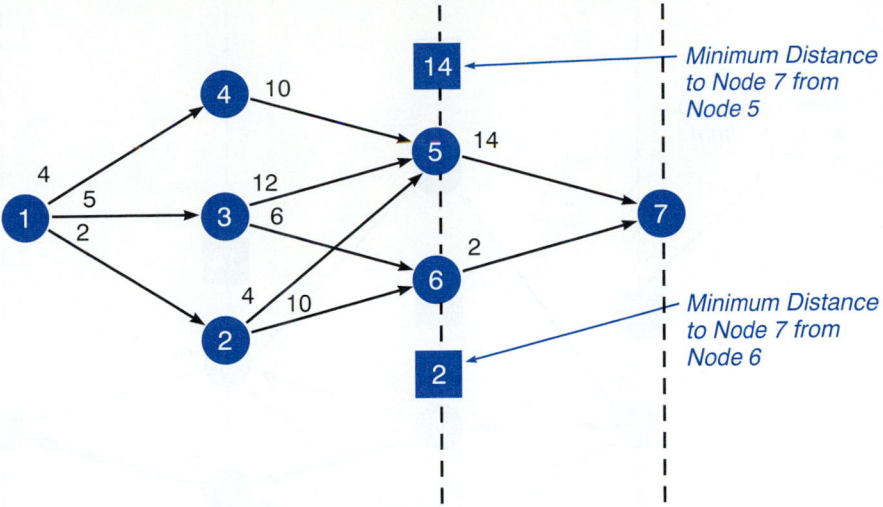

FIGURE C.3
Solution for the One-Stage Problem

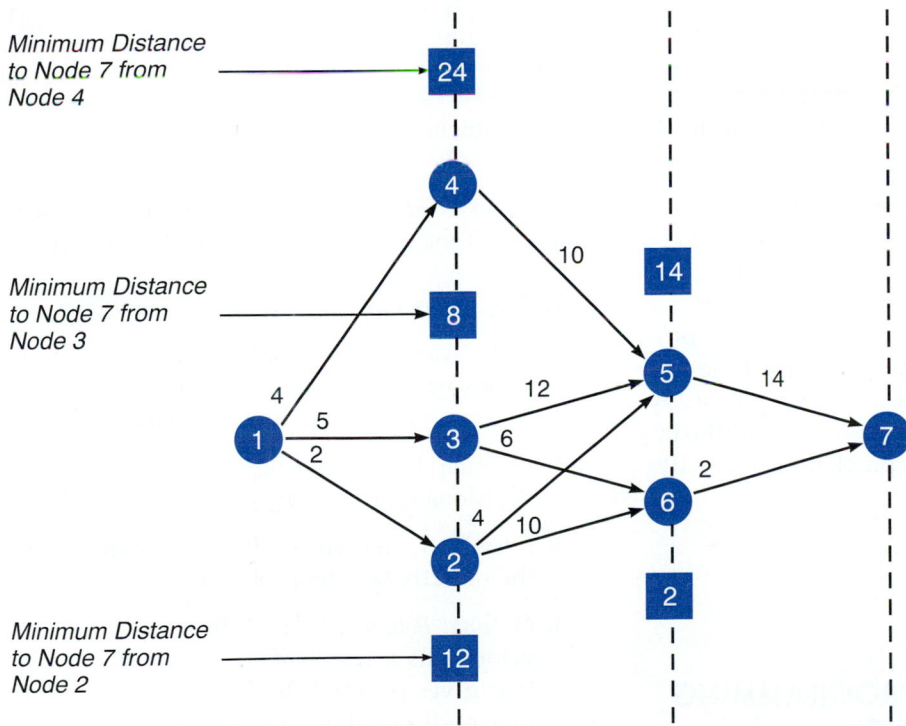

FIGURE C.4
Solution for the Two-Stage Problem

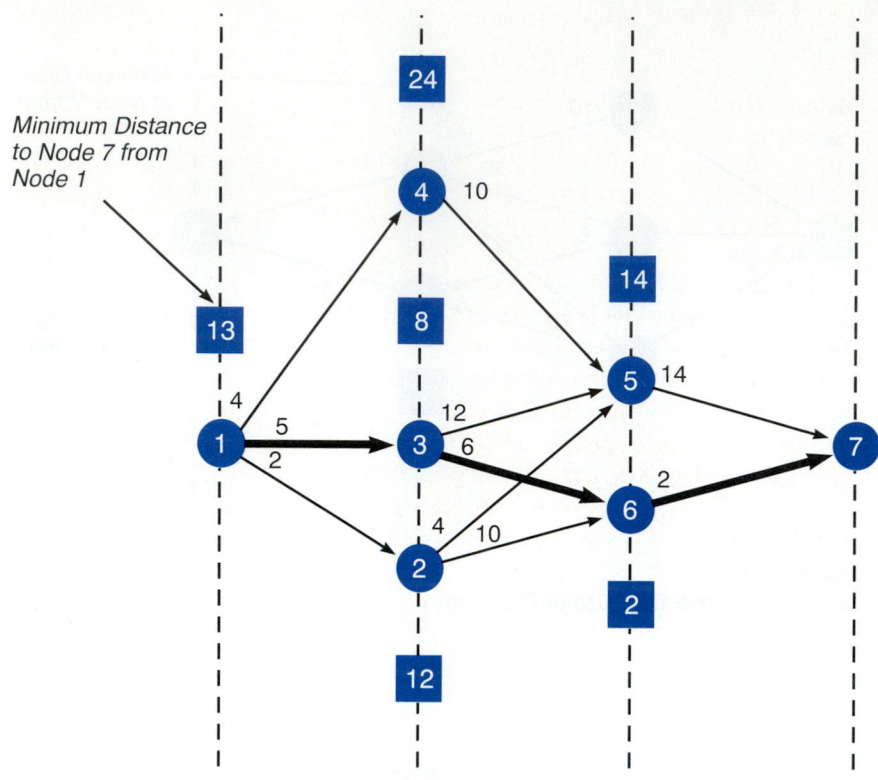

Minimum Distance to Node 7 from Node 1

Transparency Master C.3:
Figure C.5 Solution for the
Three-Stage Problem.

FIGURE C.5
Solution for the Three-Stage Problem

optimal solution at the next stage. For stage 3, we only have to consider the three arcs to stage 2 (1–2, 1–3, and 1–4) and the optimal policies at stage 2, given in a previous table. This is how we arrived at the preceding solution. Once the procedure is understood, we can perform all the calculations on one network. You may want to study the relationship between the networks and the tables because more complex problems are usually solved by using tables only.

terms and concepts that are inherent in every problem. Some of the more important ones are:

1. *Stage:* A period or a logical subproblem.

2. *State Variables:* Possible beginning situations or conditions of a stage. These have also been called the input variables.

3. *Decision Variables:* Alternatives or possible decisions that exist at each stage.

4. *Decision Criterion:* A statement concerning the objective of the problem.

5. *Optimal Policy:* A set of decision rules, developed as a result of the decision criteria, that gives optimal decisions for any entering condition at any stage.

6. *Transformation:* Normally an algebraic statement that reveals the relationship between stages.

C.3 DYNAMIC PROGRAMMING TERMINOLOGY

Regardless of the type or size of a dynamic programming problem, there are some important

In the shortest-route problem, the following transformation can be given:

$$
\begin{array}{c}
\text{Distance from} \\
\text{the beginning} \\
\text{of a given} \\
\text{stage to the} \\
\text{last node}
\end{array}
=
\begin{array}{c}
\text{Distance from} \\
\text{the beginning} \\
\text{of the } \textit{previous} \\
\text{stage to the} \\
\text{last node}
\end{array}
+
\begin{array}{c}
\text{Distance from} \\
\text{the given} \\
\text{stage to the} \\
\text{previous stage.}
\end{array}
$$

This relationship shows how we were able to go from one stage to the next in solving for the optimal solution to the shortest-route problem. In more complex problems, we can use symbols to show the relationship between stages.

State variables, decision variables, the decision criterion, and the optimal policy can be determined for any stage of a dynamic programming problem. This is done here for stage 2 of the George Yates shortest-route problem.

1. State variables for stage 2 are the entering nodes, which are:
   (a) Node 2.
   (b) Node 3.
   (c) Node 4.

2. Decision variables for stage 2 are the following arcs or routes:
   (a) 4–5
   (b) 3–5
   (c) 3–6
   (d) 2–5
   (e) 2–6

3. The decision criterion is the minimization of the total distance traveled.

Video C-2: Using Dynamic Programming to Assist in the Schedule of Operation Desert Storm Airlift Operations

APPLICATIONS OF QA

Using Dynamic Programming to Assist in the Scheduling of Operation Desert Storm Airlift Operations

The beginning of Desert Storm also marked the beginning of airlifting cargo and troops to the Persian Gulf. Each airlift mission to the Persian Gulf required three days, about one million pounds of jet fuel, and a cost of $280,000. Each airlift mission typically involved landings at seven or more airfields. During Operation Desert Storm, the Military Airlift Command (MAC) had more than one hundred such missions on average every day. This represented the largest airlift of cargo and troops in history. More than 25,000 missions had transported 774,000 tons of cargo and 966,000 passengers to the Persian Gulf region by early August of 1991.

In order to successfully manage the largest airlift of military cargo and troops in history, the MAC, along with the assistance of the Oak Ridge National Laboratory, developed a system called the Airlift Deployment Analysis System (ADANS).

The heart of the ADANS system was a dynamic programming-based airlift scheduling algorithm. Using the dynamic programming approach, the airlift scheduler for ADANS was able to produce schedules for the massive airlift based on the requirements for the airlifts, the available resources that could be deployed, and the overall scheduling of the mission.

The actual airlift operation is estimated to have cost between $3.5 billion and $4 billion. ADANS had a development cost of approximately $2 million. Even if the system was only able to improve efficiency by half of a percent, there would be an approximate 10-fold return on investment.

Source: Hilliard, Michael R., et al. "Scheduling the Operation Desert Storm Airlift: An Advanced Automated Scheduling Support System" *Interfaces* **21**, 1 (January–February 1992): 131–146.

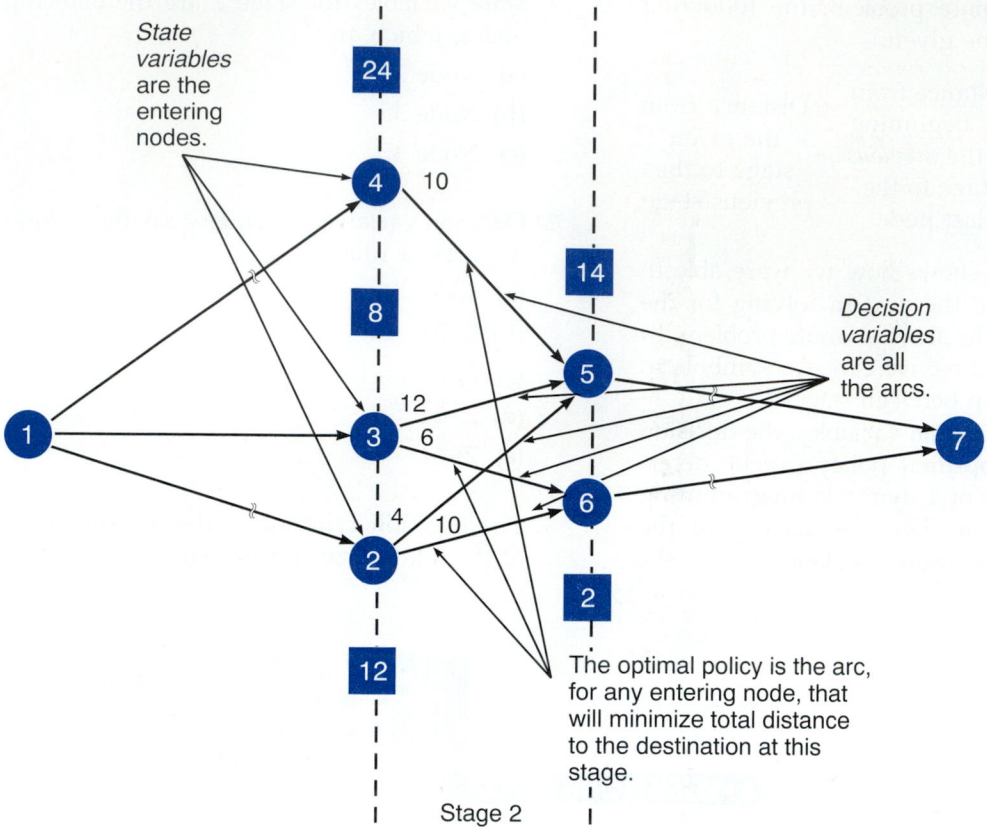

FIGURE C.6
Stage 2 from the Shortest-Route Problem

4. The optimal policy for any beginning condition is:

GIVEN THIS ENTERING CONDITION	THIS ARC WILL MINIMIZE TOTAL DISTANCE TO NODE 7
2	2–6
3	3–6
4	4–5

Figure C.6 above may also be helpful in understanding some of these terms.

C.4 USING THE COMPUTER TO SOLVE DYNAMIC PROGRAMMING PROBLEMS

The dynamic programming module included with AB:QM can handle up to 10 stages and 10 decisions, or branches, at each node. The maximum number of nodes that can be handled by the program is 75. In this text module, we used dynamic programming to solve the shortest-route problem. The input screen and output for this problem are shown in Program C.1 opposite.

PROGRAM C.1 **AB:QM's Dynamic Programming Software**

```
Dynamic Programming / Network

Problem Title :  Dynamic

          Starting Node     Ending Node      Return Value
Stage 3                1              2                2
                       1              3                5
                       1              4                4
Stage 2                2              5                4
                       2              6               10
                       3              5               12
                       3              6                6
                       4              5               10
Stage 1                5              7               14
                       6              7                2


Help  New  Load  Save  Edit   Run   Print  Install  Directory  Esc


***** Program Output *****

                          Stage    1
-----------------------------------------------------------------
S( 1)   D( 1)        R( 1)    S( 0)        f( 0)            f( 1)
-----------------------------------------------------------------
  6     6 -> 7       2.000      7          0.000            2.000
  5     5 -> 7      14.000      7          0.000           14.000
-----------------------------------------------------------------

                          Stage    2
-----------------------------------------------------------------
S( 2)   D( 2)        R( 2)    S( 1)        f( 1)            f( 2)
-----------------------------------------------------------------
  4     4 -> 5      10.000      5         14.000           24.000
-----------------------------------------------------------------
  3     3 -> 6       6.000      6          2.000            8.000
        3 -> 5      12.000      5         14.000           26.000
-----------------------------------------------------------------
  2     2 -> 6      10.000      6          2.000           12.000
        2 -> 5       4.000      5         14.000           18.000
-----------------------------------------------------------------

                          Stage    3
-----------------------------------------------------------------
  1     1 -> 4       4.000      4         24.000           28.000
        1 -> 3       5.000      3          8.000           13.000
        1 -> 2       2.000      2         12.000           14.000
-----------------------------------------------------------------
```

(Continued)

PROGRAM C.1 AB:QM's Dynamic Programming Software (Continued)

```
Final Solution
----------------------------------------------------
Stage      Optimal Decision       Optimal Return
----------------------------------------------------
  3           1 --> 3                5.000
  2           3 --> 6                6.000
  1           6 --> 7                2.000
----------------------------------------------------
Total                               13.000
```

GLOSSARY

Dynamic Programming. A quantitative technique that works backward from the end of the problem to the beginning of the problem in determining the best decision for a number of interrelated decisions.

Stage. A logical subproblem in a dynamic programming problem.

State Variable. A term used in dynamic programming to describe the possible beginning situations or conditions of a stage.

Decision Variable. The alternatives or possible decisions that exist at each stage of a dynamic programming problem.

Decision Criterion. A statement concerning the objective of a dynamic programming problem.

Optimal Policy. A set of decision rules, developed as a result of the decision criterion, that gives optimal decisions at any stage of a dynamic programming problem.

Transformation. An algebraic statement that shows the relationship between stages in a dynamic programming problem.

DISCUSSION QUESTIONS AND PROBLEMS

Discussion Questions

C-1 What is a stage in dynamic programming?

C-2 What is the difference between a state variable and a decision variable?

C-3 Describe the meaning and use of a decision criterion.

C-4 Do all dynamic programming problems require an optimal policy?

C-5 Why is transformation important for dynamic programming problems?

Problems

C-6 Refer to Figure C.1. What is the shortest route between Rice and Dixieville if the road between Hope and Georgetown is improved and the distance is reduced to 4 miles?

C-7 Due to road construction between Georgetown and Dixieville, a detour must be taken through country roads. See Figure C.1. Unfortunately, this detour has increased the distance from Georgetown to Dixieville to 14 miles. What should George do? Should he take a different route?

C-8 The Rice Brothers have a gold mine between Rice and Brown. In their zeal to find gold, they have blown up the road between Rice and Brown. The road will not be in service for five months. What should George do? Refer to Figure C.1.

C-9 Solve the shortest route problem on page 857.

C-10 Identify the state variables, decision variables, the decision criterion, and the optimal policy for the third state of Problem C-9.

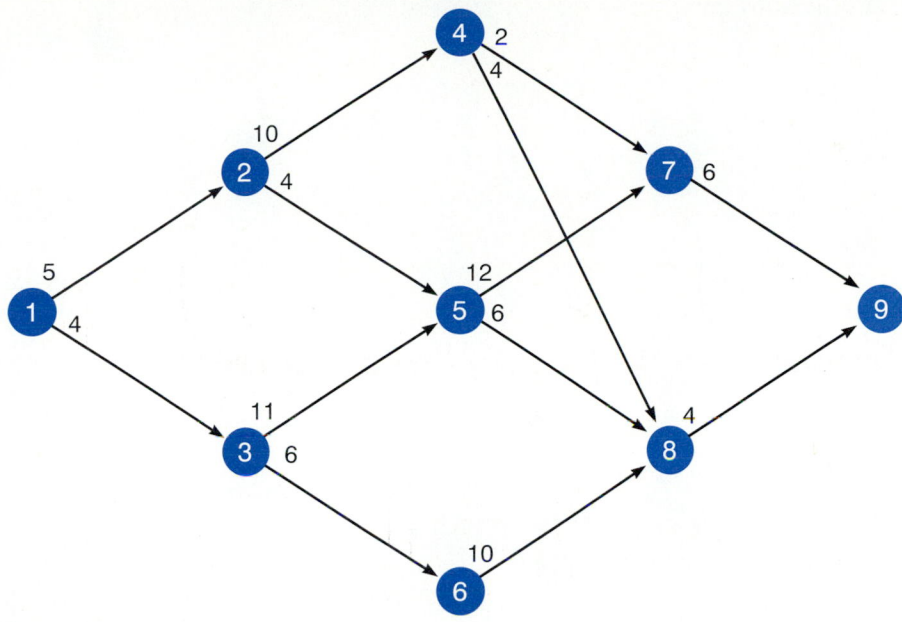

BIBLIOGRAPHY

Bellman, R. E. *Dynamic Programming.* Princeton, NJ: Princeton University Press, 1957.

Carraway, R. L. "A Dynamic Programming Approach to Stochastic Assembly Line Balancing." *Management Science* **35** (April 1989): 459–471.

Hilliard, Michael R., Rajendra S. Solanki, Cheng Liu, Ingrid K. Bushc, Glen Harrison, and Ronald D. Kraemer. "Scheduling the Operation Desert Storm Airlift: An Advanced Automated Scheduling Support System." *Interfaces* **21**, 1 (January–February 1992): 131–146.

Howard R. A. *Dynamic Programming.* Cambridge, MA: MIT Press, 1960.

Kreimer, J. "Allocation of Control Points in Stochastic Dynamic Programming Models." *Journal of Operational Research Society* **39** (September 1988): 847–853.

Lee, S. B., and P. H. Zipkin. "A Dynamic Lot-Size Model with Make-or-Buy Decisions." *Management Science* **35** (April 1989): 447–458.

Mjelde, J.W. "Valuing Forecasting Characteristics in a Dynamic Agricultural Production System." *American Journal of Agricultural Economics* **70** (August 1988): 674–684.

Potts, C. N., and L. N.V. Wassenhove. "Algorithm for Scheduling a Single Machine to Minimize the Weighted Number of Late Jobs." *Management Science* **34** (July 1988): 843–858.

Rodriguez, A., and R. G. Taylor. "Stochastic Modeling of Short-Term Cattle Operations." *American Journal of Agricultural Economics* **70** (February 1988): 121–132.

Sarker, B. R. "An Optimum Solution for One-Dimensional Slitting Problems: A Dynamic Programming Approach." *Journal of Operational Research Society* **39** (August 1988): 749–755.

Starbird, S. A. "Optimal Loading Sequence for Fresh-Apple Storage Facilities." *Journal of Operational Research Society* **39** (October 1988): 911–917.

Stensland, G., and D. Tjosteim. "Optimal Investments Using Empirical Dynamic Programming with Application to Natural Resources." *Journal of Business* **62** (January 1989): 99–120.

Decision Theory and the Normal Distribution

MODULE OUTLINE

D.1 Introduction

D.2 Break-Even Analysis and the Normal Distribution

D.3 EVPI and the Normal Distribution

D.4 Summary

Glossary

Key Equations

Discussion Questions and Problems

Appendix: Derivation of Break-Even Point

D.1　INTRODUCTION

In Chapters 5 and 6, we looked at examples that dealt with only a small number of states of nature and decision alternatives. But what if there were fifty, a hundred, or even thousands of states and/or alternatives? If you used a decision tree or decision table, solving the problem would be virtually impossible. This module shows how decision theory can be extended to handle problems of such a magnitude.

We begin with the case of a firm facing two decision alternatives under conditions of numerous states of nature. The normal probability distribution, which is widely applicable in business decision making, is first used to describe the states of nature.

D.2　BREAK-EVEN ANALYSIS AND THE NORMAL DISTRIBUTION

Break-even analysis, often called *cost-volume analysis,* answers several common management questions relating the effect of a decision to overall revenues or costs. At what point will we break even, or when will revenues equal costs? At a certain sales volume or demand level, what revenues will be generated? If we add a new product line, will this action increase revenues? In this section we look at the basic concepts of break-even analysis and explore how the normal probability distribution can be used in the decision-making process.

Barclay Brothers New Product Decision

The Barclay Brothers Company is a large manufacturer of adult parlor games. Its marketing vice president, Rudy Barclay, must make the decision whether or not to introduce a new game called *Strategy* into the competitive market. Naturally, the company is concerned with costs, potential demand, and profit it can expect to make if it markets *Strategy.*

Rudy identifies the following relevant costs:

Fixed cost = $36,000　　*(Costs that do not vary with volume produced, such as new equipment, insurance, rent, and so on)*

Variable cost per game produced = $4

(Costs that are proportional to the number of games produced, such as materials, and labor)

The selling price per unit is set at $10.

The *break-even point* is that number of games at which total revenues are equal to total costs. It can be expressed by Equation D-1.[1]

Break-even point (in units)

$$= \frac{\text{Fixed cost}}{\text{Price/unit} - \text{Variable cost/unit}} \quad \textbf{(D-1)}$$

So in Barclay's case,

Break-even point (in games)

$$= \frac{\$36,000}{\$10 - \$4} = \frac{\$36,000}{\$6}$$

$$= 6,000 \text{ games of } Strategy$$

Any demand for the new game that exceeds 6,000 units will result in a profit, while a demand less than 6,000 units will cause a loss. For example, if it turns out that demand is 11,000 games of *Strategy,* Barclay's profit would be $30,000, as seen in the following equation.

Revenue (11,000 games × $10/game)		$110,000
Less expenses		
Fixed cost	$36,000	
Variable cost (11,000 games × $4/game)	44,000	
Total expense		80,000
Profit		$30,000

If demand is exactly 6,000 games (the break-even point), you should be able to compute for yourself that profit equals $0.

---

[1] For a detailed explanation of the break-even equation, see the appendix to this module.

Rudy Barclay now has one useful piece of information that will help him make the decision about introducing the new product. If demand is less than 6,000 units, a loss will be incurred. But actual demand is not known. Rudy decides to turn to the use of a probability distribution to estimate demand.

Probability Distribution of Demand

Actual demand for the new game can be at any level—0 units, 1 unit, 2 units, 3 units, up to many thousands of units. Rudy needs to establish the probability of various levels of demand in order to proceed.

In many business situations the normal probability distribution is used to estimate the demand for a new product. It is appropriate when sales are symmetric around the mean expected demand and follow a bell-shaped distribution. Figure D.1 illustrates a typical normal curve that we discussed at length in Chapter 3. Each curve has a unique shape that depends upon two factors: the mean of the distribution (μ) and the standard deviation of the distribution (σ).

In order for Rudy Barclay to use the normal distribution in decision making, he must be able to specify values for μ and σ. This isn't always easy for a manager to do directly, but if he has some idea of the spread, an analyst can determine the appropriate values. In the Barclay example, Rudy might think that the most likely sales figure is 8,000, but that demand might go as low as 5,000 or as high as 11,000. Sales could conceivably go even beyond those limits; say there is a 15%

chance of being below 5,000 and another 15% chance of being above 11,000.

Since this is a symmetric distribution, Rudy decides that a normal curve is appropriate. In Chapter 3, we saw how to take the data in a normal curve such as Figure D.2 (p. 862) and compute the value of the standard deviation. The formula for calculating the number of standard deviations that any value of demand is away from the mean is:

$$Z = \frac{\text{Demand} - \mu}{\sigma} \qquad \text{(D-2)}$$

where Z is the number of standard deviations above or below the mean, μ. It is provided in the table in Appendix A.

We see that the area under the curve to the left of 11,000 units demanded is 85% of the total area, or .85. From Appendix A, the Z value for .85 is approximately 1.04. This means that a demand of 11,000 units is 1.04 standard deviations to the right of the mean, μ.

With $\mu = 8,000$, $Z = 1.04$, and a demand of 11,000, we can easily compute σ.

$$Z = \frac{\text{Demand} - \mu}{\sigma}$$

or

$$1.04 = \frac{11,000 - 8,000}{\sigma}$$

or

$$1.04\sigma = 3,000$$

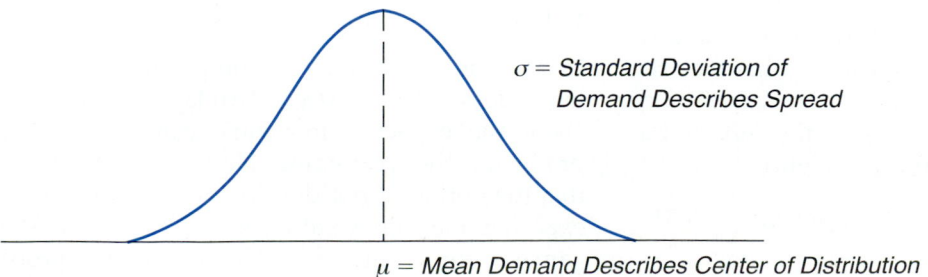

σ = Standard Deviation of
Demand Describes Spread

μ = Mean Demand Describes Center of Distribution

FIGURE D.1
Shape of a Typical Normal Distribution

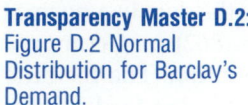

Transparency Master D.2:
Figure D.2 Normal
Distribution for Barclay's
Demand.

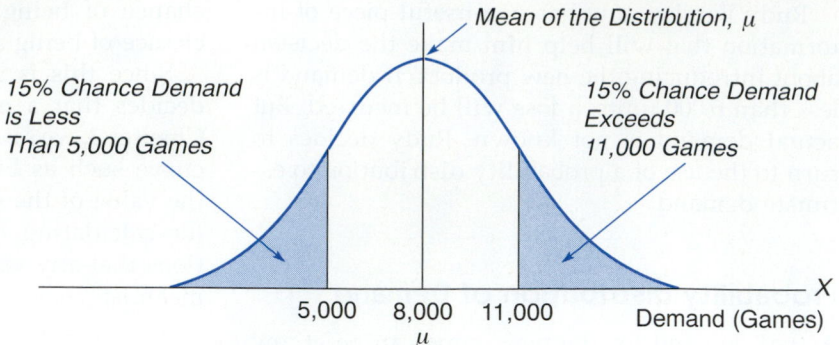

FIGURE D.2
Normal Distribution for Barclay's Demand

or

$$\sigma = \frac{3,000}{1.04} = 2,855 \text{ units}$$

At last, we can state that Barclay's demand appears to be normally distributed, with a mean of 8,000 games and a standard deviation of 2,885 games. This allows us to answer some questions of great financial interest to management—such as what is the probability of breaking even? Recalling that the break-even point is 6,000 games of *Strategy*, we must find the number of standard deviations from 6,000 to the mean.

$$Z = \frac{\text{Break-even point} - \mu}{\sigma}$$

$$= \frac{6,000 - 8,000}{2,885} = \frac{-2,000}{2885} = -0.69$$

This is represented in Figure D.3. Since Appendix A is set up to handle only positive Z values, we can find the Z value for +.69, which is .7549 or 75.49% of the area under the curve. The area under the curve for −.69 is just 1 minus the area computed for +.69, or 1 − .7549. Thus, 24.51% of the area under the curve is to the left of the break-even point of 6,000 units. Hence,

$$P(\text{Loss}) = P(\text{Demand} < \text{Break-even}) = .2451$$

$$= 24.51\%$$

$$P(\text{Profit}) = P(\text{Demand} > \text{Break-even}) = .7549$$

$$= 75.49\%$$

The fact that there is a 75% chance of making a profit is useful management information for Rudy to consider.

Before leaving the topic of break-even analysis, we should point out two caveats:

1. We have assumed that demand is normally distributed. If we should find that this is not reasonable, other distributions may be applied. These are beyond the scope of this text.

2. We have assumed that demand was the only random variable. If one of the other variables (price, variable cost, or fixed costs) were a random variable, a similar procedure could be followed. If two or more variables are both random, the mathematics becomes very complex. This is also beyond our level of treatment.

Using EMV to Make a Decision

In addition to knowing the probability of suffering a loss with *Strategy*, Barclay is concerned about the expected monetary value (EMV) of producing the new game. He knows, of course, that the option of not developing *Strategy* has an expected monetary value of $0. That is, if the game is not produced and marketed, his profit will be $0. If, however, the EMV of producing the game is greater than $0, he will recommend that more profitable strategy.

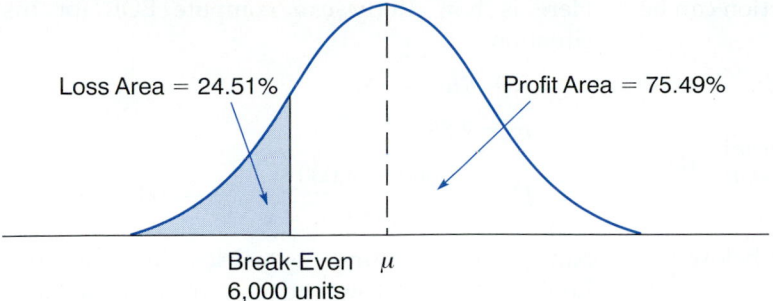

FIGURE D.3
Probability of Breaking Even for Barclay's New Game

To compute the EMV for this strategy, Barclay uses the expected demand, μ, in the following linear profit function.

$$\text{EMV} = (\text{Price/unit} - \text{Variable cost/unit})$$
$$\cdot (\text{Mean demand}) - \text{Fixed costs}$$
$$= (\$10 - \$4)\,(8{,}000 \text{ units})$$
$$\qquad - \$36{,}000 \qquad \text{(D-3)}$$
$$= \$48{,}000 - \$36{,}000$$
$$= \$12{,}000$$

Rudy has two choices at this point. He can recommend that the firm proceed with the new game: if so, he estimates there is a 75% chance of at least breaking even and an expected monetary value of $12,000. *Or*, he might prefer to do further marketing research before making a decision. This brings up the subject of the expected value of perfect information.

D.3 EVPI AND THE NORMAL DISTRIBUTION

Let's return to the Barclay Brothers problem to see how to compute the expected value of perfect information (EVPI) and expected opportunity loss (EOL) associated with introducing the new game. Two steps are involved:

1. Determine the opportunity loss function.

2. Use the opportunity loss function and the unit normal loss integral (found in Appendix B) to find EOL, which is the same as EVPI.

Opportunity Loss Function

The *opportunity loss function* describes the loss that would be suffered by making the wrong decision. We saw earlier that Rudy's break-even point is 6,000 sets of the game *Strategy*. If Rudy produces and markets the new game and sales are greater than 6,000 units, he has made the right decision; in this case there is no opportunity loss ($0). If, however, he introduces *Strategy* and sales are *less* than 6,000 games, he has selected the wrong alternative. The opportunity loss is just the money lost if demand is less than the break-even point; for example, if demand is 5,999 games, Barclay loses $6 (= $10 Price/unit − $4 Cost/unit). With a $6 loss for each unit of sales less than the break-even point, the total opportunity loss is $6 multiplied times the number of units under 6,000. If only 5,000 games are sold, the opportunity loss will be 1,000 units less than the break-even point times $6 per unit = $6,000. For any level of sales, X, Barclay's opportunity loss function can be expressed as follows:

$$\text{Opportunity loss} = \begin{cases} \$6(6{,}000 - X) \\ \$0 \end{cases}$$
$$\qquad \textit{for } X \le 6{,}000 \textit{ games}$$
$$\qquad \textit{for } X > 6{,}000 \textit{ games}$$

In *general*, the opportunity loss function can be computed by:

$$\text{Opportunity loss} = \begin{cases} K(\text{Break-even point} - X) \\ \$0 \end{cases}$$

$$\begin{array}{l} \text{for } X \leq \text{Break-even point} \\ \text{for } X > \text{Break-even point} \end{array} \quad \textbf{(D-4)}$$

where

K = the loss per unit when sales are below the break-even point, and

X = sales in units.

Expected Opportunity Loss

The second step is to find the expected opportunity loss. This is the sum of the opportunity losses multiplied by the appropriate probability values. But in Barclay's case there are a very large number of possible sales values. If the break-even point is 6,000 games, there will be 6,000 possible sales values, from 0, 1, 2, 3, up to 6,000 units. Thus, determining the EOL would require setting 6,000 probability values that correspond to the 6,000 possible sales values. These numbers would be multiplied and added together—a very lengthy and tedious task.

When we assume that there are an infinite (or very large) number of possible sales values that follow a normal distribution, the calculations are much easier. Indeed, when the *unit normal loss integral* is used, EOL can be computed as follows:

$$\text{EOL} = K\sigma N(D) \quad \textbf{(D-5)}$$

where

EOL = expected opportunity loss,

$\quad K$ = loss per unit when sales are below the break-even point,

$\quad \sigma$ = standard deviation of the distribution.

$$D = \left| \frac{\mu - \text{Break-even point}}{\sigma} \right| \quad \textbf{(D-6)}$$

where

$\quad |\,|$ = absolute value sign,

$\quad \mu$ = mean sales, and

$N(D)$ = the value for the unit normal loss integral in Appendix B for a given value of D.

Here is how Rudy can compute EOL for his situation.

$$K = \$6$$

$$\sigma = 2,885$$

$$D = \left| \frac{8,000 - 6,000}{2,885} \right| = .69 = .60 + .09$$

Now refer to the unit normal loss integral table. Look in the ".6" row and read over to the ".09" column. This is $N(.69)$, which is .1453.

$$N(.69) = .1453$$

Therefore,

$$\text{EOL} = K\sigma N(.69)$$

$$= (6)(2885)(.1453) = \$2,515.14$$

Since EVPI and EOL are equivalent, the expected value of perfect information is also $2,515.14. This is the maximum amount that Rudy should be willing to spend on additional marketing information.

The relationship between the opportunity loss function and the normal distribution is shown in Figure D.4 on page 865. This graph shows both the opportunity loss and the normal distribution with a mean of 8,000 games and a standard deviation of 2,885. To the right of the break-even point we note that the loss function is 0. To the left of the break-even point, the opportunity loss function increases at a rate of $6 per unit, hence the slope of -6. The use of Appendix B and Equation D-5 allows us to multiply the $6 unit loss times each of the probabilities between 6,000 units and 0 units and to sum these multiplications.

D.4 SUMMARY

In this module, we looked at decision theory problems that involved many states of nature and alternatives. As an alternative to decision tables and decision trees, we learned to use the normal distribution to solve break-even problems and find the expected monetary value and EVPI. We need to know the mean and standard deviation of the normal distribution and to be certain it is

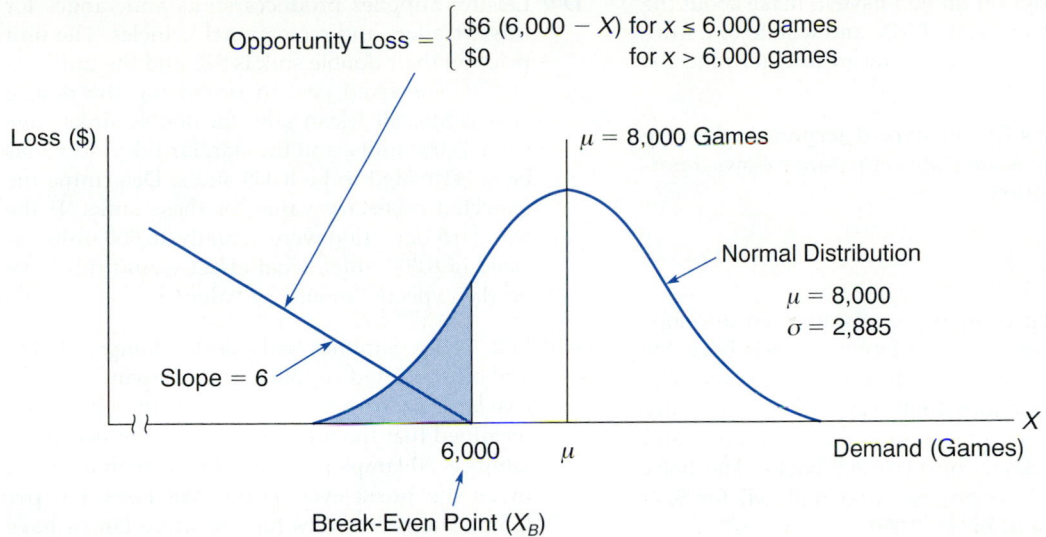

$$\text{Opportunity Loss} = \begin{cases} \$6\,(6{,}000 - X) & \text{for } x \le 6{,}000 \text{ games} \\ \$0 & \text{for } x > 6{,}000 \text{ games} \end{cases}$$

FIGURE D.4
Barclay's Opportunity Loss Function

the appropriate probability distribution to apply. Other continuous distributions can also be used, but they are beyond the level of this text.

GLOSSARY

Break-Even Analysis. The analysis of relationships between profit, costs, and demand level.

Opportunity Loss Function. A function that relates opportunity loss in dollars to sales in units.

Unit Normal Loss Integral. A table that is used in the determination of EOL and EVPI.

KEY EQUATIONS

(D-1) Break-even point (in units)
$$= \frac{\text{Fixed cost}}{\text{Price/unit} - \text{Variable cost/unit}}$$
The formula that provides the volume at which total revenue equals total costs.

(D-2) $Z = \dfrac{\text{Demand} - \mu}{\sigma}$
The number of standard deviations that demand is from the mean, μ.

(D-3) EMV = (Price/unit − Variable cost/unit)
  × (Mean demand) − Fixed costs
The expected monetary value.

(D-4) Opportunity loss
$$= \begin{cases} K(\text{Break-even point} - X) & \text{for } X \le \text{Break-even point} \\ \$0 & \text{for } X > \text{Break-even point} \end{cases}$$
The opportunity loss function.

(D-5) EOL = $K\sigma N(D)$
The expected opportunity loss.

(D-6) $D = \left| \dfrac{\mu - \text{Break-even point}}{\sigma} \right|$
An intermediate value used to compute EOL.

DISCUSSION QUESTIONS AND PROBLEMS

Discussion Questions

D-1 What is the purpose of conducting break-even analysis?

D-2 Under what circumstances can the normal distribution be used in break-even analysis? What does it usually represent?

D-3 What assumption do you have to make about the relationship between EMV and a state of nature when you are using the mean to determine the value of EMV?

D-4 Describe how EVPI can be determined when the distribution of the states of nature follows a normal distribution.

Problems

D-5 A publishing company is planning on developing an advanced quantitative analysis book for graduate students in doctoral programs. The company estimates that sales will be normally distributed, with mean sales of 60,000 copies and a standard deviation of 10,000 books. The book will cost $16 to produce and will sell for $24; fixed costs will be $160,000.

     (a) What is the company's break-even point?
     (b) What is the EMV?

D-6 Refer to Problem D-5.

     (a) What is the opportunity loss function?
     (b) Compute the expected opportunity loss.
     (c) What is the EVPI?
     (d) What is the probability the new book will be profitable?
     (e) What do you recommend that the firm do?

D-7 Barclay Brothers Company, the firm discussed in this module, thinks it underestimated the mean for its game *Strategy*. Rudy Barclay thinks expected sales may be 9,000 games. He also thinks there is a 20% chance sales will be less than 6,000 games and a 20% chance he can sell more than 12,000 games.

     (a) What is the new standard deviation of demand?
     (b) What is the probability the firm will incur a loss?
     (c) What is the EMV?
     (d) How much should Rudy be willing to pay now for a marketing research study?

D-8 True-Lens, Inc. is considering producing the popular long-wearing contact lenses. Fixed costs will be $24,000 with a variable cost per set of lenses of $8. The lenses will sell for $24.00 per set to optometrists.

     (a) What is the firm's break-even point?
     (b) If expected sales are 2,000 sets, what should True-Lens do and what are the expected profits?

D-9 Leisure Supplies produces sinks and ranges for travel trailers and recreational vehicles. The unit price on their double sink is $28 and the unit cost is $20. The fixed cost in producing the double sink is $16,000. Mean sales for double sinks have been 35,000 units, and the standard deviation has been estimated to be 8,000 sinks. Determine the expected monetary value for these sinks. If the standard deviation were actually 16,000 units instead of 8,000 units, what effect would this have on the expected monetary value?

D-10 Belt Office Supplies sells desks, lamps, chairs, and other related supplies. The company's executive lamp sells for $45, and Elizabeth Belt has determined that the break-even point for executive lamps is 30 lamps per year. If Elizabeth does not make the break-even point, she loses $10 per lamp. The mean sales for executive lamps have been 45, and the standard deviation is 30.

     (a) Determine the opportunity loss function.
     (b) Determine the expected opportunity loss.
     (c) What is the EVPI?

D-11 Elizabeth Belt is not completely certain that the loss per lamp is $10 if sales are below the break-even point. (Refer to Problem D-10.) The loss per lamp could be as low as $8 or as high as $15. What effect would these two values have on the expected opportunity loss?

D-12 Leisure Supplies is considering the possibility of using a new process for producing sinks. This new process would increase the fixed cost by $16,000. In other words, the fixed cost would double (see Problem D-9). This new process will improve the quality of the sinks and reduce the cost it takes to produce each sink. It will cost only $19 to produce the sinks using the new process.

     (a) What do you recommend?
     (b) Leisure Supplies is considering the possibility of increasing the purchase price to $32 using the old process given in Problem D-9. It is expected that this will lower the mean sales to 26,000 units. Should Leisure Supplies increase the selling price?

D-13 Quality Cleaners specializes in cleaning apartment units and office buildings. While the work is not too enjoyable, Joe Boyett has been able to realize a considerable profit in the Chicago area. Joe is now thinking about opening another Quality Cleaners in Milwaukee. In order to break even, Joe would need to get 200 cleaning jobs per year. For every job under 200, Joe will lose $80. Joe estimates that the average sales in Milwaukee are 350 jobs per year with a standard deviation of 150 jobs. A marketing research team has approached Joe with a proposition to perform a marketing study on the potential for his cleaning business in Milwaukee. What is the most that Joe would be willing to pay for the marketing research?

D-14 Diane Kennedy is contemplating the possibility of going into competition with Primary Pumps, a manufacturer of industrial water pumps. Diane has gathered some interesting information from a friend of hers who works for Primary. Diane has been told that the mean sales for Primary are 5,000 units and the standard deviation is 50 units. The opportunity loss per pump is $100. Furthermore, Diane has been told that the most that Primary is willing to spend for marketing research for the demand potential for pumps is $500. Diane is interested in knowing the break-even point for Primary Pumps. Given this information, compute the break-even point.

D-15 Jack Fuller estimates that the break-even point for EM 5, a standard electrical motor, is 500 motors. For any motor that is not sold, there is an opportunity loss of $15. The average sales have been 700 motors, and 20% of the time sales have been between 650 and 750 motors. Jack has just been approached by Radner Research, a firm that specializes in performing marketing studies for industrial products, to perform a standard marketing study. What is the most that Jack would be willing to pay for the marketing research?

D-16 Jack Fuller believes that he has made a mistake in his sales figures for EM 5. (See Problem D-15 for details.) He believes that the average sales are 750 instead of 700 units. Furthermore, he estimates that 20% of the time, sales will be between 700 and 800 units. What effect will these changes have on your estimate of the amount that Jack should be willing to pay for the marketing research?

Appendix: Derivation of Break-Even Point

1. Total costs = Fixed cost + (Variable cost/unit) (Number of units)

2. Total revenues = (Price/unit) (Number of units)

3. At break-even point, Total costs = Total revenues

4. Or, Fixed cost + (Variable cost/unit) × (Number of units) = (Price/unit) (Number of units)

5. Solving for the number of units at the break-even point, we get:

Break-even point (in units)

$$= \frac{\text{Fixed cost}}{\text{Price/unit} - \text{Variable cost/unit}}$$

This equation is the same as Equation D-1 in this module.

Multifactor
Decision Making

MODULE OUTLINE

E.1 Introduction
E.2 The Multifactor Evaluation Process
E.3 The Analytic Hierarchy Process

E.4 A Comparison of MFEP and AHP
E.5 Summary
    Glossary
    Key Equations
    Discussion Questions and Problems
    Bibliography

E.1 INTRODUCTION

Many decision-making problems involve a number of factors. For example, if you are considering a new job, factors might include starting salary, career advancement opportunities, work location, the people you'll be working with on the job, the type of work you will be doing, and assorted fringe benefits. If you are considering the purchase of a personal computer, there are a number of important factors to consider as well: price, memory capacity, compatibility with other computers, flexibility, brand name, software availability, the existence of any user groups or clubs, and the support of the computer manufacturer and the local computer store. In buying a new or used car, such factors as color, style, make and model, year, number of miles (if it's a used car), price, dealership or individual you are purchasing the car from, warranties, and cost of insurance may be important factors to consider.

In *multifactor decision making,* individuals subjectively and intuitively consider the various factors in making their selection. For difficult decisions, a quantitative approach is recommended. All of the important factors can then be given appropriate weights and each alternative, such as a car, a computer, or a new job prospect, can be evaluated in terms of these factors. This approach is called the *multifactor evaluation process* (MFEP).

In other cases, we may not be able to quantify our preferences for various factors and alternatives. We then use the analytic hierarchy process. This process uses pairwise comparisons and then computes the weighting factors and evaluations for us. We begin with a discussion of the multifactor evaluation process.

E.2 THE MULTIFACTOR EVALUATION PROCESS

With the multifactor evaluation process, we start by listing the factors and their relative importance on a scale from 0 to 1.

Let's consider an example. Steve Markel, an undergraduate business major, is looking at several job opportunities. After discussing the employment situation with his academic advisor and the director of the placement center, Steve has determined that the only three factors really important to him are salary, career advancement opportunities, and location of the new job. Furthermore, Steve has decided that career advancement opportunities are the most important to him. He has given this a weight of .6. Steve has placed salary next, with a weight of .3. Finally, Steve has given location an importance weight of .1. As with any MFEP problem, the importance weights for factors must sum to 1. See Table E.1.

At this time, Steve feels confident that he will get offers from AA Company, EDS, Ltd., and PW, Inc. For each of these jobs, Steve evaluated, or rated, the various factors on a 0 to 1 scale. For AA Company, Steve gave salary an evaluation of .7, career advancement an evaluation of .9, and location an evaluation of .6. For EDS, Steve evaluated salary as .8, career advancement as .7, and location as .8. For PW, Inc., Steve gave salary an evaluation of .9, career advancement an evaluation of .6, and location an evaluation of .9. The results are shown in Table E.2.

Given this information, Steve can determine a total weighted evaluation for each of the alternatives or job possibilities. Each company is given a factor evaluation for the three factors, and then the factor weights are multiplied times the factor evaluation and summed to get a total weighted evaluation for each company. As you can see in Table E.3, AA Company has received a total weighted evaluation of .81. The same type of

TABLE E.1 Factor Weights

FACTOR	IMPORTANCE (WEIGHT)
Salary	.3
Career advancement	.6
Location	.1

TABLE E.2 Factor Evaluations

FACTOR	AA CO.	EDS, LTD.	PW, INC.
Salary	.7	.8	.9
Career advancement	.9	.7	.6
Location	.6	.8	.9

TABLE E.3 Evaluation of AA Co.

FACTOR NAME	FACTOR WEIGHTS		FACTOR EVALUATION		WEIGHTED EVALUATION
Salary	.3	×	.7	=	.21
Career	.6	×	.9	=	.54
Location	.1	×	.6	=	.06
Total	1				.81

TABLE E.4 Evaluation of EDS, Ltd.

FACTOR NAME	FACTOR WEIGHTS		FACTOR EVALUATION		WEIGHTED EVALUATION
Salary	.3	×	.8	=	.24
Career	.6	×	.7	=	.42
Location	.1	×	.8	=	.08
Total	1				.74

TABLE E.5 Evaluation of PW, Inc.

FACTOR NAME	FACTOR WEIGHTS		FACTOR EVALUATION		WEIGHTED EVALUATION
Salary	.3	×	.9	=	.27
Career	.6	×	.6	=	.36
Location	.1	×	.9	=	.09
Total	1				.72

analysis is done for EDS, Ltd., and PW, Inc., in Tables E.4 and E.5. As you can see from the analysis, AA Company received the highest total weighted evaluation. EDS, Ltd., was next with a total weighted evaluation of .74. Using the multifactor evaluation process, Steve's decision was to go with AA Company because it had the highest total weighted evaluation.

E.3 THE ANALYTIC HIERARCHY PROCESS

In situations where we can assign evaluations and weights to the various decision factors, the multifactor evaluation process described in the previous section works fine. In other cases, decision makers may have difficulties in accurately determining the various factor weights and evaluations. In this case, the *analytic hierarchy process* (AHP) can be used. AHP was developed by Thomas L. Saaty, and published in his 1980 book, *The Analytic Hierarchy Process.*

This process involves pairwise comparisons. The decision maker starts by laying out the overall hierarchy of the decision. This hierarchy reveals the factors to be considered as well as the various alternatives in the decision. Then, a number of pairwise comparisons are done, which result in the determination of *factor weights* and *factor evaluations.* They are the same types of weights and evaluations discussed in the previous section and shown in Tables E.1 through E.5. As before, the alternative with the highest total weighted score is selected as the best alternative.

Judy Grim's Computer Decision

As an example of this process, we take the case of Judy Grim, who is looking for a new computer system for her small business. She has determined that the most important overall factors are hardware, software, and vendor support. Furthermore, Judy has narrowed down her alternatives to three possible computer systems. She has labeled these SYSTEM-1, SYSTEM-2, and SYSTEM-3. To begin, Judy has placed these factors and alternatives into a decision hierarchy. See Figure E.1 on page 872.

The decision hierarchy for the computer selection has three different levels. The top level describes the overall decision. As you can see in Figure E.1, this overall decision is to select the best computer system. The middle level in the hierarchy describes the factors that are to be considered—hardware, software, and vendor support. Judy could decide to use a number of additional factors, but for this example, we keep our factors to only three to show you the types of calculations that are to be performed using AHP. The lower level of the decision hierarchy reveals the alternatives. (Alternatives have also been called items or systems.) As you can see, the alternatives include the three different computer systems.

The key to using AHP is pairwise comparisons. The decision maker, Judy Grim, needs to compare two different alternatives using a scale that ranges from equally preferred to extremely preferred. This is shown on page 872.

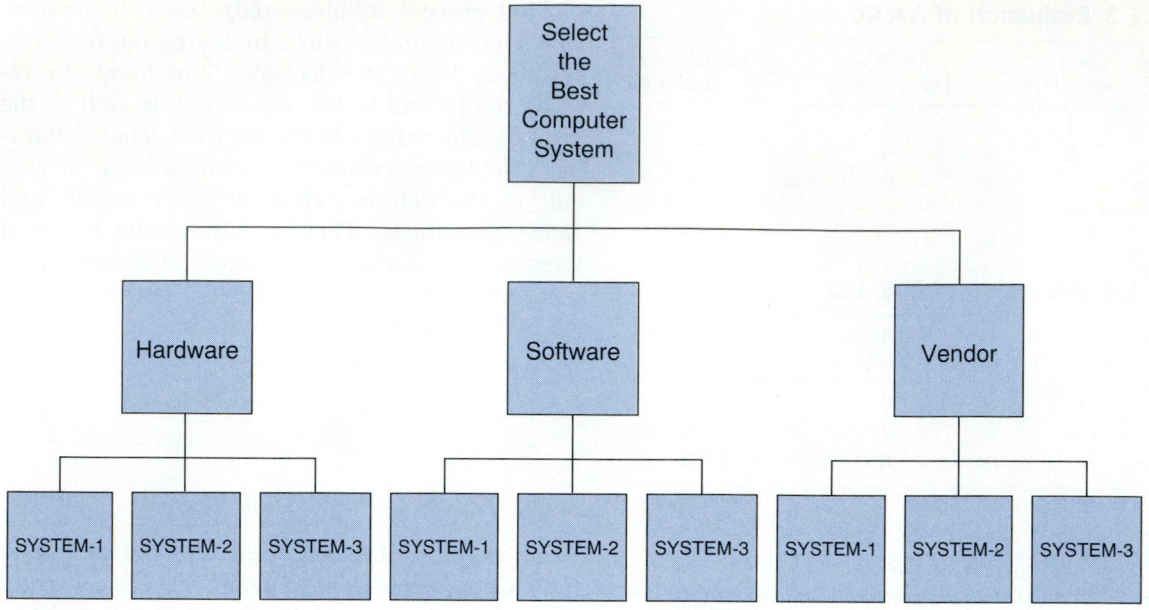

FIGURE E.1
Decision Hierarchy for Computer System Selection

Use the following for pairwise comparison:
1—Equally Preferred
2—Equally to Moderately Preferred
3—Moderately Preferred
4—Moderately to Strongly Preferred
5—Strongly Preferred
6—Strongly to Very Strongly Preferred
7—Very Strongly Preferred
8—Very to Extremely Strongly Preferred
9—Extremely Preferred

Using Pairwise Comparisons

Judy begins by looking at the hardware factor and by comparing computer SYSTEM-1 to computer SYSTEM-2. Using the scale above, Judy determines that the hardware for computer SYSTEM-1 is moderately preferred to computer SYSTEM-2. Thus, Judy uses the number 3, representing moderately preferred. Next, Judy compares the hardware for SYSTEM-1 to SYSTEM-3. She believes that the hardware for computer SYSTEM-1 is extremely preferred to computer SYSTEM-3. This is a numerical score of 9. Finally, Judy considers the only other pairwise compari-

son, which is the hardware for computer SYSTEM-2 compared to the hardware for computer SYSTEM-3. She believes that the hardware for computer SYSTEM-2 is strongly to very strongly preferred to the hardware for computer SYSTEM-3, a score of 6. With these pairwise comparisons, Judy constructs a pairwise comparison matrix for hardware. This is shown below.

HARDWARE	SYSTEM-1	SYSTEM-2	SYSTEM-3
SYSTEM-1		3	9
SYSTEM-2			6
SYSTEM-3			

The pairwise comparison matrix just shown reveals Judy's preferences for hardware concerning the three computer systems. From this information, using AHP, we can determine the evaluation factors for hardware for the three computer systems.

Look at the upper left corner of the pairwise comparison matrix. This upper left corner compares computer SYSTEM-1 to itself for hardware.

When comparing anything to itself, the evaluation scale must be 1, representing equally preferred. Thus, we can place the number 1 in the upper left corner, which compares SYSTEM-1 to itself. The same can be said for comparing SYSTEM-2 to itself and comparing SYSTEM-3 to itself. Each of these must also get a score of 1, which represents equally preferred. In general, for any pairwise comparison matrix, we will place 1s down the diagonal from the upper left corner to the lower right corner. To finish such a table, we make the observation that if alternative A is twice as preferred to alternative B, we can conclude that alternative B is preferred only one half as much as alternative A. Thus, if alternative A receives a score of 2 relative to alternative B, then alternative B should receive a score of ½ when compared to alternative A. We can use this same logic to complete the lower left side of the matrix of pairwise comparisons:

HARDWARE	SYSTEM-1	SYSTEM-2	SYSTEM-3
SYSTEM-1	1	3	9
SYSTEM-2	⅓	1	6
SYSTEM-3	⅑	⅙	1

Look at this newest matrix of pairwise comparisons. You will see that there are 1s down the diagonal from the upper left to the lower right corner. Then, look at the lower left part of the table. In the second row and first column of this table, you can see that SYSTEM-2 received a score of ⅓ compared to SYSTEM-1. This is because SYSTEM-1 received a score of 3 over SYSTEM-2 from the original assessment. Now, look at the third row. The same has been done. SYSTEM-3 compared to SYSTEM-1, in row 3 column 1 of the table, received a score of ⅑. This is because SYSTEM-1 compared to SYSTEM-3 received a score of 9 in the original pairwise comparison. In a likewise fashion, SYSTEM-3 compared to SYSTEM-2 received a score of ⅙ in the third row and second column of the table. This is because when comparing SYSTEM-2 to SYSTEM-3 in the original pairwise comparison, the score of 6 was given.

Evaluations for Hardware

Now that we have the completed matrix of pairwise comparisons, we can start to compute the evaluations for hardware. We start by converting the numbers in the matrix of pairwise comparisons to decimals to make them easier to work with and getting column totals:

HARDWARE	SYSTEM-1	SYSTEM-2	SYSTEM-3
SYSTEM-1	1	3	9
SYSTEM-2	.3333	1	6
SYSTEM-3	.1111	.1677	1
Column Totals	1.444	4.1667	16.0

Once the column totals have been determined, the numbers in the matrix are divided by their respective column totals as follows:

HARDWARE	SYSTEM-1	SYSTEM-2	SYSTEM-3
SYSTEM-1	.6923	.7200	.5625
SYSTEM-2	.2300	.2400	.3750
SYSTEM-3	.0769	.0400	.0625

To determine the priorities for hardware for the three computer systems, we simply find the average of the various rows from the matrix of numbers as follows:

HARDWARE		

$$\text{Row Averages} \begin{bmatrix} .6583 \\ .2819 \\ .0598 \end{bmatrix} \begin{matrix} = (.6923 + .7200 + .5625)/3 \\ = (.2300 + .2400 + .3750)/3 \\ = (.0769 + .0400 + .0625)/3 \end{matrix}$$

The results are displayed in Table E.6 (p. 874). As you can see, the factor evaluation for SYSTEM-1 is .6583. For SYSTEM-2 and SYSTEM-3, the factor evaluations are .2819 and .0598. The same procedure is used to get the factor evaluations for all the other factors, which are software and vendor support in this case. But before we do this, we need to determine whether our responses are consistent by determining a *consistency ratio*.

TABLE E.6 Factor Evaluation for Hardware

FACTOR	SYSTEM-1	SYSTEM-2	SYSTEM-3
Hardware	.6583	.2819	.0598

Determining the Consistency Ratio

To arrive at the consistency ratio, we begin by determining the weighted sum vector. This is done by multiplying the factor evaluation number for the first system or alternative times the first column of the original pairwise comparison matrix. We multiply the second factor evaluation times the second column, and the third factor times the third column of the original matrix of pairwise comparisons. Then, we sum these values over the rows.

Weighted sum vector

$$= \begin{bmatrix} (.6583)(1) & + (.2819)(3) & + (.0598)(9) \\ (.6583)(.3333) & + (.2819)(1) & + (.0598)(6) \\ (.6583)(.1111) & + (.2819)(.1677) & + (.0598)(1) \end{bmatrix}$$

$$= \begin{bmatrix} 2.0423 \\ .8602 \\ .1799 \end{bmatrix}$$

The next step is to determine the consistency vector. This is done by dividing the weighted sum vector by the factor evaluation values determined previously.

$$\text{Consistency vector} = \begin{bmatrix} 2.0423/.6583 \\ .8602/.2819 \\ .1799/.0598 \end{bmatrix}$$

$$= \begin{bmatrix} 3.1025 \\ 3.0512 \\ 3.0086 \end{bmatrix}$$

Now that we have found the consistency vector, we need to compute values for two more terms, lambda (λ) and the consistency index (CI), before the final consistency ratio can be computed. The value for lambda is simply the average value of the consistency vector. The formula for CI is:

$$\text{CI} = \frac{\lambda - n}{n - 1} \tag{E.1}$$

where

n is the number of items or systems being compared.

In this case, $n = 3$ for three different computer systems being compared. The results of the calculations are as follows:

$$\lambda = (3.1025 + 3.0512 + 3.0086)/3$$

$$\lambda = 3.0541$$

$$\text{CI} = (\lambda - n)/(n - 1)$$

$$= (3.0541 - 3)/(3 - 1) = .0270$$

Finally, we are now in a position to compute the consistency ratio. The consistency ratio (CR) is equal to the consistency index divided by the random index (RI), which is determined from a table. The random index is a direct function of the number of alternatives or systems being considered. This table is shown, followed by the final calculation of the consistency ratio.

n	RI
2	.00
$n \rightarrow$ 3 $\rightarrow$	.58
4	.90
5	1.12
6	1.24
7	1.32
8	1.41

In general, $$\text{CR} = \frac{\text{CI}}{\text{RI}} \tag{E.2}$$

In this case, $$\text{CR} = \frac{\text{CI}}{\text{RI}} = \frac{.0270}{.58} = .0466$$

The consistency ratio tells us how consistent we are with our answers. A higher number means we are less consistent, while a lower number means that we are more consistent. In general, if the consistency ratio is .10 or less, the decision maker's answers are relatively consistent. For a consistency ratio that is greater than .10, the decision maker should seriously consider reevaluating his or her responses during the pairwise comparisons that were used to obtain the original matrix of pairwise comparisons.

As you can see from the analysis, we are relatively consistent with our responses, so there is no need to reevaluate the pairwise comparison responses. If you look at the original pairwise comparison matrix, this makes sense. The hardware for SYSTEM-1 was moderately preferred to the hardware for SYSTEM-2. The hardware for SYSTEM-1 was extremely preferred to the hardware for SYSTEM-3. This implies that the hardware for SYSTEM-2 should be preferred over the hardware for SYSTEM-3. From our responses, the hardware for SYSTEM-2 was strongly to very strongly preferred over the hardware for SYSTEM-3, as indicated by the number 6. Thus, our original assessments of the pairwise comparison matrix seem to be consistent, and the consistency ratio that we computed supports our observations.

Although the calculations to compute the consistency ratio are fairly involved, they are an important step in using the analytical hierarchy process.

Evaluations for the Other Factors

So far, we have determined the factor evaluations for hardware for the three different computer systems along with a consistency ratio for these evaluations. Now, we can make the same calculations for the other factors, namely software and vendor support. As before, we start with the matrix of pairwise comparisons. We perform the same calculations and end up with the various factor evaluations for both sofware and vendor support. We begin by presenting the matrix of pairwise comparisons for both software and vendor support.

SOFTWARE	SYSTEM-1	SYSTEM-2	SYSTEM-3
SYSTEM-1			
SYSTEM-2	2		
SYSTEM-3	8	5	

VENDOR SUPPORT	SYSTEM-1	SYSTEM-2	SYSTEM-3
SYSTEM-1		1	6
SYSTEM-2			3
SYSTEM-3			

With the matrices shown, we can perform the same types of calculations to determine the factor evaluations for both software and vendor support for the three computer systems. The data, for the three different systems, are summarized in Table E.7 below. We also need to determine the consistency ratios for both software and support. As it turns out, both consistency ratios are under .10, meaning that the responses to the pairwise comparison are acceptably consistent.

You should note that the factor evaluations for the three factors and three different computer systems shown in Table E.7 are similar to the factor evaluations in Table E.2 for the job selection problem. The major difference is that we had to use the analytic hierarchy process to determine these factor evaluations using pairwise comparisons, because we were not comfortable in our abilities to subjectively assess these factors without some assistance.

Determining Factor Weights

Next, we need to determine the various factor weights. When we used the multifactor evaluation process, it was assumed that we could simply determine these values subjectively. Another approach is to use the analytic hierarchy process and pairwise comparisons to determine the factor weights for hardware, software, and vendor support. In comparing the three different factors, we determine that software is the most important. Software is very to extremely strongly preferred over hardware (number 8). Software is moderately preferred over vendor support (number 3). In comparing vendor support to hardware, we decide that vendor support is more important. Vendor support is moderately preferred to hardware (number 3). With these values, we can construct the pairwise comparison matrix and then compute the weights for hardware, software, and support. We also need to compute a consistency

TABLE E.7 Factor Evaluations

FACTOR	SYSTEM-1	SYSTEM-2	SYSTEM-3
Hardware	.6583	.2819	.0598
Software	.0874	.1622	.7504
Vendor	.4967	.3967	.1066

ratio to make sure that our responses are consistent. As with software and vendor support, the actual calculations for determining the factor weights are left for you to make on your own. After making the appropriate calculations, the factor weights for hardware, software, and vendor support are shown in Table E.8 below.

The Overall Ranking

Once the factor weights have been determined, we can multiply the factor evaluations in Table E.7 times the factor weights in Table E.8. This is the same procedure we used for the job selection decision in the previous section on the multifactor evaluation process. It will give us the overall ranking for the three different computer systems, which is shown in Table E.9. As you can see, SYSTEM-3 received the highest final ranking and is selected as the best computer system.

<table>
<tr><td>**E.4**</td><td>**A COMPARISON OF MFEP AND AHP**</td></tr>
</table>

Multifactor decision making has a number of useful and important applications. If you know

TABLE E.8 Factor Weights

FACTOR	FACTOR WEIGHT
Hardware	.0820
Software	.6816
Vendor	.2364

TABLE E.9 Total Weighted Evaluations

SYSTEM OR ALTERNATIVE	TOTAL WEIGHTED EVALUATION
SYSTEM-1	.2310
SYSTEM-2	.2275
SYSTEM-3*	.5416

* System-3 is selected.

or can determine with confidence and accuracy the factor weights and factor evaluations, MFEP is preferred. If not, you should use AHP. As it turns out, AHP also gives the factor weights and factor evaluations from which the final selection can be made. The only difference is that with AHP we compute the factor weights and factor evaluations from a number of pairwise comparison matrices. We also compute a consistency ratio to make sure that our responses to the original pairwise comparison matrix are consistent and acceptable. If they are not, we should go back and perform the pairwise comparison again. Although AHP involves a larger number of calculations, it is preferred to MFEP in cases where we do not feel confident or comfortable in determining factor weights or factor evaluations without making pairwise comparisons.

<table>
<tr><td>**E.5**</td><td>**SUMMARY**</td></tr>
</table>

Multifactor decision making is appropriate when an individual, group, or organization faces a number of factors in a decision-making situation. With the multifactor evaluation process, a decision maker assigns an importance weight to each factor. The weights can, for example, range from 0 to 1. Then, for each alternative, all factors are evaluated. The factor weights are multiplied times each factor evaluation for a given alternative and summed. The alternative with the highest overall score is selected.

With the analytic hierarchy process (AHP), the decision maker performs a number of pairwise comparisons between each pair of alternatives for each factor to determine the factor evaluations. A pairwise comparison is also performed between each pair of factors to determine the factor weights. This information is used to determine a total weighted evaluation for each alternative. The alternative with the highest total weighted evaluation is selected. The AHP approach also allows for the computation of a consistency ratio to help decision makers determine if their pairwise comparisons are consistent.

GLOSSARY

Multifactor Decision Making. A decision-making environment where multiple factors are to be considered in making the final selection.

Multifactor Evaluation Process (MFEP). A multifactor decision-making approach where the factor weights and factor evaluations can be accurately determined and used in the decision-making process.

Analytic Hierarchy Process (AHP). A process that uses pairwise comparisons to determine factor evaluations and factor weights in a multifactor decision-making environment.

Factor Evaluations. These are evaluations on a scale from 0 to 1 that indicate our preference for a particular factor for a particular alternative or item.

Factor Weights. These are weights that range from 0 to 1 that give the relative importance of one factor to another. The factor weights for all factors in a multifactor decision-making environment must sum to 1.

KEY EQUATIONS

(E-1) $CI = (\lambda - n)/(n - 1)$
Consistency index.

(E-2) $CR = CI/RI$
Consistency ratio

where   RI = the random index,
λ = average of the weighted sum vector divided by the factor evaluations, and
n = the number of alternatives or items.

DISCUSSION QUESTIONS AND PROBLEMS

Discussion Questions

E-1 Describe decision situations where multifactor decision making is appropriate. What decision-making situations do you face that could benefit from the multifactor decision-making approach?

E-2 Briefly describe the multifactor evaluation process.

E-3 When should the analytic hierarchy process be used compared to the multifactor evaluation process?

Problems

E-4 George Lyon is about to buy a compact stereo cassette player. He is currently considering three brands—Sun, Hitek, and Surgo. The important factors to George are the price, color, warranty, size of the unit, and brand name. George has determined factor weights of .4, .1, .1, .1, and .3 respectively. Furthermore, George has determined factor evaluations for all of the factors for the three different manufacturers of the unit he is considering. The Sun unit has factor evaluations of .7, .9, .8, .8 and .9 for the price, color, warranty, size, and brand-name factors. The Hitek unit has factor evaluations of .6, .9, .9, .8, and .9 for these factors. Finally, Surgo has factor evaluations of .8, .4, .4, .2, and .6 for the same factors of price, color, warranty, size, and brand name. Determine the total weighted evaluation for the three manufacturers. Which one should George select?

E-5 Linda Frieden is thinking about buying a new car. There are three different car models she is considering—car 1, car 2, or car 3. An important factor for Linda is the price. She has determined that car 1 is equally to moderately preferred to car 2. Car 1 is very strongly preferred to car 3, and car 2 is moderately to strongly preferred to car 3. Determine the priorities or factor evaluations for the three cars for price. What is the consistency ratio?

E-6 Linda Frieden (Problem E-5) is also concerned about the warranty for the three cars she is considering. The second car is moderately preferred to the first car in terms of warranty. The third car is very to extremely strongly preferred over the first car, and the third car is strongly preferred over the second car. Determine the factor evaluations or priorities for the three cars for car warranty. Compute the consistency ratio.

E-7 Linda Frieden (Problems E-5 and E-6) would like to consider style as an important factor in making a decision to purchase a new car. Car 2 is moderately preferred to car 1 in terms of style, but car 1 is moderately preferred to car 3 in terms of style. Furthermore, car 2 is very to extremely strongly preferred over car 3. Determine the factor evaluations for style concerning the three cars and compute the consistency ratio.

E-8 Linda Frieden (Problems E-5–E-7) now must determine the relative weights for the three factors of price, warranty, and style. She believes that the price is equally to moderately preferred over warranty, and that price is extremely preferred to style. She also believes that the car warranty is strongly to very strongly preferred over the style. Using this information, determine the weights for these three factors. Also determine the consistency ratio to make sure that the above values are consistent enough to use in the analysis. In Problems E-5–E-7, Linda has determined factor evaluations for price, warranty, and style for the three cars. Using the information you determined in this problem along with the solutions to the above three problems, determine the final rankings for each car. Which car should be selected?

E-9 Jim Locke, an undergraduate student in the E.S.U. College of Business, is trying to decide which microcomputer to purchase with the money his parents gave him for Christmas. He has reduced the number of computers he has been considering to three, calling them system 1 (S1), system 2 (S2), and system 3 (S3). For each computer, he would like to consider the price, the brand name, the memory capacity, speed, flexibility, and compatibility with IBM PCs.

In order to make the correct decision, he has decided to make pairwise comparisons for all the factors. For price, the first computer system is equally to moderately preferred over the second computer system and very to extremely strongly preferred over the third computer system. The second computer system is strongly preferred over the third computer system.

For brand name, the first computer system is equally preferred to the second computer system, while the first computer system is strongly to very strongly preferred over the third computer system. The second computer system is moderately to strongly preferred over the third computer system.

When it comes to memory, the second computer is equally to moderately preferred over the first computer system, and the third computer system is very strongly preferred over the first computer system. Furthermore, the third computer system is strongly to very strongly preferred over the second computer system.

For speed, the second computer system is moderately preferred to the first computer system, but

the first computer system is equally to moderately preferred over the third computer system. Furthermore, the second computer system is strongly preferred over the third computer system.

For the flexibility factor, the third computer system is very to extremely strongly preferred over the first computer system, and the second computer system is equally to moderately preferred over the first computer system. The third computer system is also moderately to strongly preferred over the second computer system.

Finally, Jim has used pairwise comparisons to look at how compatible each computer system is with the IBM PC. Using this analysis, he has determined that the first computer system is very to extremely strongly preferred over the second computer system when it comes to compatibility. The first computer system is moderately to strongly preferred over the third computer system, and the third computer system is moderately preferred over the second computer system.

When it comes to comparing the factors, Jim has used pairwise comparisons to look at price, brand name, memory, speed, flexibility, and compatibility. Here are the results of the analysis. Price is extremely preferred to brand name, moderately to strongly preferred to memory, strongly preferred to speed, moderately preferred to flexibility, and equally to moderately preferred to PC compatibility. In other words, price is a very important factor. The computer's memory is equally to moderately preferred to brand name, speed is equally preferred to brand name, flexibility is moderately to strongly preferred to brand name, and PC compatibility is strongly preferred to brand name. In looking at memory, Jim has determined that memory is equally to moderately preferred to speed. PC compatibility, however, is strongly to very strongly preferred to memory, and overall flexibility is equally to moderately preferred to the computer's memory. PC compatibility is strongly to very strongly preferred to speed, and flexibility is moderately preferred to speed. Finally, Jim has determined that PC compatibility is equally to moderately preferred to flexibility.

Using all of these preferences for pairwise comparisons, determine the priorities or factor evaluations, along with the appropriate consistency ratios for price, brand name, memory, speed, flexibility, and PC compatibility for the three different computer systems. In addition, determine the overall weights for each of the factors. Which computer system should be selected?

BIBLIOGRAPHY

Hughes, Warren. "Decision Making Using the Analytic Hierarchy Process: The Falklands Crisis." *Proceedings of the 1986 Annual Meeting of the Decision Sciences Institute* **2** (1986): 768–770.

Islei, Gerd, Geoff Lockett, Barry Cox, Steve Gisbourne, and Mike Stratford. "Modeling Strategic Decision Making and Performance Measurements at ICI Pharmaceuticals." *Interfaces,* **21,** 6 (November–December 1991): 4–22.

Saaty, Thomas. "A Scaling Method for Priorities in Hierarchical Structures." *Journal of Mathematical Psychology* **15,** 3 (1977): 234–281.

Saaty, Thomas. *The Analytic Hierarchy Process.* New York: McGraw-Hill, 1980.

Saaty, Thomas, and K. Kearn. *Analytical Planning—The Organization of Systems.* Oxford: Pergamon Press, 1985.

Schoner, B, and W. C. Wedley. "Ambiguous Criteria Weights in AHP: Consequences and Solutions." *Decision Sciences* **20** (Summer 1989): 462–475.

Wind, Yoran, and Thomas Saaty. "Marketing Applications of the Analytic Hierarchy Process." *Management Science* **26,** 7 (July 1980): 641–658.

Zahedi, F. "The Analytic Hierarchy Process—A Survey of the Method and Its Applications." *Interfaces* **16,** 4 (1986): 96–108.

Using AB:QM

MODULE OUTLINE

F.1 Introduction

F.2 Basic Requirements for AB:QM

F.3 Starting AB:QM

F.4 Using AB:QM

F.5 A Forecasting Example of AB:QM

F.6 Limitations of AB:QM

F.1   INTRODUCTION

In this module, we will explore the use of AB:QM. Before using AB:QM, you need to know how to boot the computer and format one or more data disks. These and related beginning steps are discussed next.

Beginning Steps

The first step is to boot, or start, the computer. With a computer with floppy disk drives, this can be done by placing the disk operating system (DOS) disk in the A disk drive and turning on the computer. At this point, the computer will ask you to enter the current date and time. After you have entered this information, you will see the A prompt or A:/> on the screen. If your computer has a hard disk drive, booting the computer can be accomplished by just turning on the computer without the DOS disk (or any disk) in the A drive. In this case, the computer will display the C prompt or C:\>.

Using the FORMAT Command

At this point, you may want to format one or more data disks. If you have a dual floppy computer system, you start by putting the DOS disk in the A drive and a new unformatted disk in the B drive. At the A prompt or A:\>, you type **FOR-MAT B:** and press the return key. This appears as follows. Note that we have typed commands that you enter in **bold.** In addition, you should press the return key after each command you enter.

A:\>**FORMAT B:**

After you have formatted the first disk, the computer will ask you if you want to format another disk. Type **Y** for yes or **N** for no. *It is important to note that the formatting process will destroy any existing data or programs on the disk. Thus, do not format the program disks.* If you have a hard disk computer system, you will need to go to the directory that contains DOS. This can be done with the **CD** or change directory command. For example, if your DOS programs are in a subdirectory called DOS, you can type **CD DOS** at the

C prompt or C:\>. Put the unformatted data disk in the A drive and type **FORMAT A:**. The process appears below.

C:\> **CD DOS**
C:\DOS>**FORMAT A:**

Other DOS Commands and Procedures

There are other DOS commands or procedures that you may find useful. You can change disk drives by typing the letter of the drive. For example, you may be in the A drive and want to go to the C drive. This is done by typing **c:** and pressing the return key. You may also want to get a list of files (data and programs) on a disk in a particular disk drive. This is done with the **dir** or directory command. For example, you may be in the A drive and want to get a list of the data on a floppy disk in the B drive. Type **b:** to get to the B drive and **dir** to get a directory or list of files for the disk in the B drive. This is shown below:

A:\>**b:**
b:\>**dir**

Another useful DOS command is the **copy** command. It can be used to copy one or more files from one disk to another. For example, to copy the data file PROB1.INV from the disk in the B drive to the disk in the A drive, you type **COPY B:PROB1.INV A:PROB1.INV.** Note that the first drive and file (B:PROB1.INV) is where the file is copied *from* and the second drive and file (A:PROB1.INV) is where the file is copied *to.*

Making a Subdirectory on a Hard Disk

If you have a hard disk system, you may want to create a subdirectory for AB:QM. The first step is to make a directory with the **MD**, or make directory command. You can type **MD ABQM** from the C prompt to make a subdirectory for the AB:QM programs. Next, you can change to this new directory with the **CD** command and copy the AB:QM files from the A drive to the new subdirectory using the **COPY A:*.* C:** command. Once this is done, you can start AB:QM by typing **QM** and pressing the return key. This procedure is shown below. Note again that commands you enter are in **bold.** Once you have performed these beginning steps, you are ready to start AB:QM.

C:\>**MD ABQM**
C:\>**CD ABQM**
C:\ABQM>**COPY A:*.* C:**
C:\ABQM>**QM**

F.2 BASIC REQUIREMENTS FOR AB:QM

AB:QM runs on IBM and IBM-compatible computer systems (including many IBM PS/2 models). It requires 640K of RAM (random access memory). An EPSON or compatible printer is recommended. A color monitor or monochrome monitor may be used. One floppy disk drive is acceptable, although two disk drives or a hard disk are recommended.

The program comes on two 5-1/4-inch floppy disks or one 3-1/2-inch floppy disk. The software can be run from either a floppy disk drive or from a hard disk.

F.3 STARTING AB:QM

Depending on your type of system, AB:QM can be started in a number of ways. In this section, we will show you how to start AB:QM with a floppy disk system, a hard disk system, and from a network. We begin with starting AB:QM on a floppy disk system.

Starting AB:QM With a Floppy Disk System

Step 1. Boot the computer system by putting DOS (disk operating system) in the A drive and turning on the computer. If the computer is already on, you can hold down the control (Ctrl) and alternate (Alt) keys and press the delete (Del) key. Once this is done, you will get the A prompt, which looks like A>. You have now booted the computer system.

Step 2. Insert the AB:QM floppy disk into the A drive. If you have a 5-1/4-inch drive, there will be two disks. Insert disk 1. If you have a 3-1/2-inch drive, there is only one disk, which you insert.

Step 3. Type **QM** and press the return (or enter) key. This will start program execution. Typing **qm** in lower case letters will also work.

Starting AB:QM With a Hard Disk System

Step 1. Boot the computer system by turning on the computer without any floppy disk in the A drive. You can also hold down Ctrl and Alt and press Del. If your computer is already on, it is not necessary to boot the computer.

Step 2. Make sure the AB:QM programs are transferred to a directory on the hard disk. This may already be done for you. If not, you can use the COPY *.* command to copy all of the files from the floppy disks to the hard disk. If you are not sure how to copy the programs, you may need to ask your instructor or a lab assistant.

Step 3. Get into the directory that contains the AB:QM programs. This can be done with the Change Directory (CD) command. For example, if you type CD QM at the C prompt, you'll be in the QM subdirectory instead of the root directory (assuming that the QM directory exists and contains the AB:QM programs).

Step 4. Type **QM**. This will start the execution of the programs.

Note that hard disk systems can be configured in a number of different ways. If you are having trouble, you may have to get assistance from your instructor or a lab assistant.

Starting AB:QM From a Network

Step 1. Log onto the network. This step will vary according to the network at your school. In most cases, you will need an identification number and password.

Step 2. Go to the AB:QM directory or menu. This step will vary according to how the network is set up. In many cases, you will see AB:QM as a menu selection after you log on. In other cases, you will have to give several commands to get to the AB:QM menu.

Step 3. Type **QM**. This will start the programs.

Note that today, many schools use a network to tie personal computers together. Networks are different, and each school will have policies concerning the use of its network. Make sure you understand the operation of the network and the policies or rules that exist at your school. After you are finished with AB:QM, it is important to properly log off the network. If you are having any problems, you may have to get assistance from your instructor or a lab assistant.

F.4 USING AB:QM

Once you start AB:QM, you will see the main menu. From this menu, you can run one of the programs, save and retrieve data from a data disk, print results on a printer or disk file, and exit from AB:QM. These important features will be covered in this section.

Menu Selections. Once you have typed QM at the A or C prompt, the menu is displayed. See Program F.1.

Running One of the Programs. Once in the menu, you can type the appropriate letter or move the cursor to highlight the application you

wish to run and then press the return key. This will start the execution of the desired program.

Every program in AB:QM has the same type of screen layout or appearance. Three areas appear on the screen. The upper area or upper window contains initial data for the particular application. Included are the problem title and other model parameters that set the overall structure for the application. The middle window is where detailed data entry occurs. Specific values for the model are entered in the middle window. Both the upper and the middle windows act like a spreadsheet. The cursor can be used to highlight the appropriate area, and data can be entered by pressing the correct keys. Changes can be made easily. Simply move the cursor to the place the change is to occur and type in the new or corrected value. The lower window contains the commands that are used for all applications of AB:QM. See page 885 for some of the most useful commands.

The commands in AB:QM are executed by typing the first letter of the command. For example, the Edit command is invoked by typing the letter E.

Use of a Data and Backup Disk. Although there is a limited amount of free space on the program disks, it is recommended that you keep a separate data disk to store the results of AB:QM. In addition, you should also keep a backup copy of all files on your data disk in case of unexpected problems.

Getting Results from AB:QM. Once you have run a program using AB:QM, you can send the

PROGRAM F.1 Main Menu of AB:QM

```
_____ Menu 1 _____
|                                                                    |
|  A      Linear Programming          J      CPM/PERT                |
|  B      All Integer Programming     K      Inventory Models        |
|  C      Zero One Programming        L      Queuing Theory          |
|  D      Goal Programming            M      Dynamic Programming     |
|  E      Transportation              N      Simulation              |
|  F      Assignment                  O      Forecasting             |
|  G      Break-Even Analysis         P      Markov Analysis         |
|  H      Decision Theory             Q      Game Theory             |
|  I      Network Models              Esc    Exit AB:QM              |
|                                                                    |
|_____|
```

COMMAND	EXPLANATION
Help	Help is used to get on-screen assistance for an application.
New	New is used to enter new data into an application.
Load	Load is used to retrieve data that have been previously saved using the Save command.
Save	Save is used to save data onto a floppy disk or a hard disk. It is recommended that data *not* be saved onto one of the program disks.
Edit	Edit is used to alter or change any of the values of the particular model. In some cases, the Edit command cannot be used; for example, it cannot be used to change the overall structure of a problem, such as the number of alternatives, or the overall size of the problem. In these cases, new data must be entered from scratch.
Run	Run is used to execute the program. This command will first display the data entered and then the actual program output.
Print	Print can be used to print results on the printer, a disk file, or both. You may print results only *after* the Run command has been given.
Install	Install is used to set various parameters for the AB:QM program.
Directory	Directory is used to get a listing of files for a particular floppy disk or a subdirectory on a hard disk.
Esc	The escape (Esc) key is used to back out of any application. Pressing the Esc key will exit what you are doing and bring you to the next highest level. Pressing the Esc key repeatedly will eventually cause the computer to exit from AB:QM and return you to the DOS level. (Note that this is similar to the use of the Esc key in Lotus and other spreadsheet software.)

results to a printer, a disk drive, or both from the Print command. By typing the letter P you will start the Print command. The computer will then ask you if you want your output sent to the printer, a disk device, or both. Of course, if you send output to a printer, make sure that the printer is on and loaded with paper. If you tell the computer to send the output to a disk device, the computer will ask you for a file specification. For example, B:LP1 could be used to save the results on a floppy disk in the B drive with a file name of LP1.

If you are using a word processor, saving the output to a disk file is a good choice. Most word processors allow you to upload or insert other disk files into a document. Thus, you will be able to include output from AB:QM directly into a professionally executed report using a word processor.

Potential Problems. When you first start to run AB:QM, you may encounter problems. Typical problems and their solutions are briefly outlined here:

PROBLEM	SOLUTION
Program title not on the screen	Check to make sure that you have the correct program disk in the disk drive and that the disk is not damaged.
Red disk light stays on	This means that the disk drive is still spinning. Do not take out the disk while the red disk light is on because this could damage the disk. Instead, reboot the computer by holding the Ctrl and Alt keys and pressing the Del key.
Messages saying invalid command or file not found	If you type QM to start the program and get either one of these messages, the computer cannot find the QM file. You may not have the correct disk in a floppy drive. If you are using a hard disk system, you may be in the wrong subdirectory.

Exiting from AB:QM. The best way to exit from AB:QM and get back to the DOS level is to first get to the menu of AB:QM. If you are in a subdirectory, press the Esc key to get back to the main menu. Then, press the Esc key to exit AB:QM and get back to DOS. In general, you can keep pressing the Esc key to get back to DOS. You will see the current disk drive prompt displayed, for example, A> for the A disk drive or C> for the hard disk. At this point, you can run another program or turn off the computer.

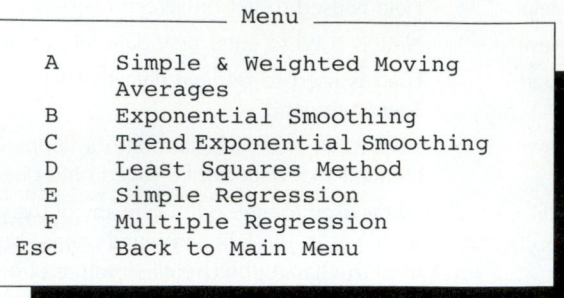

PROGRAM F.2 Forecasting Submenu

```
 _____ Menu _____
|                                                      |
|    A      Simple & Weighted Moving                   |
|           Averages                                   |
|    B      Exponential Smoothing                      |
|    C      Trend Exponential Smoothing                |
|    D      Least Squares Method                       |
|    E      Simple Regression                          |
|    F      Multiple Regression                        |
|   Esc     Back to Main Menu                          |
|_____|
```

F.5 A FORECASTING EXAMPLE OF AB:QM

To give you a better example of how to use AB:QM, we will go through a forecasting example. (Forecasting is covered in Chapter 4.) In this example, we will have the computer determine the best equation for future sales given the following data:

Vacuum Cleaner Data

SALES (Y)	ADVERTISING BUDGET (X)
23	$1,000
25	2,000
30	3,000
31	4,000
35	5,000
36	6,000

Our equation will be Sales = Intercept + (Slope) (Ad budget). Given the data for sales and ad budget, the computer will determine the best values for the intercept and slope. The forecasting submenu is letter F. Thus, we press the F key to get into the forecasting program. (See Program F.2.) Next we press the D key to get into the regression program. The computer will display a blank data entry screen. As discussed previously, the same type of blank screen is displayed for every application. The screen is divided into three areas. The top area is for general problem data. The middle and largest area is for detailed data entry, and the bottom area shows the commands that we can give.

Because this is the first time we have run the forecasting program, we might want to get information about the program. When we press the H key (for help), we will get the first help screen. In most cases, there is more help information than can fit on a single screen. By pressing the down arrow or the page down (PgDn) key, additional information will appear. In general, we can use the up or down arrow or page up (PgUp) and page down (PgDn) keys to obtain the information or help we want. The help screens for our initial request are shown in Program F.3.

When you are finished with the help menu, press the Esc key to get back to the data entry screen. Again, you will see the blank data entry screen. At this stage, we want to enter data for our problem, so we press the N key for the New command to enter data. In the top window, the computer will ask us to enter the problem title. We type VACUUM CLEANER SALES DATA and press the return key. Next, the computer will ask us to enter the number of observations. We type 6 and press the return key. Next, the computer will go to the middle window and ask us to enter the values for the six observations. When we have entered all values, the computer will beep to indicate that all values have been entered. The completed data entry screen is shown in Program F.4.

Let's say we made an error in the third observation. Instead of entering 30 sales we entered 300. To correct this problem, we press the E key for the Edit command and the computer places us in the edit mode. We move the cursor to the mistake by using the arrow keys. The computer will highlight the value to be corrected. Then we type

PROGRAM F.3 Help Screens

```
***** Program Description *****

Purpose
------

The Simple Regression Model consists of one dependent variable and one
independent variable, which are assumed to be linearly related. The dependent
variable is the variable to be forecast, and the independent variable is an
explanatory variable. This model uses the Least Squares Method to estimate the
values of slope and intercept.


Limitation of System
----------------
1. Maximum number of observations : 50


Explanation of Key Words and How to Input Data
----------------------------------------------

<< Upper Window >>

1. Type the problem title or your comment for later reference purposes.
2. Enter the number of observations.

<< Middle Window >>

1. Input the value of the dependent variable in column Y for each observation.
2. Input the value of the independent variable in column X for each observation.
```

PROGRAM F.4 Data Entry Screen

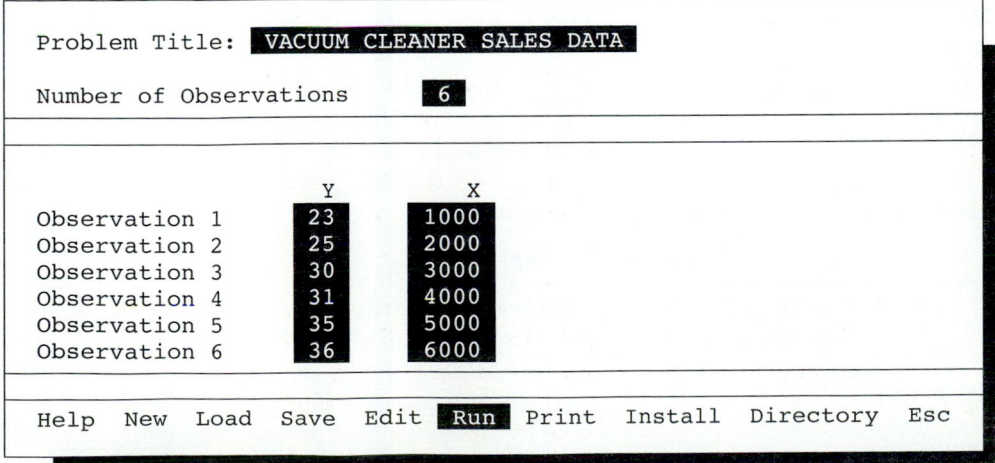

```
Forecasting / Simple Regression

  Problem Title:  VACUUM CLEANER SALES DATA

  Number of Observations        6


                        Y            X
  Observation 1        23         1000
  Observation 2        25         2000
  Observation 3        30         3000
  Observation 4        31         4000
  Observation 5        35         5000
  Observation 6        36         6000


  Help  New  Load  Save  Edit  Run  Print  Install  Directory  Esc
```

in the correct value and press the return key. Again, we will be put into the data entry screen with the correct value in place.

With the data correct, we would like to execute the program and see the results. We do this by pressing the R key for the Run command. The computer will first display the input data. By using the arrow keys or page up and page down keys, we will be able to see all of the output as shown in Program F.5.

PROGRAM F.5 Running the Program

```
Program: Forecasting / Simple Regression

Problem Title: VACUUM CLEANER SALES DATA

***** Input Data *****

Obs.          Y               X

  1         23.000        1000.000
  2         25.000        2000.000
  3         30.000        3000.000
  4         31.000        4000.000
  5         35.000        5000.000
  6         36.000        6000.000


***** Program Output *****

Parameter       Coefficient        SE B             t

Intercept         20.4000         0.9700        21.0303
   b 1             0.0027         0.0002        11.0120

Coefficient of determination :       0.9681
Correlation coefficient      :       0.9839
Standard Error               :       1.0420

Prediction Error

           Observed       Predicted
Obs.         Value          Value         Residual

  1         23.000         23.143          -0.143
  2         25.000         25.886          -0.886
  3         30.000         28.629           1.371
  4         31.000         31.371          -0.371
  5         35.000         34.114           0.886
  6         36.000         36.857          -0.857

Mean Absolute Deviation (MAD) :        0.9029

ANOVA Table

Source of
Variation              SS          df          MS

Regression         131.657          1        131.657
Residual             4.343          4          1.086

Total              136.000          5
F* =      121.263

***** End of Output *****
```

Look carefully at the output. As you can see, the coefficient for the intercept is 20.4. The coefficient for the slope (called b 1 here) is 0.0027. Thus our equation for sales is: Sales = 20.4 + 0.0027 (Ad budget). If we want to predict sales for the budget of 3,750, the equation would be Sales = 20.4 + 0.0027 (3,750) = 30.5. Thus, sales would be about 30 units.

Now, let's say we would like to save the data on a floppy disk in the A drive. We do this by pressing the S key for the Save command. The computer will ask us to enter the file specification without an extension. We enter a:sales and press the return key.

If we want to retrieve data previously saved, we press the L key for the Load command. The computer will ask us to enter a file specification (without extension). For example, we can enter a:sales to have the computer retrieve the sales data.

If we are completing a homework problem, we will want to get a printed copy of the results. We press the P key for the Print command. The computer will ask us if we want the results on the *Printer*, *Disk* file, or *Both*. Type P for the printer, D for the disk, or B for both. If you are using a word processing program, you may want to print to a disk file and then retrieve the results from the disk file into your word processing program.

AB:QM allows us to specify a default disk drive where our data will be stored. The default disk is called the *working directory*. If you have a hard disk, you may want your data stored on floppy disks in the A drive instead of on the hard disk (C drive). This can be accomplished by pressing the letter I key for Install and typing the drive specification, A:, and then pressing the return key.

The final command we will investigate is the Directory command, which gives us a list of all AB:QM files that we have saved on the working directory. At this time, our working directory is the A drive; of course, we can always change the working directory with the Install command. We press the D key for the Directory command, and the computer will display all of the AB:QM files on the A drive. As seen in Program F.6, the only file that is on the floppy disk in the A drive is SALES.FCT.—the data for the sales example. The letters FCT, which stand for forecasting, are the file extension. AB:QM automatically placed this extension on the file name.

F.6 LIMITATIONS OF AB:QM

Like any computer program, AB:QM has limitations on the size and types of problems that it can solve. These limitations are presented in various chapters throughout the book and summarized in this section. See Table F.1 on page 890.

PROGRAM F.6 **Directory Command**

```
Forecasting / Simple Regression


*** Working Directory: a

SALES.FCT

*** Disk status ***

 78.26% used.
 158720 total bytes available on disk.


ESC
```

TABLE F.1 Limitations of AB:QM

PROGRAM	LIMITATION
Linear Programming	Maximum number of constraints = 50. Maximum number of decision variables = 50.
All Integer Programming	Maximum number of constraints = 15. Maximum number of decision variables = 15.
Zero One Programming	Maximum number of constraints = 15. Maximum number of decision variables = 15.
Goal Programming	Maximum number of constraints = 50. Maximum number of decision variables = 50.
Transportation	Maximum number of sources = 40. Maximum number of destinations = 40.
Assignment	Maximum number of rows = 40. Maximum number of columns = 40.
Break-Even Analysis	This program can handle almost any size break-even problem.
Decision Theory	Number of alternatives must be between 2 and 20. Number of events must be between 2 and 20.
Network Models	Number of nodes must be between 3 and 50. Number of branches must be between 3 and 50.
CPM/PERT	Maximum number of activities = 50. All nodes must be numbered using sequential integers, starting with 1. Looping is not allowed. One source and one end node are required. All time values must be any positive real number. The optimistic times should be less than the most likely times. The most likely times should be less than the pessimistic times.
Inventory Models	Number of items must be between 2 and 50.
Queuing Theory	Mean arrival rate should be less than mean service rate.
Dynamic Programming	Maximum number of stages = 10. Maximum number of decisions at each node = 10. Maximum number of decisions at each stage = 20. Maximum number of nodes = 75. All nodes must be sequentially numbered using integers.
Simulation	Maximum number of runs = 9999. Number of categories must be between 2 and 40.
Forecasting	Maximum number of moving periods = 48. Maximum number of periods = 50. Number of periods should be greater than the number of moving periods by at least 2.
Markov Analysis	Maximum number of periods = 200. Number of "From" and "To" states must be between 2 and 20.
Game Theory	Number of strategies for each player must be between 2 and 50.

Solutions to Selected Problems

Chapter 2

2-8 .30

2-10 (a) .10 (b) .04 (c) .25
(d) .40

2-12 (a) .20 (b) .09 (c) .31
(d) dependent

2-13 .54

2-15 into Abu Ilan .384; into El Kamin .616

2-17 .947

2-20 (a) .995 (b) .885 (c) assumed
events are independent

2-22 .78

Chapter 3

3-10 2.85

3-11 $E(X) = 5.45$; variance $= 4.047$

3-12 probability ranked no. 1 $= .05086$;
probability win all four games $= .0039$

3-15 $P(11.5 - 12.5$ oz.$) = .25$; $P(12$ oz.$) = 0$

3-16 .8849

3-18 .3413

3-20 P(oven causes defect) $= .1587$; $P(460° - 470°) = .1327$

3-22 (a) 1.0, .80 (b) 1.0, .80
(c) equivalent results

3-24 (a) .2778 (b) .0555 (c) 11.4

3-26 .0668

3-27 1829.27

3-28 (b) .6125

3-29 .7365

Chapter 4

4-10 (a) 337 (b) 380 (c) 423

4-12 3 month MAD $= 6.48$; 4 month MAD $= 7.78$

4-13 weighted M.A. slightly more accurate

4-15 MAD for 2 year M.A. $= 2.22$, which is lowest

4-17 Year 1: 410.0; Year 2: 422.0; Year 3: 443.9; Year
4: 466.1; Year 5: 495.2; Year 6: 521.8

4-19 MAD for $\alpha = .3$ is 74.56; MAD for $\alpha = .6$ is
51.8; MAD for $\alpha = .9$ is 38.1

4-21 $Y = 522 + 33.6X$; 1990 sales $= 622.8$

4-23 (b) $Y = 1.0 + 1.0X$ (c) 10

4-31 (a) $Y = 1 + 1X$; $r = .845$

4-32 (b) $Y = 5.06 + 1.593X$ (c) 2,099,000
people

4-36 $130,000, $108,000, $98,000, $184,000

4-38 $Y = .972 + .0035X$, $r^2 = .479$
$Y = 2.197$, $Y = 3.77$

Chapter 5

5-9 maximin criterion: best alternative is Texan
5-11 best decision: deposit $10,000 in bank
5-14 **(a)** $200 **(b)** yes $80
5-15 **(b)** large wing **(c)** no
5-17 **(b)** medium sized facility
5-20 **(b)** back roads **(c)** $3\frac{1}{3}$ minutes
5-21 produce 300 cases and stock them
5-24 62 bottles
5-27 3016 reports

Chapter 6

6-12 construct clinic
6-13 the survey should be taken; EVSI = $11,140
6-15 if the survey is favorable, build large shop. Otherwise, do not build.
6-17 $P(\text{successful shop} \mid \text{unfavorable study}) = .25$
6-18 do not gather information but build quadplex
6-21 **(b)** use supplier A **(c)** $60 less than supplier A
6-24 do not conduct survey and do not construct clinic. They are risk avoiders.
6-27 yes. He would not conduct the study but he would build the large plant.
6-28 **(a)** Broad street–27.5 minutes
 (b) expressway
 (c) Lynn is a risk avoider
6-30 Jack should accept his kids' bet
6-32 **(b)** stock 1,500 gallons **(c)** EVPI = $1,500
6-33 do not conduct survey. Build medium-sized facility; EMV = $670,000

Chapter 7

7-6 45.034 to 46.966 for $\overline{x}$
 0 to 4.008 for R
7-8 16.814 to 17.187 for $\overline{x}$
 .068 to .932 for R
7-10 2.236 to 3.728 for $\overline{x}$
 0 to 2.29 for R
 Process is in control
7-13 62.36 to 64.54 for $\overline{x}$
 0 to 3.423 for R
7-15 .0081 to .0581
7-17 6.6 to 33.4
 Out of control

Chapter 8

8-12 $Y = \sqrt{(DC_h)/2C_o}$
8-15 $Q^* = 20,000$ screws
8-16 ROP = 4,000 screws
8-19 $D = 8$ million loads of plywood
8-23 yes; total cost = $41,416
8-24 expand to 10,000 cu. ft. to hold 100 motors; expansion worth $250 per year
8-26 $1,920 on a yearly basis

Chapter 9

9-8 $Q_p^* = 2,697$ scissors
9-9 1,217 wheel bearings
9-10 take the discount; cost = $49,912.50
9-12 30 units of safety stock
9-14 item 33CP needs strict control; no strict control for the others
9-17 maintain a safety stock of 400
9-20 order quantity = 852; total cost = $176
9-23 order quantity = 51; total cost = $1,901.22
9-25 order 300 units; total cost = $9,066.83
9-27 safety stock level is 150 units; total cost is $1,848.66

Chapter 10

10-9 40 air conditioners, 60 fans, profit = $1,900
10-11 200 Model A tubs, 0 Model B tubs, $18,000 profit
10-13 40 undergraduate, 20 graduate, $160,000
10-14 10 Alpha 4's, 24 Beta 5's, $55,200
10-17 $X_1 = 18\frac{3}{4}$, $X_2 = 18\frac{3}{4}$, Profit = $150
10-18 $X_1 = 25.71$, $X_2 = 21.43$, Cost = $68.57
10-20 5 TV spots, 68 ads, exposure of 1,535,000
10-23 24 coconuts, 12 skins, Profit = 5,040 rupees
10-27 Make all MCA 300 Baud Modems (27,750 of them)

Chapter 11

11-1 max $R = 28X_1 + 25X_2$
$$3X_1 + 2X_2 \leq 360$$
$$1\frac{1}{2}X_1 + 1X_2 \leq 200$$
$$\frac{3}{4}X_1 + \frac{3}{4}X_2 \leq 125$$
$$X_1 \geq 60$$
$$X_2 \geq 60$$
$X_1 = 60$, $X_2 = 90$, $P = $3,930$
11-6 min $C = 925X_1 + 2,000X_2$
$$.04X_1 + .05X_2 \geq .40$$
$$.03X_1 + .03X_2 \geq .60$$
$X_1 = 20$, $X_2 = 0$, $C = $18,500$
11-9 $X_1 = 26$, $X_2 = 5$, $X_3 = 6.5$, $X_4 = 14.25$, 51.75 drinks

11-10 min rolls $= 20X_1 + 6.8X_2 + 12X_3 - 65,000X_4$

$$X_1 + X_2 + X_3 \leq 17,000$$
$$X_1 \geq 3,000$$
$$X_2 - .05X_3 \geq 0$$
$$X_4 \geq .20$$
$$X_4 \leq .45 \quad \text{sell } 327,000 \text{ rolls}$$

11-11 $X_1 = 0, X_2 = .499, X_3 = .173, X_4 = 0, X_5 = 0,$ $X_6 = .105, X_7 = .762, C = \$1.75$

11-12 $X_1 = 497, X_2 = 1241, P = \$195,505$

11-14 1250 wheat in N parcel, 500 wheat in NW, 312.5 wheat in W, 137.5 wheat in SW, 131 alfalfa in SW, 600 barley in SE, 400 barley in N, profit $= \$337,862.10$

11-17 61 medical beds, 29 surgical beds, Revenue $= \$9,551,656$ per year.

Chapter 12

12-11 **(b)** $14X_1 + 4X_2 \leq 3,360; 10X_1 + 12X_2 \leq 9,600$ **(d)** $S_1 = 3,360, S_2 = 9,600$
(e) X_2 **(f)** S_2 **(g)** 800 units of X_2

12-13 $X_1 = 2, X_2 = 6, S_1 = 0, S_2 = 0, P = \$36$

12-14 $X_1 = 50, X_2 = 0, P = \$1,000$

12-15 $X_1 = 14, X_2 = 33, C = \$221$

12-19 degeneracy; $X_1 = 27, X_2 = 5, X_3 = 0,$ $P = \$177$

12-21 **(a)** Min $C = 9X_1 + 15X_2$
$$X_1 + 2X_2 \geq 30$$
$$X_1 + 4X_2 \geq 80$$
(b) $X_1 = 0, X_2 = 20, C = \$300$

12-22 **(a)** Min $C = 20X_1 + 24X_2$
$$X_1 + X_2 \geq 30$$
$$X_1 + 2X_2 \geq 40$$
(b) $X_1 = 20, X_2 = 10, C = \$640$

12-24 $X_1 = 0, X_2 = 17.14, X_3 = 34.29, P = \$582.86$

12-26 **(b)** X_5 will enter; A_3 will leave

Chapter 13

13-10 **(a)** yes **(b)** doesn't change

13-11 **(b)** $X_1 = 2, X_2 = 3$ **(b)** yes

13-12 **(b)** $X_1 = 33.33, X_2 = 33.33$ **(b)** yes
(c) no

13-15 **(a)** $\$7\frac{1}{2}$ to infinity **(b)** negative infinity to $\$40$ **(c)** $\$20$ **(d)** $\$0$

13-16 30¢, 0, $\$3.00$

13-19 **(a)** negative infinity to $\$6$ for phosphate; $\$5$ to infinity for potassium **(b)** basis won't change; but $X_1, X_2,$ and S_2 will change.

13-21 max $P = 50U_1 + 4U_2$
$$12U_1 + 1U_2 \leq 120$$
$$20U_1 + 3U_2 \leq 250$$

Chapter 14

14-14 Oak Ridge to House 2 = 30; Oak Ridge to House 3 = 10; Pineville to House 3 = 25; Mapletown to House 1 = 30; cost = $\$230$

14-16 Morgantown to Coaltown = 35; Youngstown to Coal Valley = 30; Youngstown to Coaltown = 5; Pittsburgh to Coaltown = 5; Pittsburgh to Coalsburg = 20; cost = 3,100 miles

14-19 degeneracy; need to place a zero in an empty cell (such as 2-C)

14-23 New Orleans' systems cost = $\$20,000$; Houston's is $\$19,500$, so Houston should be selected

14-27 $A12$ to W, $A15$ to Z, $B2$ to Y, $B9$ to X, 50 hours

14-29 post 1 to C, post 2 to B, post 3 to A, post 4 to D, 18 miles

14-31 total rating = 335

14-32 total "cost" = 86

14-33 overall rating = 75.5

14-34 $C53$ at plant 1, $C81$ at plant 3, $D5$ at plant 4, $D44$ at plant 2, 58¢

14-36 total cost = $\$1.18$

13-38 **(a)** 96 **(b)** 92 **(c)** Yes, score = 93

Chapter 15

15-13 $X_1 = 1, X_2 = 2, P = \$20$

15-14 $X_1 = 3, X_2 = 4, P = \$17$

15-16 $X_1 = 5, X_2 = 8, Z = 1,273,000$ passengers

15-21 $A4, B1, C3, D2$ or $A4, B2, C3, D1$; both cost $\$105$

15-22 $X_1 = 0, X_2 = 3, P = \$9$

15-24 $X_1 = 500, X_2 = 400, d_3^- = 100$

15-26 $X_1 = 10$ TV spots, $X_2 = 35$ ads, exposure = 8,250,000

Chapter 16

16-11 **(a)** .375 **(b)** .2 days or 1.6 hours
(c) .225 **(d)** .141, .053, .020, .007

16-12 **(a)** 1.33 **(b)** 4 min. **(c)** 6 min.
(d) .667 **(e)** .333

16-15 **(a)** 6 **(b)** 12 min. **(c)** .857
(d) .54 **(e)** $\$1,728$/day **(f)** yes

16-18 3, 2, 4

16-21 $\$36$ with 1 loader, $\$18$ with 2 loaders; saving $\$18$ with 2 loaders

16-22 no

16-27 4 entrances, 2 exits

Chapter 17

17-12 no

17-14 **(a)** 3 times **(b)** 6.95/week if we ignore fact that sales cannot exceed 8 per week.
(c) 7.16 heaters

17-19 **(a)** from the 15 breakdown simulation, there are 14½ hours of machine down time × $75/hour = $1,087.50. Cost of labor is 29½ hours × $60/hour = $1,770. Total cost = $2,857.50
(b) hire second worker; one repairman costs $4,320

17-21 **(a)** cost/hour is generally more expensive replacing 1 pen each time
(b) expected cost/hour with 1 pen policy = $1.38 (or $58/breakdown); expected cost/hour with 4 pen policy = $1.12 (or $132/breakdown)

Chapter 18

18-13 completion time is 26 days; critical path is 1–2–3–5–6

18-15 completion time is 19 weeks; critical paths are A–C–G and B–E–G

18-17 critical path is C–D–E–F–H–K; completion time is 36.33 days.

18-18 P(finishing in less than 40 days) = .9463

18-21 value of work completed = $181,600; actual cost = $172,000; cost underrun = $9,600; project is behind schedule

18-22 total budget/month using ES = $146,000; total budget/month using LS = $146,000

18-26 500 cars/hour

18-27 take route 1–3–5–7–10–13; distance is 430 miles

18-28 expected project length is 44 weeks; variance = 2.166; after changing activity 5, new expected project length = 47.8 weeks; new variance = 1.92 weeks

Chapter 19

19-7 **(b)** 90% **(c)** 30%

19-8 **(a)** 23.056% **(b)** 30.832%
(c) 75%

19-10 **(a)** 70% **(b)** 30% **(c)** 40%

19-11 25% for Battles; 18.75% for University; 26.25% for Bill's; 30% for College

19-14 41% that conditions will be fair; 19.5% that conditions will be tolerable

19-16 333 in Lake Jackson and 667 in Lake Bradford

19-18 new MFA = (5645.16, 1354.84)

19-19 61 will pass and 19 will fail

Module A

A-1 **(a)** 27 **(b)** 16

A-2 $X = -\frac{3}{2}$, $Y = \frac{1}{2}$, $Z = \frac{7}{2}$

A-5 $380, $440, $260

A-7 $\begin{pmatrix} -48 & 6 & 12 \\ 6 & -12 & 6 \\ 32 & 6 & -8 \end{pmatrix}$ = Matrix of cofactors

$\begin{pmatrix} -48 & 6 & 32 \\ 6 & -12 & 6 \\ 12 & 6 & -8 \end{pmatrix}$ = Adjoint of matrix

A-8 $\begin{pmatrix} -\frac{48}{60} & \frac{6}{60} & \frac{32}{60} \\ \frac{6}{60} & -\frac{12}{60} & \frac{6}{60} \\ \frac{12}{60} & \frac{6}{60} & -\frac{8}{60} \end{pmatrix}$

Module B

B-6 strategy for $X: X_2$; strategy for $Y: Y_2$; value of the game = 6

B-8 $X_1 = \frac{35}{57}$; $X_2 = \frac{22}{57}$; $Y_1 = \frac{32}{57}$; $Y_2 = \frac{25}{57}$; value of game = 66.70

B-11 $A_1 = \frac{41}{72}$; $A_2 = \frac{31}{72}$; $B_1 = \frac{55}{72}$; $B_2 = \frac{17}{72}$; value of game = −1.32; would rather be B.

B-13 maximize $\overline{Y}_1 + \overline{Y}_2 + \overline{Y}_3$; subject to: $-2\overline{Y}_2 - 5\overline{Y}_3 \leq 1$; $3\overline{Y}_1 + \overline{Y}_2 - \overline{Y}_3 \leq 1$; value of the game $= \dfrac{1}{(\overline{Y}_1 + \overline{Y}_2 + \overline{Y}_3)}$.

Module C

C-6 shortest route is 1–2–6–7; total distance is 10 miles

C-7 shortest route is 1–2–5–7; total distance is 20 miles

C-8 shortest route is 1–2–5–7; total distance is 14 miles

C-9 shortest route is 1–2–5–8–9; total distance is 19 miles

Module D

D-5 **(a)** 20,000 **(b)** $320,000

D-9 No effect

D-13 $999.60

D-15 $299.96

Module E

E-4 SUN − .80

E-8 Car-1 .4045

E-9 System 3 .3406

Appendixes

CHAPTER OUTLINE

A. Areas under the Standard Normal Table
B. Unit Normal Loss Integral
C. Cumulative Binomial Distribution
D. Values of $e^{-\lambda}$ for Use in the Poisson Distribution

Appendix A.   Areas Under the Standard Normal Table

Example: To find the area under the normal curve, you must know how many standard deviations that point is to the right of the mean. Then, the area under the normal curve can be read directly from the normal table. For example, the total area under the normal curve for a point that is 1.55 standard deviations to the right of the mean is .93943.

	00	.01	.02	.03	.04	.05	.06	.07	.08	.09
0.0	.50000	.50399	.50798	.51197	.51595	.51994	.52392	.52790	.53188	.53586
0.1	.53983	.54380	.54776	.55172	.55567	.55962	.56356	.56749	.57142	.57535
0.2	.57926	.58317	.58706	.59095	.59483	.59871	.60257	.60642	.61026	.61409
0.3	.61791	.62172	.62552	.62930	.63307	.63683	.64058	.64431	.64803	.65173
0.4	.65542	.65910	.66276	.66640	.67003	.67364	.67724	.68082	.68439	.68793
0.5	.69146	.69497	.69847	.70194	.70540	.70884	.71226	.71566	.71904	.72240
0.6	.72575	.72907	.73237	.73536	.73891	.74215	.74537	.74857	.75175	.75490
0.7	.75804	.76115	.76424	.76730	.77035	.77337	.77637	.77935	.78230	.78524
0.8	.78814	.79103	.79389	.79673	.79955	.80234	.80511	.80785	.81057	.81327
0.9	.81594	.81859	.82121	.82381	.82639	.82894	.83147	.83398	.83646	.83891
1.0	.84134	.84375	.84614	.84849	.85083	.85314	.85543	.85769	.85993	.86214
1.1	.86433	.86650	.86864	.87076	.87286	.87493	.87698	.87900	.88100	.88298
1.2	.88493	.88686	.88877	.89065	.89251	.89435	.89617	.89796	.89973	.90147
1.3	.90320	.90490	.90658	.90824	.90988	.91149	.91309	.91466	.91621	.91774
1.4	.91924	.92073	.92220	.92364	.92507	.92647	.92785	.92922	.93056	.93189
1.5	.93319	.93448	.93574	.93699	.93822	.93943	.94062	.94179	.94295	.94408
1.6	.94520	.94630	.94738	.94845	.94950	.95053	.95154	.95254	.95352	.95449
1.7	.95543	.95637	.95728	.95818	.95907	.95994	.96080	.96164	.96246	.96327
1.8	.96407	.96485	.96562	.96638	.96712	.96784	.96856	.96926	.96995	.97062
1.9	.97128	.97193	.97257	.97320	.97381	.97441	.97500	.97558	.97615	.97670
2.0	.97725	.97784	.97831	.97882	.97932	.97982	.98030	.98077	.98124	.98169
2.1	.98214	.98257	.98300	.98341	.98382	.98422	.98461	.98500	.98537	.98574
2.2	.98610	.98645	.98679	.98713	.98745	.98778	.98809	.98840	.98870	.98899
2.3	.98928	.98956	.98983	.99010	.99036	.99061	.99086	.99111	.99134	.99158
2.4	.99180	.99202	.99224	.99245	.99266	.99286	.99305	.99324	.99343	.99361
2.5	.99379	.99396	.99413	.99430	.99446	.99461	.99477	.99492	.99506	.99520
2.6	.99534	.99547	.99560	.99573	.99585	.99598	.99609	.99621	.99632	.99643
2.7	.99653	.99664	.99674	.99683	.99693	.99702	.99711	.99720	.99728	.99736
2.8	.99744	.99752	.99760	.99767	.99774	.99781	.99788	.99795	.99801	.99807
2.9	.99813	.99819	.99825	.99831	.99836	.99841	.99846	.99851	.99856	.99861
3.0	.99865	.99869	.99874	.99878	.99882	.99886	.99899	.99893	.99896	.99900
3.1	.99903	.99906	.99910	.99913	.99916	.99918	.99921	.99924	.99926	.99929
3.2	.99931	.99934	.99936	.99938	.99940	.99942	.99944	.99946	.99948	.99950
3.3	.99952	.99953	.99955	.99957	.99958	.99960	.99961	.99962	.99964	.99965
3.4	.99966	.99968	.99969	.99970	.99971	.99972	.99973	.99974	.99975	.99976
3.5	.99977	.99978	.99978	.99979	.99980	.99981	.99981	.99982	.99983	.99983
3.6	.99984	.99985	.99985	.99986	.99986	.99987	.99987	.99988	.99988	.99989
3.7	.99989	.99990	.99990	.99990	.99991	.99991	.99992	.99992	.99992	.99992
3.8	.99993	.99993	.99993	.99994	.99994	.99994	.99994	.99995	.99995	.99995
3.9	.99995	.99995	.99996	.99996	.99996	.99996	.99996	.99996	.99997	.99997

Source: Reprinted from Robert O. Schlaifer, *Introduction to Statistics for Business Decisions,* published by McGraw-Hill Book Company, 1961, by permission of the copyright holder, the President and Fellows of Harvard College.

Appendix B. Unit Normal Loss Integral

D	.00	.01	.02	.03	.04	.05	.06	.07	.08	.09
.0	.3989	.3940	.3890	.3841	.3793	.3744	.3697	.3649	.3602	.3556
.1	.3509	.3464	.3418	.3373	.3328	.3284	.3240	.3197	.3154	.3111
.2	.3069	.3027	.2986	.2944	.2904	.2863	.2824	.2784	.2745	.2706
.3	.2668	.2630	.2592	.2555	.2518	.2481	.2445	.2409	.2374	.2339
.4	.2304	.2270	.2236	.2203	.2169	.2137	.2104	.2072	.2040	.2009
.5	.1978	.1947	.1917	.1887	.1857	.1828	.1799	.1771	.1742	.1714
.6	.1687	.1659	.1633	.1606	.1580	.1554	.1528	.1503	.1478	.1453
.7	.1429	.1405	.1381	.1358	.1334	.1312	.1289	.1267	.1245	.1223
.8	.1202	.1181	.1160	.1140	.1120	.1100	.1080	.1061	.1042	.1023
.9	.1004	.09860	.09680	.09503	.09328	.09156	.08986	.08819	.08654	.08491
1.0	.08332	.08174	.08019	.07866	.07716	.07568	.07422	.07279	.07138	.06999
1.1	.06862	.06727	.06595	.06465	.06336	.06210	.06086	.05964	.05844	.05726
1.2	.05610	.05496	.05384	.05274	.05165	.05059	.04954	.04851	.04750	.04650
1.3	.04553	.04457	.04363	.04270	.04179	.04090	.04002	.03916	.03831	.03748
1.4	.03667	.03587	.03508	.03431	.03356	.03281	.03208	.03137	.03067	.02998
1.5	.02931	.02865	.02800	.02736	.02674	.02612	.02552	.02494	.02436	.02380
1.6	.02324	.02270	.02217	.02165	.02114	.02064	.02015	.01967	.01920	.01874
1.7	.01829	.01785	.01742	.01699	.01658	.01617	.01578	.01539	.01501	.01464
1.8	.01428	.01392	.01357	.01323	.01290	.01257	.01226	.01195	.01164	.01134
1.9	.01105	.01077	.01049	.01022	$.0^2 9957$	$.0^2 9698$	$.0^2 9445$	$.0^2 9198$	$.0^2 8957$	$.0^2 8721$
2.0	$.0^2 8491$	$.0^2 8266$	$.0^2 8046$	$.0^2 7832$	$.0^2 7623$	$.0^2 7418$	$.0^2 7219$	$.0^2 7024$	$.0^2 6835$	$.0^2 6649$
2.1	$.0^2 6468$	$.0^2 6292$	$.0^2 6120$	$.0^2 5952$	$.0^2 5788$	$.0^2 5628$	$.0^2 5472$	$.0^2 5320$	$.0^2 5172$	$.0^2 5028$
2.2	$.0^2 4887$	$.0^2 4750$	$.0^2 4616$	$.0^2 4486$	$.0^2 4358$	$.0^2 4235$	$.0^2 4114$	$.0^2 3996$	$.0^2 3882$	$.0^2 3770$
2.3	$.0^2 3662$	$.0^2 3556$	$.0^2 3453$	$.0^2 3352$	$.0^2 3255$	$.0^2 3159$	$.0^2 3067$	$.0^2 2977$	$.0^2 2889$	$.0^2 2804$
2.4	$.0^2 2720$	$.0^2 2640$	$.0^2 2561$	$.0^2 2484$	$.0^2 2410$	$.0^2 2337$	$.0^2 2267$	$.0^2 2199$	$.0^2 2132$	$.0^2 2067$
2.5	$.0^2 2004$	$.0^2 1943$	$.0^2 1883$	$.0^2 1826$	$.0^2 1769$	$.0^2 1715$	$.0^2 1662$	$.0^2 1610$	$.0^2 1560$	$.0^2 1511$
2.6	$.0^2 1464$	$.0^2 1418$	$.0^2 1373$	$.0^2 1330$	$.0^2 1288$	$.0^2 1247$	$.0^2 1207$	$.0^2 1169$	$.0^2 1132$	$.0^2 1095$
2.7	$.0^2 1060$	$.0^2 1026$	$.0^3 9928$	$.0^3 9607$	$.0^3 9295$	$.0^3 8992$	$.0^3 8699$	$.0^3 8414$	$.0^3 8138$	$.0^3 7870$
2.8	$.0^3 7611$	$.0^3 7359$	$.0^3 7115$	$.0^3 6879$	$.0^3 6650$	$.0^3 6428$	$.0^3 6213$	$.0^3 6004$	$.0^3 5802$	$.0^3 5606$
2.9	$.0^3 5417$	$.0^3 5233$	$.0^3 5055$	$.0^3 4883$	$.0^3 4716$	$.0^3 4555$	$.0^3 4398$	$.0^3 4247$	$.0^3 4101$	$.0^3 3959$
3.0	$.0^3 3822$	$.0^3 3689$	$.0^3 3560$	$.0^3 3436$	$.0^3 3316$	$.0^3 3199$	$.0^3 3087$	$.0^3 2978$	$.0^3 2873$	$.0^3 2771$
3.1	$.0^3 2673$	$.0^3 2577$	$.0^3 2485$	$.0^3 2396$	$.0^3 2311$	$.0^3 2227$	$.0^3 2147$	$.0^3 2070$	$.0^3 1995$	$.0^3 1922$
3.2	$.0^3 1852$	$.0^3 1785$	$.0^3 1720$	$.0^3 1657$	$.0^3 1596$	$.0^3 1537$	$.0^3 1480$	$.0^3 1426$	$.0^3 1373$	$.0^3 1322$
3.3	$.0^3 1273$	$.0^3 1225$	$.0^3 1179$	$.0^3 1135$	$.0^3 1093$	$.0^3 1051$	$.0^3 1012$	$.0^4 9734$	$.0^4 9365$	$.0^4 9009$
3.4	$.0^4 8666$	$.0^4 8335$	$.0^4 8016$	$.0^4 7709$	$.0^4 7413$	$.0^4 7127$	$.0^4 6852$	$.0^4 6587$	$.0^4 6331$	$.0^4 6085$
3.5	$.0^4 5848$	$.0^4 5620$	$.0^4 5400$	$.0^4 5188$	$.0^4 4984$	$.0^4 4788$	$.0^4 4599$	$.0^4 4417$	$.0^4 4242$	$.0^4 4073$
3.6	$.0^4 3911$	$.0^4 3755$	$.0^4 3605$	$.0^4 3460$	$.0^4 3321$	$.0^4 3188$	$.0^4 3059$	$.0^4 2935$	$.0^4 2816$	$.0^4 2702$
3.7	$.0^4 2592$	$.0^4 2486$	$.0^4 2385$	$.0^4 2287$	$.0^4 2193$	$.0^4 2103$	$.0^4 2016$	$.0^4 1933$	$.0^4 1853$	$.0^4 1776$
3.8	$.0^4 1702$	$.0^4 1632$	$.0^4 1563$	$.0^4 1498$	$.0^4 1435$	$.0^4 1375$	$.0^4 1317$	$.0^4 1262$	$.0^4 1208$	$.0^4 1157$
3.9	$.0^4 1108$	$.0^4 1061$	$.0^4 1016$	$.0^5 9723$	$.0^5 9307$	$.0^5 8908$	$.0^5 8525$	$.0^5 8158$	$.0^5 7806$	$.0^5 7469$
4.0	$.0^5 7145$	$.0^5 6835$	$.0^5 6538$	$.0^5 6253$	$.0^5 5980$	$.0^5 5718$	$.0^5 5468$	$.0^5 5227$	$.0^5 4997$	$.0^5 4777$
4.1	$.0^5 4566$	$.0^5 4364$	$.0^5 4170$	$.0^5 3985$	$.0^5 3807$	$.0^5 3637$	$.0^5 3475$	$.0^5 3319$	$.0^5 3170$	$.0^5 3027$
4.2	$.0^5 2891$	$.0^5 2760$	$.0^5 2635$	$.0^5 2516$	$.0^5 2402$	$.0^5 2292$	$.0^5 2188$	$.0^5 2088$	$.0^5 1992$	$.0^5 1901$
4.3	$.0^5 1814$	$.0^5 1730$	$.0^5 1650$	$.0^5 1574$	$.0^5 1501$	$.0^5 1431$	$.0^5 1365$	$.0^5 1301$	$.0^5 1241$	$.0^5 1183$
4.4	$.0^5 1127$	$.0^5 1074$	$.0^5 1024$	$.0^6 9756$	$.0^6 9296$	$.0^6 8857$	$.0^6 8437$	$.0^6 8037$	$.0^6 7655$	$.0^6 7290$
4.5	$.0^6 6942$	$.0^6 6610$	$.0^6 6294$	$.0^6 5992$	$.0^6 5704$	$.0^6 5429$	$.0^6 5167$	$.0^6 4917$	$.0^6 4679$	$.0^6 4452$
4.6	$.0^6 4236$	$.0^6 4029$	$.0^6 3833$	$.0^6 3645$	$.0^6 3467$	$.0^6 3297$	$.0^6 3135$	$.0^6 2981$	$.0^6 2834$	$.0^6 2694$
4.7	$.0^6 2560$	$.0^6 2433$	$.0^6 2313$	$.0^6 2197$	$.0^6 2088$	$.0^6 1984$	$.0^6 1884$	$.0^6 1790$	$.0^6 1700$	$.0^6 1615$
4.8	$.0^6 1533$	$.0^6 1456$	$.0^6 1382$	$.0^6 1312$	$.0^6 1246$	$.0^6 1182$	$.0^6 1122$	$.0^6 1065$	$.0^6 1011$	$.0^7 9588$
4.9	$.0^7 9096$	$.0^7 8629$	$.0^7 8185$	$.0^7 7763$	$.0^7 7362$	$.0^7 6982$	$.0^7 6620$	$.0^7 6276$	$.0^7 5950$	$.0^7 5640$

Example of table notation: $.0^4 5848 = .00005848$.

Source: Reproduced from Robert O. Schlaifer, *Introduction to Statistics for Business Decisions,* published by McGraw-Hill Book Company, 1961, by permission of the copyright holder, the President and Fellows of Harvard College.

Appendix C. Cumulative Binomial Distribution

n = 1

P R	01	02	03	04	05	06	07	08	09	10
1	0100	0200	0300	0400	0500	0600	0700	0800	0900	1000

P R	11	12	13	14	15	16	17	18	19	20
1	1100	1200	1300	1400	1500	1600	1700	1800	1900	2000

P R	21	22	23	24	25	26	27	28	29	30
1	2100	2200	2300	2400	2500	2600	2700	2800	2900	3000

P R	31	32	33	34	35	36	37	38	39	40
1	3100	3200	3300	3400	3500	3600	3700	3800	3900	4000

P R	41	42	43	44	45	46	47	48	49	50
1	4100	4200	4300	4400	4500	4600	4700	4800	4900	5000

n = 2

P R	01	02	03	04	05	06	07	08	09	10
1	0199	0396	0591	0784	0975	1164	1351	1536	1719	1900
2	0001	0004	0009	0016	0025	0036	0049	0064	0081	0100

P R	11	12	13	14	15	16	17	18	19	20
1	2079	2256	2431	2604	2775	2944	3111	3276	3439	3600
2	0121	0144	0169	0196	0225	0256	0289	0324	0361	0400

P R	21	22	23	24	25	26	27	28	29	30
1	3759	3916	4071	4224	4375	4524	4671	4816	4959	5100
2	0441	0484	0529	0576	0625	0676	0729	0784	0841	0900

P R	31	32	33	34	35	36	37	38	39	40
1	5239	5376	5511	5644	5775	5904	6031	6156	6279	6400
2	0961	1024	1089	1156	1225	1296	1369	1444	1521	1600

P R	41	42	43	44	45	46	47	48	49	50
1	6519	6636	6751	6864	6975	7084	7191	7296	7399	7500
2	1681	1764	1849	1936	2025	2116	2209	2304	2401	2500

n = 3

P R	01	02	03	04	05	06	07	08	09	10
1	0297	0588	0873	1153	1426	1694	1956	2213	2464	2710
2	0003	0012	0026	0047	0073	0104	0140	0182	0228	0280
3				0001	0001	0002	0003	0005	0007	0010

P R	11	12	13	14	15	16	17	18	19	20
1	2950	3185	3415	3639	3859	4073	4282	4486	4686	4880
2	0336	0397	0463	0533	0608	0686	0769	0855	0946	1040
3	0013	0017	0022	0027	0034	0041	0049	0058	0069	0080

Source: Reprinted from Robert O. Schlaifer, *Introduction to Statistics for Business Decisions,* published by McGraw-Hill Book Company, 1961, by permission of the copyright holder, the President and Fellows of Harvard College.

Appendix C. Cumulative Binomial Distribution (Continued)

P	21	22	23	24	25	26	27	28	29	30
R										
1	5070	5254	5435	5610	5781	5948	6110	6268	6421	6570
2	1138	1239	1344	1452	1563	1676	1793	1913	2035	2160
3	0093	0106	0122	0138	0156	0176	0197	0220	0244	0270

P	31	32	33	34	35	36	37	38	39	40
R										
1	6715	6856	6992	7125	7254	7379	7500	7617	7730	7840
2	2287	2417	2548	2682	2818	2955	3094	3235	3377	3520
3	0298	0328	0359	0393	0429	0467	0507	0549	0593	0640

P	41	42	43	44	45	46	47	48	49	50
R										
1	7946	8049	8148	8244	8336	8425	8511	8594	8673	8750
2	3665	3810	3957	4104	4253	4401	4551	4700	4850	5000
3	0689	0741	0795	0852	0911	0973	1038	1106	1176	1250

n = 4

P	01	02	03	04	05	06	07	08	09	10
R										
1	0394	0776	1147	1507	1855	2193	2519	2836	3413	3439
2	0006	0023	0052	0091	0140	0199	0267	0344	0430	0523
3			0001	0002	0005	0008	0013	0019	0027	0037
4									0001	0001

P	11	12	13	14	15	16	17	18	19	20
R										
1	3726	4003	4271	4530	4780	5021	5254	5479	5695	5904
2	0624	0732	0847	0968	1095	1228	1366	1509	1656	1808
3	0049	0063	0079	0098	0120	0144	0171	0202	0235	0272
4	0001	0002	0003	0004	0005	0007	0008	0010	0013	0016

P	21	22	23	24	25	26	27	28	29	30
R										
1	6105	6298	6485	6664	6836	7001	7160	7313	7459	7599
2	1963	2122	2285	2450	2617	2787	2959	3132	3307	3483
3	0312	0356	0403	0453	0508	0566	0628	0694	0763	0837
4	0019	0023	0028	0033	0039	0046	0053	0061	0071	0081

P	31	32	33	34	35	36	37	38	39	40
R										
1	7733	7862	7985	8103	8215	8322	8425	8522	8615	8704
2	3660	3837	4015	4193	4370	4547	4724	4900	5075	5248
3	0915	0996	1082	1171	1265	1362	1464	1569	1679	1792
4	0092	0105	0119	0134	0150	0168	0187	0209	0231	0256

P	41	42	43	44	45	46	47	48	49	50
R										
1	8788	8868	8944	9017	9085	9150	9211	9269	9323	9375
2	5420	5590	5759	5926	6090	6252	6412	6569	6724	6875
3	1909	2030	2155	2283	2415	2550	2689	2831	2977	3125
4	0283	0311	0342	0375	0410	0448	0488	0531	0576	0625

n = 5

P	01	02	03	04	05	06	07	08	09	10
R										
1	0490	0961	1413	1846	2262	2661	3043	3409	3760	4095
2	0010	0038	0085	0148	0226	0319	0425	0544	0674	0815
3		0001	0003	0006	0012	0020	0031	0045	0063	0086
4						0001	0001	0002	0003	0005

P	11	12	13	14	15	16	17	18	19	20
R										
1	4416	4723	5016	5296	5563	5818	6061	6293	6513	6723
2	0965	1125	1292	1467	1648	1835	2027	2224	2424	2627
3	0112	0143	0179	0220	0266	0318	0375	0437	0505	0579
4	0007	0009	0013	0017	0022	0029	0036	0045	0055	0067
5				0001	0001	0001	0001	0002	0002	0003

(Continued)

Appendix C. Cumulative Binomial Distribution (Continued)

P / R	21	22	23	24	25	26	27	28	29	30
1	6923	7113	7293	7464	7627	7781	7927	8065	8196	8319
2	2833	3041	3251	3461	3672	3883	4093	4303	4511	4718
3	0659	0744	0836	0933	1035	1143	1257	1376	1501	1631
4	0081	0097	0114	0134	0156	0181	0208	0238	0272	0308
5	0004	0005	0006	0008	0010	0012	0014	0017	0021	0024

P / R	31	32	33	34	35	36	37	38	39	40
1	8436	8546	8650	8748	8840	8926	9008	9084	9155	9222
2	4923	5125	5325	5522	5716	5906	6093	6276	6455	6630
3	1766	1905	2050	2199	2352	2509	2670	2835	3003	3174
4	0347	0390	0436	0486	0540	0598	0660	0726	0796	0870
5	0029	0034	0039	0045	0053	0060	0069	0079	0090	0102

P / R	41	42	43	44	45	46	47	48	49	50
1	9285	9344	9398	9449	9497	9541	9582	9620	9655	9688
2	6801	6967	7129	7286	7438	7585	7728	7865	7998	8125
3	3349	3525	3705	3886	4069	4253	4439	4625	4813	5000
4	0949	1033	1121	1214	1312	1415	1522	1635	1753	1875
5	0116	0131	0147	0165	0185	0206	0229	0255	0282	0313

$n = 6$

P / R	01	02	03	04	05	06	07	08	09	10
1	0585	1142	1670	2172	2649	3101	3530	3936	4321	4686
2	0015	0057	0125	0216	0328	0459	0608	0773	0952	1143
3		0002	0005	0012	0022	0038	0058	0085	0118	0159
4					0001	0002	0003	0005	0008	0013
5										0001

P / R	11	12	13	14	15	16	17	18	19	20
1	5030	5356	5664	5954	6229	6487	6731	6960	7176	7379
2	1345	1556	1776	2003	2235	2472	2713	2956	3201	3446
3	0206	0261	0324	0395	0473	0560	0655	0759	0870	0989
4	0018	0025	0034	0045	0059	0075	0094	0116	0141	0170
5	0001	0001	0002	0003	0004	0005	0007	0010	0013	0016
6										0001

P / R	21	22	23	24	25	26	27	28	29	30
1	7569	7748	7916	8073	8220	8358	8487	8607	8719	8824
2	3692	3937	4180	4422	4661	4896	5128	5356	5580	5798
3	1115	1250	1391	1539	1694	1856	2023	2196	2374	2557
4	0202	0239	0280	0326	0376	0431	0492	0557	0628	0705
5	0020	0025	0031	0038	0046	0056	0067	0079	0093	0109
6	0001	0001	0001	0002	0002	0003	0004	0005	0006	0007

P / R	31	32	33	34	35	36	37	38	39	40
1	8921	9011	9095	9173	9246	9313	9375	9432	9485	9533
2	6012	6220	6422	6619	6809	6994	7172	7343	7508	7667
3	2744	2936	3130	3328	3529	3732	3937	4143	4350	4557
4	0787	0875	0969	1069	1174	1286	1404	1527	1657	1792
5	0127	0148	0170	0195	0223	0254	0288	0325	0365	0410
6	0009	0011	0013	0015	0018	0022	0026	0030	0035	0041

P / R	41	42	43	44	45	46	47	48	49	50
1	9578	9619	9657	9692	9723	9752	9778	9802	9824	9844
2	7819	7965	8105	8238	8364	8485	8599	8707	8810	8906
3	4764	4971	5177	5382	5585	5786	5985	6180	6373	6563
4	1933	2080	2232	2390	2553	2721	2893	3070	3252	3438
5	0458	0510	0566	0627	0692	0762	0837	0917	1003	1094
6	0048	0055	0063	0073	0083	0095	0108	0122	0138	0156

Appendix C. Cumulative Binomial Distribution (Continued)

n = 7

P / R	01	02	03	04	05	06	07	08	09	10
1	0679	1319	1920	2486	3017	3515	3983	4422	4832	5217
2	0020	0079	0171	0294	0444	0618	0813	1026	1255	1497
3		0003	0009	0020	0038	0063	0097	0140	0193	0257
4				0001	0002	0004	0007	0012	0018	0027
5								0001	0001	0002

P / R	11	12	13	14	15	16	17	18	19	20
1	5577	5913	6227	6521	6794	7049	7286	7507	7712	7903
2	1750	2012	2281	2556	2834	3115	3396	3677	3956	4233
3	0331	0416	0513	0620	0738	0866	1005	1154	1313	1480
4	0039	0054	0072	0094	0121	0153	0189	0231	0279	0333
5	0003	0004	0006	0009	0012	0017	0022	0029	0037	0047
6					0001	0001	0001	0002	0003	0004

P / R	21	22	23	24	25	26	27	28	29	30
1	8080	8243	8395	8535	8665	8785	8895	8997	9090	9176
2	4506	4775	5040	5298	5551	5796	6035	6266	6490	6706
3	1657	1841	2033	2231	2436	2646	2861	3081	3304	3529
4	0394	0461	0088	0617	0706	0802	0905	1016	1134	1260
5	0058	0072	0008	0107	0129	0153	0181	0213	0248	0288
6	0005	0006		0011	0013	0017	0021	0026	0031	0038
7					0001	0001	0001	0001	0002	0002

P / R	31	32	33	34	35	36	37	38	39	40
1	9255	9328	9394	9454	9510	9560	9606	9648	9686	9720
2	6914	7113	7304	7487	7662	7828	7987	8137	8279	8414
3	3757	3987	4217	4447	4677	4906	5134	5359	5581	5801
4	1394	1534	1682	1837	1998	2167	2341	2521	2707	2898
5	0332	0380	0434	0492	0556	0625	0701	0782	0869	0963
6	0046	0055	0065	0077	0090	0105	0123	0142	0164	0188
7	0003	0003	0004	0005	0006	0008	0009	0011	0014	0016

P / R	41	42	43	44	45	46	47	48	49	50
1	9751	9779	9805	9827	9848	9866	9883	9897	9910	9922
2	8541	8660	8772	8877	8976	9068	9153	9233	9307	9375
3	6017	6229	6436	6638	6386	7027	7213	7393	7567	7734
4	3094	3294	3498	3706	3917	4131	4346	4563	4781	5000
5	1063	1169	1282	1402	1529	1663	1803	1951	2105	2266
6	0216	0246	0279	0316	0357	0402	0451	0504	0562	0625
7	0019	0023	0027	0032	0037	0044	0051	0059	0068	0078

n = 8

P / R	01	02	03	04	05	06	07	08	09	10
1	0773	1492	2163	2786	3366	3904	4404	4868	5297	5695
2	0027	0103	0223	0381	0572	0792	1035	1298	1577	1869
3	0001	0004	0013	0031	0058	0096	0147	0211	0289	0381
4			0001	0002	0004	0007	0013	0022	0034	0050
5						0001	0001	0001	0003	0004

P / R	11	12	13	14	15	16	17	18	19	20
1	6063	6404	6718	7008	7275	7521	7748	7956	8147	8322
2	2171	2480	2794	3111	3428	3744	4057	4366	4670	4967
3	0487	0608	0743	0891	1052	1226	1412	1608	1815	2031
4	0071	0097	0129	0168	0214	0267	0328	0397	0476	0563
5	0007	0010	0015	0021	0029	0038	0050	0065	0083	0104
6		0001	0001	0002	0002	0003	0005	0007	0009	0012
7									0001	0001

(Continued)

Appendix C. Cumulative Binomial Distribution (Continued)

P R	21	22	23	24	25	26	27	28	29	30
1	8483	8630	8764	8887	8999	9101	9194	9278	9354	9424
2	5257	5538	5811	6075	6329	6573	6807	7031	7244	7447
3	2255	2486	2724	2967	3215	3465	3718	3973	4228	4482
4	0659	0765	0880	1004	1138	1281	1433	1594	1763	1941
5	0129	0158	0191	0230	0273	0322	0377	0438	0505	0580
6	0016	0021	0027	0034	0042	0052	0064	0078	0094	0113
7	0001	0002	0002	0003	0004	0005	0006	0008	0010	0013
8									0001	0001

P R	31	32	33	34	35	36	37	38	39	40
1	9486	9543	9594	9640	9681	9719	9752	9782	9808	9832
2	7640	7822	7994	8156	8309	8452	8586	8711	8828	8936
3	4736	4987	5326	5481	5722	5958	6189	6415	6634	6846
4	2126	2319	2519	2724	2936	3153	3374	3599	3828	4059
5	0661	0750	0846	0949	1061	1180	1307	1443	1586	1737
6	0134	0159	0187	0218	0253	0293	0336	0385	0439	0498
7	0016	0020	0024	0030	0036	0043	0051	0061	0072	0085
8	0001	0001	0001	0002	0002	0003	0004	0004	0005	0007

P R	41	42	43	44	45	46	47	48	49	50
1	9853	9872	9889	9903	9916	9928	9938	9947	9954	9961
2	9037	9130	9216	9295	9368	9435	9496	9552	9602	9648
3	7052	7250	7440	7624	7799	7966	8125	8276	8419	8555
4	4292	4527	4762	4996	5230	5463	5694	5922	6146	6367
5	1895	2062	2235	2416	2604	2798	2999	3205	3416	3633
6	0563	0634	0711	0794	0885	0982	1086	1198	1318	1445
7	0100	0117	0136	0157	0181	0208	0239	0272	0310	0352
8	0008	0010	0012	0014	0017	0020	0024	0028	0033	0039

n = 9

P R	01	02	03	04	05	06	07	08	09	10
1	0865	1663	2398	3075	3698	4270	4796	5278	5721	6126
2	0034	0131	0282	0478	0712	0978	1271	1583	1912	2252
3	0001	0006	0020	0045	0084	0138	0209	0298	0405	0530
4			0001	0003	0006	0013	0023	0037	0057	0083
5						0001	0002	0003	0005	0009
6										0001

P R	11	12	13	14	15	16	17	18	19	20
1	6496	6835	7145	7427	7684	7918	8131	8324	8499	8658
2	2599	2951	3304	3657	4005	4348	4685	5012	5330	5638
3	0672	0833	1009	1202	1409	1629	1861	2105	2357	2618
4	0117	0158	0209	0269	0339	0420	0512	0615	0730	0856
5	0014	0021	0030	0041	0056	0075	0098	0125	0158	0196
6	0001	0002	0003	0004	0006	0009	0013	0017	0023	0031
7						0001	0001	0002	0002	0003

P R	21	22	23	24	25	26	27	28	29	30
1	8801	8931	9048	9154	9249	9335	9411	9480	9542	9596
2	5934	6218	6491	6750	6997	7230	7452	7660	7856	8040
3	2885	3158	3434	3713	3993	4273	4552	4829	5102	5372
4	0994	1144	1304	1475	1657	1849	2050	2260	2478	2703
5	0240	0291	0350	0416	0489	0571	0662	0762	0870	0988
6	0040	0051	0065	0081	0100	0122	0149	0179	0213	0253
7	0004	0006	0008	0010	0013	0017	0022	0028	0035	0043
8			0001	0001	0001	0001	0002	0003	0003	0004

Appendix C. Cumulative Binomial Distribution (Continued)

P	31	32	33	34	35	36	37	38	39	40
R
1	9645	9689	9728	9762	9793	9820	9844	9865	9883	9899
2	8212	8372	8522	8661	8789	8908	9017	9118	9210	9295
3	5636	5894	6146	6390	6627	6856	7076	7287	7489	7682
4	2935	3173	3415	3662	3911	4163	4416	4669	4922	5174
5	1115	1252	1398	1553	1717	1890	2072	2262	2460	2666
6	0298	0348	0404	0467	0536	0612	0696	0787	0886	0994
7	0053	0064	0078	0094	0112	0133	0157	0184	0215	0250
8	0006	0007	0009	0011	0014	0017	0021	0026	0031	0038
9				0001	0001	0001	0001	0002	0002	0003

P	41	42	43	44	45	46	47	48	49	50
R
1	9913	9926	9936	9946	9954	9961	9967	9972	9977	9980
2	9372	9442	9505	9563	9615	9662	9704	9741	9775	9805
3	7866	8039	8204	8359	8505	8642	8769	8889	8999	9102
4	5424	5670	5913	6152	6386	6614	6836	7052	7260	7461
5	2878	3097	3322	3551	3786	4024	4265	4509	4754	5000
6	1109	1233	1366	1508	1658	1817	1985	2161	2346	2539
7	0290	0334	0383	0437	0498	0564	0637	0717	0804	0898
8	0046	0055	0065	0077	0091	0107	0125	0145	0169	0195
9	0003	0004	0005	0006	0008	0009	0011	0014	0016	0020

n = 10

P	01	02	03	04	05	06	07	08	09	10
R
1	0956	1829	2626	3352	4013	4614	5160	5656	6106	6513
2	0043	0162	0345	0582	0861	1176	1517	1879	2254	2639
3	0001	0009	0028	0062	0115	0188	0283	0401	0540	0702
4			0001	0004	0010	0020	0036	0058	0088	0128
5					0001	0002	0003	0006	0010	0016
6									0001	0001

P	11	12	13	14	15	16	17	18	19	20
R
1	6882	7215	7516	7787	8031	8251	8448	8626	8784	8926
2	3028	3417	3804	4184	4557	4920	5270	5608	5932	6242
3	0884	1087	1308	1545	1798	2064	2341	2628	2922	3222
4	0178	0239	0313	0400	0500	0614	0741	0883	1039	1209
5	0025	0037	0053	0073	0099	0130	0168	0213	0266	0328
6	0003	0004	0006	0010	0014	0020	0027	0037	0049	0064
7			0001	0001	0001	0002	0003	0004	0006	0009
8									0001	0001

P	21	22	23	24	25	26	27	28	29	30
R
1	9053	9166	9267	9357	9437	9508	9570	9626	9674	9718
2	6536	6815	7079	7327	7560	7778	7981	8170	8345	8507
3	3526	3831	4137	4442	4744	5042	5335	5622	5901	6172
4	1391	1587	1794	2012	2241	2479	2726	2979	3239	3504
5	0399	0479	0569	0670	0781	0904	1037	1181	1337	1503
6	0082	0104	0130	0161	0197	0239	0287	0342	0404	0473
7	0012	0016	0021	0027	0035	0045	0056	0070	0087	0106
8	0001	0002	0002	0003	0004	0006	0007	0010	0012	0016
9							0001	0001	0001	0001

P	31	32	33	34	35	36	37	38	39	40
R
1	9755	9789	9818	9843	9865	9885	9902	9916	9929	9940
2	8656	8794	8920	9035	9140	9236	9323	9402	9473	9536
3	6434	6687	6930	7162	7384	7595	7794	7983	8160	8327
4	3772	4044	4316	4589	4862	5132	5400	5664	5923	6177
5	1679	1867	2064	2270	2485	2708	2939	3177	3420	3669
6	0551	0637	0732	0836	0949	1072	1205	1348	1500	1662
7	0129	0155	0185	0220	0260	0305	0356	0413	0477	0548
8	0020	0025	0032	0039	0048	0059	0071	0086	0103	0123
9	0002	0003	0003	0004	0005	0007	0009	0011	0014	0017
10								0001	0001	0001

(Continued)

Appendix C. Cumulative Binomial Distribution (Continued)

P\R	41	42	43	44	45	46	47	48	49	50
1	9949	9957	9964	9970	9975	9979	9983	9986	9988	9990
2	9594	9645	9691	9731	9767	9799	9827	9852	9874	9893
3	8483	8628	8764	8889	9004	9111	9209	9298	9379	9453
4	6425	6665	6898	7123	7340	7547	7745	7933	8112	8281
5	3922	4178	4436	4696	4956	5216	5474	5730	5982	6230
6	1834	2016	2207	2407	2616	2832	3057	3288	3526	3770
7	0626	0712	0806	0908	1020	1141	1271	1410	1560	1719
8	0146	0172	0202	0236	0274	0317	0366	0420	0480	0547
9	0021	0025	0031	0037	0045	0054	0065	0077	0091	0107
10	0001	0002	0002	0003	0003	0004	0005	0006	0008	0010

n = 11

P\R	01	02	03	04	05	06	07	08	09	10
1	1047	1993	2847	3618	4312	4937	5499	6004	6456	6862
2	0052	0195	0413	0692	1019	1382	1772	2181	2601	3026
3	0002	0012	0037	0083	0152	0248	0370	0519	0695	0896
4			0002	0007	0016	0030	0053	0085	0129	0185
5					0001	0003	0005	0010	0017	0028
6								0001	0002	0003

P\R	11	12	13	14	15	16	17	18	19	20
1	7225	7549	7839	8097	8327	8531	8712	8873	9015	9141
2	3452	3873	4286	4689	5078	5453	5811	6151	6474	6779
3	1120	1366	1632	1915	2212	2521	2839	3164	3494	3826
4	0256	0341	0442	0560	0694	0846	1013	1197	1397	1611
5	0042	0061	0087	0119	0159	0207	0266	0334	0413	0504
6	0005	0008	0012	0018	0027	0037	0051	0068	0090	0117
7		0001	0001	0002	0003	0005	0007	0010	0014	0020
8							0001	0001	0002	0002

P\R	21	22	23	24	25	26	27	28	29	30
1	9252	9350	9436	9511	9578	9636	9686	9730	9769	9802
2	7065	7333	7582	7814	8029	8227	8410	8577	8730	8870
3	4158	4488	4814	5134	5448	5753	6049	6335	6610	6873
4	1840	2081	2333	2596	2867	3146	3430	3719	4011	4304
5	0607	0723	0851	0992	1146	1313	1493	1685	1888	2103
6	0148	0186	0231	0283	0343	0412	0490	0577	0674	0782
7	0027	0035	0046	0059	0076	0095	0119	0146	0179	0216
8	0003	0005	0007	0009	0012	0016	0021	0027	0034	0043
9			0001	0001	0001	0002	0002	0003	0004	0006

P\R	31	32	33	34	35	36	37	38	39	40
1	9831	9856	9878	9896	9912	9926	9938	9948	9956	9964
2	8997	9112	9216	9310	9394	9470	9537	9597	9650	9698
3	7123	7361	7587	7799	7999	8186	8360	8522	8672	8811
4	4598	4890	5179	5464	5744	6019	6286	6545	6796	7037
5	2328	2563	2807	3059	3317	3581	3850	4122	4397	4672
6	0901	1031	1171	1324	1487	1661	1847	2043	2249	2465
7	0260	0309	0366	0430	0501	0581	0670	0768	0876	0994
8	0054	0067	0082	0101	0122	0148	0177	0210	0249	0293
9	0008	0010	0013	0016	0020	0026	0032	0039	0048	0059
10	0001	0001	0001	0002	0002	0003	0004	0005	0006	0007

P\R	41	42	43	44	45	46	47	48	49	50
1	9970	9975	9979	9983	9986	9989	9991	9992	9994	9995
2	9739	9776	9808	9836	9861	9882	9900	9916	9930	9941
3	8938	9055	9162	9260	9348	9428	9499	9564	9622	9673
4	7269	7490	7700	7900	8089	8266	8433	8588	8733	8867
5	4948	5223	5495	5764	6029	6288	6541	6787	7026	7256
6	2690	2924	3166	3414	3669	3929	4193	4460	4729	5000
7	1121	1260	1408	1568	1738	1919	2110	2312	2523	2744
8	0343	0399	0461	0532	0610	0696	0791	0895	1009	1133
9	0072	0087	0104	0125	0148	0175	0206	0241	0282	0327
10	0009	0012	0014	0018	0022	0027	0033	0040	0049	0059
11	0001	0001	0001	0001	0002	0002	0002	0003	0004	0005

Appendix C. Cumulative Binomial Distribution (Continued)

n = 12

P R	01	02	03	04	05	06	07	08	09	10
1	1136	2153	3062	3873	4596	5241	5814	6323	6775	7176
2	0062	0231	0486	0809	1184	1595	2033	2487	2948	3410
3	0002	0015	0048	0107	0196	0316	0468	0652	0866	1109
4		0001	0003	0010	0022	0043	0075	0120	0180	0256
5				0001	0002	0004	0009	0016	0027	0043
6							0001	0002	0003	0005
7										0001

P R	11	12	13	14	15	16	17	18	19	20
1	7530	7843	8120	8363	8578	8766	8931	9076	9202	9313
2	3867	4314	4748	5166	5565	5945	6304	6641	6957	7251
3	1377	1667	1977	2303	2642	2990	3344	3702	4060	4417
4	0351	0464	0597	0750	0922	1114	1324	1552	1795	2054
5	0065	0095	0133	0181	0239	0310	0393	0489	0600	0726
6	0009	0014	0022	0033	0046	0065	0088	0116	0151	0194
7	0001	0002	0003	0004	0007	0010	0015	0021	0029	0039
8					0001	0001	0002	0003	0004	0006
9										0001

P R	21	22	23	24	25	26	27	28	29	30
1	9409	9493	9566	9629	9683	9730	9771	9806	9836	9862
2	7524	7776	8009	8222	8416	8594	8755	8900	9032	9150
3	4768	5114	5450	5778	6093	6397	6687	6963	7225	7472
4	2326	2610	2904	3205	3512	3824	4137	4452	4765	5075
5	0866	1021	1192	1377	1576	1790	2016	2254	2504	2763
6	0245	0304	0374	0453	0544	0646	0760	0887	1026	1178
7	0052	0068	0089	1113	0143	0178	0219	0267	0322	0386
8	0008	0011	0016	0021	0028	0036	0047	0060	0076	0095
9	0001	0001	0002	0003	0004	0005	0007	0010	0013	0017
10						0001	0001	0001	0002	0002

P R	31	32	33	34	35	36	37	38	39	40
1	9884	9902	9918	9932	9943	9953	9961	9968	9973	9978
2	9256	9350	9435	9509	9576	9634	9685	9730	9770	9804
3	7704	7922	8124	8313	8487	8648	8795	8931	9054	9166
4	5381	5681	5973	6258	6533	6799	7053	7296	7528	7747
5	3032	3308	3590	3876	4167	4459	4751	5043	5332	5618
6	1343	1521	1711	1913	2127	2352	2588	2833	3087	3348
7	0458	0540	0632	0734	0846	0970	1106	1253	1411	1582
8	0118	0144	0176	0213	0255	0304	0359	0422	0493	0573
9	0022	0028	0036	0045	0056	0070	0086	0104	0127	0153
10	0003	0004	0005	0007	0008	0011	0014	0018	0022	0028
11				0001	0001	0001	0001	0002	0002	0003

P R	41	42	43	44	45	46	47	48	49	50
1	9982	9986	9988	9990	9992	9994	9995	9996	9997	9998
2	9834	9860	9882	9901	9917	9931	9943	9953	9961	9968
3	9267	9358	9440	9513	9579	9637	9688	9733	9773	9807
4	7953	8147	8329	8498	8655	8801	8934	9057	9168	9270
5	5899	6175	6443	6704	6956	7198	7430	7652	7862	8062
6	3616	3889	4167	4448	4731	5014	5297	5577	5855	6128
7	1765	1959	2164	2380	2607	2843	3089	3343	3604	3872
8	0662	0760	0869	0988	1117	1258	1411	1575	1751	1938
9	0183	0218	0258	0304	0356	0415	0481	0555	0638	0730
10	0035	0043	0053	0065	0079	0095	0114	0137	0163	0193
11	0004	0005	0007	0009	0011	0014	0017	0021	0026	0032
12				0001	0001	0001	0001	0001	0002	0002

(Continued)

Appendix C. Cumulative Binomial Distribution (Continued)

n = 13

P R	01	02	03	04	05	06	07	08	09	10
1	1225	2310	3270	4118	4867	5526	6107	6617	7065	7458
2	0072	0270	0564	0932	1354	1814	2298	2794	3293	3787
3	0003	0020	0062	0135	0245	0392	0578	0799	1054	1339
4		0001	0005	0014	0031	0060	0103	0163	0242	0342
5				0001	0003	0007	0013	0024	0041	0065
6						0001	0001	0003	0005	0009
7									0001	0001

P R	11	12	13	14	15	16	17	18	19	20
1	7802	8102	8364	8592	8791	8963	9113	9242	9354	9450
2	4270	4738	5186	5614	6017	6396	6751	7080	7384	7664
3	1651	1985	2337	2704	3080	3463	3848	4231	4611	4983
4	0464	0609	0776	0967	1180	1414	1667	1939	2226	2527
5	0097	0139	0193	0260	0342	0438	0551	0681	0827	0991
6	0015	0024	0036	0053	0075	0104	0139	0183	0237	0300
7	0002	0003	0005	0008	0013	0019	0027	0038	0052	0070
8			0001	0001	0002	0003	0004	0006	0009	0012
9								0001	0001	0002

P R	21	22	23	24	25	26	27	28	29	30
1	9533	9604	9666	9718	9762	9800	9833	9860	9883	9903
2	7920	8154	8367	8559	8733	8889	9029	9154	9265	9363
3	5347	5699	6039	6364	6674	6968	7245	7505	7749	7975
4	2839	3161	3489	3822	4157	4493	4826	5155	5478	5794
5	1173	1371	1585	1816	2060	2319	2589	2870	3160	3457
6	0375	0462	0562	0675	0802	0944	1099	1270	1455	1654
7	0093	0120	0154	0195	0243	0299	0365	0440	0527	0624
8	0017	0024	0032	0043	0056	0073	0093	0118	0147	0182
9	0002	0004	0005	0007	0010	0013	0018	0024	0031	0040
10			0001	0001	0001	0002	0003	0004	0005	0007
11									0001	0001

P R	31	32	33	34	35	36	37	38	39	40
1	9920	9934	9945	9955	9963	9970	9975	9980	9984	9987
2	9450	9527	9594	9653	9704	9749	9787	9821	9849	9874
3	8185	8379	8557	8720	8868	9003	9125	9235	9333	9421
4	6101	6398	6683	6957	7217	7464	7698	7917	8123	8314
5	3760	4067	4376	4686	4995	5301	5603	5899	6188	6470
6	1867	2093	2331	2581	2841	3111	3388	3673	3962	4256
7	0733	0854	0988	1135	1295	1468	1654	1853	2065	2288
8	0223	0271	0326	0390	0462	0544	0635	0738	0851	0977
9	0052	0065	0082	0102	0126	0154	0187	0225	0270	0321
10	0009	0012	0015	0020	0025	0032	0040	0051	0063	0078
11	0001	0001	0002	0003	0003	0005	0006	0008	0010	0013
12							0001	0001	0001	0001

P R	41	42	43	44	45	46	47	48	49	50
1	9990	9992	9993	9995	9996	9997	9997	9998	9998	9999
2	9895	9912	9928	9940	9951	9960	9967	9974	9979	9983
3	9499	9569	9630	9684	9731	9772	9808	9838	9865	9888
4	8492	8656	8807	8945	9071	9185	9288	9381	9464	9539
5	6742	7003	7254	7493	7721	7935	8137	8326	8502	8666
6	4552	4849	5146	5441	5732	6019	6299	6573	6838	7095
7	2524	2770	3025	3290	3563	3842	4127	4415	4707	5000
8	1114	1264	1426	2600	1788	1988	2200	2424	2659	2905
9	0379	0446	0520	0605	0698	0803	0918	1045	1183	1334
10	0096	0117	0141	0170	0203	0242	0287	0338	0396	0461
11	0017	0021	0027	0033	0041	0051	0063	0077	0093	0112
12	0002	0002	0003	0004	0005	0007	0009	0011	0014	0017
13							0001	0001	0001	0001

Appendix C. Cumulative Binomial Distribution (Continued)

n = 14

P R	01	02	03	04	05	06	07	08	09	10
1	1313	2464	3472	4353	5123	5795	6380	6888	7330	7712
2	0084	0310	0645	1059	1530	2037	2564	3100	3632	4154
3	0003	0025	0077	0167	0301	0478	0698	0958	1255	1584
4		0001	0006	0019	0042	0080	0136	0214	0315	0441
5				0002	0004	0010	0020	0035	0059	0092
6						0001	0002	0004	0008	0015
7									0001	0002

P R	11	12	13	14	15	16	17	18	19	20
1	8044	8330	8577	8789	8972	9129	9264	9379	9477	9560
2	4658	5141	5599	6031	6433	6807	7152	7469	7758	8021
3	1939	2315	2708	3111	3521	3932	4341	4744	5138	5519
4	0594	0774	0979	1210	1465	1742	2038	2351	2769	3018
5	0137	0196	0269	0359	0467	0594	0741	0907	1093	1298
6	0024	0038	0057	0082	0115	0157	0209	0273	0349	0439
7	0003	0006	0009	0015	0022	0032	0046	0064	0087	0116
8		0001	0001	0002	0003	0005	0008	0012	0017	0024
9						0001	0001	0002	0003	0004

P R	21	22	23	24	25	26	27	28	29	30
1	9631	9691	9742	9786	9822	9852	9878	9899	9917	9932
2	8259	8473	8665	8837	8990	9126	9246	9352	9444	9525
3	5887	6239	6574	6891	7189	7467	7727	7967	8188	8392
4	3366	3719	4076	4432	4787	5136	5479	5813	6137	6448
5	1523	1765	2023	2297	2585	2884	3193	3509	3832	4158
6	0543	0662	0797	0949	1117	1301	1502	1718	1949	2195
7	0152	0196	0248	0310	0383	0467	0563	0673	0796	0933
8	0033	0045	0060	0079	0103	0132	0167	0208	0257	0315
9	0006	0008	0011	0016	0022	0029	0038	0050	0065	0083
10	0001	0001	0002	0002	0003	0005	0007	0009	0012	0017
11						0001	0001	0001	0002	0002

P R	31	32	33	34	35	36	37	38	39	40
1	9945	9955	9963	9970	9976	9981	9984	9988	9990	9992
2	9956	9657	9710	9756	9795	9828	9857	9881	9902	9919
3	8577	8746	8899	9037	9161	9271	9370	9457	9534	9602
4	6747	7032	7301	7556	7795	8018	8226	8418	8595	8757
5	4486	4813	5138	5458	5773	6080	6378	6666	6943	7207
6	2454	2724	3006	3297	3595	3899	4208	4519	4831	5141
7	1084	1250	1431	1626	1836	2509	2296	2545	2805	3075
8	0381	0458	0545	0643	0753	0876	1012	1162	1325	1501
9	0105	0131	0163	0200	0243	0294	0353	0420	0497	0583
10	0022	0029	0037	0048	0060	0076	0095	0117	0144	0175
11	0003	0005	0006	0008	0011	0014	0019	0024	0031	0039
12		0001	0001	0001	0001	0002	0003	0003	0005	0006
13										0001

P R	41	42	43	44	45	46	47	48	49	50
1	9994	9995	9996	9997	9998	9998	9999	9999	9999	9999
2	9934	9946	9956	9964	9971	9977	9981	9985	9988	9991
3	9661	9713	9578	9797	9830	9858	9883	9903	9921	9935
4	8905	9039	9161	9270	9368	9455	9532	9601	9661	9713
5	7459	7697	7922	8132	8328	8510	8678	8833	8974	9102
6	5450	5754	6052	6344	6627	6900	7163	7415	7654	7880
7	3355	3643	3937	4236	4539	4843	5148	5451	5751	6047
8	1692	1896	2113	2344	2586	2840	3105	3380	3663	3953
9	0680	0789	0910	1043	1189	1348	1520	1707	1906	2120
10	0212	0255	0304	0361	0426	0500	0583	0677	0782	0898
11	0049	0061	0076	0093	0114	0139	0168	0202	0241	0287
12	0008	0013	0013	0017	0022	0027	0034	0042	0053	0065
13	0001	0001	0001	0002	0003	0003	0004	0006	0007	0009
14										0001

(Continued)

Appendix C. Cumulative Binomial Distribution (Continued)

n = 15

P R	01	02	03	04	05	06	07	08	09	10
1	1399	2614	3667	4579	5367	6047	6633	7137	7570	7941
2	0096	0353	0730	1191	1710	2262	2832	3403	3965	4510
3	0004	0030	0094	0203	0362	0571	0829	1130	1469	1841
4		0002	0008	0024	0055	0104	0175	0273	0399	0556
5			0001	0002	0006	0014	0028	0050	0082	0127
6					0001	0001	0003	0007	0013	0022
7								0001	0002	0003

P R	11	12	13	14	15	16	17	18	19	20
1	8259	8530	8762	8959	9126	9269	9389	9490	9576	9648
2	5031	5524	5987	6417	6184	7179	7511	7813	8085	8329
3	2238	2654	3084	3520	3958	4392	4819	5234	5635	6020
4	0742	0959	1204	1476	1773	2092	2429	2782	3146	3518
5	0187	0265	0361	0478	0617	0778	0961	1167	1394	1642
6	0037	0057	0084	0121	0168	0227	0300	0387	0490	0611
7	0006	0010	0015	0024	0036	0052	0074	0102	0137	0181
8	0001	0001	0002	0004	0006	0010	0014	0021	0030	0042
9					0001	0001	0002	0003	0005	0008
10									0001	0001

P R	21	22	23	24	25	26	27	28	29	30
1	9709	9759	9802	9837	9866	9891	9911	9928	9941	9953
2	8547	8741	8913	9065	9198	9315	9417	9505	9581	9647
3	6385	6731	7055	7358	7639	7899	8137	8355	8553	8732
4	3895	4724	4650	5022	5387	5742	6086	6416	6732	7031
5	1910	2195	2495	2810	3135	3469	3810	4154	4500	4845
6	0748	0905	1079	1272	1484	1713	1958	2220	2495	2784
7	0234	0298	0374	0463	0566	0684	0817	0965	1130	1311
8	0058	0078	0104	0135	0173	0219	0274	0338	0413	0500
9	0011	0016	0023	0031	0042	0056	0073	0094	0121	0152
10	0002	0003	0004	0006	0008	0011	0015	0021	0028	0037
11			0001	0001	0001	0002	0002	0003	0005	0007
12									0001	0001

P R	31	32	33	34	35	36	37	38	39	40
1	9962	9969	9975	9980	9984	9988	9990	9992	9994	9995
2	9704	9752	9794	9829	9858	9883	9904	9922	9936	9948
3	8893	9038	9167	9281	9383	9472	9550	9618	9678	9729
4	7314	7580	7829	8060	8273	8469	8649	8813	8961	9095
5	5187	5523	5852	6171	6481	6778	7062	7332	7587	7827
6	3084	3393	3709	4032	4357	4684	5011	5335	5654	5968
7	1509	1722	1951	2194	2452	2722	3003	3295	3595	3902
8	0599	0711	0837	0977	1132	1302	1487	1687	1902	2131
9	0190	0236	0289	0351	0422	0504	0597	0702	0820	0950
10	0048	0062	0079	0099	0124	0154	0190	0232	0281	0338
11	0009	0012	0016	0022	0028	0037	0047	0059	0075	0093
12	0001	0002	0003	0004	0005	0006	0009	0011	0015	0019
13					0001	0001	0001	0002	0002	0003

P R	41	42	43	44	45	46	47	48	49	50
1	9996	9997	9998	9998	9999	9999	9999	9999	10000	10000
2	9958	9966	9973	9979	9983	9987	9990	9992	9994	9995
3	9773	9811	9843	9870	9893	9913	9929	9943	9954	9963
4	9215	9322	9417	9502	9576	9641	9697	9746	9788	9824
5	8052	8261	8454	8633	8796	8945	9080	9201	9310	9408
6	6274	6570	6856	7131	7392	7641	7875	8095	8301	8491
7	4214	4530	4847	5164	5478	5789	6095	6394	6684	6964
8	2374	2630	2898	3176	3465	3762	4065	4374	4686	5000
9	1095	1254	1427	1615	1818	2034	2265	2510	2767	3036
10	0404	0479	0565	0661	0769	0890	1024	1171	1333	1509
11	0116	0143	0174	0211	0255	0305	0363	0430	0506	0592
12	0025	0032	0040	0051	0063	0079	0097	0119	0145	0176
13	0004	0005	0007	0009	0011	0014	0018	0023	0029	0037
14			0001	0001	0001	0002	0002	0003	0004	0005

Appendix C. Cumulative Binomial Distribution (Continued)

n = 16

P R	01	02	03	04	05	06	07	08	09	10
1	1485	2762	3857	4796	5599	6284	6869	7366	7789	8417
2	0109	0399	0818	1327	1892	2489	3098	3701	4289	4853
3	0005	0037	0113	0242	0429	0673	0969	1311	1694	2108
4		0002	0011	0032	0070	0132	0221	0342	0496	0684
5			0001	0003	0009	0019	0038	0068	0111	0170
6					0001	0002	0005	0010	0019	0033
7							0001	0001	0003	0005
8										0001

P R	11	12	13	14	15	16	17	18	19	20
1	8450	8707	8923	9105	9257	9386	9493	9582	9657	9719
2	5386	5885	6347	6773	7161	7513	7830	8115	8368	8593
3	2545	2999	3461	3926	4386	4838	5277	5698	6101	6482
4	0907	1162	1448	1763	2101	2460	2836	3223	3619	4019
5	0248	0348	0471	0618	0791	0988	1211	1458	1727	2018
6	0053	0082	0120	0171	0235	0315	0412	0527	0662	0817
7	0009	0015	0024	0038	0056	0080	0112	0153	0204	0267
8	0001	0002	0004	0007	0011	0016	0024	0036	0051	0070
9			0001	0001	0002	0003	0004	0007	0010	0015
10							0001	0001	0002	0002

Appendix D. Values of $e^{-\lambda}$ for Use in the Poisson Distribution

VALUES OF $e^{-\lambda}$

λ	$e^{-\lambda}$	λ	$e^{-\lambda}$
0.0	1.0000	3.1	0.0450
0.1	0.9048	3.2	0.0408
0.2	0.8187	3.3	0.0369
0.3	0.7408	3.4	0.0334
0.4	0.6703	3.5	0.0302
0.5	0.6065	3.6	0.0273
0.6	0.5488	3.7	0.0247
0.7	0.4966	3.8	0.0224
0.8	0.4493	3.9	0.0202
0.9	0.4066	4.0	0.0183
1.0	0.3679	4.1	0.0166
1.1	0.3329	4.2	0.0150
1.2	0.3012	4.3	0.0136
1.3	0.2725	4.4	0.0123
1.4	0.2466	4.5	0.0111
1.5	0.2231	4.6	0.0101
1.6	0.2019	4.7	0.0091
1.7	0.1827	4.8	0.0082
1.8	0.1653	4.9	0.0074
1.9	0.1496	5.0	0.0067
2.0	0.1353	5.1	0.0061
2.1	0.1225	5.2	0.0055
2.2	0.1108	5.3	0.0050
2.3	0.1003	5.4	0.0045
2.4	0.0907	5.5	0.0041
2.5	0.0821	5.6	0.0037
2.6	0.0743	5.7	0.0033
2.7	0.0672	5.8	0.0030
2.8	0.0608	5.9	0.0027
2.9	0.0550	6.0	0.0025
3.0	0.0498		

Index

ABC analysis, 298–299
  definition of, 298, 320
AB:QM software package, 882–890
  for assignment problems, 559
  for constant time service model, 657
  for critical path method, 763
  with crashing, 763–764
  in decision theory, 155–157, 195–200
  for dynamic programming, 854–856
  and expected monetary value, 155–157
  in forecasting, 109–115, 886
  for Game theory, 844–845
  for goal programming, 617–619
  for integer programming, 594
  for inventory control, 310–314
  for inventory simulation, 692–694
  limitations of, 889–890
  for linear programming, 353–354, 364, 390, 393,
    396–397, 417, 419–420, 496–497
  for Markov analysis, 808–809
  for maximal flow technique, 763
  for minimum spanning tree techniques, 763
  for Monte Carlo simulation, 687
  for overview in quantitative analysis, 18–19
  for program evaluation and review techniques
    (PERT), 762
  for queuing problems, 648–650, 653
  for shortest route technique, 763
  for transportation problem, 543–544
Absorbing states, 803–808
  accounts receivable applications, 803–808
  definition of, 810
  spreadsheets used in, 824
Activity, 727
  definition of, 772
Activity time estimates, 729–730
  definition of, 772
Ada, 703
ADANS (Airlift Deployment Analysis System), 853
Adaptive smoothing, 108–109
Adjoint, 830–831
  definition of, 832
AHP. See Analytic hierarchy process (AHP)
AI. See artificial intelligence (AI),
Algorithms, 7, 23
  definition of, 23

Karmarkar's. See Karmarkar's algorithm
Allyn and Bacon: Quantitative Methods. See AB:QM
  software package
Alternate optimal solutions, 368–369, 407
  definition of, 370
  in transportation problems, 542
Alternatives, 139, 158
American Air Lines, 406, 591
American Air Lines Decision Technologies, 465
American Baseball League, 556
Amount back ordered, 286
Analytic hierarchy process (AHP), 871
  compared with multifactor evaluation process, 876
  definition of, 877
  key equations, 877
Anbil, R., 406n
Andrews, Bruce, 645n
Annual carrying cost, 254–259, 279, 287
Annual holding cost. See Annual carrying cost
Annual inventory carrying cost, 259
Annual inventory cost, 254–259
Annual ordering cost. See Annual setup cost
Annual setup cost, 278–279, 280
  definition of, 320
Arcs, 848
Arrival characteristics, 639–641
Artificial intelligence (AI), 15–18, 22
  definition of, 15, 22
  expert systems, 15–18
  natural languages, 16
  robotics, 15
  vision sciences, 16
Artificial variable, 451–452
  definition of, 467
Assignable variations, 229, 238
Assignment problems 400–408, 516–517, 547–555
  algorithms, special purpose, 517–518
  and branch and bound method, 596–599
  computer applications for, 558–561
  dummy columns in, 555–556
  dummy rows, 555–556
  Hungarian method in, 550–555
  and maximization problems, 557–558
  and zero-one programming, 593–596
Assignment table, 547
Average inventory, 256–257, 267

Back ordering cost per unit per year, 285–286
    definition of, 320
Back order model. *See also* Planned shortages
    inventory model
    inventory model, 285–290
Backward pass, 733
    definition of, 773
Balanced problem, 520–521
    definition of, 561
Balking, 640–641
    definition of, 661
Barnes, John C., 642
BASIC, 703
Basic feasible solution, 438
    definition of, 467
Basic objective function coefficient, 484–485
Basic variables, 438, 467, 482–485
Basis. *See* Basic variables
Bayes's law. *See* Bayes's Theorem
Bayes's Theorem, 33–38, 40, 185–188
    AB:QM software, 199–200
    derivation of, 45
    general form, 37–38
    posterior probabilities, 36, 185
    revised probabilities, 37, 185–188
Bean, J, 348
Bernouli process, 56
Beta distribution, 729–730
    definition of, 773
Biales Waste Disposal, 719
Bias, 91–92, 118
Bierman, H., 632n
Binomial distribution, 56–59
    definition of, 71
    formula, 57
    table for, 60
Blackstone, Bill, 755
Blue Bell, 265
Bonini, C.P., 632n
Branch and bound method, 596–605
    and assignment problem, 596–599
    definition of, 621
    and integer programming, 596–605
    and maximization problems, 600
Break-even analysis, 860
    definition of, 865
    and normal distribution, 860–865
Break-even point, 860
    derivation of, 860, 867
Brisbane International Airport, 538
Brown, R., 93n
Byrn, Judson, 359

Cahill May Roberts Company, 529
C-charts, 236–237, 238
Calling population, 639
    definition of, 660
    Canadian National Railways Line, 697
Carino, Honorio F., 494
Causal forecasting models, 83–84, 100–105
    multiple regression, 83
    regression analysis, 83
Causal models, definition of, 83, 118
CD commands, 882
Central limit theorem, 230–231, 238
C_i-Z_i rows, 439–441
    definition of, 467
Charns, A., 517, 606
Chi, Uli, 849n
Churchman, C.W., 11n
Classical approach, 28, 39
Classical optimization techniques, 620
Closed path, 523
COBOL, 703
Coefficient of correlation. *See* Correlation coefficient
Coefficient of determination, 105
Coefficient of realism, 148
    definition of, 158
Cofactors, 830–831
    computing, 831
Columbus-America Discovery Group, 61
Column opportunity costs, 552
Collectively exhaustive states, 29, 40, 795
Complete enumeration, 7
Components in material structure tree, 301
Computer-based information system (CBIS), 14
Computer programming languages. *See* General
    purpose languages; Special simulation languages
Computers, role in simulation, 509–510
Computer simulation. *See* Simulation
Conch, David, 149n
Conditional probabilities, 32–33, 40, 180–188
Conditional value, 139, 158
Consistency ratio, 874–875
Constant time service model, 655–656
    computer program for, 657
    equations for, 655–656
Constraints, 338
    definition of, 370
    graphical representation of, 342–351
    linear programming and project crashing, 746–747
    nonlinear, 616–621
    in simplex method, 435–436
Consumer market survey, 84
Continuous probability distribution, 53–54
    definition of, 53, 71

Continuous random variable, 48–50, 71
    definition of, 49–50, 71
    probability distribution of, 53–54
Control. *See* Inventory control
Control charts, 227–237, 238
    for attributes, 235–237
    for ranges, 233–234
    steps in using, 234
    for variables, 229–235
Controllable variable, 6
Cook, Thomas, 465
Cooper, L., 492
Cooper, W.W., 517, 606
Copy command, 882
Corner point, 351–353
    definition of, 370
Corner point method, 351–353, 360
    compared with iso-cost method, 365
    compared with iso-profit method, 365
    definition of, 370
    and minimization problems, 360–362
    simplex method and, 436
Corporate operating systems, 702
Correlation coefficient, 103–105
Cost. *See* PERT/Cost
Cost-volume analysis. *See* Break-even analysis
CPM. *See* Critical path method (CPM)
Crandall, R.L., 591
Crash cost, 745
Crashing, and critical path method, 745–746
    definition of, 745, 773
    and linear programming, 746–747
    and objective function, 747
Crash time, 745
Criterion of realism, 148
Critical activities, 734–735
Critical path, 730
    computation of, 731–732
    definition of, 773
    locating of, 730–735
Critical path analysis, 735–737
    definition of, 773
Critical path method (CPM), 724, 745–750
    computer application for, 762–763
    and crashing, 745–746
    definition of, 745
    framework of, 724–725
    key equations, 774
Crosby, Philip, 225
Cumulative probabilities, 682
Current solution, 445
    definition of, 467
Customer dissatisfaction cost, 286

Cutting plane method, 588–589
    definition of, 621
Cycling, 464

Dairyman's Cooperative Creamery Association, 491
Dantzig, George D., 340, 465
Darrow, Ross, 591
Davis, Donald R., 108*n*
Debry, M. E., 700*n*
Decision criterion, 852
    definition of, 856
Decision making, multifactor. *See* Multifactor
    decision making
Decision-making environment. *See also* specific types
    of Decision-making
Decision-making group, 118
Decision making under certainty, 140–141, 158
Decision making under risk, 140–146, 158
    computer program for, 155–156, 196
Decision making under uncertainty, 140, 146–150, 158
    computer program for, 156–157, 197–198
Decision nodes, 178–184
    computer program for, 198–199
Decision points. *See* Decision nodes
Decision support systems (DSS), 15, 23
Decision table, 139–140
Decision theory, 138–175. *See also* Decision making
    under risk, under certainty, under uncertainty
    and expected money value (EMV), 862
    key equations, 865
    marginal analysis, 150–155, 158
    normal distribution, 860
    six steps in, 138, 158
Decision trees, 178–185
    AB:QM, 198–199
    steps in analyzing, 178–179
    symbols used in, 178
Decision variables, 6, 852–854
    definition of, 6, 856
Decoupling function, 251
Degeneracy, 463–464
    definition of, 467, 561
    in transportation problems, 522, 539–552
Delphi technique, 84, 118
Deming, Edwards W., 225
Dependent demand, 300–307
Dependent events, 33–35, 40
Dependent variable, 100
Desert Storm Airlift Operations, 853
DeSilva, A. H., 700*n*
Destination, 518
    definition of, 561

Determinants, 826–827
    definition of, 832
Deterministic approach, 724–725
Deterministic assumptions, 480
Deterministic network model, 745
Deviational variables, 606–609
    definition of, 608, 621
Deviations, 61–63
Diagram, Venn, 30, 31
DiLisio, F. J., 700n
Directory command, 889
Discrete distributions, with marginal analysis,
    150–152
Discrete probability distribution, definition of, 71
    central tendency, 51
    expected value of, 51–52
    variance of, 52–53
Discrete random variable, 48–51
    definition of, 48–49
    probability distribution of, 50–51
Dodge, N. F., 225
Dominance, 840–841
    definition of, 843
DSS, See Decision support systems (DSS),
Dual,
    computational advantage of, 494–495
    formulation of, 492
Dual in linear programming, 490–500
Duality. See dual
Dummy activities, 738–739
    definition of, 773
Dummy columns, 555–556
    definition of, 562
Dummy destinations, 536
    definition of, 561
Dummy rows, 555–556
    definition of, 562
Dummy sources, 536
    definition of, 561
DuPont, 725
Dynamic programming, 848–857
    computer application for, 854–855
    definition of, 856
    and shortest-route problem, 848–852
    terminology of, 852–854
DYNAMO, 703–706

Earliest finish time (EF), 731
    definition of, 773
Earliest start time (ES), 731
    definition of, 773
Earliest start time rule, 732

Eastman Kodak, 642
Economic lot size model. See Production run model
Economic order quantity (EOQ), 254–259, 267
    with calculus, 275
    computer program for, 311
    without instantaneous receipt assumption,
        278–282
Economy systems, 702
Ecuadorian Ministry of Public Health, 308
Edit command, 885
Edwards, J. R., 265n
EF. See Expected monetary value (EMV)
EMV. See Expected money value
Entering new data, 886
EOL. See Expected opportunity loss (EOL)
EOQ. See Economic order quantity (EOQ)
Equally likely, 147–148, 158
Equilibrium conditions, 800–803
    computations, 801
    definition of, 810
    determining conditions, 805
    spreadsheets used in, 823
Equilibrium share of market values, 800
Erlang, A. K., 637
ES. See Earliest start time (ES)
Evans-Correia K., 261n
Evans, James R., 556
Events, 727–728
    collectively exhaustive, 29, 40
    definition of, 780
    dependent, 33–35, 40
    independent, 31–33, 40
    mutually exclusive, 29, 40
EVPI. See Expected value of perfect information
    (EVPI)
EVSI. See Expected value of sample information
    (EVSI)
Expected activity time, 735–737
    definition of, 773
Expected monetary value (EMV), 141–142, 158,
    188–189, 862
    computer applications, 155–157
    definition of, 158
Expected opportunity loss (EOL), 143–144, 864–865
    calculation of, 143–144, 865
Expected value, 51, 59
    definition of, 51, 71
Expected value of perfect information (EVPI),
    142–143, 158, 863–864
    definition of, 158
    and normal distribution, 863–864
Expected value of sample information (EVSI),
    184–185

Expert systems, 15–18
Exponential service times, 644–655
Exponential smoothing, 89–94
  computer program for, 89
  definition of, 89, 118
  spreadsheet programs, 133–134
  trend adjustment, 92–94
Exponential distribution, 69–70, 71
Extreme point. *See* Corner point

FA matrix, 806
Facility location analysis, 546–547
  definition of, 561
Factor evaluations, 870–871
  definition of, 877
Factorial symbol, 57
Factor weights, 871, 875–876
  definition of, 877
Favorable market (FM), 185–187
  definition of, 374
Feasible region, 347, 487–488
Feasible solution, 347
  definition of, 370
Feigenbaum, A.V., 225
Feinstein, Charles D., 184n
FIFO. *See* First-in, first-out rule
Finite population, 639
Finite population model, 656–659
  equations for, 657–658
First-in, first-out rule, 641
  definition of, 661
Fixed order system, 261
Fixed period inventory control system, 261–264
Flood's technique. 550–555
Flowchart. *See* Flow diagram
Flow diagram, 689
  definition of, 706
FM. *See* Favorable Market (FM)
Fordyce, Kenneth, 253n
Forecastings. *See also* Times series models, Causal
  models, Judgemental models
  causal methods, 83–84, 100–105
  controlling of, 106–109
  exponential smoothing, 89–94
  monitoring of, 106–109
  moving averages, 87–89
  qualitative method, 84
  quantitative, 82
  scatter diagrams, 84–85, 86
  seasonal variations, 97–100
  steps in, 82
  table of comparison of methods, 117
  times series, 83, 85–100
  trend projections, 94–100
  use of computers in, 109–115
  weighted moving average, 88–89
Forecasting models, 15
FORMAT command, 882
Forrester, J.W., 702n
FORTRAN, 703
Forward pass, 732–733
  definition of, 773
Freeman, Susan, 642n
Fundamental matrix, 805
  definition of, 810

Gaballa, A., 35n
Gamble, standard. *See* Standard gamble
Game theory, 836–846
  computer application for, 843
Games larger than 2×2, 841
  definition of, 843
Gantt chart, 725
Garbage-in, garbage out (GIGO), 6
Gardner, E.S., 93n
GASP, 703–706
Gelb, Betsy, 606n
General Foundry, Inc., 726–749
General purpose languages, definition of, 706
  and simulation, 703
Georgoff, D.M., 116n
Gilmore, N.L., 224n
Glassey, C., 597n
Goal programming, 586, 605–616
  computer application for, 617–619
  definition of, 621
  graphical solutions in, 609–612
  simplex method for, 613–616
Goal programming tableau, 613–615
Goals, multiple, 605–609
Goeller, Bruce, 704n
Gomory cuts, 588
GPSS language, 703–705, 706
Gradient method, 620
Graphical solutions, in goal programming, 609–613
  to linear programming, 342–351
  in simplex method, 453
Greenberg, I., 631n
Gross material requirements plan, 302–304
Gusso, James, 697n

Haas, Steven, 149n
Hansen, Bertrand, 228n
Harkey, Lester, with General Foundry, Inc., 726–749
Harris, Ford W., 254
Harrison, H., 529
Harvard Total Project Manager (HTPM), and program evaluation and review techniques, 771–772
Hausman, W. H., 632n
Help screen, 887–888
Hilliard, Michael R., 853n
Hitchcock, F. L., 517
Hollorann, Thomas, 359
Homart Development Company, 348
Hooker, J. N., 464
Hosseini, Jinoos, 188n
HTPM. *See* Harvard Total Project Manager (HTPM)
Hungarian method, 550–555
Hurwicz criterion, 148

IBM, 253
Identity matrix, 829
    definition of, 832
Immediate predecessor, 728
    definition of, 772
Improvement index, 522, 527, 535
    definition of, 561
Independent events, 31–33, 40
Independent variable, 100
Industrial dynamics, 702n
Inequality, definition of, 339, 370, 374
    graphical representation of, 345–347
Infeasibility, 365–366, 462
    definition of, 365, 370, 467
Infeasible solution, 347, 462
    definition of, 370, 467
Inference engine, 17–18
Infinite population, 639
Ingredient blending problems, 415–420
    diet problems, 415–416
    ingredient mix and blending problems, 416–420
Inland Steel, 261
Input data, 6, 23
Install command, 885
Instantaneous inventory receipt, 278
    definition of, 319
Integer programming, 340, 586–596
    and branch and bound method, 596–605
    computer application for, 586–596
    definition of, 621
    types of problems, 589
    zero-one, 593–596

Intersection, 31
Inventory, 250
    usage curve, 255
    uses of, 251
Inventory analysis, and simulation, 687–692
Inventory control, 250–253
Inventory control models, 254–268, 278–309. *See also* specific Inventory models
Inventory cost factors, 254–259
Inventory decision, 253–254
Inventory forecasting, 250
Inventory management, computer program for, 317
Inventory models, 15
Inventory planning, 250–251
Inventory simulation, computer application for, 687–689
Inverse, 830–831
    definition of, 832
Iso-cost line, definition of, 370
Iso-cost line method, compared with corner point method, 365
    and minimization problems, 362–363
Iso-profit line, definition of, 349, 370
Iso-profit line method, 349–351
    compared with corner point method, 365
Iterative method, 434
    definition of, 466

JIT inventory. *See* Just-in-time (JIT) inventory
Johnson, Ross, 224n
Joint ordering, 299–300
    definition of, 299, 320
Joint probability, 32–35, 40
Judgemental models, 84, 118
Juran, J. M., 224n, 225
Jury of executive opinion, 84
Just-in-time (JIT) inventory, 307
    definition of, 307, 320

Kaintorovich, Leonid, 340
Kanban, 307–309
    definition of, 307, 320
Karmarkar, Uday, 642n
Karmarkar, Narendra, 464n
Karmarkar's algorithm, 340, 464–465
Kekre, Sham, 642n
Kekre, Sunder, 642n
Kelly, J. E., 725
Keown, A., 620n
Khumawala, Basheer, 606
Kinard, D. J., 79n

Kinard, Jerry, 477n
Knowledge base, 17
Knowledge engineers, 17
Kolmogorov, A. H., 340
Koopmans, T. C., 517
Krantz, K. T., 227
Krzysztofowizz, Roman, 108n

L. L. Bean, 645
Laplace, 147
Latest finish time (LF), 733
    definition of, 773
Latest finish time rule, 733
Latest start time (LS), 733
    definition of, 773
Lauderdale Construction Company, 750–753
Lauderdale, Melvin, 750–753
Lawrence, Mervyn, 538
Lead time, 260–261, 267
Least squares method, 95, 118
Lee, S. M., 606
Leimkuhler, John, 591n
Lembersky, Mark, 849n
Lenoir, Jr., Clinton H., 494
LF. See Latest finish time (LF)
Limited population, 639
    definition of, 660
Limited queue length, 641
    definition of, 661
LINDO software package, 353, 355–356, 401–402,
    404, 407, 412, 499–500, 502
    and integer programming, 594–595, 623
    and transportation problem, 566–567
Linear programming applications, 388–420
    employee scheduling, 400–408
    financial, 408–409
    ingredient blending problems, 415–420
    manufacturing, 392–400
    marketing, 388–392
    transportation problems, 409–415
Linear programming (LP), 338–370. See also Simplex
    method
    assumptions of, 339–340
    computer application of, 353–354, 364, 390–391,
        393, 396–397, 419–420, 496–497
    and crashing, 746–749
    definition of, 338, 370
    dual in, 490–500
    formulation of problems, 340–342, 490–492
    game theory, 841–843
    graphical solutions to, 342–353
    minimization problems, 358–363

and network flow problems, 516
    properties of, 338–339
Load command, 885
Logical approach, 28, 39
LP. See Linear programming (LP)
LS. See Latest start time (LS)
Luna, J. C., 308

Machine operations, Markov analysis of, 798–800
MAD. See Mean absolute deviation (MAD)
Maintenance policy, simulation model for, 696–701
Malcolm Baldrige National Quality Award, 225
Management information systems (MIS), 14–15
Management science. See Quantitative analysis
Management Sciences Associates (MSA), 389–392
Mangelsdorf, K. R., 308
Manufacturing applications of linear programming,
    392–400
    production mix, 392–395
    production scheduling, 395–400
MAPE. See Mean absolute percent error (MAPE)
MAP/1 language, 705, 706
Marginal analysis, 150–155, 158
    with discrete distributions, 150–152
    with normal distribution, 153–155
Marginal loss (ML), 150, 158
Marginal probability, 32–35, 37, 40
Marginal profit (MP), 150, 158
Market shares, 796
    definition of, 810
    predictions of, 798
Marketing applications of linear programming,
    388–392
    marketing research, 389–392
    media selection, 388–389
Markov, A. A., 794n
Markov analysis, 794–810
    assumptions of, 794
    computer program for, 808–809
    definition of, 810
    key equations, 810–811
    and machine operations, 798
    spreadsheets used in, 823
Material requirements planning (MRP), 300–307
    benefits of, 301
    computer program for, 318–319
    definition of, 320
Material structure tree, 301–302
Mathematical model, 6, 23, 678
Mathematical programming, 338
    definition of, 370
Mathematical tools, 836–845. See also Determinants;
    Matrix

Matrices. *See* Matrix
Matrix, 555, 827–833
   addition, 828
   adjoint, 830–831
   of cofactors, 830–831
   definition of, 832
   dimensions, 829
   inverse of, 830–831
   multiplication, 828–830
   subtraction, 828
   transpose, 830
Matrix M, 806–808
Matrix of transition probabilities, 794, 796–800,
   803–808
   definition of, 796, 810
Matrix reduction, 550
   definition of, 562
Maximal-flow technique, 726, 754–758
   computer program for, 766
   definition of, 773
Maximax, 146–147
Maximin, 146–147
Maximin decision criteria, 852–853
Maximization assignment problems, 557–558
   and bound and branch method, 600
MD commands, 882
M/D/1 model, 655n
   definition of, 661
Mean, 61–63
   of the distribution, 153–155
Mean absolute deviation (MAD), 90–91, 118
Mean absolute percent error (MAPE), 91, 118
Mean averages, 87–89
Mean squared error (MSE), 91, 118
META. *See* Model for evaluating technology
   alternatives
MFEP. *See* Multifactor evaluation process (MFEP)
Minimal-spanning tree technique, 725, 750–754
   definition of, 773
Minimax, 148–149, 158
Minimax criterion, 837–838
   definition of, 843
Minimization problems, 358–363
   and corner point method, 360–362
   and iso-cost line solution method, 362–363
   in Simplex method, 450–459
Minimum-spanning tree techniques, computer
   application for, 725, 750–754
   computer program for, 765
   definition of, 773
MIS (management information systems), 14–15
Mixed-integer programming, 589, 590–592
Mixed strategy game, 838–841
   definition of, 843

Mizrach, M., 597n
M/D/I model, 655n
   definition of, 661
M/M/m model, 650n
   definition of, 661
M/M/1 model, 644n
   definition of, 661
Model for evaluating technology alternatives
   (META), 700
Model, 6. *See also* specific kinds of models, e.g.,
   Forecast models, Time series models, etc.
   definition of, 5, 23
   types of, 6
Modified distribution (MODI) method, 529–532
   definition of, 561
   versus stepping-stone method, 529
MODI method. *See* Modified distribution (MODI)
   method
Modules. *See* Dynamic programming; Game theory;
   Mathematical tools
Monte Carlo simulation, 681–687
   computer program for, 687
   definition of, 705
   and probability distributions, 681–686
Moondra, Shyam L., 339n
Morgenstern, Oscar, 836n
Most likely time, 729
   definition of, 729, 773
Motorola, 230
Moving average, 87–89, 118
MRP. *See* Material requirements planning (MRP)
MSE. *See* Mean squared error (MSE)
Multifactor decision making, 870
   definition of, 877
Multifactor evaluation process (MFEP), 870
   compared with analytical hierarchal process, 876
   definition of, 877
Multiphase system, 642
   definition of, 661
Multiple-channel queuing system, 641–642
   definition of, 661
   equations for, 650–651, 662
   with Poisson arrivals and exponential service
     times, 650–655
Multiple-channel system, 641–642
Multiple goals, 605
Multiple optimal solutions, 368
Multiple regression analysis, 105
Murdick, R. G., 116n
Mutually exclusive events, 29
Mutually exclusive states, 795

Natural languages, 16
Natural variations, 229, 238

Negative exponential distribution, 69–70, 642–644
   definition of, 69, 71, 661
Negative slack, 450
Net material requirements plan, 302–304
Network. *See* Program evaluation and review
   technique (PERT)
   definition of, 772
Network flow problems, 516
Network models, 724–772
Neuman, John Von, 631, 836
New England Apple Products, 343
New York City Sanitation Department, 8
Nodes, 853
Nonbasic objective function coefficient, 483–484
Nonbasic variables, 438, 483–484
   definition of, 467
Nonlinear objective function, 616–621
Nonlinear programming, 586, 616–621
   definition of, 621
Nonnegativity constraints, 340, 342, 370
Normal cost, 745
Normal distribution, 61–69
   and break-even analysis, 860
   curves, 65
   and decision theory, 860–867
   definition of 61, 71
   and expected value of perfect information,
      863–864
   with marginal analysis, 153–155
   and program evaluation and review techniques, 737
   and safety stock, 296
   and service level, 297
   table, 65–69
Normal time, 725, 745
Northwest corner rule, 520–521
   definition of, 561

Objective coefficient ranges, computer application
   for, 495–500
Objective function, 338
   and crashing, 755
   definition of, 370
   nonlinear, 616–621
   in simplex function, 439
   in simplex method, 451–52
Objective function coefficient, 481–485, 491
Operating characteristics, 64
   definition of, 661
Operational gaming, 701–702
   definition of, 706
Opportunity costs, 533, 550–55
   definition of, 562
Opportunity loss function, 863
   definition of, 865

Optimal order quantity, 280–281
Optimal policy, 852
   definition of, 856
Optimal production quantity, 280–281
Optimality analysis, 480. *See* Sensitivity analysis
Optimistic decision criterion, 147
Optimistic time, 729
   definition of, 729
Order quantity, 688
Outcomes, 180–184

P-charts, 235–236, 238
Pairwise comparisons, 872–874
Parallel activity, 739–740
Parameter, 6
Parametric programming, 488. *See* Sensitivity
   analysis
Parents in material structure tree, 301
Parsons, Henry, 645n
Partition, 805–806
Pascal, 703
Payoffs, 139, 158
Payoff table, 139–140
Perry, Chad, 538
PERT. *See* Program Evaluation and Review
   Technique (PERT)
Pert/Cost, 740–745
   budgeting process, 740–743
   definition of, 773
   key equations, 774
   project costs, 743–745
   spreadsheets, 791–792
Pessimistic decision criterion, 147
Pessimistic time, 729
   definition of, 729
Physical model, 6, 678
Pilot plants, 6
Pirsig, R. M., 225n
Pivot columns, 441, 447
   definition of, 467
Pivot numbers, 441–444, 447
   definition of, 467
Pivot rows, 441–444, 447
   definition of, 467
PL/1, 703
Planned shortages, 287–292
   computer program for, 314
   definition of, 320
   solving with calculus, 333
Planned shortages inventory model. *See* Back order
   model
Planning. *See* Inventory planning
Plossal, George, 106, 107n

Poisson distribution, 59, 61, 639–640
  definition of, 59, 71, 660
"Policy Analysis for the Water Management of the
  Netherlands" (PAWN), 704
Posterior probabilities, 36–39, 40, 185
  calculating, 36
Postoptimality analysis, 8, 480–481
Predecessor activity, 739–740
Primal-dual relationship, 490
  definition of, 501
Primary diagonals, 826
Print command, 885
Prior probability, 37, 40
Probabilistic technique, 724
Probability, 26–44. *See also* Conditional probabilities
  Bayes's theorem or law, 33–38, 40
  classical approach, 28
  collectively exhaustive events, 29, 40
  conditional, 32–33, 40
  definition of, 26, 39
  dependent events, 33–35
  independent events, 31–33
  joint, 32–35, 40
  law of addition, 30–31
  logical approach, 28
  marginal, 32–35, 37, 40
  mutually exclusive events, 29, 40
  objective approach, 28
  posterior, 36–39, 40
  prior, 37, 40
  relative frequency approach, 28, 39
  revised, 37, 40
  simple, 32–35, 37
  subjective approach, 28
  types of, 28
Probability density function, 53
  definition of, 53, 71
  uniform distributions 54–56, 71
Probability distribution of demand, 861–863
Probability distributions, 50–79. *See also* Continuous
  random variable; Discrete random variable;
  Discrete probability distribution
  binomial distribution, 56–59
  characteristics, 50–51
  continuous random variable, 53–54
  definition of, 71
  discrete random variable, 50–51, 71
  exponential, 69–70, 71
  and Monte Carlo simulation, 681–686
  Poisson distribution, 59, 61
Probability function, 53, 71
Probability values, computer program for, 195–200
Problem,
  definition of, 3–5, 23

Production run model, 278–279
  definition of, 320
Product mix problem, 340
  definition of, 370
Profit, 139
Program evaluation and review technique (PERT),
  724–740
  activity times, 729–730
  computer program for, 762–763, 771–772
  critical path, 730–735
  definition of, 772
  drawing the network for, 727–729
  framework of, 724–725
  key equations, 774
  and normal distribution, 735–737
Programming. *See* specific type of programming, e.g.,
  Linear programming, dynamic programming, etc.
Project cost. *See* PERT/Cost
Project crashing. *See* Crashing
Project management, computer application for,
  763–769
Pure integer programming, 589
Pure strategy, 837
  definition of, 843
Pure strategy games, 837

Quadratic programming, 617
Qualitative factors, 2
Qualitative models, 83
  consumer market survey, 83
  Delphi method, 83
  Jury of Executive opinion, 83
  sales force composite, 83
Quality, 224–226, 238
  measuring, 226
Quality control (QC), 224
Quantas Airways, 35
Quantifying risks, 26
Quantitative analysis, 2–24
  approach to, 3–9
  definition of, 2, 23
  development of a model, 5–8
  GIGO (garbage in, garbage out), 6
  history of, 3
  implementation of, 8, 11–13
  and computer-based information systems, 14–18
  problems in, 9–12
  spreadsheet models, 18–22
Quantity column, 438
  definition of, 467
Quantity discount, 28, 320, 322
  computer program for, 312
  definition of, 320
  in spreadsheet, 33

Quantity discount models, 282–285
Queue discipline, 641
    definition of, 661
Queuing analysis with spreadsheets, 676
Queuing models, with Poisson arrivals and
    exponential service times, 69–70, 644–650
    assumptions of, 645–646
    equations for, 646–647
    and Poisson distribution, 69, 639–640
    and simulation, 659–660
    single-channel, 644–650
Queuing problem, simulation of, 692–696
Queuing problems, computer application for,
    648–650, 657
Queuing system, characteristics of, 639–644
    configurations of, 641–642
Queuing theory, 636–660
    definition of, 660
Quinn, Phil, 645n

R-chart, 229–230, 233–234, 238
Radloff, D., 149n
@ RAND command, 720
Random arrivals, 639
Random number intervals, 682–686
    definition of, 706
Random numbers, 682–686
    definition of, 706
    table of, 685
Random variable, 48–51, 71
    continuous, 48–50, 71
    definition of, 48, 71
    discrete, 48–51, 71
Range of insignificance, 484
    definition of, 500
Range of optimality, 485
    definition of, 500
Ray Design, Inc., 759, 770
Redundancy, 367–368
    definition of, 370
Regression analysis, 100–105
    computer program for, 114–115
    correlation coefficient, 103–105
    definition of, 118
    multiple regression analysis, 105
    spreadsheets, 135–136
    standard deviation of the regression, 102
    standard error of the estimate, 102
Relative frequency approach, 28, 39, 682
Reid, R. A., 308n
Remington Rand, 725
Render, Barry, 78n, 132n, 432n, 631n
Reneging, 640–641
    definition of, 661

Reorder point (ROP), 260–261, 688
    definition of, 260, 267
    and safety stock, 290
Results, 7–9
Revised probability, 37, 40, 185
    calculating, 185
Reynolds Metal Company, 5
RHS ranging. See Right-hand-side (RHS) ranging
Right-hand-side quantities, in sensitivity analysis,
    480
Right-hand-side (RHS) ranging, 489
    definition of, 501
Right-hand-side values, 486–488
Risk avoider, 191
    definition of, 201
Risk seeker, 191
    definition of, 201
Robotics, 15
Romig, H. G., 225
ROP. See Reorder point (ROP)
Row opportunity costs, 552
RSFE. See Running sum of the forecast errors (RSFE)
Rule base, 17
Run command, 885
Running sum of the forecast errors (RSFE), 106
Russell, R., 620n

Saaty, Thomas L., 871
Saddle point, 837
Saddle point game, 837
    definition of, 843
Safety stock, 290–298
    definition of, 290, 320
    and normal distribution, 295
    and reorder point, 290
Safety stock with known stockout costs, 291–294
    definition of, 320
Safety stock with unknown stockout costs, 294–298
    definition of, 320
Sale force composite, 84
Santa Clara University, 184
Satisficing, 606
    definition of, 621
Save command, 885
Scatter diagrams, 84–85, 86, 118
Schematic model, 6
Scherkenbach, William W., 225n
Seasonal variations, 97–100
Secondary diagonals, 826
Secrest, Steven, 491
Sensitivity analysis, 8, 23, 144–146, 264–266,
    480–489
    computer application for, 495–500

definition of, 264, 267, 500
    linear programming, 356–357
    project management, 739–740
    right-hand-side quantities, 480
Separable programming, 620–621
Sequential decisions, 179–184
    definition of, 200
Service costs, 637–638
    definition of, 660
Service facility, characteristics of, 641–644
Service level, 295–298
    definition of, 320
    and normal distribution, 295
Setup cost, 278–279
Shader Lane Hotel, 678
Shadow prices, 446, 488, 493
    definition of, 488, 501
Shewart, W., 225, 228
Shortest-route problem, and dynamic programming, 868–873
Shortest-route technique, 726, 758–761
    computer program for, 770
    definition of, 773
Shryock, E. G., 99n
SIMSCRIPT, 703–706
Simplex method, 434–467. *See also* specific types
    algebraic initial solution, 436
    definition of, 466
    first tableau of, 436–440, 455–456
    five steps, 440–444, 446–448, 449
    fourth tableau of, 459–461
    in goal programming, 613–616
    importance of, 434
    initial solution of, 434–440
    maximization problems, 449–450
    minimization problems in, 452–461
    second tableau of, 441–446, 456–458
    solution procedures of, 440–441
    special cases in using, 461
    third tableau of, 446–449, 458–459
Simplex tableau,
    definition of, 466
    first, 436
    fourth, 459–461
    second, 441–446
    third, 446–449
Simulation, 678–706. *See also* Monte Carlo simulation
    advantages of, 679–680
    and computers, 687, 703–705
    and cost analysis, 700
    definition of, 661, 678, 705
    disadvantages of, 680–681
    and general purpose languages, 703
    and inventory analysis, 687–692

    of maintenance policy, 696–701
    and operational gaming, 701–702, 706
    and preventive maintenance, 701
    and queuing model, 659
    of queuing problem, 692–696
    and special purpose simulation languages, 703
    with spreadsheets, 720–721
    steps of, 678–679
    and systems, 701–703
Simultaneous equation method, 352–353, 826–827
    definition of, 370, 832
Simultaneous equations, 352
Single-channel queuing system,
    definition of, 661
    with Poisson arrivals and exponential service
        rates, 644–650
    key equations, 661–663
Single-channel system, 641–642
    equations for, 646–647
Single-phase system, 641–642
    definition of, 661
    equations for, 646–647
Slack time, 734–735
    definition of, 773
Slack variables, 435–436, 606
    definition of, 466
SLAM, 706
Smith, Barry, 591n
Smith, H. L., 308n
Smoothing constant, 89–92, 118
Software packages. *See* AB:QM software package;
    STORM software package
Solution, 6–7
Solution mix, 438
    definition of, 467
Source, 518
    definition of, 561
Special issues in linear programming (LP), 369–373
Special purpose simulation languages, 703
Special simulation languages. *See also* GPSS
    language; MAP1 language
Spreadsheet models, 20–22, 23
    add-in, 21
    Bayesian analysis, 220–221
    budgeted costs, 792
    cell, 20
    copy command, 20
    database capabilities, 20
    in decision theory, 171–175
    decision tree, 219–220
    expected times and variances, 790
    file command, 20
    forecasting, 133–134
    @ Functions, 22

inventory problems, 276, 334–336
linear programming, 385–386
monitoring and controlling budgeted costs, 791
move command, 20
network problems, 790–791
print command, 20
PERT, 790
PERT/Cost, 791
@ Project, 8, 9–10, 21
quantitative analysis, 20
queuing analysis, 684
range command, 20
regression analysis, 135–136
@ Risk, 22
simulation, 721
state probabilities, 831
@ Statplan III, 22
@ What's*Best!*, 22
@ What If Solver, 22
Stages, 868
definition of, 877
Stair, Ralph M., 78n, 132n, 631n
Standard deviation, 53
definition of, 53, 71
of the distribution, 53
Standard deviation of the regression. *See* Standard error of the estimate
Standard error of the estimate, 102–103, 118
Standard gamble, 189
Standard normal distribution, 65
Standard normal table, 65–69
State of nature nodes, 178–184
State of nature points. *See* State of nature nodes
State probabilities, 794–796
definition of, 810
spreadsheets used in, 824
State, and dynamic programming, 873
State variables, 873
definition of, 877
States, 795–796
States of nature, 139, 158
Statistical process control (SPC), 224, 227–229
Statistical quality control, 224–247
Steepest ascent method, 620
Steinberg, D., 492
Stepping-stone method, 522–529
definition of, 561
versus modified distribution (MODI) method, 529
Sterk, W. E., 99n
Stigler, 340
Stockouts, 250, 252, 285, 290–298. *See also* Planned shortages
definition of, 320
Stone, Lawrence D., 61n

STORM software package, main menu, 19
and assignment problems, 560
and integer programming, 592
and linear programming, 353, 355, 410, 498
and project management, 763–766
and shortest-route technique, 769–770
and transportation problems, 545
use in inventory control, 314–319
Strum, Jay E., 495n
Subgames, 841
Subjective approach, 28, 39
Substitution rates, 438, 445–446
definition of, 467
Successor activity, 739–740
Sullivan, Gerald, 253n
Sullivan, L. P., 226n
Sullivan, Robert, 499n
Surplus variable, 450–452
definition of, 467
Swanson, H., 13n
Systems simulation, 701–703
definition of, 706

Tableau. *See* Simplex tableau
Taylor, B. III, 620n
Technological coefficients, 485
definition of, 501
in sensitivity analysis, 485–486
Tied ratios, 463
Time series models, 85–100
components of, 83, 85
definition of, 83, 118
Total expected costs, 637–638
Total opportunity costs, 552–553
Total quality management (TQM), 226–227, 238
in Japan, 226–227
Tracking signal, 106
Transformation, 852
definition of, 856
Transition probability, 796–797
definition of, 810
Transportation problems,
algorithms, special purpose, 517–518
alternate optimal solutions, 542
computer solutions for, 542–545
definition of, 561
degeneracy in, 522, 539–542
facility location analysis, 546–547, 561
improvement index in, 524
initial solution of, 520–521
modified distribution (MODI) method in, 529–532, 561
northwest corner rule in, 520, 521

setup of, 518–520
shipping problem, 409–411
stepping-stone method in, 522–529
unbalanced, 536–539
Vogel's approximation method (VAM) in, 532–536
Transportation table, 519
definition of, 561
Transpose, 830
definition of, 832
Trend projections, 94–100
Two-person games, 842
definition of, 843
UM. See Unfavorable market (UM)
Unbalanced problems, 536–539
definition of, 561
Unboundedness, 366–367, 462–463
definition of, 370, 467
Uncontrollable variable, 6
Unfavorable market (UM), 185–187
Uniform probability function, 54–56
definition of, 54
Unit matrix. See Identity matrix
Unit normal loss integral, 864
definition of, 865
United Airlines, 365
United States Postal Service, 700
Unlimited population, 639
definition of, 660
Unlimited queue length, 641
definition of, 661
Utility assessment, 189–192
definition of, 200
Utility curve, 189–194
definition of, 190, 201
Utility theory, 188–195
definition of, 200
Utility values, 192–194
Utilization factor, definition of, 646, 661

Value of the game, 837
definition of, 843
VAM. See Vogel's approximation method (VAM)
Variable. See Dependent variable; Independent variable; Random variable
defined, 6
types of, 6
Variable Annuity Life Insurance Company, 606
Variance, 51, 59
definition of, 51, 71

Variance of activity completion time, 735–737
definition of, 773
Variations. See natural and assignable variations.
Vector of state probabilities, 795–796
definition of, 810
Velcro, 227
Venn diagram, 30, 31
VISION, 849
@ VLOOKUP, 720–721
Vision sciences, 16
Vogel's approximation method (VAM), 532–536
definition of, 561

Wagner, H. M., 265n
Waiting costs, 637–638
definition of, 660
Waiting line costs, 636–638
Waiting lines, 636–660
characteristics of, 641
definition of, 660
Waiting line tables, 653–655
definition of, 661
Walker, M. R., 725
Waukesha, Wisconsin, 755
Weighted moving averages, 88–89, 118
Welch, Norman, 709n
Wellborn Cabinet Company, 504
Weyerhaeuser, 849
What'sBest!, linear programming, 353, 356, 414, 500
Wight, Oliver, 106, 107n
Winchell, William O., 224n
Wood, W. P., 265n
Woolsey, R. E. D., 11n, 13n
Work package, 740
Wynn, Tricia, 261

$\overline{X}$ chart, 229, 231–235, 238
Xcell, 706

Yanchik, Richard, 149n

Zero-one integer programming, 589, 593–596
computer application for, 593–596
definition of, 621
Zero sum games, 842
definition of, 843
Z_i rows, 439–441
definition of, 467